T⊕TAL
AIRGUNS

T⊕TAL AIRGUNS

The Complete Guide to Hunting with Air Rifles

Pete Wadeson

Quiller

First published in the UK in 2005
by Swan Hill Press, an imprint of Quiller Publishing Ltd
Reprinted 2006, 2007
Reprinted 2008 under the Quiller imprint

British Library Cataloguing-in-Publication Data
A catalogue record for this book
is available from the British Library

ISBN 978 1 84689 110 6

Printed in Malta by Gutenberg Press Ltd.

Quiller

an imprint of Quiller Publishing Ltd
Wykey House, Wykey, Shrewsbury, SY4 1JA
Tel: 01939 261616, Fax: 01939 261606
E-mail: info@quillerbooks.com
Website: www.quillerpublishing.com

Contents

Pete Wadeson is one of Britain's most highly regarded airgun hunters, and is also an established shooting correspondent and photojournalist. As a lifelong shooter and outdoorsman with over twenty five years' experience of hunting with all manner of sporting air rifles and firearms, Pete has amassed a wealth of practical and technical experience. He has certainly emerged and earned his stripes as the foremost contemporary authority on hunting with air rifles.

He regularly contributes to virtually all 'in-store' publications that cater for the airgun enthusiast. Though he doesn't 'boast' about his 'piscatorial prowess' he's also a very accomplished 'specialist' pike and predator angler.

During his time writing on airguns and firearms, he's had many very informed and respected articles published in magazines such as *Airgun World, Airgun Shooter, Sporting Shooter, Shooting Times* and many others including his regular features, reviews and articles that appear in *Airgunner, GunMart,* and *Shooting Sports*. Also others that are trad-oriented, monthlies, bi-monthly as well as being often enlisted as the 'Airgun Consultant' for various Airgun Annuals that are periodically published in any given year in the UK, such is his recognition as the leading authority on the subject. His continued and 'untiring' passion for the sport of air rifle hunting is once again shown here in the Second Edition of his seminal book – *Total Airguns*.

Foreword

I didn't by any stretch of the imagination grow up in what you could term a rural area. Even so, it was considered the norm to be given your very own air rifle as a birthday or Christmas present when you reached your teenage years. It was, in a sense, a rite of passage – an acceptance by your parents and elders that you were growing up. In today's climate of rising crime and widespread anti-gun hysteria, fuelled by confused news media, it seems difficult to believe that those days ever existed. I'm sure many hunters of all shooting disciplines can identify with that.

Looking back to carefree times – 'blatting rats' with a break-barrel air rifle at the side of the canal with my mates – I would never have envisaged the day would come when I'd be writing such a comprehensive book on the now-serious discipline of hunting with an air rifle.

As I have been given this opportunity, I hope that what follows will be seen by the sensible non-shooting public, as well as my friends, associates and peers in the shooting fraternity, as a considered and well-informed book on the sport. Because that's what it is … a sport. Additionally, there are many occasions when an air rifle of suitable power is a very effective tool for pest control, being widely used by professionals worldwide.

This book was first published in 2005, but due to the fast-moving pace of airgun technology, design, scopes, accessories, and because certain manufacturers and related companies have gone, to be replaced by equally as many new companies, I was rightly asked to revise and fully update the book.

My ethos remains the same and I still hope to dispel a few half-truths and wrong-headed ideas, and clear up what are often no more than fanciful hunters' tales. Truth to tell, even so-called airgun-hunting 'experts' like me return empty-handed, or only get the chance of one shot in exchange for a lot of effort. That's just the way it goes.

But even though there is a certain element of luck in being successful, there are many ways to help put luck on your side. Putting in the practice, time and preparation will sway the odds in your favour. On the following pages I hope to help you to achieve just that.

Air rifle hunting is amongst the most challenging and demanding of the shooting sports

Introduction

In over two decades of sporting shooting I've used a great variety of sporting guns and calibres. Although I enjoy the challenge of taking woodpigeon on the wing with a shotgun, long-range rimfire work on rabbits, or full-bore foxing, rarely is the feeling of achievement greater than when I've taken a precision shot with a 12ft lb air rifle.

As it's such a demanding but rewarding form of shooting, it's hardly surprising that many coming into the sport, and even those not so new to airgunning, eventually try their shooting skills against live quarry. You need to know the law, not only pertaining to hunting with airguns, but also governing their ownership and general use, so a chapter devoted to the law as it currently stands can be found at the end of this book. However, as legislation can change it's advisable to keep yourself up to date by checking regularly with the relevant government departments – primarily the Home Office and DEFRA – and of course the latest literature on the subject. Books aren't as few as they once were, but can still date quite quickly with regard to the law; the shooting magazines do keep their readers constantly briefed on legal changes, though.

I must emphasise that it's the responsibility of every individual to know the law pertaining to hunting with airguns. It's no use having the appropriate kit, even if you have somewhere suitable to hunt over, if you don't know the can do's and can't do's. Ignorance of the law is never accepted as a defence by the police or the courts. All reputable shooting organisations have the appropriate legal guidelines available on request, so do make a point of requesting them and – most importantly – reading, memorising and adhering to them.

It is also the responsibility of those wanting to hunt to be able to recognise the quarry species that are deemed suitable for control with air rifles. All the legitimate pest species that airgun hunters are allowed to shoot are listed in the 1981 Wildlife & Countryside Act. However, since the Act was passed, various species that were once included, now, due to a decrease in their population, are omitted. Most often this is due to factors such as a decline in habitat or a species-specific disease, resulting in the quarry becoming far lower in numbers than it once was – as is the case with the once-included starling. Certainly due to changes in the urban environment, the house sparrow is now wisely removed from the quarry list. This once numerous and most common of small birds has, in many parts of the UK, a much lower population than it ever had (although is thankfully now on the increase). At the time of writing, amongst the pests listed and appropriate to control with an air rifle with a power of 12ft lbs are rabbits, grey squirrels, brown rats, magpies, crows, rooks, jackdaws, jays, wood pigeons, feral pigeons and collared doves. There are some others you can add to the list, such as the exotic ring-necked parakeet and monk parakeet, would you believe, which in localised areas of the country have bred in the wild to the point when they're found in troublesome numbers due to pet birds being illegally released by disinterested owners or escapees from aviaries. You can even try your hand at certain waterfowl such as moorhens and coots – these two in particular being genres of duck, so only when in season.

The quarry species that most airgun hunters encounter will be fully dealt with in due course, but the main aim here is to illustrate and introduce when and why the precision accuracy of a good-quality air rifle is more suitable than the out-and-out stopping power produced by a live-round sporting rifle. First, we need to take into consideration that the kill-zone of smaller vermin deemed appropriate for control with an air rifle is relatively small. In many cases the hunter needs to place a pellet into a target area not much larger than a 10p piece and on some occasions, such as when taking a head-shot, this kill-zone is even smaller. An obvious scenario where an air rifle is the optimum tool and preferable to a more powerful firearm, is when shooting inside buildings such as barns, or around outbuildings. A more high-powered rifle could cause major damage and the possibility of dangerous ricochets.

The airgun hunter using a 12ft lb air rifle can often operate safely and legally in locations where a live-round firearm user can't. Many areas of open land just aren't deemed suitable by the police for a rimfire rifle to be used, but that doesn't mean that the area will be devoid of vermin. Often it's quite the opposite, as these places become havens for all manner of unwanted pests. Another example is in woodland, when squirrels or corvids such as magpies and jackdaws are the quarry. In many such situations you can't use a shotgun due to the damage that many shot pellets can do to the trees. A rimfire is totally out of the question due to the high power of the bullet, but a pellet fired from a 12ft lb air rifle has more than enough stopping power for tree rats and egg-thieving corvids. Some of the most challenging shots I've taken have been against these species. To be able to 'thread' a pellet through a maze of branches and twigs to hit a kill-zone on quarry such as these takes precision – precision accuracy from the hunter and precision performance from the air rifle, and there's the rub! We're already at the stage where you'll have realised that not only must the equipment you're using be up to the job, but also your personal level of shooting skills. These include accuracy with the rifle, and fieldcraft in your approach to the quarry. Accuracy comes with practice – an absolutely essential part of the airgun hunter's learning curve.

If your rifle and marksmanship aren't up to the job, then you simply won't be successful. Fortunately, modern air rifle engineering technology has come along in leaps and bounds in very recent years. Indeed, a newcomer to the sport can almost be spoilt by the fact that today's best air rifles, particular the pre-charged pneumatic (PCP) types, almost shoot themselves, needing only a helping hand or two to place the pellet exactly where it needs to go – the all important kill-zone. The air rifle is a precision tool that can do what many other sporting guns are just incapable of doing, which is to afford the shooter pinpoint accuracy without the 'overkill' factor that can be produced when using live-round sporting rifles. It's worth bearing in mind that quarry such as rabbits – a species obviously suited to the hunter using a rimfire or an air rifle – can often be encountered well within 50yds. Within that range only 4ft lbs of energy at the target is necessary to dispatch it cleanly, so long as the pellet strikes with precision within the kill-zone. Precise, low-power pellet placement is often better than greater power with poorer accuracy, but I must emphasise that using an air pistol for hunting is a definite no-no. The legal power limit for a non-licensable air pistol in the UK is 6ft lbs at the muzzle, and at typical quarry ranges that is simply not powerful enough. The only exception is at extremely close quarters, when you need to dispatch small vermin in a live-catch trap or administer a coup de grace.

Choosing an air rifle from the vast selection of those available and suitable for hunting can be a daunting prospect. Assuming you're already familiar with shooting air rifles, then beginning hunting can be a simple matter of transition, but even before choosing a gun we've not only got to decide upon the calibre – a topic which will be dealt with in the Ammo section and individually in Quarry Files, but the power source the air rifle uses to propel the pellet. Essentially, you have a choice of three types – either a traditional spring-powered rifle, one that's gas-ram-powered, or a pre-charged pneumatic-powered (PCP) rifle. Whichever you choose, as you're going to be hunting you will need a rifle that's capable of a muzzle energy of at least 11ft lbs, i.e. as close as possible to, but still comfortably within, the 12ft lb legal limit. Anything more powerful requires a firearm certificate.

As regards choosing an air rifle I'm deliberately not naming too many specific models, with the exception of certain landmark rifles and those that I feel are particularly suitable for hunters. Some models have already been consigned to the history books, and a few may not still be available by the time you come to read

Choosing an air rifle from the vast selection available and one that is suitable for hunting, can be a very daunting prospect

this, but I do mention certain air rifles because of the classic status they've achieved, which deserves credit and recognition.

I also mention established airgun manufacturers who have rifles in their stables that are well worth considering, but with so many different models being launched each year, I don't want what I've written to be out of date before it's even published. So, when I refer to particular air rifle features, you'll be able to look for those in the marketplace at any time, and choose a rifle from among those in production, which suits your needs and your budget. I've taken the same approach when I mention optics manufacturers and suppliers of any shooting-related accessories and products.

Here, I must mention someone without whom no book concerning hunting with an air rifle would be complete, by giving credit to the late John Darling. His book, simply yet aptly titled 'Air Rifle Hunting', is the seminal work on the subject, and one that can certainly help pave the way for our sport to be more widely accepted. It's packed with solid information that is as relevant today as it was when it was first published in the late 80s, and it's now a book of classic status that has stood the test of time. The air rifle hunter with a thirst for knowledge would be well advised to read it at their earliest opportunity.

Now – time to look at air rifles, their power sources and workings, the pros and cons of each type, and the necessary skills of the hunter who uses them successfully. Read on – and welcome to the wonderful world of airgun hunting!

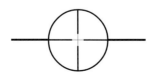

A basic but good quality 'springer' is easily capable of kill-zone accuracy out to 30 yds

Power Sources, Actions and Options

You can't see it, but boy can your quarry feel it. Of course, I'm referring to the 'ghost in the machine', the unseen, untouchable force that sends the pellet towards the target - air!

That's all it is, the air we breathe, albeit compressed to a pressure level that can project a small piece of lead effectively out towards a given target. How it's compressed is a matter of mechanics and the way we produce that to use in airguns is by compressing a metal spring in a cylinder to power a piston, or pre-charging an air reservoir that in turn lets out a measured (regulated) amount of compressed air for each and every shot. There's also the gas-ram system, first developed by Theoben Engineering but now used by many other manufacturers in their own variously named systems. This is another mechanical power source, but using a compressed air/gas filled strut instead of a spring/piston. All of these 'systems' will be explained in detail as we come to them.

As it currently stands by law, the muzzle energy that a 'legal limit' air rifle can produce is 12ft lbs, which means that you don't need a licence to own it. However, by obtaining a Firearms Certificate (FAC) you can own an 'on ticket' air rifle with muzzle energy above 12ft lbs and way up to 30, 60, 80, 100ft lbs or even more. There are now FAC-rated air rifles capable of producing incredibly high power levels, some in calibres equalling the size of centrefire rounds!

However, the majority of UK airgun hunters are content – and rightly so – with 'off ticket' air rifles that are capable of effectively and humanely dispatching quarry right out to 50–60yds, providing you've honed the shooting skills needed to achieve this. Generally, the maximum range most 12ft lb airgun hunters are comfortable with to engage their targets is widely accepted to be within 30–40yds depending on weather conditions. With dedicated practice you could eventually advance to a level of accuracy that allows you to extend that maximum distance, but only when conditions are favourable.

A few companies now produce single- and multi-shot rifles that use Carbon Dioxide (CO_2) in the form of pre-filled capsules or cylinders as a power source, and a few of these rifles are suitable for medium-range hunting and pest control – such as ratting and feral pigeon clearance. Using CO_2 as a propellant results in the rifle having recoilless attributes similar to pre-charged pneumatic- (PCP) powered air rifles but without the need for a divers' cumbersome compressed air cylinder or a manually operated stirrup-type pump.

Spring-Powered

Now to the most traditional and arguably the most popular of power sources – the spring and piston. Basic spring air rifle design hasn't really changed much in well over a century, although there have been huge advances in materials, technology and production methods. To get power from the spring, it first needs to have power put into it by manual compression – and that means you. There are three types of mechanisms (or

13

'actions', as they're known), for compressing the rifle mainspring. The most common is where the barrel itself 'breaks' at the breech (and is therefore called a break-barrel) and is used as a lever to compress the spring, or with fixed-barrel rifles a separate pivoting lever is used, either under the barrel (under-lever) or on the side of the rifle (side-lever).

By far the most popular action for a spring-powered air rifle, or 'springer' as it's often termed, is the break-barrel. As manufacturing processes are now much more advanced, a high-quality break-barrel's accuracy potential is equal to virtually any comparable fixed-barrel rifle operated by under-lever or side-lever action. Over time and prolonged use, a spring may eventually wear or even break, but most modern springs will take years of hard use before this happens – if it ever does. Even so, a mainspring is not expensive or difficult to have replaced. Irrespective of action type, the mainspring sits inside the piston, which is dragged back when the rifle is cocked and is automatically locked back in place by the trigger sear.

The break-barrel – still the most popular action for a spring-powered air rifle

Trigger Talk

The following applies to triggers on all air rifles, regardless of power source, unless stated. Any trigger mechanism in a spring gun is a high-stress component. Firstly the sear or sears are internal trigger components that fit together when engaged, to hold back the rifle piston (or hammer if a pneumatic rifle). The term 'creep' refers to the drag sometimes felt when pulling the trigger. To be strictly precise, 'creep' is really associated with 'single-stage' trigger pulls, where the entire engagement of the sear, is released by a single continuous pull to release full sear engagement. A 'two-stage' trigger unit has two movements before firing. The first stage takes up the pressure from the blade to the first engagement of the unit, whilst the 'second' stage 'trips' the sear and the rifle fires. A 'single-stage' trigger has only one movement to fire the gun. Virtually all good-quality hunting rifles are now graced with two-stage units with plenty of facility for adjustment to suit the shooter's requirement.

When the trigger on a spring-piston-powered rifle is released, the spring uncoils, driving the piston forward in the compression cylinder, which forces accumulated air in the cylinder to be compressed and forced through a transfer port, which in turn propels the pellet along the barrel. The size and strength of the spring, together with the air volume in the compression cylinder or chamber, are the major contributing factors to the power of the rifle. The main drawback of the spring-powered airgun is recoil and piston bounce on firing, created by the piston rebounding as it comes to the end of its travel. This can manifest itself as muzzle flip or mechanical recoil, both of which – if not compensated by the shooter – can cause pellets to go off target.

A muzzle weight can be fitted and to a certain extent the addition of a silencer also helps, but more importantly, accurate shooting with a spring-powered air rifle needs the shooter to adhere to a few basic set rules of good gun handling. Shooting stances and styles will be outlined as we come to the relevant section.

Although the spring-piston-powered air rifle has its downsides it certainly has its plus points. Firstly, it's completely self-contained and therefore a highly portable power source. As the rifle is cocked for each and every shot, this removes the possibility that the rifle will fail to operate due to 'running out of air' as could happen with a pre-charged pneumatic. However, a modern day, basic and good-quality spring-powered rifle is still easily capable of kill-zone accuracy out to 30yds, and dealing with most scenarios the airgun hunter will encounter.

Incidentally, it's worth mentioning here that a side effect of recoil can be scope damage. The recoil from a spring-powered rifle can be more vicious in jarring the scope than a sporting firearm firing powder-loaded cartridges. Some early models of air rifle became notorious as reticle (or 'reticule') breakers. Whatever the term, these are the crosshairs in a scope and they would actually break and be seen to split into two, or actually fall down into the eye bell. Of course, a lot of this is now history, not only due to the fact that reticles are now more commonly etched onto glass rather than actually being fine, hair-size metal wires; but the firing cycle of virtually all modern day production springers is also far less harsh than in the early days of the sport. More likely, the annoying trait known as 'scope creep' can occur. This involves the scope moving slightly in its rings or on its mounts each time the rifle is fired. But scope creep can easily be overcome by using good-quality scope mounts, a special dampened mount such as the DampaMount™ designed and manufactured by British scope mount manufacturers Sportsmatch UK, or by using scope mounts with an arrestor peg or arrestor block. As mentioned much earlier, springers aren't the 'clangy' unruly beasts they once were, and scope creep should be - and to a large extent is - a thing of the past, assuming that the scope is correctly fitted in quality scope mounts.

Virtually all hunting air rifles have two-stage adjustable trigger units and manual safety catches

The other factor of a spring-powered air rifle that needs to be considered is internal spring noise on firing. This is usually caused by the spring uncoiling, and can usually be remedied by a spring guide. Most established airgun manufacturers combat internal mechanical noise in their own ways. Special synthetic bearings and spring guides have all been used, but it was the British manufacturers Webley & Scott (R.I.P) who were the first to develop what they termed 'Silent Spring Technology' to help combat the problem. Basically, a sleeve for the mainspring was fitted inside the compression cylinder, and various bushes and synthetic parts were fitted to the piston head. The result is that the metal-to-metal contact is kept to a minimum, and all areas are lubricated to ensure a smooth firing cycle. Indeed, this is one of the reasons why, if you're serious about hunting and still want to use a springer, I'd have no hesitation in advising you to have your rifle specially tuned.

Tuning and Recoil Reducing Designs

Mechanical reactions resulting from the spring piston action can be reduced further by having the rifle tuned by a specialist gunsmith – this in effect is the hand finishing of the rifle's internal components to get a smooth and consistent action. Amongst other things, this entails piston heads being correctly sized, the mainspring being replaced with a special one, spring guides being fitted (as mentioned previously) – that is if they aren't already in the rifle - and all internals being polished to reduce friction, with all metal-to-metal parts being suitably lubricated upon reassembly.

At one time, by far the most famous custom house for tuning was Venom Arms, a partnership of airgun experts Ivan Hancox and Dave Pope. This company was responsible for inventing the famous Lazaglide tune – most often requested for the classic German-manufactured Weihrauch HW80 barrel power and its cousin the HW77.

Although Venom Arms has long gone, their ideas live on in V-Mach Custom Rifles Limited, a specialist tuning company owned and run by the highly skilled Steve Pope (Dave Pope's son).

Another highly reputable gunsmith is Tony Wall, of Sandwell Field Sports in the West Midlands. Tony shares some of his knowledge later, in the chapter on Gun Maintenance. As a 'springer fan' himself, it's no surprise that his words lean heavily towards how best to keep the traditional spring-powered air rifle working as it should.

Reduced-Recoil Springers

An ingenious gun designer, John Whiscombe, actually designed a springer that uses opposing springs and pistons so that when one travels forwards, the other travels back to cancel out recoil. The Whiscombe Rifle, first seen in the mid-1980s is probably the lowest recoiling springer ever produced. Similarly, the Ken Turner-designed Air Arms TX200SR ('SR' denoting Semi Recoilless) under-lever cocking rifle, worked on what was termed a 'sliding sledge' system; when fired, the action slid backwards in the stock, countering and reducing recoil. It was a very effective design, and I hunted with one very successfully for many years. Similarly, RWS Diana has the Model 54 Airking and the Model 56 Target Hunter side-lever action, spring-powered air rifles using a 'sliding action' to reduce recoil. I've owned both and they are very accurate, if a bit heavy. Incidentally, while on the subject of 'springers' it's worth noting that if you require open sights (or 'irons' as they're often termed) then you'll undoubtedly be buying a spring-powered air rifle. Open sights are extremely useful, especially if most of your shooting involves relatively close-range work such as indoor shooting, culling quarry such as rats and feral pigeons.

The Gas-Ram System

A straight alternative to the spring-piston system is the gas-ram-powered air rifle. Gas-ram rifles use the same cocking methods (break-barrel or under-lever) and direct barrel loading as spring-piston rifles.

Theoben Engineering were the first to perfect the gas–ram for air rifle use and their name was once synonymous with the system. Unfortunately, although once one of the UK's leading manufacturers of PCPs and the original gas-ram-powered air rifle, at the time of writing they had just announced that they'd ceased trading in the UK.

The situation at present is US-based 'Rapid Air Weapons LLC' (a precision engineering company and prior to the demise of Theoben Ltd already in common ownership), who stated that they would 'carry on with the manufacture of the company's PCP operation'. Already a few select retail outlets in the UK stock some of the main parts for original UK manufactured Rapid PCPs – these include magazines, buddy bottles etc. However, no mention has been made of Theoben's gas-ram rifles, but a lot of other companies including Weihrauch, BSA, Crosman, Gamo and Hatsan have their own gas-ram systems for powering air rifles.

The gas-ram concept gives the shooter the benefit of a faster lock time (i.e. the time it takes for the pellet to leave the muzzle after the trigger is 'squeezed'), there is less maintenance and the gun can be loaded with the gas-ram compressed for long periods with no loss of power.

When Theoben decided to throw away the spring and progressively develop the gas-ram system, they revolutionised manually-operated air rifle technology. Over the years they refined the system and used it in an under-lever as well as break-barrel action rifles. As the name implies, a gas-ram uses gas pressure to drive the piston. Specifically, this is like the shock absorber of a car, with compressed nitrogen or argon gas contained in a sealed telescoping strut. As the rifle is cocked the strut telescopes inwards, further compressing the gas it contains. When the trigger is pulled, the gas strut telescopes outwards as the gas re-expands. This means that it acts like a spring-loaded piston – pushing air before it and into the transfer port to propel the pellet.

The gas ram piston is faster than a spring-piston system generating the same power, so lock time is reduced but 'bounce back' recoil may increase. Theoben dealt with this by fitting a secondary free floating inertia piston (basically a ring), which slides independently behind the main gas-ram. As the name suggests, this ring is dragged by inertia slightly behind the piston head or gas-ram piston head; when the gas-ram reaches the end of its stroke and starts to 'rebound' from the wall of compressed air it has created after firing, the floating inertia piston behind it catches up to meet it a split second later in the firing cycle, reducing piston bounce and radically reducing recoil.

On most Theoben gas-ram rifles the letters HE were often stamped on the top of the breech. This stands for High Efficiency, and a very fitting term it is too. However, the mechanics of the system don't end there, with just using gas and secondary pistons, because the company later developed a special piston crown to complement the design. Known as the Zephyr Piston Crown, it has air channels cut into it in a 'fan' shape funnelling air towards the transfer port so most of the air can escape and isn't trapped where it can cause unwanted piston bounce.

While the level of accuracy that can be achieved with a gas-ram rifle is impressive, there certainly is a knack to firing one, just as there is for a spring-powered rifle. Granted, the gas-ram doesn't have the recoil of a springer, but it does have a definite movement on firing. This could never be termed unruly or unmanageable, but it is a side effect of the power source that needs to be taken into consideration when shooting. Now that the fundamentals of a 'gas filled' strut system have been proven, many other gun manufacturers are making rifles fitted with their own version of the gas-ram power source.

We now come to the most talked-about power source of recent times, the pre-charged pneumatic system.

The Pre-charged Pneumatic (or PCP)

Besides electronically operated air rifles, of which you'll read more later, the technology of the pre-charged pneumatic dates back to the eighteenth century when some rifles used a hollow iron rifle butt or in an iron ball as a vessel for storing compressed air. Apparently this is one of the reasons why acquiring and enforcing exclusive patents on modern PCP technology is so difficult. The major benefit of any PCP (or any other pneumatic or CO_2-powered rifle for that matter) is that it is easier to achieve a high level of accuracy because there is virtually no mechanical movement on firing and therefore the rifle has no recoil. Another bonus of the PCP rifle is that it can be rested on a bipod, fencepost or similar static object to steady your aim. Try that with a spring piston or a gas-ram and your shots could fly wide and inaccurately – PCPs are much more forgiving.

Pre-charged pneumatic air rifles are so called because you need to pre-charge (in other words 'fill') them with compressed air from an outside source – usually a larger compressed air storage vessel, such as a diver's air bottle or alternatively you can manually compress air into the rifle using an external pump. This reliance on an outside air source is what puts some shooters off PCP rifles, but it's far easier now to own and run a PCP than ever before. A small charging unit consisting of a compressed air bottle, pressure gauge and hose doesn't cost the earth, and will only need refilling depending on the amount of shooting you actually do. Divers' bottles come in various sizes, usually from 2 litres to 12 litres, which can be filled with compressed air (from a diving shop, gun shop, or industrial gas supplier) when needed.

For safety reasons, compressed air does require the shooter to adhere to a few basic rules:

- Always ensure that the connector and fill point are clean, dry and free from grit or dirt.
- Only use diver's quality compressed air, and never under any circumstances use anything else.
- Some older models of PCPs have 'fiddly' or poorly positioned fill points. Take note of this – avoid kinking or twisting the charging hose more than necessary.
- Where circumstances dictate, either have your rifle held stable in a rifle cradle, resting on a deployed bipod (if fitted) or laid down on a padded gunbag while filling.

Once satisfied the hose is correctly connected to the rifle open the valve slowly to allow the air to flow smoothly and at a uniform rate into the rifle's air reservoir. If you hear air escaping (a high pitched noise) or anything untoward, very quickly assess where the noise is coming from, stop the filling procedure immediately (close the supply valve), then tighten the leaking connection and then restart the filling process. Keep an eye on the pressure gauge and when the desired pressure is reached, immediately close the air supply valve on the bottle fully. Bleed the air out of the hose using the bleed screw or 'dump' valve, and then carefully remove the filling adaptor from the rifle. Where applicable, always refit the dust cover cap to the air rifle's filling point to keep the inlet valve protected from dirt and grime.

Note: An air rifle's user manual will clearly state a maximum fill pressure (sometimes also found on the rifle itself) but there's also a recommended fill pressure. You should never try to exceed the maximum fill pressure stated – it's potentially dangerous and will reduce power rather than increase it. The recommended fill pressure is often given as an optimum charge for a flatter power curve and also to give the maximum number of consistent full-power shots per fill.

It's worth noting that quite a few PCPs run that little bit sweeter on a slightly lower fill pressure than the one recommended by the manufacturer. You do get a slightly fewer shots, but usually you gain the benefit of better shot-to-shot consistency and a smoother, flatter power curve throughout the charge.

PCPs can generally be split into two categories – unregulated and regulated. This refers to the fact that some rifles use a knock-open valve to dispense air to the pellet on firing, whilst others have an internal air regulator. Simply put, the knock open valve literally 'knocks open' when the trigger is pulled, allowing a certain amount of air to pass through the transfer valve to act on the pellet, then closes. Alternatively, a PCP air rifle fitted with an air regulator, meters a measured amount of air to the pellet on firing. The regulated air rifle gives a very consistent level of performance and more shots per fill of air. Regulated rifles can be more costly to buy, and even so, some shooters argue that some unregulated rifles are so well developed and designed that their inherent accuracy potential is usually superior to the shooter's ability.

When it comes to the PCP as a hunting tool, in many cases it's capable of being fitted with a magazine so you don't need to load a pellet manually for each and every shot. There are many single-shot PCP air rifles on the market and some of these can be 'retro' fitted with magazine systems from the gun's manufacturer or specialist custom houses. With a multi-shot PCP the ease of the cocking and cycling operation means that at each 'throw of a bolt' another pellet can be ready to go, maximising the hunter's chances should the first shot miss. The cocking mechanism is usually a traditional rear or side-mounted ball ended cocking bolt or

Selection of magazine systems – virtually all multi-shot PCP air rifles use a removable rotary-feed magazine

an articulated cocking lever sited on the side of the rifle's action – but you may come across others, such as rifles that use an under-lever incorporated into the trigger guard (similar to a Western-style Winchester rifle).

Now to the disadvantages; obviously, the main one is the need for charging gear or access to a gun shop that provides a refill service. You also need to keep a check on the rifle so you don't run out of air while out shooting. Most quality PCP air rifles now have an on-board air pressure gauge. Whilst I personally feel these are quite handy, they should only be used as a guide. Before any hunting trip, top up the rifle to its required fill pressure so you're always running your rifle at its optimum level of performance.

Pneumania – Development and Acceptance of the PCP

Few would argue that it's largely due to Daystate Ltd that modern PCP rifles began to become popular again. Founded in 1978 by Don Lowndes, Jim Phillips, Ken Gibbon and Mike Seddon, Daystate first used a rifle with a pre-charged air reservoir to fire tranquilliser darts into animals for veterinary purposes. As the company's reputation grew they received various enquiries from pest control operatives looking for a more efficient tool for vermin control than was generally available at the time. It soon became obvious there was a market for producing a pre-charged air rifle that would fire the more traditional lead pellet projectile.

The Daystate Airwolf Tactical is one of the new breed of electronically operated PCP air rifles

This resulted in the company producing the original Daystate Huntsman, a landmark rifle which sowed the seeds for the PCP power source to become more widely accepted.

Daystate have now totally revolutionised the PCP market place with their ongoing R&D of PCP air rifles to the point where they not only produce some of the most highly desirable mechanically operated PCPs, but also fully electronically operated air rifles that use MAP Compensated Technology (MCT) and the Harper Patented electronic trigger as seen on the top level, hunter-designed AirWolf or their FT supergun.

Those terms previously mentioned aren't 'PR codswallop' but equate to how the rifle works using such hi-technology. In brief, MCT is the heart and soul of the rifle using a series of complex algorithms pre-programmed into the rifle's on-board software. The AirWolf's computerised MCT system precisely regulates its power output, eliminating the usual PCP 'power curve' discussed previously thus improving shot-to-shot consistency and returning an outstanding number of usable shots per fill. In fact, simply put, it's virtually 'driven' by an internal mini-computer that monitors every microsecond of its firing cycle making the Daystate AirWolf MCT the most technologically advanced sporting air rifle at the time of writing; and that's considering that the non-MCT version of the AirWolf, in my opinion (and of many others), is already technologically advanced enough for a hunter's needs, if not more so. When the first versions became available many hunters were sceptical (including me) that the rifles would withstand the elements of the hunting environs. However, they've more than proved they can 'hack it' in the field. Even though largely internally operated by electronic processors, capacitors and even electronic air regulators, such is the design and build quality of these PCPs that no matter what the weather, these systems still operate as they are manufactured to.

These rifles have turned the whole market place on its head due to how airgunners would now buy air rifles – a distinct change as many prefer the 'electronic' for their specific attributes (one being a totally 'dead' firing cycle). The DFC combines to afford unbelievable accuracy, and although these electronic rifles haven't taken over from the traditional PCPs, they're an option and one that definitely can't be ignored.

Their latest showpiece (at the time of writing) is the mechanically operated Daystate Wolverine 303 – yes we are talking a full bore airgun in .303" (7.62mm calibre) that puts out an FAC-rated 100ft lbs of power! Much more on this and many more powerful air rifles in the chapter devoted to FAC-rated air weapons. Throughout the 1980s and 1990s there were (and still are) quite a few independent UK designers that helped popularise the PCP power source, such as the ingenious John Bowkett, who introduced one of the first really affordable PCPs in the Titan Manitou. More recently John has created award-winning rifles for BSA, including their present flagship PCP; the R-10 Mk2.

Another legendary airgun expert was Gerald Cardew, who along with John Ford of the scope mount manufacturing company Sportsmatch, designed and produced what was to become the 'Rolls Royce' of airguns, the Sportsmatch GC2 – with its unique regulating system. To this day many believe that this air rifle took the humble airgun into a whole new era in construction, quality and accuracy. Even in the early 1980s the gun cost £1,000!

Nor can we dismiss the genius of Mick Dawes (sadly no longer with us), working in the West Midlands, who made the Brocock MDS. Although this is a rifle used purely for Field Target work, I mention it because it was Mick Dawes who, at the same time as a man named Barry McGraw (a nuclear physicist no less), was at the forefront of regulator design. For their work all manufacturers should be eternally grateful. Other names such as Joe Wilkins and his son Steve of Ripley Rifles fame, Ben Taylor and Dave Theobold of Theoben, Dave Welham of Airmasters 88, Steve Harper and Ken Turner... all had a hand in some very innovative designs, many of which are still being produced. I could go on naming names, but as this isn't a detailed in-depth look at the history of the PCP I'll leave the thread here, apart from saying that many of those mentioned above have also worked on and helped to develop top quality, spring-powered rifles too.

Rapid Fire

It was in 1990 that the Theoben Rapid 7 appeared – the first modern reliable and practical multi-shot air rifle. This 7-shot rotary magazine, bolt-action PCP rifle slowly but surely heralded the start of a trend that was to change the face of airgun hunting. Indeed for quite a while the Theoben Rapid 7 multi-shot was the undisputed champion for hunters looking for a quick back-up shot.

The 'Rapid' range of multi-shots may be named the '7' but some later models can now run a 7, 12, or 17-shot magazine depending on the individual rifle's calibre. The original Rapid 7 deserves great credit, for single-handedly establishing the popularity of multi-shot rifles for hunting. Since the mid-1990s, many other companies have turned their attention to creating their own magazine-fed rifles resulting in new repeating rifles not only becoming available but also affordable.

The Theoben Rapid 7 – this rifle single-handedly began the popularity of multi-shot PCP air rifles in hunting

Multiple Choice

All multi-shot rifles share a common factor – i.e. pellets are held in a magazine before the action cycles them into the barrel for individual firing. The benefits of a multi-shot are obvious. No need to place a pellet onto a loading channel or in a barrel for each and every shot, because another shot is ready in an instant at the throw of the bolt. If you miss, this means you can often get a second chance before the quarry does a bunk. Some quick back-up rifles are in fact 'double-shot' models, and therefore not strictly what can be classed as multi-shots, as they only have a two-shot capacity. The first production rifle of this type was the Webley Raider 2 and though not as popular as a true multi-shot, it did at the time fill a market need. Strangely enough, one of the very latest 'supergun' PCP's – the Milbro Metisse – uses an 'instant second shot' loading shuttle with just a two pellet capacity.

It's worth noting that although we're continuously reminded that hunting is a one-shot deal, and in part I'd tend to agree with that, in reality it is never that simple. In fact, I feel the majority of hunters who choose a PCP will choose a multi-shot option straight off. But how many shots do you want? Are two shots enough, or do you want as many back-up shots as you can get?

Whichever you choose, you'll immediately appreciate the benefits of that quick back-up shot, and many hunters agree they find it hard to go back to a one-shot rifle once they've experienced the ease of 'next shot' access – so you have been warned!

By far the most popular are the multi-shots of higher capacity. The rotary magazines in the majority of rifles are either spring loaded to rotate, or are indexed around mechanically by the action once the magazine has been inserted into the rifle's action block and shots are fired.

The Rotary Club

Whilst most multi-shot actions are either a bolt or lever system, what differs is the type of magazine feed employed. There are a few fixed magazines and even fewer removable straight-line or linear feed mechanisms, but by far the most popular systems use a removable rotary-feed magazine. This can either be the classic 8-shot drum magazine as first seen in FX rifles, or the 14-shot 'big wheel' as used by the now very highly regarded Weihrauch HW100 – these are just two examples.

However, as this design of magazine is open to the elements, some manufacturers prefer the enclosed types, though the drum or wheel types are easier to clean and load (at night).

Enclosed Perspex-fronted designs are used by Theoben and Air Arms multi-shots, and FX Rifles now use a version, as does the 10-shot BSA R-10 Mk2. There's also the very efficient and of course much developed Daystate multi-shot magazine.

Some very well-established manufacturers have models in their range that use the 'open' Axelsson 8-shot magazine. It's quite a simple design, being little more than a removable circular drum-shaped magazine that is loaded with pellets and clicked into the action, where it is held in place by a retaining pin. To load for a shot you simply cycle the action with a side- or rear-mounted cocking bolt for each shot until the magazine is empty, then remove the magazine, refill it or exchange it for a spare, pre-filled one, and you're good to go for another eight shots. It is a beautifully simple unit, and pretty well foolproof so long as it's kept clean and free from obstructions or fouling.

PCPs for All!

The inherent advantages of a recoilless, consistent and accurate system were primarily recognised by Field Target competition shooters, whilst multi-shot options and lightweight carbines have latterly made PCP air rifles more popular with hunters. The main disadvantage of PCPs – the fact that they had a fixed air reservoir which had to be charged up fairly frequently from a compressed air power source, usually a diver's bottle – has more or less been overcome. Rifles fitted with regulators (air meters) can easily give a full day's shooting – from 100 to 200 shots – on just one charge of air, while hunting rifles have benefited from the introduction of small to large, removable/replaceable or fixed 'on-the-gun' buddy-bottle air reservoirs, some of which can quickly be replaced in the field for a full one, with the empty one to be refilled later.

The availability of manually-operated external pumps, capable of charging rifles without the need for a diving bottle, has also helped popularise PCPs in a few areas that had limited commercial compressed air sources. Take note; an external pump can be hard work to use, and not all PCPs can be charged with them, so check before you buy one.

What of the Future?

FX Sweden show some very clever changes to the Verminator MkII 'take-down' PCP air rifle and talk of new larger calibres for various rifles they currently produce. As I write, the company have just launched The FAC-power-rated FX Boss. With a multi-shot action based on the FX Royale chassis this joins the elite of the FAC-power-rated offerings. Target cards showing sub ½" c-to-c groups have been witnessed at 100yds making this for real-time hunting what is often now termed 'a true 1½" group gun at 100yds'.

If that wasn't impressive enough, the much talked about Daystate Wolverine .303 represents yet another change in design and illustrates the now unique calibres available in FAC-rated air rifles. Much more on these multi-shot monsters and other hi-power superguns in the chapter on FAC, but I must add, these new 'exotic' calibres obviously need new ammo and very well designed and manufactured at that. Most gun companies have been working with pellet supremos JSB. Brace yourself for the ammo already manufactured for these rifles. The Wolverine uses a 50.15gr pellet, while the FX .30 calibre Boss uses a 'slug' tipping the scales at pretty much the same. FX have even designed a .35 calibre pellet and as you'll read later, hunting with FAC-power air rifles has now become one of the most talked of and very exciting branches of our sport in modern times.

Manual Pumped Pneumatics

We couldn't talk about PCPs without mentioning another type of pneumatic – the manually pumped pneumatic with its own compression lever. This includes the Holy Grail for some airgun enthusiasts; the single-stroke pneumatic. This is a pneumatic rifle that doesn't need a diving bottle or any other charging device, except the shooter himself, and can generate enough power for a single shot with one stroke of the integral pump handle on the rifle. John Bowkett invented a few such rifles including the Titan Mohawk and the JB1, production rifles that used a side-lever to pump in enough compressed air manually to produce around 10-11ft lbs of power in a single stroke. Other airgun pioneers also made working 'single-stroke pneumatics' including Richard Spenser designer of the side-lever Air Logic Genesis, a rifle capable of nearly 12ft lbs. Similarly, Graham Bluck invented the Dragon rifle, a single-stroke side-lever, which was marketed by Parker Hale. The common denominator among all these rifles is that although hailed in their time, for various reasons they are not around now, which suggests that at least commercially they were not successful. It should be noted that there have also been multi-stroke, manually-pumped pneumatics. These have been with us a long time, the most famous being the American brands of Crosman and Sheridan, and the Japanese, Sharp Innova – and now the new Webley Rebel. This type of pneumatic is relatively inexpensive and they work, but they take a lot of time to load and are tiresome to pump up to working pressure (sometimes up to 8 pump strokes for 12ft lbs). However, we now have the FX Independence, a hybrid PCP with both an air filling valve and a built-in manual pump. This Swedish manufactured multi-shot can be filled up from a diver's bottle then manually topped up in the field by the shooter using the side-lever. So to keep running on full, it's approximately 4-5 pumps per shot.

Take it Down

We now come to what are for obvious reasons known as 'take-down' PCP rifles. The original production take down was the Colchester Gamekeeper launched over 20-yrs ago and now highly sought after by collectors of airgun memorabilia. Most new models are based on already successful PCP rifles that their makers offer in full stock option. One of the most popular is the Air Arms S410 TDR (Take Down Rifle.)

Modern day TDRs usually break-down into the main butt section of stock, mainframe (action) and silencer. Read my full views on these unique and interesting rifles in Chapter 3.

The Digital Age – and Tactical Too!

From here on in, 'digital' is often the keyword to a lot of developments, be they rifles, scopes and even accessories, such as lamping kit. Furthermore, the use of digital technology takes us into a whole new realm when we come to Digital Nightvision Equipment - its operation will be explained as we come to that section. Another new term is 'tactical', obviously taken from the military, at first seen in reference to rifle models with black or camo synthetic stocks, it has now spread throughout many airgun hunting products – tactical scopes, tactical weapons cases, tactical bi-pods – the list does seem endless. With rifles, at first, it was due to the design, not always military. For instance, with the BSA Lightning XL Tactical it was the very well-designed ABS stock that this springer sits in that earned it the rather misleading title.

I must also mention Military Specification (mil-spec), for example 'made from mil-spec aircraft grade aluminium' – a term you see used for certain scopes and silencer bodies. In this case it means the grade and/or tolerances used in manufacture meet with MOD standards. This suggests high-quality components and a good level of construction. Often it does perform more effectively in the field but – to help us shoot better? That's definitely up to the individual.

Budget Priced PCPs

I'm sure many airgunners never envisaged a time when we could class any PCP as a budget rifle. Well, that's certainly not the case now. Granted, they'll always be the more expensive option, but in terms of value for money, most single-shot PCPs offer an incredible amount of performance for your investment. Some single-shot rifles can even be upgraded to multi-shot at a later date using a 'retrofit' multi-shot kit from the manufacturer or a customising house. One of the best is the Air Arms '10-shot (MS) kit' manufactured for their S200 PCP rifle. This self-indexing, add-on unit works the same as a multi-shot rifle. You'd think that there would be little point to this, but it has come about due to the popularity of HFT competition. When the competitors change firing positions, they must do so with a clear breech – much easier with a single shot.

Hardened HFT competitors use a single-shot rifle, but they also like to hunt, this gives them the option to stay with one gun for both shooting disciplines. Many multi-shot rifles (such as Daystates) now have an optional 'single-shot' clip that can be used to replace the magazine, so optimising the rifle for both hunting and HFT.

While talking budgets, when buying a PCP you not only have to budget for charging equipment – as mentioned previously - but also a scope and mounts, as very few production PCPs have open sights fitted. Unfortunately there's no avoiding this, and its here that the price mounts up – no pun intended.

So there we have it; the power sources, the actions, the magazines and the multi-shot options available. Many other new ideas and developments will I'm sure come along, and we'll be just as impressed again.

Even today, ultimately, what to choose in 12ft lb format is largely an individual matter, but there's no denying that a multi-shot gives you many benefits and the ability to capitalise on hunting opportunities like never before. But just because you have those extra shots in hand at the throw of a bolt, or side-lever remember that's never an excuse for letting standards slip, resulting in sloppy or bad shooting practice. Each shot fired should always be taken with steady care and a good aim.

Sighting Systems

Scopes, Scope Mounts, Scope Mounting and Alternative Hunting Sights

The vast majority of airgun hunters use telescopic sights – or 'scopes' as they're commonly known – for virtually all hunting applications. So it follows that almost all newcomers to the sport will opt to fit a set of optics to their very first air rifle. In fact, many air rifles, especially PCPs, have no 'iron sights' fitted as standard, so in these cases fitting a scope is a necessity.

Within this chapter you should find all the information you will need to choose a scope that best suits your needs as a hunter, but remember, like any consumer market, choosing a scope can be like stepping into a minefield. With such a huge selection available, and every company claiming their products to be better than their competitors', the decision is bound to be difficult. Even the experienced airgunner could well do with taking a little more time in choosing a new scope, and not just falling for the marketing strategies employed by all manufacturers. Scope mounts must also be considered, but this will be dealt with after we've waded through the quagmire of scope choice. First, however, a word or two about open sights.

Any Old Iron?

Open sights, or 'irons' as they're affectionately known, have been the standard and most basic form of sighting system on any gun for as long as they have been made. The basic idea is to align the target with your eye via a sight element towards the rear of the rifle and another near the end of the barrel. This should line up the bore of the rifle with the target, ensuring that you are sighting as close to the path of the fired projectile as possible – always assuming that the sights are set up correctly in the first place.

The benefits of open sights include quick target acquisition, because you have a very wide field of view, unlike a telescopic sight that tunnels a more limited, narrowly angled field of view onto the target. Also, because irons do not magnify the target, rangefinding isn't confuse' by image-enlarging optics.

See-thru mounts offer the shooter the best of both worlds

There are still many models of air rifle – all spring powered – that are fitted with open sights. These either consist of a post, bead or blade foresight positioned at the front end of the barrel, which is lined up in a U- or V-shaped notch, or a target-style aperture (hole) in the rear sight assembly (the rear sight unit is usually fitted onto the breech end of the barrel, or on the action body itself).

The rear sight will always be adjustable for height (elevation) and usually for windage too (i.e. from side to side), so they can be set for the range (zero distance) you require. Elevation and windage adjustments are catered for either by a set of thumbwheels – often numbered – or the adjusters can simply be a screw and plate.

Setting Your Zero

A matter that needs tackling before we go any further is one that relates to all sighting set-ups and systems, and that is the setting of 'zero' or 'zeroing'. Zero is the term used to refer to a pre-set point (or distance) to which the sights have been adjusted so the pellet strikes the target to coincide with the centre of the scope's crosshairs – or, in relation to an open sight set-up, the point where eye, sights and 'strike point' on the target all line up. On a 'red dot sight or the projected 'dot' of a laser sight, zero can also be adjusted.

With open sights, a maximum zero and hunting range of 15yds is more often than not the accepted and recommended norm. This can be extended to 18-20yds if the open sights are good enough and your 'iron-clad' shooting is of a high enough standard. Because this sighting system is so forgiving at close to medium ranges (because

pellet trajectory is flattest for the first 20yds or so), you can set your sights at a zero of 12yds and then, providing you do not exceed a range of 20yds, you can literally aim 'bang-on' for all ranges in between – except perhaps for the very tiniest of quarry targets.

Setting your zero with open sights is simple. Line the foreblade into the centre of the notch of the rear sight, place it over the target and have the top of the foresight element (blade, post or bead) level with the top of the rear sight. The object of accurate target shooting is to produce what is known as good groupings. A group or string of shots – usually five – is fired into a paper target and the grouping is determined by the distance measured on the target between the impact points of the most widely separated pellets in the pattern made by the shot string. For example; if this measured distance is 1½ inches between the two furthest pellets, then you have a 1½-inch group. These measurements are often taken from the outer edge of the pellet holes, because they are easier to measure, and are therefore called 'edge-to-edge' measurements; but for competition purposes they should really be taken from the

Open sights are very useful for close range rat and feral pigeon shooting

centre of the pellet hole (often termed 'centre-to-centre' or 'c-to-c'). For hunting purposes it doesn't much matter how you take the measurements, as long as you always stick to the same method – edge-to-edge or c-to-c, and, of course, be consistent in getting good, tight groups.

To find out the maximum distance at which you can hunt humanely, try shooting at paper targets set out at 5-yard intervals. The furthest target on which you can comfortably put a 5-shot group of approximately 1 inch should be your maximum hunting distance – and that applies to all sighting systems. Don't worry about measuring groups, but just draw a series of circles using a 2p piece as a template and aiming point. If your five pellets are within the 2p circle, you're on target.

Incidentally, the main problem you'll encounter with open sights for air rifle hunting is that the sights may actually obscure the target at longer ranges. This is the reason why open-sight shooting should only be seriously considered for close-range work. Whilst this makes open sights ideal for indoor shooting at rats and roosting feral pigeons, this range limitation immediately makes it apparent why a scope is such a necessary addition for the airgun hunter wanting to get the most from his rifle as regards maximum range – which nicely brings us to the subject of scopes.

Choosing a Hunting Scope

Scopes come in all shapes and sizes – small, big, thin, fat, short, long – and that's before you add on the various different features that are offered. But considering there aren't an excessive number of individual component parts used in the construction of a scope, it's still a relatively complex piece of optical equipment.

The Anatomy of a Scope

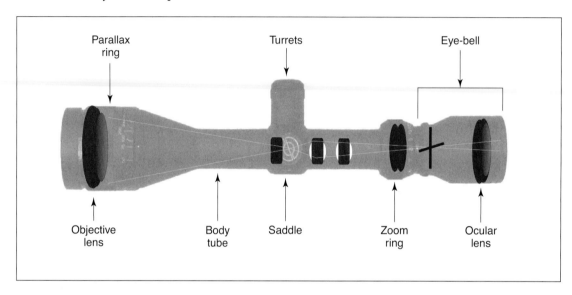

The main external features of a scope are the eye-bell (or ocular lens housing), the zoom magnification ring (if fitted), the main body or tube, the central 'saddle' or turret adjuster housing, the elevation and windage adjuster knobs, the parallax-adjusting ring (if fitted), the objective (frontal) lens bell, and, of course, the lenses and their coatings. It is logical that lens quality is of great importance, as lenses are responsible for gathering light and transmitting the sight image to your eye. Modern scope optics are coated for protection against the elements, and the scratches that can be caused by grit and dirt. They're often also specially treated with other coatings to achieve better light-gathering, more clarity, and a generally improved optical performance.

General Guidelines For All Scopes

Even relatively inexpensive scopes can be packed with eye-catching features, but the most important factors for any optic are lens quality and coatings. Good-quality lenses and coatings will not give a distorted image, will maintain edge-to-edge clarity, and will be less affected by flare (bright spots). They will also last a lot longer. A quality scope can last a lifetime, while poorer offerings can often be rendered useless in a relatively short period of time. Good glass is expensive, and with scopes you normally get what you pay for.

Apart from lens quality, other important things to look for are smooth operation of rings if fitted (front focusing or parallax ring, and rear focusing and zoom or variable magnification rings), and a positive 'click-stop' movement for each increment of adjustment on the elevation and windage turrets. This is so they only shift the reticle an equal and measured distance for each click of the adjuster turret. They also need to hold zero, so they must not move once set.

Overall build quality is also important, especially when fitting to a spring/piston air rifle. The distinctive three-way recoil of a springer has been known to wreck poorly-constructed scopes. The internal mechanisms of today's quality-brand scopes are built to withstand a lot of use. If your scope sits on a recoilless PCP then it won't be subjected to the recoil that can be delivered to it by a spring- or gas-ram-powered air rifle.

When choosing a scope, have a clear idea of your own intended uses; check these particular points:

- How often will you be shooting? A hard-used scope will need to be well made and robust.
- Will you be shooting in many different locations at varying distances? If so, you may be better off with an adjustable magnification (zoom) scope.
- Do you do most of your shooting at a fixed range? If so, you may prefer a fixed magnification scope.
- Will your scope be mounted to an expensive pre-charged pneumatic or a springer at the cheaper end of the market? Obviously your scope should be priced to suit.
- Do you intend to do a lot of low-light shooting? You'll need a scope with good light-gathering capabilities, usually with a large objective lens.

All of these questions, and others, will influence your choice, but once you've made up your mind which features you need, buy the best scope and mounts you can afford.

It's worth mentioning that one feature of a scope that many people overlook is its 'closest focus' distance. As the scope is being used on an air rifle, and quarry can often be as close as 12yds or less, you need a scope that will focus down to that distance. Many scopes don't, but with the popularity of airgun shooting, and in particular of airgun hunting, on the increase, most quality scopes for airgun use will focus down to sight-in on targets at fairly close range. If you intend to hunt regularly there are two variables you should consider – light conditions and the furthest range limit at which you expect to engage quarry.

The most popular scope specification for all-round hunting is the 3 – 9 x 40. Scope specifications are always written like this. The first two numbers relate to the range of magnifications the scope is capable of, and in this case it means the scope is a variable power scope from a low of 3 times magnification up to a maximum of 9 times magnification of the object you will be looking at. The last figure relates to the diameter (in millimetres) of the front (objective) lens. The importance of the size of the front lens will be dealt with later when we come to low-light or, as they're sometimes known, dawn-dusk scopes. As a general rule of thumb, the larger the front (objective) lens the more efficient at gathering light it will be. Therefore, large objective lens scopes are the best choice for low-light conditions. It's worth noting here that the airgun hunter also has the choice of a fixed-magnification scope. At one time the little fixed-magnification 4 x 32 reigned supreme (even for FT) and was very popular. Look around and you'll still find these little scopes for sale, and if a basic model such as this appeals, then – although it's a no-frills optic – it will suffice for a good deal of hunting work. In fact, there are some fine 6 x and 10 x fixed magnification scopes around, but by and large they're manufactured for use on bullet-firing sporting rifles. There are a few that suit air rifles, and some of the finest fixed-magnification scopes also have large 30mm diameter body tubes (one-inch tubes are the norm) and side-wheel parallax adjustment – both very tempting for the newcomer, who might like the looks and macho appeal of these types of sights.

But before we get into more specialised areas of the market let's take a look at what the general airgun hunter will require. These are: a good sight picture; reasonable and practical magnification range; and a suitably-sized objective lens to give a good balance between field of view and light gathering. A fairly wide field of view (or width of view) is vital for target 'acquisition', which simply means the ability to find the target quickly in the area you are looking at through the scope. I know this may seem just plain common sense, but using a scope with a relatively

There's a very varied selection of scope mounts to suit all rifles and fitting configurations

narrow field of view, and trying to find the quarry in your sights, can quickly become a nightmare costing you time and missed shooting opportunities. A field of view 'angle' or measurement is often given in the scope's 'Tech Spec' sheet or on the box it was supplied in. If given as an angle, the higher the number means the wider the field of view. If given as a figure – say 30ft – this means the distance that can be seen from one side of the scope's image to the other at a range of 100yds. With variable magnification or 'zoom' scopes there will be two figures, corresponding to the fields of view at the lowest and highest magnification (for example, 30ft and 12ft). The higher the magnification of the scope, the narrower the field of view will be.

Build construction is another major feature you need to consider when buying a hunting scope. For most, if not all, of its active working life it will be exposed to the elements and even on dry days it's surprising just how much the weather can throw at your equipment. Dampness, early-morning dew and humid conditions can cause condensation build-up when shooting from dawn into daylight, or in the evening chill. You'll notice the times when you need to wipe both lenses due to early-morning dew, or the rear lens catching the moisture from your breathing. It's handy to carry a lint-free cloth or, better still, a few pads of soft tissue for cleaning the lenses.

Scopes are sealed from the elements, and you'll often see that they are termed 'nitrogen purged' to expel all moisture and air before the internals are nitrogen-filled and sealed. The main areas where water or air could leak into the scope are around the front and rear lenses, any moveable adjustment rings such as zoom and parallax rings, and of course, the turret adjusters. The first barrier to the elements for the turrets is the turret cover caps or dust covers. Not only are they there to prevent turret adjusters being accidentally knocked and therefore your zero being lost, but also, and just as importantly, they offer a first line of defence against the elements. Their main duty is to offer resistance to dirt and grime, so always screw them snugly into place once you've set your chosen zero.

Personally, I wouldn't consider using a scope for hunting that didn't have turret cover caps. Certain models on the market that don't have cover caps use the so-called 'quick access' excuse, as if this was a bonus. Granted, there are some fine optics with side-wheel parallax adjustment that could well be used by a hunter who really knows his scope, but the possibility of a dial being inadvertently shifted is too great a risk to take when you're dealing in fractions of an inch, which means the difference between a cleanly dispatched animal and an injured one. Target shooters can use these scopes, and certainly use them well, but once you've set your zero on your hunting scope you don't want to have anything that can in the slightest way affect this, or accidentally alter the precisely-set pellet impact point – i.e. the zero. Uncovered adjusters that can be rotated by hand, no matter how positive and secure they seem, will eventually get moved – either by being caught or by brushing against clothing as you move, or even when the rifle is being put into and taken out of a gun bag. So be warned against the possible disadvantages of using this type of scope for hunting. The good news is that specialist scopes with side-wheel adjustment and cover caps can be obtained, and they are worth looking out for when your shooting reaches a standard where you'd benefit from such a sophisticated optic.

As for the turrets themselves, those on scopes of good quality will undoubtedly have sealing 'O' rings that prevent moisture leaking into the scope past the threads of the turret caps and the adjusters. With scope build structure, a feature I particularly favour is for the optics to have a 'monocoque build', whereby the body, including the turret saddle, is made out of one piece of material, preferably aircraft-grade aluminium alloy. Having no joins around the turret saddle means one less area to worry about for potential leakage. In any scope's specification list, look for classifications such as fogproof, waterproof and shockproof. These important three qualities, if mentioned in a scope's technical marketing blurb, mean that you're heading in the right direction in relation to build characteristics. I'm often asked if a 30mm body tube is better than the standard, more common 1 inch. Basically, it doesn't have any bearing on practical performance that should concern the airgun hunter. Thicker body tubes are likely to be stronger but this is usually due to the fact that they are intended to sit mounted on powerful centrefire sporting and target rifles.

With regard to visual inspection and careful reading of the information slip or pamphlet that may come with the scope, that's about all you can achieve. Any reasonable gunshop owner will, to a certain extent, allow you to handle the goods, and you really should look through the lenses yourself. Even though you can't fit the scope to a rifle, there are still a few basic features to check hands-on without appearing to be overly fussy or fiddly.

First try the magnification zoom ring. It should glide easily up from low to full magnification and back again. Then, if present, check the front parallax adjustment (PA), or adjustable objective (AO) ring, which are the same thing. However, now on many modern scopes there can be a side-focus (SF) dial. This won't be fitted to all scopes, but if it's present try it for operation. You'll probably find this quite stiff to turn, but once the scope is on a rifle they usually operate far more easily and smoothly. Those who say they work loose with use aren't talking sense, because they don't, and you certainly don't want things to work loose. What you might notice is that a parallax ring may stiffen up as you move it to the end of its travel towards the higher settings, which will be the longer-range marks. This is quite common so don't worry yourself unduly over it, as it'll be fine if it runs smoothly from low up to the 50- and 55-yard marks.

Now we come to the features of most contention, the turret adjusters. Whether these are finger-adjustable, target-style or 'coin-slot' operated, give them a good work-through. Listen and feel for the adjusters as they click around to the next setting. Feel for any slack or stiff spots, and give a scope a wide berth if you feel the turrets miss a click to the next station on rotation. Don't go dialling around wildly, but count the clicks left and back again, as the scope is probably already centralised, and if you buy the scope, you don't want to start off with a unit that is too far off-centre. Similarly, if you don't choose to buy, leave it as you found it for the next potential customer. In passing, I'll mention something almost all hunters I've come across don't check before fitting a scope, but FT shooters take for granted as part of their scope fitting procedure. This is what is termed as setting or checking the scope's 'optical zero'.

For the general specification of a hunting scope, I'd have no hesitation in saying that the 3–9 x 40 is the best option for most situations, and a good-quality optic with this specification will serve you well for many years. Buy a good-quality scope and it will be more than capable of handling most hunting scenarios you'll encounter. But what if you want that little bit extra?

Features, Features, Features

Before we look at the main attributes that you should consider on a scope, think about this – are you choosing a scope with lots of extra, dubiously-useful features, rather than the basic specifications you really need? I've met many people who have. They've read the advertisements, and they've been convinced that their shooting won't be as productive if they don't buy an all-singing, all-dancing mega-scope. The trouble is that such a scope usually has so many features that they'll probably only use a fraction of what the scope is actually capable of and designed to do. Following are the main features that you'll see mentioned in a scope specification, and one by one I'll explain in simple terms what they refer to.

Reticle Types

Reticle or reticule is the term for the two centrally-crossed lines (or other pattern of lines, sometimes called 'stadia', or even 'graticule') that are used for aiming – the most common simply being called a 'crosshair'. All of the terms used are recognised words for crosshairs; I prefer to use the term 'reticle'.

There are many different types of reticle, and their design and methods of use could take up a whole chapter, but on the whole, most airgun hunters are happy enough with standard crosshairs, usually in a 30/30 'thick-'n-thin post'-style format (sometimes called a 'duplex'). This is more than capable of fulfilling all the criteria needed of it from the general airgun hunter's perspective. However, certain other reticle types are worth considering. These include; crosshairs that have a central diamond, bracketed shape, scopes with illuminated reticles, and the latest favourite, the much misunderstood mil-dot reticle. All have certain attributes that different shooters may or may not feel will help them shoot better. However, in keeping with my view on specifications, I feel many are swayed towards the very latest 'must have' feature. Remember, shooters of all disciplines have hunted successfully with both open sights and standard 30/30 thick-'n-thin crosshair scopes for a great many years; FT shooters have used scopes with specialist reticles for many a moon.

Other specialist scopes with 'ladder' or 'grid' reticle types, mil-dots and even a diamond-shaped reticle have been introduced for the benefits they give a shooter for long-range shots. Most of these are only of real use for rimfire or centrefire cartridge rifles, and the mil-dot system isn't of any major use for an airgun hunter shooting out to 40yds with a 12ft lbs air rifle. However, for the specialised 'long-ranger' who has really done his homework, then the extra aim-points that ladder, mil-dot or diamond reticles offer may be beneficial. I use a scope with either a ladder reticle or mil-dot for my FAC-power-rated hunting air rifles,

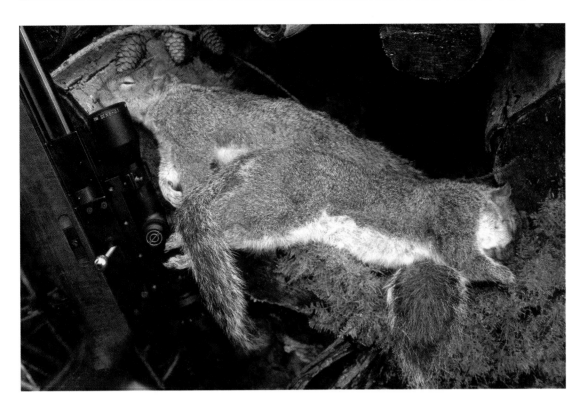

A compact wide-angle scope is the optimum choice for quick target acquisition – ideal for squirrel shooting

but only because I sometimes push these rifles to the limits of effective killing ranges. You'll find more on this in the section on FAC-specification rifles.

Scopes fitted with illuminated reticles have their admirers, and are mainly of use in low-light situations where you might lose thin crosshairs in your sight picture against a dark background. They also have a place when shooting at night with an artificial light source (or lamping, as it's known). My advice, should you choose such an optic, is to ensure that the reticle brightness control (rheostat) gives good variation from low intensity to bright without overly thickening or blurring the crosshairs on the higher (i.e. brightest) settings. While on the subject of low-light shooting, some prefer the vertical post and horizontal crosshair design or, as it is sometimes known, the 'German Post' reticle. Now to the mil-dot or multi-dot scope. You could write another whole chapter on this type of scope reticle alone, but I'll concentrate solely on the benefits it specifically affords the airgun hunter. 'Mil' in the term mil-dot doesn't derive from its military usage but is in fact an abbreviation of the word milradian. Without getting too complicated, it is the term the military gave to the system they devised to make an accurate way of measuring angles and therefore distances in optical instruments. When used correctly, this reticle can establish the milradian angle from the top to the bottom of an object (quarry or target) of a known size. This then allows the distance to the object to be calculated using that pre-determined size. The correct dot in the reticle grid can then be used as an aiming point to sight onto the target.

Two of the Most Popular Reticles for a Hunting Scope

I'm not going to get into the physics and logistics of all this 'dottiness', as an in-depth article on mil-dot systems could quite frankly send you dotty! But these systems are very accurate when used with firearms that have very long-range shooting capabilities. For airgun use, however, the mil-dot is pretty much used as a standard crosshair but with a far greater range of aiming points. So if

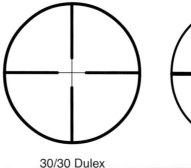

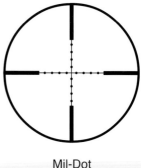

30/30 Dulex   Mil-Dot

you feel this reticle will be of use to you, then it's an option that's available. Granted, you get multi-aim-points for different ranges and side dots for wind allowance, but they're only of use if you've done your homework very carefully on the target range to familiarise yourself with the trajectory of the pellet's flight. Once you can correspond specific distances with each dot on the vertical post, you'll effectively have a zero point for a whole range of distances.

A final factor to consider when choosing a reticle is how it appears to your eye in different lighting conditions. By far the most versatile is the reticle that appears black against a light background, but a reflective gold colour against a dark background. This small feature can be found on some relatively low-priced scopes, yet may be absent on several more expensive models (especially high-magnification target models). Nevertheless, this one feature can make all the difference when it comes to being able to place a crosshair on the target, or, if targeting on a dark background, not being able to see the crosshair at all.)

Because of their lower power, air rifles tend to have a far more pronounced trajectory than cartridge rifles. Since the first edition of Total Airguns was published, certain optical manufacturers have worked on bringing us scopes with specialised reticle designs – similar to the mil-dot concept – to help cope with the steep trajectory of airgun pellets. The designs of these specialised reticules offer more aim points (often referred to as 'hash-lines' or 'dots') on the vertical line of the crosshair. This allows the shooter easy hold over, or hold under, reference points for targets that are further or closer than the scope's set zero distance. There are often other markings on the horizontal line(s) of the reticle that can be used as alternative aim-points to allow for the effect of crosswind.

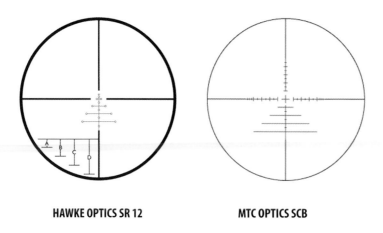

HAWKE OPTICS SR 12   **MTC OPTICS SCB**

Two Popular Designs of Multi-Aim-Point Reticles

The trend for these new reticle designs began back in the mid-80s when Hawke Sport Optics (with the help of four-time former World FT Champion, Nick Jenkinson) designed the MAP 6, SR 6 and SR 12 reticles. These were soon joined by equally useful reticles from the MTC Sports Optics range designed by HFT shooter and MTC co-owner Gary Cooper, such as the Small Calibre Ballistic (SCB), which continues to this day. The two optical companies mentioned are by far the two most proactive when it comes to the development and refinement of these designs for air rifle (and .22 rimfire) use.

It's not surprising that these types of reticles and the scopes they are installed in are already very popular amongst airgun hunters and the HFT fraternity.

The Soft Option

Due to the popularity of multi-aim-point scopes and to complement their own specialised reticle designs, Hawke Sports Optics have made 'rigging up your rig' all the easier. The reason I say this is that you can now use two free downloadable software programmes to help plot the trajectory, and work out the ranges that various aim-points correspond to for a particular hunting set-up. These can be downloaded from the company's website (www.hawkeoptics.com). Then, on your computer, you can punch in your chosen zero range, pellet weight and muzzle velocity in feet per second (fps) using that particular ammo and ... hey presto ... you can soon be printing off trajectory graphs and get all the downrange information concerning pellet drop etc. Obviously, the programmes can be used in conjunction with all the reticles Hawke offer, but the programme is also of use for any airgun hunter who wants to get a solid guide as to what to expect from a particular combo. This data can then be used in the field to fine-tune your references to suit your particular hunting combo as you range test against inanimate targets set at known ranges. There has quite possibly never been a decade that has seen so much advancement in our sport.

Magnification and Range Estimation

A major factor you should consider when buying a scope is how much you want to magnify the target. That may sound strange as a telescopic sight is, as the name suggests, capable of making a target look bigger. However, the downside is that the higher the magnification setting, the more it will appear to exaggerate the dreaded 'wobble' we can all experience when shooting from an unsupported position. A good point about high magnification is that it can be used in conjunction with the scope's parallax adjustment (or forward-placed focusing ring) to determine range. Not all scopes have a parallax adjustment facility, but those that do usually have the adjustment ring at the front of the scope, around the objective lens hood. On certain other scopes the PA may be positioned as a focusing wheel set on the opposite side of the windage turret. Whatever the design, this ring, or collar, is marked for distance, and with the magnification turned up fully, it is possible to adjust it until the target becomes pin-sharp. You then read the range off the PA focusing wheel – simple! Sometimes the distance you are actually focusing at is slightly different to that indicated on the side of the parallax ring, but you can easily put masking tape around the parallax ring and then mark each distance from 10yds to 60yds in 5-yard increments to suit your particular vision.

I'm sorry to blow away a popular misconception. A, but all this is fine in theory and, to the experienced, trained FT shooter's eye, it's the tool for the job, but how many times in a practical hunting situation is old 'big-ears' going to hang around while you fiddle around with the focus ring, then look over the top to read the distance on a dial, and then make even more movements if you decide to dial in the range from the

Bullet Drop Compensation (BDC) facility on the elevation turret? You may get away with it from a totally hidden ambush shooting position, but if not, you'll have to use some other method of range estimation.

This brings us to bracketing, a more useful method of calculating the range quickly for the hunter. As the name suggests, this is where the reticle is used to bracket the target and therefore calculate the range in relation to the size of quarry. Military snipers have long used this term, but they have their own way of using it. Basically, they estimate the closest and furthest a target could be; the difference between the two is known as the 'bracket' and they then use the average of that as an estimation of the range. To airgun shooters, both FT and hunter, the term 'bracketing' applies to using fixed marks on the scope's reticle in relation to the size of the quarry or target, in order to estimate distance to it, but this can have major drawbacks for hunters. FT shooters know that they are bracketing on a standardised 40mm circular hit-zone on a static target, so they can be fairly confident of consistent results, yet even they rarely use the method anymore because it is not precise enough for their needs, but it does work well in conjunction with the focus method, just to confirm a parallaxed range estimate.

Unfortunately, live quarry doesn't come in standard sizes, and they also move – both factors that make it far more difficult for the hunter to bracket a range accurately. Also, in the case of rabbits, although it's fairly easy to establish that you're looking at a young rabbit due to the size of its ears in relation to its head, it can be very difficult to assess if a rabbit is three-quarters or fully grown. All bracketing methods should be treated as guidelines only, and not set in stone; so once you've worked out the distances these targets appear to be, it's still only an approximation.

Obviously, different reticle types offer various bracketing capabilities. What suits one shooter won't necessarily suit the next, but many find the standard 30/30 or duplex crosshair more than useful. It's worth noting here that the reticle got the 30/30 designation as this scope, when set on 4 x magnification, is designed to measure 30 inches from point to point of the thick, outer posts at 100yds, which is the approximate chest depth of an average North American deer. This predetermined size can be scaled down on more appropriate airgun quarry, and then used quite effectively for rangefinding by the shooter who's done his homework on the target range. On this style of reticle you also have three set aim points on the vertical line for range – the central cross and the two points where the thin hair meets the thick posts at the top and bottom. You can even add the midway point between dead centre and thick post of the upper and lower horizontal as a floating, semi-fixed aim point. Using the crosshair I like to set my scope zero, then find the optimum magnification where the tip of the bottom thick post gives an aim point to hit the target cleanly at 60yds. This gives a very good reference for adjusting and 'guesstimating' holdover above my original initial zero for longer-range shots. If using the scope in this manner, always remember to change up to or stay on that set magnification, otherwise it can become confusing due to variables. In fact, only dedicated practice and field hunting experience will eventually give you the required rangefinding skills.

To recap on scope choice, here are a few key guidelines on optics, giving general specifications and the hunting techniques and situations they're best suited to.

Scope – Minimum 1.5 x or 2 x up to 5, or 6 x magnification with minimum 20mm or 32mm objective lens.
These scopes are ideal for carbine-sized rifles due to their compact dimensions. They're also the ideal choice for close-range shooting and when the target needs to be found quickly in your sights. The latter is allowed for due to the low magnification giving a wider field of view. The drawbacks of low-magnification, small-

objective lens scopes are limited range for precise pellet placement, and lower light-gathering capabilities. However, some models of these scopes are worth a look for hunting at mainly close to medium range, no matter what the light conditions. They're ideal for close-range rat and feral pigeon shooting, indoor work, and certain night-shooting applications with a lamp.

Scope – Minimum of 3 x or 4 x up to 9, 10, or 12 x magnification with minimum 40mm objective lens.
Here, we fall firmly into the 'general purpose' category and these scopes suit both carbine and full-length rifles. As I've said before, there's not much a 3 – 9 x 40 scope can't cope with. It can be mounted in medium-height mounts, and mounting shouldn't be a problem on any air rifle. They'll suit the hunter looking to try his hand at anything and everything, from stalking to roost shooting. They give a good compromise of reasonable magnification range, reasonable field of view on the lowest magnification setting, and have very acceptable light-gathering properties.

Scope – Minimum 3 x or 4 x variable up to 12 x, 16 x or 24 x magnification with minimum 40mm objective lens with parallax adjustment.
The higher magnification range means longer-range work is feasible, and the PA – if used with a high magnification facility – can be useful for estimating range. Still of use for general hunting, you may find these scopes are generally longer in the body, and mounting therefore has to be suitably catered for. These are scopes for the hunter who wants to gain optimum accuracy at long range, and they're especially handy for roost shooting and longer-range, sniper-style ambush shooting on bunnies.

Scope – Minimum 3 x or 4 x variable up to 12 x magnification with minimum 50mm objective lens.
This is the classic specification for low-light dawn/dusk hunting. Some prefer an even larger objective lens, but despite the slight benefit that may offer, many feel the 'Five-O' to be more than adequate. That big objective lens will suck in all available, useable light, and you can still wind the magnification down to take advantage of a wider field of view. The lower magnification should give better picture quality, and will certainly be more efficient at light-gathering.

There are more options, but of those mentioned this is one that will suit every hunter. Of course, there are scopes with objective lenses up to 56mm, and also a few specialist optics that can drop down a touch from 3 x in an otherwise general-purpose specification scope, but by and large, the scopes discussed above are the ones to concentrate on.

Scope Accessories

Some optics can be fitted with sunshades. These are plain black tubes that screw into the front lens housing to stop the sun causing glare across the scope's lenses. Covers can also be bought that simply slip over the front lens to protect the glass elements when not in use, and some are see-through with a tinted shade, which allow the scope to be used while still in place – a useful feature in bright sunlight. Also available are rubber eye-shades that can be slipped over the eye-piece, and the intention is to block out light that could potentially cause glare in the rear lens, again affecting the performance of the scope.

Scope Mounts and Rings

It's strange how many shooters pay scant regard to scope mounts, especially as they play a vital role, being the only attachment points for the two major components of your hunting combo – the rifle and the scope. All modern air rifles have machined grooves or raised rails to take a standard dove-tailed scope mount – the width of the grooves usually being between 11mm and 13mm.

Mounts come either in two pieces, logically known as two-piece mounts, or as a one-piece mounting unit. Usually, they're designed for scopes with 1-inch diameter body tubes but as scopes of 30mm are available it follows that suitable mounts are readily obtained for those, too. Good-quality scope mounts are manufactured from either aluminium alloy or steel. Obviously steel ones are stronger, but over-tightening the rings can easily damage an alloy scope body tube. Alternatively, alloy mounts can easily be damaged by the steel screws used to fasten the mounts to the top of the dovetails and around the scope body tube. So be careful not to over-tighten the screws when mounting your scope.

Mounts are available in low, medium and high sizes. These are to accommodate the fitting of the scope close to the bore line of the barrel without the objective lens fouling the top of the rifle. Low mounts will usually suffice for scopes

Correct alignment of the scope's cross-hairs to the rifle is very important in making your combo perform to its maximum accuracy potential

with objective lenses up to 32mm; medium ones will accept up to 42mm, while high mounts will be necessary for scopes with big front lenses of up to 56mm. It is worth noting that if low mounts can be used, then this is the better option for close-range hunting. Higher mounts are the optimum choice not only for scopes with large objective lenses, but also if most hunting is done at longer ranges. Thus, medium-height mounts are the optimum choice for general-purpose work at medium range, and will suit most airgun hunting needs. Scope mounting height is particularly relevant to pellet trajectory.

A mount comprises three main components, the rings (the lower cradle where the scope sits, and upper part that clamps it down into place), the base, or bases, (the attachment points to the rifle), and the bolts (usually Allen-head screws) that hold everything securely together. The top halves of the rings are removable, while the bottom section (cradle) is either bolted or otherwise permanently fixed to the base. Some mounts are designed with the upper rings being almost two-thirds the diameter of the scope body tube, often referred to as having a wrap-around design. Some prefer these, as they reputedly offer a more stable mount due to the fact that the upper ring pulls down and around the scope, providing more clamping area than a conventional mount involving two hemispheres. In reality, both are very well suited to airgun use.

Opting to use either one-piece or two-piece mounts is largely a personal choice. However, a one-piece mount was formerly recommended for use with a recoiling air rifle, because you had a greater length of scope mount base and therefore additional grip due to the extra metal-to-metal contact, but if you mount your scope sensibly, two-piece mounts are just as efficient. Generally speaking, one-piece mounts are unsuitable for PCP air rifles. Unless the one-piece mount fits behind the breech loading area (for a single-shot rifle) or behind the magazine housing (of a multi-shot rifle) then you can't use it, because it covers the breech, making it difficult or impossible to load a pellet, or else it fouls the magazine. Two-piece mounts are much more versatile as they can be positioned almost anywhere along the scope body and on the rifle's grooves or rail.

That brings us to the mounting point itself – the grooved channel cut into the top of the rifle's compression chamber or the machined rail on top of a PCP's action block. The former is found on most springers and this is where certain manufacturers machine special features to stop mounts moving on recoil. These can be cross-slots or shallow holes drilled between the dovetails, which engage small lugs or studs found on the base of some scope mounts. Once a mount with a stud on the base is located at this position, it isn't going anywhere. Similarly, if a recoil lug or arrestor block is fitted, with the scope mount butted up to it, this shouldn't move. Both act as a physical stop to anchor the rear scope mount in place, thus resisting movement on recoil.

If you're using a rifle with hefty recoil – say an FAC-rated springer – then anti-slip studs on the mount or an arrestor block is a very sensible precaution. Alternatively, use the DampaMount™ mentioned earlier, as it's a handy solution to stop the effects of recoil being transmitted to the scope on firing.

Before leaving mount design, it's worth glancing at the 'specials' that are available, such as adjustable mounts and risers. You can find that even though you have correctly fitted and set up the scope, you run out of movement on the elevation turret to set your zero at the required range. This usually happens when fitting a scope more suited to firearms use, and therefore calibrated for much greater distances. Even so, if you want to fit such a scope you can pack the rear mount with shims made from small strips of film negative. These go between the cradle and the scope body until the rear section is raised sufficiently to allow adjustment to be made. However, if you overdo it and try to raise the rear of the scope too much, there's a danger of exerting undue leverage on the scope body, with the potential for damage by bending forces. In this case it is much better to use a special mount raiser. These are usually one-piece mounts with the rear mount made slightly higher than the front one. Some can actually be adjusted to sit higher or lower, and even to move from side to side. However, we're really getting into rather specialised kit here, and I feel that 99.9 per cent of airgun hunters will never need to go this far. So, we'll move on to other mounts that will be more generally useful. These are 'set-backs' and 'see-thrus'.

Set-back mounts are always of the two-piece type, and can also be known as 'reach' or cantilever mounts. This is because they can be used either for mounting a scope further back on the rifle or further forward, in both cases to give optimum eye relief. This is done by one mount having the rings positioned away from the base of the mount – from the side, looking rather like an L-bracket. These mounts also allow scope mounting on PCPs that may have an awkwardly located breech, or the rails machined in such a way as to restrict positional adjustment of the scope. These mounts are also handy for avoiding any fouling of the scope's eyebell, saddle or front lens assembly against any part of the rifle. See-thru' mounts have already been mentioned for spring-powered rifles, where the shooter uses a scope but also wishes to take advantage of using the fitted open sights. These can be advantageous if your shooting takes you from normal ranges to close-up work.

So those are your mounting options. Now we look at setting up the scope.

Mounting and Setting

Even some quite experienced airgun shooters will just plonk a scope in mounts, set the middle crosshair as horizontal as possible, clamp up and then set zero. In theory, that's pretty much all you need to do, but it really needs to be done correctly. Here are some important dos and don'ts.

With suitable mounts chosen, fit them loosely but firmly onto the dovetails or rails, taking care not to obstruct the barrel's loading area or magazine housing. Then remove the top ring sections from the mounts and you're left with the cradles for the scope to sit in. This brings us to optical zero. On a new shop-bought scope the optical zero should be pre-centred, but to save time and to get the best performance from your optics it's well worth taking the trouble to check.

Basically, all you're doing is ensuring that the reticle is central in the scope body and therefore making the best use of available leeway for elevation and windage adjustments. First, dial the elevation turret all the way to the top of its travel (i.e. in the arrow direction up), then wind it fully down again, while carefully counting the number of full turns the turret takes until it 'bottoms out'. This will usually be around five full turns, so if the total is five, you should wind back two and a half turns, and then it's approximately centred vertically. Go through the same procedure with the windage turret and that will set the optical zero in both the vertical and lateral planes.

Eye-relief and Crosshair Alignment

Having done the 'centralising check', carefully tighten the base of the mounts to the dovetails or rail, and loosely fit the top sections of the rings so that the scope can't fall off the rifle, but loose enough for it to be moved backwards and forwards, and rotated. If using a break-barrel rifle, check that the front of the scope doesn't overhang the breech, which would foul the barrel and prevent it from opening fully. That's common-sense stuff, but easily overlooked.

Next, you have to set eye-relief as follows: Lift the rifle/scope combo to your shoulder, get into a comfortable shooting position, and then slide the scope gently within the mounts until you can clearly see a perfectly circular sight picture through the scope with a minimum amount of black border around it. This should be around 2½ – 3½ inches between your eye and the scope's ocular bell. You may find that this procedure is easier to do while sitting down with the rifle in a bench rest shooting position, but take care to check that you still have approximately the same sight picture when standing, kneeling or lying prone with the rifle unsupported. If not, make the final adjustments to eye-relief while holding the rifle in your most frequently used shooting position.

Once you've attained the eye-relief that's suited to you, you need to align the cross-hairs square to the rifle itself. I advise hanging a vertical plumb line (a thread or string with a weight at one end) at approximately 10–20yds distance from the scope. I have an old door to the side of my target range backstop set up with a plumb line just for this purpose. Look through the scope and make sure that the vertical wire of the crosshair lines up with the plumb line when you are holding the rifle in your usual shooting position. If it doesn't, gently rotate the scope within the mount rings until it does. Once you are certain that the scope is square to the rifle, carefully tighten the mount top rings on to the scope by nipping up the Allen screws in rotation. If using mounts with four top screws per mount, tighten those which are diagonally opposite each other. Tighten firmly, but don't over-tighten. If you're using a PCP, recoil won't be a problem in causing scope shift, so over-tightening shouldn't even be an issue. Once the scope is secured, recheck that the crosshairs are still set correctly. If not, loosen the screws and repeat the procedure until you are satisfied with the result.

A scope set slightly off the horizontal won't perform to its optimum level when using the turret adjusters. This is because of rifle cant, which I'll explain. For instance, if the horizontal line of the crosshair is only slightly askew to the rifle, then when you adjust the elevation turret of the scope – say to alter the impact higher – you could also unintentionally shift the pellet impact point to the left or right, depending on which way the scoped rifle is canted. This is because your brain will automatically make you twist (or cant) the rifle to one side or the other to make the crosshair appear square-on. If you're not shooting at long ranges the lateral variation of the aim point caused by cant may not be very noticeable, but at longer distances the deviation to right or left gets progressively greater. So as you can see, correct alignment of the scope's crosshairs to the rifle is very important in making your rifle and scope perform to their maximum accuracy potential. A scope set perfectly in line with the rifle is also important for using the BDC (Bullet Drop Compensation) facility that is a feature on many rangefinding scopes.

Now we move on to the next adjustment you should take time over – the fast-focus or reticle focus ring. Strange though it seems, this is a feature many don't bother with, but if your scope has this adjustment you should definitely take advantage of it. This feature allows you to set the scope reticle to focus for your individual eyesight. It's a simple procedure, but one that needs doing correctly. First, look through the scope at a light-coloured blank wall, or up into an overcast sky (never a sunny one). Look into the middle distance but take notice if the crosshairs are blurred or sharp. The reticle must suit your eyesight, so adjust the eyepiece until the crosshairs appear crisp and sharp to you. Many scopes have fast-focus rings and very handy they are too, but if not you may have to loosen the locking ring on the eyebell and rotate the bell itself until focus is achieved and then tighten the locking ring. Once this is achieved, you're ready to set the rifle to shoot to a chosen zero point. In addition to these manual instructions, there are commercially available devices that help you visually align the crosshairs with the bore axis, and even for the scope crosshair to be set perfectly vertical in relation to the action of the rifle. If you feel you need it, they can help.

Setting Scope Zero

Setting the zero on the rifle/scope combo is also a relatively simple procedure, but one that needs to be done correctly so that you'll always hit your mark. Note that the rifle's zero, even when set, will shift depending on your shooting position. This applies more to a recoiling spring rifle than a recoilless PCP, but if you set the zero for a standing shooting position, it will still alter slightly for a shot taken in a kneeling or prone position.

To start by getting roughly on target, first set up a large piece of paper at 12–15yds range on a suitable backstop. This target needs an aiming point, and a 2-inch black circle marked in the centre with a marker pen is ideal. Fire a string of four or five pellets, with your crosshairs trained precisely on this point. Make a note where the pellets group and then dial the turret adjusters accordingly, to move the group closer to your black dot aiming point. Repeat this until you're hitting the point you're aiming at. Next, put up another target with a 1½-inch circle on a suitable backstop and pull back so that you are shooting from the distance at which you want to zero your combo for hunting. Shoot and adjust until you're grouping your shots inside the circle on the target.

The turret adjusters on most hunting scopes alter impact by what is known as ¼" Minute Of Angle (MOA) increments. This means that the impact point is shifted a quarter of an inch per click at 100yds. At airgun distances, this has to be compensated for, so at 25yds this equates to four clicks, moving the impact point of the pellet by a quarter of an inch. Specialist target scopes often have ⅛" MOA adjustment, moving the aim point one eighth of an inch at 100yds. Which distance to choose for your zero can be debatable, so newcomers, and airgun hunters looking to undertake some general hunting, would be advised to use this as a loose guide. For a .22 calibre recoiling spring or gas-ram-powered rifle, set your zero at 25yds. For a .177 recoilless PCP air rifle set the zero point for 30yds. These zeros give you a good aim point for longer-range effectiveness, yet with a closer range reference point. With a .22 set to 25 yards zero you can also aim bang-on for 10–12yds, then slightly lower for 18yds. Then raise your aim appropriately to put the crosshairs bang on target for 25yds. After that only practice on target cards will show you how much to allow for aiming holdover at longer range. This is something we will deal with more fully in the relevant section. As you can see, the set zero is there to give you a definite aim point at your set zero range, and also a reference for closer-range shots.

Pre-charged pneumatics (PCPs) are recoilless, and the .177 calibre has a much flatter trajectory than a .22, so the whole package is much more forgiving in range estimation and assessment. You'll find on larger target kill-zones, such as a rabbit's head, with a zero of 30yds you can actually aim bang-on for ranges of approximately 20yds to 40yds and still be within the kill-zone. Incidentally, an important factor in zeroing that should always be adhered to is using the same ammo as you set your zero with. Change ammo and the zero will change. It may only be slight in relation to pellets of a similar weight and profile, but often it is enough to upset your accuracy, and therefore your efficiency as a hunter.

Although I've fully detailed how to manually – i.e. by eye – set the zero, you can purchase a gadget which is known as a 'bore sighter' or 'shot saver' that will aid the process. These can be in the form of a collimator gauge or a more hi-tech laser bore sighter. The latter fits into the barrel and actually projects a laser dot out from the barrel bore. This is all good kit, but setting up in the old-school way is by far the most commonly used method for airgun use.

Alternative Sighting Systems

With the exception of specialised night vision riflescopes, there are few alternative sighting systems for use in hunting, and none that offer a better option for all-round, precision shooting than the telescopic sight. However, for close to medium-range work, you do have a choice of sights that offer a reasonable (and in some cases better) option to obtain quick target acquisition. These are red-dot or 'holo' sights. I'd recommend a few of the red-dots that are available, but then only for rat and feral pigeon shooting, or possibly rabbit shooting when I'm sure the range will not exceed 25yds. And even then, if the quarry is further out I keep disciplined by using the sight at its optimum level of accuracy. The main reasons I'll use a red-dot are when using a PCP air rifle for close- to medium-range shooting. The sight then virtually offers all the simplicity and benefits of an open sight coupled with the obvious benefits of a multi-shot PCP.

The red-dot sight that made the biggest impact on my own hunting was the Russian-manufactured Cobra, a sight originally designed for their military for use on the AK47 assault rifle. Obviously, reliability and build construction aren't an issue. Swedish manufacturer Aimpoint have red-dots suited to hunting, as also is the Bushnell Holo-Sight. If a red-dot appeals to you and will be a suitable sighting option for the hunting you are doing, they're all worth checking out. However, I'd like to dispel the popular misconception that they're useful for night shooting. Where this myth has arisen from is anybody's guess, as they're of little use without some light. In gloomy conditions they do give you a sight point, but as for being a true night sight – they're not.

Electric Eye

Laser sights project a laser dot onto the target, but rather than being a primary sighting system they are more useful in helping the shooter estimate range in low light conditions.

I first took an interest in lasers in the mid-1990s when the American Beamshot lasers came on to the UK hunting scene. I must say my flirtations with them have been somewhat sporadic, sometimes favouring them and at others having little use for them. Though specialised, in the right situations they're handy to have.

How the laser sight is mounted dictates how you use it to assess if a target is closer or further from your set zero. The rules are simple to remember once the laser is mounted securely and has been set to coincide exactly with your crosshairs at the rifle's set zero point. If the laser is mounted below the rifle barrel, and therefore below the bore line and scope line of sight, then when the laser dot shows on the target lower than the crosshairs, the target is closer than your set zero. If the laser dot appears above it, the target is further than your set zero. Of course, the opposite applies to a laser mounted above the scope – laser dot lower = target further; laser dot higher = target closer.

A radical move in the development of lasers is that there are now models available that project an infrared dot which can only be seen when viewed through a night vision device; for instance, when wearing night vision goggles or, more commonly, when used in conjunction with a night vision (NV) riflescope. Their uses are one and the same – to help in rangefinding under difficult shooting conditions. Infrared (IR) lasers and NV sighting systems and other relevant NV equipment are very specialised, but make exciting and worthy additions to the airgun hunting scene. All these 'after hours' sighting devices and their use will be fully detailed later, in the applicable sections on hunting methods, and there'll be more pertaining to the use of both types of lasers and their benefits and usage in the chapter on Shooting At Night.

Finally, one very important factor should be remembered; even with all this hi-tech help; it's the hunter who has fully familiarised himself with his kit who will be really successful.

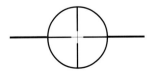

Choosing a Rifle
Combination and Usage

On first inspection of my gun rack you'd be forgiven for thinking one or perhaps two things. I've far too many air rifles and/or I'm a collector. Neither is strictly correct, because each rifle and scope combination, or to use the shortened term, 'combo', are in my armoury because each individual 'rig' is set up to serve a specific purpose.

As well as being a very keen sporting shooter, I do my fair share of pest control shooting in every conceivable situation where the air rifle is useful. It's largely for that reason that I have so many different combos, but if I were only using air rifles for sport shooting, then I would own and use far fewer. Since Total Airguns was first published, I have cut back on my rifles because new ones are now capable of multiple tasks, so if you make a carefully considered purchase, one air rifle is able to replace two or three for multiple-purpose roles. But all airgunners should have an air rifle with specifications that allow it to be used for what can be termed 'general purpose' hunting. These are the three main categories of combo most useful for hunting, and are given in more detail at the end of the chapter.

- **General Purpose Hunting Combo:** Either spring-powered or gas-ram with iron sights or, preferably and more commonly, a general specification scope. If necessary, please refer to what I consider constitutes a general hunting scope, comprehensively detailed in the previous chapter.
- **Precision Hunter:** Single or multi-shot PCP with a higher specification scope.
- **Dedicated Night Hunting Rig:** A multi-shot PCP with a night vision rifles cope on board extra IR and a laser, or if a traditionalist, a springer, gas-ram or PCP with a suitable optic and scope-mounted lamping kit.

If you don't intend to hunt regularly at night, then you can forget number three; so now we're down to just two combos. You're probably already aware, even if you've chosen all three, that there can be many permutations of mixing and matching. A rifle classed as a precision hunter could easily handle anything asked of a general-purpose rifle, even for tackling pests around the farmyard, barns and other outbuildings.

In fact, it would be all too easy just to say, 'Buy the best springer and best PCP multi-shot air rifles you can afford, get a gun-mounted lamping kit and/or NV module and leave it at that.' If I did, this would be a very short chapter and you'd not be given a reasonable number of useful guidelines to get the most from your chosen, and possibly one of the most challenging, shooting disciplines.

To have a spring- or gas-ram-powered air rifle as a back-up to a pre-charged pneumatic is, in my opinion, the least expensive option, and a very sensible and practical route to take. If you have a .22 calibre springer or gas-ram, then seriously consider a .177 PCP for your main hunting rifle. You'll notice as you progress through this book that I lean heavily towards the .177 calibre. I use it extensively and rate the smaller slug very highly, but not for every situation. Before I begin my list of things to look for in a rifle, consider this; under the current legislation you're not restricted to the number or type of 12ft lb air rifles you can possess, unlike the stipulations on FACs as regards exactly which high-powered airguns and 'proofed' silencers you may own. This absence of tight regulation means you can easily chop and change as your shooting dictates or (relevant to most shooters) as your budget allows. In other words, making a costly mistake isn't the biggest risk facing you in your purchase, as you can easily trade-in a good quality 12ft lb air rifle for a different model. Before outlining what I feel all shooters should look for in the choosing of a good all-round, general –purpose hunting rifle, I feel taking a look at the past will be of use.

Suits You

When many shooters started hunting, including me, we had limited funds, and most of us started with humble springers, such as the BSA Airsporter, Supersport or similar models from Webley. The older lads had bigger rifles, and when I mention the Weihrauch HW80 I'm sure many readers will smile as they remember it, as this is the rifle that fits the category perfectly. It was certainly a rifle that many airgun hunters eventually acquired. There was also the Webley Eclipse, an under-lever rifle that has been discontinued, but, along with the Omega model, it's a rifle that many still believe was one of Webley's finest production spring-powered creations. I must also mention a personal favourite - the now sadly discontinued Air Arms Khamsin. This was a side-lever springer that I hold largely responsible for my penchant for thumbhole-style stocks – but more on stock designs later.

Obviously, we had to use what was available, and the selection within our budgets wasn't anything like as varied as it is today. Also, we usually went for the rifle that we thought was the most powerful. The HW80 was even nicknamed 'The Powerhouse' in the advertisements, so it's little wonder that it drew us impressionable kids to it. This brings us to the first consideration because, depending on your stature and physique, you should choose a rifle accordingly. The bonus for today's shooter is that many more carbines and lightweight rifles are available that are capable, full-power hunters. These are not only handy for younger or small-stature shooters, but are also the optimum choice for stalking, hide shooting and even for use from an off-road vehicle. The primary factor concerning your first choice is - does the rifle fit you? That is the way to look at it, because although you needn't go as far as the custom-made stock tailored to suit you for FT perfectionism, finding a 'nice stick to hold' is a vital step towards becoming a proficient shot.

Stock-taking

There are three specifics of a rifle stock that need examination in relation to your personal build. The weight (including action), the reach to pull (the distance between butt pad to forward face of trigger blade) and the height of the cheekpiece or comb. The latter feature can be altered (raised or lowered) by fitting an adjustable butt pad or comb raiser, but for now let's assume that many will be happy enough with the stock in standard 'sporter' form. Also, never be fooled into thinking a nice-looking gun equals a good-handling gun. I advise you to devote some careful scrutiny and definitely request to handle the rifle you've short-listed in the gun shop and see if it really does suits you. Or, better put - to see if it feels right.

The reach to pull can be more simply explained as the reach to squeezing the trigger when the rifle is shouldered. Most traditional-style sporters hover around a length of 13 to 14 inches. If it's more, you could find it rather a stretch to reach the trigger, and nothing's more infuriating than a rifle that feels uncomfortable to hold and use. After shouldering the rifle in the standing position, (after politely asking the owner), don't be embarrassed to sit down in the shop and try the rifle from the kneeling position, resting the rifle over your leading hand supported by knee/or thigh. If you are still struggling then it's not for you because in this position you should be able to handle anything. You've much more room for allowance as the stable, rested position allows you to pull or push the rifle forwards. It's a strange phenomenon, but how a person interacts with a rifle physically does change the perception of It.

Some prefer to have chequering or stippling on the pistol grip and the forend, which should afford a much more assured hold. Unfortunately, the forend chequering or stippling on many rifles is not always in the ideal position, so in many cases this can be purely cosmetic. Granted, it is very handy if you want to carry your rifle in one hand. The method for using the forend for this is to grip the rifle under the stock and along the forend with your right hand at the chequering, allowing the unloaded rifle to point downwards at the ground when carried alongside your right leg (assuming you shoot from your right shoulder). It is a safe, comfortable hold when you have to move across ground where you may need to use your other hand to steady yourself, and it is a very much better proposition than using the scope as a carry-handle! Alternatively, of course, if you've got quick-detachable (QD) swivel studs fitted, you can quickly and easily attach a rifle sling and shoulder the gun while you negotiate the terrain.

Chequering or stippling can be useful at the pistol grip, especially if the hunter becomes a devotee of full camo, and wears gloves. Personally, I don't worry unduly about these stock characteristics, but I do prefer the stock to be of a thumbhole design and/or to have an adjustable butt pad. Some think that's strange for a dedicated hunter such as me, but I've taken these preferences from the stocks fitted to FT rifles. These features allow me to tailor the height of the cheekpiece or comb for optimum eye-relief on the scope, and the thumbhole gives me a very sure feel while handling and lining up to take a shot.

The majority of my hunting rifles have adjustable butt pads. These are often fitted after purchase, but some rifles do come ready fitted with them. If the rifle you're thinking of buying hasn't got one – and if it's a basic springer it probably won't, fitting one isn't difficult. Fitting a stock comb riser kit is more daunting, some find this another useful addition.

Next on the checklist is whether you opt for a walnut stock, or the less expensive beech or hardwood. We now have wood with a 'grippy' rubber over-moulding and even full rubber stocks with a grippy, tactile feel. I've really taken to these and some very fine hunting air rifles are now available with this type of stock as an option. However, if you are worried about the disappearance of wooden stocks (as some foretold) or them becoming prohibitively costly – don't! With the existence of many different hardwoods worldwide, most actually being the wood of fruit trees, I believe that new types of wood will eventually enter the scene, but the old, traditional woods will still be with us for a good deal longer. So, is it to be beech or walnut? I'm no 'mantlepiece' gun collector, but I certainly appreciate a nice-looking configured grain pattern on a walnut stock. Do remember that a hunting rifle will be subjected to its fair share of knocks and scrapes when in the field. If you can't bear the thought of that lovely wood getting scratched, don't buy it.

Left-handed shooters aren't forgotten and dedicated left-hand stocks are available for some models of air rifle, though generally cost extra. Fully ambidextrous stocks, with a cheekpiece on either side of the furniture to suit a right-handed or left-handed shooter, are very much commonplace in the mid-price bracket for springers, gas-rams and PCPs. Some PCP air rifles accommodate for 'lefties' even more by having a rear-mounted cocking bolt that can be altered so it can be set to the left for easier operation. As for weight difference between wood types, it's usually so minimal that I feel it's of little relevance. If there is one thing to consider it's this: a walnut stock that is kept dry after use and regularly oiled does last longer than beech. If weight-saving is a major consideration then look to the rifles that have what are known as 'skeleton' or 'profile' stocks. These are pared down to the barest minimum to save on weight, but without sacrificing strength.

Thankfully, the laminate stock is making a comeback and not only on custom specials or limited edition runs. Certain gun manufacturers have seen that airgun hunters do want these types again; for example, Weihrauch are currently offering the option to purchase the HW77K in two choices of 'seasonal identified' colour blends of laminate stock. The company have called these Summer Forest and Autumn Forest – not very imaginative maybe – but the laminate stock design is also far more ergonomic, and in Autumn Forest it would blend into most areas in whichh we operate throughout the year.

As you progress as a hunter you might decide to have a stock specially made for your particular style of hunting, a stock that your favoured hunting rifle would slip into and which would fit you like a glove. Interestingly, of all shooting disciplines, airgunners are some of the most likely to have a custom stock built and fitted to their rifle; and that's not only FT shooters, because more and more airgun hunters choose this route as well.

It was in the UK where a manufacturer excelled in the design and production of a stock that garnered praise when it was first seen on the BSA Lightning Tactical XL break-barrel springer. Designed by Jon Sykes of Hydrographics and using a 'hush-hush' formula to create the ABS mix to enable the stock to be high-impact resistant, this stock transformed any BSA rifle it was fitted to and such was its popularity it eventually became an option on most PCPs, even scaled down to suit the BSA Ultra single-shot and multi-shot.

In the right hands, a silenced air rifle is a deadly, effective tool

If you don't intend to specialise in night hunting – you won't need a dedicated night vision rig

All Important

This may sound obvious, but a general purpose hunting air rifle needs to be capable of cleanly dispatching vermin out to 30-40yds depending on your shooting ability. That's not a great distance, and virtually all good-quality, spring-powered and gas-ram-powered air rifles will be up to the job. So in that sense you don't need the recoil-free PCP multi-shot to be successful in the field. Often the rifle can be capable of achieving more than the hunter who uses it, so if you're only planning the occasional hunting foray then a basic springer or gas-ram-powered air rifle will serve you well for many years, but I must reiterate an important aspect of the sport. Not that long ago, most experienced shooters would advise you to start off by choosing a spring-powered rifle for hunting; but due to the fact that good-quality pre-charged pneumatics are now much more affordable, if you're willing to pay for charging gear, then a PCP can be a superior choice for many hunting scenarios, and a multi-shot is even better. Before we look at pre-charged or multi-shots, it's time to get back to basics and see what the hunter should be looking for in a mechanically charged and primed, single-shot air rifle.

For spring-powered air rifles, there are high-quality models with all the requisites from established British manufacturers such as Air Arms, BSA and of course the German company Weihrauch. If it's a gas-ram then at one time it would have been a Theoben; now as mentioned previously, there is an increasing number of gun manufacturers who make gas-strut-powered air rifles. Of the companies mentioned, all have rifles suitable for general hunting work. These will be no-nonsense, ruggedly built, reliable, accurate sporters. They'll handle well, and some will even be fitted with a good set of open sights. Immediately, this brings us to a feature of certain springers that makes them advantageous over others for some hunting situations. If you're intending to shoot at close- to medium-range at quarry such as rats or feral pigeons then you can't beat a basic break-barrel springer with open sights. For what I'd term 'knock-about' work it's still a very useful tool. However, whilst I still have rifles like that, I now only use them for the most basic jobs, and when many of us began shooting with air rifles, we just couldn't afford a scope!

Shooting with open sights brings its own advantages and merits. Most hunters now skip straight past these rifles and scope-up immediately. There's no denying the benefits of using a decent scope, but a whole generation of shooters have missed a very important part of the learning curve associated with the shooting of air rifles, especially if they start with a PCP. The reason is that learning to shoot with a recoiling, spring-powered air rifle instils a definite shooting discipline and, once mastered, you can then fully appreciate the benefits of the recoilless attributes of a PCP. All this will be discussed in the chapter on Gun Handling. But let's return to springers and gas-rams, and in particular to a consideration of the features that should be considered when choosing a rifle of this type.

First, if you don't want open sights, then don't worry. It may seem as if I'm contradicting myself, but if you are going for quarry at 25 – 30yds, you should be scoping-up straight from the off. Just as importantly, choose a rifle that is threaded at the muzzle to accept a standard ½" UNF-threaded silencer. Unless you're sure of the make, or you've tried before you buy, be aware of rifles with silencers that come bonded onto the barrel. In most cases, these perma-fix moderators are more than adequate for general purpose work. The rifle will also usually be shorter than a similar model that requires you to screw a silencer onto the barrel, thus increasing the rifle's overall length. This is something I'm always critical of, and it does tend to annoy me when I see a company boasting that their new model is 'ultra- short', when the reality is that you need to take the additional length of a silencer into consideration. If it doesn't slip over the end of the barrel it will usually add another 4-6 inches to the overall length of the rifle. On a carbine-sized, break-barrel springer this can be beneficial, because it will act as a cocking aid for the shortened barrel, but on a standard-length rifle it can tend to make the rifle feel overly long. The worst-case scenario is that it can make the rifle feel unwieldy and unbalanced, but this is thankfully now quite rare. Most are manageable, and you can opt for a carbine or carbine version with a silencer bonded in place, or as an outer sleeve, usually referred to as a 'bull barrel shroud'.

I've no doubt that when bull barrel shrouds first came on to the scene the intention was that they'd be cosmetic, but they function now on most rifles as an integral 'primary' silencer. Originally, as well as being cosmetic, there was no void between barrel and shroud so they strengthened the barrel. Then, they become in-vogue because the larger they were, the more they gave most rifles a macho appeal, but on full-length rifles this tended to make them feel front heavy. However, certain companies realised these shrouds could be used as a primary silencer but only if correctly fitted with silencing baffles, and a way by which air could be used most efficiently to send the pellet on its way. Excess air would be vented back down the gap that could be left in, between it and the barrel, so air exited at pre-drilled holes often found close to the front end of the action block. Hedging their bets, they still often add a ½" UNF male or female threaded muzzle protected cover cap; this often accepts a secondary silencer. The early models were quite a disappointment. On certain full-length rifles, it did work to a degree as the shroud was so long it had a deadening effect on the discharge, but to shorten the barrel and shroud was a big no-no. It was about then that I hoped companies would ditch the idea and concentrate on making more efficient silencers, which you'll soon read, they did.

On the subject of barrels, it's interesting that British companies such as BSA and, before their demise as a manufacturer, Webley & Scott Ltd, produced their own, which is a tradition that I hope BSA will long continue because these tubes are strong, accurate and well manufactured. For PCPs, however, most companies now choose to buy barrels from acclaimed German manufacturers such as Anschutz, Lothar Walther, or other quality gun barrel manufacturers.

Silencers or 'sound moderators' to give them their more accurate term, are of such importance that they'll be dealt with more fully in the chapter on Accessories, but at this stage it is worth mentioning that most serious hunters feel they're essential in attaining optimum results in the field. On a pre-charged pneumatic they are certainly a necessity, as the muzzle report from an untamed PCP is heard as a loud, sharp crack. On certain springers, the report can be quite acceptable but on the whole I would say that if you want to hunt to the optimum level then give serious consideration to the silencer already fitted to the rifle, or that which you will choose to add later.

Now to a much discussed aspect of any rifle; its trigger mechanism. The modern air rifle, even a basic model, is generally now fitted with a two-stage adjustable trigger unit. The 'two-stage' term refers to the fact that the length of travel in the first stage can be adjusted, or the length and weight of the second stage – i.e. the 'pull' or point at which the trigger trips the sear – can be altered, or both. Remember back to Chapter 1? As they come from the factory and set by the manufacturer, most triggers will tend to suit the majority of shooters, but as you come to know your gun, you'll probably want to tweak the trigger slightly to adjust its let-off. Be sensible with adjustments, read the manual that comes with the rifle thoroughly, and don't set the trigger pressure too light. Hair triggers aren't necessary or useful for a sporting air rifle, and very few hunters would advise or consider using them. Again, as for many alterations that can be done to a rifle; if in doubt get a reputable gunsmith to do the alterations.

The majority of trigger units also have a safety-catch system, either manual or automatic. These are useful because the rifle can be cocked and loaded with a pellet, ready to go, but the trigger is made safe by the safety mechanism blocking its action. However, nothing is safer than an uncocked, unloaded rifle. If you can hunt in this fashion, all the better, but there are many times when you'll need to be ready to take a shot quickly, which is best done with a cocked and loaded rifle with the safety engaged. Also, some springers can be uncocked by holding the barrel or under-lever, removing the safety, and pulling the trigger while allowing the barrel or under-lever to return under your manual control to its original position. But remember you've still got a pellet in the breech – assuming you got as far as loading. There is more to a safety catch than using it as an on/off switch, and it's up to the individual to learn to use the safety wisely, as an essential part of good, sensible gun handling.

For scope mounting, the rifle will have dovetails (and perhaps arrestor stud holes) machined atop the cylinder or action block to help prevent scope creep. This has already been mentioned, and you should check that the dovetails are well machined and are of a reasonable length to allow for a suitable scope mounting position. A new trend is, certain air rifles are even now fitted with a raised dual Weaver/dovetail rail for

An adjustable butt pad can help with shoulder fit

Larger cocking bolt handles make cycling the action far easier

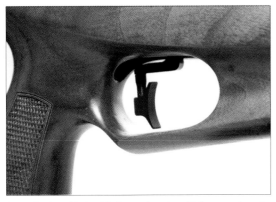

A retrofit trigger blade with shoe makes a lot of difference to how the rifle releases the shot

A standard screw cut muzzle accepts a wide variety of silencers

A retrofit adjustable barrel band can help the rifle be more accurate

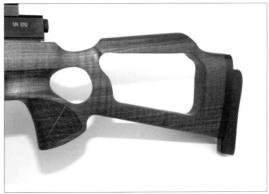

For weight saving you might want to choose a profiled stock option

traditional scope mounting or to be scoped up in mounts with a Weaver base.

Be that as it may, but team a general purpose hunting rifle with a general specification 3 – 9 X 40 or better still a 'new era' 4 – 12 X 44 or 4 – 12 X 50 scope and you'll undoubtedly have a very efficient, user-friendly, all-purpose, knockabout hunting rifle. If it's a carbine, I'd advise a compact scope of 1.5 – 5 X 20 or 2 – 7 X 32AO, the latter being a scope specification that increasingly impresses me. An original Tasco in this specification is still one that has those in the know look longingly, as does the Simmons 1.5 – 5 X 20 Compact Nightview. Either of these optics will aid fast target acquisition, making this combo suitable for snap-shooting, as well as having the capability to take shots up to and beyond medium range.

But back to the air rifle itself as by now you could well be walking out of the shop with a springer, gas-ram or even a single-shot PCP with a general-type hunting scope on board, but if you want a bit more versatility, read on.

Precision Hunter

Here the options available are innumerable. Do you stay with a single-shot or go for a multi-shot model? Do you stay with the 'mechanical animals' or go pre-charged? It's largely up to personal preference, but personally, I wouldn't consider hunting now without my multi-shot PCP unless it was punishable by law. Admittedly, I do occasionally have a wander around my shoot with a single-shot, but this seems to be getting less frequent by the season. Even so, my first choice would always be a PCP, apart from in the harshest, most grime-ridden conditions where the danger of dirt creeping near, or into, the precious inlet valve and internals would have me reaching for a spring or gas-ram-powered rifle. So what do we look for in a precision hunter rifle?

If you've served your time with the spring gun, moving up to a PCP can be a bit daunting. These days there are both single-shot and multi-shot pneumatics to suit every shooter's requirements and pocket. There are many field-proven PCPs specifically designed for the hunter, and I'll try to help you through the quagmire by outlining what a hunting PCP should have in order to warrant serious consideration.

For airgun hunters new to the PCP, the simplicity of a one-shot capacity rifle is a valid reason to stay single. Also, let's not forget that before the multi-shots took over we did very well with single-shot air rifles. In fact, hunting with an air rifle should be a one-shot affair, and there are now a host of top quality, very reasonably priced, one-shot potters on the market.

Air Arms, BSA, FX Airguns and a few other manufacturers all have rifles that are very appealing, but we can't talk about single-shot PCPs without immediately thinking of the company mentioned at the outset, and often hailed as the founding fathers – Daystate Ltd.

Market demands have dictated that even the one-time kings of the one-shot now mainly produce multi-shot rifles that are capable of being adapted back to shoot in single shot mode. There is a definite new trend for rifles to have the facility to be altered to function as single-shot, by conversion from the multi-shot models they're based on. For the present, there's a good selection of well-priced, dedicated single-shot PCPs for those who prefer a one-shot hunting rig.

The choice of a single-shot is the simplest to make. Look for ease of operation for loading the pellet into the breech or loading channel. There's nothing worse than trying to load a pellet into a fiddly loading area, especially with cold or gloved fingers. Also take into consideration the number of shots you get per charge or fill. You'll get more from a standard-length rifle than from a carbine-size PCP; but other than that, all the features previously outlined for you to consider when choosing the basic all-round springer also apply here. It's when we get to multi-shots options that you need to weigh up a few major features that will sway you one way or the other, once again depending largely on personal preference.

Bolted

One key area of a multi-shot PCP air rifle is the action that cocks the rifle, indexes the magazine around and then takes a pellet from the magazine to load it into the breech. The other, of course, is the magazine, its type and its pellet capacity. For these two features to function there are two or three other mechanical aspects to the rifle. Besides the cocking bolt or side-lever handle there's the magazine indexing system and also the pellet probe. The cocking bolt always cocks the rifle (except on Daystate electronic PCPs, I must stress), but on its rearward travel it can also contact a lever that cams the magazine around to align a pellet with the breech. Often the bolt is also responsible for pushing or 'probing' the pellet forwards from the magazine and into the breech, in position for firing.

The actual layout of the mechanical parts depends largely on the type of magazine – spring-loaded, removable rotary, or of a linear design. These were explained in Chapter 1. A matter of personal choice is the cocking bolt position and this will be either what is known as a 'short throw', side-positioned bolt action or else a cocking bolt mounted on the rear of the action block. Generally, a rear-mounted bolt action

Side-lever action PCP's are now becoming more commonplace

will have a longer stroke, while side-bolt actions are usually the slickest and quickest to operate, which is one of the reasons they're termed 'short throw'. If you do a lot of shooting in the prone position, either freehand or from a bipod, rifles with side-positioned bolt actions are often easier and more comfortable to use. To be comprehensive, I must also mention an increasing number of PCP multi-shot air rifles use a pivoting 'side-lever' for cocking and cycling the action. These are an option if you prefer them, and mostly have been developed to the point where they operate as efficiently as any bolt action design.

Now, are there any other major considerations? Obviously the price will be a deciding factor, as will the choice of a fixed air reservoir design or a buddy bottle. Again, these decisions depend on the individual's circumstances and preferences.

All Together - When Put Together

Once known as the 'poacher's gun', the take-down rifle first made its debut on the airgun scene when the Colchester Gamekeeper PCP was launched over twenty years ago. Back then it was very much seen as an oddity. Since then there have been many more take-down rifles produced and the shooting public vote with their cash as they buy them. Even today's take-down air rifles will be used by some for illegal activity but used as they should, they're an air rifle that offers true benefits for the pest controller and sport shooter alike.

A take-down is very useful when you need to be discreet such as when carrying your air rifle to an area you're allowed to shoot. A few places I shoot have long footpaths that are the only route to a hotspot for quarry and the ease of carrying the rifle in a bag that looks like a rucksack or briefcase and to wear clothing more associated with a rambler can be a huge asset.

I can climb over stiles on clearly marked footpaths, disappear on to the land to open the case and have the rifle assembled in less than a minute, and after not much longer be fully camo'd up myself. In some instances, you'll need another bag for your clothing but for my favourite take-down, the Air Arms S410 TDR, such is the generous nature of the bag that I can fit in a camo over-suit, face veil, gloves and cap or sometimes a camo net.

Without doubt, second to the TDR was the once discontinued and now resurrected Brocock Enigma, but I'd opt for the FX Verminator Mk II. It's a big shot-count, mini-carbine, which is highly and deadly accurate. For reasons of transportation the usual way the takedown breaks down is into three major component parts. The butt section of the stock can be removed from the action and barrel, and if there's one supplied, so can the silencer. It's worth stating here that for reasons of legality all reputable

A take-down air rifle can be discreetly carried over public land and then onto the shoot

Once on the land, the rifle can be fully assembled and out hunting in next to no time

air rifle manufacturers now build these types of air rifle, so when the rear section is removed the air rifle is inoperable or doesn't stray over the 6ft lb legal air pistol limit. The reason obviously being that once the butt section is removed in some cases, you have a long-barrel air pistol. Then again, such is the design of those that employ a buddy bottle for the butt section, when removed you quite frankly have no power! This simplicity shouldn't deter any shooter considering them as a serious hunting tool because once 'all together, put together', most are as accurate, handle as well and are as reliable as any standard, equal quality, full power production, full-bodied, PCP air rifle. For ease of use, it's good to see most supply cases for these rifles allow you to leave the scope in place, so there's no hassle having to keep setting zero. Even so, when you've assembled the rifle it only takes a few minutes to check it. Incidentally, as the majority of these rifles are aimed at the hunting sector, then they're mostly multi-shots. The reasons to use and own one are obvious and that's why I stated earlier that every airgun hunter should consider acquiring such a rifle. It may only get used on an irregular basis, but in my experience, at some point it'll pay its way in the amount of permissions you get to add to your list of places to shoot. That, in itself, is reason enough to own one – don't you agree?

What now follows is a guide list, to show how combos can be matched and the hunting situations to which they're most suited. Incidentally, it's worth noting that when it comes to matching size of scope to rifle, certain carbine size rifles can easily look and actually be what is known as 'over-scoped.' A rifle looks over-scoped if the optic onboard tends to overpower the rifle it sits on in terms of weight, length and in some cases, having too many features. At worst, this can affect handling but by and large compact to medium general specification optics suit carbine size rifles, whilst general specification to high-end scopes suit full-length sporters. Even then, choose wisely and you'll get far more from your combo.

Recommended Combos, The Alternatives and Usage

Single-shot, spring-powered rifle with open sights or single-shot PCP with red-dot.
Rat shooting, feral pigeon shooting. Mostly used for indoor shooting and around the farmyard and feed pens. Good quality makes medium-range, general purpose shooting a possibility, but I'd recommend a scoped rifle as follows.

Single-shot spring, gas-ram or PCP air rifle with general specification scope or slightly higher.
(See chart in previous chapter for scope choice.) The true all-rounder. This should be a full-power, one-shot potter. Good for most scenarios from shooting rabbits to shooting pigeons.

Multi-shot (including two-shot PCP air rifle option), with a higher specification optic such as a low-light scope - possibly even with higher magnification range and parallax adjustment.
This is suitable for everything, and the hunter with this is spoiled. For closer range shooting you require fast target acquisition, so look to a lower magnification scope. Again, see the scope chart in previous chapter.

A Threesome . . .

At the very beginning of this chapter I suggested that, ideally, airgun hunters should have three combos and though I recommend a few more, I still stick to the basic three in 12ft lb as a minimum. I'm asked so often about what to buy and why, and if you pinned me down and said I could only keep three rifles, I'd most probably choose the following:

- A springer or gas-ram, preferably with open sights and in .22 calibre. Depending on hunting situation, with either a compact or general spec scope fitted.
- A multi-shot .177 calibre PCP carbine with a compact scope or similar optic, with the choice of scope based on hunting opportunities likely to be encountered.
- Last but definitely not least, a multi-shot .177 calibre PCP with a Night Vision Riflescope.

If I'm travelling to another person's shoot as a guest, those three rifles are more often than not exactly what I'd take from the gun rack. Additionally, I'd not forget a selection of camo clothing, charging gear, spare pre-filled buddy bottles, a lamping kit, a plentiful supply of ammo – in fact all my other usual hunting accessories we'll eventually be looking at and why they're, in my opinion, 'Necessities not just Accessories.'

Ammo
Pellet Calibres and General Information

I think it's long overdue that we dispelled the old airgun shooting adage that says .177 for feather and .22 for fur. As a general rule of thumb that was once quite a good guide to choosing which pellet to use, but with the advances in airgun technology and the quality of pellets on offer an increasing number of hunters now recognise that the choice of hunting calibres isn't so cut and dried.

There are actually four calibres in all, because there are also the .20 and .25 to take into account, with each calibre having its devotees and its specialised uses. I personally feel that the popularity of .22 as a hunting calibre is largely due to the long held misconception that maximum power transfer on impact at the target is the major requisite for successful shooting. This is only partly true and we need to consider other factors – not the least being that the pellet must hit accurately within the kill-zone, no matter what the calibre. I mention this now, because a lot of what follows in this section can be considered quite radical when compared to the beliefs that have long been regarded as written in stone.

Any calibre of pellet hitting a kill-zone on the quarry will do the job of cleanly dispatching it, always assuming that striking energy is adequate. The .177 calibre pellet, because of its faster flight, flatter trajectory and some other characteristics which we'll examine later in this chapter, is usually more forgiving of slight range estimation misjudgements, and therefore more likely to be accurate. Yet it must be acknowledged that if a .177 is slightly off the kill-zone, it could well only wound the animal because it hasn't got the shock effect of the larger, heavier calibres. Be slightly off the mark with a .22 pellet and its heavier weight combined with a larger frontal area will still deliver a lot of energy (i.e. shock power), which means it could still result in a clean kill. This is especially the case with a head shot on a rabbit.

What we learn from this is that accuracy is the prime factor for the clean dispatching of any quarry species, but the delivery of lethal energy is still very significant. Knowledge of the quarry's anatomy and the various all-important lethal areas where one shot will be fatal are fully dealt with elsewhere in this book – along with recommended calibre options – when we look at each quarry species individually. But first let's look at the airgun pellet, its function and general design, including shapes and types available

Anatomy of an Airgun Pellet

The airgun pellet is quite a simple but clever and practical design, with four main features – the head, waist, skirt and internal profile. Each performs a specific and important function and, along with quality of manufacture, it's the pattern of these in relation to the pellet as a whole

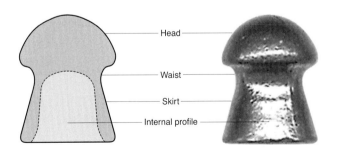

Head

Waist

Skirt

Internal profile

that dictates performance and efficiency. Pellets are manufactured from lead or lead alloy. It's been this way for years because lead is reasonably cheap, easy to work, and heavy enough to supply the weight needed to transfer the energy of in-flight velocity (kinetic energy) into weight/mass energy at the target. The softness of lead also helps to deliver energy to the target as the material expands on impact. To be thorough, I must mention that there are also pellets manufactured from zinc alloy, tin alloy and even copper. As to their 'benefits' I'll not comment other than to say that until I'm convinced otherwise – I'm sticking with lead!

Main Pellet Design Features

Head

The head is vitally important, as this is the part of the pellet that transfers the speed (velocity) and weight (mass) of the pellet into what is known as 'shock' or 'shock effect' when it hits the target. The shape of the head also helps (or sometimes hinders) the aerodynamics of the pellet, which should have a straight and accurate flight.

Waist

Pellets are waisted (i.e. pinched in to a smaller diameter roughly midway between the head and the skirt) partly to reduce the weight-to-length ratio, but more importantly to reduce friction in the barrel while separating the head and skirt sections, thereby allowing them to function as they should. The head should stay true aerodynamically in flight to the target, while the skirt expands on catching the first blast of air from the transfer port, and fills the bore. The waist acts as a hinge, so the skirt can expand to meet and engage with the rifling in the bore of the barrel.

Skirt

This is designed to catch the blast of air on firing and to expand, making an airtight seal behind the pellet in the barrel. This is the only part of the pellet

Time we dispelled the old airgun shooting adage of .177 for feather .22 for fur

that is in full contact with the bore, picking up spin from the rifling to aid accuracy. This is one reason why the skirt should be checked for deformation. It must be perfectly circular and even-edged to make a proper seal, and to engage correctly with the rifling along the full length of the bore until the vitally important last millisecond as it exits at the muzzle crown.

Internal Profile

This is the hollowed-out section at the rear of the skirt and inside it, which is designed to catch as much air as possible, thus expanding the skirt. When checking the pellet skirt for deformity it's also worth looking into this hollow section to guard against an irregular profile, which is usually caused by the skirt walls being uneven in thickness. Heavier pellets usually have less 'hollow' in relation to the overall size, due to the fact that more lead is used in their construction, which usually means that there's a thicker skirt and a more solid head. These pellets are usually designed for high-powered, FAC-rated air rifles, as they stand up better to the rigours of being blasted along the rifle's bore at much higher velocity.

Pellet Shape and Size

In the distant past, we had a valid excuse for not paying particular attention to our ammo, or 'slugs' as they were and still are affectionately known, as pellet choice was fairly limited.

However, there's now a myriad different configurations of pellets in all popular calibres, so even when you've chosen your combo and calibre of air rifle you're still faced with which type or shape of pellet to use. Fortunately, top-quality ammo is now readily available in all the main pellet designs to suit all shooting disciplines – especially hunting.

Pellet weight is given in what is known as 'grains', denoted by a 'g' or 'gr' after the numerical unit size – e.g. 20g or 20gr – and there are 3000 grains to the pound. The importance of weight in relation to pellet size is more relevant to rifles with FAC-power ratings, so it needn't concern us for the moment. More important is choosing the right pellet to suit your particular 12ft lb hunting combo.

Every airgunner should be aware that every now and then a manufacturer might come up with a new pellet type which they guarantee has better flight characteristics or power transference figures. These are intended to impress us into buying and trying them, but they are usually little more than products made for the sake of grabbing your cash. Oddly-shaped pellets invariably perform oddly!

Here are the main pellet shapes, and their principal features.

Round or Domehead

The most popular type of pellet is still the round-shaped or 'domeheaded' pellet, so named because the head has a rounded dome shape! It has all the characteristics a pellet needs and no more. All major pellet manufacturers will have at least one domehead pellet brand in their range. They may have ribbed skirts, long skirts or whatever, but they'll all still have a rounded head. From this design we've had what can be termed 'hybrids', pellets that have pear-drop shaped heads which are slightly pointed but still smoothly rounded rather than finishing with a true conical point. All stem from the good old basic roundhead design. The only true design feature that can be altered on these pellets is the sizing of the head itself, and the length and angle of skirt. To some extent the latter applies to other pellet shapes as well, but whatever the case, so long as the head is uniform and round in profile this will most certainly be the optimum choice for the hunter. The roundhead is the most accurate lead pellet design for any distance, from close-range through to long-range shooting. That is why FT shooters use nothing else but these types of pellet. Later on, more will be revealed as to why the roundhead is the optimum shape for an airgun pellet in terms of efficiency.

Hollow-Point

This terminology has been heard many times in cop films. 'The shooter used a hollow-point or dum-dum bullet.' I know I used the term 'bullet', but it's still a projectile, and the term 'hollow-point' fills us with images of a bullet that expands massively on impact, doing maximum damage to the target. In powder-propelled firearms ammunition that's very much the case, mainly because it's travelling so fast. Whether it's a live firearm cartridge or an inert lead projectile, the term 'hollow-point' refers to the fact that the projectile has a hollow or recess in the tip of the head, rather like a dimple. This encourages the head of the projectile (the pellet) to expand on impact. Whilst hollow point pellets will do this to some extent, they're not travelling with enough force to give the hunter using them any marked benefit. Although reasonably efficient at close- to medium-range, as hunting pellets they can become slightly unstable in flight over longer ranges. If using them, keep the range comfortably within 30yds and then it should only be your quarry that has any cause for concern.

Pointed

There's a long-held belief that a pointed pellet gives maximum penetration and is therefore the best option for hunting. Thankfully, this is now accepted by most thinking airgun hunters as untrue, despite which many pointed pellets are still sold to those who cling to this questionable belief. In fact, penetration as a benefit for hunting ammo is somewhat of a misnomer, because if you fire any pellet into a substance such as Plasticine from a 12ft lb rifle at 25yds, penetration won't vary greatly, regardless of the shape of the projectile.

Apart from that, the pointed pellet's design is also quite unsuitable for it to be accurate even over moderate ranges. It has poor flight characteristics and damages easily on transportation, and even on handling whilst loading. To work properly, the point of the pellet would need to be exactly coincidental with the centre line axis of the pellet skirt and the mass of the pellet. To manufacture such a pellet would be either ridiculously expensive or almost impossible.

Wadcutter

Sometimes known as the 'flat-head', it'll come as no surprise that this pellet has a head with a flat profile. The theory behind its being useful to the hunter is that the flat frontal surface should transfer maximum energy on impact with the quarry. It probably does so at close range, but it starts running out of velocity as it pushes against the resistance of the air in flight, and it can become unstable even at medium ranges. This pellet is great for 10-metre match shooters, as it is designed to punch neat holes in paper targets; but for hunting I'd recommend you give it a wide berth.

Does Size Matter?

Despite all the discussion and arguments that have occurred over pellet choice, there are still the main two to be considered – the .177 and .22 calibres. Whilst the world has mostly gone metric, we still know these pellets by their imperial increments (.177 inch and .22 inch), although their metric equivalents are

4.5mm and 5.5mm respectively. However, certain manufacturers supply these calibres in slightly larger width increments. A slightly larger pellet in the same nominal calibre, which may be only 0.1mm larger than the recognised standard, could well sit more snugly in the barrel of your particular rifle and be more efficient as it travels down the bore – i.e. shoot more accurately. This is when it really pays to experiment with various pellets to find which best suits your particular rifle. (Shooters using full-blown bullet-firing rifles find the same thing.)

The other, less widely known and used calibres, while they have their followers, do have particular characteristics that give them specific yet limited appeals, and they are therefore worthy of further investigation. The .20 calibre (5mm) pellet is often termed 'the compromise calibre' and because of all the arguments this causes it could be better termed 'the controversial calibre'. In the UK it's by far the least popular, but is much used and respected by our American cousins. It must be noted that the range of pellet choices for the .20 is limited, and therefore, in effect, it is a self-limiting calibre option. Theoretically, due to its size, you'd think you'd get the compromise of benefits – i.e. that it'd have a flatter trajectory than a .22 calibre, but hit harder than a .177. While on paper this is true, most .20 calibre pellets weigh much the same as their .22 calibre relatives, so by and large you don't gain very much. However, shooters who are seduced by this calibre can be almost fanatical in their devotion to it, especially if shooting at FAC-power levels. I can't help but feel that there is some flawed psychology in this devotion. It obviously looks bigger than a .177 and feels heavier, but, as it looks smaller than a .22, then it must be a compromise between the two. You'll note by the trajectory graph which follows that it does have some benefits, not the least of which is a flatter trajectory. But in practical situations facing the hunter shooting at sensible ranges, does wind and gravity have that much less effect on a pellet because it's 0.5mm less in diameter? I'm not convinced that it has these supposed, almost magical ballistic qualities and don't think I ever will be, but they do say, 'never say never', don't they? They also say that having confidence in your rifle/scope/ammo combo has a lot to do with your performance, and I wholeheartedly agree with that.

Now to the 'big slug' – the .25in (6.3mm) calibre. This brute has been around for as long as airguns themselves, but whilst at one time it revelled in a certain amount of infamy for its sledgehammer hit, it has by and large fallen out of favour with shooters, gun manufacturers and suppliers of good-quality ammo. The trouble is that, like the .20 calibre, it does have its devotees in the specialised uses it supposedly caters for, which are close-range rat and feral pigeon, pest control shooting. It does transmit a lot of stopping power with little or no possibility of over-penetration, thus reducing the danger of ricochets and potential damage to buildings, but at the cost of having a very pronounced trajectory curve. This is a most specialised calibre, possibly only worth considering by those who shoot regularly at close-range with a 12ft lb rifle, or the FAC-power shooter wanting extra clout, and provided you can cope with a trajectory like a horseshoe! I'm half joking, but you'll come to realise the validity of that last statement in the section devoted to FAC-rated air rifles.

Ballistics

Let's look now at the physics and facts pertaining to a lead projectile fired at a given muzzle velocity – in this case enough to produce 12ft lbs of pellet muzzle energy – which should be considered by the hunter in relation to the all-important kill-zone on his quarry.

First, it really does come down to physics, or in this case the specific branch of physics known as ballistics,

The four basic pellet types – but even these have variations

and in particular to the velocity (speed) the pellet is travelling at, in relation to its mass (weight). This in its most basic form is an explanation of how energy is transmitted or delivered to the target. The delivery of energy to the target is often termed 'shock effect' or (a term I tend to use to a lesser extent) trauma. More specifically, for a head shot, an animal or bird will die of the equivalent of what is known in human terms as 'blunt force trauma'. 'Heart failure' is a more appropriate term for when a pellet has hit any other vital organ. It's worth looking further into this because, in essence, you have four areas where vital organs are found that can be termed as kill-zones. In certain species, and due to their position in the body and the quarry's visible profile in relation to your shooting position, these can be so small they're of little use for placing the pellet, but worth mentioning nonetheless. These are the brain (skull), central nervous system (back or side of neck) heart (chest cavity) and lungs (chest cavity, and found on either side of the breast bone of a bird).

For pellet placement you're now reduced to three major areas on the quarry's body, and then only in relation to how it presents itself to you in your shooting position. These are head, neck and chest. All are dealt with in more detail in the relevant sections on the individual quarry species, but it's worth keeping the headshot at the forefront of your mind, as this is the most important of the aiming points. Deliver your hunting shots with precision into the 'napper' and you're aiming right and killing cleanly.

In considering ballistics, the smaller .177 calibre pellet delivers its shock effect mainly through its speed (velocity). Due to its smaller mass it travels faster than a larger .22 pellet fired at the same muzzle energy (ft lbs). It also retains velocity over a longer range. However, the fact that it travels so fast and is quite small has given rise to criticisms of its tendency to produce over-penetration at the target, and at medium-range this can result in the pellet passing right through the target. But a .22 calibre pellet fired at medium-range can in fact pretty much duplicate this effect of over-penetration. This is doubly confusing when you consider that a larger pellet delivers more shock value due to its larger mass, but as its velocity is slower there's less likelihood of it over-penetrating at longer distances.

But consider this. While a medium-weight .177 pellet of say 7.9g will fly faster than a heavier-weight pellet of the same calibre, the heavier pellet penetrates further into the target at the same distance. This is due to the pellet's extra weight or, better put, extra mass slamming into the target, and here's a very interesting twist: a faster .177 pellet actually penetrates less than a heavier, larger .22 calibre pellet, and that's with both projectiles fired at the same muzzle energy. This is because a heavier pellet has a better ballistic coefficient, and retains greater downrange energy. Before leaving this topic it's worth noting that, irrespective of calibre, medium-weight domehead pellets – percentage wise – retain almost the same impact energy and virtually the same velocity at 30yds as their heavyweight counterparts. This further supports the fact that weight or mass of pellet has a strong bearing on penetration at the target at this range, and helps explain why the round-head design is still the top dog for a hunting pellet.

What should we make of all this? Initially it would seem that the .22 calibre pellet is the better choice for hunting, because the facts and figures of penetration, velocity and energy retention all look good on paper. Computer chronograph read-outs of velocities, and ballistic putty or other such media used to illustrate the penetration of pellets, can only give you the base, theoretical guidelines. These are test results in controlled conditions, and not what you can expect to be exactly replicated on flesh and bone in the hunting field, which will be discussed later. Also, as mentioned before, shock or trauma is only part of the killing equation. If you hit the mark with a .177 pellet with sufficient energy, the fact you've hit the vital organ means a cleanly dispatched target. Indeed, anybody who hunts regularly with a .177 can't fail to notice how much bloodier the killing wound often is. The reason for this is that the .177 pellet will sever everything it slices into and cause a lot of internal damage to blood vessels, tissue, organs and arteries. Who says it isn't an efficient hunting calibre? It should therefore now be apparent that getting the pellet accurately to the target has priority over the size of that pellet. This brings us neatly to the facts surrounding trajectory in relation to size of calibre and weight of pellets.

Trajectory

When a pellet is fired from an air rifle, irrespective of calibre, it follows a curved path in flight, known as the trajectory. Incidentally, trajectory applies to the path taken by any object in flight fired under a given pressure. The chart/graph that follows clearly illustrates flight path characteristics of all four pellet sizes.

Trajectory Chart

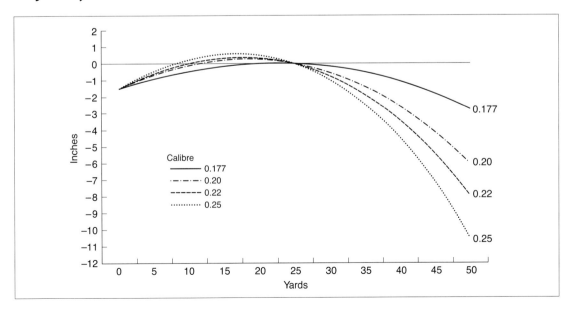

You'll notice the .177 calibre has the flattest trajectory, whilst the large .25 has the most pronounced. Of course, a heavy .177 pellet will have a more pronounced trajectory than a standard or lighter pellet of the same calibre, and this principle obviously applies to all heavier pellets, irrespective of calibre. So why mention it here? If a heavier, small calibre pellet is used, more shock effect is created due to its having a larger mass. By and large heavier pellets are designed for higher power-rated rifles, or FAC-rated air rifles as they're known. I don't want to linger unduly on the smaller calibre, but it does give food for thought that a slightly heavier .177 calibre pellet fired at 12ft lbs can be a much better proposition for the hunter, affording more heft on impact, a flatter trajectory, and better stability in flight than a lighter .22 calibre pellet. Heavyweight .22 calibre pellets are very much the choice for FAC rifles, as not only do they transfer much more stopping power but are less likely to lose shape and deform as a result of the higher pressures involved in firing. Interestingly, in general, heavyweight pellets are more suited for all benefits that they afford the shooter when fired using a PCP, whereas light to medium weights work more efficiently when fired from a spring- or gas-ram-powered air rifle.

Earlier I touched on ballistic tests – i.e. pellets being fired into a block of Plasticine or ballistic putty. The block is then cut in two to show the path taken as the pellet enters the material and slows to a stop inside it. Whilst these make for interesting study, again note that these results should still be looked upon as guidelines as to what actually happens when a pellet impacts on a live animal. Remember that a layer of fat and an outer protection of feather or fur, depending on the quarry, is added to the flesh and bone surrounding the kill-zone. These aren't uniform substances like the material used in the laboratory tests you often see. If you really want to know how a pellet performs when impacting on the quarry kill-zone, then on retrieving the kill, cut out the pellet. Distasteful as it may seem, it's a good idea to examine the wound externally and internally. Look at how the pellet has distorted on impact. Again – and this is borne out by many years of hunting – if you retrieve a pellet from your quarry, especially a bird, then more often than not the pellet will have changed very little in shape unless it has hit or smashed through bone. Internally, the wound will show extensive tissue damage leading to blood loss. But one thing is for certain and that is, whatever calibre and pellet type you choose for your hunting combo, stick with it and learn its trajectory so you are able to make the required adjustments in aim for all distances. This is known as allowing 'holdunder' or 'holdover' at the target, and even though we touch on it here, the practicalities are looked at in much more detail in the following chapter pertaining to range estimation and evaluation.

When considering the physics of pellets in flight, look again at the trajectory chart and notice how the pellets share a common factor, in that they all leave the muzzle well below the set zero before arcing upwards and descending to the zero point – predetermined by the shooter – and then drop (fall away) the further they get from the zero distance. The pellet exits the muzzle below the horizontal line of the scope due to the simple and obvious fact that the barrel is set below the fixed aiming axis given by the scope mounted above the rifle's barrel. So, in effect, you have two predetermined zero points for a pellet fired over any distance – one close to the rifle's muzzle and the other at the set zero. These are determined not only by the main zero set by the shooter, but by variables such as scope height, pellet calibre, muzzle velocity and pellet weight.

To simplify this, a medium-weight .22 calibre pellet fired at approximately 12ft lbs and zeroed at 25yds crosses through the horizontal line of aim (the 'first zero') at approximately 10–12 yards, and then drops into the set zero of 25 yards before progressively falling off until it hits the ground due to loss of momentum – or, more correctly, loss of velocity. This very basic explanation serves to illustrate why you need to allow

Smackdown! Any calibre pellet placed with precision will do its deadly duty

for what is known as holdunder (shooting lower) the closer the target is from the set zero, and allow for holdover (shooting higher) the further from your set zero the target is. As you can see, less adjustment is needed for the smaller, flatter-shooting .177 calibre. This is one of the main reasons why the smallest calibre is so popular with FT shooters, and also why it is now becoming increasingly popular with hunters. Indeed, I'll stick my neck out and say that this has only become more established by hunters as PCPs have become more accepted and used as hunting tools. The reason is that the recoilless attributes of a PCP air rifle give a much increased accuracy potential; therefore longer-range shots are taken more often than they were formerly. Once again, it seems we can learn a lot from the target boys.

Unfortunately, if the .177 has a downside it's the fact it can be affected by wind, particularly a heavy crosswind. A larger, heavier pellet does tend to fly more true, but this doesn't mean the .177 pellet gets blown around like confetti. Besides, how often do you hunt at long range in breezy conditions? You shouldn't need or want to, so in that respect I personally find nothing to condemn the smaller calibre.

The trajectory chart only applies to a shot fired along the horizontal plane in ideal conditions. When we come to shooting at upward or downward angles in the field other nuances have to be reckoned with and allowed for. Many hunters find that when shooting at awkward angles, rangefinding and pellet placement can go sorely out of the window. This will be dealt with in the following chapter – because, at times, air rifle hunting ain't easy!

Power Checker

A common misconception is that if the air rifle is more powerful then it will be more efficient at dispatching quarry. Wrong! You're now aware that accuracy at the target is the vital factor. I've often made mention of 12ft lbs being the legal limit for 'off ticket' (i.e. no FAC required) air rifles, and in the main hunting rifles should be running fairly close to the 12ft lb legal limit. But it's the responsibility of every airgun hunter who does not possess an FAC that his air rifle doesn't exceed that limit. A responsible shooter should actually be thinking of running the rifle at around the 11.4–11.6ft lb mark with medium-weight ammo. This way, if heavier or lighter ammo is used, the power theoretically shouldn't rise above the current 12ft lb legal limit. Remember, should you be stopped by the police and your rifle checked for any reason, then the powers that be are allowed to test the rifle with any ammo they choose.

So – how to stay legal? At this point, readers should make a mental note to take their air rifle to the nearest specialist airgun shop and have it checked over their chronograph. This is an electronic gadget that can measure the speed of the pellet, and by using the correct formula it will give you the muzzle energy of the rifle in ft lbs. Muzzle energy can be calculated once you know the speed of the pellet in feet per second (f.p.s) and the pellet's weight. The formula is used like this. First, square the speed of the pellet, then multiply it by the pellet's weight in grains, and then divide by what is known as the 'common factor' or 'gravitational constant' – a figure of 450240. This gives you that pellet's power in ft lbs. There are little chronographs that do the maths for you, and all you need do is punch in the weight and calibre of the pellet, shoot a few to gain an average velocity, and then read the figure off the digital readout. They don't cost the earth, and what's important is that they'll keep you on the right side of the law.

Pellet Preparation and Care

There's no use spending time on pellet preparation if your pellets aren't of a good standard to begin with. Thankfully, most of today's big brand name pellets have got the basics right. These mean good-quality lead used in manufacture, a consistent manufacturing quality control, good inspection processes and transportation and supply in suitable protective packaging to prevent pellet deformation.

As the company goes to all this trouble to get pellets in as good condition as possible to the consumer, it seems strange that many of us are still content to just empty a few into the pocket of a shooting jacket and set off for a session. Granted, airgun hunters have done this for aeons, so why shouldn't it continue? Well, it can – if reasonable results are all you desire, but if you want to achieve the finest accuracy and results you and your combo are capable of, then a little time taken preparing pellets can bring surprisingly fewer 'flyers' and save you from those infuriating, unexplained misses.

Don't get me wrong. I'm not suggesting you go to the lengths of the World Class standard FT boys, with washing, grading, weighing, sizing and lubricating. Yes, you can do all that; but just a few simpler procedures will save you much frustration in the field. First, tip your pellets out of the packaging onto a few sheets of clean brown, unwaxed wrapping paper or newspaper. Depending on the pellet brand, you'll probably be surprised at the amount of swarf (metal filings and small cuttings) that comes out with them. If the pellets have bits of swarf stuck in the skirts, you have no option than to wash them. A swirl around in a bowl of light soapy water, then rinsing and drying, will suffice. I know, it's hassle, but it's worth the trouble, and if this is a regular occurrence – find another pellet brand.

Hopefully, all you need do is pick the pellets up one at a time, and while checking the skirt for damage blow out the very few bits that may be found. If you find a pellet with a deformed skirt, dispose of it. Also check that the head is undamaged and uniform.

While checking this, ensure that the waist is central so the head and skirt are perfectly aligned on the horizontal. You could go as far as to buy a set of special scales, but you're going down a laborious road, and I've not felt the need to weigh top-quality pellets individually, so visual inspection is my main criterion for preparation. However, before returning them to the tin or box, a light spray with pellet lube is advisable. Allow them to dry naturally, and then carefully put them back in the box or tin.

At this point, I'd like to refer to the fact that some writers say they prefer to use single-shot rifles because they can inspect each pellet for every shot. This is a tad misleading. You can scrutinise each pellet just as closely while filling a multi-shot magazine as you can when loading them one at a time into the breech. The slight damage that may occur when a pellet is probed from a magazine is minimal and soon put to rights when the air blasts the pellet skirt outwards to make contact with the barrel bore. In other words, don't be misled into thinking that a one-shot rifle is the tool for total precision.

After taking all this care, a pellet pouch is a handy aid for carrying extra ammo on your shoot, and much better than just tipping a few into a jacket pocket. If you insist on just pocketing them, then make sure the pocket is clear of dirt and grit, and never put anything else – such as compact binos – into the pocket with them. Also, use a pocket that you're not likely to lean against, so there's no possibility of pellets being crushed and therefore deformed before use.

To sum up all of this, especially pertaining to initial selection of a pellet brand, I'd say choose a roundhead pellet which through careful trial and testing, you find really suits your combo and then stick with it. Incidentally, you'll find most roundhead pellets look almost identical in profile, but in actuality they will differ, and you'll find some more suited to precision air rifles with tightly-choked barrels. Only by trial and error will you discover which is best suited to your particular rifle. However, as a general rule of thumb, German manufactured pellets are a tad larger than other European ones. The best brands will even have the exact sizing written on the tin in millimetres. In that respect you can see why it really does pay to try a varied selection of quality pellets to find the brand and type that best suits your rifle. Look for a brand known for its consistency in size and weight. They'll probably be more expensive, but that's because quality pellets are more expensive to produce.

As for buying tin-after-tin, or box-upon-box, of the same batch number, it can be worth your while doing this if you do find a batch that your rifle particularly likes. This is because pellets with the same batch numbers are made from the same die set. Just a little warning though – don't go buying the shop's whole stock of them as, if you don't shoot a hell of a lot pellets, they can oxidise if left for a lengthy period of time. No amount of cleaning can sort out badly pitted pellets, and most hunters don't want to buy 10,000 slugs at a time – or will you?

Take heed – don't chop and change ammo, and do check your rifle's zero regularly. While doing that, you also need to get down to some serious target practice to attain hunting accuracy.

Gun Handling, Sighting and Firing

Shooting Techniques Explained

Air rifle engineering technology has come along in leaps and bounds in a relatively short space of time. Suffice to say that a newcomer to the sport today can be spoiled, because many modern air rifles, and PCPs in particular, almost shoot themselves! They need only a guiding hand or two and an aiming eye to place the pellet exactly where it needs to go – the all-important kill-zone. But no matter how good the gear you might be fortunate enough to use, you still need to have grasped the basics of gun handling to make full, safe and proper use of the technology you're holding.

When hunting with a rifle of any description, the more we shoot the more we tend to take the basics for granted, yet it's the basics that can mean the difference between success and failure in the field. Many, like me, probably first began learning to shoot using a spring-powered air rifle; but then as we moved up through the ranks, eventually to shoot PCPs, it's all too easy to forget those first tentative shots we fired, and what a basic rifle they were fired with.

Let's get back to basics and look at the various elements of correct gun handling and, in turn, accurate and consistent shooting.

Although airgun hunters are bombarded by stories of successful shots at quarry at 50yds and beyond, it should always be remembered these are only achieved consistently by very experienced shooters, and only when conditions allow. Every hunter should only shoot within the limits of their personal skills and ability, and always show respect for quarry.

Another important factor the hunter should always remember is that they're taking part in a sport that requires a certain level of physical fitness and that level varies depending on the demands of the hunting techniques you're employing. You shouldn't or wouldn't want to go to the gym or go jogging, for instance, if you had a heavy cold or worse. So why go hunting when you're feeling under the weather. Granted, it may do you good to get out for a spot of fresh air, but it's better to go without your rifle. Take this as a prime opportunity to go out and observe. How you feel physically – and even mentally – will affect your performance in the field. Don't drag yourself out just for the sake of going, as you'll end up missing easy shots, getting frustrated and wishing you hadn't bothered. At worse, you may even have an accident! Instead, you could brush up your accuracy at home on targets – which brings me nicely to the subject of where to practise safely, and how to set up your own target range.

Home on the Range

If you're not a member of an established gun club or don't have access to a target range, then there's nothing for it but to build your own. This is known as a 'plinking' range, and as long as you have at least 25yds of clear, unobstructed, privately-owned space from the shooting position to a secure pellet stopping/catching backstop, then you're in business. The backstop is the most important part of the set-up, as it needs to

Eye-relief and head position are vital for giving you an accurate full sight picture

be strong and secure enough to stop the pellet going through and beyond the property you own. If it isn't, you're not only shooting irresponsibly and illegally, but also inviting an accident to happen. For this reason it should be stressed that a backstop can never be too sturdy. Granted, in relation to a bullet fired from a cartridge-firing firearm, a pellet fired from a 12ft lb air rifle is very low-powered, but when pellets are continuously hitting in the same general area on even the thickest piece of wood, they will quickly start to wear a way through. This is why backstops not only need to be of a suitably strong construction but also checked periodically for damage. Many shooters use a couple of old, scrap doors with carpeting thrown over the front to help lessen the penetration of the pellet. The carpet not only helps reduce damage and prevent ricochets but also absorbs the sound the pellet makes if it is allowed to impact continuously on bare wood.

My recommendation for a backstop is at least a double layer of solid wooden doors over which you can put at least two or three layers of carpet. Fire doors are perfect, as they're made from 1½-inch thick solid wood, and like other doors you'll find them on builders' skips when they're demolishing office buildings and the like. Keep your eyes open and don't be afraid to ask if you see doors being thrown out. More often than not, the previous owners will be glad to see the back of them, and if you remove them it means less rubbish for them to shift. A word to the wise concerning the carpet used: although you might think it best to pile umpteen amounts onto the doors it's actually better to use just two or three layers, and when these show signs of too much damage, replace them with fresh layers. This prevents an excessive amount of carpet becoming waterlogged and gungy, and therefore almost impossible to remove come the time to replace it. If you've a garage or large shed, you can store old, spare carpet, and never pass up the chance of an unwanted door or two. I use my backstop so often that I've even built a wall of bricks and mortar that the doors lean against. This is approximately 6ft in height by 8ft wide and gives me total peace of mind because the pellets are never going to pass through to the neighbouring garden. Even so, I regularly check the condition of the carpet, the wooden doors and even the wall behind.

With a backstop sorted, what do you shoot at? Well, there are the obvious paper targets, which I mount onto heavy-duty metal bulldog clips hung on metal cup-hooks. A simple idea, but the clips make changing targets very easy. The same goes for reactive targets such as chalk discs. These are simply hung on small nails that I tack onto the backstop itself. Chalk disc targets give a satisfying feeling of achievement as they shatter on pellet impact, and they really do help keep you practising for longer periods. There are many other reactive targets readily available, such as spinners, and resettable fall-flats (knockovers or knockdowns).

Knockdown targets are nothing new, and have been the norm in FT competitions for almost as long as the sport itself. However, the size of the plate that needs to be hit to knock it over bears no relation in shape or position on the target to the kill-zone of the quarry it mimics. This is because the mechanics of design oblige the makers to position a circular hit-zone in the centre, rather than at the head, for optimum target operation efficiency. Other similar-principle targets, but more realistic to the hunter, are the kill-zone profile fall-flats from AirgunSport. These not only represent a true kill-zone but are in profile as well. The rabbit fall-flat consists of a profile of a rabbit's head, while the rat fall-flat shows the profile of the first third of the body. These are realistic target areas – especially the latter – as hitting the real thing here would result in a clean kill.

Whilst I use both knockdowns and fall-flats, it must be said that while your neighbours might put up with a dull thud of a pellet hitting a sound-deadening backstop, how tolerant would they be to the continuous 'ting' of an airgun pellet on metal? Even now, I prefer to use these targets by taking them along to any reasonably-sized field on one of my shoots, to practise in different shooting positions. This type of real-life practice will also be dealt with further in the chapter on Shooting at Night. Here you'll really appreciate the ability to duplicate a hunting scenario under controlled conditions, but without targeting live quarry. It's much better for the hunter than continuously putting shot after shot down a range from a bench rest. Later in this book there'll be a clear description of setting out a field course to help you hone your rangefinding and accuracy. My garden range is mainly used for setting up my hunting rigs, and setting and checking zero. Again, it must be remembered that safety needs to be at the forefront of your mind at all times when preparing or actually shooting. Here are a few safety rules that all shooters should adhere to:

- Never leave a loaded rifle unattended. This applies to the private target range just as much as it does at a club or in the hunting field.
- Never point a gun at anything that you don't regard as a legitimate target – even if you believe the gun to be unloaded.
- When loading a break-barrel, under-lever or side-lever action rifle, always hold onto the barrel or lever while thumbing-in a pellet.
- Never dry-fire a spring or gas-ram-powered air rifle – i.e. cocking and firing without a pellet being loaded into the breech. It can cause extensive internal damage as the piston slams forward unbuffered by a pellet, as it should be pushing against one in its effort to propel it from the barrel.

Getting a Grip

Successful air rifle hunting is a combination of many factors, but correct gun handling – thus giving a consistent level of accuracy – is one of the most important. Then there's experience and fieldcraft – and even just good old common sense. Correct gun handling means what the term implies – how you handle, or hold, the rifle while you take a shot. This is all about consistency – i.e. holding the rifle in the same way for every shot. Correct, consistent handling is even more important when using recoiling rifles such as springers, as they have a definite firing cycle that is mechanically the same for every shot. What the shooter has to do is work with this cycle, rather than against it.

First let's deal with the way you hold the rifle. It shouldn't be held too tightly; rather, it should just be snugly supported or cradled by the shooter, allowing it to go through its firing cycle unrestrained. In other

Practice in the standing position as many times you'll need to take shots such as this

words, you need to let the rifle 'breathe'. The object is almost to work with the rifle, acting to give it stability while equally instructing it through your actions of steadily aiming it and ultimately guiding the pellet towards the target. Follow-through is also important, and this means keeping the gun in aim and on target after it is fired. This is very important because moving the rifle, even slightly, after squeezing off a shot will have pellets flying all over the place. Remember that even after you've slipped the trigger, the pellet is – for milliseconds – still travelling along the barrel, and thus still affected by your actions. Incidentally, follow-through is also needed for a recoilless PCP, as the lock time (the period between squeezing the trigger and the pellet leaving the muzzle) is usually longer than the lock time of a springer or gas-ram rifle.

A problem that can affect any rifle is can,' or tilting. Once a rifle/scope combo has been zeroed for a particular range, if you hold the rifle differently, leaning to one side or another, even if the rifle is only slightly askew in your grip, the impact point of the pellet will be off the original set zero. This is called 'cant', and can only be remedied by practice and consistency in your gun handling. You could fit a scope-mounted spirit level or an electronic level aid which visually helps you line up the rifle squarely on the target, shot after shot, but it's far better to begin by learning correct gun handling without these aids. Another thing to remember is that you can't rest a spring or gas-ram-powered rifle directly on a solid object while taking a shot. The rifle will literally bounce off as it goes through its firing cycle, with accuracy being badly affected as a result. You can, however, rest the rifle cushioned in your hand, which can then be rested on a solid object such as a branch, gate or fencepost.

Because many PCP air rifles use what are known as free-floating barrels, don't make the mistake of resting the front of the barrel or the silencer on any solid object. If you need to, always rest it using the underside of the air reservoir, buddy bottle or preferably the underside of the stock. Resting a rifle on a free-floating barrel will have the weight of the air reservoir, or buddy bottle – and of course the stock – weighing down and therefore lifting the barrel upwards, badly affecting accuracy.

Another recommended support is to shoot in a seated position with your left knee pulled up towards your body with your arms forming a brace around you. The left hand should hold your upper right forearm so that the rifle can be rested over your forward arm. Of course, for left-handers the opposite applies. This is an established FT shooting style, but one the hunter can adopt when the opportunity arises. Unfortunately, it's only of use if you've previously had time to take up an ambush position, but as long as you don't have to stay put for hours it's a surprisingly comfortable position to adopt.

A relaxed grip and steady follow-through are essential to consistent

Shots up at birds in trees are fraught with many variables – one being to ensure the pellet has a clear path to the target

accuracy with a spring or gas-ram-powered air rifle, and also major considerations for shooting with any other type of air rifle. Whilst the following applies to most shooting positions, in the main they apply to shooting the rifle freehand, or from a standing position.

If you're using a spring-powered rifle it should be held firmly enough to keep the rifle on aim, rested in your hold as you sight on the target through the scope or along the open sights. Also, any rifle, irrespective of power source and with or without a scope fitted, has a point of balance. Your leading hand should be positioned approximately 2 to 3 inches in front of this balance point. Adopting this shooting grip while standing is known as the offhand stance, and many opportunist snap-shots will be taken from this position. This is fine if you're using a light- to medium-weight rifle such as a carbine, but if using a hefty full-length sporter it can become a strain and cause you to wobble, the longer you hold on aim, due to your arm muscles taking all the weight. If you do have more time to take the shot, pull the elbow of your leading arm round to rest into your hip – another stance favoured by FT shooters – as this affords a much more stable aim.

Even better, if the situation allows, is to adopt the kneeling position. In this position the leading arm can be rested on the left knee with your bottom sitting on your right foot, heel tucked under the body and with the right knee rested on the ground. Of course, the opposite of this applies to lefties, which involves resting your leading arm on your right knee, and sitting on your left foot. There's a slight variation of the kneeling position and, if the ground isn't too muddy, it is one that is even more stable. This is to kneel lower with the right shin almost flat to the ground, ensuring that you're sitting comfortably on the lower leg, with your right foot tucked under your bum. This allows you to rest the upper forearm of your leading arm along your left thigh, rather than only the elbow. A much more relaxed and therefore stable shooting position can be achieved by sitting in this way. More detail for changing shooting positions is outlined later, when we come to combining fieldcraft and shooting techniques in the field.

When on the target range, and whichever shooting position you use, don't pull the rifle butt-pad too tightly into your shoulder, as this will have the same effect as gripping the stock too tightly, because it causes tremors. Another factor that needs to be considered is that the impact point of the pellet shifts off zero when you alter the position you're shooting from. For instance, if you set zero in the kneeling position, don't expect it to be the same when shooting in the standing or prone position. Again, judging these zero shifts is a skill which, like all aspects pertaining to your shooting technique, can only be achieved with dedicated and applied practice.

When shooting prone (i.e. lying down), where possible I prefer to deploy a bipod, especially if waiting in ambush. Often this isn't possible, and if you've decided to go stalking you might not even have the bipod in place, and for most airgun hunters out for a spot of general hunting, the shot taken from the prone position is more often than not at the end of a stalk. You'd think the shot would be the easy part as you are well within range, and taking the shot should be a matter of course. Often it is, but after stalking a twitchy bunny you'll be pumping with adrenalin and this, coupled with the physical and mental exertion, means your nerves will probably be sending tremors around every muscle and fibre, with your breathing being laboured, heavy or both!

The technique of stalking is dealt with in full in the chapter on Hunting Techniques, but the prone shooting-style needs further discussion here. For a recoilless PCP then as long as you're comfortable, the main difference you'll notice is that the scope will seem closer to your eye, because lying prone tends to push your head further forward than when you are shooting either kneeling or standing. It doesn't take much to adopt a style that will allow for this, and the optimum way to combat it is to let the rifle out of the crook of the shoulder to rest in the upper arm, pulled slightly back. In this position your shooting (trigger) hand is holding the grip and rifle squarely onto the target, whilst your leading arm should act as a rest for the rifle's foreend.

Shooting a recoiling rifle such as a springer or gas-ram from the prone position is a different matter altogether. This is because in this position both arms holding the rifle are in direct contact with the ground – i.e. a hard surface. The rifle will therefore tend to jump off zero, either to the left or right. Some find the muzzle is more likely to flip, causing pellets to fly higher than the set zero. There's no way around this but to familiarise yourself with the particular zero shift and keep a mental note of it while you target your quarry and 'aim off' accordingly. Again, only practice will give you the ability to shoot like this and, like the standing position, this is one you need to master fully. I'll reiterate the fact that you can't always get away with using a bipod with a PCP, as many times it won't be practical to have the 'pod in situ. One aspect of the prone position is that strain is soon felt on the lower back muscles. To combat this you can raise yourself up more on your elbows with your back slightly arched, so you're not cricking the back upwards at the waist. There are some situations that allow the body to fall into a more relaxed position for prone shooting, such as when lying over a slight hillock or from a ditch. These are usually prime areas for ambush shooting, and more information for body positioning can be found in the relevant sections pertaining to shooting using a bipod. Always remember that an unduly uncomfortable shooting position isn't conducive to accuracy.

It's worth noting here that of all shooting positions, the seated position is the one that offers most variations on a theme – almost like a fine-tuning of the body position to achieve the most stable and comfortable hold. You will find which suits you by trial and error, and simply by practising. As examples, you can sit with the left leg half outstretched and your leading arm rested along the thigh, with the left leg raising or lowering to adjust height of shot. Alternatively, you can form a brace for the arms. Sit with your bottom flat on the floor, and half raise both legs at the knee approximately a shoulder-width apart. Then rest the elbows of both arms into the lower inner thighs or alongside the knees of the corresponding leg to arm. It sounds confusing, but is a very comfortable position and one that can be held for quite a lengthy period of time.

Then there is another particularly stable seated position, which is found by keeping the bum flat to the ground but drawing the right leg towards and across you into the half-lotus position (no sniggering!) and drawing the left leg inwards and upwards to form the front support. Rest the elbow of the leading arm on the lower thigh of the left leg, just behind the kneecap. Obviously, for left-handed shooting from all positions, the opposite leading arms to raised legs apply. You don't need to take yoga classes, but do take the trouble to experiment with the seated position because many times it's the body position that will keep a shot steady.

Sight Pictures

For open sights the sight picture relates to the position of the foresight within the rear sight, and those two superimposed on the quarry. For telescopic sights it relates to the clearer view you see as you look through the scope.

Although many hunters will go straight for a set of optics on their hunting rifle, for reasons of thoroughness I've already dealt with open sights. In relation to shooting with a scope I've also explained the distance known as eye relief, but it is worth re-capping here in relation to your shooting technique.

Eye relief means the distance your leading (aiming) eye is positioned rearwards from the scope's eyepiece. This varies with individuals (and also depends on the scope being used) but for most shooters it's usually around three inches or so, a distance that gives you a full sight picture – i.e. you can see the full circle of the front objective lens through the rear lens. Once you've set your scope in the scope mounts you'll probably feel you've got it just right, and more often than not you will. However, a little trick to ensure correct eye relief is to close your eyes for a few seconds, bring the rifle up to your shoulder and hold it in the most comfortable aim position with your head resting on the cheekpiece, then open your aiming eye to look through the scope. If you need to move your head forward or backward, even slightly, to attain a full sight picture through the scope, then you've not set the scope eye relief correctly to suit your natural hold. Also check that the scope crosshairs are still in line with the plumb line on the backstop you originally used to centre the scope. They too could be slightly out. Try it, as you may well be surprised to find that the eye relief and scope setting you've previously been shooting with is incorrect. If so take the time to adjust the

Many times during a hunt, it'll be possible to adopt the more stable kneeling position

77

The 'over-knee' F.T. position is very stable to use but not always practical

scope accordingly. Listen to your body, because while your eyes are closed it will naturally adopt the most comfortable position that is best for you when holding the rifle. Get it right, and you'll soon notice the difference in your accuracy and your success in the field. Do set up the eye relief for the standing shooting position if you are sure most shots will be taken from that stance. It's worth noting that scopes that have a longer degree of eye relief often prevent the shooter having to waste precious time in adjusting head position for awkwardly angled shots.

When adjusting the power ring for different magnifications on a variable-power scope, you'll find that a scope with a longer eye relief always gives you a full sight picture, as long as you've mounted the scope correctly. Scopes like this are also one solution for a rifle that may otherwise need to have more conventional optics fitted in set-back mounts to obtain correct eye relief.

Allowing For Range and Other Variables

Rangefinding and estimation have already been discussed in the chapter on Scopes, but a scope can only help you determine the range if you know how to use that particular optic's reticle to do so. Also, most hunters using the 30/30 or duplex-style reticle will use what is known as 'holdover' for a target further than the set zero, and 'holdunder' for a closer target.

Now for the nitty-gritty of considerations relating to shooting at live quarry. In a perfect world the target would be perpendicular to your aim and within a yard or so of your set zero. In reality, what is more likely is that after hours of waiting in ambush or careful stalking you either virtually trip over a bunny, or a woodie pitches into the trees at well beyond your set zero. Here you have two obvious range differences and two vastly different angles of fire to the target. So what to do? I'm sorry to harp on, but only practice and familiarisation with your combo will give you the experience to allow the correct amount of holdunder or holdover. These allowances will also vary depending on whether you're shooting the smaller .177 or larger .22 calibre pellet. Less adjustment – i.e. less aiming-off allowance – is needed for the .177 calibre and that is one of the main reasons why many hunters are now switching to it. It does not allow a sloppy shooting technique or bad range estimation, but by and large it is far more forgiving of slight errors on the part of the shooter.

As I've recommended, hunters to have a selection of rifles at their disposal in at least the two main calibres, I must also stress the importance of relearning those aim points for holdunder and holdover when you switch rifle combo. Even the occasional flirtation with the smaller calibre will have you feeling overconfident at longer range with the .22. In other words, it's back to the target range before you shoot at live quarry, so that you're back in tune with the trajectory and particular qualities of the rifle/scope/ammo equation that makes up the combo. Yes, it is a combo because all three (indeed four, including yourself) make up the final 'team' you use to cleanly dispatch your chosen quarry; and always, repeat, always stick with the same ammo you used to zero your rifle and scope for the hunting trips that follow.

Earlier I touched on the angle of fire. This is the angle at which the barrel is pointed towards the target, whether upwards or downwards. It seems that even experienced hunters disagree on the allowance that needs to be made for awkwardly angled shots. Even now I'm not a great fan of the longer-range shot into the tops of trees, the reason being that there are so many variables to contend with besides gravity. At the top of a tree the wind will be at its strongest, and will therefore affect your pellet in flight. You can, of course, watch the upper branches and twigs for indications of any wind strength and direction. Those who say they can regularly judge a shot on a swaying bird are usually not giving the full story. It can be done, but should only be the type of shot you make when you have become fully accustomed to virtually every shooting situation and angle, and have experienced what gravity, wind and even your confidence can do to a pellet's flight path. The same airgun hunters who brag about these shots might admit to clean misses, but they're certainly not admitting to the times they've downed the bird but only wounded it. This is worse still if it has flown off to die, rather than retrieved at the foot of the tree and swiftly dispatched. So if unsure – don't take the shot. Wait until a shot within your capabilities presents itself – and don't worry, because it will. While on the sensitive subject of wounding, it's a situation that will happen to even the most experienced shooter, and it is wise to be prepared for this eventuality. Should you wing a woodie from the trees then the best way to kill the bird is by a swift, solid blow to the head with a priest, or by swinging it around by the head to break the bird's neck. I have seen many fancy methods that allegedly dispatch birds more humanely – but they don't! It's either a pellet in the kill-zone, a sharp knock from a priest, or the neck twist. If you think this barbaric, then don't hunt, because you will at times need to get your hands bloodied.

But we mustn't stray from the main subject of how to shoot accurately and compensate for elevation. First, you need to appreciate the relatively low speed at which a pellet fired from a 12ft lb air rifle travels. For instance, a medium-weight .177 calibre pellet of 7.9g travels at approximately 825 f.p.s and a medium-weight .22 calibre pellet of 14.3g calibre travels at approximately 612 f.p.s. These figures might seem fast, but when you consider that an average .22LR calibre 45g sub-sonic, medium-weight, rimfire bullet travels at approximately 1050 f.p.s (which equates to approximately 100 ft lb) I think this clearly illustrates why an airgun pellet loses trajectory in flight rather rapidly, due in part to gravity dragging it towards the ground.

A pellet fired horizontally will behave differently from a pellet fired at an angle, simply due to the effects of gravitational pull. For instance, let's say that your rifle is zeroed for 30yds. If a shot is taken horizontally at this distance the pellet will travel 30yds under the pull of gravity over all of that distance, but your zero has already been compensated for the expected drop (i.e. the trajectory), so you aim dead-on. But if the target is in the top of a tree (or the bottom of a gully) and you judge it to be 30yds from rifle to target, you will have to aim slightly lower in both cases. The reason is that while the target is 30yds away, the horizontal distance the pellet will have to cover will be less than 30yds so the pellet's trajectory will effectively be less, and you have to act as though the target is closer. Hence you aim lower.

I know this might fly in the face of what you've possibly read previously in various publications on the supposed fact that a pellet travelling upwards is affected by gravity pulling more towards the rear of the pellet. That's not strictly true, and it's in the field that you'll realise that steeply-angled shots are awkward to calculate. But by following the simple guide I'll outline, you can counteract the difference in trajectory you will experience. To determine the exact amount of holdunder necessary would take a degree in trigonometry (or at least a calculator), as you would need to know the distance to the target, the exact angle of the shot and the height or depth of the target from the horizontal plane of the shooter, and then how all these and other factors would affect trajectory. Phew! Basically, you just judge the range of the target from the rifle as usual, and then aim slightly lower than you normally would for that distance if it were horizontal. Try this out on high and low practice targets before you attempt such shots at live quarry, in order to know your own required point of aim accurately. These can be twigs or leaves high up in trees.

As a starting point, try aiming a half an inch or so low at the target with a .177, and around threequarters of an inch low with a .22 calibre rifle. If the angle is particularly steep – say for instance you are at the base of a tree – you will have to use even more holdunder. This is because you will probably be much closer to the target so pellet drop is far less.

To recap, and as a rule of thumb – the steeper the angle to the target then the more allowance is needed as the pellet arches upwards instead of following the more traditional horizontal trajectory line. But this only applies if the angle of fire you're shooting at is 45 degrees or higher and the range to the target is close to your set zero. Should you be lining up for a longer shot, much further than your set zero, and the bird is high in a tree then you'll probably now need to allow for holdover, as the pellet will be affected by gravity over a longer distance. This can get confusing, and only practice will help you master the art of awkwardly angled shots. Usually it's the high ones that will present themselves and be the most difficult to assess. In fact, it's only when the angle gets to around 60 degrees and above that you should have to consider compensating for the change in trajectory. Most upward shots into trees are at roosting birds, or those alighting into sitty trees. It is a skill that needs mastering, should you choose to tackle quarry in those situations. (Incidentally, I'll dispense with vertical shots, as they're nigh-on impossible and virtually never worth taking because the bird is likely to be in a position that offers no clear kill-zone).

As for downward-angled shots, particularly if taken at a slightly downward angle and either in the standing or kneeling position towards quarry on the ground, most times you won't need to allow for any compensation for the change in trajectory from its horizontal line as the angular distance isn't very great. But if you're shooting from a high seat, a tree position or an upper window of an old building (where the situation is allowed, and opportunity arises) then it certainly does need consideration.

To all this we must add the need at times to compensate for a crosswind so, as you can see, the subject of elevation compensation is fraught with many variables, and only experience using the information given as guidelines will help you to be consistently successful.

On the subject of shooting in very breezy conditions, I'd always advise the relatively inexperienced shooter to avoid this if possible. But shooting in a light wind can be beneficial, especially if stalking, as to a certain extent the wind carries away your scent and any sounds you might make. However, if it's only a light cross-breeze, a shot taken over a medium-range of 25 yards shouldn't be duly affected. If shooting at ground level near hedges, the strength of the breeze will be less than if shooting over an open field or into trees. Even a moderate crosswind will create the need for what is known as 'aiming off' (to one side or the other, (depending on wind direction) in order to allow for the wind to drift the pellet back into the kill-zone. Again, only practice and a great deal of experience will help you determine just how much lateral allowance to give for any given wind conditions. The shooter who forgets to allow for these variables is the one who has the smallest game bag.

These variable factors lend more weight to the .177 slug as being a better option for the hunter. The pellet is lighter and flies faster. It zips through the air, and a light crosswind affects its smaller mass less, but remember that the greater the distance your pellet has to travel, or the more disturbed the conditions it has to contend with to get to the target, then the more it is affected and the less 'oomph' it delivers when it gets there. So in inclement weather I'd never chance a longer-range shot, and all will be taken with 30–35 yards at most. You might think this sounds close for an experienced shot, and it may well be; but it's a more responsible attitude than to risk injuring your quarry.

Trigger Control

Consistent trigger control or 'trigger release' is a technique neglected by just as many live-round shooters as airgunners. Many are seemingly quite happy to just hook their finger around the trigger blade and pull. Maybe that's a crude description, but it suits the crude trigger control and hand grip positions I've often seen many so-called 'experienced' airgunners adopt. For optimum trigger control your trigger finger should be square to the trigger blade, and the only part of your finger touching the front of the trigger blade should be the pad of your forefinger. When ready to take a shot, you should gently squeeze the trigger, almost feeling your way through the shot until the trigger mechanism trips the sear to send a pellet zinging along down the bore. Also, at the pistol grip, the stock might have a channel allowing you to adopt a thumb-up hold. Many feel this helps with trigger control, as the hand is in a more relaxed and natural position. Personally, I prefer this hold when catered for, especially if the stock has no thumbhole for my big digit!

Before leaving this important aspect of shooting it's worth thinking about the thorny subject of breathing in relation to taking the shot. I know some who take a deep breath, hold it in, and then shoot. Wrong! I know it can be very hard when the adrenalin is pumping, but try consciously to calm your breathing into a slow, easy rhythm. Then breathe out gently and fairly fully, pause and shoot. In most hunting situations you'll probably think you don't have time to do this, but apart from snap-shooting, where you don't have time except to aim and fire, you do. Once you get experienced in this breathing technique it will become second nature, and you'll do it subconsciously before every shot is taken. Then just watch the tally of your hunting bags grow. And it doesn't end there as let's not forget that once you've tripped the sear,

Practice shooting in the prone position as more often after a long stalk you'll need to take the shot like this

you need to allow for follow-through. Personally, after squeezing the trigger I hold the sights on aim and watch through the scope, almost willing the pellet to impact where I'd placed the scope's crosshairs before I'd squeezed the trigger.

Incidentally, most of this relates to the basics of shooting with a recoiling rifle, but most also applies to shooting with a PCP. I'm sure you can guess what I'm going to say now. If you're a hunter who's spoiled themselves by recently using a PCP air rifle but still have a springer lurking in the back of the gun cabinet, or in a case at the bottom of the wardrobe, then why not really get back to basics? As you blow off the cobwebs against paper targets, chalk discs or knockdowns, you just might be very surprised to discover just how much you've been taking for granted about your shooting, and maybe even just how much you've forgotten about the essentials of the very art of shooting itself.

Field Technique

Practice is the only way you will achieve a consistent level of accuracy. I can't stress enough the importance of making yourself fully accustomed to the capabilities of your rifle, scope and ammo combination. Everything should become second nature – bringing the gun up to the shoulder, aligning the eye and taking care not to cant to left or right before shooting; and, of course, a consistent and smooth trigger release. Before attempting to shoot any live quarry, it's imperative that you achieve an acceptable level

The seated position is the most versatile and offers the widest variations

of accuracy at inanimate targets. In other words, it's back to the target or plinking range until you can consistently make good groups of approximately an inch out to 25 or 30yds, depending on your set zero. Practice should ideally involve shooting at different ranges and angles of fire, and from different positions. Remember that in many cases when out hunting, your shots will have to be taken in the standing position. Although it's not the most comfortable of stances, do take time to practise shooting from this position. It may sound obvious, but the way you stand will affect the accuracy of the shot. When we naturally stand, say in a queue, most people lean on one leg more than the other. It's a similar comfortable position that you need to adopt for taking a standing shot. Your feet will be a shoulder-width apart, with most of your body weight transferred to the left leg, which should be forward of the body. For lefties, the opposite applies. You should be standing almost side-on to the target with the rifle across the front of your upper torso, and squarely lined-up at the target.

The standing shot certainly needs mastering, but in the field you'll often get the chance to adopt the kneeling or even prone position, especially if you're targeting a rabbit. Only experience will tell you when you need to act quickly with a standing snap-shot or when the quarry is sufficiently comfortable to let you take a little more time to rest yourself into a more stable position. When the adrenalin is pumping it's all too easy to rush, but experience has taught me that I can more often than not get myself into a rested or supported position. Even at your most comfortable, you'll probably become aware of the reason why shooters miss, and that's the simple fact of your body moving with your breathing and your pulse. You'll find you can never actually hold a rifle stock-still in any position except off a bipod or similar rest, and even then natural body movements can affect the shot. The most important art is learning to control that movement as mentioned earlier, with your breathing and basically by calming your nerves. It's not easy when under pressure, but it's this technique, when mastered, that has won many FT competitions and filled the biggest game bags. Learn to take the shot only when your timing is right, the cross-hairs are on the target, and your body is under your control.

With the standing shot there are times when you need to shoot upwards into trees. We've covered the need to allow for the angle of fire, but this is also when you will need to slightly adapt your stance and rifle hold. Your body should be leant slightly back to transfer your weight onto the right (i.e. rearward) foot. The opposite applies for lefties. Whichever the case, avoid leaning back from the waist as this will result in straining the back muscles and accentuating any wobbles. Your leading hand should be allowed to slide back naturally along the forend to hold the rifle at the optimum point of balance. Basically, as the rifle is elevated, the combo's point of balance moves back and so should your hand accordingly. Let the rifle fall more onto the upper shoulder, and all other aspects for physically taking the shot remain the same. Where possible – and often it is because I'm shooting in a predetermined ambush point waiting for birds to come in to roost – I'll stand or sit with my back to a tree trunk as a rest, and to disguise my form on the woodland floor from eyes up above.

As regards changing position when encountering ground level quarry, should you be in a standing position when you encounter it, you can be almost certain that if the quarry isn't overly twitchy, it'll be far more appropriate for you to lower yourself slowly to one knee or even flat out on the ground. Often a rabbit will have spotted you, but by lowering yourself you can fool the animal into a false sense of security because, in effect, you are adopting an unthreatening posture. Try this and you'll soon discover that rabbits will resume feeding, so you have time now to either move slowly forward, or just rest, before gathering yourself and calming your nerves ready for the shot.

Some of the advice I've given may initially seem unfamiliar, but the more you shoot and hunt it will become obvious why you need to hold, stand, sit or lie down on the job like this. Before leaving the subject of the shot, it's imperative before trying your hand against any live quarry that you make yourself fully familiar with the vulnerable aim points of each individual quarry species, or as it's known – the kill-zone. On any species this is the area on its body that when hit with a pellet with sufficient force will cleanly dispatch it. Only when you have the ability and knowledge to achieve this should you embark on your first hunting foray. The aim point is always quite small, usually a headshot, neck-shot or into the heart and lungs. This is why consistent, accurate performance is essential. Never overestimate your ability to shoot accurately at various ranges. In the field with adrenalin pumping even the relatively experienced can make hasty and, to your quarry, painful mistakes. You should always strive to dispatch your quarry effectively, as quickly and humanely as possible. There are also as many times when you'll need to be disciplined enough not to shoot, for risk of wounding quarry due to the animal not presenting a clear kill-zone. Similarly, there could be foliage or twigs between you and the target. In most cases only patience will solve the problem as, more often than not, rather than move position and risk being spotted it's better to wait until the animal turns so that a kill-zone is clearly visible. Also, although the target may look clear through the scope, look to the side or carefully peek over the optic and you'll often clearly see twigs or plant stems that could possibly cause a pellet deflection. In this case, slightly shifting your shooting position to your left or right might just find a pathway for your lead.

As for the kill-zone, different angles presented by your quarry in relation to you give different degrees of size in terms of both surface area and shape. By this I refer specifically to instances when the quarry is facing you, standing sideways on, sitting or standing. All kill-zones are fully explained later as we deal with each quarry species, but as a rule of thumb a full-on shot presents a larger horizontal line for you to drop the pellet into.

As I'm sure you can now appreciate, airgun hunting can be one of the most infuriating of shooting sports but, due to the demands put on the hunter, when you make that successful shot it's also one of the most rewarding. Before leaving the subject of taking shots, I must comment on shooting at a moving target. It may well sound enthralling that you can get to a level of accuracy with an air rifle that affords you the ability to shoot quarry that's running for cover. I've been shooting for many moons, and the only quarry that I regularly shoot 'on the hoof' so to speak is rats. One of the reasons is that the rat is a crafty critter that often doesn't keep still long enough for a studied, measured shot; but when it's on a regular run across a beam or along the foot of a wall, then you can (with experience) give the shot enough lead to put the pellet into the front one-third section of the rat's body, which gives a clean kill.

Shooting at running or even moving rabbits is another matter altogether. I'm not being biased, and my advice is born of years of experience. I feel the responsible shooter should never attempt to do this, for a few specific reasons. A moving rabbit rarely runs in a straight line, or with its head (or for that matter enough of any exposed kill-zone on the body) perfectly level. A rabbit can scurry, scamper, hop, zigzag or bound to safety. Loosing off a pellet in its direction serves no purpose other than to educate the rabbit to the danger of the raised rifle, the muted muzzle report and the subsequent whistling sound from the pellet flying past it. If you do fluke it and hit the animal, it's more likely that – through pure adrenalin and momentum – it will get into cover or down a hole to meet a painful, lingering end. Do you want this? No, and your quarry deserves much more respect. Both rats and rabbits are regarded as vermin, and this attitude might seem like a case of double standards, but whilst the rat is little more than a walking disease, the rabbit is quite a noble little creature. If you want to shoot quarry on the move – get the official police paperwork sorted out and buy yourself a nice-handling 20-bore or 410 shotgun.

Finding a Shoot

Finding a suitable area to shoot over is without doubt the hardest part of getting started as a hunter, and especially as an airgun hunter. From the start I feel I should fully clarify this. Farmers understand the need and use of the shotgun, and are usually grateful for the shotgunner's help in the ongoing battle with the woodpigeon. However, we have to admit that the airgun has had a lot of bad press in various ways, and is perceived by some as not really being a 'proper' gun for general vermin control. So before you even start, the odds are rather stacked against you, as you may have to convince your prospective hosts as to your effectiveness, as well as your responsible nature and attitude.

All land in the UK is privately or publicly owned. You can't shoot over public land, and for private land the permission of the owners is always needed. Without permission to shoot on somebody's land, you are poaching. There's no middle ground or grey area because the law sees it like this. In law, you can be charged with armed trespass, and in these increasingly gun-sensitive times, the penalty for being where you shouldn't be are quite severe. Pleading ignorance isn't going to do much to get you a reprieve or pardon – so how do you go about obtaining permission to shoot on somebody's land?

If You Don't Ask You Don't Get

Finding suitable land to shoot over – the most difficult hunt of all

Do your homework – the search begins here

That pretty much sums it up. A good way to start is really to get to know your local area. Not just where the farms, fields and woods are, but more importantly who owns them and employs the people who work there. You can begin by asking at your local gunshop, and they will be more than happy to help you with any queries and questions. They will possibly be able to supply contact numbers of known rough shoots already established in the area. Indeed, it's in their interests to point you in the right direction because the more you go shooting, the more ammo and shooting kit you'll need to buy. Although I don't want to dampen enthusiasm before you get started on searching, they'll have been asked many, many times by others before you. Also, whilst rough shooting often comes available for the shotgun shooter, the airgun is still seen by many as the 'boy's toy'. Of course we know otherwise, so that's one of the factors you should keep in mind when asking and looking for land to shoot over. An area that's unsuitable for a shotgunner or firearm sportsman may still be riddled with vermin, and many areas that are unshot can get overrun with pests. Finding yourself in the right place at the right time, asking the right questions, can bring surprising results. So even though it may just be a few fields and hedgerows covering little more than a few acres, don't ignore it as a possible place to begin your quest to find a shoot. As they say, 'from small acorns …'

To make the most of your shoot area it's essential to obtain the relevant Ordnance Survey (OS) maps. OS maps show all the roads, footpaths, farm tracks, buildings, features and even the contours of the land, and you need to know the type and lie of the land if you are going to hunt certain species. For instance, if it's rabbits you intend to target, then you will be looking for fields surrounded by hedgerows. If it's woodpigeons, magpies and other corvids, you will be looking for land that contains at least a small wood, at the very least one copse, or better still, scattered clumps of trees. As for rats, collared doves and feral pigeons, any farm with a barn or a few run-down outbuildings should fit the bill. Once you've marked the particular farms that meet with your requirements on your OS map, you've still got some homework to do before making your initial contact.

First, go along to the farms you have picked out for an initial reconnaissance of the area, but do keep to the public access routes. I know I shouldn't need to say this, but do leave your gun at home. Don't trespass, even if only jumping over a gate to get a better look at a far hedge line or wood, as you could blow your chances of getting a shoot before you start. Keep a record of the farm, its land and any quarry you see during your recce, as this will be useful later when – or indeed if – you get to talk to the owners.

Check out whether the place is still a fully working farm. Look for signs of farming activity, such as farm machinery, livestock or crops in the fields – anything

A feature such as a dead tree will stand out on the landscape – as a potential sitty-tree it's an area worth noting

that indicates the land is being worked. If none of these are in evidence, then the farm could have changed hands and may now just be a private dwelling. If that's the case, then this is usually not the place to find your shooting ground. The owners will probably have little interest in the land in terms of land management, and they'll probably enjoy seeing the 'cute fluffy bunnies' in the morning – as long as they tolerate the critters hammering their lawn and garden. In other words, they'll have bought the house and land for its scenic attraction and the privacy it affords them. Unless they realise the benefits of controlling certain vermin, an airgun hunter won't be high on their list of priorities.

However, always keep that in mind about smaller bits of land that are unsuitable for shotguns or firearms. Market gardens, plant nurseries and the like can often bring a surprise or two in the form of acquiring shooting permission. Also – bizarre as it might seem – don't ignore built-up areas. Find out who owns the run-down industrial mill or commercial units where you've seen feral pigeons hanging around. The chances are that they roost in the buildings at night and are causing a hell of a mess. It's always worth asking if there are any problems like that which you can help with, and even though this sort of shooting may not be your first choice, this can have a knock-on effect in that your name is passed on to other people who may have land more suited to the kind of shooting you prefer.

First Contact

After a few trips out, you will soon narrow down your list quite drastically, but when you've located suitable farms that fit your criteria, then it's time to make contact. In the first instance, contact the farmer or landowner by letter, not forgetting to enclose a stamped, self-addressed envelope, and also your home telephone number (and your mobile number, if you have one). Take the trouble to have your letter neatly typewritten. Explain your request in a manner that shows you have an understanding of what working a farm entails. Stress that you're responsible, will leave no litter, cause no damage, and will respect crops and livestock. If you belong to B.A.S.C. (which I advise you should) or a similar organisation, mention it, along with any insurance cover you carry. Tell them that you can and will supply at least two independent references as to your good character, as a couple of good references can make the difference between securing a shoot or missing it. Remember that you are, in effect, asking the owner if you can walk around his property with a loaded gun. Ask yourself this: would you let someone who appeared dodgy hang around, let alone shoot an air rifle in your back garden? I think not. Don't expect a quick reply. Farmers are very busy people, and if you start phoning too soon or too often you'll probably put them off.

Obviously the number of letters you've sent out will govern how many replies you can expect to get. For instance, if you've sent out two dozen requests, you'll be doing well to get two or more replies, even with a stamped, self-addressed envelope enclosed. You might think that's a small percentage, but that's the way it is. We live in a world where people are always asking for something. Unfortunately, the farmer will probably have been asked many times before, and all too often your request will get put on the same pile or end up in the same bin, but don't be disheartened. At your first positive lead, which is almost certainly going to be because you've telephoned to follow up a written request, follow it up immediately. That hopefully means you'll be arranging your first visit.

Know your quarry – woodies can cause devastation over farms growing cereal crops

A few collared doves and the like are often tolerated around farms – listen to farmers and only shoot what they specify

Attitude

So you've now got to the all-important point of first contact, and it will possibly require subsequent phone discussions before a face-to face meet. During your initial conversations, don't be pushy. They might not have fully made up their mind, so be diplomatic. Mention you have some knowledge of the farm; tell them you've seen and studied the relevant ordnance survey map and that you're aware of the surrounding land and main features, but don't sound as if you've been spying! Try to convince them that you can offer a free, efficient service that will help in the control of vermin. Though many hunters understandably want to get stuck into quarry such as rabbits, ask first if he's having trouble with rats or feral pigeons. Controlling these species for a farmer can often be a quick route to being accepted on the property for other quarry with your air rifle. Whatever you've noticed about his farm, comment on it if it is relevant to vermin control and something that may be causing him problems. Being forearmed with some knowledge of the pests that are on his land is where your initial recce will pay off.

Be prepared for rejection at any time, but once a positive reaction has been received, which it eventually will, don't waste the opportunity. Ask when it's convenient to visit the farmer personally and be prepared to meet him anywhere of his choosing, usually on the land. Don't presume that you can visit the house immediately. This meeting will be at an arranged time, not just a 'come round to the yard' sort of invitation. Why do I mention this? A farmer is a businessman, and his business is farming, so it follows that you need to be businesslike in your approach and attitude when you turn up for a meeting. That doesn't mean you need to wear a suit and tie – I've never worn one, never have, and never will – but you can easily dress smartly and project a responsible, respectable image. When you finally get around to meeting the farmer this really is a situation when first impressions do count for a lot. Whatever you do, don't turn up fully camo'd up with your rifle slung over your shoulder. Believe me – I know people who've done this and, incredible as it sounds, they are actually surprised when they're turned away. During your visit be polite, have a friendly manner, and let the farmer dictate the pace of the conversation. At this point he'll probably be 'weighing you up', so to speak. Just in case, take along your gun in its bag but leave it in the boot of the car and out of sight. The farmer might want to see what type of gun you intend to use on his property. As I've said – don't be pushy. But, due to the modern hi-tech look of certain PCPs, I've often found that this in itself can be an ice-breaker, as the farmer usually remembers the old springers and might well find your new-fangled piece of kit quite fascinating, and if a conversation develops on this – all the better.

If the meeting has gone well and the farmer has time, he might show you the area you are provisionally allowed to shoot over. You won't (or very rarely) be given carte blanche to go wherever you like, whenever you like. More likely he'll steer you to an area where he's having specific problems with a particular vermin quarry species. This is where it pays for you to know your stuff. Nothing impresses more than a good knowledge of the quarry and what it will be doing that's making it such a headache for the farmer. If you get to shoot, early results are even better, because the farmer will soon realise that having you around is mutually beneficial. On the subject of primary areas you may be shown, and specifically told you can shoot over, pay particular attention to what is said. In fact, don't take it for granted that you can shoot anything that's legally deemed suitable by law for air rifles. Ask the farmer if he wants anything left untouched. Some tolerate and even like to see a few collared doves or squirrels about the place, so don't blow it by shooting something his wife or relative has been feeding for years! Listen to him carefully when he outlines the boundaries of his land. It helps to have a notebook handy, because a hedgerow pointed out on a visit can, if not noted correctly, be mistaken for the next one along when you visit the next time, and you could quite easily find yourself straying inadvertently (but still illegally) on to a neighbouring farmer's land. Ideally, these are the neighbours you will want to impress in the fullness of time. Eventually, they too will hopefully realise that your services are very useful.

When all is sorted, and before you take your gun from its case, get your shooting permission in writing as soon as possible, with the farmer's signature. You'll need to carry this with you at all times when on his land. It goes without saying that you should treat the farmer's hospitality with respect, always closing gates behind you, leaving no litter, and taking care not to shoot so as to spook his livestock. This is specialised shooting you might have to undertake eventually, but not one you should even be thinking of doing at the outset.

Only shoot at times that have been agreed, and if you want to shoot at night make sure this is allowed, and always let the farmer know when you'll be there 'after hours'. If you bag a few rabbits or woodies, always offer them to the farmer first, if you see him. A bottle of something at Christmas will certainly be a nice gesture, and is looked upon as a country tradition.

A Word to the Wise

Even now when I secure new land to shoot over I feel I've achieved something. That's because it's the hardest hunting of the lot, and as the years go by it seems to be getting harder. Another factor that many are shy of stating publicly is that, by and large, the shooting fraternity can be very cliquey. More often than not, when you finally acquire your shoot, you'll be shooting over land that already has an established group of shooters present, perhaps rough-shooters or game shooters. They will – rightly or wrongly –

guard their own shooting permission with varying degrees of acceptance of your presence or, quite frankly, of resentment. Don't get me wrong, because not all people are like this; but it's all too easy to upset an applecart, no matter how unwittingly, especially in a close-knit community where the shooters may have ties to one another through marriage or even direct bloodlines. You will always be the new boy, and last in really does mean first out. I'm not trying to put a dampener on the matter, but do heed those words as you go about your shooting, and never become complacent. If you hear of another possible shoot, try to get your foot in the door there as well. If it means more travelling than you'd expected you should still pursue it, because you never know when permission to shoot on a farm can be withdrawn. If it is, it isn't necessarily due to something you've personally done as a shooter, and usually isn't.

Opportunities to Shoot and Learn

Another avenue to try for what can often result in shooting permission, and one that will certainly help you develop your field craft, is to help a fox shooter. Accompanying an experienced fox shooter on nighttime hunting forays can bring a mass of opportunities and knowledge. Occasionally, you'll either hear through the grapevine or even see an advert in a gunshop or broad-based shooting publication that a person is looking for someone 'enthusiastic' to help him with fox control. Invariably this will mean carrying the battery pack and operating the spotlamp. This might seem to have little relevance to airgun hunting, but you can and will learn a hell of a lot. Watch the way they move over the terrain at night; listen when they give you tips on using the lamp, take note of their gun handling, watch the way they use the wind to their advantage, and marvel at the way they can actually 'call in' their quarry. It's all fascinating stuff, and much will be relevant to the use of a lamp for your nighttime hunting exploits on bunnies. Often for your help, your 'payment in kind' will be an invitation to a farm where the fox shooter has permission to shoot. Here you'll possibly get chances to use

Shooting feral pigeon can often have a knock-on effect into gaining contacts to the kind of shooting you prefer

your air rifle at suitable-sized vermin. The fox shooter rarely has time to keep on top of the rabbits, crows, and squirrels that pester most farmers, but it's his duty as a pest controller on the land to help his host to cull all vermin. More often than not the fox shooter will be grateful for your help, as you're doing a part of the pest control he either has little interest in or, more likely, he's not got enough time to do justice to. Also, many shooters in rural areas double up as part-time gamekeepers. They'll be well practised in setting traps and snares, and this could well be another area where you'll be asked to help out. You may or may not find this of interest, but it pays to offer help to pest controllers undertaking trapping or snaring campaigns – especially in spring, when it can be a very time-consuming operation. Take an interest in all you see as you progress as a shooter, and always offer and be prepared to help on the land.

So what can you expect, once accepted into these inner circles? Usually, you'll first go out for a walk around the surrounding land with your newfound shooting companion. He'll show you the area and watch to see if your shooting, gun handling and safety are of a sufficiently high standard to warrant you being trusted to operate on your own. Eventually, he'll introduce you to the farmer and maybe, just maybe, you'll become a trusted part of this shooting fraternity and get written permission for a piece of land to shoot whenever you wish. Always be grateful to that first contact, and to those you meet along the way. By now you'll have come far, and you may even progress to be invited to accompany a deerstalker in his quest for the noble antlered beast. You might be the one who has to drag the culled beast off the hill, but watching a deerstalker is not only an experience, but also your chance to watch and follow possibly the finest form of stalking. The relevance of stalking to the airgun hunter is an obvious one – a basic part of field craft and one you'd always do well to learn more about.

But a word of caution is timely. When you've been lucky enough to be invited as a guest on to a shoot, it'll probably be pointed out to you, but don't ever presume that you can go back unaccompanied unless you are specifically allowed. Don't take it for granted that you can 'nip on' once in a while. Hopefully, it will mature into a fully-fledged shooting opportunity and relationship, but be patient. Let your hosts weigh you up, and let them dictate your progress into their shooting world. It's all too easy to blow these opportunities due to over-eagerness, and remember that the shooter who first invited you to join him will probably have spent years gaining the trust of the farmer or landowner. He'll certainly have earned his right to shoot, so be prepared to do the same. Always respect those chances to shoot on 'borrowed land', because soon it may be a place where you can go and shoot on your own.

This is even more basic, but before you even take your first shot against quarry on a shoot remember that it's your responsibility to be able to identify all legal quarry species in a variety of different situations and from even the most obscure angle. In fact, a handy saying that has served me well and is worth remembering when out hunting is this – 'If in doubt, don't shoot!' Finding a shoot can be difficult, but one thing's for sure: when found, you'll have damn' well earned it!

Observation and Quarry Location

As a hunter, I used to believe that to be out in the field without a rifle was about as much use as going fishing without a fishing rod. That was until I became involved in wildlife photography and from there on I began my ongoing learning curve and understanding of wildlife behaviour. Not only did I learn the comings and goings of quarry deemed suitable for the airgun around the shoot, but about animal and bird behaviour in general, and I can now say that time spent just watching animals will pay the dedicated shooter back ten-fold.

This is of such importance that I'm going into detail on how to observe properly the land you intend to shoot over, no matter what hunting technique you employ at a later stage.

Observation can be as simple as leaning on a wall looking over the fields, or sitting or lying in a comfortable concealed position or hide studying a particular hedge-line or group of trees. As I said earlier, getting to know a particular area usually entails many hours spent out there, preferably without your rifle, but using your eyes and ears. In other words, simply looking, listening, observing and learning. If you wonder why I'm stressing 'you leave the rifle at home', it's because it will be all too tempting to shoot quarry that comes close, and while this may bring 'instant results', it may just as likely be the reason that there's little or even no quarry in that area should you go for a full campaign at a later date. Without a doubt, observation is one of the most important but often overlooked factors that contribute to successful hunting. This preparation really is the key to hunting success and, to borrow a biblical quote, you'll eventually be able to 'reap as ye have sown'. Even just meandering around with your eyes and ears open is a start, but ideally you should be much more methodical in your approach to observation.

Map it Out

Following on what we considered in Finding A Shoot, take into consideration that once you've secured that elusive shooting ground you should also make yourself fully familiar with its overall layout by walking the area, and noting all the specific features that may be of interest to particular quarry. In Quarry Files you'll be given information to help determine which animals inhabit which types of terrain and what areas of the land. Pick out these key areas, and lie up under camo or in a suitably hidden position to watch and learn. Granted, at times it will seem boring, but at others very interesting and eventful; and try to learn from everything you see, including the animals and birds that aren't on your hit list. These too will be using an area of the shoot for reasons associated with your quarry. Usually it's because the area is rich in foodstuff, is relatively undisturbed by man, or both. For animals, a combination of the two will represent a safe place.

After the first few visits, draw up a map of the area you are allowed to shoot over. Obviously, you don't need to be a master cartographer, but don't think you can get away with just making a quick sketch on the back of a beer mat! Use at least a decent-sized notepad while out walking around the shoot, and transfer

Locate a particularly 'favoured' sitty-tree and you could well find yourself with a steady stream of potential targets

this in the comfort of your own home to an A4-size sheet of plain paper. A Dictaphone is also a good aid for keeping verbal notes, and much easier to use than continually scribbling on a pad of paper – especially if it's raining or your fingers are numb with cold. As for the map itself, make a few photocopies of it as standard maps. Then, when you've got an idea as to which quarry species are active in certain areas, mark them on one of the copies using symbols or name abbreviations. Then it's easy to keep them regularly noted by using a clean sheet to amend for any change in quarry activity or locations. The map will need to be updated every couple of months or so, depending on your particular area, the time of year and of course how often you go shooting.

The main priority of your map is to show the boundary, which should clearly indicate the perimeter enclosing the area where you are legally allowed to shoot. Unfortunately, at least part of the land probably won't be nice and neatly fenced off. The boundary could be a stream, an old broken wall, a small tree line or even a ditch. Even at this early stage, make a note of these permanent landmarks and features that clearly define the limits of your shoot.

Once you've established the boundary on your map, you can then start to mark in the places that will be of interest to various quarry species – which are, of course, the places that you should also make your first target areas. Begin by marking any wooded areas, no matter how small, and even if they are only a couple of trees standing together. These could well prove to be what are known as 'sitty-trees' (trees used by birds for perching to rest or watch the surrounding area before moving on), that – if approached stealthily, or better still to be hidden up by, within range – could well see you bagging a few pie-filling woodpigeons, or ridding the land of a bonus nuisance corvid or two once your hunting begins in earnest.

Just Watch

Note down areas that may be appropriate for siting a hide, which will be useful when you've mastered hide-building, the technique of which will be outlined later, and any other spots that offer you natural cover for ambushing and laying bits. All these specific hunting styles will be dealt with in the relevant chapters, so rest assured that you'll be well informed and prepared when the time comes to put it all into practice.

Once you've made the map, do keep it regularly updated. By this I mean keeping notes on where you've seen various species. For instance, this may include rabbit activity (e.g. droppings, runs, burrows), or maybe you're lucky enough to have an area of woods used by quarry birds for roosting. Even if you haven't, you're likely to have times when birds will fly over your area on the way to feeding areas or back to roost sites. These, when established, are known as flightlines, usually of woodpigeons but crows also use regular flight paths. You certainly won't be able to shoot them on the wing as the shotgunner can, but you can tempt them down on to the ground using decoys, or for the corvids a carrion bait. Also, many forget or don't realise that birds, as well as having flight lines, also have regular stop-off points along them. These are usually the sitty trees, areas to feed, drink, rest or even to await others of their kind before moving on – usually and unfortunately out of your allotted shooting area.

Take time and trouble to prepare yourself properly, and don't underestimate the importance of reconnaissance. An absolutely invaluable piece of kit is a pair of binoculars. A good pair of compact binos, e.g, with a specification of 8 x 21, are light and extremely handy to carry at all times. If waiting longer, then a pair with larger magnification and larger front objective lenses will be less of a strain on the eye. Incidentally, whilst I prefer a monocular while shooting as it's smaller, compact binos are a good compromise for using if you're doing a bit of reconnaissance and shooting. For more serious use then a larger pair of binos is the optimum choice. You can even get them in camo!

Creatures of Habit

Now we've established that animals – and especially birds – have set behavioural patterns which they generally stay faithful to, according to season, come spring, summer, autumn and winter. They do say that only mad dogs and Englishmen go out in the midday sun, and they should say that only mad airgun hunters go out in potentially bad weather conditions, but sometimes, taking a chance – and as long as the weather isn't forecast to be extreme – to wait up in ambush in the right position can be well worth the effort. This is because crows and magpies seem unbothered by inclement weather, and even during lengthy spells of light drizzle they move around pretty much as normal on their daily routine. Heavy rain, though, is often the cause of birds disappearing into the woods, and animals, especially rabbits, sitting well under cover out of sight. The point is that weather can and does affect how an animal's behavioural pattern changes, but, like us humans, at some point they will need to feed and drink. So, in general, certain animals or birds use some areas more than others for food, to rest and, in the case of the weather, to find shelter. Knowing this and using it to your advantage will put you in the right place at the right time.

Some areas are certainly heavily frequented by wildlife because they are secluded or relatively undisturbed by humans, and only prolonged observation of the shoot will reveal key areas such as this. For instance, with a flock of birds such as woodies, crows and jackdaws, their stop-off points could be a clump of trees in the middle of a field, or a quiet corner of the field itself, where they might only be grubbing around looking for an early feed or late snack. Whichever the case, and I again stress the point, be there at the right time and it could well be their last supper! Correct, dedicated observation and preparation quickly show just how important they are to successful hunting.

Look also for nest sites (in winter, when trees are bare) that betray the areas frequented by magpies, crows and rooks. Corvids return to the same ones year in, year out. The magpie's nest is unmistakeable by its football shape, whilst the rookery will be obvious by its sheer number of nests, and is often heard before it's seen. Crows, though usually in paired twosomes during nesting time, are just as likely to be found nesting in loosely grouped colonies rarely exceeding half a dozen nests – a sort of 'crowery', as I like to call them. These tend to be found in twos or threes, with a few in the same tree, quite high but certainly not as high as rooks' nests. Whilst these birds build in the very top of the tree, entwining their bulky structures around the small twigs of the treetops, crows favour the clefts of branches for a more stable base. The same applies to squirrels' dreys, which are often mistaken for crows' nests. The drey, however, is shaped like a small magpie's nest and will have more leaf litter in the structure. Squirrels like their own space so the drey will be on its own, and in a position that allows them good views of the surrounding area. Look, too, for the smaller 'nut store', once thought of as fanciful; but a squirrel in an established territory can use an old drey above or below the new, usually larger drey to store food. But enough on dwellings and nests, as this is just an example of what you can find by keeping your eyes peeled and knowing what to look for. In-depth quarry behaviour will be dealt with in suitable sections devoted to the individual quarry species.

The best times for watching for signs of activity are usually early morning and late evening – and not surprisingly, these are also the optimum times for hunting. When you walk around your shoot, looking for signs of life, it's very important that you go at the times you will be intending to hunt in the future. It's no use you being in the right place at the wrong time, so to speak. In relation to this, if you do spot areas used as stop-over points or sitty trees, note down the time the birds are more often there. It could well be a relatively small localised group only stay for 10-15 minutes in that area at the same time each or even every other day. Then again, locate a particularly favoured sitty tree and you could well find yourself faced with a steady stream of potential targets and be able to reap the rewards if waiting in a carefully chosen shooting position.

There's no way I can advise which quarry species you should target first. Obviously, most hunters want to get stuck into rabbits, because that's something for the pot and in many areas abundant enough to be bagged in good numbers, but the initial recces of your shoot should already have indicated what is where, and what is where most often. Young guns should start with rats. That's how many of us started, and even now every time I go ratting it seems to bring back a memory of a trip from my youth, but remember, in those days we could largely go where we wanted. Restrictions on airgun use weren't as draconian as they are now, and many a session was spent walking up the cut (canal) on a summer's evening potting rats on the opposite bank or towpath. Today, the newcomer will usually find a shoot with a good few rabbits and certainly woodies and corvids.

If there are trees, then squirrels will also be on the list of possibilities, and for some reason they can be quite oblivious to your presence and the threat you pose to them, at times – that is until you've started to make serious inroads into their population! This is when another major skill comes into play, which is fieldcraft, and knowing how to get within range or fool the quarry; and also knowing when to leave a particular area undisturbed for a while.

This might sound like a complete contradiction in terms, but almost as soon as you start over a new shoot you should be considering which areas to rest (stay away from) first. No hunting ground has an unlimited supply of suitable quarry. Granted, there are areas that seem plagued with rats, rabbits and crows, but you'll be amazed how, at the slightest disturbance, that very same area can soon appear to be devoid of all life. Of course, if you haven't been there on a major pest control cull they'll probably still be there, and in good numbers. They'll just be more wary or even have moved to a safer spot. Sod's law intervenes again, as often that safe place will be somewhere you aren't allowed to shoot. Experience will show you when it's time to rest an area, but it will probably be blatantly obvious, because you'll not see hide nor hair of anything, even at the most opportune times and in ideal weather. It's called conditioning, and the animal responds and reacts to adhere the basic rules of self-preservation in the wild. The importance of 'rotating' your shoot, especially in relation to the time of year, can often be made simple by looking at the options each season brings. This 'airgun hunters calendar year' – as it can aptly be termed – can be very useful in order to know what should coming soon, or be just around the corner in terms of monthly behaviour in relation to shooting opportunities.

Preparation and General Fieldcraft

No matter what the hunting method, the hunter must have a plan – even if only a very basic one. In fact, all successful hunters will follow a generally similar line, and this applies to airgunners just as much as to deer stalkers. Depending on the weather and time of year, you'll have to plan according which areas are most likely to be the most productive. For instance, ratting can be a very slow affair in winter, and in some cases useless unless shooting indoors and where such enclosed areas are relatively warm. Alternatively, rabbits can be out of their burrows for much longer in mild and warm weather, while on very cold or hot days they're either holing up underground or relaxing in a hidden sun-trap. If it's raining your best target quarry species will be of the feathered variety that will be seeking shelter in trees and hedgerows which afford a decent canopy of foliage from the elements. If it's windy,

Rabbits betray their presence in many ways – none so obvious than rabbit holes into well-used warrens

then look to the leeward side of the woods, especially for woodies and crows. But even with the best laid plans, things do at times have a tendency to go pear-shaped, so do have what the army would call a contingency – i.e. an alternative back-up plan.

For instance, if you've been keeping your eye on the weather and you've noticed plenty of signs of rabbit activity around a certain area, and even if all seems fine for an early morning bunny bash, you should still be prepared to have another area pencilled-in to target. In other words, have a few decoys and extra camo net in the rucksack and at the ready should you get rained off. It could well be that moving to another side of the shoot will bring down a few woodies, or bag a few sheltering from the rain should you scour the outskirts of a wood. Remember, if you've been sitting near a warren, even if the weather has been ideal since early morning, and nothing has stirred, it could well be that in the small hours ol' Reynard has been out and about running rabbits into burrows, and more than likely nabbing a few overnight for himself. In fact, foxes can leave an extremely distinctive aroma – trust me, because you'll know it when you smell it. If even we humans can detect this, with our limited sense of smell, just think what it must be like to a rabbit – a veritable aromatic air-raid siren! Knowing when to move and change the original plan is possibly one of the hardest matters for a hunter to master. Experience will certainly help you decide on a move, but even now I've lost count of the times I've thought, sod it, there's no way any pigeons are coming down to a decoy pattern' and then, sure enough, I emerge from the hide just as a flock has started to come in to the pattern. Sod's law, I think that's called!

Quarry Location

Walk along any public footpath and you'll see clear indications of where and how recently a walker has been that way. Unfortunately you're just as likely to find litter, which definitely is a sign that humans have used the route; but this amply illustrates how all creatures leave signs, indication and 'calling cards' that they've passed that way. In the case of humans and litter it's inevitable, alas; but hunters should know the country code and never act so irresponsibly; but back to the quarry we seek and the tell-tale signs to read off the land.

Each specific quarry leaves a part of itself or some other indication that it has used an area, and rabbits are the most obvious. Runs, holes to warrens, gaps under square wire-fencing mesh, hair on low barbed wire or the ground, scratchings in the soil or 'scrapes', nibbled grass, bare patches in grass due to heavy urination, bark stripped from the base of trees and shrubs, and of course paw prints. In the heart of a warren, where entrance and exit holes are most abundant, if the warren is heavily populated the surrounding grass and earth will even smell of them! In fact the smell of rabbits will permeate from the burrows – what a temptation for the local fox population!

Squirrels also leave marks of their activity, and usually these are the teeth marks where they, like the rabbit, have gnawed away to keep their ever-growing incisors in check. Similarly, rats are just as big if not more of a nuisance in this respect. Woodpigeons and other birds leave their white droppings on leaves under sitty trees; you'll see the stalks of berries where the fruit has been plucked off, and downy feathers caught on brambles and around trees means the woodie has been there. Spent kernels, half-eaten nuts, berries, etc. scattered on the ground below can also be signs of squirrel activity, and these are just a few of the signs to look out for as you walk your shoot for observation purposes. All living creatures leave evidence of their activities, whether it be tracks, droppings, ground disturbance including scrapings or 'runs', and,

Rabbit droppings

Fresh soil outside the burrow – obvious sign of recent rabbit activity

Discarded husks and empty shells

Nibbled fir cones – obviously the doing of squirrels

Classic rabbit damage – bark nibbled and stripped at the base of this sapling

A chewed hole in a feed hopper – typical squirrel damage

of course, their dwelling, be it nest, hole or burrow. It's essential that you know the general type of terrain where these more specific calling cards can be found.

This is fieldcraft at its most basic. Always keep in mind the main elements that your quarry needs to live and thrive. Think like them, and you'll soon be finding the areas they favour. Locating quarry isn't an exact science, but more a case of common sense and a little applied detective work.

Birds and animals differ in two main respects when choosing to hole up. Birds favour areas that afford shelter from the elements and, just as importantly to them, a good view of the surrounding area. The only mammal that also does this is the squirrel because, like birds, it is mainly a tree dweller. The rabbit, the main mammal quarry species for the airgun hunter, isn't worried about holing up in an area it can observe from; instead, it relies on its deep, safe burrow for protection. All woods will hold birds and sometimes squirrels, and most farm buildings will also appeal to birds such as collared doves or feral pigeons – and often rats.

Here are ten things to look for when locating quarry.

- Animal tracks and well-worn natural paths. Obviously this relates mainly to land animals such as rabbits, rats and to a lesser extent squirrels.
- Half-eaten discarded foodstuffs, empty fruit or nut shells, and droppings.
- Burrows, holes, scrapes, and runs.
- Nest sites, old and new.
- Squirrel dreys and (although harder to spot) the smaller nut stores built from twigs.
- Freshly cropped (nibbled) grass and crops. Crops broken by wings and 'strimmed' by birds eating from the outer edge into the field.
- Scratch marks and partly-stripped bark.
- Tufts of fur or remnants of hair on low barbed wire and brambles.
- Watch for regular flight lines and roosts.
- It may sound obvious, but look out for the animals and birds themselves, as well as listening for their calls and other noises.

Basic Instincts

At the risk of stating the obvious, every wild animal is driven by basic instincts which include the need to find food, water and shelter. The latter varies in accordance with the species and the conditions, but generally during the day an animal may seek shelter from either danger or the weather. Alternatively, it could be to digest food and, especially in the case of birds, a place to rest – i.e. their roosts in the evening. These, plus the drive to procreate (again depending on the seasons) are its basic survival instincts.

Feeding areas are chosen not only because they are rich in the appropriate foodstuffs, but also because they allow the animals good visibility of their immediate surroundings. In other words they feel safe. For these reasons, certain safe, food-rich locations become regular, favoured feeding grounds. So – find this, and you'll find the quarry. There are a few exceptions to the rule because, at times, quarry can be uncharacteristically clumsy and carefree when it finds food. Typical examples are when woodpigeons are competing with others of their kind and crashing around in the trees gorging on ivy berries, but the same rarely applies to the birds when feeding on the ground. Similarly, a group of magpies squabbling over a rabbit carcass can be totally oblivious to a sniper in a well-chosen position. Carefree and careless to the point of foolhardiness, they often don't realise that their numbers are diminishing with well-placed shots as they bicker and compete for the tastiest morsels – the rabbit's eyes.

As for feeding areas, locating these is usually the easy part, whereas getting within range of the quarry using them is quite another. This is where the hunter needs to use all his fieldcraft skills to enable him to get within effective range. As mentioned, food is the main driving force at all times of the year for all wild creatures. Whether it is to satisfy their own hunger or for rearing their young, finding and gathering food takes up a large part of their daily (and sometimes nightly) routine. This is when thorough knowledge of your particular shoot pays dividends. Knowing the seasons, which fields have just been sown, which wild fruits and berries are likely to be ripening, where nuts and acorns will be falling etc., are all basic requirements for quarry location. Most of this knowledge can be obtained first-hand if you are a country dweller or spend a lot of time on your shoot, but most don't have this luxury, and even those that do will benefit from obtaining good reference works on countryside flora and fauna. These should include naturally-growing trees, shrubs and seed-bearing plants as well as farmed crops – grasses, cereals, vegetables and tree plantations. If you have a good rapport (which you should) with the farmer who owns the land you shoot over, even though he's a busy man, when you get the opportunity, do pick his brains. Ask him at what time of the year he seems most pestered with certain species. He might not know the specifics, but he will be able to tell you to the week what has been sown, where has been or is to be ploughed or cut – and he'll also tell you what he can expect to see in and around that field at that time and immediately afterwards. Another tip is that even if you don't own the necessary paperwork and an appropriate rifle to shoot foxes, still listen to what he has to say about their movements. If they're seen regularly in a certain area near a specific warren you know it may well be that those rabbits are getting seriously thinned out or ultra-twitchy, and certainly worth considering as an area not to concentrate your precious time and effort – at least until the foxing lads nail that particular Basil.

Reference books are important, and I still enjoy reading this sort of material. To some it'll seem like an unnecessary task, but do make the effort. Then you'll be able easily to identify nuts that have been nibbled, pine cones that have been stripped and the shattered shards of beech mast – and, more importantly, by which species. A book I can highly recommend for this is *Nature Detective* by the renowned naturalist and countryman, Hugh Falkus. This particular book is excellent for identifying tracks and other clues as to what has been going on when you are away from the shoot. There are many other very good books on this subject, so the words 'library' and 'go immediately' apply!

Rabbit runs are well-used pathways that can run for quite a distance between burrows and the animals' feeding areas

Just as there are seasonal feeding areas, so there are also those that are sources of food for living creatures all year around. These are the grain stores, domestic animal feed troughs and other food sources around farm buildings. Rats soon learn that pigpens and hen coops contain a ready supply of free handouts. Likewise, grain storage and distribution points are a magnet to collared doves, woodies and feral pigeons. Early and late in the day you can be sure that one or more of these quarry species will be paying a visit to such places. Corvids, of course, are never far behind, just usually a bit more cautious; but in some parts of the country the jackdaw can be as brazen as the starling in its search for food amongst the sheep and cattle feed troughs, both indoors and out. These are the man-made feeding areas, whereas the natural larders are the other main areas to look to, because this is where your quarry is going to feel safest, in its own habitat.

Another requirement for all creatures is water, and both animals and birds have their own favoured sources. This could be a pond, stream, cattle trough or even just an area of ground that regularly becomes waterlogged. Personally, I don't favour specifically targeting these unless otherwise advised, as I haven't found them very productive in the short term. However, if you're the very patient type, lying up in ambush near one of these could well produce the goods, especially during times of low rainfall.

Gimme Shelter

Like humans, most wild creatures – especially birds – don't like being out in the wind or rain if they can avoid it. Therefore shelter is another major factor on your quarry's list of priorities. A cold, wet animal can soon find itself in difficulty, so whenever possible they avoid getting themselves into that state in the first place. There are two types – temporary weather shelter during the day, and roost areas at night. On a windy day it's virtually certain that quarry such as pigeons or corvids will be on the leeward side of the woods, and even more so if the wind is driving a significant amount of rain. Although the hunter may not be particularly fond of being out in such weather, the one who does is more than likely in for a productive foray – assuming he's done his homework – and with the quality outdoor wear now available there's no reason it should be a hardship. It's also worth noting that after a good blow in autumn and winter the woodies and squirrels are often found rooting around in the leaf litter for fallen goodies. There is more of this in the chapter on seasons, but in damp, drizzly weather both these species – especially woodies – can also be found perching much lower down in the trees. I'm sure this is to keep the rain off that would soon soak them should they stay high in the uppermost exposed branches. Crows seem to be able to weather the rain well, as the water runs off the glossy black plumage.

Rabbits are notorious for their dislike of rain, but if it's not too heavy look for them along hedgerows and stone walls rather than out in the exposed open fields. The same applies when targeting them at night. The leeward side of the wood is also the warmest area, and appeals to them. The denser the tree growth the more sheltered and cosy it is, and, on the subject of wind, I've found that cold north and north-easterlies early in the day are the kiss of death for a good airgun hunting session. So pay attention to the weather forecast the night before your proposed outing. I know they're not always spot on, but wind direction and the movements and localities of cold fronts are usually dependable. This relates more to winter shooting, of course, but it can help you choose your optimum shooting time. If the forecast is for a drop in temperature and a cold front sweeping the country, or your particular area, you can be sure that the creatures of the fields and woods are out feeding, knowing that leaner times are just around the corner. In other words, try to be there when they are, and not when they've gorged themselves, at which stage they go and find the nearest

No matter what hunting technique you employ – observation is always the key to success

shelter and sit out the bad weather to come. Squirrels in particular seem to know just when to be out eating, so as to be tucked up snug in their dreys once those biting winds pierce through the trees and soaking rain sweeps with it. Wind direction might not seem so important, but in relation to your particular hunting area it can make a lot of difference. In some areas such as mine – the grim North-West – a west wind coming off the coast will bite hard, whereas a warm inland breeze could well heat up the surrounding area, even in winter, if the temperatures haven't already dropped too low.

It follows that when the weather is adverse, look to areas that afford shelter, as the quarry won't be keen to feed in these circumstances, unless driven to it by necessity. However, should the rain subside and the sun come out, their thoughts will turn to food and your attention should again therefore be turned towards the feeding areas you've found from your time spent observing previously. As we've seen, finding your quarry is mainly common sense, and not a science.

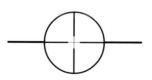

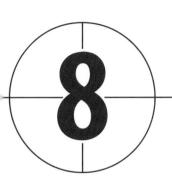

General Fieldcraft, Camouflage and Clothing

Despite all the hype, you don't need to wear the latest hi-tech camo pattern clothing to start hunting with an air rifle. Having said that, effective camo will have a dramatic effect on your performance in the field. Whereas you can certainly hunt with some degree of success in drab clothing, or preferable the military DPM (Disruptive Pattern Material), I'm a firm believer that the modern, new-era camo wear definitely does give you the edge when it comes to fooling your quarry. Camo clothing isn't the be all and end all, and that's one reason why this chapter deals with general fieldcraft in association with camouflage and the various apparel that is now readily available to conceal us. I'm approaching this subject in this way because camouflage is of little use if the wearer doesn't know how to move and act in the field. You'll also notice that the term 'camouflage' links with the word 'concealment'. You may think they're one and the same but, by definition, camouflage loosely means, 'to make something hard to see or interpret', whereas conceal means, 'to hide or make something secret'. Consider those definitions and the next descriptive usage of words will be more useful in helping you to understand camouflage in relation to what it is used for and the intention behind its use. In other words, we may hide using camouflage to help conceal us, but camouflage by itself cannot totally conceal us, although it can make us less noticeable if used correctly.

Camouflage works because it creates visual confusion. It disguises the recognisable human form by blending the mass or shape of the human body into the surroundings and to some extent by breaking up your outline. The need for effective camouflage clothing for the airgun hunter is obvious, because the rifle used has a limited range, and the hunter needs to get within close striking distance so that the shot cleanly and humanely dispatches the pest species targeted, but camo wear is an aid to your concealment, and not a cloak of invisibility. Getting within range also requires fieldcraft, which in part involves camouflaging the body so that you can move across land without being detected. This is a major skill that will be continuously mentioned and explained throughout this book as we come to various situations where it is needed. To be thorough, at the end of this chapter there's a piece that charts the development of the new generation of hi-tech camo patterns that are now so popular and readily available.

Nature's Own

Animals, and to a certain extent most birds, have a distinct advantage in the fact that they have a natural outer protective skin (fur or feathers) of a coloration that helps them blend into their habitats. Naturalists have concluded that brown is the most common colour for any form of wildlife in the natural world. Similarly, and more obviously, green is the predominant colour of foliage plants, but also including brown and other similar earth-toned colours of a darker hue relating to the surrounding cover plants, and depending on the season.

This is taking it to the extreme but camo is an invaluable aid to the airgun hunter

In relation to our main quarry species, we can immediately look to the rabbit as a direct indication of how effective brown actually is in helping an animal to blend into the great outdoors. Just try to pick out a rabbit against a dark background such as an earth bank, under a hedge line or general ground cover. Even amongst a relatively strong colour of green foliage such as grass, if the rabbit remains motionless it can be very difficult to spot with the naked eye from a distance. A situation such as this reminds us how limited our senses are, but thankfully, optical technology gives us binoculars of such quality that we can scan areas we'd otherwise not be able to look at, or survey from afar. Even then, as we scour near a hedge line or taller rough grass at the field's edge, often only the pale creamy colour of the animal's inner ear gives its presence away - and then only if it twitches them a few times. So, whereas the green used in camo designs is obvious, you can now see why brown (an earth tone) is still used widely as a base colour for many modern designs. Backtracking slightly, note the use of the term 'motionless', which brings us to another and possibly the most important factor relating to good concealment, and that's movement. For both quarry and hunter, movement is the biggest giveaway. Next on the list after sight for the human predator is sound, and then smell - the latter two changing in importance depending on the quarry species targeted and how far you are from the target. You may think I've used a strange description, but that's what we are when we're hunting

– we are predators, and it is like a predator that we need to think and behave so as to bag our chosen prize. Humans aren't naturally coloured to blend into their surroundings. Strip us naked, and unless we have a few bob to spend on frequent exotic holidays we're mostly a pasty white. Okay, maybe I speak for myself, but I think you get the gist. In society, we wear clothes for decency, modesty and warmth, whereas in the field we wear appropriate clothing that not only protects our rather fragile outer skin but also keeps us warm and dry. As hunters in particular, we use clothing with a suitable colouration to help to conceal ourselves.

The optimum words there being 'help to conceal', as other factors come into the equation such as light values, angle and direction of the light which depends if the sun is low or high in the sky, not forgetting if it's summer or winter. This may appear to be a conundrum but all will be revealed (almost literally) as the chapter progresses.

Military Man

For sport shooting, camouflage clothing was originally adopted from the Army, firstly because 'used fatigues' such as combat pants and jackets were readily available from army surplus stores and established mail-order companies. The bonus was not only the hard-wearing nature of the material the clothing was made from, but that the material was in the army's long-used and effective DPM (Disruptive Pattern Material) camouflage - in other words it was appropriate, rugged, weather-resistant clothing in a suitable blend of colours and pattern. The army have long known the importance of effective camouflage in relation to their person, their kit - including weapons - and even vehicles. In the history of warfare, we can see how the armies of the world first saw a distinct need to have specific patterns on battledress. During and shortly after WWI, the armed forces of most countries developed their own camo designs, mostly based on standard issue khaki. There are many variations of these camo patterns, as different countries have different foliage and terrain specific to their regions.

Being hidden isn't just about the camo you wear but also how you use the terrain as you hunt

Also, due to the fact that battles can and would possibly be fought even in arctic climates, the British Army saw the need to develop patterns to suit all eventualities they might face some day. This was the reason we saw the widespread issue of the familiar DPM for use in temperate European surroundings. Other types include designs of jungle, desert, and urban camo. Interestingly, the original Laksen camo (the Swiss Army camouflage) was once quite popular with UK hunters. This is neither a copy of foliage nor fauna, but rather an amalgamation of dappled, coloured blotches. This is a good example of a camo that's effective; not due to directly imitating the foliage in which the hunter is operating, but because it uses the disruption and blurring of the overall image of the human shape to achieve the desired effect. A pattern that uses this same effect is the German Flecktarn camo. Of the military patterns, it's long been established that British DPM, French Central European and US Woodland are the best suited to the countryside environs of the UK.

In relation to camo for hunting, certain forward-thinking individuals had noticed that army issue camo wasn't suited to some terrain. Indeed, whereas DPM confuses the eye, the new age designs - often termed 'photo-realistic' - actually imitate your surroundings. It was this basic idea of imitating the surrounding foliage that spawned the glut of hi-tech, photo-realistic camo wear that the UK hunter from the beginning of the Millennium back then, and through various new designs, has to choose from even now. Many will be aware that it was in America that these designs originated, the most famous being the first Advantage® camo pattern, which was readily adopted by hunters and outdoorsmen. This pattern was designed by a hunter himself, Bill Jordan, and has grown into a worldwide phenomenon in hunting and eventually in the UK amongst specialist anglers, to becoming a billion dollar industry that is moving ever-forward in

The hunter, if using the right camo design, can blend into even the most sparse of surroundings

the new designs it offers. Another, but less popular camo, and one of the first alternatives to DPM to enter the UK, was a camo pattern called Mossy Oak, and there was also Trebark – launched here at the time as Superflauge.

Back in 2005 I stated: 'It's hard to predict how this type of camo clothing will progress. New patterns will emerge, but I'm sure we're reaching a peak in terms of optimum colour blend and effective pattern type, if we haven't peaked already.'

Well, in hindsight I don't feel I made that bad a job of predicting how camo patterns would progress. New ones emerged, some 'came, didn't sell as well as expected and they were gone, but another design soon followed that was of more general appeal. Not surprisingly, it was Advantage/Realtree who always maintained a strong presence here in the UK; after a relatively lengthy hiatus they eventually came back with a vengeance, boasting new patterns such as Realtree AP (All Purpose and APG (All Purpose Green). Then, of course, we have the HD (High Definition) variants thereof. Currently, as I write, Realtree has launched Xtra Green, and Realtree Xtra. Both are seasonal patterns, the former being a summer design the latter being autumnal. Their biggest rival, if that's the correct term to use, is Mossy Oak and they have not been idle as they came back relatively recently with Break-Up Infinity, Brush, Obsession and a incredibly realistic 3D variant of their Shadow Grass pattern called Shadow Grass Blades.

With the amount of other clothing design giants now pitching designs into the arena, particularly the Scandinavian-based companies, it's now a very saturated market. Danish clothing giants, Deerhunter, initially launched the 'Innovation' camo pattern in an attempt to pry loose of having to pay 'under licence', always to use the established and most favoured, known camo designs from Advantage/Realtree and Mossy Oak. As I write they're championing a very interesting new camo called Equipt. They claim pixilation of the colours almost blurs the garments; jacket, trousers etc ... to break up any outline, and therefore help you blend in with your surroundings. There is now much debate over which is the better option, photo-realistic camo patterns or those that are termed as digitalised. These patterns are generated by computer software that calculates all colours in the general outdoors without allowing the pattern to be terrain specific, therefore being more versatile in its use.

A company who stand out or 'blend in' you could say that do need mentioning because they were the first UK company to design a pattern specifically for the autumn in particular the Autumnal Woodland and areas where bare leafed hedgerows met equally barren looking fields, is Jack Pyke of England, who took the bold step and launched a pattern called 'English Oak'. A mix of brown leaves with dark to slightly lighter brown shades, broken up by branches, twigs and autumnal foliage that is highly effective. This was followed by a summer pattern when the woods are in full leaf and the hedgerows and fields are in full greenery. This was 'English Woodland'. Their first design actually outsells the latter as it is still a favourite with UK airgun hunters for the seasons of bare cover. They released yet another camo pattern known as 'Wild Trees Grasslands'; a pattern suited to marshland with its mix of reed stems and bulrush heads, wild rye grass stems and lighter foliage mostly found in such areas. To a certain degree, I feel it fills a niche for use while hunting near certain terrain. The blend of foliage mentioned is very terrain-specific but I can see Its usefulness, when the seasons change and certain areas where hedges, fields and particularly moorland look barren of any specific colouration. So too, when the stubble fields start to look bare of any colour as the cut crop stems die back. They now have a wide range of apparel available in all three patterns. Also, in my opinion, they've designed a unique system of clothing, best described as a hybrid ghillie suit/mesh oversuit with what is termed 'edge relief' (die-cut leaves that break up your outline, which Is also used on

Loose-leaf camo systems such as the LLCS build-up system are extremely effective when used in the right circumstances

certain camo netting and pop–up hides). Their LLCS (Loose Leaf Camouflage System) is available in both English Oak and English Woodland. Both patterns work remarkably well as long as you use them correctly - i.e. don't forget fieldcraft. They also market separate strips of very realistic die-cut leaves which you can wrap around and secure to your rifle using No-Marc tape. If used accordingly, you can almost reach invisibility if staying static and in the right terrain that the pattern is designed for.

Scandinavian manufacturers such as Harkila/Seeland have begun to design their own camo patterns and it's here we see the change, as these use what can be termed a 'colour blend' found in nature. You could say these designs are a modern alternative to DPM! Most noteable patterns are X-Invisible, Erase XT, Opti-Fade, with others even as I write being talked of. Also, JahtiJakt's (yes you read that right) own design, 'Invisible', camo pattern is very popular, but this isn't a book devoted to all camo patterns so I have to leave off at some point and here's not a bad place to do so. I leave by mentioning that infiltrating the hunting scene, we are now seeing military patterns such as the Multi-Cam, designed by Crye Industries for US Armed Forces. It's described as a 'digitalised non-terrain specific camouflage.' First indications are that some clothing manufacturers are offering it to civvy street, but the general airgun-buying, cam-clad hunter isn't stampeding towards it or others of its kind.

Mix 'n' Match

I'd taken a personal interest in camo long before the new-age designs arrived, having been experimenting with military patterns as diverse as urban camo and desert camo, and they proved very usable. In hindsight, it seems my findings have proved interesting because the base colours of these patterns are browns (desert camo) and combinations of greys and black (urban). It came as no surprise that brown would become a predominant colour for many new commercial patterns, not only because it's a natural colour in nature, but also because my experiences with different army camo showed this. When the early Advantage® pattern arrived, with its base brown colouration, I wasn't surprised at its effectiveness. I also remember thinking as soon as I saw Realtree Hardwoods® 20-200, a pattern largely made up of dark colours including greys, browns and even black, that it would prove very useful. It did, and the rest is history. So my experiments and findings had shown that I was at least heading in the right direction in my thoughts on the colours most beneficial for camouflaging myself in the field. Even now, I'll mix-and-match different camo designs in my overall kit. For instance, camo that's predominantly heavy with browns and darker tones suits the woods, and certainly if sitting amongst leaf litter it's wise to wear suitable camo trousers of, say, a bark and leaf litter heavy pattern such as Advantage Timber® or Xtra Brown, and of course English Oak – a highly-effective design for the autumnal woodland..

However, because the foliage growing from the ground up is often ferns and suchlike, it can often be wise in certain instances to cover the upper body in a green-based camo, such as the older designs of Realtree Hardwoods Green® or Mossy Oak Breakup. Interestingly, the American manufacturers themselves recommend this mix 'n' match approach.

Another factor that should also be considered when matching camo to terrain is the angle from which your quarry is likely to spot you. If shooting up into trees, ambushing birds coming to sitty trees, or roost-shooting then, as you're concealing yourself from eyes above your position, a more uniform, darker hue 'branch and bark heavy' autumnal -coloured camo pattern suited to the leaf litter and woodland floor is the best option. The reason is that you'll probably have your back to a tree trunk, green foliage will most likely be sparse, and you'll also probably (and preferably) be amongst the shadows; and remember to keep your pale hands and face covered with suitable gloves and a face veil.

This illustrates the importance of carefully considering your shooting position and studying the terrain you normally shoot over, and then tailoring your camo to suit. As the seasons change so does the foliage, so a hunter should change and adapt his camo accordingly. There are many permutations for this mixing and matching concealment technique. I'll often wear DPM Gore-Tex™ over-trousers because I'm sitting on wet grass or foliage, while my jacket can be anything from Realtree Hardwoods Green, Advantage Timber, or a Mossy Oak pattern. Whatever suits the conditions and helps me to blend better into the surroundings is what I'll wear. It is also worth mentioning that the US duck hunters' one-time favourite camo, Advantage Wetlands Camo® was probably one that got the least interest from the UK shooting fraternity, especially airgun hunters, but I found it very well suited for the autumn fields and conditions when ground foliage has died back around tall wild grass stems, and sparse hedges if I was keeping close next to the edges, especially if stalking near the barren-looking stubble fields. Maybe this is the niche that Wild Trees Grasslands will fill.

There's also the Advantage ® Max-4 HD™ pattern to choose. Although it sounds like a computer game, this camo with its brown/ochre base overlaid with reed- and rush-type stems will suit the autumn and, of course, wetland areas heavy in rushes and reeds. Basically, it's not that popular but at the time, the angling fraternity switched on to camo big-style, fell for marketing campaigns and started to wear green-based, photo-realistic, camo design – yes, the craze was now fashion.

To an extent I feel the camo industry has reached a point where all terrain and seasons are catered for, and yet I think some hunters are increasingly trend-orientated in their choice. As time moves on, so will the designs that become available, and once again a safe bet to say this is one area of the market that will continue to impress the consumer rather than leading to the ultimate downfall of more vermin! Clever marketing campaigns will try, and possibly succeed in convincing many people otherwise, but the selection of camo we already have basically caters for all terrain – until we hunt on Mars, that is!

So, how does basic camo such as DPM now rate in its use for airgun hunting? I still wear DPM combat-style trousers, because this pattern is useful for the foliage and fauna of the UK. I've also now taken to wearing 'Marpat' combat style trousers, again, as they cause visual confusion, the new digitalised patterns we are now seeing are actually being designed with computer software as a random camo pattern to suit most terrain with ground foliage of certain colours, variations thereof and hues. If they're waterproof, and over-trouser design, all the better as they are very practical for the sitting, kneeling, and crawling involved in many situations that the airgun hunter encounters. I find it strange that so many hunters overlook them, as they're relatively cheap and easy to come by; understandably, in the present climate, which is still one of predominantly photo-realistic patterns.

Certain elements involved in the promotion of all the new imitative camo designs working within the industry still actively try to discredit DPM as a pattern. Granted, these designs look more realistic to the foliage we sit amongst, but what of moving across bare grass fields and open land - both largely uniform, blank areas of one colour? This shows that the matter is not as simple as just putting on the latest 'must have' camo gear. I feel the matter needs further, more detailed explanation and certainly how quarry rather than another human being sees you.

It's now accepted that quarry doesn't have half the amount of colour receptors in the eyes as a human, so it basically sees any object as shades and shapes. If you're blending in and not moving, depending on how close you are to the targeted quarry, it more than likely knows something is around - but there's always something else around. Keeping downwind, movement to a minimum, and keeping quiet are the major requisites for being 'unnoticed. You may now be saying that this blows everything you've thought or heard of in relation to the effectiveness of any photo-realistic camo pattern out of the water. Well, in a way it does, but in others it doesn't. They were first created in the US for bowhunters who would wait amongst certain terrain to hide near a known ride to be much closer to their quarry (usually the whitetail deer) than someone using a powerful firearm, so the reason these types of camo works for them is very valid. As the 12ft lb airgun hunter also needs to be concealed to get or wait within the relatively short range, a 12ft lb air rifle is capable of cleanly dispatching legally deemed quarry species. I feel this is one of the major reasons airgun hunters in the UK welcomed them with open arms.

We shouldn't forget that DPM is still useful when used as a base pattern – the military once added foliage cut from the land they were operating over. This all helped the soldier to blend into the terrain.

I use the military again as an example, because the infantryman also realised that white faces and hands stood out because they reflect light, but this was soon remedied by the use of 'camo cream' – either green, black, or the American-style, multi-colour face cream. Granted, that is for the army, and often the use of camo becomes a life and death situation; but the hunter who realised that his hands and face gave him away would also use this cream even though he'd more than likely receive sniggers from other hunters if he mentioned using it. The truth is that he was better prepared to conceal himself from his quarry. Now, as clothing and designs have advanced, manufacturers have seen the benefits of full concealment and made apparel available to the public that negates the need for big splodges of cream, and these take the form of face-masks or veils. I swear by the use of these camo aids, including gloves.

I also feel the dedicated hunter in some instances should wear these at night, as even when there is little moonlight, a white face and hands at close quarters can stand out like beacons.

As I'm sure you now realise - the use of full camo when required is something I feel strongly about, and the only times I think of not using a camo mask or gloves are when indoor feral pigeon bashing, and certain ratting situations – all techniques that are dealt with elsewhere in this book.

Now we specifically look at a part of the body that gives everything away – the eyes. Your eyes are a big feature of your face and I have little doubt that the eyes, or maybe the movement and whites of the eyes, can allow another animal or bird to realise that you too are an animal and not the harmless inanimate object you are trying to resemble with the aid of camo. A peaked baseball-style cap or, if you prefer, a 'boonie hat' can be used to part-shield or obscure the eyes. You shouldn't look directly at the quarry, but rather look up under the brim of the hat or peak of the cap, especially when observing quarry in the trees. The trick is to look up - without making direct eye contact - while you determine the bird's demeanour or state of awareness. Once it settles, you can then slowly move to adjust your position, or whatever it takes to sight in on the target, but it must be said that if the quarry is totally tuned into its surroundings and on high alert, the slightest movement will have it off and away. Even though this can be terribly frustrating, a tip in such situations is simply to wait for it to settle or for a better opportunity to present itself. It is definitely better not to shoot, so as not to risk scaring other potential quarry that may arrive on the scene.

Alternatively, if you're in position and you know the general area where birds are to pitch into the trees, you can have the rifle raised or part-raised towards the target area beforehand. Then you only need make the minimal movement necessary to put the cross-hairs onto the quarry's kill-zone. You're only able to do this if you've got into a comfortable sitting position to begin with. If the ground is uneven or rocky, use a shooting mat, or a specialist seat such as a turkey seat to avoid 'numb bum syndrome', and if the shooting mat or seat is black, drape a piece of camo net over it. You may think this a case of camo-overkill, but it's not so, because a bare patch of black on the ground with you looking like a bush in the middle could attract curiosity then alarmed attention from quarry up above.

Cap, face veil and gloves are a necessity when shooting up into trees or when shooting at close range

The optimum position for this style of shooting is to be sitting comfortably, slightly leant back and using the trunk of a tree as a backrest, while your leading arm rests on your raised left knee and holds the rifle pointing upwards in the general direction of the area where quarry is likely to present itself. Obviously, if you're a left-hander then use the raised right knee as support. This means you're not straining muscles by holding a rifle up, as it's already rested and little movement will be needed on your part once you decide to take a shot. Another and sometimes better way to adopt this shooting position is to rest the rifle forend on a set of height-adjustable, two-leg or three-leg shooting sticks. Positioned correctly for the particular hunting situation, you can pull back on the sticks and the rifle will rise; pushing them forward has the opposite effect, though to a lesser degree.

This again illustrates how movement is the biggest giveaway, and one you should always be aware of to keep one step ahead of your quarry. Still on the subject of the 'whites of your eyes', you can wear American-design shooting glasses that are transparent from the inside but have a camo pattern printed on the outer. These allow the shooter to see out but the quarry can't see in. I tried these when they first emerged in the UK as a camo accessory and they do work - something to consider if your quarry has become ultra-twitchy, or you're relatively close. However, to my knowledge, they didn't sell well and aren't available in the UK any more but I bet you'd find them on the Internet!

All this might seem like going overboard, but the hunter who pays attention to this sort of detail at times is more often than not the most successful. It's interesting to note that many very experienced hunters agree that the ability to blend into the surroundings is most important when at closer ranges, whereas the longer the range (i.e. the distance from your quarry to your position), the more care has to be taken in the prevention of showing your outline. More on this later as having established the benefits of good camo, I'll now sidetrack slightly to mention another factor relating to fieldcraft.

If you're a smoker you run a higher risk than a non-smoker of being scented when you try to get close to your quarry, and the same applies if you use too much aftershave. A rabbit's sense of smell is legendary, and its nose is seemingly constantly twitching. When really alert, the animal sits up or stretches higher on its hind legs, not only to get a better look around and to listen, but also to smell the air. I'm not coming down on smokers, but if I can smell a smoker - and my sense of smell isn't a patch on an animal's - what do you think? Some advocate the use of the American sprays, or as they're known, 'scent inhibitors.' Those who use them swear they work, and on that matter I'd say if you feel they help cover up unnatural smells then use them, because they'll boost your confidence if nothing else. Also, don't use heavily scented soaps before you go hunting. Just because the good lady was kind enough to leave hers handy in the shower is no excuse. Use it when you come home by all means, but before you hit the field - it's not recommended.

We've now dealt with reducing sight and smell, so what about sound? To mention the obvious rattling zips and buckles is all too easy, and most will realise that needs dealing with. Boots that squeak and clothing that rustles are also out, and nothing in your pockets should make any noise when you move. A major gripe I also have is the use of Velcro. At night and/or when close to quarry, you might as well shout as use large strips of this material. Small tabs are acceptable for added security on pockets, but if you need to open anything and it is fastened or attached with large strips of double-sided Velcro, either do it before getting near to your chosen hunting area or don't use it at all.

Now, with everything covered, concealed and silenced, hopefully at this point it's now understandable why we go to these lengths to conceal ourselves!

Summer and Winter Wear

Camo clothing, like general outdoors country wear, is available in two distinct categories – lightweight summer wear, and heavier jackets and trousers suited to the temperatures and weather conditions of winter and colder weather.

Likewise, experienced outdoorsmen will say there's no such thing as bad weather – just bad clothing! When it comes to purchasing clothing for cold and/or wet weather, this is when you'll discover if the manufacturer's claims are true or not. Always buy from reputable companies with established, tried and tested products. As many companies now produce quality garments, some will be named as I mention individual garments, while other manufactures will be listed at the end of this book.

The former and warmer seasons often only involve the airgun hunter wearing a breathable, long-sleeve T-shirt under a lightweight jacket and combat-style trousers of a suitable green-based, photo-realistic camo design.

At present Realtree APG and APG HD pattern clothing seems to be all the rage. However, due to our unpredictable weather, no matter what time of year, you still need to think of worst case scenarios. The jacket should be at least showerproof, with a detachable hood and have a wick-away mesh inner lining. Likewise, the trousers, but a mesh inner lining isn't as important as stowage so that's why standard 6-pocket combats still rule the roost for most hunters. A poncho should definitely be in your kit bag, which for summer can be one of the rucksacks known as 'hydration backpacks'. These have become very popular in a relatively short space of time, as have waist bags. I use this term as they're much more featured than single-pocket bum bags, and many a time you can carry everything in your waist bag rather than have the hassle of a backpack – even though it might have the in-vogue water bladder hydration system installed. All will be explained in the chapter that follows on the Kit and Accessories that I recommend any airgun hunter consider.

You'll often be stalking one period of the hunting foray and ambushing the next, so dress accordingly, and if ambushing it's always useful to take a suitable-size and design of camo net. If intending to shoot from ambush a gun bag/shooting mat can be very useful, but again, all will be revealed in the chapter that follows. Light faceveil and cap, boonie with veil, it's up to personal choice but don't forget gloves and always take a spare pair of them.

Mesh suits are often used in both summer and winter, they can be slipped over existing clothing and, when not in use, pack away easily for carrying and storage. These now come in most of the new patterns, and the better types are even shower resistant. When the weather's warm, they certainly offer the optimum solution for comfort, and they're also handy should you need or wish to change camo patterns quickly. A case in point is when stalking hedgerows and then deciding to wait up in ambush, if moving to another different foliated area. It is handy to have a suitable alternative pattern in a large enough size to throw over whatever your main camo wear is at such a time, in summer or winter. Incidentally, using a mesh suit in this manner doesn't afford you much protection from sharp objects or foliage, due to the lack of padding in this lightweight, almost skimpy wear. They offer little comfort when sitting or kneeling on rough ground, or when crawling into a shooting position, so wear something more substantial underneath, and perhaps gaiters to protect the lower legs. There are other forms of over-wear which I rate highly, and these are traditional-style ghillie suits, as previously mentioned, and their modern equivalents. Now, we must look at outdoor camo wear suited to cold, damp, inclement weather.

Most of the main garments you wear such as jacket and trousers should be made up of several different materials, typically an outer protective shell to withstand wear and tear, an inner membrane or laminate for total waterproofing, and in many cases fixed or removable inner thermal or fleece linings for added warmth and comfort. Different manufacturers have their own trade names for these membranes and insulation linings, with Gore-Tex™ being one of the many and most respected brands, and probably the best known, but all are very effective. In relation to the style of jacket, different people have different preferences in the type or even the cut. Personally, I don't like parka-style garments, preferring three-quarter-length field jackets, and in summer wherever possible I'd opt for a bomber-style or similar with hood. At risk of contradicting myself, I'm not usually a great fan of using a hood on a jacket, because they can obscure hearing and vision, but if it's removable, either by zip or stud fasteners, then it's certainly useful to keep it in a side pocket should you need to sit out a downpour. Even I am not so stupid as to get wet, but when possible I prefer to use a baseball-type cap to protect me from showers. Some hoods are effective if they have integral peaks and come far enough forward over the head to shield the eyes partly by putting them in shadow, and if this is more appealing than wearing a separate item for full-face cover, at least you are using something useful. In relation to hoods, many are constructed as they feature 'volume adjusters.' These are often seen as three adjustable drawstring cords with ABS toggles, usually found either side and at the top and/or back of the hood. These ensure a perfect fit should the rain come down in buckets. However, I've usually found hoods a hindrance, not only to hearing but also if you are looking around, as the hood can obscure vision to the sides. Adjustment means more movement, and that's something we're trying to keep to a minimum. The jacket's collar should be of the high, stand-up, 'storm' design, to protect the back and sides of the neck from wind and draughts that can sneak into exposed areas.

Front fastening is usually by a zip or double zip and, as added protection, a stud fastened over-flap or storm flap. The jacket should cater for a snug fit around the wrist, with knitted ribbed cuffs or an adjustable wrist strap. All do the job they're designed to do, and that is to keep out the elements; but do remember to put your gloves on first before fastening up the wrist adjustments. The jacket's outer material is also important because it needs to be silent. Saddlecloth and Shikari Cloth were amongst some of the first to combat the dreaded 'rustle' but others are now taking their place. Manufacturers often now use the phrase 'made out of a silent outer fabric.' Many more will be developed as this side of the sport continues to expand. Talking of 'expansion,' that's another area addressed by clothing manufacturers for the active hunter. The inner waterproof laminate is termed 'stretchy' obviously meaning it doesn't hinder movement. Laminates such a Deerhunter's 'Deer-Tex' are testament to this. Also look to specifications such as water-resistant. This often means that although it does offer some protection from the rain it can't claim to be 100% waterproof, simply because the seams are not sealed. However, virtually all quality outdoor wear is now breathable and fully windproof.

The season, and especially the prevailing weather or time of day or night when you're actually going hunting will dictate what you wear underneath a jacket. This may only need to be a light fleece, but at other times something more suitably substantial will be needed. As I'm sure many already know, several layers of progressively thicker clothing are preferable to one big thick woolly jumper - no harm in reminding ourselves of that. The reason being, they allow the air to circulate so that you're not as prone to sweating, but the layers trap warmth when it's needed. If you're too hot, removing a layer of clothing is the easy solution; but if you only had the one thick garment under your jacket then you'd not be able to regulate your temperature as efficiently or at all.

Layer Cake

The 'layer' principle of clothing should be adhered to, but also what is used in the build-up of the layers and also what the individual item's main properties and attributes are.

For clothing closest to the body I recommend the following; a lightweight, breathable fleece with a three-quarter, zip-up neck opening. This helps to regulate heat retention. If this type of garment is worn, then combine it with a neck warmer that has a longer bib-style front to hide the bare white flesh of the neck. However, at this stage it isn't that crucial as you can zip up an outer garment over the exposed area if necessary.

In colder weather the quantity of clothing needed is one of the reasons I take a rucksack when I go hunting. I store extra clothing that may be needed in it, so leave it at a known position as I go about my hunting, then when needed I can go back to get another layer or safely store something I might have removed. If I need another layer due to the temperature dropping, a fleece top with high collar and full-zip front opening, or an item many airgun hunters don't consider, a fleece gilet. These are very versatile as an outer alternative to a full fleece or even extra last layer of your system - especially useful are ones with zip-up side pockets.

All extra layers are stored separately in the main pack in compression bags so they're not as cold as the surroundings and will be dry as a bone when you need them. Extra pairs of dry socks (both under-sock and outer if it's cold to the point a layer system is used for your feet) are always stored in the pack, as are a spare facemask and gloves. These are very important items if wearing full camo for concealment, and if you hunt regularly in them you'll know how a facemask can become sweat-soaked quite quickly, even in relatively cool conditions, and depending on your exertions. Gloves have a habit of picking up dampness as you put a steadying hand down on the ground. It will always seem to find any wet patch of grass, bare-earth or area of waterlogged ground.

As for the thermal underwear - thanks to the hi-tech new materials used in manufacture, we don't have to make do with those old-style cotton thermals that left you feeling sweaty and clammy after the slightest exertion. Those 'old-school' thermals once wet, stayed wet, leaving you feeling chilly and uncomfortable. Clothing has developed to the point where there are thermals that are constructed to allow moisture to pass through from your body – or, as it's known, wick away to an outer layer where it is held. The really hot new designs (no pun intended) use a polypropylene/cotton mix that allows any moisture to wick out, keeping you dry, warm and comfortably mobile. Stop! Then why have I still not found any that are 100% reliable; my opinion is because they are too tight-fitting to the skin. Those are just my views on the subject. Then again, we don't hunt in almost Arctic conditions in the UK do we – well not quite yet anyway!

The key words that are stated for a large percentage of hunting garments, both summer and winter, particularly suitable for all outdoor activities in inclement weather are; breathable, waterproof and windproof. Three words that mean a lot in respect of how a garment has to be made and what materials are used to achieve this.

It's obvious why we require these attributes but the breathability of a garment isn't easily achieved, depending on design and of course what is worn over it. This is very important in very cold conditions when building up a layer system of garments for warmth; regulation of the temperature that can build up when worn under a suitable waterproof and windproof jacket – note the lack of the word 'breathable' in that last statement.

Also, tailoring the clothing you wear to the hunting you are intending to do has to be a major consideration as to what you wear. If actively seeking out or pursuing quarry, you'll be amazed at how much you actually do perspire under all those layers. In the cold, you will quickly warm up, but stop, wait and watch a while in a known hotspot for quarry, and you can begin to shiver all too quickly if you get the layer system wrong. This is because you've unwittingly blocked the flow of air from base layer to outer, so know now the importance of breathability. Your base layer, no matter how supposedly hi-tech of build will retain body sweat to some extent. The fast build-up, even though some of the damp perspiration is wicked away, is the main reason you will feel clammy and cold, so the garment you wear closest to your skin is very important. I've used top brands that we should be able to rely on, but upon calling it a day (or night), as soon as I've been able to remove the base layer it was completely soaked with sweat. In certain weather conditions, nothing can change this happening even if you wear the right layers; only going to the motor or rucky to change it solves the problem. In the cold, it isn't ideal stripping down to your bare upper torso to change the first layer, so if not sitting or lying in ambush this isn't as critical because you're not exerting yourself and therefore sweating.

What follow are my personal views. Use them as a guide to what suits the hunting you normally undertake and, of course, the weather conditions.

Base Layer - Should be a very light garment, loose but not an overlarge fit, that's breathable. Preferably, it will have air vents or open mesh at the underarms or upper sides and have a three-quarter-length, zip-up neck. This allows you to regulate manually the air trapped under the garment, and some will be if wearing other garments on top.

Mid Layer – This is the garment many get wrong and most just put on a long-sleeved T-shirt or sweatshirt – WRONG! It needs to be a more substantial, looser fitting garment such as a light fleece with three-quarters- or full-length zip front opening, but have the same properties as the base layer detailed previously. If windproof as well, all the better.

It has to be very cold for the next layer so choosing again isn't easy as your body temperature fluctuates. A heavier fleece, full zip opening and high, stand-up, storm collar, with elasticated cuffs is certainly the least you require. Alternatively, as mentioned previously, you could wear a gilet - basically a body-warmer with no arms and full zip-up front. Both can quickly be removed should the need arise and I've found myself wearing these more and more in the colder months.

Pay particular attention to the jacket you wear, be it one colour or camo. The reason being if it has a zip-out fleece lining I'd say if it isn't too insulted, remove this as it's easier done before setting out than having to remove it in the field, and store it or your top layer worn underneath.

The jacket will preferably be breathable, and needs both a separate waterproof and windproof laminate, preferably with regulating arm and body vents that you open or close with rain-protected zips. They work, as when open they will reveal a more open mesh, this keeps out heavy rain, and are positioned in areas that aren't as easily exposed to the elements. The number of cargo pockets, or other-style outer pockets, is up to personal choice but better to have more outside than continually opening what should be a heavy-duty, full-zip front with storm flap and stand-up collar with integral or removable hood. Also, strong, adjustable,

Velcro strap fasteners are needed at the cuffs to cinch the jacket tight, when needed, around the upper part of the gloves you should be wearing.

The trousers I recommend are pretty much standard combat-style for summer and come winter, combine these with a heavier-duty, pull-over, breathable, waterproof and windproof over-trouser. The latter may or may not have pockets, but one or two are favourable as are side access openings to your inside pockets. As for the ankle area, you'll often find that combat trousers have drawstring bottoms. If not, they should, as there's nothing worse than those with a nondescript straight-leg cut. For the over-pants, these usually are elasticated at the top and/or have zipped-leg, open bottoms so they can be pulled on over boots. Then zip up the lower area, and on better-quality garments there'll also be ankle adjusters of either the Velcro strap design or press stud fasteners allowing at least two settings to cinch tight around the ankle of your boots. We'll come to footwear later, but in my experience anything with a zip is an area that needs to be considered in relation to it being a stress point, and the amount of use it receives. Usually, good-quality garments have heavy-duty zips, so there shouldn't be a problem. You'll need to clean these ankle zips regularly so that they don't become clogged with dry mud and earth that will be picked up in the field. A tip is, once the zip is clean and dry, rub the teeth with candle wax as this help to keep them lubricated and working as they should, and to some extent it also helps to limit the picking up of dirt. The same applies to the zips of jackets and pockets.

Since the original version of my book, a superb all-in-one zip cleaner/protector and lubricant called E-Zip has been developed and is available in aerosol form. It's a 'Napier of England' product and I make no excuses for their products being recommended throughout this book because, certain products they design and have manufactured in the UK are very innovative, and in more recent years they've been pro-active in producing more products for the airgun user and of course developing kit that impresses.

Wash Out!

Camo wear should never be washed in normal washing liquid or powder. It infuses the clothing with ultraviolet, accentuating the pattern in turn, rendering it much less effective. Clothing should be given a lukewarm or cold water wash with no detergents. I leave mine for as long as I can, but I do wash them when needed so that the camo is still effective, and doesn't turn into a bland-looking splodge of mud. Similarly, if over-washed, and although the camo designs are printed using inks and dyes designed to be as colourfast as possible, eventually all fabrics will fade. A faded camo pattern loses both colour and contrast, and this undermines its ability to create visual confusion necessary for it to be effective. To delay fading through washing, wash the garments turned inside out, using cold water and allowing them to hang-dry naturally, and not on a hot spin-cycle. Although it's not easy when sharing your living accommodation with others, don't worry unduly if your clothing smells of the outdoors. That's the smell of Mother Nature and God's own earth, and it's the best human scent inhibitor you'll ever find to cover natural body aroma, which is especially important for an airgun hunter needing to get closer to quarry. If you can leave them without washing, keep the clothes in a sealed bag or somewhere hung off the ground. The place should be dry, and it's ideal if you happen to have a roomy garage - but do bring them indoors before going hunting. It's surprising how cold can permeate a jacket to the point where it seems you can never get warm in it, especially if it hasn't been properly dried and aired before use.

Leg It

At the leg area, gaiters used to be popular but are now very much left to deerstalkers and rough shooters. If you don't like wearing high-leg boots then gaiters are worth considering, as they do offer calf and upper leg protection when walking through tall, wet grass, prevent nettle stings, and when operating in an area where ticks can nip up a trouser leg ... and yes - camo gaiters are available!

For face and hand cover I recommend the Cap with Veil (Arctic Outdoors). Garlands supply some excellent garments for face/head and hands and I particularly must highlight Jack Pyke of England. It really does seem that JP's sister company, Thatchreed Ltd, have exploded on to the scene with all manner of clothing in their own specific camo designs; gloves, head/face covers and much, much more. 'From small acorns', as they say ... no pun intended.

Obviously, it's light gloves for summer, and heavier waterproof gloves for winter. In warmer weather, I prefer to use light gloves with dot grip palms, but in winter I'll opt for the heavier camo neoprene gloves, again with the dot grips. I certainly now prefer the neoprene stretch-fit gloves with fold-back trigger and thumb. Whatever the season though, it's beneficial to have gloves with extra-long cuffs for full wrist concealment and protection from the elements. Most airgun hunters will have light gloves for summer, stretch neoprene with fold-back finger and thumb, Fingerless mitts, with or without overflap, sturdier neoprene cut-fingers and, of course, any all-weather airgun hunter should have a suitable pair of MacWet Gloves.

A useful tip for any full-finger, heavier neoprene gloves is to cut the tip off the forefinger and thumb of the glove for the shooting hand. This allows the shooter to feel the trigger and to load pellets into barrels, loading channels or magazines easily. For the latter I'll also sometimes use gloves on which both hands have the specified finger and thumb tip severed. This is often preferable for holding magazines while refilling and refitting them to the rifle. With heavier gloves, even if they are what are termed 'cut-finger' types (meaning that you can fold back the first two fingers and thumb, which are split and have a Velcro fold-back) I often still cut the finger and thumb tips off the shooting-hand glove.

This is because the folded-back tip of the glove may foul on the rifle's trigger guard, and they have the annoying habit of flipping back over to their original positions - usually at crucial moments. But I must admit that on the left hand I find them useful, and often leave them unmodified. Incidentally, for hunting at night I often now wear a pair of strong yet tactile fingerless-mitt-style, tactical shooting gloves - more on night attire in the relevant section on Shooting At Night.

Although we've talked head/face cover, I'd like specifically to address the lightweight facemasks you pull over your head and tie at the back. I don't feel the camo pattern to be crucial in your selection, but do ensure that it's not of a type that could move as you turn your head and start to hinder your vision.

There's also the head-over sock or stocking-type headgear, similar to a stretched leg of nylon stocking as used by bank robbers. These come in a basic camo pattern called Spandoflauge®. I've used them, they work, but you don't see them as much and I'd not recommend them if you tend to feel claustrophobic.

If it's cold, you can add an extra insulating layer, which I prefer than wearing one heavier-duty, knitted balaclava design, camo pattern, fleece-fronted face mask. These are camo fleece face covers that go on from the front, covering the forehead, have eye-slits, nose-piece with vent and mouth vent. These can easily be kept in a jacket pocket and quick and easily fit around your faceveil or mask to fasten at the rear usually with a strong Velcro tab.

As for caps or hooded garments with integral drop-down face veils, these are notorious for shifting position and exposing part of the face. This can be remedied by stitching in a couple of tabs of double-sided Velcro, so long as you don't overdo it, but by and large I prefer to cut these out and use a mask. There's always a 'but' - drop-down face veils do actually conceal the eyes more effectively, as well as the face, as they often cover the whole of the facial area with a see-through mesh similar to the material used in pop-up hide shooting windows. So, if they can be modified to suit your shooting style then so much the better.

The head and shoulders of the human form are unmistakeable, no matter how they are covered. Strive never to show your head or upper torso in silhouette against a contrasting background, because as I've continually driven home as being proven fact and discovered by myself and many others, the best camo in the world won't hide your outline. Even though the body is covered by an imitative camouflage pattern against suitable foliage, if you're not positioned correctly you will still stand out.

A Case of the Ghillies

The best concealment to break up the outline of the human body shape is 3D leaf-effect over-suits, or as they're commonly known, ghillie suits. The loose 'leaves' protrude irregularly from the straight edges of your body, thereby blurring the outline. The origin of these suits is commonly attributed to the US military in Vietnam, as it was around the 1960s that they began to be issued and used by military snipers. Even earlier, they were certainly used by some British soldiers in WWI. However, there has been some fanciful speculation as to their invention and first use by the sport shooter. The name would have you suppose there is a link with Scottish deerstalkers and countrymen of the same name – ghillie. The link seems to be a tenuous one, but it could be that the name was adopted because Scottish ghillies mainly wore - as they still do - traditional tweeds of a colour that makes them less obtrusive on moorland heather. There's also a 'tree fairy' of Celtic folklore known as the Ghillie Dhu, which disguised itself with leaves to play pranks on those who ventured into the woods. That's a nice twist to the tale and a play on words, but not wanting to get embroiled in a controversy over the garment name's true origins, I feel that's one for military historians.

The suit itself is of great benefit, firstly for the soldier; the military version is used by snipers who need a large, baggy, comfortable suit or universal, effective camo covering that they can move in and rest under. They also needed one they could swiftly remove when they needed to leave an area in hurry, and these soon became standard sniper issue. Early ones were little more than strips of dark hessian and strips of khaki-coloured cloth stitched onto khaki fatigues. As the availability and types of clothing advanced, the military designs were usually manufactured from more modern materials in dark olive, charcoal and even black. Interestingly, the more recent military versions seem to have reverted to the 'hanging cloth' design, using strips of burlap and jute on a mesh suit to obtain the desired effect. There are now many loose-leaf systems available and also rifle covers that use the same design and do an excellent job of concealing a rifle/scope combo.

For hunting, a more formal style of the ghillie suit is now available in a small selection of new-age, imitative camouflage patterns. Any ghillie suit will probably provide better concealment than flat cloth camouflage, because the first function of a ghillie suit is to add a sense of depth to the otherwise two-dimensional human outline. No printed cloth in the world can duplicate this, even though some HD (High Definition) patterns are now almost reaching a level where they have 3D characteristics. As well as creating depth, the second essential purpose of a ghillie suit is to make the resulting three-dimensional form blend as undetectably as possible into its immediate surroundings, whether that happens to be ground characteristics or vegetation, or both.

Much of the effectiveness of a modern hunting ghillie suit is due to the loose leaf design, as the texture of the outer material won't look flat or block-cut. In the natural environment few things have clean-cut edges. In certain cases I would choose a ghillie suit, but only if not moving through heavy undergrowth or sitting up in tangled vegetation, as brambles in particular have an annoying habit of catching in the loose-leaf build of these suits. Some manufacturers have tried to remedy this by using a half-and-half design – i.e. loose-leaf for the edges of the suit, while the back is of flat cloth camo so that you can push yourself backwards into undergrowth. Fine in theory, but there's always a stray branch or twig that'll catch on the side of the suit, so if you're going to move about regularly use a more conventional design of camo wear. If lying up or sitting still in ambush, they can be deadly effective. Interestingly, as you've seen earlier, you can purchase part ghillie-type garments that just conceal the head and shoulders, and these do go some way to eliminating the problem of getting snagged on foliage as you stand and move position.

Use good camo, fieldcraft techniques, knowledge of quarry and the right accessories and you'll be successful

One downside of military-type burlap and jute ghillie suits is they can be heavy and warm, and unfortunately, if they get wet they can absorb a lot of water, rendering them uncomfortable and even heavier to wear. No matter what camouflage you've chosen to help conceal yourself, let's take an example of a scenario that facilitates its use with the terrain you're operating over to stress the importance of body positioning, and the part your use of other cover plays in concealment.

Always try to position yourself, when seated or even when moving, with branches or other such objects half-obscuring your body from the area you're targeting. Branches and low foliage that runs across the front of your outline, as long as they don't obscure your view and shot to the target, are helpful in breaking up the unmistakable human form. Remember, there are no straight lines in nature, especially ones that move like we do, so anything that helps you blend into the surroundings should be used. Branches, small shrubs, a patch of high nettles, ferns - anything that's there, use it as cover.

Good camouflage will help conceal you, but using it with the terrain also allows you to make small, slow and subtle movements, especially when in a position to make final adjustments for your aim - the crucial moment for any successful shot taken in the field.

Suited? Now Booted!

We can't discuss clothing without mentioning the importance of good quality footwear. For most, a strong pair of hiking boots will suffice, and a pair of mid-height flexible boots and flexible outer soles. This type of boot I favour for stalking in summer.

You'll be surprised how quickly you can amass a selection of boots, including high-ankle field boots and even camo boots, to cope with the terrain and situations you hunt over. I've got as many different pairs of boots as there are months in the year, and I swear I've a use for them all. I think … ?

The two main specific types of field boot are mid- or high-leg design. Lower-cut boots give more flexibility for slow, stealthy stalking while high-leg, as the name implies, affords better ankle support to avoid sprains and similar injuries should you go over into a rut or when negotiating rough ground. Also, these are often more insulated and therefore ideal for the colder months. Another important feature of any boot is the sole or, as the treads are known, the cleats.

Whilst a stalking boot requires a soft, flexible sole, boots with a harder, tougher and more rigid, thick rubber cleat are more suited for wet, muddy fields. A word of caution is that some cleats and the material the sole is manufactured from are notorious for being slippery on wet stone.

I always prefer to wear field boots that offer ankle support, and as camo boots are now available, these are often tempting to the airgun hunter who needs to get closer to the target. In my view, it's not necessary, but a nice selling ploy as they're intended to give more confidence to the wearer.

Some prefer to wear traditional Wellington boots, and I personally wouldn't recommend these for airgun hunting due to their lack of flexibility, but there are alternatives that I do wear, especially the field boots manufactured as a half Wellington/half field boot. These have rubber soles that come midway around the ankle, providing superb protection in waterlogged fields, tracks and ditches. The special sole is stitched onto a more typical leather or Cordura field boot for better flexibility of movement.

Whichever you choose, don't skimp on the quality of the socks you wear underneath, as I touched on previously. Frankly, some socks sold as thermals are about as thermal as my chest hair! A couple of pairs of thinner, good-quality socks are better than one pair of poor-quality thick ones. As with underwear, you can obtain socks to be used on the layer principle, and these give an impressive performance in terms of comfort and heat retention.

The technological advances in footwear suited to the the hunter and the serious outdoor pursuit devotees is amazing in what now can be built into a modern hunting boot. Not only insulation but shock absorbing soles, heat retaining and heel to toe supportive foot beds and shanks, Achilles heel flex panels at the rear for comfort – I could go on and on as the specifications of most footwear is now bewildering!

Removable hi-tech insoles, higher and more toe and heel protection with front ridging to help you walk up muddy or slippery wet terrain and equally the design at the outer rear, rising up the heel section can be ridged, and in most cases it's part of the sole. This design reduces slippage or slows down an unsteady descent in the same slippery conditions. All manufacturers have their own names for the design that protects or supports, and the different membranes and materials used for the boot to be waterproof, insulated and that now much mooted, but hopefully now due to what you've previously read, important attribute, breathability. That oval, orange, rugby-ball-shape found underneath the sole is often an indication (if you see the name and logo) that it's a Vibram design - the world's leading designer and manufacturer of one of any boot's most important areas. The outer sole and cleat layout has to offer good traction, flexibility and comfort.

So as you can see, the choice is huge, but the dedicated hunter needs to be prepared for all situations. That includes, like clothing, the fact that your footwear will need cleaning especially in winter. If muddy or wet after a hunting foray, put them in a boot bag, so you don't unnecessarily dirty your motor.

Once home, let them dry naturally (if not raining, out in the open) as I often do, in the garage or shed, but bring them in to warm up slightly before the next stage. Once mud is dry, carefully knock it off with a rubber-headed mallet; don't bang them together, bash them on your concrete or brick-paved drive, and certainly not against an outside wall. Remove laces, the rest of the mud and any clods of soil with a firm-bristled shoe brush – not forgetting to clean lugs and cleats of the soles of any debris they've picked up. Then clean with the appropriate cleaning products advised by the company, or those you favour. It's always wise to treat leather to prevent cracking, with the suitable leather replenishing cream or foam.

Follow the instructions of any cleaning agent you use and that applies to boots as it does to clothes. Loosely replace the laces, and if advised by the manufacture spray a light covering of water-repelling liquid onto them and store back in the boot bag until your next trip out.

Hardware

Most hunters will have seen full camo-covered hunting combos. They look very appealing to certain airgun hunters, and in the field can be really effective for concealing a weapon, as I've detailed previously.

Long before these were available, many like me, had taken a leaf (no pun intended) from the military handbook and we were concealing our rifles with strips of tied-on scrim scarf and patches cut from worn out DPM combats. Useful as it was at the time, you can now make use of camo tape such as the No-Mar (No-Mark) Camo-Tape made by the American company, H.S. Camo (Hunter's Specialities), to break up the outline of the stock, action, scope, barrel or silencer. Even if you only wrap it around the barrel and put

There are various coverings for your hardware – some are permanent finishes, others semi-permanent

intermittent stripes on the stock, you're going along the right path to concealing your kit. Another bonus is that tape can easily be changed for another pattern, thereby adapting to suit a particular terrain. In fact, the best camo I once used was while shooting where there was minimal cover at the side of a barren field. To remedy this I used camo tape around the silencer and the appropriate dark brown pattern camo netting draped around the rifle and over me! The army realised the importance of camo on weapons and scopes, as everything you carry or use (not forgetting yourself) all needs to be concealed at certain times, as in effect, you and your kit, if seen, are a foreign object often classed as dangerous in the terrain you're operating over. The camo you employ will imitate the surrounding foliage, and does break up those give- away straight, black outlines of a mainly black-coloured object with well-defined lines and edges to the action, barrel, silencer, scope mounts and scope. Some think this is going too far, and many feel it's unnecessary. In some ways I can agree, as a rifle with a matte finish and dull colour stock is very much like a branch - as long as you're not waving it around - but on the subject of movement, move your combo, say to raise it to your shoulder, and it does give off some glints no matter how much it seems to be matted down. Also, nothing in the natural environment is made of plastic or metal, and everything is more noticeable when it's moved. You'll also not often stumble across a luxurious piece of quality, hand-finished, oiled walnut stock wood whilst on your shoot.

We've noted the importance of movement as a give-away of position, but consider this. Slowly moving a rifle combo that's been camo-covered is less likely to be noticed than an untreated one, so in situations such as relatively close-quarters hunting - and especially if shooting from cover below aiming up into trees - I'd say having the rifle combo covered in camo definitely gives you an edge. If you're really serious about this aspect of cover, you can go the whole hog and have the combo specially dipped in the camo pattern of your choice by the specialists in this field, as I mentioned earlier – Hydrographics. Yes, the very same as run by the superb stock designer, Jon Sykes. This company can cover virtually anything by the ingenious dipping process of immersion coating. The item to be covered, be it rifle action, stock, scope, mounts etc., is immersed in a liquid which has a film of the desired camo design floating on the surface, and that adheres to the item when immersed. Ater coating, a finish is applied to give the camo a protective skin. This is so fine-tuned that it can be made matte or, even more useful, a final finish called 'soft touch' can be applied.

As the name implies, this gives a sure grip and another bonus is that once treated the outside of your rifle and scope are waterproofed. Even accessories such as spare buddy bottles, scope mounts and bipods can be treated – in fact, your whole kit and caboodle.

However, choose your camo pattern with care as this is a perma-cover, (permanent covering) that to remove would need sanding off and another pattern put on to replace it.

You can choose now to have other coverings, as I touched on earlier in my views on disguising hard outline; some permanent, semi-permanent and different types of non-permanent camo finish. Permanent obviously means that if you want to change back, you can't. The reason being, to treat a rifle by dipping, or by having special custom paint jobs done, they first attack it with a rotary wire brush to scuff up that lovely walnut stock and deep blued or blacked finish so that the sheets of camo,or special paint used, depending on the one you choose to have done, can adhere properly to your kit. The only way back from this, if you do want to change colour, is to use suitable LLCS loose leaf strips and change as the seasons do, or it's a case of having a completely new pattern camo dip. Personally, my dipped rifles were very well considered choices, and used only after testing clothing in the camo pattern until I was satisfied that it was efficient enough for a high level of concealment. Only then would I choose which pattern to have my complete rig given the dipping treatment. The plus side, though, is it protects the rifle from rust, (except the inside) – so you still need to keep up your maintenance routine periodically of barrel-cleaning, lubing and oiling where necessary.

If you feel competent at DIY, then I'd say, why not try the camo cover kits from USMC Military Supplies. You can use templates or just experiment. I'd say try earth tones, obviously, unless shooting over snow! When you want to change back, you spray it with a solution that doesn't harm metal or wood but quite literally changes the dry paint into a non-residue-leaving liquid. It works, and that's a reason many prefer it.

Those with less artistic skills can choose the alternative non-permanent measures; these include using the No-Marc camo tape or a military-style rifle wrap as previously detailed.

Be warned. Non-permanent measures can easily give you a false sense that the rifle is protected. Not so. I've seen rifles covered with both materials; they've got wet or just taken on the moisture that is around at morning and night, and if you're rifle gets wet, you MUST TAKE OFF ALL CAMO MATERIAL you've applied. If you don't, under that superb camo job you did you'll find, to your horror, a rifle that's now begun to rust. Worst case scenario is you'll need to have the rifle re-blued and blacked. If you are not now put off concealment for hardware, have it camo-dipped at Hydrographics. They'll remove all pitting and any rust residue and dip it in the camo pattern of choice which now seems to be a never-ending selection; not only Bill Jordan's Advantage Realtree patterns but they also license a couple of what I feel are very useful Mossy Oak photo-realistic patterns.

The latest to hit the market and one I can recommend is from a company called CAMO IT. This comes in kit form in a Jack Pyke camo of choice. That company do keep cropping up don't they? Anyway, you get different size strips of adhesive-backed, special camo material, and instructions of how to apply. I've done one myself and can say they aren't easy; they're certainly more difficult the more intricate the stock design is, such as thumbhole stocks. However, take time and effort and the benefits are that the material, does protect the metal from the elements.

There are also different colours of special paint available that come in aerosol form, that you can use to create your own camo job for your rifle/scope combo. These paints dry hard and don't rub off. Surprisingly, they're removable using a special cleaning/removing solution that can be bought from the same companies who offer these paints. So, get it wrong and you can redo it Those who have used these say you get better the more you experiment and I've seen some very good examples. As a guide, use drab green as a base layer and add touches of brown and black; that should be sufficient, and come autumn, if you've done this for summer's lush greenery, change to an overall more autumnal colouration. You never know, you might discover an artistic side in you! Incidentally, something you really need to consider is that any custom work done specifically to you, and particularly a permanent camo finish, will make it more difficult to sell the rifle as it won't be as generally desirable as it once was. The amount of money you spend on that cherished, unique air rifle, can actually devalue it should you come to want to trade it in or sell on.

The History, Origins and Ethos of Mossy Oak...

In the mid 1980s an enterprising young man named Toxey Haas came on to the scene, due to a love for the outdoors installed in him by his father. So strong was his ambition that he took the sound biyte of 'building a business from the ground up' quite literally. Using inspiration from the natural surroundings of the woods, in 1986 he founded Haas Outdoors, Inc. and the brand we all know as Mossy Oak was born.

Some of Mossy Oak's first products were manufactured in his mother Evelyn's sewing room in their attic. Now, products bearing the Mossy Oak logo can be found all across the States and far beyond.

To quote the company's website: 'It began with a fist full of dirt in 1986,' (an even niftier sound byte), but one that goes to illustrate that the same hunting and outdoor lifestyle still exists at the company to this present day. This love of the outdoors and MO's commitment to sustain that lifestyle drives them to team up with other companies that share their values.

This has resulted in the Mississippi-based company working to support programmes and various organisations that are committed to the outdoors, as well as building relationships that complement what they term as 'The Mossy Oak brand lifestyle'.

Beginning with a 'desire to get closer to critters,' Mossy Oak's first patterns were Bottomland®, Greenleaf®, Treestand®, Full Foliage® and Fall Foliage®. These all used natural elements and colours, effective and terrain, or situation specific, designs that helped the hunter blend into the natural surroundings.

Their development team soon realised that shadows are the most common element of nature. The first in their shadow series of camo patterns was Break-Up®, which revolutionised the way people thought about camo. Break-Up was much more effective at concealment and in so many different hunting situations it quickly became a best seller. Other specialty patterns in the shadow series included Shadow Grass®, Shadow Branch®, Shadow Leaf® and Forest Floor®.

As technology improved in digital imagery and printing techniques, so did Mossy Oak patterns. Come the Millennium their patterns became much more realistic with an enhanced 3D effect. New technology was put to work on their most popular pattern at the time, the very effective Break-Up and the redesigned pattern was introduced in 2002 as New Break-Up®. This was soon followed with New Shadow Grass®. Then in 2004, came their latest pattern for springtime, Obsession®.

Mossy Oak Brush® was the first pattern to use an all-new background other than Bottomland.

Then, launched in 2007, Duck Blind® incorporates elements from all flyways from coast to coast. In 2008 the launch of all-new Treestand® gave hunters a pattern that works specifically for hunting from an elevated position.

Building on the success of Break-Up, in 2010, they introduced Break-Up Infinity®. This features six layers of depth, giving the illusion that you are actually looking into the pattern as if you were looking into the woods - or to quote the company: 'with depth, detail and definition.'

Mossy Oak is first and foremost a camouflage brand, as you'll soon read, like Realtree, they manufacture camo patterns not clothing, and like Bill Jordan's Realtree empire they are proud that their products are worn by people as a representation of their love for the outdoors, and the hunting lifestyle in their daily lives. Mossy Oak always state that the very same appreciation for the outdoors and passion for hunting exists within their company and is consistently communicated through various channels.

The History, Origins and Ethos of Realtree...

Many hunters recognise the brand, Realtree, with their popular, distinct camouflage patterns used successfully worldwide, but not everyone understands the humble beginnings of the brand, and the fascinating story behind their global success.

The Realtree story started 27 years ago in 1986, in a front garden in the USA. It was in his parent's front yard that Realtree founder, Bill Jordan, sketched his first camouflage pattern. Bill discovered that he could create a three-dimensional appearance that would match different terrains, by layering the images of twigs and leaves over a vertical bark background.

At the time, Bill was trying to find a way to separate his first company 'Spartan Archery Products' from its competitors. Spartan manufactured and sold T-shirts to large retail customers across the US, but it was tough going with low profit margins and high volumes, and Bill was forced to scrimp, penny-pinch, and compete in fishing bass tournaments to provide an income to keep the business up and running in these tough times.

Bill took his newly-created design to local mills and navigated the printing process so he would have a set of camouflage clothing to photograph. However, the invisibility power of the camouflage was proving too effective! Trying to get the camouflage pattern to stay on the fabric without rubbing off proved to be a major challenge.

Ever resourceful, and recognising the importance of promoting the patterns from the beginning, Bill resorted to sending photos, every month for eight months, to buyers of hunting clothing across the US. There was increasing pressure for garment samples from interested parties, and Bill recalls, "I didn't have any garment, but I couldn't tell them that, so I just sent them some more photos."

The first Realtree-patterned samples were finished just hours before their official launch at the annual Shooting, Hunting, and Outdoor Trade (SHOT) show in 1986. The SHOT Show is renowned as the largest, most comprehensive trade show for all professionals involved with the shooting sports, hunting and law enforcement industries; currently attracting buyers from across the US and the world.

Anxiety levels were high; with no manufacturer, no money, dressing mannequins at midnight just before the start of the show, and unable to pay for the cost of the booth in full, Bill found himself ducking out the back every time the organisers visited the stand looking for payment! Although, Bill did find a way to pay his obligation by the end of the show.

Bill's huge risk was about to pay off. By 10am on the opening day of the show Bill was standing in good company, with the buyers from Bass Pro Shops, Oshman's and Wal-Mart's, the largest retailers in the world.

Wally Switzer of Wal-Mart could clearly see Bill's passion and determination. Unable to fund a clothing manufacturing business, a relationship was built with Eastbank Textiles where Wal-Mart would buy the fabric from Eastbank, who would then, in turn, manufacture the garments and see how well they sold - and this is how Realtree and its licensing business was born.

The Realtree story is truly inspirational with Bill and his then small team celebrating every small success. Today there are over 1,500 licensees and 10,000 products, with Realtree employing more than 80 people in Columbus, Georgia.

Technology for producing the camouflage designs has moved forward significantly; with sophisticated computers, digital cameras, and photo-realistic printing, light years ahead of Bill sketching designs in his parent's front yard!

The licensing business model is reliant on volume; Realtree receive a small commission every time one of their camouflage patterns is used in manufacturing approved products, such as tools, equipment and clothing for the hunting and lifestyle markets.

A global enterprise, Realtree understands that each international market has its own unique requirements and commits to working with their partners to provide a valuable connection to the outdoor pursuits sector.

Most importantly, Realtree aim to be much more than a brand; they aim to represent wearing Realtree as a way of life and a badge of honour, promoting good hunting practices. Bill Jordan says, "Our patterns not only allow the outdoor enthusiasts who wear them to be more effective in the woods, they also allow them to show their love of the outdoors in their everyday lives."

Footnote: Both companies have a camo for hunting in snow. Not as popular or readily available in the UK, but should you require it Realtree offer AP Snow, and Mossy Oak has Winter.

As you can see, there's always a camo to suit the season and terrain, so choose wisely and wear with confidence.

Hunting Accessories
Kit Bag Essentials and Useful Extras

As you progress as a hunter you'll soon come to realise the need for certain accessories and to carry a few essentials, besides the obvious such as extra ammo, but caveat emptor, as some accessories are just vying for your cash and offer little by way of practical field usage. So, where I do make mention of specific items it's because I now use them and appreciate the benefits they offer.

Accessories generally fall into two distinct categories; those that are small and compact enough to fit into a jacket pocket, and those of a size that come in their own larger, padded carry cases, or for extra protection, warrant you buying a suitably sized rucksack, or a fully- featured waist bag.

Fortunately, the accessories you will find of most use, to have immediately to hand, will fit into a pocket of your jacket, but be warned; it's all too easy to start adding more and more to your hunting kit until you start to overburden yourself. The general airgun hunter should be more concerned with items that can be classed as 'kit bag essentials' which will easily fit into a small to medium-sized rucksack of 30 – 35 litre capacity. For most of the year, I use rucksacks or backpacks, as they're more often termed, but in summer

Most people carry accessories onto the shoot in a rucksack or specialist waistbag

and for shorter sessions I now prefer to use a waist bag.

The former is a well-thought-out design that affords maximum stowage without hindering movement. The latter is designed as a waist bag with enough pockets to store essentials discreetly and securely, including an integral, fold-out, waterproof, heavy-duty, nylon-lined roe-sack-style/sized bag that, when not needed, sits neatly behind the carrying system. This is configured as an adjustable/detachable double shoulder harness. Before going any further, let's not forget that there is, of course, the all-important factor of the gun itself being carried; even while in a vehicle it needs to be in a gun bag.

If that's the only journey it makes, from your house to the vehicle, and then you're fortunate enough to be able to step straight onto your shoot, then you can use a gun slip. These cover a rifle but offer little in the way of protection. Whichever you choose, it's required by law that you carry your gun in a gun bag at all times if travelling in or through a public place.

Most good gun shops will stock a range of gun bags of one sort or another. Also, virtually all gun manufacturers have bags manufactured for them and 'badge' them up as their own. These range from simple gun slips, as outlined, to padded cases with extra external pockets for kit, and some even have special carrying attachments.

In that respect, the amount of various designs of gun bags is a seemingly endless list, but on the whole they share very similar properties depending on classification. Have a clear view of what you want from your gun bag, and you'll easily find exactly the right one for your needs and not have to search that hard.

In the long run it's often better to opt for a specialist type of padded case, granted it'll be more expensive, but it's ideal for gun protection, stowage (external pockets) and the versatility it can offer given the amount and/or types of carrying options.

Feature Creature

Main features to address are: It needs to be manufactured from tough, weather-resisting synthetic or canvas material with high-strength fittings and preferably have reinforced stitching. Where applicable, clips should be metal or at least toughened ABS and all zips need to be heavy-duty.

On some brands, you'll find an inner fleece lining with a waterproof liner but better still, look for a gun bag that has close-cell, high-density foam padding with an internal waterproof liner and adjustable internal retaining straps so the rifle can't move around in transit, plus a muzzle protector and/or a butt retainer.

The features detailed are installed to ensure that maximum protection is given to the rifle in transit. Many bags have external cargo-style pockets or zipped outer sleeve-type pockets – some more than others depending on type. These are handy for carrying extra kit.

Most hunters these days go for a fully featured bag from the off. Even so, if possible, once on a shoot I leave my bag in the vehicle or in an area where I know it's safe, on my permission and out of plain sight.

There are more specialised bags known as gun bag/shooting mats for use when the hunter is specifically setting out to shoot off the bipod, from the prone position and lying comfortably on the shooting mat that the gun bag has transformed into, so that waiting in ambush is not dictated by the terrain beneath it.

Incidentally, if more protection is needed for the journey in transit, there are semi-rigid ABS carry cases with egg-box-type foam linings available from Flambeau and Plano, even aluminium, strengthened, lockable, airline-approved flight cases from such trusted brands as Napier or Peli. So as you can see, the choices for keeping that valuable rifle/scope combo safe in transit are many.

Semi-Detached

One piece of kit that I feel is essential, and which hunters should consider fitting to the rifle from the outset, is a set of quality sling swivel studs. Not only to use with a sling and Quick Detachable (QD) sling swivels to ease the burden when walking around your shoot, but equally of use for attaching a bipod. This is a very useful addition to your equipment for ambush shooting if using a PCP air rifle and there'll be much more on these rests later. Many hunters, as I do, feel the best by far are the QD sling swivels and swivel studs manufactured by Uncle Mike's, a company which also makes a variety of rifle slings. Even so, you have other makers of specialist slings that offer other benefits such as slings with thumb loops, for ease of carrying and ensuring that it stays in place on your shoulder when your thumb is in the loop. There are stretch slings that can be used as a single sling but can be split into two halves, due to a very discreet yet very heavy-duty zip that runs up the middle so you can wear the rifle like a backpack and be hands-free – again, for negotiating rough terrain or climbing up slippery slopes in

The hunter who chooses and uses the right accessories is better equipped to be more efficient in the field

woodland where you may need to use the tree trunks as supports as you climb up any steep rises; another accessory where the list is seemingly endless.

The downside is that they can snag on clothing when you shoulder the rifle, catch undergrowth as you move, and swivels 'click' making noise at a crucial moment, or the strap itself rubbing against the body can be a potential noisemaker. However, don't forget that QD sling swivels allow the sling to be removed in an instant should you need to be dangle-free. e I find a sling to be of most use when I need to carry the rifle and be hands free for negotiating very rough terrain.

Suffice to say a suitable quality rifle sling fitted with QD sling swivels is very handy to have.

Backpacks

Since I first began hunting, seriously, I've taken my bits and bobs in a rucksack (or to give it the now 'in-vogue' name, backpack) and carried off my game in a heavy-duty plastic bin bag. In the early days, I used ex-army 'ruckys in DPM, then I began using various sizes of Bergens, and even a selection of ramblers' waterproof packs.

There's a seemingly ever-growing selection of top quality 'ruckys' now available to suit every eventuality. Manufacturers such as Deerhunter, Harkila/Seeland, Jack Pyke, Viper, Ridgeline and, my personal favourite for this type of gun luggage, the Ranger series of backpacks from Napier. There's a comprehensive range of different sizes and configurations – even a very unique pack,

Quick detachable (QD) sling swivels make removing a rifle sling an easy task

which I'll detail later in the chapter, devoted to hi-power, FAC-rated air rifles. As a teaser I'll just say it allows you to carry a 3L diver's bottle on to your shoot held securely within the rucksack itself.

Hydration packs, as they're known, have become far more popular and can be purchased in various camo patterns. The main leaders in the manufacture of these packs are Camelback and Geigerrig, amongst others. Hydro backpacks all have a facility to carry an internal hydration bladder (usually with a capacity of 2-3L), with the feed hose running down attached to one of the shoulder straps for ease of wearer use.

As you can see, we've really come a long way, even in view of the type of luggage available that we can carry accessories in.

One feature you'll find useful which is incorporated in many well-designed ruckys, is a strengthened and moulded rubber or heavy-duty rubberised base; this ensures that the contents inside at the bottom keep dry when placed on the ground. A simple but clever way of keeping out the water from damp grass should you inadvertently plonk the pack down in a puddle. The size of pack you choose depends on how much gear you intend to take with you, but as with a gun bag it can be left in a safe area, to return and get larger items when needed, such as extra clothing or even food. Look for ergonomic and well-padded shoulder straps, a sternum strap and a strong, well-appointed waistband (all adjustable of course).

If you intend walking far with it on your back, a rucky with outside cargo pockets and/or strong, elasticated, side mesh pockets are handy so you can access certain items quickly without having to rummage through the bag. One factor pertaining to rucksacks is that I recommend you don't leave them on while you are actively shooting. Not only will you find this tiring but it will also interrupt and hinder the shooting stances and holds you've taken the trouble to master. Even a small bag can catch a slight crosswind, knocking you off balance usually at the very moment you are going to take an opportunist shot; shoulder straps catch, and some hinder the rifle held at the shoulder. Numerous problems can be encountered. As with most accessories, though, they can be useful. As they now come in very effective camo designs, I often use a pack as a rest and as part concealment, forward of my shooting position. Even so, and as I've recommended earlier, it's best to take out the kit you need and leave the bag in a set safe place. Just don't leave important items such as wallets, car and house keys, shoot permission or your FAC licence in it.

There are even backpacks with the facility to hold your rifle on the outer rear of the pack, being held secure and protected until needed. Useful if making a long walk, and I certainly see the potential for their use for some airgun hunting situations I've found myself in, particularly when you might happen across a shot along the way and need the rifle to be quickly and easily accessed.

Generally, though, they're quite specialised kit with the exception of those 'yomping' to far away shooting positions over treacherous ground.

I've already mentioned waist bags but the smaller bum bags are handy for taking a few extras with you. They're especially useful if wearing a ghillie suit or mesh oversuit that has few or no pockets. They're handy for ammo, spare magazines, spare face veil, gloves,

There are specialist rifle slings for specific hunting situations

quarry calls, your shoot permission and other personal items including your mobile phone. More on these accessories later, but suffice to say; waist bags, bum bags and backpacks or hydration packs are all very useful for the situations they're designed for. Personally, I feel at times they're another essential.

Before looking at what you should be carrying in your pack, a quick word here of carrying game off your shoot. You've probably read many times how you can carry rabbits in a rucky after you've shot them. I've done this but even three, and certainly four, full-grown rabbits get very heavy and a rucky soon starts to whiff. As I've already said, I don't continually 'yomp' around my shoot with the pack on my back but the rucky is a convenient way to carry kit further towards the shooting area – for me it's an extension of the off-road vehicle. In relation to shot quarry, rabbits are usually hocked and hung on a branch. Woodpigeon are placed above ground, wrapped in a small swing-bin-liner bag to keep off the flies – and if actively hunting, all are collected as I return to my starting point. Other non-edible species such as crows and magpies are thrown in ditches for scavengers or if there are a fair few I'll bag them up and take them to an incinerator. Fortunately, the main shoots I frequent have incinerators on site, meaning I have easy access for the proper disposal of the carcasses and my hosts see how much I'm helping to alleviate their vermin problem. Unfortunately, on a bad day they see that I've not done that well – but as they say, 'c'est la vie!'

Kit Bits

Some of the following are essentials while others can be added when finances allow or indeed if you feel you need them. Also, not everything will be needed every session – so you can tailor your pack to suit the circumstances but always be mindful of

Hydration packs are becoming more and more popular within the hunting fraternity

the unexpected eventualities that could occur. Another factor in choosing what to take is the duration you intend to stay in the field; the weather forecast and, of course, the season of year will dictate what extra you'll need, or should consider taking, in terms of clothing. In no specific order here's a run-down of accessories that I'd consider for virtually all hunting sessions.

An observation aid such as a pair of compact binoculars or a monocular is a must-have piece of kit. Scanning around using the scope isn't the most advisable way of observing your shoot. It's better to have a dedicated observation aid for scouting the land up ahead or looking up to scour the treetops. Compact binos are most popular, but as optical technology has improved we now have many compact models with a specification of either 8 X or 10 X 42 with rubber-armoured outer casing to help protect them from knocks and scrapes. A good quality pair won't cost the earth and most optical manufacturers offer good quality product including small, rubber-armoured monoculars. Usually, they come with a quality carry case and have a lanyard for hanging around your neck. If you've read through the previous section on observation then you'll certainly realise that binos are essentials, but when observation is done, when on the land shooting, I'll as likely and more often than not choose a monocular.

I advise the use of a compact monocular as they're very small and can be stored to the side in a pocket, and taken out for a quick scan around when needed. It amazes me how small and powerful some are, and since acquiring an ultra-compact Luger 6 – 18 monocular, it's usually on its neck lanyard, tucked into my top until needed. There are many other handy monoculars and compact optics so I recommend you go and see which type you prefer.

Double Vision

Almost everything that applies to a scope as comprehensively detailed in Chapter 2 also applies to virtually any optical piece of equipment we, as hunters, use to magnify a target, but in the case of a binocular, there is a definitive difference of types, which is the internal optical construction. While a scope has an internal prism that is used to reflect light and turn the magnified image the right side up, with binoculars you also have to decide if you want a pair that are of roof prism or porro prism design. Binoculars work by using a prism to lengthen the light path between the objective lens and the eyepiece. Lengthening the prism, therefore, can increase the magnification without increasing the length of the binoculars. Porro prism binoculars have objective lens tubes that are offset from the eyepieces; the prisms angle from the eyepieces to the objective lenses. Roof prism binoculars have two straight tubes, so more often than not this enables them to be smaller and more compact in size. Therefore, many assume that porro prism binoculars are going to be more expensive because they're bigger and more substantial, but roof prism binoculars can actually cost more to make due to the more complicated manufacturing process for the internal angled prism. However, porro prism binoculars score again because they often give a higher quality image due to less internal light loss – in turn this makes the sight picture clearer and often more defined. Although roof prism designs can have a comparable optic, their compact design and complex prisms make the higher-priced roof prisms a better bet for those looking for a higher quality binocular. In my opinion, for the airgun hunter, it's not an easy decision to make as to which type to choose; do you want the more compact roof prism binos, or the less expensive quality of the porro? Consider this; when you factor in the range over which the 12ft lb rifle is effective, , you'd think it an easy choice.

However, check back at the chapter on observation. Then you'll realise we can't always get away with lower price observation aids if we really want to scour the land from a good distance away, so as not to disturb quarry we are intending on finding and eventually targeting.

Here are a few guidelines to look for in relation to observation aids such as your binos and/or monocular;

- **Lens coatings** – Check the specification sheet for level/amount and quality of coatings as you would your scope.
- **Eye-cups** – Check the eye-piece twist-up design and/or if they have them fitted, the rubber covered or extended, shade design eye-cups. Ensure that they suit your eyesight and feel comfortable. Some designs, even if they do allow the shaded portion to be folded back, won't suit everyone – particularly spectacle wearers.
- **Objective/Front lens size** – Check if this will be of sufficient size and good enough quality to suit the light levels you usually hunt in.
- **Sight Image Quality** – Check the sight picture viewed in several lighting conditions, but if only one is available during your visit to access this, look for blurring towards edges of the sight picture. Ideally, it needs to be as clear and bright as possible to the very edges of the image viewed through the eye-piece – again, just like your scope.

Just as useful is a fixed magnification, laser rangefinder monocular. There are some models which are very good value for money, should you require them, and, if anything takes the guesswork out of range estimation then, in my book, I reckon it has to be a useful aid. Granted, you should be sufficiently skilled in range estimation before even attempting hunting, but there's no law saying you can't add a rangefinder to the kit list. Some have gimmicky features an airgun hunter would never use such as 'incline to target', but those that have impressed, even though I still use my old faithfuls, Bushnell Scout and MTC Rapier, are the Nikon models and NV specialists, Thomas Jacks, have some excellent rangefinders of monocular or binocular design.

Send and Receive

Even the most hardened traditionalist must realise the benefits of carrying a rangefinder. Compact, highly portable and at the push of a button the ability – if used correctly – to give us a range to a target that is usually +/-1yd precise. All rangefinding devices that use a laser work on the same principle; a pulse of invisible laser light sent out to a target which then reflects back to be received by a receiver lens. The unit then calculates the distance due to the time it takes for the light to do this round trip from unit to target and back again. In the simplest way this is how

a laser rangefinder works. Most popular models are those from Bushnell, Hawke Sports Optics and of course the one that many are judged by, the models Leica produce. They're obtainable as compact, monocular-style devices, or binocular design, but whichever one is chosen, the workings are the same. Some models are rated for higher distances and these are of most benefit for deerstalkers and daytime fox shooters.

However, there's the problem; a laser rangefinder will only work in daylight, or if used at night, it has to be used in conjunction with a light source. Even in daytime, if the light levels are very low, laser rangefinders struggle to give accurate readings. Whenever you can take two or three separate readings of the target, this will ensure that you achieve positive range estimation.

A compact hand-held laser range finder takes the guess work out of longer range shots

The airgun hunter doesn't need a top-end expensive rangefinder due to the ranges at whichh he is able to take a sensible shot, but quality kit is nice to have. Moreover, a compact and highly accurate one out to 250-300 yards or so will be very reasonably priced and you can purchase them more often in a monocular style, or usually and more expensively in compact binocular style.

Next up is a basic first aid kit. This doesn't need to be overly comprehensive, but the contents should be kept safe in a watertight container and at least should include; wet wipes, antiseptic wipes, a small bottle of antiseptic cream or spray, painkillers, a selection of plasters, sterile gauze, a small roll of bandage. An army field dressing kit is a very useful addition as are tweezers and small scissors – the usual basics. Even this has now been addressed by certain manufacturers and you can purchase First aid kits in waterproof pouches – some in camo! You can add what you need as to what you feel is missing, but the pouches are a great aid for keeping everything together relating to first aid.

Spare ammo is an obvious requirement. You can tip a few in a jacket pocket (not advised), or better still use one of the quality pellet pouches I mentioned in Chapter 4. If you're a longer session hunter, take a cold drink for warm weather, but avoid sugary drinks and certainly no alcohol, they'll make you thirstier, the latter also of course impairing judgement. A water bottle is simple basic kit, not only to hold water to quench a thirst but also to rinse hands and obviously to clean any cuts you may accidentally suffer. There are quite a few different sizes around but include a small container of liquid soap or hand sanitiser, not forgetting a small hand towel, along with the obvious uses you might have for tissue and/or some toilet roll. Some take rubber or disposable surgical gloves for messy tasks such as gutting. If you use these, keep a few zip-lock plastic bags handy to put them in when used and take them home to dispose of correctly.

If out and about in cold weather it's certainly very advisable to carry a hot drink and it's advisable to pack a spare jumper or fleece. Neck warmers are also useful to keep out draughts.

An ex-army poncho is often ideal and rolls up to a compact size for storage. Incidentally, another bonus of a poncho is when out hunting and a sudden shower does come over your area. Afterwards, if you intend to lie on the ground in ambush, use it as a groundsheet so as not to get damp due to pressure transfer through contact with the ground. It'll usually open out further and offer a solution to lying on the gun bag.

Typically a first-aid kit should contain the basic necessities

Now, while many cover themselves, they forget to treat the rifle with similar respect. You should immediately put it back in the gun bag, but if caught out away from the bag then I now use a rifle-wrap, as they're termed. These cover protectors are designed to roll up into a very lightweight and discreet size to be kept on your person.

Next up is a knife. A traditional and now familiar Swiss Army-style knife or Opinel penknife is not always the most useful to take into the field – although many still do. Essentially, in the field you'll need 'field cutlery' of various types, especially for paunching or preparing baits. Ideally, have a folding lock knife and a small (3 – 4-inch) fixed blade skinner, and don't forget the sharpener as knives have an infuriating habit of losing their edge at the least opportune moment. Like all accessories mentioned, we're spoiled for choice, but for quality, look to brands such as Gerber, Leatherman (Buck Knives) and suchlike.

Now to the many useful pocket-size multi-tools: So many have emerged since I first wrote Total Airguns that this is again a very saturated market, but on the whole, stay with the named brands and you won't go far wrong. They're handy for field repairs and all manner of tasks that can face you as you go about your shoot. It's surprising how often you'll find the pliers, wire cutters and the various knife-edges and screwdriver heads they contain of use. However, I'm sure others have seen it written, 'they're useful for nipping up screws on the rifle.' That makes me cringe. There's no way you should need to be doing quite intrusive work on your rifle body or action while in the field, hunting. If so, you've not been keeping the rifle maintained properly. Screws don't just suddenly decide to become loose so that you notice them while out hunting. Look to the Chapter on Gun Maintenance for advice on combating potentially troublesome hunting session faults before they start.

A selection of multi-tools, folding lock knives and a small blade sharpener – are all useful pieces of field cutlery

Tips for Choosing the Multi-Tool Most Suited to You

- Scrutinise all dimensions and weights of these tools. Remember, they're designed to lessen your load.
- Carrying options – suitable for your needs, non-existent or optional-extra type of pliers head required – regular or needle nose and gape (width) of pliers-head when open.
- How the handles/tool feels when held in operation. This applies to pliers and other tools, particularly the main ones you feel you'll use most.
- Are the other tools the 'multi' features that you require.
- Check what type of pivot points are used, how they and the lock-out mechanisms work.
- Do they suit the build quality of the other features? Remember, these areas take a lot of strain.
- Select a specific knife design that you want the multi you choose to have as a main feature.

Stay Sharp

A blunt blade on a folding lock knife or multi-tool/knife is not a good blade; in fact, it often can be a dangerous one. Since the launch of the superb and acclaimed original Blade-Tech Pocket Knife Sharpener hit the shops, they've now developed an improved version – a MkII. Featuring a tungsten carbide edge, it's now capable of sharpening the dullest blade and due to the design it can be used on more tools and takes far less time in helping you to stay sharp, as it works on both sides, sharpening them simultaneously. It comes in a heavy-duty canvas carrying case with a Velcro flap closure and belt loop. If your bladed tool has a serrated or part-serrated knife edge then the sharpener can be used on these as well. Secateurs are handy as is a compact, folding wood saw; ideal for trimming hides or cutting foliage to use as cover.

Just as handy to have in the kit bag is a reasonably-sized camo net. Even if you don't initially intend to build a full-size hide, you need something that packs down small and will still

At one time the airgun hunter would have chosen to use a Swiss Army-style knife or an Opinel

fold out to offer a reasonable amount of screen should you find yourself requiring the use of extra cover. Many companies offer a handy-sized piece of net and the correct pattern of camo netting has often saved the day, just draped over me to disguise my static position. You often need to cut a few slits here and there for shooting through, but throw it over your person, or some branches and foliage, and you've got yourself an instant, covered shooting position. More on the use of netting will be found in Hunting Techniques.

Also, let's not forget how handy a roll of camo tape is, indeed, H.S No-Mar tape is a must if you want to cover or break up the outline of your rifle action, stock or barrel.

Even if you don't intend to hunt at night, dusk soon turns to dark and a small torch such as a Mini-Maglite, or better still a small LED headlamp, is very handy to have. It not only makes the walk back to the car less hazardous but light sources are also very useful if you spill pellets in a hide. You'll hardly find the lion's share in the gloom, but the lead will glint in torchlight meaning that more can be found. I mention the more up-to date multi-function LED headlights as these, more often than not, have variable white beam ,and other colours to switch over to if you're wanting to save your natural night vision when out after the nocturnal quarry species.

Also, the better brand name manufacturers such as Cluson, Gerber, Petzl and Fenix have flashing modes for signalling for help and many other features that are useful in the field at night.

Always carry a copy of your written permission to shoot and although many feel them intrusive, a mobile phone is a valuable friend to have. You can always turn it off when not needed, but don't rely on the phone exclusively for help should, God forbid, you have a hunting accident while out on your own. What if the battery runs flat or you can't get a signal? So take a back-up, a few coins for use if you can reach a public phone, but for safety's sake, an emergency whistle is the least you should have.

There are of course many other accessories to aid the hunter such as Paracord rope, quarry calls, a bipod or shooting sticks, and bulkier items such as decoys, pop-up hides and traditional hide poles. However, I feel strongly on the use of pop-up hides and the benefits they offer the airgun hunter, and there'll be much more on these superb pieces of kit and what to take inside in the chapter on Hunting Techniques.

Silence is Golden

Without a doubt, one of the most popular accessories, which I feel is a necessity, is a silencer or as they're more appropriately termed, a sound moderator. Some rifles come with integrally fitted silencers whilst most others, especially PCPs, have the muzzle threaded or have an adaptor to accept their own optional silencers, or another company's as long as it has a standard ½" UNF thread.

Now, the reason we as hunters use a silencer on any rifle, but more so on an air rifle, has I feel become mystical and the facts somewhat distorted. In truth, you'd hit your quarry with an unsilenced air rifle because almost instantaneously after firing, if your accuracy is of the required level, then your quarry should be dead! But the reason silencers are beneficial is that they allow the airgun hunter to go about his business without overly disturbing the area. The trouble is, this doesn't hold much weight when you consider the sound a pellet makes on impact with a rabbit's skull. It can often be as loud as an unsilenced air rifle and what has to be considered is that the sound is usually right next to quarry feeding or sitting alongside the one targeted. Also, modern quality-manufactured silencers are generally quite efficient at taming muzzle report. I've used a decibel meter set down-range and the pellet zipping through the air towards the target, even at 25-30-yds out, is louder than the muted muzzle report.

Baffling

Almost all brands and sizes of silencers work on a similar and often a relatively simple principle. The air that exits the muzzle directly after firing a pellet hits what is known as 'still air' and it's this that causes the crack heard on firing, not because the pellet is emerging from a 12ft lb air rifle faster than the speed of sound. You could term this as the after-shock. To combat this, silencers need to utilise internal chambers (baffles) to help deaden or deflect the blast of air following the pellet as it travels through the silencer without reducing the pellet's velocity or flight path to a degree that is unacceptable for it to be effective at cleanly killing the target. Simply put, the pellet exits the muzzle as it should, while the air following exits the muzzle at a much reduced pressure.

These chambers inside the silencer can be what are termed 'active' or 'passive' baffles. There's also the relatively new (for airgun use that is) reflex design of silencer.

Before technology progressed to the level it is now, manufacturers would cram as many baffles inside the silencer as they could, often even making overly long silencers so they could add even more. However, any traditionally designed silencer adds extra length to the rifle (reflex designs add much less than conventional types) so in general it's a balancing act of design; placement of baffles, number of baffles and length of silencer, that dictates its effectiveness. Also, the effectiveness of the sound deadening felt that is wrapped around the workings, or better put, the open/honeycomb cylindrical portion of an internal baffle to combine with the complete internal layout to try to create a unit that really is able to reduce muzzle report.

Active baffle types originally used a piston to absorb and cushion the air, now they more commonly use springs to 'revers-abrate' (that's my way of describing it and should be in the Oxford English Dictionary), the blast back towards the muzzle, in turn cancelling forward momentum of the exiting blast of released compressed air.

Alternatively, passive baffles are basically stacked inside the silencer body with spacer washers to enforce the distance each baffle is set away from the one next to it.

The major plus point of the silencer is that it doesn't betray your shooting position, so once the quarry has scurried for cover or flown off after a comrade has fallen, the specific area they've vacated is the place the quarry is watching, not your shooting position. Should both remain undisturbed, by you not giving away your position, say by movement – and in some cases it only needs to be a matter of minutes – quarry will return, especially if it's a favoured sunning spot or has rich pickings. This often allows you more shots at quarry in approximately the same area and at the same range as the first. Because of this behaviour, it's also one of the reasons you shouldn't be in too much of a hurry to retrieve shot quarry, only if it has fallen badly in an untidy manner or you need to administer a coup de grace. Also, a rabbit lying on the ground doesn't seem to deter others from returning back out to feed. Indeed, I've had rabbits come out and actually go over to sniff and nose around the deceased scut tail. Many times I've had crows and magpies fly in to take advantage of the freebie meal giving me even more quarry to target.

The subject of which silencer is best is very much down to personal choice, as the quality and choice of name brand quality silencers is, as you'd expect, far greater than it was only a few years back.

Sandwell Field Sports manufacture a range of remarkably quiet moderators as do V-Mach and all on request will custom-make virtually anything you care to order. To name a few of the many highly-regarded sound moderators at the time of writing; Weirhauch's own moderator originally designed for their HW100 PCP surprised many, the Milbro Huggett is a much muted silencer and comes in a wide range of configurations to suit many popular hunting PCPs. There are so many others worth considering. For instance, calibre specific 'cans' were once just available from custom houses but BSA have now created a VC (Variable Choke) Silencer. Just by changing a grommet at the end of the silencer to reduce the aperture changes it from being suitable for .177 to .22 and it does work quite noticeably better.

Daystate have progressed so fast that they've adapted their Airstream moderator, completely redesigned the internals and taking their cue from our centrefire cousins, have manufactured off-the-shelf reflex moderators that sleeve back over certain models of their rifles; these are incredibly quiet and light and add barely 3" in overall length to the rifle. In fact, initially the development of their carbon-fibre models came from an idea Tony Belas had after discovering one of the quietest silencers he'd heard – this was the Manders Silencer manufactured in New Zealand.

Unlike most silencers that screw onto the end of the muzzle and increase the length of the rifle, the reflex silencer only usually adds half its overall length as the rest neatly sleeves back over the muzzle and barrel, attaching internally in the middle of its length. The air escaping from the muzzle is then defused towards the back of the silencer, while any air still travelling forward behind the pellet travels over a series of (you guessed it) baffles. The result is a silencer that protrudes less from the muzzle but gives a full-sized silencer effect. As the muzzle screws directly into the baffle, machined from solid aluminium, and the distance to the end of the silencer is much shorter, tolerances can be much tighter. Daystate say that this completely removes the chance of misalignment and a pellet clipping the end of the silencer. The outer body of the silencer is manufactured from carbon-fibre so as well as being light in weight, it's also cosmetically attractive and is given an anti-glare matte black finish.

Needless to say you'll soon come to appreciate the need for a silencer on a PCP and the benefits of using a silenced air rifle – especially when hunting at night.

Something I feel is a much overlooked accuracy aid when shooting over certain terrain are height-adjustable shooting sticks. Long associated more with fullbore shooting, used wisely, all rests such as shooting sticks or monopods can be invaluable aids to help steady your aim.

Although I mention the benefits of traditional shooting sticks, there are now various configurations so they can either be deployed more quickly, or adjusted far easier and faster due to the height adjuster for the legs being set at the head.

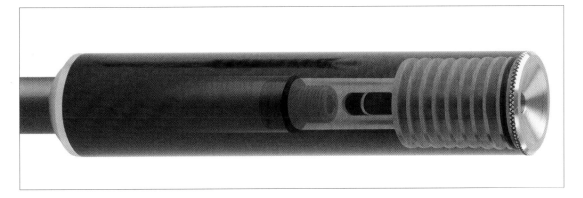

Some companies are now producing silencers of a reflex design such as the Daystate Airstream MK4, as shown

For the airgun hunter, in my opinion, nothing is more useful and handy than the bipod. Again, there are so many different bipods that the mind boggles which to buy. The Harris is very much an industry standard while some favour the B-Square brand as it utilises a different method for deployment.

A bipod is a detachable unit comprising a mounting plate and two stabiliser legs that attach to the rifle to form a rest to steady your aim, usually while shooting in the prone position, but extendable models allow more height and can be used for shooting from a sitting or kneeling position.

The basic bipod available is little more than two toughened ABS or high-grade, black, anodised aluminium legs attached by a hinge with a half-open cup that clips onto the barrel. More beneficial are bipods with spring-loaded legs that fold up out of the way when not in use, plus adjustable legs.

These usually fit to the rifle by attaching to the front sling swivel stud. In fact, sniper shooting from a hidden ambush position with a PCP on a bipod and using a silenced rifle enables the hunter soon to put a good bag of bunnies together. Used this way, these are two accessories that perfectly complement each other – especially with the aid of good camouflage and fieldcraft.

Before we leave this section, a quick word or two on other accessories often mentioned for use in a hunter's pack. You'll probably have read that it's wise to have a space blanket, a compass, mirrors for signalling and other such boy scout-motto-fuelled paraphernalia. Take these if you must, if they help make you feel secure but why this advice continues to be foisted around is anybody's guess. Granted, if hill walking, they can save your life, but, the average airgun hunter will probably never venture so far that he'll need these survival aids. In fact, more in your mind should be to hunt sensibly and safely and certainly don't venture into or on to areas that are ridiculously remote or so obviously unsafe. I've hunted over some very rough terrain and I've never once felt under-equipped or ill-prepared, but then again, I've not stalked the banks of the lower Zambezi or in a Peruvian rain forest – yet!

Having said that, I must quantify my statement by mentioning that the Bear Grylls endorsed range of survival tools and knives manufactured and marketed by Gerber have caused great interest in the airgun hunting community, not least because the knives, multi-tools and other such kit are very well designed and highly practical for field usage.

To wind up this chapter, I must reiterate; do take the basics, the essentials and at least have a spare full change of clothes in the car, spare shoes or trainers, a car travel blanket should you get snowed in, and a folding shovel is handy if you need to dig out the back wheels.

Keep safety as a watchword for your shooting, and equally, be watchful to your own well-being as you go about your sport.

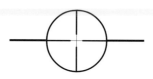

The bipod is a very useful accessory, especially when shooting prone from behind cover

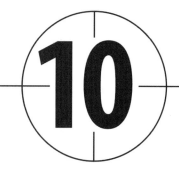

The Changing Seasons

An Airgun Hunter's Year

Now it's time to examine the changing landscape and weather that the different months bring, with the effect this has on the quarry you seek. Also outlined are the year's countrywide farming and agricultural landmark times that indicate where, when and why airgun hunters should be actively using certain hunting methods and targeting specific quarry species. As seasons seemingly aren't as cut and dried as they once were, we can even have summer-like conditions in late September, and winter weeks that are so mild you'd be forgiven for thinking it was spring. Take prevailing conditions into consideration when planning specific hunting trips, but use the following as a guide to what is most likely to be happening through the months of the year.

January – February

The calendar year starts in January, of course, and as the airgun hunter isn't currently governed by any game laws or close seasons, unless he is shooting seasonally protected quarry, I'll start here. Most if not all parts of the country will certainly have experienced not only their first hard frosts of the year, but the more northerly areas will also have had snow. Hunting in these conditions isn't impossible, but it is impractical enough for me to advise only the extremely dedicated to try their hand in such extreme conditions. I've been out late at night fox shooting 'on the lamp' and been amazed at the lone rabbits that venture far out into frost-ravaged fields. Why they're out and what they find to eat is a mystery to me. The rabbits I've shot at this time of year aren't on my most frequented shooting areas, but when I've been kindly invited to join others shooting over moorlands with all-round rabbit activity, and areas with large rabbit populations. It seems the rabbits that inhabit the upper parts of the Pennines and both the Highlands and Lowlands of Scotland are a hardy breed! It goes without saying, at this time of year, that if I'm hunting in these situations I'll be very well wrapped up, but to be up and out in time to witness a bright wintry sun breaking through a clear blue sky over snowbound hills or frost-tinged fields is a wonderful sight to behold. When shooting in such extreme conditions, I'll hole up in ambush near any natural cover. Usually dry-stone walls or hedgerows are favoured locations, but then only if I've been told by my host that it's near a spot that rabbits regularly frequent for their brief spell in the early morning sunshine. It's not uncommon to encounter crows or magpies, and this is a time of year when baiting them with a slit-open rabbit carcass will do the trick. Corvids are used to finding carcasses, especially if the weather has been particularly harsh.

January must be amongst the worst, if not the very worst, of times for planning any hunting trip. Woodies can be found huddled in sitty trees, but you'll have to hope you can get near them, or preferably have done some serious planning so as to be hiding in ambush and waiting for them to fly in and seek shelter.

By February, if your land has pheasants on it you might have to put woodpigeon roost shooting on hold until the pheasants have left the trees. Not only do you not want to disturb the 'stubby-winged ones', but also it doesn't help your relations with the keeper if you shoot one by accident. The air rifle is often the best option for dealing with certain types of vermin in the woods, and although the shotgun is still widely used, at this time of year many keepers are coming to realise the benefit of the air rifle, because it's almost silent. Nothing is so sure to have pheasants high-tailing it to live in another wood than shotgun blasts! Rooks will be returning to re-establish themselves at favoured nests in the rookery, and the young that escaped the previous year's short springtime brancher cull will swell their ranks, building nests anew.

At this time of year, my outdoor shooting is usually limited to roost-shooting woodpigeons, wandering around the woods for opportunist shots at squirrels, and shooting corvids over baits or, where possible, on feeding areas. Crows will still be flocking together as they move around fields in search of food, usually in the company of other corvids such as jackdaws, and they'll be finding food in the creep feeders that are put out in the fields to fatten up the sheep. If you get within range of one of these areas in a suitable hide, a good few sessions can be had before the birds move to steal feed from a safer feeder.

Even magpies seem unusually sociable in February, hanging around together in small and sometimes very tight-knit groups, but by the end of the month it's typical to see that some will have paired up and be back repairing old nests in preparation for the coming breeding season. Note where their nests are and keep watch for activity around them. However, if you're not overrun, don't disturb magpies too early as there can be opportunities later in the year to bait-up nearby, as soon as the young leave the nest. Alternatively, you can annoy the whole family with a strategically placed little owl or kestrel decoy, which they will mob. As February progresses, you'll see them less frequently over open areas of land, as the pairs will be staying close to the nest areas, often with another noisy suitor in tow.

Don't ignore the open fields for chances of shots at other vermin. Stubble fields and set-aside areas left from autumn can see a glut of flying felons, and for the shooter in a well-chosen hide position they can yield surprising results. Typically, in the woods the woodpigeons will be stocking up, probably feeding on the last of the ivy berries and the like before eventually moving on to rape fields later in the year. (There'll be more to consider on berry feeding woodies towards the end of the year.) If it's windy, you'll find them sitting out the bad weather on the lee side of the woods, and depending on how severe the weather is, they'll sit lower in the trees because they don't like getting bashed around by the stormy elements. Rainy conditions will also see them perching lower than usual. Squirrels can often be found scratching around in leaf litter on the woodland floor, and at times they're even seen foraging alongside the woodpigeon which will be frantically pecking around the bases of the trees. The squirrel can be taken by surprise by the soft-footed shooter, as it may have its head so deep in the leaves that it won't hear your approach. The woodie, on the other hand, is never so obliging or foolhardy when on the deck.

February is definitely a month of change. Many airgun hunters of my acquaintance – and I must generally agree with them – feel this to be one of the best times of the year for hunting, mainly in wooded areas before the branches become covered with leaves. Walking these areas comes high on the list, as you can encounter a variety of species ranging from most of the corvid family to the woodpigeon and grey squirrel. If you're fortunate enough to be able to shoot around old buildings in rural areas, you can often encounter jackdaws, and in some areas certain broad-minded representatives of the clergy will allow airgun hunters to take discreet walks around their churches and grounds, as they know that vermin do not respect such places. They can be havens for feral pigeons, crows, jackdaws, rooks and squirrels, to name only a few.

Obviously, in places such as this you need to use your discretion as to when to go shooting. It is not good practice to be seen sauntering around in full camo just before or after worship, but go when people have gone home, and your quarry will still be there. Many a productive afternoon can be spent walking around taking opportunist shots.

By the end of the month, spring will definitely be in the air and the daffodils and snowdrops will already be well on their way to flowering, a sure sign that a change of season is underway.

March – April

With more light to shoot by in the mornings, and a little more in the evenings too, the countryside is waking up for the airgun hunter. It's a good time to be out and about as the fresh smell of spring hangs in the air. The typical weather is more accurately described as pleasant rather than really nice, but on the whole, a vast improvement in conditions will be seen as we progress through the month. The weather may still change suddenly, and it can catch out those who are too optimistic and not prepared for variable weather. During these months rain can be the hunter's downfall.

The 'mad march hare' of lore and fact will be seen in certain parts of the country, and although it is a legitimate species to be tackled with a powerful FAC-licensed air rifle, many now recommend the animal best left for the .22 rimfire rifle or the shotgun. If you want to try your hand with an FAC hi-powered air rifle and there are plenty of 'long ears' around, I say keep the range sensible – and don't forget your game licence!

Come early spring, corvids such as magpies are already paired up and in many cases rebuilding or building new nests

Corvids will have paired off and be getting ready to lay the first clutch of eggs, while the first young rabbit kits will be out, very innocent and foolhardy as they learn the ways of the natural world. Many fall as easy prey, being mopped up by foxes, stoats, weasels and buzzards. The sporting shooter will leave them until they're of a size worth preparing for the pot, but take note of the area as it's a place to target later in the year.

Generally this is the busiest time of year for serious pest control, because the adult rabbits are easier to target before the foliage starts to green and thicken up. Rabbits will also now be much more active at night, and at dawn and dusk. You'll notice that the burrows are starting to be redug and run through. Fresh scrapings and earth near entrance holes shows that the rabbits are back in business. They're likely to be much more active during the night, and the optimum times are the first couple of hours before and after dawn, which comes earlier as the weeks pass. If you're targeting them at night, it can be very cold and temperatures can quickly drop below freezing, just as happens in autumn, even though the days may have been pleasant and at times very sunny.

Tackling the corvid population before they breed is important. Unfortunately, you'll have to rise early, as the dawn still seems to be trapped in the night and it can be hard to get up in time to be in position to catch these earliest of risers. Try baiting or ambush tactics for both crows and magpies, although you will find that these will decrease in effectiveness as the birds find mates or re-establish acquaintance with old flames, and go off to do what comes naturally. Baiting can be done again with a vengeance, though, once they've raised a family. The woodie roost shooting will have all but dried up by now, not only as the trees get their leaves but also as the birds pair off and leave established communal winter accommodation to find individual nest sites.

By this time in the season, if not earlier, you should have either repaired natural hides, or be building new ones for reaping rewards from summer into autumn. If you see rabbits establishing a new warren, now's the time to build a hide within comfortable striking distance, and by late summer you'll have a hidden shooting position just waiting to be used.

May – June

They say 'don't cast a clout until May is out'. Many will have heard this old saying, and it's one that usually holds true. Rain can come at any time, but those fresh spring mornings can also still bring a chill, as will the evenings, but on your shoot this is definitely a key time of year to hit vermin hard. Corvids are preparing to raise further broods of potential problems. Gamekeepers cull magpies with Larsen traps, and even large crow traps nab their share throughout the breeding season, but where possible airgun hunters should use their rifles to help eradicate those birds that dodge the traps. The first rabbit kits you saw not many weeks ago will soon be ready to breed themselves. Everywhere you look the countryside is growing greener. Bluebells erupt into full bloom, forming carpets of colour wherever they're found along hedges and the woodland floor, while the fields are getting full of long grass and tall stalks of barley, wheat and oilseed rape. Land animals have plenty of cover now to hide in, and tree dwellers have much more foliage from which to call and watch.

May 12th is still known by many as 'brancher day', and the annual beginning of shooting young rooks preparing to leave the nest is part of the tradition in many country areas. Although the young branchers in many areas can now be seen to emerge as early as April, May 12th is still the particular date that many

When the weather starts to warm up, time can be better spent during the day shooting around the farm buildings

choose to go out and stand underneath a rookery waiting for a youngster to venture forth. Rook shooting is a controversial subject, however, and some are now of the opinion that there should be some control over this practice, especially if the species isn't in plague proportions locally. It seems that more and more 'officers of the countryside' are deeming rooks the farmer's friend, not that I've met many farmers – especially sheep farmers – who'd miss their presence on their land.

As for activity in the fields, this is my favourite time of year for hunting rabbits with dedicated night-vision equipment. Early summer nights are very appealing, and this is an exciting branch of our sport that is certainly worth trying once you're proficient enough. Rabbits are very much more active by this time of

Young rabbits are naïve to the ways of the world and betray the presence of warrens

year. If the weather is fine, they'll be spending a lot more time above ground, both day and night, and that means many more shooting opportunities. Ambush shooting near warrens, feeding areas, and the sides of crop fields they're invading is very productive, and at times it can seem as though you're almost tripping over them. At others, they're very wary; but look for signs that they've been around and it could indicate nocturnal activity.

During the day, woodpigeons in particular might seem to be quite thin on the ground, although there will actually be many about. Rather than settling into flocks to feed on the fields, they'll now be raising their young. The birds feed sporadically to produce the regurgitated pigeon milk that is food for the young. Magpies that have escaped your attentions or the gamekeepers' Larsen traps and gone on to breed will now be seen in family groups. Often the adult birds will fly along hedgerows with the brood following in an undulating line. These are opportune times to lay baits, and often you can make a good bag, especially before the young birds get too educated and wary. This also applies to young crows, which can be quite comical as they make their first solo flights.

Many grassy fields around the countryside will now have had their first cut of grass for silage, or will soon do so, and this makes rabbits easier to get at once they stray onto the freshly-mown, lawn-like expanses. With a keen eye, the shooter should be able to see them right up until last light; but many rabbits will stay near the rye grass that always escapes cutting. They frequent these areas to feed as well as to utilise the little bit of cover it affords on otherwise flat fields. If the grass has been swirled around and left by the cutter, you'll find good sport spotting them between the rows of cut grass left in the fields to dry. Alongside hedges that border crops, especially alongside rape fields, the rabbits can cause havoc. This damage often goes undetected until the end of May, when the crops are cut only to reveal large semi-circular patches of barren ground, because ever since the seed was sown the rabbits will have nibbled their way out into the field. The airgun hunter should take opportunities to watch for the beginnings of this damage before the rabbits get too established. Carefully walk the edge of a field, looking for signs of rabbit activity, and you can then ambush them over these well-frequented feeding spots, saving the farmer costly losses.

As we come into June the morning light really does break much earlier and the sun goes down far later in the evening. The longest day is approaching, and high summer is just around the corner. All those lovely daylight hours to hunt in! But in reality, especially during a sudden warm spell, quarry can be quite scarce over the fields, while only the dedicated will rise to be out before dawn. That means 3am starts (or even earlier in far northern Britain) to get into position if we're ambushing, and not many will endure that for long. Time is better spent in the longer evening bunny-bashing sessions, while a mooch around the farmyard and outbuildings can often be the most productive way to find quarry during the day, especially as we get into the progressively warmer months that follow. Birds regularly visit farms and outbuildings to feed or drink at this time of year. Collared doves, feral pigeons, woodies, jackdaws, crows – they'll all gravitate to the outbuildings and areas holding livestock, and corvids especially will hang around cattle and sheep pens. Sit in the open-plan, 'hangar-type' barns, maybe using some form of hide, and await intruders. Many a time when it's sweltering in the fields, time spent sitting indoors in the cool shade produces a steady stream of winged quarry throughout the day.

In some places I've had superb sport shooting jackdaws coming to steal the protein-rich pellet feed put out for livestock. Uncannily, they know the exact time it'll be spread into the troughs, and in some places they'll perch outside on fences, telegraph posts and overhead power cables waiting to descend, after the farm workers have left the building after putting out feed. Be in there, hidden and waiting, and you can have some very hectic, fast-firing early morning action.

Take care on your way to and from the shoot as you travel the country lanes, as farm machinery will be coming and going at all hours to get the many seasonal jobs done. If bales are left bagged-up on grass fields, you can often find magpies and crows pecking around the base and even attacking the plastic, and a cluster of bales is possibly a place to consider hiding up to ambush them in the early morning. If well hidden in ambush at the side of a newly-cut field, don't be surprised to see corvids dropping down to sift through scattered hay if it hasn't been baled.

At the end of June, and certainly as we reach July, they have their young with them, often two and occasionally only one juvenile bird that follows the adults, cawing to be fed. The adults busy themselves picking through the freshly cut grass for anything edible to stuff into the cackling young bird's eager beak. If you're there hiding up in ambush, make the most of this and put something else in the way of its bill!

If you have an appropriate vehicle and the weather is fine – and, of course, if the farmer or landowner gives you permission – now's the time to drive around picking off rabbits at the side of the hedges backing on to the cut fields. You can usually shoot without the aid of a lamp until it's quite late in the evening. Alternatively, if you're fortunate enough to own or have access to one, you can be out roving those inaccessible areas on an ATV such as a quad bike. Yes, summer's here and it really is getting close to the time for reaping the rich harvest of shooting opportunities that are not only just around the corner, but have also already begun. With the longest day past, you're now hunting in high summer.

July – August

Warmer weather should be predominant, but as this is the UK our unpredictable climate can throw up many surprises. The only sure feature of these months is that there's more day than night, and the sun lingers low in the sky during the evenings. Woodpigeons have bred, and you'll start to see the young birds (squabs) flying with others of their kind, which are recognisable by the lack of a white neck flash. The squabs aren't too cautious, and if you encounter them away from the more worldly-wise adults they can easily be picked out of trees and off the ground if they land amongst decoys. As the crops will now be standing tall, it's time to try decoying birds on to set-aside fields.

At this time of year, it can seem as if the fields are alive with rabbits. Depending on the weather, geographical location, and when the seeds were sown, grassy fields could still be being mown.

This is a busy time on the land, and you don't want to be getting in the way, or putting anybody working on the land at risk. Let them know you're there, because with modern camo you can literally disappear in the undergrowth. Remember that many accidents occur on farms, and you don't want to be one of them. If fields are being tended, keep well out of the way, as you don't want to be a hindrance. You're there to help the farmer and the other people whose livelihoods depend on the land.

August can be a strange month, with autumn just around the corner. Quarry creatures can be found anywhere and everywhere as they search for food, with their numbers boosted after the breeding period. The mornings can be surprisingly chilly, as can the late evenings, especially if aided by a chilling breeze combined with little cloud cover to help the earth retain the warmth of the day's sun. As the month ends, spring-sown cereal crops such as barley, oats and wheat will be harvested. The long-stemmed, drooping ears of the crop first take on a rusty appearance and soon thereafter ripen, and then, as if the fields were never green, they'll soon be turned back to stubble.

September – October

Fieldfares will by now have begun to arrive, and it can often seem that these members of the thrush family are bobbing around everywhere. Whilst September must rank amongst one of the busiest months of the year for the farmer, for the airgun hunter autumn yields many opportunities, but due to the unpredictability of the weather it can also be very frustrating. The weather can drastically change and ruin any hunting plans you might have. Squalls, rain, freak gales and thunderstorms are always a possibility – certainly, at this time of year they're never far away. So expect the unexpected!

Farmers will be cutting late crops, and ploughing ready to sow others. Most will have harvested all their rape, wheat, barley and other cereal crops, and by the end of the month the new seeds of winter oats, barley and wheat will be back in the fertile ground. Grass fields will have had yet another cut, and probably been tilled for another. These are the ever-continuing cycles of the agricultural calendar, and the airgun hunter needs to learn them so as to be in the right place to ambush and target quarry.

With all this harvest and sowing activity, it's hardly surprising that September is woodpigeon time as they descend like locusts to feed on freshly-cut and freshly-sown fields alike. This is always a time that the shotgunner looks forward to, and the same should go for the airgun hunter. The woodpigeon is a worthy adversary and, better still, is very tasty. By this time of year I'm nearly fed up with eating rabbits, and a bit more woodie is a very welcome change. Decoys used under flight lines and over the fields the birds are visiting

Know the times crops are sown and you'll find the quarry that visits to feed

are the way to target these crop-guzzlers. I've learned many of my pigeon shooting tricks from watching experienced shotgunners, and I recommend airgun hunters to do the same. It pays to keep an open mind and remove the blinkers, because the keen pigeon shot will possibly have years of experience, so watch and listen – and when the opportunity arises, join in. Shooting over stubble can bring all manner of sport, with rabbits, crows and woodpigeons being the most common.

Planting and harvesting are a never-ending cycle for the farmer, and as I'm sure you're now realising, often open up many opportunities for the airgun hunter. These windows of opportunity are at times relatively small ones, as in many

As autumn comes down in the woods – it's not only rabbits that forage in the leaf litter

places no sooner is the corn cut to stubble than it's ploughed in again and promptly planted with rape or winter barley. Similarly, grass fields once harvested are superb areas to go lamping over, but within weeks the farmer could have tilled them again to get another crop of grass, or the lush new growth won't benefit from much pounding, so there's no more rattling across the bowling green-like surface in your 4 x 4 vehicle. Whilst we need to take advantage of the opportunities, also be mindful of what the farmer has done. He'll not take too kindly to you tramping over freshly-seeded fields, and your muddy boot prints or wheel tracks will always give you away. If you are continuing your shooting around these fields, then 'around' is the key word. Shoot quarry on the edges of the field, and when moving your position walk around the edges, keeping well off the seed.

If myxomatosis hasn't reared its ugly head, rabbits will be plentiful. However, if they've been shot regularly during the year, by now they'll be very twitchy. Once the crops and grass are cut at least you have a quick chance at getting at them before they dive back into cover. Ambushing them in the early mornings and the short evenings, once you've established the areas they still use, can be productive, but the evenings start to close in very quickly now, with shooting time being reduced steadily with every passing week. At times, you can shoot by moonlight, and if positioned correctly you can shoot woodies that are silhouetted in the treetops. It's not always possible or practicable, but it can be done. Also, at the end of September into October, woodies will be feeding heavily during the day around and actually in the trees that hold acorns, beech mast and rowan berries. Again, this is one of those small windows of opportunity the forward-thinking airgun hunter can take advantage of. Find the right area and wait up in ambush and a good bag can be put together. Shooting will be demanding as the trees will still be in almost full leaf. Alternatively, put a few deeks out around the base of these trees and try to entice them down onto the deck.

Many hunters now see autumn as the start of the lamping season, the time to 'turn the lights on' and focus your attention on shooting rabbits at night with the aid of an artificial light source. This can be done either by going out in pairs, with one holding the lamp, while the other shoots or, as I prefer to do, go it alone with a gun-mounted lamp.

Once again, remember that as the farmers are busy, cutting and baling there will be more activity on the country lanes, so be careful on the way to and from your shoot. Remember my earlier warning on weather – note too, that September days can go from one extreme to the other as regards temperature. The afternoons can be gorgeous and even hot, and you may be sweltering under camo when decoying pigeon, yet shivering when dusk comes and you ambush rabbits. It often feels very chilly during night-time lamping sessions.

If grass fields have been left after the first cut they could be cut again as late as the first week of October, before rain becomes more frequent. Winter corn, barley and oats will all be sprouting in the fields – a good time to watch for flying vermin visiting. The rabbits will be hefty, having now put on body fat in anticipation of the lean winter months ahead. As for weather, rain will sometimes put paid to shooting, and may curtail a lot of hunting plans when we have lengthy periods of wet weather. Trudging across sodden fields isn't ideal or fruitful, but for those who have indoor shooting opportunities for quarry such as rats and feral pigeon – go to it! Alternatively, look around the woods and even small pockets of trees or copses. Now's the time when you'll see squirrels as they go about their daily routine of eating and travelling the routes they use along branches which will by now be starting to lose their foliage. They'll be preoccupied with gathering food, especially beech mast. This is as much a favourite with squirrels as it is with woodpigeons, as it has a high protein and fat content – just what wild animals need to help sustain them in harsh winter conditions. As we saw at the start of the year, you can once again find squirrels amongst the leaf litter frantically gathering up the nuts that fall from split husks to stash away for use at a later date. The same applies to jays and woodpigeons too. The best tactics are to find where your quarry is making regular visits to feed, and then wear full camo, sitting quietly with your back to a tree to hide your silhouette as you silently wait in ambush.

Woodpigeons will still be around, but those that are will be very wary. If they've escaped the shotgun or your airgun they'll be more difficult to decoy than ever before. Try deeks on set-aside fields that look barren, as a well-placed deek pattern might just fool them down to investigate if their brethren have found food.

As the foliage starts slowly to disappear, tall ground cover also dies away. Now you can target rabbits under hedges that are usually impenetrable during the summer months. Night frosts will more likely than not increase by the end of the month, and the trees will definitely be looking increasingly bare.

If September has been particularly mild you can be pretty sure that October will see winter arrive with a vengeance. Rainy conditions will be the norm, with much colder temperatures in the mornings and evenings as well as during the day. Cold, strong winds are usually most prevalent as well, but if you head for sheltered areas such as copses and woods you might be pleasantly surprised at what can be found sheltering there. Dawn breaks later, so an early morning session can be profitable if you can stand the cold. By the end of the month it's dark soon after teatime, and as the clocks go back, another hour of light is lost in the evening but gained in the morning.

As food becomes harder to find, you'll discover that corvids are easier to entice to baits. Woodpigeons will readily come down to deeks placed almost anywhere, especially as they'll be visiting set-aside areas in search of wild flowers, shoots, seeds and clover.

By the end of October we'll have done well not to have a smattering of frost over nearly every field in the country, and that means swapping from lightweight camo wear during the day to insulated jackets, trousers and gloves at night.

November – December

Nowadays, the climate is such that in late autumn and early winter we almost have what can be considered a rainy season. A prolonged period of rainy days will not only affect you while it's raining, but will also quickly turn many fields into muddy bogs. It can take up to a week for the land to dry off afterwards. Indeed, in some years it's only dry when the weather has turned cold enough to harden the soil by freezing the water it holds. When these rains come, which can be earlier or later than November, you can be sure of one thing – that they'll put a huge dampener on your sport, unless you've got access to indoor shooting. These will be lean times for your trigger finger until the rains lessen and the cold, sharp frosty mornings herald a return to outdoor shooting for the hardy hunter who can go back out into the fields and woods in search of sport. Even then, quarry will be hard to find on the ground, and the targets will be mostly corvids, pigeons or squirrels.

Again, baiting is a favourite method for corvids, but now is a good time to establish a baited area for squirrels, although wood-walking among the bare trees can also yield a nice bag of 'tree rats'. Decoys still work for woodpigeons, especially lofted deeks near sitty trees; but as much thought as goes into hunting should also go into your own welfare – in other words, keeping warm and dry in the cold weather. If you're cold or wet, not only are you uncomfortable but you won't hunt efficiently either. There's no shame in admitting that it's too cold and admitting defeat. Far better to go home and come back to hunt another day, than to end up with short- or even long-term illness.

Come December, the woodies will be even easier to target in trees with very sparse foliage, and easy to spot against ivy-covered tree trunks. They can become uncharacteristically quite careless of their own safety as they take

When the colder weather arrives it's time to head back indoors to catch up on the rat and feral shooting

the opportunity to gorge once again on ivy berries, so if you find trees they're regularly visiting, being in the right place at the right time can produce results. You only get the opportunity of a few sessions at them in these situations, as they'll soon wise up to the danger and visit other more inaccessible areas to feed.

As the weather closes in, especially when cloud is very low and it's damp and drizzly, squirrels will come down from the trees and be much more active on the woodland floor again, searching for food. The same applies to woodies which can often come down onto glades, clearings and tracks alongside the trees, and not only in the search for food. I side with those who believe they also come down from the upper branches to escape the damp air. If an animal or bird gets wet through, it can have disastrous consequences so it follows that a small animal such as a squirrel or a downy-feathered woodpigeon would be susceptible to saturation and chilling. The weather can be downright miserable and will steadily worsen, and unfortunately, it will tend to remain much the same until late January … and that's where we came in – at the start of the year.

Now that we've reviewed the seasons, I'm sure you've realised that both the beginning and end of the year can be very dour times, and unproductive to be out on your shoot. But these are opportune times to take advantage of the lull in activity by making a thorough check of all your kit. If your camo clothing's looking worn and battered treat yourself to some new garments. Even though regular routine maintenance of your rifle should be done periodically throughout the year, most shooters opt for a thorough annual check-up. See the chapter on Gun Maintenance for useful advice on keeping your rifle in tip-top condition. If you've spent all year hunting regularly with a PCP air rifle, now's the time to seriously consider having it sent into the manufacturer or a good specialist airgun-smith to have it properly serviced. That way, when it comes back, it'll be working as well as ever to take on the fresh crop of vermin that each new year brings.

There's no way I can be described as a fair-weather hunter, but when winter has gripped the land, with hard frosts the norm, possibilities of snow and the Met Office issuing the familiar stormy wet weather warnings, there's not much to tempt even the hardiest or most optimistic out into the fields. When this happens, I do as nature indicates and head indoors with my rifle, and that means catching up on feral pigeon clearance jobs and late-night ratting sessions. Remember, in colder weather these are the times when the rat will seek shelter from the elements and will be getting well established in places where the farmer doesn't want it. It's time to prove your worth as an airgun hunter and earn your right to shoot on the land when more conducive weather returns. When I do occasionally venture forth at the back end of the year for sport, it's really for the challenge and I recommend that anyone who does the same should keep sessions short.

11 Quarry Files

The back of the head, neck and between the shoulder blades – a crow shows the 'Achilles' heel' kill-zone of all flying felons...

As mentioned at the very start of this book the airgun hunter has a specified selection of quarry species classed as vermin that are deemed legal to shoot with a 12ft lb air rifle on land where permission has been granted to shoot.

It's the responsibility of every hunter to be able to Identify quickly and easily all quarry species in all conditions and from a variety of angles. In fact, if you take time to study the quarry species as a naturalist studies the behaviour of animals and birds, you'll soon notice your hunting tally grow. You will realise why certain creatures react and behave the way they do pertaining to variation of seasons, weather conditions, even their tolerance to sensing danger.

For instance, the first crow you examine close up (which will be the first one you shoot) will remind you of every Hammer horror film you've ever seen. The bird's gargoyle-like features, its 'reptilian-esque' legs and almost demon-like claws all betray the bird's lifestyle and true character. There really is nothing to like about the crow. The only thing to respect is its wariness and intelligence. Whilst a magpie's curiosity can often get the better of him most times a crow will never be so stupid, neither will the adult rook or a large gathering of jackdaws. It really is amazing to watch a flock of jackdaws descend into the treetops as they fly hither and thither on their daily search for food. Hardly have they alighted on the trees than one of their number spots something untoward below and the flock take noisily to the skies. In fact, further in the chapter on Hunting Techniques you'll soon come to appreciate that you'd rather be in a position worrying if one pair of eyes has spotted you than three or even four. So, imagine how you'd cope worrying on upwards of a hundred!

Even the humble rabbit can be a source of endless fascination. There's always something to be learned from just watching your quarry even without a rifle in your hands. Granted, you'll be amazed at the animal's voracious appetite as it nibbles and gnaws its way over the ground. These fluffy 'Hoovers' seemingly do nothing but eat, but as often as not they'll sit motionless seemingly doing nothing but listening and watching. Then, in the blink of an eye they can either start to groom themselves, resume feeding, start to doze in the sun, huddle down against the rain or just simply leg it to the nearest hedge cover.

Observing animals equally shows their destructive sides, which is the reason they've become classed as vermin. Rabbits chew, eat, nibble and scratch at everything, squirrels similarly so and they climb. Rats are possibly the most abhorrent – the urine and droppings being a particular cause for concern due to the health aspect. This is where birds come into the equation. Droppings from feral pigeon and collared dove spoil grain; woodies eat masses of it and are responsible for other cereal crop damage, as are corvids, particularly crows. Those who suppose crows only scavenge for carrion should forget the first 'C' in the birds' Sunday name, as along with the woodies this is the biggest cause for concern on barley and wheat fields at certain times of the year. Its wings easily beat down crop stems and left unchecked they can strim the fields from outside in, or inside out within a matter of weeks. Even in a few days, a mass of destruction can be caused by a large enough concentration of these pests. So, when you see this destruction, you know the financial burden this puts on to the farming community, and realise that you are doing a service. Although pursuing a very absorbing sport, you do put a lot back to your hosts who allow you to shoot on their land. Before going any further a word on the importance of kill-zones and the knowledge needed of what is, in essence, each and every animal and birds' Achilles heel.

Some of what you have probably read in certain publications is tempered with caution or inflated with flowery prose to make up for a lack of practical know-how.

It must be remembered that quarry rarely presents itself perfectly side-on or fully facing you. This is sometimes referred to as a quartering target, meaning it will often be at a slight angle. However, in some cases this can work to your advantage as it can help you place the shot past protective feather, fur or bone into a specific kill-zone area. As we come to each individual quarry species you'll clearly have it detailed where and when each kill-zone is a viable and suitable area to aim for.

This will ensure that you hunt as effectively and dispatch your quarry as humanely as possible. This is of the utmost importance as you need to have respect for your quarry until the very end, and although I have a favoured calibre, I'll detail which are suitable to use for each.

Not wanting to get too bogged down with the ultimate result, it is time now to look at each quarry species in turn. In other words, a closer in-depth view into the lives and behavioural patterns of the 11 most wanted.

Rabbit (Oryctolagus Cuniculus)

What better animal to start an in-depth look at our main quarry species than with the rabbit? Unquestionably, the rabbit is the mainstay of the airgun hunter, and why not? It's usually found in abundance, it can often be a very challenging adversary and to top it all, it's very tasty.

The rabbit belongs to the family of mammals known as lagomorphs, which actually means 'hare-like'. In actual fact, they belong to the same family as the hare, which is leporidae. Despite what some presume, they're not true rodents, as rodents such as mice and rats have four incisor teeth whilst lagomorphs have six. However, it does share a major similarity with any rodent; when in large numbers it can be a great pest. Everybody knows what a rabbit looks like but commonly, rabbits are covered in a grey-brown colour fur, with an orangey patch on the nape of the neck and an off-white underbelly, and not forgetting the little brown topped, white tail known as the scut – often seen disappearing before the hunter's had chance to take a shot. In some areas, black rabbits aren't uncommon but albinos and piebald are very rare. Rabbit can be distinguished from its close relative, the hare, by the fact that it has smaller ears, shorter hind legs and is much smaller in build.

The rabbit is the airgun hunter's major quarry species

When to target the animal is very much up to the population on your shooting ground, and the farmer's or landowner's instruction. Usually, you need to make inroads into a large population in early spring, but if not totally overrun, use your discretion and don't overshoot the land. Their numbers will soon dwindle under heavy shooting pressure even though they are prolific breeders giving rise to the familiar phrase, 'breed like rabbits'.

Due in part to the fact that a sexually mature female can produce up to 30 offspring in a year, it's no surprise that the rabbit is an animal that farmers and estate managers keep a weather eye upon. Breeding can begin as early as January and continue into early autumn. At the start of the season the female rabbit is continuously fertile; in less than half a day after giving birth, the female is fertile once again. Hence the ability to breed in such large numbers as it's not uncommon for a healthy doe to produce over six litters a year, each containing on average, half a dozen kittens.

Even in certain urban areas it can cause havoc on cricket pitches or bowling greens – sports centres being a particular favourite as for some strange reason best known to 'ol bugs' it just loves to gnaw on the very expensive all-weather Astro Turf. In the countryside, in badly hit areas, cereal farmers have been known to experience a 20% reduction in crop yield. Despite its numbers, the rabbit can at times be perhaps the most infuriating quarry to bag, quickly wising up to the methods you employ.

Habitat

Rabbits can be found almost anywhere. A very adaptable mammal, it's found amongst hedgerows, fields, and scrubland; certainly over most arable land and amongst foliage that provides the requisites for survival, those being cover and a plentiful food supply. Basically, its diet consists of anything that's green and edible ranging from grass to seeds, berries and in deepest winter when other foodstuff is hard to come by, even the bark of bushes and trees. By and large, they prefer soft, sandy soil to build warrens that are usually found on slopes to provide drainage. Contrary to popular belief the rabbit isn't the world's best burrower, and that's the reason loose sandy soil is ideal for them to excavate and build the warren, its communal home. It is an accomplished climber, scrabbling up saplings to get at shoots, quickly clambering over dry stone walls and has even been known to swim short distances when the need arises.

It's an extremely sociable animal, which in many areas generally spends most of the daylight hours underground. Depending on population, it can be seen at any time of day but the early morning and late evening, especially in spring and summer are times to turn your attention to a spot of rabbiting.

Where population is at a reasonable level the rabbit serves as an important part of the open countryside's eco-system, but left to its own devices it can become a disastrous nuisance, particularly to the farming community. This is when it needs to be kept in check and the reason it offers such widespread sport to the shooter of all disciplines.

Location and Behavioural Patterns

Finding rabbits is relatively easy as like most animals they leave clues as to their presence. These are holes or burrows, dense round pellet droppings and runs. Runs are basically flattened pathways rabbits regularly use to move around to and from a feeding area. If left undisturbed rabbits tend to be quite unadventurous travellers preferring to use the same route day in, day out as they venture from their burrows to feed. Feeding areas are easily identified as closely cropped grass or bare patches in newly sown crops at the edges of fields. Also bits of fur on low, barbed wire fencing or at the edges of brambles will indicate areas of rabbit activity.

Rabbits don't like the wind on them, so on blustery days you will normally find them in a sheltered position. Look for them on the leeward side of anything that offers a windbreak; stonewalls, hedgerows and high embankments all fit the bill very nicely indeed.

The rabbit has many natural enemies so has developed a high level of detection systems. These are, in the following order – ears, nose and eyes, the three Ss of sound, smell and sight. Reputedly, a rabbit can smell a predator, especially a human, from up to a hundred yards away and its hearing is even more acute. Little wonder it can make such challenging quarry, especially when you consider, due to the eyes being positioned at the side and towards the top of the head, that a rabbit can virtually see all the way around and above its position. The animal is usually in a constant state of alertness, so the only time you can stalk up on them successfully is by approaching downwind, keeping low and hoping the animal is either dozing in the sun or preoccupied with feeding. Interestingly, it's now known that a rabbit's status of alertness changes depending on its location. If close to cover you'd think it'd be more relaxed, but not so, as here it realises that a predator could spring from the same cover it can take refuge in. Also, when far away from its burrow it'll also be very alert as it knows it's got a longer distance to travel to safety. The animal will only relax in areas it has found to be relatively undisturbed and when in such a position it feels comfortable. If you regularly observe rabbits you'll soon recognise that their body language is a giveaway if they are anxious or untroubled. This is when being out and watching animal activity can reap dividends for you as a hunter. Just watching lets you see the animal in its natural state going about its business, and if you remain as unobtrusive as possible you'll be surprised at how much you can learn and how close they'll come. The body language of a rabbit is also the biggest giveaway to the way it reacts to its surroundings. Once the ears droop onto the back of the head, it has relaxed one sense, the next are the eyes which won't actually close but like a dozing human it will half close them and then it will drop its head onto its chest or even lie flat out on the ground. You often see this behaviour during hot weather and through the longer summer evenings, but it only takes the slightest hint of danger for the situation to change. Whether that is because it has detected a suspicious movement, foreign smell or sound, it'll prick up its ears, and get up onto its hind legs in readiness to bolt for cover. Learning the body language of a rabbit is very important as it can often save you a lot of wasted effort in maybe stalking a rabbit that just isn't a suitable candidate for your attentions.

Methods to Use

The rabbit is a candidate for virtually every hunting technique. You can come across one while opportunist shooting or wood-walking. You'll most certainly need to stalk closer to take the shot and ambushing them in appropriate areas can be a very productive method. They can be targeted at night with the lamp or dedicated night vision riflescope. If you are allowed and can drive around a particular area of the shoot you can shoot them from the cab or passenger seat of a 4 x 4, or going solo on an ATV such as a quad bike.

In most cases stalking can be productive and is a skill that needs to be properly learned. There are times when it's unstalkable and this is when you should try lying up in ambush, but one thing that we have in our favour is its habit of freezing when it first senses danger. This can either be its saviour from predators, or if we spot it, its downfall. To have any measure of success with hunting rabbits it is essential to know where they are likely to be at certain times of the day and/or night.

Ambushing is a much more relaxed way of shooting rabbits and can be very productive as long as you've chosen your shooting position with care. Always reconnoitre the area you intend to shoot over and establish where the rabbits are found and at what time of day. Get into position before the rabbits usually appear and a good bag can be on the cards.

As a hunter, I feel there's nothing like the first adrenalin rush when after watching a hedge line for a lengthy period, you see a flicker of movement. It could be a twitch of an ear or the tentative first sight of the animal's twitching nose, slightly poking out from the undergrowth to sniff for danger. Alternatively, it can just suddenly lollop out into plain view to sit and survey the scene or even start to spruce itself up. Sometimes, however, that flicker of movement that sets your pulse racing can just as likely be a robin or wren searching out insects. On more than one occasion these busy birds have charged me up to have my head on the cheekpiece getting ready to sight in on what I have thought to be the first potential bunny of the day.

Lamping can also produce when the rabbits are active at night. Alternatively, if the rabbits are wary of the lamp (lamp-shy) more and more hunters are realising the benefits of using dedicated night vision equipment such as NV scopes to target quarry in total darkness. Suffice to say, in the relevant chapters to come, all these hunting techniques are outlined fully to help you deal with this most rewarding of quarry species, and, at some time or another, the airgun hunter will thank it for the sport it offers.

Calibres and Kill-Zones

As I used the rabbit as an example of where pinpoint accuracy is of paramount importance in placing a pellet into a kill-zone, way back in the chapter on pellets and calibres, it's now the place to explain the reason for that and to explain kill-zones in general.

While choice of calibre is a hotly debated subject amongst airgun hunters, nobody can disagree, that if you hit any animal correctly in the kill-zone with any calibre 'slug', it'll be dutifully dispatched. Therefore, all calibres will be more than a match for the rabbit as long as your accuracy puts the lead into the areas detailed here. Incidentally, it's very fitting that we begin with the rabbit in Quarry Files pertaining to kill-zones, as this animal's vulnerable areas are surely the most misunderstood.

With a legal limit 12ft lb air rifle, more often than not, when targeting the rabbit, this is where it's advisable to adopt an all-or-nothing attitude in your hunting and take only head shots. A wounded rabbit can quite easily get to cover and perish in its warren or similar area of safety. This is an unacceptable situation that you must strive to prevent from happening at all costs.

To say glibly, 'head shot' isn't explanation enough, as a more detailed look at rabbit anatomy is needed to describe exactly where the pellet needs to go. Although the head of an adult rabbit looks quite large, the kill-zone of the brain is approximately only the size of a walnut. To hit this area with deadly effect, imagine a line from eye to the base of the rabbit's ear. The area to aim for is just off centre behind the eye, on that line towards the ear. This is why I mentioned the need for precision with the smaller .177 calibre pellet. Hit dead-centre with .22 or even slightly further forward or back and it's also fatal. Move further to the front with .177 and you could actually go into the nasal passage of the animal. Now, I'm not purposely trying to be controversial, and I know this has never been written about before but I feel a book intended to be highly comprehensive should address these matters. I've shot rabbits that have obviously recovered from these wounds but is it fair that they've been injured in this way? No, and I'm sure the majority of responsible hunters agree. So that's the 'side-on' head shot fully explained. Now, if the rabbit presents itself 'head-on' facing you from the front, we can take a line from just above the eyes to just below the neckline and again achieve a clean kill with any calibre from a 12ft lbs legal limit air rifle. Sometimes, especially at night while lamping, the rabbit can infuriatingly turn its back on you, adopting a position where it can move directly away from you, and usually this is when they're near cover so they face back into it. If they do, put one straight into the back of the 'napper' or base of the neck before it does a runner.

Now to the thorny subject of the body shot, and it is one that some shooters take with a 12ft lb rifle and feel is a valid kill-zone. That's fine if it works for them, but personally, it's a shot I'd only take using a high-power .22 calibre air rifle of say 22+ft lbs.

If the rabbit is facing you and if it is standing on its hind legs you can shoot directly into the centre of the upper chest to place the pellet between the front forelegs. From the side, it isn't as easy. Here you follow the line of the foreleg to where it meets the animal's body. Then place the crosshairs so the shot will impact the rabbit approximately a third of the way back on the body. This will place a shot straight into the boiler room – the heart and lung shot. These shots are acceptable due to the fact of the rabbit's rib cage not being overly strong at this point, coupled with the lower amount of body tissue surrounding these organs. But in autumn when the rabbit has usually piled on the pounds with extra body fat, you do have more to contend with. This is where I'd not take this shot with anything but a hi-power air rifle and then only when necessary. There is a section devoted to hi-power (FAC) rifles much later in the book, also as you work through Quarry Files, you'll notice that a hi-power air rifle gives you more options on pellet placement for a variety of species. But I digress. When a rabbit presents itself full-on, sitting up and looking in your direction, a hi-power, FAC rifle really does give you the edge, allowing a very specific shot. Imagine a line drawn across the head just above its eyes and one drawn down the centre of the animal's body – making a cross, the centre of which being just above the rabbit's eyes on its forehead. From here (the brain) to approximately 3 inches on the vertical line down its chest to the heart and lungs is all exposed kill-zone. If your rangefinding isn't the best, that's a fair drop of allowance and certainly a reason some choose to use

FAC air rifles for rabbits, but as this is for the majority who hunt with 'off-ticket' rifles, the head shot is still the optimum kill-zone.

Incidentally, for those who really want to understand the reason these body-shot areas are effective; when you shoot a rabbit, dissect it by slitting straight up the front and middle with a sharp knife or game shears. Cut up the sternum to expose the chest under the rib cage and look to see exactly where the heart and lungs are. This also applies to other species; dissect them and you'll have a better understanding of the quarry's anatomy, giving you better insight into these vulnerable areas known as kill-zones.

Myxomatosis

You can't talk about the humble rabbit without having to mention the horrendous plague that all but annihilated them in this country in the 1950s, that being the insect-carried virus, myxomatosis.

Myxomatosis or 'myxi' was used to clear Australia of their plague of rabbits, and it was introduced here in the early 50s, some pin it down to 1953. It was brought to Europe by a French physician called Dr Delille to control the rabbits on his country estate near Paris. Many presume that it was brought and introduced here intentionally, and granted, it has been put down in some areas; sometimes legally, others not so. When farmers realised how effective it was in eradicating pesky scut tails, they moved infected rabbits to other areas where the rabbit flea just went about its business spreading the disease, but it's not just the rabbit flea that carries the virus, most other blood-sucking insects can also to some extent spread the plague. It can take up to two weeks after being bitten for the rabbit to contract the disease, which manifests itself on your shoot when you see misty and swollen-eyed rabbits. The eyes stream with mucus that they continuously rub and scratch, often until they bleed. The rabbits quickly weaken and eventually die of starvation or lung infection. Rabbits carrying the disease can look healthy up to a few days before death when they show characteristic signs of lethargy, blindness, stumbling and weak movement. Unfortunately, the disease still rears its ugly head today but tends to crop up in localised pockets and then will not totally wipe out the area because more rabbits survive as generations have developed a tolerance. The fleas still carrying the disease can over-winter with the rabbits in burrows ready to infect the next generation. Pet rabbits can now be vaccinated against it and as it's highly contagious they should, but for the wild coney, shooting a rabbit in this state is an act of mercy as if not picked off by natural predators, they otherwise meet a lingering and unpleasant end.

Brown Rat (Rattus Norvegicus)

The woodpigeon, magpie and carrion crow surely top the list of farmers' most unwanted feathered pests, but undeniably the brown (or common) rat is surely the most detested of all terra-firma-based vermin. Not only does it eat anything, but it also carries all sorts of infectious diseases, including the potentially fatal Weil's disease. It's caused by the leptospira virus hence its other name, leptospirosis. It is carried in the rat's urine, so humans only have to come into contact with something it has soiled and they can become infected. For this reason, never touch any that you've dispatched. Handle them only with protective gloves or tongs. Dispose of them properly, preferably by burning, or bury them with a shovelful of quicklime.

Despite, or because of, its deplorable ways, you could say that along with the feral pigeon, we have it to thank for the public accepting the valid use of airguns as a tool for controlling vermin numbers. Virtually all airgun hunters have a tale to tell and I'm sure you've heard the 'rats as big as cats' stories. Well that's a bit of an exaggeration, but adults can weigh up to 2lbs and be up to two feet in length, from the tip of its whiskery nose to the end of its scaly tail. Its ability to survive and thrive is staggering.

Habitat

Wherever there is human habitation you will find the rat, living in unhealthy (for us) harmony with its unwitting hosts. During the summer months they, like all mammals are spread far and wide across the countryside. When the colder weather comes they head for barns, grain silos and outhouses, in search of warmth, shelter and of course, food. Although they are found in sewers or beside drainage ditches and canals, they aren't the greatest lovers of water – preferring

Man's mortal enemy – the brown rat

warm dry accommodation. Farms make ideal rodent environments; spilt grain, chicken and pig feed all make a ready food supply for the rat, whilst outbuildings, barns and chicken coops make ideal homes. In fact, your average farm could be considered a five star hotel for a rat. There's little more to say on the subject other than they can live above or below ground; the holes and runs they use can at times seem too small for them to pass through or use, and they are everywhere they are not evicted from.

Consider this: As they have no breeding season or seeming limitations to breed here are some frightening facts: The brown rat becomes sexually mature in little under three months and most females produce at least five or six litters each year, each containing up to ten young. This means that in an ideal habitat, a pair of sexually mature rats can easily produce over 60 offspring, as a pregnancy can last as little as 24 days. Taking into account the relatively short time it takes them to reach sexual maturity, this knock-on effect can mean a pair of rats, including their offspring in one year can theoretically be responsible for creating well over a thousand rats - a staggering thought! There's also the widely held belief that rats can sense disease in a potential mate so healthy rats don't mate with poisoned rats. A reason they say, that modern poisons are becoming less and less effective.

Incidentally its close relative, the black rat (Rattus rattus) responsible for the Black Death, is now a protected species (cough!) and thankfully only found on the Island of Lundy.

Location and Behavioural Patterns

On the farm, the first sign of rats is usually amongst the pigpens, cattle feed troughs and hen runs. Later, or simultaneously, they'll appear in and around grain silos and hay bales. You'll probably catch sight of one out of the corner of your eye as it scurries along the base of a wall, across a beam or girder making its way to food, or back to an entrance to a communal home. Hundreds of these rodents can occupy an absolute labyrinth of tunnels and 'scrapes'.

Rats just love dark, gloomy places – all the better if they contain straw such as the aforementioned hay bales stacked in storage over winter. Any of the animal pens or outbuildings are worth a try for locating them, but as extreme caution is needed if shooting near livestock, first check if you can target them elsewhere.

Within the confines of the farm buildings and outhouses, rat holes can often appear as if overnight, when the rat is usually finding its way in from the fields. In fact, I'll take this opportunity to dispel the popular misconception that the rat lives indoors all year around. You'll more often than not find a few in and around the farm all year long,

The rat can be incredibly wary but at times unashamedly bold

but come late spring and the onset of warmer weather it returns to the fields. Often then only returning to farm buildings because of the food it can find. Once the food source is taken away, in the case of grain, used and sold, then so too will the rat, like Elvis, 'leave the building' until the colder weather once again returns.

The rat is an unwelcome guest around the farm due to two major problems it will cause. One is damage and the other is the foodstuffs it will spoil. Granted, it will eat a lot of grain but the major problem is the droppings left on top and the faeces that permeate down into the valuable stored cereal. The other damage is the rodent's penchant for gnawing into anything that it comes across – electrical cable, sacks, wood and particularly its burrowing into bales of hay, not only to rip out material to take away for nest building, but also to find a cosy spot to raise yet another brood.

Incidentally, be warned: indoor close range shooting isn't as easy as it first seems. No sooner will you see one, than it will disappear into the little hidey-holes they use for safety. Despite its abhorrent nature, the brown rat is a clever, intelligent and at times infuriatingly cautious critter. It's also a socially structured animal that can pass on information quickly to others concerning areas that hold food, or once you've shot a few times, the area that carries danger.

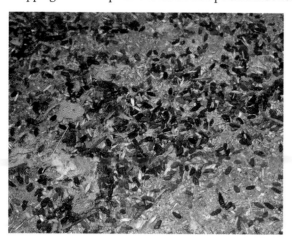

Rat droppings are unmistakable and betray areas of heavy infestation

Methods to Use

By and large the brown rat is a nocturnal creature, spreading its nastiness under the cover of darkness. There are two ways to bag them, both involving shooting at night using some form of artificial light source. However, now with the availability of hi-tech, night vision equipment the true specialist has even more options.

First the tried and trusted traditional methods: the most widely known, being baiting out. Before going any further it must be said that although this method works, and works well to some extent, it isn't half as effective as targeting them on their established runs and self-appointed feeding areas, which will be dealt with in the chapter on Shooting At Night.

As the name implies, 'baiting out' is a method whereby the shooter puts out a suitable bait into an area with the objective of establishing a feeding area the rats feel safe visiting. Similar in reasoning is a dead rabbit left out to bring in carrion feeders.

The baiting process is quite straightforward. Food should be left out regularly for up to a week before any shooting is done, and anything will suffice, from bread to rotten fruit. Most who've done this type of shooting prefer certain foodstuffs, but the experienced agree that putting out bait that can't be dragged away and eaten out of sight is far better. Some favour bread or a chicken carcass in a net bag suspended a few inches off the floor. The rat has to work to get at the food above its head and to get into the bag. Similarly, a big tin of pet food with holes punched in the side so the rat has to struggle to get its nose in is another good bait, but if there's one treat they can't resist it's grated chocolate and peanut butter. Peanut butter is ideal as it sticks to the area you place it and the rats have to stick around to nibble and lick it up. As an added incentive the grated chocolate is like icing sprinkled onto the cake, and the combined aromas waft around to be easily picked up by the whiskery rodent's nostrils. There are other baits used, including grated cheese or groundbait used by anglers; this small crumb bait keeps the rat nibbling away on the spot.

The kit, and employment of the method, is simple. You need to choose a hidden position within range with a shooting angle that gives you a sturdy backstop behind the target. If needed, put a big piece of heavy wood covered with carpet behind the bait to absorb the impact of pellets. For many situations such as this, you don't need a gun lamp as you can shoot by the illumination of the low-power light near the bait. In these cases, I'll opt to use a springer with open sights or preferably a multi-shot PCP with red-dot for the fact that they allow you to get a quick fix on the target. However, I'll more often than not use a scope with a gun lamp onboard so as to target those detected in the areas out and away from the baited area.

As well as preparing the area with bait, it should initially be illuminated with a low light on a regular basis so the rats become accustomed to it. Most barns have a power source for illumination so all you need to do is put a low wattage bulb of no more than 40W in a suitable holder such as an old bedside lamp or car inspection lamp. I set the light to the left of my intended shooting position and no more than 12 yards from the baited area. The light source is then blocked out from my direct view so I'm never able to look directly at it, thus saving my 'night vision'. Baiting-out tactics can bring quick results when first employed but soon lose effectiveness after a few shooting sessions.

This is when you need to search the rats out in the runs they're using to and from the natural food they've discovered. In fact, it's often the case that where rats have established food and a way to and from shelter they'll not respond well to baiting-out tactics anyway. In this situation, you'll need some extra and specialised accessories other than rifle and pellets. These other methods will be detailed in full in the relevant sections.

Calibres and Kill-Zones

Though I'm a great fan of .177 calibre, I must admit it wiser to opt for the .22 calibre slug when targeting rats, especially if taking them 'on the hoof' so to speak. Usually, a pellet into the front third of the rodent's body will dispatch it but if it's moving, that's a very small target. The .22 allows you more leeway from the exact point of kill whereas a .177 pellet needs to go straight into the brain or heart. If the rats are hanging around, then I would use .177 calibre but take full-on head shots and preferably the best shot by far is directly into its whiskery snout, from the front as it peers down or up at you. However, if the range is within 25yds I choose to use .22. Some even advocate .25 but though you're getting a pellet giving extra weight and mass, I don't feel the pros outweigh the cons. So that brings us back to the two most popular calibres and equally as important where to place the lead. Obviously, head shots are preferable and with the .177 calibre essential. However, with larger calibres and at closer range, If you hit the rat in the front third of the body it isn't going to go far!

Ratting can be very challenging and yet satisfying as every time a scaly tail snuffs it, you've done a public service – no arguing with that.

Know your Voles

When hunting near rivers, streams, lakes, canals or any body of fresh water, make sure that you don't confuse the brown rat with the little bank vole or larger water vole. Both are becoming quite scarce in some areas, they do no harm to the environment and are largely protected.

It's easy to distinguish between rats and these friendlies. A full-grown bank vole is only about 8-10cm in length, including its furry tail – more the size of a mouse than a rat. The water vole is a lot bigger, with head and body about 20cm in length and a hairy, ringed tail of about 10cm. Its head is round and blunt in appearance (vaguely similar to a guinea pig), with tiny ears. In contrast, an average-sized rat has a head and body length of 23-28cm, a pointed whiskery nose, prominent ears and long, scaly tail.

Grey Squirrel (Sciurus Carolinensis)

A prolific inhabitant of our forests and woodlands, the grey squirrel has been nothing but trouble to our forestry industry since its introduction to this country from its native North America in 1876. It's a busy little rodent that will gnaw and nibble at anything, and it has a penchant for biting the growing shoots from young saplings, resulting in a stunted, unsightly tree. It also has another particular annoying habit of stripping the bark, even though it doesn't eat it.

The grey squirrel is little more than a tree-rat

Most of these random acts of destruction are due to the fact that like other rodents it needs to wear down the incisors due to the continual growth of these effective gnashers. It eventually was recognised as such a huge problem that in the 1960s a bounty was put on its head as the Government actually paid people to shoot them. Incidentally, it's approximated there are now over two million greys in the UK at any one time, despite the pest being well and truly classed as vermin.

Easily distinguished from our native and protected red squirrel, it has a uniform grey fur coat, with a dirty-white underbelly extending up to the throat and face, and it has a characteristically long, bushy, silvery grey tail. Its small almost indifferent ears are a big contrast to the red's ear tufts which are, in relation to the ears of the animal, large and very distinctive. The grey is also much larger, stockier and even in silhouette has an unmistakable outline. Come spring before new foliage fully takes over the trees, the squirrels can feed on buds or gnaw to get at sap just under the bark. This is where, when and why they cause such a problem to plantation owners, but it's not only due to the damage they inflict on trees, because come the breeding season for birds, they're notorious egg thieves and fledgling killers. Often we punish and blame corvids such as magpies and crows but just as likely the culprit is the squirrel.

They're also a nuisance on keepered estates where they will steal the grain spilled out for game birds, and in harsh winters will even chew holes at the top of the feed hoppers to get inside. As you can see, definitely not a fussy eater and couple this with the fact that it serves no constructive natural purpose at all to the woodland eco-system, and you have on your hands a right royal pest!

Habitat

Where there are trees, there will usually be grey squirrels – especially in deciduous woodlands. An extremely resourceful creature, it is equally at home in a town park or urban garden where it delights and thrives in raiding bird tables for nuts, fruit and seeds. A popular misconception since its arrival on these shores is that this larger alien species of squirrel has ousted the more timid native red squirrel. This is only partly true. The red was actually in decline before the introduction of the grey. Also, it's now coming under threat from the parapox virus and to top it all, our native species prefers coniferous woodland – a habitat in somewhat of a decline in most lowland' counties. Another misconception is that squirrels hibernate during the winter months. Again, this is definitely not the case and one of the reasons it provides excellent sport for the airgun hunter during the colder months is that it can be seen out foraging even in the snows of deepest winter. However, it does prefer the warmth of the drey during harsh wet weather but if hunger dictates it must feed, it will be out rummaging around in the leaf litter. The drey is usually quite a modest-sized, ball-shaped construction of twigs and leaves, usually built in the cleft of a tree. In the safety of its lair, two litters of one to seven young are reared between January and June.

Location and Behavioural Patterns

Signs of squirrel activity in the woods on your shoot will be easy to spot. They usually have a particular branch or stump from which they keep an eye on the trees around them, and this can often also be a favourite feeding spot. Around the bottom of these areas you will find pieces of stripped bark, broken husks, chestnut shells, split and gnawed fir cones etc. The drey is also easy to identify and locate once the trees have lost some of their foliage. This can look like a small nest but will often only be a scruffy collection of twigs, dead leaves and even pieces of bark jammed into the fork of a tree. Usually, they're not very high up, maybe midway up the tree as the squirrel isn't keen on repairing wind-damaged dreys perched in the upper branches. Occasionally, you'll find established dreys with nut stores close by, usually higher up and smaller in size than the main drey, like the animal's separate outhouse-cum-larder. Sometimes the squirrel just takes up residence in an unoccupied crow or magpie nest adding fresh building material when needed. In fact, find a drey in spring that has had some recently added fresh vegetation with green leaves showing in the construction, and you know it's being used.

Squirrels, like rats, have no difficulty in finding food. They have an acute sense of smell – one of the reasons they easily find hoppers full of grain and any spillings or leftovers that are freely on offer. Then again, the squirrel is so adaptable and intelligent it can soon work out a way into most containers of food storage – usually by chewing its way in. As with any form of hunting, location and patience are the key to success. A quick walk around a small copse or wood will soon have you find the tell-tale signs of squirrel habitation. If near coniferous trees, you'll find the fir cones neatly stripped, gnawed down and discarded like an eaten apple core. Small scratchings at the foot of trees in any wood betrays their presence especially if accompanied by signs of bark being stripped. These signs aren't always aloft; as squirrels often have a favoured fallen log or branch they'll gnaw away at like hungry little beavers.

It's the feed hoppers themselves that come regularly under attack and regular replacing, even the toughened plastic types, is a troublesome chore for keepers, not forgetting an extra expense. Find these areas and you'll undoubtedly have some squirrels. Look aloft as you walk through the trees and you'll soon find its bulky home.

But it's not only outdoors that squirrels can be found as they can cause a right problem when they've taken up residence in the roof space of country houses, or even in urban areas. They can ruin loft insulation by scratching, and gnaw through wiring; all potential fire hazards.

Methods to Use

The airgun hunter can target them in the trees, and where possible, bait them down to a natural or artificially created feeding station. There is a technique known as drey-knocking. This is more often used by shooters working in pairs whereby they knock the drey with lofting poles to send the squirrel out to meet an end with the shotgun. Though some airgun hunters try this method, by and large I'd leave this for the shotgunner as we want them to be still, rather than running for cover. However, the method is detailed in Hunting Techniques, for reasons of thoroughness.

Wood-walking is just as the name implies and can be allied with opportunist shooting as the technique involves you walking slowly through woodland scanning the trees for signs of activity. These methods are outlined in the appropriate chapters. Needless to say, the best time to hunt squirrels is from autumn through to winter.

When beech mast is ripening early on in the autumn, squirrels will stay in the trees, but once the split-open husks fall, they'll follow the food source to the woodland floor. It's plentiful food and the trees are bare so take the opportunity to reap results until the buds start to green the trees up come the spring, and squirrel shooting becomes nigh on impossible due to the foliage.

However, it's at this time of year you can sit up near an area where you've found they're feeding and wait in ambush. Sitting quietly within range in full camo is the way to succeed. If it is a feed hopper they're visiting, then they'll come down to feed near it, but it often pays to give them an extra incentive to bring them to the shooting position.

Spend time in a place frequented by squirrels and you'll soon notice they have favourite walkways to and from areas. They'll come down or go up the same trees and use the same branches to keep moving around while still keeping off the deck.

Whether it follows its own scent or just knows its way around a familiar area is debatable but they certainly do show a preference for travelling along the same routes. They also definitely have favourite positions to sit and eat foodstuffs. These can be in the fork or cleft of a tree, anywhere that gives them an easy place to sit on their haunches as their front paws are busy holding and manipulating the food for getting their greedy chops around. Alternatively, in spring they'll go to the very tops of trees to get at the most succulent buds.

I don't think there's any animal or bird classed as vermin with the exception of the rabbit, that can't be tempted by a free meal. An animal's inquisitive nature can often be its downfall which is one of the reasons they're sometimes easily trapped, but squirrels are very clever and soon learn to avoid the cage traps that are regularly set in any one particular area for them.

Usual baits for traps include corn, any cereal grain, ground or whole peanuts and would you believe, some swear by chocolate. Use ground-up nuts, assorted nuts and raisins or cheap brand breakfast muesli and put it out at the base of a feed hopper or favoured tree they use for descending from the canopy. Then carefully select a spot, under another tree within range and just sit and wait for events to unfold.

Make yourself comfortable and prepare for a long wait. I'll use the same tactics I employ when sitting up near a sitty tree waiting for woodies; that's full camo, including facemask and gloves but ready to take shots along the horizontal as soon as the squirrels come to the feeding area. When shooting in this way, I prefer to use a low-light scope, with the magnification wound down to its lowest setting so as to take full advantage of a big objective lens's light-gathering capabilities. Even on the brightest days it can get quite gloomy under a tangled canopy of even quite bare branches. When the squirrel does make an appearance, and don't worry, it will eventually, aim carefully depending on how it presents to your shooting position and you'll have ambushed the first of hopefully many bushy tails.

Incidentally, in my experience it doesn't pay to leave shot squirrels near a baited area so although you need to break cover, look to check that there aren't other potential targets around before removing it.

Like any animal, squirrels soon sense danger and wise up to the fact that hanging around on the deck isn't a good idea once a few have been shot. Thankfully for the shooter, they're predictable little varmints and if they don't sit and hold on the ground, they might nick a piece of the tasty treats left out and high-tail it to sit high up on a branch nibbling the prize. Once up aloft, in familiar territory, a squirrel's confidence rises dramatically, even to the point of arrogance.

Calibres and Kill-Zones

For squirrel shooting, any calibre be it .177, .22 or the less popular .20 will suffice as long as your accuracy is up to the mark. Targeting these rodents isn't easy because the kill-zones aren't that large and if it's aloft the shot could be a tricky one.

If the squirrel is sitting side-on, the prime spot to aim for is the head down to the shoulder but if it presents full-on the little white chubby underbelly is a very exposed tempter. The squirrel is a deceptively tough critter and even here the pellet can't be allowed to drop below the animal's front paws or else you'll miss a vital organ. If facing away, flat to a tree trunk, drill one right into the back of the head or neck area and it won't be clinging on for long.

The Collared Dove (Streptopelia Decaocto)

The collared dove is a relatively recent visitor to our shores, but has now become firmly established as a most common and abundant breeding bird. It's hard to believe that it was once strictly a bird of the Balkans (the hilly region encompassing Bulgaria, Greece etc.) and lowlands of mainland Europe. The first reported nesting pair in the UK was in Norfolk in 1955 and its colonisation of this country since that time is staggering. There can't be a farm, park, garden or urban estate roof that hasn't been graced with its deceptively pretty presence at some time or another. The main reason for the amazing population expansion is largely due to its ability to breed all year round if the food supply is plentiful. Not to be confused with the protected and slightly smaller turtle dove, the collared dove is distinguished by the black and white edged half collar around the back of its neck – hence the name. This collar, which sets off the creamy grey brown to buff neck and body plumage make it a very attractive member of the dove family. Unfortunately, appearances can be deceptive, as left to its own devices this bird will eat a store of winter grain.

Habitat

Whatever the species, bird population usually declines due to the fact they either can't adapt or they are too shy to live in close proximity to humans. The collared dove, however, is perfectly designed to live near urbanised areas and feeds on anything from grain, corn or poultry feed to household scraps and bird table offerings. In fact it's now officially classed as a bird of town parks and gardens. In areas where dairy farming is the norm, the collared dove easily adapts to live further out into the fields on anything from weed-seeds and young shoots to elderberries.

Why are collared doves so unpopular then? Well, they can actually steal the feed from free-range hens, where they are often seen feeding right amongst the domestic fowl. Even though it's a prolific breeder, its nest building skills leave a lot to be desired; the usual nest structure being little more than a flimsy platform of woven twigs high in a tree, on a ledge, on a fluorescent tube light fitting or in the rafters of the barns and outbuildings. An insight into its self-procreating potential from some recognised ornithologists states that in the case of collared doves living in a high yield food enriched habitat, female birds can be in

The collared dove is a deceptively pretty pest

a state of near permanent fertilisation. Somebody really should tell them about birth control.

Location and Behavioural Patterns

The collared dove is a very easy bird to find, due to the fact that it never strays far from its food supply. So it follows that its need to be close to a regular source of suitable foodstuffs is the key to this pretty pest's location. This is why they, like feral pigeon and in some instances, woodpigeon, have taken to frequenting town parks and gardens. For obvious reasons the law prevents you from shooting them in these public places, so the main place for the airgun hunter to target them is around the farmyard and surrounding buildings. Short observation

Hardly sport – but the collared dove is now so common partly because it can breed all year round

recces will soon show where it prefers to feed. The bird absolutely detests bad weather, and will always be found sheltering from the wind and rain. The unmistakable relatively high-pitched double 'coo', so common to doves of all varieties, or the repeated 'cu-coo-cu' call will usually betray their presence. The collared's call is also a quite lengthy repetition of this set pattern. It has another quite raucous 'crying' call which is used when flying off or landing – it's used as both an alarm signal and telling all and sundry it's arrived on the scene. Like many other feathered felons, it will also have favourite sitty trees, ledges or beams where it will sit and digest large meals. In a sitting, this relatively small dove can get through an enormous amount of seed, corn or grain. In fact, when they are in this digesting mode after a good feed they can be quite easy to sneak up on.

Methods to Use

Firstly, it must be said that although the collared dove is a pest in certain areas, similarly when targeting other quarry species use your discretion as to what exactly constitutes a threat to the farmer's livelihood or health. I only consider shooting collared doves when they are present in seriously large numbers and known to be spoiling or taking an unacceptable amount of grain. I say this because shooting collared doves is relatively simple and in my opinion an act of sheer pest control, not sport. Their trust of humans is their downfall and they will hang around much longer than any other quarry species, apart from established feral pigeon colonies.

If you are asked into an area to shoot them, then the three main methods of dealing with or dare I say 'hunting' this prolific dove are roost shooting, stalking (around the farm buildings) and baiting-down with grain. As soon as the dawn starts to break they'll probably already be out and about feeding. Although the bird tolerates human presence, it still has keen eyesight and if it does sense danger from you it will flutter up to move on to another part of the farm to feed. This can be infuriating but it still won't be as shy or wary as any of the other legitimate quarry species. Roost shooting isn't anywhere near as productive as the other two methods, as collared doves tend to roost in very small numbers, usually twos or threes. However, this is also the most unsporting, and again a method to use if shooting for sheer pest control. In fact, when the birds have paired off, especially when they have eggs or young they often roost together on the nest. In the day, the female sits on the eggs, the male hanging around outside the barn in a tree or on the building roof. At night he comes in to snuggle up against the female but the birds often sit facing in opposite directions. The sitting arrangement is presumed so the birds can defend the nest from rats that will also be up there in the rafters and roof space. The collared dove is very brave for its size and they'll fly at magpies and even rats keeping them away from eggs and chicks. Unfortunately, in the kafuffle they often knock their own eggs or even fledglings out of the nest so they achieve little. However, such is the prolific breeding pattern they soon have another clutch of eggs, usually two laid shortly after they lose any. They're also, once paired off, very affectionate to each other, preening one another and generally sitting and staying close together. But I digress and back to shooting methods.

Baiting-down is the most efficient method of making inroads into the bird's population where it has become troublesome. Once you have established an area that the birds frequent regularly, it's just a matter of putting out feed for them and leaving them undisturbed for a few days. This form of ambushing obviously necessitates the use of shooting from cover. This can range from a perimeter wall, from inside an outbuilding or from behind any type of static farm machinery. I stress the term 'static' as it's no use if the tractor gets driven away on the morning you plan to shoot. Large bags can be built up shooting this way as the collared dove, even when scared off, will usually return quite quickly. Whether this is pure greed, or they are just plain dumb is anybody's guess. I reckon it's a combination of both with a liberal sprinkling of plain old gluttony! However, a trait they do display which is their downfall is they tend to stay together in pairs and even when you shoot one, often the other won't fly far sometimes only fluttering up to immediately settle back down strutting around near the fallen comrade. These are the times a double-shot or multi-shot rifle are a godsend as a quick back-up shot will usually end in you bagging a brace a time. As I said, shooting collareds is hardly sport.

Once you've shot a few birds, these can be used as decoys, using chin sticks set up as you would using shot woodpigeon as natural deeks. Try to sit the birds in a head down, feeding position. Unlike decoying woodies, the pattern you lay collareds out in isn't critically important. One tip though is to arrange the birds as if feeding in a loose circle, heads facing inwards towards each other. This seems to be the dove's natural feeding pattern when congregated in a small group.

Stalking is the most demanding method for dealing with the birds. Even though the doves might at times seem to be untroubled by the human presence, a person intentionally sneaking up on them is something else altogether. If the weather has been inclement for a few days then this could well work in your favour, as the doves will shelter amongst the buildings and surrounding trees. When moving around the farm buildings themselves, stay close to the wall and move slowly. Plan your route in an anti-clockwise direction so as to approach corners with the ability to peek around them rifle half-mounted at the ready. This allows you to keep most of your body concealed. Of course for 'lefties' the opposite direction will apply. For once, full camo gear isn't needed, but do wear drab clothing to suit the farm buildings, rusting metalwork of silos and outdoor machinery as well as the darker areas in shade. Whichever attire you choose, when sneaking quietly around the outbuildings in this fashion, be mindful to the possibility of coming across any other people who might be working in the area. Remember, safety at all times!

Calibres and Kill-Zones

I'll always choose the small .177 calibre pellet, time in and time out for the dove but any of the popular calibres will suffice. Head shots and full on breast shots will see this bird cleanly dispatched. Remember though the head shot is very small. This takes accuracy especially shooting at awkward angles so more often than not I'll always take this bird with a shot that punches straight into the upper part of the chest cavity.

When you've shot your doves, don't waste them as the breast meat is quite tasty. Tougher than woodpigeon but cooked slowly and for a longer period it's worth the trouble of breasting enough to make into a stew or casserole. Mixed in with a bit of woodie, rabbit meat and root vegetables you've got a tasty meal and the farmer gets to 'lose' yet another cause of potential loss of earnings.

Woodpigeon (Columba Palumbus)

On a dull overcast day the woodpigeon, or as hunters affectionately know it, the 'woodie' can appear to be little more than a plump, large grey bird with a patch or two of black and white. When the sun hits the plumage, marvel at the attractiveness of its beautiful pink/mauve breast feathers, the brilliance of the white neck patches and glistening iridescence of the green/blue feathers that surround those attention-grabbing neck flashes. Even the bold black bars of the wings are etched with broad white bands giving the woodie an almost regal appearance. Yes, the collared dove might beat it hands down for cuteness but you can't deny the woodie its place in the countryside as a very distinctive and attractive bird.

Unfortunately, it's the scourge of every cereal farmer, crop grower and market gardener in the land. The woodpigeon may be a dreaded agricultural pest, but it's a firm favourite with the shooting disciplines of shotgunners and airgun hunters – and as an added bonus it's very tasty. In fact alongside the rabbit it surely now rates as the airgun hunter's staple quarry species for year-round sport. With thought and know-how, decent bags can be achieved as you pick them out of the trees as they rest, or off the fields as they feed. Wherever and whenever you encounter the woodie, you can be sure it will prove a very worthy and wary adversary.

The wood pigeon is a major agricultural pest

Habitat

As its name implies, this is primarily a bird of the woods although depending on season it will feed and readily move over and on to fields. Due to its massive population figures, it can also be found even in relatively treeless areas, including towns and even some cities. Like the collared dove it's becoming a much more common sight in urban areas. I suppose it's safe to assume it realises it's not under threat from the gun there. For nesting, it usually builds a small platform of twigs high up in the trees and will raise two to three broods. Unlike most other birds, the adults feed the young on pigeon milk they produce during and throughout the breeding season. This can start as early as March right through to October but depending on availability of food they have been known to breed even in winter. The young birds are known as squabs and can be seen over the fields come summer. They're easily distinguished from adults due to the lack of white neck patch and of course are a lot smaller. Some shotgunners consider it unsporting to shoot these naïve, inexperienced birds but I don't think a farmer in the land would thank you for giving them a reprieve. The reason being that woodies can eat an amazing amount of food, stuffing their crops to bursting at every opportunity – especially when feeding on oilseed rape, corn, wheat, young pea or bean shoots and ivy berries in the winter. Woodies feed three or four times a day, so ambushing them can be a very effective tactic when you've learned the areas they use as flight lines to the fields they feed over. Unlike a lot of other birds, its habitat is not in decline or under threat. Although some woodies are lost to foxes and cats, it has few natural enemies – most commonly those being the sparrow hawk, peregrine falcon, kestrel and buzzards. The latter especially can cause havoc when decoying, as the buzzard will spook the birds but as it's nature's way, we have to put up with the goings on around us as we hunt and adapt accordingly. Needless to say, if a buzzard is soaring and gliding around the area, the woodies aren't likely to be feeding confidently. However, none of these raptors pose a major problem to the bird's population figures.

Location and Behavioural Patterns

The movements of woodpigeon are very much dictated by the seasons and their need to find food and shelter. They can usually be found over fields during the daytime and around woods and copses in the evenings where it will return to roost, and depending on season, not forgetting weather conditions, it will often spend a lot of time in the woods. This is when the bird's distinctive and repeatedly used throaty 'cooo, coo, coo – coo, coo' call will more often than not give its presence away long before you see it. The woodpigeon's voracious appetite and specific dietary preferences, coupled with the annual availability of those foodstuffs, are the definitive key to its location. Basically, if there's grain on the soil or crops growing in the fields then you'll find pigeons on them. It pays to know when the farmer is sowing, as the birds will descend like a plague as soon as the grain is on the ground. This is because, unlike some other birds, the woodpigeon isn't keen on scratching about deep in the soil; it rarely if ever will dig into the soil for food. It prefers to take easy pickings of seed kernels and grain off the top where and when it can find them. It also doesn't like getting its feet wet or muddy so when conditions dictate, look to the sitty trees for sport, the edge of woods or dry areas of fields with good drainage – a factor to take into consideration when choosing an area to set out decoys.

It stands to reason that to ambush them effectively you need prior knowledge of potential feeding areas, and the flight lines that the birds regularly use. A few days watching the land will soon indicate which 'lines' the birds fly up and along. They often follow hedge lines, a line of trees – even along roads.

In winter the birds really do have to search for food and can from day to day be found either foraging on the woodland floor, or around the bases of trees and hedges before they get the chance to descend on the winter rape fields.

Methods to Use

The successful pigeon shooter must be organised, well informed and disciplined in their approach and methods. Although major methods are decoying and roost shooting, the airgun hunter can have superb sport if favoured sitty trees are located. You can also encounter the birds while out wood-walking or opportunist shooting but more often than not as you sneak stealthily around, the first indication that any are near is the sound or sight of them clattering out of a nearby tree.

Talking of trees – when the birds are preoccupied, feeding on ivy berries in the colder months you can often, with prior knowledge, be waiting for them to arrive – well concealed to pick the birds off when they're gorging themselves. Or if they're staying deep in the wood because of wet, harsh or cold weather conditions, know the areas they frequent when this weather arrives and carefully slip from tree to tree until within range. This is particularly challenging but very rewarding if successful.

Ambushing near watering holes isn't a method I'd rely on but if the birds have been feeding on cereal, especially corn, they seem to get quite thirsty. Discover a place they use to take on water, which unlike most other birds they actually do by sucking it up and you could well have a few good sessions. It could be a pond, stream or water trough, but I'd rather recommend you find the feeding fields they're coming from or going to and ambushing them there with the aid of decoys. If you want to get serious about woodies, then check the crop of the first few birds you shoot in a session, as this will give you good indication of where the birds might be feeding. Decoying, roost shooting and my preferred method of picking them out of sitty trees – they're all very productive methods for bagging a few birds.

Calibres and Kill-Zones

Either .177, .20 or .22 calibre is suitable to cleanly dispatch woodies at sensible airgun hunting ranges but the pellet needs to be placed with precision in one of three major kill-zone areas, depending on how the bird presets in relation to your shooting position. Crop shots shouldn't be taken as the foodstuff in the bird's onboard storage tank can be packed so densely that it can deflect or stop a shot being fatal. First and foremost is the side-on shot at the head and neck; next is the upper chest cavity, but only if you can slip the pellet up between a wing fold from below, and the angle into this area also has to be right so that the pellet enters the heart and lungs. If the bird has landed on the ground, aim for just forward of the shoulder/upper wing fold to put a pellet into the chest cavity. Alternatively, if shooting from behind, put one right between the shoulder blades, into the neck, or crack it in the back of the head.

If you don't mind spoiling or bruising some of the breast meat then there are times a hi-power, FAC-rated air rifle in .22 calibre would be my rifle of choice. This doesn't mean you can let power override sloppy shooting technique, but it does allow two very different target zones and when you've not that much time to select the kill-zone it's handy. To save continually repeating myself I'll mention here that when using a hi-power air rifle, these kill-zones also apply for all the larger members of the corvid family. These are; a side-on shot in the frontal chest area where a pellet can actually crash through the front of the wing doing deadly damage to the bird's heart and lungs, and similarly, the full-on chest shot, aiming from the lower neck to just below the crop. For corvids, aim slightly off centre to the right or left of the upper chest.

A heavyweight .22 calibre pellet fired at 28-30ft lb out to 40 – 50yds retains a lot of energy meaning the lead projectile really can smash through the bird's protection to enter the chest cavity causing massive internal damage. Some might think this not the most sporting way to tackle the birds, but then again, what's the difference in that or a shotgun blast?

Feral Pigeon (Columba Livia)

As unlikely as it seems the feral pigeon's original ancestor is the protected rock dove but nowadays the ferals are just as likely to be related to domestic pigeons escaped from medieval dovecotes, or wayward homing pigeons. The word 'feral' simply means gone wild. Due to this, the coloration of the plumage can be extremely variable. It could be brown, slate-grey, black or even dove white. Any combination of these colours can be found, but the pigeon will usually still have double black wing-bars and traces of an iridescent purple green front/side neck patch and/or white rump, proving its rock

Indoors or out, the feral pigeon is a terrible nuisance

dove ancestry. Don't be too worried about mistaking a feral for a 'rocky' as the latter is now very rare, confined to a few colonies on the sea cliffs of Scotland and the West of Ireland. More likely it could be mistaken for the stock dove, or a bedraggled racing pigeon.

The stock dove is usually more uniform grey with no white rump patch. The 'stock' also has a double grunting call rather than the traditional cooing of a dove or pigeon. In the case of mistaking it for a racing or homing pigeon, check that the bird has no rings on its legs. If you're unsure and you don't have a clear view of the bird's legs, then don't shoot.

Habitat

Feral pigeons are found everywhere and anywhere. A veritable avian avalanche of these flying rats flood our every town and city, so you'd be forgiven for thinking these felons stay around the streets all year round – not so! Like their close relatives (woodies, collared doves etc.), they move where the food supply is most plentiful. In winter they do stay in the cities and towns where they feed on scraps of food, usually fast food leftovers disposed of onto the floor by the thoughtless. Come the spring and summer, many birds periodically head out for the country to feed on freshly sown grain as well as general farmland stubble. It's also not unusual to find them in the company of woodies and I've shot countless ferals over the years that have landed amongst decoys. Although they usually nest on beams and amongst the roof space of disused buildings, they're not fussy where they site their sparsely built nest of twigs; any hollow, or sheltered ledge will , but they do prefer it to be indoors.

Location and Behavioural Patterns

Due to the bird's ability to adapt and its inherent nomadic nature, ferals can crop up almost anywhere on your shoot. More likely than not around farm buildings where they can often be found in the company of collared doves. When you find them in the open country, the best time to try to thin them out is in the spring before they drove back to the towns to breed.

For pest control purposes, this is the main place you'll be able to shoot them in any great numbers when they colonise abandoned buildings, factories and industrial units. Gaining access to shoot here isn't as difficult as you may think as any small business owner with a feral problem is worth approaching – as long as you do so in the right manner. If you gain permission, wherever practical and possible shoot them off the roof as inside work is specialised stuff, but not beyond the capabilities of the practised and disciplined shooter – more of which later. Before going inside to find them, though, you'll first see them sitting around the same areas for most of the day. The same applies to the barns and outbuildings on your shoot. Look to the ledges, ridging tiles and the sheltered, sunny side of the roof. They certainly seem to have favourite sitty areas, especially in the colder weather when they can take advantage of the expelled warm air from chimneys and factory extractor fans.

Step inside a disused building and you'll have no trouble locating the birds as under the areas they roost and rest the floor will be a quagmire of droppings. This is one of the main reasons you'll be asked and allowed to shoot inside an old building they've taken over and you'll have to take them out; and depending on the building you're in, you could find yourself in some pretty nasty conditions.

Methods to Use

It's hard to believe that you need official sanction to dispense with feral pigeons. According to DEFRA (Department of the Environment, Foods and Rural Affairs) it has to be confirmed that they are causing a major problem, as specified by the department. Usually they are, but you are only authorised to shoot them with the building owner's permission, and the fact that other methods such as scaring and netting are failing to contain or evict them from the premises.

Obviously, the main qualifier for culling is that they present a major health hazard which they undoubtedly do, due to their droppings containing a multitude of dangerous pathogens and diseases, and it goes without saying, like rats, when you shoot any don't pick them up without gloves, and dispose of them in the correct fashion by burning.

We're now getting very much into the realms of serious pest control and a situation the majority of sporting airgun hunters won't ever want to be in, or find themselves asking to do. However, it's worth remembering that doing such a favour can have the knock-on effect that your name is passed on to somebody who might have some land. Word of mouth usually means another feral clearance job, or some rat shooting is in the offing. If the latter is around a farm barn or outbuildings this could well score you some field shooting, depending on how you conduct yourself.

As we're back at the farm, around the farmyard the method for dealing with ferals is exactly the same as for collared doves; stalking around the outbuildings and even baiting them down with grain or even bread, but we still come back to the fact that most serious feral bashing and rat shooting for that matter will be done indoors. Due to this, I'm purposely going to deal here, as a prelude to the chapter on Hunting Techniques, how best to go about your shooting inside old buildings, barns and around the farmyard itself. Take note of the latter as ferals are partial to sitting around on the farmhouse roof so we'll check out the etiquette of shooting around the farmyard. First, forget ferals for a moment and consider the opportunities of being allowed to shoot inside the big main barn on the land you've maybe recently gained permission to shoot over. This is a big chance for you as an airgun hunter to prove yourself. No live round sporting gun is needed here, just the precision, modern-day air rifle, running within the 12ft lb legal limit, in your hands. That's why you're here looking at a feral job, so before you go lumbering in, double check your zero, your accuracy, your kit – everything. Most of all be sensible and show how responsible you are as you go about your sport. Firstly, though, the C & Ks of the feral pigeon.

Calibres and Kill-Zones

As I've stuck to a formula for these Quarry Files, and although the feral is a nasty, disease-ridden pest, it still deserves to be dispatched correctly. Incidentally, it's worth mentioning, some shooters use detuned (lower power) rifles due to the fact the birds are shot at such very close range, especially indoors. This is to lessen the possibility of over penetration at the target. That's a specialised route, and one to consider, but for the majority of airgunners who get the chance to go feral felling, a standard hunting combo will be more than adequate. Though I favour .177 calibre for most hunting situations, for this work I prefer a good old .22 slug. This is also one of the only times I'll mention the .25 calibre as an option. Here it can be useful as if a building hasn't been cleared for a while, targets will more often than not be encountered well within 20yds and that big piece of lead drops them like a stone.

Kill-zones apply exactly the same as they do for the woodpigeon but with one big exception. If you think the woodie a tough bird then this is the 'Arnie' version. OK, somewhat of an exaggeration but it is true to say whilst the woodie has soft downy feathers the feral has a relatively thick layer of full and very strong feathers all over its body, a sort of avian armour plating. These feathers can absorb quite a lot of the pellet shock value, so place those pellets carefully, especially if using the chest kill-zone.

Shooting Specifics – Indoors and Outdoors

First Up – Indoors: This form of hunting opens up a whole new range of opportunities for the shooter. Invariably, you'll be shooting for pest control only because your targets, as we've outlined, will mainly be feral pigeon and, of course, rats. However, at times when the weather isn't very conducive to outdoor work, having the opportunity to shoot legally indoors can be a welcome and challenging alternative. In some cases you could get the chance to cull collared doves but in most cases you'll be evicting feral perils and scaly tails.

The first major factor to take into consideration when shooting 'ndoors is your own personal safety. Ricochets can have dangerous consequences and if shooting inside abandoned industrial units and even places you are unsure of, always note if you see bare wires. You can't be a hundred per cent sure a wire isn't live until it's too late so don't go near them. Also watch for rotten floorboards, rubble underfoot, rickety stairs and dodgy ceilings. As this isn't a manual on feral pigeon clearance I'll stay on the sporting side of advice but even so, In the years I've been shooting indoors I've been into buildings that quite frankly should have been condemned, so be warned. Also, you always need to pay particular attention to what lies behind the target. Airgun pellets punch nice neat holes in corrugated or plastic roofs and no farmer wants his outbuildings to have roofs like colanders.

If you walk in during the day and there's still a few about, then that's fine – shoot them off the beams they perch on. Until they wise up they'll sit there thinking you're a farmhand or factory worker depending on location of shoot. At night it's a different matter altogether and, of course, you'll need a lamp. Incidentally, a word on the use of lights for indoor feral pigeon shooting: under the 1981 Wildlife & Countryside Act, it's an offence to use a device for illuminating a bird to shoot it. However, provision is also made in the act for the grant of an annual licence that allows feral pigeon, amongst others, to be culled with the aid of an artificial light source and sighting device for purposes of pest control.

The aftermath! The scene after a feral pigeon cull – not a glamorous job, just sheer pest control

So, once all legalities are satisfied, before getting in there to shoot you need suitable clothing. A disposable boiler suit and a dust mask are sometimes needed, such are the conditions, but many times an old pair of combats and jacket will suffice. If it's a factory unit, presumably it won't be too disgusting and the occasional walk around, with the permission of the owner, to curtail the numbers is good to tone up your shooting practice. Incidentally, in many old outbuildings and disused industrial units there'll be no light, hence the provision for the use of a lamp. Some opt to work with another person, one shooting while one 'spots' and operates a hand-held lamp. Others prefer to go in solo with a gun-mounted lamp. If unsure of the area, the building and even if you feel more at ease, I advise you go with another shooter, but if in pairs or alone, the correct way to deal with pigeons at roost in buildings are the same. That is to enter the building sweeping through the areas or rooms methodically, then after shooting all those you pass, move out to rest the area for a while. After a reasonable amount of time, repeat the procedure until the ferals are sorted. The entry points they've used which are often broken windows, holes in the roof etc. need to be covered or else they'll be back in before you've finished showering at home. After shooting, collect all the dead birds, using gloves, and sack them up to be disposed of properly by incineration. Those that drop stone dead up on the beams should be retrieved or else you've provided free rat food.

I know, it's not sport, it's not exciting, but it's a job that at times needs doing and with the air rifle you have the perfect tool to do it. Talking of which, this is an ideal situation to use a quality springer with open sights or gas-ram-powered rifle with a quality red-dot sight. No messing around finding the target in your sights and you won't need to magnify the target anyway. Even if using a multi-shot PCP I've often been thankful of the super-fast target acquisition the red-dot sight affords and believe me, get amongst a colony of established ferals and the action can be fast and furious! Similarly, if using a scope. a laser is useful for giving a quick ranging reference.

Incidentally, this brings me to a much-overlooked nuance of indoor shooting and another reason to use these alternative-sighting systems. As with shooting outdoors at night, enclosed areas can play havoc with rangefinding. Shots can seem closer or further than they actually are. In fact, optical illusion will make upward shots seem closer and shots along to quarry on the floor will appear further than they actually are or vice-versa. And that's with the building lights on. So as you can see, ranging difficulties aren't something you'll only experience when using a lamp.

Outdoors – Close To Home: Usually, unless stipulated the farmhouse will and should be out of bounds unless you're invited in for a brew and a chat. Remember this is your host's home. By all means, when allowed, stalk around the barn, storage units, pigpens and cattle sheds but respect the farmer's privacy. If you are going to be shooting around the farmyard always ask and let the farmer know. You may be lucky enough eventually to be given carte blanche on the land, but near the farm and inhabitants take no liberties with your host's generosity. Also, farmers and their workers start early, and that means there'll often be people around from first thing in the morning to possibly late evening. Sundays are better as even the farmhands at most times of the year can be scarce on this day. Even so, never take a risky shot; don't presume someone won't walk around a corner. Let the lads in the yard know you're there even though you may have told the farmer, and always let them know which part of the farm you'll be going to next. Again, ricochets can be a problem if a misplaced pellet deflects off a concrete wall. Watch while taking upward shots, plastic guttering, lead flashing, asbestos roofing, security lights – all are no-no's if near or behind the quarry targeted.

As outlined in 'Seasons …' many quarry species will be found around the farmyard, especially in summer. Corvids can crop up anywhere looking to scavenge food, especially around dung heaps. Woodies stop over at any time and of course the collared dove is virtually guaranteed to be around. It's not only opportunist shooting, though, as for the flying felons you'll often need to plan your trip with more care and more often than not build a hide. Yes, a hide isn't only of use in the open countryside. You might even need to build one in a barn itself if targeting feed-stealing jackdaws, collareds or ferals. Luckily, there'll be plenty of materials in the outbuilding to use, such as wooden pallets, sheets of corrugated iron, heavy-duty cardboard sheets, old empty grain and feed sacks … anything that blends in with the surrounding area. My preferred material if present, and more often than not they are in abundance, are hay bales. With a bit of ingenuity, a few hide poles or garden canes and a suitable amount of camo netting, you can construct a hide that allows you to be fully hidden yet affording a good view of the marauders' comings and goings, but, I must again stress the importance of letting others know where you are and what you're doing. If there's the possibility that the area will be used by people, the utmost caution is needed and every precaution taken to ensure the safety of those concerned.

Every so often the farmhouse garden may even need a periodic ridding of pests. Squirrels and magpies that come to a bird table are easy targets and need evicting if becoming troublesome. With you, the airgun hunter, around they won't be there for long and you'll earn yourself some brownie points with the boss.

There are a few tricks to shooting around farm buildings that have been detailed in the section devoted to the collared dove so all that was written there obviously applies here. Another tip though is when shooting around machinery; if resting your rifle on anything to steady your aim, take care not to knock the rifle on anything so as to cause any noise. In the early morning, metal-to-metal contact of an air reservoir, cylinder, barrel or silencer on the side of a tractor can be all that's needed to give your presence away. As for the birds that don't tumble off the roof but lodge in guttering, ask to borrow a ladder and get them down. There's nothing worse than leaving quarry in this situation as it'll cause blockages where it lodges, and the owners won't thank you for a blocked drainpipe should it wash into one after a downpour.

Shooting Near Livestock

Whether shooting indoors or outdoors, when faced with this form of shooting there are obvious safety aspects that need addressing. It certainly needs a degree of shooting discipline as there are many times, infuriating ones at that, when you'll need to hold off taking a shot because the quarry targeted is too close to livestock, or the backstop behind the target isn't safe. Whenever possible, always shoot away from livestock and try to avoid even shooting over the top of the animals. Obviously, there are times you'll need to shoot over them but use your commonsense and discretion. Don't ever drop your rifle too low and don't think you can skim over the animals. Upward angles are fine but, as always, consider the likelihood of ricochets. Animals in pens will be unpredictable, sometimes they'll stay put and at others walk to the far side of the pen. If they start getting too twitchy, stop shooting. Some animals, such as pigs, can be quite tolerant to you shooting near them, others not so. The farmer won't thank you for scaring his prize heifers or having his sheep constantly jumping around. Be sensible, and always think before you shoot.

Carrion Crow (Corvus Corone Corone)

Reputedly capable of living for up to 20 years, it's little wonder the crow is so wily and cautious as it has plenty of opportunity to learn that humans pose a major threat to its survival. It's undoubtedly got very keen eye-sight, which it uses to scan continually for feeding opportunities or danger, but don't discount the bird's uncanny ability to detect dead carrion. I'm not the only one of the belief that it does so ,due to an acute sense of smell. Seemingly the bird can home in on carrion not clearly visible from hundreds upon hundreds of yards away. Little wonder that baiting-down with a slit-open rabbit is so effective at drawing them to a shooting position.

The carrion crow is the largest of the corvids (crow family) that airgun hunters are legally allowed to shoot. With a large, thick-set stocky body, uniform blue/black plumage and a lighter, shiny black bill. Older birds look bedraggled and often have white feathers in their plumage. I've even seen all-white crows that couldn't be classed as albinos.

I'm sure most hunters have heard the saying 'lonesome crow.' Well, study the behavioural pattern of this corvid and you'll soon come to realise this is only partly true. Crows will gather, move, feed and roost in large numbers at various times of the year – especially after breeding in summer and in autumn into winter. Although generally it doesn't flock to nest, like

The carrion crow is the wiliest of the wily

its close relative the rook, it can sometimes be found nesting close to others of the same species, and on the outer limits of large rookeries, but by and large, when breeding, crows prefer their own space and both noisily and aggressively guard the territory around the nest.

Habitat

The carrion crow is at home over fields with a few trees as it is in dense woodland, moorland or even close to the seashore. At the shore it takes on characteristics more attributed to the familiar gull, beachcombing the estuary and sand flats for foodstuffs such as small crustaceans, lug and ragworm. This is one of the reasons it has been so successful in colonising areas and becoming so plentiful. It is just at home scavenging on an inland rubbish tip as it is in the woods, over farmland and on the coast. All but absent in Ireland, and not too common in parts of Scotland where it's replaced by the hooded crow (corvus cornix), it is nevertheless, widespread in the rest of the UK. Incidentally, whilst it was once supposed the 'hooded' was a sub-species of the 'carrion' it's now widely acknowledged that they're both species in their own right.

During late spring, unattached crows pair off (apparently staying together for life) and will then move regularly in pairs. During the colder months they cover quite a distance between feeding areas and the communal roost. Although it roosts in numbers, on the whole it can often appear to be quite solitary and at times single birds (hence the 'lonesome' saying) seem to wander lazily and aimlessly over the land, especially in the daylight hours of winter. In that respect, despite the obvious similarities, it is not like the rook. In fact its behavioural patterns ally more closely to the magpie than any other corvid. Indeed, it's quite common to see a few magpies moving around or feeding with a crow noisily bringing up the rear.

Having said that, when it comes to being with its own kind, the carrion crow does display a very complex social infra-structure, especially when large numbers descend to feed over fresh cut grass fields, cropland or amongst pasture land, used for the grazing of livestock in the summer months, and the behaviour of the crow is very much dictated by the seasons. For instance, large numbers can be seen in the company of jackdaws and rooks feeding over fields in summer. Similarly loose packs join up on their way back to roost, a place where once again the bird's complex social behaviour is very evident. Interestingly, it's believed that certain individuals take it upon themselves to act as sentries sitting on the outskirts of the roost or feeding area to watch out for any potential danger. I've noticed this and it does have some credence. It's also worth noting that when crows are found in small groups these gatherings are known as a murder of crows, and taking the birds loathsome nature, a very fitting term it is too.

Location and Behavioural Patterns

Look over the five-bar gate to the far fields where the sheep or cattle are grazing and the black dots strutting and pecking incessantly around are more often than not crows. Indeed, if there is one certainty, where there are sheep, you will always find crows, jackdaws and to some extent rooks. The stories told of crows sitting on the backs of a young sheep pecking at their eyes are based on some truth. Not only do they sit on sheep to peck at ticks and insects in the sheep's wool, but they'll also attack the new-borns, sick and weaky.

The birds will attack the lamb, first pecking out the eyes then attacking the soft flesh of the throat. Once the hapless lamb is debilitated to the degree that it cannot stand, the crow, singular or in groups, will descend to finish off the animal, pecking at any soft areas of flesh. They certainly seem to have a liking for the tongue. Needless to say, lambs or adult sheep that die by natural causes are absolute magnets to these birds.

It will, however, more readily kill and eat other small animals such as frogs, voles and even young rabbits, using its heavy, big black beak as a formidable instrument of doom, and whilst the crows' varied diet does consists of grain, seeds, worms and beetles, it will always prefer to take eggs, nestlings and gorge on carrion of any description - hence its name. It's not all carnage when they're next to livestock. They follow flocks of sheep around primarily to pick up anything edible that the grazing sheep might disturb. This is also the reason that they follow cattle.

Finding a roost isn't difficult either, as when evening starts to draw in they will come lazily flapping over the fields making a beeline straight to their communal roosting site. Hence the origin of the phrase: 'as the crow flies'.

During autumn, you can almost set your watch by them as they fly home to roost. If you're lucky enough to have a roost site on your shoot then you'll be in for some cracking crow action come the colder months when hundreds upon hundreds can often be found heading back to stay at the same roost. Be warned though, as the crow learns very quickly and seeing a few of its own tumble from the trees will soon cause it to rethink its sleeping arrangements, probably never to return to that area of the wood again.

Its feeding areas tend to be much less localised. In summer when the younger birds have paired off for the first time they establish and stick to their own definite territories.

When the crow is nesting, even if it hasn't as yet got chicks to raise, both adult birds still only tend to search for food within a few hundred yards or so of their nest site. This is quite a small territory but it serves the birds well at this time of the year.

Crows display very strong parental instincts towards their young during early summer. They feed them on the ground and show them how to feed; the young cawing incessantly for attention and food. The adults peck around the ground near the young bird encouraging it to do the same. The birds will frequently stop to preen the youngster eating the ticks that infest the bird's coarse, thick feathers, but this cosseting doesn't last long as the adults soon start to ignore the sibling, realising that it needs to become independent in order to survive.

When the young are reared, then they all wander far and wide and this is a time when most hunters can encounter them and attract them within range of a shooting position. A very productive time is late summer after the young crows have started to fly and follow the parents. Large flocks of adult and young birds can descend onto fields of barley, corn or flailed maize. They will also, like the woodpigeon, take advantage of flat spots caused by wind or rain. They can even flatten low growth areas and cause even more damage as they progressively tread down the crops as they eat out into the field. Find an area such as this and set up a suitable hide and you could well score yourself a couple of memorable sessions before the flock decides to move to safer feeding areas. In built-up areas, like the magpie and in some areas the jackdaw, it's found in and around human habitation. All scavengers know that they get easy pickings in these areas but obviously these are not the places for the hunter.

Methods to Use

For hunting this particular corvid you have quite a few options. Baiting-down, ambushing them from a hide next to a feeding area or an established sitty tree, or an opportunist shot when hiding up in or next to woodland awaiting squirrels or woodies. Forget trying to stalk up on the bird; it's the wariest of the wary even if in the trees, so stick to the methods outlined in full later in the book if you don't want to be ripping your camo gear off in frustration.

Like the magpie it's the early riser of the bird world. That means whether ambushing or baiting-down you need to be up well before dawn and in position to reap the rewards.

The daily nomadic scavenging nature of crows means they can crop up unexpectedly anywhere on your shoot – just one of the reasons an opportunist shot can always be a possibility.

The crow's scavenging and curious behavioural patterns can sometimes be its undoing. Often when using decoys to bring woodpigeon within range shooting in autumn over stubble fields, and especially if using a 'confidence crow deek' I've had crows drop down for a quick look. They don't stick around long but if you've downed a few woodies, you should be tuned in enough to sight in on the kill-zone and successfully take the shot. To bag a crow or two is always a true test of your fieldcraft, hunting and shooting skills. They don't call 'em 'crafty' for nothing you know!

Shooting Techniques Specific to Crows

During the summer into autumn, shooting crows over feeding areas can be very time consuming – specifically in relation to how long you need to wait in the hide between shooting spells. This can vary depending on how frequently the area has been shot. Now, whilst they come to fields holding sheep where they raid the creep feed troughs, they also like bovine company. Take advantage of this by setting a hide near an area of a cattle field they're known to frequent. They will systematically work over a field pecking through cow dung; this distasteful habit shows the carrion crow for what it is. The birds will appear from the roost to congregate in the tops of trees and on power lines and pylons adjacent to the field they intend to feed over. As if a switch has been turned, the birds will then land in the field in twos and threes, with a continuous flow of birds arriving and most, if not all, will land next to the birds already feeding. They'll be seen to land almost on top of one another seemingly looking to take the other bird's food and squabbling over the foodstuff found in that area. Slowly but surely, they'll work their way over within range but you need patience as sometimes this can take quite some time. Once the birds are within range, shoot the one that seems the most dominant; easily distinguished if there are younger more inexperienced birds near it. Once you've downed a crow the rest will take up to the sky, but more often than not, some birds can often hop over to peck at the downed bird whilst others wheel around in the sky cawing loudly from above. This affords another shot and if successful even more will come to harass the dead birds. While this can happen, alternatively, after maybe a minute, but it always seems a lot longer, the birds will eventually leave the area to sit high up in nearby trees or on power lines to survey the scene from a safe distance.

From here they'll eventually return – hopefully for you to pick more from the flock. In fact, if you shoot with a partner it can be very productive for one shooter to be positioned hidden at the side of the wood, within striking distance of the sitty trees and one in a hide adjacent to the field they're feeding over. This can often keep them moving but they don't fall for this trick too many times before feeding on safer areas or infuriatingly coming down to feed again but always keeping out of range.

At times, action can be hectic as you knock one crow over, then another. A magpie might zoom in as if from nowhere to stand stock still next to a dead crow. This peculiar behaviour is only displayed by members of the corvid family, but is certainly one that the airgun hunter should be aware of so as to take advantage when it presents itself.

As fast as the birds are seemingly oblivious to danger and preoccupied behaving in this uncharacteristically reckless manner, one shot more can see the birds vanish to safety. In this and other situations it seems that corvids, and I specifically include the crow, rook and jackdaw, all display a very complex pattern of social interaction. One minute they will squabble over the feeding area but quickly establish a pecking order, and the next, it can appear to be a mass free-for-all during which the shooter should take advantage of this confusion. After many, many years spent watching and shooting all the black corvids, I reckon there's still a lot to learn of their complex behavioural patterns.

Calibres and Kill-Zones

The main kill-zones on this wily old bird have to be the head or heart/lung shot. When possible take a side-on head shot or full-on neck to upper chest shot. If the angle presents itself, a slug in the base of the back of the skull is equally effective. One of the traits the bird shares with other corvids is, when sensing danger it will turn around showing its back, while looking over its shoulder, usually just before it flies up and away. It's at this point you have a chance of the deadly kill shot into the back of the neck and between the shoulder blades. If shooting from below, slipping a pellet up into either side of the bird's upper chest under the wing fold will find another weak spot. It has little protection here at the chest under those heavy wings.

Some say .22 only but place a .177 or .20 in these kill-zones and it's goodnight Vienna for this crafty corvid. When using hi-power air rifles, the same alternative kill-zones apply as outlined earlier in full for the woodie.

Jackdaw (Corvus Monedula)

Of all the quarry species airgun hunters are legally allowed to shoot, the jackdaw must surely rate amongst one of the most intriguing, with that grey neck-cape giving them a look of a balaclava-clad burglar ready to get up to no good. Despite its noisy, troublesome behaviour the jackdaw is quite a pretty bird with its glossy black plumage, grey neck and head feathers and when seen close up you can't fail to be charmed by the pale blue iris of the bird's very keen eye. Their 'coughing' call is quite unique to this bird, seemingly being an alarm call as well as a call for general location and contact between individuals. This metallic 'tchak' or intermittent 'tcha-ak' sounding call usually heralds the bird's arrival on the scene but equally if being cautious it can almost appear as if from nowhere. Being one of the smallest of the corvid family, when keeping quiet, they're equally expert at unobtrusively going about their daily routines, but during the breeding season, especially during the mornings or evenings the birds can put on fascinating, acrobatic aerial displays as they fly, flit, glide and soar, twisting this way and that around a church spire, or high above a group of tall trees on the wood's edge.

The jackdaw is a very intriguing bird

Habitat

Jackdaws are nomadic in nature but will flock readily with their own. Primarily a bird of woodland it ventures out to feed and in many areas to breed. This is when the jackdaw often presents itself as a problem when nesting in buildings in rural areas – doubly so if they've taken to regularly visiting farms with livestock and large outbuildings. When near human habitation, the jackdaw's fondness for nesting in dark crevices often has them nesting in chimneys or ventilation outlets of houses. This means they are a potential fire hazard not forgetting the raucous racket they make eventually having the most tolerant of homeowners in despair. In fact, in many rural areas, the chimney outlet is covered with mesh to prevent birds nesting. Church spires often have ledge spikes installed by professional pest control companies, primarily to prevent the intrusion into the holy building from feral pigeon. Unfortunately, the smaller jackdaw can easily slip through these and sometimes they actually use them to secure their untidy bulky nest to the building.

Although all viable hunting methods are discussed later, I must make mention here of the correct procedure for dealing with a situation where a pair or group of birds are nesting in an urban or rural dwelling. It must be stipulated that even on a one-off localised house shoot you need the property owner's written permission. Targeting them in these situations isn't difficult as long as you adhere to a few basic rules of safety. Firstly, ensure no stray pellets leave the area you're shooting in, which by and large can be a medium to even a large estate garden. Also, be thoughtful to the neighbours. Without fail, go around the houses that overlook the property or those nearby to let them know the situation. This has not only assured the people that all is above board and safe but can also even gain the responsible airgunner a few extra jobs. These can range from dealing with pesky squirrels to eviction orders placed on other unwanted neighbouring jackdaws and magpies.

In respect of problems for the crop farmer, they cause damage to newly planted cereals but they have to be present in large numbers. Like crows, they're drawn to the presence of sheep; not only in the fields, but also where the sheep are fed on sheep pellets the jackdaws can acquire a taste for this high protein foodstuff. It's not uncommon for the birds, by learned behaviour, to know when the feed is being put out and be there ready and waiting to descend suddenly to steal the amount they need. They'll also invade the farm outbuildings if the sheep are inside at lambing, and if left to their own devices will swarm over the sheep pens picking at anything that looks even remotely edible.

Location and Behavioural Patterns

An unfussy feeder you'll find jackdaws anywhere they can find food. Scavenging for scraps around picnic tables, walking amongst pedestrians in

Pairs and even small flocks of jackdaws can put on fascinating acrobatic aerial displays

the rural areas picking over fast food leftovers, or out in the country – hanging around the creep feed troughs in sheep fields – yes, they know where life is easy. That's why when they find a free meal, they'll regularly come back to it.

Locating the roost sites around buildings is simple as you only need find the white splashings familiar to all roosting birds. It applies to some extent for woodland roosts but these are more readily found by observation in the evening. The birds coughing call rings out over the fields as they fly into the woods to flock tightly together in chosen trees. Roosts can be well established, deeper in the woods than a woodpigeon's and often shared with crows, but as with other roosting birds, once disturbed by shooting they'll very quickly move to a safer area.

Come the spring and jackdaws are easily located due to their untidy nest building. Underneath a church spire, house roof space or tree with dense foliage you'll find thick twigs and sheep wool littering the ground; the two main materials the bird uses to build its very bulky home. In areas near human habitation, the nest is also padded out with any manner of litter it can find in the area, such as bits of plastic, crisp packets, bits of cloth – the jackdaw isn't house-proud.

Although the birds pair off for breeding, and to some extent nest alone, they will often be found in localised groups. Unlike the crow, seemingly no dominant birds have a specific territory, rather they share the feeding areas around them and seem to communicate and move as a flock especially after breeding and when out feeding when the juvenile birds boost the group these can number considerably.

They feed liberally amongst other corvids, particularly rooks and crows. It's also not uncommon to see them feeding over pasture with woodies and even starlings.

Methods to Use

The time to target jackdaws, like other members of the crow family is in the spring as they prepare for, or are actually raising young. However, the sport with the birds in jackdaw plague areas can last all year around and once you've found areas the birds regularly visit to feed you can be sure of some satisfying yet challenging shooting. If the jackdaws are visiting these feeding stations, whether outside or inside buildings, you need to be in position and shooting from a hidden position, or if outside using a hide, wearing full camo clothing and using all and any natural cover that's available. The birds will noisily arrive very early in the morning in large flocks to initially gather on sitty areas close to the source of food before dropping down to dine. Then they'll leave to return sporadically throughout the day in twos, threes or fours.

Not all the birds will disappear over the fields or back into the woods after the early morning feeding raids. In fact, even during the hottest of summer days a steady but dwindling procession will visit the area throughout the day. By mid-afternoon the birds will usually show up very infrequently, and when they do, it'll be in very small groups.

Outside, you need to wear full camo wear, and if there is any hedge cover to shoot from, use this or alternatively erect a hide near the sitty area. Small, portable, pop-up hides are great for quick concealment at times and in situations such as this. When shooting in this manner, better to have the birds come in small numbers, especially pairs as often you can shoot one from the sitty area or feed trough, whilst the other will at first fly up but circle around the area calling down to the fallen bird. Sometimes it will land on the sitty area, which will be high structures such as telegraph poles, overhead wires, rooftops etc., still calling to its mate. The second bird will only land briefly to survey the scene below before flying off, rarely if ever landing near the shot bird, as can be the case with crows or magpies. If the second bird is going to land, it will almost certainly land up aloft so keep your eye on the circling jake, while keeping your rifle raised towards the area you expect it to land. The reason being, in this agitated state it won't tolerate the sight of any movement on the ground, so as soon as it folds its wings to land you want to have the muzzle pointed in the general direction, positioned so as to be able just to take aim carefully and shoot.

Roost shooting isn't as profitable due to the shorter time slot you have to shoot them and their intolerance of intrusion when disturbed, but again, this is an area where they can be targeted.

Calibres and Kill-Zones

Like the jay and magpie this is a relatively small bird, therefore the kill-zones are equally small. Any popular calibre placed with precision into the head or upper chest cavity will see it cleanly dispatched. The chest shot will be most practical as the bird hardly keeps its head still, constantly searching this way and that for something of interest to see or find. If shooting when they've entered a building then all safety aspects (dealt with in the relevant section pertaining to indoor shooting) apply. It's the same for when shooting near livestock.

Jay (Garrulus Glandarius)

It's debatable whether the jay should even be on the airgun hunters hit list as it's not nearly as common as it once was in many parts of the country, but as it's deemed legal vermin for control with the air rifle, and considered one of the main target species, it warrants inclusion here in Quarry Files. Personally, I rarely shoot these birds but I presume it's been tagged as vermin on the list for pest control because of its somewhat tenuous links to the rest of its relatives in the corvid family, but rather than preach my own belief, I'll say the decision to shoot this species is best left up to the individual.

Originally, there's little doubt, the bird was targeted for its plumage which was used for decorating hats, and still is used for the making of fishing flies for sea trout. A pity its coat of many colours then has put it in our sights, but it does cause some upset in a habitat where it is in over-abundance.

However, the bird's beautifully coloured plumage belies the fact that it's a member of the corvid family at all; so unique that it's hard to describe the bird with its almost peach/pink, brown-coloured body, white bib, with thick black stripes leading from each side of its beak. The wings are the most prized for fly tying, with the striking blue side flashes with white patches and black wing trims and broad black tail feathers.

The jay – a technicoloured corvid

Habitat

Found in both broad-leaved and coniferous woodland there's no doubt the jay is at home in the heart of the wood. Now resident throughout the UK except in Northern Scotland it rarely leaves the protection of the trees. It favours established oak woods but is equally at home around beech and hornbeam woods.

In the areas these habitats are being reduced it will then move into suburban parks and gardens. Interestingly, the resident population figures fluctuate quite wildly because at times, large numbers of Central European jays migrate here during early autumn.

Location and Behavioural Patterns

A shy and cautious bird, the jay must surely be one of the most difficult quarry species to find intentionally. In summer, you'll most likely only hear its harsh screeching call as it sweeps through a glade, or alternatively, in autumn through winter, you can often see them flying in their characteristic bouncy fashion across your path with an acorn in their beak. Like the squirrel, in autumn the jay will bury acorns for retrieval later when food is getting scarce. Obviously, they don't remember where every one is, so the upside for the natural environment, is that the jay is one, if not the most important, natural planters of acorns, and therefore helping to conserve and distribute natural oak woodland. This, in itself, leads to why in some areas the jay is best left to its own devices.

Even though it's so colourful, a jay can miraculously disappear in a tree, even one with sparse foliage. Whilst it will steal the eggs of small finches and songbirds, it's nowhere near as bad as the magpie. It can easily thrive without thieving and pillaging due to its love of acorns, hazelnuts, beech mast, seeds and insects.

Methods to Use

Of all species the jay is probably only ever going to be encountered while opportunist shooting and wood-walking. Whilst at times quite nomadic, make note of an area you see jays frequenting as the bird is very territorial and staid in its ways, staying within its own territory to feed and breed. During the breeding season it can be annoyed with a little owl decoy placed within its territory. Be in position and it could well show itself for a clear shot.

Alternatively, at other times of the year due to their habit of carrying off food to bury, you can wait around these areas and pick them off as they go about their business. In fact, when feeding, they often carry food in their beak up to a favourite tree branch to pick out the kernels. Again, locate one of these through very dedicated and careful observation and this can be an area to wait in ambush for that lone solitary bird.

As this is a very shy but busy bird, the first indication a hunter has that a jay is close by is often only when the technicoloured corvid flies past to disappear into the trees and foliage.

In winter, this gives the bird away and those who are quick and keen of eye can watch the bird land amongst branches then flit upwards until flying on, hardly before pausing for breath. Jays hardly keep still. This is the main reason this bird is so hard to target. Also, it has the uncanny habit of keeping twigs and branches in between you and it.

In spring and summer, the only time you get to take a shot is when it pops its head up above the leaves to take a look around before flying off. In fact, truth be known, hunters targeting squirrels deep in the woods will often be the ones who encounter most jays.

Calibres and Kill-Zones

As this is a relatively fragile and small bird; the same kill-zones apply as with the jackdaw and magpie, as do calibres. If you do shoot these birds, at least know someone who will use the feathers for fly-tying or a retailer who will take them off your hands for this purpose.

The Magpie (Pica Pica)

The most notorious of the corvids, the magpie can't be mistaken for any other bird native to the British Isles. With its iridescent blue/black and white plumage, long narrow wedge shape tail and raucous call, it is bold, brash but very wary. Like other members of the crow family, landowners and gamekeepers persecute it due to its fondness for the eggs of game birds. Equally, it can totally decimate the songbird population of an area that it is becoming a nuisance in. However, a born survivor, it'll just as happily feed on grain, seeds and insects which in actuality at certain times of the year make up the greater part of its diet.

There's no disputing the fact that the magpie is undoubtedly a nest raider, taking eggs as well as chicks of all species. This behaviour is thought to be the reason it builds its own nest as a doomed roof structure so birds flying over cannot see into it, but that doesn't mean it's totally safe as I've personally witnessed other magpies invade and plunder another magpie's nest.

The 'maggie' is widely credited with hoarding food, and to taking a liking to shiny objects. Again, this is largely based on truth. In old England, the bird was known as the 'maggot pie'. Supposedly, maggot alludes to the name Margaret and pie is derived from pied, an allusion to its black and white plumage. For the airgun hunter this bird will, at times, test your fieldcraft skills to the full, not to mention your patience to the limit.

Habitat

In recent years the magpie, like the fox, has adapted well to urban existence, and is a common sight around housing estates as well as city-centre parks and gardens. In its natural habitat of deciduous woodland and hedgerows, it's perfectly designed to prey on the weaker, smaller inhabitants. It is active throughout the year, but will retreat into woodland in harsh winters and come the breeding season in spring into early summer, will haunt the bushes and hedgerows that surround the woods. The magpie is most commonly found moving around areas in a seemingly non-stop search for food in small and even quite large groups. The latter gatherings are more commonly seen in winter, when like its relative the carrion crow

The magpie is a notorious egg thief

it can flock with its own kind or mingle in with crows to feed over grain fields. The birds will eventually pair off to breed, which can be as soon as late January when they start to build, return to repair old nests or take over nests of others. The usual breeding and laying takes place in April or May.

As mentioned before, the magpie will eat virtually everything and anything, be it animal or vegetable, and although predominantly a scavenger, it will, like the crow, kill its own prey when the need arises. Chicks of song and game birds present no difficulty, but on rare occasions, a pack of them has been known to kill a young rabbit.

As for an agricultural pest it can be a nightmare. Although it isn't a problem over cereal crops, the time it really causes damage is at baling time. When the bales are wrapped in black plastic, in many areas the farmers need to get these off the fields as quickly as possible because the magpie, and to a lesser extent the crow, will peck holes in the covering thus allowing the elements in to spoil the hay. It's presumed that the bird sees its reflection in the black shiny plastic and attacks it. As it makes a hole in one area, as soon as it catches sight of its reflection in another, it pecks at this. As both birds are very territorial this explanation seems a very valid one. Either way, the magpie, like the crow, is a major pest species that needs to be kept under control.

Location and Behavioural Patterns

Finding magpies is an easy task. Not only are they highly visible birds when moving but also they can initially betray their presence by their distinctive 'chack, chack, chack' alarm call. When caught out in the open or suddenly alarmed the response from the bird is usually a noisy one. However, in wooded areas, they are more likely to slip silently from tree to tree. The magpie is very sharp-eyed and will not stick around long, especially if it suspects even the slightest hint of danger. This, coupled with its preference for sitting high up in trees to survey the surrounding area, makes it almost impossible to sneak up on. In fact the birds have favoured sitty trees or areas in trees where they can regularly be found watching. If you're patient and know these areas you can hide up in ambush but it's still not the easiest of ways to target this corvid.

Nests are easy to find and are usually returned to year after year. These bulky, domed structures are sometimes taken over in winter by squirrels and a fair kerfuffle can be heard and seen whenever the twain shall meet.

Methods to Use

The two main methods of dealing with magpies are wood-walking and the more effective and dedicated method of baiting-down. Both these techniques will be outlined in full in the relevant chapters, but it's worth noting that as with all hunting methods, prior knowledge of the area to be shot over can pay handsome dividends. The birds will more often than not be active at set times of the day, and being in position at the right time can save hours of fruitless searching or waiting. Birds of a certain area will tend to have localised feeding spots and routes to and from them. Indeed, as the woodpigeon establishes a flight line, more often than not you'll find magpies seem to use the same route as each other. Sometimes birds will follow other birds in five to ten minute intervals. Some naturalists presume they're birds from the same brood but whatever it is, they're definitely moving and searching around in the same areas as a form of connected team. However, as the corvid is a scavenger it can stop off anywhere it sees that may provide a likely source of food, whichh is one of the reasons that baiting-down is so effective. Like the crow, the magpie is definitely one of the earliest risers of all flying quarry species. They are often active on the shoot a good half hour or more before dawn breaks, starting their scavenging activities, looking for leftovers from other predators from the night before. Also, some believe they're active so early because it gives them the opportunity to search out nests to raid, as sitting female birds or fledglings calling out to males for food are easier to hear at this time. Whichever it is, if targeting these wary adversaries you need to be out on the shoot or even in position if baiting-down at least an hour before sunrise.

The black 'n white terror has a varied selection of calls from the familiar chack, chack, chack call to the chattering, cackling call not dissimilar to the sound a box of matches makes when being quickly shaken. Indeed some use the rattling box of matches trick to entice or annoy the bird within range, but as for the bird itself, like any other clever scavenger, they can when they prefer be silent and quite discreet in their movements.

Calibres and Kill-Zones

The calibres .177 and .22 including .20 are suitable for dealing with this crafty corvid, and in most situations, to cleanly dispatch the bird you have two choices of kill-zone – depending on its attitude to your shooting position. If it presents itself side-on then a head shot or just forward of the wing fold will give an instant kill. But like all corvids it rarely stays still and the head shot is a very small kill-zone. Alternatively, a full-on chest shot in the upper chest cavity is my preferred area of pellet placement and deadly effective

Though they don't have an overly strong breastbone, care should still be taken in placing this shot accurately. It's easy to see where the shot should go as you can't fail to see the bird's large black bib extending from head and neck down to end approximately mid-point on the chest area. Directly below, you'll clearly see the bird's strong muscular legs as there's a clear defined line that centres down from the bib. I mention this to illustrate that anything below the bib is a wounding shot, ideally half an inch up into the black of the bib in the chest is straight into the heart and lungs. Another fragile area on the bird is from the back and like other corvids this is a position it often adopts when alighting in an area it isn't too sure of. It puts its back to potential danger, but with its keen eyes watching around and behind. This is so it can fly off in the blink of an eye, or if on the ground hop quickly away in the opposite direction. Little does it know, again like other corvids, that it's offering its weakest spot. A well-placed pellet into the base of the neck, between the shoulder blades to even approximately an inch down its upper back will quite literally break its back and result in a clean kill. This is quite a large kill-zone for such a deceptively small but fragile-framed corvid and a superb kill-zone for any other flying felon.

On the subject of size; the magpie isn't much bigger than a blackbird. Like other feathered predators, it belies its size by fluffing out its plumage and sitting bolt upright.

Rook (Corvus Frugilegus)

Few sights or sounds so epitomise the traditional view of the British countryside than the raucous activity that surrounds an established rookery set in a lush woodland setting. High in the treetops, large bulky nests of twigs can at times seem almost to merge into one because of their close proximity, while great black birds circle high above the treetops cawing incessantly to each other. This rural scenario even extends to the old traditional country recipe for the dubious culinary delights of rook pie. There can't be many more birds that have steeped themselves so firmly into our countryside's heritage and lore. Whilst crows and magpies are treated with the disdain they so rightly deserve, the rook seems to have slipped through the cracks to earn the airgun hunter's respect. It's a clever, almost noble-looking bird with purple-black glossy feathers and that characteristic grey white bill. Contrary to popular belief, the bird is actually a tad smaller than the carrion crow, and arguably much less gregarious in nature. Its cawing is also of a higher pitch than the crow and it seems to have a much wider range of calls.

Habitat

The rook is a bird of the wood – only leaving the sanctity of the rookery to search the fields for food. Deciduous woodland with farmed cereal fields lying on the outskirts makes for a prime rook environment. An extremely social bird, it nests in the colonies known as rookeries. Some can number over a hundred nests, but in each season a lot will

The rook is a noisy but noble looking bird

be uninhabited, although on record there are some absolutely astronomical examples. One rookery in Scotland was once reputed to be home to nine thousand pairs of birds! Now that's what I call communal accommodation.

Although the rook is extremely sociable, with its own kind, living in such large numbers, and in such close proximity, it still defends the small territory around its own bulky dwelling. In fact, this communal life is so well developed that it has given rise to fanciful stories of 'rook parliaments'. It was once actually believed that if one bird in the rookery had been, for want of a better phrase, out of order in some way then the others would sit in judgement and dish out appropriate justice.

Although responsible for attacking freshly sown fields when it digs up shoots and seeds, not all the rook's activities are harmful to the farmer's livelihood. Due to its taste for leatherjackets (crane fly larvae) and wireworms, it can serve a very useful purpose, but like all other members of the corvid family it'll pretty much eat anything, and this is the major problem. Unfortunately, like crows, they batter down the stems of growing corn and barley with their wings or simply land and walk forward primarily to get at the grain and seeds, but the flattening damage to the crop left uneaten means it can't be picked up by the combine harvester. Over fields they dig around for worms and larvae and scavenge for the eggs of nesting ground birds. They're also attracted down to freshly-cut grass fields; ploughed crop fields, and areas with an abundance of molehills showing can attract birds on a regular basis.

Why, you ask, have I not mentioned carrion as part of their diet? Well, although it does eat carrion, it isn't as keen on meat as its other close true carnivorous flesh-eating relatives.

Location and Behavioural Patterns

Most deciduous woodland will have a rookery or two; so established woodland especially with tall oak, birch or yew trees is the place to look. Finding a rookery is easy. If the birds don't give themselves away with their non-stop cawing, then sooner or later, walking through a wood scanning the tree tops, you'll spot those big, bulky, untidily built nests that the birds return to year after year. In winter the rookery can be an eerie place with all the blobs of nests dotted above you, and an uncharacteristic silence as the birds are feeding elsewhere. In fact, by midsummer, once the young rooks have left the nests, the birds form into huge flocks and leave. They usually roost in another location but in some parts of the country, as early as January, the birds start to return to the rookeries. At first they tend to use the trees nearby as sitty trees as if getting used to the area again. Then in preparation for breeding they start to repair or rebuild a nest for the season's brood. This can be a clutch of up to five eggs, and are laid so that the fledglings don't all hatch together. This way, more are likely to be able to go on to survive – unless you're there to knock them from the trees.

The rookery in winter can be an eerie place

Methods to Use

Methods for hunting rooks aren't as simple as those for other corvids, such as baiting-down. You can find very few birds opportunist shooting as you 'wood-walk' but more likely and more traditional amongst the shooting fraternities of all disciplines, the main method for controlling population numbers is what is known as brancher shooting.

Brancher shooting takes place around the first couple of weeks in May. For some reason, certain country folk like to pin this down to a specific day, that being May 12th. Well, we all have out little foibles, but whatever you term it or date it, brancher shooting is a very short season. To be there at the right time you need to keep a close eye on the rookery so as to take advantage of the young rooks clumsily emerging to hop about near the nest, but, it's widely recognised as the only worthwhile method of curtailing their numbers. Before we deal with that tried and trusted method, I'll explain my previous declaration as to why the rook doesn't fall to the usual corvid curtailing techniques.

Of all the corvids (jay excluded), the rook has the keenest of eyesight, and that's saying something, as all the corvids seem to have bionic 20/20 vision on the worst of days. However, whereas a magpie's curiosity will sometimes get him nailed, the rook will never be so foolish. Also, although you'll regularly see them feeding over fields in summer, autumn and winter you'll often not get within a bazooka's distance of them.

If you're fortunate to get on to land where they haven't been shot at, you could well bag a few before they give the area a wide berth. This can also apply to when the rooks are sitting tight near the rookery early in the year. Again, you'll only have a few chances before they immediately fly up on your approach and not settling at all, unless sitting atop a nest out of sight.

Suffice to say, the rook is a crafty and very challenging adversary for the airgun hunter. However, don't let me mislead you into thinking it has got supernatural powers. It has not. Like any living creature it does have to sleep, so yes, what would we do without the chance of roost shooting? Even then you'll only get the chance of a few shots and only a few sessions before they move on to roost elsewhere in the wood or maybe even a wood in the distance.

In fact, it's worth me relating a couple of behavioural patterns of rooks when at the rookery that makes them so difficult to target even when repairing nests and, indeed, when roosting there.

Firstly, all the birds are seemingly constantly wheeling over the area, never still except for some which will be sitting on the uppermost branches, as high as possible, and amongst a labyrinth of potential pellet-deflecting twigs. You'll rarely see adult rooks sitting low in the trees or in plain sight. They're far too clever and wary to make that mistake.

When the birds are actually back roosting at the rookery, depending on the season they'll only come back late so the light is all but gone by the time the main body of birds arrive. Also, such is their cleverness and wariness of character that as the birds fly in droves into the rookery, virtually all will land in the top of the single tallest tree giving them the best view of the rookery. Even here they're on their guard, the treetops black with hundreds upon hundreds of rooks. This would be the shooters' only chance of a shot when they're behaving in this manner, as after the birds are satisfied that the area is safe, and as if given an order, they then split up and spread out throughout the rookery to sit out the night in the security of either the nest they're re-building or a handy abandoned one. Within minutes, hundreds of birds can disappear into the bulky structures leaving the rookery as quiet as the grave. Once in the nest, no amount of normal activity on the woodland floor will spook them out until they're ready to rise before dawn to repeat the season's particular routine. This can be to leave the rookery to wander around and feed, or to establish with mates in the mating ritual, and rebuilding and re-establishing their position in the colony high in the trees.

I'm sure you're now beginning to see why shooting the young birds (branchers) in spring is the most practical hunting method. Basically, if you've done your homework you'll know the time and place to employ this tactic. So how do you tackle it?

Brancher Shooting

When the young rooks first leave the nest, taking their first clumsy steps onto the branches, as the name implies they hang around the nest on the surrounding branches. That's why they get the nickname of 'branchers', and while in this fairly vulnerable position, they're sitting ducks for the shooter below. Although we have a yardstick, the brancher season can actually start sometimes as early as the end of April into mid-May, depending on which part of the country you live in and how the year's weather conditions have affected the colony during the early part of spring.

The only reliable method to catch the branchers napping, as it were, is to keep a regular watch on the rookery at this crucial time. Only then will you be ready for the young, inexperienced birds' emergence. Don't get the impression that's it's overly easy though, as the shots are often very challenging. After shooting you'll have a crick in your back and a pain in the neck from continually looking upwards, but done correctly, brancher shooting is by far the only effective method of keeping the rooks' numbers in check.

Though some might scoff – I recommend that you wear full camo with gloves and facemask. Anything that helps you blend in below is a useful aid and don't go crashing about in the undergrowth beneath the rookery as you shift shooting position. It will keep the birds twitchy and have adults less likely to settle back. They'll constantly be calling an 'intruder alert' which the young rooks take heed of.

Shooting upwards at awkward angles is difficult at the best of times, but couple this with the fact that the type of trees the rook inhabits means the twigs are plentiful, and starting to bud and sprouting leaves makes it even harder. There's plenty of opportunity for a pellet to get deflected off a branch or twig on its way to the target, so always be aware of this and place your shot carefully. A recoilless multi-shot PCP air rifle will be a godsend as you can rest the rifle on the side of a tree trunk to steady your aim and there is no need to keep loading after each and every shot. Choose a rifle you can shoulder easily and one that won't be too straining to lift up. Also, as you begin shooting, the adults will noisily take up, with the branchers scrabbling to higher branches or clumsily hopping back into the nest. There often can be relatively long periods when you can't find a target, so rest by sitting down for a while until things settle, which they eventually will. Even take shots from this seated position; it's much easier on the back muscles and a steadier hold and aim can often be achieved

A tried and time-tested method, but it's certainly not as easy as you might think.

Calibres and Kill-Zones

As with the crow, it's often said that the prime kill-zone is the head. This is usually credited to the fact the bird has a strong breastbone (keel) easily capable of deflecting a pellet, so head shots should be the name of the brancher and rook shooting game. After much hunting experience this is yet another myth that I feel can be dispelled. Whilst the crow and rook have fearsome, solid, heavy-duty beaks for smashing young fledglings and digging around in the ground their skeletal make-up is nowhere near as robust as the head and beak. The skull of a corvid is reinforced and is certainly thick to accommodate the proportionately large heavy bill, but the chest bone is only as strong as a bird of a similar size such as the woodpigeon. Its ribs being just as prone to damage, so heart and lung shots can be taken if the bird presents itself at the correct angle. Obviously a pellet will deflect off a heavy bone such as the central chest bone or keel. Look under those heavy wings of the corvid and there's a lot of flimsy unprotected flesh. Place a pellet of any calibre up into the chest area of these birds and it will result in a clean kill so don't be fooled into thinking you only need try for a head shot.

So whilst the rook is a quarry species to have on your list for spring, and the chance to shoot it as a brancher short, you will encounter adults atop trees.

While we're now at the end of Quarry Files, I'll just reiterate that although an FAC rifle shouldn't ever be thought of as a tool for getting longer range, what it can do is give you less to worry over with awkward angle shots and trajectory allowances. When the birds are high, and you're taking these shots then this is certainly a case where the hunter shooting an FAC-rated air rifle could get the chance at shots which hunters using a 12ft lb air rifle couldn't dream of attempting. Look to the same kill-zone areas mentioned for the woodpigeon in relation to using a hi-power air rifle.

Other Species

Before the Quarry File is fully closed, I feel I should briefly take a look at what other species are legally classed as vermin and still deemed suitable for air rifle. The reason I feel they should be dealt with in this way is due to the fact that you may encounter them as you go about your shoot and might be asked to deal with them when and where appropriate. Although there's a specific section at the end of the book detailing the law pertaining to airgun use as it currently stands, it's still worth a few cautionary words to the wise on the subject, in relation to your shooting and the land you hunt over.

Responsible Attitudes

Firstly, remember that we are only allowed to hunt any species because permission is granted to us by the powers that be; in other words, it can just as easily be taken away from us. As a responsible airgun hunter this should always be at the forefront of your mind and while out in the field we should all act accordingly. Just one stupid reported incident or action could have serious repercussions, not only for the perpetrator, but also for the whole of the sport.

It's easy to fall foul of the law inadvertently while out hunting. For instance, you can get so engrossed in stalking that you stray 'out of bounds', as it were.

Always – repeat always – keep aware of the possibility of others in your vicinity. Whilst you may know the boundaries of your shoot, ramblers and the dreaded inconsiderate dog walker can have the nasty habit of appearing as if from nowhere. I'm sure others have experienced this. A pellet will travel with sufficient energy in flight to inflict possible serious injury for up to 200 yards or more, and that's from a 12ft lb air rifle. Before you shoot at anything, carefully consider where a missed shot might go. If shooting around buildings, that's a usual worry, but in the open fields are you sure the hedge line is thick enough to stop the shot, or is it so sparse that a pellet can fly straight through?

Know the footpaths and rights of way across the land you shoot. Although some may hardly, if ever, be used, there's always the possibility that they will at some time attract the walker. With the 'public right of way' law, even I'm surprised at areas being opened up that I presumed closed indefinitely to unauthorised persons. In that respect, even if shooting in your allotted area you can still technically commit an offence if you are shooting within 50 feet of a public footpath, roadway, bridlepath etc, and there is the current mentality of the non-shooting public to think that a man with a gun is up to no good, especially if clad head to foot in camo!

One of the major reasons that DPM camo first fell out of favour was due to incidents giving this attire and 'look' a bad public image. In turn, this tarnished those who were seen wearing it, but in part, we can be thankful that this helped to inspire the wider acceptance of the new-era, non-aggressive camo patterns most airgun hunters now use.

On the subject of the general public, and the fact that they might just appear on your shoot, my own personal code is a simple one: If I can see another person, in any direction from my shooting position, I don't shoot. This applies to anybody who might not know who I am, what I'm up to and why. In fact, I'll lower the gun and wait for them to pass, then phone the farmer to enquire who is on that part of the land. It could be a disoriented walker but also maybe even a poacher.

Fur and Feather

Of the eleven quarry species fully detailed in the previous pages, you can of course add a few other birds and animals to this list depending on time of year (season) and status of both yourself and the situation you find yourself operating under.

Vermin such as the mustelids, including weasels, stoats and the mink, are also animals that can be dealt with by air rifle hunters, but, despite the times, wherein non-thinking, animal rights activists free mink from farms, they're still generally not a common sight. However, when they do emerge over an area it can be very localised and their presence felt very suddenly.

Mink are best left to be managed by a dedicated trapping campaign

Usually, a well thought out and deployed trapping campaign sorts these vicious destructors, but if caught in live catch traps, the air rifle is the tool for dispatching them humanely. To hunt them is very, very challenging and more often than not will prove a pointless exercise. I have shot mink, but in over 20 years probably not enough to make a decent hat!

The airgun hunter is also allowed to shoot the hare which I've made brief mention of in the chapter on Changing Seasons. Even so, it's a point of contention if the 12ft lb air rifle is up to the job in hand. Personally, it's one to consider with an FAC rifle, but largely best left to the rimfire shooters and shotgunners. In fact the hare isn't as common as it once was in many areas, so the hunter will have to use his discretion, but consider this; anatomically the skull of a hare is much stronger and thicker in bone than a rabbit's. Not only that, but the chest area is also generally covered in a thickish layer of fat and of course muscle; body shots therefore being out of the question to responsible airgun hunters.

Waterfowl

Most hunters don't realise you're also allowed to shoot both moorhen and coot. Many might not consider these waterfowl suitable airgun quarry, but they are a legitimate species, when in season. These closely-related water birds come under the Game Laws which means the close season is from February 1st to August 31st. This allows them, like game birds, to nest and breed unhindered. This 'royal' pardon is strange as they were originally shot in truckloads by river keepers as vermin, due to the damage they do to nesting ducks. The coot will rob ducks' nests and even kill the young. Some say it's aggressiveness, other say it's because they are competing in the same territory with the more timid duck, and in comparison, though slightly smaller than an average mallard duck, coots are very aggressive and territorial. Just watch the birds in the breeding season – 'mad as a coot' – no surprise why that saying came about! Interestingly, of these two birds, the moorhen does venture into the fields and meadows to feed in winter, especially over waterlogged areas.

You'll often see them in moderately-sized groups of four or five, scavenging over muddy ground. This is when one might just well present you with an opportunist shot; head- or full-on breast shots being suitable for both species.

I'm reliably informed that coots and moorhen can be quite tasty, and the dish is still a favourite in parts of the Norfolk Fens. So maybe this is why they originally became classed as game? If this has sparked your interest in these birds, bear in mind that they are mainly only ever found on or near water. If you do have a duck pond or some such waterway running through your shoot, then do take precautions when shooting around water. Specifically, be aware of the risk of ricochet from the water's surface.

In some parts of the country waterfowl such as the coot is considered a tasty dish. And when in season lawful quarry for the airgun hunter

Real Game

While the law doesn't stipulate that game birds such as partridge, pheasant and grouse or some species of duck can only be shot with the shotgun, many feel the airgun hunter partaking in the shoot is little more than a poacher. The reason for the 'unsporting' label is certainly due to the fact that these game birds especially, aren't very clever while on the ground so offer little sporting challenge as a static shot. To take them on the wing with shotgun, flushed up by beaters and dogs, is the way to take on these birds as it does give them a sporting chance. If your shooting ground has wild pheasant, then ask the farmer, landowner or gamekeeper if you can take the odd one for the pot should you encounter it. This sensible attitude to the situation, shooting etiquette and commonsense will be duly noted and you'll probably be allowed to do so. A pheasant is a big, stocky bird and rather than get myself embroiled in controversy I'd say head shot only at medium range, but do ensure that you're not upsetting any shooting syndicate-linked apple carts.

As I've said way back in an earlier chapter, finding a shoot is the hardest hunting of all, and the easiest one to lose! If ever in the slightest doubt – don't risk it.

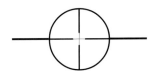

Hunting Techniques

The tactics and techniques you can employ when hunting with an air rifle are pretty much the same as they have been for years. However, as air rifles have become more accurate, and pre-charged pneumatics much more affordable certain hunting methods can be used that weren't viable in the past. Also let's thank the gods for the sound moderator (silencer) and of course multi-shot air rifles.

Even if you're a traditionalist, once you've been hunting a while you'll soon realise the benefits a 'multi' affords. Not only those extra-quick, back-up shots, but also the fact that you don't need to fiddle around to load a pellet for each shot. In that sense, and definitely from a personal perspective, I'm achieving results in my hunting I'd have never thought possible. But back to the matter in hand and techniques you can use to bag quarry.

Whilst there are many variants, no matter which method you employ it will fall into the major classifications of either active or sedentary. Active: which obviously means actively pursuing quarry, such as opportunist shooting. Wood-walking or stalking: to the sit-and-wait, sedentary methods such as ambushing or hide shooting. Some techniques cross into others, such as baiting-down corvids while using a decoy placed near the bait to lull the birds into a false sense of security, or decoying woodpigeon to a shooting position and then shooting them from a hide shooting position. As you can see, the possibilities are wide ranging. So let's take a look at the basic tactics and the main quarry species they can be used for. Firstly, those that require a bit of legwork.

Opportunist Shooting

By far the most suitable way to acquire more knowledge of your shooting ground and probably give you the most chances of targets is a method known as opportunist shooting. This can range from something as basic as a walk around the farmyard and outbuildings, right up to the outermost fields and hedge lines of the land you're legally allowed to shoot over. Contrary to certain misguided belief, it's not just a case of wandering aimlessly around your shoot in the hope that you'll get the chance to take a pot-shot at whatever presents itself. Rather it's about reading the land, watching, listening and taking advantage of any opportunities that may present themselves. I realise that many readers will probably want to get straight into sneaking up (stalking) on feeding rabbits they see out in the fields, but to get within effective range takes fieldcraft and much of what is outlined in this section will be relevant to those scenarios.

As outlined in the chapter on Observation, when out 'oppo shooting' always be aware of what's going on around you. If you see the woodies landing in the next or a few fields away, plan your route accordingly, and using whatever available cover there is, make your way over there. Don't worry, the specific methods of using cover to mask an approach are outlined further in this section.

If bunnies are appearing out of the hedge line adjacent to the one you're shooting along – carefully stalk

Tread carefully, quietly and slowly when opportunist shooting and stalking

over to that area. Incidentally, I think it worth stressing that the word 'stalk' refers to walking with slow, careful deliberation and upright, just as it does in the half-stooped position. You'll come to realise which posture suits the situation.

So back to the theme – getting to quarry. This will mean plotting a route, often not a direct one, and using any and all natural cover as an aid, along with your camo clothing for concealment. You can see how hunting methods can cross over; one moment slowly and attentively adopting the role of an opportunist hunter, and the next, purposely moving towards a target. Needless to say, this is stalking at its most basic, so keep low and always try to prevent yourself showing as a silhouette. Approach from downwind and move slowly and quietly. All are basic requisites of good fieldcraft.

There are times when you need to go out with a specific plan, but sometimes even the best laid plans can go badly wrong. This is when the hunter who notices and takes advantage of the opportunities that arise can score over even the most careful tactician. For example, if you've planned to lie up in ambush near a feeding area, or woodie or corvid sitty tree, the prevailing weather conditions could well dictate whether you have a productive or non-productive foray. Therefore, always be adaptable. If you think you'll be wasting your time waiting around for something that isn't going to show then it's definitely time to become an opportunist hunter.

Doing this has resulted in some of my most challenging and memorable hunting forays. One moment you might come across a twitchy rabbit that takes all your fieldcraft skills to stalk up on, or you can be carefully walking through woods and spot a cocky squirrel sitting well within range on a branch thinking it's untouchable until you drop it with a well-aimed shot.

Alternatively, on a walk around the farmyard, just what might be sunning itself on the far side of a barn roof or outbuildings, and what might be mingling in or hanging around near domestic fowl looking for a quick feed – get the picture?

You may think it strange that Hunting Techniques has seemingly dived in at the very deep end, as this method of hunting tests your shooting skills and reflexes to the full, but as I said earlier, this method employs fieldcraft techniques that apply across the board. One such is to never let your concentration wander. It's uncanny that just when you stop for a breather and turn your attention to wiping a blade of grass or dirt off the rifle barrel, a rabbit bolts out from well within range or a woodie leaves the trees nearby. If you'd taken more care, been more attentive, maybe you'd have seen them, who knows? Maybe an opportunist shot was on the cards. You'll always get caught out like this, but just pay more attention to the job in hand and you'll start to find you're not caught out as often.

Also, and this is something that is dealt with in more detail later, there's the need to avoid direct eye-to-eye contact with your quarry until ready to shoot, and then you should be looking through the scope, crosshairs locked on the position, to send a pellet into the kill-zone. The reason for this is the animals' uncanny ability to sense danger. There will be times when a magpie will let you walk past, usually when you're out walking without a rifle, but still keep an eye on you and it can let you stray unusually close. Now slowly raise your hands as if pointing a gun, and the same bird will be away. This is the animal sensing and reacting to what it has come to learn, by inheritance of genes from previous generations, as a threatening gesture.

 Threatening postures will be outlined further but the one that can give you away, especially with wary rabbits and corvids is direct eye contact. They know that you looking directly at them is a prelude to potential danger. Add a threatening posture of the body – stopping with arms rising – and that's one legally deemed vermin species that will live to cause problems another day.

The next bit of advice may sound odd, but in certain cases it does work. If you catch sight of a potential target out of the corner of your eye, don't whip your body and head around to look but try to act as if you haven't noticed it. Still be ready, and when you get within range to take a shot, try to walk up to the quarry without overly changing direction. Have the rifle pointed down but in your shoulder, so you can position yourself to take the shot. Squirrels are particularly susceptible to this technique. Even though most hunters, like me, will try to adopt a more stable kneeling, sitting or prone position, when opportunist shooting, a high proportion of shots invariably need to be taken while standing. There's a reason to be well-practised in all shooting stances and holds before targeting live quarry. Another factor to take into consideration with this form of hunting is not only quick target acquisition, but also recognition. From certain angles the sparrowhawk can look uncannily like a wood pigeon; the green woodpecker can in silhouette be mistaken for a jackdaw, jay or even juvenile crow. Books on British birds are commonplace so invest in one. It'll pay you back in terms of the knowledge you will learn from it, even though only a few it contains are legally classed as vermin. Incorporate knowledge such as this with what you observe in the countryside yourself and it will help to make you a better countryman, let alone hunter!

Remember also the importance I've placed on movement in a previous chapter being the hunter's biggest giveaway. So move slowly, stopping at regular intervals, but only stopping if you're sure that there are no potential targets near the position you decide on for this studied position. Look up ahead; look around and even back along the track or hedge line you've moved along. The key watchwords are concentration and observation. Even if walking over ground that in your experience hasn't produced much during other hunting forays, don't discount it by rushing through. With opportunist hunting you just never know. This time there could well be quarry everywhere, and that's part of the thrill and challenge. You don't know what you could happen across next.

For this form of shooting, like many other experienced airgun hunters, I favour a carbine-sized air rifle. The reason is obvious; its compact dimensions and light weight make it ideal for carrying around and it is fast handling. I also now choose to use a PCP multi-shot as it'll give me the opportunity to access quick back-up shots and if quarry has stuck around longer than is wise, sometimes it can be 'two down' in double-quick time.

It goes without saying that full camo wear is the order of the day. Also, holding the rifle at all times is preferable, so unless I'm 'yomping' any great distance to a specific area, I prefer not to have a sling fitted, or remove it. Thank heavens for QD sling swivels.

For scope choice you need an optic that allows you to acquire the target quickly when spotted. This is definitely when you'll appreciate a wide-angle scope. There are a few very good, compact optics on the market, but a general specification scope is often just as handy wound down on a lower magnification setting for optimum width of view. Then, if you require, you can wind up the magnification for a more studied, longer-range shot if the situation allows. Also, let's not forget the fact that you'll often walk into a dull area or be operating under a canopy where the light is low. As most optics have good coated lenses I'm not saying opt for a specialised low light scope, but one with good light gathering capabilities should always be at the forefront of your selection list. Although you'll often take quick 'select and fire' shots, never take chance shots. If there's the slightest possibility that the quarry may be wounded and get away, be disciplined and leave it until another day.

As I'm sure you now realise, Opportunist Shooting requires a high level of fieldcraft, shooting skill and, of course, experience brought on only by actively practising the method. Importantly, address your body language; the half-stooped slow walk is exactly the right way to move once you've sighted a target such as a feeding rabbit which, of course, you intend to get closer to. However, moving across any ground in such a way will be sensed and seen by other quarry species as threatening. Anything that spots you moving along a hedge line or through undergrowth instinctively knows you are a predator switched on to hunting mode. This might sound bizarre but consider thi; animals such as rabbits, and to a lesser extent birds, will quite happily carry on feeding or hold position as a deer or even a cow ambles past them. The reason being, the deer or cow will not only be familiar to the animal but has always behaved in an unthreatening manner, so this reaction and acceptance is learned behaviour. Not that I'm suggesting you dress up as a cow or deer but as you should be fully camo'd up, walk with an unthreatening posture as you try to almost 'drift' over the ground. Stooped with rifle half at the ready isn't always the way. I know I've used a few military references in this book already, but the army adopt a walk in sensitive areas that allows them to appear unthreatening, but ready to respond should the situation dictate. That is, rifle across the chest, muzzle pointed slightly downwards held in half-folded arms, walking slowly, while their eyes study everything around and above them. Adopt this alert but seemingly relaxed posture and you're halfway to blending in with your surroundings.

Pay particular attention to the ground you walk over. This obviously also applies to stalking when you've spotted a target you want to get within range. Stepping on a twig can make a sharp, quarry-alerting 'crack'. Noise can be created if stepping on gravel, loose stones, pieces of tree bark, dry leaves … the list is endless. Virtually every writer on hunting has commented on how the shooter should place his feet when walking. The basics are: move slowly, and step forward, first placing the ball of the foot down on the ground, then carefully roll the weight forward onto the sole of the foot, then step forward again and repeat the procedure. You need to feel the ground beneath your feet as you look at the ground you're walking over. This is all fine in theory, but only experience and practice will enable you to walk as quietly as possible over a variety of terrain.

The footwear you choose also makes some difference. Although, as a rule of thumb, a soft-soled, trainer-style shoe can be useful for stalking in summer, in the winter every hunter should wear a pair of suitably heavier-duty field boots. Most offer a good compromise of support, grip and flexibility. Again, you'll discover which suit you as you progress as a hunter. By and large, following the basics will help you to adopt the style of walking that best suits your build and agility. Firstly you walk an area with your eyes. Look at the five yards forward of your position, making mental note of what lies on the ground, and the consistency of the terrain, and then slowly use the ball, sole, forward rolling movement. If you feel anything on the ground underfoot about to slip or snap, stop and look at what it is. Carefully retract that foot and place it suitably in another place and progress on your way looking ahead, around and in many cases above for any sign of quarry. Again, remember you still need to stop at regular intervals again to inspect the area that you're about to walk over or around. While doing so, take this opportunity to check around your position for any signs of life. It may seem nigh on impossible but this slow, drifting walk will eventually become second nature.

Walking over soft, long, damp grass is much easier than any woodland floor. That is until the frosts have the ground scrunch with a sound as if you're walking on cornflakes. You'll soon come to realise that stalking in the frost is a definite no-no. My experience of walking over frost-ravaged fields at night, lamping foxes with a fullbore, has made me realise that trying to get within range with an air rifle for any suitable quarry is nigh on impossible. Know when it's impractical to walk up on quarry. This is the time to use other methods such as hide shooting, using decoys, and/or ambush techniques with bait for corvids. Again, even though we've come away from the main thread, the fact that hunting techniques often complement each other or blend well together is an all too obvious one.

Back to 'hoofing it' around the shoot actively searching out quarry. Now, as the way you move around your shoot on foot is of such high importance so is the use of cover, and the rules apply as much to opportunist shooting as they do to stalking. I detail movement because this is a very important part of fieldcraft and in actuality, stalking is by definition different for the deer stalker, as it is the airgun hunter trying to stalk closer to a rabbit to take an effective shot. It's only the last but very stressful distance, whether it be as many as 60 or only ten yards to get to the final shooting position, usually crawling on your belly on the final approach until you are within range.

I'll further detail how to think about planning your route and how to use hedgerows, small copses or tree lines, using the cover these natural features provide. I've nicknamed this technique 'hedge-hopping', which is simply slowly stalking or walking along hedges, walls or any other perimeter that will offer cover, and keeping an eye out for quarry in front of you, that you may walk up on, or even come across on the other side of the cover you are using. Whenever possible, always walk away from the sun, into the wind and keep in the shaded areas, and that applies wherever you're moving around looking for quarry. When stalking around hedgerows, do so in an anti-clockwise direction (clockwise if left-handed) as this allows you to have the rifle mounted in the shoulder to be ready for a shot should you spy an opportunity as you round a corner. This is opportunist shooting in its most applied and dedicated form.

Applied Opportunism

At certain times of year, an area that could have been relied upon to hold a few likely targets may suddenly seem to become devoid of all legitimate quarry species. This is dependent on how much disturbance it's been subjected to, either by too much shooting pressure or by other factors such as an increase in natural predators; foxes, stoats, weasels, feral cats, birds of prey etc. Waiting around for quarry to turn up in this sort of situation can be fruitless and one occasion when ambushing techniques are nigh on useless in these areas, but this will be dealt with in the relevant section. So as I'm sure you can realise, this is when a hedge-hopping, stalking technique can come into its own, as you are actively seeking out a shot.

Creatures of the outdoors survive on their wits, so they will soon start to avoid areas you've had a field day in only a few days before. This is very noticeable amongst rabbit that have been over-lamped at traditional times of year, and yes, lamping is another technique that will be covered in detail later, so back to the matter of opportunist shooting. Due to disturbance, they can become much more wary, becoming reluctant to stray too far from their burrows or cover. This is especially the case if you share your shoot with other airgun hunters, rimfire shooters and/or shotgunners. In the main you'll find that at first light 'twitchy' rabbits will remain close to home. More often than not these will be sited under hedgerows or shrubbery or right inside bramble thickets – favourite haunts for rabbits in many parts of the country. If rabbits are your main chosen quarry species, look for sandbanks or soft disturbed soil leading up to these hedgerows or shrubbery. Similarly, the well-used runs through the grass; these flattened grass pathways lead out to feeding areas and the regularity of the quarry using these routes can often be their downfall, not only because you can ambush them as they come and go, but also they're clear indications that there may well be a hidden burrow system in the heart of the bramble bushes, or whatever dense cover the runs lead in and out of.

The following information could have been put in the chapter on Observation, but opportunist shooting is as much about observing and learning from what you see as it is about getting more quarry in the bag. In that respect, be advised that around an active warren, rabbits can be found feeding on the grass near the cover of hedges and bushes at most times of the year. This is because it will probably be more lush and nutritious, not being as exposed to the elements and the feet of grazing livestock as much as the grass further out in the fields. Plus, and perhaps most importantly, they also feel safer near their homes.

Note that the grass can be quite long near the hedgerows, so when taking a snap shot in this opportunist way, although I've advised where possible to adopt the kneeling position for extra stability, the downward angle of a standing shot may sometimes be the only and optimum option. The rabbit's head may be all that's visible when it stands up to peek around. In that case, the only sure route for an unobscured flight path for the pellet to the target is when the shot is taken from the standing position. In the section on stalking, we'll further deal with 'eyes from above', feathered quarry that may spot you from the trees. Suffice to say that woodies and magpies can be an awful nuisance, even though legitimate and challenging targets, if your attention is always on the ground they will give you away when they spot you approach. Woodies are canny creatures and almost invisible amongst the branches, with the annoying habit of suddenly taking off, wings clapping, alerting everything in the vicinity as to your presence. So by and large, if opportunist stalking around hedges for rabbits, and I know the woodies have taken a liking to a particular area of hedgerow or copse, I'll usually steer well clear. I know this may sound contradictory, as you are supposed to be opportunist shooting and looking for any quarry, but unless working through a wooded area, I'll keep away unless I've decided to lay-up in a pre-dawn ambush for them. The reason being, it's very difficult to sneak up on birds unless you've decided to attempt the seemingly impossible. Further in this section there are a few tips to help you assess the worth of targeting a bird spotted while opportunist shooting in the woods. So if the intruder alarm goes off, bang go your chances of coming across land-bound and ground-feeding quarry.

Rabbit on the alert, sitting bolt upright, ears pricked up

However, by slowly and stealthily making your way along or around the perimeter of hedgerows and bushes, it's a fair bet you'll find a bunny or two, and when I say 'near', I really do mean as close as possible. Once again, a word on the shooting position: If a rabbit is spotted close up under the hedge it's likely that shooting alongside will be deflected by a straggling branch as much as a tall heavy piece of undergrowth. Here, depending on terrain, you have the option of lowering yourself to the floor to take a shot under the canopy of the hedge cover that can often be very bare. The rabbit could just be sitting outside its warren watching or even dozing. Worst-case scenario is, the cover is such that you need to move out from the cover you've walked along to take a shot inward to the rabbit's position. This is fraught with variables. Firstly, in no way can you step out. You need to make yourself as low as possible and move slowly, usually crawling flat to the ground on your belly, moving side-ways out into the field. It may only be a few yards, maybe even a few feet, but the rabbit will notice any movement as it will more likely be side-on to your original position. Once far enough out, you then still have to contend with ensuring that the pellet has a clear path to the target. The words 'challenging' and 'why do we put ourselves through it' come to mind, but when you get it right and the end result is a bunny down with hardly a twitch of a back leg, then it's worth every drop of sweat on your beaded brow.

A word here on using areas of low light to your advantage, or you could say, 'lurking in the shadows'. Every natural predator knows the importance of staying in the shaded areas, be it a lion in the African grasslands or a fox scouring the English hedgerows. There's also the use of shadow in the woods, which we'll come to later. So in respect of using the shadows of the hedges and low foliage, notice which side of the hedge the sun casts the shadow, and stalk up this area. It may well be that the rabbit is sunning or feeding on the other side, but as you'll soon appreciate, you'll stand a better chance coming up in these darker areas.

Typical hedgerows that suit this technique have to afford you enough cover (be sufficiently thick and dense in foliage or branches) to prevent your silhouette being spotted by quarry feeding further out in the field. Again, we are already coming to a juncture where, as I mentioned in the introduction to this section, hunting techniques can often merge or be used together for a successful outcome. Incidentally, this cover-hugging technique works well when stalking/walking slowly along old dry stone walls overgrown with ivy or other creeping cover plants. Even plain dry stone walling can be used to conceal your silhouette, providing at these areas you stay low. While opportunist shooting in this way there are many times you need to move low and slow. Breaks and gaps in badly maintained walling offer the chance to scour the field on the other side. If there's no quarry on your side of the cover, periodically take a peek over the other side to see if there's anything around in the field adjacent. This must be done very slowly, your eyes leading the way, with only the slightest amount of your head showing above to allow you to look over. This way, if you spot quarry, you can watch its demeanour as you bring the rifle over to sight-in on the kill-zone. If the quarry begins to look twitchy, freeze, and as soon as it relaxes, leave it at least a minute before resuming bringing the rifle into position. Rarely, you might just surprise a group of feeding woodpigeon. Magpies and crows will more likely be off and away at the first glimpse of your eye, even the top of your head, but pigeon especially, and, of course, rabbits and squirrels can often get totally lost in the urge to feed and the wall allows a nice, steady rest to shoot over. In fact, when and wherever possible, take the opportunity to look around and scour both sides of the cover you're using. Stopping at frequent intervals to take stock of the situation is of great importance if you are to reap dividends from such an applied approach to this method. Ideally, you are striving to spot quarry before it has chance to spot you.

Unfortunately, when you do encounter quarry it often has noticed something amiss, and in many cases it most likely is aware of your presence. I can't stress this highly enough but movement is the hunter's Achilles' heel. If you sight quarry and it has also seen you then all you can do is completely freeze. I know I'm repeating myself but patience is of the essence in this situation. It can be infuriating, almost like a battle of wits, who will break first, but never be tempted to carry on sighting in or moving when the target is so tuned in to your position. At this stage it probably isn't recognising you as danger, but is certainly realising that you're something to keep an eye on. All you can do is remain totally motionless, avoiding direct eye contact, hoping that the quarry will soon relax and resume whatever activity it was engaged in before being attracted by your seen, or sensed, presence.

If you have a shoot that includes unmanaged hedgerows which have had the opportunity to grow to a decent height, these can be a nightmare to stalk along. Woodpigeon can be uncannily invisible even in sparse foliage. If you do spot a bird dozing, sleeping off a good feed, a rare opportunist shot this is indeed, so in this situation, slowly raise the rifle, assess range by eye then take the shot.

I'm sure you're now thinking that for this form of hunting you not only need eyes in the back of your head but the top as well. If a bird does suddenly strike out and you are close to hedge cover, then keep still. Quarry around that hasn't seen you and is near cover itself will possibly hold position or only nip into the very edge of cover. It won't necessarily disappear for the day. This watch-and-wait tactic has paid off for me many times and it may well seem fruitless to spend any amount of time in this position but surprisingly, if the area isn't usually shot over, quarry can be surprisingly tolerant. You'll discover in the Stalking section that quarry is rarely as tolerant when out feeding away from cover.

Natural breaks in the hedgerow and man-made passes, such as gates, should be approached with particular care, as these give the hunter the opportunity to take a studied look into the adjacent field. More often than not, rabbits also use these areas to cross between fields, so they are also areas to consider as an ambush point. In these breaks in cover, again look for rabbit runs and beats (narrow pathways with flattened or bald patches in the grass) going out into the field. These will usually cross the hedge line close to the hedge itself or at the base of gateposts and either side of broken dry stone walling. As for those strange rabbit runs that disappear at the base of a wall – no, the rabbit hasn't walked or maybe I should say 'hopped' back on itself, it's probably gone over the wall. Until you see it you probably won't believe it, but rabbits are good climbers and will when necessary go over such an obstacle. They'll even swim; something that has surprised many countrymen who've seen the phenomenon. Then again, it's usually when being chased they'll do this and not a regular route they'd prefer to take. So, in respect of opportunist shooting for the land-borne quarry it's very much a case of expect the unexpected. The prize you seek could be just at the other end of the hedge you're walking along. Tread carefully; walk quietly, and keep your wits about you at all times.

All scenarios mentioned have lent more to shooting around cover and along the hedgerows that form borders to fields - now to opportunist shooting in the woods.

Wood-Walking

It's hard to categorise some methods as they're a mixture of elements taken from the others. One such is wood-walking which can be construed as a form of stalking. This is used when opportunist shooting squirrels, magpies, woodpigeon etc., as they go about their routine in the woods. Also, don't neglect the perimeter (sides) of the wood. Here you can find a variety of quarry from rabbits to woodies at the edge of fields, to corvids in the tops of the bordering trees.

Again, this is a very challenging form of shooting that needs stealth, keen eyesight and good marksmanship. It is best carried out in the months between and including October and March because the trees have less foliage for quarry to hide in, making spotting much easier. If you're looking for squirrels at this time of year, a walk through an area will usually send a few squirrels scampering back up into the trees. A wood-walk can be described as an alert but leisurely stroll, slowly walking through the woods and stopping at regular intervals, keeping eyes and ears open to the sights and sounds around you. Often, all you'll see is the flick of a silvery-grey tail, enough to give away the squirrel's presence. At others, dead branches can mysteriously fall from the trees on windless days, or you'll hear scuffling sounds coming from the forest floor which could be a squirrel foraging amongst leaf litter. Soft-soled shoes are the norm if it's not too muddy, and full camo wear including face veil and gloves is a must.

Once a squirrel has been sighted, you can be 99.9% certain it has spotted you no matter how well camo'd you are. As you freeze in position, the camo creates the effect of blending you back into the wood giving the squirrel a false sense of security as it will be unsure what to make of what it thinks it has seen. Either way, it will have seen you and will react in one of two ways. It will either stop perfectly still or scamper up a tree to a position where it thinks it's safe to observe your intrusion. If you have stopped still at this point, you're in with a chance of a shot. Continuing towards the squirrel as it watches you will see it disappear higher up or into heavier foliage if available, or even into a hole, crevice, small hollow – anywhere it can to give it cover from you. In squirrel shooting, patience is a virtue as eventually, with you keeping quiet and motionless, it will carry on feeding. The squirrel's habit of freezing is usually its downfall, as if he's within range you should slowly raise your rifle, aim and have dispatched the tree rat. Often they scamper around the tree to put it between you and itself. Sometimes it will scurry up the tree only a few feet, then poke its head around again to check if you're still there. This curiosity can also be its downfall, and is possibly the reason that they can respond to special calls.

Here a quick word on quarry calls: If you can't spot any squirrels, or one has gone from view, try one as it might fire the animal's inquisitiveness to the point that it shows itself. These calls, when used correctly, emit barks and chatters similar to the animals. I don't particularly think you're talking 'squirrel speak' but it does seem to interest the rodents enough for them to take a closer look.

An old trick often recommended is to drape your coat over a small bush, and then walk around the other side to confuse it, but in practice, this is utter 'BS' as the squirrel isn't completely stupid. Anyway, who wants to take take their jacket on and off every time a squirrel is spotted? This is when shooting in pairs is beneficial and is one of the few times I enjoy the company of another shooter.

When stalking the woods, even in autumn, keep the sun behind your shooting position so you're not squinting when aiming at targets. There's no need to worry over it casting your silhouette forward as your quarry is likely to be above you. Stop at regular intervals to scan the trees, and ground, ahead. In fact, when walking the woods it's worth keeping an eye on the woodland floor for spoor (tracks) in the woodland loam. Also, gnawed fir cones or scratchings may indicate that the area is well inhabited by the 'grey ones'. Looking aloft as you walk through the woods, you'll possibly find the squirrel's bulky home – the drey, not dissimilar to a magpie's nest but smaller. In fact, it's not uncommon for squirrels to take over old magpie dwellings. If shooting in pairs, one can poke the drey using lofting poles, there's even an attachment unimaginatively called a drey attachment to put onto the end of the poles instead of the wire arm used for deeks. The technique is a simple one; assemble the sections of the lofting poles together until you've got enough height to reach the drey, then knock the drey or poke the pole right into it. Incidentally, if

The correct way to hold the rifle as you belly crawl into final position to get within range of the target

there is any breeze or even if there isn't, the guy using the poles should stand away from the tree so the dead leaves and debris that knocking the drey will create isn't continually falling into his eyes. The shooter then stands ready in preparation of a shot when the tree rat emerges. They'll sometimes leave the drey very lazily, or they'll come rocketing out. Sometimes they'll stop within a few yards, in plain view, trying to suss out what has caused the disturbance. This is the time to take the shot as they'll soon head straight for the treetops clinging to the thinnest of branches or disappearing far out of view. Just a few important pointers on drey knocking; Ensure that there are no overhead power lines. It only takes a brush with one of these and your hunting days are over. Also keep a check on the ferrules where the poles join together. Make sure the spring-loaded ball catch (if fitted) is strong as losing a lofting pole amongst the branches might sound unfeasible but it's easily done. Although I've detailed this technique for reasons of thoroughness, by and large I leave this for the shotgunner.

Now, a major problem facing the wood-walker is sound on moving through the wood. Dry leaves are impossible to walk over without making a noise, but that doesn't mean you can't cut down on audible disturbance. Like other forms of stalking, don't drag your feet; don't scuffle the leaves unnecessarily, but lift and place your feet carefully, being ever cautious to avoid those ear-splitting, dead twigs that can send a 'crack' echoing through the trees. Wet leaves can also be treacherous so watch your step. Consider each footstep as you stealthily move through the wood. There's no hurry and I recommend the hunter stops at more frequent intervals to take a studied look around than when out on open ground.

You need to look all around your position at all times, at what could be on the woodland floor, flat against the tree trunks, sitting on limbs and branches. From the ground up, everywhere around you has the potential to produce targets. Shooting in woodland holds many different attractions to the open fields and can be quite exhilarating. If you're lucky enough to be able to walk through a large, old, mature wood in this way, give thanks to the owner as every time you visit you're entering a magical place, full of things to see and hear. A jay flits across between the trees to disappear into even the sparsest of cover. How the technicoloured corvid manages this is a mystery, until you realise that it uses shadow, cover and remains motionless. A magpie chack, chack, chacks from a position high above, squirrels scamper busily around doing squirrelly things – it's an airgun hunting heaven.

For the challenge and variety of targets you'd be hard pushed to find better hunting for the air rifle than the English wood. Not only do you need almost extra-sensory senses but also remember, there are particular tricks to employ when a potential target is spotted. For instance, if a bird pitches into the trees it'll head straight for the area where the twigs, or whatever foliage is available, is most dense to give itself as much cover as possible. It depends on the species of bird, and any can do this, but more likely corvids, such as the jay and magpie mentioned will head for the upper branches before flying out. Woodies usually just head straight out. A tip for targeting an opportunist shot such as this when the scenario arises is, don't try to scan the foliage where the bird entered the tree but train your scope to scan the top of the tree where the branches are barer. Here you might just get a crack at the bird as it makes its way up, before heading out. If not alarmed, it could sit up there looking around. However, should another follow it in, don't start dithering over which to sight on; choose the area you feel one particular bird will appear from and stick to it. Sweeping your rifle from left to right will only have you unready and miss the small opportunity you have. If it's a pair or lone woodpigeon that's flown into a heavily foliated tree, chances are it'll just flop right out again anywhere, so don't waste time waiting for this to climb the tree because it won't. Jays and magpies are birds that use the 'climbing' tactic but woodies will land in a tree to rest or feed. If they're resting after feeding, these trees can be known as sitty trees and for a woodie it can return to the same tree time and again. These are easily found by the amount of bird droppings, or 'splashings' as they're known, found around the base of the tree along with the birds' downy feathers. To sit or stand quietly and patiently within range can produce good sport.

Other areas to hang around are feed-hoppers. These can be found in woods for game birds and those that have duck pits. Everything will come to know that these bins are packed with food. Indeed, squirrels and even rats will gnaw their way in to get at the food inside, especially during a harsh winter.

Another form of shooting I find very enjoyable around the woods is shooting woodpigeon when they've taken to the thick, ivy-covered trees to feed on the ivy berries. The birds can become so preoccupied as they jostle each other for the berries that they sometimes don't notice the first few shots, or birds dropping from the tree, because birds are continually crashing into trees near them to feed. Once you've found a place this is happening, stand with your back to a tree in full camo and wait for the best shot to present itself.

For once, the birds are easy to spot in the bare branches and also stand out against the lush green of the ivy leaves. The best time to shoot these birds is before they've been disturbed. Birds new to the area are cautious, but not as cautious as ones that have seen comrades fall, or you walking beneath the tree canopy picking up your hard-earned prizes. When birds are new to an area, they're flitting around looking and generally taking over the trees. They'll barge anything out of their way to get at ivy berries because in a harsh winter the fruit can really be their saviour. Unfortunately for them, but fortunately for the well-organised and observant airgun hunter, finding woodies feeding in this manner can result in challenging and exciting sport.

Again, don't overshoot an area, just take what you need for the pot as depending on region, weather conditions, and density of pigeon population in relation to the food supply, you'll have a good few months at them. When it's over, an area can be completely stripped of berries, leaving just bare stalks, the downy feathers below bearing testament that they've been there. In fact these are signs to look for amongst the berries that remain to indicate that the birds are frequenting and feeding confidently in the area. Some use lofters (see Lofting) to encourage birds to the shooting position, or install a feeling of safety so they land near the shooting position. However, when the birds are feeding in this way, I've never found that deeks were needed because the birds are coming and feeding anyway.

Stalking

The word 'stalking' has already been used quite frequently in this chapter as generally it's the term used to refer to the way we stealthily walk up on quarry,undetected, in a myriad circumstances. Many will know the word in association with a sportsman hunting deer. A deer stalker, of course, being a hunter who purposely walks up undetected within suitable range to shoot a deer with a suitable calibre of firearm. In relation to airgun hunting, 'stalking' is specifically used as the term to describe a technique widely accepted and employed for targeting rabbits; basically, walking up undetected within range to shoot the rabbit with a suitable power of rifle – in this case the 12ft lb air rifle. This requires the shooter to get much closer to the quarry, due to the relatively limited effective range and it's one of the major reasons why stalking up on feeding or 'sunning' rabbits is by far one of the most demanding of hunting techniques that the air rifle hunter needs to master.

Most usually, this method is employed during the spring right through to late autumn. Incidentally,

The crucial moment at the end of any stalking situation – taking the shot

although stalking is in essence 'sneaking up' to your quarry without it seeing or sensing you, we shouldn't kid ourselves, as the truth of the matter is, most times it probably has. However, the secret of effective stalking is to get within range without your movements overly alarming your quarry with the result that it bolts for cover.

The basics of stalking are: Whenever possible, approach from downwind, keep as low a profile as possible, move slowly and quietly taking advantage of every bit of available cover, including shaded areas, on your way to the target. The use of natural cover will be dealt with in greater detail later.

Camouflage clothing is by far one of the most useful aids in the airgun hunter's kit bag. In summer, lightweight over-wear such as a mesh suit is ideal, but as you'll be walking and then crawling through and over rough ground, it's always advisable to wear something more substantial underneath. Incidentally, the pattern of camo isn't overly important as long as you're using an appropriate colour blend suited to the summer hues of the open fields and hedgerows you'll be stalking along. As we've touched on previously in the chapter on Camo and Fieldcraft, obviously soft-soled, dark green trainers or lightweight field boots are a must for feeling your way across the ground, and importantly, the whites of the body (hands and face) should be covered if you're to get up close and personal with ol' bugs - and that means facemask and gloves.

Any quality spring-powered, gas-ram or PCP air rifle with general specification 3 – 9 x 40 scope will suffice for this method. Although I always prefer to use a PCP carbine with a good low light scope as you'll often find stalking most productive in the early morning or late on a summer evening when the light values fade.

One of the first mistakes the novice bunny stalker makes is to attempt to creep up on rabbits that are so obviously to the experienced eye, 'unstalkable'. Let me explain that further: Firstly the ground may be unsuitable for a stealthy approach, the rabbit may already be on high alert or there are other factors to contend with such as ground feeding or nesting birds interspersed amongst the feeding rabbits. If so, leave them be and move on until you find rabbits that are stalkable.

As for the ground you're going to have to move over, stalking often needs to be done on ground that is completely or relatively flat with no cover. Rabbits that are feeding out in a freshly-cut grass field during daylight hours might appear confident, but don't mistake their apparent nonchalance as foolhardiness. It's anything but, as the animal's every sense is ready to detect anything approaching that resembles danger. This is why you need to adopt the stalking walk and learn how and when to use the various stages; those being to half-stoop, then to lower yourself progressively as you draw near. On sensing your approach the rabbit will freeze, and could immediately bolt for cover, or lie flat to the ground. If its ears are pricked up, it's heard you and is listening for danger. If it has stopped feeding you can be sure it's also looking in your direction.

Going the Distance

Here's the right way, to get within range to make the telling shot: If there are bushes or trees behind you, use these to prevent showing yourself as a silhouette; basically, don't allow the rabbit to see you in outline. If there is no backdrop to use, then you only have one option and that is to reduce your size to distort what the animal can see. Whilst camouflage works and works well at breaking up or disguising the unmistakable human outline, unfortunately, against a blank or uniform background of either sky or the field behind you, even if wearing the best camo available, you will show a certain amount, if not all, of your body shape in hard outline. This is a situation when you need to break up the human form and still move forward, and it sounds impossible, but it isn't. Also, you can never put a definite range to target that you should change to these different levels of approach, but there are basic guidelines to follow – these are:

The closer you get to the target the smaller you must try to make yourself appear. This means that almost as soon as you've spotted quarry, you should adopt the half-stooping posture as you begin carefully to make your approach.

Once you get closer, continuously watch the animal's demeanour. Is it showing signs of being worried at your approach? If so, stop. If not, then the closer you get to the target, reduce yourself lower, walking as low and close to the ground as you can. This is straining on the thigh muscles and you'll soon need to get down to your hands and knees to crawl closer to the target. Certainly, towards the end of the stalk you will have to belly crawl into a final position, using your elbows and knees to move forward.

While making the final approach, you should adopt a 'move, stop and look' procedure. Keep an eye on all rabbits, especially the closest to see if it has sensed or is disturbed by your presence. If all is well, choose the rabbit in the feeding group that presents the best shot, and then when within range, take careful aim and take the shot.

The golden rules of engagement are to check; a rabbit on the alert will sit bolt upright, ears pricked, nose twitching as it uses its exceptional hearing and sense of smell to detect danger. They really are wary little critters!

Now, in a perfect hunting world all would go according to plan, you would reach a distance to take an effective killing shot, and the rabbits would remain perfectly still to let you achieve this end, but it's hardly ever that text-book simple.

For a start, the most infuriating factor of stalking is that not only have you to be mindful of the quarry you are stalking up to (old bugs), but also quarry that might spot you on the way there. Rabbits in the field that you haven't seen may bolt for cover, bobbing up as if from nowhere.

Similarly, as mentioned before, woodpigeon can suddenly crash out of the trees with clapping wings sending your intended quarry scuttling for cover. Likewise, the magpie can be an infuriating nuisance shouting its alarm call to all and sundry that an intruder is in the area. If you're hunting over or around a field in spring into summer that has nesting lapwings, forget it. The peewits aren't deliberately spoiling your sport, only thinking of the family by trying to divert you away from the nest or the flightless chicks that you will encounter scurrying across the ground. It can be frustrating but all these factors need to be addressed and taken into consideration in a stalking situation. Even unseen song and game birds could flush out of cover to signal your presence to everything in the area and beyond.

If that weren't enough to contend with, there's also the possibility of birds flying over at the last minute. This can be a nightmare, in summer especially. Crows can drift over at the most inopportune of moments, their raucous 'kaarr, kaarr, kaarr' cawing alerting anything within 'crow-shot' that everything isn't as it should be down below. Even woodies flying over the same field; if they veer off their flight line close to the feeding rabbits, they will notice and carefully look around for danger. If you notice birds flying into the area don't look directly at them for any reason as they will invariably react to your attention. In these situations, you can only freeze, and keep your eyes and head lowered. As rabbits are creatures of habit, if they do bolt at this type of disturbance they'll often only nip into the nearest cover or lower themselves flat to the ground. Whatever the reaction, freeze; keep totally still. If you don't make any undue movement, the rabbits, more often than not and if they aren't worried by the 'blob' lying on the ground (you), will soon resume their previous activity.

Stalking isn't only a long distance option and mostly, just as many times it can also be adopted in situations when you might encounter rabbits quite unexpectedly, often while opportunist shooting. Usually, they'll bolt on your approach as your sudden appearance in the area will have surprised a small group or a solitary feeder – a case of being 'too close for comfort', so to speak. If you aren't too close, and the rabbits aren't too twitchy, they'll probably hold on the alert or hop further down the hedge line or field. As they have not bolted for cover, it means they know you're there but haven't particularly identified you as representing danger. In this situation, you could try the disappearing act of slowly lowering yourself down to your knees, then onto your stomach, eyes facing the floor. Again, it's nigh on impossible to put a time-frame on moving closer in these situations because the behaviour of the rabbits will dictate your next move. Always bear in mind that you should never rush. The speed of your approach isn't only dictated by the proximity of the rabbits, but also the terrain you're moving over. It could be smooth, fresh-cut grassland or uncomfortably rough pasture, both obviously have their own particular nuances for using the stalking technique.

Over rough, hilly ground you can at times travel quite quickly between areas, using hillocks and clumps of foliage to mask your approach, then slowing once again to a belly crawl to peer carefully over to see what may be feeding over the brow of the hill. Unfortunately, in this type of terrain, a rabbit can seemingly hide behind the smallest clump of grass, suddenly darting off in a zigzag to disappear into the distance. The times this will happen will far outweigh the textbook stalks. Also, a rabbit when flat to the ground, even on a relatively flat grass field, can be virtually invisible, only being seen when it bolts. You might think it incredulible how they manage to make themselves so invisible, but remember, this is how and why they survive detection and capture from natural predators such as foxes and stoats.

Whereas some would look over a set of fields on land relatively flat and see nothing but a few trees and hedges, the experienced stalker's eye will notice every bump, bush, nettle patch or fencepost. These are all objects to be used to mask an approach. Using a row of fence posts you can get surprisingly close to a rabbit feeding on even the flattest field. Move when the rabbit is relaxed stopping at each post. Stand side-on to disguise your shape and if downwind from the rabbit it will find it difficult to detect you as long as you remain completely motionless. Whilst the rabbit will notice movement, as you get closer it will also detect your approach felt as vibration on the ground. Remember, rabbits signal to each other by thumping their hind legs on the ground as a danger signal. They're tuned into the vibration of anything unnatural or running. Sheep that run across a field on your approach will send rabbits to cover, and a flock of sheep moving in such a manner is thunderous to a rabbit. This illustrates the importance of your footsteps and how quietly you walk on a successful stalk, and as your movements need to be slow, steady and fluid, so do your footsteps need to be light, carefully chosen but purposeful.

Walking on long, damp grass can be done quite quietly, but as always there's the possibility of a broken branch or twig if near hedges, so still pay attention to the terrain as you move. If walking over marshy, sodden ground, place your feet on the highest clumps of grass as these are the driest and will make less sound. Don't step into deep mud if you can help it. The sound of your boot coming out will make more noise than when it was carefully placed down into it.

Stalking is also very strenuous and will test the level of every hunter's fitness. In fact realising your own limitations, and certainly knowing when not to stalk can save valuable time in the field.

Another factor is how much movement the rabbits will tolerate. Rarely will they be unaware of your presence. As we've established, movement is the hunter's biggest give-away and when in a position to take a shot, bringing the rifle on aim correctly is crucial if you don't want to blow it at the last minute.

Presuming that you are now in a prone position, and have read the chapter on shooting positions, then you'll be manoeuvring the rifle forward of your position to sight onto the target. The rifle must be kept low, flat and side-on to the ground with the right-hand side of the rifle uppermost. This is so you don't catch the cocking lever. Few PCP air rifles have dedicated left-hand bolt actions so I'm sure most will have to use this method of bringing the rifle to bear. Alternatively, if you've stalked along a wall or hedge and are now in a kneeling position, there's another factor to address in bringing the rifle on aim. That is to bring it slowly up to your shoulder directly in front of your body; this way your body acts as a backdrop behind you so the movement of the rifle is screened. That means not allowing even the tip of the muzzle to present itself forward of your position outside your outline as you bring the rifle to bear.

You may feel foolish but the best way to practise this procedure is while watching yourself in a big mirror – full length if possible. Stand in front of the mirror and practise bringing the rifle up to your shoulder to shoot from different angles: kneeling, sitting, lying prone and even standing.

Also, remember that when lying prone you're at the same level as quarry on the ground. Many wonder why at the end of a stalk and in this position, the quarry spooks. It can be the simple fact that it's alarmed at the movement of the rifle along the floor. Alternatively, the rifle catches on something and makes a sound; it can be that simple. This is one of the reasons that I rarely use a rifle sling when hunting in this way.

Another factor that can make or break a successful stalk is how you observe the target as you approach. As mentioned previously, when looking at any animal, if it detects you try to avoid making direct eye contact. Keep the rabbit in your peripheral vision but don't stare intently at it as it will more often than not realise you're another animal and combined with any movement, smell or sound it may have detected, will act accordingly. In other words, 'leg it'. Only when its body language shows it's relaxing and, for instance, it has resumed feeding should you continue the stalk towards the target.

How a rabbit 'sees' the stalker can only be imagined. Obviously, it hasn't got the benefit of seeing you as a standing, average-sized adult would. This is why a ground-dwelling animal such as the rabbit relies so heavily on its other senses of hearing and smell. I'm sure the fox is detected by smell more than being visually detected. If you get the opportunity, watch a fox stalk a rabbit and you'll not be far wrong copying the way it carefully chooses a path, hugging the ground using all cover before launching forward to grab the bunny.

The effort needed to stalk is not only a strain on the muscles but on the nervous system and the adrenalin will have you shaking. As you reach a position where you feel you can make an effective shot, lie perfectly still and rest. Calm yourself before even attempting to put the scope crosshairs on the target. Once within a reasonable range, which for most airgun hunters should be within 30 yards, you should always go for a head shot.

Another of the last checks you need to do before taking the shot is to ensure that the path from muzzle to target is clear. At ground level a mound of earth could deflect the pellet as could coarse, heavy grass or foliage.

Slightly tilt your head to one side of the scope to visually check the terrain. The scope can often give you a false sense of security at this stage so double check all is as it should be. Don't lift your head above the scope as that'll show more of your body. A quick but studied look should be all you need to do, then settle those crosshairs on the kill-zone and it's yours.

There are times though when stalking within range of rabbits is impractical, nigh on impossible or both. This could be due to many factors; the terrain is unsuitable, the wind isn't in your favour, or just the fact that the rabbits have become very, very wary. There is no need to despair as the airgun hunter should be a king of adapting to the situation he faces, and for times such as these, there is at least one other technique at his disposal, which we will look at next, that being the art of ambushing.

Incidentally, another challenging method for targeting rabbits is not only shooting at night with a lamp but also stalking with a night vision riflescope. These nerve-wracking techniques will be dealt with in the coming chapters, so suffice to say, practise hard and long during daylight hours and you'll soon find yourself wanting to take on the challenge at night.

Ambush Shooting

Sometimes known as 'static hunting', this requires the airgun hunter to wear full camo clothing, use some form of hide or make use of natural cover, and usually a combination of all three. The ambush shooting position obviously needs to be chosen or built within effective range of where the quarry is known or expected to move, frequent or feed. Ambushing from a hidden shooting position is used in conjunction with many other methods to bag wary quarry. These can range from decoying, baiting-down and in some instances, even indoors rat shooting. So it follows, the most important requisites of successful ambushing are a well-chosen shooting position, good camo techniques and sometimes a well-constructed hide.

Ambushing gives the hunter the advantage of surprise and in most cases if you choose your shooting position correctly you'll also know the approximate range of the species targeted. This is most prevalent when baiting crows or magpies down at a known fixed position. Further details for shooting corvids are in the section devoted to that technique.

Ambushing can be a very productive hunting method

Similar ambush tactics can be used to set up in wait near a rabbit warren. If you've located the main entrance holes and runs to a large, well-populated warren, this form of shooting can be very productive. Again, cover and concealment is your major concern. In many cases you should be able to position yourself under a hedge or heavy cover within range of the target. If you've got a sling swivel stud attached to the forend of your rifle, and it's a PCP, you can take advantage of this and shoot using a bipod. Otherwise, use a camo rucksack as a rest. This can also help to partly conceal you from the forward position. Whilst, by and large, ambushing is a set 'hidden and sniping' technique, depending on what quarry species you intend to take by surprise there are certain factors pertaining to various situations that need to be addressed if you want to operate to the optimum level. Ambushing our main land-borne quarry, the rabbit, is a much more straightforward affair than sitting in wait for flying felons. Typically, what you can get away with in the form of what can be usable cover for sniping rabbits will often be totally unsuitable for crows or woodpigeon. Often, you only need a camo screen forward of your shooting position to pot rabbits as they emerge from a warren or a hedge line, but if you don't have complete cover around you and are completely hidden from prying eyes from up above, then you'll not stand any chance of ambushing quarry landing in trees. A crow's eyesight is legendary and the woodpigeon's equally keen. They're as much on the lookout for danger as they are food.

Firstly, we'll deal with the animal that hops and jumps – the rabbit. Although knowing quarry movement around an area is essential to successful hunting, to reap the best rewards from this method, you really must know the movements and specifically the time of day most rabbit activity can be expected in a given area on your shoot. You don't want to be lying or sitting up for hours on end with no activity. Often, you need to be up before sunrise to get into position and many times within the first half hour or so of daybreak you can have a couple for the pot. It goes without saying then that in summer when dawn breaks very early, only the dedicated regularly get up at such ungodly hours. By and large though, when the sun is hot and up high in the summer sky, the fields aren't the best places for the airgun hunter but that's been dealt with in the chapter on Seasons – I mention it here as a reminder.

They say that patience is a virtue and nothing worthwhile comes easy, and that's never so true than when you've made the effort to ambush on a summer's morning, but whatever the season, it takes careful planning, fieldcraft and a disciplined shooting technique if you are to achieve optimum results. Note the use of the word 'discipline' as this is only second to patience in order of importance when ambushing. When you've stuck it out and waited three or even more hours and not had a sniff, it can be tempting to take on a dodgy long shot or one that tempts you to try the impossible at an awkward angle. In the right circumstances, in ideal conditions, you might well be lucky enough to hit the mark, but luck should never be relied upon when you're at the moment of slipping the trigger. After sitting or lying for hours on end, then at long last to spy an opportunity, it can be all too easy to grasp at straws. For instance, shooting rabbits as they emerge from hedge lines can be very rewarding but challenging. You've got to drop the rabbit where it stands, as one kick off those powerful hind legs will see it lost in the undergrowth or straight down the hole it emerged from. Wait a while and it'll more likely than not move out a little further to present a clearer shot. That's the one to take and the one you should wait for.

Even when you've chosen a suitable shooting position, the nature of ambush shooting means it can be very frustrating just sitting or lying in wait. It's best to allocate time spent ambushing, especially in winter, to shorter applied sessions, and I know that from bitter experience, as I've sat, or that should be 'lain prone' for well over five hours on a bitter cold, February day waiting for a solitary bunny. The reason I remember that particular month and session is that although the rabbit did eventually appear – which I duly missed – in hindsight, I now realise I also experienced the first stages of hypothermia and believe me it's no joking matter. I'll recount the tale because it's certainly a cautionary one.

After forcing myself to stay awake and I'm sure I must have at some stage started to doze, I eventually got the chance of a shot. Although well within range, again with the advantage now of hindsight, I realise my clumsy clear miss was due to tiredness and the fact that my co-ordination was affected by the cold weather's effect on my body. Stubbornly, I carried on waiting in the vain hope that I would get another chance before nightfall. Eventually, it became too dark to see with the scope so I finally relented and admitted defeat. As I tried to move, not only was I numb and shivering, but also for a second or two nothing moved. No, I wasn't paralysed but rather my clothing had frozen to the floor. When I peeled myself up off the deck, a layer of soil was stuck to the front of every part of my body that'd been in contact with the ground and in the gloom you could clearly see the outline of my prone shooting position in black soil on the surrounding hoar-frosted floor. It looked eerily similar to the chalk outlines you see of a dead body in the movies. If I'd stayed there any longer, who knows? Some unlucky farmhand could have found me the next morning, and that, as they say, would have been that. Needless to say, take warning from that story.

So with the doom and gloom out of the way it's high time we now get into the nitty gritty of successful ambushing. Also, I reckon it's worth you having a quick re-read of the section on Observation – a very important requisite to all methods of airgun hunting.

Previously, I've mentioned how an overly uncomfortable shooting position isn't conducive to accuracy, and this certainly applies to the shooter waiting in ambush. Experience has taught me a few major factors pertaining to this form of shooting. Firstly, prepare for the unexpected and be ready to adapt accordingly, and while waiting, adopt the most comfortable and relaxed shooting position you can. It may sound obvious, but if leaning on anything for any length of time, put padding between you and the hard surface. This is where shooting mats or cushions are a godsend. Also keep strain off the arm muscles until you need to use them to alter your aim. As I've mentioned previously, holding a rifle up for any length of time has been dealt with in Shooting Techniques, where possible use a branch as a rest until you need to take control of the rifle to place the crosshairs on a selected target. A typical scenario for this being those potentially long waits for birds coming to sitty trees. More specifically, here I'll address the use and positioning for using and correct deployment of a bipod.

Give it a Rest

Some are of the opinion that you plonk the rifle down on the ground on the pod, lie behind it and wait for a shot. All fine in theory, but body positioning and even height of bipod need to be considered for both shooter comfort and effective use of this super-accuracy-aiding accessory. For instance, if shooting out of a ditch or over the brow of a hill, there is one very important reason to use a bipod. You are already able to lie in a way that puts your upper body in a natural angle so you can comfortably look around the area you're observing.

Also, the rifle is already elevated high enough off the ground so you're not tempted to lower it, as could happen if holding it, too near to the ground when you take the shot. At longer range, there's no reason to keep yourself too flat to the ground. If you do, the pellet could well be deflected by something on the way to the target; a sod of earth, or foliage, or other such ground obstruction. In fact, where possible I always recommend the use of a bipod over propping-up the forend with your leading hand. Talking of propping-up, this nicely brings me to the importance of your body posture and position behind the rifle. You'll not always have a handy ditch to drop the lower half of your body back into, so don't be tempted to overly arch or bend your back to lift your body to look through the scope. If you have to do this, you've adopted the incorrect shooting position. The strain might not be felt within the first hour but you'll pay for it when you try to move later the same or next day.

You can easily damage back muscles lying or sitting in awkward positions. Optimum body position for bipod use is to lie with the forearm of your leading arm flat to the ground at 90 degrees facing across the body or bent slightly inwards, but comfortably forward or at shoulder level to the ground. This supports the weight of your raised upper torso. The other hand can rest naturally by the side, underneath the rifle while waiting for quarry to appear, letting the rifle's butt pad sit in your shoulder under its own weight. Then, when a shot presents itself, slowly raise your trigger hand to take the grip, line up the scope crosshairs and gently squeeze off a shot. Pay attention at this stage. Even though the rifle is steady on a rest, your body behind this fixed point needs to be equally stable; no flinching on taking the shot, dropping the shoulder, or moving the head. You're steady at the forward position, but you need to keep just as steady at the rearward position to achieve the ever-important follow-through. The shooting position may be different but the theory and physics for firing a rifle always remain the same. Lock onto the target, squeeze the trigger and freeze while you watch the pellet slam into the quarry's kill-zone. A tip for those having trouble in keeping the shooting hand steady is to bring the leading arm hand up to support the wrist of the shooting hand or underside of the rifle butt, thereby forming a secure cradle for the rear of the rifle. You'll soon discover which works best for you.

Incidentally, some bipods come with leg extensions for extra elevation and there are even extra-long-legged, specialist bipods that allow you to adopt a sitting position and still shoot the rifle off a steady rest. Whilst there are various heights of bipod, you can even obtain steadying aids that allow you a rest while standing. These are shooting sticks such as monopods, extra-long bipods or tripods. Although you might find these useful for rare occasions, or if you're standing shooting stance is particularly shaky, I'd recommend that you don't start to rely on one as it means carrying extra kit around and more to sort out before you take a shot; at least when not in use, the bipod folds flat up to sit neatly under the forend of the rifle. Choose a lightweight model and it won't unduly affect handling when shooting off-hand and you can still fit a rifle sling to the bipod's extra sling attachment point. So in that respect, you tell me – can any airgun hunter ignore the benefits a bipod affords?

Where and When

As different quarry species have different routines it follows that there are better ambush areas for specific species. Here are some examples and ways to tackle the areas from a perspective of ambush:

A good ambush point for rabbits is obviously, and as outlined earlier, near their warrens but I also favour surprising them as they emerge from hedgerows or as they cross farm and dirt tracks. The obvious signs to look for are well-worn runs out from cover; as well as flattened grass stems, look for soil worn flat and shiny under a hedge, wire fence or side of a vertical wooden fence or gatepost.

In these positions, they cross where they have the best view to the front and to either side, but hold up within range near a well-used crossing point and you could reap rewards. When they've decided to leave cover, they'll either bolt straight across the track or and this can often be the case - most often they'll either just sit on the edge of the track or sit almost in the middle. The reason for this behaviour I presume is because they're weighing up the area , deciding if it's safe to enter the field they're facing or move to the area they're intending on feeding over. This is the opportune moment to snipe them from cover. The optimum shooting position is to conceal yourself on the nearside of the hedge line next to the track so the rabbit has left cover before having any chance of spotting your position. If the undergrowth is thick and tall, position yourself within this cover but with a clear path for your pellet from muzzle to target. This ensures that there are no mistakes shooting alongside dense undergrowth and it also gives you a better angle of fire.

Utilising Natural Cover

Cover you've walked beside while opportunist shooting the fields is also typical cover you can use for hiding in while waiting in ambush. I'm sure after a few walkabouts you've established the warrens so you'll know where best to settle down to await your unsuspecting quarry. Not to put that big a deal on it, but this form of hunting isn't for the shooter who might be wary of scratching their treasured rifle or getting the odd knock, scratch and scrape themselves, but if you want the results … no pain, no gain, as they say. Seriously though, getting amongst thickets, brambles and even thick ground cover with stinging nettles isn't the easiest of tasks, but quarry – specifically rabbits – are often found in these inhospitable areas because they realise that these places afford them the safety they require, so you can be pretty sure they won't be far away. A note of caution, though, when moving through nettles; don't presume to use even gloved hands to move them aside. Light summer wear will often be too flimsy to afford your skin protection against the aggravating nettle stings. Instead, use your rifle, or if wearing a suitably padded jacket, the back of the forearm. If settling into position amongst foliage with nettles, avoid applying body pressure onto the plants unless suitably padded. In this situation a padded gun bag can be used as a seat, as can a shooting mat, rucksack or one of the specialist padded ground seats.

As always, stealth and slow movements are of vital importance. Even though you plan to use 'sit- or lie-and-wait' tactics, don't go stomping straight into the undergrowth or trampling the cover down as this defeats the object of entering the cover. Take the least disruptive route you can, and this way you're less likely to get too many scratches or scrapes, not only to yourself but it also helps to avoid damaging the rifle and snagging your clothing. This is where a pair of secateurs can be very handy for making a pathway that can be regularly pruned for future and continued use if the site proves a good point of ambush. Unfortunately, there's no chance that you won't disturb the area to some extent, as you invariably will, but once in position in the thicket or bushes you've chosen, you're in one of nature's very own hides. If you think it strange to choose these areas for ambush, once again, consider the fox that will lie up in this cover, awaiting a rabbit to emerge from the very same area.

Try to position yourself for optimum manoeuvrability, so that you won't have to make too much noise when you want to change position. This is more important should you be choosing a smallish thicket of foliage or bush in a wooded area, when you may be using it as a completely self-contained natural hide from eyes above. For this, ideally the thickets you choose should be smallish so you have what is, in effect, natural cover surrounding you and a canopy of foliage concealing you from above, but not so much cover that you can't virtually do a 180-degree turn with your rifle if the need arises. Also, and I know I stress this, but ensure that shots out from this cover aren't in danger of being deflected by long grass, twigs and the like. Similarly, if shooting upwards at anything that may pitch into trees, always ensure that the path to the target is clear. Other forms of utilising cover can be as simple as shooting from behind fallen or uprooted trees, dry stone walls, or even out of drainage ditches found on the sides of fields. The idea is to hide or conceal yourself, and you can even do this in plain view using suitable camo in conjunction with a large enough backdrop, such as a hedge, bush or even a large tree trunk. The objective is to shield your figure being silhouetted so that light doesn't show your upper torso or body as a hard outline as it would if you were backlit, so to speak.

Another tip is, while holding up in ambush always use your ears as well as your eyes. You'll notice that I often mention this – 'hunt with your ears as well as your eyes'. Rabbits will be heard moving through or underneath thickets, scratching or plucking grass from the surrounding area and you'll likely hear woodpigeon land in trees. Granted, they can slip in undetected, but often the clapping sound of the wings as they seemingly clumsily alight into the trees gives them away. Don't look up immediately as you'll be seen. Wait a while, until the birds have done their initial neck-craning, eye-scanning recce of the area, then slowly look up to try to spot the tell-tale white patch on the neck. They'll be hard to spot, no matter what the season, as even in trees with sparse foliage the bird isn't one that's easily detected. Choice of rifle for ambush shooting is again a matter of personal choice, but as it's a static method, standard length rifles give extra shots and they also balance out nicely for bipod use. Carbines can also be used off a bipod and for shooting freehand; they can be more manageable in restricted spaces, especially useful in the confines of a hide.

The construction of a hide is detailed soon, but first, to one of the most basic of hides – the use of a suitably-sized piece of camo netting. Camo net has progressed a hell of a lot since the days of the heavy tank mesh used by the army to conceal vehicles and positions from enemy planes flying above. The theory of the use of camo net is exactly the same, that being to disguise and hide that which lies behind or beneath. Modern camo net is lightweight, offers some water-resistance and is very, very effective. A length of net approximately 10ft x 5ft (although 12ft x 56 inches is a commonly found and available size), is sufficient for covering the human form whether thrown over branches or just over the shooter lying prone. The more net you use, then granted if you're constructing a hide, then the larger the interior can be, but the more you'll need to carry. In many situations I prefer to use a stalk-and-sit technique. A cross between stalking and then sitting up in ambush as you wait in a likely position. This is when full camo wear and/or a suitable piece of camo net is very useful. If it can be rolled up to fit in the rucky, all the better.

Here are just a few instances where camo net really produced for me when there was little natural cover to use:

One of my most useful ambush tricks is to use a suitable dark pattern of camo net thrown over myself, with my rifle on a bipod. Alongside a freshly ploughed field it completely breaks up the outline even though you'll appear as a 'blob' on the landscape, you're still accepted as an unthreatening object.

Another method I learned to use was due to a problem I encountered one autumn and which I eventually solved. There was a huge warren teeming with rabbits, and it had been built in the most inaccessible of areas. A tangle of roots surrounded the warren and bramble and ferns littered the entrance holes and runs to other areas. There was no cover to snipe the rabbits from, with the only shooting position that would afford a direct shot being from the open field, unfortunately in plain view. For a time, a pop-up hide did an excellent job. Left for a few days it was accepted and a good few fell to the lead before they began to question the Tardis-like object. Then I discovered the desert sand-coloured camo nets. Pigeon shooters swear by these for putting across or around a few bales to form a hide in autumn. The way I used one was to lie within range, in the prone shooting position actually in the stubble field facing the warren. The net was draped completely over me like a blanket and this was amazingly effective as birds flying over ignored me because they couldn't make out a human shape. Rabbits had no idea where I was, and the trick to consistent, continued sport was to regularly change my shooting position. Another tip I found for comfort was to use a shooting mat. The reason being, after my first session with the thick-cropped stalks of stubble digging into me it felt like I'd been lying on a bed of nails.

Talking of Positions …

If looking to do some general pest control, then setting up ambush within striking distance of a feed trough can be very fruitful. Virtually all the flying quarry species will come to visit a feed, or indeed water trough at some point during the day. Corvids, woodpigeon … even rats and squirrel can put in an appearance, and considering the fact that rabbits use the paddock for grazing and the gate access as a crossing area, you could possibly find everything here at one time or another, dependent on season. It's always a good area to try especially if you've had limited time to recce the whole area.

There is also ambushing in a way that gives you two options or better, put two arcs of fire into two different areas around your shooting position. A double-whammy approach, you might say. Obviously, this can only be done for those with the luxury of two rifles, but referring back to my chapter on combos, if you have two set-ups and you've taken my advice and fitted at least a front sling swivel stud, then another combo can be employed to use in the double-shooting ambush technique.

There is a myriad options in setting up two rifles, but the basics are the same no matter how you're shooting. Firstly, and obviously once again the ambush position needs to be chosen with great care. Both rifles need to be set on bipods and preferably and I'd now say by necessity should be pre-charged pneumatics, unless you have the option to hold one when shooting. You can lie up in full camo in the undergrowth with rifles pointed to either side along opposite lines of the hedge you're lying up in, or both out to the front at different angles, or in a few cases, if you can find the appropriate spot you can lie up in ambush with a rifle set in front and at the back of your position. The method is quite simple but does take concentration as you're watching both areas and, depending on what presents itself, you need to get behind the rifle to take the shot. It can be difficult shooting, but very productive for covering a wide arc of ground once you've mastered the method.

Roost Shooting

Basically, this is just another form of ambushing as you're waiting for the birds to come back to an established resting place in the woods for the night. By and large, winter into very early spring are the optimum times for roost shooting, the reason being that there's less foliage on the trees. When it's particularly cold, woodies have a crafty habit of preferring to roost in conifer trees meaning targeting them here is impossible. Incidentally, note the chapter on Seasons and the advice given therein on roost shooting, particularly the months that the method is least productive.

Once again, observation is the key to success as you watch where the birds fly out from the wood at dawn and return to in the evening. You need to be out in good time to see the birds on their early to late evening flights back to their chosen areas. This will probably be on the lee side of the wood amongst large mature trees. Other favoured spots are where conifers, ivy-strangled

The author blends back into the wood and takes careful aim on a woodie at roost

larches and oak trees are sited, any of which break up the usual sparse foliage of the season. Even when that's established, I recommend you enter the wood shortly after midday without the rifle to find the trees they will be actually using. Watching from outside the wood, the trees you presume they're landing in might not be the ones they settle into. The usual white splashings at the base of the trees give this away. When these are established, locate the best spot to sit or stand which gives you the optimum shooting position when they do return. There's nothing more infuriating than to be there waiting and find a few gangly bushes or trees in your line of fire, or be 50yds to the left of the best position. There's no point going and walking around spooking the birds before you begin, so cover all the options. Once you've established this, enter the wood, this time armed, at the same time as your initial visits and take up position in the area you now know gives you the best chances of bagging a few. In many areas, the birds can be quite obliging and the perfect roost site can be right on the edge of a wood. I say 'perfect' as this allows the shooter to take up position within the wood, the gloomy inner woodland floor often helping with concealment.

Preferably sit or stand with your back to a tree to disguise your body and, needless to say, as a backstop for concealing your outline. Your head and hands should be covered, as uncovered they will stand out like white warning beacons from the woodland floor. To prevent a fruitless wait, whilst the shotgunner prefers blustery days to carry away the blast, we do not want to contend with shooting in those conditions, so check the weather forecast before your trip.

Don't think the birds will only come back in the evening, as a steady trickle of birds can start to return depending on how they've fed during the day as early as mid-afternoon, and as often as they do, don't expect them always to announce their arrival on whistling wings or by clattering into the branches. They can just as likely alight above and around you with hardly a sound. Many times, after taking a shot on what I thought was the first bird to come home to roost, an eruption of clapping wings set up from the branches of trees all around me.

On textbook days, a few will arrive and one will present itself perfectly. Let the bird settle, take careful aim, checking the path to the target is clear of twigs. Even a thick leaf can deflect a pellet enough for you to miss the vital kill-zone. Then once certain of the shot, squeeze the trigger and the bird crashes to the deck.

Don't be in a rush to pick up as others could be coming in within minutes or less. For the airgunner that's how it works best. On other days a whole flock could come whistling in, fly around the back of you and then settle into the roosting trees.

It's an exciting moment as you anticipate the challenging shots ahead, and although you'll be eager to take the first shot, you really have to let these birds settle because you now have many eyes that could detect your movement as you sight in on a bird. However, when the woodie has come into roost in such a way, even if a few birds notice your first movement as you take aim, if you see them getting twitchy, as long as you hold the position and no single bird flies up to take the others off with it, they'll tolerate this as something natural on the woodland floor and carry on to settle down to roost. This really is one of those 'heart in your mouth' moments as you freeze, wondering and waiting for them to settle fully so you can train the crosshairs on the bird you'd already picked out, and hopefully bag it. Then they will be up and away, but that's the name of the game in roost shooting.

In most woods you don't need a hide; if anything, a hide restricts your movement and angle of fire on the birds in the trees. Like many other hunters, I often prefer to stand while roost shooting as this allows you to edge around into a better position to take shots on birds alighting into the upper branches. However, if you are certain that birds will land within an area you can see comfortably and target while seated, this is less strenuous and more comfortable on the neck muscles as you wait.

Once you've become adept at roost shooting, which is a very skillful form of airgun hunting, you could shoot on into the night if there's light cloud backlit with bright moonlight. These conditions give you an ideal backdrop to sight the roosters against. Only target those showing as full body outline silhouettes, as these will more likely have few twigs to deflect the pellet. This is exciting and demanding shooting, the birds often more unwilling to fly off as is usually the case when they've only just settled in, but note: never shoot with a gun lamp as this is illegal.

Once you've shot a particular roost site, leave it a good few days. If you can, best to wait a full week before returning because the birds wise up quickly and will find another suitable area to roost, and Sod's law says, usually an area off limits for the shooter as they'll be further into or away to another wood.

A very important part of the kit for the roost shooter is the choice of scope. A good quality 3 – 9 x 40 will suffice but a special low-light scope is handy for when the light begins to fade, and during autumn and winter the light is gone all too quickly. Sometimes you have a very limited amount of light for shooting. Granted shooting at silhouettes can be done but as I've outlined, only in perfect conditions when you are very experienced at this form of hunting.

Another factor to contend with is judging the range of the bird. Judging distance is hard enough at the best of times when you have objects near your target to relate to. However, when all you have is a blank sky behind and around your quarry, range estimation becomes very tricky indeed.

That aside, presuming you've nailed those upward angle shots and are confident in your aim points, roost shooting involves little else except common sense, fieldcraft, a steady nerve and an even steadier aim! As for roost shooting corvids, this is similar but has its own perils and pitfalls. If you thought woodies are hard to target then crows are more so. However, at times, because of the racket all the birds make as they come into roost, you can take the birds from trees and the sound of others joining easily overpowers the resultant crack of lead hitting crow kill-zones. Whereas the crow is a noisy rooster, jackdaws can have loose roosts but in total contrast are almost silent as they flit into what they feel to be a safe area for the night. Targeting jackdaws at a roost site can be almost impossible. There are much better places to tackle these corvids as you'll have read in Quarry Files.

Sitty Trees

Whilst there's no denying the effectiveness of shooting woodpigeon at roost during the evening, many airgun hunters won't even have a roost on their shoot. However, woodies also have routes (flight lines) to get to and from the various feeding areas, but most importantly to the airgun hunter looking to nab a few for the pot, in-between times the woodpigeon use what shooters affectionately term sitty trees.

Not only found in woods or amongst small copses, these trees can be a small standing group amongst fields or even a lone tree on a landscape all offering the airgunner this accessible alternative to roost shooting. In fact it's surprising how the birds can often prefer a lone single tall tree in the middle of fields or a dead tree with hardly any leaf cover. It's safe to presume this is because both afford such a commanding view of the surrounding area.

Optimum times for shooting in this manner are in autumn through to spring before the trees leaf up as the woodies can be picked off the bare branches with a precision shot, but if it's a dead tree with no cover, it's a perfect place to shoot all year around as long as you don't overshoot.

You can only establish the areas and specific trees the birds use with dedicated observation by scanning

Find yourself a sitty tree and you'll be in for some good sport

the fields and trees of the shoot with a good pair of binoculars, preferably from a reasonable distance. It won't take long to spot the trees the birds favour and note the times they're used. A quick recce on foot around the trees should show bird droppings and downy feathers, dead give-aways that woodies are alighting here with some regularity.

Incidentally, whilst sitty trees are used by woodies to sit in to either rest and digest food, they are also as much used as an observation post, or stop-over point before flying on to another area, or simply await others to catch up and join them. A good 'un' is likely to attract other species such as crows, but never be tempted to raise your sights on these until they've fully settled into the tree. While woodies can sometimes zoom straight into the tree the crow is never so foolish, and on seeing anything untoward near the area will veer away, cawing loudly. Crows can indeed be a good indicator as to the effectiveness of your camo or the hide you've built.

That brings me to the next important issue after establishing the sitty trees, to determine a shooting position for the relatively limited effective range of the air rifle.

Whenever possible I prefer not to shoot from the confines of a hide, even though there are times when that's the only way to keep you concealed from the woodpigeon's incredible eyesight. Thankfully though, there are times when full camo wear or a modern ghillie suit and face veil will do the trick, but the white of the face and hands must also be covered with facemask and gloves. Next give-away is movement: If you're constantly raising your rifle or craning your head up and looking around you'll be spotted immediately.

Similarly to roost shooting, ambushing woodies coming to sitty trees can be done standing or sitting, the former is only viable in dense woodland where you can stand with your back against a large tree trunk to disguise your silhouette and remain under any foliage canopy, to hide in the gloomy area on the woodland floor beneath. Usually in copses and amongst or near a small group of trees, a seated shooting position offers the better option for being able to blend into the surroundings. If seated on the ground, rest the rifle on your knee so that a minimum amount of movement is needed to place the crosshairs on the bird's kill-zone.

Another tip is, before the birds arrive, and this can apply to roost shooting, take a few shots at chosen small branches. Hit these and this will give you a confidence boost that you've sussed the correct adjustment of hold-under needed for the different angles of fire.

Patience is the name of the game and you'll often hear the birds come into the trees as they whistle in, or the clapping of wings as they clatter into the branches to waddle along into a comfortable resting position. Unlike roost shooting, the bird isn't going to be as relaxed once it has landed. Even before looking up, give the bird time to settle; you'll probably hear it call or be joined by others. It can seem like an eternity, but wait until the birds are in position until you slowly look up to seek the giveaway white neck patch in the

Watching and waiting – patience can be a virtue in airgun hunting

branches. When spotted, slowly raise the rifle and sight the bird through the scope. Again, and I know I'm sounding like a stuck record, ensure that the path to the target is clear of twigs or leaves that could deflect the pellet. Incidentally, an amber colour front lens cover for the scope is useful to prevent the possibility of any light reflecting off the objective lens and possibly spooking the bird. If a few have arrived, choose the one offering the optimum shot or closest to your set zero. Done correctly, the slipping of the trigger should be followed by a satisfying 'thud' as the bird tumbles from its lofty perch. If the tree is surrounded by undergrowth there's no need to retrieve the birds as more could be coming in.

Now, there's an important trick you can employ to bag more birds in these situations and that's as follows: When you shoot a bird, don't drop your rifle when the others clatter away out of the tree. Woodies are notorious (as are crows) for looking behind and down at any movement as they fly away.

If they spot you, and they will if you move your rifle, then they can mark your shooting position. This might sound far-fetched but believe me when I say I've had woodies fly out to come around and land in a tree behind or to my side but well out of range, plainly sitting and craning their necks, watching me. This still might not sound important but any birds alighting afterwards are likely to quickly spot their comrades staying away from the tree and quickly fly over to join them. I speak from experience as a lapse in concentration like this once bagged me one woodie while I had to watch bird after bird land in the tree on the opposite side of the field, clearly watching my position. This is just one example of the various tricks you'll pick up yourself through experience out in the field. You will make mistakes but as your fieldcraft and knowledge of your quarry increases you'll know instinctively by your target's behaviour whether it's going to sit tight, settle or fly! Incidentally, as we've been discussing the tactics for taking birds from trees, it's worth remembering those variables for upward angle and longer-range high shots we covered in the chapter on Shooting Techniques. Not that easy is it? So, that's the shooting method, but there is still more to say on this subject as anything that helps fool the birds into the optimum position for your shot is useful. This is where a technique known as 'lofting' could well boost your bag.

Lofty Aspirations

I'll mention this technique here, but it could equally be at home in Decoy Techniques or even previously in Roost Shooting. The reason being, a few lofted birds near an established roosting tree can often keep the birds coming in even though others have flown up after a shot indicating danger. The technique is not as widely used by airgun hunters as some would have you believe (it's a trick borrowed from the shotgun shooters), probably due to the kit required and whilst the shotgun shooter often has a few poles and a T-bar, the airgun hunter may only have plastic deeks. We'll come to decoying later but the intention and basic reason to use any decoy is to give the bird a false sense of security. It sees what it thinks are its brethren and has the confidence to come in to join them.

Although I prefer to sit and wait within range of an established natural sitty tree and wait for the birds to arrive, there are times when it can be beneficial to use a few carefully placed decoys in this manner to pit the odds in your favour. The intention in using these birds is the same in theory as why decoys are used on the ground; it triggers the bird's flock instinct. Where it sees others, it presumes that place must either be safe or there's something there to interest them. The difference in this example of using decoys being that the birds are 'lofted' up into the trees, and birds flying over within range see these plastic pretenders, and drop in to join them in what appears to be a nice cosy area to rest. The method is a simple one as long as a few basic rules are adhered to.

First, the decoys are placed on a T-shaped cross-bar, but they must be secure as you don't want to have to keep bringing the birds down to re-adjust them because they've drooped or shifted into an unnatural position in the breeze. Lofting poles are usually 5 – 6ft in length and made from aluminium, painted green to disguise the shiny alloy. They have a spigot at one end that fits into the next, where a spring-loaded pin locks the poles together. The next procedure is a bit tricky, especially if breezy as you loft the arrangement higher. A tip is to find a fork in a branch to use as a rest then lift the first pole with the T-bar and decoys attached. Once high enough, the next pole can be slotted into the underside of the first and this pushed further up until another pole can be inserted into the underside of this. Once the required height is achieved the deeks should be positioned facing into any breeze and the pole leant onto the tree and pushed into the ground for added security. Don't be tempted to loft them too high as decoy birds obscured with a few branches look very realistic and a pigeon's keen eyesight won't miss them in the bare branches. Anyway, in a breeze or when resting up, woodpigeon tend to sit lower in the trees.

There are decoys that have eyelets on the back that are used for hanging the birds onto branches with wire. Alternatively, fishing line can be tied to a brick and the brick thrown (or catapulted) over a branch. The brick end of the fishing line is then tied to the eye on the back of the deek and the bird pulled up into a position in the tree with the line being secured to keep the bird in place. Although this method means you don't have the encumbrance of carting lofting poles, it's a poor alternative as you need a calm day else the birds will likely swing unnaturally on the line or wires. I mention the method here only for reasons of thoroughness.

Hide building – Hide Shooting

Of all hunting methods, hide shooting can probably be classed as one of the most productive, but only by having a very good knowledge of your shoot will you be able to select the best area to build a hide to gain the best from it. These 'buildings' can take the form of the simplest structures of a framework of thick branches leant against a backstop such as a large tree trunk or thick hedge, using extra foliage for front cover, or a few hide poles draped and surrounded with camo netting or even permanent sited structures resembling little purpose-built bungalows.

Alternatively, natural cover can be embellished and made more impenetrable to quarry with a suitably patterned, well-placed piece of quality camo netting. There are even commercially available portable hides. All types will be detailed later and all have their uses. Suffice to say, a hide is often more substantial than just throwing a piece of camo netting over the surrounding foliage or your body, even though as you've read previously the latter can at times be very effective. The reason being that modern camo nets, both in pattern and design, are far superior to what was once available. Choose wisely and you really can be hidden from view even in places quite scarce of natural vegetation, and that's the main purpose of any form of hide; to allow the hunter to get within range of wary quarry in situations where there is little or even no natural cover.

Where, When and What Type

One of the major considerations of choosing the hide position is where the sun will be in relation to the time of day you'll be shooting. I know of more than one person who's built an extremely good hide, got into position only to discover the sun coming up to rise in their face and stay shining at them all morning;

an ideal shooting position for dusk, but at dawn – big mistake. So, firstly plot where the sun rises and sets on your shoot, including where it will be most intense midway through a bright, sunny summer's or even winter's day. Remember, the sun in winter can be even more harsh than summer, and don't build where the sun in summer can keep baking down on you – you'll swelter inside. You should be avoiding this already, as you search for an area that affords natural shade to build the hide. You'd be surprised when you look around an area at how many places fit this description due to surrounding bushes and/or the position of nearby trees.

Once you've established the basics, observation, which has been dealt with previously, will have given you all the information you need on the quarry activity on your shoot. Preferably, the hide should give you control of the shooting situation, so you are well within range of the quarry targeted. Once you've taken everything into consideration, it's time to build the hide.

Unless building a permanent hide, the first important factor to address is to judge how much the building of it will disturb the area. Some quarry will tolerate quite a reasonable amount of activity whilst others won't want to see you around at all. Similarly, depending on species targeted, you need to take into consideration at what time of day you undertake construction and how long you take in building the hide. For instance, if building a semi-permanent hide within striking range of an established woodpigeon sitty tree, then build in short sessions and use sparingly. Don't use it every time you go out on your shoot, no matter how tempting. However, build a hide near an established crow roost or feeding area and you'll be lucky to have more than one, or at most two sessions before the crows will move on. If it's a field they use for feeding, they soon wise up and just move further out into the field, and infuriatingly always just out of range. A tip here is to build the hide near the trees they use to sit before dropping into the field to feed, but I'm sure you're now realising, winged vermin are always more confident off the ground.

Alternatively, rabbits can often be quite quick to accept even a crudely built hide in their area. Woodies are more aware, but the corvid family really will notice any structure so the hide needs to be the best you can build.

Obviously, if it will only be of use for a short period, or if you have a short period of time to build it, you'll need the most basic of structures, but always remember that any hide is only as good as the amount of concealment it affords the shooter inside. It's always better to overbuild a hide even if it does take that little extra time and effort.

If building near a warren, build when the rabbits are least active. If possible have another hide built so you can alternate shooting positions. If you're tactful you'll be able to cover most of the major entrance and exit points from both shooting positions, but when the rabbits decide to move on because of over-shooting, they'll be gone as if overnight. A semi-permanent hide – say built for decoying woodies you've noticed that are feeding over a particular area – should be quick and easy to build. Some hides, especially for rabbits need only to screen you from the forward position. There are even portable camo screens with poles attached that stretch out to form a wall of cover. If this will suffice for a few sessions, then they are very handy, quick and simple to set up.

Incidentally, a hide can be built anywhere, including around the farmyard, or even within a farm outbuilding or barn. If building around or in the barn, then obviously certain factors need addressing such as other people's safety and the fact that they need to know you're there and when you are there shooting. There's more on building hides around the farm in the relevant section, but I mention it here to stress that it's not only over open land where a purpose-made, hidden shooting position is of use.

Hide shooting can often be the only way of getting within range of targets

Size Matters

Spend any length of time in a small and cramped hide and you'll not want to use it again. The hide needs to be large enough to accommodate you and some essential equipment comfortably, be roomy enough for you to move around (within reason), and take different aiming positions, but it also should be small enough so that it doesn't overly stand out from the area it's built in.

When looking to build any hide, ideally look for a natural recess or gap in a hedge line; one that you can blend a structure back into. It's always better to build around a natural feature. When you've chosen such a position sit on a hide seat in the area that would be the centre of the hide and, using the rifle, swing through an arc of fire. If building with hide poles, place the front poles that will form the framework to the sides and forward in relation to your sitting position so you have a comfortable and acceptable field of view. It needn't and more often than not won't be 180 degrees, but do allow yourself room to manoeuvre to shoot. Also, you'll probably have your gun bag, some other utility carryall such as a rucky and small hide chair in there with you, so allow for this when building the hide. Once you've decided on the internal size of the hide, don't forget to allow yourself enough headroom when sitting. Use an extendable hide pole and stand it next to you at head height, then extend above that whichever height you feel comfortable with, then you can use this as a yardstick when building.

Also look to see if there are points that could be useful to shoot up into. If there aren't any and you only have the forward area as a firing zone, then begin building. Clear what will be the floor area of any runners and straggling branches from the hedge or cover near where you're building. The reason being that you don't want to trip on anything while in the hide, and you certainly don't want to stand on anything that may snap to cause noise, and kneeling on brambles or nettles is never recommended. If you're going to sit on the floor rather than a hide seat, clear the area of stones as afterwards you can sit on a small camping mattress, preferable green but definitely a dark-coloured one. This will keep out the cold and wet, and help to prevent you from getting a numb bum, but do make sure it doesn't cause any noise when you move.

At this stage, consider which position you will use as the entrance. This should preferably be from the side and to the rear, but discreet enough so you can drape a piece of camo netting across as a door blind when you're in residence. Equally, though, it needs to be large enough for you to take equipment in, and for you to enter and exit with ease.

As we are now at the building stage, you'll hopefully recall in Hunting Accessories that I mentioned the kit that would become useful once you progressed as a hunter. This is one such situation as for hide building you need a few basic tools and equipment. Firstly, a pair of garden secateurs, a wood saw, twine, camo tape, and the obvious such as hide poles and camo netting. If building a permanent hide, add to that your toolbox including hammer and a plentiful supply of nails, but this is the extreme; for most structures it's the basics you need and always the basics of correct hide-building that you need to remember. Another factor to consider is that before you even think of building a hide, although you have permission to shoot on the land, don't take it for granted you can go building on it. If it's a permanent hide you'll obviously need the permission of the landowner, but in some counties they can even be classed as a dwelling. It's common courtesy to ask the farmer if you can construct anything on his land, and more times than not he'll gladly agree if it helps you to eliminate more vermin. Also, he might just have a few pieces of material that could help in its construction such as old fence posts and even railway sleepers, the latter being ideal for the building of more substantial hides.

Here, I'll stress the importance of the hide needing to have a solid, impenetrable back section. If not, quarry can see you clearly as you move inside, as you cross the chinks of light passing in from the back. This is where many new to hide building make their first mistake. It's all well and good wanting to be able to see all around your shooting position, and if shooting from natural cover you can often achieve this, but it will be to the detriment of total concealment. So, when hide shooting, there are sacrifices that have to be made for the cover it affords. It follows that the hide needs to be built with the base knowledge from the outset of which way you will be facing to shoot. It's here that you'll need small openings in the foliage to shoot from, or gaps in the netting you poke the barrel through. Note here not to have too many shooting positions. It may seem like a good idea, but if you can see out, wary quarry is just as likely going to see in and the shooting slits or holes you make shouldn't be overly large; no more than fist-size in a hide built from natural cover. Far better to have them closely covered with camo net with the intention of just poking out the barrel to shoot. This means less foliage is needed so as not to obscure sighting the target through the scope, but enough to conceal your movements – a case for compromise.

Now we come to choice of cover materials for the hide, and net types. Firstly, natural cover: If you find dead branches lying around, use these and if possible leave them without trimming. Nothing looks worse than a regimented row of cut sticks. For weaving into this framework use weed trees of alder and hazel, but whenever possible, as camo netting has become so much more advanced, I often prefer to use extra natural cover only to embellish the netting.

As for netting itself, the best nets in my opinion are what are known as cut-leaf, open weave. These already have openings wide enough for you to shoot through and the leaf design has a natural break-up effect around the open weave. This means maximum visibility outwards, allowing you to gain a sight picture while the shooting opening is still quite concealed. Once built, stand away from the hide and visually check to ensure that there are not any unnatural-looking straight edges formed by either framework or netting. If there are, disguise them by using natural foliage you can add from the surroundings. Also, when gathering natural foliage, take it from a reasonable distance away from the hide rather than at the sides. If you don't, this will make the area look less natural and will have the hide stand out rather than blend in.

What you build depends not only on the time you can spend in construction, but also the time of year you've chosen to construct it. For permanent hides, it's widely accepted that early spring or even earlier are prime times as then, when the surrounding foliage springs into life, the natural growth actually adds to the hide, and over the years, if you keep a hide maintained, a very natural look will eventually be achieved. So, let's look at the hide options to build or buy.

Natural

A framework is always needed and like a house has walls, these are the supports that hold the structure up and give it strength, so use thick branches. Once in place, as you're going to use what nature provides, dead branches that easily snap off or are found on the ground are useful for shoring up at the front, sides or even building a roof, but if you need to cut flexible branches for weaving into your framework, you need to know which trees to cut. It's not good practice to cut everything you see that looks useful as, in effect, you're damaging the woods you should be there to protect. If you're going to use live trees, know which ones that are known by some forestry workers as 'weed trees'. These include most soft woods such as elder or hazel as they common in most areas. These woods are nice and flexible, and you'll find enough straggly branches to use in the construction of your hide, but take note to ensure that the leaves stay the natural, dark way up. Most leaves have pale undersides and even this can be just enough to deter quarry from coming in closer.

If the farmer has removed any old dying trees or just cut back an area for any reason, this is the time to ask if you can use the dead wood as he'll only probably burn it for disposal. You can, in fact, do the farmer a favour in clearing the cut wood, and although this is mainly a natural-built hide, if necessary I'll also use old camo netting as extra concealment. Incidentally, if you've left a natural hide for a while it'll more often than not need some repair, and you'll possibly also notice the dead wood will have dried up and look different to the natural live foliage growing around the area. In that respect, a bit of titivation with some fresh greenery will soon have it spruced up and looking like new.

Semi Permanent – Using Poles and Netting

This is the most popular and versatile as you can have a hide erected quickly in any area you choose. The ability to build where you like is made all the easier thanks to the large selection of quality hide poles and effective camo netting easily and commercially available. One item definitely to add to the kit are cross support bars which means a firm framework for the roof can be formed once the camo net is draped over. This will help prevent the net sagging down into the hide. Hide poles can be lightweight or heavy-duty, standard fixed sizes or extendable. Some come with kick plates for pushing into hard ground. So as you can see there's a large variety to choose from. All are useful in various situations. Similarly, there are many types and different patterns of camo netting to suit the varied terrain; usually these are either autumnal colours or more 'green heavy' for summer foliage. There are sand-coloured nets, and these are ideal for using over stubble fields, more often by pigeon shooters and draped over a few hay bales. You'll often be building against a hedge so use the appropriately coloured foliage netting. I've already mentioned my preference of net design but with the additional use of natural vegetation, a hide such as this can be erected in no time at all.

A word of warning though: When you add foliage to make the hide look more natural, don't weave the foliage and branches into it unless you want to spend a day removing straggly branches from a net you need somewhere else shortly afterwards. Only do this if it's to be left in situ for a fair amount of time. If not, lean the natural foliage against the netting – it's just as effective.

Permanent

The beauty of a permanent hide is that it can be built to a much higher standard and in some cases be able to fully withstand the elements. Also, as the seasons progress, if built near growing hedgerow of bramble or hawthorn, nature really will soon encroach onto and around the structure blending it into the natural background, and one built in a well-chosen position can often offer all-year-round sport. The ideal places to consider for these hides are within range of where quarry crosses from one area to another. For positioning, the usual type of areas such as natural gaps in hedge lines that might accept a hide into the surroundings as a continuation of the hedge, are ideal. As it will be there, in some cases for years, you need to build from much more substantial materials. Thick fence posts make an ideal framework and should be driven well into the ground. The lower base surround of wood ideally needs to be made up of substantially-sized logs or old railway sleepers. They can also usually be much larger than semi-permanent hides, and even have enough internal space to accommodate two shooters. A seating arrangement such as a small bench can easily be made and I certainly recommend that you build a fixed strong roof of either weatherboard, or shiplap construction, with a slant to allow rain to run off. You can even build a proper doorway, but let's not forget the outside. This should always be repaired to suit the seasons.

No matter what the main construction, even it was made from breezeblock, the outside still needs to resemble the outside vegetation that surrounds it. Think along the lines of a birdwatcher's hide, but one that blends in with its surroundings. The longer an object is in situ on the landscape, no matter what it is, be it a hide, tractor trailer or discarded oil drum, the more it will be accepted by the local wildlife. This is a major bonus of permanent hides that work in the hunter's favour as they are there much longer and therefore have more time to be considered just part of the scenery.

Portable Hides

The main benefits of using portable, or as they're often known 'pop-up' hides, is the fact that you can erect a hidden shooting position in literally seconds. Some even fold down into a carry bag the size of a very large pizza. Arrive on the shoot, pop-up the hide and use it.

If you've chosen a bad position or you spy a better area to shoot from, it can be moved just as quickly, so you can constantly take quarry by surprise, vermin never knowing where you could strike next. These hides have given me some excellent shooting and have proved to be very usable for many hunting situations. Set up and leave it in an area for quarry to become used to it for a few days, arrive before dawn, get settled into position and reap a few hours of quick-fire action. They come in a small but useful variety of camo patterns and designs. Whichever you choose, all have windows for shooting out of that can be opened or closed depending on how much or little you want to see out. All come with pegging points, guy ropes and pegs and most are quite secure until it really gets windy. If this sort of weather is forecast best to take the hide down, rather than leave it set up, or a good blow could see you traipsing over the other side of the fields to collect your hide next time you arrive to use it.

Another downside is that these one-man hides tend to be quite small and cramped inside, good for short sessions but you'll feel the strain on your back the longer you sit in there, waiting to see what is going to appear. They're always handy for when you spot an area where pigeons or crows have suddenly started feeding over, though – so don't discount this option.

Pop-up hides are extremely useful when you require a fully covered shooting position

The Hide Shooting Technique

Once you've finally built the hide, depending on type, a few words on maintenance: If it's a natural hide or even a permanent one, before entering give it the once over. Check to see that it still blends in with the surroundings. Hopefully, vegetation will have grown up in front or over your hide helping to make it blend more into the surroundings. If all's well, fine. If it looks a bit shabby, give it a spruce up. If you haven't used a hide for a while certainly check that the shooting points aren't obscured. Embellishing slightly with a bit more naturally growing cover is no bad thing, but to the point of obscuring your vision – no way. If the foliage needs trimming back then do so with secateurs or adjust the netting accordingly. After that check that the back is still impenetrable to light. Incidentally, if you're after the dawn feeders, you'll almost always have to be in and settled a good half hour to an hour before dawn.

Before even starting to use a hide, a routine check that I advise shooters do, and one that can be done on a day prior to shooting is to range certain objects from the shooting position. You can do this from inside with a laser rangefinder, or purposely pace out and set markers at different positions from the front of the hide. Markers can be stones or even wooden pegs. You can be as frugal or comprehensive as you prefer, with range markers set out at your set zero, then at 5yd increments closer and further out from this mark. I'm sure you will realise the benefits of this and that ranging can be used when just lying prone in ambush near a warren.

However, specifically in relation to hide shooting, depending on the field of fire you can comfortably target, you'll possibly want to set out markers to the left and right of the hide as well as directly in front. These will form a semi-circle around the front of the hide. Don't put out too many as they'll become confusing – too few and you'll not get a reasonable indication of a range should quarry present itself too far to the left or right of a set range marker. The way you set this out is up to you, but try to envisage the effective shooting area you have as a block grid map of set ranges. When quarry is within a grid reference on the area, you'll know the approximate range to target. Once you've assessed the ranges, it's time to use this knowledge and the concealed shooting position you've now created.

The two major requisites that will aid success and your enjoyment of hide shooting are the need to be organised and comfortable. You're likely to be in there for some time, so set out the gear you need so everything is to hand. That way you'll not have to rummage through a bag for extra ammo or to get a drink. Also, there's nothing more infuriating than settling down in position, waiting patiently for first light, and then suddenly to remember something you've left in the car. As you progress learning and developing your skills as a hunter you'll soon realise the accessories that are useful to you. We've dealt with the general accessories available in the relevant chapter, but certainly as you do more hide shooting you'll know which accessories suit the task.

Obviously, unless you've built-in some form of seating, or are sitting on the ground, a small lightweight, portable folding hide seat or pigeon shooter's bag combined plastic tub seat will certainly be a must. The latter being very handy as these holdall carry bag/seats will accommodate poles, netting and your deeks. A small rucksack or carryall will still be needed to carry extra ammo and other bits and bobs such as a flask, food, extra clothing … anything you might need during your stay as you work under cover. Incidentally, although the hide should ideally be built in the shade, inside it can still get hot in summer and certainly cold in winter. As you're not moving around much, in winter it can be very cold indeed, so take appropriate drinks depending on the time of year, and certainly consider a soup flask for some warming nourishment in winter. Don't be tempted to take too much gear into the hide as what at first may have seemed to be a fairly roomy construction can soon become crammed with kit.

Different shooters want different things in the hide but there are basics. Have a checklist so you don't forget something obvious. If you've a bad memory, there's no shame in checking the list before you start a session. It'll certainly be a better proposition than having to leave the hide for something you've forgotten – usually just as a woodie or two are about to drop into the area you're decoying over.

In fact, leaving the shooting area to retrieve a kill can be infuriating. If dropping birds from trees and the grass is quite long around the base you might get away with leaving them. Sometimes, it'll be a necessity and need to be done immediately after the kill, especially for birds that fall unnaturally in the open to be seen by others flying in.

However, just as many times it pays to hold off a shot for the fact that the bird, or for that matter a rabbit, lends itself to being a natural decoy. A scraggy, lone feral pigeon in the trees isn't that worthy a target, but wait a while and it could soon be joined by woodies. Similarly, a crow you hear just out of sight behind or directly above isn't worth spooking by undue internal hide movement as it'll probably soon drop down into the field in front, especially if using baiting-down tactics. Also, it can possibly attract others into more suitable shooting positions. That brings me to mention that even though you are supposedly fully hidden, don't think the cover of the hide allows you to move around freely; try to stay as quiet and still as possible at all times. This is often known as 'hide discipline', adhere to it and it will pay dividends.

Now, even though you're hidden I recommend the use of full camo wear including facemask and gloves. No matter how good the hide, no point in taking the risk of blowing it due to your leading hand flashing white across a shooting area. Don't go looking out of the hide showing hands or face because even though concealed, your movements will be noticed. Too many get impatient and look over or around a hide, even putting their face right up to a shooting point – don't. It's easy to become inpatient but this is a waiting game. Remember, hide discipline at all times.

When it comes to rifle choice, carbines are the optimum rifle type as they are suited to manoeuvring in smaller spaces. Even so, when pushing the rifle through to shoot, do so slowly and only far enough so you can sight in on the target. Only the very end of the muzzle should need to poke through as sometimes you don't need to push the scope right up close to the inside of the netting or front cover foliage to see out. If so, this is also a situation when once again the front scope lens can be a cause for concern, even on dull days a bird, especially one as wary as a corvid, can see the sky reflected off the front lens and even catch a glint from the finish of a rifle barrel. Use an amber scope cover or piece of loose 'see-thru' camo material wrapped and secured with a rubber band around the objective lens to prevent this.

I recommend camo tape around the silencer and maybe a bit on the barrel immediately behind it, and if using a rifle with a buddy bottle, cover that as well. Slip-on covers of brown or camo can be bought for the major rifle models, and I'm sure quarry can spot the black outline of a barrel or even tip of a silencer moving in or against camo. No use blowing it for something so trivial. Another bonus of shooting from a hide is, you often have more time to take the shot. Without fear of detection you can take more time in waiting for the quarry to present itself better, so you can put the pellet smack bang into the kill-zone.

As with other techniques, you hunt with your ears as much as your eyes. The magpie will often noisily herald its presence, to the more discreet rustling of a rabbit. Alternatively, the sound of it plucking grass from the ground can be quite loud and tell you there's one close by. Another give-away is the clapping of a woodpigeon's wings as it lands in the trees, and crows usually can't help but start harshly cawing to see if one of their own is about.

Depending on the size of your shoot, the permission granted and the length of time you've been shooting over the area, I'd advise most hunters to construct at least one permanent hide and maybe one or two semi-permanent ones on their shoot. More hides means you can rest areas and rotate the use of the hides so as not to overshoot an area.

Now to the subject of using a rest in a hide. An old camera tripod is useful for this. A camera beanbag or shooting beanbag on the head of the tripod will allow you to slide the rifle back and forth and swivel it right around. If you had the rifle on a bipod, even with extended legs and swivel facility you'd not get this level of movement. Then again you could use a small compact monopod.

Going for a slash? Sorry to sound crude but it's a natural bodily function. You can bet Sod's law says you've waited three hours and as soon as you leave for a call of nature, quarry will appear in a position you could have drawn an easy bead on. A funnel into a length of plastic pipe, set to the back and running from inside to out, is better than using an old container and throwing it out the back door. I know it may sound unpleasant but you need to take these things into consideration. That's hide shooting.

Decoying

As the name suggests, decoying is a way of attracting (in some cases, distracting) a bird with an imitation known as the decoy, or deek, of the same species, so that the intended quarry targeted is brought within range. In the case of the woodpigeon, the bird most associated with this method, attracting them down to an area is nothing new, as shotgunners have been doing it almost since they first seriously began targeting the crop guzzlers. Alternatively, using a crow deek positioned near suitable bait, such as a slit-open rabbit, works to give the corvid a sense of safety near the food, and the same applies for magpies. For corvids, there is the alternative decoy method where a bird is used, such as a little owl or raptor, placed in their territory or near a nest sight to annoy the corvids to show themselves as they mob the intruder. Those peripheral and off-shoot decoying methods will be dealt with as we come to the relevant section, but, there's no doubting that both methods work well, at the optimum times of year in the right locations.

First the use of decoys for our most popular pie filler – the woodpigeon. The theory behind the method is quite a simple one. Arrange a pattern of decoys in a field to look like feeding pigeons so the real ones flying over will come down to join them. Then hole up nearby within striking distance, more often than not well hidden in a purpose-built hide. Eventually, pigeons flying over, see the imitation birds, assume their brethren have found some grub and come down to join the feast. Sounds easy if you read it quickly doesn't it? Well, obviously it isn't, because unlike shooting with the shotgun, as you're using an air rifle you need the pigeon to land and stay still long enough for you to take a shot. This is the main problem that faces the airgun hunter using this technique. If they've come in en masse, always let a good few settle amongst the deeks before choosing a target. There are times when small groups or even lone birds will land with more confidence, and as I often say, fewer eyes to potentially see you is much better than numerous ones. So now, let's go through the stages to set up the woodies for what is, in effect, a most crafty deception. As with other hunting methods, observation is of major importance. You need to watch and learn where the pigeon feed, but more importantly, learn the regular flight lines the birds use to and from feeding areas. Once you've established a pattern of behaviour in your local woodie population you can make a start, but take advantage of any sudden feeding areas you observe the pigeon use. They might even be off a regular flight line because they've found 'lays' in the corn or barley. These are flattened patches caused by wind or rain, and even tramlines caused by the tractor, left after spraying, are wide enough for the birds to drop into. Watching from a distance you'll see the woodies drop like stones to disappear from view gorging and ruining more of the crop field. If left untroubled by shooting attention, woodies and, of course, crows and rooks can strim crop fields from inside out and vice versa. Like other methods of hunting, make the most of the opportunities you see and get over there as soon as you can, set up a hide and put out the decoys. That is if you can get to the position without trampling over precious crops yourself! If you can't, you need to wait until the fields are harvested. It's not only a method for the autumn, though, as decoying can work at any time of year when crops are cut. You can even decoy birds down onto the barest set-aside field. A few decoys and hide-building material will get you started. If you get the bug, you'll soon be buying all sorts of paraphernalia; floater poles, bird cradles, possibly even one of the electric rotating pigeon attractors or 'whirligigs' as they're often referred to. Let's take a look at basic decoys, the types available, and patterns to set them out in.

Although the art of decoying hasn't changed much since its early use, the types of decoys available to the modern shooter most surely have. In fact, back in the very early days of the sport, keen pigeon shooters made do by making their own from bits of wood and feathers or either used dead birds, or carved wooden ones. Trouble was, you had to either shoot a few first to set out in a pattern or lug heavy wooden ones on to the shoot. Fortunately, the decoys you can buy today are much more user-friendly, and are either plastic full body, plastic or rubber shell, or EVA-foam, outstretched wings, silhouette-types. The latter are for use as floaters or to put on a whirligig machine if you haven't already bagged a few birds to use as naturals. Methods of usage will be outlined presently. Incidentally, there are plastic decoys that are treated or flocked, this is the term given to the fact they're covered in a soft, felt-like material or 'flock'. This makes them very realistic-looking and in situations of bright light and direct sunlight, they can often work better as they don't glint or shine unnaturally. In fact, flocked decoys are now available for most species.

The Art of Deception

Decoys should be placed out in the field under an established flight line, and set out in little groups or patterns, as they're known, always facing into the wind. Don't position them too close to your shooting position, but obviously keep the nearside edge of the pattern well within range.

Unfortunately, birds often come in textbook fashion but veer away because there's something not quite right about the set-up. Maybe they caught a glimpse of you, the hide doesn't blend in well enough with the area, or the decoy pattern just isn't quite right for the day. However, you'll not have long before woodies do land, but they often don't hang around long before they realise their mistake. As soon as the bird settles and raises its head, take the shot, slightly poking the muzzle of the rifle out of the hide netting; an adrenalin rush of a moment as you'll be willing the bird not to move or catch sight of you.

At first, this shooting technique can be very frustrating but very challenging. If all goes according to plan, the shot bird will have dropped and is hopefully not showing breast feathers or with wings outstretched. If it has, leave the hide so as to retrieve it, or better still, if it's not during a warmer month set it out as a natural decoy. I mention the season as birds will soon get fly-blown if left out in the field. For setting out dead birds as decoys, you can either use a special cradle that supports the bird on the ground, or simply tuck its wings into its side and lay its head out at a right angle, or better still prop it up using a chin stick. Don't have the head stuck up too high as this is the posture of an alert or unnatural-looking bird. When used correctly, shot birds certainly do make the best deeks.

Incidentally, even though hide building has been dealt with already, the importance of a hidden and well-constructed hide can't be overstressed. It must obscure you from prying eyes, especially from above as birds fly over, but, so good are the new camo nets that I've had birds land in the pattern spook at something, or they're twitchy from past experience and fly up into the trees on my left or right, clearly visible from my shooting position. Due to their position in relation to the hide, they can't see into the gloom beyond the net as you've got a full dark-colour backdrop – the ground. Many times I've taken them from the trees shooting through the net roof of the hide.

Now, as this is not an in-depth look at advanced decoying techniques. but more a guide to help you try your hand at the method, I recommend that anybody who seriously gets into this form of airgun hunting gets a quality book on the subject of pigeon shooting. Knowledge is power in this game and even then, the reason behind employing certain tricks will only become apparent after much experience.

The basic patterns I use are variations on a theme that most shotgunners use, and that's what can best be termed as a loose horseshoe, a staggered L-shape, or a pattern in the shape of a comma; all so named due to the appearance of the pattern from above. In all cases, the deeks at the front of the pattern form a barrier to the front so incoming birds drop into the open space behind, but watch how birds react to the pattern. Have a bad pattern out and they'll let you know, they'll hardly give the area a second glance on their way over. It could be that they're determined to get to a specific area, but often a good deek set-up will turn them in. So don't be scared to experiment with the pattern, slightly enlarging it, narrowing or even changing its shape.

Also, when setting the deeks out, if there is any wind, face the birds into the breeze. Don't make the pattern too regimented or have birds too close together. Have some at a slight angle to the others, some with heads up and some with heads down as if feeding.

Now, specific to this form of shooting with the air rifle, and not to cause problems further down the line, the decoys shouldn't be overly spread out. I set them out so that the closest birds in the pattern are

20yds and the furthest edge of the pattern of birds are at approximately 40-45yds out from my shooting position. The pattern itself is no longer than approximately 40yds from front to back. The reason for this is, when you're in position, even in a hide, movement is your biggest give-away. Unless you're totally concealed, even carefully moving the rifle to the left or right will spook them and up and away they'll go. Using a more tight pattern usually brings the birds, or at least a reasonable amount, down as close as possible to where you're ready to train the scope. This should be towards the back of the pattern. This is probably the major difference between setting a pattern for air rifle shooting instead of targeting them when using the shotgun.

Remember, of all quarry, woodies are amongst the wiliest, and unlike a rabbit that knows it can bolt to run for cover, the woodpigeon on sensing, hearing or usually seeing anything untoward will just fly up and away – and not always to a tree where you can pick it off. It won't sit there thinking on the ground. This means shooting is very demanding. Often, as soon as the bird lands and stops moving you've got to take the shot. However, the plus points the air rifle hunter has over the shotgunner are that shots can be taken at greater distance and using a silenced airgun there's very little sound to disturb the peace. In fact, many times I get the bonus rabbit or two that comes out of the nearby cover to my shooting position while pigeoning. I presume they see deeks in the field and it gives them confidence to come out as well.

As an alternative, and whenever possible, I relish the opportunity to shoot over decoys from natural cover. It'll be obvious that there aren't many times you will find an area with an ideal shooting position ready prepared such as this. Obviously, you need to wear full camo wear and it needs to be somewhere where you can get right back into the hedging at the side of the field, under overhanging trees to use the hunter's friend – shade.

If you've found an ideal spot where you don't need the encumbrance of a camo screen then not only have you been very lucky or been vigilant in your observation, but you can also adopt a shooting style very similar to the shotgunners. Once you spot a bird or two are coming into the decoys, and you really do only want them to come in small numbers for this technique, put the butt of the rifle into your shoulder and follow the bird keenly with your eyes as it drops into the pattern. As it is landing, slowly raise the rifle, pointing it in the direction of the bird and drop your head onto the rifle cheekpiece to sight alongside the scope. Incidentally, this is the only time the bird will tolerate movement from your position, although you should strive to keep it minimal, as its eyesight at this moment is concentrated on the landing area.

If you've smoothly followed the bird's path on landing you should only have to shift the rifle slightly to sight through the scope and the woodie will be in the sight picture. This is the ideal scenario as there's nothing worse than waving the rifle around trying to spot the bird. If you haven't got it in your sights, carefully look to the side of the scope, find the target, line up the muzzle and look again. Hopefully, the bird won't have spooked, but as they're so inconsiderate, it probably has! It will certainly by now be walking and moving, wondering what's going on. This is the most nerve-wracking moment because it'll feel like an eternity until it stops still or lingers in a feeding position long enough for you to line up on the kill-zone. If hide shooting or using alternative cover, I recommend that you take heart/lung shots as believe me, head shots are almost impossible unless it does what I've now termed the 'vacant stare'. Watch woodies feeding, or even when in sitty trees, every so often they just stop with the head slightly cocked to one side with the most vacant look in their small, yellow-rimmed, black-spot eyes. However, don't be fooled, as the bird's anything but vacant; at this moment it's using all its senses to take in everything going on around it. That's why you can't be moving around or even wavering with the muzzle. If it catches sight of you, a glint off the barrel or the scope lens and it'll be off. At this point, you should be on target and it's definitely only during 'vacant stare' moments that I'll consider taking a head shot on a woodie that's landed.

There are also times when you can get back in heavy cover, or under a camo net shooting from a prone position. This is one of the only times shooting lying down, when I often prefer not to use a bipod because the pigeon can land anywhere and, for once, the bipod would be an encumbrance.

In these situations, some natural cover could well be needed to be cut from foliage placed in front, anything so those keen eyes don't spot you as the woodies pitch in.

Incidentally, if lying prone, or shooting from a ditch at ground level a woodpigeon doesn't stand very tall as a target. To be most flexible, you should whenever possible find a position where you will be slightly above the shooting area. In this situation there's no following the bird or birds as they come in; it's 'head down' and let them land, and then slowly sight a target and take a shot.

It's worth mentioning that if the birds are not coming to decoys, also keep your eyes peeled as many times a lone buzzard, kestrel or sparrowhawk will spook them. If so, it's time to switch plans. I'll usually opt to go for a spot of opportunist shooting because if they're really twitchy they'll not land in the pattern when there's a predator around.

Nothing's ever cut and dried with any hunting technique. It can be a long wait or at others you can have just put out the deeks, turned on the pigeon machine and entered the hide when they come flying in; and that brings me nicely to the subject of rotating pigeon machines, or as they've become affectionately known 'whirligigs'.

Decoying woodies in autumn is now as traditional for airgun hunters as it is for shotgunners

Magic Roundabout

I first became interested in the use of pigeon machines through their use in shotgun shooting but primarily, as an airgun hunter, I noticed a few things pertaining to how the birds reacted towards them. Admittedly, when the machines were first used, birds absolutely zoomed into the area. Presumably, they work because of the movement of the whirling birds on the machine, in theory resembling birds circling maybe to land or lifting off jostling for position over an area heavy with feed. The pigeon machine is used with traditional deeks on the ground and where you set it in relation to the pattern is personal choice or judged by experience. Most set it to the rear and to the side. Now, the thing I noticed was birds that snuck in under the noses of the shotgunners without detection would actually fly at the machine and land underneath. Strange behaviour, or some natural feeding characteristic, or both? I prefer to think the birds come zooming in to get under the flying birds circling above, to get at what is presumably a food-rich area underneath. Birds that do this will often sit longer, possibly because they're puzzled at the birds that are still circling overhead and the fact that there's probably nothing much of interest where they've landed.

So if using one of these machines, watch for this, but also watch for birds landing more conventionally into the pattern. It's now generally accepted that the machines, in some areas, are losing effectiveness. I think this will come and go with seasons and as new birds come along with each and every year. In other words, like other quarry species, some birds have learned to stay away because they associate them with danger, they've possibly been shot at in the past, but are ones that have been lucky enough to be missed. The pigeons soon wise up. If you're keen, get yourself one as they don't cost the earth and at times they certainly will work, but as with most things, experience will show when, and when not, to use them.

Incidentally, the rotary pigeon machine often attracts crows. Unfortunately, crows tend to lazily float over the area watching more than the sometimes foolhardy woodie, and can infuriatingly glide off just as lazily as when they first arrived. However, let's leave the machines, and return to more traditional decoying methods. A crow decoy placed well back at the outside edge of the birds can often bring woodies down to a pattern. This is known as a 'confidence deek' and works to give woodies a feeling of security, as it does to fool the crow that one of its kind has found something edible. It gets the nickname of confidence deek as every animal knows how wary the crow is, and if woodies see a crow looking comfortable on the ground then the area must be safe.

Another useful device to use with decoys is a floater. This is just an extending pole that has a cradle on the end. Onto this you set a dead pigeon with wings outstretched as if it was floating down to join the others on the ground. You can also use an EVA foam silhouette deek if you've no naturals. You can even mount a crow on the floater. Whichever you use, in any sort of a breeze, they bounce and sway about, resembling a bird about to join the flock below. Needless to say, it pays to position the floater to the back, even quite well behind the main decoy pattern, depending on conditions and the area being shot over.

Come October, those that have survived will have probably seen a lot of pigeon machines and been shot at by traditional methods so will associate them with danger. This is where a very small tight decoy pattern and a couple of floaters can be very effective. While on the subject of floaters, it's this movement that attracts other birds in when using these decoys as the wind raises and lowers the floater giving it a natural look. That's why you can often see these decoy set-ups referred to as 'bouncers'. You can now get electronically-operated floaters that even flap their wings as if landing, and some can be set with a timer to flap every so often. Also there are 'peckers' which, as the name suggests, peck at the ground, operated by battery – all clever stuff, and I'm sure other ingenious deeks will be developed and designed and all will be

Great care must be taken when shooting around or near livestock and if they start to get twitchy – stop shooting!

useful at times. Even simple half-body, shell deeks placed on their stakes rocking in the breeze can often be enough to trigger a response from birds flying overhead.

Although at times infuriatingly difficult, decoying woodies down to the air rifle is now amongst my favourite forms of airgun hunting, especially through autumn into winter. I can't describe the buzz you get as you'll need to be out there and experience the feeling for yourself as they fly over, then circle around to take another look at the deeks on the ground. Your heart will be in your mouth as you wait for them to drop into the pattern. Sometimes they touch down but take off as soon as their feet hit the ground, but they'll do another circuit of the field before returning to land, hopefully this time, with more confidence. Don't try to watch them fly around, just follow them with your ears as you'll soon know when they've come back. It might be the clapping and whistling sound of wings or a glimpse of shadow and dark shapes sweeping overhead, but then they're back and it's your opportunity to put the pellet into the target.

Though using established and traditional decoy patterns are a good starting point and will produce results, experiment with your own if you're not having much luck. One of my favourites is to huddle a small group of no more than half a dozen together near the base of a sitty tree or in a quiet corner of a field. Be in a hide within range and birds often fly in but veer away from the pattern to sit in the nearest tree to watch the area from above, that's if they don't land next to the deeks. Remember, it's natural for the birds to be seen feeding at the base of trees, especially come the autumn into winter when berries, beech mast or nuts are falling. If coming in, but preferring the safety-first approach and landing in the tree, a good bag can be had taking them from the branches in this way. In effect, you've created an artificial but inviting sitty tree. If you prefer, a few lofted birds in the closest tree to the pattern can be used as an added attractor.

Annoying Habits

As mentioned at the very start of this section, another method to use with decoys is one of annoyance. This is used to trigger the attack and mobbing instinct familiar to all corvids, especially magpies, crows and to some extent, jays. The method couldn't be more straightforward as you simply locate a nest area or territory that you've seen birds regularly frequent after feeding, and position a little owl, kestrel or similar raptor. Some have even had success with teddy bears, the target trigger presumably being the big glassy eyes staring out of the trees. You can position the deek on a pole, which I prefer to put close to cover in a position where the corvids will have chance to sit on a branch to call angrily at this intruder. It's at this stage you can pick them off and, of course, it hardly needs saying that you need to shoot from a well-hidden shooting position. This is also a shooting situation where the use of the suitable quarry call can be employed to agitate the birds further into making a foolhardy mistake. There'll be more on the conventional use of decoys for corvids in the Baiting-down section.

So as you can see, many uses for decoys and I'm sure many will agree that it's definitely a case of 'never leave home without your plastic!'

Baiting-down – Corvids

This is the most popular method for bringing wary corvids such as crows and magpies within range, but in lean, hard times, even woodies, collared doves and squirrels can be brought to suitable bait, as of course can rats which has been dealt with in Quarry Files. As a matter of interest, some reckon they have success using baiting techniques for rooks, but in my experience, the rook is too clever for that and can seemingly always find a meal somewhere safer.

In its simplest form you put out suitable bait, which for corvids is most often a slit-open rabbit, wait in a well-hidden shooting position (usually a hide) and pick them off as they come to the bait.

However, a much more methodical and thoughtful approach is required if the hunter is to reap the most for his efforts, which in the case of baiting-down corvids is the fact that you need to be up well before dawn as the magpie and crow are surely, like their close relatives, veritable insomniacs of the bird world.

To get up to use this method in the depths of winter takes commitment, and it's during this period that the method really comes into its own because like other species, corvids find food harder to find. Don't despair; if you enjoy a lie in, when the birds have reared young it becomes very effective again from midsummer onwards at any time of day. Evening sessions can also be very productive in summer before the sun drops too low.

In fact, starting a baiting campaign again once the birds have reared young can be deadly. Young magpies and crows are surprisingly naïve and can be caught out nearly as soon as they've sampled their first-found free meal, especially if you're waiting to greet them with some lead!

The reason for the lull in early springtime before the method becomes 'killer' again in the summer, is that although it seems maggies and crows are everywhere you look on your shoot, come late February and certainly by early March, both species will have paired off and not be spending as long over the fields looking for food. Much of their time is spent as breeding pairs, rebuilding nests and preparing to rear young, and more and more of these nest sites are in town gardens and cities, a major reason that you now generally see fewer of them over the open countryside.

Incidentally, in some parts of the country, at certain times, rabbits can be quite hard to target and shoot, especially for use as bait. To save the effort or indeed the waste of good rabbit meat, you can use pet food or Chum mixer. Unfortunately, these make easy pickings for the birds to grab and quickly fly off with, so better still, when I can find them, I'll use road-kill rabbits as bait. However, you can try a makeshift bird's nest using straw or scrunched up dying foliage and put out a few hen's eggs. Corvids are used to raiding any nest including ground-nesting birds so it isn't unnatural for them to find food like this. A trick that's worked for me is to use at least one white duck egg with a couple of hen's eggs; the duck egg helping the bait become more visible. Also, a trick is to put down Clingfilm and crack open one of the eggs to expose the contents to make it even more appetising. If there's one thing these egg-robbing corvids detest it is another of their kind getting to the spoils first. Alternatively, a piece of raw, bloody liver, the rubbery the better, nailed down onto a log or fence post so it can't be dragged off, also brings in the corvids. The texture of the meat isn't easy for them to break up so they have to work to get pieces off, giving you more time to target them.

It must be said, a dead rabbit is by far the best, though. Preferably bait-up in an area already regularly frequented by the targeted species, and you need to bait an area for a good few days before shooting; better still, a week or more so the corvids will get used to finding free meals, but just as importantly, be confident feeding there. Then, when you've got the birds feeling the freebie dining area is a safe place, you simply get yourself into position before feeding time to pick off the carrion-eating critters. A major advantage of this method is that it allows you to dictate the range at which the quarry is to be targeted. Obviously, before the baiting-out process begins, you'll need to have either built a semi-permanent, natural hide or have left a pop-up, portable hide in position in readiness for use. This has to be accepted by the local corvids as a natural part of the scene, and as both the magpie and crow are always moving around looking for food very early, this means you need to be ready and waiting in the hide with fresh bait in position even earlier.

Once you're in position with your crosshairs trained on the bait, you shouldn't have long to wait until a chack, chack, chack will herald the magpies' arrival, but at times they can arrive as silently as the crow. Whichever way they come, they will usually land away from the bait then hop up to it when they've had a look around to check the area is safe. As magpies rarely travel solo, they don't often come to the bait alone, and it's best to let a few start tucking in before starting to shoot. When using slit-open rabbit, don't empty too much of the rabbit's innards out onto the ground. If you do, the birds can get at it too quickly and be away with the dissected delicacies, leaving a gutted and less attractive bait. The eyes seem to be a particular favourite and once taken, a dead rabbit can soon become spent, and the bait rendered quite ineffective. There also seems to be a pecking order amongst a group of magpies. A few birds may dig into the rabbit but often one will stand nearby as if waiting its turn. As the other bird or birds will be moving and ripping at the bait the static bird is the one to target.

You can also use decoys to make the scene look more natural, but I feel rather than setting a scene, what you're actually doing is creating a pack mentality, a situation where the birds arriving want to join in before everything has gone. Whatever it is, a few sensibly placed magpie deeks can work wonders.

When I use a magpie deek, I place it right next to the bait with its beak in the open slit. This can have others flying straight onto the bait to join in for the easy meal as their greed seemingly overtakes their usual cautious nature. Alternatively, position one in a nearby tree.

Now, the crow is a different matter altogether. The crow will more often than not just appear silently as if from nowhere to land upon the bait, filling your scope with a black flurry of wings. At other times, it's deafening as you hear them calling from around the shooting position but there are none in plain view.

Then again, you might experience what I term 'the long walk' approach. This is when you'll see the birds land out in the field and walk slowly forward, pecking at nothing in particular, and then walking back on themselves in a very strange display of behaviour. Whether this is because they're not that hungry or are suspicious, which can be the case if the bait is positioned too close to heavy cover such as a thick hedge or tree line, is debatable. In this and other similar scenarios, the hunter needs to be patient and wait.

Just as infuriatingly, they might circle overhead, incessantly making that distinctive 'kaarr' call, with eyes scanning the area for anything untoward down below. If you're experiencing these situations of hesitancy, there are ways to give the black stuff a feeling of security. The best by far is to use the confidence deek trick, but anything that seems wrong with the decoy, usually the fact it doesn't look quite realistic enough, will put the birds off. In the past, I'd weather my traditional plastic deeks so that they lost their shine, but now we have deeks including magpies, and of course woodies, covered in a soft fibre that makes them look remarkably realistic. As previously outlined, these are known as flocked decoys, but even then, when specifically targeting the crow, unlike the magpie, positioning can have a marked effect on how other crows react. Some advocate putting the deek right next to the bait, others say it works better put well to one side, but both ways work on their day. Maybe the crow's not in the mood for a scrap so it won't go near the bait until the other leaves, or if hungry enough, isn't fussed so decides it wants to dive straight in. Whatever you're experiencing, wherever you place the decoy, stick with it as there's no way you can leave the hide and expect any more action in a hurry – not from crows that's for sure.

When it works, the extra attraction obviously instills false security in the crow flying over, proof that the crow is even seen by other crows as the cautious creature it is. If you really take to crow shooting you can put out a pattern of crow deeks, but not unlike woodies, crows don't give each other much room to feed as if one has found food, the others want to get to it as well. Some have success using this trick by using a smattering of crow deeks, and also placing a rabbit or even using dead pigeon as bait near the pattern. Again, all are methods that are worth trying, and as with decoying woodies, there are pecking decoys and flappers available for the dedicated crowman; and let's not forget that there's no better deek than a dead natural, so if you shoot a crow, set it out using a chin stick.

I've already mentioned the use of calls for squirrels, and some shooters swear by crow and magpie calls. If used correctly in conjunction with a deek they'll even be answered, and they do work. Overused and used incorrectly, though, the corvids soon know that the sound wasn't right. Calls are designed to either reassure quarry that it's safe to land, or annoy by imitating the territorial challenge call of the species that the call is intended for. Some imitate distress calls of the quarry's prey, such as a young rabbit or mouse, and could possibly lure a crow or magpie into range. They're not only for fox shooters and are another accessory to consider for the kit bag, but until you're sure you've got the knack of using them, stick to the deeks and bait.

Baiting down is a deadly effective technique for bringing corvids such as crows within range

Another trick if you have one on your shoot is to position yourself under an old tractor-trailer; farmers often leave them out on the side of tracks. The bonus of this is it's something already accepted by the birds on the shoot. No problems from being seen from above, but obviously, you'll need to build a screen of camo to conceal you totally, hidden beneath. In this scenario, I use another trick, which is to put out the main bait as usual, but also to put a few, and I mean a few, scraps of pet food, bacon rind, Chum mixer … anything that only acts as an appetiser, on top of the trailer. Then I can hear birds landing above me. They will then more often than not move onto the bait. While magpies can make their familiar noisy arrival, a thud above usually signals that a crow has arrived. Fast, galloping 'footsteps' (or should that be claw steps) mean that magpies have arrived quietly yet are clattering quickly around as they compete for the scraps you've left out above. As mentioned, one of the bonuses of this method is that you can position the bait at the exact same zero of your combo. Over this distance of 30 – 40yds, I choose a pre-charged .177 with a low-light scope for the early morning work, as in winter it seems to take an age for the light levels to rise.

Now, all this is fine on arable land but what of airgunners who have land devoid of much cover, such as moorlands? Don't be deterred, as I've found baiting-down to be just as effective, if not more so.. Magpies, and especially crows, can be found in great abundance, living off the dead of the land, so to speak, as they're used to finding stillborn lambs, dead sheep etc.

When shooting on barren landscapes such as moors, cover for the hide can be difficult to find, but a few hide poles with some of the darker, autumnal pattern, camo netting leaned against a dry stonewall, or even around fencing, will usually conceal you well enough to make the effort worth your while. Needless to say, I'm sure you can appreciate that baiting an area for suitable quarry can reap rich rewards for the patient hunter.

So there you have it – Hunting Techniques. In this chapter I've outlined more methods than most hunters will ever get to try, and in some cases depending on the type of land you're allowed to shoot over, some methods aren't going to be viable to use. In fact, it's fair to say that most airgun hunters shoot over pasture land, and if lucky enough you might get the chance of a shoot through a large mature wood. Some are unfortunate in the fact that they have mainly moorland at their disposal, often harsh and bleak areas especially in winter. I've shot all over the UK and due to my geographical position, I regularly get up onto the Pennines, down to the lovely lush land of Shropshire, over to the rolling and wonderful country of Wales, and back to the relatively flat, open mixed countryside, or even the industrial wastelands that scar some parts of the North West. Although I have my obvious preferences, each area sets the airgun hunter a challenge which it's always up to the individual to accept and make the most of.

Even if you don't get to try all the techniques mentioned, you'd surely get a chance to try your hand at most. Hopefully, as you become more proficient you'll quite possibly start to develop tactics of your own, and we haven't even looked at shooting after hours yet!

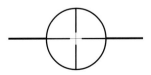

Shooting at Night

The night hunter now has a choice to target quarry either with an artificial light source (lamping) or a Dedicated Night Vision (DNV) riflescope.

Both lamping and night vision equipment have moved on in leaps and bounds in a relatively short period of time. In relation to the former, lamps now use LEDs and battery packs are smaller and lighter.

With the introduction of the first dedicated digital night vision riflescope, NV kit has also changed out of all recognition. A lot has happened since the original version of this book was published in terms of the options that are available for night hunting.

However, despite the relatively new technology of rechargeable, long-life, Li-ion batteries and powerful, compact, LED-illuminated beams (replacing Halogen or Zenon bulbs), it would seem from a certain perspective that lamping seems to be at an all-time low. Also, no one could have predicted how digital night vision units (more on these in the relevant section) would suddenly captivate the interest of both airgun and firearm hunters. The result is lots of new NV kit has been made in a relatively short period of time. This has certainly slowed sales of lamping kit, but the established gun light manufacturers still have a lot to offer and are fighting back with some of the best lamping kit the sport has ever seen.

Many night shooters are now switching over to the more compact and user-friendly tactical torches

Lighter and Brighter

Most of the leading names in lamping gear have shifted emphasis towards the 'tactical torch', especially for airgun use, offering lightweight, self-contained, gun-mountable units with no heavy external battery packs and trailing leads. Some allow us to see right out to 200yds+. Over-powered? Not really, as most have variable power modes and depending on the unit or quarry being targeted, at the quick push of a stock-mountable, multi-function remote unit the light can be dimmed so as not to alarm quarry within sensible hunting range.

Build-quality is at an all-time high; battery management systems are fitted to virtually all units that are gun-mountable, all use high-quality, industry standard Cree LEDs and have multiple mode/power settings that you operate with suitable remote switches. The design of these units is compactness, lightness and in many cases more power, and ease of use.

Lamping

Firstly, the traditional method using lamp and gun, because the hunter, except in very specialised circumstances, still hunts quarry after hours using time-proven methods and basically, it's the equipment we can use that's got far better.

Sport shooters and pest controllers have been using lights to target quarry at night for many years. In the early days, these were homemade light sources; from big searchlights mounted on ex-Army Land Rovers, to cumbersome torches strapped under barrels and gun lamps made of bits acquired from old motor vehicles or motorbike headlamps.

In those early days, the night shooter was always striving to find kit that worked more efficiently. Many a hunting apprenticeship was learned from a son carrying the battery pack for father's lamping trips.

It must be remembered that to the non-shooting public, a lamp seen scanning over a field at night must be the work of a poacher or ne'er-do-well. Remember, always inform the landowner or farmer if you are planning a trip at night, and in certain cases, even put a call into the local police station. It's courtesy and prevents a time-wasting trip out for the local bobby to investigate.

The countryside after dark is a completely different world to the one you see in daylight. Sounds are not only magnified but also as certain animals and birds go about their nocturnal activities, strange noises can at first be unnerving for the newcomer to night shooting. If so, go with a shooting partner, but never be complacent. Consider this saying - 'always be properly equipped to shoot and hunt effectively, efficiently and safely'. That could never be more appropriate than at night. In fact, for reasons of safety always let someone know where you are going; a relative, friend, wife or girlfriend, and tell them when you expect to be back. Unfortunately, accidents can and do happen, and at night if you're not prepared it could have disastrous consequences.

Required Kit

We mainly have both Deben Group Industries Ltd and Cluson Engineering Ltd to thank for many of today's lamping innovations, as they are the major players who've pioneered the design of lamping kits. There are lighter lamp heads or gun-mountable torches and the much lighter external batteries or on-board, hi-tech, rechargeable batteries, lamps/torches of varying intensity, some with optional dimmer switches, stock-mountable on/off switches, with or without dimmer control.

We'll see later in this section, that whilst in some cases using a dedicated Night Vision (NV) riflescope is a better option for night shooting, or to use another term, shooting in a lightless area, the traditional night time walk with lamp and air rifle searching the autumn fields for rabbits is still a very challenging and most rewarding experience.

As we're dealing strictly with air rifles, there are more shooting techniques and opportunities available to the airgunner using the lamp than just shooting at night over fields for rabbits. These include close-range indoor shooting for rats. Due to this, in the following sections I'll deal separately with lamping over fields for rabbits, and using a compact gun lamp or tactical gun-mounted LED torch for rat shooting in and around farm buildings. Also due to the fact that lamping is done outdoors for rabbits, and often indoors for rats, I'm segmenting this section so it fully details lamping technique for each species, including methods specific to both outdoor and indoor use.

As we progress, you'll notice that I often make reference to the use of night vision equipment with your lamping kit of choice. The airgun hunter has the opportunity to take advantage of such useful accessories as a handheld, pocket-size NV monocular and where possible, I feel they should. I'm sure that even the hardened traditionalist will realise the benefits of observation in an area without disturbing it with light - both indoors and out.

Compact head torches are a necessity for the night hunter – as useful for loading magazines as they are for finding downed quarry

Green Day

Stepping way out of the box, but still within the realm of light, we have what is claimed to be the 'ultimate alternative to night vision' in the form of the ND3 Subzero Laser Designator, from Laser Genetics. This uses patented technology to create, in their words, 'true night vision' and turns a day-scoped rifle into a night hunting rig. It's not a true night vision unit, rather it uses a powerful eye-safe light emitted by a green laser diode. It's capable of projecting an intense green beam out to 250yds. Powered by a single CR123A battery, it comes supplied with a fully adjustable 1" and 30mm scope body tube mount with windage and elevation adjustment, remote on/off pressure pad switch, a binocular and spotting scope mount, Weaver mount with dual-size mounts (3/8" and 5/8".)

The adjustable scope mount allows you to fine-tune the torch to illuminate exactly the range you require it to be set, and the beam can be quickly changed from almost pin-spot to flood by turning the ridged and conically shaped adjuster (Rotary Optical Beam Collimator) positioned at the rear of the torch head.

Operated by tail switch or remote pressure pad and lead, they're still somewhat of a specialist piece of kit in the UK. However, at times, they can be a solution to knocking down twitchy hares or rabbits with a hi-power, FAC-rated air rifle as the green laser diode light doesn't seem to bother them as much as a normal or even filtered beam of light. It could be that they're momentarily puzzled, or even dazzled, but you'll easily pick out eyes and the animal itself for clear identification through the scope when using one. Scan an area with it on whatever setting you feel is best, as you would when using any gun-mounted light, then nudge the beam around to a very tight laser spot almost 'painting the target' for a smart bomb!

In the Spotlight - Rabbits

A major consideration for using a lamp with an air rifle is range, and choosing a suitable lamping kit isn't all about candlepower. This is the term pertaining to the power given off from a lamp that uses the more traditional Halogen or Xenon bulb, whereas in the case of an LED, this is rated in lumens. Remember, more often than not, you only need to spot quarry at 80-100yds at the most, not dazzle everything out to 200! For the airgun hunter, gun-mounted lamping kits are plentiful as there are a reasonable amount of companies now making this equipment, and although all have various models, they're basically very similar. Their job is simply to illuminate the target, whereby enabling the shooter to take an effective shot.

The lamp needs to have a tight, controllable beam, not overly intense even without a filter. If gun-mounted, you want the lamp to be lightweight and as unobtrusive as possible so as not to affect the handling of the rifle and, of course, easy to use. The last thing you need to be doing is fumbling around searching for switches or controls at a critical moment. Similarly of concern, is loose-fitting filters that may fall off at the least opportune moment and lead attachment points that can easily become disconnected. This is why many now favour the gun-mounted, rechargeable LED torch design lamping kits.

An alternative way to scan using the gun light is to have the rifle held in a specialised rifle sling and set high on the body

In relation to lamping kit, buy from the reputable brand leaders and you won't go far wrong. As part of any hunter's standard lamping kit, if you're still not using a lamp which has an LED, I'd always recommend that you take along spare bulbs, battery fuses, and a couple of different coloured lamp filters for diffusing the light down if rabbits are twitchy or difficult to spot on a dimmed, unfiltered white beam.

There's also another very good reason to use a red filter on a lamp. While white light to some extent shines back off the rabbit's eyes, you'll see a much more pronounced red glow from the animal's retina when using a light with a red filter. This makes rabbits far easier to spot amongst scrub and when within range, aids you as a useful reference point to put the pellet into the head shot kill-zone. So, filters - very much as essential for spotting as they are for diffusing a harsh white light.

Now to the powerhouse: Always ensure that the battery has a full charge before setting out, and remember,-a 6 volt battery pack and lamping kit gives less run time-than a 12 volt, but the larger battery does, of course, tend to be heavier. If possible, take a spare battery pack and leave it in the car in case it should it be needed.

If your lamping kit can be boosted with one, take the vehicle charger out as well. Apart from that, there are other pieces of kit you'll find useful for all manner of night shooting. I highly recommend that you keep an LED torch in a pocket, or on a lanyard (tucked into your shirt) around your neck, so it's close to hand at all times. Small, button-size LED lights or compact LED torches are very handy for changing/

refilling magazines or reloading a single-shot in the dark, but I must say a multi-shot air rifle at night is a big bonus. Carry a few pre-filled spare magazines and you'll be sorted for all but the longest of forays. A small roll of camo or insulation tape is useful for securing trailing leads out of the way if you are still using the lamp to battery connection leads, and if you get a troublesome connection on your kit, it'll be handy to bind it together. Here again, your multi-tool will come in handy, not only because a sharp blade and scissors are always useful, but also the pliers can help you sort out electrical connections.

For the rabbits you bag, you'll need a knife, string, and Paracord or a game carrier to aid carrying. That is if you haven't mastered the art of hocking; this is threading a back leg through a slit carefully cut in the lower part of the other back leg, which allows the rabbit to be hung on a branch to cool. If you haven't mastered this trick in daylight, tie the back legs up with string or Paracord and similarly, hang the rabbits to cool on a gate or fence post until you pass back that way.

Of course, once you've done your rounds and collected them up, a rucksack with a plastic bin bag liner is very useful to carry them away in. Some recommend that you paunch (gut) them in the field as this is less weight to carry off the shoot. If you don't shoot everything that hops within range, and only take a few for the pot, then a rucksack with a waterproof lining is a suitable option.

Keep some wet wipes in a jacket pocket to keep your hands, knife and gun clean. These are useful for removing fresh blood splashes off metal, but once home, use a suitable silicone oil wipe. Talking of which, never forget cleanliness when dealing with any situation where an accidental cut or spilt blood is involved, and yes, here's when you also might welcome the antiseptic spray and plasters in your first aid kit; and remember - a mobile phone can be a life-saver. You can switch it off when actively hunting, but it's your contact for help should it be needed. An emergency whistle is another back-up safety measure and contact device to have with you. So, there's the kit, but before we look at its use a quick word on something that many shooters tend to forget.

As the traditional lamping season passes through autumn into winter, the temperatures at night can drop suddenly and surprisingly low - so dress accordingly. Whether you wear a facemask and gloves is up to the individual. At night, during the colder months, there is reason to use them for keeping warm as wind can soon chill the face and numb the hands. As for concealment, on a dark, relatively moonless night they're not essential, and I may or may not wear them depending on the situation, but I do tend to find that they help focus me into hunter mode, and in turn, help me to shoot with more confidence. However, and I know I'm getting ahead of myself, if using a night vision scope on a moonlit night, that I would recommend you do. A thermal, black balaclava and black fingerless gloves will suffice; it doesn't need to be camo, but certainly dark enough to hide the white face and hands.

As sound carries much further at night, even more care must be taken with your movement. Zips and buckles you hardly notice in the day can sound like metal gates rattling in the wind in the still of the night. Another no-no is clothing that rustles.

Also, the only sure way of walking more quietly at night is to lift the feet higher than normal, lessen your stride and place the feet down slowly and carefully. The reason is that you can't be as sure of the terrain as you can during the day. Walk cautiously, there's no need to rush and you want to know the ground is still flat. Walking over terrain as unobtrusively as possible really is an art form in itself, but one that can and should be mastered! What should be addressed here is not to overexert yourself in the process of your night hunt. If you do, by the time you reach any quarry, your pulse will be racing and you'll be breathing heavily, resulting in a very unsteady, shaky aim. Always be prepared to rest when needed before carrying on, and certainly know when to call an end to a hunting foray. Also, don't try to cover too much ground. Better to cover a reasonable amount well, while shooting on top form than cover a lot, but shooting and generally performing well below par.

Now a note on practising with the lamp: As familiar as you are with your combo, it will at first feel strange shooting at night with the light illuminating the target. First problem will be head position to look through the scope and the next will definitely be rangefinding. I don't recommend that you shoot on your back garden range after dark as neighbours won't take kindly to this, even if they tolerate some daytime zeroing and practice sessions. Preferably, get out on a quiet part of the shoot, one usually barren of rabbit activity, and practise at night on a few knock down targets. Set out a small course with three or four put out at staggered intervals, and don't give yourself the added bonus of knowing ranges from set positions or range markers. This defeats the object. Once set, start from approximately 100 yards from the first target, walking up and actually practising your lamping routine. Once you feel you're within range, try a shot. Don't take forever in taking it because few bunnies just sit there as if dazed by light. Shoulder the rifle, put the lamp on, take aim and shoot. This will soon get you up to the required skill required. You may think this a waste of time but believe me, not half as much as going out night after night only to miss every opportunity that presents itself.

As you practise and familiarise yourself with the lamp and shooting in these simulated real-life conditions, you'll begin to appreciate that judging range can be very deceptive with artificial light. This is because light is being directed at the target from your shooting position and not coming from all around, as in daylight. This tunnel of light can make targets look further away than they actually are. Some experience the opposite; targets seem closer than they really are. Obviously, lamping conditions can affect different people's senses and perceptions of distance in different ways, and practice is the only way to master this visual distortion.

Another trick is to use a laser in the set-up, as detailed earlier in the book, as a reference for quick range estimation. I must admit that I use these in certain indoor shooting situations and especially with NV scopes, I find them a godsend. Before leaving the subject of range, a big no-no is to try long-range shots at night. It is irresponsible and unsporting. If you can't stalk closer, leave them until another night.

Here a reminder on safety and safe shooting practice; All that holds true in the day must be strictly scrutinised more closely when shooting at night. Although you are using a relatively low-powered rifle, always ensure that the backstop is safe behind the target. Although tempting, don't pot a rabbit on the brow of a hill if you aren't 100% sure that there can't be any person, or for that matter a domestic or farm animal ,over that hill. Know your shooting ground, paths thoroughfares, anywhere someone might 'just appear' don't go there at night. Remember, safe shooting at all times.

So now – the method: Firstly, I'm presuming you know your shoot well and have a good idea of where the rabbits feed. Even so, go at dusk without the rifle and observe the area. Watch from a distance and you'll see the rabbits and which fields they venture into. If you want to really reconnoitre the area at night, then invest in a pair of NV binoculars.

The knowledge you'll learn observing various areas of the shoot with NV is priceless. A small monocular is handy to have with you while out shooting, but a pair of good-quality Gen 1+ NV binos, or the digital equivalent, is far better for this type of dedicated observation.

First major no-no is, never overuse the lamp or go clumping straight into a field you presume will contain rabbits. For this reason, I always recommend the airgun hunter use an NV observation aid such as a compact monocular; either analogue or the lighter, and often better priced and performing digital alternative, to examine the area he's planning on operating over. At risk of sounding like an NV sales rep, believe me when I say, in the time I've incorporated one into my lamping kit and routine it's revolutionised my night hunting.

Not all areas will be overrun with nocturnal feeders, and a few hours at various times of the night, if you can spare the time, will show if you should be out an hour after last light or the wee early hours of the morning. Then, once all is established, it's kit together and off into the area where you've assessed rabbits are most likely to be feeding.

Everything you've previously read about stalking holds true when lamping – if anything doubly so. Be especially mindful of wind direction because at night the rabbit will be relying heavily on its sense of smell and hearing. Before you use the lamp you should have one major bonus on your side; they most likely haven't seen your approach. This is where stopping at regular intervals for a quick look through the NV monocular can be a great advantage. When you spot the feeding rabbits, your approach should begin with even greater care. Incidentally, when looking through an NV device, quarry can look a lot closer or even further away than it actually is, so don't over-rely on it. Let the observation unit aid you in two things; spotting the rabbits that appear to be stalkable, and to plot your route across the area between you and a suitable shooting position. Never try to get too close without quickly scanning the area with the lamp. This may seem strange as you have the opportunity to watch undetected, but this first quick sweep 'light on, light off' will allow you to determine how twitchy the rabbits are and where they will now be in relation to the distance you've travelled. Whether using an NV device or not, the optimum way to use the lamp for detecting rabbits is the same. Don't, as some advise, continually bring the rifle up to the shoulder, switching the lamp on, scanning around looking through the scope to observe. Not only will this quickly become tiring on the arms, but you'll also miss spotting a lot of rabbits, even if using a scope with a good width of view.

In the dark you might think you're heading in the right direction, but unless you've also picked out a landmark on the horizon, clearly silhouetted in front of you, it can be surprisingly easy to stray off the line of approach. So, on first pass of the light, look for four major things; closest target to set zero, other potential targets close by, the state of alertness of all the rabbits in the bunch, and of course check the terrain.

This is a most crucial moment. I always recommend that the hunter, quickly switches off the lamp and stops to gather composure and calm nerves as adrenalin will be pumping. If you've approximated 60, 70 yards or beyond to the target, when ready to move on, count your steps until you've counted off enough to bring you approximately within 25 yards of the target.

Then, move forward a tad further depending on the initial range judged. When you flick on the light you'll more often than not still be at the range you thought you would be before you moved forward. Because you're moving slowly, the distance of your pace is less, so you cover less ground than when walking in the daylight. Also, rabbits, even if not overly twitchy, have a habit of shuffling around and moving away from anything detected in the field. I'd recommend you steady yourself, adopt the standing or preferably the more stable kneeling position, if the terrain allows, bring the rifle up to your shoulder, flick on the lamp, choose your target through the scope and without too much dithering take the shot.

Okay, you missed or hopefully you've knocked your first rabbit over, but as soon as you see 'miss or hit', as long as it isn't a wounding, turn the lamp off immediately. This is where an NV monocular comes in handy again as you can use the unit to assess the situation with other quarry. If other rabbits were in the proximity, they can have fled for cover, whilst some might even hang around bolt upright, ears pricked up, wondering what happened. Your actions at this moment could give you another chance of a shot or a short stalk for a shot. Experience will show whether that's on the cards or if you need to retrieve the prize and hang or hock it for collection later. Don't wander off aimlessly in another direction in search of any other rabbits before retrieval, as you'll not find the first rabbit you've shot, not without much searching and disturbing the area with light, anyway.

So a quick recap: Never overuse the lamp, to prevent spooking quarry and save your own night vision. A tip on regaining the latter if you inadvertently catch a flash of the light is to look at the sky, look at the floor and then look at the horizon. Try it - it works!

When rabbits are running and twitchy don't follow; it's more often than not a pointless exercise. Try another area or tactic. One is to cut off the rabbits' escape route. This may sound strange but rabbits really are creatures of habit. Why do you think they make such well-worn runs out into the fields? If really late, the rabbits could well be a long way from the main warrens or boltholes so if the wind is in your favour approach from the warren along the rabbit runs. Incidentally, the direction of the flattened grass in the run will often help indicate which way the rabbit headed, and experience will even help you to determine how fresh a rabbit run is.

So, when you find the 'far feeders' this method of approach and the light hitting them from your position will cause confusion. Often, rather than risk bolting past you for the cover which you are cutting them off from, at seeing the light they'll often squat down low and as flat to the ground as possible.

Another factor that will have bearing on results is the weather conditions. If there's the risk of fog, or even a light mist, coming down that night, at ground level this can cause infuriating bounce-back from the lamp, making spotting very difficult. Most say that ideal conditions are a cloudy, moonless night with some wind and a light drizzle! Well, as for the latter, living and lamping in the North of England, drizzle can often be the norm at night, especially during the latter part of the year. Whether it does help mask the sound of your approach is debatable, but you shouldn't need to rely on anything overpowering the sound that you shouldn't be making anyway, and on nights with drizzle, rabbits aren't troubled and go about their nightly routine - they're used to the elements.

As for cloud cover, I'm not convinced that a sky heavy with cloud is of such high importance. For a start, ambient light from a partial moon and a few stars can be a bonus, especially when using the NV monocular. Obviously, you don't want a crystal-clear, cloudless, still night with a full moon, but you certainly don't always need a total blackout. Consider this: Years ago, there weren't as many streetlights, factory and workplace security floodlights, or even house lights to light up a night sky, and in some country areas, streetlights used to be switched off very late to conserve power. Now with rising crime, lights are everywhere, and for people's security and safety that's a good thing, but when the cloudbase is really low all those lights actually reflect down, making the ground lighter and creating an orange-tinted glow. Unless you're in the Outer Hebrides you're then faced with being seen quite easily from a rabbit's ground view as your silhouette is visible in the glow no matter how well you conceal yourself.

Other variables to consider are; which fields hold sheep or cattle, and it is no use shooting fields with long grass or over land with two many ridges to cross. Also know what the farmer has planned, no use walking carefully over to a far field to discover the tractors out late with the roller flattening grass, or he's working late cutting or trimming hedge-side foliage!

Favourite areas are freshly-cut grass fields, with a lovely scent in the air and the rabbits relatively easy to spot at medium range even without the lamp. Stubble fields are hard to walk over silently but do attract the rabbits. If you can, walk around the perimeter of the stubble field and you might well spot a few and be able to keep a hedge or some such cover behind you, thereby helping to conceal you're appearance in silhouette.

Now to other ways with lamps: The airgunner can even use a simple headlamp, either powered with batteries in a head-mounted pack, or for longer duration, attached to a belt- mounted battery pack. If you're fortunate enough to be driven around the shoot in a 4 X 4, there are remote-operated, vehicle-mounted lamps, or simply use the gun-mounted lamp to scour the area within range, out from the sides of the track or fields you're travelling over.

As mentioned earlier, if unsure about going it alone, then shooting with a partner is an option; one operating a hand-held lamp while the other shoots. By pairing up in this way you can take it in turns to take the shots. If you try your hand at this method, then establish a set working routine with your shooting partner. Lamp man spots – shooter shoots. The lamp man should keep the main beam off any rabbit spotted until within range, so the shooter has a clear and straightforward shot when they arrive. He should never walk behind the shooter as this can cause the lamp to produce glare in the eye-piece of the scope making targeting nigh on impossible. Slightly to the front, but obviously out of the line of fire, and keeping to one side, usually the left, is the name of the lamp man's game. Most cordless, rechargeable hand-held lamps will have enough power for the duration of a usual session. If not, take at least one spare fully-charged battery, and leave another at a convenient pick up point to swap over if one runs low. It's also useful to communicate with hand signals to cut down the need to tell each other of opportunities spotted, time to stop, or change a line of approach. If verbal communication is needed, do so in whispers.

Incidentally, although scopes have been dealt with in previous chapters, it is worth looking at a few factors pertaining to optics best suited to lamping. You've probably read that you need a scope with a large objective lens. This isn't strictly true because any quality scope will afford you enough light transmission to target your quarry when using a gun lamp.

It is more important that you have a scope with a wide field of view and one that doesn't have a reticle with overly thin crosshairs that can get lost in the sight picture. If using a general specification 3 – 9 X 40 scope, winding the magnification down to 3 or 4 X will give a reasonably wide field of view enabling you to quickly find the target in the sight picture.

Although we have scopes with multi-aim-point reticles, I'd recommend hunters stay with the 30/30 duplex, German post design, or if you use it for day and are very accustomed to it the standard mil-dot. Also preferably choose one that can be lit using a rheostat with a dual (red/green or red/blue colour) illumination facility.

Now to a subject of some contention: Personally, I'd say never take a shot at a rabbit on the move. I cringe when I hear people brag about how they can regularly shoot running rabbits with an air rifle. Always go for the head shot, a clean kill is imperative as you'll never find a wounded runner at night without a dog. Don't get frustrated as you will find rabbits that hold in the lamp. So why educate them into putting the equation together that 'you + light + sound of pellet whistling past' = danger? They'll be much twitchier the next time you go out. Talking of which, if the rabbits do seem overly twitchy or there's few around where your observation has told you otherwise, it could well be that a fox has been out that night already. As I mentioned in a previous chapter, foxes at times can leave an extremely distinguishable aroma much worse than cat wee, and trust me, you'll know when you smell it.

Unfortunately, on occasions such as this rabbits can be very unpredictable. They could re-emerge from

Hunting at night is as challenging as it is rewarding

their burrows sooner than expected or stay hidden for a good few hours. When faced with this situation, depending on how much time you have, I'd recommend that the hunter try a totally different area or it maybe better to return another night. Don't get too complacent or lackadaisical, know your hunting area and watch how you go. Stumbling into a ditch or tripping on rough ground isn't recommended with a loaded rifle. One very experienced airgun hunter of my acquaintance did this and got away with snapping the lovely walnut stock of his favourite hunting rifle. He was lucky, as it could have been his leg, or worse!

Well, that's it for rabbit shooting with the lamp, but of all hunting methods, when you get it right it can be one of the most rewarding.

In the Spotlight - Rats

Shooting rats with a gun lamp is even less about candlepower (or lumens), than lamping rabbits, usually because it's done at much closer range, but before altering your rifle's zero, it's advisable to have a recce of the shooting location to assess the ranges where you'll be most likely to encounter targets. In some cases it can be as close as 10yds or even less, others 20yds, or if the barn is a high, hangar-type you might well be best leaving your zero set as normal.

Invest in one of the gun-mounted lamping kits with a variable power control to dim the lamp or torch. If you want to use the same lamping set-up you use for rabbits, then certainly get a coloured filter that really does diffuse the brightness of the lamp - red or amber filters being the preferred colours of most hunters and again, it'll help you spot those beady eyes.

As for an NV monocular, for rabbit shooting you don't strictly need one, and neither do you for rat shooting, but once they've become very skittish to the lamp, for giving you an edge, I reckon you do. They've come down in price dramatically since they first came available on the civilian market, so you won't need to pay a fortune for a good, compact, Gen 1 model or more favoured now, a hand-held digital unit. A basic hand-held compact device will suffice for ratting but you do require it to have an infra-red (IR) illuminator which allows you to see in total darkness, and the IR light projected reflects back off the rats' eyes, this time seen glowing whitish/green when viewed through a traditional, tubed NV device, or piercing white in the monochromatic sight image that a digital (more on this technology later) unit creates. Whichever you use, you have no problem spotting them in even the furthest, darkest recesses of the most cluttered building.

Again, a multi-shot PCP air rifle is the ideal choice coupled with a scope with good light-gathering properties and, of course, a wide field of view. Also, a standard red laser sight with rear-mounted, push-button on/off switch or the more versatile stock-mountable, pressure pad design switch can be useful.

Before we get into the pros and cons of the laser in the set-up, firstly, a look at the method with traditional gun-mounted lamp. As always, location is the key to success. Even a quick look around will show where the rats have been visiting; the signs of rat infestation are droppings, scratchings, teeth marks, chewed sacks or materials, and other such damage.

As you are shooting rats indoors in the farm barn, you need to be mindful of your personal safety. Check the place over during daylight or with the lights on before you settle in for the night. It's all too easy to walk into a piece of angle-iron or trip over a wooden pallet or a welding-torch hose.

If actively searching around the inside or outside of the barn, have the rifle half-mounted with the butt in your shoulder and the leading hand in a position to hold and both operate the lamp switch and direct the beam. Holding the rifle in this manner means you're able to react more quickly once you spot a rat, or just catch the red glint off those beady eyes. Then you can fully mount the rifle and shoot. Rats rarely give you time to think, so quick range estimation and careful aim are needed. Now, that can be as difficult as it sounds or easy depending on how much activity the rats tolerate, the population present, and if they've been shot at before. If searching inside, scan all the beams, girders, nooks and crannies. Rats love overhead structures that can provide off-the-floor routes to and from areas of interest to them.

To establish which beams or girders rats use to get to and from a food supply, simply get into a position that allows a good view of the barn interior and just quietly stand or sit, carefully watching and listening. Yes listen, as more often than not you'll hear their sharp claws scratching around in the grain silos, or storage bins, and the odd scrabbling or squeaks as they pass overhead on a run along a beam. You might actually only see them at the points they enter (drop) into the grain bins or make out the unmistakable silhouette when they travel along the top of beams and girders in the gloomy roof space, and whilst you can target them searching with the gun lamp, a more productive and less tiring method is to employ an NV device into the technique.

Using the NV monocular you can spot scaly tails without disturbing them with the light. At first you'll get 'sitters'. Sitting up aloft on their little perches they'll either be nibbling something or just hunched up, watching. Once a static rat is spotted through the NV monocular, carefully put the hi-tech sighting device to one side, and bring the rifle up to the shoulder but angle the rifle higher than the rat's position so when you switch the lamp on, the beam doesn't hit the rat full-on. Ideally, you want the light to point above, not shine directly at the rodent as it may immediately run for cover. The optimum way is to bring the beam down slowly to the point where your crosshairs reach the rat's kill-zone, then fire.

When you get into the swing of lightless sighting, and this particular lamping and gun handling technique, you'll soon have scaly tails thudding down onto the barn floor, but they'll not hold in the light for long and the shooting will become even more demanding as you eventually need to tackle them on the move.

In fact, when shooting, take regular breaks to lull the rodents into a false sense of security so they might come out once they've settled again after the initial disturbance. Remember, few barns are over-large so, in effect, you're continually shooting the same area.

If trying your hand at rats on the move, you need to get into a position that allows you the best view of the rat as it travels the beam or girder. Usually, the main beam in a roof space will be crossed and met with other beams, or angle-iron strengtheners. At these points, the rat will slow down to negotiate them and often, if wary, will pause momentarily here before moving on. These are the areas to take the shot but you often only get a split second to take a snap shot of the target. Shooting them in this manner requires pinpoint accuracy, coupled with the discipline of knowing when not to shoot.

If they're not pausing, then shooting really is demanding. As long as they're not moving too quickly, you can track the rat in your sights and actually shoot as it is moving along the beam, or alternatively at ground level along the base of a wall. You need to establish that the backdrop is safe and you have to be skilled enough to give the rat just enough lead, as once you slip the trigger, like the shotgun shooter you need to keep your rifle moving with the target so the pellet keeps on line to go into the kill-zone on impact. As you can imagine, this isn't easy but once mastered it is very rewarding. Similarly, establish a point where the rat enters another area or climbs up or down an adjoining beam. The rat may also pause at this junction and if you can time your shot as the rat passes through the area, you're in business. Again, this takes skill and until it is acquired be prepared to waste a fair amount of ammo, but, once you get the timing right, it's very gratifying. Eventually, tracking the rats this way with a beam of light from a gun-mounted lamp will have them running more quickly and the rat really can shift when it needs to. If they're running this fast then it's even unsporting on the rat to try to shoot them in this fashion, but there are still a few tricks you can employ.

The obvious one is to diffuse the light even further with a filter and if your lamping kit has one, which I advise, bring the brightness of the light down with the dimmer switch as low as you possibly can, but still see to target the quarry.

When shooting in pairs, a trick at stopping a rat in its tracks is for one hunter to track it with the gun lamp, and then the other shooter, using a gun lamp or hand-held, suddenly illuminates the area the rat is heading for. This can often cause the rat to pause for a second or two, deciding whether or not to dash through the light to safety. This hesitancy can be just enough for the first shooter to take a shot, but when they're becoming overly lamp-shy and scurrying for cover at the slightest disturbance, it's time to target them using dedicated night vision riflescopes, a particular specialised form of shooting and one we're now ready to look at for both rabbits and rats.

Just before we do so, a few words on lasers; If the situation has had you set the scope zero at 20yds, the laser can be set either as an aid for quickly assessing range, or as a secondary sighting system for the rats that really do appear too close for comfort. Often while you're scouring the beams or sitting quietly watching an area, one will cross the barn floor, even appear from a grain funnel, or from under cover no more than five or six yards away, and there can be enough ambient light in the building for you to see the rat in the gloom, especially if positioned close to a large open entrance. Even with your scope on the lowest magnification, you'll have no chance of even seeing it through the lenses, let alone assessing the holdover that very close-range shots require. With the laser set for a range of eight yards or so, without using the scope, you can put the dot on the front third of the animal's body, resulting in the smack of a solid hit or the 'zing' of a clean miss. However, I must quantify this technique by saying that I only use this set-up shooting .22 calibre, and I only set up the laser in this manner when experience of an area has indicated that rats are often coming in this close. Also, the laser in these cases isn't scope-mounted but rather fixed in a special mount on the barrel or silencer, to be as close to the axis of the barrel bore as possible. As you can see, lasers are very versatile. The setting up of them was covered in the latter part of Chapter 2, but there's more on these devices to come in the next section.

Night Vision

Advancements in Night Vision technology have been huge in recent years. Many airgun hunters know that digitally operated night vision equipment is now a reality, widely used and accepted by many who prefer the stealth of hunting without a conventional lamping set-up.

This chapter has been revised in part to explain the difference between traditional NV units or as they're now termed, analogue and digitally operated ones. Also, there are other sighting systems that use digital technology so they can be for both day and night use. Even so, it's still of great relevance that I begin by charting how NV equipment first came into the UK. Please be aware that what follows refers to the origins and use of early analogue units, so called because they use an Internal Image Intensifier (IIT) to create a sight picture.

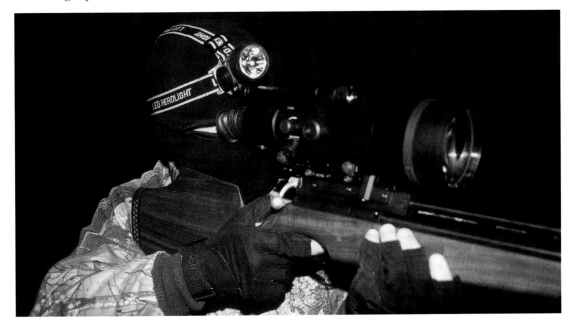

Hunting with Nightvision is an exciting branch of the sport

In the Beginning

When night vision equipment first became available to the UK sport shooter, it caused some interest but didn't have immediate mass appeal due to the comparatively poor performance in relation to cost. Also, the very early models of NV riflescopes often had unconventional reticles, basic adjusters for windage and elevation, and in many cases were heavy and gave a poor or grainy sight picture.

Not surprisingly, the shooting fraternity at the time was divided on this new see-in-the-dark technology. On one side there were those who felt it would have limited appeal and fade away into obscurity, but on the other, the more open-minded who hesitated at the beginning, still watched from the sidelines, read the reviews and eventually decided to try NV when it had proved itself and become more established as an alternative to gun-mounted lamping kits.

Night vision equipment was originally designed by the military for detecting, and ultimately in terms of a NV riflescope, was designed for shooting man-size targets without detection in the dark. Later, the export models were designed for sport shooters targeting large animals, such as bears, wild boar, elk etc., and this is one of the reasons that reticles weren't very subtle, usually being little more than a thick-lined, inverted chevron. Also, the grainy, green image produced inside by the IIT was not really up to the standard required and 95% of units were poor-quality Gen 1 scopes with pitifully weak built-in infra-red illuminators. Some factories were producing new second generation intensifiers, and these offered more range and better performance but weren't of high build quality. The internal 'noise' of the picture was poor, slightly fuzzy and a bit like a television set not tuned in properly.

I realise many will feel there have been too many other military references in this book, but this is an area that can only be fully clarified by charting the development of NV technology for the armed forces, before we can appreciate how it began to become accepted into our sport.

Night Vision – The Full Story

In the 1960s, military officials predicted battles would be fought at night. No surprises then that both superpowers, the USSR as it was then known, and the USA, and NATO pact countries, had a programme dedicated to the development of observation devices and riflescopes that could be used in the dark. The early devices, used technology that dates back to the end of the Second World War, which to some extent can be termed Gen 0, and were operated by bathing the target in infra-red light. The observation aid, or scope, had an IR projector and an IR detector that picked up this light and, coupled with the IIT, produced a sight picture.

Though usable and effective, they had one major drawback for the military and that was, if you sent out an IR beam of light, the enemy watching using a similar NV device could spot your position. This was because they were 'active' (emitting a beam) and not 'passive' as with the more advanced equipment that followed which doesn't use IR. Immediately, the boffins got tinkering and moved up to what is classed as Generation 1 equipment which is basically where it first becomes of interest to the sport shooter.

This was the first passive system that could actually use natural ambient light provided by the moon and stars to produce a sight picture, negating the need for the IR give-away. Even so, some had an IR facility to boost viewing range when needed, and gave the benefit of being able to see into areas of total darkness. One of the most important facets of these early Gen 1 devices was that they were cascaded. In their construction they had three Gen 1 intensifier tubes butted one against the other to create a cascade effect. Each tube had a gain of approximately 50 times the outside night-time screen, so this gave 50x50x50

= 125,000, and this brings us to one of the downsides. These early analogue units, especially NV riflescopes, tended to be big, heavy and often cumbersome because they required a large body casing to house the three intensifiers and a large objective lens, both of which helped to overcome the primary need for the IR booster. By the late 60s the development of even more hi-tech gadgetry meant that image intensifier tubes could be made smaller, but with higher gain and therefore offering a much better sight picture.

The heart of any analogue NV unit is the intensifier tube, and it's the quality of the tube or the grade, or 'generation' as it is termed for classification, that gives a better sight image, and will often be the reason that the unit is much more expensive than lower generation equipment. As technology moved forward, the devices then progressed to Gen 2, 2+ and then SuperGen®. It was the advent of the Micro Channel Plate (MCP) that was the breakthrough. The MCP gave the necessary high gain, negating the need for three Gen 1 cascade tubes, which in turn allowed the construction of a single, small intensifier tube and the construction of small and effective, man-portable, night vision devices.

Gen 2 devices have a fibre-optic window where the night-time scene is focused; in Gen 2+ technology it was replaced by anti-reflective glass giving more resolution and gain. SuperGen technology made even more improvements to the intensifier tube and increased the lifespan to 10,000 hours. The installation of fibre-optic input windows meant that anything butted up to the fibre-optic window is in focus – such as the reticle. The main advantage of Gen2+ is the fibre-optic bundles in the MCP that gives the unit much higher sensitivity and better edge-to-edge resolution of the sight picture. Most agree this gives 20% better performance up from Gen 2 because the image is literally being projected straight into the intensifier tube through the glass input window.

The British and American military have Gen 3 units but interestingly, like sporting shooters, are exploring the possibilities of what digital technology can do. American Gen 3 units with traditional image intensifiers, although of a very high quality and grade, are banned for sale to civilians, but there are dodgy units available, often on the black market, that claim to be Gen 3 and you'll find that these are often of Chinese manufacture, or actual Japanese military devices. What is of more importance is that generally there's no escaping the fact that these devices are specialised pieces of kit and you really do get what you pay for, so it pays to be informed.

So, back to the introduction of these scopes into the civilian market for the use in sport shooting: After the Cold War and the demise of the Berlin Wall in 1989, quite unexpectedly a quantity of what was, in effect, ex-Russian military night vision equipment became available to the western commercial market in the early 90s. Those early devices had limited use in a sporting market, though; in particular, the lack of precision because the windage and elevation adjustment of the riflescopes was very crude. Whereas the sport shooter is used to one click on a scope turret for ¼" movement at 100yds, military night vision was imparting movement of approximately 4" per click at 100yds. They were also heavy, and required a lot of getting used to.

However, certain forward-thinking importers of optics realised the benefits and began to develop and also modify existing equipment so it would be of use to the hunter. Expectations were initially high, but unfortunately, quality wasn't, as we were still seeing ex-military equipment coming from the Eastern Bloc. Feedback from people who field tested the devices before they came into the UK had companies address the problems. These were to install better-quality intensifier tubes; more precise windage and elevation adjustment, and some even changed the reticle for a more traditional crosshair. The latter usually being a more precise and acceptable red, illuminating cross that would show up in the ghostly green-glowing sight picture familiar to all analogue NV equipment. So whilst we now have usable scopes, in lower Gen classification they still do have certain limitations, but be aware of those and the airgun hunter has very usable analogue equipment for specialised hunting situations.

I now feel it's very fitting that I should detail how a traditional analogue NV unit works; the workings of digital night vision will be fully explained when we come to these devices.

How Does Analogue NV Work?

Whilst a conventional telescopic sight, or 'scope' as we know them, uses light from the sun during daylight hours to produce a sight picture, night vision equipment, be it a sighting device or observation aid, uses the invisible photons of light both inside and outside the usual spectrum.

The main difference is, it uses an image intensifier tube held within the main body casing and with the help of an IR illuminator to create the sight image viewed, the intensifier tube amplifies and changes these into electrons, and finally back to light when they hit a phosphor screen at the back of the intensifier tube. Thus, a window of green light is formed inside the tube and miraculously, the dark is pierced and we can, in effect, see through and into the night. Check out the cross-section diagram of a typical internal set-up of a Gen 2 NV riflescope. Incidentally, Gen 2 has been used for this due to the fact there's a less complicated internal structure, but it also amply illustrates the major components of an NV riflescope.

ANATOMY OF AN ANALOGUE NIGHT VISION RIFLESCOPE

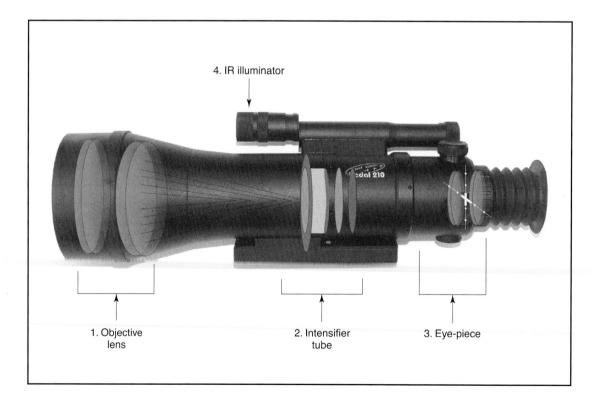

4. IR illuminator

1. Objective lens

2. Intensifier tube

3. Eye-piece

With reference to the night vision riflescope diagram: the objective lens (1) used in a night vision device has a very high light transmission factor, much higher than a normal daytime scope. This allows more light to be gathered for amplification by the intensifier tube. Also, special coatings allow better transmission of the infra-red spectrum which is something greatly utilised by the tube.

The intensifier tube (2) is situated at the heart of the night vision riflescope. It has a thick anti-reflection coated input window composed of either glass or fibre-optic. The highly light sensitive coatings of the photo-cathode are situated here. This converts rays of light to the particles known as electrons. In a Gen 2 device, these electrons then stream through a thin glass microchannel plate full of fibre-optic strands – several million of them. This is where the amplification of light takes place by a cascade process, resulting in even more electrons being knocked off the internal surface of the individual fibre-optic, causing a chain reaction; this is known as the 'gain' of the tube. The intensified electrons leave the microchannel plate and strike a phosphor screen completing the intensification process. This results in the eerie, green-glow sight picture, familiar to all analogue night vision devices, be it riflescope, monocular or binocular. The sight picture sent back through the small screen of the intensifier tube is magnified by the eye-piece (3) of the night vision riflescope which is positioned just behind the intensifier tube and before the ocular eye-piece. The illuminated (lit) reticle is usually situated at this area.

The IR illuminator (4) is a very powerful torch that shines supposedly invisible light in the IR spectrum. The torch doesn't use bulbs, rather IR diodes that are many times more powerful than conventional light bulbs. The IR beam is invisible to the naked eye but visible through the night scope and also reflects back from the eyes of animals making detection of quarry much easier. It is this that makes the IR illuminator invaluable in very dark conditions supplying the intensifier tube with a light source to amplify. Even in zero light conditions, utilising the IR, the intensifier is able to create a sight picture allowing the shooter effectively to see in the dark. Incidentally, traditional (analogue) image intensified night vision has pretty much reached a plateau in terms of development. The only possibility is that US mil-spec Gen 3 tubes may be made available for export, but many would say that's a long way off or even something that won't happen.

Note: I use the term 'supposedly invisible' in relation to IR - it isn't if you look directly at the emitter. which you shouldn't do even if the unit is classed as eye-safe, you'll see the diodes glowing red.

The Next Generation Alternative to Analogue NV

Many airgun hunters will already know that the very exciting news on the night vision scene was when, at long last, digital NV riflescopes and observation units finally became available in the UK in March 2010. It had long been rumoured that it was due, and the airgun hunting scene in particular was buzzing with anticipation. So much so, that many waited and held off buying more expensive analogue Gen 2+ scopes.

The first Digital Night Vision (DNV) scope sold out on back-order and Thomas Jacks Ltd the importer of the Pulsar brand (part of the massive company - Yukon Advanced Optics Global) initially struggled to meet the demand.

The first true dedicated digital night vision scope that became available in the UK and many other EU countries was the Pulsar D-550 Digi-Sight marketed in the UK by NV specialists Thomas Jacks Ltd. At the time of writing, the upgraded version, designated the N750, is now with us, and a seemingly ongoing flow of other high-quality digital kit has also begun to be seen on these shores.

How Does Digital Night Vision Work?

Digital night vision units use a CCD (Charge Coupled Device) that's specifically optimised (calibrated) to the IR spectrum. This is because approximately 70% of starlight is infra-red so the unit can utilise this ambient light source to the highest level. Because they use a CCD, and not a traditional IIT, they cannot be damaged by exposure to bright lights; for instance, a high-power beam from a lamp, a flash off a distant

The Pulsar 5 X 42 Digital Nightvision Scope - one of the new breed of Digital Dictators

street light, car headlights etc. Many digital NV products also offer a Video Out (VO) facility so that you can record from them, and some even have a built-in recording capability. Another major difference that many need to adjust to is, at present, digital NV shows a monochrome sight picture, not the ghostly-green image we have become used to with analogue devices.

History in the Making

Loaded with features, the Pulsar Digi-Sight N550 digital night vision riflescope, has several switchable pre-loaded reticles of various shapes, and it also has the facility to allow the owner to upload optional reticles from the Yukon website. Reticle inversion (colour change from white to black and vice versa depending on the target colour) and the enhanced contrast facilities are very useful too. The riflescope also has a jack performing two functions; video out, to conduct video recording to external devices without the use of additional adapters and camera or camcorders, and Video In (VI) which can be used to display information on the riflescope's LCD screen transmitted from remote cameras via radio channel.

It's resistant to bright light exposure and a nitrogen-purged optical channel allows the use of the Digi-Sight N550 in rapid-temperature-drop conditions. It is also capable of detecting fox-size targets out to about 300yds when used with an eye-safe Laserluchs IR laser illuminator, equivalent performance to entry-level Gen 2 scopes when used with the recommended externally-mounted IR illuminator available as an optional extra. For the airgun hunter, the onboard, fully-adjustable IR, is certainly more than adequate for the unit to be of great use for the 12ft lb airgun hunter.

The unit is also very sensitive to artificial IR light sources and can see further into the light spectrum than units using image intensifier tubes, so can see covert IR greater (>) than 900nm. The term 'nm' denotes nanometer and is a billionth of a metre measurement of light.

Digital night vision has plenty of potential for development; sensitivity and resolution will improve; the use of OLED (Organic Light Emitting Diode) screens giving colour images is very possible, and as they reduce in price, other opportunities will open up.

Digital Dictators

Not content with bringing us the first digital NV scope and its higher resolution, higher magnification offspring, Pulsar shocked us yet again with the launch of the incredible Pulsar 5 X 42 Photon. A true 5 X fixed magnification, NV riflescope that mounts using conventional 30mm rings to any standard air rifle dovetails. The built-in IR is of high enough power to give you an observation range of up to 80-100yds and for airgun use and the ranges at which we engage targets, it is yet another breakthrough in digital devices to choose from. Powered by 2 X AA batteries with a run-time of approximately three hours, the Photon has a fast-focus ocular and uses an illuminating red-centre-dot, German, post-type reticle. Fine focusing for ranges is catered for by the front position main focus ring, operating very much like an Adjustable Objective (AO) does on a conventional day scope. It has a brightness control to adjust the in-view OLED screen to your required intensity level, and even has a video out recording facility for use with a compatible external recording device. The illuminated red dot of the reticle is powered by a single CR2032 3V Lithium battery.

The Nite-Site NS50 has proved very popular since its introduction to the airgun hunting scene and gives a novel heads up TV viewing experience that works very well at sensible ranges

Now for the unit that took the airgun hunting scene by storm; the Nite-Site NS50. Developed in the UK, it is powered by a stock-mountable 12V battery. This system uses two modules which easily attach to a normal day scope. The module that enables you to see the viewed image through the scope is attached to the top of the scope like a gun-mounted lamp. This module comprises a 3" LCD TV monitor facing the shooter with an integral infra-red illuminator facing away toward the target. The second module is a camera unit that attaches to the eye-bell of the scope and picks up the image illuminated by the IR beam, which is then displayed on the top-mounted, rearward-facing TV screen. Because the NS50 is relaying the image produced by the IR through your scope there is no shift in zero, meaning you can use a scope with front or side parallax adjustment, and even a scope with an illuminated reticle. Range is approximately 50yds depending on ambient light and for the most part it's ideal for many ratting situations. The Nite-Site is easy to fit onto virtually any scope and the stock-mounted battery pack gives approximately five hours run time. The heads-up shooting position isn't to everybody's taste, but you do soon become accustomed to it. Smaller, longer-life battery packs and screen filters are now available. This is the digital device that many feel could lead to even bigger and better things.

Bonus Points

The major benefits of digital units are that unlike analogue devices it's safe to use them in daylight hours. Generally, they're much lighter than their analogue counterparts and as you've read, they're available now as dedicated NV scopes, as well as there being front- or rear-mounted units that you can use with your existing daytime scope. These are an option if you don't want to dedicate a rifle to being solely scoped up with the NV riflescope, but remember, the beauty of digital is the ability to use it in the day or at night. To side with modules (add-ons), they do solve a problem and most rear-mounted units are actually hand-held monoculars that can convert the scope for use in darkness, as they attach at the correct distance for you to use the scopes reticle and side or front PA focus dial or ring. Also they come with, or have the facility to mount, an IR illuminator to give the much needed IR light that enables any form of NV equipment to work.

Since the N550 and N750 (2012) became available, others are now entering the UK, not forgetting alternative sighting devices such as the NS50 mentioned previously.

Time now to look at the devices in relation to our sport and why the airgun hunter doesn't have to have the highest Generation grade of analogue device to hunt effectively, or the latest comparable digital offering – at present, that is. So what follows applies to both analogue and digital NV, but still leans heavily towards analogue due to the fact that many airgun hunters still use them.

That brings us back to the reason airgun hunters can use these units more readily than any other shooter. Firstly, the limited effective range of the air rifle leant itself to the fact that early Gen 1 and even Gen 1+ had a similar targeting range. Using the IR illuminator that was fitted to these devices also helped to target quarry as it actually made the sight picture brighter and clearer; not forgetting that the infra-red light would bounce off the eyes of quarry, showing up as white-ish/light-green dots, or with the sight image produced by digital equipment, the eyes look white.

Even under the darkest areas at night, direct an IR torch into the area and the shapes may at first be hard to pick out, but the eyes will always give the quarry away. From that initial sighting you can concentrate your vision, focus-in using the scope's fine-focus dial and soon fully see the quarry. On certain models of NV riflescope, an extra IR torch won't be needed as the onboard one will be sufficient. However, if you need one it will often have variable intensity control and the facility to tighten the invisible beam from spot to flood.

Even with extra detection ability, the shooting range always has to be kept within the realms of the ability of the shooter, but having success with these units soon realised that the .177 calibre was the better choice due to its flatter trajectory and therefore more forgiving of errors in rangefinding. Determining range successfully and precisely will only come with practice or by using a laser in the set-up, which will be detailed soon. Most Gen 1 analogue units are only 3 X or 4 X magnification, and some have a narrow field of view. Be aware of this and if possible, try before you buy!

You might think rangefinding is hard enough at night with a lamp, but flashback a moment and consider this: Certain early NV riflescopes had large objective lenses meaning there was a notably increased distance between the axis of the rifle bore and that of the sight. Try judging holdover or holdunder at varying ranges, and those new to these devices soon become frustrated at the regular misses.

Thankfully, the major NV manufacturers and importers knew this was a problem that needed addressing and all the early pitfalls have now been fully rectified.

Observation Devices

These can range from a compact hand-held monocular to a more substantial pair of binoculars. All quality units obviously have IR facility, invaluable as it extends viewing range and also reflects back off quarry's eyes to up your detection rate.

If you want to be hands-free, there are models of monocular that fit onto a head harness. These are designed so the monocular can be flicked down to look through, or when not needed, flicked up out of the way so you can sight through a scope. More advanced, higher Gen equipment is available as head-mounted goggles that cover both eyes when in the deployed position. I've used both types successfully. There will be more on head-mounted NV when we come to those accessories I alluded to earlier - lasers.

Night Vision Riflescope

Classification and specification Generation of equipment has already been explained in full. If looking to enter this exciting branch of the sport, an entry-level digital scope or analogue Gen 1, or better still Gen 1+, unit is more than suitable for air rifle use. However, as with virtually all equipment, you do get what you pay for and if staying with analogue equipment, if possible I'd recommend you do go for the slightly higher Gen 1+ or even Gen 2. Most at this level will have powerful IR integrated into the unit, some with two-stage power settings.

Nightvision binoculars are a far better option when observing open areas for longer periods at a greater distance

How to Mount and Zero the NV Riflescope Correctly

Most NV scopes, even the first digital units, are designed to fit a Weaver-style of mounting rail, so for airgun fitting you need the appropriate adaptor to fit it to dovetails or scope rails. The mount specialists B-Square makes these mounts to suit virtually all air rifles, even for mounting to multi-shot rifles which have magazines that protrude quite high from the action.

Other specialist companies can supply adaptor rails for mounting to rifles with fixed scope mounts such as on the popular Rapid series of multi-shot PCPs that Theoben used to manufacture when they were still actively working and trading in the UK.

Once this is sorted and the scope is mounted securely, like a conventional optic you need to set zero. Due to the sensitivity of the internal circuitry, a traditional (analogue NV scope) can only be used in daylight with the front lens cover cap left in place. The lens cap will either be a camera screw-on type or more often a push-fit, heavy-duty rubber cover. This will have a small pinhole through the centre that lets just enough light in for you to use it safely in daylight, allowing you to switch on the unit and initially set zero to test your shooting.. However, once set up in this way, always double-check and if necessary reset zero in the night, as this prevents image shift problems and ensures zero is set accurately for the lightless conditions you'll be hunting in. Incidentally, the mount adaptor elevates the NV scope higher than a more conventional optic, but now the devices themselves are of a more reasonable build, rangefinding, although an art that needs fine-tuning for using these units, isn't the almost impossible task it was with early equipment. In fact, certain manufacturers have seen the popularity of Gen 1 with air rifle hunters and are also offering them a conventional dovetail mount instead of the Weaver base. Unfortunately, it still doesn't solve the problem of mounting to a multi-shot PCP with a protruding magazine.

Thankfully, these days, few Gen 1 analogue riflescopes have low-power onboard IR illuminators. However, if this is the case, for upping the observation range, then it's certainly worth investing in an additional IR torch – particularly to the add-on units

NV Stalking

Just because you think you're not going to be seen due to you not using a light, it doesn't mean that you can let your fieldcraft lapse. Using NV means you can hunt in the dark with more stealth, and indeed, when practised, you'll be surprised at how close you can get to your quarry, but the major issues such as, keeping sound to a minimum, feeling your way with your feet across the ground, taking care to prevent showing as a silhouette and, of course, walking up to quarry from downwind all need to be considered. Take the time to familiarise yourself with the control layout of the NV riflescope.

There are two ways to stalk quarry with NV; either walking forward scanning the area continuously with the rifle up to your shoulder, or alternatively, only bringing the NV scope up to the eye to scan for potential targets, then moving forward and stopping and scanning again. Once within range, you compose yourself, choose a shooting position, and put the scope up to your eye and take the shot. The latter method is less strenuous on the arms as you're not continuously holding the rifle up, but if using a very lightweight carbine, the former can be a better option for short search periods, especially if actively looking for rats around the side of outbuildings. Ratting will be dealt with soon, but I will say, this method tends to strain the eye and play havoc with your own night vision.

When using this method, it's easy to get totally absorbed scanning for targets as you move, and while moving you can easily stumble over rough ground, or something lying on the farmyard floor. Much better is to sweep the ground ahead with the NV and IR illuminator switched on, looking first to locate quarry with the tell-tale reflection from the eyes. Once spotted, slowly move forward, ideally approaching from downwind until within range. The inexperienced will usually chance longer-range shots, but be as patient as you can and with practice you will be able to stalk to a position well within your set zero. Once in position, take careful aim, slip the trigger and the rabbit should roll over dead. Using a silenced air rifle, the sound of the lead impacting the skull will seem very loud in the darkness, even louder than when lamping – or so it seems. Other rabbits in the vicinity will prick up their ears, but many times they'll hold position wondering what's happened. In these cases you'll be able to get in another shot or possibly two!

Needless to say, a multi-shot PCP is the optimum tool for the job; the lighter the better and one that handles well with the NV rig on board. When using NV scopes in this way, it's also a time when I use one of the specialist slings to hold the rifle in the optimum position. The one I prefer is the Cheater Sling, but some specialist mail order military equipment stores have tactical slings that are suited to the job. The Cheater doesn't attach to conventional sling swivel studs, as Is usual, but due to the design, uses elasticated loops that can be fixed virtually anywhere on the rifle. Whilst I often recommend an NV monocular for observation, for this particular stalking technique I don't find it necessary. However, if planning on stalking but waiting up in ambush during the hunting foray, a compact NV device slipped in the jacket pocket is always handy.

Whilst on the subject of accessories, there are other items that are useful and necessary. As always, safety first, so pack the mobile, and although you're hunting without a conventional light source (gun lamp) to illuminate the target, as with other night shooting techniques, you will still need a light source for other necessary tasks in the field. I recommend a small head torch, especially one with a multi-LED facility. Use the lowest LED setting for reloads or hocking rabbits, then use the multi-LED facility or main beam for locating and retrieving shot rabbits before moving position. Now to one of the most overlooked essentials for any night hunter, a good pair of shooting gloves. At night, your hands have a nasty habit of finding every nettle on the ground, every rusty nail sticking from a wooden post, or discarded piece of barbed wire. I often wear a pair of SOLAG fingerless mitts, by Blackhawk. These are strong but flexible, they offer a tactile feel and as they're fingerless there are no problems loading pellets, changing magazines or twiddling dials. In fact, they're ideal for lamping as well as lightless NV hunting. Indeed, virtually all accessories that have been mentioned for lamping apply, but definitely don't forget the spare batteries for the night vision riflescope, and extra ones if using other devices such as a laser or IR torch.

I've probably made stalking rabbits with NV sound a bit complicated, but it isn't. Once you become experienced, you'll find this a very exhilarating branch of the sport and whilst I've outlined the plus points of shooting with NV, let's accept and address the downsides.

Assessing range is without doubt the major obstacle to overcome. Whilst you can quite easily pick out the targets with the sight, as your view through the scope is very tunnelled, the view of much of the ground from your position to the target is virtually non-existent. Granted, this is the same when using a conventional scope in the daylight but consider how many times you weigh-up the target with the naked eye before putting the scope to your eye to shoot. Basically, you've assessed range well before you begin placing the crosshairs on the kill-zone, but with NV your first sight of the target is through the sighting device. The only and best way of determining range to the target is by one of two means; using the reticle as a guide and bracketing, as you would with a conventional scope, or to use a laser in your NV rig. This can either be a conventional red-dot laser or a truly invisible IR laser. The latter only being visible when viewed through an NV device.

Whichever you use, I first recommend you practise in the following way: Draw and cut out from a thick piece of cardboard the profile of an average-sized rabbit and place it upright on the ground. Walk 25yds from the target and using the NV scope reticle, assess a reference point as you would if using the reticle of a standard daylight scope to bracket the target. Some reticles will help you to some extent to bracket the head, others the body. As the scope will be on a set, fixed magnification you can then use this as a starting point for ranging.

However, accurately judging the size of a rabbit through NV equipment is almost impossible so I'd say use this as a very rough guide and rather use a laser in the set-up as will be outlined in full later.

You're still practising in daylight, with the protective cap covering the objective lens. Now, as we've covered before on setting a field course for lamping, do the same but now attempt it with the NV. On your first practice runs in the dark you'll probably be quite dismayed at your results. There's no peeking over the scope as in daylight hours, or using a lamp to illuminate the way. Don't get too disheartened, though, it will come and you'll eventually become adept at rangefinding in what must surely be the most difficult hunting scenario of all. Now, with a laser in the set-up, you obviously need to set the laser to coincide with the set zero of the scope reticle. More on my personal preferences for this later, but the basics for proper usage still apply, which are: Depending on how it's mounted, either above scope or under the barrel any laser set-up will give you the reference you need to assess range, and as you're stalking in a very stealthy manner whenever possible, it will be practical more often than not. Stalk carefully up to the target until the laser coincides exactly with the reticle crosshair aim-point (that is if set conventionally) and take the shot, safe in the knowledge that you can aim bang-on as you're at your set zero from the quarry. Incidentally, as I use both IR laser and traditional red-dot laser, I don't have a preference to lasers for NV shooting, but one thing I certainly now do is to set the dot mark of the laser to one side of the centre of the crosshairs at the set range that my scope zero is set for. Let me explain why: The image intensifier will magnify the dot of either IR or conventional daylight red dot, and I've found that the dot, when set to coincide with the centre of the crosshairs, can obscure precise aiming. It's worth mentioning that, if you are using digital NV – a conventional red-dot laser can be too bright because the internal circuitry of digital equipment is sensitive to the laser wavelength and intensity. However, you can reduce the brightness of these scopes' sight picture to compensate, or better still use an IR laser of which you'll read more soon.

Staying with conventional red-dot lasers: Although I use a pressure pad switch just to dab the laser on to determine range, it isn't always shining there to obscure the crosshair, but I do ensure that I've set the laser to the NV scope so it precisely hits the horizontal line of the reticule at the set zero point. Now while this suits me it may not suit you, but try it. I think you might just find setting any laser up this way is better for integrating one into your rig.

Now to the practicalities and my recommended method of actively pursuing and seeking out quarry when stalking with NV, and presuming it's on a specialist sling, the way is as follows: The rifle combo should be hanging in front of you as previously outlined, but only with your neck through the sling – not including a shoulder. The sling supports the weight of the rig and the rifle is steadied and angled slightly away from the body, with the right hand cupped under the forend, and the majority of the stock just resting on the underside of your right arm. The opposite obviously applies for left-handed shooters.

The reason for this is that if the eye-piece is allowed to rest against clothing, or to direct back in the direction of your body, the intensified light image that's created by analogue NV (the green glow) will be reflected off your clothing or face. If this is allowed to happen, you might as well be walking around holding a green torch. The rubber eyecup shields the glow from the side, but not when put slightly askew at the side of a solid object. It's equally important not to pass your hand or part of the arm over the eye-piece if reaching for something as this gives a solid surface for the green light to reflect from and show forward of your position. Because of this problem, you should also adopt a set routine for bringing the rifle up to your eye for scanning and aiming. When bringing the rifle to bear, whilst moving the rifle upwards, also push it out to your right (opposite again applies for left-handers), and then bring the gun up fully until the butt is in the shoulder, ensuring that the eye-piece is facing over the shoulder. When ready to scan or take the shot, bring your aiming eye into the eyecup from the side, carefully but purposely, without too much delay.

However, you can forget all I've said on using an NV scope that has an open, more conventional rubber eye-piece, if you can obtain what is termed a gated eye-piece to replace the original. These are closed (the inner rear at the back is designed so when not in use it actually fully covers the ocular lens), but press/push your eye into the rear of the eye-piece and the covered inner opens, so you can see through to obtain a full sight picture. I prefer these if using an analogue unit, so check if there is an option for the NV riflescope you choose. Incidentally, you'll notice that some have a habit of catching condensation more easily than others. This can be annoying as you need to wipe the rear lens, and depending on conditions, this can be infuriatingly all too frequent, and don't forget; if anything goes near the eye-piece the green light will reflect so take this into account when clearing the lens with a suitable lens cloth.

If you thought magpies a pain in the day, spoiling a stalk, or calling out to all and sundry, when they catch sight of a lamp you should hear them when they spot you skulking near the hedges at night – and you think NV makes you undetectable? Magpies aren't the only problem, trust me, a covey of partridges suddenly flushing-up as you stalk towards a target can bring on minor heart palpitations! Also, if you surprise a rabbit and are too close for a shot, don't use the 'backing away' technique as is more useful with rats. Stand stock-still and the rabbit will in most cases shuffle around, or hop away, but often stop and sit within range. Now you can target the quarry and as you're operating with much more stealth, you usually won't be crawling within range as on a daytime stalk. You will have to stop at times, but this is usually so you don't show your silhouette.

The bonus of hunting in this way is that you are more relaxed and can easily adopt a more stable kneeling shooting position. This allows you to steady the rifle and the forward knee supports the weight of the combo for the shot. If you do take the shot standing, tuck the elbow of the leading arm into the hip for support. Some analogue scopes are still hefty, but the extra weight does have a benefit in that it can at times help steady aim.

It must be noted that actively hunting with NV can be very tiring both physically and mentally. As with lamping, rest when needed, there's no need to rush because, in effect, you have all night!

Now to the subject of the clothing you wear: Granted, foliage patterns aren't needed, but dark, non-reflective, rustle-free clothing is a must and in my experience so too is a facemask and gloves; the latter not only for concealment but also for reasons given earlier in this chapter. Incidentally, many experienced pest controllers operate at night in black boiler suits and black gloves and masks. It can sometimes be the more appropriate form of clothing to wear.

It's often said that animals can't detect infra-red light, but if you continuously switch a powerful IR illuminator on and off the animal does seem to notice it and will eventually get wise to it. Use the IR sparingly and set on the lowest setting that you can still clearly identify the target. Never forget, no matter what is stated - as a matter of safety – never look directly at any IR emitter or laser, be it a conventional red-dot or a truly invisible laser projector. Your eyes are very precious, so don't take risks such as this!

NV Ambushing

The method is exactly the same as for daylight ambushing and with the added advantage that you're able to target them in darkness with the highest level of stealth, but you must adhere to a few strict guidelines to have the best results. Firstly, you need to position yourself within range of a well-used entrance point to a warren or a passing point from field to field (usually an area of hedgeline), or a place where they sit out near a warren before they move further into the fields to feed. As rangefinding is the biggest pitfall of NV use, I recommend you choose the main entrance hole and pace 25yds from that to a position downwind to use as the shooting point. I'll more often than not put two stones either side of this entrance point, setting these at 5yds beyond the entrance and 5yds closer to my position. This gives two clear range markers at 20 and 30yds. In effect, you've chosen a 10yds long killing-zone. If you've chosen well, there's a lot of traffic that can pass through that corridor.

Items you'll find useful for ambushing in this way are a pair of NV binos or an NV monocular, and to use a multi-shot PCP on a bipod. Incidentally, using a pair of NV binoculars or a monocular is preferable as they give less strain on the aiming eye as you diligently watch the area for activity. Don't be tempted to use them too often, though, as you ruin your personal night vision and yet again, remember if they're analogue the bounce back of the green sight picture can possibly bathe your face when you bring them up or take them away from the eyes. When you do use the binos, only switch them on when you're looking through them, and when you take them away from your face do so in a swift fluid movement preventing the green sight picture in the eye-pieces finding anything solid to reflect off. While lying in wait, use your ears as much as your eyes. You'll hear rabbits plucking at the grass, scratching and generally moving around in cover. If your eyes have become accustomed to the dark, not 'spoiled' by overusing the NV, then you'll possibly see their shapes move out into the designated shooting area. This is the ideal scenario, as once spotted you can put the rifle in your shoulder, eye in the rubber eye-piece and switch on the NV scope.

As the sight image develops there should be rabbits in your sights and if all has gone according to plan, one within range and soon in your bag. No need to rush the shot as ideally you're operating totally undetected. Take careful aim, and shoot. Once you've shot one, don't rush to pick up as long as it's a clean kill. At night, and shooting in this stealthy manner, more rabbits soon appear and are certainly not troubled by the fallen ones you've dispatched.

Incidentally, while watching and ambushing rabbits in this manner, I've discovered an unusual trait of rabbit behaviour that you, too, can put to good use. That's actually to use a fox call, one that mimics the distress call of a small rabbit or vole, to entice rabbits out into the open, even towards your shooting position. For some reason, the rabbits are drawn to the sound rather than repelled. I've had rabbits come running in to a 'squeaker' and standing like knock downs well within range. It can also make them move further out from cover, presumably so nothing can pounce on them - strange behaviour, but a trick to use if they're keeping out of range or too close to tall cover.

NV Rat Shooting

All the above information and tips for NV use apply to ratting except that you'll be shooting indoors and around barns and outbuildings. Therefore, the safety aspects remain the same for indoor shooting, and targets will more often than not be closer. As you can get close to your quarry anyway using NV then I'd advise you to reset zero down to 20yds maximum, maybe even less at 15yds. Stalking around the farmyard at night can be particularly productive. If circuiting the perimeter of buildings, where possible walk the same distance as your set zero from the walls, continually scanning the base of walls and along the top of any materials stacked near it for scaly tails. Once you spot one, position yourself as near as possible to the set zero and shoot. If you come across one much closer than your set zero - don't attempt to adjust your aim for the range, rather physically back away until you're at the required distance, as close as possible to your set zero, and then take the shot. Indoors, you can patrol in much the same way, scanning the interior, especially the beams and girders, anywhere above that can provide the rat with a walkway. Alternatively, use baiting-down tactics without a light and shoot them with the NV riflescope when they come to feed. Also if you know an area that has a lot of rat activity, make yourself comfortable on a chair or bale of hay and sit and wait. This is when using an extra aid such as an NV monocular for spotting is very advantageous. This negates the need for you to hold the rifle up continually, to use the riflescope to survey the roof space. Using an observation aid keeps the strain down to a minimum, but be mindful that when you spot a potential target you make the least disturbance when swapping over from observation aid to riflescope.

As mentioned in the section on lamping, using these devices gives you the edge on the quarry. With the IR illuminator switched on, work along the areas the rats are known to frequent. You'll soon spot the animal, even if it only pops its head out of a hidey-hole, by the infra-red light reflecting off its eyes. Once you spot a rat within range, put the observation aid down and carefully sight-in using the NV riflescope.

IR and Conventional Laser Sights

The introduction of IR lasers that emit an invisible beam and a dot (aim point) on the target are fascinating. Even the projected dot is invisible to the human eye until viewed through a device incorporating an image intensifier. These can be either a head-mounted monocular, NV goggles, or by looking through the NV riflescope. The supposed benefits aren't as cut and dried as you might think though. You can, albeit in a limited manner, use the IR laser as a primary sighting device, but it must be remembered that this has very limited accuracy potential. Some use them by setting the dot to a range of 20 or 25yds and shoot rats 'from the hip' as they spot and sight targets through head-mounted NV equipment, place the dot on the kill-zone and shoot. In theory all's well and good, but the reality isn't nearly as good as it sounds.

How the laser is mounted also has a bearing on the accuracy. If you're intending to use an IR laser in this manner, the laser should ideally be positioned as close to the bore line of the barrel as possible, so it follows the pellet path more closely until trajectory drop takes over. Also, the range that the laser's set for needs to be strictly adhered to, I recommend 20yds maximum. Even at this range you'll only have a few yards either way of set zero until the dot (set aim-point) is inaccurate. So if you use an IR or conventional laser in this manner, use a special mount to attach the device to barrel or silencer, and be very disciplined in your shooting and well practised in estimating range.

As I've previously outlined, I personally feel lasers of both types better serve the shooter when used as rangefinding aids. The way it works with an NV riflescope being the same for how a conventional laser is used with a conventional riflescope. Incidentally, when viewed through analogue NV equipment the aim point of both IR laser and conventional red-light laser appear as a very light green, almost white dot. Sighted through digital it will appear as a white dot. As I've mentioned previously, rangefinding is very difficult with NV riflescopes and this is the area where shooters will find lasers to be of most benefit.

Because rabbits are once again a major agricultural pest and rat numbers are reaching ever-higher levels, night shooting is a part of airgun hunting that will always thrive as long as we're legally allowed to do it. The air rifle is often the optimum tool for cleanly dispatching them, and yes, that includes rats because even with so-called 'designer' poisons and clever traps, the rat can build up immunity and can easily learn to avoid a trap after a near miss.

With lamping kit at an all-time quality high, and NV devices becoming more affordable, the opportunities

Ambushing using an 'add-on' NV module fitted onto the eye-bell of a day scope

for the night hunter are many. Indeed, where NV goes from here is anybody's guess. Certainly better quality equipment will become available as long as its sale to the civilian market isn't restricted by sanctions.

Whilst writing this book I've seen many more thermal imagers to come into the UK, the price far exceeding the practical use they have for airgun hunters, but these are yet another device that will detect animals at night and pick up the heat given off by them. There's little use for these expensive gadgets in our sport, though; more so for gamekeepers, professional deer stalkers.

We should remember one important factor pertaining to this branch of our sport and that is, if there's one thing guaranteed to get an air rifle hunter granted permission to shoot on a farm, it's the initial offer to sort rats which are causing destruction in the barns and grain stores, and rabbits destroying the fields.

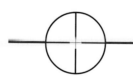

FAC Air Rifles, Options, Ammo and Accessories

Throughout this book I've made mention of FAC- (Firearm Certificate) rated air rifles, usually with the slant that they give more kill-zone options on quarry encountered, but this is only one benefit. Others include a harder hit at a given range, a flatter trajectory over that range, and they can be used with more safety and in more situations where a live, round-bullet gun (such as a rimfire) is either too powerful or unsuitable due to other factors.

Not only that, but the interest in FAC air rifles has undergone a huge surge in popularity from both the specialist airgun publications and, in turn, airgun hunters alike, driven by an increasing number of gun manufacturers shifting emphasis towards the development and promotion of a new breed of what can best be termed 'hi-power-super-guns.'

This has resulted in much change in relation to the air rifles themselves, specifically the power levels they are designed to run at. Coupled with this are the new larger calibres with ammo specifically designed and manufactured for them. I'm sure you can realise, the whole genre is now an even more specialised sector of the airgun hunting scene than it ever was before.

The High-Powered Air Rifle

I still stand by original statements as written in the First Edition – 'most airgun hunters may never want to own or use an FAC-rated air rifle, but it's a tool in the armoury for the all-round airgun hunter and at times can be very useful, albeit in reality it's still a very specialised piece of kit.'

First, though, you obviously need to go through the process of applying for a Firearms Certificate (FAC). This is usually what puts most people off, but don't be deterred because after filling in the relevant application forms (Form 101), as long as you can satisfy your local Police Firearms Department that you are a fit and suitable person to own a firearm, it's just a matter of going through due process, and you have your FAC. Of course, the fact which will be addressed after your initial application and visit by your Firearms Liason Officer (FLO), Is that you need secure storage for the firearm. That means that a gun cabinet will be needed because, yes, that's what an FAC air rifle is – a firearm. That's a factor that should always be remembered when and where you use it, and before and after using it, it stays where it belongs, inside the gun cabinet, locked away secure and safe.

Now, even after that very brief overview to obtaining an FAC, you'll probably be asking yourself if it's worth the hassle of applying and satisfying the responsibility of ownership criteria, just to have an air rifle with a bit more 'puff!' Quite frankly, if you're content to hunt at 12ft lbs then, no – but a resounding, yes, if you want to broaden your shooting horizons and experience air rifle hunting to the absolute max and eventually, maybe even move into other shooting disciplines. Notice that I've refrained from saying, 'if you're serious about shooting, you'll get one' which is something I've heard many times from FAC-holders in relation to non-FAC shooters. That's nonsense because a hunter using a 12ft lb air rifle can be just as much, if not more, serious about his sport than a fully certified, ticket-waving, power-blessed one..

The Power Game

In previous chapters of the book we've dealt with hunting with a rifle of legal limit. That's why a good phrase to use for 12ft lb air rifle hunting is 'precision over power', but what about when you can have precision with power? That brings us to address one of the most popular misconceptions surrounding FAC-power-rated air rifles, that extra 'oomph' gives you some sort of super-long-range ability. It doesn't, but depending on how powerful they are, they do hit far harder at ranges right out to 80yds and in some cases well beyond, but the rifle still needs to be fired accurately. Also, weather conditions, strength and direction of wind etc … need to be favourable for longer-range shots. In reality, the benefits an FAC-rated air rifle gives are a flatter trajectory, a harder hit when the pellet reaches the target, and the winning fact that at times it can give you more kill-zones to aim for, depending on quarry and its position to your shooting position.

Indeed, mention hi-power rifles and it does seem to bring out the dreamers. Shooters with ridiculous claims that 'such and such' rifle running at 'such and such' ft lb puts pellets straight as a die out to 'X' many yards. This is nonsense. If anything, the FAC air rifle is too specialised for most shooter's requirements. Let me explain that statement.

Overkill, especially at close to medium range, can easily come into the shooting equation with a bullet gun, and that's why the hunter using a 12ft lb air rifle fills a niche. He can operate where other types of guns are unsuitable and the shooting situation requires them – for instance inside barns, around outbuildings, land with footpaths on or around it, smallholdings with little land, dense woodland etc. Now, taking this statement forward, the FAC air rifle shooter has a firearm that to some extent, and to coin a phrase, bridges the gap between a legal limit air rifle and a live round rimfire. A .22 calibre air rifle with 30ft lbs of muzzle energy is still only starting to nudge up to a .22 rimfire, short in terms of power level, but even so, the hi-power pellet is certainly not as potentially dangerous as a bullet fired from a rimfire. Even at medium range, a hi-power FAC air rifle can be too powerful for the job in hand. Incidentally, despite popular misconception, ricochets aren't as nearly dangerous on open land as some suppose. The reason being, a deflected pellet soon runs out of steam even if fired at high velocity. More so, you should be mindful of what lies behind the target; the major consideration for any shot taken with any sporting gun.

So, that brings us back to the fact that, in effect, it's only out to a certain range that the big power air rifle delivers the big power punch. After a set distance, as you'll read further in this piece, even a pellet fired at hi-power is already dropping, quite radically and eventually like a stone, whereas a rimfire bullet continues for up to a mile if unobstructed. See how the FAC air rifle can be most useful, and the situations in which it caters for a much safer type of firearm to be used?

Incidentally, mechanically operated rifles such as springers or gas-rams specifically manufactured to be capable of hi-power are few and far between. Granted, most springers can be tuned-up to run at higher power above the 12ft lb legal limit, but unless you're only notching it up to 16-18ft lb, it's best the rifle is built to achieve those power levels from the outset. Also, higher power in a springer often means more recoil, thus accuracy can be affected. So that brings us to the PCP power source and this is where you'll really appreciate the hi-power capabilities with no recoil.

However, a downside of a hi-power PCP is that it gives fewer shots per charge than its 12ft lb counterpart, so that small bottle you use for home fills is best now taken into the field for top-ups, and an even larger diver's bottle kept at home. If you don't have access to your own filling gear or a diving centre close by for filling the larger bottles, you could opt to acquire a rifle that uses buddy bottles, but always remember to take enough pre-filled spare buddy bottles into the field. However, for the design of air rifles that use a forward- or rear-mounted bottle to store compressed air, the bottle is more likely these days (except on older rifles) to be fixed, so is filled on the rifle like many 12ft lb air rifles. There are certain accessories and kit that will help you top-up in the field and there's a section devoted to those and others later in this chapter.

Another point pertaining to hi-power FAC rifles is that most are full-length. Not only due to the capacity of the air reservoir being limited in a carbine, but also a short barrel of a carbine doesn't impart enough spin to the pellet due to lack of rifling. For a 12ft lb

The FAC power rated air rifle is a very specialised piece of hardward

air rifle, all carbines are suited to impart enough spin on the pellet for optimum accuracy, but for a hi-power heavyweight slug it benefits from having more barrel to travel along. Some FAC rifles even have longer barrels than their standard length, legal limit counterparts.

Now to a very important aspect of hi-power and indeed for legal limit air rifles, which Is is the need for a top-quality, highly-efficient sound moderator.

As you've seen mentioned much earlier in this book, the muzzle crack (report) from a PCP is loud when unsilenced – well, it stands to reason this is more pronounced from a hi-power rifle. Here you really need to make an informed and well-considered choice.

Production or Custom

All gun manufacturers of hi-power air rifles produce or have produced for them silencers that they recommend for their 'on-ticket' air rifles. Many now actually have specialists in the field to design moderators for specific rifles. For instance, Daystate excel in producing some of the finest hi-power air rifles available, but make no secret that they recommend the Twink Silencer, from A&M Custom Gunsmiths or the special FAC-rated Hugget, from Milbro. You need to make this a priority when considering purchasing a certain manufacturer's hi-power air rifle, but generally any of the company names you've heard mentioned for being established at air rifle customising can build a silencer to special order.

I mostly use John Bowkett's custom silencers. He first began developing special reflex designs, which are superb, and amongst the quietest you can purchase. I now have them on most of my customised FAC air rifles. If you have a silencer especially made to work almost in harmony with the rifle, then you will have the best you can get. No silencer can cope with all the power levels and calibres now becoming reality so if the sound on discharge is a factor that concerns you, please take heed of the advice given.

Don't forget you need to have provision to own one and it needs to be included on your licence when you are granted one.

Some of the quietest sound moderators for FAC air rifle use are often manufactured by the specialist custom gunsmiths

Choosing the rifle itself can become an issue because you don't want to make a costly mistake. Most FAC air rifles won't hold value bought from new because the resale market for them in the UK at present is still relatively small. Good for those looking to pick up a bargain, but if you're set on a new rifle be warned that, as with buying a new car, once you leave the showroom your luxury new 'boy's toy' becomes a very expensive loss.

I'd advise most shooters new to FAC after getting the relevant paperwork sorted (and of course if they have one in their armoury), to have a rifle tuned-up to a suitable power level by a reputable gunsmith. Alternatively, buy a good quality, used PCP air rifle suited to tuning and have that powered up. Just remember to get it put on your ticket. This is the less expensive route into the FAC power game and will help you assess if your hunting really requires one.

As for choice of sights: Any of your favourite hunting scopes will suffice but many soon require optics with a bit more power which more often equates to a scope with a magnification of either the now accepted 4 - 16 X or 6 – 24 X range. Also, the more you come to realise the nuances of the hi-power pellet's flight path, then you'll probably come to feel a scope with a multi-aim-point reticle could be very beneficial to you.

Scope Options

I once mainly preferred the mil-dot reticle, using scopes that utilised this design almost exclusively on virtually all my FAC air rifles. Don't get me wrong, this is still a good option but there are now far better designs that many will find much more to their liking.

Choosing the optic to marry up to your hi-power air rifle is also very much dictated by personal choice, so I'll only briefly outline the two models I currently favour as I find they work best for me in a variety of calibres. The requisite I favour is that there is sufficient information mostly on the lower stadia of the reticle, because after you've set a zero, due to the pellet then dropping, depending on pellet weight and calibre this can be relatively slow or a quite pronounced change (drop) in trajectory after the set zero.

I've begun to favour two reticles based on the standard mil-dot package; the AMD (Amended Mil-Dot) as used in the MTC Optics Genesis LR 5 – 5 X 50 SF IR, and the half-mil dot reticle as seen in certain scopes from the Hawke Sports Optics stable. The 4 – 16 X 50 Sidewinder SF IR I find is a hard spec' optic to beat for 12ft lb as well as FAC-rated air rifle use and like the MTC offering is a fully-featured scope.

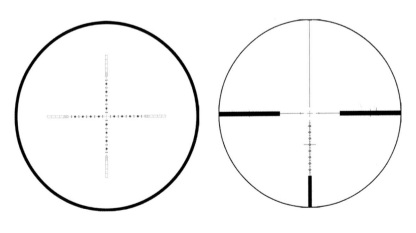

Hawke Half-Mil Dot   **MTC Optics AMD**

As their names suggests, set on 10 X magnification both scopes are a true mil-dot design, the Hawke giving lots of alternative aim points and can be used for rangefinding using the bracketing technique. It offers masses of aim points for both holdunder and holdover, and for aiming off, if you are confident judging wind. Alternatively though, the AMD can be used as a conventional mil-dot if required – obviously due to most of the aim points being set on the lower stadia - not for bracketing. Therefore, this scope is a more dedicated long-range optic offering lots of very useful aim points for holdover. As you'd expect there are now many other reticle designs that you might find more suited to your particular liking.

As we're now dealing with choosing hardware, I feel this is a good place to look at the accessories to help you in the field when shooting FAC.

Accessories for the FAC Airgun Hunter

Many accessories that the hi-power hunter will find useful have already been fully detailed in Chapter 9 because of their benefits for 12ft lb legal limit air rifle use. Due to this, I'll only mention them briefly as a reminder. These are; a shooting bag/gun mat, bipod, a good-quality rangefinder, and a pair of binoculars or a monocular. In relation to rangefinding or estimation, some find a laser incorporated into the set-up also helps – refer to Chapter 2 for its usage.

Of equal and even more importance to the FAC hunter is the need to keep the rifle topped up with air. In that respect, lugging heavy diving bottles into a field isn't an option, but taking a smaller filling bottle is. The accessory to transport a 3L bottle for in-field fills has never been bettered than to use the specifically designed Ranger 6 Combo-Pack from Napier. This enables you to carry the bottle, as it sits securely inside the rucksack which also has pockets for various accessories you'll find useful for helping you top up the rifle. Best-Fittings are a one-stop shop for kit that helps you fill your PCP more efficiently. No surprise then that they also supply mini-compressed air bottles complete with fill line and air gauge, and for a few top-ups they're so portable that they'll fit into the large pocket of a gun bag.

If shooting from a hide, use a set of triple-leg shooting sticks that you can comfortably sit behind and have a stable forward rest to take precision shots. Your seat can be one of the many rucksack chairs. Most seats they employ fold inwards so they form a frame for the rucksack attached when used for transportation, and then when you need it, allow the seat to open ao you have a quick and useful seat. A gadget that some very ardent FAC shooters are now integrating into their kit is a windometer. As the name clearly suggests, this measures wind speed. If you think a device such as this may help you then its there to be made use of. More so I'd say, learn to judge wind speed, and only experience on the range or dedicated in-field practice can help you attain that.

We now come to the major bone of contention, that being what calibre to choose and at what power? If you thought 12ft lb airgun hunters were divided on calibre choice then add another variable such as power in relation to calibre and you really do open up another can o' worms. While some swear by .22 calibre at 40ft lb, others are equally smitten with the same calibre fired at 24, 26, 28 or 30ft lb. To throw even more

Kit required for the long-range FAC shooter – note the laser rangefinders, binos and shooting mat – bunnies an optional bonus

controversy into the pot, some would say you cannot beat .20 calibre at 24ft lb or .177 calibre at the same, or at 18 or 22ft lb. The truth of the matter is once again, not only is it very much up to personal choice, but also there is a simple equation of what I term, 'balance of power.' This, we are coming to, but basically it's the relationship between the weight of projectile fired to the power it's fired at.

Incidentally, don't discount the much-maligned and misunderstood .20 calibre of which I now have much experience and regard for, since adding one to my armoury. I've had many memorable hunting forays using this calibre since I acquired a Daystate AirWolf running at 26ft lb in this calibre using 13.73gr JSB Exacts – it was a very considered decision but one I'll never regret making.

Balance of Power

As previously established, any calibre pellet fired from an FAC-rated rifle has a flatter trajectory over a given range than its 12ft lb counterpart. Also, if the pellet has been placed with accuracy, it transfers a mighty 'whack' at the target. Power, as I said at the beginning of the book, is somewhat of a misnomer and definitely in the case of the FAC air rifle, all too easily misunderstood. Many experienced FAC air rifle shooters recommend power levels of 18 – 24ft lb. Some might feel it's not worth the trouble getting an FAC for this rating, but remember, this is approximately giving you double the power of a 12ft lb off-ticket air rifle.

This is where the term 'balance of power' becomes very apt. In respect of power (ft lb) in relation to pellet weight (grains), to gain optimum performance from the set-up becomes somewhat of a balancing act; matching the weight of ammo and power of air rifle. As selection and choice of pellets in .22 calibre is greater, then this is probably the best calibre to use as an example to illustrate this phenomenon.

If shooting an air rifle with a power level up to and including the mid-20ft lb bracket, you have a far greater choice of pellets that will withstand this power. I could compile a list of my current recommendations for various calibres and power levels, but I've no doubt that new ammo will have come along before or shortly after this is published. However, what does hold true is this: step beyond the 30ft lb power mark and many that are capable at 26ft lb become more and more unstable in flight. Initially, you must think this a power band that is a barrier – but ...

Old Dog New Tricks ...

I'm sure most airgun hunters realise that they are on a never-ending learning curve. Personally, my initial views of ammo weight to power rating are now much more open. However, these views still relate to what I term the balance of power. Let me explain.

After writing the first edition of Total Airguns, I was fortunate to have out, for quite a lengthy test period, a rifle that in many ways opened my eyes to the possibilities that are available when using higher power levels than 12ft lb. The rifle was the Air Arms S410 Xtra FAC, and at the time it was quite unique due to it being one of the few rifles that allowed the shooter to vary the power by turning an external, serrated-edge adjustment dial. This is situated on the right of the action, and allows the power to be adjusted from approximately 10ft lb up to about 32ft lb. This was quite some time ago and the reason that I use approximations, but it didn't take long until I began to realise that the facility to vary the power of this rifle wasn't a gimmick, and it had great potential for the open-minded airgun hunter.

Once, we only had a few options of pellet that could withstand hi-power air rifle use. The most widely used was the one-time heavyweight champion of the FAC-pellet world – the Bisley Magnum. At 21.4gr this is the heavy slug that will withstand being ejected from the air rifle at 40ft+ pounds of power. Fantastic for the time and still is in the right circumstances – like the H&N Barracuda which is almost identical in weight and profile.

Now, with new hardware and superbly manufactured pellets if you try a variable-power air rifle such as the one previously mentioned, or its successor, the S510TC FAC then it will enable you very much to begin to realise that the gap from legal limit to any rating up to 30ft lb is a fascinating journey of discovery.

Just one of the many up-graded features of the side-lever action S510TC FAC variant is an even more precise power adjuster. In fact, I can fully understand and appreciate why this rifle can be classed as the most versatile air rifle currently on the market in either .22 or .25 calibre. Considering the latter, I have to admit that it enables hunters to use the big old ¼" slug to the best of its ability, and for the most useful purposes that this calibre can be used. Powered down and set at a suitable zero using a pellet chosen from the many new types of .25 calibre ammo available, it then becomes a rat-clobbering and/or feral-pigeon bashing tool par excellence, and safe to use in an enclosed area. Power up, change ammo, re-zero and you can be knocking down rabbits at ranges out to 60yds+ as long as your shooting ability is up to it.

When running at full power you're just getting into the area, in my opinion, that a .25 calibre slug shows the reason it was intended for. You've still got a quite loopy trajectory to get to grips with, but it's certainly one to consider for the sensible and most useful way to use a .25 calibre air rifle and for some, a .22 calibre.

I feel the need to highlight the S510TC FAC as it's possibly now the most versatile of the new breed of air rifles in FAC format currently available. Now, back to what I feel is of more general importance pertaining to the FAC airgun user who chooses a rifle in one of the more traditional calibres.

At one time the heavyweight Bisley Magnum in .22 calibre was the one to beat for FAC rifle use...

Be Sensible ...

I feel I've more than established that power isn't everything, neither is it all about the weight of the projectile. We must also consider the downsides and for most FAC-rated, PCP air rifles these are a low shot count per fill and the fact that they are noisy. The reason being, they expel a high volume of air with each shot. In fact, I feel the real bazookas that have come on to the scene may become a niche within a niche, as most made in the UK are destined for export but some professional pest controllers will, and do, find them useful – more on the very hi-power rifles at the end of this chapter.

Consider this statement: 'There is much more involved than just brute force when you have an FAC air rifle at your disposal.' That sentence is even more relevant now and one I fully came to realise the meaning of after testing various weights of pellet that could withstand being fired at 30ft lbs – a power level that I have already detailed is a very popular power rating in .22 calibre.

Obviously, when I began experimenting with pellet weights to power rating, a lighter pellet than the bruisers I was initially advised to use was needed to fully appreciate this. After listening to experienced shooters who also sought more versatility from this power level, I eventually discovered a handful of pellets in what can be termed the 'upper- mid-weight' bracket that could actually cope with the rigours of that heft without showing too many flyers or blown-out skirts. These were the Air Arms Field Diablo, Crosman Dome and Webley Accupell, and of course JSB Exacts, amongst only a very few others.

What I'd proved to myself and what actually happened was, I'd hit on a good level of consistency with a far flatter trajectory. Let me explain.

Speed Limit

After chrono checking the power, Bisley Magnums were generating an average of 800 f.p.s at the muzzle. A .177 calibre 12ft lb air rifle isn't travelling much faster and the trajectory isn't that different, the bonus, of course, being the hitting power at the target! But remember this, an air rifle with a power level of 12ft lb only needs to deliver 4ft lb at the target for the much required humane kill on a rabbit at practical distances. It followed that stepping the pellet weight down, certain pellets did indeed show they could retain accuracy and still have more than enough whack at the target to dispatch any legal pest species cleanly.

Despite the apparently impressive figures for FAC-rated guns, never lose sight of the fact that the lead pellet does not offer the ballistic efficiency of a rifle bullet, which in comparison will be less influenced by exterior forces.

This became apparent when going over 1000 f.p.s with certain pellets because accuracy suffered considerably. However, if you keep the speed sub-1000 you could find a lot that offer better performance suitable for your rifle and requirements in this calibre and power level.

Air Arms Field Diablo (16-grain) immediately showed a remarkably flatter trajectory and accuracy. It didn't go supersonic as a lighter pellet would and left the silencer with the lowest report, but had enough robustness of construction to withstand the power level it was subjected to.

The Air Arms Field Diablo Plus weighs 18-grains (gr) and I use this example as that extra two grains does make a marked difference. The muzzle velocity dropped as expected which translated to approximately only ½" below the standard Field Diablo at the previous set zero range. Granted, not too shabby, but a slower pellet is more susceptible to wind-drift and this means the shooter has to contend on certain days with factors that result in the pellet not performing that much better over the 16-grain Field. Also consider this: With a zero range of 45-yards, only 15-yards further out, then should the wind blow it will result in a miss or wounding.

As previously mentioned, there are other pellets to consider, but now using these, my 30ft lb .22 calibre combo has become for certain situations a much more versatile and accurate tool. I hope you can see that in FAC, the key words can be 'versatility' and 'accuracy'. Test and try other brands around the weights mentioned as there are many more than you'd first expect; mostly dome heads or what are often termed 'air bullets'.

The FAC air rifle often allows you to take kill shots you can't otherwise take using a 12ft air rifle

Air bullets obviously get their name due to the shape, not the fact that they actually use a powder charge to propel them. A typical example of this is another heavyweight pellet the Logun Penetrator (still around and packaged as such, when you can find them) but also known as the Exterminator under another brand. At 20.5gr in .22 calibre and 9.5gr in .177 calibre this air bullet is very efficient in certain rifles.

Another is the H&N Rabbit Magnum II, at 15.74gr in .177 calibre and 24.7gr in .22 calibre they're obviously designed for FAC use again having a profile that many class as air bullets.

The H&N Rabbit Magnum II is a typical air bullet design

Closer inspection of the twin-ribbed outer shows that they're actually chamfered steps where the bullet head size tapers slightly back to meet the first step, which then angles (chamfers) back up to match the head size, and then it tapers back again a shorter distance to meet the second, which uses the same design then continues as per head size until the rear. Preceded by the highlyregarded and hard to find Eley Magnum (40gr), the H&N Rabbit Magnum II certainly aren't copies but pretty much the closest you'll find to replace it. Due to the higher-precision manufacture, they give better accuracy but still deliver a mighty clout. Many report good results up to 22ft lb in .177 and 40ft lb in the larger calibre – this as usual depends on the rifle. If you feel these will suit your barrel, these niche market 'bunny bullets' should certainly be given a go. As with selection of ammo for any power of air rifle, try the ones available and find the one best suited to your rifle and power setting.

In general I still feel most UK shooters are content to run their air rifles at 18 – 22ft lb in .177, 22 – 26ft lb in .20 and 30 – 60ft lb in .22 calibre – any higher power above this and it really is time to look to the .25 calibre rifle.

So, before the 'big boys' take over I stress the point that these observations aren't grabbed from thin air but born from my own personal experience and many others agree with them. In fact, some shooters think an FAC air rifle the choice of the lazy shooter. Granted, if you're set on .22 calibre and you are never fully confident in your rangefinding, keep the distances reasonable and you really can enjoy the benefits a flatter trajectory hi-power air rifle affords. Also, the need to allow or take into consideration the effect wind has on the pellet is less. Obviously, this only applies to sensible ranges, and you can be more confident in the flatter trajectory for taking awkward upward angle shots as well; the reason that when roost shooting, I sometimes prefer to use an FAC air rifle. Also, I'm sure you can see the benefits of using a hi-power air rifle for both lamping and when using NV riflescopes.

Remember in Chapter 4 on Ammo, we looked at checking pellets? Well, while it's important to use quality undamaged pellets in 12ft lb, when using a FAC air rifle the slightest deformity or damage will render it very unpredictable and should be discounted. Whilst pellet choice is always important, correct pellet choice and scrutiny of the quality is vital for using in a hi-power air rifle.

Interestingly, and I still agree with the many other hunters, using a .177 calibre rifle running at 18-24ft lb recommend the Bisley Magnum pellet, and at 10.5gr it does seem to be the optimum choice for the small calibre FAC fan. As proof of its popularity, it's available in a few slightly different head sizes in both the popular calibres. Without wanting to seem like I'm contradicting myself, you really can tailor those heavyweights to suit your particular gun, and as I'm sure you're now aware, taking the trouble to find exactly the right one that suits your rifle barrel will certainly show itself in the accuracy you're able to achieve.

However, as we are soon to look at the much talked of bigger calibres, I feel that nicely brings me to the next factor to address in relation to FAC rifles, and calibre size is the misconception of power or 'hitting force' at the target being the main requisite for effective hunting. Once again, go back to the Ammo Chapter and you'll see this particular mistaken belief is more than dismissed for a pellet fired from a 12ft lb air rifle and so it equally applies for FAC rifles. It's accurate shooting that puts the pellet into the kill-zone not power, although power does offer better accuracy potential under certain conditions. Consider this fact: A .177 calibre 22-24ft lb air rifle still delivers approximately 12ft lb of muzzle energy at the target and at 60yds, that's some clout! So with calibre size and weight in relation to power out of the equation, what other reason is there specifically to use an FAC-powered air rifle?

Some areas of land might be certified fit for an FAC air rifle but not necessarily suitable for rimfire. As the law is continually becoming more stringent there are no grey areas pertaining to responsibility of gun ownership. In other words, land is either passed for rimfire or it isn't. If it isn't, then more likely it will pass for FAC air rifle and in these cases, if you feel the need of the extra oomph, the FAC air rifle is the tool for the job. I'm sure you can now realise that it's all too easy once you get your ticket to get carried away and go for the most powerful rifle you can find. You need to weigh up your needs and abilities, the ranges at which you're likely to encounter quarry, and the reason you needed or wanted the extra power in the first place; and to return to the subject of kill-zones, more areas of vulnerability on quarry targeted are now open.

To steal a rifleman's phrase of 'putting one in the boiler room', which is possible with an FAC air rifle, as it means the centre target mass, that will usually be the heart/lung area. Heart/lung shots not dared possible shooting at 12ft lb, are acceptable with a hi-power rifle. So are the side-on, smash-through hits on the chest area of corvids and pigeon.

For the latter, though, you do risk bruising at least one side of the breast meat, but if this is the only way to tackle them, if you own an FAC the tool is at your disposal. Consider this example of the opportunities that having a FAC air rifle can open up for you. If shooting from a reasonable-sized hide, I often take in both a standard 12ft lb air rifle and a hi-power rifle. For quarry that presents at medium range, the FAC can often be too much gun for the job so the 12ft lb does the duty there. For wood pigeons or crows that sit further out or higher up at longer range in trees, the FAC rifle is the one to pick up for that shot. With my Theoben Rapid MkII allowing me to have 30ft lb at my disposal, pigeons in trees drop out like stones when hit in the alternative kill-zones that the hi-power air rifle can offer. Another bonus is, I don't need to worry about small leaves or twigs, as that heavy weight pellet will brush those aside and still crash with deadly duty into the carefully targeted and selected kill-zone. Another reason I'd pick up the FAC is for other legal avian quarry species that roosts or generally sits higher than usual in trees, sometimes now even for brancher shooting.

Super Hi-Power FAC

Though what follows are tales of air rifles with jaw-dropping raw power, I must say very hi-power air rifles are nothing new. Renowned airgun designer, John Bowkett, was making incredible weapons to special order for the USA way back in the early 90s with Stalker Air Rifles and his own bespoke designs as J. B Custom Air Rifles. Can you believe these included .45 and 50 calibre PCPs with power levels of 200 - 300ft lb?

Yes, the Americans like to go large, and in their homeland they've now launched a beast; the jaw-dropping monster very suitably named 'The Benjamin Rogue.' It's electronically managed by what the company (Crosman USA) term 'ePCP' and it shoots - wait for it - .357 (9mm) calibre bullets. They've made their own ammo weighing a whopping 127-gr, there's a .35 option from JSB, and the highly-respected bullet manufacturers Nosler specifically manufacture a 145-gr, polymer-tipped, .357 calibre air bullet for it!

It's only right to mention the Daystate Air Ranger 80 as this leans more towards what the UK has had in the past in .25 calibre, but with more accuracy. A firm favourite, particularly in the USA, I was fortunate enough to try one and it does have to be said, there's a real buzz when you trip the sears of this high-power behemoth.

There are so many other specific FAC air rifles that warrant a mention, but due to space constraints I must add here, the specialist shooting publications now fully cover all the latest and notable major air rifles irrespective of power level, such is their impact on the scene.

Even so, this chapter certainly wouldn't be complete without including the Daystate Wolverine .303. It's caused the biggest buzz in the industry I've known, especially here in the UK. As attractive as it is unique, with an automatic pressure switch that prevents the rifle from being fired when the pressure in the reservoir is too low, all the action is built from expensive and new types of materials needed to withstand the almighty power this unleashes. It also uses a blow-back system to cycle the 9-shot magazine.

As an example of the reason this rifle is of use in the UK, who better than Jerry Moss, full-time ranger with the Red Squirrel Conservation Society at the Whinfell Forest Red Squirrel Refuge to inform us? He uses the rifle on a daily basis in his work protecting our native endangered red squirrel.

FAC air rifles often allow a flatter trajectory to the target; just one reason many prefer to use them for shooting at awkward upward angles

Jerry Moss: Ranger and a Trustee for the Penrith and District Red Squirrel Group.

'Amongst other duties, I monitor the red squirrel population in a 5km buffer zone of Whinfell Forest, as well as the forest itself. A major concern is the control of grey squirrels and for this, like the other rangers, we use various methods - often these include shooting or trapping.

The Daystate Wolverine 303 was launched at Greystoke Castle in July 2012. Afterwards Tony Belas, of Daystate, asked me to use one, as he wanted to see how it got on under real-time field test situations. The next day, after putting three tins of the huge

Jerry Moss in action with the Daystate Wolverine .303 in the Whinfell forest

The Daystate Wolverine .303 running at over 100ft lbs is a very specialised but highly capable pest control tool

50.15gr Daystate Rangemaster Emperor through it, I discovered it gave 18-20 useable shots which is easily enough for most days on my rounds.

I decided on a maximum range of 50yds as most of my work is within woodlands. 30, 40, 50 and 65-yd targets were set out and I was achieving groups over these ranges with a 50-yd set zero within one-inch. Since then, I've shot numerous grey squirrels from 20yd out to 60yd, so many might immediately think, 'Why use the Wolverine running at 100ft lb, and not a 30 or 40ft lb FAC air rifle?' Well, the grey squirrel is a tough little critter and it's imperative I get the all-important clean dispatch, so I'm working at greater distances a lot of the time and every shot has to account for one fewer non-native pest species.

Who would have thought that FAC hi-powerewd air rifles would be used in the protection of some of the UK's native species (Sarah McNeil photographer)

Standard FAC air rifles are very useful, but I'm so impressed with the rifle that it is now my weapon of choice in the situations I know it will serve me best. Advantages are, it's very hard hitting with the large pellet over greater distances, so it's very accurate and the pellet has a very quick fall-out so elevated shots at grey squirrels are a 'go', as long as the background and distances are suitable.'

J.M 2012

There is so much more that can be said on this subject but I have to end the chapter at some point. Jerry has more than ably conveyed the pertinent fact that specialist pest control situations do, at times, require specialist FAC air rifles. Where this leaves the FAC airgun hunter is simple. Once armed with the facts about these rifles, make a very considered judgement of whether you really need such a specialised rifle, or not. Also, I feel his comments have helped put a lot of what was written by me , into a very apt context.

So at last - there you have it. The FAC air rifle may well be a specialised tool, and have specialised uses, but should the situation be encountered, the rifle fulfils its role admirably.

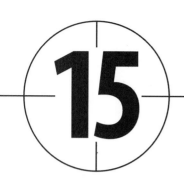

General and Routine Maintenance

Many moons ago when I got my first air rifle, kids such as myself borrowed a tin of WD40 and 3-in-1 oil from our dad, and some furniture polish from our ma, and that was how we looked after our slug guns. Of course, it isn't the best way to do it but strangely enough, as basic and in many ways as unsubtle as it was, it was at least an attempt at keeping the rifle clean and corrosion-free. Amazingly, it didn't do half bad a job either. WD40 isn't the best but is good at preventing rust, and while furniture polish did clean the stock it left it 'slippy', but at least it did smell nice!

Had we known then, what we know now, that those lubes and oils can actually have an adverse effect on the finish of chemically-blackened parts, I'm sure we wouldn't have been so enthusiastic about their use.

Obviously, as we grew older and learned by way of magazines and books, we took more time and effort in looking after our guns. Even now though, you'll see it written – 'wipe over with an oily rag, put it away in a gun case and place in a safe, dry place'. To a certain extent, I feel that's better than nothing but it's advice that's of little more use than what we did way back when we first shot springers on the cut for rats.

Most shooters have their own views on what are the requisites for gun maintenance – some, most or all being done on a regular basis. For reasons of thoroughness, in this chapter I'll not only give my recommendations but I've managed to persuade a well-respected gunsmith to contribute some sound advice, that being Tony Wall who you heard mention of, way back at the start of this book. He's somebody I not only rate highly for his knowledge on the subject and hunting prowess in the field, but also someone I owe a great debt of gratitude to for advice and other such help in this sport of ours.

Firstly though, my thoughts on gun maintenance and the very basic dos and don'ts of DIY 'gunsmithery.'

The Basics

Firstly, a word or two of caution: If you buy your air rifle new, consult the manual and associated literature; the rifle, more likely than not, will have a recommended 'lube' list with guidelines.

Follow these to the letter as if you don't and the rifle needs major repair, it will need to go back under warranty. If the manufacturer sees you've ignored the guidelines and used inappropriate lubes or have just tinkered, then the warranty will be void and you'll probably end up having to fork out much more than expected for what could be a very simple fault, even one you've maybe unwittingly had a hand in causing.

A basic set of tools is needed, and a more substantial set being all the better. At least you should have a reasonable-sized tool box containing various sizes of slot- and cross-headed screwdrivers, a selection of standard-size Allen keys, both imperial and metric, long-nosed pliers, scissors (for cutting cleaning patches and swages), small mole grips, small adjustable spanner, multi-tool, a ratchet multi-bit head set, barrel pull-through, barrel cleaning rods with brushes and jags, scope lens cloth, and of course, the correct oils and lubes are definitely needed. In fact, a good selection of the lubes in suitable dispensers will enable you to

Portable workstations make rifle maintenance easy and allow the storage of essential tools, lubes and oils

have a full service and maintenance kit for the air rifle, you might say.

There's a wide selection of lubes and oils on the market but you really do need to know which to use for what part of the rifle, or else you can end up doing more harm than good. Incidentally, whilst a simple plastic tool box for keeping everything together will suffice, one of the portable rifle maintenance centres incorporating a cradle rest to secure the gun while you're working, including storage areas on a box or tray is a much better option. These workstations don't cost the earth and make working on your rifle much easier, and they can even be used for setting up the scope and zeroing. I use one manufactured by MTM with an accompanying shooters' accessory box. This allows me to store everything in the same place. Small items that are needed frequently store at the top section and larger cans of oils and tools in the accessory box. Invaluable if you take your sport seriously and care about the rifle you shoot.

Now a look at what lubes your maintenance box should ideally contain and where the various types can be used.

As we now know, it's definitely not wise to spray the whole rifle liberally with any aerosol lubricant or cleaning spray, as we did in the past. In fact, when applying anything (and that means anything), spray it onto a clean cloth and then apply to the rifle. So with that in mind, here's what you should have at the ready.

A silicone cloth for wiping down metalwork and the stock: Have one for metalwork and a lint-free cloth will suffice for the stock wood. Incidentally, always carry a cloth in the field and should blood drip or splash onto the metalwork, wipe it off immediately, and then clean properly and oil when at home. Nothing attacks the metalwork as viciously as blood, moisture or rust.

This wiping maintenance routine should be the first and last thing you do to the rifle, before use and certainly after use in the field. Talking of which, if the rifle is wet after a hunting trip, initially wipe over with disposable absorbent kitchen towel, and then leave it to dry fully and naturally at room temperature in an airy place before lubing and storing away.

If your rifle has a non-lacquered stock, be it walnut or other such wood, then make sure you have the appropriate stock wood oil and use it regularly to keep the stock wood replenished with the natural oils that the weather and your hands will remove.

Now, as I've already mentioned silicone, I must follow that immediately with the warning that it's fine for protection and the initial wipe over, but any oil or grease that uses silicone as a base substance should never be applied to a load-bearing surface such as breech, jaws or pivot pins. You'll find it's available as a silicone spray and silicone grease, but of all the lubes this is probably the most specialised. It was wrongly thought by some in the past, to be a wonder-lube for lubricating any metal surface – it's not! It has no uses except to protect external metalwork from moisture, including the acid in perspiration from your hands and fingers, so therefore helps stop the onset of rust. That is its primary job; to dispel moisture, and it does it well. As for silicone grease, this is even more specialised and should only be used for lubricating plastic surfaces.

Grease that can be associated with silicone is Molykote 33. This is silicone with lithium base and its function when used sparingly and properly is to lubricate O-ring seals such as the breech seal, buddy bottle O-ring seal, and on the seals of pellet probes, but words of caution – use very sparingly and wipe off any excess.

Grease that is the most useful is Molygrease. This is usually a thick, dark grey paste and is the one to apply to the large, load-bearing surfaces such as breech jaws and springs. For the pivot pins and linkages, it's best to use a lighter lube such as Molyoil. If you are wondering, 'moly' is the airgun's friend, as when you see the name it's the shortened reference term for the substance known as molybdenum disulphide.

Now you may think it strange that I leave it until last to mention one of the most useful and usable, but I once again want to stress that all lubes, even and including molybdenum should always be used sparingly. Another magic lube is good-quality, light machine oil. Remember that good old 3-in-One oil we've used for years? Well, forget it because there are special light gun oils that are more suited. Light oil in itself does no damage wherever it is applied, but always remember that nothing, repeat nothing, should be put either in front of the piston, and in a PCP never put anything in the air reservoir. Do not put grease on or near the inlet valve, either. Keep it clean but do not have anything near it that could have cause to be transferred into the reservoir on filling.

Talking of which, I'm sure you'll have noticed most of the maintenance advice pertains to spring-powered air rifles, rather than PCPs. As you'll read further, even the experienced advise that you have a PCP serviced by an expert. Of course, barrel-cleaning can be done, as can exterior work, but for the valving and other such mechanics of the PCP – leave it to the experts. Incidentally, for more in-depth info there are books on the subject but we're fortunate here to get a few tricks of the trade from a professional. I now hand the platform over or maybe that should be the 'oily rag' to Tony Wall, of Sandwell Field Sports.

From the Man who Can

Tony Wall – Gunsmith: After many years in the trade I know all too well how the elements can soon affect a lovely new rifle. Even as soon as it leaves the shop, and after you've put your hands on the metalwork, it's already under attack from corrosive elements. Even the moisture from your touch will start to eat away at that lovely lustre of the metalwork, and after saving hard-earned cash, and after many weeks of deliberation over which to choose, it's only fitting you look after what is, in effect, a precision instrument.

So, like many others who enter the sport, you've been keenly shooting it, on and off for about three months with no problems and everything is rosy, or is it? Now you've done your bit to keep the nasty rust monster at bay by wiping the gun over with an oily rag as Mr Wadeson so succinctly puts it, and putting it back in its bag to protect it from bumps and scratches that will inevitably occur over its coming lifetime, but have you thought with all that vibration and recoil (by-products of the internal operation of a spring-powered or gas-ram air rifle) that maybe the stock screws have come a little loose? Now then, that may explain the inaccuracy of the gun all of a sudden!

How do we cure the problem of loose screws? Simple; degrease the threads with a quality degreasing agent or methylated spirits, and apply a very weak thread lock. If no thread lock can be found then a small dab of nail varnish will suffice, failing that because not every bloke has nail varnish in his gun maintenance kit, (I'd be worried if he had!), a bit of cotton thread wrapped around the screw threads will do the job equally as well. Loose screws not only cause inaccuracy in a gun, but in the case of a recoiling gun can potentially cause split woodwork as well.

While we're checking over the gun for loose screws, it's always worth checking the tightness of the scope-mounting screws as well, although on a recoilless PCP air rifle, if you've mounted the scope correctly, this is rarely a problem. Just a gentle tweak is all that's needed; don't go like a bull at a gate and tighten it so that you need a length of scaffold pole for leverage to undo it again, but just enough to hold the clamps securely in the dovetails without them being damaged. If you do re-tighten, always re-check zero.

If you own a break-barrel recoiling gun then pay close attention to the area of the breech jaws as all sorts of problems can occur if left to their own devices. First of all, check for the biggest killers of all airguns – dirt and grit.

Grit has the annoying habit of actually shaving metal away when compressed and making what was once a wonderfully smooth gun into an old clapped-out banger. So what do we do about it when we see a fair amount of dirt and the like, accumulated in the said area? Well, I'm afraid there's no way around it really, apart from a full strip-down, but if there is only a small amount to be seen then there is an easier method to apply. If you know someone with a compressor then give it a quick low-pressure blast around the area, pointing away from your person. (Note: You should only attempt this method while wearing appropriate safety goggles. Also, do this under the guidance of someone who has intimate knowledge of how pressure equipment works.)

You'll now be feeling pleased with that job, but when you jetted away the unwanted grit and dirt, unfortunately, you also unintentionally disposed of the oil and grease that the manufacturer put there to lube the area. You guessed it, now we have to put it back again. So, what lube is best? Well, I wish I had a penny for how many times I've been asked that question! There are many lubes out there and I could write reams on that subject alone, but I'll condense it to specify a few lubes that I use and recommend.

Around the breech area, if stripped down, I'll use a thick, synthetic molybdenum paste as made by a company called Lurbo Teknik. If you don't feel competent enough to strip your gun down then pop along to a good motor accessory shop and ask for a can of non-silicone motorbike chain-spray oil. This can be termed oil or grease as it comes in aerosol form and leaves the can as a liquid spray to dry as a viscous greasing and protecting agent. Use it very sparingly on the inside of the breech jaws, pivot pins, at the barrel detent and just about any area where there is a high load factor. Also check your breech seal for signs of wear, if there is the slightest of nicks in it then replace it as it will only get worse with use and as Sod's law dictates, will fail you when you're on that long weekend hunting trip, or squeezing the trigger on what could have been a shot of a lifetime. Breech jaws and shims need checking for wear as does the breech axis pin for working loose. That's the big screw bolt that holds the barrel onto the breech jaws.

The spring and piston powerplant will periodically need care and attention, eventually even replacing

If you feel confident enough to take the action out of the stock then do so, and wipe away all the debris that has accumulated underneath the action and in the recess of the stock. Then, using the chain-spray oil, spray a little onto the coils and spring guide if your gun sounds particularly 'boingy', but for more dedicated spring-dampening, change lubes and use a cotton bud to smear some thick Moly grease into the cocking slot and between the coils. When all is complete and nicely oiled, be it pneumatic or a springer, before putting the action back into the stock, sparingly spray the motorcycle chain oil onto the underside of the action to protect against the elements.

Probably the most important part of an air rifle is the trigger unit, not only has this component the laborious task of releasing the piston or valve spring hammer, time and time again, but it has to do it with the consistency of a Swiss clock over a good many years of use. If any foreign object or debris finds its way into a trigger unit, a multitude of problems can arise. This is an area I personally pay great attention to, cleaning it meticulously when I service or tune a gun. A word of caution though; if you're stripping down to clean a trigger unit you really need to know what you're doing. One small misalignment of the components upon reassembly and you've got a dangerous gun on your hands. The golden rule is, 'if you don't have a mechanical mind, then leave well alone'. Take it to a reputable gunsmith who for a very modest fee will only be too glad to do the job for you. If a trigger is to be lubed (which is very rarely needed), then use a very small amount of the lightest oil you can find, but I must stress the importance of careless hands and fiddly fingers in relation to trigger units. Over the years, I've had cause to put right many DIY-bodged-up and tampered with trigger mechanisms, the air rifles' owners thinking they were doing the right thing and adjusting the trigger to suit them as well as cleaning it. In fact, I'd always say for safety's sake and the peace of mind it will give – do leave this area to the experts.

So, although I've warned against tampering with triggers, I'm presuming you've followed my advice and taken the action out of the stock and carried out all the other routine lubing. If so, when you put the stock back onto the action again, you will see a slight gap all around where the action seats into the woodwork.

This is an area where rain can and does run to the underside of the metalwork, and in extreme cases can cause the woodwork to swell and split, so smear a good dollop of petroleum jelly into the gap all around and wipe away any excess with an oily rag. Oops, nicked that one from Pete. Anyway, pay particular attention to the butt pad where it joins the woodwork, again smearing petroleum jelly into any gaps where rain can get in, and in time do its worst.

If any dents or bruises have occurred to the stock, any competent gunsmith can sometimes repair them if it is an oiled finish, but on a lacquered one I'm afraid then you'll just have to live with them. For cosmetic repair of an unlacquered stock, I use an electric kettle with a narrow spout that emits a small jet of steam, which I hold the dent over until it has raised then I 'cut it' back with very fine wire wool and oil it again so that it looks like new. On some lacquered stocks, which have scratches, I've successfully used boot polish to hide the unsightly marks, but this is more of a temporary measure rather than a long-term one.

We've now covered the protection of the external metalwork and woodwork, but what about the insides of the gun? Well, here comes the controversial part; do we clean the barrel or not? There are many trains of thought on this matter and I'm afraid I live in the camp of clean it, be it with a phosphor bronze brush and rod, or a pull-through. A barrel can never give its full potential if it is dirty and I always clean mine every 200-250 shots, whatever the gun, while FT shooters on average swear by cleaning theirs every 80-100 shots. Then again – some just swear!

Although modern pellets are a lot better made than they were in Grandpa's day, and even though they may look clean in a tin, believe me they are, in fact, very dirty with minute lumps of swarf and oils on them. OK, we can wash and lube them in many of the pellet lubes that have become fashionable these days, but the truth is, lead is a very dirty material (you only have to look at your loading fingers at the end of a long practice session to see that) and coupled with the speed of the pellet travelling up a choked bore you can see why a barrel becomes dirty quite quickly. So how do we clean a barrel, then? I favour two methods, the first is to scrub the bore with a good-quality phosphor bronze brush and rod to loosen up any lead fragments – I promise you it won't damage anything. Then I pull the bore through with a lint cloth with a few drops of airgun barrel cleaning fluid on it (NOTE: Don't use the solvents intended for the cleaning of fullbore rifles; these solvents are very corrosive and if allowed to trickle inside a pneumatic air rifle valve or come into contact with any synthetic material, over a period of time it will dissolve them. Only use cleaners intended for airgun barrels; if in doubt contact your local gunsmith or manufacturer of the gun.)

I then proceed to use the barrel pull-through, replacing the patches until they appear clean. When you are satisfied it's clean, fire a few shots through the gun to settle the barrel down again.

If you have a silencer fitted – which most hunters should have – then it can be very frustrating trying to get a pull-through wire into the front of a barrel through a long silencer. If it's a screw-on silencer, no problem, just unscrew to remove, clean the barrel, then after refitting the silencer, check the zero. If it's a push-fit silencer held in place with a grub screw, it can be time-consuming and quite a struggle to remove, and nigh-on impossible if it has been bonded in place! So how do we overcome this problem? Well, a simple little trick I use is to insert an ordinary plastic drinking straw into the silencer until you feel it bottom out (come up against resistance), as it touches the muzzle or crown of the barrel itself. Then place the pull-

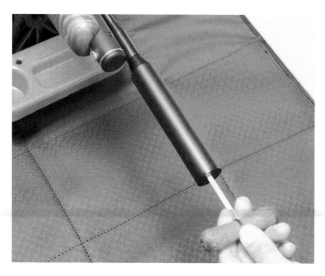

Tony's straw and pull thru' trick for cleaning a barrel with silencer fitted

through wire into the protruding straw's hole and feed it in until it shows at the breech loading area. Then fit with a clean patch and pull through as usual. On exiting the barrel, the patch catches on the drinking straw and, hey presto - all come out of the silencer together.

Talking of silencers, unlike on powder-burning guns (live-round bullet guns), airgun silencers don't really need cleaning inside as there's no real residue discharged by the airgun to get rid of, so on this matter I'd say leave well alone. If it ain't broke, don't fix it, and as the internal baffles are precisely set for the airgun silencer to work at its best, there's no point risking upsetting this harmony.

Pellets

As for pellet care – do we lube the pellets or not? If you've washed them then I say a resounding, yes! The reason being that after washing, pellets have nothing on them to protect them from oxidisation and so if left to the elements they turn white and 'scabby' and don't shoot at all well. If you shoot unwashed pellets in a pneumatic then I would also say again, lube them because quality lubes cut down the need to clean the barrel as often, while I find spring guns don't really like a lubed pellet at all. I have a theory about that because when a springer shoots, it disperses a tiny amount of its own lube up the barrel, therefore adding any more oil to the equation seems to upset the equilibrium, causing the odd flier to occur and so spoiling an otherwise good group. To help prevent this, for my springers, I use a wax-based lube very, very sparingly on the washed pellets so as not to cause any dieseling.

As many hunters like Mr Wadeson now prefer to use a multi-shot PCP air rifle, a word or two on the maintenance and care of pellet magazines. These little ingenious but relatively simple units can be an area where all sorts of muck and grime can accumulate so a good cleaning session wouldn't go amiss here as well. Cleaning some magazines such as the removable 8-shot drum ones can be done with relative ease, whilst others such as those with an outer casing and inner drum 'sprung or free moving' have to be stripped down or disassembled. You'll either see through the perspex cover if dirt is accumulating, or for closed-face types you'll actually feel the grit as you rotate the inner drum of the magazine while filling with pellets. This isn't an uncommon occurrence; especially if you've dropped your magazine in the mud a few times, or keep them in dirty jacket pockets, or even pay scant attention to the ammo you load into them.

I clean these types of magazines with a product called 'Gunk-Out' made by Kleanbore. This is a quick evaporating degreaser and cleaner. If you can't get this excellent product, then once again, pop down to the local motorist spares shop and get a good-quality brake and clutch cleaning agent. Spray the magazine liberally inside to get rid of all the nasty debris and place on one side for this inner pellet carrier to dry naturally. Then lube lightly with a good pellet lube or Teflon-based lube, and never use a gooey, thick grease otherwise you'll find after assembly that the internal carrier soon gums up, catching more dirt than it did before. (Note: The above is a base guideline and will suit most removable rotary feed magazines currently in use. However, check with the rifle manufacturer for advice on lubing their particular magazine, not all magazines work well with lubricant.)

As for specific maintenance of a PCP, I'd recommend that you always take it to a reputable gunsmith. Most work done is commonsense and not difficult, but it can be very dangerous for 'Fred In The Shed' to go willy nilly at it.

Before I hand back to Pete, I'd like to stress the point that as responsible airgun hunters it's our duty to ensure that the air rifle in our possession is running within the UK legal limit currently set at 12ft lb. As I do much custom-tune work on rifles, the most common request is to make the rifle as powerful as possible up to the limit. I don't do this for a specific reason; if an air rifle is set dead-on 12ft lb with one pellet brand, use a different, say lighter pellet and then the rifle will stray over the limit – rendering it, in effect, a firearm and if you haven't got an FAC with this on your ticket, you're breaking the law. I always recommend and set the rifles up at approximately 11.4-11.6ft lb depending on the rifle. Small, basic chronographs aren't costly, and if you can't get to a specialist dealer who has one, although in my mind all gunshops should have one, it's no great task to keep a check of the rifle power output at home. This helps you to ensure that you're legal, and importantly for your hunting, that the rifle isn't dropping in power for any reason.

All air rifles are meticulously checked over a computer chronograph before leaving the gun manufacturer – it's every shooter's responsibility to ensure the rifle's power level stays within the legal limit

I'm sure Pete's pointed this out, but I still feel it needs clarifying from a gunsmith's point of view. Everybody is an ambassador for the sport and we want all who take part to do so safely and within the law.

So that's about it – everything I've outlined is within the capabilities of the most DIY-phobic, but there are times when the rifle, be it spring-powered, gas-ram or PCP will inevitably have to go to a reputable gunsmith for repair or service. Beware; not all gunsmiths have the knowledge of the intricacies of modern air rifles. They may be expert at repairing shotguns and superb at servicing fullbore rifles, but airguns are a totally different matter. If you are unsure to whom you should entrust your prized possession, look at the adverts in one of the many airgun magazines and you'll find certain companies who advertise as experts in the field of airguns. They'll know how to breathe new life into your pride and joy. Failing that, you can in most cases send it back to the manufacturer, after all they built the darned thing in the first place, didn't they?

Tony Wall.

Gun Storage

We've had some very wise words from Tony on gun maintenance so time now to look at a subject that is equally important – the safe storage of the air rifle.

Like me, Tony and many others of my acquaintance believe that storing your gun should be as important as cleaning it. What's the use of spending all that time meticulously oiling and cleaning your pride and joy only to put it in your bag and stand it in the corner of a damp room or garage?

Do this, and leave it in there for any amount of time, and you'll come back to a brown and black-coloured gun that resembles a patchwork quilt with moss growing on it! OK, maybe I'm over-dramatising that a little, but how do we stop the dreaded rust from attacking the gunmetal in the beginning? Well, this is where we come back to the oily rag. Yes, wiping the metalwork over is a help, but there are now numerous lubes on the market these days and they all claim wonders and miracles for keeping a gun rust-free, but depending on how the rifle is stored, oil often isn't by itself good enough to protect a rifle. The reason being, oil is easily absorbed into some gun bag linings and so the rifle is soon rendered dry. If the rifle is not going to be used for a while then more protection is needed. A popular one with collectors is to smear a thin lining of grease or petroleum jelly onto the metalwork. Also, guns that are not being used very often should preferably be stored lying horizontally. This mainly applies to springers as internal oils will only run one way – and that's downwards!

Now, as for storing rifles that are used with some regularity, without doubt the best place to store a gun is in a gun cabinet or enclosed gun rack. Not only does this protect the rifle from the bumps and bruises that can occur in a soft gun bag, but it also allows it to 'breathe' and equally importantly – it's away from prying eyes. If young children are in the house then it certainly should be in more substantial storage than just being put away in a bag at the back of a wardrobe. If you can afford it then go for a lockable gun cabinet for scope with rifles (these are deeper to accept the scope), not only can you store your gun in it but you can put small personal valuables in there as well.

You will never buy a sounder investment as a shooter, but first, I will detail the important legal requirements for airgun storage in the UK and my own advice on what is your required duty. Of equal importance is the fact that the laws on gun storage are now being fully enforced by the authorities. The Home Office in the UK has issued a leaflet on storage of a 12ft lb air rifle. The magazines and our

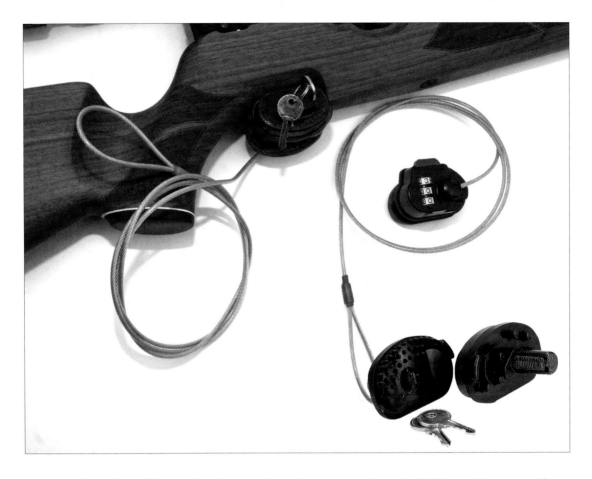

Just two examples of what the HO accept to be used as reasonable security precautions as long as the air rifle is secured to a permanent fixture in the house and is also kept out of plain view

organisations are also keeping us fully briefed on what the police don't want to see when they may have to visit. Recommendations are quite strict, but with children and underage teenagers potentially getting a hold of a relative's air rifle, we need to be careful. Boys will be boys, as they say.

However, no matter what, our air rifle is our responsibility so in the eyes of the law we should lock it (mechanically) away. Not necessarily in a gun cabinet as there are many padlocks with cables for attaching the rifle to a permanent fixture in the home, or for locking the access to them. These range from the most basic trigger locks, cable and lock types which are now supplied with all new air rifles sold, courtesy of the airgun manufacturers. You also need to keep ammo in a separate safe area. All this is not a change in the law, but more a case of strictly enforcing the law as it stood.

Personally, I feel the Home Office guidelines as fully detailed (as they currently stand at time of updating this book) are sensible, and what every responsible airgun user should have been adhering to in the first place.

Lock Down

By law you don't need a metal gun cabinet to store a 12ft lb air rifle, but the Home Office recommends the following sensible precautions:

- Store your airgun out of sight and separately from any pellets.
- Use a robust, lockable cupboard and keep the keys separate and secure.
- Always store your airgun inside a house rather than any type of outbuilding, such as a garden shed.
- Never store the airgun cocked and/or loaded.
- When using your airgun, keep it under close supervision and never leave it unattended.

The full Home Office guidelines are in a free HO leaflet, available from your local police station or the Home Office website. The term is, 'take reasonable precautions'. In other words, don't leave your airgun uncovered, lying around in plain view or where little Johnnie can play with it when you're out, or a burglar can easily find it and make off with it. Everybody's situation will be different, which is a major reason why there are various different options to suit your particular requirements. Incidentally, another factor to take into consideration is that ammo (pellets) should be stored separately from the airgun and preferable locked away. A little lock safe, strongbox or lockable filing cabinet will suffice for their storage.

Trigger Locks

Standard types of what are known as 'trigger locks' are the minimum level of security you should use as they render the rifle inoperable. Generally made of toughened steel, they come in two parts, use rubber panels to prevent scratching the rifle and fit easily through the trigger guard, and here they mate-up by a securing and ratchet spindle to be locked in place. They can be either key-lockable or of a combination lock design. Use these if you do have a room or place in the house that is inaccessible to anybody but you. Always err on the side of caution though, and if possible have a lock fitted to the access points to that room or space. Trigger locks are best used in conjunction with some form of cable lock, as the airgun is always safer when attached to a permanent fixture in the home.

Many companies supply high-quality trigger and cable locks. Specialist Firearm Security Company – F.S.C. – I feel are amongst the best on the market and supply HO-approved security of all types to suit virtually all requirements.

Gun Cabinets

The optimum way of safe storage is to go for a quality gun cabinet; rifle plus scope designated. They come in various sizes, so you choose in accordance with how many guns you want it to be able to store. However, you could well eventually want an FAC air rifle and then go on to live round firearms so you definitely will need one. Try to be sensible and consider what you may add at a later date to your armoury of sporting guns, as it's best to buy one that'll hold more than you have at the time of purchase. I'm not urging you to buy a bigger one than you need, but you'll be surprised at how the bug can bite, and the bonus is, if you don't add that many, there's still more room in the cabinet so you're not running the risk of scratching rifles standing on each side as you take the one you want for a particular hunting session.

I have two storage areas; one is for the 12 ft lb air rifles and is in actuality a purpose-built, floor to ceiling, lockable cupboard that outwardly is designed to look like a built-in wardrobe. Inside is a custom-built gun rack that holds up to 12 rifles and has storage space and drawer units for various airgun associated accessories, except ammo, as these are kept under lock and key out of view elsewhere in the house.

Here, the rifles are safe and secure, ready rigged with scopes, zeroed and ready to be picked up and slipped into the appropriate gun bag for use when needed. My other storage facilities are locking, police-approved gun cabinets. These house my FAC air rifles nestling alongside live-round firearms.

Before leaving the whole subject of gun maintenance, I'll end on this thought. While we think nothing of having our cars regularly serviced, why is it so different to put our springers, gassers or PCPs in for servicing by trained personnel? Personally, I say a yearly tune-up or service should be considered for your most used hunting rifle. At the very least, now armed with the information in this chapter, you have no excuse for giving it the close scrutiny every four to six months or so, but certainly, in the case of a PCP, read the manual to see what the manufacturer recommends. Many have their own in-house service departments and do, in fact, recommend either a yearly or 18-month service. Don't think they're just after more money – they're not, as no service is over-expensive and surely it's worth the cost to have the rifle back up 'n' running at peak performance.

As they say – Stay Clean and Keep Safe!

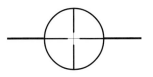

The Airgun Hunter's Larder
Preparation of Game

Although hunting with an air rifle is done primarily for pest control of vermin, there are obvious benefits besides it being an absorbing, challenging and enjoyable sport. A major plus being the fact that certain quarry species is very tasty to eat.

I've now come to a point in my shooting career when I feel that if edible quarry isn't taken for the table, it's a waste of good food. Even if it's not to your taste, or maybe you've no room left in the freezer, then you likely won't need to look far to find somebody who will welcome the nutritious meat on offer. If you really get into cooking your own game, then it's wise to invest in a small fridge freezer; a large chest freezer stored in the garage being even better. That way it stops the arguments with the missus that you've taken up valuable freezer space, and you can store a lot more game at any given time in various forms of dress. By that, I mean there are times you might only gut a rabbit but want to freeze it, and leaving the fur coat on means the rabbit meat is protected from freezer burn and tastes just as fresh once you defrost it to skin it and prepare for cooking. Also, if you really take to the technique of baiting-down crows and magpies, save the rabbit heads and the carcass with guts. Freeze in strong freezer bags to use as bait at a later date. Corvids aren't fussy and off-cuts and dissected heads work just as well as a whole rabbit at bringing them in - and in the long run who wants to waste too many good rabbits?

Now, unfortunately, in this age of processed, pre-packaged, ready-prepared food there are many who wouldn't know 'one end of rappit from 't'uther', as they say in old Lancashire. If I have the time, which I rarely seem to have, I gladly prepare fresh game for the pot for friends, and I feel all who can prepare for the table should show those willing to learn how. If not, then that's yet another traditional country way of life lost.

Of course, it can be messy because fresh game preparation requires gutting, paunching and jointing. The cutting of flesh and cleaning out of a carcass is unpleasant to some, but many hunters will find some dissection educational. Just check out the crop of a woodpigeon and discover what it had been feeding on. It'll indicate where to look for more at that time. Also, I'm of the opinion depending on foodstuff, especially as I've noticed the difference in woodie by the season, that these different foodstuffs can slightly affect the flavour.

When gutting a rabbit as a hunter, check out where those vital organs in the body are. Yes, they are small and as I've mentioned in the section devoted to the rabbit in Quarry Files, the heart and lungs are very high up in the chest. As you slip the sharp blade of the knife up, notice how easily that rabbit comes 'unzipped'. There's not much protection at the top end where the ribs are either. You're now discovering these critters' vulnerable areas for yourself and you might well be surprised at just where they actually are in relation to their outward profile; but enough about biology and animal skeletal make-up because of all meat available the game we shoot is amongst the most nutritious you can find, being low in both saturated fats and cholesterol. This is true, untainted, wild protein and all wild meat has an unrivalled

Game from the airgun hunter's larder is amongst the most nutritious you can find

quality as during that animal's existence it lived as nature intended, in most cases eating a natural diet. Not being fattened up and pumped full of growth hormones or fed high-boost animal feed. Yes, no dangerous chemical additives to worry about, no excessive salt or the dreaded E-numbers. Once prepared, you're left with good, flavoursome, wholesome fresh meat.

Before leaving the subject of taking for the pot, although I rarely shoot jays, if I'm shooting where they are in large numbers I will take one if the shot presents itself. The reason being, I know of several people more than grateful of the feathers for fly tying, and that in turn will result in a friend catching a sea trout, and again the basis for a fresh, healthy meal.

The edible game we shoot is rabbit, woodpigeon, collared dove and squirrel; yes, even the grey, bushy-tailed ones cook up to make a tasty meal. Rook pie – sorry, not for me, so here follows how to prepare my favoured quarry for cooking with a recommended recipe or two thrown in for good measure. Game cookery books are widely available and you might be surprised how interested you become in the subject. Even to the extent that you obtain reference works to help you identify edible wild mushrooms and natural vegetables and herbs.

Also, you can easily adapt most recipes that use game to utilise the meat from the airgun-hunting larder. You can even use a few types of meat in the same dish to make stews, casseroles or pies – my 'Airgun Hunter's Game Pie' recipe at the end of this chapter being a prime example, and let's not forget the fact that any meat here can be used in a curry, kebab and even cut in strips for a stir-fry. The adventurous amongst you can have a field day, but, whichever way you prefer to cook the meat, you'll first need a few essential tools to prepare it.

The knife is the most versatile tool in the hunter's accessory kit and shows itself to be very useful in game preparation. Most hunters should have at least one good-quality, compact, folding lock knife. You can skin and paunch and fully joint-up a rabbit with such a knife as long as the blade is strong and sharp. Nothing's more useless or potentially dangerous than a blunt knife, so always keep those knives sharp.

However, a few more specific utensils are required if you want to prepare the game more easily and efficiently. A small skinner, a sharp, fixed-blade preparing knife, a meat cleaver and/or a heavy, serrated-edge, boning knife is handy as are a strong pair of game shears. Chopping boards are a must, as is a sharpening tool for keeping a keen edge on the knives you use for preparation.

Now, to our staple quarry species and the candidate for many a culinary delight – the rabbit.

Rabbit – Preparation

While it's traditional to let some game hang for a time, there is no need to do this with the game that airgun hunters will bag; rabbits need only be allowed to cool fully before being prepared for the pot.

There are two ways to deal with the rabbit; paunch in the field or wait until you get home. Now, I'll usually take rabbits home whole, and gut the rabbit prior to skinning, but only after it's cooled for up to 24 hours. I prefer to do it this way as long as I've not got a lot to carry around before leaving the shoot. A word of caution though: Don't allow them to stay intact too long before gutting as the insides can start to go off and possibly taint the flavour of the meat. While on this subject, while it's not very appetising, they say you'll come to no harm eating a rabbit that has myxy. Personally, it doesn't appeal and a way to spot the disease if signs aren't too obvious externally are by white spots on the animal's liver and occasionally, you'll find them on the other internal organs. These can go to the dogs, ferrets or people who fly hawks – so even these needn't be wasted.

First job is to empty the animal's bladder. This is done by holding the rabbit with stomach facing away from you, the hind legs pointed towards the floor while running the thumbs down either side of the animal's lower abdomen towards the lower thigh joint. Do it this way to avoid getting an eye-full of rabbit pee when skinning!

Most shooters who regularly prepare their own rabbits for the table have a set way of doing it and though all are similar here's the way that suits me.

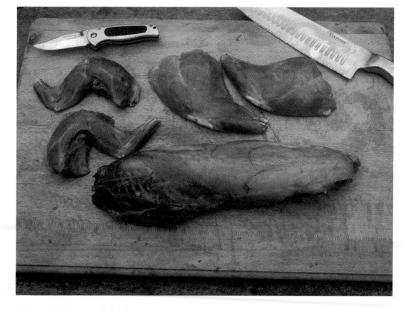

A jointed rabbit – ready for the pot!

Once I've purged the rabbit of its last 'widdle' (and of course gutted it), I'll then pinch the fur of the rabbit across the middle of the back with the thumb and forefinger of my left hand and using a sharp-pointed blade held in the right hand, I push this through the pinched fur to pierce between fur and rabbit body, taking care not to go into the animal's flesh. In effect, what you are doing is slitting the fur across the back to facilitate the skinning process. To make the next step even easier, using the same sharp blade and cutting away from you, cut the fur downwards towards the animal's belly on one side, then turn the rabbit over and repeat the procedure. This now will have created a long slit right across the rabbit's coat.

At this stage, you can if you wish, as I often do, cut the head off at the base of the nape of the neck. It's now time to pull the fur off the rabbit. Take hold of one side of the open slit across the back in one hand, and the other side in the other hand. Then, pull apart in opposing directions whereupon the fur coat will quite literally, and relatively easily peel off the carcass. It's at the hind and front quarters that you'll need to manoeuvre the legs out of the rabbit's coat, and if you haven't first cut the legs off, once you do this you'll be left with a skinned rabbit still wearing furry little boots. I leave it until now to cut the feet off as this shows the natural point to cut, keeping as much meat as possible on the bone.

Jointing is done by cutting off both hind legs and thighs from the body and then removing the front forelegs and shoulders. The body can be left whole but most cut in two or into a section of three for ease of cooking. Also, at this stage you can now carefully pare and cut away the sinewy clear tissue (this is a layer of white sinew or clear skin) use a very sharp filleting knife or dedicated fixed-blade skinner.

After removing the tail, and all excess skin and any remnants of fur, the meat needs a thorough rinse, and you now have one rabbit, ready for the pot. Should you wish to freeze it at this point, dry it off with kitchen roll, then wrap in cling film or use freezer bags to prevent freezer burn on the exposed flesh, and always date the bags so you know which to use first.

Flash frying any meat sears in the taste

Some say the meat of young rabbits is very tender and succulent, but obviously there's little meat on a small rabbit. Only the hind legs are worth jointing and I'm not one for taking such young, unsporting game unless specifically working to a strict pest control directive. I am told though that glazed and dipped in flour and then pan-fried the legs are delicious! That's for you to find out if you happen to have call to deal with a very large rabbit cull operation.

Here's a couple of my favourite ways with rabbit, and although I might call them casseroles, soups or pies, the recipe differs for various tastes and all can be modified to suit. Look upon them as guidelines. That includes how much you add in terms of seasonings such as garlic or black pepper. They are certainly adjustable to suit your own particular taste, including the amount of ingredients, but the recipes as stated are more than enough to serve two generous hunter-size portions.

Recommended Recipe – Rabbit Stew

Ingredients:

2 large onions, diced
2 tbsp olive oil
2 cloves of garlic, chopped
1 large rabbit – cut the meat off the bone into manageable but chunky pieces
3 large carrots, sliced
8oz mushrooms, sliced
2 vegetable stock cubes
Worcestershire sauce
Black pepper
Gravy granules, for thickening

How to Cook

Using a large stew pot, fry the onion in the oil until starting to soften, add garlic and further fry for no more than a few minutes. Then place vegetables and meat into the pot.

Mix the stock cubes in a pint of boiling water and pour over the contents. If you need more water to cover the ingredients, add now. If you like garlic – add another clove on top at this stage.

Add a dash of the Worcestershire sauce and sprinkling of black pepper.

Bring to the boil, place lid on stew pot and turn down to simmer stirring occasionally. Cooking time may vary but should be approximately 3 hours. Towards the end of the cooking time add gravy granules to thicken the dish and test meat to check if it is tender and fully cooked.

Once cooked – serve with mashed potato and winter vegetables such as broccoli, cauliflower and cabbage. Incidentally, if you fancy a rabbit and pigeon stew – you simply add some woodpigeon meat. Simple isn't it?

Recommended Recipe – Simple Rabbit Soup

Ingredients:

1 rabbit, jointed
1 potato, diced
1 tin of sliced carrots
2 tins of Heinz chicken and leek big soup
Dried mixed herbs
Black pepper

How to Cook

This is the easiest to prepare and one that's surprisingly tasty due to the tang of the leeks in the soup – not forgetting the mixed herbs.

Firstly, the rabbit should be pre-cooked by roasting or boiling and the meat allowed to cook until it falls easily off the bone. Strain off the liquid and juices from the cooked rabbit and put into a dish to cool. This can be frozen for use at a later date as stock in other dishes.

Now remove all bones from the cooked rabbit and chop meat into chunky pieces.

The potato should be boiled in a separate pan until just beginning to fall. Then drain off the water from the pan the potatoes were boiled in and add the tins of soup, drained tin of carrots and the rabbit cubes. Add a liberal sprinkling of mixed herbs and black pepper and simmer for 4-5 minutes stirring regularly.

Serve with crusty bread of choice.

Recommended Recipe – Rabbit and Onions

Ingredients:
6 rabbit leg and thigh pieces, whole
2 large onions, sliced
2 vegetable stock cubes
Celery, diced
Salt and pepper to taste
Gravy granules, for thickening

How to Cook

Put the onion in the casserole dish and place the rabbit thighs on top. Mix the stock cubes in a pint of boiling water and pour over the contents in the dish. Place lid on dish and pop in a pre-heated oven at 180°C/350°F/gas mark 4 for 2 hours.

After this reduce the oven heat to 160°C/325°F/gas mark 3, adding celery, and cook for a further 3 hours. The casserole should be removed from the oven every hour or so for stirring and to check liquid content.

Towards the end of the cooking time, add gravy granules to thicken the dish and test meat to check if it is tender and fully cooked.

Serve with mashed potatoes and seasonal vegetables.

Woodpigeon – Preparation

This really is a simple job and requires little or no plucking if you are only using the breast meat.

A tip before commencing to breat the pigeon is to cut off the wings as close to the breast as possible with game shears. This makes the task of breasting much easier, not having to contend with floppy wings getting in the way as you carefully cut the skin away and peel back before cutting the breast meat from the keel of the breastbone.

Firstly, place the pigeon on a worktop such as a chopping board, facing breast up, then starting from the top just below the crop, pierce the skin and carefully slice down the centre with the blade, following the top of the breastbone. A tip is to pluck a few downy feathers off to find the skin for the blade. Once you've made the cut, carefully tease the skin back from the flesh and cut away to the side if necessary, peeling this back with your fingers to expose the dark breast meat found on either side of the large, solid breastbone.

As a hunter, marvel at the size and strength of that keel and consider now why full-on chest shots are so easily deflected? Once you've exposed the breast meat carefully, slice down the side and against the keel, and then follow the natural guideline of the breast meat around and under the wings. Repeat for the other side of the breast.

You should now have two large, chunky, teardrop-shaped pieces of meat. If not using immediately, rinse, dry and wrap in cling film or a freezer bag and freeze for future use.

Incidentally, the same process applies to breasting a collared dove, and don't discount this dove as the meat, though a tad tougher, is considered by some to be even tastier than woodie. It does require a longer, slower cooking time, and to moisten and soften the breast meat it benefits from being marinated in olive oil and herbs for 24 hours.

Recommended Recipe – Wonderful Woodpigeon

Woodpigeon makes a fine addition to stews, casseroles and game pies, but if you like to taste the pigeon as it should be tasted, I recommend that you prepare it as a starter because it makes a lovely dish on its own. It has a strong, distinctive flavour and one that deserves not to be hidden amongst other meat, or covered up with rich sauces or heavy seasoning.

I can't take any credit for this as I only discovered it when fortunate enough to be served it as a starter at a posh do. After tasting the woodie on its own, I was hooked and I must admit this is certainly the way I prefer it.

Ingredients:
2 woodpigeon breasts
2 tbsp olive oil

How to Cook

The cooking process is a simple one. First, heat a heavy-bottom frying pan then add a little amount of oil. When the oil is hot, carefully place both halves of the pigeon breast into the oil to flash fry on either side to seal in the goodness. Cook for approximately 3 minutes a side. When done, leave whole or carefully cut into thick slices.

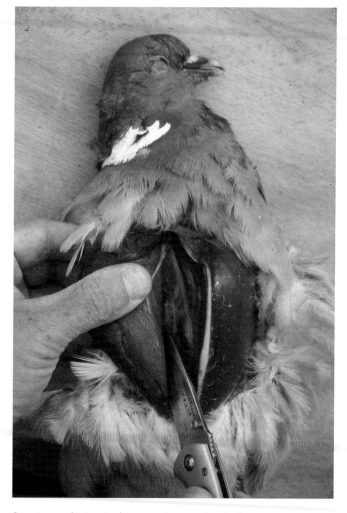

Breasting woodies is a simple matter – but use a sharp knife

Serve with a light salad of mixed leaf, cherry tomatoes and cucumber with a few mixed herbs. Depending on personal preference, liberally drizzle on a balsamic vinegar dressing or a generous dollop of garlic mayonnaise – wonderful.

Incidentally, even if the woodpigeon is to be put into a stew I still prefer to sear the meat by flash-frying to keep in the flavour before fully cooking. If using in a casserole or pie, cut the half breasts in two before searing – when done, remove and place in the casserole dish with other meats.

Everybody seems to have a recipe for pan-fried pigeon, and I'm no exception, but if cooking this way, and the same advice applies for most meats, don't overcook or else the meat goes rubbery.

For another succulent way with woodie I recommend the following

Recommended Recipe – Woodpigeon, with Roasted Peppers and Mushroom

Ingredients:

1 red pepper, sliced
1 yellow pepper, sliced
1 large onion, thickly diced
4 large grilling mushrooms
2 tbsp olive or vegetable oil
6 pigeon breasts (whole halves)

How to Cook

Place peppers and onion on baking tray and pop into pre-heated oven at 200°C/400°F/gas mark 6. After 20-25 minutes prepare mushrooms, place on a baking tray, brush with oil and pre-heat grill. While grill is heating up, place pigeon breasts in hot oil in a frying pan. Now put mushrooms under a medium heat grill. Cook mushrooms and pigeon breast for 4-6 minutes depending on taste.

Remove everything from the oven and grill and serve as follows.

Either as a mixed dish on a bed of rice or alternatively, as a starter with a mixed crispy leaf salad. Garnish with vinaigrette dressing and serve with rustic wholegrain bread rolls.

Squirrel – Preparation

Though not something you'd expect Jamie Oliver to whip up, or indeed find in a supermarket, squirrel is quite tasty, and if you've shot a few it's a pity to waste them. In fact, I don't know why it's frowned on so much in the UK as our American cousins are very partial to a bit of squirrel. The main problem that deters most people is how to prepare them. The best way is to think of it as a small, skinny rabbit. First gut as you would a rabbit, and skin as you would with rabbit but only worry about fully pulling back the fur off the back legs and the skin up to the forelegs. Then cut the body, straight across two thirds up along towards the head. This leaves you with two hind legs and some meat on the lower carcass – the saddle.

Incidentally, you'll see recipes with names such as; squirrel fricassee, deep-fried squirrel or just plain and simple, pan-fried squirrel, similar to the one I show below. They're all very much of a muchness, but with slight changes in ingredients or coatings. As you'll read at the end of the section, with squirrel, I prefer to cut the meat into pieces and add to other off-cuts of game to make a nutritious and mouth-watering game pie or casserole, but I will here give a couple of simple squirrel dishes.

Recommended Recipes - Pan Fried Squirrel in Breadcrumbs

Ingredients:

3 squirrels, use only legs and thighs
1 egg, beaten
2 tbsp olive oil
Breadcrumbs

How to Cook

Obviously, as the squirrel is so small you need at least three per person, preferably a half dozen medium-sized bushy tails, and the only meat needed for this recipe are the back legs and thighs.

Coat each leg and thigh in the beaten egg and then coat in the breadcrumbs. Place these in a pan of hot oil, turning frequently to avoid burning. After the initial browning, turn the heat down and fry slowly for a good few minutes to ensure that the squirrel is thoroughly cooked and crispy.

When done, serve with a salad garnish and add a dip such a garlic mayonnaise or sour cream and chives.

Recommended Recipes – Quick & Easy Squirrel Stew

Ingredients:

2 squirrel saddles, meat cut off the bone into small chunks
2 tbsp of olive oil
1 beef stock cube
1 small tin of stewing steak
1 large onion, chopped
2 cloves of garlic, chopped
1 small tin of garden peas
1 tin of sliced carrots
Dried mixed herbs
Worcestershire sauce
Black pepper
Cornflour

How to Cook

In a deep, heavy-bottomed pan, fry the squirrel chunks in the hot oil until brown, to seal in the taste. Then add onion and garlic and cook until soft. Add the beef stock mix and simmer for approximately an hour.

When meat is tender, add the tin of stewing steak, tin of garden peas (drained), tin of sliced carrots (drained), Worcestershire sauce, dried mixed herbs, and liberally sprinkle with black pepper. Now simmer adding cornflour to thicken the stew. If you've cooked correctly, there shouldn't be too much liquid left so it should thicken easily.

Serve piping hot in a dish with rustic rolls or crusty fresh bread.

With all that game at our disposal, when you've prepared other dishes what to do with those frozen off-cuts you've saved – or should have? Simple – make the ultimate airgun hunter's game pie, and believe me, once you've tasted this it'll make you more determined to fill that game bag!

Airgun Hunter's Game Pie

Ingredients:

One rabbit – jointed, and cut off the bone into chunks

4 woodpigeon – breast halves cut across into chunks

4 collared dove – breast left in halves

2 jointed squirrel, off the bone cut into chunks

2 large carrots, sliced

8oz mushrooms, sliced

2 cloves of garlic, chopped

Worcestershire Sauce

Gravy granules

2 large onions, sliced; in fact, add any root vegetables you prefer. I sometimes add some thick cubed potato for good measure.

Frozen puff pastry (saves hassle and I'm no Hugh Fearnley-Whittingstall!)

Airgun Hunter's Game Pie – now who wouldn't want some of that?

How to Cook

Mix together the raw vegetables and put these with the mixed meat pieces in separate layers into a large casserole dish. One layer of mixed vegetables, then a layer of mixed meat, and repeat the process until all ingredients are layered in this manner in the dish. In between layers add a dash of the Worcestershire sauce and sprinkling of black pepper, not forgetting the garlic.

Mix the stock cubes in a pint of boiling water and pour over the contents into the dish. If you need more water to cover the ingredients, add now. Place the lid on casserole dish and pop into a pre-heated oven at 180°C/350°F/gas mark 4 for 1 hour. After the first hour, reduce the oven heat to 160°C/325°F/gas mark 3 for a further 3–4 hours. The casserole dish should be removed from the oven every hour or so for stirring and to check liquid content.

During the cooking period, take out a portion of the frozen pastry for defrosting.

Towards the end of the cooking time, add gravy granules to thicken the dish and test meat to check if it is tender and fully cooked. If it is, turn up the oven to 220°C/425°F/gas mark 7. Now it's time to roll out the pastry following guidelines on packet, and then place pastry on top of the casserole. Return to oven and cook for a further 25-30 minutes, whereupon the pastry should have risen to form a crispy, golden brown crust.

Serve with mashed potato and extra vegetables of choice.

So there you have it, my recipes might only be basic but they're a good basis for you to try what you've harvested from the land yourself with the air rifle. In fact, nothing tastes better than a rabbit taken after a long, nerve wracking stalk, or a hard tricky shot on a woodie in the trees. Bon appetit!

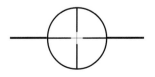

The Law, Safety and You!

There are actually a selection of laws that govern the use of air rifles. By and large, misuse an air rifle, or any firearm for that matter, and you are governed by the same rules of conduct. These are found in the Firearms Acts of 1968–1997 and the Wildlife & Countryside Act 1981. Add to that the penalties that can be imposed on you for breaking the law under the Criminal Damage Act 1971, Public Nuisance Act, or Anti-Social Behaviour Bill et al and you're going to suffer the consequences.

Also, the law on the use and purchase of airguns has changed since the first edition of Total Airguns was published in 2005. These changes were included in the 2007 VCR (Violent Crime Reduction) Act – one being that individuals must be 18 in order to buy an airgun legally.

The Act also changed the way in which airguns could be bought from shops. From 1st October 2007, shops selling airguns as part of their business became Registered Firearms Dealers (RFDs) and you can now only buy from them direct, and not by mail-order.

This restriction only applies to airguns and silencers, not to scopes, mounts or any of the huge range of airgun-related accessories available from gun shops; neither does it apply to private airgun sales.

Sale of an Airgun from Person to Person

The bill requires that all sales be in person. This applies when a person sells an air weapon by way of trade or business to another person in Great Britain who is not registered as a firearms dealer. It does not apply to transfers, so airguns that have been repaired need not be returned in person, but can be sent by carrier. The restriction does not apply to sales that are completed outside Great Britain, for example, when air weapons are sold by a person in another country by mail order or via the Internet and then posted to someone in Great Britain. Where this section applies, the buyer and the seller or his representative (the sellers' servant, another RFD or his servant) must be present in person so that the final transfer of possession is face-to-face.

We must always remember that when used unlawfully, an airgun carries the same legal status as shotguns and live-ammunition guns. Misusing airguns will result in huge penalties, including terms in prison.

So here, as they stand, are the laws. Whilst all shooters need to adhere to them, I leave it up to the individual to decide if the law is indeed an ass!

The Wildlife & Countryside Act 1981

It's meaning and relevance to the airgun hunter: The quarry we are allowed to shoot with an air rifle of a suitable power had remained unchanged for many a moon – longer than the Act itself (the Countryside Act, not the one passed in 1981). It has been changed in relation to what is deemed legal quarry for the airgun hunter using a rifle with a power not exceeding 12ft lbs.

Be aware that this may change again. The Scottish leadership have more than once shown their willingness to require all air rifles (irrespective of power) be put 'on ticket'. However, the voices of our sport keep us informed; any updates are immediately put on the BASC website, so if in doubt always head there for the most recent news and information.

Incidentally, according to the act, all species of bird, their eggs and nests are protected, but every year the government issues what is known as the 'Open General Licence' that allows certain species of bird - deemed pests - to be killed. It also makes reference to animals on the unprotected list due to the fact that their population is in need of management and/or the animal is classed as vermin.

All have been listed at the beginning of the book but I mention them in entirety here with pertinent notes to their culling. The corvids (crow family) including magpie, rook, jackdaw, crow and jay – the latter, however, is currently protected in Northern Ireland.

Now to a genus of bird much more straightforward to deal with in terms of our rights, well even here I must add 'use your discretion', the winged felons being pigeons and the dove family. In the W&C Act this makes mention of woodpigeon, feral pigeon and the collared dove – the latter like the jay being a protected species in Northern Ireland.

As some pest species of birds do resemble protected species, especially from certain angles and in poor light or weather conditions, as I always say; err on the side of caution and don't shoot until certain. It's every airgun hunter's responsibility with all animals and birds to ensure that he can clearly identify all protected species, as it is the unprotected ones you target. Before we leave feathered felons, the law doesn't say the airgun hunter isn't allowed to shoot certain game birds but the practice is deemed by many to be unsporting.

Personally, I say if the landowner or gamekeeper allows you to take the odd one or two for the pot, if shot cleanly, then it's acceptable albeit a little out of the norm. However, you must hold a game licence and the following species can only be shot within the season allotted to them; they are pheasant, partridge, grouse (red and black), ptarmigan, common snipe, woodcock and golden plover.

In respect of wildfowl, while these don't require a game licence, they can only be shot during their allotted season. These are ducks including; mallard, tufted duck, teal, wigeon, shoveler, pochard, pintail, goldeneye and gadwall.

We are also allowed to shoot geese, including; Canada goose, greylag and pink-footed goose - I bet that surprised a good few readers! - and let's not forget the troublesome twosome dealt with in Quarry Files, the coot and moorhen. Incidentally, I feel that some comment should be made on areas of the country where local restrictions apply, such as the Norfolk Broads, where it is illegal to use airguns on areas of water and land controlled by the Broads Commissioners. So if in any doubt, as always – check your local byelaws.

Now, whilst I will refer over to shooting organisations at the end of this section it's worth noting that the BASC does actually recommend that wildfowl only be shot with shotgun. My views are, certainly any legal quarry species when in flight should only be tackled with shotgun, but as for a 'one shot, head shot, clean kill' on a stationary bird - why only let the 'scatter blasters' have duck or pheasant on the menu?

Now to the furry animals on the list, and whilst the fox is included but only for suitable calibre and power firearm, I'll not comment other than to say this crafty predator certainly needs a bullet or buckshot; although many feel they can clear up cubs with a high-powered air rifle, I'd still say use a .22LR silenced rimfire in the least, and at sensible range. However, with the new calibre of super high-power air rifles coming on to the scene, that's not as cut-and-dried in some situations where a live-round bullet gun might not be allowed.

Now to the vermin we can cleanly dispatch with a pellet fired from a 12 ft lb air rifle.

These are; rat, rabbit, most species of mouse (not including the dormouse family) the grey squirrel, weasel, stoat, mink, feral cat (not including the Scottish wild cat) and the hare. Now we've come to a few species that often cause some controversy. These being feral cat and the hare because although legally deemed quarry species, they aren't encountered that often, and particularly in the case of the hare, still not as widespread or as plentiful as it once was in many parts of the UK. However, specifically in relation to the hare, if the odd one crosses your path, let it go on its way as it adds to the variety of wildlife and is a noble animal that has a tough enough time living all its life above ground. However, if they're plentiful and encountered by the airgun hunter using a hi-power FAC air rifle – that's certainly a powerful enough firearm to dispatch it capably at sensible range. Stoats and weasels hardly ever keep still, so they're certainly better served by the shotgun or trap, and as for the mink - I've mentioned previously I've had cause to shoot them but mainly when dispatching them after they've been caught in live-catch traps.

Now to the legalities of the actual shooting of all quarry species deemed as pests.

Pests can only be shot if you have the landowner's permission to shoot on the land he actually owns or presides over. If you don't, you can be charged with armed trespass and if you shoot any quarry, charged and prosecuted with poaching. Both carry hefty penalties – especially armed trespass!

Armed trespass carries a hefty penalty

Add to this the fact that even if you have the landowner's permission to shoot you can only do so if the species is actually a pest – this is what the powers that be say on the matter

The species is classed a pest if:

1. It's threatening other protected wild bird populations.
2. Endangering public health and/or spreading disease.
3. Causing damage to crops, livestock, fisheries, young trees or waterways.

Sift through those classifications outlined , and you can be in no doubt why we can target rabbits, rats, wood pigeon, feral pigeon, magpies and crows, to name but six, now can you?

A very important point is that there are laws not in the W&C Act that govern cruelty to animals and the purposeful wounding of any animal – even those classed as pests. Again, prosecution can carry heavy penalties. I'll outline a hypothetical scenario to illustrate this point.

Say you legally shoot a woodpigeon or magpie in your garden or on your shoot, and it flies off and lies wounded in a neighbouring garden or on private land you have no permission to be on. Should it be found, and the finder takes it to the authorities – such as the police or RSPCA - with an accusation that you shot it wilfully - you could, if found guilty, be charged with a crime.

In fact, it's a very contentious subject to shoot birds in your own garden as being able to prove they are a pest species causing damage in the garden is very difficult. Also, few if any neighbours would accept someone shooting birds in gardens – remember, the majority of the non-shooting public don't know what is considered, by law, to be 'a pest' – except maybe the feral pigeon.

Consider the following; shoot a rabbit and it goes under a fence on to private land that you have no right to shoot over. Say it is injured to the point where it can run no further, but needs a coup de grâce for merciful dispatch, and you nip over the fence to administer the final shot and retrieve it. If you do go over with your air rifle, you can be charged with armed trespass. If you go over and just retrieve the animal, legally it's still trespass and you could be called to prove that you weren't poaching! What of the rabbit that kicks its last on a public footpath after legging away from a wounding due to an unfortunately misjudged shot? Woe betide you If you're the one accused of shooting it and it has been found by an animal lover. You might think these scenarios mentioned very unlikely or judge them as grey areas, and in some ways, they may be, but in reality these are situations that can so easily happen. To avoid straying into these minefields I feel it is advisable here to remind hunters never, no matter how tempting it may seem at the time, to venture on to land where you don't have a right to be.

Certainly, if you're the airgun hunter who leans over another farmer's gate to nab an early morning rabbit with a naughty shot as it sits on a dirt track on another's land – you poached that rabbit – no grey area there, and in the process you committed several offences in the shooting and retrieving of it.

Even when on land you have a right to shoot on, never - repeat never - shoot any species of legally deemed vermin unless you have a clear, safe shot and one that to the best of your knowledge should cleanly dispatch the intended target - as always – if in doubt – then don't shoot!

That basically covers the W&C Act as it stands at present, but remember it's possible that these laws could be amended. Certain quarry species may be added, but certainly more likely taken off the list governed by the Open General Licence. So consult the relevant literature, organisations, authorities and websites.

Age Restrictions and Laws Pertaining to Ownership, Transportation and Other Use

These are quite clear-cut and need little if any comment from me.

- If you are under 14 years old you cannot buy, hire, be given or own an airgun or airgun ammunition – that's right – even pellets. However, an under-14 can use an airgun but only if supervised by someone 21 years or older, and you must only shoot on land that you have permission to shoot on, or at an approved shooting club and the rifle is only used for target shooting at that club.

Now I did say I wouldn't comment, but here I must have a say on what I feel is a great loss to the sport. This law is quite frankly not only unfair (what's new?) but doesn't work! Few under-14s, unless they have older brothers, will be able to shoot, and, lets be realistic, those older lads have little time to help little Johnny when they're at an age they could well be more interested in cars, girls and having a drink than family matters. To be totally realistic, that older sibling will have a life of his or her own and quite frankly, have zero interest in air rifles or shooting. Also, we now unfortunately live in a social climate of part-time parents, particularly fathers – that's if they're on the scene at all. In that respect, some under-14s will never get the chance to try shooting with an air rifle, and that comradeship of youthful shooting we enjoyed is also effectively removed. Then again, this law is supposedly designed to stop kids getting up to no good with an air rifle; it's a pity that it won't stop them sitting around on a street corner scaring elderly people and smashing something out of boredom. To think, a large part of the reason we were given our first air rifles was so that our parents knew what we'd be up to, and it gave us something to be interested in, gave us a pride of ownership and something to respect using. Hell, we got air rifles to keep us out of mischief!

When we were kids, getting our first air rifle was part of growing up. You got a fishing rod, an airgun, then you discovered girls and the first two went out of the window. Okay, I'm only half joking, but what I'm trying to illustrate is that a large part of the culture of growing up has been lost. When people like me were kids, we could go anywhere, with some exception but not anything like the Draconian rules that govern freedom of movement now, and with our air rifles to shoot rats. We did no harm. Obviously, there was always the idiot who did something daft with his airgun, but by and large, he grew out of it or if not, just grew up and did other stupid things often resulting in committing further crime. In other words, that person would have done something stupid or malicious no matter what he had his hands on or was involved in.

Back to the law as it now stands, and the reasoning of 'keeping guns out of the hands of youngsters!' The knock-on effect of this law pertaining to youngsters may seem to have little importance to long-term shooting adults, but think on this: The law effectively prevents a whole new generation of youngsters from being able to grow naturally into shooting, as we did. If it was your thing, you carried on shooting; if not you looked to another sport, hobby or pastime. It's that simple. Robbing generations to come of the experience of shooting in their formative years is a terrible pity, and they won't go on to discover it at a later age. Quite frankly, even back then we grew up too quickly. As you approach 17, shooting air rifles is probably going to be the last thing on your mind. Don't be misled; they're chipping away at our sport from the ground up. Sorry that turned into such an issue but I think we should all be aware what is happening. Now, back to the law …

- No person under 18 can be given an airgun as a gift. On the outset that seems sensible enough, but consider this. Parents or relatives, who give their under-18 an air rifle, are themselves breaking the law, but reach the magic age, and between 14 and 18 you can be given, or loaned an airgun and ammunition but you can't buy or hire one yourself. Now doesn't all that make sense? Right, from now on I won't comment because I'm getting far too opinionated and importantly, if I carry on we'll never reach the end!

If you don't have permission to shoot on the other side of the fence and take a shot, even if you miss you're breaking the law

- If an air rifle or pistol is used on private land including the garden of a private dwelling the pellets mustn't stray outside the boundaries of that land. This is the reason we need solid backstops for the home-target plinking range. If it does go 'zinging' out of bounds, this is now also an offence under the Anti-Social Behaviour Act, carrying a maximum £1000 fine as a penalty.

- An air rifle can only be carried or transported by someone of the appropriate age, or one who is properly supervised, in a public place when covered with a securely fastened gun cover – this means a gun bag - which should be zipped closed at all times.

- Never carry a cocked or loaded gun in a public place out of or inside a gun bag. Now this is one to be very cautious of as a rifle is deemed loaded if it has a pellet or even a cleaning felt in the barrel and for a multi-shot if it has a magazine - even an empty one - in the action. Always remove the magazine from a multi-shot and store separately while travelling to and from the land you are legally allowed to shoot over. As for the former, you should never have cause to carry a cocked rifle and/or a single-shot rifle with a pellet in the breech; a simple rule of safety. The magazine of a multi-shot should be empty even when not with the gun as this in itself is deemed a loaded weapon!

There are more but they come under a broader rule of gun law that we will now try to decipher, but to recap: Generally speaking, for the under 14s, very strict rules apply to airgun use. Between 14-18 years of age, for all practical purposes, you must be supervised by a person over 21. However, when 18 you can purchase an air rifle and ammo - the air rifle not having a power exceeding the 12 ft lb UK legal limit. It can only be used on land over which you have written permission from the owner to shoot, and don't take it for granted that the person who signs your written permission is the owner - double check! I'm not saying go behind any body's back snooping, but do take the trouble to ensure that written permission is as it should be – correct and legal!

Now to something that doesn't affect hunters as they're virtually all too low-powered to use for hunting, but should be borne in mind if you happen across one. The law has now deemed airguns that use the self-contained air cartridges such as Brocock, Saxby & Palmer etc., need to be on an FAC. If you own one and didn't get an FAC for the time limit stipulated in April 2004, or hand it in – well, you're now breaking the law and can be sentenced under the Criminal Justice Act 2003.

The next set of guidelines are taken from the Firearms Act and are relatively straightforward as they pertain to responsible usage of an airgun or firearm. Also others that follow are now in force as they're included in The VCR Act passed in 2007

- It's against the law for anyone to have an airgun in a public place unless they have some proper reason for doing so. Public places are any areas where the general public have legal access. These are roads, footpaths, canal towpaths, and public parks - any such areas, and in relation to this, never presume a bridle path or footpath is not used just because you rarely see anyone on it. The time when you do could be the time a costly and dangerous mistake is made!
- It is an offence for anyone under 18 to carry an air weapon unless: they are under the supervision of a person aged 21 or more; they are on private land and have permission from the occupier; they are shooting as a member of an approved club; or they are shooting at a shooting gallery for miniature rifles.
- It is an offence for any person, regardless of age, to be in possession of an air weapon in a public place without a reasonable excuse, which might be carrying a gun to and from a target shooting club, or to and from land on which you have permission to shoot. It would also include taking a gun to and from a gunsmith for repair or service, or taking a new gun home from the dealer.

Always know the exact location of footpaths, bridleways and any public thoroughfare on the land you shoot over

It is an offence to fire an airgun or any firearm within 50 feet of the centre of any roadway or public thoroughfare, which includes the pavement. This is seemingly straightforward but there is one exception. If you shoot in your back garden on a plinking range you will likely be within this distance. This being the case, you should be out of view from the public, behind a tall screen of hedge or fence. You should also be shooting away from the road. If in doubt about your plinking area, consult your local police force; they can advise on your rights. While on the subject of plinking, never presume that your neighbour is accepting of your participation in the sport; some will, but more likely just as many won't. Shoot at reasonable hours and don't shoot for hours on end. This may seem like an infringement on your rights, which in some ways it is, but have consideration for others and uphold neighbourly relations. The continuous sound of a pellet striking a backstop can become unnerving and irritating and is as annoying as any loud music. Think on that carefully in relation to the times when you practise.

That's how the law stands at the moment. Whether it will change is up to the governing bodies and unfortunately, these changes are usually driven by public acts of stupidity.

Hopefully, commonsense will prevail and Whitehall will realise that the general shooting public go about a satisfying and challenging sport responsibly, and that airgun hunters and sport shooters alike perform a helpful and necessary service to the country community, helping to maintain and protect the natural balance of the great outdoors.

Although a few basic rules of safety have been outlined elsewhere, here are the important ones to which we must all adhere for safe gun use.

- Always treat an airgun as if it is loaded and cocked. Never presume it isn't.
- Always store an airgun securely in a safe place, always storing it uncocked and unloaded. Ensure that they're out of sight from prying eyes and never let young children near them. Please refer back to the section on the Home Office Guidelines as they were fully explained in Chapter 15.
- Never load or cock an airgun until it is safe to fire it.
- Never point an airgun at anyone – even if unloaded.
- Never touch, pick up, or attempt to use someone else's air rifle without their permission.

As a matter of course, whether you are hunting or getting kit together, make a point of always checking that a rifle is safe and unloaded before putting it in a gun bag. Also check again immediately that you remove it from its case.

Never shoot beyond your seeing distance; for example past the end of a building, wall and if in open country, past the end of solid hedgerow.

So, at last that does bring this section to a close. However, I will mention that you should always carry your written permission with you whenever you go shooting on the land it relates to, and remember that although the statute laws previously stated apply to you, you also have to bear in mind that should the unexpected or unimaginable happen due to mishap or accident, you could find yourself facing a civil action for damage to property or, worse still, unintentional injury to persons or livestock.

In my opinion, every shooter should have third-party Public Liability Insurance. You can obtain this privately, but upon joining one of the associations that represent shooters interests you can gain insurance as well as being part of a public voice on the sport. These are the British Airgun Shooters Association (BASA) or the British Association for Shooting & Conservation (BASC)

These are currently the two main associations representing airgun shooters within their ranks, along with other sport shooters.

I'd also like to mention and give credit to the Airgun Education and Training Organisation (AETO) for the good work that they do in educating and training people in safe shooting practice in relation to the use of all airguns.

Farewell and Thanks

Now updated, once again I can say: "So there you have it – *Total Airguns*". I hope you have enjoyed this version and found much to interest, encourage and enhance your airgun hunting. I again make reference to the demanding sport of Field Target (FT) shooting, and although no section is devoted specifically to that discipline, because the book mainly concentrates on the use of air rifles for hunting, I've always realised and recognised the shooting skills required to be successful in that sector of the worldwide airgun shooting community and I pay due respect to those who compete.

At the time the original version of 'TA' was launched, Hunter Field Target (HFT) was pretty much in its infancy, but due to the impact it has had with many airgun enthusiasts, HFT needs to be credited as it has done so much good for the sport of airgun shooting. Indeed, as an established shooting discipline in its own right, the fact that it has retained a firm 'hunting' slant is, I feel, a great credit to all those who organise, sponsor, participate and attend any HFT meeting. This time around, I can also appreciate the many unsung ambassadors of our sport, including the almost 'left-of-field' air rifle shooters, who use airguns not only for sport but also in their work, including the FAC hunting pest controllers who need specialist air rifles whichh the trade can now supply. On reflection, I feel I am continually realising just how far I have travelled and progressed in my own shooting career. It has been one that has seen much change in the quality of air rifles, scopes and equipment due to advancements in all manner of technology that is readily available for us all to use to help us have greater success in our chosen sport.

Now this newly-updated book really is at an end, so I'll sign off by saying this: Respect the countryside, respect the people you shoot with, the land you shoot on and especially those who are kind enough to let you do so, and no matter what the situation – indoors or outdoors, ambush shooting or stalking – shoot well, shoot wisely and most of all shoot safely! Before I express my thanks to all those who have helped and encouraged me in so many ways, I'd first like to offer an extra special 'No Thanks' to certain elements of 'the system', and those who tried to pull me down, hassle, stress, annoy or hinder me in any way. You know who you are. It hasn't worked, has it? Nice throw, but you still missed!

I'd like to give a very heartfelt thanks to the following: (names and places appear in no particular order):

Personal thanks: Pat Farey (diamond geezer), Peter Moore, Andrew Johnston (who's patience I've tested to the limit and beyond – thanks for keeping the faith) and of course all at Quiller Publishing who've gone 'above and beyond' to make all this possible.

Colin McKelvie (R.I.P.) sub-editor of the first edition of *Total Airguns*, a life-long outdoorsman, sport shooting enthusiast and a greatly missed spokesman for the countryside, its wildlife and all it encompasses.

Tony Wall, Steve Pope, Glynn E (MIA), Chris A, Richard A, Howard H, Terry Almond, Dave Mills (AETO), Sammie & Gary Cooper, Dave and Derek Rose, Ben Taylor, Richard Bingham and of course a very special thanks go to Tim McAvoy, Jan and family who've helped more than they've ever needed, or I suppose ever expected or wanted to! In fact, huge thanks go to all at T & J. J McAvoy Gunsmiths. Cheers Tim.

For contributing and supplying info and images in Ch 14: Jerry Moss of the Penrith and District Red Squirrel Society - the good work he and his fellow workers do shouldn't go unnoticed: www.penrithredsqurrels.org.uk.

My gratitude still holds for James Marchington for that first-ever acceptance slip for a magazine article.

Who can forget Richard North's impact on the airgun scene? Even though no longer actively in the airgun industry he still remains one of the true inspirations that fewer by the year seem to follow. Thankfully, however, there are others that still have drive not dissimilar to his.

Bill Sanders (R.I.P.)

Tony, Bob and Trace at Sandwell Field Sports; John 'The Guru' Bowkett, Steve Rowe, Paul Sim and all at 'N.o.L,' Jamie Ransome, Tom Whitman and all at 'DGI Ltd', Glenn Lewis, Tony Belas (a man always worth listening to), Jamie Garland, Simon Esnouf, Lloyd and all at Blackpool Air Rifles and Team Wild Media.

Matt Clark, Terry Doe and to all magazines and their editors, who not only have time for my scribblings and wittering, but even sometimes put up with my downright ranting! Also, not forgetting the fact that they continually support and serve the sport and trade.

For moments in time, captured on picture, film or tape … Oops, I suppose that should include 'any digital media' to be more in-keeping with the book.

Portmeirion (The Village) – friends made, and all there for helping me and 'A.N. Other' have magical, happier times that have now become very treasured memories – the likes of which I'll never see again.

My thanks and feelings of gratitude that are way beyond special go to my sister.

Feelings I know the meaning of the more that time passes and ones that no one else deserves to know go to my mother and father – God rest their souls.

In fact, to all those who've now gone, from loved ones, cherished ones, friends and the 'fallen over' with ones – yeah, you will always be remembered.

If I've forgotten to list anyone who deserves a personal mention or further after an acknowledgement all I can do is apologise, but in my defence – blame it on far, far too much rock 'n' roll.

Acknowledgements: Photos: Pete Wadeson, Glynn Eatock, Chris Aldred, Tim McAvoy, Howard Heywood, Richard Alty, Sarah McNeil. Basic Graphics: Julian Marsh, Debbie Harley.

Gun Companies: Air Arms, Crosman & FX Airguns (ASI Ltd), BSA Guns (UK) Ltd, Daystate Ltd, Gamo, Ripley Rifles, Weihrauch (Hull Cartridge Co). No longer trading but for their support during the time they were: Falcon, Theoben Ltd, Logun, Webley & Scott Ltd and all the team at The Webley-Venom-Custom Shop.

Shooting Accessories & Clothing: AimfieldSports, Arctic Outdoors (Jahti Jakt), Cluson Engineering Ltd, Deben Group Industries Ltd (incorporating Hawke Sports Optics), Edgar Brothers, The Photon Shop (Fenix), Garlands Ltd, Gerber & Silva Ltd, Knockover Targets Ltd, Harkila/Seeland International, Henry Krank and Co Ltd, Highland Outdoors Ltd, John Rothery Wholesale Ltd, Milbro Ltd, MTC Optics, Mac Wet Gloves, Napier of London, Thatchreed Ltd (Jack Pyke of England, Viper and Web-Tex), Whitby and Co, Range Sports, Keen Footwear, Allen Outdoor Equipment.

Specialist Companies: Sportsmatch UK, Best Fittings, Hydro Graphics, Brattonsound Ltd, Dr Bob, FSC Ltd, Rowan Engineering Ltd, Starlight NV Ltd, Thomas Jacks Ltd, V-Mach, Airmasters 88.

Index

POLAR BEARS FROM SHEFFIELD

A MEMORIAL TO THE OFFICERS AND MEN OF THE

HALLAMSHIRE BATTALION

THE YORK AND LANCASTER REGIMENT
WORLD WAR TWO

BY

DON SCOTT

TIGER & ROSE PUBLICATIONS
ENDCLIFFE HALL, SHEFFIELD

Copyright   : *Don Scott 2001. 'Polar Bears from Sheffield.'*
Copyright   : *Mary E. Hart Dyke. 'Letters to Mary.'*
Copyright   : *Doreene Somers. 'The Diary of Capt. A.C. Somers.'*

Design   : Don Scott

Publisher   : Tiger & Rose Publications
              RHQ The York & Lancaster Regiment
              Endcliffe Hall
              Endcliffe Vale Road
              Sheffield
              S10 3EU
              Tel: 0114 2662279

Printer   : Paper Kapers
              280 Queens Road
              Sheffield
              S2 4DL
              Tel: 0114 2721759

ISBN 0-9541261-0-6

First Published in 2001

e-mail
General exchanges (on any subject within this book and perhaps identification of un-named individuals in the photographs to add to the Regimental Museum Archive records) are welcome until December, 2001, by which time it is hoped that most of the research material will have been passed to the York and Lancaster Regimental Museum, Rotherham, South Yorkshire. There is no guarantee that all such enquiries can be answered and this will depend on the level of response. No help can be given in respect of Individual Personal Records of Service and this type of enquiry should be placed with Army Records Office. Furthermore, access to such World War Two records may only be available to next of kin.
e-mail address <donscott@beeb.net>

CONTENTS

DEDICATION

The first fifteen years of my life were in the care of my adoptive Grandparents, John Wilkinson Kirtley and his wife, Elizabeth Oswald Kirtley, who brought me up in their most quaint, endearing and Victorian way. They meant so much to me that I have often wished that their blood flowed in my veins. That is sufficient reason in itself for this book to be dedicated to them but, there is another which stems from my childhood memories of their suffering on two occasions during 1944, when these very dear people lost both of their sons.

Bob (Petty Officer Stoker, R.N.) went down with his ship, "HMS Penelope" off the west coast of Italy and his brother Billy (Signalman, Royal Signals), also buried at sea, died as a prisoner of war when being transported on a Japanese ship.

It is for this reason that the book is dedicated to my Grandparents, and all others like them, who have suffered the lingering agony and grief brought about by loss of their loved ones in war. For many, that suffering has been life long.

ACKNOWLEDGEMENT

This book is largely the spoken, written and photographic works of a number of people but it has been particularly pleasing to bring together the writings of three men who were not only fellow officers but also known to be very great personal friends. David Lockwood, John Marsh and Chris Somers could never have envisaged that their separate works would one day become part of a single tapestry of evidence. It seemed sometimes during the weaving of it all, that something a little stronger than coincidence had brought this about but, due to my own lack of religious conviction, the claim would have to fall somewhere short of divine providence. It is doubtless, however, that such a coming together would have pleased those three men which has in turn been of great satisfaction to me, the mere instrument of it all. A very special thank you is extended to Mary Hart Dyke and Doreene Somers for the invaluable help they have given in connection with documents relating to the wartime service of David and Chris.

One other person deserves mention here in that he provided the first material in the form of an audio taped interview, which sparked my idea and enthusiasm to collect more and write a book. It was he who provided contacts and introduction to many of the other sources as well as having some direct input into early research of the casualty list and identification of photographs. That man is Arthur Green of Sheffield, to whom I would like to give special thanks.

A number of those others who subscribed material for this book are now passed on. It is hoped that families and friends will accept my deepest thanks on their behalf and be proud that the individual stories will live on in the minds of many other people. I am indebted to those who may or may not appear in the main text but subscribed to this work in very many ways. All are named below, as they are or were known to me or others, without title and in no particular order.

Individuals...
Arthur Saunders, Arnold Whiteley, John Wollerton, Trevor Hart Dyke, Ivor Slater, Maureen Boulter, George Robins, Les Gill, Jesse Mitchinson, Bert Murray, George Linley, Albert Binns, Cliff Campin, Tony Jaques, Les Dalton, Ray Langdale, Cliff Lister, Sam Woolley, Les Sewell, Roy Simon, Dennis Townsend, Bill Jackson, Jack Haslam, Ken Godfrey, Doug Catley, Wilf Fisher, Harry Furness, Graham Roe, Geoff Cooper, Joe Beckett, Bert Green, Harry Dinnigan, John Swift, Arnold Bracewell, Tom O'Connor, Joe Penn, Arthur Naylor, Bill Ashby Jr., John Ellis Jr., Charlie Denton, Doug Redmond, George Pape, Harry Portas, Pat Strafford, George Learad, Ray Jenkinson, Geoffrey Norton, Francis Huijbrechts, Kate How and Alfred Dow.

Lastly, I would like to thank my wife Margaret who provided the encouragement and so very much more.

ORIGINS OF PHOTOGRAPHIC AND OTHER SOURCE MATERIAL.

(YLRM)	The York & Lancaster Regimental Museum.
(HFC)	The Hallams Fontenay Club Collection.
(IWM)	The Imperial War Museum.
(PRO)	The Public Record Office.
(SNL)	Sheffield Newspapers Ltd.
(AFPU)	Army Field Photographic Unit.
(CGR)	George Robins Collection.
(DEL)	David Lockwood Collection.
(THD)	Trevor Hart Dyke Collection.
(ACS)	Chris Somers Collection.
(DCB)	D.C. 'Joe' Beckett Collection.
(DWS)	Authors Collection.

WITH COMPLIMENTS TO

The York & Lancaster Regimental Trustees
who ensure the preservation of
Battalion History

AND TO

The Commonwealth War Graves Commission
who ensure the preservation of its
Memorials

FOREWORD

David Lockwood, my first husband, attended Charterhouse School where he had been a member of the Officer Training Corps. He was later commissioned in the Hallamshire Battalion of The York & Lancaster Regiment, when Gazetted as a Second Lieutenant on the 5 November, 1930. The Battalion became his life and gave him the opportunity to serve his country. Being a true countryman, he enjoyed country pursuits and developed a deep appreciation of English Literature and Poetry. Very well known for his sense of humour, wit and art of mimicry, his talents were always in great demand. His loss in Normandy was very great but he lives on in our hearts forever.

Many years later, I married Trevor Hart Dyke who had commanded the Hallamshires in Normandy and led them into the very battle at Fontenay le Pesnel in which David Lockwood died. At about the time of my second marriage (1965), a club of 'Fontenay' veterans was formed which drew many of them together in a large family of comradeship. I know how much it meant to Trevor when he was invited to become President of that close knit fraternity. It made him feel appreciated and satisfied that his efforts to prepare the Battalion for Normandy had not been in vain. He and others had been warned when he first took command in Scotland, that there would be sad consequences if the 49th Division was not brought to high efficiency, which in turn, triggered a rigorous programme of discipline and training. Trevor came to know the sterling worth of those officers and men in the Hallamshire Battalion and his confidence in them was fully justified at Fontenay. In return, they were to place complete confidence in him after that first and testing encounter with the enemy.

Don Scott has been known to me for some years and his book is a special source of pride to me, for obvious reasons. There is considerable achievement in this remarkable history of the Hallamshire Battalion in World War Two. Although he insists that a work of this type can merely scratch the surface, it has been painstakingly compiled over many years and his utter devotion to the subject as well as to those it represents, has immortalised the Hallamshires for posterity.

Finally, some words from Tennyson's 'Morte D'Arthur' come to mind as I reflect upon a more recent age now past, but one to which I very much belong.

The sequel of today unsolders all
the goodliest fellowship of famous knights
whereof this world holds record. Such a sleep
They sleep - the men I loved.

Mary E. Hart Dyke

APPRECIATION

There have been at least two books written before about the Hallamshires at war.

Captain D. P. Grant - at times the Adjutant of the 1/4th (Hallamshire) Battalion in the first World War - recorded the experiences of the battalion in France where they were among the first to arrive in April 1915.

Normandy to Arnhem - a story of the infantry - written by Brigadier Trevor Hart Dyke is written from the viewpoint of a battalion commander. This is a book which, to this day, should be required reading of any one who aspires to command in the army at any level as it covers all aspects of the infantryman in battle.

Polar Bears from Sheffield, which Don Scott rightly describes as a memorial to the officers and men of the Hallamshire Battalion, is very different to the other two. This is the experiences of the soldiers who served with the Hallamshires and shared its moments of fear and boredom. It is a story of those who volunteered to serve their King and country and others, called up, who may never otherwise have chosen to be in the army.

As a Territorial officer with 25 years service - the first 17 of them in which I was privileged to be in the Hallamshires - I can well understand the problem of converting enthusiastic amateurs into a disciplined fighting force which the Hallamshires undoubtedly became, with no distinction between those who chose to belong and those who had to. Not only did it touch many peoples lives for the six years of war, for many it became the highlight of their lives. This is a story of those people.

Although I did not join until 1951, it would have been impossible for me not to have become a true Hallamshire because of the training and help I received from many of those who appear in this book. Their inspiration made those who continued to serve, when their war time colleagues had all retired, an example to others who recognised the qualities which the Hallamshires had given to us. It shines through this book as it shone in Captain Grant's book of 1914-1919 and Brigadier Trevor's book of his time with us in 1943 - 1945. It is that spirit that made this the book that Don Scott had to write.

Colonel I. Geoffrey Norton TD JP DL
Vice-President
The York and Lancaster Regimental Association

INTRODUCTION

These are stories about the Second World War, held in the memory of a mere handful of people who served with the Hallamshire Battalion, a Territorial Army unit of the York and Lancaster Regiment. Throughout that War, the Battalion was a part of the 146th Brigade of the 49th (West Riding) Infantry Division. This Division adopted the image of a Polar Bear for its insignia as a result of two years service in Iceland (1940-42). This explains the reason why the Hallams, with a peacetime base at Endcliffe Hall, Sheffield, came to be wearing such an unusual image on the upper sleeve patch of their uniform (cover picture).

The purpose of this book is to document aspects of the history of a World War Two Infantry Battalion by using the evidence provided in a number of ways by only a small cross section of officers and men who served within its ranks. It has to be admitted at the outset, of course, that if stories had been related by another group from within the same Battalion then they might have painted an overall picture quite different from the one uncovered here. It is also natural enough for some stories to have become embellished with time and the telling, particularly if they tend to place the teller on a higher plain. All that accepted, the stories etched on human memory which are the subject of this work are, for the most part, revealed in print here for the first time and have not always been stamped in the mind by positive time and place. For this and other reasons, the cart will appear to preceed the horse from time to time and the main storyline may go astray now and then to add a little extra flavour or information. It is hoped that such meanderings do not upset the reader or the chronology too greatly and apologies are also offered at the outset, with regard to attempts made in conveying the spice of Yorkshire dialect in some of the quotes.

So as to stitch these stories together in a chronological way, there will be some attempt towards an ordered sense of place and time through the use of War Diaries and other historical records. Most of the stories, however, relate to individual experiences and thoughts of men who served with the 'Hallams' in various capacities during World War Two. These memories may have been seldom aired in the past sixty years, even in family circles, but must have been brought to mind on many occasions in all that time. They may be of little interest to a modern and sometimes indifferent world, but will hopefully help to place the magnifying glass on part of a generation that was required by the warmongers of that period to sacrifice millions of youthful lives in five years of bloodletting.

Many of the accounts were recorded on audio tape over the past ten years or so and during sessions it was stressed that differentiation should always be made between those events personally witnessed and those of a secondhand nature. Hesitation was often experienced where names had to be linked with unpleasant occurrences but the good and the bad were revealed wherever possible. Some of the names connected with stories that came to light in this book are not recorded here so as not to cause any offence or embarrassment to relatives, although some names are sure to be recorded elsewhere. Even some of the collected stories have been omitted that shed a poor light on the words and deeds of some individuals who are no longer alive to defend themselves or their actions. All too often, the accounts of war are tempered with a sense of caution in an effort to veil the truth about the less attractive nature of man. The nature of man, however, is much affected by his immediate environment and circumstances. It is not for others now to judge the actions of these men who, more than half a century ago, were thrust into the pit of horrors that mankind calls war.

The truth, of course, can be shocking but if it appears anywhere in the following pages it will be simply to put war in its proper perspective and to relate what are believed to be simple and honest accounts by men who were there. War itself is shocking and any written account of it should shock it's reader just to show that the so called 'paths of glory' are paved with the most grotesque injuries and indescribable suffering. At the other end of the scale, British soldiers are renowned for making light of the serious business of war. This book may not be without some occasional ill timed humour and sick joke, both of which can be used to cushion the reality of war. In part, it is the essence by which some soldiers have been able to shield their minds from the trauma of it all. Having said all that, any reader expecting a blood and guts account of war might be disappointed.

The Hallamshire Battalion may henceforth be referred to as the Hallamshires, Hallams, the Battalion or just Bn. As the story unfolds there will be reference made to other battalions, units and formations with which the Battalion was involved or formed a part. For this reason it is felt that a simple breakdown should be given of the Brigade and Divisional Formation to which the Hallams belonged for the duration of the war. This will be found in Appendix I at the back of the book and may help those who are unfamiliar with the structure of a British Brigade or Infantry Division of the period. There is also another breakdown given in Appendix II which attempts to explain the basic structure and content of an Infantry Battalion. It should be remembered that some slight variations may have existed from one unit to another in terms of numbers of men, material and internal organisation. These would generally be governed by operational requirements, modifications as the war progressed, or as a direct result of shortages caused by active service losses, etc.

The photographs used in this work are from very many sources and acknowledgement is given wherever possible, but the vast majority were taken with cameras which leave a lot to be desired by modern standards and are mostly attributed to the 'Hallams Fontenay Club'. Many were copied from tiny prints of obscure origin and some were quite battered, but all of them are gems because they have not previously been published. Others have the ability to illustrate a story, so well in places, that a reader can go straight to the scene without having to conjure up inaccurate visions. At one end of the scale the Icelandic episode is well catered for, but there is an understandable paucity of photographs in some areas, particularly in the post Normandy Landings period that relate directly to the Hallams. This is taken care of by using modern photographs from the authors collection (all are prefixed thus ❖) which are able to link with recorded memories of the past. Visits to continental battlefields and memorials over a ten year period during holidays or on tours were often in the company of veterans who were sometimes able to pinpoint scenes of action and relate a story on the very spot where it happened. This was particularly true of Fontenay le Pesnel, where the Hallams fought their most costly battle, and Tessel Wood where they were committed to slit trench, static warfare for three weeks.

Because of its nature, this book can not paint a detailed picture with regard to cooperation between units or even a blow by blow account of all operations, but it should be remembered that the Hallamshires did not work and fight in isolation. At all times they were surrounded by, or operated in conjunction with, various other units. These were mainly within their own Brigade and Division in the immediate areas to left, right, front and rear. In a general account, more mention would have been made of them but this book concentrates on individual stories as opposed to strategies which are better found in some of the works listed in the bibliography. The fact was that most individuals in battle were hardly aware of what was going on in the next slit trench let alone the next field, unless it directly affected them! In these pages will be found mainly the thoughts and deeds of men fighting their own personal war but who could not, of course, ignore the fact that a much larger war was raging all around them.

Many people supplied information for this work, mostly veterans who are no longer alive to read it. That is something I deeply regret and I sincerely hope it will be worthy of them. Although it has taken over ten years to compile, it can never be complete because of the many stories left untold. However, it is also hoped that its words and pictures will impart at least some of the feeling and atmosphere of an age now passed on. If just one of the following pages is able to draw some emotion from any of its readers then he or she will have ventured into the realms of the mind visited by the writer on many occasions during the writing and researching of it all. That alone might be sufficient justification for producing this memorial, as well as inducing a very private and personal tribute to a group of people for whom the shedding of tears seems hardly enough, especially for those who lost their lives. Those wasted, youthful lives with everything to live for, all taken in a carefully planned yet mindless slaughter on both sides. There will never be words or memorials sufficient to express the pity of it all.

After having turned the last page, you may feel the need for something in the way of follow up. If that is so, then you could do no better than to set out on a journey of remembrance and visit some of the places mentioned in this book. Such a journey will inevitably take you to some of the burial grounds. Many of these will seem more like gardens than the dour places you might have expected but, unless your heart is made of stone, they will have a marked effect.

As you walk around these silent places, you will recognise some of the names engraved on headstones that have become familiar from the book. In each of the war cemeteries visited you will raise your head and gaze at row upon row of identical stones, each one a public testimony to untold private grief.

Sooner or later, an uneasy feeling will stir within you as the mind formulates a simple question that contains only one word, to which there is no answer... ...Why?

RIFLE VOLUNTEERS

Since ancient times the threat of invasion, both real and imagined, has weighed heavily on the British mind. When Julius Caesar invaded the South Eastern shores of Britain in 55 B.C., he became the first man in recorded history to do so. He retired only to repeat the exercise a year later but failed to consolidate any gains he may have made. It was left to the Emperor Claudius in A.D. 43 to launch a successful invasion, resulting in the occupation and settlement of this land by the Romans that was to last for almost the next 400 years. The more recent and perhaps best known invasion to take place was that perpetrated by William the Conqueror in A.D. 1066. There have been numerous attempts both before and since with varying degrees of success and failure.

Most readers will be well aware that the Roman and Norman attacks were both launched from the shores of France. Since then and up to the middle of the 20th century, the threat of invasion has been seen to come mainly from that shore. The French and English have long been unable to live side by side with any ease due in the main to their strong competitive nature, particularly in the area of Empire building. However, reactions to such threats have usually been followed by a quick appraisal of home defences that were invariably found to be wanting (it would seem that things have remained little changed in that area of our history). Such was the case in 1859 when the Emperor of France, Napoleon III, flexed his muscles and all England quaked.

Officers of the Hallamshire Rifle Volunteers, c.1861/62. They are from left to right standing : F.T. Mappin, A. Bright, Sgt. Major Leve, M. Flockton, Cockburn?(Adjutant), W. Prest. Seated : T.E. Vickers and A. Vickers.(DWS)

To counter this threat, wheels were set in motion, on a countrywide basis, to build a volunteer force. It was hoped that this might contain the situation in the absence of Regulars, the majority of whom were busy policing a far flung British Empire.

On the 18 May, 1859, a notice was placed in local newspapers by a Mr. Wilson Overend, Deputy to the Lord Lieutenant of the West Riding of Yorkshire, with instructions to the effect that arrangements should be made for a unit of Rifle Volunteer Corps (RVC) to be formed in Sheffield. After a general meeting held in the Town Hall, committees were appointed to put in motion the raising of the Corps. On the 8 June a Deputation from Sheffield, received by the Secretary of State for War, was followed on the 27th of that month by selection of Officers, Senior N.C.Os. and men for two newly formed Companies. The 'Hallamshire Rifle Volunteers' had come into being and after a number of Drills at the Collegiate School and Bramall Lane Cricket Ground they paraded, for the first time in uniform, on 20 August, 1859, at the latter venue.

Early uniform consisted of a light grey tunic with scarlet facings (collar & cuffs) with an Austrian Knot in black cord to the lower sleeve. Trousers were also grey with a thin scarlet band running through the centre of a wider black stripe down the outer seams. The grey, peaked Forage Cap had a black Oak Leaf band and the waist belt was also black. Officers and Serjeants wore a black sword belt and crimson sash. Both wore a grey Shako similar to that of Line Infantry. This information, dating from August 1859, is basic and may not reflect the minor changes occurring in dress even at this early date but is considered enough to wet the appetite of those interested in military fashion of the day.

A Company of the Hallamshire Rifle Volunteers assemble outside the Bagshawe Arms at Norton, c.1860. An officer (just right of centre) leans on his sword and the tall man to his right, wearing a light coloured apron, is the Pioneer. He has an axe in his left hand and what appears to be a machete strapped to his waist belt. (YLRM)

By 3 December, 1859, four Companies had been raised for Sheffield, which was sufficient to allow full Battalion status. The aforementioned Mr. Wilson Overend was appointed Major Commandant and Mr. W. Prest as Adjutant of the 2nd Yorkshire West Riding (Hallamshire) Rifle Volunteer Corps, to give it the correct title. This was something of a mouthful and a more wieldy 'Hallamshire Rifles' fell into common usage.

The Sheffield Directory for 1860 states that the Headquarters of the Corps was based at 75 Eyre Street, the site of which must now lie beneath the North East slip road at the roundabout junction of Arundel Gate and Eyre Street. This address was large enough to accommodate a glass roofed Drill Hall to the rear with various rooms to the front, including the Headquarters office. Number 19 of the same street was occupied for use as an Orderly Room and Quartermaster's Store. Spare land at the junction of Matilda and Arundel Street, opposite Deakin's Silver Works, was adopted for the purpose of an open air parade ground. The first shooting range facility was located at East Bank Road, Heeley, although it seems that some sort of small bore target practice was available in the Drill Hall itself.

Lord Wharncliffe was elected Lieutenant Colonel of the 'Hallams' on 7 March, 1861, after Major Overend had resigned his Command. In the same year Captain John Brown, who had raised one whole company at his Atlas Steel Works, was made Mayor of Sheffield. In 1862 scarlet uniforms with purple facings were adopted and the Battalion was presented with its first Colours. These were well cared for and gave 48 years of service before being finally laid up in Sheffield Parish Church where they remain to date.

A small booklet entitled 'Rules of the Hallamshire Rifle Volunteer Corps' gives a fair insight to organisation in the early years. Item 15 covers the establishment of companies that were required to consist of a Captain, a Lieutenant and Ensign aided by one Serjeant, two Corporals and a Bugler. Company strength was not to exceed 100 or be less than 60 men of all ranks.

Senior officers in command were empowered to inflict various fines on defaulters. For loading a rifle without orders or firing out of turn the sum of one shilling (5p) fine was imposed. Pointing a rifle, loaded or otherwise, at any person without orders incurred the massive fine, in those days, of five shillings (25p). Non serving Honorary Members were a means of supplementing Corps Funds to the tune of £10.10s.(£10.50) as a 'one off' life payment or an annual subscription of £2.2s. (£2.10). Enrolled or serving members were also required to subscribe on a sliding scale up to the rank of Captain, who paid £5 per annum.

National fervour grew to such a pitch by May, 1861, that no less than 170,000 men had become volunteer soldiers. It was now left to this merry band to settle into some 40 years of home soldiering with few, if any, shots being fired in anger. Needless to say the French threat never materialised. It should be said, however, that many lives must have been enriched by the training, discipline, annual camps and perhaps more than anything else, the feeling of comradeship thus generated. Such was the peaceful lot of those early Victorians.

Three Active Service Companies were formed for duties in South Africa by men of the 1st and 2nd Volunteer Battalions of the York and Lancaster Regt. This is part of the half company (Hallamshires) formed in December, 1899, under Capt. E.A. Marples (centre). Photo taken at the Hyde Park Barracks, Sheffield. They sailed from Southampton on 16 February, 1900, in the S.S. 'Guelph'. (YLRM)

3

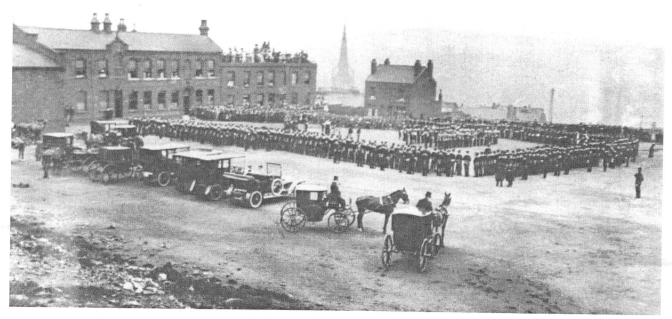

Early 20th Century scene from Hyde Park Barracks before the Great War, when the men were still parading in scarlet tunics. On this occasion it was to be presented with new colours. Note the mixture of carriages in the foreground, both horseless and horsedrawn. These will have brought families to watch the spectacle who can be seen in front and on the roof of the barracks. Some idea of industrial pollution at that time can be gained by the spire and other buildings which are all but lost in the smoke filled, hazy background. C.1909 (YLRM).

The original title was retained until 1883 when the Cardwell Reforms of 1881 took effect and the RVC was amalgamated with the Regular Army on a County/Recruiting Area basis. The Hallamshires then became the 1st (Volunteer) Battalion of The York and Lancaster Regiment. It was shortly after this (1886) that the Battalion moved to new barracks at Hyde Park and a fine rifle range was constructed at Totley in 1900. It was not until very nearly the end of Queen Victoria's long reign that the Hallams were able to prove themselves in battle. A number of its officers and men were given the opportunity to take part in the Boer War by joining specially formed Volunteer Companies, one of which was sent to South Africa in 1900 and another the following year. In 1908, Army restructuring (the Haldane Reforms) changed the Hallams title yet again to the 4th (Hallamshire) Bn., Territorial Army or T.A. as it became known.

Overseas service reached new heights during the Great War, 1914 - 1918, when the Hallams, then housed in Hyde Park Barracks, raised an additional two Battalions, such was the eagerness of young men to take part in the Great War for Civilisation. The existing Battalion was renumbered 1/4th and saw active service on the Western Front as part of the 49th

The Hallamshire Battalion leave Sheffield after mobilisation. August, 1914.(YLRM)

4

Division and was present on the first day of the Somme Battle (1 July, 1916) in support of the 36th Ulster Division at Theipval Wood. The two additional Battalions were raised for the duration of the war with the 2/4th being sent to France in January, 1917, as part of the 62nd (West Riding) Division. The 3/4th remained at home, acting as a feeder unit and supplying trained reinforcements to the other two.

Shades of the 'Good Old Days'. Pre war view (1934) of Endcliffe Hall, Sheffield, during what appears to be a garden party with the band in attendance. This was the home of the Hallamshire Battalion from 1916 but, whilst the hall exterior has changed little, the grounds have suffered down the years. Traces of the original formal garden layout can be seen to the right of the marquee where the band sits but this area is now a large concreted vehicle park. Since disbandment of the Hallams in 1968, this place has been home to the Yorkshire Volunteers, The Duke of Wellington's Regiment and now a Field Hospital Unit. Few British Army 'territorial' units have been able to boast of such splendour but the place is now just a shadow of its former glory and scenes like this may well have become a thing of the past.(YLRM)

A final change in title came in 1924 when, with special permission from H.M. King George V, it dropped the prefix '4th' and became known simply as the 'Hallamshire Battalion'. The Battalion was also allowed to continue the privilege of wearing the 'Hallamshire' cloth shoulder title, as it had done in the Great War, rather than that of the York and Lancaster Regiment, to which it belonged.

It was during the Great War period that Endcliffe Hall, in Sheffield, was procured for use by the Territorial Army. This building had originally been the private home of the Hallamshire Battalion's early benefactor, Sir John Brown. That fine old mansion might well have sunk into dereliction but for the timely intervention of Col. G.E. Branson when he secured its use as a permanent base for the Hallams. Headquarters moved there in 1916 but it was not properly occupied by the Battalion until November, 1919, when it returned from Germany.

If this place could speak, it would tell a thousand stories dating from its construction in 1865 to date. It would tell of the first fifteen years of happiness that turned to grief with the death of Brown's lifelong companion, Mary, and how his life and industrious nature began to deteriorate rapidly until he could no longer bear to stay in the place any more. He never recovered from the loss and died in obscurity somewhere in London. His body was brought from there and placed with that of his wife at All Saints Parish Church, Ecclesall.

There could be no other place more fitting than Endcliffe Hall to harbour the ghosts and memories of Sheffield's Hallamshire Battalion. It was the very heart and soul of this territorial unit and strangely linked from the moment that its very first stone was laid by John Brown. Since disbandment of the York & Lancaster Regiment in 1968, military activity has continued there as new units have come and gone, but later incumbents with any sense of history, right up to the present day, may often experience the distinct feeling that they are standing on hallowed ground.

The Hallamshire ghosts reign supreme there now but, to set the scene for this story, the clock must be turned back to the hot summer of 1939. Endcliffe Hall was then, very much a hive of industry as the whole Battalion put finishing touches to preparations for proceeding on what was to be the last peace time Annual Camp for some years to come, as the skies darkened over Europe.

Men of the Hallamshire Battalion embark on the S.S. 'Tynwald' as they proceed to their last annual summer camp (Bibaloe, Douglas, Isle of Man) before the outbreak of war. August, 1939 (YLRM).

DRAWING SWORDS

War loomed on the near horizon but the impending cloud, as yet, was insufficient to cause any cancellation of the Annual Summer Camp which was this year planned to take place on the Isle of Man. Because of the large increase of Territorial Army recruitment at this time it was decided that, for the first time since the Great War, it would be impossible for the whole Brigade to go to camp as one unit. For this reason the Hallamshire Battalion and its recently raised duplicate 6th Battalion were to proceed to Douglas on the 13 August, earlier than originally planned, returning on the 27th of the same month.

The man that would be taking the Hallams to their Summer Camp was Lieutenant Colonel Christopher George Robins who was known to his fellow officers as 'George'. A regular officer, he had seen service with the 2nd battalion of the York & Lancaster Regiment during the latter part of the 1914 -1918 war and was now Officer Commanding, The Hallamshire Battalion. If he could be summed up in three words then those words would be 'firm but fair'. He was also seen as something of a father figure to many of those who served under him. With these qualities, there was probably no better man to lead the Hallamshires because they were a very close knit group, especially the officers who could almost be described as a family in that many of their forefathers had served in the same unit and also the fact that many were inter-linked through local industry and commerce.

C.G. Robins. c.1935. He wears the rank of Captain and the collar insignia (Tiger and Rose) of The York & Lancaster Regiment. He is also carrying ribbons of the 1914 - 1918 War and Victory Medals.(CGR)

That same sense of family could not help but rub off onto most of the Non Commissioned Officers (NCOs) and Other Ranks, all of whom were part time volunteer soldiers of anything up to ten years service and more. This togetherness also instilled a sense of pride within all ranks which united them in such a way as to make it rather difficult for the newcomer to be quickly accepted. There was certainly a sense of difference between the volunteer soldier and his regular counterpart, especially among some of the officers which seems to have manifested itself in the attitude towards methods of maintaining discipline among the men. Some territorial officers were convinced that a volunteer did not require the whip and this would cause some strain later when 'outsiders' took command of the Battalion who had a tendency towards strict discipline.

Sheffield man George Learad must have been among some of the last to 'volunteer' for Army Service rather than wait for 'call up' on a compulsory basis. By doing so, he had more chance of getting into the unit of his choice, the Hallamshire Battalion! Even so, there was to be no guarantee of being able to stay with it and a few of his pals that joined with him were later transferred. His own 'Hallams' service in the pioneer platoon came to an abrupt end when he was seriously wounded by a mine near Venlo in Holland, towards the end of 1944.

George Learad...

I was born in Sheffield near Arundel Street at Court nine, House nine on the ninth of the ninth, 1919. When the war broke out, I moved up to Parsons Cross and got together with a few of my mates up there and we all decided to join up. Walt Neil joined up with me but he was later transferred to the 50th Division and was killed in Normandy. Bill Coe was another and he finished up as a mortar platoon officer. Syd Nowell and I joined up together at Endcliffe Hall and we also finished up there at the end of the war. We were exempt from army service as we were both in a factory making aircraft parts but we decided to join in May, 1939, before we were called for Militia Service. We started off in the 6th Bn. but they transferred us to the Hallams and went to the summer camp in the Isle of Man. The war was just starting then so when we got back to Sheffield we never got back home so to speak. We went straight into barracks at Endcliffe and slept on the floor!

A great deal of additional training was required prior to summer camp due to the influx of many new recruits. This was achieved by having as many as four drill nights per week in addition to range firing and weekend camps at Totley, all of which were very well attended.

In the July issue of the Regimental Journal 'Tiger & Rose', it was reported that the Commanding Officer, Adjutant and Quartermaster, together with their opposite numbers in the recently raised duplicate 6th Battalion, went to the Isle of Man on Friday, 23 June, for a preview of Bibaloe Camp. It was noted that a certain member of the party spent most of the train journey to Liverpool preparing himself for a rough crossing of the Irish Sea. He had armed himself with various types of sea sickness remedies, amongst them being such simple cures as parsley and newspaper! No light can be shed on the origins or potency of this curious concoction but on arrival at Liverpool, it was found that such preparations were wasted as the sea turned out to be perfectly calm. Bibaloe Camp was situated about two and a half miles from Douglas and was on the main road with a good bus service to the town. It therefore presented no problems for anyone who wanted to enjoy the pleasures of local civilization.

Prior to the Annual Camp, July had been a very wet and busy month. A Divisional Exercise was held on the 8th and 9th during which the 146th Brigade (of which the Hallams were a part) was temporarily commanded by the O.C. Hallams, Lt. Col. C. G. Robins and the Battalion itself, by Major W. M. Dixon. The Annual Weapons Training Course was completed by the 15th and the standard of firing and Bren Gun handling was reported as being extremely good. The Officers Annual Shoot was held at Totley on Sunday, the 16th, where the competition for Officers Cup was won by Major John Hunt and the Visitors Spoon by Major J. Derby. Mrs. Holmes and Mrs. Marshall tied for first place

R.S.M. Harold Marshall takes Roll Call at Midland Station, Sheffield, prior to the men boarding the train for Summer Camp, 1939. The Sgt. looking towards the camera is George Linley. Apart from the side caps, the uniform pattern is still the same as that worn by their predecessors when they marched to war in 1914. (YLRM)

in the Ladies Shoot. Overall, the weather won the day when conditions deteriorated and rain prevented any firing from the 500 yards range positions. There were, however, sufficient gaps in the weather to allow some visitors to fire the Bren Gun and others to have rides on the tracked carriers. Promotions were announced in Sergeants Mess Notes as follows : To Sergeant : L/Sgts. G. H. Elwood, T. F. Bridges, G. W. Stocks, Cpls. G. W. Steel and L. H. Codd. To Paid Lance Sergeants : Cpls. H. Moore, A. W. Green, J. W. Brown, E. Braham, A. Boucher, F. K. Horner and G. E. Major.

'C' Company was chosen to be inspected by Col. G.E. Branson (Honorary Colonel) just prior to the whole Battalion, with a strength of 31 Officers and 600 Other Ranks, leaving Midland Station, Sheffield at 8.30am on the 13 August. Upon arrival at the Heysham ferry port around lunch time, they were delayed for nearly three hours before being finally embarked on the S.S. 'Tynwald' at 3pm, bound for Douglas on a flat calm Irish Sea. The newly formed 6th Battalion was also on board sporting the equally new (to Territorials) battle dress uniform which must have upset some of the Hallams 'old sweats', most of whom were still wearing tunics of the pattern used in the Great War. Any ill feeling may have been moderated, however, as they all relaxed on deck for the crossing and were serenaded by the excellent Band of the Hallamshire Battalion, conducted by Capt. H.L.Cole.

The Regimental Journal 'Tiger & Rose', ceased publication for the duration with the August issue which was a mixture of bright and gloomy news in the Hallamshire section. It contained an extract from the 'Isle of Man Weekly News' headed 'Hallamshire Territorials Defeated - By Fog' which is the only written evidence of the Summer Camp which has so far come to light...

Three hundred and fifty officers and men of the Hallamshires, one of the Territorial battalions encamped at Bibaloe, had to acknowledge themselves defeated on Thursday when, after waiting at the Edward Pier in their 'troopships' for the fog to lift, the assault on Ronaldsway airport, which necessitated a sea voyage to Derbyhaven, had to be abandoned.

But the Hallamshires, under Col. C. G. Robins, rose to the occasion, and at about 7 a.m. the Harbour Board's barge 'Sirdar' and their dredger 'Mannin', laden with troops, together with the diving boat, landed men on the Tongue and on the south side of the harbour for an assault on the 'enemy' petrol depots at these points. These were captured and the railway station was 'blown up'. At the Tongue, where the 'Sirdar' went, the troops quickly occupied strategic points in the neighbourhood. The approaches to the Douglas Stone Bridge were all guarded. Men with fixed bayonets, others with Bren and Lewis guns, a detachment with the new three-inch mortar and a range-finder, were ready for any eventuality.

At the other objective near the Douglas Swing Bridge, much the same thing was happening. Men guarded the Swing Bridge and others were posted at the steps leading to Douglas Head, where there was concentrated the main body of troops entrusted with the task of capturing the petrol depot and other vital objectives in the neighbourhood.

Officers and men buzzed about in the fog in the baby Army cars and Douglas might have been mistaken for a town in a war zone. Army trucks and 'commandeered' civilian lorries were drawn up on the quayside. Officers consulted their maps to get their bearings and it all looked very much like the real thing, even down to the stretcher-bearer parties.

Major J. Hunt had charge of 'A' and 'B' Companies on the Tongue, and Major W. M. Dixon was in command of 'C' and 'D' Companies which proceeded to Douglas Head and captured the railway station and the Douglas Head Hotel in the course of their operations. These were almost successful and came as quite a surprise to the 'enemy' who had only a few armoured vehicles which, in one or two cases, caused considerable consternation at Battalion Headquarters. The excellent arrangements made by the Harbour Board were very much appreciated by Col. Robins, his officers and all ranks.

Note : The baby Army cars mentioned above were almost certainly Light Utilities such as the 10 Horse Power Austin which was to become known affectionately as the 'Tilly'. In theory anyway, each of the Company Commanders were issued with one these, directly replacing the 'charger' which had been the previous mount of officers at this rank. The horse, as far as the infantry was concerned, was now becoming a thing of the past except perhaps on some very special occasions. There must have been mixed feelings among those officers concerned, at having to exchange living flesh for metal boxes on wheels, and who now found themselves sat astride these new steeds, each with the power of ten horses!

The operations lasted until about 9 a.m., after which the men went back to camp after a very tiring morning. They had been roused at 3 a.m. and left the camp about half an hour later, getting to the Edward Pier about 4.30 a.m. At that time, the fog was just beginning to settle in and there never afterwards seemed any prospect of the trip at Derbyhaven taking place. At 6.30 a.m. the planned operations were definitely cancelled by Col. Robins and the minor attacks were substituted. Many people in Douglas that morning thought the international crisis had taken a more serious turn overnight. Visitors in the boarding houses saw the men in full battle order marching along the promenade about 4 a.m. with lights carried in front and behind the troops. A rumour quickly spread that they were embarking for England.

The major scheme, the assault on the airport at Ronaldsway, was probably unique in the history of the Territorial Army. The men were supposed to leave Douglas at 5 a.m. and the attack was timed to begin at 6.30 a.m. Defending troops were being rushed there by road in lorries. The Harbour Board had erected a temporary landing stage at Derbyhaven, and altogether had gone to a great deal of trouble in their co-operation with the Hallamshires.

A rebellion was supposed to have broken out on the island, the rebels wishing to break away from the British Empire. To the Hallamshires was entrusted the task of quelling it and, as the airport was in the hands of the rebels, that was a very important objective. Orders were to seize it and destroy all planes. The fog altered all that, but at least the men got some experience of embarking and disembarking, even if they didn't go very far to do it.

At this point it might be in order to stray from the narrative a little so as to introduce another man among many who were not soldiers at the beginning of the war but who were nevertheless destined to become drawn into it.

Arthur Green wearing a pre- battledress Tunic with brass buttons and the Tiger and Rose collar dogs of The York & Lancaster Regiment. He also wears the Field Service cap and a lanyard.(Mr. Arthur Green)

Arthur Green was living with his parents in Sheffield in 1939 but, by sheer coincidence, was on holiday in the Isle of Man during the same period as the Hallams Summer Camp although he was not aware of it at the time. At the outbreak of war the Hallamshire Battalion, being a Territorial unit, was seldom up to full strength and made up of part time volunteer soldiers who had normal civilian jobs. However, its numbers were soon to be increased by people like Arthur who was about to be 'called up' or 'conscripted' as it is better known today.

Arthur Green...

I was working in the metallurgical department of Daniel Doncasters, Sheffield, when I was called up. My Mother and Father had a fish and chip shop in the city. We only lived five minutes walk from the Somme Barracks on Glossop Road where I was given a medical examination but eventually received orders to report to The York and Lancaster Regimental Depot at Pontefract Barracks.

I got a railway warrant and travelled from Sheffield Victoria Railway Station. There were numerous others on the platform and I got talking to one lad called Anderson (Andy) from Attercliffe and we stuck together for the day. We were given Army Numbers and had stew for dinner and I always remember being issued with various clothing. Size six boots I took and this Andy was only a couple of inches taller than me and he asked for size ten! I couldn't believe it and looked at him gone out. I said, 'You never take a size ten', and he said, 'Yes', and he had a size ten. I thought, 'He's going sailing in them damn things, he's not going to war'. I thought, 'He'll never get round barrack square with them things on', you know!

Just inside the gates of the barracks there was a tower and in it was the Armoury. We went in there and they issued us all with a rifle and I've never seen so much grease on a rifle in all my life. We had to clean these for a parade the next day and they were 1914 -1918 rifles, the old S.M.L.E. (Short, Magazine, Lee Enfield). Anyway the Sgt. (possibly Wallace) came in when we were cleaning these things. There were two lads in our billet who were wanting to be Dispatch Riders and were real enthusiastic about it. The Sgt. asked if anyone could ride a motorbike and these two lads jumped up and nearly went through the roof. The Sgt. produced a bayonet and scabbard from behind his back, thick with grease, and gave them each a piece. 'I want that scabbard in the morning so as you can see your face in it and I don't want to see a speck of grease or dust on the bayonet!' They were on till 'lights out' cleaning the damn things, which was all as a result of being able to ride a motorbike!

Sgt. Wallace was a regular soldier recently returned from overseas living in Pontefract with his wife and children and on Saturday mornings, when I should have been on parade, he would tell me to go to the Company Stores and collect a bicycle and go for his rations. He used to say, 'When you've picked up the rations, I want you to go to this address and I don't want to see you back here while dinner time after the parade is over.'

After six weeks training, I was put into driver training at Pontefract Racecourse where there was snow on the ground and no heating in the Totes where we were billeted. They'd boarded all the little betting windows up and there were rats running all over you during the night. Anyhow, we finished our training there and passed out as drivers in civilian cars and then transferred to the Hallamshire Battalion at Thirsk.

This is just one example of how some conscripted men would eventually find their way into the Hallams, not all of them necessarily doing their initial training with the Parent Regiment as in Arthur's case. As the war progressed, reinforcements were taken in various numbers from many different sources to the point where, in August, 1944, a whole Company was transferred to the Hallams (from the South Staffordshire Regiment) to make up for losses in Normandy.

Meanwhile...
The Battalion sailed from Douglas at 9am on 27 August in the S.S.'Manxman' and upon return to Sheffield was almost immediately mobilized. Everyone became so busy that their annual camp in that summer of thirtynine soon faded from the mind, even though most had enjoyed their short stay on the Isle of Man. Col. Robins reflected that the great open spaces of the camp had

Hallamshire swords were drawn very shortly after the outbreak of war but on this occasion without aggression when the newly married David and Mary Lockwood walked from St. Peter's Church, Hope. At the reception, they were toasted by fellow officers including : Phil Young, Chris Somers, Stephen Bartolome, Douglas Bell, Joe Beckett, Charles Strong, Derek Webster and others. The Battalion band played medleys throughout the day, very ably conducted by the bandmaster and also by the bride.(DEL)

been a very healthy exercise for all and, judging from a number of quick reconnaissances to the sea front, few khaki clad figures appeared there after the first night without a female companion. The weather had been so hot that shirt sleeves were the order on many occasions, the sun being so intense during the first few days that some men began to suffer from sunburn and swollen faces. The new Field Service forage cap gave little protection from the sun, which added to the discomfort and noticeably so for those inclined to baldness. Lt. Col. George Robins concluded his last report in the 'Tiger & Rose' with the following words... *May I, in conclusion, say that when the great hour comes I feel assured that both Battalions will worthily uphold the great traditions of The York and Lancaster Regiment, and they will not be found wanting in any way.*

A happier event reported in the last issue was the marriage, on 6 September, of Capt. David Eadon Lockwood to Miss Mary Eliot Roberts at Hope, Derbyshire. Later, on the lawn of 'Brookdean', Thornhill, Bamford (home of the bride's parents), the Battalion Band, under the leadership of Capt. H. L. Cole (and partly the new Mrs. Lockwood!), played a number of tunes during the Reception. All but two of the Officers attended, the latter remaining on duty at Endcliffe Hall having presumably drawn the short straws.

In conclusion, the article stated... *The bridegroom and best man, Capt. R. W. West, needless to say, wore uniform and carried their gas masks slung over their shoulders, strictly in accordance with the orders issued...   ...in the far distant future, when the bridegroom sits in his easy chair talking of 'those were the days', this item may grow into one of importance as marking something strange and novel.*

Almost five years later, the Battalion was to find itself on the outskirts of a once quiet little village to the southeast of Bayeux in Normandy. As in the Isle of Man exercise during the annual summer camp, a thick fog would pervade the scene, but would now be the prelude to a real battle. It would culminate in the full justification of Col. Robins words about upholding Regimental Traditions. Many casualties were to be sustained on that day, one of

12

which would deprive a certain young officer of his *far distant future'* and those pleasant armchair thoughts of bygone days.

A Message Form dated 1st September from 146th Brigade H.Q. to Hallams simply reads 'Mobilize'. Another of the same date and in reply states 'Mobilize Received'. The time on both documents is given as 16.10 hrs. With the order to Mobilize, came instructions for the first 28 day programme of activities for the Battalion. It was calculated that a total of 156 hours per man were available during this period for all types of work and training and it gave a breakdown of just how many hours should be expended on each task. These included 20 hours each of Weapons Training and Section/Platoon Training, 14 hours each of Route Marches, Fieldcraft and Company Training, 8 hours each of Trench Digging and Drill. The rest was made up of Kit Inspections (6 hrs), Lectures (4 hrs), Physical Training (6 hrs), First Aid (1 hr), Church Parades (4 hrs) and last but by no means least, Gas Training (2 hrs).

A more detailed programme of work for week-ending the 9 September, 1939, contains the ominous instruction:-
1) Gas Chamber will be allotted to Coys. for 1 hour each during Thursday and Friday. Position of the Gas Chamber will be notified later.

In the absence of any contemporary description of this particular piece of training from any of the Hallamshire veterans, the author can shed ample light on the detail of having been placed in a gas chamber during military service training in the post war period, an experience that will never be forgotten...

Gas Training was little different then (1939) to that which stands out in the memory of the author when based at R.A.F. Padgate, Lancashire, in 1956. The 'lead up' to being sent into a Gas Chamber (that part of the training to help you know what to expect in a real gas attack) filled everyone with dread and was almost more terrifying than the actual 'gassing' because of the frightening rumours about it, spread with relish by those who had already experienced it. When the time came we were led into a sealed concrete block house and locked into a dank, dimly lit room accompanied by a tough old Sergeant. We were then made to stand in a big circle in the middle of which was set what looked like a Bunsen Burner under a small tripod which held a tin lid. We had each been issued with a gasmask and told to obey the order of command as to its use. It should be remembered that although we were only recently recruited, we were already extremely well disciplined and had a genuine fear and respect for superior rank. When we were ordered to do something - we did it!

The Sgt. then placed a substance on the hot tin lid which almost immediately gave off fumes that spread quickly throughout the room and affected the eyes, nose and lungs. The Sgt. shouted, 'Gas! Gas! Gas!' which was our cue to put on the gasmasks, but when the gas fumes got to their most pungent we were given the order to remove the masks! Then we were bullied into running around in the circle, singing the chorus of one of the current top ten tunes of the day - Davy Crocket, for which everyone at that time knew the words! This we did, but things were not going too well as the gas was causing eyes and noses to stream, not to mention the panic beginning to well up in our minds as lungs struggled for fresh air which was now almost totally absent. The words to Davy Crocket began to turn into sounds of panic which could only be described as something akin to cattle bellowing in fear and terror.

At last, double doors were flung open and somewhere in the region of 30 youths aged between 18 and 20 years attempted to exit at exactly the same moment in time. This was no orderly old time English bus queue, but a nasty cattle stampede in the best of Western Movie traditions. Friendships that had been cemented in recent weeks suddenly lost any significance as a block of humanity passed through the doors, three or four bodies wide and two high! We fell about on the grass outside in brilliant sunshine gasping for clean air to repair heaving lungs, with tears streaming down our faces. The ordeal had come to an end and that bit of training that terrified us all, was over.

A War Office document dated 2nd August, 1939, clarifying the use of forms required when implementing Section 108A of the Army Act was received by Battalion H.Q. This Section laid down the rules governing the requisition of Billeting. It was not long before the Commanding Officer found it necessary to exercise this authority. On the 1st September, Lt. Col. Robins informed the Chief Education Officer, Mr. H. S. Newton at Leopold Street, Sheffield, that two buildings were to be annexed. These were Nether Green Council School on Fulwood Road and Broomhill Council School on Beech Hill Road. The need for the Broomhill establishment was subsequently cancelled by a letter dated 5th September.

It would seem that some individuals were well informed of the pending need for Billeting requirements. A letter dated 29th August and received by Battalion H.Q. reads... *Dear Sir, Should necessity arise, we would be willing, at short notice, to place this good type guest house with all its facilities at the disposal of the military or public body... etc.* The guest house referred to was 'Ashdell Grove' on Westbourne Road and there is, of course, no reason to suspect this offer as being anything less than a patriotic gesture but it was very well timed. There is no evidence of this accommodation being accepted then or later but the scheme allowed for reimbursement to owners of such requisitioned properties.

One of the intriguing aspects of any World War Two study, is the amazing attention to detail that can be found in British Army documents such as Operational Orders, etc. This statement will no doubt incite laughter in many of those who were ever subject to the demands of such documents. The blunders which occurred at the most crucial times cannot be denied but it was seldom for the want of well planned, timed and detailed instructions on paper even though these would, in many instances, be allowing for the inevitable casualties. The slow turning wheels of a peacetime unit of the Territorial Army now geared itself to the needs of war in terms of the trickle of paper orders which would soon lead, on a national scale, to the demise of whole forests.

New Code Words were introduced and a £5 Embodiment Gratuity ceased to be paid for Commissions or Enlistments taking place after midnight on the 23 August. Voluntary Service was now no longer a real option so there was little need for the War Office to offer cash incentives. Even before the Battalion returned, a number of Key Personnel were 'called up' for service at Brigade and Divisional level. All of these men proceeded on the 9am. ferry from Douglas to Liverpool on 25 August where they continued their respective journeys by train to report at their places of duty. These movements were as follows... *To proceed to HQ. 146th Brigade, Doncaster. Capt. J. R. Daykin; Ptes. 4744683 A. Downs (Batman), 4746078 B. Hartley (Batman), 4746332 C. B. Hand (Driver, I.C.) and 4746329 F. Priest (Orderly for Signals Section). To proceed to HQ. 49th Division, York. 4742940 Sgt. C. Attwood (to assume acting rank of C.Q.M.S.), 4744734 Cpl. W. Bradford (Clerk) and 4537611 Pte. C. I. Daine (Batman).*

Another man from the Yorkshire area was soon to become acquainted with the Hallamshire Battalion at around this time. Arnold Whiteley, a man who lived in the Huddersfield area, had already had his newly married life disturbed when his 'call up' papers dropped through the letter box.

Arnold Whiteley...
I was first to report to the Drill Hall in Huddersfield for a medical and were rather pleased to come out A1, not realizing what it was going to lead to afterwards. The Interviewing Officer asked me what unit I preferred to join and I said, 'The Black Watch', as that was the only previous family connection with the army that I knew of.

However, he received orders to report to Pontefract Barracks in July for six months training. On arrival he was given the choice of two queues to line up in and these were either the King's Own Yorkshire Light Infantry (KOYLI) or The York and Lancaster Regiment (YLR). Arnold hesitated.

Arnold Whiteley...
There were Officers and R.S.Ms. waiting to greet us and I stood there with my leather case so one of them said, 'Come here laddie. What are you in?', and I said, 'Black Watch!' He looked at my papers and told me to join the York and Lancaster queue. So that were the last free words spoken and we were then kitted out. It wasn't a hard regime and we were soon made really fit as they marched and drilled us all over the place. We had one or two characters, the odd one who couldn't keep in step or another who always cut himself shaving and looked as though he had been in a battle.

We'd been on a church parade on 3rd September and got back to barracks to be informed that Mr. Chamberlain had announced that we were in a state of war with Germany, so then we knew that our six months training was going to be somewhat extended.

In late September, myself and others were taken to Endcliffe Hall at Sheffield to bring the Hallamshire Bn. up to fighting strength. Well, there was a lot of friction before we integrated with them. We thought we'd been through the Regular Army drill and better soldiers and of course, they were more like a family unit with a great band that they were very proud of. Anyway, friendships were struck up after a while even though there was a bit of a language barrier between the people of West Yorkshire and South Yorkshire. South Yorkshire was 'Na' then thee!' and West Yorkshire was 'We're t' goin' t'neet!' and things like that but eventually, unity prevailed. Most of the officers were business men from Sheffield and it was an outlet for their energies. In the end, they turned out to be exceptional and extremely good officers. The Commanding Officer then was Colonel Robins, a fatherly figure and rather a nice man.

Les Sewell wears the curious combination of a 1937 pattern battle dress and a 1908 pattern webbing belt. No doubt the early issue of battle dress was down to the fact that he had been initially recruited into the 6th Battalion.(Mr. Les Sewell)

Leading up to this period, Les Sewell of Intake, Sheffield, a Lithographic Printer with Greenup & Thompson, attempted to join as a volunteer in the Barrage Balloon Service along with his brother.

15

Les Sewell...

...we rather fancied joining the Barrage Balloon Service of the R.A.F. as there was an airfield quite close to us at Norton, so we all queued up one day at a recruiting office in Attercliffe to join. When it got to my turn, I was asked what I did for a living and it was decided that I was in a reserved occupation and could not be accepted so off I went. I sort of felt that I had done the dirty on my brother because he was accepted, so when I saw posters for recruitment into the Hallamshire Battalion I applied, went for an interview at Normanton Springs and was later given a medical examination. The Doctor said, 'cough' and I was in! A day or two later I was officially 'sworn in' with a few others by a Major Marsh at the little village school at Normanton Springs.

Les had initially joined the newly formed 6th (Duplicate) Battalion which was also recruited in many places outside of Sheffield including Wath, Bolton on Dearne, Ecclesfield, Dinnington and other places. At the outbreak of war, however, these contingents were congregated at a big school in Woodhouse. A number of these men, including Les, were subsequently transferred from this Battalion to Endcliffe Hall, where they became part of the Hallamshire Battalion.

Les Sewell...

We lined up on the parade ground in front of R.S.M. Burns and he was a bit frightening to some of us. We were told that we could be in whichever Company we wanted and I ended up in 14 Platoon, 'C' Company, which was commanded by Captain Lockwood as he was then. The Platoon Commander was Lt. Somers.

We were sent to High Green School where 'C' and 'D' Companies were based and billeted in a classroom along with others, some of whom had been posted in from basic training at Pontefract. So, our platoon was made up of ex 6th Bn.(Territorial Volunteers) and so called Militia Boys (conscripts from Pontefract). Our Section Commander was Cpl. Powell. Then there was Andrew Machin and his pal Ernest Whyatt. There was Frank Smith who became a Bugler. He worked in the Sheffield Gardens Department before the war and after it he and his wife fostered many children.

In October, the 49th Division received orders to concentrate for training in the Yorkshire Wolds and it was on the cards for the Hallamshires to move to Thirsk Racecourse for that purpose. On the day before the move was to take place, the Battalion was required for duties in an anti-invasion role and was transported to Louth in such transport as was available.

Les Sewell...

We went by buses to Louth for a week on Coastal Defence and we were billeted in a skating rink. During the week we were there, we played an R.A.F. team at football on one of their airfields. Of course we all had to go, if not to play, then to support! It was quite cold at this time and we were issued with some very large long-johns. Two lads, who were very small, one called Arthur Warren and the other who was a bit deformed (should never have been in the army) started dashing about and performing wearing only these long-johns and it was so funny, very funny! Anyway, we were soon relieved by the Northumberland Hussars (they had motorbikes!) and off we went to Thirsk.

Another Sheffielder, Wilf Fisher, also remembers being transported to Louth but his journey was not quite so luxurious as that of Les Sewell.

Wilf Fisher...

We left in open coal lorries at night from Nether Green School, the worst journey I've ever had, to Louth Skating Rink. Believe me, when we got there, I thought I were going to die on that lorry in the middle of the night, no sides on it - nothing. We were there for a couple of days but on the second night there we were called out to go down to the estuary at Hull as there'd been word that parachutists had dropped. So we went out on this and it was absolutely farcical, wading about in this water and reeds and we hadn't a clue what we was looking for. We came back because it was all a false alarm, evidently.

Arnold Whiteley...
Then we moved to Louth and the convoy was very slow as they hadn't yet got it down to a fine art and it took us quite some time to get there in the night. There was a huge warehouse with a concrete floor (skating rink) and it wasn't very pleasant but we were only there for a day or two. It was here that we first made a complaint about food. We'd been travelling and they hadn't been able to get things organized and all we had was a packet of army biscuits, a piece of butter, a mug of tea and a tin of sardines between four or five men, you see.

An old soldier in our party said, 'We're not having this for a carry on!' So, we complained and they sent for the Orderly Sergeant and we told him that we were not having it. Then the Orderly Officer came with his King's Regulations and read the bit about tea in the army not being of a necessity but a privilege. Then one of the lads without thinking said, 'This is a F...... sacrilege! never mind a privilege.' Needless to say, it didn't alter matters and I swore that I would never complain again about food.

Theoretically, a War Diary should have been raised, and probably was, by the Battalion from the moment of Mobilization on the 1 September. However, the Public Record Office at Kew, Richmond, Surrey, does not seem to have any evidence of one for the period up to the end of 1939. War Diaries held on deposit there, begin 6 January, 1940, as far as the Hallams are concerned. The events for the closing months of the year are therefore very patchy especially in

Officers at Thirsk. Front Row : Mumby, West, Hunt, Strong, Robins (O.C.), J.Marsh, Lockwood, Dimmock, Dobson. Row 2 : Newton, Palmer, Brown (RAMC), Beckett, Murray-Smith, Cave, Wells (RAMC), Blake, Bell. Row 3 : Turrell, Slack, Randall, Moorwood, Somers, Firth, Longridge, Sandford. Back Row: Young, Lonsdale-Cooper, Morris, Bartoleme, Good, Jenkinson, Willis-Dixon, Ridley. (YLRM)

the absence of the 'Tiger & Rose' which, it will be remembered, had been suspended for the duration after the August issue.

ROLL OF OFFICERS ON EMBODIMENT

Hon. Col. G.E. Branson. V.D.
Lt. Colonel C.G. Robins. O.C.
Major W.M. Dixon. 2 i/c
Major C.C. Strong. Adjutant.
Major J.P. Hunt.
Captain D.E. Lookwood.
Captain H.J.W. Marsh.
Captain K.W. West.
Captain R. Mumby.
Captain J.P. Dobson. Q.M.
Lieut. J.T. Rankin.
Lieut. R.I. Slater.
Lieut. D.C. Beckett.
Lieut. P.W. Marsh.
Lieut. D.B. Webster.

2/Lieut. P.S. Newton.
2/Lieut. D.R. Morris.
2/Lieut. J. Firth.
2/Lieut. P.M. Young.
2/Lieut. W.G. Blake.
2/Lieut. J.F. Martin de Bartolome.
2/Lieut. M.B. Elliott.
2/Lieut. W.L. Cave.
2/Lieut. D.R. Bell.
2/Lieut. L.M. Lonsdale-Cooper.
2/Lieut. C.R.S. Sandford.
2/Lieut. C.A.B. Slack.
2/Lieut. R.N. Longridge.
2/Lieut. A.C. Somers.
2/Lieut. S.J.D. Moorwood.
2/Lieut. S. Martin de Bartolome.

Capt. David Eadon Lockwood. 1938.(DEL)

On the 15 October, 1939, Capt. David Eadon Lockwood wrote a letter to his wife from the Royal Station Hotel at York, where he was attending a training course. His wife, Mary, has treasured all of his letters to the present day and has very graciously allowed the author to use this and extracts from many of the others which provide a testament to the nature and feelings of just one man among many thousands who were sucked into the awful conflict that was now brewing. From the many letters he wrote to her during the war it would seem that he seldom missed the chance to be with her at home or make some provision for her to visit or stay with him wherever the Battalion was based. Here, he was making arrangements for them to spend a weekend together in York, where he was attending lectures, as he could not get home. His words hint at the Battalion's imminent move to Thirsk which would eventually take place in early November.

David Lockwood (Letters to Mary)
Just a quick one to say how I'm longing to have you with me here. It's a comfy bed and the food's good and although the bedroom's not large its got a lovely view over the garden with the Minster in the background - I swapped it for a bigger room with no view at all. Dawn will be there to meet you at 5.38 and we shouldn't be working long after that. Three lectures this morning and all four of us going to Thirsk this afternoon for a look round.

Les Sewell...
For a few days we were under the stands - a horrible place! Damp and cold but we had bed boards to lie on. However, the following weekend was Armistice and there were races on so they sent most of us home out of the way for a long weekend. We had a training area and I rather enjoyed it there because it was such nice country.

18

What I do remember, and I've pointed it out to my children and grandchildren many times since, when we've been past that way, was that 14 Platoon actually captured the White Horse of Kilburn! There's a white horse cut in the hillside there that you can see from miles around and we had the job of capturing that during an exercise. Often, at weekends, I used to walk for miles around that countryside because it was so nice. Through the little village of Kilburn (which later became famous for the oak furniture maker 'Mouse' Thompson, so called because of his practice of carving a mouse on all his produce) and another village where the author of 'Tristram Shandy' Lawrence Sterne, had lived.

It will be remembered that Arthur Green was posted to the Hallamshire Battalion from basic training and driver instruction at Pontefract Racecourse.

Arthur Green...
When we got to Thirsk they had no army vehicles there either. They had all sorts of civilian vehicles, ice cream wagons, coal lorries, bakery vans, all commandeered vehicles in a great big field.

Anyhow, when we arrived we were sent on a three-quarter mile walk from the entrance to the racecourse with our kit bags and finished up at the stables where we were billeted! There were two, two-teared bunks in each stable that normally housed one horse! Stone floors, whitewashed walls and one stove in each and my god you needed it. There was a space of about four inches between the roof and the wall for ventilation.

The next day I had inoculations and it knocked me out completely. You were excused duties after it for 24 hours and I think I was in bed for three days and daren't move. Cpl. Oakley, as he was then, kept me alive by fetching me grub, cups of tea and what have you. He kept me alive. My arm was like a pumpkin and I wouldn't allow anybody near me for about three days!

There wasn't much to do for the first few days there, except to get your meals and cleaning your stable out and then eventually we got some military vehicles, Morris and Bedford 15 cwts. Anyway, Cpl. Oakley took me out one day in a Bedford and said, 'Come on, I'll take you for your test!' I said that I'd already passed out at Pontefract and he said, 'I'll pass you out!' So we had a nice ride round on a lovely sunny day and I thought - 'this is the life.' He took me to the nearby Sutton Bank, about one in four gradient, and made me pull up and I jammed the hand brake on to hold it. He took out a Captain Webb matchbox and put it under the back wheel of my truck and said, 'You see the shape of that matchbox Green, if it's not the same shape when you've pulled away from here you've bloody failed!' I gave it all I'd got in first gear and we shot off up that hill like a rocket. Of course there was no traffic about in those days, early 1940.

Wilf Fisher...
I remember most, the route marches. I never had such bad feet in all my life and sometimes my socks were just drenched as though you'd took a knife and cut all my feet and blisters - terrible! But the thing was when you were coming back about a mile or so from the race course, the band and drums used to come and meet us and it's amazing the effect it had on you. You used to get new life from somewhere just as though you were setting off at the beginning of the day. It's amazing the effect that that music had.

I slept in the ladies toilets in the stands and there was race meetings and during these we were not allowed in there but had to swill it all out afterwards before we could sleep in it again. It used to smell horrible.

'C' COMPANY. (Thirsk) O.C. Capt. David Eadon Lockwood.(DEL)

George Learad...

We slept in the Cocktail Bar at Thirsk and there were two race meetings while we were there. I backed Gordon Richards on 'Maneater' and he won. He rode the same horse the next day and it won again but I wouldn't chance backing it again. We used to sit around the hut with a penny 'Oxo' each to drink because that was all we could afford. Then we'd sing songs together with harmonizing, 'Goldmine in the Sky' and songs like that. That was the way we entertained ourselves because it was a dead and alive hole there. There was nothing much in Thirsk itself either and we didn't even have any cigarettes except what we got in comforts from home and that.

Arnold Whiteley...

We did some very hard training at Thirsk although perhaps as regards weapons we may not have been very expert, we just had rifles and Bren guns, 2 inch Mortars and every day we were out marching and at the end we were all really tough, you know. If we had been harshly treated, then we were able to get our revenge. Up the racecourse itself there were some small stands which had been boarded up at the back to turn them into huts and the Company Stores was in the first one. The Sgt. Major Grant had a coke stove in there and it was a severe winter. We used to cut a sod of

'D' COMPANY. (Thirsk) O.C. Capt. Kenneth W. West. (HFC)

20

turf from the racecourse, walk up on the roof and put it on the chimney. Then we'd go back to our huts and wait for the result. Afterwards they'd come out coughing and choking and kicking the stove shouting, 'Get this bloody stove seen to!' After a while we would go and take the turf off again and they never twigged. They never found out that we were getting us own back.

Jack Haslam, a Wakefield man who did his basic training at Pontefract (Minden Block), joined the Hallams at Thirsk.

Jack Haslam...
They put me in the band, and I was supposed to learn to blow bugle. The lads I was with were all buglers and a few side drummers. They even wanted me to play the big drum but I said, 'No way!' I think we were officially Ack-Ack (Anti - Aircraft) Platoon. We used to have a Bren on a tripod for firing at aircraft. We were in a big wooden hut near the main entrance at Thirsk Racecourse, on the left just inside the gates and it were all mud and duckboards.

Les Sewell...
On one of his Saturday morning billet inspections, Col. Robins stopped at the bedside of a Corporal called Leasily who was an older man and had been a regular soldier. The Col. spoke to him by another name and the man said, 'No Sir, Leasily!' and the Col. said, 'Well you used to be this other name!' which was just one example of the remarkable memory of Col. Robins because it transpired that this man had served in the 2nd Bn. way back under another name. For some reason he had changed his name and was now in the Hallamshires. He wanted to get lost I suppose!

I volunteered and went with a special platoon under a Sgt. Gandy to Ripon for training as anti-tank gunners. We were supposed to train on a French 25mm gun but I never got to see one, it was all theory. However, we did get some practice in company with the Duke of Wellington's Regiment. The gun was an old 2 pounder and set up in a large greenhouse where, at the other end, there was a model Hornby train on lines in a big circle and on one of the wagons was a cardboard tank. On the top of the barrel of our gun was a .22 rifle fitting. We went through the normal loading and firing drill with the 2 pounder using a dummy wooden round, but actually fired a .22 pellet! So if you put a hole in the cardboard tank you knew you were on target.

On 6 January, 1940, Lt. P.W. Marsh, A/CSM G.W. Steel, Sgt. C. Attwood and Cpl. T. Leaper all left the Hallams to be attached to the 1st Battalion of the Regiment (York & Lancaster) for duties as Instructors. The 1st Battalion at this time was a part of the 15th Brigade, 5th Infantry Division, British Expeditionary Force (BEF) in France. Also during this first month, a number of men were either released or discharged to industry. These were by no means the first nor the last to be lost to the Battalion in this way. By the end of January, a grand total of 64 personnel had left the unit by this method since mobilization in August the previous year. A notable arrival on the 16th was that of Capt. N. Murray-Smith who replaced Capt. H. McIntyre as Chaplain to the Hallamshires. These comings and goings are the only occurrences reported in the official War Diary so it would seem that little else of any interest took place during the first few weeks of 1940.

Arnold Whiteley...
We had one truck per Company but the rest were all commandeered civilian transport with tradesmen's names on them and once we went to a church parade at York Minster in a convoy of these here tradesmen's carts and what not. The winter was severe and all the wagons were frozen up until they got some anti-freeze and gradually we got organized and onto a good footing.

There's another thing I should say... The main toilet amenities were down in the racecourse complex and it were a long walk to go down there but there was a small wooden shelter into which they'd put one of these here massive buckets, you see, for a urinal. The lad whose job it was to empty it got fed up so he took a six inch nail and made a few holes int' bottom so it were like a colander. Well, it got so soggy down there that you had to stand about two yards away and try to hit it, yeah!

Our Coy. Cook used to do everything in the same pot. He only needed a set pot and a broom handle and everything went in, you know, even his sweat went in and a bandage once. Well, when you've marched about ten miles up Sutton Bank and been out in the cold and frost, his soup used to be delicious. Yes! he'd been a railway driver before the war!

The War Diary for February is equally sparse in respect of any interesting Battalion activity but this would probably have been denied by the men who were granted their second period of leave since mobilization. Such a release had to be staggered, of course, and the whole of 'D' Coy. were first to go on the 12th for seven days. These were followed by various groupings made up from parts of the rest of the Companies. The last to go, 'A' and 'B' Coys. plus half of HQ. Coy. drew a short straw when their leave was cut short to just four days because of preparations for the Battalion to proceed abroad. Instructions for such a move were received by the C.O. on the 12 February.

Wilf Fisher...
We got ten days embarkation leave and with me being the Coy. Clerk, I was invited by Sgt. Major Harold Marshall to meet with other NCOs at the Westminster Hotel on Sheffield High Street for a drink. Later, as we came out, we were all stood on the pavement (one of the other Sgts. was George Lindley) and who do we see coming down the street but two red caps (Military Police). Now Harold always had his hands in his pockets and you couldn't see the crown on his sleeve. One of these police came right up and said, 'Get your bloody hands out of your pockets!' Then Harold turned round and he looks at them and says, '...and when you speak to me Cpl., stand to bloody attention!' pulling his arms out of his pockets with the crowns on. The Cpl. was very apologetic but still reported the incident which was brought in front of the C.O. when they got back to Thirsk.

During this month also, there were many comings and goings. 2/Lts. G.L. Woolass and L. Bilton joined from Infantry Training Command (ITC Pontefract) on the 10th, and the officers and men who had been attached to the 1st Bn. on Instructor duties returned on the 26th. On the 27th, 2/Lt. M.B. Elliott plus 50 Other Ranks (ORs) awaiting Medical Boards, etc., were transferred to ITC Depot for final disposal although it is thought that this particular officer was either retained by, or returned to, the Hallams at some later date. These losses had already been pre-empted on the 20th when a draft of 100 ORs arrived from the Depot. It is doubtless that most of these would have had very little soldiering experience and may only have completed their basic training plus some trade training in the form of signals, transport, etc. They were now being posted to a unit which was on the brink of being sent abroad to an as yet unknown destination. Anyone with access to the February War Diary may, however, have spotted a clue in the form of a War Office General List officer who became attached to the Hallams on the 26th. His name was 2/Lt. C.J. Jurgensen!

By the end of the month it was found that the Battalion was still 130 ORs short of the number required to bring the unit up to full War Establishment for service abroad. The strength now stood at 34 Officers and 706 ORs with 7 Officers and 21 ORs attached from Technical Units, etc.

Arnold Whiteley...

There was one incident that should go on record although I'm not making fun of anybody, this is a fact. There was one boy who got discharged later and shouldn't have been in the army because he had a throat impediment and a kind of nervous affliction, you see. He'd start with Ah, Ah, Ah, Ah, and then he would try to cover it up by bursting into song!

Well, we had a visit towards the end of us training from the Field Marshal, Lord Milnes or Milner? Our 'A' Coy. formed the Guard of Honour outside the racecourse and we were lined up with the

Hallamshire Bugles. The officer is 2/Lt.R.N. Longridge and Jack Haslam stands on the left of the back row.(Mr. Jack Haslam)

band. The outriders came and then a car with a pennant on the bonnet pulled up in front of us and a very tall officer got out, resplendent in Sam Brown (leather belt and shoulder straps), knee breeches and leggings. The band struck up a slow march and the Field Marshal, a very old man in his seventies, got out and we were called to attention and presented arms. He started to inspect the guard but when he got past 'Whoopsy Doops' as we called him, this here lad couldn't control himself any longer and burst into song! Of course, he was immediately run off to the Guard Room but all was explained later and he wasn't punished for it. The song incidentally was a Bing Crosby number 'When the bbbbbblue of the night meets the gggggggold of the ddday'.......

On the 1st March, the O.C. 146th Brigade, Brigadier C.G. Phillips, D.S.O., M.C., inspected the Battalion and declared himself well pleased with the 'Turn Out' and on the 7th another 120 ORs joined from the Depot at Pontefract which virtually brought the Hallams up to full strength. There now began a series of Movement Orders and subsequent cancellations which must have proved very frustrating to both officers and men in terms of the wasted effort of preparation.

The first instruction received on the 13th was to move for service abroad on the 15th, but this was postponed the next day and the Battalion placed on 24 hours notice of movement readiness but the Movement Order was cancelled altogether on the 16th. It was as though someone in high places with a knowledge of Julius Caesar had avoided any invitation for the Fates to decend on the Hallamshire Battalion on the Ides of March, but fates were being decided much further afield in Finland as will be seen later.

The void left by the cancellation was ably filled on the 16th by what must have been a hastily organized visit and inspection by the Battalion's Honorary Colonel, G.E. Branson V.D., T.D. who had recently been confirmed in that appointment for the duration of the war. Next day an order was received from Brigade HQ. stating that conditions were returned to normal and that all entitled personnel could be granted Easter Leave. This was allocated during the period 19th to 27th of the month.

On the 18th, a letter was received by the C.O. from Colonel Branson. It read...

I must thank you for one of the most cheering days of my life on Saturday. The Honour of receiving that salute on the road from Battalion, practically on its way to war, was to me the Crown of my connection with it. I left with the impression, to use a Naval simile that the Battalion is a 'Happy Ship', a description which comprises efficiency and cheerful working together. I feel very proud of it. I am sure from what I saw yesterday that the men will live up to its old reputation and come back from the war having added substantially to the honours gained by their fathers in the past.

Jack Haslam...
We always used to know if there was something afoot and if we were going to move. Orders used to come around - 'Empty your Palliasses!' Well, we must have emptied our Palliasses about four or five times and then we'd have to organise us kit - Full Marching Order, ready for moving off. Then order would come - 'Go fetch your straw and put your straw back in your Palliasses, its cancelled.' I was in HQ. Company.

Yet another Movement Order was received on the 26th to be in readiness as part of the 49th Division to take over the duties of the 42nd (East Lancashire) Division by the 1st April but these orders were cancelled on the 30th. The next day, instructions were received to prepare for a move abroad and that all personnel on leave or otherwise should be recalled by telegram. It seemed now that the War Office was finally getting to grips with decision making even though situations were still being largely dictated by circumstances beyond its control. The Battalion was about to be cast into a campaign which was to be very poorly provided for in terms of backup, a situation which the men involved were as yet blissfully unaware. However, the Hallamshires were to fair better than most of the other units that were committed, although they would not come away entirely unscathed.

VIKING SPRING

At the outbreak of war, there was sufficient reason for Britain to be troubled by the situation in Norway. This country was still providing what had been a legitimate peacetime rail and sea route by which Germany could receive three quarters of her import requirements of iron ore from Sweden. By late 1939, Norway was seen by Britain as the possible route by which a relief force could go to the aid of a beleaguered Finland which had suffered an unprovoked attack by Russia on 30 November. Plans for such an operation were not finalised until 5 February, when it was already too late for a rescue attempt. Due to these extended delays in decision making, the justification for setting foot on Norwegian soil was lost when, on 13 March, 1940, Finland surrendered to the Russian Army.

Some justification for landing a force in Norway was still needed, however, for the obvious reasons of denying the use of Norwegian ports and landing grounds to the German war machine, should the latter decide to occupy that country. The great difficulty at that time was the question of what kind of reception would be given to a British landing in the prevailing circumstances of no invitation having been received from the Norwegian Government. A secret document of the period went to great pains in laying out the ground rules for behaviour of British troops in the event of any hostile reception.

A decision was made to go into that country by both Britain and Germany at about the same time and in the early stages things went fairly well for the British. The German Navy suffered a bad reverse at Narvik but British efforts further south were ill fated from the start, even though the Norwegian Army welcomed the help offered.

The first objective of 146 Bde. (which included the Hallamshire Battalion) as part of 'Avonforce' was to take Narvik. However, plans were changed on the sea voyage and the force was split, with roughly half of it holding to its original course. The other half with a new codename 'Mauriceforce' which included 146 Bde., sailed south with orders to take Trondheim in a pincer movement by landing 146 Bde. to the north and 148 Bde. to the south of the objective. The former made landings at Namsos and Bangsund and the latter at Aandalsnes.

Things started to go wrong immediately when 148 Bde. was persuaded by the Norwegian Army to come to its direct aid in trying to stem a German push from the South, thus allowing itself to be diverted from the primary objective. For this it suffered heavy casualties but may not have faired any better had it stuck to the original plan. Another British force, the 15th Brigade of the 5th Infantry Division, comprising troops removed from B.E.F. in France and of which the 1st Bn. of the York and Lancaster Regiment was a part, also suffered heavy casualties in this area south of Trondheim. The Hallamshire Bn. was fortunate to be a part of the 146 Bde. northerly pincer and escaped the brunt of the fighting, although it had to dodge a number of attacks from the air, the last of which was to cause the only fatal casualties suffered by the Battalion during the withdrawal from Norwegian waters.

Two, blue backed exercise books (of the type commonly used in schools during the war period) were found in a pile of unregistered documents at Endcliffe Hall. These contain a not always easy to read, hand-written account of the period April - May, 1940, and the introduction reads as follows…

This story was written in September, 1943, three and a half years after the events took place. No official account has yet been published of the Norwegian Campaign and such accounts as have been published by journalists, escaped Norwegians and others have had little bearing on the Hallamshire adventures.

I am writing it to put on record my own memories of what took place, which may help an official historian of the Battalion at a later date. I was Adjutant of the Bn. and saw and knew as much of what was going on as anyone except the Colonel. I have by my side the Bn. War Diary, most of which I wrote myself; dates and times given in that are accurate, any others I give are from memory.

Capt. John Marsh (late 1940 at Krossastadir Camp, Iceland). This officer was more a man of peace than war and very highly respected by all who knew him.(CGR)

Major Harry John Wilson Marsh M.C. (John Marsh to his friends) was the writer and, as Captain and Adjutant of the Bn. at the time of the Norwegian Campaign, perhaps better placed and qualified than anyone to give a broad account of the events which took place as far as the Hallamshire Battalion was concerned. Sadly, he was killed in action on 12 September, 1944, in Italy whilst serving with the 6th Bn. Ironically, he died in the process of accepting the surrender of enemy soldiers who were emerging from a bunker. At that moment, one or more of them changed their mind and opened fire with automatic weapons. These men forfeited the privilege of surrender and died for the life they had so treacherously taken. That life belonged to a man who, by his pleasant nature and from all accounts, truly epitomised the word gentleman in its purest form… a gentle - man.

Over sixty years later and as a tribute to John Marsh, all of what he wrote will form the basis of this chapter unabridged. John used the word 'emity' on two occasions in his original script. This word will not be found in the English dictionary and its meaning has not yet come to light even after consulting a number of 'dyed in the wood' Yorkshiremen from the Sheffield region. It had undoubted meaning for this officer and so has been retained in the text to wet the appetite of any would be sleuth. Given the context in which it is found, it could easily be equated, in both cases, with the word 'exciting' but this is pure guesswork.

Additional material from other eyewitness accounts and later works will be found which merely punctuate the very comprehensive account given by John. Some of the anecdotes related confirm that most of the men who landed with the Hallams knew little or nothing of the odds against them or what was happening beyond their immediate surroundings. This happy state of ignorance was perhaps the key to some of the stories which, on occasion, verge upon the comical but add much flesh to the bone.

The M.S. 'Chrobry' in which the Hallams were embarked for Norway was a Polish vessel that could best be described as a small passenger liner which must have been 'at sea' or otherwise escaped capture when Germany invaded Poland in August, 1939. Still retaining its Polish crew, the vessel was now being used as a Troop Ship and had made crossings of the Atlantic Ocean in this role. This note adds a little background to the ships origins.

Capt. D.C. Beckett (Transport Officer during the Norwegian Campaign) emigrated to Canada after the war and in 1962 found a fascinating newspaper article written by a man called Gregory Clark (a Canadian Infantry veteran of the First World War and a war correspondent in the Second). In December, 1939, Clark sailed from Canada to Britain in a convoy that was escorted by such vessels as the battleships H.M.S. *'Revenge'* and the French *'Dunkerque'*. It was 5pm. on Christmas Eve in a rough sea and Clark was travelling on a ship called 'Chrobry' contemplating what was, in his mind, going to be a pretty miserable Christmas in the middle of the Atlantic Ocean, when he and others were approached by the ships master, Capt. Deschaikowski. He invited them to a traditional Polish Christmas Eve Dinner! *Gregory Clark...*

...later, we went down the corridors, down the stairways, among the crowd of soldiers. Ahead we could hear the din of men in meeting. When we craned our way into the great saloon, there it was - Christmas!

The Poles had gone ashore in Halifax and laid in an enormous stack of fir and spruce, three times life sized Christmas trees that lined the war-bared dining saloon of the ship, hiding its iron bones. The trees were decorated with lights, tinsel, bright coloured objects of every conceivable shape that would shine; tin, brass, clipped metal from the ships stores. The long tables of a troop transport, unlovlier than political picnics, were bright with white cloths, starred with clusters of candles and - Flowers, yes sir!, real flowers in vases...

...it's rather wonderful. These Poles, this ships company, inviting us all for Christmas dinner! They haven't had a word from their homes, their wives, children, for four months. Since September, they have been wandering the sea like pilgrims, like the Flying Dutchman, homeless wherever they go.

The sad part, however, was the fact that some of them would never see their loved ones again nor the ship another Christmas...   ...but for now it was April, 1940, and M.S. *'Chrobry'* was setting off on another voyage from an anchorage off Gourock (Tail of bank) on the Clyde, with the Hallams on board.

A Diary written by Sgt. George H. Linley (a Sheffield man who had served with the Hallams since February, 1921) has an interesting entry for the 10 April. As the *'Chrobry'* moved down the Clyde he had helped with the task of issuing extra kit to the men which was begun just after midnight. It was laid out in the dining saloon where each man received...

1Pr. Rubber Boots, 1Pr. Ankle Boots, 2Prs. Gloves (less trigger finger!), 2Prs. Mittens, 9Prs. Socks, 2Prs. Snowglasses, 2 Sweaters, 1 Pullover, 1 Sheepskin Coat, 1 Sheepskin Cap. This was not a very good omen for some of those on board who were convinced that the Battalion was bound for warmer climes. George noted that he didn't get to bed until 3.30am as the ship steamed on its way to rendezvous with others at Scapa Flow.

During the two day stay at Scapa Flow, someone had the bright idea of lowering the Chrobry's lifeboats in order to exercise the bodies and minds of the troops on board and a 'Grand Regatta' was held in which platoon teams competed with each other. This noisy, wild and hilarious exercise did not go unnoticed by the Divisional Commander, Major General P.J. Mackesy, who sent a signal of congratulations! This officer was a realist and led his men by a simple but practical and effective motto - ' We do what we can! '

At 1230 hrs. on 12 April, the *'Chrobry'* moved out of Scapa Flow to join the *Empress of Australia* (which was carrying other elements of 146th Brigade), *Monarch of Bermuda* and *Reina del*

Pacifico off Cape Wrath. These now made North for open waters in company with other transports and a naval escort. 'Avonforce' was under way…

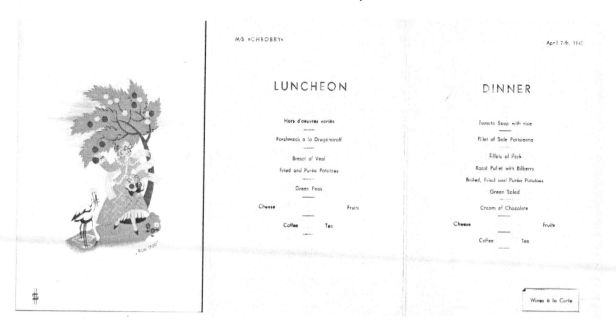

Cover design and menu from the dining saloon of the M.S. 'Chrobry' dated 7 April, 1940. It can be seen that there was no erosion of quality and standards aboard this ship just because there was a war on. Chrobry had been operated by a company called Gdynia - America Shipping Lines, Ltd. at the outbreak of war and must have had a good stock of menu cards (printed in Warsaw) still available. Where else, at this time on the U boat infested high seas, could such mouth-watering delicacies such as 'Roast Pullet with Bilberry' and 'Forshmack a la Dragomiroff' be even imagined - let alone served? (CGR)

John Marsh…
We now had a C in C, Admiral the Earl of Cork and Orrey (Ginger Boyle) in H.M.S. Southampton. In her too, were Major General Mackesy, the Military Force Commander and two companies, Scots Guards, to whom we had transferred some ammunition; also my brother as cipher officer. 'Southampton' was to go ahead to Harstad, north of Narvik to investigate the familiarities of landing there…..with the object of occupying the port and its railway link with the Swedish ore fields. There was believed to be about 3000 Germans around Narvik with transport and six destroyers.

Meanwhile the remainder of the convoy under Commander Hornwell was to rendezvous East of Ando about 69 degrees North by 16 degrees East. Brig. Phillips (O.C. 146 Bde.) had transferred to M.S. 'Batory', taking with him our interpreter Lt. Jurgensen whom we were sorry to lose for personal reasons as well as his services.

The usual ships routine of inspections and so on occupied us and we all started to learn navigation from Capt. Currie. Philip Young, our Intelligence Officer (I.O.) and I spent hours tracing the routes from all our possible ports of disembarkation to Narvik, an endless pastime. On our photostatic maps it was very difficult to tell various roads and contour lines apart. All the roads in that part of the world include ferry crossings and we continually found ourselves following rivers and fjords instead of roads.

The ship had a loudspeaker apparatus and on this I broadcast Orders several times a day, quite one of the features of the voyage I think, and also practiced bugle calls for various eventualities. 'Come to the cookhouse door' would signal an air-raid with other unauthorised uses for familiar calls. *Another diversion was giving the names of the naval vessels which came in sight. These varied from battleships to destroyers and we felt in strong hands.*

13 April was fine and enjoyable. In the morning we heard from the 4th Destroyer Flotilla that they were in Aalesund with no German force nearer than Bergen and Trondheim. We all hoped to have our course altered for Aalesund, but in view of the misfortunes of the 148th Brigade and later the 15th Brigade we were lucky not to do so. In the evening we had several messages giving the progress of the naval battle in which seven German warships were destroyed off Narvik.

A heavy swell in the morning considerably reduced cheerfulness and activity on board. About mid-day we crossed the Arctic Circle. In preparation for this event the Naval C.O. on board and I produced a certificate from Father Neptune which was printed and distributed to all on board. At 1610 hours an enemy submarine was sighted away to starboard and destroyers dropped depth charges. This meant more than the normal changes in course and by this time we had all come to know well the various signals for this manoeuvre.

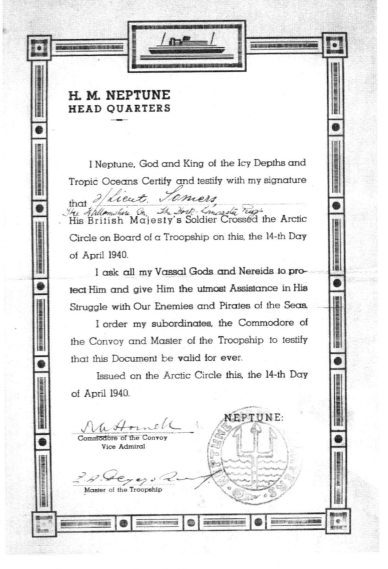

After dinner, which we had very early in accordance with Polish custom, orders were

Arctic Circle 'Crossing' Certificate. (ACS)

received for 'Chrobry' and 'Empress of Australia', with two cruisers and destroyer escorts, to change course from 15 degrees to 190 degrees and proceed to Namsos. No one on board had ever heard of this town but a hurried look at the charts showed its whereabouts. There were no details of its harbour or fjord on the charts but I managed to produce some facts about quays and depths from the W.O. Intelligence Reports.

A signal of explanation came at 0518 hours (15 April) 'To Chrobry, Empress of Australia from C.S.18 (18th Cruiser Squadron). Reduced opposition expected Narvik and securing of Trondheim urgent. 146th Brigade will now be diverted to Namsos area where it comes under command of Major General Carton de Wiart who should arrive Namsos by air early today, Monday. If no orders are received from him, Brigade Commander will endeavour to establish his force ashore as early as possible in Namsos area so as to cover the disembarkation of further Allied troops. Decision regarding locality for landing to be made with senior Naval Officer. Suggest localities (a) Bangsund (b) Namsos. Arrival of transport will be timed as late in the day as possible consistent with safety of navigation and every effort will be made to disembark troops during dark hours using every available craft. Troops will probably transfer to destroyers for this purpose.' Brig. Phillips having been carried on north in M/S 'Batory', Col. Robins assumed command - we had no idea at this time what troops were in the Empress, though it transpired that she had on board the remainder of our own Bde. under Lt. Col. Newton of the Lincolns. At 1000 hours the Col. gave out his orders for the Bn. to land at Namsos in destroyers. Whilst he was doing so a submarine was sighted, a zig zag course adopted, and depth charges dropped. A further diversion was that we were all feeling very sea sick, Young obviously so, whilst the Col. only just held out to the end of his orders. His very handsomely appointed cabin was right in the bows and got the full motion of the boat : full length mirrors in the walls added to ones queasiness. By chance this cabin was distempered a hideous finish, exactly the colour which we had tried some years before on the walls of our ballroom at Endcliffe Hall - a colour which had reminded our then C.O. of a brothel in Algiers - a comparison few of us could verify.

My zeal in overcoming seasickness sufficiently to commit these orders to writing was wasted, however, as at 1400 hours we got a message that 'Chrobry' could proceed up the fjord with a pilot close in to Namsos. Namsos lies some 60 miles inland up the Namsen Fjord. Obviously, however, these enclosed waters would not suit the Empress.

Col. Robins accordingly issued fresh orders. The Hallamshires were to land in boats from the 'Chrobry'. 'A' Coy. on the right and 'B' Coy. on the left leading, followed by Bn. H.Q. and 'C' and 'D' Coys. We had no idea at this time whether Namsos was occupied by the enemy or not and no maps to show the size or shape of the town or nature of the terrain. The Colonel's orders comprised the necessity of effecting a landing even if the leading companies were sunk. The other two Bns. were to follow in destroyers. Just as he finished his orders at 1425 hours when we were mentally braced for a gallant but cold bath, a message was received to alter course to 340 degrees - again almost an about turn. This was expanded by orders to anchor next morning at Lillesfjona in Sjonen Fjord, 66 degrees 14 minutes N. by 13 degrees 0 minutes E.

The morning of the 16 Apr. accordingly found us in a narrow fjord, its sides covered with snow. There was no town near but a few fishermen's huts. This was the 25th anniversary of the Bns. leaving York for France in the Great War - I imagine I was the only person who was present on both these occasions, although my memories of the earlier one are far from clear.

At breakfast time Maj. Gen. Carton De Wiart V.C. arrived in H.M.S. 'Somali' from Namsos. He had arrived there by seaplane the previous day with two or three young officers and found it unoccupied. The navy had then proceeded up the fjord after being heavily attacked from the air and landed 400 Marines at Namsos and 70 at Bangsund.

M. S. 'Chrobry' transfers the Hallamshire Battalion to three 'Tribal' class destroyers for the landings at Namsos and Bangsund. H.M.S. 'Mashona' can be seen alongside taking off the C.O. with 'A' and 'B' Coys. and others. This photo was taken from H.M.S. 'Matabele' which had already taken off 'C' and 'D' Coys. Most of the transport personnel and rear party came across on Chrobry's second trip but did not land. (DEL)

A conference was held in H.M.S. 'Somali' and the Hallamshire Bn. was ordered to transfer to destroyers. This transfer commenced about 1130 hrs, the destroyers coming alongside M/S 'Chrobry'. The C.O., Adjt., 'A' and 'B' Coys. transferred to H.M.S. 'Mashona' ; Bn. H.Q. and H.Q. Coy. to H.M.S. 'Nubian'. We took with us from H.Q. Coy.- the Coy. H.Q. (Comd. Capt. Mumby) Q.M. and staff, Signal Pl. complete, A.A.Pl. complete (2/Lt. Longridge), about 12 drivers and a fighting pl. made up of Carrier Pl. personnel with their bren guns, (2/Lt. Palmer). The rest of this Coy. made up the rear party with the transport, under Capt. Beckett, following us. The 2nd in Command, Maj. Strong, with 'C' and 'D' Coys. to H.M.S. 'Matabele'. In each case, only personal kits, weapons and a proportion of ammunition was taken, the heavier stuff was left in M/S 'Chrobry', Capt. Cave staying on board with a rear party.

Whilst the transfer was taking place, several air attacks developed and hampered things considerably. Each time, the destroyers cast off from alongside to free themselves for action. This was done very quickly and the chain of loaders broken between the 'Chrobry', companionway and destroyer. A certain amount of stuff got lost overboard in this way. I had fun giving the practised bugle calls and other instructions on the loudspeaker.

The last attack before we left was pressed very strongly and bombs fell between 'Chrobry' and 'Empress'. Only the 'Mashona' was still loading : most of the men had transferred but the C.O. and myself, Maj.Hunt (O.C. 'A' Coy.) and his C.Q.M.S. plus some weapons were still on 'Chrobry'. The destroyer captain was unwilling to tie up again and was only persuaded to send a boat because one of his ropes was still attached to the 'Chrobry'. As an act of grace, he allowed four of us including the C.O. to use this to join the Bn.

Meanwhile the other destroyers had set off down the fjord and we followed at high speed. More bombers came over and chased us, diverting their attention to the laggard 'Nubian'. It was very inspiring to watch the handling of the destroyer from the bridge - we waited until the plane was running straight at us and the bombs could be seen released and then heeled sharp over. This manoeuvre was not too easy in the narrow waters of the fjord and within a day or two the German planes resorted to counter it by attacking immediately after one another from different directions. Watching this on the bridge was emity; but for one attack I was in the Ward Room, this was less pleasant - first came the shattering noise from a 4.7 inch gun above our heads - then when we heeled, all the lights went out and everything loose slid down the floor including ourselves.

Les Sewell…
'C' Coy got on the 'Matebele' down two decks out of the way and I didn't like it being bottled up below… …we seemed to be going for a while and we heard action stations and a manhole cover was removed and we could see sailors below, shoving the shells into the hoists, we were right above the magazines and I thought, 'Well, we're all right here if anything hits us.'

John Marsh…
The voyage was picturesque and exciting : we were going at a good speed inside the islands with snow covered mountains on our left and every now and then deep fjords appearing. We passed the mouth of the Namsen Fjord in daylight and then put back just at dusk. As we went up a signal was sent from 'Somali' to 'Matabele' for that part of the Bn. to land at Bangsund whose lorries should be waiting to take them down to Beitstaden road junction. Unfortunately, half way through the signal they turned off right for Bangsund and passed behind an island so never got the part about getting the lorries. We arrived at Namsos about 2000 hours in the dark and put in to the quay in the order 'Mashona', 'Nubian'. The ground down at the harbour was under snow to the depth of about one foot and our first care was not to make new tracks in it. We were met by

31

the Marines from whom we were taking over and who turned out to be from H.M.S. 'Sheffield' - the Hallamshire and Sheffield's officers had exchanged courtesy visits and we had presented a set of tankards to their wardroom when she was commissioned a year or so previously. Under their guidance 'A' Coy. proceeded to take up positions guarding this road bridge on the Namsen river some two miles above the town. 'B' and H.Q. Coys. with Bn. H.Q. moved into the school. There was no blackout and we were for the moment without maps which had been left still on 'Chrobry' when the destroyer put off, but we got an idea of the position by candle light with the aid of a school atlas. The unloading of the destroyer was completed by 2300 hours and most of the night was spent in carting stores, taking care not to leave tracks. The lack of tpt. made this a tedious job.

Jack Haslam...
We had to transfer to a destroyer, H.M.S. 'Nubian', down nets and as we were about to cast off to pull away we were attacked by two German aircraft. I remember the sailors using axes and chopping through ropes to get us away but one of them they couldn't chop so they rived half the ship away.

After landing we were in a school and when we went to the toilet you always had to take a sweeping brush with you so that when you came back you swished the snow over your tracks because they (German aircraft) were always over looking for us.

Most of the transport found in the area had been rendered unusable by the removal of parts. The few that were left could not carry out all the tasks required and frequently came to grief on the treacherous road surfaces. This one is typical of those that were available and is being recovered by men of the R.A.S.T. Troops soon became exhausted through struggling around on foot in very bad conditions.(DEL)

Wilf Fisher landed at Bangsund and remembers the strong smell of pine coming from the timber yard on the dockside. 'C' Coy was disembarked from H.M.S. 'Matabele' and the troops moved away from the docks at once.

Wilf Fisher...
I was walking down this road and I saw this line of vehicles and every one was knocked out. I saw Jack Firth looking at each vehicle, lifting the bonnets and as I walked down he said, 'Ah! Fisher, I'm looking for one with a bloody rotor arm in and there's not one of them got one in.' He did the whole line of vehicles on this road because he was trying to get some transport for us.

I'd been carrying one of these big glass flasks of rum for about three days and when we met up with these French Chasseurs they were absolutely starving, no food and one thing and another, we gave them a case of corned beef and this flask of rum... ...I wasn't very pleased about it.

Les Sewell...
It was dark when we landed at Bangsund and on the right hand side we could see stacked timber so there must have been a sawmill of some kind. There were already Marines there, in blue, waiting for us (H.M.S. 'Sheffield') and they said, 'It's all yours!' We marched to a little village and

32

my section was billeted in one of the houses, all of which were empty. I was with Jack Staniforth, a stretcher bearer/bandsman and we were put on guard on this bridge. Later on, another chap and myself had a walk round these houses and all we came back with was an atlas which was a god send as we had no maps and Major Lockwood made use of it.

I was No.2 on the 2 inch Mortar but we left the ammunition for that on board (M.S. 'Chrobry') so I became No.2 on the Boyes A/T Rifle - 'Ginger' Robinson was No.1. He was a bit of a character, I remember he used to save his rum ration and mix it with his tobacco to make it nice and juicy!

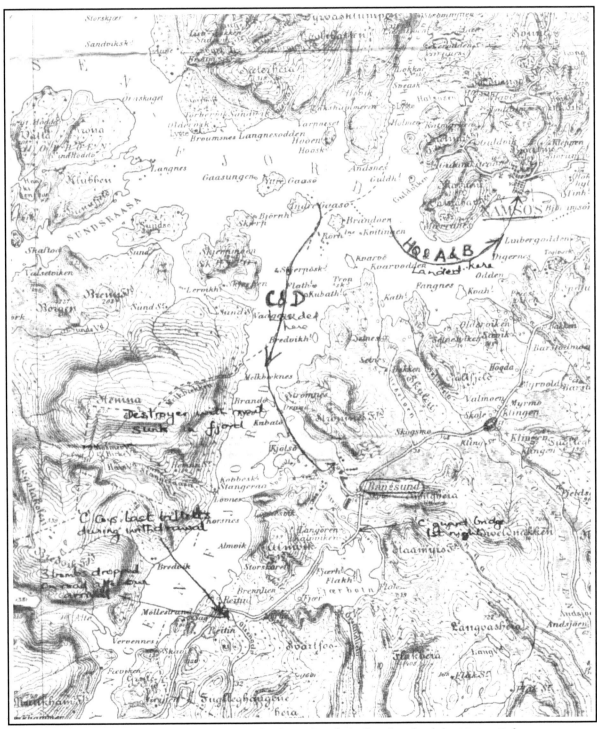

Section of map annotated by Chris Somers, showing the places where the Hallamshires landed in Norway. Reference to :- ['destroyer' with mail sunk in fjord] is thought to be the sloop H.M.S. 'Bittern'. Other notes are ['C' Coys last billets during withdrawal] [3 bombs dropped on road after our arrival] and ['C' guard bridge 1st night]. (ACS)

Meanwhile John Marsh and his contingent had carried on to Namsos.

John Marsh...
Bde.H.Q. (less the Brigadier and B.M. who had been carried on to Harstad) had come up in H.M.S. 'Somali' and established themselves in a house near us. First thing in the morning the Col. and I went round there, previously giving strict orders that nobody was to show themselves in the town in daylight. One chief concern was to keep the knowledge of our landing at Namsos from the Germans as long as possible to gain us a chance to get as many men and as much stores and ammunition ashore as possible before bombing began.

Battalion HQ. at Bangsund. They are from left to right : Lt. Col. C.G. Robins (C.O.), Major C.C. Strong (2i/c), Capt. H.J.W. Marsh (Adjt.), Lt. C. J. Wells (R.A.M.C.), Jack Randall?, Setta (Norwegian Army), Capt. A.P. Currie, Glasgow Highlanders (Intelligence). (CGR)

Peter Heming, the writer and explorer, had landed by air with the General and had woken me up at dawn. At his suggestion we sent a lookout party up to an observatory on a high hill above the town. He went with us to Bde. H.Q. and from there he and I went down for breakfast at the Grand Hotel on the quayside where we found the Naval Officers, who were to form the base, installing themselves. Conversation at breakfast was chiefly about how soon bombing would begin and we all agreed the Grand Hotel would get it first. In point of fact it did and several of the Naval staff, including Capt. Blake R.N., who had become a great friend of us all, were killed.

Amongst other things, Heming had brought up all the white fabrics in the town the previous afternoon, and I took a lot of this off him to use as camouflage. It was he who had met our Bangsund party but he had been unable to lay on the transport to take them inland. Their destroyer had gone on up the fjord in the gloaming at full speed and tied up alongside the quay. Bangsund was a small fishing village perhaps four miles off by sea and fourteen by road to our south.

The Col. got a car and went off to Bangsund. 'C' Coy. had taken over the guarding of the road bridge there from the Marines. 'D' Coy. was now to go forward. This they did the same afternoon in lorries, two pls. with Coy. H.Q. in Steinjaer and one pl. (2/Lt. Lonsdale-Cooper) forward at Vist. These places were both on the railway which made a wide sweep inland before going south to Trondheim and the forward pl. made itself a munitions fort with the help of railway sleepers. Their move was completed by 2300 hours (17 Apr.).

When I got back to the school, I gave a resume of the facilities to the H.Q. Coy. officers and I remember the main point being that the Germans had complete control of the air and control of the sea in the Trondheim Fjord, which was the fact which concerned us. I didn't think I really knew our objective but we all presumed it to be Trondheim. As far as I remember I was completely optimistic although we all realised it would be a struggle but I am afraid my summary of the

34

situation, which may have had a cynical touch or two in it, rather opened the eyes of the others to the difficulties which lay ahead.

The chief of these was the snow, which was about four feet deep as soon as one left the edge of the road. Through this we had one direct road south via Bangsund and Namdalseidet and the road and railway via Grong and Kvam. The two routes met at what became known as ABP junction thirty miles due South as the crow flies but nearly twice that distance even by the direct road. The snow was still crisp and hard, but the roads were already beginning to soften. Trondheim was sixty miles on from Steinkjer, both road and rail running alongside the fjord all the way. Small inlets including the Beitstadfjord were still frozen over but the ice was beginning to melt.

'B' Coy. also marched forward this evening by road, going along the north side of the fjord. Coy. H.Q. and two pls. went to Malme with our pl. forward guarding the station at Follafoss. They were also to guard the crew of a German merchantman stranded in the ice (until it melted) near Inderoan.

After dark, the 'Chrobry' came in again and we got off the ammunition and most of the stores we had left on board. Every care was taken not to give away our presence. A note was made of everything on the quay at the end of the day and exactly the same things were left for the morning German air patrol to see. Patrols were coming over regularly, morning and evening, and occasionally during the day. This took up all the hours of darkness.

This was the last we saw of 'Chrobry', which had been a real home to us. She later went to Harstad and was sunk off Bodo by a bomb which fell in the saloon where our officers had spent so many hours listening to the news (and in other ways). In the meantime she had been up to Namsos again with our own rear party on board.

Next day, 18 April, we again avoided all movement by day. In the evening 'C' Coy., leaving our platoon to continue guarding the Bangsund bridge, went forward to a village at the head of the Beitstad fjord which we called Beitstad or later 'New' Beitstad, although 'Old' Beitstad was shown on the map a couple of miles further south west. The village, like all others, was almost completely deserted, the people having gone to their summer houses in the hills. A few farmers came down each day to look after their houses. We established ourselves in the village hall and a cafe on the road side, with the R.S.M.(A. Burns) comfortably lodged in a coffin in the undertaker's shop opposite. A few air patrols during the day again failed to discover our presence.

The following evening, 19 April, Bn. rear H.Q. moved up with the rest of H.Q. Coy. and all the stores we were likely to want except a small amount of Mortar ammunition. When I say 'moved up' it gives little idea of the complicated process involved. The whole day was spent by Capt. Curry and Setta our interpreter, a Norwegian officer who had met our party at Bangsund and stayed with us giving invaluable help till the last night, telephoning round and procuring lorries. We had brought with us our M.T.O. J. Randall and about 15 drivers, the remainder having stayed behind with all our transport under the Carrier Platoon Comd., Capt. D.C. Beckett, to follow us. They mostly drove the lorries though occasionally the Norwegian drivers helped. Loading and unloading in strange places in the dark and cold were bad enough but driving on unknown roads, very bad with narrow surfaces, with ditches and snow drifts on either side, without lights, had to be seen to be believed. The road surface rapidly broke up under our movement and lorries often had to be manhandled out of holes in the middle of the road.

During these nights the rest of the Brigade, 4th Lincolns and 1/4th KOYLI had followed us ashore and leap frogged us by trains to positions south of Steinkjer. 'D' Coy. accordingly was moved back by road into reserve at Elden, up the road in the hills between Bn. H.Q. and 'C' Coy. at Namdalseid. 'A' Coy. also this night moved forward by trains to Steinkjer. They had not time, however, to load all their stores on the train between dark and its departure and 2/Lt. W.R. Jenkinson with a party was left at Namsos to bring the remainder.

From breakfast time the next morning, 20 April, German bombers in flights of three passed continually overhead, going north and returning south. At first we could hear no sound of bombing and hoped they were going up to Harstad as the British landing there had already been announced on the radio. It gradually became apparent, however, that the target was Namsos and this was confirmed by General Carton De Wiart when he passed through at about 1230 hours. By that time most of the block of the town which lies in a square shape by the side of the fjord had been destroyed. The German planes finished off for lunch and resumed their activity in the afternoon.

The first party of French had landed the previous night and some said it was they who had disclosed our use of Namsos first by opening fire on the reconnaissance planes. Others blamed the British wireless for announcing our landing. At all events by nightfall Namsos was little use as a port. Fortunately the French had moved straight into the woods on disembarking and escaped with few casualties. Fortunately too, our rear parties from 'A' and H.Q. Coys. escaped without casualty although having a very bad experience. In the morning the Germans contented themselves with destroying the port and town, moving steadily up the hill from the quays as succeeding waves came in. In the afternoon, however, they bombed and machine gunned the surrounding woods where our men were hiding. Few, if any, civilians were killed as the town was pretty well empty.

The desolate scene at Namsos after German bombing raids which left many dead. The mostly wooden structures were destroyed by fire but left their chimneys pointing skywards and described by Jack Haslam as looking like totem poles. With no Allied air cover, the Luftwaffe was left to attack ground targets almost at their leisure but it was a different story during the withdrawal at sea when these aircraft came within the firing range of naval anti-aircraft guns. (CGR)

As soon as dusk fell I set off in a car, followed by Randall with three lorries, for Namsos to collect our parties and any of our belongings that remained. I ditched the car twice on route but got on the road again. The first time after a bit of hard work and the second more easily thanks to the ready assistance given by some Frenchmen nearby. The flames of Namsos could be seen from the hill top when I got there, ten miles away. Before I reached the town I passed a party of men marching away which I thought were our people but, being in the car, went on into the town to investigate.

The road leading out of the town was arrayed with the French, who had all their weapons, ammunition and other stores on the side of it. As soon as I got to the outskirts it was clear that little was left. Some isolated houses in the fields still stood, but all that remained of the town was chimneys (the only part of the house normally built of stone) and a few charred remains. I went on to the school but all I could find were a few mangled remains of our band instruments. For the occupation of Trondheim we had been told (a) To make every effort to impress the local people and (b) that we could expect no NAAFI stores for a month and must make our own arrangements. We had lost in Namsos : Our band instruments and clothing, all our football and sports kit and some £200 worth of chocolate and cigarettes. Still, we had been very lucky to get out ourselves with all our fighting equipment though it was largely due to the care we had taken not to be seen.

I felt sure that the target for the next day, Namsos having been destroyed, would be Bangsund with its long narrow bridge; so I hurried back to find my three lorries and ferry everything I could over this bottle neck. After over shooting them twice we found our men with Brigade H.Q. sleeping the sleep of the exhausted and recovering from a great night in some farm buildings. I am afraid I woke them somewhat unceremoniously and hurried them on. By daylight we got the whole party to Beitstad including our two R.A.P.C. officers who travelled in my car. All of the cash for the expedition had been destroyed in the bombing so we could pay for nothing till more arrived. I have never been so tired as about 0500 hrs. that morning and rarely so dirty. I staggered into our R.A.P. where they sat me on a chair with a cup of cocoa. I am afraid I fell off fast asleep with the cocoa on the floor. I had had a fairly busy and emity time on board ship and really no sleep since, what with plans and conferences by day and movement of men and stores by night. This was typical of all our H.Q. officers though most of the rest of the Bn. could sleep by day when not on sentry duty.

During the night 'A' Coy. moved from Steinkjer to relieve the 'B' Coy Pl. at Follafoss, leaving an N.C.O. and thirteen men in Steinkjer. The Bn. was at last more or less grouped together again instead of being spread over 80 miles of country, much to the Colonel's relief, and some good work by the Signal Pl. (under 2/Lt. J. M. de Bartolome) got all Coys. connected with Bn. H.Q. on civilian telephone.

Not Bangsund but Steinkjer was the bombing target for today, 2 April, again we had just got 'A' Coy. out in time. Again, Brigade H.Q. was in it, as they had moved on in the early hours from Beitstad to Steinkjer - the lift for them in my lorries had not proved a very good turn. However, they had no casualties.

The previous afternoon the Col. and I had taken a walk across the fields to old Beitstad, from where one could get a view down the fjord where the ice was melting rapidly. A few trial steps off the track showed me that the going was too soft, and from then on the snow would not bear movement and we were confined to the road and farm tracks.

During the morning I took 2/Lt. Jenkinson and his party out to old Beitstad, partly to act as a look out across the fjord for us and partly with an idea that new Beitstad on the road would be bombed and it was their turn to be out of it. A good many planes flew over us as we moved out, but we escaped their notice and I left them more or less comfortable in some farm buildings.

Early this day it had been rather foggy and Maj. Hunt of 'A' Coy. had telephoned more than once from Follafoss reporting the daily movement, seen in the mist, of one or more German naval vessels. We had expected their landing at Strommen (the Beitstad Fjord or Hjelleboten was still blocked with ice) and it was partly with this in mind that Jenkinson was sent as a look out.

Another patrol under 2/Lt. Palmer (personnel of the Carrier Pl. with Bren Gun) had also been sent out on Jenkinson's left.

Actually, the German warships put in on the main road down the east side of the Trondheim Fjord. Fighting was known to have taken place between troops they landed and the 1/4 KOYLI and the Lincolns. Late afternoon found these battalions cut off from us, beyond the enemy and out of communication.

Arnold Whiteley...
There were two brothers from Sheffield, Thomas and Lawrence Ryecroft, and they had to position this 2 inch Mortar in the snow near the edge of the fjord and Sgt. Major Codd said, 'Now then Ryecroft. If they land, can you hit them from here?' and he said, 'Well, I think we might do if we had any ammunition Sir!' Codd was furious so he spoke to them very confidentially and said, 'Wait till they land and get near enough, then throw the F...... Mortar at 'em and run!' Luckily, the Germans didn't land there.

John Marsh...
What with the fog, the bombing and the uncertainty of the situation this was a rare day of alarms. Two I remember. An anxious message of German L.M.G. fire a mile or so away. We moved up a couple of platoons who found the sound was caused by Norwegians breaking firewood. Then a party of Germans was reported digging Mortar positions, but this proved to be Norwegians pulling a cow out of the snow. They had taken the unfortunate animal out of a barn for her weekly constitutional and she had strayed off the track, much as I had done the previous day. Afternoon found us all on the move again. The Bn. was to take up a position on the line Hjellebotn - Snaasevvik, through which it was hoped the other two battalions might withdraw up the road via Kvam to Grong and reinstate themselves.

Owing to the emergency, 'C' Coy. was moved in daylight from Namdalseidet to Foling. With the snow beginning to melt they had put on their rubber boots. They had not had time to change nor sufficient transport to take any kit with them. A day later when they got back their leather boots they could not get their feet into them, a lesson for us all. This daylight move brought our first machine gunning from the air, resulting in great excitement but no casualties.

Les Sewell...
We loaded the kit on lorries and some of us were balanced on top of the kit bags when we came to this tunnel and I was frightened to death of lifting me head up. The next morning we were stopped at some crossroads (Namdalseidet-Asp/Beitstad-Foling?) and we could see all the German aeroplanes flying around, just like pigeons, over Steinjaer and it was burning in the distance. We later stayed in a place like a village hall near a 'T' junction (Asp?) upstairs in a large room, I remember there was a big chest with old clothes in it.

Les and his platoon then moved in a direction away from Steinkjer to a place where they began to fortify some workshops using sacks of grain against the walls. Looking at the map and following the description given by Les this was probably Foling, and it was a line between here and Beitstad that the Hallams were required to hold. During their stay here, a German aircraft flew over...

Les Sewell...
We'd got a Brengun on an anti-aircraft mounting and a lad ran out and started firing at it and kept hammering away at it till it flew on, that was a young chap called Stephenson who left us after Norway. Then they decided to move us again, but instead of going by road to the junction we went across country. The story was that the Germans were not far away. We did an all night

march across country and everybody was really knackered and there were chaps staggering, you know, like a defeated army. We stopped one night in a schoolhouse at Sprova and there were a big stove in there with a fire guard. Ginger Robinson was cleaning the gun again, he'd never used it, and he got a piece of rag jammed in the barrel and couldn't shift it. So, he knocked one of these rods out of the fire guard and hammered the rag out of the barrel with it. We were in a panic in case the Germans came!

John Marsh...
At night 'A' & 'B' Coys. moved, leaving most of their kit behind, from Follafoss and Malme to positions astride the road south of new Beitstad. Bn. H.Q. we also moved about a mile inland as we again felt sure that Beitstad would be bombed. This proved very inconvenient however and next day we moved most of the ammunition to some houses in the edge of the woods but adjoining Beitstad village. Our reserve rations and ammunition we sent off under the R.S.M. up the proposed route of withdrawal to Kvam. 'Sent off' again is a poor description of the search for transport and the work of loading and unloading in the dark. 'D' Coy. was the only one not to move this night, remaining in reserve at Elden.

George Linley had also landed with the contingent at Bangsund where they seemed to do little else but keep on the move from one place to another and all the time harassed by German air attacks.

George Linley (Diary)...
21 April. 7am. getting packed up to move at a moments notice. Must be expecting an attack from Steinkjer... 3pm. Get moving in private lorries towards Tranjeen (Trondheim?) about 25 miles south. Aircraft catching us on the road came down and machine gunned our lorries, very lucky no one gets killed. I was told our destination is Steinkjer but when we get to Asp we see Steinkjer up in smoke so it seems we are too late. Get our rations in a school room at Asp and move back to Thurling at 7pm. Still 'stood to' at midnight and then another ride to Steinkjer to get put up in a barn, not knowing what we was up against - got bedded down by 3am.

22 April. Up by 6am. A German aeroplane comes over our barn and nearly pulls the top off. These fellows seem to do just what they want. If only we had some aircraft to keep them busy. As a matter of fact it would be a sight for the lads to see any aircraft with a ring on the wing instead of a black cross! 4.30am. Aircraft sounds and five Gerries are over and gave us the biggest pounding we have had up to now. Swooping down, drilling holes in the roof where we was and keeping it up for three hours. Our job was to keep under cover if any aircraft came over but one of the lads couldn't stand for that any longer so he engaged them with the Bren Gun and that made him stay longer than he would have done. We only get two slightly wounded with all the bombs he dropped. 9.20pm. Move north about 12 miles through Asp, on the way we could see buildings burning where Gerry had been in the afternoon, lighting the sky up for miles through the darkness. Marching through the snow and in rubber boots was beginning to tell on all of us. Everybody flopping down in the snow each rest we had, for the last two miles some of the lads was beat to the world - a lot in the rear walking as if they was drunk. Reaching our destination about 2.15am we just slumped down anywhere and then, fast asleep.

John Marsh...
Next day, 22 April, was an anxious but amusing one. Continual rumours came through of the surrender of the 1/4 KOYLI and the annihilation of the Lincolns. Steinkjer was most thoroughly bombed with much of our stores and fourteen of our men still in it. All of us who moved about were machine gunned. Amazingly, the only casualty was 2/Lt A.C. Somers when a bullet passed through the windscreen of his lorry between him and the driver, slightly scratching his hand.

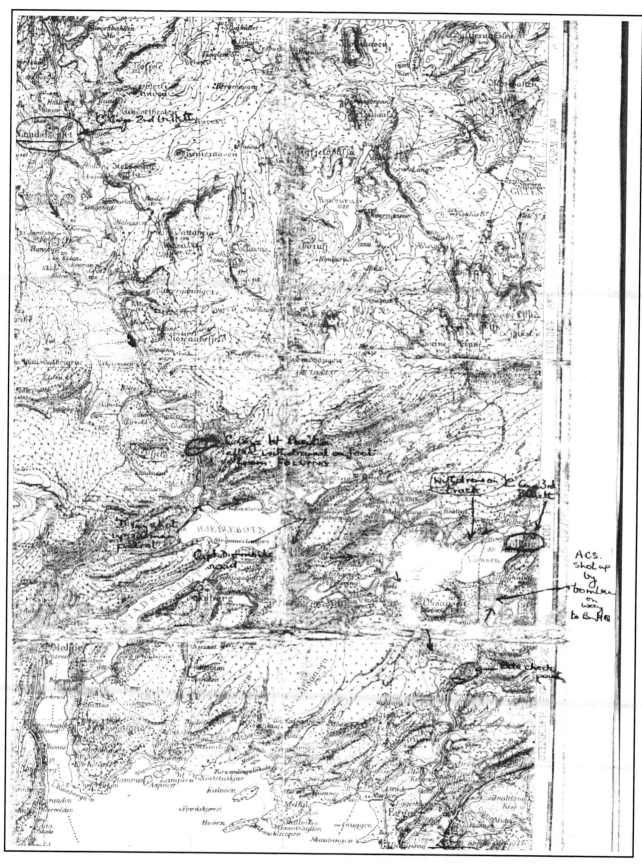

Map of Norway showing area between Namdalseidet (top left) and Steinkjer (bottom right). Although in poor condition it is worthy of inclusion as it has been overwitten by Chris Somers with some interesting information which compliments the stories of John Marsh and Les Sewell. Both maps in this chapter are from Chris Somers scrap book. Another officer, Raymond Jenkinson, confirmed that these maps were campaign issue. (ACS)

40

The O.C. H.Q. Coy. (Capt. R. Mumby), the doctor (Capt. C.J. Wells) and the M.T.O. (2/Lt. J. Randall) went out in a car, got shot up, and took refuge in the snow under a tree. They were harried by a plane until it ran out of bullets but no one was hurt.

The C.O., Currie, the I.O., Bartolome and I set off to find a new H.Q. Bartolome and I got out of the car, had a word with 'A' Coy. and set off across to Foling over a track through Roseg. On arrival we practised our Norwegian and arranged billets for 80 men of H.Q. Coy. As we went on some planes passed over and I remarked that they were misfiring badly. They were not misfiring but machine gunning us and we were in the middle of a snow field a mile from the nearest tree. However, we walked on with all the nonchalance we could muster and pretended it was not our war. At Foling we found 'C' Coy. with some Norwegian troops. We still had orders not to disclose our presence and consequently not to fire back. We accordingly took shelter first in a cellar and then in a barn or stable. This latter was a mistake as the panic stricken horses were more frightening than the machine gunning.

Here we met Col. Robins who in turn had met the General. The Col. and Currie had also been machine gunned. The only result had been that our car now stopped every quarter of a mile or so and we had to get out and push. Pushing a car up steep hills and watching out for planes that are trying to shoot you is not so funny.

The General had issued new orders. The Grong road was congested by the Norwegian Army trying to mobilise, not very successfully as all their clothing, weapons and equipment were in German hands in Trondheim. A French half brigade was advancing to our assistance down the Bangsund road on foot, as we had all the available transport of about 4 cars and 4 lorries. So, the Bde. was to withdraw north through Beitstad.

We got all this at Foling and so could make arrangements for 'C' Coy. immediately. They moved that night to Sprova, a group of farms just behind 'D' Coy. at the Malm road junction (at the head of the Hjellebotn).

On the way back I called in to tell 'A' Coy. They had been out in the snow for some reason and got machine gunned too. Several of them have told me since that seeing me walking up the track to the farm swinging my stick pulled them together again. I had arrived after their machine gunning was over! Major Hunt was in pyjamas, having at one stage dived head first into a clump of bushes and got wet through. He, Cave and I had a most hilarious tea party. The rest of the Bde. was lost, the Germans were just ahead in overwhelming numbers, so we finished off all the best items in their Coy. Mess Pannier.

When I got back, I found a rear Bn. H.Q. was being formed under Major Strong at Elden. I sent back my clerks to this with all the documents and full instructions as to how and when to destroy them as I was convinced they should have to do. Our Battle H.Q. were moved back into our old Cafe on the main road where it was far more convenient and had not yet been bombed.

During the night about two thirds of the Lincolns came through, having been shelled from the sea and attacked by German landing parties, but they were far from being annihilated let alone demoralised.

Next day, 23 April, was one of anxiety for the rest of the Lincolns and the 1/4 KOYLI. There were many rumours of enemy advance in our front and flanks now that these were completely exposed, except for the protection given by the melting snow.

George Linley (Diary)…
23 April… Had no letters from home since we landed in Norway. We are now the forward platoon of the Battalion waiting for the KOYLI and the Lincolns to come through. 10pm: The King's Own came through our post and what a sight they were, everyone nearly dead with the long tramp and fighting. One hour after, the Lincolns came through. I have heard them talk of the retreat from Mons - If it was worse than this lot, God help them. I can see about five men with their shoes tied together and slung round their neck, walking in their socks.

John Marsh…
The Bn. had been ordered to withdraw this evening if the 1/4 KOYLI came through. In view of the situation just described the C.O. asked the Brigadier for permission to withdraw from our present position to a more comfortable and stronger one at the head of Hjellebotn. The Brigadier came down to join us to await the arrival of the KOYLI, snatching four hours sleep in our Cafe. It should be understood that the latter was just a building entirely deserted and empty.

While the desirability of closing up was still being debated, 'B' Coy sent a signal that the 1/4 KOYLI were just passing their position. They had been met near Foling by 2/Lt. G.J. Good with a patrol which had been sent out to try to make contact and guide them in. They had marched a hundred miles or more round behind the Germans through the mountains but had had to leave behind everything including 2 inch Mortars and Bren Guns but retaining their rifles. With them came our R.S.M. and three men who had taken the Bn. reserve ammunition to Kvam when we expected to move that way. They had been cut off from us when the Norwegians retired north from Foling.

One of the main regrets at leaving Beitstad was that we were unable for reasons of security to give warning of our intention to the telephone operator. She had been most helpful and loyal, working the exchange for us night and day in spite of the danger (from which all the other civilians had fled) but had on several occasions asked for warning before we left.

Before leaving we tried to fire the petrol tank at the garage but found this more difficult than we expected. However, Randall finally succeeded and got cursed by the Brigadier for giving our intentions away for his pains.

It was now possible to draw back 'A' & 'B' Coys. and the remainder of H.Q. Coy. with Bn. H.Q. which was done in the order given. By day light, 24 April, we were strung back along the Namsos road still depending on the melting snow and the ice on the fjord to protect our flanks. 'C' & 'D' Coy. were in front at the Malm road junction, the former covering the Beitstad road and the latter that of Malm.

Major Strong had found a tiny cottage well back from the road in the woods for Bn. H.Q. He met us where the track left the road with a broom and industriously swept away all traces of our tracks behind us. I am afraid this amused the Col. and me but a few weeks later when we heard how a 1st Bn. withdrawing to Andalsnes had had its H.Q. bombed on several occasions half an hour after occupation, we saw his point.

42

This evening we sent patrols forward into Beitstad and to Kvam to collect baggage which we had had to leave behind for lack of transport. Our reserve ammunition and rations was becoming a problem with our supply base so thoroughly bombed and ships also being constantly attacked.

I went first as far as Beitstad to see how the land lay. We never had any idea of the German strength or whereabouts but held a vague notion that they were stronger than us and advancing round about Steinkjer. I had with me a fighting patrol under 2/Lt. J.T.D. Moorwood, but finding all quiet, went ahead in my car. To my horror I found the lights on in the first billet I approached. I crept cautiously up with revolver cocked but found it empty, the lights having been left on by our men that morning.

I expected no success for our patrol to Kvam. Apart from the probability of German opposition it had nearly thirty miles to go over roads which had been blocked by the Norwegians when they retreated. However, they met with no Germans and were back with most of the ammunition before dawn. They had come across 14 road blocks but scarcely been delayed by them.

25 April was a quiet day of recognition with no air authority. In the evening 'D' Coy. took over both roads in front and 'C' Coy. withdrew a mile or so to a group of farm buildings known as Sprova. A further patrol was sent out to Beitstad and Roseg to receive stores and a fighting patrol under the command of the I.O.(2/Lt. P.M. Young) as far as the Asp road junction which proved to be still clear of the enemy. This patrol went on a lorry and took a bicycle. One man was given orders in case of trouble to 'have away' on the bike to tell the tale. On his return he said something about it being lucky he had not had to use it as it turned out he could not ride one! He might have said so earlier.

During the morning of the 26th, a party of Lincolns came through bringing with them 'A' Coys. Corporal and 13 men who had been left in Steinkjer. The Hallamshires were now complete again.

About mid-day 'D' Coys. forward post got a phone message from friendly Norwegians that a German patrol was approaching the town of Beitstad. The post was in a shop between the road and the fjord side with a section well forward up the hillside designed to cut off the approaching patrol when it hit the road block. A further telephone message said that the Germans were on bicycles and had stopped in Beitstad, some two miles from our post. So the platoon stood down for dinner and the forward post came in. Just then the Germans rode up on bicycles.

A Sgt. opened fire with a Bren from the shop window and killed one man. Another fell off his bicycle as he turned round and was captured. This was the first blood we drew and I arrived a few minutes later to find the platoon, commanded by 2/Lt. Lonsdale-Cooper, very pleased with themselves. I ultimately asked questions and pointed out that some of the patrol had got away and that we must now get the C.Os. permission to move our road block forward.

Later in the afternoon a Fleet Air Arm officer who had been shot down in the mountains after bombing Trondheim came through. We had not yet seen a single British aircraft so it was encouraging to know they were functioning as far as possible. Some Norwegians also came along who had escaped from the Germans and told us of a store of explosives at Follafoss. They also told us the Germans were using as their H.Q. in Trondheim, the same hotel as we had for ours.

At night we sent another patrol to Kvam and Foling to obtain stores, the most important item being reported as the Brigadier's suit case. They achieved their objective without incident.

The B.B.C. was reporting that the Germans were digging in around Steinkjer which was hailed on the news as being an open admission of defeat on the part of the Germans! We scarcely could agree but were glad of the information.

Next morning, 27 April, a daylight raiding party went to Follafoss, found it unoccupied and brought back the remainder of 'A' Coys. baggage and 15 cwt. of explosives. Unfortunately, no one knew how to handle this - even the name was new to us - Melignite. I put it in the barn at the back of Bn. H.Q. and the detonators in my pack in case they should come in useful later.

After tea, the Brigadier suggested a further patrol to the Asp road junction or if not, then to Kvam in order to maintain the initiative. I must admit, I looked upon this as a highly dangerous undertaking as we had done this now for four nights and the Germans had been fifteen miles our side of the road junction, only thirty-six hours earlier. After all, we had retrieved his suit case! The matter was settled by a report of an enemy patrol about 12 strong on the far side of Beitstad. To attack was very difficult owing to all movement having to be along the main road. Capt. R.O.S. Dimmock therefore took a Pl. of 'B' Coy. to ambush them on the southern edge of Beitstad village. He went out at dusk having discovered they were spending the night in a barn by the roadside which had been his own Coy. store and which still held much of our kit. It was decided to await their movement at dawn but they had not stirred by 1000 hours so an attack was made. Capt. Dimmock left the bulk of the Pl. under 2/Lt. C.R.S. Sandford and went for them himself accompanied by C.S.M. Howden and a few men. As soon as they were seen by the enemy, he and Howden threw No.36 grenades killing and wounding some of them. However, it had been impossible to surround the barn and the bulk of the German party got away into the trees. One German soldier had been wounded in the stomach and died a few hours later, another was captured.

Both Dimmock and Howden were also wounded, both in the buttocks when taking cover after throwing their grenades. Both men were later recommended for decoration, Howden receiving the M.M. and Dimmock the Norwegian decoration. Dimmock, unfortunately, had to be evacuated to England and was taken out by Sunderland flying boat. Capt. D.R. Bell now took over command of 'B' Coy.

I took the prisoner to Bn. H.Q. Both I and Bartolome spoke some German and chatted with him but in accordance with orders sent him back to Bde. H.Q. for interrogation. It subsequently transpired that no one there spoke German, so no interrogation took place. Meanwhile, on the previous evening (27 April), orders were received for the relief of the Bn. by the French. For this purpose the Bn. came under their command (Chef du Brigade Brethhovard). He first attached to us a couple of platoons of ski troops and very glad we were to have them covering the hills on our left flank. Here the snow was now melting rapidly whereas our right was to some extent covered by having the fjord in front of it.

On the morning of 28 April, we moved back a convoy by lorry, for the first time in daylight. It got bombed and machine gunned but had no casualties. By now we were very familiar with the German air timetable which was never varied due, perhaps, to the paucity and bad quality of airfields available. A Heinkel float plane was always the last flight at dusk (about 1730 hours) and first at dawn (about 0500 hours). Between those times we could be sure of our movement unobserved, at least from the air. Sorties for bombing and machine gunning were made between 0600 and 1800 hours with a break for lunch from 1230 to 1330 hours.

In the evening, the French took over our positions (13th Regt. Chasseurs Alpins). They brought with them some light field guns which made us very jealous. They also had some real transport including troop carrying vehicles but at about this time fifteen British 15 cwt. trucks were landed of which four were belonging to the Hallamshires. These and the usual two or three lorries helped with baggage movement but the Bn. had of course to march and set off by road to Bangsund. By a little wangling with lifts, H.Q. Coy. managed to get there by day break having had a start of some 8 miles and several hours. The other Coys. were strung out along the road when dawn came and so took shelter for the day in barns. My morning was spent in finding them and getting them rations.

A good deal of air activity during the day, 29 April, was directed at Namsos. Huge clouds of smoke told us that the sloop, H.M.S. 'Bittern' had been hit. Being irrecoverable, it was sunk by the Royal Navy during the evening using torpedo. At dusk the march was resumed, several parties having by now provided themselves with handcarts. I went back with some of the transport to glean more of our heavier belongings which had been left behind the previous night, mostly under camouflage on the roadside. By this time the road had really broken down under the thaw and conditions were unsuitable for driving in the dark.

During this night, preliminary orders for the withdrawal of the Force were received, it now being impossible to land further troops or supplies at Namsos. With this in view, we also handed over some of our weapons and arms to the KOYLI and Lincolns. The first idea was to withdraw by land northwards in conjunction with the Norwegians on our left, but there was no road through to the north and it was given up. However, this was not before our 2 i/c had done some recce and nearly gone into Sweden in the process.

H.M.S. 'Bittern' (photographed from M.S. 'Chrobry' on the latters second trip to Norway with transport and rear party on board). Shortly afterwards, this escort sloop was badly damaged by air attacks near Namsos and had to be sunk as unrecoverable. (DCB)

Arnold Whiteley…
When the withdrawal started we hid mostly in barns and isolated farms during the day and then as soon as it got dark we got on the road again marching. We found a pony trap in a barn but no pony so we were the ponies with so many to each shaft and we put the heavy gear on it, machine guns, ammunition, stretchers and things. If anybody fainted on the march they were thrown on this here cart until they came round and then they were made to start walking again.

In one barn we were in, there was one of these brand new Opel cars that were just beginning to flood the market and it must have been the farmer's pride and joy. Sgt. Maj. Codd said, 'We'll see this doesn't fall into enemy hands,' and put a sledge hammer through the cylinder block.

John Marsh…
30 April was a quiet day with less aerial activity than usual. We thought at the time this was due to a few Bofors guns having arrived but actually I think the Germans were busy strafing the Andalsnes evacuation (including our own 1st Bn.). Opportunity was taken of this lull to

45

reorganise the Battalion. We now had the French in the front line, then the KOYLI, Lincolns and ourselves round Bangsund, nearest Namsos. We were to stay put whilst the remainder of the force withdrew through us. We made what defensive dispositions we could though digging was out of the question. At Bangsund, most of our officers had a bath for the first time in Norway in a charming house which was also used as Bn. H.Q. The lull in aerial activity had made us reckless again.

That night we made a further gleaning expedition for stores which we hated the Germans getting although we knew we had little chance of taking them away ourselves. We stayed out rather late with the truck and knew we should be caught by 'Henry' the recce plane before we got back. However, we managed to spot him coming and got into a wood.

These nights of 'flitting' I shall long remember, very cold but bright starlight with the most glorious scenery. Our drivers were having a hard time of it due to night long operations in unfamiliar lorries over shocking roads. They were having two or three ditchings on every trip. Still, they got most of the daytime in which to sleep, a luxury for which I envied them. Our signallers too had been working like Trojans in order to get communications going after every move, then cutting the wires each time we withdrew. Our S.O. became really expert at climbing poles and cutting wires although his motor driving still left much to be desired!

1 May brought another quiet day with definite evacuation orders. The French and the other two battalions were on the move before these were cancelled about midnight, presumably owing to lack of shipping. For some reason the consultation took some time to filter through to all of the French who spent the dark hours passing through us, in both directions! The other two battalions, however, got safely into the Namsos area and we were left in the front line once more.

It was now hoped to evacuate the rest of the force from Namsos and us from Bangsund, but our ships were unable to come in, I am afraid they were sunk in the attempt. The morning brought the first and last issue of Force Orders - half a sheet of promotions for staff officers who had arrived the day before!

The evening of 2 May brought a final conference for the intended evacuation. Whilst it was on we heard the Prime Minister announce on the wireless that allied forces were evacuating southern Norway. He said our troops had got away from Andalsnes without a single casualty. We felt little confidence in the same good fortune after this warning to the enemy.

The other two battalions and the French embarked first and we were all to be on board by 0100 hours. We had 14 miles to do and only transport enough to do a little ferrying although the French transport had been handed over to us during the day. I issued written withdrawal orders in English and French at about 1900 hours taking them round to Coys. in a fine Pontiac with one flat tyre. We finished with quite a dinner party, our batmen doing marvels with our rations and what we found in our luxurious billet.

Our invaluable interpreter, Setta, went back to his home which was next door to our old H.Q. at Elden. His mother's wireless had given us most of our news for two or three days.

The Bn. moved more or less simultaneously, although we got a good deal of H.Q. Coy. down to the boat early. Between us and the enemy, a party of French engineers remained till the last minute with Capt. Cave acting as Liaison Officer with them. They blew a road bridge between Bangsund and Namdalseidet first, then soon after midnight the big bridge over the Strumen at Bangsund. The Colonel, Currie and I stayed to watch this, packed the French into their truck and set off after them in two cars. Cave and I were right at the back and about half way the engine stopped. There was no one behind us and we were due on the last boat in ten minutes. A few minutes agitation, however, and it started once more.

Arnold Whiteley...
We marched all the way back to Namsos and when we got to the outskirts there was a huge ravine with a road viaduct. When we got to it we had to stop and the French Engineers mined this bridge and we waited for some time. Then they sent some trucks up from the docks to fetch us and Col. Robins was with them. We went to the other side of the viaduct and stopped as the plunger was pressed to demolish it and it was the biggest explosion I have ever seen. This entire viaduct lifted up, disintegrated into the ravine so as to hold off the Germans for some time.

John Marsh...
On our way we passed any amount of abandoned transport, more than we had seen during the whole campaign. Also a big R.A.S.C. dump on the north side of the Namsen bridge. As the troops had passed they had been issued with rations and taken whatever they liked in the way of chocolate, cigarettes, etc. Unfortunately we were too late to share in this.

On arriving near the quay we left the car and heard a staff officer ahead calling to anyone left to run for the boat which was just leaving. By chance Currie and I ran one way and got on the 'El Djezair', the Colonel and Cave and others onto the destroyer 'Afridi'. I actually had to jump for my ship which had already put off when I arrived.

We had left everything we possessed in Bangsund except what we could carry in our arms. We had had little time to destroy all these stores and most of them fell into German hands intact, although I had spent a long afternoon burning papers, etc. Even our arms we had to leave on the quay, except for rifles. There may have been a good reason for this decision by the staff but it was a bitter blow to us after carrying Bren Guns, Mortars, etc. so many miles. When the 'Afridi' put off she fired a few rounds into the row of transport and equipment on the quays.

Les Sewell...
A rumour that we were pulling out was spread by a lad called Ted France. I don't know where he got his information from but he'd always got it. He said, 'You're on your way home tonight lads,' and no one would believe him. Anyway, we moved on again at night and the next place was Namdalseidet in a farm barn over the top of the cows. This was the last place we called at and, after a one day delay, we went on to Namsos at night and had to run to get aboard the 'El Djezair.'

Jack Haslam...
When we came back to Namsos, all that were left were chimney stacks which were made of brick and all wood had gone. They were like totem poles and just reminded me of a Red Indian settlement. As we were coming away they were bombing us like mad, dive bombing, aerial torpedoes and the lot they were throwing at us. Where I were, we were just lying down in a gangway and we got a big bang and then there was all this water coming at us and lads started panicking. 'We've been hit! We've been hit! We're going down!' I says, 'Give o'er, if we're going down, I don't mind. This is hot water!'

They'd hit us, because he'd knocked one of propellers off back and when we got this water we all went up on deck and watched 'Afridi' go down... ...as we were laid on deck there were rats, I'm not joking, these rats were yellowish coloured rats, they were pushing us out't way to jump into water. Big yellow rats, pushing us out't way to jump over the side. They said they were bilge rats.

They say rats always leave a sinking ship, so we were getting worried then...   ...we were transferred to another ship, a luxury liner at Scapa Flow and...   ...when we got back to Glasgow the ship we'd come over on from Namsos (Al Kantara?) was in front of us and when we saw it we nearly died. It were right over on its side.

Wilf Fisher...
We finally climbed aboard this French ship and it was absolutely jam packed and I always remember there were some American correspondents sat there and there was two of them sat there cool as anything, sketching what was actually happening. I couldn't believe it!

John Marsh...
The 'El Djezair' was packed. It was built for the run from southern French ports to Algeria overnight, and to take perhaps 500 passengers. Now we were packed like sardines, about 50 officers in the small saloon and men lying two abreast along all the passageways. Besides ourselves there were a lot of French on board. The whole force except for a few stragglers on the destroyers were packed on this and two similar French boats. There was no water on board for drinking, let alone washing but luckily I had some in my water bottle. Those who had taken the chance at the R.A.S.C. dump to fill up with rum regretted it! I had also managed to squeeze into my flask pack, a tin of bully and a packet of biscuits. This lasted me till the evening of the 5 May and was, I think, typical of most peoples position.

I slept like a log on the floor of the saloon (the last four nights in Bangsund we had slept in beds, but the previous billets had inured us to hard lying) and was woken by the air raid alarm. It was a calm day with a clear sky and beautiful sunshine. The Germans started on us early, their first attack being made on the transports. All their bombs missed these as luck would have it as we could not have had life boats for more than a sixth of those on board and few life belts. Now they turned their attention to the destroyer escort.

The first ship they hit was the French destroyer 'Bison'. Oil poured from her and more men were lost in the burning oil on the water than from the bombs. 'Afridi' stayed behind to pick up survivors and after circling the 'Bison' for nearly two hours, had to sink her. Before she caught up with the rest of the convoy she got hit herself, with a bomb on the forecastle mess just as some of our men were having their dinners. Thirteen of the Hallamshire Battalion lost their lives and several others were injured. Many had narrow escapes having to climb through the hole in the ships side. The destroyer sank in 20 minutes at about 1345 hours.

A destroyer has already turned back to go to the aid of the stricken H.M.S. 'Afridi' which can be seen as a speck on the horizon to the right of the cruiser H.M.S. 'York' (centre). As a matter of interest, the 'York' was abandoned later in the war (25/5/41) after being struck by an Italian explosive motorboat at Suda Bay, Crete. (DEL)

George Linley escaped on the 'El Djezair' and describes the air attacks on 3 May...

George Linley…(Diary)
…everybody on deck and here we see at least a dozen aeroplanes dropping their stuff and the battle is on in true earnest now. The sky is full of smoke, aircraft diving down and machine gunning, then up and dropping bombs. The guns barking off the 'Afridi' hit their mark and down one comes into the sea… The 'Afridi' gets hit right in the middle and gets hit again. On deck, four bombs fall at once and up the ship goes, oil and smoke all over the place. The ship goes down inside half an hour. I think there are some of our lads on it. The two destroyers that had been alongside the 'Afridi' pull away now and resume the attack. After two hours things quieten down. 11.30am. Over they come again and this time a French destroyer gets hit, how bad we don't know. Three more Gerry planes fall into the sea.

John Marsh…
Air attacks continued all day with usual break for lunch from 1200 to 1330 hours, but no one else was hit. Next day, 4 May, we were pretty well out of range and at about mid-day a Blenheim patrol arrived, a very welcome sight. Other naval vessels came to escort us including a hospital ship for the survivors.

Early on 5 May, the convoy anchored in Scapa Flow. Our first orders were to continue in our present transports down to Glasgow, but we quickly made it known the unpleasant conditions on board, dirt, overcrowding and no food or water. At about 1100 hours we got permission to transfer to the Duchess of Atholl and I went over in a lighter with the last party at about 1500 hours.

Lockheed Hudson makes low pass over the stern of 'El Djezair' as she nears home waters, with 'Al Kantara' and naval escorts following in her wake. Even a Sunderland Flying Boat turned up on the scene to greet the convoy as it made its way towards Scapa Flow (DEL).

When the 'Afridi' had been hit, rumour had gone round that some of our people, including the Colonel were on board, but no one knew if this was really so or not, let alone whether they had been killed. Great was our joy, therefore, on nearing the 'Duchess' to see the Colonel waving to us. This was soon dashed by the news of other of our friends having been killed.

George Lindley had also been transferred to the 'Dutchess of Athol' where he saw all the men that were saved from the 'Afridi' and wrote in his diary…
6 May, 9pm. Had a Service in the Ball Room for those that went down on the 'Afridi', 127 were lost. The C.Q.M.S., Gilbert Rodgers, has a nice tuck in his head and broke his collarbone. He tells me a man was trying to escape through the port hole and got fast. He went mad and they had to shoot him. Gilbert says the destroyer broke in two and he got some falling steel on top of him.

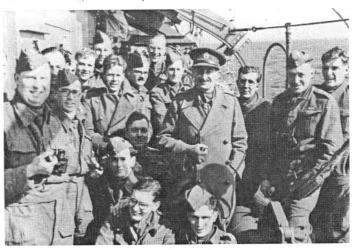

The faces of these Hallams Officers on board the 'El Djezair' show natural signs of relief at having withdrawn from Norway safely. They are from left to right (standing) *Hunt, *Murray-Smith, two men obscured from view, Bartolome, *Young, —, *Good, Bell, *Wells, Strong (wearing SD Cap), Marsh, *West, Lonsdale-Cooper. Those kneeling in lower picture are from bottom in clockwise direction - *Mumby, Blake, *Moorwood, Cave. (DEL)
— = unidentified
* = wearing side cap

John Marsh...

The contrast between the 'Duchess' and the French transport was indescribable and all we asked for was a drink of water and a biscuit. We were met by a steward at the gangway who issued every man with two cards giving his berth and his place at table. Lunch was still on and consisted of the usual peacetime fare - six or seven courses with a choice of some thirty dishes each more desirable than the one before. The Colonel had met me at the gangway with the news that he was O.C. troops and I, ships adjutant again, but I found time for a quick lunch.

A tender comes alongside the 'El Djezair' to take off the Hallamshires and other troops aboard, in order to transfer them to the 'Dutchess of Athol' where conditions were very civilised and good food was waiting. (DEL)

The job, however, was no sinecure. Word had come from the War Office that we could not sail till we had sent them a full list of those on board. They amounted to some 3,000 persons which included our own Brigade, attached troops (all arms), naval and merchant service survivors from the 'Afridi' and 'Bittern', trawlers etc. and a few Air Force. Actually, I never got them all totted up till the following day although everyone was most helpful. Units kept cropping up that no one knew were on board. However, we were allowed to sail after sending casualty lists only at 2000 hours.

In the evening we celebrated the 21st birthday of my cousin, Stephen Bartolome (S.O.), which had occurred on 4 May while aboard the 'El Djezair'. I had remembered it and taken a sip of water in his Honour but now could do better.

Next day, 6 May, was fine again and we had a glorious trip down inside the Hebrides and anchored off Gourock about midnight. Apart from boat drill, my only unusual business was to hold a court of enquiry into the absence of a gunner who, at the last moment, had preferred the arms of a Norwegian girl to the calls of home.

We spent the 7 May anchored off Gourock enjoying the good fare on board and the sight of a snowless land once more.

Arnold Whiteley...

We were wined and dined by waiters with white jackets on and when we sailed up the Clyde there were people picnicking at the lower reaches and we were sat on the rails waving to them and that. We got up to Glasgow and as we came down the gangplank we were greeted by CQMS McCredie, sat by a tea chest full of Black Cat cigarettes. Our reward was a packet of twenty Black Cats each and somebody in the Hallams christened them 'McCredie's Death Warmers' and that name stuck with them ever since! We were then taken into a big warehouse and given a talk by Sir Edmund Ironside who told us that we hadn't been driven out of Norway. We were told that we were going on leave and that we mustn't tell any despondent stories so as not to upset people. We came back in what we stood up in and we'd lost the band instruments. Anyway, we were all rekitted in that warehouse and off we went on leave.

John Marsh...
On the 8 May, we moved up the Clyde, another fine trip especially as viewed from the towering bridge of the 'Duchess'. Arriving in King George V docks at 1630 hours we immediately marched into the sheds to be addressed by the C.I.G.S. General Sir Edmund Ironside. His address, to the affect that we had come away out of Norway under orders and not just run, fell rather flat. We had all heard it the evening before on the wireless when he gave it to the troops back from Andalsnes and greeted it, I fear, with some derision.

After that we went back on board and there occurred the most memorable event of the war. The R.A.O.C. filled the transit sheds with clothing and necessaries and we were allowed to file through and take what we liked - no check of any sort. We were also invited to return any Arctic Clothing we cared to, but again with no compulsion. We little guessed we should get it all back a month later on our way to Iceland. A great reunion took place in the docks that evening. Our rear party were now at Bellahouston Park and Capt. Beckett came down to swop experiences and find out who was still alive. (A summary of their days is given in the war diary). I think our main feeling was a wish to go back to Norway as soon as possible and have a chance of getting to grips with the enemy on land - preferably with a little air support!

Canadian Pacific

Breakfast.

Grape Fruit

Apples   Oranges

Compote of Prunes   Preserved Pears

Oatmeal Porridge

Puffed Wheat   Force   Grape Nuts

Fried Fillet of Whiting
Grilled Kippered Herrings

Eggs: Boiled, Fried, Turned, Buttered
Omelettes : Plain, Parsley

Broiled Breakfast Bacon
Grilled Pork Sausages

TO ORDER - 10 minutes
Devilled Lamb Kidneys with Bacon

COLD
Prime Roast Beef   Pressed Ox Tongue

White and Brown Rolls   Cinnamon Buns
Toast : Plain, Buttered

Griddle Cakes with Quebec Maple Syrup

Jam   Marmalade

Coffee   Tea   Cocoa

A. (046)
Tuesday, May 7, 1940

An almost unbelievable Breakfast Menu from the 'Dutchess of Athol' dated 7 May, 1940. It would challenge any so called 'full English' that could be offered today. It would also, then, have challenged the waist belt of any man who attempted to do it full justice! (ACS)

So ends this fascinating account by John Marsh and others.

It will be remembered that Capt. D.C. Beckett had remained behind with the Rear Party and very few of these, if any, had managed to set foot in Norway. They had been ordered to follow the main body of the Battalion from Thirsk at very short notice but, due to various changes in plan brought about as the situation developed, found themselves moving to and fro between east and west coasts of Scotland. Arthur Green, a driver with the Rear Party remembers travelling by road in convoy to Rosyth whereupon the M.T. was loaded onto a cargo ship, the S.S. 'Blackheath'. Personnel were afterwards sent off to Glasgow by train. They were then brought back again to the east coast and embarked on board S.S. 'Orion'. The assumption was that they would sail in this to join the main body of the Battalion in Norway.

Arthur Green...
We got on this boat called the S.S. 'Orion', it hadn't even got its war paint on. It had just come from Australia and on board was loads of cheap Australian wine at fourpence a glass and of course we soon made short work of that. The food wasn't too clever but we survived for about three days when they decided we needed a bath or shower, so they ferried us off to shore by sections to the submarine dock. Of course, there were sailors getting their showers as well. We were raw recruits and we could see these old sailors with tattoos all over 'em. There were big tattoos and hairy chests, regular sailors, some with beards on in the showers and that. There were no where to put your soap and there were just pipes above with pull chains for warm and cold water - nowhere to put your soap, you daren't put your soap down, you were frightened to death! I'll always remember there were one sailor come in and he had an eye tattooed on each cheek of his behind, I'll always remember and across the top was written, 'I see you.' You didn't know whether to smile or what and you thought, 'Right lads these sailors' but anyhow we got back on the S.S. Orion...

They were taken off again and back they went to Glasgow by train to be embarked on the M.S. 'Chrobry', the latter having already transported the main body to Norway. This ship returned once more to Namsos where she narrowly escaped another bombing attack. On the outbound voyage, sea conditions were a bit rough.

Arthur Green...
We were right in the bowels of the ship where they used to put anybody who had been misbehaving. We had to sleep down there in those cells but I didn't sleep very much. I used to sleep up on deck and you've never seen seas like it - waves I should think twenty feet high and the destroyer escorts used to disappear for a period and you thought, 'It'll never come up again.' Anyway we managed it and I was very fortunate not to be sea sick. Most of the lads were and one particular fella, Tommy Collier from Bolton, Lancs, was sick as a dog and green as a cucumber all the way across. I kept him alive on dry bread and he lay all the time in a life raft on deck with a tarpaulin cover over him.

Very little was disembarked in terms of men or material but a number of officers and men from the 1st Bn. who had evacuated through Aandalsnes were taken aboard for the trip home. In the meantime, the S.S. 'Blackheath' carrying the Hallams vehicles made the voyage and moved up the Namsen Fjord in order to unload at Namsos. Only four of the Battalions 15 cwt. trucks were unloaded and used by 146 Brigade but these were later abandoned in the evacuation.

By the time the Rear Party arrived off the Norwegian shore the situation was already much deteriorated and the bulk of these troops and equipment were returned to Scotland. An amusing incident occured as masses of men started pouring through the sheds after disembarking by the King George V dockside. The crowd of soldiers moved at a snails pace and almost unbelievably H.M. Customs men began to single out individuals for kit bag searches! Someone started making the sounds of sheep being herded along - Baaaaaaaa! Baaaaaaaaaaa! This noise of disapproval was now taken on by the whole 'flock' and according to Arthur... *You never heard anything like it in your life.' A senior N.C.O. was running around shouting, 'I'll give you bloody Baaaaaa... when I get you on parade.'*

These troops comprising the Rear Party were the first back and went under canvas at Bellahouston Park, Glasgow, there to await the arrival and disembarkation of S.S. 'Blackheath' with the rest of M.T. which was to be followed later by the main bulk of the Battalion.

The Battalion was disembarked at King George V Dock from 'Dutchess of Atholl' at 1230 hrs. on 9 May and proceeded to a place called Stobs Camp near Hawick in two trains. The first train left at 1330 hrs. with all but 'A' Coy. and Carrier Pl. on board. The latter followed at 1430 hrs. and the two arrived at 1732 hrs. and 1837 hrs. respectively. The Battalion was granted 10 days leave from the 13th.

The whole Norwegian Campaign can be looked back upon now with shock and horror at the sheer lack of overall back-up for the operation and the dangerous position in which the infantry was placed, because of the almost total absence of artillery and air support. The whole effort could be summed up in the old phrase 'too little, too late'. It is perhaps understandable, if not forgivable, for some dithering to have occurred when gambling with the amount of material to put ashore against its possible loss in the event of a quick retreat, especially in this case where the German Army had already beaten us to the post, so to speak.

Transport had been in very short supply and movement off the roads was almost impossible due to the snow. Given these serious shortcomings, however, the Battalion did the best it could in the prevailing circumstances and the casualty rate on land could be described as minimal with no one killed. The order to evacuate was none too soon but it was perhaps soon enough to save 146 Brigade from a fate similar to that suffered by the other half of the pincer movement on Trondheim, which had landed at Andalsnes. This was the 148 Brigade which was so badly depleted that it could not continue as an operational part of the 49th Division. It was replaced later when the Division was serving in Iceland.

Casualties for the Battalion amounted to 13 O.R.'s killed and 11 wounded (H.M.S. 'Afridi'), and 1 Officer and 2 O.Rs. wounded on land. The Hallamshires had also drawn first blood in their war, the victim being a very young German soldier who died from his wounds. Only fate could have decreed that his blood should have been drawn by a man with the most inappropriate name. He was a Sergeant from 'D' Coy. and his name was..... Innocent !

By the evening of the 12 May, the vast majority of Battalion personnel had dispersed on leave for a well earned 10 days. The Rear Party and Transport Drivers of the Battalion who should have followed the Bn. into Norway but never actually disembarked there, arrived at Stobs Camp on the 15th from Bellahouston Park, Glasgow, to act as an Advance Party for the Bn. on its return from leave. A/Capt. D.C. Beckett was in Command of this group with Lt. D.R. Morris as his Transport Officer.

Stobs Camp, approximately 3½ miles from Hawick, was constructed on part of 3,600 acres purchased by the Government in 1902 and had seen its heyday during the Great War when it was used as a training camp for British and Commonwealth troops of all types. Part of it had also been enclosed for use as a Prisoner of War camp with its own graveyard. Total accommodation was said to be in the region of 20,000 at its height. Between the wars it had been used for little more than military summer camps and up to 1938, most groups that used it were under canvas. By the end of 1939, however, a major building programme was underway which included Nissen huts and an electricity generating station to add to some of the original structures still remaining, such as the mess halls, recreation hut and hospital, set in the central part of the complex. Very little remains above ground of this once vast camp today, although many building foundations can still be detected. Much of the area now seems to have been given over to farming activity.

Arthur Green…
Stobs Camp was about four miles outside Hawick. It was an old 1914-1918 Army and Prisoner of War Camp. There were wooden huts on two sides of a valley with a little river running through it. It was lovely weather and I always remember it was one of the best months we had in the Army.

When I was driving to Stobs Camp, we were travelling at night and hadn't a clue where we were or where we were going. It was pitch black and I remember I was following a 15 cwt. Guy truck and I had lost sight of him. I couldn't see his rear light and I was belting like hell down this road to catch him, turned round this corner and there he was, I swerved but bashed him in the back, bust all my front end in and there was hardly a mark on his truck.

Stobs Camp near Hawick c.1940. The Hallams stay in Scotland was quite brief at this time but they were destined to be back two years later for some very intensive training, surrounded by some of the most beautiful landscapes around Loch Fyne and the Kyles of Bute.(HFC) ❖ Below : as it looked in the mid 1990s.(DWS)

Cliff Lister was born in Cockermouth, Cumberland. He had completed his basic training at Pontefract Barracks and had been posted to the Hallamshire Bn. ('A' Coy.) prior to its move to Thirsk in October of the previous year.

Cliff Lister…
I remember going into one of these big huts at Stobs Camp and there were mail there that were a month old perhaps, food parcels, and there were rats and mice and everything running around in there. The first lot of blokes in had ransacked the parcels, you know, looking for their own mail and oh! it was a terrible sight. Jars of jam and cake and things like that - all gone rotten. So, a lot didn't get their mail.

When we first got to Stobs we inherited gardens with vegetables and stuff growing in them from the previous lot. We used to go on what they called Rabbit Piquet. It were lovely weather and we used to sleep out at night in the gardens to keep the Rabbits off the cabbages and that. There were more night Piquets on the gardens than there was guarding Camp!

Jack Haslam…
In Transport, there were this army shooting brake (see photo of C.Os. staff car in Iceland) and they called it 'Sheffield Flyer'. Some of the lads were running it back and forward (unofficially) to Sheffield but they got caught one time when they ran out of petrol. They were Court-Marshalled and ended up paying for the petrol they'd used.

During the month of May there were two tragic accidents both involving army trucks in the area. Two young boys from Hawick, Henry Scott aged 15, and John Gillies aged 9, both died from injuries in separate accidents when hit by trucks from Stobs Camp. The younger boy was struck by a vehicle belonging to the Hallams when he ran onto the road from a gap in the hedgerow where he and some other boys were playing.

The main body of the Bn. returned from leave on the 23rd and the total Bn. strength noted at this time was 30 Officers and 812 O.Rs. All weapons and equipment were now withdrawn from the unit so as to allow for a complete renewal. The Brigade was now in reserve and, as with all troops in the border area, available for Home Defence duties in the event of an emergency. New equipment and arms began to arrive and by the first few days in June the Bn. was still re-equiping when it received orders to be prepared for a posting overseas.

Meanwhile, Home Defence Duties continued in the following roles. In case of Air Raid, it might be called upon to aid the Civil Authorities, especially in the Edinburgh or Glasgow areas. One quarter of the Battalion, however, was to be always ready at 2 hrs. notice to move out as a Mobile Column in case of attempted landing by Parachutists. Such attempts were practiced, as revealed in a letter written by David Lockwood to his wife…

David Lockwood, Stobs Camp. (Letters to Mary)
We stood-to at 3.45 this morning and at 4.15 George (Robins) came out and said that a milkman had come in and said that he had seen some parachutists landing on the moor about seven miles south of here - the 'enemy' were actually some Hallamshires under Phil Young, John Marsh and Jenkinson - twenty of them.
We eventually found one party 'blowing up' the tunnel on the Carlisle line and caught another party as they arrived at the railway viaduct at Shankend and I myself got the remaining two during a reconnaissance on the moor in a Carrier....so we got them all!

The remainder of the Bn. was to be at 4 hours notice in Scottish Command Reserve to oppose any attempted landing by the enemy in force. On 2 June a platoon was sent out to take over a Road Block from 69th Field Regt. R.A., near the Shankend Viaduct on the road between Hawick and Carlisle. It was manned night and day and designed to keep a check on normal traffic for 'aliens' or any suspicious circumstances as well as preventing its use by enemy forces landing by air. A similar Road Block was manned one mile north of Teviothead on the A7 road Carlisle to Edinburgh.

Lt. Peter S. Newton rejoined the Bn. at about this time having been ill when it embarked for Norway. On 6 June a number of other officers were posted to the Hallams from the 1st Bn. York & Lancaster Regt. and elsewhere (The 1st Bn. was stationed close by at Galashiels having also recently returned from Norway to lick there considerable wounds and, like the Hallams, to re-equip). The newly arrived officers were 2/Lieuts. E.G. Sheppard, P.H. Froggatt, J.E. Crook and C.R.A. Tong (the latter formerly of the 6th. Bn. York & Lancaster Regt.).

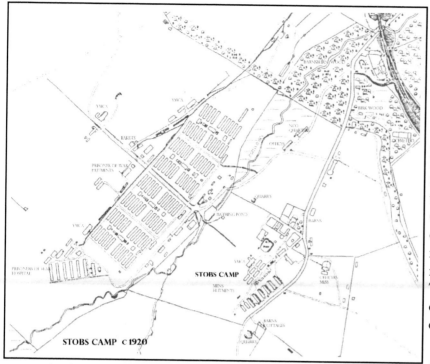

STOBS CAMP c 1920

Layout of Stobs Camp c.1920 in its heyday. Almost all of these buildings have been demolished and the land given over to farming. Traces of foundations can be plainly seen and the stream still flows under the bridge in the central area. In 1962 the bodies of German prisoners from the 1914-1918 War were disinterred from the cemetery here and placed in the military graveyard at Cannock Chase, Staffordshire.(After Hawick Archaeological Society Transactions 1988 modified)

On the 8 June at 1100 hours, a demonstration was given on the proper actions by troops holding Road Blocks to approximately 400 Local Volunteers from Hawick & District. On the 10th, six W.Os. and N.C.Os., who had seen long service with the Bn. and found to be too old for Administrative Services in Norway, were posted to Infantry training Command (I.T.C) Pontefract. On the same day a Draft of 150 ORs. were received from I.T.C. These were mostly militiamen from Yorkshire Towns who swelled the strength of the Bn. to 35 Officers and 957 other ranks.

Albert Binns was born in 1917 at Birstall.
Albert Binns…
…I was called up in January of 1940 and I was still at Pontefract when they (BEF) came out of Dunkirk because I remember having to go to the station to help people who were coming back to the hospitals. We'd heard about the Hallams coming out of Norway earlier and I was one of many sent up to Scotland (Stobs Camp) to make their numbers up to strength. I remember the train stopping about two miles outside of Hawick and we had to get off the train, up a little embankment and there was the Camp all under tents. There were no Nissen huts (for us) and that was the first impression I had of joining the Hallamshires.

The C.O. and Adjt. carried out a reconnaissance under orders of Major General M.O. Curtis D.S.O., M.C., who was the newly appointed G.O.C. 49th. Division. This Division was now under a whole pottage of orders amongst which required it to be prepared to move to France immediately, to be in U.K. reserve for Home Defence, to be in Scottish Command Reserve for Home Defence and, whilst awaiting orders under any of these three headings, to prepare a Defensive Position, in case of enemy landings on the East Coast of Scotland which might be followed by an attempted advance on Glasgow. The reconnaissance was on a two Brigade Front from Perth up the River Tay to Dunkeld. The Hallams were allotted work on this front including Perth, with River Tay as a F.D.L. This Front was approximately 8 miles in length and expected to be held by a brigade in case of attack.

A Warning Order was received at 1500 hours on 17 June to move in accordance with the above mentioned reconnaissance and next day an Advance Party of 20 other ranks under Maj. C.C.Strong left by Road, followed later by 'C' Coy. and part HQ.Coy. The remainder of the Bn. left by train from Hawick on the 19th, the transport proceeding under convoy via Stirling later the same day. The Bn. dispositions, mostly under canvas, were as follows… Bn. H.Q. in the Village Hall at Almondbank, three miles N.W. of Perth. HQ.Coy. at Almondbank and

Pitcairngreen, half a mile further North. 'A' & 'B' Coys near Tibeermore two and a half miles West of Perth. 'C' & 'D' Coys. at Redgorton four miles North of Perth.

Arthur Green...
...I remember one place called Pitcairngreen......we were on our own on this village green with trees all round and there was this old cottage with barn doors on, typical Scottish house, stone built, and this woman, she used to bake scones every day and she used to say, 'Just come in in the morning and help yourselves to these scones.' They were on this scrubbed table in the kitchen and you could help yourself. There was always a pile of scones and you could make a cup of tea.

On the 17th day also, Col. Douglas S. Branson, D.S.O., M.C., T.D., D.L., A.D.C., was appointed Honorary Colonel of the Bn. in place of his father who had died earlier in the month.

The Hallams short stay in Scotland was now coming to an end even though a detailed reconnaissance of the new area was being carried out. All of the Companies were now spread along a Front Line Area of some one and a half to two miles from right to left A/ B/ C/ D and HQ. The digging of trench positions and weapon pits began on the 21 June with much of it completed on a greater part of the front by the next day, when a Warning Order was received for 146 Inf. Bde. to move overseas on 22/23 June.

On the 22 June, 'C' and 'D' Coys. with part of HQ.Coy. under Maj. C.C. Strong, left by train from Lungarty station and embarked at King George V Dock, Glasgow on H.M.T. 'Andes'. At 0345 hrs. and 0745 hrs. the next day, the remainder of the Bn. under Lt. Col. C.G. Robins left by trains from Almondbank Station to embark on the same ship. On board were the G.O.C. 49th Division, Maj. Gen. Curtis D.S.O., M.C., with the 146 Inf. Bde. (less transport) consisting of the 4 Lincolns, 1/4 KOYLI, the Hallamshires and attached troops commanded by Brig. C.C. Phillips.

Soldiers line up on the station platform at Perth. The glum faces seem to suggest that some of these men already knew that their destination was Iceland, but few could have guessed that their stay would last for the next two years. (HFC)

Very recent previous experience may have had a lot to do with army command structure on this voyage which once again saw Col. George Robins designated as O.C. Troops and Capt. John Marsh as Ships Adjutant.

At 1400 hours, H.M.T. 'Andes' slipped out of King George V Dock and moved about fifteen miles down stream to an anchorage opposite Gourock known as 'Tail of Bank' at about 1700 hours. She lay there until early morning waiting for other ships to gather in convoy which was to set out for a destination, as yet unknown to many of those troops on board.

*King George V Docks in the shadow of sunset and somewhat better days, Summer 2000.
(DWS)*

58

H.M.T. 'Andes' weighed anchor at 0030 hrs. on 24 June, 1940, to begin the journey to Iceland under an escort of two destroyers and the aircraft carrier H.M.S. 'Argus'. The weather started off dull and calm but by evening the ships speed was reduced to 6 knots due to high winds.

Albert Binns...

There were that many of us on the ship, some had to sleep on deck going across. It were quite rough and there were a lot of chaps got sea sickness and I managed to go two days and two nights, but then I had to go and do a four hour duty keeping watch on the bow. As I was going on duty I came across one of the blokes coming off and he was green... he was green! Then of course seeing him set me off. I'd been on duty for about half an hour when one of the night watch came round and asked me what was the matter. I told him I felt awful so he said he'd go and

Charles Strong and John Marsh relax on the sun drenched deck of H.M.T. 'Andes' in the Clyde. The cruise would end in Iceland to begin a two year tour of duty for the Hallamshires. June, 1940.(CGR)

fetch a pot of tea. About ten minutes later he came back with the tea and a sandwich. I had this sandwich and me tea and I felt a lot better after that and he said, 'Do you know what you've just had?' and I said, 'No.' He said , 'You've had a sandwich of fatty bacon , all fat and you won't be sick any more,' - and I never was!

Postcard showing the 'Andes' in her civilian role and colours. This ship was almost new (built in 1939) and was later fitted out as a Landing Ship Infantry (Large) .

At 1200 hrs. a conference was convened by 146 Brigade Commander. Information and instructions were issued to the various Commanding Officers with respect to the pending landings in Iceland of those on board. 147 Brigade plus a Canadian battalion were already established on the island (since the end of May) but were now in need of reinforcement which was about to be supplied by H.M.T. 'Andes'.

Those officers attending the meeting were reminded of the size of Iceland (slightly larger than Ireland) and that the general purpose of the exercise was to deny the enemy any use of the island as a base for submarine warfare or jumping off place for invasion of the British Isles. Disembarkation was to take place at Reykjavik, Seydisfjordur and Akureyri, with 146 Bde. H.Q. being established at the latter on the north side of the island. The immediate task was to occupy the most likely places of use to the enemy and to observe, monitor and control any movement by land, sea or air.

On the 25 June, 1940, the Battalion strength at sea was as follows...

O.C. - Lt.Col. C.G.Robins; 2nd i/c - Maj. C.C.Strong; Adjt. - Capt. H.J.W.Marsh; I.O. - 2/Lt. P.M.Young; M.O. - Lt. C.J.Wells; Chaplain - Capt. N. Murray-Smith.

HQ.COY. O.C. Capt.R.Mumby, Lt.P.S.Newton, 2/Lts.S.Martin de Bartoleme and J.Randall, Capt. & Q.M. J.P. Dobson D.C.M., M.M.

'A' COY. O.C. Maj.J.P.Hunt, A/Capt.W.L.Cave, 2/Lts.G.J.Good, R.N.Longridge and W.R. Jenkinson.

'B' COY. O.C. A/Capt.D.R.Bell, 2/Lts.M.J.A.Palmer, W.G.Blake and C.R.S.Sandford.

'C' COY. O.C. Maj.D.E.Lockwood, 2/Lts.A.C.Somers, S.J.D.Moorwood, H.W.Ridley and P.M. Willis-Dixon.

'D' COY. O.C. Capt.K.W.West, 2/Lts. L.M. Lonsdale-Cooper, C.A.B. Slack, P. Turrell and J.E.Crook.

Bn.HQ.	RSM. A.Burns, RQMS.C.H.McCreadie, 46 ORs.
HQ.Coy.	CSM. C.Curzon, PSM. J.Whitham, CQMS. E.Peek and 170 ORs.
'A' Coy.	CSM. L.H.Codd, CQMS. E.Candy and 120 ORs.
'B' Coy.	CSM. J.Howden, PSM. T.F.Bridges, CQMS. C.Heath and 119 ORs.
'C' Coy.	CSM. H.Marshall, CQMS. H.B.Tunstall and 120 ORs.
'D' Coy.	CSM. F.Colley, CQMS. J.G.Rodgers and119 ORs.

Also on board but with HQ. 146 Brigade were Capt. J.T.Daykin (Staff Capt.), Capt. R.I.Slater (I.O.), 2/Lt. J.Firth (Assist. Staff Capt.), Lt. P.W.Marsh (Cipher Officer), 11 ORs.

Capt. D.C.Beckett (O.C.146 Inf. Bde. Details) had remained in Perth, Scotland, in command of Lt. D.R.Morris and 68 ORs. plus all Transport and Carriers of the Bn., and the first batch of reinforcements.

Although Capt. R. I. Slater (Ivor to all who knew him) was a Hallamshire Bn. officer from before the war, he had spent most of his time attached to Brigade HQ. and could not add much to the immediate Hallams story thus far. However, he was standing close to George Robins as they all leaned on the rails of the 'Andes' as it approached Iceland.

Half truck/half bus transport of the kind described by Arnold Whiteley as being used for the overland trek from Reykjavik to Akureyri and not unlike those which had been resorted to in Norway a few weeks before. Fortunately, the Battalion's own vehicles would soon be on their way out to join them in Iceland.(CGR)

Ivor Slater...
As we came into sight of Iceland, George Robins just happened to be leaning on the rails nearby and he said, 'Well, just look at that. Miles and miles of bugger all!' I'll always remember him saying that and how true it was.

There were no special facilities for unloading the 'Andes' when she arrived (first at Reykjavik) and it was estimated that total unloading time for all three ports of call would take about eight days. Disembarkation would be effected by the use of two destroyers and the 'Andes' own life boats. Basic stores for the Akureyri contingent which included the Hallams was listed as eleven days composite rations, sixteen days bulk rations, three blankets per man and tents.

However, it was instructed that all arms and ammunition should be unloaded first, plus equal amounts of any other supplies as time allowed. Much general information was revealed at the conference and it was learned that H.M.S. 'Argus', the aircraft-carrier, would be putting in at Reykjavik where some bomber aircraft would be based. The Hallams were later to become involved with the location of one of these aircraft, a Fairey Battle, which crashed in their area.

The 26 June was a fine day when the ship arrived off Reykjavik at 1900 hrs. where unloading began immediately. This continued through the night in very light conditions due to the time of year. An advance party was organized to proceed overland to Akureyri consisting of Maj. J.P.Hunt, 2/Lt. G.J. Good and 19 other ranks of 'A' Coy. Travelling with this group was Arnold Whitely.

Arnold Whitely...
We went overland in these half truck/half bus transports to Akureyri on very rough road surfaces with river crossings and it took us about two days. We were all issued with a sealed tin of chocolate as part of emergency rations and instructions on the tin read 'Only to be opened with the permission of an officer'. As the journey progressed tins were opened and people started nibbling away at their blocks of chocolate. We were eventually put under canvas at Akureyri and after a while an officer noticed that many of the tins were being used as soap containers! He had a snap inspection and discovered that most men had eaten their chocolate. He shook my tin and it rattled because I'd still got chocolate in mine, but there was only one square left. So we all got an hours pack drill for disobeying the instructions on the tin. I said that I shouldn't have got an hour because I only ate half of mine! He (the Officer) said, 'Did anyone give you permission to open the tin?' I said, 'No Sir, but what if the officer had been killed and there was nobody left to tell us we could open them?'

The 'cross country group' were accompanied by a similar force from 4 Lincs which included the O.C.Brigade - Brigadier C.C.Phillips. A larger force had been envisaged to seize Akureyri but it was learned that a platoon of 147 Bde. had already occupied the town. It would seem that some of the Icelandic people were, understandably, not very well disposed towards an occupation of their island by British Forces. The most militant of them, however, had already been interned prior to the arrival of the 'Andes'. The Hallams do not seem to have been welcomed by the inhabitants of Akureyri (about 2,000 strong) with open arms. The British Army were at best, uninvited guests to this land and it would take a little time for at least some of its close-knit community to accept the situation. For many others, the British presence must have always remained, quite understandably, an unacceptable intrusion into their daily lives and customs. By all accounts, this manifested itself in the occasional skirmish.

Meanwhile, with escort destroyers H.M.S. 'Punjabi' and H.M.S. 'Firedrake' , the 'Andes' sailed on with the major part of the Hallams from Reykjavik at 1700 hrs. on 27 June, arriving at Akureyri on the 28th at 1500 hrs. which coincided with the arrival of the overland advance party. 'A' Coy. was chosen to act as ships unloading party and continued with this task through the night. In the meantime, 'C' & 'D' Coys. proceeded in transport to billets in a fish factory at the nearby Krossanes. 'A', 'B' & HQ. Coys. were encamped on the north side of the town and Bn. HQ. was set up at 35, Strandgata on the waterfront.

(note on escort destroyers : H.M.S. 'Punjabi' [F.21] - lost in collision with H.M.S. 'King George V', North Atlantic, 1/5/42 and H.M.S. 'Firedrake' [H.79] - Sunk by U211, N. Atlantic, 17/12/42).

Above : Hallams being put ashore at Akureyri using small fishing vessels with the destroyer H.M.S. 'Punjabi' (F21) standing by.

Below : One of the first tasks was to issue the men with weapons/ammunition and provide accommodation which, for all ranks during the first few months, would be in Bell tents of the type seen to the right of the central building.(HFC)

Albert Binns...

We landed at Akureyri in small boats and set up camp there on a piece of ground in tents. The first night I was on duty with an Ack-Ack Gun, you know, a Bren Gun mounted on a tripod and there were about eight round the camp and at about three o'clock in the morning it was still like daylight. We were right on the seashore more or less. We stayed about two or three days and then 'B' Coy. were sent further North to a little place called Saudarkrokur. There were another place called Vahmalid. It had swimming baths with hot water fed by the geysers and we used to do our own washing in a local wash house. We kept a Platoon there on a rota basis. We were in tents at the start but I remember the officers slept in spare bedrooms at the school caretakers house when they were at Vahmalid but Coy.HQ. were at Saudarkrokur.

At 1600 hrs. on the 29 June, 'A' Coy. was redeployed with Coy. HQ. and two platoons to Dalvik and one platoon under command of 2/Lt W.R.Jenkinson at Hjalteyri. The next day, 'B' Coy. was moved out to cover road junctions north of the town with platoons being spread out some two miles distant from one another. S.S. 'Salonika' arrived at Akureyri on this day with accommodation and canteen stores.

On the 1 July, the Battalion dispositions were as follows...
Bn.HQ.   35, Strandgata, Akureyri.

'A' Coy.   Camping Ground on north side of town.
'B' Coy.   Junction of roads to Akureyri from Reykyavik and Dalvik, 5 miles north of the town.
'C' Coy.   Krossanes - less 1 platoon which was at Oddeyri (North Quay of Akureyri).
'D' Coy.   In the hills covering the north and west exits from Akureyri.

Major C.C. Strong and 2/Lt. Randall had been on a 2 day reconnaissance of the countryside as far as Hraun via Saudarkrokur and Hof, returning on the 2 July. This was all in connection with the better establishment and dispositions of the Hallamshire Battalion in its new environment for what was to become a two year stay in Iceland.

On 5 July, two vessels were sighted by the detachment off Dalvik in the mouth of the Fjord described by the spotter as looking like a 'liner' and destroyer. The sighting was in very misty conditions but it was enough to create sufficient panic for 146 Brigade to order a 'stand to'. It may not have been a coincidence that the very next day saw 2/Lt. C.R.S. Sandford and No.11 Pl. ('B' Coy.) leave for Saudarkrokur where an Observation Post was to be established with the intention of challenging and inspecting foreign shipping coming into port. At 8pm. on the same day, two Walrus seaplanes arrived to assist with patrol work and later still at 10.45pm. 2/Lts. Lonsdale-Cooper and Turrel with 16 Pl. ('D' Coy.) sailed in S.S. 'Heingar' for Siglufjordur. This was to be one of five Control Ports at which all ships and boats visiting Icelandic waters must call and obtain a Clearing Certificate. 2/Lt. L.M. Lonsdale-Cooper was given the title of Port Control Officer here. An Observation Post was set up at Siglufjordur, one of those five Control Ports and 2/Lt. Jack Firth became Port Control Officer at Akureyri.

Bn. Headquarters was initially set up in this building, No.35, Strandgata, which overlooked the bay at Akureyri. It was soon to be vacated when orders were received to move into the Horga Valley about 12 miles to the northwest. Early conditions there would best be described, on a Youth Hostel grading, as Primitive(CGR)

Small adjustments were being made now in order to place various contingents of the Bn. in the most effective places with regard to protecting and defending the ground for which it was responsible. The North Quay of Akureyri (Oddeyri) was vacated by 2/Lt. W.H. Ridley and his platoon of 'C' Coy. when it was handed over to the 4 Lincolns. His new orders were to move to Ytri-Baegisa to act as guard for a new R.A.S.C. Dump. Many other adjustments and moves were made, all leading to the re-siting of Bn. HQ. and the main force away from Akureyri to be established in less exposed positions away from the immediate shore line. The state of flux which hung over the first half of July gave way to consolidation, as discussions took place about the best programme and dispositions for the recently arrived troops in order to retain a secure hold on their area of responsibility.

Arnold Whitely...
Most of us were on small detachments of Companies with one or two Platoons spread out from there and (in that situation) the idea of being in the army sort of breaks down. We were under canvas to start with then the Nissen huts were built around the September under the supervision of the R.Es. and activities were mainly guard duties. In the summer we had a lot of freedom, we could hire a boat or go pony trekking and things like that.

Albert Binns...
We did various things, regular things like route marches, drilling, guards and competitions to keep occupied. We used to do a bit of fishing off the pier end because there were plenty to catch, especially cod.
At one part between Saudarkrokur and Siglufjorder there were a bare stretch of land and we got set on to building mounds of rocks over an area of about three miles by one mile to stop aircraft landing and it took us about four or five months to complete. Two days after we'd finished there was an aircraft came over, a small one that the Icelanders used for spotting fish, and down he

came and landed! So next day we were out again, putting more stones down and it was funny because it was the first time we'd seen an aircraft up there.

In a letter to his mother, David Lockwood painted a picture in words that gave an overview of the strange but intriguing place in which he and Hallams now found themselves.

David Lockwood...
(Extract from letter sent to his Mother from Iceland)
9 July, 1940 (Krossanes)...
Two things that strike you most are the bird life and the wild flowers - both simply fill the place. I should think this must be one of the finest bird sanctuaries in the world. They are all extraordinarily tame and their nests are everywhere - snipe, curlew, golden plover, oyster catcher, arctic terns and every kind of wader and water bird you can think of... ...as for the flowers, I wish you could see them - all alpines of course and enough wild thyme and saxifrage to stock all the rock gardens in the world...

This is believed to be the Farm house called Krossastadir at the entrance to Bn. HQ. and from which the new camp took its name.(CGR)

...The people are very decent but very independent and we had a very stoney reception, but they're warming to us now. It started after three or four days by the children copying the troops and saluting us. We saluted back of course, and now I see the troops getting off with the girls - who, incidentally, are extraordinarily well dressed and very different from the Eskimo women we expected.

Early scene showing the Officers Quarters at Krossastadir. Their mess (Endcliffe Hall) can be seen to the right of centre at the foot of the hill. The small shack behind, was where Dummer (mentioned in one of David Lockwood's letters) did such wonders with the Bully Beef contained in standard rations.(CGR)

64

The troops seem happy enough and morale is good - they've got a picture house and several pubs in the town which is about 25 minutes walk away and they get one night off in three.

HQ. Coy. moved on 13 July and set up camp on the River Clera about two miles west of Akureyri and quite near to 'D' Coy. but 10 days later made its final move to a new site in the Horga Valley, some 15 kilometers distance from Akureyri on the Saudarkrokur road. It was here, near a little farm called Krossastadir from which the camp took its name, that Bn. HQ. was to become firmly established for the next two years. It was here that a major part of the photographic record was made of the Battalion's stay in Iceland, much of it to be found in these pages.

On 23 July, Bn. HQ. moved out of 35, Strandgata, to its new camp site at Krossastadir which straddled the road mentioned above and where a great deal of work was needed to be carried out before the winter set in.

The camp was approached on a road from the southeast (Akureyri) for about eight miles which then turned west into the Horga Valley. A few miles along this road was Krossastadir Farm on the left and a small bridge spanning a stream which formed a natural boundary on the east side of the camp. The whole site was set on a slope that fell away from the ridge on the south side of the road behind the officers quarters and down to a river (Horga) on the north side. Beyond the

Above : Construction begins on the new 'Endcliffe Hall' in the Horga Valley and is finished, complete with fireplace and chimney. Below : The NCO in charge was Sgt. Jack Walker but none of the men have been identified. George Learad and his pals, Strutt and Coe, were a part of this team so they should all be in this picture.(CGR)

river, the land rose steeply to form a huge barrier of mountain peaks which, according to Arthur Green, became popularly known as the Five Sisters. On the west side, the camp just petered out and left the 'public' road to wind its lonely way into the interior towards a place called Ytri Baegisa.

Interior furnishings and layout inside Endcliffe Hall. The cupboards and bookshelves seem to be made from modified boxes and the seats would probably fetch good prices on the Icelandic antique market today. There is a matching set of four chairs and settee which appear to have elaborate carved and turned wooden frames with boldly embroidered covers, piping and tassels. The shield above the fireplace contains a carved York & Lancaster 'cap badge' in the centre with the words 'Hallamshire 1940'. The magazine lying on the settee is 'The Sphere' which has, like many of the books on the shelf, no doubt arrived in a parcel from home.(CGR)

The Officers Mess and domestic site seems to have been well chosen by utilizing a gully in the hillside which was situated on the south side of the road not far beyond the bridge. It had a sufficiently flat and wide enough base to establish the required number of Bell tents which was at this time the only available shelter. A series of photographs were taken at about this time which gives a fair idea of the layout of this particular area. They also reveal the resourcefulness of a Commanding Officer of 'territorials' who was prepared to utilize the industrial skills of his mainly part-time soldiers to good effect. Whilst waiting for the arrival of more permanent accommodation in the form of Nissen

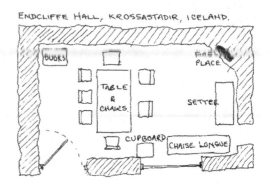

The floor plan at 'Endcliffe Hall' derived from various photographs.

huts, a structure took shape which was to become a veritable home from home, certainly for those longer serving Hallamshire Officers.

Only the C.O. could have authorized the building of such an ambitious little structure that was destined to be named after its much grander counterpart in Sheffield. It was built by a team of men under the supervision of a Sergeant who may not have been endowed with all the dry stone walling skills but nevertheless produced a very solid structure that was destined to become the Officers Mess, complete with some very interesting none government issue furniture which could only have been acquired from local sources. Luckily, the work was recorded on camera and internal snap-shots enable a good guess at the layout of the cramped but homely conditions inside the alternative - Endcliffe Hall! All or most of the officers of that period must have visited the place at some time or another to eat, drink and rest a while. Surprisingly few O.Rs. knew it was there or ever saw it but this is easily explained in that officers quarters are normally out of bounds for the men. Another reason was quite simply that it was situated in a gully which led to no where else except the officers quarters. It is wondered if there is any trace at all of that building today.

Battalion transport, in this case a Bedford MW 15cwt Truck, is offloaded from H.M.T. 'Ulster Prince' onto the Akureyri dockside.(HFC)

George Learad...
We built the officers mess in Iceland and at about that time, Strutt, Learad and Coe were all put into the Pioneer Platoon. The pioneer Sgt. in charge of the work team was Jack Walker and he got wounded early on when we got to Normandy. Some of the other lads that helped to build it were Tommy Marshall who were a bricklayer and also played football for Southport. Then there was Harold Garner, Johnny Paget and Bill Coe. We'd got bricklayers, joiners and even a blacksmith so there were plenty of people with the skills to do the job. We lived in tents when we first arrived there and we'd no bath for ages.

On the same day that HQ. Coy. moved to Krossastadir, H.M.T. 'Ulster Prince' had arrived at Akureyri bearing the Carrier and Transport personnel under the command of Capt. D.C. Beckett. Also with this group were Lt. D.R. Morris, 2/Lt. C.R.A. Tong and 21 O.Rs. Captain Beckett and his men (which included Arthur Green) had arrived ahead of their transport but they did not have to wait long for delivery. Ten Carriers, two Water Carts and four 15 cwt. General Service Trucks were unloaded from S.S. 'Adjutant' on 15 July.

Arthur Green...
We were Rear Party to follow the rest of the Bn. later. Myself and a few others somehow got separated from the rest (after Stobs Camp) and landed up with the Holding Bn. at Doncaster Racecourse. However, we'd been there for a couple of weeks to a month doing nothing, as you might say, then we were sent out to rejoin the Bn. We got to Glasgow and boarded a Dutch ship which had been a pre-war cross channel steamer. Going across the North Atlantic to Iceland was

Stephen Bartolome, Philip Young, John Marsh and the Reverend N. Murray-Smith take advantage of the Autumn sun. The date must be around August, 1940, as they are still living in tents here at Krossastadir. The Padre was affectionately known to his fellow officers as 'Nicotine Norman' because, like David Lockwood, he was never very far away from his pipe.(CGR)

no mean effort for a boat of its size. Anyhow, we were eventually arrived at Reykjavik, stayed in a transit camp for a few days, then left aboard another ship (H.M.T. Ulster Prince) for Akureyri.

HQ. Coy. was up a valley at a place called Krossastadir way out in the country and the Companies were billetted at various places on the coast, some of them with very funny names. I always remember, I think it was 'A' Coy. that was at a place called Glaesibaer (Glass-a-beer) which seemed amusing to us because we never had a glass of English beer for ages. We knew about it when the first stuff came though, it was Canadian beer in quart bottles and they were rationed at the NAAFI. My mate, Doug Redmond, didn't drink so I bought his ration and I got these two quarts of Canadian 'Dow' but I don't remember much after supping the first one. They got me back to the billet about two hundred yards from the NAAFI and all I remember was them putting me on the bed and me just laying there and the Nissen hut was just floating. Oh! it was strong stuff, I've never tasted anything as strong in my life.

During this period, Lt. J. Firth was appointed A/Staff Capt. with Bde. in place of Capt. J.T. Daykins when the latter was evacuated to Reykjavik for an operation. Another two Observation Posts were established at Dalvik and Skagastrond, the latter position being some sixty miles from Bn.HQ. although it was more like one hundred miles by road. In all, the Hallams were allotted about one hundred and twenty-five miles of coast line to watch and defend.

David Lockwood...
(Extract from letter sent to his Mother from Iceland)

29 July, 1940 (Krossanes)...
The sea fishing is extraordinarily good here and I generally organize a competition for the men off the local jetty on Saturday afternoons. We get a lot of very good plaice and one of the rules of the competition is that the Company Officers Mess has the pick of the catch! One of my sergeants has just come in with a six pound cod he has caught from a boat this evening. A knock on the door just now as I wrote the last sentence and the sergeant in question put his head round the door and said would I like a cod steak for supper - but we had some very good steak and onions cooked by Chris Somers batman an hour ago and I'm full...   ...The officers mess is really attractive and overlooks the fjord from the top of a cliff.

I ride a motorbike permanently now as my beautiful truck has been given away to someone in England and worst of all, Simpson (his batman) has gone too. Motorcycling here is a real art on these roads which are nothing better than cart tracks in places and never better anywhere than our worst un-tarred third class roads - full of holes and covered with loose stones.

On the 1 August the Hallamshire Bn. dispositions were as follows :-

Bn. HQ. & HQ. Coy.	KROSSASTADIR
'A' Coy. (less 2 Pls)	REISTARA
1 Pl. of 'A' Coy.	LITLI-ARSKOGSSANDUR
1 Pl. of 'A' Coy.	HJALTEYRI
'B' Coy. (less 1 Pl.)	SAUDARKROKUR
1 Pl. of 'B' Coy.	VARMAHLID
'C' Coy. (less 1 Pl.)	KROSSANES
1 Pl. of 'C' Coy.	GLAESIBAER
'D' Coy. (less 1 Pl.)	DJUPARBAKKI
1 Pl. of 'D' Coy.	SIGLUFJORDUR
O.P. at DALVIK (Sgt. Wingfield and 4 men)	
O.P. at SKAGARSTROND (Sgt. Lees and 4 men)	

On 7 August the 'Konigen Emma' steamed into Akureyri harbour with considerable reinforcements aboard. These included 2/Lts. J.A.N. Sim (to 'D' Coy.), A.C.F. Stewart (to 'B' Coy.), R.H. Canter (to 'C' Coy.), J.L. Hall (to HQ. Coy.) and C.A. Mackillop (to 'A' Coy.) with ninety O.Rs. of whom forty-two had seen previous service with the Hallams. The men were deployed - ten to HQ. Coy. and twenty each to the Rifle Coys. to form a fourth Pl. in each of these. This influx now brought the establishment to thirty-six Officers (two attached), eight hundred and thirty Other Ranks (four attached). Of these, sixteen were attached to 146 Brigade HQ. in various capacities.

The sun was now retreating to the southern hemisphere and at last the nights were giving way to some darkness. The weather continued rather fine but slight frosts were creeping in at night with some snow falling on the hilltops. Not before time, a start was made on the erection of huts to replace the Bell tents before the winter really set in.

Arthur Green...
There were about ten of us to a Bell tent and when you've got all your kit and ten of you in a Bell tent believe you me its just chaotic, you know, all your kit, your kit bag, wellies, everything! They were supposed to 'sleep' twenty-two, one to a panel and I think the panels were about fifteen to eighteen inches wide at the bottom. How we used to manage that I do not know.

Anyhow, eventually a ship came in with Nissen hut parts and I was detailed to go down with others to unload these sectionalised buildings. We'd been building the foundations for some time before, because we already knew the base dimensions required and we received a good quota of huts that gave us plenty of room, about twenty men to a hut. We just managed to get them up before the winter started. There was no furniture and we had to scrounge wood to make whatever we wanted. We were issued with double sleeping bags and why they issued blokes in the army with white sleeping bags, I don't know. After we'd had them for a fortnight they were black and you couldn't wash them at all. We eventually had three blankets and if you were still cold you could use your greatcoat.

Jack Haslam...
It was a twenty-four hour job building Nissen huts because of the light nights. They put us on eight hour shifts with a R.E. in charge of eight man teams. So the work went on continually day and night.

The first ten Nissen huts erected at Krossastadir were taken over and occupied at 2 pm. on 1 September, one of which was built near 'Endcliffe Hall' to accommodate the C.O., Lt. Col.

69

Most of the men were required to put some of their time into the laying of Nissen hut foundations . The team on the left is led by Sgt. Walker and includes Arther Green, who can be seen far left (kneeling).(HFC)

Robins and other members of his staff. How long it took him to complete the furnishing of his own room is not known but one piece, a chair that was probably acquired in Akureyri, cost him no less than £3 and 10 shillings (£3.50), a princely sum in those days. The Bn. meanwhile continued with other tasks such as defensive works, wiring and rivetting, as materials became available.

Transactions were taking place elsewhere which did not seem to involve any money changing hands but doubtless leaving participants well satisfied. An amusing 'bill' made out to David Lockwood during the previous month for services rendered was presented by a local man at Krossanes who was most eager to receive his payment 'by next Saturday'. Such luxuries would be in short supply at this time and just the thing to spice up Mr. Jorgenson's forthcoming Saturday night.

David Lockwood...
(Extract from letter sent to his Mother from Iceland)

2 September, 1940 (Krossanes)...
We get a two penny bar (chocolate) issued free per week but it's fairly gritty but useful in an emergency - but the Terry's (he had just received some in a parcel) is a luxury here. We take choc always on our climbing expeditions. We've made two attempts in the last fortnight (Chris Somers and I) on the highest mountain in this part of the island - a mountain called Kenling which is 5000 odd feet, but each time have been defeated by snow and loose stones... ...We've got a mobile cinema here now in a motor van run by the NAAFI and they are giving their first show in our Recreation Room next week.

On the night of 3/4 September, a billet at Saudarkrokur which housed the Men's Canteen at ground level and a Radio Station on the first floor, was destroyed by fire which could easily have taken the life of Douglas Catley. A Rotherham man, Doug had worked in the Tailoring departments of two well known shop names in the town, Muntus and then Waddingtons before being called up.

Doug Catley...
We had the upstairs of this building as our Wireless Station with all our equipment in it and underneath was used as a canteen. We used to sleep upstairs through a trap door and one evening when we went to bed a lad we called 'Jock' stayed up on watch and was writing a letter. About one o'clock he needed to go for a pee, so he opened the trapdoor and realized that something was on fire. He woke me and the other man, then went down ahead of us but made

the mistake of opening the downstairs door which immediately fed the flames with oxygen. We just managed to get our trousers on and jumped through the window in our bare feet. We lost all the radio equipment, personal belongings, everything! There was some bandolier ammunition in there as well and when the fire got going it was banging away. The C.O., Lt. Col. Robins, just happened to be on a visit at the time and he took the photograph from his hotel accommodation across the street.

Doug was born in James Street, Rotherham and before the war he worked at Waddingtons Taylors and Outfitters, and was being trained to manage a new branch to be opened in Doncaster but the war stopped all that. After preliminary training he was sent out to join the Hallamshires in Akureyri (Konigen Emma) and eventually ended up at Saudarkrokur as a signaller.

S.S. 'Goteborg' arrived at Hjalteyri with British military personnel on board who had been repatriated from Sweden but it was sent on to Reykjavik under an armed guard commanded by 2/Lt. J.L. Hall and 7 O.Rs.

This 'Bill' for wire installation at Krossanes must have been the result of some shrewd bargaining and did not involve cash payment.
'bringing electric light in your little white house = 3 boxes of plaiors'
(Players Cigarettes)
'for lent you 9 lamps = 1 bottle whiskey'
These items have been amusingly totalled below so as to leave no margin of error or possibility of misunderstanding of the agreement.(DEL)

Canteen and Signals hut at Saudarkrokur after the fire had caused serious damage. An armed guard has been placed on the building, much to the bemusment of curious onlookers who can only wonder why the English would want to place such high security on a burned out shell. There was, of course, probably still some signals equipment inside waiting to be retrieved.(CGR).

Arnold Whitely...
One of us tasks was to observe at the mouth of the fjord all the shipping that came in. We had a list of any ships that was due to come in apart from fishing vessels and what colour it would be and superstructure, and this , that and the other, and further up the fjord there was a detachment of Marines with artillery pieces. One day a ship came up that wasn't on the list and of course we

rang the Marines who fired a blank warning shot across it to stop it. It wouldn't stop immediately so they put a live shot across and it stopped dead and it turned out they were exchange wounded prisoners.

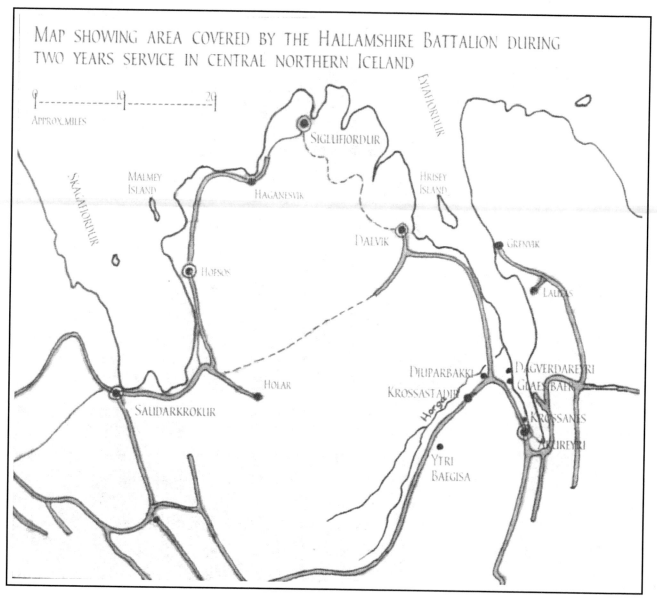

MAP SHOWING AREA COVERED BY THE HALLAMSHIRE BATTALION DURING TWO YEARS SERVICE IN CENTRAL NORTHERN ICELAND

Map showing the position of Krossastadir (Hallamshire Battalion HQ.) in relation to the various detachment locations and some of the platoon outstations mentioned throughout the text.(DWS)

On 7 September, the first snow fell in the valley, covering Krossastadir Camp with a thin carpet of white. Major John Hunt escaped from the worst of it when he was granted three months leave to return to industry but as it turned out, was not destined to rejoin the Hallams in Iceland. In the meantime, the weather continued mainly fine and mild with only a few falls of snow during the month with occasional frosts at night. This enabled work to progress well on the preparation of winter camps and all troops except a few guards were in proper hutments by the month end. In many cases, however, conditions were very cramped and without the luxury of separate dining accommodation. The winter dispositions were being finally settled before the Hallamshire Bn. was gripped by the oncoming Icelandic weather.

72

David Lockwood...
(Extract from letter sent to his Mother from Iceland)

10 September, 1940 (Krossanes)...
All the trawlers are returning now and the local harbour is full of masts again. The boats from the Faroes, hundreds of them, come in here before going home and the town today was full of Faroe men - great big toughs with thigh boots on and jack knives in their belts and furry red and black striped caps on their heads like the top of a stocking folded over and sewn down...

I'm looking forward to seeing a garden again. The only thing you see here is a few lupins and some quite good stock in one garden. One fellow in town grows stocks and sweet peas in window boxes - inside his window. They'll give anything for English seeds here and we gave a farmer a few packets we'd brought with us from our garden at Stobs Camp (Hawick) and we had free eggs for weeks!

Major John Hunt was perhaps the first of a number of officers that were called away to industry but did not return to the Battalion until after the war when he became its Commanding Officer. (CGR)

Early winter view (northwest) from the window of George Robins Nissen accommodation near 'Endcliffe Hall' at Krossastadir, late 1940. The rest of the camp sprawls away to the west beyond buildings on the left and the Horga Valley floor can be seen in the middle distance on the right. The mountain chain beyond is part of the range called 'Five Sisters' as Arthur Green called them - or was it three?
The road leading out of camp to the right (off picture) crossed a bridge over a stream which formed the eastern boundary. The farm called Krossastadir was at the junction of road and stream.(CGR)

Distribution of the Battalion on 1 October was as follows...

Bn. HQ.; HQ. Coy. (less 3" Mortars.)	KROSSASTADIR
O.P. Sgt. and 4 men.	DALVIK
'A' Coy. HQ. and 2 Pls.	BRAGHOLT
2 Pls. of 'A' Coy. + Det. 3" Mortars.	FAGRISKOGUR
O.P. Sgt. and 4 men.	LITLI-ARSKOGSSANDUR
'B' Coy. HQ. and 1 Pl.	SAUDARKROKUR
1 Pl. of 'B' Coy.	VARMAHLID
1 Pl. of 'B' Coy.	SIGLUFJORDUR
Reserve Pl.	YTRI-BAEGISA
'C' Coy. HQ. and 3 Pls.	KROSSANES
1 Pl. of 'C' Coy.	GLAESIBAER
'D' Coy. + Det. 3" Mortars.	DJUPARBAKKI

David Lockwood...
(Extract from letter sent to his Mother from Iceland)

4 October, 1940...
We're really very spoilt with papers and Mary keeps sending bundles of them so that we've got heaps now. In addition, the subalterns have collected about fifty or sixty Penguin books and we've swapped some with the officers of a warship that called...

Our new mess is a great success and I've got a very nice room with a communicating door into the mess....the front door is about ten yards from the shore of the fjord.
We've got electric light (see 'Bill' on earlier page) which is a great blessing and the house is a wooden one built in the Norwegian style and I wouldn't swap this or the men's billet for any other I've seen in Iceland... At the moment there is no electricity in the men's place but we're hoping to get it soon when we get some cable...

David Lockwood on the jetty at Krossanes with the tabby he called Caroline. He awoke one night to find that she had crawled into his sleeping bag with him and produced four kittens.(DEL)

We've built a most super latrine for the men for the winter with turf and timber and corrugated iron and a concrete floor with some cement we pinched from the R.Es. We've also built an incinerator and are now just completing a terrific washhouse for the lads to use, instead of a stream, with a proper army wash bench and six brass taps, and the first water came out today. I've made drawings for all these erections and have made each of the subalterns into a foreman with their platoon as the gang and we have taught them to work to a drawing.

A neighbouring battalion of ours actually ran a private dance last Saturday and George Robins, Bill Cave, James Moorwood and I represented us. It was a very good party once we got going and we taught the locals to Paul Jones and Palais Glide and Lambeth Walk - they loved it. It was a nice change anyway and if it hadn't been for the language difficulty, might easily have been a Territorial dance in Sheffield. I got quite a shock when I walked in and saw it all going on - it was so unlike anything that has happened here before.

On 21 October, General the Viscount Gort, V.C., K.C.B., C.B.E., D.S.O., M.V.O., M.C., Inspector General of Training, visited the area accompanied by Major General Curtis, G.O.C., Alabaster Force. His Itinerary included...
1030 hrs. Inspection of 'C' Coy. at Krossanes as they manned battle positions.
1330 hrs. Lunch at Bn. HQ. Mess, Krossastadir.
1430 hrs. Observation of Field Firing exercise carried out by 18 Pl. 'D' Coy. commanded by 2/Lt. C.A.B. Slack.
Next day the Lord Bishop of Aberdeen confirmed 71 men of the Bn. with 20 others at Djuparbakki and lunched with 'D' Coy. Officers. At the end of the month, the C.O. and Adjt. travelled by sea on the S.S. 'Disco' to Siglufjordur on a tour of inspection.

Under control of the Signals Officer, the Battalion Meteorological Station opened on 1 November equipped with all the necessary instruments to gauge the oncoming weather. Even better news came on the 3rd, when new Band Instruments arrived which were presented to the Bn.

'anonymously' by Mr. Firth. These were to replace those which had been lost in the Norwegian Campaign when they were stored in a building which took a direct hit in an air raid on Namsos.

During the latter half of November, additional transport arrived in the form of three 15 cwt. and five 30 cwt. trucks and educational classes became available for both special and general subjects. On the 29th, Sgt. Pearson (Provost Sgt.), and Sgt. R.C. Wingfield (Int. Sgt.), went to Reykjavik, the former to take instruction at Detention Barracks and the latter to attend an Intelligence Course. There was a spell of very cold weather with slight snow in the middle of the month, but the end of the month was milder with all snow melted except on the hills. Work continued throughout the month on Camp Sites, especially pipe laying, drainage and road making with parties of R.E s. attached to the Coys. for this purpose.

Arthur Green...
There was a bridge at Krossastadir and anything over 30 cwt. you couldn't get over because it was on a bend and a very tricky job to get through. We were issued with some of these 30 cwts. secondhand from another unit when theirs were replaced with new ones. They all had names painted on the sides and mine was called 'Hotazell' and I remember the C.O. examining these vehicles and saying, 'Get these names off!' Evidently, he'd had a bit of a brush with my particular vehicle a week or two earlier in his Humber Snipe Staff Car. I later discovered the reason for this truck having that name was because it was continually blowing core plugs and we often ran out of the things. We used to use old pennies specially modified by beating them with a hammer to replace them.

Lt. Col. C.G. Robins was suddenly thrust into a world of sheer luxury compared to his meager quarters at Krossastadir when he was required to stand in for the 146th Brigade Commander whilst he attended a conference in Reykjavik. This involved temporary accommodation in the Brigadier's flat for approximately ten days. The C.O. took some photographs of this place which still retained the decoration it had when it was hastily vacated by a German who, before the war, was claimed to have been some sort of ambassador of the German Government. Whatever his position in life, he had certainly been able to afford to surround himself with, what would seem to any ordinary soul of those days, the trappings of a prince. On the 13th of the month, the dream came to an end and the C.O. was back in the real world of Krossastadir, back to his share of a Nissen hut out in the wilds of Iceland. For him, however, it must have seemed as near to home as a man in his position could feel in that place, which was about to be engulfed in the desolation of winter.

Compare O.C. Hallams meagre quarters at Krossastadir (above) with those of the O.C. Brigade at Akureyri (right). The Flat was thought to have belonged to a high ranking German diplomat before the war started and furniture/decoration was very much as he had left it.(CGR)

David Lockwood...
(Extract from letter sent to his Mother from Iceland)
17 December, 1940...
I can't believe Christmas is a week tomorrow and we had a meeting of 'C' Coy. officers and sergeants after lunch today to decide what we were going to do. We're having a sing - song in the billet in the evening of Christmas Eve. On Christmas Day, George is coming down to see us at 12.00 and we're having the sergeants in here to crack a bottle of your fizz with them. Then at 12.30 the men are having their Christmas Dinner and we shall wait on them as we did last year when Mary helped to dish it out (Thirsk). George is coming in to wish them luck.....
....we've got some pork in cold storage in town and are hoping some stuff for plum puddings and mince pies will arrive in time by sea. Also the beer is due but not here yet, we haven't had any for some weeks now........George has got a packet of sweets or chocs. per man from home and 50 cigarettes per man from the 'Telegraph' (very kind) and Mary has sent 1000 Players for them which I thought was very sweet of her. So, they'll have a pretty good Christmas.

Nurses from the Hospital Ship 'Leinster' seen here visiting 'D' Company. Their names were not recorded but known officers from left to right are: —, Mike Lonsdale-Cooper; —, Brian Slack and Ken West (O.C. 'D' Coy.) (HFC)

We're running a couple of officers dances in January and I find myself representing the Battalion on the Brigade committee......We've got a Hospital Ship here now and this is being run mainly for the benefit of the 'Nannies'. We've got one of them on the committee, the second matron who is as tough as old boots and has got an India N.W. Frontier medal ! - but is a very good sort and actually wears lipstick !   ...but they talk English which is something to hear - an English woman's voice. They come to church with us in the Cathedral on Sundays now.

David Lockwood (Letters to Mary)
18 December, 1940 , Iceland.
(Writing after news of the Sheffield Blitz)
So far I've heard of one unlucky man - a soldier in HQ. Company whose wife and child have been killed. Poor devil, he's in the Hospital Ship (Leinster) having just had an operation and the Padre went down this afternoon to break it to him. Maud Robins sent George a cable about it...

...You would have laughed the other evening - Eddie was standing by the stove in the mess and said, 'You know, there are all the characters in Winnie the Pooh in this mess.' When we came to think of it , it was true so now we've started a system of officers code names !

Chris	'Piglet'	(Somers)
James	'Rabbit'	(Moorwood)
Tony	'Baby Roo'	(?)
Paul	'Wol'	(Willis-Dixon)
Eddie	'Eeyaw'	(?)
Me	'Pooh !!'	

....We rang Tony up last night and told him that for purposes of secrecy all officers were being given codenames - that his name was 'Baby Roo' and that all messages, etc. must be signed that way in future. I'm afraid he's seen through it now ! Aren't we teenies ! (this word was used regularly in David Lockwood's correspondence - it means 'childish' or 'children')

...I'm still enjoying the Herries books so much in bed at night and find it helps me to go to sleep if I read a bit first. It's so refreshing and such a complete change to read a book like this after Iceland and the army all day long - it simply breathes England - and you my darling...

This Christmas Card seems to suggest a shortage of fresh meat, but there was hardly any danger of Polar Bears prowling around the camp except for the human kind, now that the image had been adopted as the new 49th Divisional sign. It seems obvious here also that 'George' Robins was more popularly known by his first name within his own family circle.(CGR)

The last month of 1940 was drawing to a close and the seasonal thing was about to begin. Two NCOs. were destined to miss these proceedings when they were embarked for U.K. to attend courses. 4745831 Sgt. C. Laughton to attend Small Arms School at Hythe Wing, Bisley, and 4745171 Sgt. E. Wells to Central NCOs. School at Strensall, near York. They embarked on the 18th, so in all probability they would have managed to get home in time to celebrate Christmas with their families.

On Christmas Day the Commanding Officer, George Robins, together with his 2 i/c Charles Strong and John Marsh (Adjt), visited the Coys. and Detachments to serve the men their dinner as was the custom. They were also accompanied by Capt. & Q.M. J.P. Dobson. (as an N.C.O. in the Great War, this man had already done his bit for King and Country having been awarded the D.C.M. and M.M. He was popularly known by everyone in the Bn. as 'Dobby'). Their itinerary was as follows...

1230 hrs. to HQ. Coy., 1315 hrs. to 'D' Coy., 1400 hrs to 'C' Coy.(Krossanes),1600 hrs. to 'A' Coy. (Fagriskogur), 1630 hrs. to 'A' Coy. (Bragholt) and finally at 1730 hrs. HQ. Sgts. Mess - always a good place to finish!
At 1300 hrs. on 26 December they visited 'B' Coy. at Ytri-Baegisa and at 1700 hrs. 'C' Coy. at Glaesibaer. Each man was provided with a Christmas Dinner of pork, Christmas pudding, mince pies, together with beer and gifts of cigarettes and sweets.

Winter had still not taken a real hold and the Christmas period was described as warm with a little snow. The roads became considerably worn, but were quite easily passable throughout the month. Various types of training and education were carried on together with the usual camp chores as the year came to a close for the Hallamshire Battalion who were about to experience their first winter in Iceland. No one may have realized it then but they were setting a record of being based in the most northerly place the York & Lancaster Regiment had ever served.

Iceland 1941

The year got off to a brisk start with quite a number of movements both in and out of the Battalion. These movements are well documented in the War Diary with names of both Officers and NCOs proceeding on various courses, etc. However, to aid the better flow of this text it is not proposed to list all of them.

On the first day, Lt. P.W. Marsh and 2/Lt. J. Firth were transferred (the latter was already attached) to HQ. 146 Bde., the former as Cipher Officer and the latter as Staff Lt. Both were struck off Bn. strength with effect from the 19 November, 1940, but it would not be long before they rejoined the Battalion. Ivor Slater left his position as Intelligence Officer with 146 Brigade to become the Hallams Adjutant on 4 January, 1941, when John Marsh relinquished that post and was given command of 'A' Coy. at Bragolt. Ivor now found himself at Krossastadir where he claimed that he had wonderful meals at Battalion HQ.

Ivor Slater at Hopton, Spring 1944 (HFC)

Ivor Slater...
I went back to the Hallams as Adjutant in place of John Marsh, a super chap. The whole of the time I was Adjutant, I mounted the guard at six in the morning and dismissed them at night except on one occasion. There was a blizzard one morning and I couldn't find the way from my hut to the Guard Room and there were sheets of metal flying all over the place, tin coming off the Nissen huts and I just couldn't get there. Other than that, I never missed a day.

George Robins decided that everybody (officers) would wear a thing which was like a cravat. In effect, you put it round your neck and tied it through as tight as you wanted it and turned it round with the 'bib' tucked in at the front. It was very smart and jolly good because it saved you from having to wear a collar and tie. (see photo - page 68)

The last thing at night, George and I always boiled up some tea in our mess tins. He was a great whiskey drinker and he always laced his tea with it but I didn't enjoy the stuff, never have done. I must admit that when it was very cold I did put a drop in mine. However, more of my whiskey went on my feet because I used to get cold feet and hands and rubbing whiskey into them warmed them up very quickly. George used to think it was an absolute waste.

On the 5th, Sgt. J. Pearson returned from a course at the Detension Barracks at Reykjavik and 2/Lt. R.H. Canter returned to U.K. to resume his career in Medical Studies.

A new draft arrived which included two men who had been put ashore and hospitalized at Reykjavik when the Bn. first came to Iceland in June the previous year. The draft, which included two officers and 51 O.Rs., was absorbed by HQ. Coy. (13 O.Rs.), 'A' Coy. (2/Lt. W. Holmes and 13 O.Rs.), 'B' Coy. (12 O.Rs.), 'C' Coy. (2/Lt. J. Wollerton plus 5 O.Rs.) and 'D' Coy. (8 O.Rs.).

John Wollerton had joined his father's decorating business in Sheffield when he left school but barely a year had passed when he contracted lead poisoning. He then turned his mind to architecture, spending the next five years in concentrated studies at Sheffield Technical College, no less than five nights per week. When war broke out, he went shopping around the recruitment offices to see what was on offer.

John Wollerton...

When war broke out, first of all I tried to join the Navy and they took the 'Mickey' out of me. Their office was opposite the Cathedral on Church Street. I walked in and said, 'I want to join the Navy,' and a chap with a lot of malice said, 'Oh Yeah! Well, to join the Navy you've got to be very fit and you've got to have very good teeth and you can only join for 7 and 5' (a reference to the number of years a man would have to sign on for service and reserve). *I said, 'Well I can't do that because I've only got half a crown with me!'* (This joke will be lost on anyone who is too young to remember pre-decimal currency !).

John Wollerton, Holland, 1945.(HFC)

Then I went to the R.A.F. recruiting office in West Street. I'd cottoned on to the humour of the services and I walked in there - this was September the fourth, the Monday morning after war had been declared. I've come to join the R.A.F.' and he said, 'Oh Yeah, do you want to do anything in particular?' and I said, 'Well I'd like to fly.' He said, 'Any particular 'plane?' and I said, ' Well yes - a Spitfire!' You have to remember these were being advertised all over the place in Sheffield. Then he said, 'Do you want any particular markings on this Spitfire?' The conversation was reduced to a good humoured laugh but it seemed that there wasn't a chance at that time for me to get in as a pilot. Even qualified pilots were being refused because of the clamour to sign up.

Eventually I was called up in February, 1940, and proceeded to Pontefract Barracks. At twenty-two years of age I walked through the gates completely undaunted, to me it was a new experience. We got our various issues of the usual kit and then we were taken for a haircut. Afterwards, everybody looked the same above the eyebrows! It wasn't long before I got into trouble with my sense of humour. I was walking along the serving hatch in the mess one day with these two dumplings in my mess tin and I said to the server who was about to put my meat on, 'If you were to drop these two dumplings on Berlin the war will be over tomorrow!' I was immediately sent to the back of the queue and put on a Charge...

John was eventually selected for a commission and was sent to Colchester for training at the O.C.T.U. after which he returned to Pontefract. After putting his name forward for duties abroad in a hot climate, he found himself together with 2/Lt. W. Holmes (John calls him 'Leslie' in the taped interview), on a ship bound for Iceland.

John Wollerton...

We landed at Reykjavik and stayed in transit there for a week where I met Padre Thomas for the first time. We then went on board 'Lochnagar' and sailed for Akureyri in an anti-clockwise direction round the island and arrived after a pretty rough passage. We had to pull in to a fjord on the way round for shelter where I tried to tidy the draft up by getting them to wash and shave and had them formed up on deck as we approached the quayside in Akureyri. There was an officer that I couldn't recognize, waiting there to greet us, who returned my salute. Unfortunately, I think I lip read him correctly and his words were, 'What a bloody shower!' That officer turned out to be the Commanding Officer, Lt. Col. Robins.

Of course, in the end, I discovered what a marvellous fellow he was, typical regular soldier, a disciplinarian through and through, but always fair. I think I learned not only a lot from him but a lot from all the officers in the Battalion. The fact that they'd all come from a civilian background apart from the C.O. and a few others, my immediate impression was what a fine Battalion I had joined.

We made our way up to Bn.HQ. (Krossastadir) but soon I joined 'C' Coy. where David Lockwood was in command, a very affable, very pleasant man indeed...

...The officers mess was in a house at the shore end of a jetty with the toilet very conveniently placed on the jetty itself. Two of the officers that come to mind were Chris Somers and James Moorewood. The men were in Nissen huts near a fish factory and the whole place was infested with rats because of the waste left over from what was mainly fish oil production.

As I approached the Platoon Hut that had been assigned to me, I noticed a man standing outside holding a home made fishing rod with a bit of string on, dipped in a bucket of water. They were trying to send me up but they didn't know I had been a Private soldier a few months before and knew the ropes. As I passed the man, I said, 'Stand up,' which he did and I said, 'You won't catch any fish that way,' and he said, 'Why not Sir?' to which I replied, 'Well, you haven't got a hook on.' They never tried that again although they did occasionally mime my walk because I've got a bit of a funny walk - that amused me and it was good for the Platoon to have a bit of humour.

It is a pleasure to include this photograph in that all those appearing can be named. They are from left to right : Thorpe, Gillat, Greenwood, Rodgers, Lees, Lt. Wollerton, Cartwright, Hirst, Slater, Powell, Ellis, Whyat and Ogden. These are all members of John Wollerton's Platoon but the man who fished in a bucket without a hook on his string can not be identified. (HFC)

Ray Langdale also left with that draft of men from Pontefract barracks and sailed to Iceland on a ship, manned by Newfoundlanders, called 'Chitwell'. He remembers the draft officer i/c was John Wollerton and the draft included 'Bunny' Whiting and John Ellis.

Various courses at Force HQ. were attended by officers during the month of January which included Tactics (Lt. Morris with 2/Lts. Lonsdale-Cooper, Sandford and Somers) and Signalling (2/Lt. Turrel). Cpl. R.C. Wainman and L/Cpl. F. Priest went on a Signal Instructors Course. Lt. P.W. Marsh rejoined the Bn. when he was replaced as Cipher Officer at Bde. HQ. by 2/Lt. H.W.

Ridley. CSM Howden of 'B' Coy., embarked for home when he was granted compassionate leave and returned to I.T.C. The York & Lancaster Regiment, at Pontefract.

More transport was supplied during the month in the form of Morris Commercial 15 cwt. Trucks, three of which arrived on S.S. 'Skagen' (8/1) and two on S.S. 'Zaanstroom' (17/1). The usual routine inspections took place at some of the Coy. detachments and one, not so routine, at the newly completed Detension Barracks at Krossastadir. The inspection was carried out by Lt. Col. Beam (R.A.M.C.) who recommended that a number of improvements should be carried out before he would consider it to be of an acceptable standard.

The Commanding Officer, Adjutant and Medical Officer travelled by air on a tour of inspection to Saudarkrokur and later from there, by sea, to Varmahlid and Siglufjorder in the 'Koralen I'. The aircraft they used in the first leg of the journey can best be described as a high wing, single radial engined float plane of which a snap shot was taken by Lt. Col. Robins. It was a civilian aircraft believed to have been used by the local fishing industry for fish shoal spotting but no doubt also used as a very convenient means of transport and communications.

This is the actual aircraft used by Col. Robins on the tour of inspection which he carried out at Saudarkrokur. Painted bright red, it was described as a Northrop Floatplane and seems to have been 'hired' from the local fishing industry. (CGR)

Three tractors and two snowploughs arrived on the scene which were all allocated to the Bn. in plenty of time to deal with the rigours of a winter which had not really taken hold yet. One of each of these was located in a Camp at Lons where a Dock Operating Coy. of the R.Es. was based and the rest were established at Krossastadir. Capt. D.C. Becket took over the temporary command of the Dock Operating Coy. pending the arrival of an Officer of that unit from Reykjavik.

By the end of the month, Standing Orders for the operation of the new Military Detention Barracks at Krossastadir (for use by the whole Akureyri Garrison) were issued and Capt. R.I. Slater was appointed Commandant. The erection of a Miniature Range which was begun on the first of the month had to be temporarily abandoned on the 29th due to shortage of men and materials. A/Capt. P.W. Marsh with 12 O.Rs. of 'D' Coy. Ski-Platoon, sailed to Siglufjorder for two weeks

Siglufjordur (HFC)

81

to gain early experience there, as no facilities were available around Akureyri. It can only be assumed that the reason for this was lack of snow fall in the latter area although some light snow falls were reported with bitterly cold winds at times.

In a monthly summing up of progress with camp site work achievement, it was reported that the installation of electricity had taken place in the Orderly Room, P.R.I. Hut, Signal Office, Q.M. Store, Detention Barracks, HQ. Coy. Office and Stores, Diners and Canteen along with nine Sleeping Huts.

On the 4 February the C.O. convened a conference to discuss future policy regarding Coy. dispositions, training for the Spring and Summer and other general matters. On the same day, Bde. HQ. imposed thaw precautions restricting operational movement of vehicles which in turn caused the cancellation of a Battalion Inter - Coy. Boxing Tournament organized for the next day. These restrictions were lifted later in the day but orders came too late to revert to the original programme, so arrangements were made to hold this boxing event on the 12th.

Arthur Green...
We were told that we would have to train and were given a talk by the C.O., Lt. Col. Robins, that we would be trained to a fitness never known before in the British Army because we were going to be Mountain Troops. Believe you me, we were fit and we could go up mountains like they were nothing. The mountains opposite the camp we used to call the Five Sisters, we used to set off and go up there through the valley across the river and up the other side and right to the top in no time. That was part of the schemes and exercises and we used to sweat cobs but we carried gansies (jumpers) in our kit so that when you got to the top sweating, you could put them on in the icy wind.

On the 7th, Capt. P.S. Newton disembarked from M.V. 'Esja' at Hjalteyri to take over temporary command of 'C' Coy. during Major Lockwood's temporary tour of duty at Krossastadir. On the same day, another ship (S.S. 'Sudin') arrived at Hjalteyri with the three Officers on board that had been on the Tactics course at Reykjavik during the previous month.

L/Cpl. Cavill wears the 1937 Pattern Battle dress Blouse with all insignia attached separately (Mr. Cavill)

A Brigade Commander's inspection took place at Dagverdareyri on the 8th after which he proceeded to Krossastadir to inspect HQ. Coy. Camp, Transport lines, Carrier lines, Detention Barracks and Ration Stores. Some of the buildings that were constructed in connection with the transport section were just another example of additional skills possessed by men of a territorial battalion. One of these which was given the name Carrier Cottage, for obvious reasons, was constructed from blocks of peat and timber framing. The gable ends and some other parts of this building were then given protection from the wind and weather by being clad with large flattened ration pack tins. This structure was the brainchild of Sgt. Moore and was recorded on camera by the C.O., who described the building as a workshop.

Another interesting event this month was the enforcement of new Dress Regulations regarding the positioning of cloth shoulder titles, etc. It is assumed that the head down Polar Bear was worn from this date to accompany the 'Hallamshire' shoulder title above it and the single Brigade seniority stripe just below. This red (infantry) stripe denoted that the Battalion was a part of the Senior Brigade within the 49th Division (it should be remembered, however, that this Division was known as Alabaster Force whilst in Iceland!). The white metal rose was to be worn further down the sleeve just below the main group of cloth insignia. In the photograph of L/Cpl. Douglas Cavill, which gives a good idea of the layout, it can be seen that all of the parts were stitched on the sleeve as individual patches. This was tidied up at some later date as can be seen from the front cover picture, where all the parts were machine stitched onto a wedge shaped piece of khaki cloth and issued from stores like that.

The reader might appreciate the mess that must have been made by a large proportion of about eight hundred men, with varying needlework skills, trying to hand stitch even one patch on their uniforms squarely. For most, three would have been out of the question. The later made up patches were guarded very jealously by the Battalion and had to be removed from the uniform and handed in by anyone who was leaving the Hallams on a permanent basis. Only a few of these patches have survived to the present day. Whilst on this subject, it is interesting to note that the Battalion 'shoulder title' was unique in that it carried the word 'Hallamshire' in red on a Khaki background. As far as is known, all other infantry battalions of the British Army carried their 'Regimental' title, mostly in white on a red background. Furthermore, it is believed that the Hallams were the only infantry battalion to have a 'name' rather than a number. This dates from 1924, when special permission was granted by King George V, to drop the number (4th) from its title.

Members of the Carrier Platoon with their O.C. Capt. D.C. Beckett. (front row with two Sgts. on his right and one to his left)(DCB)

Warning that an enemy aircraft had been reported to be operating in the Hallams area caused a bit of a scare with special watches and anti - aircraft guns being set up. The latter would no doubt have included Bren Guns mounted on fixed tripods and also on special posts fixed to the Bren Carriers so as to give some degree of mobility. It is thought that some considerable skill would have been required by the operator to hit, let alone bring down any aircraft that might be sent over by the enemy at this time. If a German aircraft was indeed overflying the area, it would have been in all probability, a high flying, long range reconnaissance machine known as a

Focke-Wulf Condor. Although this aircraft had some offensive capability it would almost certainly be operating in the role of spy plane, trying to locate British installations in Iceland by use of aerial photography.

During this month, Capt. D.C. Beckett returned from his attachment with the R.E. Coy. at Lons and a group of Officers and NCOs. were given a very instructive talk on the subject of Unit Boxing, Cross Country Running and Ski-ing. The speaker was Capt. Harris of the Army Physical Training School, who came to Krossastadir at the request of the Lt. Col. C.G. Robins. On the 9th, a Canadian Officer, 2/Lt. P.S. Whaley became attached to the Bn. for a course of instruction in Regimental Duties. He seems to have been the first but certainly not the last of such Officers to do so, as will be seen later.

S.S. 'Tordenskold' had arrived on the 8th with only one of those travelling on board posted to the Hallams. On the 10th it sailed away again carrying with it two Officers, Major C.C. Strong, bound for the Senior Officers School at Devizes and Major H.J.W. Marsh, who was granted six months leave to return to industry. This man was someone rather special as revealed in conversations with many of the veterans and also somehow by his writing style (see the Chapter on Norway). Sadly, John Marsh was not destined to return to the Hallams after his six months stint back in Sheffield. Instead, he somehow found his way into the 6th Battalion only to be killed in action with that unit in Italy. No. 4746259 L/Cpl. E.A. Buttress left on the same ship to attend No. 13 Signal Course at Catterick Camp near Richmond, North Yorkshire. The leaving of Major Strong caused a bit of a reshuffle in responsibilities when he was replaced by Major D.E. Lockwood as 2 i/c. This then necessitated the replacement of David Lockwood as O.C. 'C' Coy. which was ably filled by Capt. P.S. Newton.

The postponed Boxing Tournament took place on the 12th in the Town Hall at Akureyri. Preliminary fights took place during the afternoon with semi-finals and finals being fought in the evening. The Bde. Commander, Brigadier C.C. Phillips presented the prizes, the winning team being 'A' Coy.

John Wollerton...
I found the local people, the men particularly, a bit off hand because they didn't want us there in the first place. The girls were very beautiful and hard working at the same time. They'd be up to the eyes in fish scales one minute and dressed dramatically the next - in the summertime that is. The men weren't all that keen on us at all and there was occasional trouble. Later on when I had a spell at Siglufjorder, things came to a bit of a head when our Sgt. told me he was going to send eight of our toughest lads to meet eight of theirs and they went and knocked each other about a bit... ...we had no more trouble after that.

On the 13th, an armed guard consisting of one NCO and five men embarked on a trawler at Hjalteyri to be taken out and board a ship, the S.S. 'Goteborg', which was lying off a place called Hrisey Island. This ship was apparently loading a cargo of fish bound for some other country and the orders were to prevent any verbal or close contact between its crew and Icelanders, who were helping with loading or otherwise in the vicinity. The guard took with them two days rations, kit and sleeping bags, but the task was soon accomplished as they returned the next day. A report was received from 2/Lt. M.J.A. Palmer at Saudarkrokur on the 17th, that one of their 15 cwt. trucks had come off the road and ditched whilst travelling between Varmahlid and Blonduos.

Akureyri harbour looking north. (HFC)

Doug Catley…

I was sent from Battalion HQ. to Hrisey Island in the mouth of the fjord to do a job which was concerned with the monitoring of shipping to and from Akureyri. There were two converted trawlers, the 'Viking Dis' and 'Dorothy Grey' with six pounder guns mounted on their sterns and they used to sit off this small island which was mined on one side. This forced shipping to use a channel down the other side and every ship that came in to Akureyri had to report to the naval vessel on watch. These passing ships were checked out by the latter and given flags to fly and their details like ships name, cargo etc., was signalled by Aldis Lamp to us on the island shore. We then relayed that

Vehicles often skidded (ditched) in treacherous icy road conditions. Here, a Bedford MW 15cwt. Truck (possibly the one reported by 2/Lt. Palmer) has come to grief. A Morris Commercial Field Artillery Tractor has come to the rescue with its 4 Ton winch. (HFC)

information by wireless to a place about thirty miles up the fjord, where there was a coastal defence battery. They then watched for ships passing and if any tried to pass that were not notified by us, the shore battery had the means to stop them. We used to get a rum ration every day on that job - the same as the Navy. The locals would give anything for this rum like, and the navy lads used to put a few tots of rum in a bottle, top it up with cold tea, and they'd get about £4 a bottle for it!

We also had R.A.F. signallers there to control aircraft which occasionally came out submarine hunting in our area and when that happened we were requested to switch on a beacon on the *island which they could home in on as they flew out from Akureyri. I'll always remember the automatic signal that was transmitted. It was Sugar, Sugar, Seven (SS7). We used to go out from the island in a small motor boat and sometimes fish all night. There were particular types of fishing lines we would use that had one hundred and twelve baited hooks on them and we'd leave them tied to a buoy in the evening, and by morning there'd be a fish on almost every hook - Cod, Catfish, Plaice, but mainly Cod.*

David Lockwood
(Extract from letter sent to his Mother from Iceland)

17 February, 1941(Krossastadir)…
I've removed and am now living at Battalion HQ. some miles from where I was before and in the wilds of a huge valley, very like Glencoe on a larger and less beautiful scale - the mountains go up to 3500 and 4000 feet almost from sea level on both sides in huge sweeps.

I'm now acting second in command of the battalion in place of Charles Strong who has gone to England for four months on a senior officers course.....At the present moment I've taken on the running of the Junior Commanders School that we've organized here for young officers and senior NCOs, both from the Hallamshires and other units in the neighbourhood.....Ivor Slater is back with us now (from Brigade) as Adjutant permanently and is making a first class job of it - its just the thing for his methodical brain.

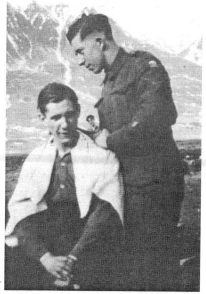

It's an open air 'short back and sides' for Doug Catley. He made some good friends in Iceland and was one of the few who returned there after the war (Mr. D.Catley)

Saudarkrokur (HFC)

We live in Nissen Huts here and George and I share one with a partition across the middle. They're very comfortable really except that they're usually either too hot or too cold. One of the snags is an inch gap under the door and snow blows underneath but I'm getting South (his batman) to make a sausage thing to keep it out. We use, as an anti-room, another hut about 50 yards away and feed in a stone built home-made shack called 'Endcliffe Hall'. Food is extraordinarily good as we've got a chef called Dummer who we enlisted at the beginning of the war from the Connaught Club and although we live on rations just the same, he finds such marvellous ways of doing things. One of his great dishes is bully beef in batter - grand. How he cooks in the home made kitchen built of turf and corrugated iron is a mystery.

Capts. W.L. Cave and D.R. Bell, Lt. S. Martin de Bartoleme and 2/Lt. C.R.A. Tong all proceeded by sea to attend a course at No.4 Force Tactical School, Reykjavik, at various times during the month. On the 18th, the M.O. and Padre (Capt. N. Murray - Smith) sailed on a visit to Saudarkrokur in the 'Disko'. They were accompanied by Sgt. Lees and L/Sgt. Raynor, both of whom were returning from a Junior Commanders Course at Bn. HQ.

Arthur Green...

I think we were the first in the British Army to have string vests, they were experimenting with string vests and I remember putting mine on for the first time and going on a scheme with it and my shoulders were like raw meat when we got back. Terrible they were, if you were carrying any weight for rubbing like, but they did keep you warm. We did get some Parker type jackets later, with cold weather hats to which was fixed the Regimental Cap Badge on a back patch of cloth. Things like woollen gloves, socks and balaclavas, we used to have sent in parcels from home and of course we were issued with a cap comforter. (a khaki, woollen tube stitched at both ends that could be folded to form a very warm head cover)

A detachment moves by sea to Saudarkrokur in the 'Disko' (HFC)

The M.V. 'Esja' arrived again in Akureyri at 1500 hrs on the 20th, bringing 2/Lt. Turrel back from Reykjavik and left in the evening of the same day carrying away with it the following personnel...

4604137 CSM. L.H. Codd.	Medical treatment on H.S. 'Leinster' at Reykjavik.
4746020 A/CSM. B.(Bunny)Whiting.	Course at Hythe Wing, S.A.S. Bisley.
4745283 Sgt. E. Battle.	Course at NCOs. School, Strensall.
4739595 L/Sgt. H. Oakley.	Course at School of Driving and Maintainance,Harrogate.
2/Lt. P.M. Young.	Sniper Course at Netheraven Wing, S.A.S. Bisley.

By now, the weather was starting to get wild and stormy with road blockages near Ytri-Baegisa (cleared by the detachment there) and between Akureyri and Dalvik, at the junction leading to Hjalteyri. One of the snowploughs was sent out from Krossastadir to clear the latter, which it did very successfully. The weather continued to worsen with very cold winds and drifting snow, accompanied by poor visibility that all together caused Communications to be temporarily suspended with Bde. HQ. By the end of the month, in spite of continuous work performed by the snowplough, serious drifting took place and various roads became blocked. Now, the snowplough from Krossastadir got stuck in a ditch on the road to Ytri-Baegisa and the one at Lons with the R.Es. could only operate in the vicinity of Akureyri. Another 15 cwt. ('A' Coys. Ration Truck) left the road near a place called Sponsgerdi. What it was doing there will have to remain a mystery as the place name does not appear anywhere else in this story amongst all the other *'funny names'* as Arthur Green called them.

The continued high winds, at times reaching gale force, created a severe blizzard on the 28th which caused further drifting of snow and atmospheric conditions which interfered with R/T. Many roads became blocked and even the snowploughs had difficulty in operating, one of them ditching at Ytri-Baegisa. The expected weather had at last arrived with a vengeance to concentrate the mind on what must have been one of the main subjects - keeping warm. It was at these times that pot-bellied stoves were teased into a state of overheating that caused some of them to glow like the metal drawn from a blacksmith's furnace.

Arnold Whitely...

Iceland was really a pleasant relief you know, and we were comparatively safe. They got us into Nissen huts before the outbreak of winter and it was severe in the winter. There were people frozen to death in one unit after being caught in a storm. On detachment, discipline tended to be relaxed as no one could spring any surprises. We were issued with a double sleeping bag, four blankets, and these big Canadian coke stoves in the middle of the hut. During winter the Bugler used to sleep with his bugle at his side. When it came near time to blow 'reveille' he would put it beside him in the sleeping bag to warm it up. He would then get up, quickly run and open the door, rush back to the warmth of his sleeping bag, and blow reveille call - laying in his sleeping bag!

Reveille is best described as a sort of military alarm clock. Soldiers have always associated the notes of this call with the appropriate words... *You've got to get up! You've got to get up! You've got to get up in the morning!*

March was a tale of battling against the weather with various degrees of success. The ditched vehicles were recovered, including the snowplough, with negligible damage and routes were cleared where possible by working parties. Rations could still be delivered to the main Company detachments by sea but in at least one case, the outpost at Ytri-Baegisa, it was delivered by sledge. John Wollerton mentioned that when he first arrived in Iceland and sailed from Reykjavik to Akureyri there were Husky dogs brought on board but it is not known whether these were used to deliver rations as in the case just related.

Arnold Whitely...

There was one incident when they were bringing our rations up in a Bren Carrier, our CQMS McCready called at detachments with his rations and he'd been transacting his corned beef for eggs and things on his way round and we were the last stop. There were quite a lot of eggs in this Carrier and it ran off the road onto some rough ground to turn around. Ken Rispin was the driver and it started to slip out of control on the ice and he had to abandon it as it slipped into the sea. The CQMS was seething, not so much about the Carrier but at the loss of his eggs. (Many years later this same driver, Ken Rispin, was to become a Mayor of Barnsley)

Ivor Slater related the fact that David Beckett was responsible for an idea which eventually lead to the modification of many carriers within British Army units in Iceland. This involved the removal of tracks and the reversal of every fifth link which was then turned inside out so that its drive tooth was on the outside. In winter conditions these 'spikes' gripped the compounded ice and snow, whereas previously the carriers had tended to slide all over the place as in the case of Ken Rispin's vehicle.

David Lockwood (Letters to Mary)

7 March, 1941 (Battalion HQ. Krossastadir)...

First, thank you so much for your very sweet letter (No: 73 - Feb. 19th) that arrived at lunch time and just when I needed it most....and now for the great news that has literally knocked me sideways. George sent for me this afternoon to show me a postal telegram from the War Office ordering the release of Capt. (T/Major.) D.E. Lockwood, York and Lancaster Regt., T.A., to work of 'vital national importance' at Newton Chambers and Co. Ltd. 'This officer to be released at the earliest opportunity to disembodiment - indefinite release' in other words out of the army for good, unless there is an unexpected national emergency i.e. civil war or a rebellion.

...George was upset I am afraid and though I don't flatter myself I'm any great loss, I know how it feels to lose an officer and this now is three Majors in succession, plus Charles (Strong) on a long course...

...George and I went off in his car yesterday afternoon to David Morris's detachment to ski, about 6 miles away. It was the most perfect day again with the bluest sky you ever saw and the skiing slope was the best I've ever seen. We had such a lovely afternoon....I've learnt how to 'stop' in skiing now which is most important, almost more important than 'going'! George and I both came some terrific croppers yesterday but without damage and I actually tried a three foot jump! Of course, I landed on my bum so that was the end of that!

Later. 10.45 pm.

Just been playing chess with George again and dammit, he's beaten me again! He's the only person in the mess that I never seem to beat - very nearly sometimes but that's as far as it gets!

2/Lt. P.H. Willis-Dixon had assumed the appointment of I.O. when Philip Young went on the Sniper Course but he proceeded to Bisley himself on the 8th, relinquishing his position to 2/Lt. W.R. Jenkinson. 2/Lt. Willis-Dixon embarked on the M.V. 'Esja' accompanied by 4747561 Sgt. A. Kirby who was on his way to the NCOs. School at Strensall. On the same day, the C.O. had a meeting with the O.C. Bde. in connection with the latter's impending departure to pastures new.

Three views of the C.Os. Staff Car. It was based on a Humber Snipe chassis and the picture opposite shows it with the name 'Eyre Coote' painted on the side. It is the name of the first Colonel of the old 84th Regt. (c.1760) of which the 2nd Bn. The York & Lancaster Regiment was a direct descendent. It can be safely assumed that this was the choice of George Robins (having served with the latter unit). Bottom right shows the vehicle shortly after receipt in Iceland with a Pelican motif on the front nearside mudguard. Those in the photograph from left to right are : R/C Padre (name unknown), Cpl. Seaton (C.Os. Driver), Philip Young and C.J. Wells (Doctor). Below shows the same vehicle with the Polar Bear now painted on the front. Other markings are the Hallams unit sign (57 in white on a red background) and the Bridging Plate denoting the vehicles bridge weight limit of 2 tons. Vehicle Identity Number is M4111169 and the tyres are Dunlop Tracgrip! (CGR)

David Lockwood (Letters to Mary)

9 March, 1941 (Bn.HQ. Krossastadir)...

The stream that flows past our hut and mess is now a raging torrent outside, but fortunately in a deep gully as it passes our hut. The flood gets bigger every hour and the roar of it is like the noise of the falls at Yorkshire Bridge, just outside my hut - very soothing at bed time, I find!....

....the water runs over the top of the ice and this of course raises the level a good deal and it looked this morning as if it might soon wash 'Endcliffe Hall' away as it bends round behind it. So George

and Dobbie and I decided to have a game with it and got three Mills Bombs (grenades) and threw them in under the ice to break the ice up and let the water away. We threw them in one at a time into a deep pool through a hole in the ice and then ran away behind cover and then the bang and great chunks of ice a foot thick were thrown into the air - grand...   ...later on we played cricket with snow balls and an army shovel and, of course, the game was to hit the batsman with the snow balls - teenies! - but great fun!

George invited the local Medical Colonel to dinner last night so I asked Ken as my guest. Later, Seaton (George's driver) and I, took Ken home in George's car and on the way back got on a patch of road that was completely smooth ice and on a slant. We were going about 5 m.p.h. I should think and just slowly slid sideways getting faster and faster until we'd gone right off the road with the car at an angle of about 30 degrees and petrol pouring out. Trying to drive it out only made it worse and the car was at such an angle that there was no weight on the higher back wheel at all and it just spun round. I Thought she might go over any time so made Seaton climb out of the passengers door on the top side and he and I walked home about a mile and a half. It was a lovely night with a moon and clouds rushing across it in the lovely balmy southwest wind that is so pleasant after all these weeks of almost continuous frost...

David Lockwood and Seaton must have approached the camp that night from Djuparbakki, further down the Horga Valley where Ken West was based ('D' Coy.). As they approached the bridge which formed the eastern entrance to the camp, they would have been able to see much of the camp in the moonlight with the Five Sisters towering away to their right across the river. To get to the officers huts, David would have had to turn left over the bridge. It would then have been only another fifty yards walk up the gully towards the Nissen hut that he shared with George Robins, close by the stone built 'Endcliff Hall'. By the time he got in, of course, George may have already laced his tea with a drop of whiskey and retired to his bed.

Carrier cottage. The Ancient Romans would have instantly recognised the construction method! (HFC)

The ground at the edge of the main road through the west end of Krossastadir Camp fell away steeply on the north side and the rear of the garage/workshop, named 'Carrier Cottage' was set into it. This structure was purpose built with a basic timber frame (a scarce commodity then in Iceland) reinforced with very thick walls made up from peat blocks in the same style as that was used in the construction of many of the nearby farmsteads. The roof and upper facings were covered with discarded petrol tins beaten flat to form a sort of tiling. The rest of the carriers were housed alongside in a row of individual, smaller sheds of similar construction to Carrier Cottage. These at first, had consisted of low earthen walls without roofing but sufficient to give a lot of protection from the wind and weather. As materials became available, these were also given a timber roof, clad with flattened petrol tins. None of these buildings could be approached directly from the main road and so a smaller service road was constructed, which ran parallel to it but on a lower level. The Carrier and MT lines lay sandwiched between the two. The carrier

90

lines were west of the main Motor Transport area and close to the bakery at the far western end of the camp. These were the last group of buildings on the side of the main road that carried on west into the interior wasteland up the Horga Valley.

HQ. 146 Brigade issued orders that all transport must come off the roads which left one or two vehicles and groups stranded. The Ski-Platoon ('D' Coy) returning from training at Siglufjorder by sea, had no alternative but to take accommodation at Bde. HQ. hutted camp at Akureyri. On the 10th they were ordered to march from Akureyri to Djuparbakki, their kit being transferred later by a currently stranded 15 cwt. truck at the docks.

Next day Lt. Col. Robins assumed command of the Bde. and Major D.E. Lockwood took temporary command of the Hallams. Capt. K.W. West was granted the Acting rank of Major. The weather around this time was fine but dull with increasing winds, becoming cooler. Large pieces of pack ice were seen drifting down the River Horga past the camp at Krossastadir, where they slowly came to a standstill without hindering the continued flow of water below.

On the 19th of March an order was received from Bde. HQ. that a special vigilance must be kept at this time in the Hallams sector. Reference was made to particular operational Orders in connection with this and all efforts were made to relay the message to all outposts as quickly as possible. Some units were informed by Special Dispatch Rider, while some were informed directly by HQ. 146 Brigade. It can only be assumed that some intelligence had been received possibly concerning enemy naval movements in the area. It was in these waters that some of the larger German battle cruisers prowled that had already sent the aircraft carrier H.M.S. 'Glorious' to the bottom of the sea in June, the previous year. Another prize was awaiting them in the very near future... H.M.S. 'Hood'.

Promotions were received on the 20th which made War Substantive Lieutenants of the following Officers...

73883 2/Lt. M.J.A.Palmer	73901 2/Lt. P.M.Young
74027 2/Lt. W.C.Blake	79990 2/Lt. L.M.Lonsdale-Cooper
62413 2/Lt. C.R.S.Sandford	89120 2/Lt. C.A.B.Slack
89104 2/Lt. R.N.Longridge	89123 2/Lt. A.C.Somers
89110 2/Lt. S.J.D.Moorwood	89131 2/Lt. P.Turrell
93130 2/Lt. C.R.A.Tong	

On the last day of the month, Lt. Col. Robins returned from temporary command of the Brigade and Major Lockwood not only stood down from temporary Command of the Battalion but also relinquished his position as 2 i/c when he embarked for Reykjavik on the first leg of his journey home. This was on relegation to Disembodiment with effect from 21 February, 1941, which might sound to the lay person almost like an end to this Officer's army career for at least the rest of the war. However, David Lockwood was not yet finished with the Hallamshire Battalion.

He had plenty of travelling companions for the first part of his journey on the M.V. 'Esja' as it pulled away from the dockside in Akureyri harbour. Also on board were Capts. R. Mumby and P.W. Marsh, Lts. C.A.B. Slack and J. Firth, 2/Lt. G.J. Good and three batmen, all bound for No.6 Force Tactical School at Reykjavik. Others on board were being sent to the General Hospital there, pending Medical Boards. They were 4740503 CQMS J.G. Rodgers and four ORs.

On the 1 April, the now well established Ski-Platoon consisting of one Officer and 23 ORs. moved to Logmanshlid for further training with the Detachment of the Norwegian Army. Arnold

Hallamshire Battalion Ski Platoon. (HFC)

Whitely mentions them and, although he himself was not a member of the Ski-Platoon, was given snow-camp and ski training, along with many others of the Battalion.

Arnold Whitely...

Arnold Whiteley (Mr.A. Whiteley)

We used to go marching and then they started a school to train with these Norwegians, where we used to climb mountains and sleep out for up to five days at a time in these two man tents but we had good equipment for it then. They were all in one piece, skewered to the floor, and you lifted a flap in the floor to scoop snow out the bottom to melt down for food. We used a heater like a tin where you took the top off and pulled it up and it became a little stove. It contained a sort of solidified metholated spirits so you lit it and melted your snow down.

Your food was all in cubes like, there'd be so many cubes to make porridge and you put it in with your water. Then there was tinned milk, butter and biscuits all to last for five days. Of course you didn't wash or shave or anything like that when you went on those expeditions.

Jack Haslam...

We used to go ont' mountains for a fortnight, training in the snow, and you couldn't put your haversack on yourself because it were so heavy. Two of you worked together and one would carry all food and paraffin and the other one would have sleeping gear, tents, bedding. Then you'd have skis and snow boots. We used to make igloos or snow holes and things like that. When you put a two man tent up, you'd take your boots off and put them under pillow because they used to freeze if not. You had your Primus stove int' middle and most of the food was block rations, hard tack biscuits and that. Me and my mate, unknown to the big bosses, used to go and buy a loaf and potatoes out of canteen and we used to do chips! You were n't allowed to take towel, soap or razor on these schemes.

Jack and his mate were not the only ones who indulged themselves in the making of fish and chips.

92

George Learad…

A lad called Billy Bird used to tickle trout down there and catch fish in the stream. We used to have to send two men to the cookhouse every day to peel spuds, so what we used to do to save time was to all go down and do the job together, but each of us would put a couple of spuds in us pockets. We'd come back, go to the end of the pier where it was easy to catch fish and then go back to the camp and get the cook to do us fish and chips at night. I'll get put in jail for this! We used to take a few tins of stuff when we were guarding the rations and then bury them. Later, we could get together and say, 'Right, what are we going to have tonight?' And we might have sausage and chips or bacon and chips or whatever else was in the tins with chips. We'd just go and dig a tin up when we wanted one.

We did get on each others nerves at times in Iceland and we used to put boxing gloves on then and, we'd be back to being friendly after that. I remember old Bill Coe and me had a go one time and old Arthur said, 'Right, I'll referee this,' and we were right as rain after that because we were big mates. What we used to do then at night, we used to have a good Solo school because otherwise it was really boring out there. When this strong Canadian beer came over, we went mad and when we got any news of a victory at sea, they used to bring us rum. I used to swap my cigarettes for other peoples rum ration. We used to go mad then and the officers never bothered us and stayed well away!

On the 4th, a young 2/Lt. stepped ashore at Akureyri from S.S. 'Tordenskold' who was newly posted to the Hallams from the Depot, The York and Lancaster Regiment, Pontefract. His name was J.A.H. Nicholson better known to his friends as Tony. This Officer was destined to be decorated on active service by Field Marshal Montegomery himself, one of the very few to be so honoured, when he was awarded the Military Cross in Normandy.

Work had been carried out for some time now on the construction of Dummy Gun Positions on the coast line at Fagriskogur and Dagverdareyri in co-operation with the R.Es. They were built using concrete bases and sandbagging systems accompanied by O.Ps. To complete the deception at the latter installation, it was arranged for a Carrier to come and churn up the ground and create tracks between the Platoon area and the Dummy Battery positions. The new Brigade Commander, Brigadier N.P. Procter M.C., was no doubt impressed when he inspected the works in company with the C.O. on the 8th at both of these sites. The inspection also took in Djuparbakki, Krossastadir and Bragholt.

On the 10th, the weather was described as hot and sunny with good visibility and, although it turned dull with light drizzle the following day, did not prevent the Unit football Competition taking place. This was a six a side affair but no less than eight teams were raised with two each from HQ, 'A', 'C' and 'D' Coys. Only one of the matches was left to be played the next day.

A place of worship had been established earlier in one of the newly erected Nissen huts at Krossastadir and on the 13 April, a Memorial was unveiled there by Col. Robins, dedicated to those men who had lost their lives when H.M.S. 'Afridi' was sunk by German aircraft on 3 May the previous year. It was in the form of a plaque, painted by one of the men, with a list of names of all those thirteen men who had died in the withdrawal from Norway.

H.M.S. 'Galatea' and 'Arethusa' made visits to Akureyri and Siglufjordur respectively. The former ship entertained two officers and 15 ORs. from the detachment at Krossanes and forty-seven ratings visited Krossastadir. All the troops at Siglufjordur were able to visit the other ship during the day. During the following few days, however, a major alert was declared to the effect that an enemy convoy was believed to be near Iceland and in sufficient force to pose a threat of

invasion. Various contingency plans were put into operation and all troops were ordered to 'stand to' in the early hours of the 21st, but were stood down at 0500 hrs. All was quiet and no ships had been spotted.

Things were soon back to normal and on the 23rd, two officers on a visit to Iceland collecting publicity material, came to the Hallams HQ. at Krossastadir, where a special exercise was laid on for them. One of these officers, a Captain Taylor, was a photographer who recorded a number of scenes during the manoeuvres performed by the carriers, both in and around the River Horga.

On the 25th, two Fairey Battle aircraft gave gunners on the ground a rare opportunity when they flew up and down the Eyjafjordur in order to allow anti-aircraft practice to be carried out. It must be said, however, that this practice fell short of actual firing so no one was able to boast of any 'scores'. On this same day, permission was given for the platoon based at Varmahlid to dismantle their two Nissen huts so as to transport and re-erect them at their new base at Saudarkrokur. During the whole month, both officers and men continued to come and go, mainly in connection with all manner of military training courses at Reykjavik and in the U.K.

Early May saw the arrival of Major R.O. Sclater who immediately assumed the duties of both 2i/c and O.C. HQ. Coy. This month was also an exciting time for many in the Battalion because the first batch of leave was authorized. On the 9th, contingents from various Companies and detachments had converged at Akureyri by way of boats, buses and on foot and were gathered on the dockside ready to embark on the S.S. 'Lochnegar'.

Hopes were dashed when the men were told to return to their various camps as the sailing had been cancelled indefinitely but on the 11th, they were back again. Five officers and ninety-six men climbed aboard to begin their journey home for a well earned period of leave. The rest of the men had to wait their turn and find whatever pleasures they could on this side of the ocean.

One of the photographs taken by Capt. Taylor during his visit to Krossastadir when the Battalion Carriers were put through their paces in and around the River Horga. The vehicles in the foreground 'NIVE' and 'PENINSULAR' were, like the others, named after pre Great War Battle Honours. (HFC)

Wilf Fisher…

We had a certain SNCO who had a lady friend, no names! no pack drill! This particular morning he wasn't in the Coy. office where he should have been. So the 'skipper' sent me to find out where he was. He said to me, 'Do you know where he is?' and I said, 'Yes! He'll be in his billet.' So I went down there, down to this room and when I opened the door of this room it was like some queer film. The only thing I could see was all black cobwebs, everything was pitch black and there was

all these black cobwebs hanging down everywhere. He was in bed with this female and they were absolutely covered, they were, in this black soot and cobwebs. Apparently, what had happened, they'd got a paraffin heater and it must have gone wrong and the whole room was just one mass of long black threads.

Then we had a film. We only had one film there and I'll never forget it, it was Nelson Eddy and Jeanette MacDonald in 'Rose Marie' and for about three months afterwards you could hear blokes singing, 'I'll be calling You..ou..ou..ou, ou..ou..ou!' Oh! it was shocking that, it just got on your nerves, you know.

Morris Commercial 15cwt. Truck adapted for the transportation of water. The name is curious as 'Nelson' is not known to have had any connection with The York & Lancaster Regiment! On the other hand, if one of the other vehicles at Krossastadir was named 'Jeanette' then all would be explained! (see Wilf Fisher left) (HFC)

(On the back of the original photograph, the name J.S. Peel is printed.)

A story was related by one soldier (Arnold Whitely) that an officer of the Battalion, who shall remain anonymous, was very fond of the bottle. On one particular evening he had partaken of excess liquid and strayed too near the edge of a loading jetty whereupon he tripped and fell into the water. The only witness to this occurrence was an Icelander who had some smattering of English. He ran some distance to the nearest Army post and in an out of breath voice uttered the immortal words, *'One of your officers has gone to sea!'* The retrieval, in shallow water, was not carried out hastily as it was thought that a slightly prolonged dip in the extremely cold ocean might have some sobering effect.

Sgt. R.C. Wingfield and L/Cpl. A.H. Oates were both interviewed and recommended for O.C.T.U. training by a panel of officers at Brigade HQ. in Akureyri and later in the month, a Handicrafts Exhibition was held in the town. A number of Hallams men entered their work and prizes were won by Sgts. R.Crookes, E.Goodliffe and Pte. W.Farnell. Special mention was made of entries by Ptes. W.Whittaker, D.Newman and J.Lynch.

In a place like Iceland, especially in the winter months, boredom must have been quite a problem, but handicrafts and hobbies could help to stave it off. It has already been said that some men had literally made their own furniture. Some of

Very smart turn out of the guard in glorious Icelandic sunshine. The large pouches were designed to carry Bren Gun magazines but these would have been lined with cardboard and stuffed with paper to give them perfect shape. Blanco wasn't used by the Hallams in Iceland and all Mills Webbing equipment had to be scrubbed clean. (HFC)

the them had even constructed beds from packing cases and cable wire but many continued to sleep on the floor. As far as is known, steel framed beds were a luxury which found little or no

space in the holds of ships that were bound for Iceland. It is doubtless that many were acquired from the local people but at a price, perhaps, that few ORs. could afford. One example of the finer side of craft work in the Battalion was a tapestry hand grip bag which was made by David Lockwood and sent home to his wife. She was no doubt very thrilled with it and even had her photograph taken holding it. That small bag is still in her possession today and in its original condition.

Never let it be said that the men of the Hallamshire Battalion were lacking in their ability to combat boredom. Wilf Fisher found that one of his friends had found a more gruesome cure for it, which was not altogether Wilf's cup of tea !

Mary Lockwood with the handcrafted clutch bag made by her husband, David, in Iceland.(DEL)

Wilf Fisher...
One night Sgt. Rose came to me and he said, 'Wilf, come out tonight with me and I'll show you something you've never seen in your life.' I said, 'Oh! Good.' He said, 'I'll call for you and we'll go down to the mess and have a walk after.' We got

Typical billet interior, where most men continued to sleep on the floor. Some made their own bed frames from packing cases and signal cable. Storage consisted of a single shelf which ran the length of the building and clothing was hung on it between bed spaces. The stove has a large kettle perched on it to provide the brew that was necessary for most Englishmen when far from home. A rifle rack on the end wall contains both rifles and shovels. The latter saw far more service than rifles, both for clearing snow and 'ratting'.(HFC)

down onto this main street and he says, 'Here you are, there's a stick there,' (like a scout pole) and I said, 'What's that for?' and he said, 'Keep it, you might want it!' We got down to the Bakers and walked at the side of it in a little passageway into the back. Well, you've never seen anything like it in your life. I mean we'd seen rats but this... ...there was just one massive swarm of rats. Not small things, I mean huge things and all colours and they were all going on top of one another and there's Ernest Rose giving it this with his stick. Well, you know what I did don't you? I just turned around and I said, 'No way am I stopping here!'

But Wilf's association with rats didn't end there...

Wilf Fisher...
I was Cpl. in charge of my Nissen hut and my bed was long ways at the side of the stove. When I got in this night there were all these blokes all lying about. Of course I'd made my own bed out of signal wire and one thing and another and the blokes were lying around on the floor. I gets in there and we'd got double sleeping bags and gets in this sleeping bag and everybody's fast asleep and its quarter past eleven, you know. I gets in and puts me foot inside this sleeping bag and I thought, 'What's that!' I'd a flaming big rat inside. Well, you can imagine can't you, you know (high pitched scream). Then everybody's shouting, 'Shut up! Shut up!'

What they used to do round our Nissen hut where the stove was, it's hardly believable but this is true - I've seen them do it. You could hear them biting the floorboards and they used to make holes and come up to get into the barrack room to take paper or anything. Instead of us having the normal kit inspection on a Saturday we used to have a campaign where all the Company surrounded a Nissen hut at a time, with all the fire fighting appliances, you know, spades and pick handles and all this sort of stuff. All the Nissen huts were piled at the sides with peat and this is where they were nesting and we used to pull these away, little by little, and they couldn't possibly escape because we'd got a circle around it. As they came away we used to get them and you'd be surprised at what they made their nests with - chocolate paper, bits of rag, four by two, cigarette packets. Anyway, that night when I got in my sleeping bag and I put my foot on this damn thing, I was out like lightning!

On 23 May, information was received from Brigade that extreme vigilance was to be observed owing to the fact that an enemy warship was in the neighbourhood. No one in the Hallams knew it then but the ship was 'Bismark' accompanied by an escort cruiser 'Prinz Eugen'. The commanders of these German warships were stalking what must have seemed to them, a much bigger prize than anything that could have been gained, from a sailors point of view, on the shores of Iceland. The next day, they engaged the pride of the British Navy south of Greenland and H.M.S. 'Hood' was struck a

The Hospital Ship 'Leinster' surrounded by ice in Akureyri harbour. Besides the care she provided for the physical well-being of the troops in that part of Iceland, there was the added taste of home in the form of nurses and good food. (HFC)

Group of officers enjoy the open air and Canadian beer in quart bottles. They are from left to right standing : Lt. Morris, Mike Lonsdale - Cooper, Chris Wells (Doctor), Peter Newton, Ivor Slater. Seated : Capt. Dobson (QM), George Robins and Ken West. (CGR)

mortal blow in the first few salvoes. When this ship was sunk on 24 May, the Hospital Ship 'Leinster' received a coded emergency message to pull out of Akureyri immediately to collect and provide care for any wounded that might be found.

Ivor Slater...
The Dental Officer for the Akureyri land sector had his surgery installed on the 'Leinster' and he was given just twenty minutes and no more, to rip out as much as he could and get it onto the quayside which he managed to do. The 'Leinster' then steamed up the Eyjafjordur and went off to rescue whoever she could from the 'Hood'.

That was quite an incident and did make people think a bit about how close the Germans were coming to Iceland.

Arnold Whiteley recalled that the Hospital Ship 'Leinster' had been brought up to Akureyri Harbour and in mid winter they decorated it with fairy lights and people were skating around it on the frozen sea surrounding it. Wilf Fisher remembers actually going aboard this ship to visit a friend...

Wilf Fisher...
On the 'Leinster' they'd got bread and some good food and I went to visit someone I knew, but I was always very feeble about smelling ether and when I got on, I passed out on the gangway. Next thing I knew, I'm lying in bed nicely tucked up in white sheets feeling smashing but they said, 'Oh! You've got to stay overnight.' Next morning I had white bread, lovely fresh baked bread, egg and bacon. Oh! Beautiful marmalade and the lot. Of course you can imagine when I got back to the Coy. - there's Harold Marshal.

'Where the F... have you been?'... 'I had a bit of bother,' I said... 'I know where you went!, you went to get the bacon and eggs and some bread!' I said, 'No Sir!' and he said, 'Oh! Yes you did, You're not the first so and so who's done that. Don't you try it again !'

On the 26th, a message was received by the Hallams asking if anyone had seen or heard a Fairey Battle aircraft overflying the area. The aircraft was overdue at Kaldadarnes and was feared to have crashed or made a forced landing somewhere in the surrounding mountains or valleys. The Recce Platoon (newly formed from the renamed Ski Platoon) was now required to operate from a base at Bakki and send out patrols in search of the aircraft. Ray Langdale was a member of the Recce Platoon at this time.

Ray Langdale...
One thing I remember was a Fairey Battle aircraft went missing over our area so they turned us out to search for it in the mountains and valleys. Of the three groups that went out, it was eventually spotted by a man called Colin King. The method used was for individuals to set up in

prominent positions and scan large areas with powerful field glasses. His group were on the other side of the valley in which the aircraft came down. They guided us onto the scene by wireless and we found the wreck in a basin at the head of the valley. All the crew of three had been killed so we came down the mountain to a school house where we had a meal. Eventually, two Padres, an RAF officer and four Sergeants arrived with a large wooden cross about six feet high. We took them back to the scene and we mounted this cross on a cairn, close to the wreckage. We had a Catholic and Church of England service at the site.

Fairey Battle at R.A.F. St. Athan, South Wales. This aircraft also crashed in Iceland during the war but the wreckage was recovered and brought back to U.K. in 1974. Restoration was completed by the author's brother, Malcolm, in 1990.(Mr. M. Siddle)

There were apparently no 'recoverable' bodies and therefore no individual burials as the crash had been a bad one with the armed aircraft exploding on impact and wreckage scattered far and wide. The few remains found at the crash site were placed under the cairn.

…they brought us down and a few days afterwards an RAF bus collected us from camp and took us to their camp. They gave us a smashing meal and we were thanked by their Commanding Officer. They then paid for us all to go to the cinema in Akureyri. The film was a comedy about the army starring Bud Abbott and Lou Costello!

Work during the month consisted of weapons training, field firing and improvements to Dummy Coastal Defences (DCD). The latter were inspected by the Brigadier and a bit of realism was added to the visit when real guns were fired from the C.D. at Hjalteyri. This was spiced up by the R.E. who set up a charge that provided a resultant explosion just in front of the dummy positions. All went according to plan!

On the first day of June, the erection of a Recreation Hut begun in May, was completed. It was shaped like all the rest of the Nissen huts but very much bigger in length, width and height. All it needed now was a lick of paint, the outside of which may well have been influenced by a newly arrived visitor. This man, a Capt. Moody, was an expert in camouflage and came to Bn.HQ in order to conduct training exercises and demonstrations in the 'art' of concealing vehicles, equipment and men. The whole Carrier Pl. and many other vehicles were employed to show the use of new methods and materials and no one was lost in this exercise! Then, the first leave party arrived back from England, having been away from the Battalion for exactly one calendar month. On the 12th, a Falling Plate Competition was held by Brigade HQ. and teams from the Recce and Rifle Platoons were entered.

Sergeant J. Thomas arrived at Krossastadir on the 14th and took on duties as the new Physical Training Instructor, but he had what might be termed a compulsory settling in period. This was because his equally new Recreation Hut was being used for a couple of days by ENSA who were putting on a show for the troops at the base and, presumably, any other personnel in the area who could get to the camp.

No. 8 Platoon. 'A' Company. Sadly, no names came with this photograph. (HFC)

Arthur Green...
I remember the Sgt. P.T. Instructor. He would get us all in a circle and stand in the middle swinging a pair of boxing gloves around his head and then let go of them. Whichever two blokes the gloves hit had to box each other and one day I was picked against this lad who was not the boxing sort and made me look good. Just then, the CSM came in and thought that I was Joe Lewis! He made me box in a later round of fights which were put on in the Recreation Hut to entertain the officers. I was put in with this lad who had been a good amateur boxer in Leeds and he put me down with the first punch. I wasn't going to have anymore of that so I stayed down!

Eight MMGs were received on the 19th which were presumably unusable due to the fact that not one of them came complete. Later on the same day, a gale blew up and ripped the roofs off two garages, one of which struck a civilian telegraph pole breaking it in half but without severing the cables. 'A' and 'C' Coys. changed places on the 28th, in order to allow the whole of 'C' Coy. to train together at Djuparbakki and a combined course for the Bn. Intelligence Section and prospective snipers was held during this month at Krossastadir.

Very little was reported in the July War Diary other than weather conditions which were generally warm and bright with good visibility. One occurrence, the arrival of some U.S. Marines in Iceland, was probably the first indication of a future plan that was to eventually replace British forces there. One other event of note was a football match which took place on the 13th, between HQ. Coy. and a team of sailors from the cruiser H.M.S. 'Devonshire' which was on a visit to Akureyri and which was won by the Hallams, two goals to nil.

Lt. W.R. Jenkinson assumed the appointment of Commandant, Sector Detention Barracks vice Capt. R.I.Slater on the 24 July. Two days later, the Second UK leave party returned to Iceland and it can be seen that once they disembarked at Akureyri, each had various methods by which they had to get back to their individual detachments. HQ. Coy. had no bother by bus to Krossastadir and 'A' Coy. marched to Krossanes. However, some 'B' Coy. men had to go by sea again to Siglurfjordur whilst others of the same Coy. travelled by road to Saudarkrokur. 'D' Coy. also went by sea to Hjalteyri.

A pattern seems to emerge of one warship per month visiting Akureyri and it was the turn of H.M.S. 'Shropshire' on the 1 August when representatives of all ranks were entertained on board. One Platoon of 'D' Coy. 1/9 Manchester Regt. (MMG), pitched camp on the same day at Djuparbakki, which seems to be the start of a policy to back up rifle battalions with special support units armed with Medium Machine Guns. The Manchesters would be replaced in June, 1943, when the 2 Kensington Regt. took over this role, normally one Company per Brigade, as part of 49 Division.

Left : Sgt. George Linley ('C' Coy.) outside 'The Magnet Hotel' at Saudarkrokur, where one of the cooks sports a well risen Yorkshire Pudding (a welcome change from Shepherds Pie! - see page 104). Many of the Nissen huts were named after their more grand counterparts in Sheffield although some of the originals did not survive German bombing raids in December 1940. Sadly, none of these cooks at Krossastadir have been identified but it is sincerely hoped that some of these men and others in the book may be recognised by family or friends. (HFC)

John Wollerton...
One day a very big warship came down the fjord and hit a whale, which eventually came ashore outside our mess. How they dragged it ashore I don't know, it was an enormous great thing. The Icelanders began cutting it up and selling off the pieces at so much a kilo until most of it was gone - I had a bit but didn't like it very much. The snag was that they didn't clear away the carcass and the smell for months was abominable.

Col. George Robins and Capt. C.J. Wells (RAMC) were at last given the opportunity of some home leave on the 8th August. They embarked with the third leave party on the SS 'Lochnegar' which would take them on the first leg of the journey to Reykjavik. Here, they would board a larger ship for the sea crossing to Glasgow. The constant comings and goings of both officers and men also continued and took up much of the War Diary coverage at this time, there being not a great deal of other things to report. Major C.C.Strong (now returned) assumed temporary command in the absence of George Robins, which was closely followed by a couple of inspections from Brigade, of the Detention Barracks, Transport and Carriers at Krossastadir.

On the 31 August, the Bishop of Aberdeen and Orkneys administered Holy Communion in the Church Hut at Krossastadir and had breakfast at Bn. HQ., probably in 'Endcliff Hall'. Later that same morning, he confirmed no less than 76 members of the Battalion in the Cathedral at

Akureyri. Doug Catley was one of those confirmed and kept his certificate all these years. It was signed by the Bishop himself and the Battalion Padre, Capt. N. Murray-Smith.

The Hallamshire Battalion march into Akureyri on a church parade with Major Charles Strong at the Head of the column. Behind him is Ivor Slater followed by the larger than life character of CSM Codd. Both officers and men appear to have something painted on their helmets which may be an image of the York & Lancaster Regimental cap badge. The Regimental Museum Collection contains a stencil made from part of a World War II steel helmet and probably dates from this time. (HFC)

Wilf Fisher...
The Germans had built a new church (Cathedral) at Akureyri as well as bridges and roads. Everything had been done by the Germans pre-war and that's why people were so anti-British, because it was only the Germans that had done anything for them. Anyway, we used to come on this rough track from Krossanes into the town and we used to have the Catholics who were not on Church of England parade, waiting at the edge of town with dusters and brushes for us all to clean our boots before we marched our way to the church.

We got in there and it was particularly hot this day, summertime, and there was Sam Woolley and Sgt. Parler went up the stairs where they used to do the baptisms. The font was there with the water and it was so hot. Sam said, 'Well, I'll have to have a bloody drink.' Next thing I saw was Sam drinking this holy water out of the font!

As has already been mentioned, many of the buildings erected by the Hallams, incorporated tried and tested methods long used by the people of Iceland. Even these, however, did not always stand up to extreme weather conditions. During September, force ten gales did serious damage to a number of turf buildings at Krossastadir and also to huts at Djuparbakki. This did not stop the construction programme though, which had continued since the Hallams arrival where weather allowed. No less than twenty-five huts were erected during August and

September, 1941, which were now sufficient to allow the vacation of all requisitioned and hired buildings at various detachments and outposts.

During the early part of October, a Battalion Military Tournament took place which included competitions for rifle, and no doubt other weapons and equipment. This was held over a number of days and in the middle of it all, the battleship H.M.S. 'King George V' sailed into the harbour of Akureyri. The usual exchange invitations took place and a ship's company football team played Hallams teams at Krossastadir, Krossanes and Djuparbakki.

Whilst on the subject of entertainment, an ENSA group was doing the rounds in this sector with a show entitled 'Swingtime Follies'. It laid on a show at Bragholt and two at Krossastadir on the evenings of the 10th to the 11th. When Arthur Green was asked about these shows he could remember very little except that one was interrupted by a young lad who was invited onto the stage by a female part of the act and had to be physically removed when he overindulged himself by the laying on of hands. Enough said!

These shows did not have the polish, attraction or publicity of those laid on by the likes of Bob Hope and Vera Lynn during World War Two, but they did reach the parts where others failed to tread. What they lacked in 'billing' they must have more than made up for in bringing a tiny slice of home to the troops in Iceland. Echoes of such songs as Bless 'em all, Bless 'em all, the long and the short and the tall! must have lingered in the recreation hut many days after they had left the place. For their ability to brighten the hearts of even a few young men, far away from their loved ones, the ENSA shows were well worth their keep.

ENSA shows were not the only entertainment to be had as some individuals could lay on there own brand of 'Follies'. Whilst on detachment at Bragholt, Ray Langdale heard about the panic in the officers mess when the resident cook went sick. A temporary stand in was found, who was full of enthusiasm even though totally lacking in cooking skills.

Unnamed group stand by the sign near the eastern entrance of Krossastadir Camp.(HFC)

Battalion Drivers. Back Row from left to right : Tom Fowler, Edgar Gill, Joe Powers, Jack Paris, Ron Harding (of Shepherds Pie fame) and Sgt. Jack Oakley. Front Row : Harry Dinnigan, Bert Green, Duggy Redmond, Arthur Green and Bill Himsworth. (HFC)

Ray Langdale...

We were on detachment at a place called Bragholt and the officers mess cook went sick, so Ron Harding volunteered to stand in. He took up his place in the cookhouse and the Armoury Sgt. had made an oven for them. It was a sort of biscuit tin on stilts and underneath was a Primus stove. On one occasion when he was preparing a weekly menu, Lt. Longridge came in and said to Ron, 'Harding, do you think we can have Shepherds Pie?'. Well, Ron hadn't a clue what Shepherds Pie was. The officer said, 'I'm sure we can have it because we've got plenty of Bully Beef and POM (powdered potato). What mummy used to do, she used to get a dish and put in a layer of potato, a layer of meat, a layer of potato and so on until the dish was full with a last layer of potato.' So Ron did it and it was met with approval by the officers.

The following week, Lt. Longridge came in again and said, 'Look here Harding. That Shepherds Pie you made last week was so good, I'd like to put it on the Menu again for one day this week, but you know, when mummy made it, there was always a nice brown crust on the top. A nice crispy brown top on the potato. Do you think you could get it like that?' So Ron said, 'I'll have a try Sir.' So he made some more of this Shepherds Pie and he couldn't get the top to crisp up and it was getting near to dinner time in the officers mess. He went and saw the Cpl. Mechanic and said, 'Hey, Archie! Have you got a blow lamp?' and Archie said, 'Yes!' and Ron said, 'Fetch it round the mess will you?' Then he got this Shepherds Pie out of the oven onto the top and gave it two quick flicks with the blow lamp and created the perfect, crispy, brown crust!

There was another officer who always liked seconds and the Coy. cook was getting a bit fed up with the plate always being brought back into the kitchen and the officer saying, 'Are there any seconds?' Well, on this particular occasion the dinner was M&V (meat and vegetables) and of course you could get gristle in that meal and various other things that you couldn't always identify. The plate came in again this day, 'Lt. so and so wants to know if there are any seconds?' The cook went and got every plate with scraps on that had come off the tables and put all the gristly lumps he could find onto this blokes plate and covered it with gravy! Then he took it back out to this officer, and by, that bloke did enjoy it! He cleared his plate!!

Temperatures fluctuated during October with some quite warm days followed by raw, frosty mornings. Snow fell on the mountains but was often melted in a quick thaw that caused the valley streams and rivers to swell. Groups of men were still coming and going in connection with U.K. leave, with the Sixth Leave Party embarking in the 'Leinster' on the 25th. Many of the men travelling on the ship may have been anxious in recent days about the lack of news from home. If they had still been around the Bn. HQ. on 1 November, they would have known the reason why, for no less than thirty bags of mail arrived which were, on average, one month old!

John Wollerton...

I used to write letters for some of my men who couldn't write for themselves. We had problems with some men's wives sending letters to their husbands relating to what they were up to at home which caused not only distress to the recipient of the letters but to me also. I helped to write letters back which the men wanted to write themselves but which would have been too vulgar, but I could understand their feelings.

Anyone who was up and about at 0730 hrs. on the 11th, would have been quite surprised if they had raised their weary heads and gazed over the mountains to the north. A Barrage Balloon had broken loose from its moorings and was now adrift and destined to wonder through the heavens until the gas depleted. On the same day, the Carrier Platoon were due to practice firing from moving vehicles and would have probably given up their eye teeth or cigarette ration for a chance to let fly at the balloon. Towards the end of the month, an Inter-Coy. Open Boxing

Tournament was fought over a two day period and ended in triumph for 'D' Coy. The prizes were presented by Brigadier N.P. Proctor. The U.S.A. became closer involved in Icelandic affairs when some of their Army Staff Officers visited Akureyri.

Col. Robins called for donations to the newly created 'Afridi Christmas Fund'. The purpose of this fund was to bring a little happiness to the widows and children of those men who had been killed and to give officers and men of the Hallams an opportunity to do something collectively by way of remembrance of their friends and colleagues.

Capt. R. Mumby. This officer was to die at sea on the 27 February, 1943. (HFC)

December came in with a bang in terms of orders. On the first day, Winter Training commenced with all Rifle Coys. being required to do 140 hrs., with Bn.HQ. and HQ. Coy. doing 70 hrs., of mountaineering! A special Training Card was issued for each man so that he could record and total up the number of hours he had spent marching or ski-ing. There may have been some relief in it all, by the fact that the Battalion had until 28 February to complete the task.

Capt. R. Mumby left the Bn. on the 3rd, to take up a second period of duty as Ship's Adjutant on vessels sailing between Reykjavik and the U.K. The 'Leinster' arrived once more at Akureyri with a returning Leave Party. Also on board were 2/Lt. F.R. Tett and 15 ORs. who were newly posted to the Hallams. The wintery weather was beginning to close in now with a mixed bag of cold winds, snow, rain and hail although there were still a few 'fine' days. These conditions will have been just right for the testing of two vehicles which were delivered to the Bn. On 23 December for experimental purposes. They were described at the time as 5cwt F.W.D. (Four Wheel Drive) cars or American Blitz Buggies. They were to become known later by a far more familiar name and without doubt, became the most famous of World War Two vehicles. The Hallams were most privileged because they had just taken delivery of two of the very first examples of the 'Jeep'. They were eventually to be developed and used in just about every theatre of that war and were in such great demand that no less than 639,245 were mass produced by the Willy's and Ford motor companies.

Les Sewell had been with 'C' Coy. at Krossanes since his arrival in Iceland but in late 1941, he volunteered for transfer to the Carrier Platoon based at Krossastadir.

Les Sewell...
Krossanes was a fish factory with a caretaker's mud house. There was no village there. There was a little house perhaps a quarter of a mile on the Akureyri side that was Coy. HQ. and we had to make a pathway to it.

Just before Christmas, 1941, they were asking for volunteers for the Carrier Platoon which was based at Battalion HQ. and they had a NAAFI there and better grub and all this helped to pursuade me. They didn't have an anti-tank section then, but they were extending Support Coy.

We had three carriers in each of three sections commanded by an officer and one Sgt. with their own carrier. There were three men to each vehicle - the driver, the NCO and the gunner. We also had one dispatch rider (DR) and a 15cwt truck. So, we had 10 carriers and they all had individual names taken from previous Battle Honours. (see appendix for names)

When the strength was increased in 1942 we got four Jeeps, another three DRs and the number of carriers rose to 14 vehicles. We were eventually to be issued with a newer model operated by four men when we got back to England, and three of these were converted to mobile flame throwers known as the Wasp.

Each carrier driver had certain tasks to do on his vehicle every day using a servicing log book, so that they were always kept in condition. We had a REME fitter in the 'garage' and one vehicle was always off the road in the garage being completely overhauled, engine out, the lot. In the winter, every night, the guard had to keep going round and starting the engines to stop them freezing.

The Seventh Leave Party must have been feeling a little downhearted when they walked ashore on return to the Bn. on Christmas Eve. Accompanying them on the same ship was a Draft of forty five re-inforcements and one hundred and two bags of Mail which must have included many parcels of presents, cakes and other good things. Most of it was delivered to various detachments before noon the next day except for some of the more remote outposts.

On Christmas Day, George Robins with his 2 i/c, Adjutant and Q.M., visited and served the men at their dinner table in the traditional way. They were able to get around the camps and detachments at Krossastadir, Djuparbakki, Fagriskogur, Bragholt, Krossanes and finally back to the Sgts Mess at Krossastadir. Someone must have drawn the short straw and stayed sober for all that driving, whilst the passengers would have had every opportunity to test the strength of their legs and stomachs in their effort to sample the 'good cheer' offered to them in abundance at every port of call during their strenuous tour of six separate dinners in one day.

The Northern Lights

In this Christmas Card for 1941, the Northern Lights have taken on the familiar 'Victory V' sign, made famous by the finger gestures of Winston Churchill on his rounds of the hard pressed people of Britain at that time. Meanwhile the Hallams nestle cosily in that happy little valley of the Horga in the comfortable knowledge that a guard is watching over them! (CGR)

One of the last but most enjoyable tasks of the year was a vehicle trek over the mountains to test their capabilities. Col. Robins joined the team which included the Transport Officer, the O.C. Carrier Pl. and four ORs. in the two 'Jeeps' and one Carrier. This Carrier had the special track 'modification' (mentioned earlier) that allowed it to grip icy surfaces and without which it could not have negotiated the road to Saudarkrokur which had been closed for weeks. The performance of the F.W.D. 'Jeeps' in mud, snow and ice was reported to be remarkably good.

As the year drew to a close, the weather warmed a little and the men must have pondered what might be in store for them in the coming year. Few may have known of it then, but the officers of the Hallamshire Battalion had served their last Christmas Dinner in Iceland.

George Learad...
I started getting headaches and whatnot at the end of 1941. Anyway, they wanted the three of us to go into the NAAFI to give them a song and I didn't want to go because I felt horrible. Anyway, I went and fell off the stage after I'd sung and I was working my way back to the billet. Later on, the lads came back shouting and bawling and realized how sick I were like, so they quietened down.

I reported sick and they said that I'd got tonsillitis and the M.O. said, 'Go and fetch your bed.' Eric Goodliffe, who were in charge of the M.I. Room, looked after me there.

I remember banging my head and then waking up and I didn't know where I were. They'd taken me to the Hospital Ship 'Leinster' in the harbour at Akureyri. I had a beautiful lady, she were a Queen Alexandra's Nurse sat on the bed next to me and she said, 'Oh! You've come back to us then!' They hadn't given me any hope of surviving because I had Meningitis and the padre had been round to see my mother at home in Sheffield. The nurse stayed with me and looked after me every night. This nurse was called Dyer and she was given the title 'Lady Dyer' and while she was looking after me, my mother died.

January, 1942, began quietly enough but by the end became a tragedy for the Hallams. It started with a fire which occurred at noon on the 23rd in one of the Nissen huts at Krossastadir. Apparently, there was not a great deal of damage to the building but Pte. Fredrick Heald sustained severe burns and was taken to No. 81 General Hospital in a dangerously ill condition. Three days later, at 1100 hrs on the 26th, a 15cwt. truck came off the road near the Horga Suspension Bridge. The driver, Private Thomas Hateley, suffered a fractured skull and was also admitted to the hospital mentioned above. Sadly, both of these men succumbed to their injuries on the same day, Pte Heald at 1215 hrs. and Pte Hateley at 2335 hrs. on the 26th. A Memorial Service was held for them both in the Church Hut, two days later.

In February, fifty-two ORs. were struck off the strength of the Battalion as being unfit for the future role of the unit. The Hallams had already been earmarked for the role of mountain warfare, which was a strenuous task to say the least. It can only be assumed that these men, who were otherwise designated medically A1, were posted to other units where physical fitness was not of such high priority. This would no doubt upset some of the men, especially those who had been with the Hallams for some time and had become part of the 'family'. They certainly could not have been quite as upset as ten others who had set off on UK leave on the 11th and who had been turned back in disgrace from Reykjavik, just before embarking for home. No details are given as to their misdemeanour of contravening regulations governing the taking of NAAFI property to the U.K. The word 'theft' is not used in any context and therefore a reasonable guess can be hazarded in view of the fact that these men were about to spend a few weeks at home.

Their misdemeanour probably amounted to no more than purchasing more 'NAAFI Stores for H.M. Forces' in the form of alcohol and cigarettes, than was allowed per man. Such may have been the common practice for men going home on leave in those days and in this case, the only 'crime' was in being caught at the game. If their crime was of a similar nature, it can only be said that the punishment was extremely harsh and would certainly not have required anything in addition. Leave was one of the most precious things to officer and man alike and those ten young men must have been devastated.

The two 'Blitz Buggies' were out again on the 26th to carry out further tests in traction and grip on frozen surfaces. Col. Robins must have enjoyed his first trip out in them because he was there again with his personal driver, Pte J.A. Bertram, in one vehicle and Lt. Morris and Pte. A Whittaker in the other. They were accompanied by Lt. Mackillop with Ptes. W.W. Bramald and E. Myers in a Carrier. The carrier was given a one hour start and in that time covered about nine and a half miles. Shortly afterwards, it stopped at a place called Bakkasel and was joined only ten minutes later by the two Jeeps. In their journey from Krossastadir to Saudarkrokur and back they covered a total of 148 miles. In reports afterwards it was stated that the Jeeps suffered no mechanical failures of any kind and little difference was experienced in performance between

two and four wheel drive. At some part of the journey the Carrier shed a track which took twenty minutes to replace and this vehicle was also noted to have gobbled up one gallon of petrol for every 3.1 miles travelled!

The beginning of March saw much shuffling of 'A', 'B' and 'C' Coys. and some of their platoon detachments which, if nothing else, would have given the men a slight change of scenery. Little else took place during the month other than examinations over a two day period for those who had been indulging in various educational courses. The whole Bn. was given a treat on the last day of the month during an exercise, when everyone had to spend forty-eight hours in the open air and sleeping in two man tents. The dangers of camping out in the open was brought home very sharply to the 2nd Bn. Kensington Regt. on, of all days, the first of April when three men died in a blizzard. Their tents had been blown away and they died of exposure.

The Hallamshire Battalion must have been one of the first units of the British Army to try out the new 'Blitz Buggy' which was to become far better known as the Jeep. The Willys and Ford Motor Companies combined, were to produce almost 650,000 of them by the time the war came to an end. It is possible that the man in the first vehicle is Capt. Douglas Bell. (DCB)

Jack Haslam...
The 'Kensingtons' (Machine Gun Battalion) had been up ont' mountains back of our officers quarters to test oils used on their weapons that wouldn't freeze. They thought they were going camping and they'd stuck their tents on top of snow, like int' middle of a field and they'd just blown away and left them exposed. They tried to come down but we had to go and fetch some

and they were frozen stiff and some had come down to let us know what was happening and all their bootlaces had broken and they'd come down in their bare feet and frost bitten. Some of them died up there and ponies were used to bring the bodies down.

There began a very big thaw on the 12th with the rivers becoming swollen. The Horga, which flowed through the valley at Krossastadir, reached its highest flood level.
Four new officers arrived on the 19th. These were Lt. Leslie Gill ('A' Coy.), 2 /Lts. O.F. Wilson and A.C. Chadwick ('B' Coy.).

Capt. Les Gill with 'A' Coy. Cross Country Team that won the Northern Sector Inter Unit event in June, 1942. (Mr. Gill)

Leslie Gill was born between Selby and Market Weighton on the 25 June, 1917. He joined The York and Lancaster Regiment as a Private soldier but was soon selected for officer training and went to Sandhurst where he also won a Light Heavyweight Boxing Championship. On receiving his commission he went to 11 Bn. at Doncaster and was still with this unit on Yorkshire Coastal Defences - HQ. at Hunmanby, near Filey when he received orders for transfer to the Hallams in Iceland during early 1942. He was placed with 'A' Coy. and the first person he met there was the company cook (Foss?) who had slept in the next bed to him at Pontefract Barracks during basic training, prior to his being selected for Officer Training.

Les Gill...
Captain Jack Firth was Company Commander, Gordon Good his 2i/c and the other officer was Jan Sim, a most wonderful cross country runner. We had a most wonderful Sgt. Major Codd, an expert on bayonet fighting.

Some of the most memorable times was during ski training. There were three officers and about twelve others on one particular ski camp, high on a mountain slope and each person had to carry his own equipment, food etc. up there and it was a real tester. The Norwegian instructors camp site was a little higher up the slope than ours and one night we were invited up there for a drink so, off the three of us went. Eventually it came time to leave again, but one of the officers couldn't even put his skis on. We managed to get them on but after setting off for our camp below, one of his skis came off after about twenty yards and there he was trying to slow himself down and his ski passed him. We never found that ski ever again.

George Robins was obviously impressed by the Jeeps as he went off on another trip over the mountains to Saudarkrokur, this time taking with him, the Medical Officer (MO) and the Signals Officer (SO). He was able to 'show them off' to the full, however, on the 30th when he, Capt. D.R. Bell and Lt. Elliott motored across to Blonduos. They went there to liaise with a Capt. Shrewberry of the American Garrison Corps and this was the first operational contact that had been made between the Hallams and American Forces. They had a discussion on what was termed Mutual Defence, which must have hinged on the subject of preliminary arrangements for the planned withdrawal of British troops from Iceland, a move that few members of the Hallamshire Battalion would have regretted. Never the less, they still had a few more months of soldiering left to do in this land of the midnight sun.

Very little was reported for the month of May, other than the usual comings and goings of both officers and men on training courses and leave but June saw a number of interesting occurrences. Bn. Exercise No. 5 was carried out using 'B' Coy. and the Carriers as the enemy. In co-operation with this exercise, an American Douglas B18 landed at the aerodrome near Akureyri. These were originally designed as bomber aircraft before the war started, but only two variants of this twin engined aircraft were in use during 1942. One was an American conversion which operated in an anti-submarine role and the other was used by the Royal Canadian Air Force for maritime duties.

On the 12th, a series of tests were conducted which involved the firing of weapons from the so called Godfrey Sledge. Accompanying copies of the Hallamshire War Diary in the Public Record Office is a group of photographs which show various adaptors allowing the fixture of a 2 inch Mortar, Bren Gun and the Boyes Anti - Tank Rifle to these sledges. On closer inspection of the photographs, it can be seen that the demonstrator, even though wearing cold weather clothing and a balaclava helmet, is none other than Col. George Robins. Many other interesting documents are to be found in this particular part of the War Diary, including Care of Arms and

Motor Transport in Cold Climates, Tent Techniques and a drawing of Arctic Bivouac, Sledge Packing (Nansen type) and finally, Care of Arctic Kit.

All this may sound like music only to those steeped in the subject of military history and keen to know every detail that can be found on the most obscure items of unusual equipment. It is listed here only for those who have a taste for it and may not otherwise have been aware of the existence of such things.

The smiles on these unidentified faces may be caused by the knowledge that the tour of duty for the Battalion in Iceland was drawing to a close and they would soon be going home.(HFC)

Whilst on the subject of music, the North East Sector Orchestra left Akureyri on route for Reykjavik on the 18th for a two week stay. The purpose was to make radio broadcasts on Tuesday, 23 June, for a Forces programme. The Hallams were well represented by Sgt. J.H. Cole (Trombone), Pte. A.R. Graydon (Clarinet) and Pte. N. Peel (Singer).

An Iceland Disposition List for the Battalion and its detachments was given for the last time at the end of June, 1942...

Bn. HQ., HQ. Coy. (less 1 pl., Recce Pl. and 1 OP)	KROSSASTADIR
1 Pl. of HQ. Coy.	YTRI - BAEGISA
'A' Coy.	DJUPARBAKKI
'C' Coy. (less 2 Pls.)	DJUPARBAKKI
'B' Coy. (less 1 Pl.)	KROSSANES
1 Pl. of 'B'. Coy.	SAUDARKROKUR
1 Pl. of 'C' Coy.	SIGLUFJORDUR
1 Pl. of 'C' Coy.	DAGVERDUREYRI
'D' Coy. (less 2 Pls. and 1 OP)	BRAGHOLT
2 Pls. of 'D' Coy. and Recce Pl.	FAGRISKOGUR
OP of 'D' Coy.	DALVIC
OP of HQ. Coy.	HRISEY ISLAND

On 7 July, an accident at the Firing Range near Bragholt, resulted in the death of Sgt. Eric Douglas Seymour from a gunshot wound. It is believed that he was working in the 'butts' at the time, when a round either ricocheted or passed through the banking. His funeral took place on the 9th at Akureyri Cemetery, where he was buried close to Ptes. Hateley and Heald, who had died earlier in the year. Their graves are in a remote place but well cared for to this day, as are all the other British Military Memorials throughout the world, dating from the Great War, which are accessible due to the good works of the Commonwealth War Graves Commission.

During the month, both the heaviest rainfall and the hottest day (71 Degrees Fahrenheit) were recorded at Krossastadir since the arrival of the Hallamshires on 26 June, 1940. The last ENSA show was performed, entitled 'The Gypsies' and another group of 'wanderers' left the Battalion in the form of an Advance Party to U.K. Capts. R.I. Slater and G.D. Good, Lts. S. Holmes and

L.M. Lonsdale-Cooper with thirteen ORs. made up this group which set off at 1500 hrs. on 23 July. Their destination, Leominster, close to the Welsh border would, at this time of the year, have seemed like the Garden of Eden compared to their stay in Iceland over the past two years. Whilst they were gone, a very sad departure took place in the form of Lt. Col. George C. Robins. He was struck off the strength of the Battalion on 6 August when the command passed to Lt.Col. J.J. Packard (East Yorkshire Regt.) although Major K.W. West was given temporary command, pending the whole Bn. moving to their new quarters in England.

Major 'Dobby' Dobson, known also as 'put that tent peg there' by some of the men because of his obsession with discipline and attention to minute detail, was a key figure when it came time for packing cases, etc. When the Bn. was preparing to return to U.K., one of his instructions to John Wollerton was to pack the bottled spirits by completely surrounding them with packets of Blanco so as to foil any dockers who might accidentally drop and damage the package and then get curious as to its contents. They would have little interest if they thought the case was full of Blanco (normally used to treat all the items of Mills Webbing Equipment). There must have been a lot of this in stores as it was not generally used in Iceland.

Above : This was the bridge at the eastern entrance to Krossastadir Camp which Arthur Green said had an awkward angled approach road. The farm was just off picture to the right. The vehicle is a three tonner of the type driven by him and other drivers in Iceland. Right : Battalion motorcycles similar to those he was transporting to Akureyri when the Hallams began the job of packing up to come home. (HFC)

On 16 August, an accident occurred at Grotgardup Bridge on the road from Bn.HQ. to the dockside in Akureyri in which Arthur Green was involved as a driver. Although the War Diary only mentions some superficial damage to the load he was carrying, it was fairly traumatic for both Arthur and a passenger who was travelling in the back of his truck. The load was eventually taken down to the town and loaded along with other heavy baggage onto a ship with the most unlikely name of the SS 'Bug'.

Arthur Green...
Shortly before the day we left Iceland, I had to take four motorbikes that would just go in a 30 cwt. down to the docks. They were Nortons and I had a Dispatch Rider in the back to keep them steady like. The roads were like 'Rubbing' boards (a reference to the slipperiness of a board used for playing a game called Shove Ha'penny). Anyhow, it was getting late and I set off, but as I was approaching a bridge I gave way and moved too far over for a vehicle coming the other way. As I pulled onto the bridge my back wheel didn't quite make it onto the bridge and I upturned the

vehicle into the ravine - panic - upside down in this ravine and not much other traffic on the road. I had the Dispatch Rider trapped under these four motorbikes and I was covered in acid spilled from the batteries.

I managed to get around the back and I could see the man lying on the trucks canvas canopy which was keeping the water from him. Where you get the strength from I don't know, but I could only see his greatcoat. He said, 'That bike you've got your hand on, it's on me chest.' Of course they're all mingled together - four bikes. I lifted them up and he says, 'That's all right I can breath now'. This lad, we used to call him Rudolf because of his red nose, didn't want me to leave him but I could hear a truck coming. I had to go and get some help, so I dashed up this bank and waved this 15 cwt. down. Anyhow, there were about four blokes with it and we got him out unscathed, nothing wrong with him. The transport Officer came and he said, 'Are you all right Green?' and I said, 'Yes sir', so he said, 'Right, get in that 15 cwt.' I said, I'd be all right but the nerves and shock was setting in a bit. 'Get in the 15 cwt. here,' he says. I'll always remember him, Mackillop they called him - Grand fellow - Captain Mackillop. Anyway, it was only a few days later that we, the Rear Party, packed up and were on the boat back home.

On 20 August, H.M.T. 'Batory' anchored in the harbour of Akureyri with a shipload of U.S. Army personnel on board. Various parties of these came ashore and proceeded to all camps for the final hand over of the Hallams sector.

This Kit Inspection layout seems to confirm the use of a cap badge motif on the steel helmet. The tin just above and to the left of the boot heel is the container for Emergency Ration containing the 'forbidden' chocolate. (see Arnold Whiteley at start of Chapter.) (HFC)

Wilf Fisher…
I'd been looking after all these rations very, very carefully because food was at a minimum and we had two cases of tea which was in the original old ply, Ceylon Tea boxes and two cases of dried apricots. As I was handing these emergency rations over to this American Capt. he said, 'Throw those in the bloody fjord.' Well, we knew what the situation was in England as regards food and tea, etc. Here's this bloke saying, 'Throw them in the fjord!' I thought he was joking but he wasn't and these blokes got hold of these two casks of tea, took them down the road and threw them and the dried apricots into the sea.

One of the last duties to be performed was the destruction of all Secret Documents that were no longer required and the area was left in the hands of the 3rd Bn. 118th Regt. under the command of Lt.Col. MacSwain of the U.S. Army. On the evening of this same day, the Hallamshire Battalion embarked on the same ship as the Americans arrived on.

At noon the next day, H.M.T. 'Batory' weighed anchor and slipped slowly down the Eyejafjordur and out into the open sea. As that part of Iceland disappeared over the horizon, some of those on board must have looked back and pondered on the two years of their lives it had kept them from their loved ones. Even though there must have been plenty of good times to be remembered, they were going home at last and would soon have turned away. Only the collective spirit of the Hallamshires may have lingered for a moment longer, to take a last fleeting glimpse of the place called Krossastadir, but then it too would be gone. That little slice of England, Endcliffe Hall, would never be the same again.

Endcliffe Hall. (CGR)

On the 22 August, the 'Batory', having made her way around the coast to Reykjavik, joined H.M.T. 'City of Bermuda' and H.S. 'Leinster' now gathered in convoy for the journey home. A few young hearts on the quayside may have been broken as the ships turned away at noon, but the fact was that many of the Icelandic people would not have been sorry to see their uninvited guests leaving at last. It is also true to say, however, that very many good relationships were cemented in those two years of occupation. This was manifest in many ways, not the least of which was evidenced by a few recently married brides on board. One or two of them may have shed a tear right then, as they watched their homeland fading away into the distant haze and, doubtless, wondering what their future held in store.

The convoy was escorted by three destroyers and some Catalina Flying Boats, the latter of which shadowed the group as far as their fuel tanks would allow, before having to turn back to Iceland. By 0900 hrs on the next day, the ships had made good time and Iceland was now three hundred miles to the north. They reached the Clyde at 2100 hrs on the 24 August.

Ray Langdale...
On the boat coming back from Iceland, Lt. Sims called us all together and said that he was very sorry but the Recce Platoon would cease to exist when we got back due to reorganization and that we'd all have to go back to our respective Companies. Four of us from 'A' Coy. had originally volunteered for the Recce Platoon in Iceland and when they asked for volunteers to form the new

❖ *Against the spectacular backdrop of heavy rain clouds, a modern ferry moves down the River Clyde off Gourock (right). H.M.T. 'Batory' would have anchored off the Tail of Bank, a large open area of water beyond the ferry opposite Greenock, which lies just around the headland.(DWS)*

115

Anti-Tank Platoon at Leominster, nearly all the old Recce Platoon were back together again. Tom O'Connor, Jack Salkeld, Franky Perkins, Colin King, Joe Pennington among others.

Ivor Slater (Advance Party) came aboard the ship when it anchored off Greenock on the morning of the 25th and eventually, two parties disembarked and left by train for Leominster. 'Dobbie' Dobson and John Wollerton stayed on board with a working party to oversee the unloading and entrainment of the Heavy baggage which, in all probability, included the bottles of spirit that they had so carefully packed in Iceland. They would be particularly vigilant to see that no one suddenly became abnormally interested in acquiring a few hundred tins of Blanco! There was an extra bonus for the three members of the Battalion who had married Icelanders when they were allowed to proceed immediately on leave. Of course, this 'privilege' may have had more to do with international relations than anything else. It would not have gone down too well with some of the others who had not seen their wives and sweethearts for months and would have seen this as little else but preferential treatment.

Arthur Green...
We boarded the train at Gourock. Crammed full! No idea where we were going - hadn't a clue! Nobody tells you anything in the infantry and the poor bloody private gets to know nothing. Rumours galore! You go to the toilets on the train and get to know a lot more there, than from any official sources. Anyhow, we were given sandwiches to last us for the journey and managed to get a drink from somewhere as we travelled through the night. We kept stopping in sidings, half an hour here, an hour there but eventually arrived at our destination in the early morning at a small market town called Leominster in Herefordshire. We stepped from the train and were told to leave our kitbags in a pile at the station and then marched to our billets about half a mile away. We were in civilian houses on the streets of the town. They were mostly big, rambling, Victorian type houses and all the furniture had been taken out, leaving just the bare floor boards and blackout frames in the windows.

The trains arrived at 0115 hrs. and 0400 hrs. on the 26th and the men were marched to requisitioned billets in the form of civilian buildings throughout the town, with one exception. 'A' Coy. and No.4 Pl. were taken to a place called Eaton Hill, about a mile out of town. Three new officers joined the Hallams at this time in the form of Lt. H.E. Poyner and 2/Lts. T.F.H. Pethick and A.A. Adams, all from 60th (Welsh) Holding Unit, which brought the officer strength up to forty two. Major Ken West proceeded up to the 'real' Endcliffe Hall at Sheffield to retrieve all the officers Mess Kit which must have been in store there for the past two years. The officers may have taken such clothing to Iceland but it is unlikely that the Battalion would cart such trappings around the world when on a war footing. The officers were now determined to get back into the swing of things and be dressed correctly for the part.

Arthur Green...
We soon got to know where the boozers were, what the beer was like and if there were any birds! I found out about dance halls because I was pretty keen on dancing at that particular period. We noticed that there were a lot of Land Army girls in the neighbourhood and it was that time of year when the fruit was full in the trees. There were apples, pears, plums and we hadn't had any fresh fruit for a couple of years and we were just making pigs of ourselves. We went 'scrumping' and took our pick in the orchards and, of course, it was cider country so we made ourselves poorly. Nearly all of us had stomach trouble for a week or two until we got used to things.

Arthur's close linking of Land Army Girls and the picking of ripe fruits, almost in the same breath, lends itself to mind reading, but it has to be said that these men would have needed superhuman will power to pass by an orchard, laden with all that forbidden fruit! There had

116

been no Land Army Girls in Iceland and any fruit to be had, came in tins. Leominster was a 'scrumpers' paradise!

Ivor Slater...
A few of us went into this pub and there were quite a few chaps in there and we said, 'We're new to Leominster. What do you drink here?' We knew it was cider country and we started off with this stuff and it was pints all round. We later left the pub and went across the road to our accommodation where the whole lot of us passed out.

South Street. Leominster. C.1942 (HFC)

Les Sewell...
Battalion HQ. was in some Georgian buildings down Etnam Street and Support Company HQ. was across and further down the same street. I remember one Company was in a premises called Sugar King and the rest were scattered about town. There was a huge market shed that was used for fruit and we messed in there, Batemans Buildings it was known as and the NAAFI was housed in a cinema.

On the 29th, the Reverend H.G. Thomas, R.A.Ch.D. became attached to the Battalion and attended the first unit Church Parade the next day. Major R.O. Sclater took the Salute outside Bn.HQ. which was located at No.18 Etnam Street.

Arthur Green...
We had parades out on the front street and Bn.HQ. was in a house similar to ours. The Dining Hall was a big warehouse where they used to store fruit. It could house the whole Battalion at one sitting although they normally did it in two sittings in order that the cooks could handle it. We were issued with more modern equipment and vehicles and these were garaged in yards. We got all brand new Jeeps, 15cwts, 3 Tonners and were sent on all sorts of courses for various things.

The new Commanding Officer was Lt. Col. J.J. Packard (East Yorkshire Regt.). This officer has been described as one who did not seem to be on the same 'wave length' as a group of men who had just spent two very sparse years in what was a veritable wilderness, compared to the place they now found themselves. The strict discipline, which no one would have denied was needed after Iceland, fell like a sudden hammer blow instead of it being delivered in a steadily measured and progressive way. Independently, Ray Langdale and John Wollerton tried to sum up this obviously brilliant man whose skills would have been far better placed, and later were, at a much higher level, elsewhere.

Ray Langdale...

Our new C.O., Col. Packard (East Yorkshire Regiment), was immaculate in his dress and I was told that he was an administrative man, a Rhodes Scholar and spoke about four or five different languages. He must have been a very, very, clever man.

John Wollerton...

Col. Packard was a very intelligent person and could speak many languages but he wasn't well liked. He was too intellectual and didn't have both feet on the ground. I was in trouble once from him for not running when he called me over in the presence of a General and I didn't even know there was one with him. The next day I had a strip torn off and was given seven days extra Orderly Officer duties. He was a disciplinarian but I think he had difficulties in communicating with others who weren't of his own intelligence and I can't think of any better way of putting it.

Men on the receiving end of hard discipline are usually more blunt but Arnold Whiteley, like many others, could still see the amusing side of having to run everywhere at the double.

Arnold Whitely...

When we got to Leominster and with it being summer, the fruit were coming out and it were like heaven. It was like another world to us after Iceland. Of course the battalion was split up a bit and we weren't all in one building. We were in various commandeered buildings. Bateman's Buildings was one and some over shops, but it wasn't bad. There was one fly in the ointment, however. We lost Col. Robins and we got another Colonel and I don't think he'd been told who the enemy were. He thought we were the enemy and set about to make a soldiers life as miserable as he could. He filled the Glass House with minor offences that would normally have been admonished.

No.18 Etnam St. (white fronted building - centre) was the Bn.HQ. and next door (left) (No.20) was used as offices for No.1 Platoon and Transport. Mission Hall (where the 'Spotters Cub' used to meet) was just off picture to the right. (DWS)

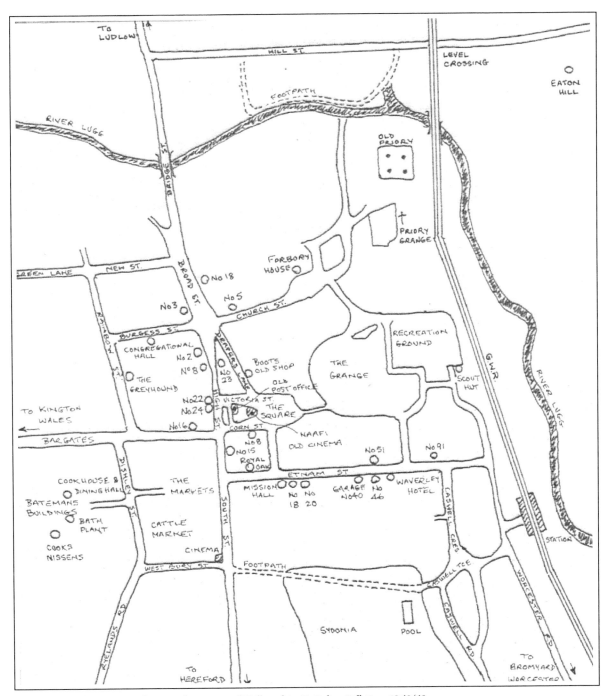

Sketch Map of Leominster showing disposition of Hallamshire Battalion Billeting, 1942/43

'A' Coy. & 4 Platoon. at Eaton Hill.(4Pl. later based at Ashfield House)

'B' Coy. at Forbury House, Church St., 3 & 18 Broad St.

'C' Coy. at 8, 22, 23 and 24 High St.

'D' Coy. at Old Post Office, Boots Old Shop, Greyhound, 2 High St. & 8 Corn St.

H.Q. Coy., Company Office, P.R.I., Messing Office & Administrative Officer at 51 Etnam St.

1 Platoon & Transport at 20 Etnam St.

Nos. 2, 3 & 5 Platoons, Stores & Workshops at 46 Etnam St.

QM at 15 South St. & Scout Hut.

Medical Inspection Room at Congregational Hall.

Armourer at 16 West St. Bn. Diner & Cooks at Batemans Buildings.

Lecture Room at Mission Hall.

Officers Mess at the Waverley Hotel. (now demolished)

Bn. HQ. at 18 Etnam St.

Sgts. Mess at 91 Etnam St. (now demolished)

Transport Garages at 40 Etnam St. & the Royal Oak Hotel. (DWS)

Then he started a cross country run every Friday afternoon and everybody had to go on this run you see. Then he put a boxing ring in the open fruit market and we were all introduced to it. The Sgt. Major would be Master of Ceremonies and if you were within a couple of stones of each other, you were deemed to be about the same size. Then you had to put your Blues (gym shorts & vest) on and box. Of course, some didn't like that sort of thing as a public spectacle. Everybody would be sinking down in their seats. Then it was your turn...'You there lad, come on!'

The First and Second leave parties went off at the beginning of September and little more was reported in the first two weeks. A trial run was made on the 13th of the local Assault Course by a squad of officers and they found it to be adequate, provided a few minor alterations were made. Exercise of a different and probably more enjoyable kind was had by thirty Hallams men beginning on the 18th, when they were placed on loan to local farmers and helped with the harvest and fruit picking.

Les Sewell...
The Carrier Platoon was first based in Eaton Hill, outside the town with very large grounds where there were several Nissen huts built. We were only there for a few days when we went on leave and on return were moved to Ashfield House at the top end of the town and the carriers were parked in a builders yard called Norgroves. In the corner of this yard was a Nissen hut that served as a guard room and we had to mount a guard there every night.

We started training there in earnest and the corner of Norgroves yard was hit quite a number of times by learners trying to get in with the carrier. We got a new C.O. there too, Col. Packard, and he was dead keen. We started cross-country runs every Saturday afternoon and it had to be done in a certain time or you did it again in your own time.

During the month, seventeen officers and one hundred and sixty five men went to Hereford to see a demonstration of both British and German Tanks, the latter probably being the product of fighting in North Africa. The C.O. gave a talk to all officers on the subject of new organization within British Infantry Brigades as well as the new Coy. Battle Drill. There began a series of cross country runs at this time, the first being held over a short distance and won by Lt. F.J.F. Jones. The second over a longer course on the 25th, was won by Pte. Bird of 'D' Coy.

An interesting event took place on the 24th, when an inaugural meeting of the 'Spotters Club' was held in the Mission Hall on Etnam Street. The object of this newly formed club was to enable members, by various means, to take an interest in current military aircraft and more importantly, for them to recognize types from various angles. The benefits of such skills in those days are obvious and in addition to available silhouette pictures being made available, Pte. Allott volunteered to build some models with the help of others. Pte. Moreley agreed to produce some poster drawings, again with the aid of anyone else who was interested and these would be displayed in the N.A.A.F.I. and W.V.S. as a decorative aid to recruitment of more members to the Club.

Les Sewell...
We went on this training scheme one day, without any food, chasing all over the countryside. It was about September and, of course, we went through orchards where we did find some food but we weren't supposed to. The majority of our training in carrier platoon, however, was driving various types of machines which included motorbikes, jeeps, trucks and our own carriers. It was very pleasant really because after Iceland, Hereford and the Welsh border was very pleasant, quite a change.

The first exercise (ALAN) was laid on towards the end of the month and the Battalion moved to Dolyhir in Radnorshire in troop carrying transport for this purpose. On arrival, the Hallams debussed and marched to Gladestry where No.4 Pl. provided personnel to act as the 'enemy'. The rest of the Bn. were unable to defeat the enemy by nightfall and had to spend the night in bivouacs. The attack was resumed early the next morning when the enemy were surrounded and succumbed by 0830 hrs on the 28th. Then the Bn. was marched back to billets, a distance of twenty one miles. At noon the same day, Lt. A.B. Cowell who was to command the new A/Tk. Pl., with Cpl. Wathall ('C' Coy.), L/Cpl Rose (HQ. Coy.), Cpl Langdale ('A' Coy.) and Cpl Salkeld ('D' Coy.), went to 88th A/Tk. Regt. at Llanidloes to attend a course of instruction on the Q.F. 2Pdr. A/Tk. Gun. On the last day of September, the Battalion took part in a Drill Parade on The Grange.

October started warm and bright and anyone who was paying attention to what was going on may have been slightly confused when they noticed that a Mr. Harold Gibson was giving a lecture to the whole Bn. on the subject of 'Russia'. Then three days later, Capt.C.G. Wells, RAMC, proceeded on a course to the School of Tropical Medicine. On the 8th, John Wollerton was appointed Assistant S.O. and transferred to HQ. Coy. The 'Spotters Club' was very active and the subject of a meeting held on the evening of the 14th was entitled, 'Introduction to Aircraft Recognition'. A film show was given on the 17th at the local 'Clifton' cinema and may not have gone down too well because of its implications - the title being 'Next of Kin'. The following day, one hundred ORs. attended the same cinema and sat through a film on the subject of Aircraft Recognition! The Spotters Club was going to be swamped with new members at this rate. Lt. Leslie Gill and thirty two ORs. must have felt rather proud of themselves when they left for Llanberis to act as Demo Pl. at the War Office Advanced Handling and Field Craft School on the 21st. The Battalion strength at the end of the month was given as 38 officers and 819 ORs.

A Glider crashed at Brinshope on 4 November for which the Bn. had to provide a guard of one NCO and six men, a duty that was to be repeated in December when the same thing happened, this time at Knapton Green. The Grange seems to have been the ground used for major parades and inspections and in company with the local Home Guard and British Legion, the Battalion attended the Armistice Service at the War Memorial there on the 8th. Capt. Wells said good-bye when he was posted to 165 Light Field Ambulance, Kilmarnock, and on the same day, Lts. Mackillop and Tett were admitted to hospital.

Officers and NCOs left on what appears to have been a day course on Street Fighting which was set up at a special school in Birmingham. The Hallams took in a number of films at the Clifton Cinema which included the titles 'Everybodies Business' and 'Baptism of Fire'. Lectures were delivered on the subjects of 'Why Democracy failed in Europe' and 'Psychiatry'. The talk on Democracy was given by an Austrian, Mr. Carl Egger. The Psychiatry talk must have been the subject of repeat performances because David Lockwood attended one of these later (1943) and was obviously impressed, judging by his description of it in a letter. A lecture on

❖ *The Clifton Cinema on South Street (now a Bingo Hall) where the Hallams were introduced to various lectures and training films during their stay at Leominster.*

the 6Pdr. A/Tk. Gun was given to all officers this month. It had been decided to create a War Information Room earlier in the month and this was opened on the ground floor of 46 Etnam Street on the 25th. Capt. Morris and Lt. Hinshelwood gave instruction to the local Home Guard in Battle Drill and Street Fighting.

Some embarrassment was caused on the 7 December when two prisoners, under close arrest, escaped from the Guard Room under cover of darkness whilst the guard was being changed. An old friend, Col. C.G. Robins, made a brief appearance on the 13th when he took the salute on the march past of the Church Parade. On the 22nd, the newly formed Hallams Dance Orchestra made its debut at a dance given by the W.V.S. and on Christmas Day, all officers and Sgts. waited on the men at dinner. The officers were very pleased with themselves the next day when they beat the Sgts. at football, four goals to nil. In the evening, an 'all ranks' dance was held in the Drill Hall. It was noses back to the grind stone for part of the Battalion on the 28th, however, when they were ordered to spend the night in bivouac under a new training scheme. This was going to require every man to sleep out for one night per week. Bn. HQ. and the A/Tk. Pl. organized a special 'Night Out' on the 30th and another all ranks dance was held in the Drill Hall on the last night of the year.

The Officers Football Team. Those identified are Peter Newton (cricket jumper!) Ken West (centre with black shirt) and Mike Lonsdale-Cooper (extreme left with white rolled sleeve shirt). (HFC)

January got off to a slow start with not much happening other than sports fixtures with units in the surrounding area. The Rugby team beat 4 Lincs (23 - 2), R.A.F. Shobden (17 - 14) and 146 Field Ambulance (22 - 6). Lt. Tony Nicholson left for the School of Infantry at Barnard Castle and Lt. John Wollerton attended the School of Signals at Catterick. An Army Concert Party put on a show called 'Norton Follies'. Everyone has to lose sooner or later and the Rugby XI blotted their copy book on the last day when they played 1/4 KOYLI. The score was 8 - 16.

February saw the beginning of various schemes and the first one to take place was an exercise 'ONWARD' which involved the Bn. HQ. in Battle Procedures. A Battalion exercise, code word 'WALKER' came next on the 8th which involved tactical advancing, the crossing of a river in assault boats and an attack on a hastily defended position. The Bn. played the part of the 'enemy' when they took part in a Divisional exercise 'FILLDYKE' which focused on bridging and was carried out over a four day period, beginning on the 15th. Lt. R.J. Hinshelwood sustained severe spinal injuries during a Divisional Battle Course and was taken to a Birmingham hospital. Capt. Douglas R. Bell assumed command of HQ. Coy. on the 21st. On the 27 February, the Hallams loaded all their carrier vehicles onto special trains for a rail journey to Buckinghamshire and the whole Battalion went by road the next day in preparation for a major scheme. Exercise 'SPARTAN' was about to begin and the Hallams were encamped about a mile to the west of Chalfont St. Giles where they were issued with sixty-six bicycles which 'A' Coy. used to form a mobile patrol.

On the first day of fine weather and brilliant sunshine, no 'enemy' action took place but there was an attempt the next day by would-be saboteurs to damage transport by putting earth in the fuel tanks. It can only be assumed that this was part of the exercise and not actual damage, in which case the saboteurs would probably have left labels on the fuel tanks to say that they had been! On the 4th, the Bn. moved to its defensive area an Monks Risborough by way of a fourteen mile route march and from there, by troop carrying vehicles to Warborough. Some embarrassment was caused here when two 'enemy' Jeeps passed through, right under the noses of Bn. HQ. 'C' and 'B' Coys. were now moved out to forward positions with 'A' Coy. in reserve.

Ray Langdale...
There was an incident in Chalfont St. Giles, a beautiful town what I saw of it, and we were on the outskirts with one A/Tk. gun. It was a Sunday morning and the sun was shining and the houses on either side of us were real posh residences. We were armed with Thunder Flashes (pretend shell fire) and up the road came this Canadian (enemy) armoured car and as it got to us we threw one at him and scored a good hit. The driver must have got a shock because he turned straight into this private driveway, did a three or four point turn on this immaculate lawn, came back out and shot off in the direction he'd come from. Well, if you'd seen the state of that lawn.

The 'enemy' were reported to be crossing the Thames at Sonning the next day and the Hallams were ordered to move forward to contact by way of a route march to Henley, via Checkenden. It was reported that 'B' Coy. lost a Platoon in a very sharp engagement and during the day, a Lt. Col., one carrier, two Jeeps and two Machine guns were captured by the Battalion. 'A' Coy. then got into the action on the 6th and returned to Bn.HQ. on their bicycles after having blown bridges at Days Lock and Shillingford. The same Coy. was attacked later in the day but drove off the 'enemy'. The Bn. then withdrew to High Wycombe and managed to serve at least one hot meal by the side of the road, en route!

Ray Langdale...
We had strict instructions not to beg, buy or accept any extra food. You had to exist on the rations provided for the exercise but our driver had got hold of four or five pork pies and Reg Bratley hit upon the great idea of heating them up on the exhaust manifold on our truck.

From a newly established HQ. in High Wycombe, the Bn. was ordered to evacuate the town and hold the right flank so as to allow for the withdrawal of the Buckinghamshire Brigade. There now began a movement through Clements End, Leighton Buzzard, and finally to Battlesden, just before which the C.O. narrowly missed being captured. A cease-fire was called at 0900 hrs on 12 March and after a few days clean up and reorganization the Hallams returned to Leominster at 1800 hrs on the 15th.

An order which landed on the C.Os. desk on the 20th must have come as a bit of a shock because it required the Bn. to Mobilize ready for service overseas by the 15 April. Col. Packard was called to the War Office in London the next day and Capt. Douglas R. Bell assumed temporary command. Towards the end of the month, 2/Lts. A.D. Howard and T.M. Murray were posted to the Bn. and at the Western Command Cross Country Finals, the Hallams team secured 2nd place for the Division.

Early in April, 1943, 2/Lt. G.H.R. Jackson joined the Battalion and on the 6th, a Major A.F. Welsh arrived to interview those applicants who had applied for transfer to the Parachute Regiment. The whole Bn. was inspected at Eaton Hill by Lt. Gen. E.C.A. Schrieber, C.B., D.S.O., where he presented Polar Bear medals. On the 9th, all Ford transport was withdrawn and replaced by Bedfords. Things carried on as normal in the first half of the month during which there was an

All Ranks dance held in the Drill Hall on the 10th and an officers pistol shoot on the range the next day. On the 13th, Lt. P. Turrell left the Bn. on a six months course at the Small Arms Training School, Stoke on Trent, and Lt. Wollerton was appointed Bn. S.O. It was on this same day that the Hallams received a movement order for Exercise 'Soudley', which required the Bn. to move to Creiff in Scotland.

The Advance Party arrived at Crieff the next day and over the next few days the Battalion was taken there by both road (Transport under Capt. D.C. Beckett on 15th) and rail (Carriers under Lt. S.J.D. Moorwood on 20th). The main body left Leominster by rail at 0415 hrs. and arrived at Crieff at 1535 hrs the same day (under Capt. Morris). Capt D.R. Bell remained at Leominster with a Rear Party of two officers and twenty men. During all this time, Col. Packard (accompanied by Capts. J. Firth and D. Sandford) was with the 69 Field Regt. at the Artillery Practice Camp, Redesdale. Then on the 28th, a veritable bombshell dropped when the whole Battalion was ordered to return to Leominster.

Ivor Slater...
Crieff was the first time where the Battalion was all under one roof during the war. I went up there to take the place over and had just got sat down and about to sign the receipt of acceptance when an order arrived by motorcycle to return to Leominster. At that particular time, some of the Canadians, who were in the south of England, were very obstreperous... Ivor had heard that these men had declared that they had come over to fight and not to sit around twiddling their thumbs in England - or words to that effect. This story can not be verified, however, but Ivor went on to say... *It was decided that they would be sent to Scotland to take over the Hydro in our place and, after they had been there for about three weeks, they were sent out to Africa.*

It seems odd that the Hallams had been warned in March for 'service overseas' and then subsequently sent to Crieff on the very day designated for that move, the 15 April. It is wondered whether the unit from Canada took over, not only the place of the Hallams at Crieff, but also the move shortly afterwards to Africa. Be that as it may, the Hallams were all back at Leominster on the last day of April and fell back into the old routine. Few would have complained though, about being sent back to a place which was both familiar and pleasant, not to mention the return to close friendships that had been bonded there. A few of the latter were to blossom into marriage eventually, and a number of Hallamshire men were to settle in Leominster after the war had ended.

May saw its fair share of the usual comings and goings, training films at the Clifton Cinema and various sports activities. Major Ivor Slater left for Edinburgh to attend a Coy. Commanders course. There was a Cross Country Race between the Officers and Sgts. Mess which was won by L/Sgt. Liptrot, and a two all draw when they played each other at football on the pitch at Eaton Hill. The Bn. cricket XI defeated Stoke Prior by twenty-two runs in the first game they had played since 1940. Then a cricket game was played on the 21st between Officers and Sgts. Mess on the Grange with the latter winning by thirty-four runs. A return match was played on the 23rd and the officers lost again, this time by four wickets.

Tragedy struck on the 25th when a child was accidentally killed during weapons training on the Grange. It is difficult to understand how or why live ammunition was being used in such a place so near to public areas and could not possibly have been intentional.

John Wollerton...
Life at Leominster was super because it was almost a civilian life. I really enjoyed it because my hobby was cross country running. Otherwise we did a lot of running there, in fact the local

inhabitants thought we'd been sent there for punishment because we went everywhere at the double and we got very, very fit. It was a lovely place to be though. One or two things happened that marred it, however. One incident occurred when a group of men went out to practise firing and accidentally killed a child through unknowingly having a live round in the weapon instead of all dummy rounds. That had a very upsetting effect on the local population.

John mentioned that one or 'two' things happened to mar the joy of being in that place. Indeed, there was a second occurrence which must have shocked and affected everyone, both civil and military alike, as deeply as the first. Sergeant Cliff Lister was directly involved in the immediate aftermath of a crime that some might describe as one of 'passion'. His account is given here but without naming the soldier or woman concerned.

Cliff Lister...
I used to sleep in the same billet (attached to the dining hall) as a Sergeant who had shot this young lady. This particular night when I came in he'd buzzed off somewhere and left her lying there. I got our ambulance to take her away and gave them my field dressing to put round her. She'd been shot through the stomach and died later in the Cottage Hospital. I'd had a few drinks but I soon sobered up and wondered where he'd gone to. I could hear this kind of a moaning coming from the dining hall.

❖ *Part of the complex known as Bateman's Buildings, this oversized 'Nissen' type structure was normally used for the storage of fruit in peacetime but was requisitioned for use as a Dining Hall by the Hallams. It was here also that a young woman was seriously injured by a gunshot wound from which she later died. (DWS)*

Some instinct told me it was him and he were a big fellow, six foot odd you know, and I was a little bit apprehensive. It was him and I just sat there and looked at him and I said, 'What have you done Bill?' He says, 'I've shot Ruth, haven't I?' and I said, 'Well, apparently you have.' Then he said, 'Would it be possible to see her?' and I said, 'I don't know.' Then I said, 'What do you want to see her for?' and he said, 'I want to go and ask for forgiveness and pray to God that she doesn't die.' So then I said, 'Right, but you ought to go to the Police Station first and give yourself up.' I wasn't going to argue with him. However, he says, 'Well, will you go to the Hospital with me and see if we can see her?' So, I walked across with him and there were soldiers and police stood at each side of the corridor as though they knew who we were but nobody challenged us.

He knelt down at the side of her bed and asked God to forgive him and I don't know whether she actually died there and then or afterwards but I said, 'Right we'll have to go down to Police Station now Bill. I can't make you go but you ought to.' Anyway, he did. We walked down, nobody stopped us and he gave himself up. I visited him a few times in Shrewsbury Jail and every time I went, there were cigarettes from some of the lads to take, you know, they still felt sorry for him even though he'd done that. Eventually, we had to come down from Scotland for the trial. At the end of summing up, the judge put the black cap on and said, 'Sergeant .... you will hang by the neck until you are dead'. Later he asked to see me at Hereford Cells...   ...A later appeal was upheld and he got seven years penal servitude.

The shot was fired from a .303 rifle and there were two rounds discovered at the scene of the crime. One spent case was on the floor and the other live round was still in the weapon. They had both been highly polished and on the spent case was inscribed 'R.I.P. Ruth'. The live round was in the breech and marked 'R.I.P. Bill'. *Cliff ... he'd intended to shoot himself by the look of things.*

On 24 May, Capt. S. Martin de Bartoleme rejoined the Bn. after special duties with the M.O.I. Another officer came back to the fold in the form of David Lockwood, who reported for duty on 3 June. It will be remembered that he had been released to industry from Iceland in the early months of 1941. From that time, he had been very much involved in the production of Churchill Tanks at the Newton Chambers works at Sheffield but now he was free to come back once more to the old Battalion he'd joined way back in 1930. Although he was reported in the War Diary to have rejoined on the 3rd, he must have got to Leominster on or before the 2nd because his first letter is dated then and he has already had time to take stock of the situation and reacquaint himself with old friends. Most, if not all, of his letters from Leominster will probably have been written in his room at the Waverley Hotel (Officers Mess) on Etnam Street.

David Lockwood (Letters to Mary)
2 June, (Leominster)...
Things have changed a lot in detail but not really in the main things. There are hundreds of old faces and everyone I know, both officers and troops, have been awfully decent and there has been much handshaking - quite a second home - though a pretty poor second!
Today has been a case of finding my way around the town and seeing billets and talking to people. Interview with Packard this morning who has been very charming and seems pleased to have me and as I said this afternoon (on the phone) wants me to go to Barnard Castle (on a course).
As far as my job is concerned at present, I am 2i/c 'B' Coy. (the old Coy. I joined under Milo (Dixon) in 1930) and it will be the best way to getting a Coy. of my own which Ken assures me I shall get and Packard has hinted at without committing himself.

Not a bad journey down (from Sheffield) bit long and tedious, and finished up in Worcester in a funny little two coach farmers train with Ken's old Company cook, Craven, who I know well and heard all the gossip. This (Leominster) is a nice little town, you'd like it, much better than Thirsk and right in the heart of rural England at its best - nothing but farming and the country looks grand. I have borrowed Ivor's batman, another old friend and am after one, Whittaker, George Robins ex-batman who is in my Coy. Got a nice airy room with big window overlooking the main street and a proper bed but of course use my own bedding - the mess as a whole is poor and pretty grim - the Waverley Hotel !
James Moorwood has arrived back from leave just now - Stephen Bartoleme is back too with a parachute on his sleeve - 5 jumps! No one knows what he's doing but I gather his job has fizzled out. I'm glad I got with Oscar Sclater (O.C. 'B' Coy.) as we have something in common - he's tall and very quiet (just like me!)

David very quickly became aware of the strict discipline that was now being instilled into the Hallams and noted the effect it was having on at least two of his fellow officers.

David Lockwood (Letters to Mary)
3 June, 1943 (Leominster)...
(Officers wives, Vera West and Pam Newton, were staying at a nearby Hotel to be with their husbands)....*as they are here, Packard has suddenly decided that the whole of Bn. HQ., including Ken (West) and Peter (Newton) shall bivouac out every night till Monday - they've gone out tonight*

126

and left their grass-widows at the Royal Oak. Ken is convinced it's intentional on Packard's part and he and Peter are livid, naturally.

Bn.HQ. left for a four day exercise which was for the purpose of gaining experience under active service conditions. It may have been at about this time that Arthur Green was required to be detached for a few days to an Artillery Training Camp, some thirty-eight miles WNW of Leominster, as the crow flies, but considerably more by road.

Arthur Green...
I was sent to this place in Wales called Llanidloes with a Ford 3 Ton Truck that had a front end on it that looked like a whales snout and the bonnet kept coming up, it wouldn't stop down on the catch. I was attached to an Anti-Tk. unit during an exercise and I have never in all my service been with such a shower. The officers had no control over the men, there was no discipline and I don't know how they got away with it. Anyway, we set off on this scheme with a load of stores and we were 'captured' after only about six hours and spent the rest of the time on a farm which was designated a PoW camp. The poor old farmer never had any eggs for a week because the lads used to be at the side of the hens waiting for them to lay and when some Canadians turned up, even the hens were disappearing. They didn't give two hoots!.

David Lockwood (Letters to Mary)
5 June, 1943 (Leominster)...
Last night we went to a Hallamshire Sergeants dance and I went along with Vera, Ken, Pam and Peter, also Packard who I find is only 33! - I feel more able to cope with him now I know he's only two years older than me...

❖*Above : Retirement home now stands on the site of the Waverley Temperance Hotel which was used as the Officers Mess. Both this and the Sargeants Mess at No 91 were demolished some years after the war.* ❖*Below : The Chequers, a fine old timber framed building just across the street from the Waverley and the place where Ivor Slater and others were first introduced to the powerful local brew! (both DWS)*

...your Ted got pounced on by a married woman... ...James Moorwood introduced me as she had tagged herself on to some of the subalterns in the Talbot on the way there and before I knew where I was, I was doing the Palais Glide with this woman on one side and Pam Newton on the other. Well, she really was a number! and could I get rid of her, not likely!

Of course, we were down to Christian names in about five minutes and after palming her off

during a Paul Jones, found her back again expecting me to sit with her after it! Several of the lads warned me against her and of course after another dance or so (I hate being rude to women) she as good as asked me to see her home. I escaped to the bar and got another chap who was in the plan to dance with her while I slipped out and away home to bed - very thankful! Well at lunchtime one of the mess waiters came in to say a lady wanted me on the telephone - my God it was her! to apologize to me for 'missing' me after that dance and would I come to tea tomorrow!! I said no apology was necessary and that I had a tea date tomorrow (a lie) - well then could I come to tea today? - No! thank God I couldn't as we had the Battalion Sports this afternoon. Phew! Eventually I shook her off. No credit to my will power, darling, the woman isn't a day under 45, has henna-ed hair and isn't the least bit attractive!! Great joke in the mess of course and various offers of a bodyguard when I walk the town.

Capt. Joe Beckett (centre with moustache) raises his sherry glass at a stag party, in honour of his impending marriage. Those identified are standing (left to right) 1. Capt. Morris, 2. Maj. Sclater? 4. Maj. Dobson. 5. Capt. Newton, 6. Capt. Beckett, 7. Capt. Lonsdale-Cooper, 8. Maj. Slater. (DCB)

David Lockwood (Letters to Mary)
7 June, 1943 (Leominster)...
Tomorrow evening, Joe Beckett and I with two signallers, two wireless sets, a truck, a driver and the Frog-Boy (his batman Pte. South) are off to Monmouth for 24 hours to join a Field Gunnery Battery and do a real shoot with them in the mountains. Joe and I will represent the infantry and give targets to the gunners over the wireless - of course I'm tickled to death and looking forward to it no end. I am in command of the little party. We leave after tea tomorrow and spend the night with the Battery and shoot on Wednesday.

David Lockwood (Letters to Mary)
12 June, 1943 (Leominster)...
We left here at quarter to eight this morning, picked up by the R.A.M.C. on their way through here and went out through Presteigne right into Wales about 30 miles away to the west. Got to the rendezvous before nine and climbed a hill and there was one of the most marvellous panoramas I have ever seen. We were on top of Radnor Forest - a grassy moor - and at our feet was the most beautiful valley Cwm Aran (the valley of the River Aran) all rich farmland and looking like a patchwork quilt in every shade of green and the brown plough and here and there a field of mustard shining in the sun like brass - lovely woods too and the river Aran winding in and out down towards Builth Wells to the west and then rising up beyond the valley, row after row of green hills into real mountains perhaps thirty miles away - Plynlimon (towards Tal-y-Llyn where we went, do you remember?) in the north, round in a great semi - circle to the Black Mountains (where I was on Wednesday) and the Brecon Beacons in the South.....

...we went to see a demonstration of infantry in action and lots of other weapons joining in, all with live ammunition, wireless, etc. Very good, and done by the Divisional Battle School. Chris Somers was there as a control officer and we met and had a long talk. I gave him half my lunch

and we shared the last two chocky bics. you gave me to bring down here - hunger got top side of sentiment!

The General was there dressed like Montgomery as usual! - he's a rum chap, about my height with a face rather like Malcolm Fisher. Terribly keen and fit - we were spectators of course, about 50 of us, and usually walk from one view to another - not so the General (Barker) who said, 'Where do we go now? Right! Come on you chaps, double!' Whereupon he sets off at a run with Brigadiers and all of us tripping over the moor after him, just like Beagling - my God it was hard work!! He is an incredible man, and a great change from docile old 'Uncle Harry' Curtis.

On the 15th, The Carrier Platoon was concentrated at the Divisional Battle School, Norton Manor, Presteigne, about twelve miles west of Leominster.

Les Sewell...
The Battle School was formed there and I had a fortnight of it which nearly killed me because everywhere you went you had to double carrying Brenguns, PIATs and everything. Always at the double! I remember at the end of the course we had to go round crawling through trenches with a Brengun firing just over the top of us and if you'd stuck your backside up, you would have had a bullet in it. Of course, the cows used this field normally! Then you were over a wall and down a ditch, across a river at the other side of which there were officers firing 'Tommy' guns around you. Then you'd to go down a hill with a hedge about five feet high at the bottom, a thick thorn hedge which you had to get through somehow. You couldn't get through it, you had to go fast enough to go over the top of it! Then it was up the hill again and finish off charging with fixed bayonets at these dummies, yelling, then you'd got to dig slit trenches which had to be a certain size, exactly! It were about ten o'clock when I finished and the officer had to 'pass' each slit trench and when he'd passed it you could go back to the billet and get some food and that was the end of it. It was pretty tough!

David Lockwood must have had a course at Barnard Castle brought forward at short notice as he does not mention such an early date in his last Leominster letter. He travelled to Barnard Castle by train via Darlington in the guards van to a camp, Humbleton, four miles on the Darlington side of Barnard Castle on the 14th.

David Lockwood (Letters to Mary)
16 June, 1943 (School of Infantry, Humbleton Camp, Barnard Castle)...
I've just had dinner in the huge dining hall run in the cafeteria way (fetch your own food from A.T.S. at a counter) about 250 officers sit down to dinner - and I am now sitting in one of the three ante-rooms with a wireless going and every chair taken. The food here is much better than at Leominster (so far) and the ante-room's comfy though crowded. The whole place is very well organized, the course has started with a bang today, absolutely first class with good lecturers and first class demonstrations showing the wrong way(which is very funny) and then the right. Our chief instructor is a Colonel Stewart who commanded a battalion of Argyll and Sutherlands in Malaya - a grand chap. We are divided into syndicates with an instructor (Major) in charge of each. Tony Nicholson is not an instructor on the Tactical Wing but I expect I shall see him in due course - they live in a different mess. The camp is run by A.T.S. and C3 men - my firsthand experience of A.T.S.
This place corresponds to Woolwich for Sappers or Larkhill for Gunners and is absolutely the 'top' - all new theories are tried out here and the infantry tactics of the British Army are largely worked out here - what Barnard Castle says and thinks today, the infantry do tomorrow. So you see I couldn't have come to a better place and I think I am lucky to have got here - the sort of 'Oxford' or 'Cambridge' of the infantry.

...It's incredibly cosmopolitan and so far I've seen Polish, American, Norwegian, Dutch, Belgian and Dominions officers in our class. In our hut alone there is a Pole (next bed to me!) an American, a Belgian and a Canadian but the British are still a majority, thank God!. Our aristocracy is also represented by the Honourable somebody (Scots Guards) in our hut - pale-blue pajamas! There are three other Polar Bears here on various courses but I don't know any of them.

Meanwhile back at Battalion, the A/Tk. Platoon had been sent to Harlech for field firing but Ray Langdale remembers similar training at Barmouth from a base in the Artillery Training Camp and Llanidloes.

Ray Langdale...
We went to Barmouth on the coast of Wales and we must have been in a bay where the sea used to go well out at low tide. There was a little miniature railway which was a shooting range for our 2 Pdr. A/Tk. guns and the tracks went all over the area. There was a man at a desk who controlled the whole thing with levers and the targets, about three feet (1m) high, had silhouettes of tanks on them and moved on the tracks. They could be

❖ *Above : No. 40 Etnam Street had a considerable parking area at the back for Battalion Transport but could not contain it all.* ❖*Below : The back yard of the Royal Oak Hotel at the other end of the street was also used. (DWS)*

crossing from left to right, vice versa or straight at you, head on and you were told which targets to go for. Tom O'Conner was pretty good at it and rattled them off. You pulled your gun onto a firing point and then at a given signal, the man at the controls started to operate the system. Then there'd be an Umpire standing behind you shouting, 'Action right!'. So we went for a tank in that direction. We were firing tracers at it and it was quite exciting was that. Damned good!

Les Sewell had undergone similar training at Thirsk but on a much more primitive scale. Now he was involved with more mundane things that had to be performed back at Leominster and found himself on the inevitable Duty Roster. This would see most of the men having to occasionally stand on Night Guard, Fire Piquet, Orderly Corporal, etc.

Les Sewell...
I got in one night and looked at the Roster and there I was, detailed as Battalion Orderly Corporal. The Orderly Sgt. was a certain Sgt. in the same platoon as I was and before I went to bed I went to look him up in his bunk but he wasn't there. So the next morning I got up and put my belt and bayonet on and he hadn't turned up but I knew where he spent his nights. I got his belt and bayonet and I went down this particular road where there were two houses in each yard and I wasn't certain which house it was he was in. It was about five o'clock in the morning, dark, and I went up one passage, threw stones at the window till somebody came out and I said, 'Is so and so

130

here? 'No! He's not! He doesn't live here.' So, I went to the next passage and did the same there, 'Is Sgt. so and so there?' Then I heard some whispering 'What's up Les?' I said, 'You're on Orderly Sgt. and you'd better get a move on!' Well, he got dressed quickly and came down, put his belt and bayonet on. He didn't have a wash, didn't have a shave, but luckily it was dark in the mornings and first job was with the Orderly Officer to the Diner to see if there were any complaints and that sort of thing. Then we were dismissed till a bit later on. Well, he got through that all right and he dashed back to the billet and sorted himself out. I had saved his bacon!

Anyway, he carried on like that until one day somebody went into the Sgts. Mess to see him and said, 'Thee wife wants to see thee, she's outside!' She'd come from Sheffield and Oh! Dear! He was in a fix. She were eight month gone and apparently he had a rough time. Anyway, she insisted on going to see this woman. They had a heart to heart talk and he promised never to see her again and he kept his promise. He got another las in t' next village! They called him Casanova!

David Lockwood (Letters to Mary)
29 June, 1943 (School of Infantry, Humbleton Camp, Barnard Castle)...
...we climbed to the top of Melsonby Church tower (about 8 miles SW Darlington) *to get a view of the ground, up a pitch dark spiral stone staircase and took a wrong turning half way up and landed amongst the works of the clock! I hit my head a hell of a crack against the pendulum box (wood) but no damage - afraid I swore and then remembered I was in church - but perhaps the belfry doesn't count! The biggest tragedy of the day was lunch - we'd taken sandwiches and as it was pretty warm and we had all been looking forward to going to the Black Bull (the only pub) for a pint. By about noon, our tongues were hanging out and we were the first syndicate to arrive at the boozer! But the door was locked. We knocked and the landlady came and told us she hadn't a drop of beer or even minerals left in the house. Catastrophe! So a party of very hot, thirsty and disappointed officers started to scan the village for liquid. We eventually found a little grocers shop and he had some orange and grapefruit in bottles and we drank his entire stock!*

At about the same time as David Lockwood and others were quenching their thirst in the little village of Melsonby, the officers back at Leominster were in deep discussion on the Role of the Dive Bomber, and to what extent the R.A.F. could displace the R.A. in provision of Close Support to advancing infantry.

David Lockwood (Letters to Mary)
2 July, 1943 (School of Infantry, Humbleton Camp, Barnard Castle)...
The psychology lecture the other night was simply magnificent and without any nonsense about 'complexes' and 'repressions' and so on. I honestly think it was one of the best lectures I've ever heard on any subject. It lasted one and a half hours - twice as long as any other lecture should last - but I could have sat on my hard wooden seat till midnight listening to that chap. We all agreed about it and I've never heard a lecturer get such applause as he got at the end - its not usual to clap at military lectures at all. It was simply that he put into words what one has always known and felt but has never been able to express. Every officer in the army ought to hear it - it would do some of them a hell of a lot of good....
...Went for a walk yesterday evening with my pal Wright, and helped the local farmer to stack some hay. It was a grand evening and we thoroughly enjoyed ourselves - afterwards the usual coffee and bun in the YMCA.

It was perhaps through working on the farms or more likely at the dances in Leominster that the Hallams got to meet girls from the town and also the Land Army girls that Arthur Green said were numerous, because of the fact that their kind of labour was much needed in the surrounding countryside. Many of the latter, coming from a town environment, must have been quite shocked at some of the farming practices which they witnessed and in some cases had to perform. Of course, these would eventually become commonplace to them, but for Wilf Fisher and some of his friends, the shock was still to come.

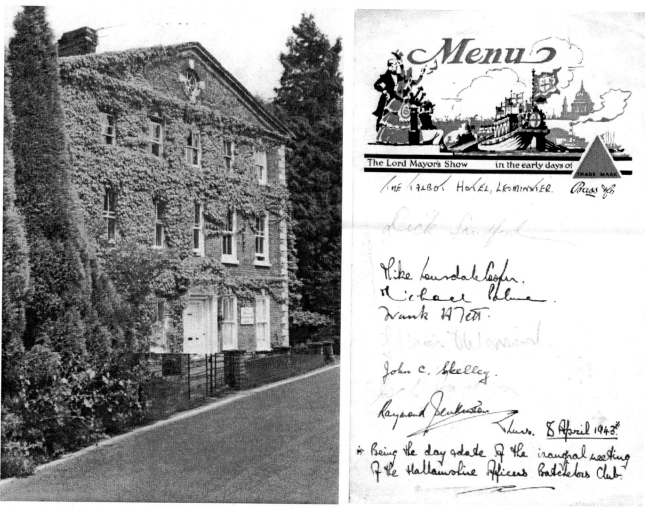

❖ *Left : Forbury House in Church Street is now a residence for the elderly but then housed 'B' Company. (DWS) Right : Signatures of the officers who formed a 'Bachelors Club' at the Talbot Hotel. They are - Dick Sandford, Mike Lonsdale-Cooper, Michael Palmer, Frank Tett, James Morwood, John Skelly, Jack Jackson and Raymond Jenkinson.(HFC)*

Wilf Fisher...
There used to be three of us Walt, Sam and myself and we got talking to these Land Army girls and we said, 'What you doing?' and one said, 'Well! In the morning we're mating the bull,' and I said, 'Are you?' and she said, 'Yes, have you never seen one?' and I said, 'No, I've never seen that happen.' So, she said, 'You come down, we're doing that tomorrow,' and I said, 'Get away!' Anyway, we got down there and there she was, not a bit afraid - and this bull, I've never seen anything like it. She was helping this bull... Well! and before it was halfway finished it came out, didn't it, and we was all splashed, it were horrible!

Another farmyard story came to light which was probably no shock to the system, but none the less embarrassing when related to an officer on a temporary duty at Bn.HQ. When John Wollerton was appointed S.O. he became part of HQ. Coy. and on one occasion had to do stand in duties for the Adjutant who was absent for one reason or another.

John Wollerton...
I did a stint as Adjutant and I had a woman came in front of me to claim maintenance for a child that she was pregnant with. I asked her who the father was and she said that she didn't know because it could have been any one of three men. I said, 'When?' and she replied, 'Oh! All on the same night on a haystack!'

On 3 July, the Battalion Team won the Brigade Sports at Hereford by just one point and were presented with a cup by Brigadier Proctor. This was followed by Divisional Sports which were held on the 7th and this time, the Bn. came away with second place. On the same day, a draft of forty men arrived and was placed with 'D' Coy. David Lockwood returned from Barnard Castle the next day and Major Ken West came back from the same course on the 12th.

On the 11th, the whole Bn. had taken part in a cross country run of four and a half miles which was won by Pte. Aistrop of 'A' Coy. in twenty-six minutes. This was more or less the final act as far as the Hallams were concerned with Leominster, because an Advance Party under Ivor Slater left on exercise 'Overdo'. They were bound, once more, for the Crieff Hydro in Scotland, about sixteen miles west of Perth.

Ivor Slater...
Word then came that I was to go and take over Crieff Hydro again and when I got there, there was not a single wash basin in any bedroom, anywhere in the entire building that had not had the butt of a rifle through it and was useless. It was done by the Canadians through sheer devilment on the last night they were there, and they did their utmost to destroy everything they could lay hands on. All we had then was a tin basin to put in the wash basin and that's what we washed in all the time we were there. Absolutely scandalous.

David Lockwood led the Road Party on the 24th and travelled by way of Shrewsbury, Preston and Carlisle. As usual, he had pencil and paper close at hand.

David Lockwood (Letters to Mary)
26 July, 1943...
I'm sitting in my car by a dutchbarn almost on the shore of Solway Firth a few miles south of Gretna - nine o'clock, a grey drizzly evening of the kind one always seems to get on the Solway - through the windscreen with its camouflage net over it I can see the low ridge that is Scotland across the Esk - lovely and peaceful and I do wish you were here to share the fun.
We arrived here about six and had our hot meal - I went over to Brigade on a motorbike (you should see me in a crash helmet) for my orders for tomorrow and now I've finished for the day and this is my first real chance to do what I've been looking forward to - write to you, my love. We're off at 7.45 in the morning which means reveille 5.00 breakfast 5.45!! Tomorrow is our longest day and we finish our great journey at quarter to seven - eleven hours!

The transport is drawn up in a lane outside the farm here and I've pulled my car into the stackyard with its back under the barn. I've told the lads to get to bed early and am turning in soon myself. South and I have got the sleeping game down to a fine art and we lay my Lilo out in the back of the car (the same one that took the pram to the Talbot - Kens!) and put the passenger seat down flat - so my head is by the tail-board and my feet in the front - extraordinarily comfy and I've slept like a log. He generally 'kips' on the floor alongside the car - my bodyguard! Tonight he'll be in the haystack behind me.

While I was having a wash here, a little lad toddled into the stackyard just like Benjie does - a moment later its mother, the farmers wife, came shouting, 'Billie' - I said, 'How old is he?' and she said he was fifteen months! - I told her about our Billie and she said hers was always up to mischief! He has fair, very curly hair and of course is filthy and wears teeny clogs with no socks - his trousers were coming down just like our Billie! I've just heard him being taken to bed, yelling - nine o'clock! There's been a good deal of argument in the farmyard about which child goes to bed first - there are thousands of them from a girl about Olives age down to Billie! ....It's one of those low white washed farms with a slate roof like one sees up here and should think they all sleep in one bed! When I says 'turn' we all turn!!

The midges are biting a bit! but it's 200% better than last night when I slept in the car park of Preston Northend football ground, stinking of petrol, hundreds of trucks crammed together and all the noises of a Lancashire town on Sunday night! Terrible! I've been looking forward to tonight... ...I really have enjoyed this trip up to now - things have gone well (touch wood) and we've arrived each night dead on time like a train, as laid down by Brigade in their timetable, with all our trucks intact. Up early and bed early and I feel awfully well and happy - happier since I spoke to you.

It really is grand to be away from the Bn. with a command of my own again for a short time - 150 men, 60 trucks and Jeeps, and 12 Dispatch Riders - quite an impressive array on the road that stretches for two whole miles! The Dispatch Riders ride two abreast behind me and our trucks are all newly painted and look terrific....

At Wellington we slept in the grounds of a big house, Apley Park, and that was a good night but busy for me as it was our first night out. We send the cooks on in two trucks with the cooker (petrol) and the quartermaster-sergeant each morning and when we arrive in the evening our hot meal is ready.

Today has been a bit tricky as we met another convoy coming over Shap too fast and a man at the rear end of the KOYLIs was killed about a hundred yards in front of me. He was stationary and was hit and knocked out of the driving seat by a damned fool in a big lorry (RASC) - I was furious. The details are ghastly and I won't inflict them on you, except to say that he was in more than one piece when we picked him up - literally - sorry!! Quite unnecessary and just damned bad convoy discipline and bad inexperienced driving on the culprits part. He'll be for it, the convoy commander should be too.

The new officers, Cowell, Howard and Jackson that are with me have done their stuff well and are becoming Hallamshires. Great excitement this morning between Carnforth and Lancaster where the railway runs alongside the road, the Hallamshires train passed us and they recognized us - result, terrific cheering and waving from every window and some chaps seemed to be almost half out of the carriage! Wasn't it a coincidence!

The worst thing that has happened so far is that I've snapped the stem off my best Dunhill pipe that you gave me - very sad! However I'm using my reserve which is quite an old friend and I must see what I can do with the Dunhill when I arrive. The swallows on the telephone wires on the Gretna road at the end of the stackyard have all gone to bed and I really must too...

The convoy left on time the next day and travelled a distance of approximately one hundred and fifty miles to reach Crieff at about 1830 hrs on the 27th. The Carriers had left by rail under Lt. Les Gill on the 25th and the main body of troops under Major R.O. Sclater, also by rail, the next day. All of the Hallams had arrived by the last day, including the Rear Party but the odd straggler was still adrift.

Doug Catley...
I always seemed to land for these odd jobs. They wanted a party to go up on the Yorkshire Moors around Whitby there, on an artillery shoot. There were a couple of officers and signallers, Sandy (Arthur Saunders) was on the same do with us, and we stayed in this empty house in Robin Hoods Bay. We were only there for a couple of days but it was interesting because we practiced on the moors with the artillery using the wireless to range guns and specify targets to be fired upon. I remember we went on to Scarborough from there and then directly to Crieff Hydro in Scotland.

In the middle of it all, two new officers had joined the Hallams. These were Lts. G.A.G. Bedward and R.V. Findley who may have felt slightly neglected until things settled down a bit in this huge building in which they now found themselves. The Crieff Hydro was a kind of 'Spa Hotel' where, as Arthur Green put it, people used to 'come for the waters'. Curiously enough, the Hallamshires had also 'come for the waters' but with a whole new meaning and in much greater volume. It would be no splash in the bath for them when they got to the shores of Loch Fyne in October.

❖ *Leominster, Summer, 2000. (DWS)*

A SPLASH IN THE BAY

Originally known as the Strathearn Hydropathic Establishment, Crieff Hydro was opened in or around 1870 and was described as being set in a place containing some of the finest and most picturesque scenery in Scotland. The setting has never changed but the Hydro was eventually developed into a prestigious resort hotel offering the best range of facilities combined with healthy climate, most delicious cuisine, together with a welcoming atmosphere and attentive service. The Hallams could not have expected all of these things, now that the place had been turned into an army barracks for the duration, but many found the surrounding area very much to their liking.

David Lockwood (Letters to Mary)
28 July, 1943 (Crieff Hydro)...
We had a glorious run from Gretna - blue sky and white clouds, very clear and the hills of Dumfrieshire past Lockerbie (do you remember?) and over Beattock Summit. Lunch by Lanark Racecourse and then up between Edinburgh and Glasgow through Stirling (the Castle looked marvellous in the evening sun) and so over the hills into Strathearn and here we are. Arrived about 6.30 and I really was sorry to have finished the journey.......nearly 400 miles and we came in on time with every truck and every motorbike having gone at 15 miles an hour all the way! The Brigadier was down in the town to wave to us as we came in - I like old Proctor.

This (Crieff Hydro) is a colossal pub and holds 350 people in peacetime - or maybe more. Our Coy. Office is in Room 365 at any rate, but of course that doesn't mean there are 365 rooms. Very forbidding, Scottish on the outside and inclined to be Victorian within - dressed stone and slate with little round towers in the Scottish style. It stands well up above the town facing south and the mess is colossal with a palm in one corner, a billiard table complete, a verandah and a cocktail

South face of Crieff Hydro, c.1942. It was large enough to billet the whole of the Hallamshire Battalion. (HFC)

137

counter! Really most impressive and more like Endcliffe Hall than anything we've had since then. We now live more like gentlemen again!

The town is quite nice though of course very quiet and I went down this afternoon to see if some barrels of beer had arrived at the goods station - no luck! The two new officers have come, both full Lieutenants, one Y&L and one Sherwood Foresters - names Bedward and Findlay. We have sent for Sgt. Cole (an ex-bandsman) to come here from Leominster to run the Officers Mess.

31 July : There is a steep hill behind us up to 900 ft. known as the Knock of Crieff which is the popular walk for the town. Yesterday evening we went up there after dinner, all officers, for a short map reading exercise run by Ken (West). It was lovely on top except for the flies and we sat among the bilberries and looked over pinewoods at a most beautiful panorama of the Grampian mountains - the country called Breadalbane....

As a matter of interest : One of the most intriguing items in the York & Lancaster Regimental Museum Collection is a richly embroidered 'Pipe Banner' dated 1777 and a relic of the American War of Independence. It is directly related to the York & Lancaster Regiment in that it belonged to the Royal Highland Emigrants, a unit raised by the British in Canada from mostly Scottish settlers there, to fight against the 'Americans'. The R.H.E. was redesignated as the 84th Regiment of Foot which eventually became the 2nd Bn. of The York & Lancaster Regt. in 1881.

This banner was 'discovered' in the Crieff Hydro some years ago and subsequently gifted to the museum. It remains a total mystery, just how it made its way back to this country or how it came to be in that place. Someone may have found their way back to Scotland after the war and brought the banner home. Equally intriguing is that the legendary Flora MacDonald, of Jacobite Rebellion fame, later became married to an officer of the R.H.E. She now rests in peace on the Isle of Skye, but that is another story...   ...Well! I did say that I might add a little extra flavour occasionally !! Back to the Hallams...

Arthur Green...
We'd to go to this place called the Hydro there, an enormous building used in pre-war days for therapy. There was a small indoor swimming bath and people used to go there 'for the waters' as they used to say, the same as Bath. All the Battalion was billeted inside so I'll leave you to guess the size of it but it was a fantastic place.

Les Sewell...
In the 'Hydro' each Company had its own corridor and down below there was a large N.A.A.F.I. There was also a big dance hall and we had dances there every Saturday night.

E.N.S.A. was on the scene very quickly and gave two performances in the Hydro at 1830hrs. and 2030hrs on the evening of 4 August. David Lockwood must have had some responsibility for the welfare of this group during its stay with the Battalion, but he doesn't seem to have been very impressed with one or two of them.

David Lockwood (Letters to Mary)
3 August, 1943 (Crieff)...
Yesterday we worked a normal day (Bank holiday) but had an E.N.S.A. show in the canteen in the evening - quite good and very much better than we expected when we first saw them! As soon as they arrived (late!) Doug and I met them and we were told the leading lady was off ill and one

of the dancing girls was lame - what a start! A moment later a hunchback with some fingers missing - the pianist! - got out of the bus and came up to me, looked at the stock round my neck and said in all seriousness, 'Got boils?' Well, Doug (Bell) and I nearly died! I kept a straight face and said no, I was just keeping my neck warm, and he never realized what he'd said. The mess was convulsed when I told them!

The 'stock' referred to by David, is thought to be the same item of clothing described by Ivor Slater in the Iceland Chapter as a 'cravat' and was introduced by George Robins for casual day use in place of the collar and tie. This is interesting because if he is describing the same item, then it had survived well considering it was an unofficial piece of clothing. Its use can be seen in a photograph taken in Iceland, late 1940.

David Lockwood (Letters to Mary)
5 August, 1943 (Crieff)...
Packard ordered a conference tonight after dinner at which all Coy. Commanders and Peter Newton (back tonight) and I were ordered to be. He said he had decided in the interests of the Bn., to reorganize its command and after much pre-amble and me wondering what was coming, gave us the 'result'.

HQ. Coy.	Douglas Bell as before.
Support Coy.	Me instead of Ivor Slater.
'A' Coy.	Ivor Slater instead of Gordon Good.
'B' Coy.	Oscar Sclater as before.
'C' Coy.	Dick Sandford as before.
'D' Coy.	Peter Newton instead of Joe Beckett.

So Gordon Good and Joe Beckett lose Coys.
Naturally, I'm tickled to death as Support Coy. is the biggest Coy. in the Bn. and contains four platoons instead of three as in the others and big platoons at that, and I reckon it's the best job in the Bn. I've got the Carriers (Les Gill), the Mortars (Jim Moorwood), the anti-tank guns (Arthur Cowell) and the Pioneers who blow things up (Dick Longridge, who will act as my second in command). Four damn good lads.

After the conference each Coy. Comd. was seen separately by J.J.P. (Col. Packard). He told me that from what he had seen of me in the short time (five weeks - four at Barnard Castle) he reckoned I was 'going to be a pretty good officer!?!' So here we are. I told him I had commanded the Support Coy. way back in 1935 when it was machine guns and mortars only, so I knew a bit about it - thought I wouldn't let him get away with it altogether!

Things have been happening since I spoke to you on the telephone last night - and I do hope your throat is better poor lamb - first I was hauled in to see Packard (10 p.m.) and congratulated - yes actually congratulated! - on the success of the transports move up here from Leominster - I nearly collapsed! And then I was told to go off on a Divisional Exercise (four days) that starts this Sunday and act as Battalion Commander with a skeleton staff representing the Hallamshires. Taking Raymond with me as Adjutant and Stephen Bartoleme as Intelligence Officer, some signallers, cooks and the Frog Boy! Well that nearly knocked me sideways too! We return here on Thursday, 12th, and I go on leave that weekend, grand! It'll help to make the time go quicker next week when I shall be looking forward so much to the weekend as well as being a nice trip down to Troon in Ayrshire, and that part of the world - expect you know it. Things are looking up.....

....Today has been absolute hell and quite the most unpleasant I've had since Iceland. We set off at 8.30 this morning (whole Bn.) to Glen Turret, a wild spot in the mountains very like Iceland, to rehearse a demonstration we are giving to the rest of the Brigade tomorrow. It started to rain as we started off in a biting cold north-east wind and the higher up the side of the glen we got (the windy side!) the harder it blew and the rain came horizontally. A tin hat saved some of it but I was wearing a ground sheet cape like the men which is a useless thing in a wind and flaps about and wets you more, and by ten o'clock my bum was wet through and it was running down my legs inside my trousers. Added to this, it was cold as March and we were standing about with no shelter, Foul! The men took it jolly well and at noon we got into a bit of a wood for a sandwich where it was blowing a little less and only dripping off the trees. We were at it all afternoon until four when we set off for home and it stopped raining! I cursed Scotland and scotch mist and everything belonging to the place - it was a devil!

I was commanding 'B' Coy. as Oscar is not so well. Tomorrow will be my swan song with 'B' Coy. and we are praying for a fine day.

Although David does not mention it here, the demonstration rehearsals were on the subject of 'Assault Landing Drill' for which the Battalion had only received instructions on the previous day.

Les Gill...
I was given responsibility for the Carrier Platoon in Scotland. Captain Beckett had the carriers before me and was a great favourite with the Carrier Platoon, very efficient. He was a brilliant fellow and technically he could have eaten me. It was quite a change for me because I had always been with a rifle company. The make up of this Platoon was such that I had the most amazing bunch of lads who were outstanding mechanically and in many other respects, and I was really proud to work with them.

On the 7th, a group of ten men under David Lockwood and the I.O. went on an exercise called 'CONTACT II' and stopped at various farms on the coast and inland, south of Glasgow. On the same day, Lt. J.A.N. Sim left the Hallams and was posted to Airborne Forces Depot. In the evening an 'All Ranks' dance took place in the Hydro.

'CONTACT II' ended on the 10th somewhere in the Tinto Hills but the group did not return until the 12th. They may have got back in time to get smartened up for another 'All Ranks' dance in the evening, but must have missed the Shooting Competition between the Hallams and the KOYLIs which was won by the Battalion. The highest individual score of ninety-two points from a possible one hundred was gained by Pte. J.W. Hames. No less than ninety-four personnel were posted in to the Bn. between the 14th and 17th of the month, very many of whom were men who had recently returned from overseas service.

Roy Simon was yet another man who joined the Hallams at Crieff, perhaps with the influx mentioned above. Born in Mexborough, he grew up there and later worked as a miner at Barnborough and Cadeby Main Collieries. He hadn't been at Cadeby long when the war started.

Roy Simon...
How I got to know that war had broken out - I were camping at the back of Cadeby pit with two mates of mine and we didn't know anything about war. Then, all of a sudden, me twin sister came on her push bike to tell us we'd got to come home because

Roy Simon. 1943.(Mr. R.Simon)

140

there was going to be a war. I said, 'No! We're not coming home.' So me mates, Joe Gorchard and Cyril Riley, stayed and when we got up in the morning we got a knife and marked on a tree 'War'. Just then the sirens went and we panicked a bit and ran home.

I eventually got my call up papers and went to Huddersfield for a medical and I rather wanted to go in the Army as a lot of us did at that time. I was 18 on the 14th of November, 1941, and I got notification to report in January, 1942 to The Durham Light Infantry at Branspeth Castle in County Durham, and that's where I met me 'muckers', Les Tebbs, Jody Pedel and Clifford Hargreaves. None of us smoked and we all seemed to get mated up together.

Then we got posted to the Green Howards at Richmond. It was nice marching around Richmond and we used to do training on the race course. Eventually we were posted and put on a train for Scotland and ended up with the Hallamshire Battalion at the Hydro in Crieff. It was a massive place, you could get lost in it and because of that there were painted signs on the walls. We were upstairs and it were a smashing view over the town to the hills beyond and I used to like going out there.

❖ *The busy rear entrance of the Hydro as it looks today. (DWS)*

I remember we did a right march from there once and it was comical, more or less, at the end of it. We were right up ont' moors with transport and they were going to introduce us to the artillery. We were going to do map reading and all that kind of thing. We eventually came to this range and we'd to take up these positions in front of these big guns and they fired some blanks and we were shown how they were handled and ranged and that. Then we marched back until we comes to this kind of an escarpment, and we could see this path right down in bottom with all transport there and we all shouted, 'Hurrah!' We all sat down and had a right thick cheese sandwich with a great big onion, and we used to enjoy it. I looked down right in bottom and there was a cottage right down to the left and it always reminded me of Kingsley's 'Water Babies'. There's a scene in that where Tom is at the top of this escarpment looking down and there was a woman in this cottage, just like the book, hanging clothes up. When we got back to the Hydro, not being a drinking man, there was a double rum ration but I thought, 'Right! I'm having this.'

I remember little 'Totty' Wood, a right comedy act, and 'Dusty' Rhodes and lots of people from around where I lived and it were like family. Then there was Pickersgill, Cyril May and Ronnie Coulson. Then there was Jody Pedel, a stocky little chap and we'd come from Durham together with Les Tebbs who came from Northumbria. Little Jody used to be always saying, 'Roll on death!' he used to say, but I don't think he knew his future though. He were a right good pal of mine.

Out of the blue, Lt. Col. J.J. Packard called the whole Battalion together at 1200hrs. on the 19th, said farewell, and was gone.

Les Sewell…
We went on a scheme and it was supposed to last two or three days. Anyway, Gen. Anderson came to see us and something went wrong. Everything was cancelled and we got the word that everyone had to return to billets. We got back to billets and there's Col. Packard in his best service dress bidding us all goodbye on the Battalion parade in the hall, and that was it!

Roy Simon may have been on this scheme which he said was rounded off by an E.N.S.A. concert show. An E.N.S.A. concert did take place on the 20th when a first class performance was given by a group known as Morgan Lloyd & Co.

Roy Simon…
When we came back from one of these schemes, they said, 'ENSAs coming! and they're going to give you a concert.' So we all got down into our seats in the ballroom and we were all sat there waiting for them to come on when all of a sudden they lit this stage up and there were bars like a prison. I think it might have been a scene from Rigaletto. Anyway, we were there, and we hadn't seen this man at first and this woman came on… Big woman she was, she'd a chest out here and everybody started laughing at her, you know, it were like them comics you see when that clucking hen comes out and sings. She just looked like that. She were getting on as well, she were no spring chicken, she must have been about sixty and everybody were laughing.

Then the light went up and you saw this bloke appear behind the prison bars and he was as old as Adam and they were laughing at him. Then she started singing and boy, when she started singing it went as quiet as a mouse. She had a beautiful voice and he was just the same and they didn't half cheer her off that stage. Everybody were clapping them when they went off. They were really good and I always remember that.

Col. Packard was not replaced immediately and it was almost another month before a new C.O. arrived on the scene. Major Ken West had to assume temporary command in the meantime. A number of letters were sent by David Lockwood between 7 August and 6 October and it was during this period that he mentioned for the first time, the presence of the Hallams new C.O., Lt. Col. Trevor Hart Dyke (Queens Regt,) and that he himself had been promoted to Major and promised his own Coy.

In the meantime, a Battalion Sniper Course was commenced on 23 August and a Weapons Training Exhibition was opened in the Information Room at the Hydro the next day. Sadly, the Hallams witnessed the departure of a long-standing member of their fraternity when Major J.P. 'Dobbie' Dobson, D.C.M., M.M., relinquished his position as Quarter Master. After fifteen years service with the Hallamshire Battalion, he was being posted to No.2 Northern Command Infantry Depot. The officers did not let him go before they had wined and dined him in the Officers Mess at a grand farewell celebration. Lt. A.F. Gibbs was chosen to become the new Q.M.

142

On the 29th, a Polar Bear medal was presented to CSM E.Gandy by Brigadier N. Proctor and in the evening, the men were treated to a film, shown in the Ballroom, entitled 'The Fleet's In'. A 12 mile route march took place the next day and a cloth model 'exercise' was held in the officers Ante Room. The subject was 'Assault Landings' and all the officers were required to attend.

On 4 September, the whole Battalion was treated to a demonstration by the 'A' Group of the 2Bn. The Kensington Regt. in live firing of 4.2 inch Mortars and MMGs. Lt. A .C. Somers was appointed T.O. in place of Lt. C.A. McKillop who moved to 'A' Coy. which was about to be taken by road to Leith Fort, Edinburgh, for a weeks course in the art of Street Fighting. All of the Coys. took it in turn to attend tank demonstrations at Blackford. Capt. J.C.S. Jones joined the Bn. and was placed with Support Coy. A number of small exercises were carried out during the month, some only with the use of table models and cloth 'mock ups'. One of these was code named 'Carry On' in which 'A' and 'B' Coys. took part on the 24th!

On 25 September, Lt. Col. Trevor Hart Dyke (Queens Royal Regt.) arrived at Crieff, and the officers laid on a welcome dance in the officers mess, to which all units within the Brigade group were invited. He introduced himself to the Battalion at 1230hrs. on the 27th.

Lt. Col. Trevor Hart Dyke. D.S.O., 1944. (THD)

In 1994, the author was invited to visit Trevor Hart Dyke and his wife at their home, a charming old stone built farm house on the side of a hill, overlooking Hope Valley in Derbyshire. Trevor was asked to give a brief summary of his life prior to taking command of the Hallamshire Battalion in Scotland.

Trevor Hart Dyke…
I was born at Chaman on the Afghan Frontier, that's in Pakistan now, and my father was commanding a Company of the Indian Army, The Bluchers. We went home to England when I was about five and I didn't see much of my parents for three years as I was with my brother at school. I used to stay with an aunt. My father retired in 1922 and I was back out in India in 1924 with The Queens., having been through Sandhurst. I was told I was going to be a soldier from when I was born, I think! My mothers family were all sailors, so my brother went into the Navy and it was his son that lost his ship in the Falklands War, 1982.

I was in India for two years and the Sudan for one, then back to England and did two years. I had a perforated ulcer which was the result of getting hookworm and malaria in the Sudan. Then I did fairly well, getting a distinguished in my promotion exams and small arms school. You couldn't have a Captaincy before you were thirty, so I went out to the Kings African Rifles. Then my insides played me up a bit, so I went to Uganda where my battalion was, and became Adjutant. Not very long after, I was made Principal Staff Officer of the Brigade at Nairobi and also made Secretary to the Defence Committee of Kenya and Uganda, at the age of twenty-six. After six years out there I came back to England and was sent to the War Office to write books on Africa, and then I got into Staff College after the third try and then back again to the War Office.

Then I was made a Brigade major with the 18th Division in Norfolk. Having settled down there, I was sent to the Secretary to the Defence Committee for Gibraltar. It was very interesting because

143

France had then fallen and we were expecting the Germans to come through. So, we had to put everything underground and had two tunnelling companies, one Canadian and the other British. The former did the hard rock and the British did the soft. All the spare soldiers were used to get the earth out and make an airfield. It was very interesting. I was sent home again with stomach trouble. After about three months and sick leave, I had to write the Light Scales for the British Army landings in North Africa. I was told later by Gerald Templar, that those Scales were used also for Sicily, Italy and 'D' Day. Then I got back to my regiment and was afterwards sent to the Hallamshires.

Arnold Whiteley...
On his arrival, Col. Hart Dyke had all the Battalion on parade there and he gave us a pep talk and started by telling those on his right to stick their left arm up, and all those on his left to raise their right leg and then declared that we were all half asleep. However, he was a fair officer. He were keen but he were fair and all the officers had to toe the line as well. We trained at Crieff and then moved to Inveraray, then Rothesay, Kyles of Bute and that was so as we could practise seaborne landings. We used to go over to the mainland from there and drop the ramp and practise running ashore. We were firing mortars and the lads charged up this beach but there were casualties when one fell short. What had happened, the base plate of the mortar had sunk into the ground and as a result a shell fell short.

John Wollerton...
Hart Dyke was very, very keen and I think he was right, but at the time we called him all the names under the sun. I think he was right in what he did and that was to sort us out, and sort us out he did! His intent was to improve discipline in the Battalion. He said it was being run by people who would have been better running a civilian establishment rather than an army one. Whilst that might have seemed unkind, you can understand how important it was to instill that discipline throughout the Battalion for when we went overseas. I think all the officers, in the end, felt that way, no matter what they may have called him before we went to Normandy. I could see his side of it and he had a formidable task to get us into shape in such a short space of time. Bill Ashby, his new Adjutant, struck me as being a typical regular soldier, a first class officer. He didn't mince his words and that's how I liked him.

Ken Godfrey was born on 14 March, 1925, at Long Eaton, Derbyshire. He was originally trained on 3 inch Mortars after basic training, and posted to the Hallams in Crieff around the middle of September, 1943, when a number of others were drafted in.

Ken Godfrey...
I was part of a new intake and was stood there when Hart Dyke came across and spoke to every one of us. When he got to me he said, 'Who are you?' and I said, '214578371, Private Godfrey T. K., Sir!' and he said, 'What are you?' and I said, 'A first class mortar man! Sir.' He said, 'How old are you?' - 'Eighteen and a half, Sir!' Well, I remember him looking me up and down and saying, 'Mmm, eighteen and a half. Well, we're going overseas shortly and you will be too young to go so we'll put you in 'D' Coy.'

I thought the Hydro was absolutely magnificent, a wonderful hotel and we weren't allowed to wear army boots because of the floor, and had to wear soft shoes as often as we could. We were billetted in the hotel rooms and I thought Crieff was a lovely place to be. Don't forget, I was only eighteen years old then and there used to be notices put up by some of the local people to say that we were invited for tea and cakes and one day a group of about six of us went to this little house, and that's where I had my first appreciation of classical music.

144

I was shortly afterwards transferred to the Intelligence Section because of my ability in compass and map reading, which was really gained through doing quite a lot of pre-war cycling, walking and Youth Hostelling and things like that. I was in that Section then until we got to Belgium.

I remember when we were on a scheme, I was put on guard one night outside a house that was an HQ. and this lady came out in the early hours of the morning with a great mug of cocoa and some hot, home made scones, and said, 'Here you are, have this you poor lad.' Well as I was drinking and eating, the RSM walked by and he looked and she said to him, 'You leave that lad alone while he's drinking!'

Sgt. Tony Jaques. 1945. (Mr. Jaques)

At the Inveraray camp (Shira), we were on parade one day and there was a Sgt. Major Gandy, the men used to call him 'snake hips' but I don't know why. Anyway, he told everybody to fix bayonets and I didn't. He glared at me and much to the amusement of the others he said, 'Why haven't you fixed bayonet?' I said, 'Sir, they told us at the Depot that it was obsolete and would not be taught!' He just said, 'Watch the others and do it!' At the finish everybody had a good laugh. The names I remember in the Intelligence Section with me were 'Wag' Ellis, Phil Haley from Sheffield, Arthur Bownes and Arthur Jepson the D.R. Then there was Cpl. Jim Metcalfe who later became a sniper.

1456616 Pte. Anthony Jaques also joined the Hallams at Crieff Hydro and the first officer he met, Major Newton, on discovering Tony had previously worked in an office, placed him in 'D' Coy. office. At some time afterwards he must have transferred to Bn. HQ. Orderly Room. He had been there for only a couple of weeks when he suffered his first trauma...

Tony Jaques...
A bell rang four times in the office which I understood to mean that Lt. Col. Hart Dyke required a man to go to his office to take notes in short hand. The man who normally responded to these calls was Stan Hunter, but he was out of the office at the time so I was persuaded by the rest in the office to take his place, as I had some knowledge of short hand.

As Tony got to the C.Os. door, a particular bugle call was sounded which was the signal for a gas attack alarm. Everyone had to put on their gas masks when these alarms went but this did not prevent Hart Dyke from dictating the whole of his memo, on the subject of the Bren Gun, with his mask on! Whilst relating this story, Tony rendered an hilarious imitation of Trevor Hart Dyke dictating the memo with his gas mask on. It is a pity that such a funny rendering can not be transmitted in this text but it sounded rather like the muffled voice of a Spitfire pilot over an intercom. Tony, who claimed that he found it difficult enough to understand the C.Os. accent under normal conditions, missed large chunks of dictation and went back to the Orderly Room a worried man. His pals did their best to fill in the missing phrases but there were still gaps in the text. By the afternoon there was nothing for it but to go to the C.O. and admit the problem....

Tony Jaques...
He went mad! 'I'll get you transferred to a Rifle Company!, I'll stop your trade pay!' Well, I must have looked at him rather oddly because he said, 'You do get trade pay don't you?' and I said, 'No Sir' - I didn't even know what he was talking about and that must have taken the wind out of his sail because he just said, 'Oh....Oh, well let's have a look at the memo and fill it in.' He told me again what he had said and so I was able to type the memo.

Doug Catley...
One thing I remember that Hart Dyke brought in at Crieff, we had to get up in the morning, on us honour, and go and have a run. Only just a mile or something down the road, you know, you weren't paraded and he had everybody doing that.

Some of the higher ranking officers were not so happy, again it seems, about the tough measures that were almost immediately brought in by the new Commanding Officer. Eventually things came to a head. It must be said that there seems to have been similarities to the problems that were experienced with the previous C.O. and to do with, in part, the attitudes of 'Territorial' officers towards 'Regular' officers, and vice-versa! However, the problem may not have been all together confined to the Hallamshire (Territorial) Battalion. Part time 'volunteer' soldiers which formed a major part of the Hallams, including the officers, were needing to make a lot of adjustment before they could knuckle down to soldiering that contained very little of the 'fun' element which was undoubtedly present during a peacetime role.

Ivor Slater...
We approached John Mott and informed him that we, the Company Commanders, were not prepared to go to war with Hart Dyke and we told him that he had better do something about it. I think he went to Divisional HQ. and reported the situation after which the C.O. was brought before the Corps Commander. He was eventually sent back to Battalion to inform us that he was to remain, and the sooner we changed our ideas and conformed, the better.

The main problem was that the officers objected to what they saw as unnecessary 'Bull Shit' which was a term to describe over-indulgence by those in command in trying to make everything look ultra smart, clean and polished. One of the 'flies in the ointment' in this particular case was that officers and men were required to use white 'Blanco' on all their webbing instead of the usual green. The white was particularly messy in that, as it dried, it created powdery deposits over uniform and elsewhere. Because of this, it took a great deal of time and effort but was claimed to be all in aid of instilling discipline into the Hallamshires. The officers who were making the complaint, all 'dyed in the wood' Territorials, were not convinced. They had always done it their way and, of course, were now confronted by an equally 'dyed in the wood' Regular soldier who was quite determined to use his much more strict methods. Ivor Slater summed up the whole episode in these words...

Ivor Slater...
I will admit that we were wrong. In the field, he was outstanding,... a brilliant commander!
Enough said!

Tony Jaques...
I remember we did a twenty-seven mile route march and that takes a bit of doing. Many of those miles were up hill walking through bracken and you had to lift your legs up the whole time, consequently you got tired out. Even so, going up the hill back to the Hydro one day, the man in front of me, a little Scouse man whose name I can't remember but he was a tough little so-and-so. He just collapsed like that - went out like a light. What struck me was that there was so many NCOs saying, 'I'll take care of him,' but what they were really saying was that they were as tired as I was but they were getting out of walking up the hill.

Ray Langdale...
I remember Col. Hart Dyke addressing some reinforcements from the 2nd Battalion under a verandah at the Hydro, one man was called Nicholson (later a Sniper Sgt.), and complimented them on the fact that they'd come back to England and would be able to take part in the Second

Front. There was one or two grumbles because some of these lads had been in Tobruk and had already seen 'action' in the desert.

A Brigade cross country run was won by the Hallams team on 27 September, just a day after Capt. D.R. Bell and Pte W. Fozard had been awarded the Polar Bear Medal for their success in previous Divisional Sports.

Ray Langdale. C.1942.
(Mr. Langdale)

On 2 October, the Battalion left Crieff by road for exercise 'BRIDGEHEAD' and was concentrated at Townend, Dumbarton, that night. A Bn.HQ. was established at Symington, just east of Troon, and remained there until the 5th. when the Bn. returned to Crieff. It may have been during this scheme that Roy Simon found himself lying in fields with others, all soaked to the skin and about to be made an offer that few could refuse.

Roy Simon…
One scheme we were on and we were dug into this field position near some semi-detached houses. We were dug in and it were very foggy and you could have a dry coat on in Scotland and when it began to get dusk it would start going foggy and it didn't matter how well you were wrapped up you were wet through. The old 'Scotch Mist' used to come down. No rain, just this mist and it used to go all through your clothing and it were like that till dawn.

Now when we were digging in on this scheme, all of a sudden a voice came through this hedge, 'Are you there soldier?' with a real Scotch accent you see.. There were 'Tishy' Porritt and Sgt. 'Knocker' Lees and they said, 'What's the matter?' 'I brought you these,' and there were these two middle aged ladies and they'd got these trays with cups of tea on them. Knocker said, 'I'm sorry love, I appreciate what you're doing but we can't accept it, we're on a scheme.' Sgt. Lockwood was there as well. Now they kept coming out, so to pacify them Knocker Lees went into the house and when he came out he said, 'It broke my heart has that. They're there, they've taken us in four houses, they've got mattresses down ont' floor and everything, and when it gets dark we've to go in and sleep in there!' They were right generous people and then when I were coming back, I got the job of traffic directing and I was about the last one to be picked up. We came to this road junction and there was a pub on this junction where I was stood, and this old chap comes out and he says, 'Are you alright?' 'Aye!' I said, 'We're all right'. 'Do you want a drink?' I said, 'No thanks, I don't drink,' so this other lad had one. Anyway, we were eventually setting off and he came out again and shoved this parcel in me hand. In the parcel was a beautiful fruit cake and all the rest were these Scotch scones that they used to make.

On the 7th, an Advance Party left the Hydro for Inveraray and Major Mott joined the Bn. ('C' Coy). At this time David Lockwood had found some accommodation for his wife and young son, to come and stay for a while in Crieff in a house belonging to a Mrs. Duff. It was rather unfortunate that the heavy programme of schemes laid on for the next two months or so, would prevent him from being with them for a large amount of the time they were there.

David Lockwood (Letters to Mary)
7 October, 1943 (Crieff)…
A double room for us (twin beds I'm afraid but wait till you hear the rest!), a small room for Benjie with single bed and an upstairs sitting room with bay window facing south-west (like Slayleigh) and a piano(!) for Benjie! A grand modern bathroom and an all electric kitchen downstairs. Coal fire in the sitting room and a good sized garden back and front. She keeps fowls and says we

❖ *Ardnahane today - the home of Mrs. Duff in 1943. Her family still run a taxi service in the town. (DWS)*

can have eggs. She drives a taxi for her husband who has a garage in town and is out most of the day, so I had to say you'd look after yourself I'm afraid..... .....It's only four minutes walk from the Hydro and the house is a semi-detached, but nothing like as cramped as Slayleigh and is on a hillside between here and the town - much the nicest part. There are nice walks in the country within a few minutes for you and a Dalmation dog of hers who she says loves children and will go walkies with Billie, but lives in a kennel outside. She has a Siamese 'tiss' too!

Most important of course is Mrs. Duff - a most awfully nice woman... ...She has two sons both prisoners from the 51st Division at St. Valerie and a daughter who is a Ministry of Agriculture inspector in Morayshire. Mrs. D. was one of the first Field Army Nursing Yeomanry to go to France in 1914 - had her own horse which she supplied herself and took to London with her, but they wouldn't take the horses overseas, so they drove cars instead and has had a licience for 31 years! She was present at the Battle of Loos in 1915 with the Belgians...... .... (in respect of the house) I'm certain we couldn't have found anything nicer in every way in the whole town.... ...there is a church opposite the house!

...we go to Inveraray by road tomorrow (address by the way, Shira Camp, Inveraray, Argyllshire) till the 29th, then on the 31st I take the Coy. to the Divisional Assault School at Callendar till Nov. 5th. Then we return here till the 22nd of Nov. when we go to Kilbride (Kyles of Bute) till Dec. 2nd.....

...I think you'll like it here, the air is so crisp and clean with glorious views. Today has been gorgeous - such a change.

On 9 October, David Lockwood wrote to his wife from Shira Camp, Inveraray, having probably arrived on the 8th, and describes the journey to get there from Crieff. This route was followed in glorious sunshine by the author and his wife in August, 2000, and found to be every bit as beautiful as David described and probably very little changed in all these years.

David Lockwood (Letters to Mary)
9 October, 1943 (Shira Camp, Inveraray, Argyllshire)...
We got here at tea time yesterday after a really lovely run right across Scotland through the Highlands. We started up Strathearn through St. Fillans (saw the pub where you had tea and thought of you) then along Loch Earn and up Glen Ogle, very wild, over the pass into Glen Dochart above Loch Tay. Saw Ben Lawers and Ben More, I believe the two highest after Ben Nevis, with clouds blowing angrily round their tops, one minute hidden the next moment bursting out with a great black head towering above us. And so through Crianlarich and up Strath Fillan to Tyndrum. We stopped to eat our sandwiches just short of Tyndrum and enjoyed the view though it was cold in the wind and grey skies but the atmosphere was clear and the country looking its wildest.

❖ *Inveraray as it looked in August, 2000, from the pier. When the sun shines on the western coastal region of Scotland, there is no better place to be. (DWS)*

At Tyndrum we left the Fort William road and went down Glen Lochy to Dalmally and Loch Awe. I think Loch Awe was one of the most perfect sights Iv'e ever seen and I did wish you could see it - hundreds of little tree covered islands and on one of them the ruined Kilchurn Castle with creeper on it. The Loch was very full and the trees every possible shade of green, gold and brown and above it all the mountains - on the far north west shore were many lovely houses and I thought of the holidays people must have had there. As my driver said, 'You can't appreciate it as we're fixed wi' t' war now!' But I must say I did appreciate it.

From there we came on a new road over the pass into Glen Aray and down into glorius beech and pinewoods round Inveraray - the Duke of Argyll's estate at Inveraray Castle in whose grounds we now live. And there, as we came out of the woods, all of a sudden was the little dour old county town and the sea, Loch Fyne - the Fjord as we call it! - and all the ships and amazing craft. Ssh! Very secret! By then it was raining of course as it does here, I'm told, every day of the year and the mud in camp is indescribable.

❖ *Shira Camp as it looks today. This view is taken from the other ranks quarters where traces of Nissen hut bases can still be seen. The little stone bridge lies in the shadow of trees (middle right) which led to the officers quarters across the river. The edge of the fresh water loch can just be seen to the left. A stone cottage at the head of the glen is reputed to have been the one time home of Rob Roy. (DWS)*

149

Shira Camp is about a couple of miles from the town and is at the foot of Glen Shira between a little fresh water loch and the sea - the sea being Loch Fyne. The camp is part of the grounds of the Duke's Castle and there is the most magnificent avenue of colossal beeches through the middle. We are in good Nissens and if it would only dry, it would be a good camp. The officers lines are over on the opposite side of the Shira river from the rest of the camp - a lovely river between the loch and the sea and we cross a little stone bridge to our huts.

Loch Fyne hasn't the beauty of Awe but is still very lovely. The shore is fringed by woods which are a perfect picture now with the mountains above up to two thousand feet from the sea, then sides covered with bracken at its best golden brown and red.
We are watching a demonstration on the beach this afternoon and for a moment the sun came out a very rare moment for Argyllshire! And what a sight it was! There is rain in the wind always but mild west coast wind like Devon - I feel sleepy here and have a terrific appetite.

The main body of the Battalion doesn't arrive till Tuesday evening. We are here to learn the job and are doing a course of lectures, demonstrations and films, so that when they arrive we are 'au fait' with everything. We are getting incredibly nautical! The C.O., Ivor (Slater), Peter (Newton) and a few others are here plus a lot of NCOs. We three Coy. Comds. are sharing a hut at present and Ken (West), Mott and Jonas will be in here when they arrive. Mott is getting 'C' Coy. from Dick Sandford (now a Capt. and 2i/c of 'A' Coy.) and Jonas has taken over Support Coy. from me as a Captain. Both are regular York and Lancasters. Mott has been a Major all through the war and was at Sandhurst with Packard! My crown hasn't come through yet. We have left Oscar (Sclater) at Crieff. He has no Coy. now and is waiting for a medical board to grade him out.

I wrote to your friend the Teddy Bear (Branson) the other night and told him we'd got a good C.O. - also about my impending crown. Thought he'd like to know.

Its awfully interesting here and we're enjoying ourselves. There is such a different atmosphere…
…and one can talk to this chap (Hart Dyke) like we did to George Robins. Ivor has got his wireless set by his bed and we're a very happy hut. We have a lot of fun about the Regular Army and say we are going to have Territorials at one end of the hut (Ken, Ivor, Peter, Me) and Regulars (Mott and Jonas) at the other with a notice up 'Amateurs' and 'Professionals' or better still 'Gentlemen' and 'Players' as they say in county cricket! Supper Time now.

Later… Been playing darts tonight - the Colonel and everybody, great fun. John Mott has arrived tonight and we find we know each other - he was at Pontefract in 1935 and knows the Battalion well. A nice 'little stiff chap' about my size!, dark moustache and has just returned from India where he has been 2i/c of 2nd Battalion. I think he'll be an asset here. He's just putting his pyjamas on at the moment! Must finish this before the lights go off at 11.30…..

David Lockwood was soon to go on a boat trip on Loch Fyne to see a demonstration which was the prelude to intensive training for seven days and due to start on the 14th. The training itself was that which would be necessary to prepare assault troops for the Normandy landings in June of the following year but that would remain top secret for many months yet.

The main body of the Battalion left Crieff at 0800hrs. on the 12th, arrived at Inveraray to take part in Combined Operational Training and were concentrated at Shira Camp on the edge of Loch Fyne, less than two miles from Inveraray.

Roy Simon...
The whole Battalion went to Inveraray for invasion training and when we got to the camp it were rough, just a load of huts laid out and it were all mud. Talk about the First World War! We had to start building roads and bridges on the camp and I rather enjoyed it - not big bridges, just over dykes like, tree trunks covered with earth that could take the weight of vehicles. You used to go over one as you went through the main entrance past the Guard Room on the right.

On 14 October, 1943, David wrote another letter from Shira Camp giving Mary the address of Mrs. Duff at 'Ardnahane', Stratheam Terrace, Crieff, and arrangements for Mary to move there. He was worried about his batman, South (Frog Boy), who had announced that he was going blind! Apparently he'd been to Perth to have treatment and had been told he was suffering from eye strain. The trouble was that David would lose him as a batman if the problem persisted and he couldn't bear the thought of that. The eyes were apparently better and South's wife was expecting a baby at any time. On this same day, the Battalion said goodbye to another longstanding member when RSM Burns was replaced by RSM F. Hallam! The former had been posted to Northern Command Infantry Depot where he would no doubt meet up with Major Dobson, who had gone there earlier.

Training commenced in earnest on the 15th and all Coys. practised Platoon training with water craft and scrambling nets. Drivers also practised the loading of vehicles onto craft during the day.

David Lockwood (Letters to Mary)
16 October, 1943 (Shira Camp)...
This evening I'd bicycled two miles in a Burberry, gumboots and tin hat to Inveraray in the usual rain and wind specially to telephone (you) and had then waited half an hour in the post office for it to come through - and after all that being cut off, bicycled back, still in the rain in a rather bad temper!

❖ *Left : Part of the private estate of Ardno, which survived all the live firing exercises nearby and is now in fine condition. During 1943, it was right on the edge of a number of regular objectives 'attacked' from the landing beaches (❖Right) during assault training on Loch Fyne. Inveraray can only just be discerned on the other side of the Loch in the far distance. (see Sketch Map on Page 152) (DWS)*

The training here is pretty hard but it really is grand fun playing with these boats and of course the troops love it. ......I have the Frog Boy out with me to fire my signal flares and he's very good at allowing for wind (of which there is plenty). I generally stand on the stern platform of the motor landing craft with the coxswain and naval officer and with nothing between us and the sea. Tried to look very professional using my glasses without hanging on to anything and nearly fell overboard this morning!

Yesterday afternoon we took the troops out in naval cutters for rowing instruction under naval coxswains and it was so funny. I had the tiller of one boat with twelve sweating soldiers in front of me with huge oars in the most hopeless tangle and I laughed till it hurt. You know those drawings in the 'Tatler' by Oakley-Buettler - well, this was just like that !

On the 17th, all Coys. practiced training with craft and fifty officers and NCOs attended a demonstration of 'Landing of the Beach Groups'. Drivers practised night loading their vehicles onto craft. The C.O. held a T.E.W.T. (Tactical Exercise Without Troops) on Exercise 'NEWTON BAY' at the Brigade Cloth Model Room. Next day, Coys. carried out dry shod landings with live ammunition and training films were shown to the Battalion in the afternoon.

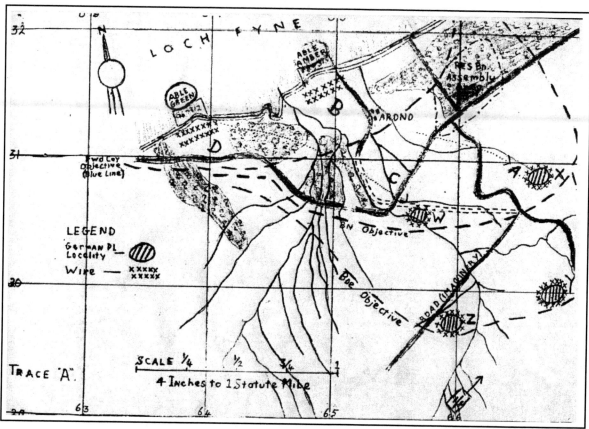

Above : Sketch Map made during beach assault exercises carried out on Loch Fyne during October, 1943. The farm buildings known as Ardno still survive after being in the middle of live firing.(PRO) ❖ *Below : Evidence of training was found on the shore line, in the form of a concrete ramp and imitation seawall made up from cement filled bags. It was here that Pte. Spurley Harper was killed by a stray mortar shell during one of the exercises. (DWS)*

Arthur Green...
I was on some sands with me truck at Inveraray and the lads were coming in on Infantry Landing Craft (LCI) and they had to wade through the water onto the beach. They'd all come ashore dripping wet through and I had to take them back to the camp. It was quite

152

shallow at this particular spot and I remember seeing the ramp go down at the front and I could hear them shouting and they seemed to be a long way out. The Naval Officer was telling them it was all right to jump now, but they wouldn't jump because they thought it would be too deep and asked for the boat to be taken further in. He had to do something drastic to convince them that it wasn't too deep so he jumped in himself and disappeared below the waves with just his hat floating on the surface! The LCI took on water and settled onto the sand bank and they all had to come ashore.

David Lockwood (Letters to Mary)
18 October, 1943 (Shira Camp)...
Thank you so much for ringing up Munks - amazingly enough, three caps arrived on approval today. Peter, Ivor and I have had a good deal of fun in the hut tonight choosing one, and I've eventually settled on the size 7. I've packed up the other two with a cheque for 22/6 - what a price! - but blue ones are 32/6. My blue one is all right. (these prices amount to £1.12 ½ p. and £1.62 ½ p. respectively!)

Today has been fine - such a relief after yesterday and last night. We set off at 8.0pm for a night operation with craft on the loch in sheets of rain. The troops were grand as usual in the rain and when we got to the landing beach found a young river in flood, roaring down it which didn't make embarking in the dark any easier. The Colonel and Ken were out with us and I got a 'rocket' quite unjustly in connection with training for which he afterwards apologised when he found I was right. He's like that though, very quick tempered but soon cools down and the 'rocket' might never have been delivered. We all get 'rockets' fairly frequently. However, with my usual luck the weather cleared soon after we put to sea and the moon came out - a really lovely sight over the loch and mountains and most romantic, had the setting been less warlike. We got in about midnight and had a rum issue - good!

Today 'A' and 'B' Coys. have been doing an exercise with live ammunition and I was very anxious about the outcome as I hadn't seen 'B' Coy. in action with ammunition before. I went to a good deal of trouble yesterday to get it all taped with my officers and NCOs and believe it or not, got a big bouquet from the Colonel after the show - so 'B' Coy. are Mondays blue-eyed boys. I was very relieved to have got through also without killing anybody!

On the 19th, 'C' and 'D' Coys. did an assault landing with live ammunition at Newton Bay. On the next day, more landings took place at Ardno, Ardnan and Slaite, observed by the Divisional Commander, Maj. Gen. E.H. Barker, C.B.E., D.S.O., M.C., at Inveraray. Afterwards, he visited Shira Camp.

John Wollerton...
Shira Camp wasn't much of a place and was on a flood plain to the base of some of the Nissen huts. We marched to the landing craft and we went across the Loch and marched down the ramp and got soaked well above the knees. Then we marched about ten miles around the Loch to the craft again, got on and repeated the whole thing.

On 21 October, the Hallams embarked on an Infantry Landing Ship (LSI) for Exercise 'ARDNO 5' and carried out Battalion Assault Landings. The exercise continued next day but five casualties were sustained when a 3 inch Mortar Shell fell short and dropped onto troops coming up the beaches. One of them, Pte S. Harper, died of wounds at Inveraray Hospital at 1655hrs.

David Lockwood (Letters to Mary)
22 October, 1943 (Shira Camp)...
Last night I spent with the Coy. (only us) on board a converted oil tanker - a big ship in Loch Fyne. We got on board about 8.0 in the evening and had to climb up the side in the dark on rope ladders in pouring rain with arms and full equipment - I was glad when we got them all on. Landing craft came alongside about an hour later and after stowing our gear in them for morning, and having a conference and supper with the troops on their mess deck (jolly good!), got to bed about twelve. Gordon, Dick and Doug (who was with us for the exercise) in a four bunk cabin with sheets and pillowcases!!

We were called by the ships watchman at quarter to five, had breakfast and then once again went over the towering side of the tanker in pitch dark and the usual rain at 6.30 - everything was wet. After that we did a dawn landing with the rest of the Battalion and the exercise finished at noon. We've been doing a bit of revolver shooting here, and often take one or two empty bottles out on the bank behind the mess after lunch (when we're in), and have a crack at them. There's something very satisfying about hitting a bottle.

David Lockwood (Letters to Mary)
25 October, 1943 (Shira Camp)...
Great news, the Frog Boy has got a son!! He got a wire this morning and has gone off by the lorry this evening to Arrocher on Loch Long where he gets a train to Glasgow and will be in Sheffield in the morning. I've given him 72 hours compassionate leave and he'll rejoin at Crieff on Friday a.m. when we arrive back in the evening.

Ivor, Peter and I decided to break out last night to get away from soldiering for an hour or so and bicycled into town for dinner - very nice.

There's precious little news here except that a private soldier in 'A' Coy. was killed in training on Saturday. He was an old Hallamshire from Sheffield, called Harper. His body is being sent home and the Padre going with him.

Roy Simon...
They used to take us in trucks and sometimes we used to march to where these landing craft were and you didn't do much sailing, just learning where your position was in the craft. Now I always carried the 2 inch Mortar with me and I carried Mortar bombs in each of these two respirator cases strapped to my sides. They weren't issue but I could carry eight bombs that way. I usually took position behind the Corporal, Bill Goodall, and there was also 'Tishy' Porritt. He was also a Corporal at this time. He came from Heckmondwyke, his father had a paper shop there. We used to do practice landings and often I'd end up in the front. I used to get off that boat sometimes sodden wet and I'm surprised I didn't catch pneumonia. No matter what state we were in though, on our way back we used to always march through them gates, we were as good as any on 'em. The officer used to just say, 'Right! straighten yourselves up lads,' when we were coming to gate, and we always marched in.

We started training with live ammunition and we were going through rows of barbed wire with a Bangalore Torpedo and when we got to a certain spot we had to shove it under the barbed wire. All this was observed by adjudicators and one came up to me and said, 'What do you think you're doing soldier?' and I said, 'I'm pushing this Bangalore Torpedo through here.' He says, 'You're supposed to do it sitting up!' and I said, 'Aye! and you're supposed to get shot, aren't yer?' He says, 'Do you know who you're talking to? You're talking to an officer.'

154

Then we got going and one of these officers came up to me and said, 'Right, you've got a wound in your ear!' So he shouted for stretcher bearer and I was going to get on this thing when this other officer walked up and he says to this adjudicator, 'Wounded?' and he says, 'What's wrong with him?' and he says, 'It's just up your street this, your specialty, he's been shot int' ear!' and they were talking to each other as though I had actually been shot int' ear.

The Exercise continued, still with the use of live ammunition on the 25/26 October but some bad weather caused cancellations and the Battalion did some 18 miles of route marching. Drivers carried out wading exercises on the 27th and the main exercise came to a close the next day. The Hallams returned to Crieff on the 29th. Jesse Mitchinson arrived at Crieff about this time and reported for duty to the Battalion Adjutant, Capt. Bill Ashby, as a brand new commissioned officer.

Jesse Mitchinson…
I came from Doncaster and left school there at fourteen to become a railway apprentice with the L.N.E.R. (London North Eastern Railway). I couldn't see any future in that so I studied to join the Police Force although it wasn't easy to get in during the 1930s. I joined Gravesend Borough Police in Kent during 1938 and was present there when the war rumblings began. When war started I saw a lot of the Battle of Britain from the ground and the bombing of London when the German Airforce used the River Thames as a guide for their bombing runs over the City.

The Police Force was a reserved occupation then but in 1942, policemen under the age of 27 years were allowed to be called up for military service. I was to report to an establishment in Newport on the Isle of Wight where we underwent basic training at a General Service centre. After six weeks basic training I was asked to consider the possibility of becoming an officer which was a little bit of a shock to me coming from a working class background. In the meantime, I was posted for training to the Royal Armoured Corps at Catterick in Yorkshire as a driver/wireless operator but was asked again what I thought of the idea of taking a commission. The pre O.C.T.U. unit I was likely to attend was in Kent where my wife was living and, if I was going to be subsequently knocked off, she would get a better pension. So, with that and the prospect of being together with her for at least a short while, I accepted.

Main training took place at Douglas on the Isle of Man where I discovered that I was already too old, in my mid twenties, to be a tank commander and so I opted for the Infantry. We had to decide which Regiment we would like to join and were allowed to choose three. I was given my first choice, The York & Lancaster Regiment and was posted to the Hallamshire Battalion in Scotland when I finished Officer Training. I was very apprehensive about meeting the other officers at Crieff Hydro but when I got there, I was placed in 'C' Coy which was then under the temporary command of Mike Lonsdale-Cooper. I was given my own platoon and another platoon commander, George Jackson, was very willing to show me the ropes. Of course, you couldn't have a nicer individual than Mike Lonsdale-Cooper to keep putting you right, and I looked upon this period as very much of a learning process.

The Battalions own Corps of Drums was reformed at the beginning of November and on the 5th, Capt. W. Ashby (Queens Regt.) joined the Hallams on the 5th, and assumed the position of Adjutant in place of Capt. W.R. Jenkinson. Both 'C' and 'D' Coys. proceeded to Dunblane for a course at the Assault School and the C.O. travelled to Barnard Castle on a Battalion Commanders course. Yet another officer, Lt.S.J.D. Moorwood, left on a permanent basis when he was posted to an Airborne Division, no doubt as a result of the calls for volunteers to this service earlier in the year.

Capt. William 'Bill' Ashby.
(Mr. W. 'Bill' Ashby Jr.)

On the 10th, an Advance Party left Crieff for Hamilton and were joined the next day by the rest of the Hallams. The Bn. was concentrated on the Racecourse except for 'C' and 'D' Coys. which found accommodation in the Barracks. Roy Simon was among this latter group.

Roy Simon…

I had my 19th birthday at Hamilton Barracks and it was a queer place, as ancient as Adam. We were in these cold, stone blocks. We used to have to come out and wash in these long narrow places and you could get an electric shock off the water when you turned tap on, it were dangerous. Some of the light switches were the same. We weren't there very long but it were a bad place.

David Lockwood (Letters to Mary)
15 November, 1943 (Racecourse, Hamilton, Lanarkshire)…
I'm sitting writing this by the telephone extension in the quarter occupied by Chris Somers, Mike Elliott and Phil Young who are all out - very convenient! Where I'm sitting now is just on the edge of the paddock - the hut cuts into the ring fence - and its funny to think that hundreds of racehorses in the balmy days of peace must have walked through where I'm sitting! I am so glad you saw Crieff and I do hope it has done you a bit of good.....   .....heres to the next trip and may we be as lucky with digs as we were at Crieff!

❖ *Only the gate and Guard Room of Hamilton Barracks are left now, not far up the road from the racecourse (below) where John Wollerton was injured by a grenade. (DWS)*

After having been able to spend some time with his wife at Mrs. Duff's house, David had seen his wife off on a train (possibly Edinburgh) for home. It seems that he then travelled by rail himself, direct to Glasgow on his way to Hamilton. Travelling in the same carriage was Anne Ziegler and Webster Booth (possibly part of an E.N.S.A. group) in company with what David described as *'a crowd of line shooting theatricals'* whom he would not have recognized but for the confirmation given by a Capt. sitting next to him.

He had obviously made prior arrangements for someone to pick him up at the station.

David Lockwood…

…I found the C.Os. driver L/Cpl. Bertram (one of my old Ecclesfield lads) and another driver waiting for me at the barrier and to my great relief a 'bread van' instead of a draughty jeep…… …I was in bed just after twelve and the Frog Boy had lighted my stove which was a grand welcome! (Missed a lecture on Sicily)

David Lockwood (Letters to Mary)

16 November, 1943 (Racecourse, Hamilton)…

I'm off to Tighnabruaich on Friday to reconnoiter the ground with the C.O. and other Coy. commanders. Going in my Jeep and I think it will be pretty parky if this cold spell is still on. From Friday to Tuesday we shall be at Kames Hotel, Tighnabruaich, Argyll…. …..Then on Tuesday we join the Battalion at Rothesay, and 'The unit, Rothesay, Isle of Bute' should find me until December 2nd when I go to Dunblane…. …Hart Dyke and John Mott return here from Barnard Castle tomorrow so we are expecting a real father-and-mother of a training conference tomorrow night! I gather from Ashby that Hart Dyke was always known as 'Dark Night' in the 13th Queens - rather amusing.

I'm feeling rather pleased with myself today as I had my annual T.A.B. and Tetanus injections last night - one in each arm - and have been up and about all day. Apart from a slight arm stiffness and a suspicion of feeling I've had a night out I'm absolutely fine. This is something new for me as you know because at Thirsk and in Iceland I was flattened out next day completely - do you remember? - you were so sweet to me….. ……After my inoculations last night, Ken, Peter, Mike Cooper, Chris and I went into Hamilton to see 'Gone with the Wind' and then walked back about one and a half miles and it may have been the walk that put me right today - who knows! I did enjoy it so (the film) and have never known four hours go so quickly - I could have sat through it a second time quite easily. All the cast seemed to be at the top of their form with Vivien Leigh and Clark Gable the best I thought. But Leslie Howard and Olivia de Havilland were excellent too…. …..I must say it exceeded anything I'd ever dreamt of - I did wish you were there, it seemed all wrong that you weren't.

It's still freezing here and feels worse because it's damp but I've got a grand fug on in here (my room) with the stove tonight. My Coy. Office under the stables with a concrete floor and wooden sides, one board thick, is like a workhouse with one small paraffin stove!

The Rear Party arrived on the 16th and two days later, Major J.H. Mott was appointed 2i/c in place of Major Ken West. On reflection, Ken West seems to have been an officer with very broad shoulders in that he bore a great deal of the burden in assuming temporary command of the Hallams on a number of occasions at difficult times. He is often mentioned in the War Diary.

Between the 19th and 20th of November, various elements left Hamilton to take part in a number of exercises in and around the Isle of Bute. A Battalion Recce Party comprising Trevor Hart Dyke (C.O.), John H. Mott (2i/c), Intelligence Officer and four Coy. Commanders were the first to arrive by road at Tighnabruaich. Then an Advance Party made their way to Rothesay on the 20th.

David Lockwood (Letters to Mary)
20 November, 1943 (Kames Hotel, Tighnabruaich, Argyll)...
This is a marvellous spot, far nicer than Inveraray as it's not so shut in by mountains and the training areas are better too. They've cleared the population out of the part where we train including the whole of one small village and the place has a very deserted look with all the windows broken by the blast!

This afternoon I put up three hinds when I was alone walking along a hillside and they skipped away like a flash, moving wonderfully gracefully with their snow-white bums showing as if their skirts were up, showing a pair of white knicks!

❖ *Kames Hotel, close to the beautiful shore line on the Kyles of Bute and just south of Tighnabruaich. It was here that David Lockwood stayed prior to the exercises conducted from a main base centred on Rothsay, Isle of Bute. (DWS)*

This is a funny little pub just above the shore and south of Tighnabruaich and with a lovely view up the Kyles of Bute which looked simply grand in the sun today. Bute of course is just across the water about a mile away.

We're looked after by three old girls whose one concern is that we shall be in for meals punctually and they feed us jolly well - plenty of everything and fresh butter...   ...they make their own electricity and it goes out about a dozen times every night! You always know when it's going out because it suddenly goes very bright and then fades out and the three females roar round the house with candles shouting, 'Has somebody touched a switch?!'

Wasn't it a good call we had last night! I liked the old boy on the exchange - did you hear him say 'The lady at Bamford says you're worth three shillings' (15p). I did enjoy it and you sounded so grand and cheerful. (David had an arrangement with Mary's parents at Brookdean, Bamford, to reverse the charges and settle up later. This saved problems with coin operated telephone boxes)

Peter's truck killed a cocker spaniel coming down Loch Fyne yesterday. It wasn't their fault, the dog jumped off a wall in front of them but the unfortunate thing was that the owners children and nurse saw it happen and they were all very upset. The owner was very decent, but the nurse insisted on screaming all the time and all the kids cried and had to be led away - awful business. Fortunately it was killed outright so we didn't have to finish it off with a revolver as we were preparing to do.

During the last few days prior to the Hallams move to Rothesay, John Wollerton was extremely lucky not to have been killed, when he was injured during weapons training on the firing range at Hamilton Racecourse.

John Wollerton...
We were doing weapons training and I went range firing which was being organized on that day by Capt. Bell. I had walked round with CQMS Gandy when somebody threw a hand grenade

which hit my left shoulder and I got hold of it, threw it away and ran. Unfortunately, I wasn't quick enough in going to ground, rolled over and that was it. Gandy ran up to me, saluted and said, 'Sir, you haven't been hit, you've just been mesmerized!' Well, I'd already checked that I'd still got the most important parts of my body intact but I discovered in the end, that my left leg wasn't right when I stood up. I undid my left gaiter and blood gushed over the top as it was running down the leg from my thigh which had been hit.

I was losing a lot of blood and they took me around to the Officers Mess on a stretcher, and it was all quite amusing because there was no pain as it had just gone numb. The immediate treatment was hot sweet tea but they hadn't got any sugar in the Officers Mess, so they rushed me round to the Sgts. Mess where they had! Then the ambulance got lost and I spent some time in that by which time I was feeling dreadful. The doctor was from a country in South America, and when I got to the hospital after lunch time he said, 'I will operate on this officer,' and this lady said, 'No you won't, I will because I'm the senior surgeon here,' and I said, 'Thank God!' That doctor didn't speak to me for ages afterwards.

There was a question afterwards as to whether or not Capt. Bell should have been court marshalled as the red warning flags were not flying at the time I was injured, but I'm very glad he wasn't because he was a very good friend of mine. The thrower didn't count to three before he threw the grenade either. If he'd done it properly I would have been dead now!

The whole Battalion moved from Hamilton to Rothesay on the 23rd, to take part in a number of exercises in connection with Combined Operational Training over an eight day period.

David Lockwood (Letters to Mary)
23 November, 1943 (Kames Hotel, Tighnabruaich)…
We're off to Rothesay across the water this afternoon to join the Battalion who arrive today and the field officers at any rate are staying at the Glenburn….
…John Wollerton has been wounded back at Hamilton with a piece of hand grenade in the bottom! Not serious and should be back in 10 days.

I'm losing Phil Young once more as he is going to some air photograph interpretation unit - the thing he applied for when he left Brigade….   ….and I hear two new 2/Lts. have arrived in the Battalion….. ….the officer problem is serious.

Peter and I found such a nice cottage on our travels yesterday in the evacuated area. It had obviously belonged to someone who had quite good taste and was awfully well fitted up - I thought how well it would have suited you, Benjie and me. It had a drive up a hill through a little wood and fields to the south where the sun was, and glorious views over the Kyles of Bute and Arran and Loch Fyne to the west. A really lovely spot, but it was emptied and troops had shot through the windows and bullets had lodged in the plaster on the other side of the sitting room and in the ceilings. The windows were all broken of course and the front door had been opened, and cows had got in and made pats all over the dining room and sitting room - you never saw such an incredible mess with broken glass and plaster everywhere. It was all so unnecessary and I thought so very sad - if the windows had been boarded up and the doors properly locked, none of it need have happened. I wondered where the owner was and how heartbroken they would have been to see it. It made me very annoyed to see it. You would have loved that little house.

The first exercise, on the 26th, was code named 'BLINDMAN' and involved assault landings, which were carried out in the presence of the Divisional Commander. Three more exercises took place up to the 30th, and included those code named 'KILBRIDE', 'MILLHOUSE' and

❖ *The ever popular Glenburn Hotel perched high near the waters edge at Rothsay, with fine views overlooking the Kyles of Bute to the east and Loch Striven. (DWS)*

ending with 'KAMES', a night attack using live ammunition. All of these names were taken from place names in the surrounding area and were conducted both on water and inland areas. A number of officers had joined the Hallams, again during a very hectic period. These officers were 2/Lts. J.W.Michinson, D.C. Braithwaite, D.Newton, F.T.Pierce,P.Turrell, O.Watson-Jones and P.M.Bendall, the latter of whom was one of only two Battalion officers destined to become Prisoners of War.

David Lockwood (Letters to Mary)
26 November, 1943 (Glenburn Hotel, Rothesay, Isle of Bute)…
This is far more hectic than Inveraray ever was and that's saying a lot - but thank god we're only here for 10 days! We leave for Hamilton next Thursday (Dec. 2nd).

…now I am in for tea for the first time since we arrived - very good - in the lounge with a lot of people simply oozing money around me and about 50 per cent services. There is a band (trio) playing soft music in the hall and the whole show is very snakey! The life here is quite the most extraordinary I've ever struck as it's a really very slap-up hotel, as I told you (like the 'Station' at York) and yet we live a sort of camp life as far as the training goes…. …this place is awfully like Douglas, Isle of Man.

Ivor, Peter and I share a double room with me in a little bed in extra. It's pretty crowded but the lounges here are lovely and the food excellent. Rothesay is a funny place - nice bay with a lovely view onto the Argyll coast up Loch Striven opposite…

Jesse Mitchinson…
I remember the training at Bute where all the invasion divisions went for manoeuvres on the island and assault landing training. I remember the latter very well because just about everybody on my landing craft was sea-sick! I wasn't, but I came to the conclusion that when you're in charge of a group like that, you're so taken up with the responsibility of it all and trying to remember what you have been told to do, that you don't have the time to succumb to those kinds of things. I found that to be the case in a number of situations later on.

I remember my batman who was a little chap called Parkin, a lot older than the rest of them. He was also my wireless operator and carried an 18 set on his back with a long whip aerial on the top. I remember doing a landing in waist deep water from an LCA (Assault Landing Craft) and wading in towards the shore when he stepped into a hole and disappeared under the surface. Only the aerial was sticking up like a submarine periscope, and he slowly emerged as we moved towards the beach. He never said a word! He was a lovely little fellow and had about six children but he was later killed in Normandy during the advance to the Seine.

David Lockwood (Letters to Mary)
28 November, 1943 (Glenburn Hotel, Rothesay, Isle of Bute)...
Yesterday morning.... ....we got up at 2 a.m. and had breakfast at 2.30 then set off in lorries across the island. After waiting on the beach for two hours in sleet and a perishing east wind, wet through at the elbows and down the neck. We embarked and after getting lost in the darkness and sleet at sea, eventually landed in the early light having had to jump out of the boats into three feet of Atlantic ocean - up to our waists. Not satisfied with this, running off the beach, your Ted tripped on a trip wire and losing my balance, did a complete somersault and landed on my back in mud and water! Imagine! as if wading a hundred yards through breakers on a November morning in full equipment wasn't enough!!.... .... I don't think I shall ever forget that moment when frozen stiff in the boat and feeling slightly sick (a lot of the troops were sick) I felt the boat ground on a sand bank and the navy said, 'sorry, can't take you any further'. I being the Coy. Commander was honour bound to jump first and the worst of it was, I couldn't see how far away the bottom of the sea was - all I knew was that we seemed to be a devil of a long way from the beach! The troops were damn good though and of course its all part of the game.

I suppose you'll have heard all about the Regiment being given the Freedom of Sheffield and being allowed to march through the city with fixed bayonets like the Royal Marines and Guards in the City of London. The Colonel and Ken and several troops are going to Sheffield on Dec. 4th, at the Lord Mayors invitation, for the ceremony. Rather nice idea I think and a great honour for us of course.

A whole lot of new subalterns have arrived at last and I have been given one of them - George Watson-Jones by name from Birmingham. He's the only full Lieutenant of the bunch and has been in since 1940 in the 11th Bn....He's a very nice lad and I took to him as soon as he walked into the office... ...took his platoon out for the first time on yesterdays exercise - what a christening, as I said to him! - and did extraordinarily well, so much so that he was congratulated by the C.O. at the conference on the exercise this morning - and that is something.

Great news! H.D. has decided to take all the rifle Coy. Commanders to Sheffield for the show on Dec. 4th and about 30 - 40 men, all Sheffielders. We shall travel on Friday and stay with our families on Fri. and Sat. nights and travel back to Hamilton on Sun. - Isn't it grand!!! I'm so excited at the thought of seeing you again so soon... ...I gather the Teddy Bear and George Robins are on the job and want plenty of us there - what luck!!

The Battalion returned by sea and rail to Hamilton, which was just in time for a chosen few to take advantage of an invitation to travel to Sheffield and take part with other contingents in a 'Freedom of the City' being conferred on The York & Lancaster Regiment, to be followed by a march through the streets. A party of 34 ORs. under the command of Lt. P.H. Willis-Dixon represented the Hallams and Lt. Col. T. Hart Dyke, Majors R.I. Slater, D.E. Lockwood and P.S. Newton also attended. On the 4 December, the Lord Mayor of Sheffield (Councillor S.H. Marshall) presented the Scroll (Dated 1 December and now in the Regimental Museum, Rotherham) to Lt. Gen. M.G.H. Barker, C.B., D.S.O., and took the salute.

David Lockwood (Letters to Mary)
7 December, 1943 (Racecourse, Hamilton, after Sheffield Freedom parade)...
We're fearfully busy getting 'pansied' up for Monday and H.D. is running round in small circles! South has wangled me a new suit of Battle Dress today for nothing. He took in my oldest one (Thirsk) which was literally in rags after removing the crowns and exchanged it as his own - free! The new one is utility, I'm sorry to say, with outside buttons but not too bad looking.

Old Michael Barker seems to have worked the oracle all right at the War Office and the Battalions train arrives at 9 a.m. Monday, but leaves again at 3 p.m.

The Lord Mayor is taking the salute at the War Memorial and D.S.B. (Douglas Branson, the Hon. Colonel) is trying to have the City Hall steps, opposite, reserved for Hallamshire families. We'll produce some tickets from here....   ...we leave Sheffield by road on Tues. a.m. and have told D.S.B. there will be eleven of us available plus wives for a party on Monday night. H.D., John Mott, Ivor, Peter, me, Joe, Raymond, Mike Elliott and one or two others. I'm getting very excited about the whole thing!

The Lord Mayor of Sheffield, Councillor S.H. Marshal is escorted by Lt. P.H. Willis - Dixon during the inspection of the Hallamshire Battalion on 4 December, 1943. The well known figure of CSM Conway (Codd) stands nearest to the camera (SNL)

The Hallams at this time were on the brink of being posted anyway, from Hamilton to Hopton-on-Sea, Norfolk, so they took an opportunity to stop off on route by train at Sheffield, so as to march through the streets once again and exercise the Civic Honour as a whole Battalion, the first in the Regiment to do so. This, of course, also gave the men belonging to the city and surrounds another chance to have a brief moment with loved ones. They left Hamilton on the 12th and arrived in Sheffield at 0330hrs the next morning and those with homes in Sheffield, were allowed to detrain at once and go home for a few hours. The rest left the train at 0700hrs. and marched to Edmond Road Drill Hall, where they were joined by the Road Party of which, Arthur Green was a member.

Arthur Green...

When I set off from Hamilton, we'd been travelling for about three quarters of an hour and somebody in the wagon in front started waving like hell. Anyway, a Dispatch Rider (D.R.) came alongside and waved me down in such a panic and when I stopped and got out, I was on fire in between the cab and the body. Apparently, the person that had been using my wagon whilst I was on leave, had been doing underneath with an oily rag and left it on the exhaust pipe. There were flames shooting up through the gap where the spare wheel was mounted with a camouflage net on top, but we were lucky and caught it in time as the fuel tank was just forward of that position. I thought there would be an inquiry later but nobody said anything more about it.

We got to Edmond Road Drill Hall on the day before the march through Sheffield and it was only ten minutes walk from where I lived. My father and sister were there waiting when I got there but I couldn't leave the wagon outside because it carried a valuable load (designated G1098), so it was decided to get as many vehicles as possible in the hall. Well, we wondered if a 3 Tonner fully loaded could be supported by wooden floorboards but we managed to do it with much creaking of timber and I managed to get home for the night and sleep in a decent bed.

The morning of the 13th was spent cleaning up and the march through Sheffield began at 1200hrs. with Bayonets Fixed and Colours flying. The Battalion was led by the Band of The York & Lancaster Regt. and marched past the saluting base in Barkers Pool. The City Hall steps were reserved as a stand for relatives of all ranks. Trevor Hart Dyke notes in his book that... *it was a very stirring experience and did much to bolster up the already high morale of the Battalion. The Sheffield W.V.S. and Home Guard entertained us at (Edmond Road Drill Hall), and after the march through the city, wives and families were allowed into the Drill Hall and a happy time was spent by all.* After lunch, the Regimental Band stayed for a while and entertained everyone with a selection of music and the place was visited by many past serving members of the Hallamshire Battalion.

Arthur Green...
It was a nice break but we were off again the next morning and my father and sister came down to see me off. I could see tears in me fathers eyes, he'd never been a soldier and was never really a sentimental fellow but I could see tears in his eyes when I left.

Arnold Whiteley...
We broke our journey at Sheffield to exercise our Freedom of the City and stayed at (Edmond Road Drill Hall) for the night. I managed to get a message to my wife and she came to Sheffield. On the march through the city next day, I got on the outside rank and she was walking down the road with me so as we could have a chat. We took the salute outside the City Hall and, after lunch, marched down to the railway station and we just had time for a little cuddle then on to Hopton on Sea where we started further training...

It was only the Road Party that had the pleasure of lingering a while at the Drill Hall where their vehicles were parked ready for the second leg of the journey to Hopton the next day. Meanwhile the rest had boarded the train and, in a cloud of the usual smoke, soot and steam, chugged out of Sheffield's Victoria Station at 1530hrs. to begin their journey to Hopton-on-Sea. The majority of these men would soon find themselves billeted in a pre-war holiday camp known in those days as 'Golden Sands'.

❖ *Ettrick Bay, Isle of Bute (one of a number of beaches used for practising amphibious assault landing during 1943). (DWS)*

ON GOLDEN SANDS

David Lockwood had sat down to a wet, foggy and cold journey to Hopton via Newark and Sleaford. When he got there he found things a good deal better than was expected and the officers mess was in a house. The house had been the 'Club House' of Golden Sands Holiday Camp and he declared it to be the best mess since rejoining the Battalion at Leominster. He and Ivor Slater were sharing a room which had two windows and a view over the sea front with a balcony outside.

David Lockwood (Letters to Mary)
15 December, 1943 (Hopton, nr. Great Yarmouth)...
The more I see of this place the more I like it. It's such a joy to start with to walk about on dry ground and not perpetually in mud as in Scotland. The camp is really very good value for money and, I should say, extremely immoral in peacetime!

The sea is full of interesting things and the beach is littered with warlike things such as paravanes and bits of aeroplanes - but of course we're not allowed on the beach and I for one am not going to disobey the order as I don't want to go up on a mine!

I've been for a run round in my carrier this p.m. looking at training areas with George Watson-Jones and it's lovely country inland, a funny mixture of Broads and windmills and then little hills and pinewoods. I've never seen so many windmills - Benjie would love it.

George Learad...
As pioneers, we cleared mines off the beach at Hopton and blew them up but I don't think we got them all and in my opinion there's still plenty there yet under the sands. They were our mines and by this time we were fairly sure that the Germans weren't going to invade, so we started clearing them. It was a nice walk into Yarmouth but you had to be careful walking back at night. They might be firing at Gerry aeroplanes and all the anti-aircraft shrapnel would come falling down at the side of the road.

Jesse Mitchinson...
I was on the advance party from Hamilton and was in charge of the half dozen vehicles in my convoy which stopped off at my home town of Doncaster for the night at the racecourse. I was able to sneak off and spend the night at my mother's home which wasn't very far away. Next morning we set off and passed through Retford where my grandparents lived. I stopped the convoy there and to their delight, they were able to give all the lads a cup of tea as we were on our way to Hopton on Sea. When we got to Hopton I was transferred to the Support Company and made 2i/c to Capt. Les Gill who was in command of the Carrier Platoon. I didn't last very long in that as they had an influx of other officers amongst whom was an officer who had trained on carriers so he joined the platoon and I went back to a rifle company.

If any of the men thought they were on their holidays, the bubble soon burst when only two days before Christmas they were treated to a Minefield Clearing demonstration by the R.E. at Kessingland. Then another R.E. team brought their mobile unit to the camp on the 29th, which they termed a 'circus' and more demonstrations took place. This time it was to allow the troops to become familiar with an array of various types of German mines, no doubt to ensure that everyone would be able to identify such things if they happened to come across any in the near future. For those who were still around on Christmas Day, the Padre gave a service in the Recreation Room and afterwards the officers became servants for a day as the men sat down to what was always the best dinner of every year.

Les Sewell...
I travelled to Norfolk with the carriers and it was pitch black when we got into Lowestoft. When we got there somebody said, 'There's some Germans there,' These people were on the roadside and it was the Poles, they'd been in the camp before us because there were all Polish words all over the toilets, and some German words! Anyway, I went straight on Christmas leave then because I hadn't had a Christmas at home so far in the war. When I came back, the Company Office had been burned down. I think there was a reason for that, somebody were covering their tracks because there'd been that much fiddling! Support Company was based at Rogerson Hall Holiday Camp and there was a long shed there where we kept the carriers and we were billeted in a row of chalets. The Battalion was at Golden Sands Holiday Camp.

Doug Catley...
Three parts of the Battalion got Christmas leave but I didn't and I'd not had a Christmas Leave in the Army. There were lots of younger, newer blokes all off on leave but Douglas wasn't! My mate, Syd Nowell, and I were both courting girls in Leominster so we decided we were going to go off there, so we went. We jumped a train and got back to Leominster and we had our Christmas there. We just took off, the pair of us!

We went back to camp after Boxing Day. They didn't have to fetch us back but they wouldn't have known where to find us anyway. We reported in and were placed on Company Orders the next day. We were on this Charge and marched in front of the officer and he said, 'What's all this?' I just said, 'No excuse at all Sir, I've been with the Battalion all these years and never had a Christmas leave and very aggrieved about it. I just took the law into my own hands to go to the girlfriends in Leominster and I went.' 'I'll stop you from doing that in future,' he said, 'I'll hit you where it hurts.' He stopped me nineteen days pay and I didn't even get C.B. (Confined to Barracks) and I thought I'd be over the wall to be quite candid.

David Lockwood (Letters to Mary)
30 December, 1943 (Hopton, nr. Great Yarmouth)...
Poor old Joe Beckett has just been in here to ask my advice as to where to go - he wants to leave at any price now he's a subaltern again and I don't blame him. It's all very sad, Tony Nicholson coming in as a Captain has meant that some other Captain had to go down.... ....My latest bombshell is that I've lost Gordon Good who has gone to command 'C' Coy. I'd seen it coming for some time and it's now Chris who looks like being my 2nd i/c..... ...it looks as though Ivor and I will be the sole survivors of the regime..... ....The old Battalion seems to be passing away from before ones very eyes day by day, and with it goes the old spirit that was always so good and can never be the same again.

I went to Lowestoft this morning for a lecture but had to come back as soon as I got there as they telephoned me to appear before this medical board. It was a lovely morning, cold with blue sky and we saw an absolute mass of Fortresses setting off on a daylight raid, wheeling round in the sky like a huge flock of geese - a wonderful sight.

The medical exam was the most thorough I've had in my life and having a strong attack of that after-leave feeling and missing you very much I really felt I wouldn't mind if they found I'd got hammer toes or leprosy so that I could retire to some nice cushy job like so many people seem to have in England!! But that was naughty of course! Well, I stripped down (cold) and did knees bend and stretch, deep breathing and was listened to and tapped all over back and front, had my legs and feet examined like a horse, had my blood pressure taken, had my pulse felt, jumped on and off a box for three minutes (!) had my pulse taken again, rested for three minutes and had my pulse felt again (back to normal), lay on a bed and had my tummy pummelled all over, was asked millions of questions, had my throat and teeth looked at, tested my eyes and finished up spending a penny into a bottle (!) after having my knee joints tapped with a little hammer to see if my legs jumped - and after all that was told I was as sound as a bell, A1. and fit for anything!!......so there you are, I suppose good health is worth a whole heap of cushy jobs as a crock.

It had been long understood that the 49th Division was being trained for the purpose of carrying out Beach Assault Landings but news was beginning to filter through that it was Gen. Montgomery's intention to use another unit for this purpose that had been tried, tested and toughened in battle. For this reason the 50th (Northumbrian) Division, with battle experience in North Africa and Sicily, was brought home to retrain. The 49th Division was now required to assume a follow up role.

Just watching the first 15 minutes of the film 'Saving Private Ryan' is enough to give most people an idea of what can happen to troops in an Assault Landing, although the portrayed action on OMAHA beach was particularly bloody. With this kind of hindsight and knowledge, it must now seem difficult for anyone to understand why the Hallamshire Battalion, or any other unit of the 49th for that matter, could express disappointment at being prevented from dying 'en mass' on the beaches of Normandy. The fact was, of course, that few people in the 49th Division at that time had any real vision of what, exactly, might be the happier consequences of having to take second place! It would have been seen then, simply as the 50th Division being given the privilege of leading the way to victory. The extended and automatic privilege of dying in much greater numbers may not have loomed large then. If this was so, it might just be possible now, to understand their disappointment then.

Trevor Hart Dyke...
At Hopton we started to do the training for a follow-up role, which was rather different, so it was marches to training areas some miles away and then carrying out attacks with live ammunition, supported by either medium or field artillery. We were interested to see how close up to our own fire we could get and I was a bit dubious about the Medium Regimental Commander so he said, 'Right! You and I will walk in front of the chaps' which we did and found it was quite safe.

On the first day of 1944, a weeding process began by the creation of another Coy. designated 'E' into which all personnel of a low medical category were placed. The fine tuning was now underway that would see to it that only the fittest would be sent into battle. The REs 'circus' came around again, no doubt for the benefit of those who had gone home for Christmas and missed the first one. A few days later, all available drivers went to attend a 'mine lifting' demonstration at Bungay and a Brigade exercise 'CENTIPEDE' took place the next day. This practised the organization and movement of whole Brigades over bridges.

Ken Godfrey...
We went on a number of schemes there with pick axe handles and things like that when the platoons went out and fought among each other where some represented the 'enemy'. They used to end up with a few bruises and black eyes in the scuffles and then all would march back together to the general area of Hopton on Sea. I was fortunate because I never got belted.

HALLAMSHIRE BATTALION OFFICERS AT HOPTON, LATE SPRING, 1944.

Back Row: Elliott, Watson-Jones (kia), Wollerton, M.C. (w), Sneath, Mitchinson (w), Crook (e), Turrel (sw), Tett (kia), Abbott (sw), Jackson (w), Gibbs (e).

Middle Row: Cowell (sw), Birch (e), Willis-Dixon (w), Somers, Gregory-Dean, (M.O.) (w), Gill (w), Mackillop (w), Lonsdale-Cooper, M.C. (w), Nicholson, M.C. (w), Thomas, M.C. (Padre), Morgan (e), Bedward, Bendall (prisoner of war).

Front Row: Good (w), Bell (dow), Lockwood (kia), Newton, M.C. (w) Mott (w), Hart Dyke, D.S.O. (C.O.), Young (kia), Slater (w), Brinton (sw), Sandford (sw), Jenkinson (w).

There are six other officers that should be included here. Four were absent from the photocall . They are Pearce (kia), Poyner (kia), Firth (dow), Ashby (dow).

The other two might both be described as detached to other units. They are Mumby (died at sea) and Marsh (kia).

(kia = killed in action dow = died of wounds sw = seriously wounded w = wounded e = evacuated for any other reason . (YLRM)

The main pastime was bussing down into Gorleston at nights, dancing and Saturday nights out into Yarmouth and queuing up for the last bus with five of us getting six pennyworth of cold tripe, pepper, salt and vinegar and sitting on the bus getting back to billets at Hopton. No end of us would eat it because we all liked cold tripe! We didn't go into Yarmouth that often though because Gorleston was a lot nearer. There was a pub there called 'The Feathers' and I believe the forces were banned from it because they had some wild nights and a couple of A.T.S. girls did a strip on the tables. I was still growing up and I learned to dance there.

Capt. Raymond Jenkinson now assumed command of Support Coy., vice Capt. D.R. Bell, who became 2i/c to David Lockwood in 'B' Coy. At around this time David was looking for accommodation with the help of a local vicar (Scott-Adams) so that his wife and son could come and stay with him in the Hopton area. Also at this time, John Wollerton rejoined the Battalion after recovering from the hand grenade injuries he had sustained a few weeks before, on the Hamilton Racecourse.

John Wollerton...

At Leominster I had become the Signals Officer (S.O.) on the strength of a course I had done at Catterick from there. When I got to Hopton I'd said that I wasn't very keen on being the S.O. really and I was given a test message in Morse code to decipher. I said, 'I just don't understand what it says,' and they said, 'That's it, that's the message!' Then we did the Aldis Lamp and I said, 'That's worse than the Morse Code,' and he said, 'Well, you've got that right too!' and I was still the Signals Officer! So the whole thing was a complete con so I did my best from then on but was never able to send or receive Morse, except for very simple messages. Luckily, we were using 18 and 38 sets exclusively so it was all audio messaging by then.

The Signals SNCO, Sgt. Priestley, was extremely good. He'd been a shopkeeper in Sheffield and he'd got everything organized and he could pack more in a truck than was possible. He had a very good Cpl. who was also his brother-in-law (Putnam) and a group of lads who were all good at their jobs. They were split up between the companies with some platoons like the Carriers, Mortars and Anti-Tank had their own individual signaller and the C.O. had his own - Arthur Saunders. We had our own store keeper, a man called Andrews, and my job was to supervise them all which was easy in training but not so easy in action.

BATTALION HEADQUARTERS. LATE SPRING, HOPTON, 1944.
Front Row : 1 Philips, 2 Birch, 3 Bamford (kia), 6 Scott, 7 Warren?, 8 Smith?, 11 Genders?
Second Row : 1 Bedward, 2 Thomas, 3 Jessup, 4 Gibb, 5 Mott, 6 Hart Dyke, 7 Ashby, 8 RSM?, 9 Gregory-Dean, 10 Bennet.
Third Row : 4 Marsden, 6 Bertram, 7 Shelton, 11 Nowell, 12 Stenton.
Back Row : 1 Clifford, 2 Field (kia), 3 Hague, 4 West, 5 Lees, 6 Nicholson, 7 Naylor, 8 Haley, 9 Cole, 10 Badger, 12 Metcalf. (YLRM)

David Lockwood (Letters to Mary)
4 January, 1944 (Hopton)
(Still searching for accommodation)...
Yesterday afternoon I worked a new area (having drained Corton Village absolutely dry) north of here about two and a half miles away on the Yarmouth side, Warren Hill by name, but with no more luck than before and eventually finished up being recommended to a place that turned out to be practically no more than a railway carriage in a field!! It's so difficult here, almost impossible...... .....There are so many more of the services here to the square mile than anywhere we've ever been before - all sorts of peculiar units for defence on the coast.

Practically the whole of 'B' Coy. were inoculated last night and a lot of them have been flattened out today including Laughton, my C.S.M. Frog Boy has a stiff arm only!

HEADQUARTERS COMPANY. The photograph has been enlarged and presented in overlapping halves to aid the identification of some individuals. Front Row : 1 Bannen, 2 Griffiths, 5 Peel?, 12 McIntosh, 14 Stenton, 16 Howard. Second Row : 1 Warren?, 2 Paris, 3 Priest, 4 Rochford, 6 Jackson, 7 Beduard, 8 Thomas, 9 MacKillop, 10 Hart Dyke, 11 Jenkinson, 12 Langdale, 13 Wollerton, 15 Gregory-Dean, 17 Oakley, 18 Bennett, 19 Saunders, 20 Garfitt, 21 Rose, 22 Taylor, 23 Saunders. Third Row : 5 Hartley, 6 Shaw, 11 Naylor, 12 Allison, 13 Powers, 16 Jaques, 17 Andrew, 19 Marshall, 20 Sutcliffe, 21 Higginson. Fourth Row : 2 Calverty, 3 Bramwell, 4 Storr, 5 Brook, 6 Riley, 7 Godfrey, 8 Holgate, 10 Scott, 11 Warren, 12 Redmond, 20 Sladdin, 21 Haley, 22 Tolan. Fifth Row : 3 Wragg, 4 Denton, 5 Holmes, 8 Bownes, 10 Jackson, 14 Penn, 15 Gloster. Sixth Row : 1 Collier, 4 Nowell, 5 Knight, 6 Shipley, 8 Scott, 11 Heathcote?, 12 Thompson, 14 Himsworth, 15 Johnson, 17 Peel. Seventh Row : 1 Houghton, 3 Hobson, 4 Jackson, 6 Garner, 8 Garbett, 9 Metcalf, 17 Badger, 18 McGrath, 19 Godfrey, 20 Davies.(YLRM)

170

Les Gill...

Another officer and myself used to like getting away out of the mess and enjoy ourselves and we used to go to the Gorlestone Golf Club. We got down there one night and this other officer always got a bit obstreperous when he'd had a few. To get back to quarters we had to walk over this golf course and we were just waltzing along, chattering away and he was a bit noisy. Anyway, I said, 'Hey! Shut up Dave, there's somebody coming up behind us.' He said, 'Let's get down behind these gorse bushes.' So we dived down behind these big gorse bushes. Anyway, instead of him keeping quiet, the twit, he burst out laughing when they were nearly opposite us. Then their was voices, 'What's going on in there?' Anyway it turned out to be a couple of Hallamshire Sergeants and they had a laugh and invited us into their mess for a last noggin.

So off we went to their mess and, sitting at this bar, there was the most luscious girl. So off my mate went with the conversation and he got really close, talking away and then the door opened and the RSM came in. 'Captain so and so, what's going on?' and he answered, 'I'm talking to this lovely lady,' and the RSM replied, 'Yes! She is a lovely lady, she's my lady!' We were then quietly escorted from the Sgts. Mess.

David Lockwood (Letters to Mary)
9 January, 1944 (Hopton)...
I went off to Hopton House to see old Col. Walter (ex Regular), the Welfare Officer of Yarmouth, to see what he could recommend. We talked a bit about various places, a dear old boy, very tall and humorous and told me one or two very good stories! - and then went off to see his wife who came in to see me. He is over seventy but she must be much younger, is also very tall and equally nice and I took to both of them straight away.

Well, to cut a long story short, they've got a huge house in very nice grounds and part of the house is not used and she eventually said. 'Why not come here?' I was a bit taken aback when I'd never seen them or they me before. It was entirely their idea and they obviously meant it....
....they can give us a couple of bedrooms and a sitting room upstairs and I'm going round in daylight tomorrow to see the rooms and discuss details....

Went to Yarmouth with Gordon yesterday p.m. and had tea and dinner and saw a very good flick called 'Heaven can Wait' in colour - most amusing and very clever....   ....had a very amusing voluntary church service this a.m. Our Padre ran the service and played the organ himself and the senior chaplain of his Division preached. In the middle of the sermon the local bell ringer got up in the belfry over the pulpit and started ringing the one bell for civilian service so the Padre had to climb up to stop him as we could not hear a word! Most amusing to hear the Padre and the bell ringer arguing overhead in the belfry during the sermon - the bell ringer was deaf!! The senior chaplain is an oily little devil and very affected. I like our Padre, Thomas, more every day - a really fine chap and a true Christian if ever there was one...

Arthur Green...
It was well into wintertime and it was very cold and we were in chalets meant for two. Of course the army couldn't have that so we had a pair of two teared bunk beds in to sleep four and hadn't room to swing a cat hardly. The electric supply to these chalets was by overhead cables and most of us had managed to buy, steal or borrow a two bar electric radiator and they were all tapped into this here cable. We used them to keep warm and have a bit of toast in the billet but one night Sgt. Jock Henderson came tearing in. 'Switch your electric radiators off, it's going down the line!' The rubber insulation on the cable wire was melting and dripping down and the bare wire was glowing red hot in the dark due to the overload.

NO.? PLATOON OF 'A' COY. The officer is Lt. H.L. Morgan. Middle Row: 1 Bert Murray, 2 Gallagher, 3 Denton. Back Row: 4 Clifford, 6 Clark, 7 King. (HFC)

12 PLATOON, 'B' COY. The officer is Lt. Oliver ('George' to his friends) Watson-Jones. Front Row: 3 Sgt. Robert Haynes Middle Row: 3 J.A. Bunting. (HFC)

Roy Simon...
Shortly after we got to Hopton Camp, they split us up and I went with Les Tebbs and Clifford Hargreaves to 'C' Coy. and Jody Pedel stayed in 'D' Coy. I was sorry to lose him but he stayed there.

The Coy. Commander was Capt. Good and the platoon Commander was Lt. Bendall and we did a lot of weapons training and range firing, lots of route marching. I remember we'd been on this scheme and it was a long one and it was getting to us. Then this drummer lad, Gabbitas, who had come out with the band to bring us in gave us a beat and made such an impression and kept it up for so long that the C.O. commended him.

We even trained in this Kipper factory at Yarmouth, swinging on ropes where they used to hang the kippers and we also did swimming and life saving in some baths around Gorleston. We really got ourselves into peak condition there.

We did a lot of sports at Hopton and I was on the boxing team and 'Knocker' Lees used to be us trainer. When we went fighting he used to be my second. There was one bloke in the boxing team and he was a southpaw heavyweight and one day he said to me, 'You think you can fight you, don't you Simon?' He said, 'Stand up and I'll show you how to fight'. So, we were just playing around, acting daft and we were dodging and this, that and t'other. Then he left himself wide open and I hit him with a straight left and his legs buckled. It hit him ont' chin end and his knees buckled. Then he got up and said, 'I'm going to kill thee' and I was saved when Knocker came round the corner and stopped it. They were all laughing and somebody said, 'Simon nearly put him down Sgt.'

David Lockwood (Letters to Mary)
10 January, 1944 (Hopton) in respect of accomodation)...
We have got a sort of corner of the house on the first floor facing east and south and we'll be right away from their part of the house really.... ...Our sitting room used to be Mrs. Walters bedroom and is really awfully nice and gets all the sun. The bathroom is most modern and a damned nice setup. Our room has a good looking old fashioned bed which is either a 'small double' or 'very large single' and I said it would do fine!!.... ....the great thing is the communicating doors for the whole suite. The fire in the sitting room has had a stove like Mrs. Duff's sitting room but that has been removed. However, they go to Yarmouth on Tuesday (tomorrow) and are going to see if they can get another - failing that we can make it an open grate and I said the Frog Boy and I can fix it! He is going down at 9.30 tomorrow to do some cleaning and shift some furniture with Mrs. Walters.....
....she said this morning, 'I do want to make her happy' (you darling) - rather nice I thought. She suggested next Monday - a week today so of course I jumped at it and said I thought you'd agree.....

❖ *Morris Commercial CS8 15cwt Office Truck (restored during the 1980s by the author and his brother, Gordon) which is now in the Museum of Army Transport, Beverley. This mid-thirties vehicle left the driver exposed to the elements because of its 'Tiger Moth' style windscreens. It is the same type as that described by Harry Dinnigan. (DWS)*

14 PLATOON, 'C' COY. Foreground : 1 Roy Simon, 2 Ripley? Front Row : 2 Timlin, 3 Freeman, 4 'Knocker' Lees, 5 Lt. Bendall, 7 'Tishy' Porritt. Second Row : 1 Betts, 2 Cutts, 7 Clifford Hargreaves, 10 'Totty' Wood? Back Row : 1 Perkins?, 2 Pickersgill?, 4 Cyril May, 8 'Dusty' Rhodes?, 9 'Paddy' Burns (HFC)

17 PLATOON, 'D' COY. The officer is unknown but may be one of the Canadians, possibly Lt. F.J. Pearce who was with 'D' Coy. when the Hallams sailed to Normandy. Two of the men on the back row are Les Dalton (2nd from left) and Bill Jackson (5th from left). The first was involved in the capture of a German Half-Track, the second was involved in being captured by the Germans!

The drivers did a lot of practice travelling in convoy down a road between Acle and Great Yarmouth which was dead straight for miles, except for one bend, and ideal for the job. At night with all the normal vehicle lighting switched off so as not to be seen from the air, they were able

174

to judge the distance between trucks by the 'diff light' on the truck in front. This was a small, narrow beamed light fixed to the underside rear of each vehicle to shine forward onto the differential housing which was painted white.

Arthur Green...
We did a lot of map reading at night. The Transport Officer, Mackillop would give us a six figure map reference then he would be at that the place at a certain time later to check us in. A lot of the lads never arrived because they hadn't a clue on how to use a map so, they used to get lost and end up in a boozer.

Arthur's Truck was designated G.M.1 carrying G1098 stores. This included a number of large wooden cases filled with rifles and spares, boots, gaiters and all manner of clothing, webbing and other personal equipment, steel helmets and anything that the individual might need in the way of replacement.

Even though much of the motor transport was recently issued, some of the vehicles were still quite antiquated and all but obsolete, particularly those that still had open cabs with only small glass screens to protect the driver and passenger from the elements. One such machine had an 'Office' body fitted but was seldom if ever used for this purpose.

Harry Dinnigan...
We had a special vehicle as an Orderly Room truck. Bn. HQ. never used it for its correct purpose but whenever we moved it went with us and one of us had to drive it. It was on a 15 cwt. chassis and in the back were bench seats in two compartments separated by a central desktop with drawers and cupboards for documents and paperwork. It had special canvas awnings that could be unfolded on either side but they were never used. As far as I can remember it came with us to Normandy and stayed with us to the end. We could never get rid of it because it was on battalion strength!

During the month, Exercises 'CENTIPEDE', 'THRUSTER' and 'DUN' were carried out. These were to practise movement of the whole Brigade over bridges and night attacks. There were demonstrations of mine lifting at Bungay, and Street Fight training in Yarmouth. On 27 January, a training directive was issued on the subject of selection and training of Snipers. It is not known how many snipers were available to the Battalion when the unit eventually went into action in Normandy, but the allocation on paper seems surprisingly large. This allowed for eight men at the level of paid L/Cpl. operating directly under the I.O. at Battalion HQ., two each to the Rifle Coy. HQs., and one to each Rifle Coy. Section. If this is understood correctly from the War Diaries, then the total strength would have been thirty-eight! It is thought very unlikely that battalions were ever able to boast that many on actual strength in the field.

Initially, only four special rifles were allocated to Bn. Snipers and one each to the Rifle Coys. It can only be assumed that by the time the Hallams went into action later that year, that no individual sniper would be without his own special equipment, including the most important part - the correct weapon for the job. Sniper suits were provided for, at both Bn. and Coy. levels, but it was suggested that these could be improvised by using them as reversible garments. Disruptive patterns could be painted, light on one side and dark on the other! Each man was to carry a light camouflage net to cover the body and main training was to consist of 'stalking' and the 'art' of camouflage.

The men to be chosen for this very special task were required to be courageous and resourceful, physically fit, observant, alert and patient. They had to be able to make good use of ground, be capable of working alone and, last but not least, be good shots! Many of the people who were eventually chosen for this work were to become a lot more proficient than this basic outline required. They would have to if they wanted to survive. Even though the highest rank establishment was L/Cpl. at the time of inauguration of a sniper platoon or section, there would be plenty of promotional opportunities for men of the right calibre.

Tragedy struck on 6 February, when Pte. Reginald Baker was accidentally killed during a liaison exercise 'WICH', with the 79th Medium Field Artillery Regiment, R.A.

SIGNALS PLATOON. Front Row : Calverley?, C.Storr, Brooks, Arthur Thompson, Henry Branwell, Fred Taylor, Eric Scott, Robert Knight, Arthur Warren, Jim Riley. Second Row : Arthur Saunders, Johnny Rose, Arthur Garfitt, Frank Priest, Lt.John Wollerton (O.C.), Bernard Rochford, Tommy Holgate, Raymond Sutcliffe, Tom McGrath. Third Row : 'Dukie' Gloster, Norman Peel, Alf Jackson, Albert Wragg, Ken Davies, Fred Andrew, Marshall, Walter Jackson, Godfrey, Heathcote. Back Row : Johnny Houghton, Cecil Griffiths, 'Porky' Hobson?, William Hosker, Banner?, Tom Garbett, Jim Tocan, Harry Shipley. (HFC)

Training was now gathering pace with all manner of exercises, lectures and films, in cooperation with various other units that would be a steady build up towards the invasion of Normandy, planned for June but still top secret. On the 12th, the whole Battalion went to a training camp at Culford for a one week scheme alongside tanks. Then the Carrier Platoon, under Capt. Gill, was inspected by Gen. Sir Bernard L. Montgomery. The A/Tk. Pl. went to Sotterley Park with similar platoons from the rest of the Brigade for field firing practice. Two other exercises, 'TILT' and 'REMEDY II' were carried out. The first was to rehearse rapid occupation and digging of defensive positions, which was soon to become extremely useful, and the other was a scheme to test Medical and R.E.M.E. services.

On the 21st of the month, copy number one of a newspaper was printed and issued. It was given the title 'Hallamshire Herald' and priced at one penny (the best way to give an idea of its modern value equivalent is to say that there were 240 old pennies to the pound!). The aim of the paper was to create a common bond of interests, entertainment and news for the men, their families and relatives. It must be said that some of the latter would have found it rather difficult to understand army humour because much of it could be described as 'in jokes' which only the soldiers themselves could fathom. For instance, in this first issue was a reference to Wintery Weather where it was stated that - 'some of us at any rate have learned the difference between snow and rice pudding in the dark.'

Recent marriages were announced...
Lt. P. Turrell   Sp. Coy. - 22 January, L/Cpl. Wortley   'A' Coy. - 7 February,
Sgt. Mellor   Sp. Coy. - 7 February, L/Cpl. Green   Sp. Coy. - 9 February,
There was also a large coverage in the sports section which included Hockey, Soccer, Rugby, Basketball, Tug of War and Boxing. One of the last entries was made by the P.R.I., who was anxious to buy mouth organs in order to brighten up some of the marches which were presumably those ones not otherwise supported by the Corps of Drums or Regimental Band.

'B' COMPANY. O.C. Major D.E. Lockwood. (Officers seated on Front Row - have open necked collars and can all be identified from earlier officer group photograph - Page 156) (YLRM)

'D' COMPANY. O.C. Major P.S. Newton. (Officers seated on Front Row - have open necked collars and can all be identified from earlier officer group photograph - Page 156) (YLRM)

Douglas Catley was one of a number of Hallams chosen to form what was being called 'First Line Reserve' and he was very much less than keen to be taken away from his Battalion at this stage and sent to Aldershot. It seems that these groups were being formed to fill the gaps which were bound to occur in the ranks of those units who were part of the 'D' Day assault landings. It also seems logical that such reserves could only be found from the designated follow up Divisions like the 49th which were well trained and fit for the job.

On 6 March, Lt. P.H. Willis-Dixon and 14 ORs. of the Pioneer Pl., commenced a one week course on the subject of Knotting, Lashing and Watermanship. Only one exercise 'HERRING' seems to have taken place this month but plenty of other training schemes were run, which included a demo of enemy AFVs. at Chobham and a sniper course at Kessingland. The Battalion cross-country running team won the Divisional Championship on the 18th, for the third time in succession. There was little else reported for this month.

Ray Langdale...
Whilst we were at Hopton, there was some new system came out whereby one complete Company went into First Line Reserve. They didn't land with us in Normandy and Capt. Bell was the C.O. I was promoted to Sergeant Major at that time and we were close to leaving for Normandy and I remember two things happened. We went into Norfolk onto a big country estate and formed a hollow square. It was a brigade thing because the Lincolns and K.O.Y.L.I. were there also and the King reviewed us. I thought it was most unusual really in one respect. On parade you had two 'line' infantry battalions and one 'light' infantry (K.O.Y.L.I.) with rather different methods of 'present arms' and, although it wasn't a shambles, it wasn't far from it!

The C.O. had given orders that all men with medal ribbons had to be in the front rank and I remember the King stopping at a man who was just to my left. This man had three medals - the Africa Star, Palestine Medal and one other. Anyway, the King stopped and spoke to him and I heard him ask the man where he was in the troubles in Palestine and this man told him about that and about his third medal (might have been N.W. Frontier). Then the King turned, and was about to walk on, then he turned back to him and said, 'Do you realize my man, you have your medals on in the wrong order?' I came to understand much later that George VI had made a study of medals.

The Ceremonial Parade mentioned by Ray Langdale above, took place at 1045 hrs. on 27 April, at Somerleyton Park. A number of exercises were also carried out during this month under the code words 'PHONEY', 'DAWN', 'BUMP' and 'PLOP'! Again there was little reported in the War Diary for this month but the one for May seems to have been destroyed or lost altogether, because no copy of it is held by the Public Record Office

Arnold Whiteley...
Once we were marched to the football field, stood in single file and wondered what was happening. A police car pulled up and a young woman got out and she was walking around trying to identify someone who'd interfered with her or something like that. She didn't recognize anyone from our Coy. so I don't know what the outcome of that was.

Somebody pinched the payroll while we were at Hopton on Sea. There used to be this little Coy. office and when there was a party going on leave, they'd bring the money from the bank the night previous and lock it up in the Coy. office, then pay them out the next morning before they went. Somebody must have been watching this carry on and sometime in the night had taken all this cash. They had us all in the dining room and told us what had happened. Anyway, they searched that camp with a fine tooth comb but they never found out who it were.

My wife was able to come down for a holiday there in some cottages and a very old woman lived in one of these. There were no polished furniture but a white topped table and everything scrubbed

and spotless clean. You washed in a hand basin with a big jug of cold water but it were a good holiday. We went to see this woman a few years since but she had died. There were some good kind people there.

Training was mostly marching... ...we finished up there with a really long march and slept out in the open one Saturday at Dulwiche in Suffolk and after a morning exercise, we did a 25 mile forced march all the way back to Hopton. The full band met us outside the town and marched with us back to the camp and not one man dropped out. The Col. thanked us for that and I think he knew then that he'd got some fairly good lads under him.

Bert Murray, born in Preston, was 'called up' on 4th Nov. 1943, and did initial infantry training with the Gordon Highlanders in Aberdeen, which was completed at Carlisle with the King's Own Border Regt. After a number of moves, one of which almost ended in a posting to Italy, he was transferred in the latter half of April, 1944, to the Hallams which was at that time based at Hopton on Sea. Here was a typical example of men being conscripted into an army unit with no regard to individual, regimental or county roots, but more on the basis of gap filling. At standard infantry training establishments, men were being drawn into what became known as the General Service Corps, from where they were posted to units as required. Before and after the war, Bert worked for the Post office and retired after 46 years service as Sub Post Master at Bamber Bridge, just south of Preston, Lancashire.

Bert Murray...
I recall sharing a chalet with two old soldiers, 'Nobby' Clark and the other a big guy whose surname I think was Clifford. They became my friends and mentors in the Hallams and were going to look after me. However, they unfortunately became two of our first casualties in France due to a shooting accident.

NO.? PLATOON OF 'D' COY. The officer is Lt. Frank Tett, who was to become the first fatal casualty among the commissioned ranks. It is thought that he died as a result of sniper fire when patrolling an area to the east of Audrieu in Normandy. (HFC)

Roy Simon...
I reckon we were just about ready for leaving Hopton because for the simple reason we started having our photographs taken. That's when I thought, 'Well, there's something going off,' but we knew by then that we were not going to be on the initial landings. We then began to pack our tackle up and hand a lot of stuff in to stores that we'd normally carry ourselves and then we were shipped off. I can't remember whether we went by train or wagons.

Jesse Mitchinson...
A Reserve Coy. was formed to which I was transferred as 2i/c to Capt. Jack Firth. We were taken away from the main Battalion and went into a camp near Redhill where we waited for instructions to embark for Normandy. There was a N.A.A.F.I. at Redhill and I went there to get a couple of footballs to keep the troops occupied while we were waiting to be called forward. We eventually sailed from the same port as the main group of Hallams which was Newhaven. Later, when we reached Normandy, we were broken up and fed back into the Battalion where I became a platoon commander in 'A' Coy.

On the 3 June, 1944, Advance Parties moved out of Hopton and made their way to the vast marshalling areas of men and machines beyond the Thames, where the assault waves were already boarding their respective sea craft. The Battalions marching troops were placed in a camp which was situated between Newick and Chailey, whilst the vehicle parties went initially to Epping. 'A' & 'B' Coys. travelled on the 6th and the rest the next day, so that all were assembled in these so called 'sealed camps' by 1700 hours on the 7 June. Arthur Green travelled with the vehicle parties.

'A' COMPANY. O.C. Major R.I. Slater. (Officers seated on Front Row - have open necked collars and can all be identified from earlier officer group photograph - Page 156) (YLRM)

Arthur Green...
We hadn't a clue where we were going but, eventually, ended up at Tilbury Docks. We were loaded onto this big ship with all our fuel tanks and cans full of petrol.

Arnold Whiteley...
We knew what was going to happen. We were taken down by trucks but where we were, we couldn't say. The signposts were taken down all over the country, the Post Office, Co-op signs, everything.

George Learad...
When we set out to the south, I thought, 'Ay! Ay! This is the big do this! This is it!' It didn't worry me really and I never had any thoughts about us ever losing the war. I always had the feeling that we'd never lose the war even when things weren't working out. The only thing is that I thought, 'You've got to look after yourself. Life is precious.'

John Wollerton...
We did the waterproofing of our vehicles at Hopton and then went down to a place near Newhaven where we camped in a wood and were threatened that if anyone tried to leave the enclosure, we'd be shot. There were sentries posted all around in wooden towers and we were given so many French Francs to spend, God knows where, and that was it!

Les Sewell...
When the Battalion was leaving Hopton, I was on the rear party and we were detailed to clean the camp up as soon as the Battalion had gone. I went into the Sgts. Mess and there was a pile of records and a couple of wind-up gramophones, so I brought those into my billet that I shared with the R.E.M.E. chap. Anyway, the Battalion came back as things were postponed for a day and the RSM came round the billets and he said, 'What you doing with them?' I said, 'Well, I brought them here sir, to protect them from being lifted.' He said, 'That's right! Take them down town, sell them and give me half of what you get!'

The amount of stuff we found left behind, shoes, boots, scarves, pullovers, stacks of old socks. All the old woollens went down town and fetched quite a price. Of the band instruments, the big base fiddle disappeared. Nobody knew where it had gone, although several transport chaps knew where it went, but they weren't talking. It must have been somebody with a truck because you can't put a big base fiddle under your arm and carry it away.

Anyway, the rear party all moved out of Golden Sands into the workhouse at Yarmouth under Capt. Bell. Two or three days later, part of the rear party, myself included, set out in a Brigade Convoy for the docks. We didn't know where we were going, of course, but we finished up in East Ham where there were tented camps in areas that had been cleared of blitz damaged housing. Next thing, we were on Liberty ships going down the Thames and we passed the Straights of Dover in the night.

Trevor Hart Dyke (O.C. Hallamshire Bn.)...
The camp we took over had just been evacuated by units of the assault waves. We were there for a couple of days and received briefing which informed us of the beach assembly areas and the information was passed down to the Coy. Commanders, etc.

David Lockwood (Letters to Mary)
4 June, 1944 ('Sealed Camp' near Newhaven on South Coast - between Newick and Chailey)...
It's a lovely day and we clocked in about 3 p.m. after a good run. I wish you could see the country and the rhododendrons - hills and dales and the thing you and I missed so much at Hopton, a view - this is a lovely part of the world and one that I've not seen since I was at school. The houses too are sweet and all so neat and clean - many of the converted cottage variety that one sees in 'Ideal Homes' and that sort of paper. More about our surroundings, I can't say!

Things move in a mysterious way and one realizes what small pawns we are in the big game on these occasions....   ....but I do miss you so and when it came to tea time, I did so long to be with you both, with Billie saying 'More jam!' - I was eating roast beef and two veg. at the time - 4.30 p.m.....   .....There's a cinema show in the camp tonight and I'm thinking of going to the second house - I can hear the talkie part from here at the moment.

Quarter to seven - you'll just be putting Billie to bed and he'll be leaping about and wanting 'Gee - Gee!' Bless him...
How I hate saying good-bye! I hope we never have to do it anymore now - and I don't see why we should. What a waste it seems having to leave anyone as sweet and lovely as you alone...
....it seems all wrong that you and I who are always so happy together with you such a grand companion and such a cheerful sweet thing should be parted. But the cause at least is good if it gives us peace for the rest of our life together and for Ben and Susan (?)...

Roy Simon remembers being under canvas and, feeling at a loose end, decided to darn some socks...

Roy Simon...
I came out of this tent and got sat down on a box and were darning these socks. I'd just about done when I heard this Yank voice from over the fence, 'What ya doing?' and I told him like. He says, 'You don't do a stupid trick like that.' I said, 'We do in this Army!'

The American soldier then disappeared for a few moments and returned with some new pairs of socks, chocolate and other goodies which he threw over the fence to Roy!

David Lockwood (Letters to Mary)
5 June, 1944 (South coast - sealed camp)...
We're using these troops envelopes as we hear that they are the only ones which are being delivered....   ...Ivor and I are sharing a room and have just come back from the camp cinema, Fred Astaire in 'You were never lovelier' - quite good - there's a different film on every night, aren't we spoilt?! I'm using the Padres pen as mine is out of ink. We're very comfortable here with good food and beer on tap. Of course we aren't allowed out of camp so make our own amusements here. The lads are all in great form and the weather's been reasonable so far.

Lt. A.C. 'Chris' Somers has been mentioned on a number of occasions, particularly by David Lockwood in his letters. Chris wrote a Diary which is almost a parallel to Trevor Hart Dyke's book 'Normandy to Arnhem'. Chris made this Diary available to the author some years ago and it is an invaluable source for much of the following chapters in that it covers periods for which no other evidence is available except in the official War Diaries in the Public Record Office, but more will be said later.

Chris Somers (Diary)...
6 June, 1944, 'D' day at last!
I forget where we heard the news but we were now in the South of England in Transit Camps awaiting our turn. Each of those three days we waited, we watched the shuttle service of fighters landing and taking off from a nearby Aerodrome. The wireless told us that the landings had been a success and everything was going according to plan. I still hoped that by some miracle our turn would never come. The landings seemed so easy when one listened to the news but one wondered at what they really went through. It was not such a picnic for anybody on the spot.

David Lockwood (Letters to Mary)
6 June, 1944 (South coast - sealed camp)...
What a day this has been and I've thought about you such a lot and wondered how Hopton had received the great news! The first news we had was when a rumour started in the camp that the landings had started and as all the wireless sets in the camp seem to be out of action except the N.A.A.F.I. one, I went to see the manager who told me it was true. Everybody's spirits went up about 200 per cent and we've spent the day listening to news bulletins and then the King's speech and the various commentaries just now - fancy poor old Howard Marshall having a wet landing! Everyone is in great form and Chris has just gone upstairs having announced that he is about to wash his smalls! We've done a lot of laughing today.

We've been to see Noel Coward in 'In which we Serve' this evening in the camp cinema - a really first class film and awfully true to life - I've wanted to see it for a long time. I heard a nightingale the other night - lovely - and it reminded me so much of the times we used to listen to the broadcasts of it when we were at Slayleigh Avenue - do you remember?

David Lockwood (Letters to Mary)
8 June, 1944 (South coast - sealed camp)...
Just been in the N.A.A.F.I. listening to the nine o'clock news and things sound quite good - there is an absolute bedlam in there tonight and the barrel is nearly empty - the lads are in terrific form but there'll be some thick heads in the morning!

It was lovely here this morning and hot, but this afternoon it turned to drizzle which rather spoilt a camp race meeting which we held - you know the kind they have on board ship with dice and people moving the 'horses' round - with a tote double and everything run very well by the permanent staff. Great fun, and I finished about all square.

John Wollerton...
When we went down to Newhaven, there were people going out shopping normally and having toasted tea cakes and coffee and I thought, 'Oh, dear!' We were in billets there for a short time, some semi-detached houses that had been commandeered.

The men were all fit and ready to go now and the unit that they would soon be taking over from in the Normandy front line was already fighting hard to the east of Arromanches. The 6th Bn. Green Howards of 69th Brigade/50th Division had landed on King - Gold Beach at La Riviere (Ver sur Mer) on the morning of 6 June, and were now moving towards Crepon. The Hallams were about to follows in their footsteps, but first there was the matter of a short boat trip across the channel to the beaches. A few miles inland from that landing place, Destiny was waiting patiently for their arrival so as to put all their previous training to the deadly test. The little village of Fontenay le Pesnel was far and away beyond anything they had yet experienced.

It was to cost them very dearly.

FAR AND AWAY IN FONTENAY

At 1615 hrs. on 9 June, the Hallamshires were embarked on a journey from which many would never return, although they might have faired even worse had they been included in the initial 'D' Day assault landings for which they had originally been trained on the west coast of Scotland.

Early post war view of Newhaven and the jetties where the main contingent of the Hallams were embarked. (THD)

The Battalion Flag after the war and much action. It had been hastily stitched together using various remnants just before crossing to Normandy. It now hangs in Endcliffe Hall. (THD)

Trevor Hart Dyke...
We were embarked on five small ships, Landing Craft Infantry(LCI) and when I came up to the HQ. ship, a midshipman commanding it came up to me and said, 'We had damage when we went across last time with enemy fire' and he wondered whether it was safe to go over. I said, 'Well, it's your job to get us over and not for me to say whether it's safe or not'. Anyway, he seemed to think it would be all right and I asked if he would mind us flying our battle flag at the mast, which he agreed to do. We were told to expect a dry landing and so the special canvas trousers were not used. Our landing, however, turned out to be very wet and it took some time before we could get properly dried out...

Arnold Whiteley...
...we went across on these LCIs. It were a bit upsetting, half of the life jackets had been saturated with blood you know. Some of those that had gone before must have been killed and wounded. They were dragging that floating harbour across on that day. I might be exaggerating but only to make a point. The ships that were on that sea, if you'd fallen off one ship you'd have fallen onto another. No air raid could have touched them.

185

John Wollerton...
Then we got on this boat which had a great big hole blown in the back of it and we went across in that. We were given hot drinks in cans with a self heating device and you'd to pierce the top and take the lid off and that gave you a scalding hot drink of soup. When we got off at the other side, I must have stuffed about ten of these in my trouser pockets either side, saved for when we got to the other side for some of the lads who were ill at sea and couldn't drink them then. When we got there I jumped over the side, thinking it was shallow, instead of walking off the front and got into deep water and I thought I'd never get out. We marched ashore and got bikes. We didn't bicycle very far and when we heard firing in the distance we were given the order to sling them away. They were useless!

Chris Somers (Diary)...
Then it was our turn: We sailed from Newhaven on the night of the 9 June in two LCIs. David was in command of our boat - the C.O. and Battalion HQ. and 'A' & 'D' Companies in another. They flew the Hallamshire flag from the masthead for the crossing. The five officers on our own boat shared a small cabin. As it had bunks we settled down to sleep. Luckily, it was a calm crossing and when we awoke next morning the invasion coast was in sight. I expected to see shells and bombs falling all over the place but apart from a few loud bangs from the guns of battleships nothing happened in that respect.

Soon, we were transferred into a smaller landing craft and made a semi wet landing on the beach which then appeared to be in a state of chaos. Quickly forming up, we marched off up a rough track leading inland. Every moment I expected shells to be landing all around - all was peaceful - in fact if only I'd known, the enemy was miles away.

There are differences in the accounts above, as to the type and number of vessels the Hallams were embarked in at Newhaven, although it must be said that there were many different types in use at the time. All of the personal and War Diary accounts differ and although it will not matter too much to the casual reader, an attempt will be made to sort it out for those with an inquisitive mind.

Trevor Hart Dyke states that five vessels were allocated to the Battalion and in his book he calls them LSI (Landing Ship Infantry), but just one of this type was capable of carrying the whole Battalion (it may be remembered that the 'Andes' was later converted to a LSI after it brought the whole Battalion back from Iceland). Chris Somers remembers only two vessels and that they had to transfer to smaller craft for the beach landings. John Wollerton remembers jumping over the side of his into very deep water! He would have had a very long drop from a LSI but, of course, these things are all down to memory and this is not a fault finding exercise.

The Bn. War Diary states that the vessels were LCI(L) - Landing Craft Infantry (Large). These were purpose built, full sea going (crossed the Atlantic under their own steam) ex-U.S. Navy craft on Lend/Lease to the Royal Navy. Each was able to carry approximately 190 troops under cover, right to the shore by beaching the bows, ideally on a rising tide. It seems almost certain that the Hallams did indeed sail in five of this type which would have been just right to carry a whole infantry battalion. These craft had a displacement of 234/384 tons, 158 feet long by 23 feet wide and had a crew of twenty-four. They were powered by two diesel motors developing 1,440 B.H.P. and giving a speed of 14 knots. Armament was in the form of four, single 20mm MGs and two, single .303 inch MGs. Finally, they were of a normal shipshape with pointed bow, but these were scarped to allow troops direct forward access, from narrow gangways on either side, to the two steep ramps down to beach level. Dry landings depended on weather conditions, gradient of the shore line and how far the bows could be driven onto the beach.

Trevor Hart Dyke recalls that, on the strength of a predicted 'dry' landing, he and the others dispensed with the use of specially issued canvas trousers. He chose to be first ashore and sank up to his waist, soaked to the skin!

Arthur Green, who landed two days after the rifle companies, was with the transport and in a different type of vessel which embarked from the Thames. He could not remember the type or its name, only that it did have one...

Arthur Green...
I couldn't tell you the name of the ship we were on but eventually we had to be lifted into Tank Landing Craft (LCT). The vehicles were fitted with these special flanges on the wheels for hoisting by crane. With the swell and that, I thought they were going to damage the sump on my truck. It nearly hit the anchor that was strapped to the LCT. I thought, 'Good God, that anchor's going to go through the bloody sump next.' Anyway, I'm sweating like hell and we had to climb down into this here LCT and that's when your heart begins to thump. You can hear the shelling in the distance although they weren't shelling the beach. Then I thought, 'Let's hope your water proofing has been done right.'

The waterproofing referred to by Arthur was a special kit of parts applied to the military vehicles prior to embarkment which enabled them to be driven the distance between ships ramp and the Normandy beaches in the event of a so called 'wet landing' without the engines being 'drowned' in the shallow sea water. The kit consisted mainly of a waterproof material that had the consistency of 'plastercine' modelling clay wrapped around electrical parts and a special watertight extension tube to the carburetor which allowed the engine to 'breath'. The wet landing was achieved by selecting bottom gear and anything up to full throttle for the whole run from ships ramp to shore so as to have the best chance of preventing a stalled engine. Arthur remembered doing tests in a purpose-built water-trough near the sea front at Gorleston when the Battalion was based at Hopton.

Arthur Green...
There was this Yank in charge of the boat and he's sat on a little platform at the back and he hadn't a care in the world. He's got his head down into this Readers Digest and just sailing away towards the beach. Anyhow, when they lowered the ramp we rolled straight off onto a jetty and never even got me wheels wet!

Instructions were that the first thing you do on landing was to get your bonnet up and remove the waterproofing and this plastercine stuff was all over the place, you were knee deep in the damned stuff for about half a mile inland. Six days had gone by so things were quiet on the beach but we had to make for our allotted place in the Battalion assembly area which we did by following each other and the direction markers.

❖ *Part of 'Gold' Landing Beach at Ver-sur-Mer where the Hallams came ashore. The concrete ramp is considerably larger than the one constructed on the waters edge at Ardno, Loch Fyne.(DWS)*

Bert Murray (Rifle Coy.)...
I recall landing in Normandy on the 10th June, our landing craft missed all the obstacles and put its ramp right on the sand. Before we had time to cheer, the Padre, carrying only a prayer book, bounced down the ramp pushing us backwards and the rest of us with all our battle gear waded ashore. Apparently, there was a wager amongst the clerics of the Brigade as to who would be first in France.

Narrow lane used by the Hallams leading south from Ver sur Mer and the beaches which would eventually lead to Crepon and Rucqueville.(THD)

Arnold Whiteley...
There were one or two shells falling on the beaches here and there and men up against the sea wall. I don't know if you knew or not but we had a label tied onto us when we went over. It was a double label and one was taken away when you landed to prove that you'd crossed. Our landing was quite peaceful and we walked straight off the beach, across the road, and into Normandy.

The thing that sticks in my mind was this middle aged lady in a tweed costume and pushing a battered old bicycle. One of the lads jokingly said, 'Mademoiselle, how are you?' and she replied, 'Oh, I am much better now that you are here.' Then I saw the partly soil covered bodies with rifles stuck in the ground with helmets placed on top, you could see there'd been fighting. Then there was this French peasant in denims and wooden sandals who, for our benefit, started dancing on the dead bodies of some Germans who had been left uncovered.

The sands of 'Gold Beach' in front of Ver sur Mer had already been passed over by 50th (Tyne Tees) Infantry Division. These troops had already carried the raging battle well inland and left the beaches in a relative state of calm except for naval gunfire, some distant shelling, and the drone of mostly friendly aircraft overhead. The shore line, however, was strewn with all manner of disturbing wreckage and expendable equipment.

The following officers landed with the Battalion in Normandy...

Bn. Headquarters: Lieutenant-Colonel T. Hart Dyke (C.O.), Major J. H. Mott (2 i/c),
     Captain W. Ashby (Adjt.), Lieutenant C. A. G. Bedward (I.O.).
H.Q. Company : Captain W. R. Jenkinson (O.C.), Captain C. A. Mackillop (M.T.O.),
Lieutenants J. Wollerton (S. O.), A. F. Gibbs (Q.M.) and P. Turrell.
'A' Company : Major R. I. Slater (O.C.),Captain C. R. S. Sandford (2 i/c),
     Lieutenants H. E. Poyner and C. Nosieux (Canadian Army)
'B' Company : Major D. E. Lockwood (O.C.), Capt. P. M. Young (2 i/c),
     Lieutenants A. C. Somers, O. Watson-Jones and M. B. Elliott
'C' Company : Captain G. J. Good (O.C.), Captain L. M. Lonsdale-Cooper,
     Lieutenant G. H. R. Jackson
'D' Company : Major P. S. Newton (O.C.), Captain J. A. Nicholson, Lieutenants F. H. Tett,
     H. L. Morgan and F. J. Pearce (Canadian Army)
Support Company : Major J. Brinton (O.C.), Lieutenant D. A. Abbott
Carrier platoon   : Captain L. Gill, Lieutenant L. G. Sneath (Canadian Army)
Anti-Tank platoon : Captain A. B. Cowell, Lieutenant H. J. Birch
Pioneer Platoon   : Lieutenant P. H. Willis-Dixon
Attached   : Captain A. A. Gregory-Dean (M.O.), Captain H. S. G. Thomas (Chaplain).

Initial Battalion landings were made on 10 June to the east of Arromanche where preparations were being made to draw together the parts of a massive floating harbour which had been code named 'Mulberry'. The whole idea was based on the premise that if it could not be guaranteed to capture one of the nearby harbours like Cherbourg in reasonably usable condition and quickly, then the next best thing was to transport one from the British mainland! This was a monumental feat of engineering and one of the most daring and secret operations of the war, a one which could hardly have been envisaged by the German High Command. The very fact that no natural harbour existed along that stretch of the Normandy coast was reason in itself for the Germans not to expect a full scale invasion from that quarter and so there was delayed reaction to what was thought to be a lure from the main assault, more likely in the Pas de Calais. The whole plan, however, almost came to grief in a bad storm shortly after its installation at Arromanche and a similar artificial harbour, further west off the more exposed American beachhead, was so badly damaged in the same storm that it had to be abandoned.

❖ *The small village of Crepon was on route to Rucqueville from the beaches. It had already been passed through by the Green Howards a few days earlier although they had to take it by force. This fine memorial to their 6th and 7th Battalions was unveiled in 1996 and also commemorates the Victoria Cross award to Sgt. Major Stanley Hollis on 'D' Day, 6th June, 1944.(DWS)*

In the meantime things were not running too smoothly for the 49th Division as certain landings had not yet been completed. Divisional and Brigade Headquarters were still at sea, as was the Advance Party and Battalion transport. In their absence it was decided to deploy and move inland via a dispersed march by companies across the fields and byways. The Battalion arrived at their designated concentration area in the village of Rucqueville where Bn. HQ. was set up in some farm buildings with the men billeted in any buildings in the surrounding area that were available for their first night on French soil. Most, if not all, were able to sleep above ground in these early stages but would soon have to resort to digging slit trenches in the not too distant future and continue to do so for some considerable time to come.

Top : Aerial photograph taken shortly after the war of the farm buildings used as the first Bn. HQ. at Rucqueville. (THD) ❖*Below : Part of the outbuildings where David Lockwood may have written his first letters home. Little has changed today but often, French farms have that bare look of neglect. Two of the original six palms along the farm house front (seen in the above picture) survive, although no trace could be found of the fig tree mentioned by David Lockwood in his letter dated 12 June, below.(DWS)*

Ray Langdale...
We had a jeep and it was loaded with our kit plus a lot of small Divisional Signs with arrow heads and the drill was that I had to peg out the route from the beach to Battalion HQ. at Rucqueville. Then I was sent to a crossroad with a list of all the Battalion fighting and 'B' Echelon vehicles and tick them off as they arrived.

Les Gill...
Because he wanted his car sooner than anybody else would want a car, knowing him, the C.O. had it put aboard with my carriers at Tilbury. Our landing on the beaches was preceded by a German aircraft dropping a bomb on the sands in front of us where we were about to disembark. The ramp was lowered and the C.Os. car went out first into what was, initially, shallow water. As the car (believed to be a Humber Heavy Utility) approached the beach, it progressed into much deeper water. The driver, Cpl. Bertram, had to open the door and stand up with his head and shoulders out of the cab to keep above the water whilst keeping his left foot on the accelerator. It had to be abandoned and as a consequence, the C.O. often used one of my carriers.

We had a loading chart for every vehicle so in the carriers we had this, that and the other. However, on my carrier I also had to reserve a space for the C.O. because it was his second line of transport, especially with it having tracks. I occasionally put things into that particular space which was not on the loading chart. You could drink it! Without doubt, I do believe we were the first people to have a little noggin when we arrived over at the other side because I had it in the carrier.

Les Sewell... (may have landed later than most other transport - probably on 13/6)...
When we reached the beaches it was late on and we anchored off the beach. Next morning landing craft came alongside us and the trucks were hoisted over the side and we had to get down scrambling nets. When we came off the landing craft, the water came up to about the foot boards then we were guided well ashore and into a field where we had to take all our waterproofing off. We went via Bayeux and were directed to the area of St. Leger by some Redcaps who told us that the Hallams had just gone into the front-line near there. Along the road we eventually spotted our water truck driven by a Rotherham chap called Tucker and we followed him and finally reached the Battalion. The first chap I saw at carrier platoon was Fred Trigg (he was always called 'Jimmy'), a R.E.M.E. fitter, and he and some others were fiddling about with a German vehicle. Then I reported to Capt. Gill who sent me back to 'B' Echelon.

Prior to Les Sewells landing, the Hallams were still centered on Rucqueville and awaiting orders to move into the front line...

Roy Simon...
Somebody were talking about having a bath, and so they said, 'Oh Aye, there's some big tubs here,' and they got these women to boil this water up and fill these big tubs. Then somebody says, 'Aye! Officers first and then all t'other ranks'll have to get in amongt muck!' I discovered there were some girls hiding behind these bushes and heard them giggling. I never said nowt to anybody and just left it as it was - I didn't have a bath meself!

The War Diary for this period mentions the consumption by the Battalion of many hens eggs. The farm at Rucqueville may have been a collecting point or storage depot for German Army food supplies in that area. It is generally believed that the eggs had already been paid for by the Germans but were now resold to at least some of the Hallamshires by the French occupants of the farm.

Trevor Hart Dyke...
I had my Head Quarters at the farm and we found there was a large quantity of eggs which had been sold to the Germans and then, of course, the French wanted to sell them to us which we, having just landed, weren't very pleased about. We thought we might have been given them.

The price charged remains unknown but can only have amounted to pure profit. To this day the surviving veterans have remained, jokingly, unimpressed by the seeming ingratitude to men who were about to bleed heavily in an effort to liberate France. However, it must be said that feelings at the time may not have run very high as blood had yet to be drawn from the Hallamshires. Anyway, here was their first opportunity to spend some of the FF100 pocket money which had been issued to the men before they embarked. By a number of accounts, it would seem that not everybody had been issued with these French Francs and not everybody was having to pay for the eggs either!

It wasn't long before David Lockwood was able to put pen to paper and write home in his easy style that almost painted pictures with words. His first two letters set a tranquil scene in the midst of a typical Normandy countryside, but it was merely a brief calm before the storm which was about to swallow him and many others. The letters he wrote in the last few days of his life reveal much about a man who was very eager to play down the dangers for the benefit of his wife's peace of mind. He was, of course, very much aware of the real situation but still able to keep separate the two worlds in which he undoubtedly lived. The world most dear to him was the private one in which his wife Mary was the centre and made so obvious in the letters he wrote, the very personal side of which will not be found in these pages. The other world was his military one which had, up to now, only been an occasional hindrance in respect of keeping them apart. But now, as Trevor Hart Dyke had feared, it was about to become a terrible threat to this man who knew no other way to lead, save from the front!

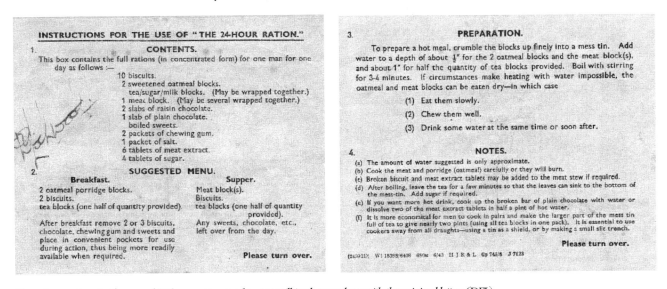

These instruction for the use of 24 hour ration packs were still in the envelope with the original letter. (DEL)

David Lockwood (Letters to Mary)
11 June, 1944 (Rucqueville, Normandy)...
Well, here we are sitting on a pile of hay (my bed) in the granary of a farm in France - yes I am allowed to say that - it seems hard to believe we're really here after all the months and weeks of waiting and anticipation but with a pocket full of francs and the locals talking French I suppose it must be true - and to my surprise I find I can make myself understood in my school French too!

Life seems to go on quite calmly here - the country people are friendly and seem pleased to see us - a fowl in the stable below has just laid an egg and there are two of the sweetest calves in a shed next door. The countryside is beautifully green and surprisingly English looking. The weather is just like our English summer, dull today with an occasional shower! - not too hot to wear a jacket at present.....

I finished my midday meal about an hour ago and South and I cooked it between us! I'm sending you a direction card out of one of our ration boxes as I thought it might amuse you and there's nothing secret about it as the whole thing was written up in the papers about a couple of months ago. The whole box is just a bit bigger than the paper and about two and a half inches deep and in that there are about 500 more calories than we eat in a normal day at home. The tea is surprisingly good also the porridge excellent but I can't say I enjoyed the 'meat block' which even with meat extract in, tasted more like straw than meat but I ate it because of its calories! The biscuits are like shortbread and contain butter in dried form. The whole thing is very cleverly done and we cook in our mess tins on a little folding stand which holds a special 'hexamine' fuel tablet, all of which plus water sterilizing tablets goes into a very small space. Nothing has been left to chance and like the whole of the rest of this colossal operation has been organized marvelously down to the last fine detail - most impressive. No one is going to tell me after this is over that the British are a nation of muddlers - but perhaps the Americans had a hand in this!!

Some 'very' fresh food was also available on site but this was still walking around! To get it in the pot required some additional effort on the part of Ken Godfrey and others.

Ken Godfrey...
I was chasing this chicken around and I'd got a big stick. There was a Cpl. there and somebody else and I whacked the chicken, missed it and hit the Cpl. right across the shins but we finally got there and he said to me, 'Go, pluck it!' I'd never plucked a chicken in my life so I hung it on a door and started on it. Just then, the door opened and there stood the Regimental Police and I thought, 'Well, I've had it now'... 'What you doing?' 'Mm, I,m, I'm'.... 'Right! you better send some down to us then!' Anyway, we used the old 'Benghazi' stove, you know, with sand and petrol in a big tin can. Then we got a biscuit tin with some water, found some green potatoes and stuffed them all in with the chicken and had something to eat.

David Lockwood (Letters to Mary)
12 June, 1944 (Rucqueville, Normandy, France)...
It's a gorgeous day here and I've just had a huge lunch of pork and veg. stew (tinned) and marmalade pudding (tinned) both excellent and your Ted is now very fat, full and comfy! It's incredibly peaceful here apart from artillery (ours) and the eternal noise of planes (also ours) and most of my boys are asleep this afternoon. 'La belle France' is certainly looking 'tres belle' today - wonderfully green. Chris, Tommy (Padre) and I have been lying on a ridge above here before lunch in the sun with the larks singing over a marvelous field of green wheat - not at all my original idea of the 'Second Front!' - and I fancy it's not what you are thinking I'm doing either - but I told you war was like that didn't I!

Went out in a jeep this a.m. with Trevor, Ivor, Peter and Gordon, and I drove - very funny to be driving on the right hand side of the road and I found myself wondering which way to go every time anything came in the opposite direction - however, with a jeep having a left hand steering wheel it does make it easier.

Mike on his bed of hay in the corner has just woken up from an afternoon nap and sends his love to you and Ben. George also is asleep. Poor old Chris is having a shocking time with hay fever and is having to hang out his hankies today!

We do awfully well for choc and boiled sweets on these rations of ours which suits me as you can imagine!....... ....whenever I look at boiled sweets I always think of you and Billie - and of him saying, 'Like a sweet - like one ! like one !' etc. etc. etc. and so on until he gets one!

Tommy took a rather nice short service in the company area yesterday evening and gave a very good little talk to us when he said something I thought I'd pass on to you my darling for what you think it's worth. He said that he knew we should be asking God to look after our wives and families during these months to come while we are away but, he said, ...'having done that, don't then start worrying about them because if you do it is as if you snatch away the care of your family from God when you have already asked him to look after them.' I thought that was rather good and that it also applied to you worrying about me, my love - don't you think it does ?

We're in shirt sleeves today and everyone is getting very brown - the sun is absolutely brilliant outside and I can almost watch the figs getting bigger on the tree up the stone wall opposite. A couple of swallows have got into our loft here and are twittering round my head. In the yard below the farmer is just feeding a couple of calves in a shed and they're asking for more - his wife is there too, a fairly heavy-weight in a large blue dress and sabots - it's all incredibly like the pictures in the French books at school of 'La Ferme' - you know the sort of picture with as many objects crammed into it as possible for you to learn the names!
P.S. I forgot to tell you we got lashings of fresh eggs and milk here thrust upon us by the locals . I gather the Boche had collected eggs in this area here for the past few weeks to send to Germany but the consignment never went so we are having them instead!!

The people mentioned in the above letter were *Chris* (Somers), *Tommy* (Padre Thomas), *Trevor* (Hart Dyke), *Ivor* (Slater), *Peter* (Newton) and *Gordon* (Good), the last three being Coy. Commanders at that time, like David himself. The man he refers to as *'George'* is Watson-Jones although this officers Christian name in Commonwealth War Graves Commission records is stated as Oliver! It can only be that *'George'* was a nickname given him by his close friends. Chris Somers also uses that name in his diary.

Most of the 146th Brigade transport had disembarked by the 13th and a decision was now made to move into the front line where the 50th Division were badly in need of relief. The Hallams approached from the direction of St. Leger and moved into woods between the villages of Loucelles and Ducy St. Marguerite where they took over that part of the line being held by the 6th Bn. Green Howards (The Yorkshire Regiment). These and other 50th Division troops had done well since their early morning landings on 'D' Day, 6th June. Fighting as they had done, from the minute they hit the beaches, it could be said that they had attempted far more than should have been expected of them. However, the situation was now such that a weakened 50th Division had fallen back from their most recent gains leaving a lot of ground unoccupied and in a state of flux, which the Hallams and others would now have to retake. This situation was one that the opposing forces could and did take advantage, in the way of consolidation and in the exploitation and selection of good sniper positions. The so called Bocage type of hedgerow (field boundaries formed by earthen banks topped by hedge which left many of the narrow lanes apparently sunken) were almost designed for the latter activity in that they afforded good cover for movement and retreat.

Roy Simon remembered this early period moving into ready dug trenches during the changeover where 6th Green Howards of the 50th Division withdrew through the Hallams Lines.

Roy Simon...
They were saying, 'We're glad to get out of this lot!' and then one looked at me and said, 'It's Roy Simon isn't it?' I said, 'Ay!' and it was a lad called Morris, Harold Morris. He said, ' Remember Ronnie Atkins?' and I said, 'Ay! I ought to do, I went to school with him.' and he said, 'He's just got killed.'

Meanwhile, back at 'B' Echelon...

Arthur Green...
On a misty morning, a day or two after arrival, I'd just got back from Bn.HQ. to 'B' Echelon and was stood on top of the truck canopy (tilt) fixing me camouflage netting and there was suddenly a hell of a rattle of machine guns, anti-aircraft guns banging away and I thought, 'What the hell's this?' Directly above us came these two Gerry aircraft and by the time I saw them, they'd gone! I reckon they were recce planes because the next day that orchard had been shelled heavily and there was hardly a tree left standing. Luckily, we'd already moved out of there!

The Hallams were now required to advance in a southerly direction towards the village of Audreiu over ground that had obviously already been fought over but which now needed to be retaken. In some places, the 50th Division had in fact advanced much further than their present front line but had fallen back in the wake of German counter attacks, leaving many of their dead behind. The dead from both sides lay strewn around in this unoccupied area awaiting recovery and the normal procedure of temporary burial until later placement in a proper Military Cemetery. It seems doubtless that at least some of those men whose names appear on the Bayeux Memorial to the Missing were 'lost' in this way. However, it should be said that many of those men declared 'missing in action' are to be found lying in Commonwealth War Graves containing unidentified remains with headstones that contain the simple phrase, 'A Soldier of the Second World War'.

Left : Audreiu Railway Station shortly after the war (looking towards Caen). The Hallams were in the fields on the left side of the track and crossed it to move into the village on the right to make their first contact with the German Army. No opposition was met in the village itself. (THD)

❖ *Right : View from platform looking towards Bayeux today. All the buildings are gone and the track has been electrified. The station has the appearance of being little used except, perhaps, by commuters to the two cities. (DWS)*

Roy Simon...

Then they said, 'Right we're moving,' and we started to move up the side of this field and we had the Pl. Commander with us, 2/Lt. Bendall. We used to call him 'Nodder' and he had a little moustache and he were only small but he were all right. Anyway we walked up this field on a cart track and then a bloke says to me, 'Look at all them Gerries there,' and I turned round and looked and I said, 'Are you colour blind?' and he says 'Why?' and I says, 'Them are not field grey uniforms, they're khaki.' Then we stopped a minute as Bendall went over to have a look at them. They were Green Howards and they were all dead. One were a Sergeant and I'll never forget him and he were sat there and the top of his trousers had been ripped and he had a bandage wrapped

Left : The Hallams walk through the village of Audrieu, unopposed, but they were about to see some action on the east side where their first casualties were suffered. A few hundred yards further up the road, they would come to the Chateau Audrieu.(IWM)
❖*Right : This is the same place today but, due to a great deal of rebuilding work, hardly recognizable. Even the roof structures have been reworked and are now set at much steeper angles. (DWS)*

round and he was sat there, nothing supporting, with his hands up and smiling. I said, 'Excuse me sir, can I go and have a look at that Sergeant?, I think I know him!' and I went and looked at him and it was a Sergeant that was at Richmond (where Roy had done his basic training). There were about seven or eight of them lying dead together.

We then turned left down the side of this wood and Ronnie Coulson and I later recalled an incident that we thought very dangerous at the time. Lt. Bendall came down and we were walking down the side of this wood looking into it and there were three Gerries, dead! Two of them were sat up and one crouched down and Bendall says, 'Just a minute' and climbed over this fencing and went to where these blokes were. Now one of these chaps who was sat up against a tree was equivalent to a Sgt. Maj. in our army was holding the stump of his leg with a pad in his interlaced fingers. Then Bendall took his knife out and clipped his epaulettes off and put them in his pocket. We said to him he shouldn't have done that because there might have been some mines there.

On the 14th June, having crossed a railway track (connecting Bayeux with Caen) near a small station that served the local villages, the Hallams began a move to clear Audrieu which was taken without a shot being fired. However, contact was made with the enemy in woods and fields just east of the village.

Roy Simon...
We went down into this village (Audrieu) and I remember marching through t'street and there were Gerry dead all over the place. They just looked as though they had been assembling up and

the artillery had caught them and they really did look bad. I remember one chap who did stand out in my mind and whatever had hit him... He didn't seem to have a mark on his body but his body was crushed right in and his head was as flat as a pancake... oh! he did look bad and I just kind of flipped him from my mind.

Chris Somers (Diary)...
The next day 'C' & 'D' Coys. cleared Audrieu, not meeting any opposition till they were through the village. Here we suffered our first casualty. Lt. Tett was shot when advancing across a field and killed. Poor old Frank - he always said he would be the first casualty in the Battalion. The same day we moved up into Audrieu and got our first sight of dead corpses - Germans thank goodness - lying here and there up the main street. Unpleasant sights too as they had been lying there for a few days and the air around was not exactly pleasant. I always wondered how these gruesome sights would affect me at first. Perhaps my mind was too preoccupied because they hardly registered and one was glad to think that they were a few less Germans to kill.

It was at this time that the Hallams suffered their first Officer fatality when Lt. Frank H. Tett was killed just to the east of Audrieu during a sweep from west to east to clear that area. This officer was blind in one eye but still accompanied the Battalion into action in Normandy even though such a disability might well have excused him from such front line duties. He was on patrol with his platoon when he was hit by small arms fire and fell back into a ditch from which he had just emerged.

Arnold Whiteley...
I wasn't a witness but evidently he was shot with a bullet and he wasn't killed. If he'd have stayed down he'd have been all right but he got up and started ploughing forwards saying, 'Come on lads,' and they got him second time.

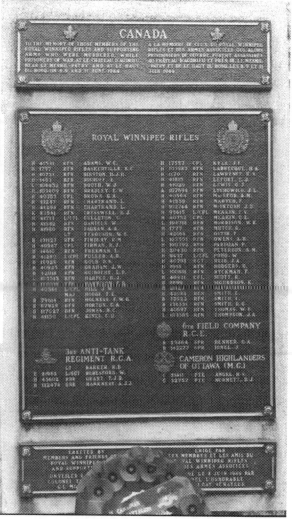

❖ *Chateau Audrieu and the memorial plaque (50 yards to the north of the main entrance) commemorating the lives of 66 Canadian soldiers who died here and elsewhere. As far as is known, all of the men listed here were killed after capture in contravention to the rules of war prevailing. Those people responsible were duly tried at Nuremberg after the war, where the Hallams Padre Thomas gave evidence. These were not the only soldiers to be 'murdered' in war and many died on both sides - after capture! It is strange that mankind has imparted such special rules of chivalry to screen the brutal act of killing his fellow man in war, no matter which side of capture it occurs. (DWS)*

196

This account of fearless determination is echoed in David Lockwoods mention of Frank in a letter of the 19th June. This early period would prove deadly for many of the men as they slowly learned the habit of keeping heads down and out of sight from very accurate sniper fire.

Chris Somers (Diary)...
The next morning (15th) after spending the night in shallow slit trenches in a field - 'B' Coy. was to do their first minor attack. David went forward with the C.O. to recce and I followed with the Company. We sat waiting in a narrow shell torn lane - the time seemed to drag - we made fatuous remarks to one another and laughed. An easy disguise to the fear that was within us - my throat felt as dry as a bone. Then suddenly there came a burst of firing from up the lane where the recce party had gone. They returned with some speed apparently as they found that our start line, to be, was a forward German Coy. HQ. and had nearly run into a German sentry!

The farm behind Chateau d'Audrieu which was occupied by part of 'B' Coy. on the night of 15 June, 1944.(THD)

The northerly end of the village of Audrieu was not far from the railway station mentioned above. At the other end of the village stood the Chateau d'Audrieu around which the Hallams spent the night of the 15th and in the grounds of which Pte. Colin King (recce platoon) discovered the bodies of 14 O.Rs. of the Canadian Army who had been tied, lined up and shot through the head. It may be remembered that it was this man, also, who had discovered the wreckage of the crashed Fairey Battle in Iceland.

Ray Langdale...
The lads were scrounging around the Chateau when Colin King found these Canadians. Then he fetched Tom O'Connor and they both came for me. I went back to have a look and all their pockets had been emptied, their paybooks, letters and what have you were scattered about and I don't think there were many of them with any boots on. They'd taken their boots off. The padre was eventually brought and I understand that it was he who later gave evidence in the war crimes trials.

These murdered Canadian soldiers were reported in the Battalion War Diary as belonging to the Regina Rifles but in fact were subsequently identified as men of the Royal Winnipeg Rifles. They were not the only Canadian Troops to be killed in this way as others were later found buried in the grounds of the Chateau and elsewhere. It would seem that this place, a HQ. of the 12th S.S. Recce Bn., was also used for a very short period as a place of interrogation and execution until its very early capture by the allies.

A much more recent Canadian casualty was that of Lt. C. Noiseux, a French speaking officer on so called 'Can-loan' to the Hallams with his obvious interpretive skills. He was killed in action on the 15th when taking part in an attack with 'A' Coy. on woods to the east of Audrieu. Cpl. John William Payne was also killed, the first Hallamshire Battalion non-commissioned man to die in the Normandy Campaign, and Sgt. Wheelhouse was wounded. The next day Capt. C.R.S. Sandford was wounded when his Jeep ran over a mine. The practice of lining vehicle cab floors with sand bags no doubt saved his life but his injuries were still bad enough to require the amputation of one foot.

Chris Somers (Diary)...

My platoon was situated that night in a walled in kitchen garden with the corpses of the Canadians on one side of us and a pile of dead animals in the farm yard on the other. The air was foul to the extreme and I didn't find tinned meat very easy to consume! Some chaps in the Coy. found a lot of champagne and got a bit tight, I believe I could have done with a bit myself! One of my platoon got a bit jumpy and kept on imagining men jumping over the wall which rather aggravated me because I had to keep going to check up with the other platoon in that area.

The Hallams were now required to advance further south where Bn. positions were centered on a place called Le Haut Audrieu. It was during this period that plans were being finalized for an attack on Fontenay le Pesnel and a feature beyond called Tessel Wood which was all part of a much bigger operation code named 'EPSOM'. This was to be a major push forward in an effort to encircle and capture the stubbornly held city of Caen.

Chris Somers (Diary)...

Next day we moved up to Haute Audrieu for what was intended to be a Battalion attack on Fontenay. When David came back from the recce with this story that we had to cross a long forward open slope in full view of the enemy, my heart sank into my boots. However, we began forming up on the start line among the cornfields on that hot summer afternoon. Scattered here and there amongst the corn were the dead bodies of the gallant men of 50 Div. who lay where they had fallen in an abortive attack. The legs of dead cows and horses could also be seen all over the place pointing stiffly skywards.

We lay on the start line waiting for the word 'Go'. It is hard to describe the agonies which ones mind goes through during that time of waiting - though it wore off as one became more experienced. My throat became parched and I became drowsy and practically dozed off lying there in the sun. However, a few mortar bombs and snipers bullets soon awoke us to the fact that this attack was going to be no picnic. However, in the nick of time it was suddenly called off and we were saved from what I'm sure would have been a very disastrous attack. 'B' Coy. consolidated round the ruins of a nearby farmhouse and dug in, Coy. HQ. being situated in a large barn with a thin slate roof. Just as well nothing hit it!

We spent a few days here patrolling and preparing for a real attack on Fontenay. Luckily we didn't get stonked in our Company area though some moaning minnies fell right on the Battalion HQ. just behind us and burned out the signal truck. The gunners had set up an O.P. well forward overlooking Fontenay, so I went out to visit them once or twice. Maj. Hudson very kindly put down some air burst for me on what I considered a likely enemy playground. I did my first patrols in this area, luckily a very easy one - merely to patrol down to the edge of Fontenay so that I could recognize landmarks during the attack itself

I took a L/Cpl. and Pte. with me. The Pte. turned out to be a bad choice as he appeared unduly windy and breathed too heavily! We stole down in the darkness through the open cornfield. A shell landing short just to our right was the first thing that made us jump! Then as we got down near the bottom of the valley we heard something coming towards us through the corn. We lay flat on the ground, it came nearer and I could see a dim shape in the darkness looked like at least six Boche. The movements stopped just in front of us. Had they seen us? The shapes then dropped to the ground as well. I crept forward to see what was what. It was only a horse!!

Things were not going too smoothly for some contingents operating in the vicinity of the Hallams. Although 1/4 K.O.Y.L.I. had fought a very tough but successful clearance of the village at Cristot, the 6th D.W.R. received a bloody nose when taking over positions from another unit during attempts to take a feature called Parc de Boislonde, a little further south. This move had barely been completed when a massive shell and mortar attack was put in by the Germans followed by a counter attack which overran D.W.R. forward platoons and drove a number of others to withdraw from their positions. Many of these men poured through the Hallams lines and also through the supporting guns of 185 Field Regt. R.A. (70 Bde.) which must have been somewhat disturbing! In recent years a letter sent to Arthur Green by a man from this artillery unit, who witnessed the occurrence, said that his C.O. had drawn his revolver when calling on infantrymen to return to their lines but to no avail. It must be said that the 6 D.W.R. (147 Bde.) suffered such high casualties in this action that the unit was shortly afterwards withdrawn from the line and replaced by the 1st Bn. Leicestershire Regt. It has been said in the past that it was left to the 7 D.W.R., a part of the same 147 Brigade, to uphold the 'honour' of the Duke of Wellington's Regiment by retaking the position. However, it can hardly be claimed that any honour had been lost simply because a group of men were unable to hold ground against overwhelming odds. Advance and withdrawal are elements in all wars but some of the latter are strangely frowned upon if not carried out in a planned and orderly way. The 'honour' of 6 D.W.R. will be found to be well upheld in the nearby Military Cemeteries.

David Lockwood (Letters to Mary)
19 June, 1944 (Le Haut Audrieu, Normandy)...
At last there seems to be a reasonable chance of being able to write you a decent letter but I mustn't speak too soon, one never knows what the next hour will bring and life is full of surprises and changes!

...Who do you think joined us last night as a reinforcement - Jack Firth! - also a subaltern of ours called Mitchinson. Jack has gone to 'A' Coy. as 2i/c to Ivor as poor old Dick Sandford went over a mine in a truck and we're afraid he'll lose his left leg - he's probably in England by now....

Above : A poor but the only picture of Le Haute Audrieu from the same series taken in the early post war period. It was here where David Lockwood wrote his last letters. (THD)

.....Ivor has scratched his nose on some barbed wire and is going about with a large piece of plaster down his dial!
We've had a bit of bad luck with subalterns in the opening stages and Frank Tett and Noiseux (a French Canadian whose wife had presented him with twins only a couple of weeks before) have both been killed. It was always sort of V.C. or nothing with Frank you know.
I'm in a big stone barn with nice clean straw on the floor and chaps who've been up all night sleeping all around me - Chris is just at my feet and John Brinton who has called in for an hours peace from Bn. HQ. is on my 'bed' in the corner - I picked a place where there were no holes in the roof!

THD (Trevor Hart Dyke) is certainly much more human and I think he'll make it now - he came down to see me yesterday evening to have a chat and told me the Brigadier (who is very quick tempered too) had sacked him in the heat of the moment the day before yesterday but had come round the next day to apologize - what a party!! I must say THD has done very well up to now and

I think one or two spells of good honest 'wind up' which we've all had, has mellowed him a good deal.

...I've got Chris as 2i/c at the moment but THD rang up this morning to say he is sending me Bill Ashby which I'm glad about. Bill hasn't been much of an Adjutant but he's the right type for a rifle Coy. and should be a great asset. Anyway, it's a great weight off my mind that I've got an active and sound 2i/c again... ...they took Phil Young away from me for a special job as soon as we got over here though he's still with the Battalion. George Watson-Jones is turning out all right - I thought he would.

This farm we are in now has been deserted by the inhabitants but all the livestock is still here and even the dogs and cats - the yard is full of fowls and ducks and geese some of which have come to a sticky end already I'm afraid and are now in the pot. I had new potatoes for supper last night which the Frog Boy had dug up and cooked himself - lovely.

The last place we were in was a chateau (must have been Chateau d'Audreiu) or rather in its grounds, and there I had some of the best strawberries I've ever had ! Their kitchen garden was the finest I've ever seen... ...this chateau was a wonderful spot though the war had knocked a lot of holes in it unfortunately. The owner must have had a packet of money and the furniture was lovely. The scene inside was of indescribable confusion and the people must have left in a hurry because everything was left - even washing in the laundry. The smells are so interesting too - I noticed an extremely naughty perfume, probably Chanel, in one room. The house itself was magnificent - what we should call a Hall in England, not a castle - built on three sides of a square just two storeys high and the walls stuccoed white - lovely big windows and a wonderful air about the whole place. I gather the owner was a Baron and I'm sorry for him when he sees his house again. His wife's furs are full of plaster dust and his best glass is smashed. How I hate the sight of war !

This is reminiscent of similar feelings for 'owners' that David had, on discovering a damaged cottage near Kames in Scotland during training. As for the damaged mansion found here in France, he could never have guessed that the man he imagined to be a 'Baron' and owner of the Chateau d'Audreiu was at that very moment serving as a Navigator with the Royal Air Force. This man was to become an almost legendary figure on both sides of the Channel for his exploits during the war. Squadron Leader Philippe Livry-Level received awards of the D.S.O., D.F.C. and Bar besides decorations from his own country and the U.S.A. His story is well worth reading in 'The Times' dated 19th and 22nd of December, 1960, which contains further references.

David Lockwood (Letters to Mary)
20 June, 1944 (Le Haut Audrieu, Normandy)...
I've just written a note to Fred Neill to thank him for the 2000 razor blades that arrived yesterday in the nick of time before everyone started growing a beard as of course the N.A.A.F.I. isn't with us yet... ...Had a letter from Dobbie (Major Dobson the old QM) too, who said he was thinking about us all and wishing he was with us - wish he was.

One of the farm dogs who refuses to leave - a sort of white Setter - is doing a lot of barking outside. Poor things, they do hate the guns but I think they're getting used to them now. The farmer returned today to fetch some bedding in a handcart and was rather distressed to find that a lot of his fowls had disappeared. I knew that the lads had had some of them so we had a whip round and raised 400 francs which sounds a lot of money but actually is £2 ! However, the farmer seemed satisfied.....

Bill Ashby arrived with me last night and is certainly a tremendous asset and has already taken a tremendous load off your idle husband! It's such a joy to be able to give an order and know that it will be carried out and not be wondering all the time whether things are all right as I was latterly...

Dunlop, by the way, has had a nervous breakdown as a result of the past ten days when I gather he never went to bed (quite unnecessary) and has departed. Johnnie Walker has taken his place and should be very good we think.
It's certainly a healthy life this and we feed awfully well - the most delicious tinned treacle puddings are my favourite that really stick to your ribs! I eat like a horse here.

Jesse Mitchinson...
All the time we were sent out on patrols, probing forward so as to gain information about the enemy. I remember going out on my very first one around Audrieu and I was told where to go and what compass bearing to use but foolishly, didn't trust my compass. I knew better than my compass! I remember cattle lying around that had been killed and all blown up with gas and then being completely lost. Everybody relies on you even if you're only a junior officer so they followed me and we eventually came out near some 25 Pdr. Royal Artillery lines. In the end we got to our own lines where I was debriefed but didn't tell the whole truth. We'd fulfilled our purpose but not quite in the way that had been instructed.

We were dug in and every morning between about five and six o'clock, we were stonked by Nabelwerfers (multi-barrelled mortar projectors). They were dead on time every morning and one of these mortars burst into a tree in our lines and there were cries from some men who had been hit. I went over to where this happened and found one of these men with splinters of wood all over his face just like blackheads, no other physical injuries, just these pieces of wood. He was the first casualty suffered in my platoon.

Bad weather that damaged the artificial harbour also caused delays in the landing of supplies needed to continue the advance and this in turn delayed the offensive for a few days. Although this gave the 49th Division time for a breather and in some willing cases, a much needed bath, it was also allowing its German opponents to reinforce their own positions which were now just south of the road Tilly - Caen and centered on a village called Fontenay le Pesnel. This place was about to become very much a part of Hallamshire Battalion history.

David Lockwood (Letters to Mary)
22 June, 1944 (Le Haut Audrieu)...
Yesterday was a gala day - I had a hot shower! Wilfred Tyzacks boys are in an ex - German billet and the Boche had installed showers for his chaps with a boiler. John Brinton, Peter Turrell (now Adjutant) and I went down and mucked in with the troops in an incredibly steamy, smelly room with a wet muddy floor of tiles. It was absolutely marvellous to feel clean again...   ...then in the evening Tommy came down and gave us a Communion Service which I found most soothing - the one thing that remains the same as home in a very strange world.

There is a sweet little goat kid in this farm which trots about just like the Welsh Regiment's mascot at the Northern Command Tattoo. It has two priceless little horns about a couple of inches long and is a great pet with the lads. They do love playing with animals. Ben would love chasing it around.

The following letter is the last written by David Lockwood, a man with only one more full day of his life to live. For reasons in addition to family grief, the loss of such people as David Lockwood could be ill afforded by this country and, together with the carnage of two World

Wars during the 20th century, has cost us very dearly. In future studies those wars may yet prove to have been far more damaging than this once great country could bear and from which it never did, nor ever will recover. Those finest hours are long past.

David Lockwood (Letters to Mary)
23 June, 1944 (Les Hauts Audrieu)...

My very Dearest One
Just as I thought! after saying I hadn't heard from you since you got home, I got a letter this morning written the day after you arrived, bless you!... ...I was afraid it would be a bit of a wrench for you leaving Hopton when the time came darling, I know just how you'd feel. As you say I don't think we've ever been happier anywhere together and I do feel we were so awfully lucky.

I did love that room of ours so, didn't you? As I told you in an earlier letter, having you there just made all the difference to my life and changed it from mere existence to a colourful, happy time with someone always to look forward to. I shall always remember Hopton with you as very happy days and so different from the early days at Hopton before you arrived. We had our ups and downs of course as is only natural with a war in the background but apart from the inevitable bombshells we always expected, how very, very happy we were... ...I do feel that it is such a good sign for the future for us and our young family - we shall always live happily together now, I know that so well, and I do feel we've got so many happy years before us with Ben and Susan (?) - Ben is such fun and Susan is bound to be - I should love to have a girl who was like you, angel - but if it turned out to be a boy, I should be equally happy as I feel Ben would love a brother.

❖ *One of a number of buildings belonging to the group known as Les Hautes Vents. It was from here that the Battalion moved onto the start line for the attack on Fontenay le Pesnel. Barking dogs still abound here but this one played a passive role for the cameraman (author) and made no advances (see letter dated 20 June) (DWS)*

It's a glorious day today with warm sun and I've got my pullover off for the first time for four days. I took Bill Ashby and my platoon commanders out this p.m. for a bit of a look round us and apart from the occasional shell burst the country looked extremely peaceful with its thick woods and very green fields. Cattle were still grazing in no-mans-land but no one comes to milk them - except our lads! Some of the cattle have been killed by shellfire or bullets and lie stiff on their sides, smelling appalling - there has been much burying done lately, thank God. At some farms we have found calves tethered and horses too, and in some cases pigs, rabbits and goats shut up and all without water for some time. We release them and turn them loose as there's plenty of water about and plenty to eat. But some of the horses have been pretty dangerous as the poor devils were so thirsty. However, I haven't seen any animals that have died naturally or from thirst yet so I think we've been in time. The farmers must have left in panic in a great hurry, and there's no doubt that a running fight must have surged inland for many miles on 'D' Day and the day after. The difference now of course is that what we have we hold as opposed to a general mix up of both sides in the early days.

We're having a very welcome pause in the proceedings just now and we and the lads are getting lots of sleep and are all in very good form. Morale is grand - I've never known it better - far better than it was in training days in England. Of course the rations are jolly good and the weather now, so what more could you wish on this side of the Channel !

Dinner has just arrived in the barn from the cider vat room opposite which is our cookhouse. Time, quarter to six. You'll be thinking of putting Billie to bed now and perhaps he'll be looking at Quillo's on your knee or splashing you in the bath. Did he remember Gang-gang and Dad-dad ? Just had dinner - jolly good ! Steak and kidney stew and very spicy date pudding - all tinned of course. We are not on bread yet as the appointed time for the field bakery to get going hasn't come yet but the biscuits we have instead are very good.

Thinking about my letter to you yesterday, I'm afraid it may have been a bit gloomy - I think it was the weather and that I was wanting a letter from you - rather a teeny ! - but now your letter has come and it's sunny I'm fine again. I find letters make such a difference. Let me say quickly, no one else had had any mail for a day or two - it wasn't that you hadn't written, bless you!

We do very well for papers and got Mondays London papers today (Friday). Just been listening to the 6 o'clock news and wondered if you were listening too. Knowing Brookdean, expect you had to!! Hope my letters are reaching you all right, my love.

Tell me all your news however small it may seem to you - I do so long to hear about you and Ben. All my love to you both and big kisses and a hug for my own darling one - I love you so,

x x x x x x x x x x x   Ted.

Operation 'EPSOM' was the first large scale offensive to be mounted following the costly establishment of a broad foothold off the Normandy beaches. Its mission was to smash through German defences to the West of Caen, thus affording an anti clockwise encirclement of this stubbornly held city. Various contingents of VIII Corps were chosen to provide the initial muscle with its central thrust based on Cheux which was meant to eventually bridge the rivers Odon and Orne in the intended movement. General Montgomery was, perhaps unwittingly, only just pre-empting a massive planned German counter attack designed to drive the Allies back into the sea just as soon as a number of armoured divisions arrived by rail from the Russian Front and elsewhere. However, on the 25th June, the Hallams front was opposed by elements of the Panzer Leher Division (a much depleted unit through earlier fighting) and the 12thSS (Hitler Youth) Division. The latter were slightly to the left of the Hallams front line but it became necessary for some 12thSS armoured vehicles to become involved in the Panzer Leher area in the next few days.

Much has been written about the 12th S.S. (Hitler Youth) Division including that story of some of its members being issued with sweets instead of cigarettes in field rations on account of their low age. Never let it be said, however, that the Allies were opposed by children. These people were well trained and perhaps even more eager to prove their worth in battle than most. Weapons are just as deadly in the hands of the young and these people gave a good account of themselves, much to the cost of the Hallamshires and others.

Part of the main task was to take and hold the small village of Fontenay le Pesnel and the high ground which lay immediately to its south. This was entrusted to the 49th Division and supporting units now poised and ready to strike from higher ground to the north. Fontenay lies in a depression hemmed into the 'Y' fork of two converging roads, one from Tilly ser Suelles and the other from Juvigny, both to the west. Control of these roads, which met at the eastern end of the village and continued as a single road to Caen, was vital. The lowest points of the village are traced by a stream which enters the village from the south via a bridge under the Juvigny road and then turns westwards, winding through the older half of the village.

❖ *View of Fontenay le Pesnel from a position that may be just a little forward of the original Form Up Point (FUP) that was laid out with guidance tapes early on the morning of Sunday, 25 June, 1944. The Caen - Tilly road runs from left to right and just this side of the water tower. Most of the village is hidden from view because it lies in a depression. It can be seen that no attack would have succeeded across this open ground in broad daylight. The results would have been even more devastating for the Hallams and other troops advancing. Trees on the right horizon are part of the feature known as Tessel Wood which was to become very familiar to the Hallams during the next three weeks. (DWS)*

The Hallams were assigned this western half of the village and would be required to cross the stream and both roads mentioned in order to reach their first objectives. These objectives were to take and hold orchards and farm buildings immediately to the south of the Juvigny road. The 11 R.S.F. and the 4 Lincs were to advance in the same manner on left and right flank of the Hallams respectively. The 1/4 K.O.Y.L.I. were to move up in support and later pass through the Hallams so as to take and hold the North end of a feature called Tessel Wood.

Chris Somers (Diary)...
Everything was now set for the attack on Fontenay early next morning. It was my unfortunate luck to have to spend all the night sitting out with a standing patrol in the now familiar cornfield, to ensure that no Boche patrols interfered with Jerry Bedward the I.O., who was taping the start line for the attack. It was cold and damp lying in an open field all night, made all the more unpleasant by the thoughts of the impending attack and the realization that I should get no breakfast before it!

From the assembly point at Le Haut Vents, those companies designated for the assault moved forward to the start line tapes which had been laid down earlier by a team under the command of Lt. C.A.G. Bedward (I.O.). It was 03.15 hrs on Sunday, 25 June and still dark at the Form up Point (FUP). The men had been ordered to place their white hand towels in a trapped condition under the flap of their small packs with a part of it hanging down at the back. This would enable each man to be easily recognized from the rear by other members of the unit and hopefully prevent casualties through mistaken identity.

> This was reminiscent of similar practice adopted during the Great War when special coloured patches were stitched onto the collars and back panels of tunics for the same purpose. (As a matter of interest, all ranks of the Hallamshires in that war had worn a small red rectangular patch on the back collar with an additional similar sized and shaped white patch just below on the back panel worn by officers).

If the men had been stood there in daylight they would have been gazing down open, gently sloping fields to the Tilly-Caen road with the village of Fontenay beyond but partially obscured by the fact the it lies in a hollow. They would certainly have seen the spire of St. Aubin's church which was centred on the objective by the second road (Juvigny-Caen) and beyond that, the rising ground towards Tessel Wood on the horizon about a couple of miles away. This battle was going to be bad enough in terms of casualties but a daylight advance (which had been intended a few days earlier) down this open, forward slope would have been disastrous.

John Swift...
I was the Forward O.P. Wireless Operator with 'F' Troop, 69th Field Regiment (25 Pounders) supporting the Hallamshires. I would be there with an officer in the advanced positions taking notes of the co-ordinates of wherever an attack was going to go in so we had a much better idea of what was happening than the rest of the soldiers. We would direct fire for our 25 Pounders but if the battle was so heavy, you could ask for further and heavier guns to be trained on the area. In the case of Fontenay, a large number of enemy tanks were concentrated there and the officer asked for additional support for a 'Victor' target which was the code that could call on additional fire power from much bigger guns which included those of the monitor H.M.S. 'Roberts' in the Channel. You knew when those shells came over because they made a noise like no other, a sort of sucking noise that created a vacuum!

Chris Somers (Diary)...
At about 0345 hrs the heavies and mediums opened up on the German rear positions and about quarter of an hour later, I withdrew back to the start line. The companies were all lined up ready as far as one could see in the dim half light of a misty morning. I quickly joined my platoon just as the word to advance was given at 0415 hours - Zero Hour. This was the 49 Div. first full-scale attack and the forward battalions were lined up in extended order, three paces or so between each man. The 4 Lincs were immediately to the right of my platoon and 'B' and 'C' were our forward companies. This was at last my first real attack. What awaited us down at the bottom of that valley? Down came our close supports barrage about 100 yards to our front. We advanced up to it, paused for it to lift another 100 yards then on slowly again. The noise was deafening.

Whatever my feelings as we advanced down the hill, they were soon forgotten as I realized that my platoon was splitting in half. The right trying to keep in touch with the Lincs and the left with the centre of the Coy. One gun firing short immediately to our front was also causing a bit of annoyance as this part of the line tended to hold back a bit.

We were now entering a thick mist and in my last attempt to get my right hand section to move across to the left a bit, I suddenly found myself completely and utterly alone. My first attack and I have lost my platoon! Keeping my direction from the barrage I plunged on into the thick mist and suddenly bumped into Cpl. Neal with my batman Hanson and a few others. I made them stick in close single file behind me, while I tried my compass. It was too wet and misty to read it though, so had to steer by instinct and aimed well to the left to hit the I.O. laying the axis tape. I was lucky - I bumped into David with the I.O. and our Coy. HQ. They were also lost and relying on Jerry and his compass!

Ken Godfrey...
We were all given great big rolls of tape. I don't know who was with 'Bull' Bennett to lay the central tape but they went first and we followed. It was dark at that time and you could hardly see a thing. When the fighting companies moved off from the FUP we walked ahead of them and unrolled the tapes as we went all the way down to the first road.

The line of the FUP was not parallel to the first road but seems to have been governed by the front line held by the Division at the time, which could very roughly be drawn between Parc de Boislonde on the left flank and St. Pierre on the right, the latter having been recently taken and held by the D.L.I. (22/23 June). This was very close to the first road. However, the field boundary strips and crop alignment were at right angles to the road and this may have caused some confusion as the advance progressed. The troops moving forward were consequently walking diagonally across these fields only to converge with furrows and lines which the troops may have had the tendency to follow. In the dark, and for whatever reason, many of the men began gradually to veer to the right which caused some of the Hallams to get mixed with 4 Lincs and some 11 R.S.F. to cut right across the Hallams front. It must be assumed that the tapes were laid on the correct alignment so the men were either missing them or ignoring them. This confusion was heightened when, just before light, a thick fog came down which became mixed with the smoke of explosions caused by an artillery barrage laid down in front of the advance by 500 guns of various calibre. Visibility was now less than five yards as the men made their way down the gently sloping fields to the first road...

Arnold Whiteley...
They laid a tape as far as they dare go to give you guidance and talking to your mates you knew that some of you were going to catch it. They brought us our breakfast up, haversack rations to do us the day and I think its the only time I remember, they gave us about half a pot of rum apiece. Neat, strong rum you know, so we knew then when we were lined up on this tape. It started and I have never heard or witnessed a barrage like it. It was as though all hell were let loose and we'd to walk as close as we could to this here barrage. We moved forward as close as we could to it in a straight line with your rifle held at port across your front.

Jesse Mitchinson...
There was a lot of noise, particularly the shelling coming in over our heads from our artillery support and from warships in the Channel. There was a young lad and he came and grabbed me round the knees and said that he couldn't go on. Fortunately, there was a stretcher bearer walking alongside and I said to him, 'Take him away!' I could see that this lad just couldn't take it and I just couldn't let it spread to the rest of the men and it was lucky that I could get him away.

We then got down the slope and into the German forward positions where there were some in slit trenches. This was the first time some of us had seen the enemy and as soon as we fired some shots these fellows put their hands up straight away. Then we got to the first road and quite a few people had got lost and I had a couple of Lincolns in with us that had strayed too far to their left. I left the platoon Sgt. in charge and moved along to see if I could find a place to get through the thick hedge. I'd gone about 30 yards when there was an explosion fairly close to me and I went up in the air. I thought I might be riddled with shrapnel or something like that but I wasn't. I couldn't walk but I dragged myself back to the platoon and then I was taken away by stretcher bearers back to the RAP.

I didn't want to be taken away all together and so I was able to join Johnny Mott who was 2i/c and was filling Brengun magazines at rear Bn. HQ. My leg got worse and when I tried to stand up I just fell over. So, John Mott said, 'You can't stay here, you'll be in the way and we can't look after you.' He took me back to the M.O., Gregory-Dean, who told me that I would have to be sent back. I went back to England in a LCT, which was full of stretchered casualties including Ivor Slater, my Coy. Commander, who had a wound in his cheek. I remember him reprimanding me for not having handed my binoculars in before I left the RAP. The strap was still around my neck and the binoculars were tucked inside my battledress blouse! Anyhow, I didn't get back to the Battalion again until they had reached Nijmegen.

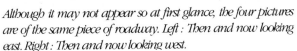

Although it may not appear so at first glance, the four pictures are of the same piece of roadway. Left : Then and now looking east. Right : Then and now looking west.

Above Left : The abandoned German A/Tk. Gun barrel aims at a 'Sherman' tank down left side of the road and there is a German 'Panther' on the right. Both are knocked out.(IWM) Above Right : Men of the Durham Light Infantry coming out of the line from opposite direction, pass the same 'Sherman' on their right and the 'Panther' is partially obscured by the tree on left. (IWM). ❖ *Lower Photos : The only buildings left today are the long barn (left photo) and the house among trees (right photo). The car in the right picture is in the position where the A/Tk.. gun was standing. Beyond it on the right is the ditch where Roy Simon lay after having walked down the fields from the FUP to the right. The Panzer Grenadier lying dead in the road may even be the one who Roy heard moaning. The Battalion crossed this stretch of road seen in the right picture from right to left in the attack on Fontenay le Pesnel. David Lockwood was killed in a field after crossing the road as troops were entering the village. (DWS)*

Roy Simon...
We had to follow these yellow tapes and we set off in extended order and it was still dark and as it got light a fog came down, it were right foggy! Capt. Good were in front of me and he told us to keep close with hands on each others shoulders until we got down to this road. Our objective was a small bridge in the western end of the village. As we turned onto the road there was this shadow in the fog and somebody shouted, 'Gerry' and then all of a sudden I heard this blinking Brengun behind me and I made a dive into this ditch and this Gerry copped it. Then all hell broke loose.

I fired some rounds up the ditch but I couldn't see what I were firing at. There was a lot of screaming and I heard somebody shouting, 'Oh! Mother, take me pack off it's hurting me,' and this poor Gerry in front of me kept moaning and groaning. Then I heard a voice and I gathered afterwards it was Sgt. Lockwood, 'You lot, you Gerries, come out and fight us right. We're from Sheffield come out and fight us right.' Next thing you know he got it in chest, he was on the opposite side of the road to me. I will say this that there wasn't a shot fired (small arms fire) until we opened up at Fontenay.

Capt. Good shouted for me and two other men behind me (one of them were Cutts and the other was Clifford Hargreaves) to crawl up this ditch we were in so we set off till we came to this fallen tree over the ditch. I tried to go over the top of it but got a burst of fire and it were Brengun fire, so I tried to dig under it. Then Cutts said, 'We,ve gone far enough.' Then I kept seeing these explosives dropping nearby and every time one came down Cutts was grabbing me feet and trying to drag me back. I was laid there and it was beginning to get as you can see and I could just see this Gerry on the other side of the road and he was throwing these 'tattie mashers' (stick grenades) across but they were going right over our heads into the field. He must of thought we were other side of hedge and I must have counted nine going over and I kept thinking, 'God, don't let any of them fall short,' and I were scared stiff.

Then somebody came running up and sits with his back to me and I put me bayonet to his back, 'Move,' I says, 'and you've had it!' and he said, 'Don't be so stupid, it's me!' and it were 'Knocker' Lees. So he goes to the side of this tree and he says, 'Cyril May is coming over and he's bringing a Brengun, so you two on Bren.' Then Knocker says to us, 'I'm off. Count ten and follow me,' and off he went along the ditch with Cyril May behind him. I was just about to set off when something hit me and it was Cyril May coming back. I said, 'What's the matter?' and he said, 'They've got me in't knee and I think they've got Knocker.' Next thing I know I sees this bloke crawling towards me along the ditch and it were Knocker and he looked in a terrible state with a wound to the side of his nose. Then Bill Goodall was at side of me and he used my penknife to cut away the webbing straps so we could drag him through under this tree. We got him through and I saw him a little later slumped up against a post and he was muttering something about not wanting to go on the stretcher.

Leslie Dalton (17 Platoon, D Coy.)...
On the morning of the attack, we was all in lines and I was with my two mates, Lovell and Eastwood. As we were walking down through the mist, one thing stands out, every now and again you could hear a buzzing like bees and this was with bullets. You could hear them zipping past and I was amazed that nobody seemed to get hit with them.

German Halftrack. SdKfz 251, similar to the type captured by the Hallams and used to evacuate casualties from the battlefield. (DWS)

All of a sudden I was on my own and I finished up with another Regiment altogether (4 Lincs) and there was about a hundred of us. A 2/Lt. took charge and we was all in a group and he made us stand in a big circle facing outwards and as the mist cleared at the far end of the circle from me there was a German half-track. Our lads saw them first and they captured or killed them and took the half-track. Eventually they used it as a first aid truck because I remember Thomas the padre, he went out to rescue 'B' Coy. once and bring the wounded back.

The half-track, thought to be an SdKfz 251 of the Panzer Leher Division and one of a number captured in the area, was commandeered by the Hallams and eventually found its way back to 'B Echelon' (best described as the Battalions 'mobile field depot' in the rear) where it was given a check over and found to be in a good reusable condition. It was during this initial servicing that two packages made of sacking were found underneath the vehicle, tied to the chassis. Each of these contained a fur coat with a Paris label which were no doubt destined to adorn the wives or sweethearts of the German vehicle crew if they ever got back to their home land. Sgt."Jock" Henderson (R.E.M.E. attached to Hallams) and Jack Shaw carried out the vehicle inspection and it is believed that the contents of the packages eventually found their way to Aberdeen and Bradford respectively.

Doug Catley, (mentioned in the previous chapter as having been transferred to the so called First Line Reserve) had been eventually disembarked at Arromanche. From there he passed through Bayeux only to be sent further east and reunited with the Hallams around the Audrieu area but was not destined to be with them for long. He was given back his job as a signaller and now found himself on the FUP.

Doug Catley...
We were marched onto open ground over these tapes on the start line and I was with Henry Benwell carrying an 18 set on my back which we took in turns to carry... ...we went down until we came to this ditch and road and everybody seemed to be lost really. We didn't know what were happening and we got in this here ditch and I could hear voices and I remember saying to the Coy. Commander that it were Yorkshire voices we could hear so we're all right. Then, when the smoke started clearing and the mist started to lift you could see all along this road, as far as you could see either way, all the troops were mixed up, all British. 'Bunny' Whiting was alongside and he was in a different Company to us! Major Newton then ordered us to advance across this open ground and we got so far and he ordered us back.

Ray Langdale...
I was with Battalion HQ. and I got separated from the C.O. for some reason but I had a message to pass to Major Lockwood. Now, I went up to him and if you knew him, one thing would stand out in your mind - he had his pipe in his mouth and very seldom would you see him without his pipe in his mouth. It was shortly afterwards that they went into the assault in which he was killed.

Chris Somers (Diary)...
We eventually reached the lateral road and quickly got across it. As we got in the ditch the other side, a Spandau (actually firing from a Tiger Tank) opened up down the road. We then moved into a field where we linked up with the C.O. and his advanced HQ. He told me and Sgt. Gallagher to scout forward in the mist to see if we could locate any enemy. I bumped into Mike Lonsdale-Cooper and Jock Jackson around the end of a wall and we nearly shot each other up. Neither of us had seen anything so we reported back again. This time he told me to collect what men I had and make for a house down a track. He told David the same thing so we joined forces. He had the 18 set and I had six men including a Bren gun and 2 inch mortar!

We strode down the track in front of our little group with Bill Ashby and the wireless just behind us. We thought there was no enemy about in this particular area but were soon mistaken when a burst was fired straight at us out of the mist. We flattened on the ground, staring into the mist ahead to try to see what was there. Those tense few minutes seemed like hours. The mist was gradually clearing and we could discern the faint outline of the house about 30 yards ahead.

I suggested to David alongside me that I should throw a grenade as if we waited much longer we should be lying in full view of whoever was in the house and without a bit of cover. He was about to give me some order but the order never came. Another shot from the house and David uttered a groan and his head fell forward, blood running from his mouth. The first man I had seen killed was not only my company commander but also my best friend. I was filled with rage and an impulse to rush headlong forward into the mist and put a quick end to whoever was there. Then I heard Bill Ashby shouting to David. I told him what had happened and he told me to take a section round to the right. I looked around to find only the signaller behind me so began to crawl back for some men at the back.

❖ *The bridge objective of Chris Somers platoon looking in a southeasterly direction. Not far away, Graham Roe found the body of Arthur Longford by the stream and thought he was having a drink. The church stands on the north side of the Caen -Juvigny road and a sunken path beyond the bridge leads up to a T junction at the top.* ❖*Below : The farm at this T junction became the Bn.HQ. but was abandoned soon afterwards when some of the buildings caught fire due to enemy shelling. (DWS)*

However, Bill didn't wait and charged forward with David's Batman. His grenade however bounced back wounding South. We were now all around the house, but the bird had flown. We collected the few men we had together, a mere half dozen and pushed down through the orchard to some farm houses. Luckily these were all clear and on coming out of the other side saw the stone bridge, my platoon objective, a bare 100 yards in front. I ran down to it covered by the few men I had and here again I was in luck. I decided not to run over the bridge but to wade the stream. How right I was, because as I attempted to push through the hedge up the steep bank, I was welcomed by a short Spandau burst.

Leaving Cpl. Watkins to watch this side I waded under the bridge and tried the other, again without luck, so consolidated as I was with two men on the bank either side of the bridge. 'D' Coy. had now come up on our right and were able to push up the hill onto the second lateral road. Soon 'B' Coy. received the order to move up to the second lateral road. We went quickly up the hill over the open field but luckily the Spandau was no longer there. On reaching the second road we halted temporarily by some bomb craters and were then ordered to push Eastwards along the line of the road and on the far side.

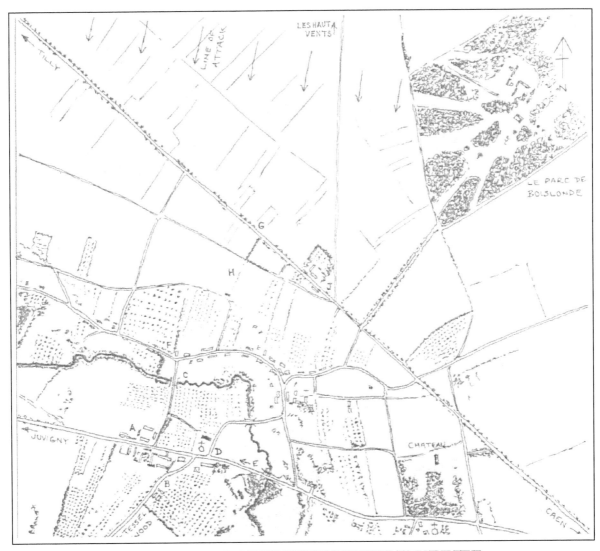

MAP OF FONTENAY LE PESNEL SHOWING VARIOUS POSITIONS REFERRED TO IN THE TEXT.

(A) Farm where Bn.HQ. was first established. (B) Orchard where S.B. Cpl. Joe Penn saved many lives which almost cost his own. (C) Bridge objective and approximate position of second Bn. HQ. position. (D) Position from which Hallams A/Tk. platoon knocked out Panther tank. Arnold Whiteley took cover in the lane here and spoke to Lt. Jack Firth just moments before he was fatally wounded. (E) Arrow showing direction from which the tank approached. It was just south of this spot that Bill Ashby stalked a tank with a P.I.A.T. and Pte E. Hanson died. (F) Position of the knocked out Tiger tank where Pat Strafford found the motorbike and sidecar full of cigarettes. (G) Ditch where Roy Simon counted the stick grenades being thrown over his head. (H) Approximate place where David Lockwood died. (J) Position of knocked out Sherman and Panther. (DWS)

Sometime earlier, Roy Simon and his group had gathered themselves to move off the first road and down towards the village after having lost Sgts. Lockwood and Lees.

Roy Simon...
...we crossed the road into the fields and moved towards the village in extended order and we were going through a bit of an orchard and there were a barn burning and then somebody amongst us opened up with a Brengun and somebody shouted, 'Stop that man,' and somebody gave him a rugby tackle and he went down. We moved past this burning building and there was this little black dog and it were whimpering. I didn't say nowt to it but it came running across and I bent down and tapped it and half of its ear was missing. We went on to a place where there was an open space beyond which was a wood, someone said it was Tessel Wood, and we started to dig in. Some of the older blokes came around and said, 'You did all right you young 'uns!' The next thing there was this German tank and it was firing towards us and it blew up and there was stuff flying

all over the show and the next thing, 'Oh! Dear, they've got me, they've got me leg!' I looked down and I could feel all this wet on me leg and noticed then that it was me water bottle split completely. Some time later I was near to Lt. Bendall and someone said, 'Simon's wounded sir'. I said, 'I'm not it's only water down me leg!' He said, 'Have you seen your arm?' So I looked and all me arm was full of blood here and I didn't know until that lot told me. Then I was off down to Casualty Clearing Station in this Jeep and the bloke said, 'Do you want to see where Knocker Lees is buried?' and I said, 'No!' We ended up back on the beaches.

Roy was then sent back to England with a nasty gash down his arm caused either by the ripped water bottle or the piece of shrapnel which had caused damage in the first place. Roy was to rejoin the Battalion later only to be wounded again in the attack on the Depot de Mendicite in Belgium.

Dennis Townsend...
When we went into Fontenay with the Mortar Platoon, I think we'd got seven Carrier vehicles, we went into a small field and of course there was a lot of mist about and we saw there were a lot of trenches that the Germans had left. So, we got out of our vehicles to mount the Mortars and thought we were in lucks way, because there were trenches (ready-made). The Germans started shelling us and we went into the trenches and they hit about five of the Carrier vehicles and they went up in smoke and all the ammunition and our rifles and that were in them. When the firing stopped I went back into the next field from where we'd come and I went into a trench and there were three of us in this trench and one was wounded. We'd lost a lot of our lads in the shelling then the other lad that wasn't wounded said, 'I'll take this one back and you stay here Dennis.' Of course, I was only eighteen years of age and we'd set off very early in the morning and with the shelling and that, I must have been exhausted, I just fell asleep....You probably don't want to know this!

.....I suddenly woke up and I wondered where I was because everything was so quiet. So, I thought, 'Well, there's only one thing for it to do and that's to go the way that I came from,' so I went back and I hadn't walked back through these fields for more than about 50 yards when one of the Sergeants from the Mortar Platoon had got three or four other lads with him and he was bringing them back into the action and they were complaining. They were saying, 'Sergeant, we haven't got any rifles, it's no good us going forward,' and he was saying they'd got to go forward. He said, 'The lads up there want some help and you've got to come and I'll find you some rifles.' So, I just attached myself to them and nobody was any wiser that I'd fallen asleep.

The devastating fire which caused so much destruction to the Mortar Pl. carriers also wounded it's Commander, Lt. D.A. Abbott. Meanwhile, Dennis Townsend must have moved on down towards the stream.

Dennis Townsend...
Then as I came forward, there was Col. Hart Dyke. He was in a slit trench and he was having a shave as if nothing had happened. In England he'd always been a disciplinarian to get the Battalion fit and that, but on this occasion after so many casualties to the day, he was a father like figure and spoke to us as though we'd been friends all our lives.

Dennis may have seen the C.O. in the second Bn.HQ. position at Fontenay which was in relative safety down the hill near the stream. The first position in farm buildings up on the road near the church had been evacuated when it was stonked and barns caught fire. It is thought that this was where CSM Stanley Morton was killed and Major John Brinton (O.C. Sp.Coy. - a South African officer) was wounded.

212

Graham Roe was moving down towards the stream when the Carriers blew up behind him and turned back to see their contents going skyward with the help of exploding ammunition. When he reached the stream he saw a man lying prone near the edge who appeared to be having a drink. He warned the man about the dangers of drinking water direct from a natural source but got no answer. On closer inspection, Graham noticed that the man's face was under water. He was Pte. John Arthur Longford, one of the carrier drivers, and he was dead.

George Learad...
Arthur Longford was killed by a sniper and because I used to go to school with his wife, I wrote to a woman who I knew that lived next door to her on Easter Avenue. I just wanted her to go round and tell her how sorry I was that her husband had been killed. I found out later that when she went round to see her, Arthur's wife didn't even know that he was dead. The neighbours knew about it before she did and this was about a fortnight after his death. Her 'nee' name I remember was Mary Wragg, a relation of the jockey, Harry Wragg.

Arnold Whiteley...
We were on a road to the right of Fontenay so we turned left and small arms were chattering then. We went in by the church and they were shouting for 'C' Coy. to go down by the side of the church and dig in by an orchard and that's where Lt. Firth spoke to me. There was an anti-tank gun on the road in front of church and we got caught in shelling down that road and if you'd have stood up you would have been killed. My friend said, 'Don't move,' and we stopped there and they landed int' road, they were hitting side of church and when it eased off we got where we had to dig in and there were lads there wounded, dying. I remember some and we tried to comfort them and we laid with them and talked to them, you know, 'You'll be all right,' but you knew it, you can tell by that pallor, you know when death's coming to them...

Ivor Slater...
Jack Firth was my second in command ('A' Coy.) and I gave him morphia when he was badly wounded. We were in a ditch with no stretcher bearers around at the time and just after that an enemy anti-tank gun turned up and started firing at us. We and other troops around us whipped into a farm building and some ricochet from that knocked my tooth out and gave me shrapnel wounds. I made my way back to Bn. HQ. to see Hart Dyke and he said, 'Get out of here!' He wouldn't have anybody who had any sign of a wound or blood on them, anywhere near his HQ. I went back to the RAP where Padre Thomas was and after they put a dressing on I was quickly sent on my way to the coast.

Ivor was evacuated and some time after recuperation, teamed up with Peter Newton, who had by this time also been sent back to England. At Seaford near Brighton, they were given the task of retraining various groups on updated methods of warfare in a scheme they called 'Red Rosa'. Red Rosa was the name they had bestowed on a small, wooden, ships figurehead which they had picked up in a local antique shop. This was strapped into a Jeep and used as the objective on exercises which the troops had to home in on, and capture, by the use of map references and stealth. Ivor did not get back to the Hallams and was eventually posted to the 1st Bn. The York and Lancaster Regiment as 2 i/c to Charles Strong when it was based in Brunswick, Germany, after the war ended. Jack Firth was seriously wounded and taken back to a Field Hospital in the vicinity of Bayeux where he had a leg amputated, but died shortly afterwards with other complications.

Meanwhile, Chris Somers and Bill Ashby had been ordered to clear an area across the Juvigny - Caen Road to the south east of the church. It was in this area that Cpl. Joe Penn, a keen rugby player, was operating as a Stretcher Bearer and may even have been one of those mentioned by Chris Somers. Many men were being hit by sniper and machine gun fire here at this time and Joe continually went into the orchard behind buildings opposite the church and dragged the wounded to relative safety. During his final rescue attempt he was hit by Spandau fire down one side of his body, arm and leg. Joe was awarded the D.C.M. for his bravery in being involved in the rescue of 32 men, 11 of whom were brought out under enemy fire. He was recommended for the Victoria Cross which would have been richly deserved. The leg was amputated later but he spent the rest of his life with little complaint, a fierce guardian of his independent ways.

Arthur Green...

There was one lad in particular that I know, Joe Penn, he was a stretcher bearer and during the action at Fontenay he fetched out a dozen or more wounded lads whilst under fire. He was dashing back and forth with the wounded and eventually got hit by machine gun fire down his left hand side and his arm and left leg were shattered. He is reputed to have said to the wounded man he continued to help from an orchard across the road from the church of St. Aubin, in the village, 'We better get out of here or else that bugger'll kill me!' His leg was too badly gone to do anything about and it had to be taken off. He was decorated with the Distinguished Conduct Medal (D.C.M.) for that particular action.

Chris Somers (Diary)...

We moved at a quick speed through the first few farm buildings until we came to a road (this must have been the road leading up to Tessel Wood). Here Bill Ashby told me to do a 'right flanker' with what men I had through some buildings to the right. My platoon was now nothing more than its HQ. plus a Bren Group. We rushed round at top speed in the true Battle School manner. Fortunately there were no snipers in the building or we should have 'bought it' properly. As we crossed an open field the other side of the buildings I found that there was only Cpl. Neal with me, the others having lagged a bit. So I told him to collect them into the ditch the other side of the next hedge while I chivied up those at the back. He must have paused as he got through the hedge, because a shot rang out and he fell in the ditch, the other side wounded in the arm. So I got the remainder in the same ditch through another gap and then proceeded to 'pepper pot' across the open orchard using a rifle group and myself and 3 and a Bren Group consisting of Sgt. Liptrot and Cpl. Binns. L/Cpl. Wainwright manned the 2 inch mortar with Hanson and stonked a hedge on the right where I suspected we'd been sniped from. Unfortunately the movement was spoiled by the Bren jamming. Something was firing at us from the front every time we moved but it was quite impossible to see and our odd rifle shots failed to locate it (later I assumed it to be a tank over the other side of the small Valley).

Eventually, by making short dashes and dropping to the ground every time the bullets started flying, I got across the track with McCartney and one other, leaving Cpl. Watkins in a track the other side with L/Cpl. Chapman. From here I tried to locate movement over the open ground in front but without success. Soon Hanson joined me with the 38 set. I had hardly told him that he would perhaps be better off the other side of the bank when a burst rang out and Hanson said they'd got him. How the bullets missed me I don't know because I was lying half in front of him and right against him. They must have just caught his back. Luckily there were two SBs close at hand and we managed to drag him out of the exposed position and behind the bank in the track, though it was very painful to him. The SBs dressed his wound which was in his back and then they went down to a nearby house to try to find a stretcher as we couldn't move him without.

They hadn't been gone long when an almighty 'stonk' came down right on top of us. I pressed myself hard to the ground thinking it wouldn't be long now! Branches and all sorts were falling down on top of us and the noise was deafening. Eventually, after what seemed hours, the barrage

214

lifted and I realized it must have been in error. Actually I believe it was the opening barrage of mediums for the KOYLI's attack on Tessel Wood.

This was indeed a creeping barrage which was being laid down by Canadian Artillery to allow the KOYLI to pass through the Hallams and go on up to the North side of Tessel Wood. The FUP was on the second road where the Bn. was consolidating. Unfortunately the first artillery shells had been laid on the start line instead of 100 yards in front. One of these KOYLI men, Pat Strafford, had already had one shock as he passed through the lower part of the village where he was suddenly confronted by a Tiger tank. Luckily, its crew were in no condition to man it. Pat stepped through a hedge and found them in the adjacent lane, all lying dead but seemingly without a mark on them. It struck him how very young they all looked. The only man alive was their wounded officer who lay on a stretcher near a motor cycle, the sidecar of which was brim full with packets of cigarettes. In a nearby house there was a table set for their meal, with food still warm on the plates, like the 'Marie Celeste'. He then had to move quickly up the hill to the FUP where all hell was let loose. Doug Catley was caught in the same 'stonk'.

Doug Catley...
We eventually went up there behind the church and I remember all up them orchards there were these horses and cattle on their backs and blown up and killed. Then I saw the first dead Gerry and that was just behind the church as we moved into an orchard on the other side of the second road and started to dig in. Another thing that stands out in my mind was seeing this carrier coming along with Hart Dyke on it which made me feel good to be honest. The next move was a creeping barrage by the Canadian Artillery to be put down in front of us and moving towards Tessel Wood the KOYLI to come through us. This barrage started to come down and instead of it being in front of us, it was on top of us and we had a lot of casualties from that. We'd started to dig and Henry was down in what we'd dug so far with the 18 set and I went across and laid by a stone wall. It was a terrifying experience and I remember moving back across the road into a ditch at the side.

Chris Somers (Diary)...
When I had disentangled myself from the mass of foreign branches I found I was apparently alone. Hanson was quiet now, so I decided to go down to a large house about 100 yards away to see what had happened to the rest of my chaps and the SBs. There I found a room full of groaning wounded being attended by other SBs. Some were 'A' Coy. and others from George's platoon. I then learnt that poor old George (Watson-Jones) had been killed while charging across a nearby orchard.

I suddenly began to feel terribly tired now which was not surprising really, having been about 20 hours without food or sleep. So while I chatted to a chap manning an O.P. upstairs, I lay on a bed for five minutes and ate a packet of sweets. These seemed to fill me with renewed energy, or it may have been just relaxing for a few minutes. As I went outside again I ran into Ivor Slater who had just about lost all his Coy. so I told him where I had seen a lot and where my chaps were. This was the last time I saw him because he was shot through the mouth just afterwards.

I then heard Bill Ashby shouting for me to join him back the other side of the orchard. As I went back past a farm yard I looked inside a barn to see if it had been occupied and happened to glance through the window on the other side. I could hardly believe my eyes. There was a large Tiger Tank with about 8 Germans just jumping off the top. At that moment a shot from our A/Tk. gun rang out and hit the wall behind which they were crouching. They had their backs to me and were barely 80 yards away. I couldn't miss! But there was a snag, the window was about a foot too high to fire out of. I searched frantically for something to stand on. I found something which

❖*Left : Lane leading up to the junction with Caen - Juvigny road. Arnold Whiteley and others took cover in a ditch up the side of this church wall here (now filled in to make the lane a little wider).(DWS)* ❖*Right : The junction (at top of lane - left) where the A/Tk. gun was sited (just this side of the road sign) which knocked out a 'Panther' tank coming up the road. Bill Ashby and Chris Somers cleared the area on the right side of the road down to a bridge in the position where the car is parked. (above left photograph used as basis for mural now hanging in Endcliffe Hall) (DWS)*

would just do, but my target now had moved and the tank had backed over the road. I saw two standing together and took careful aim. They dropped, the one I shot at a little quicker. I reloaded and saw another lying on a bank. He likewise dropped down.

I shall never know whether I hit them or not. The A/Tk. crew say they reckoned that someone from 'B' Coy. had shot some of the Germans after they had left the tank and there are three graves there now, one of which no doubt contains one of the tank crew. I felt I had something to revenge having lost one of my best friends and 'Happy' my batman during the past few hours. I then had to join Bill Ashby quickly who was quite rightly in a hurry to reorganize with what men he had as soon as possible. Shots from another tank were whistling up the road and some barns where I had been were now on fire. There were about 30 men left in the Coy. Our Carrier was still down the road as the crew had been knocked out by a tank which they met around a corner just after we had gone by. The carrier was still working and Bill drove it around to the small orchard where we were digging in.

I was worried about my missing men so Bill said I'd better look around where I had last seen them. So I went forward to the track again to find them lying in the same ditch where snipers had been making them keep their heads down. L/Cpl. Chapman had been shot through the neck and was in great pain. However, he asked us to leave him there till dark as he didn't think we should be able to lug him over the open with the odd bullets flying about without causing him much greater pain and said he would wait for a stretcher after dark. Hanson, nearby, had passed away before we could do anything for him, much to my regret.

We ran back and rejoined the Coy. and got busy digging. Luckily we found a ready dug hole for the 18 set into which four of us could squeeze. We had now been reinforced with 'B' Echelon personnel. The excitement was not over however, as a tank started to maneuver around the orchard where we had left L/Cpl. Chapman. We had nothing apart from rifles to defend ourselves with, and one P.I.A.T. Unfortunately the platoon near the tank didn't have it. It came up to the neighbouring hedge but came no further. As darkness fell it started to move away again which was indeed fortunate as it could have run us all down. Bill went after it with the P.I.A.T. and reckoned he hit it twice without much effect.

Soon after the CQMS had brought a meal up, we were well and truly stonked by mortars but didn't suffer any casualties. Digging continued in the darkness and pouring rain and a standing patrol went forward to my track. They couldn't locate L/Cpl. Chapman though and he wasn't found till next morning as he had rather foolishly moved from where we left him. An unexploded mortar bomb had pierced his leg too, but he survived the ordeal.

We remained here next day which was reasonably quiet apart from occasional mortaring. The next night I went out with the standing patrol and brought Hanson's body back with the object of burying him in our area next morning. However, we moved forward at first light and the burial was performed later by the padre. Unfortunately I was unable to attend.

Wilf Fisher...
I'd got to take these reinforcements down towards Fontenay and when I got down to the road at the bottom, they were all young lads that were with me, and I don't know what happened. Something dropped at the side of me and Boom! The next thing I knew, I was in this first aid place lying on a stretcher and the bloke on the left hand side of me was 'Knocker' Lees and next to him was Jack Firth. To tell the truth, I didn't know whether I was alive or dead and I thought, 'Am I imagining all this?' I must have passed out because the next thing I remember, I was on a boat. When I came round and finally knew where I was, I was in Crumpsall Hospital, Manchester. I couldn't talk and one arm was in bandage and my right hand, I couldn't keep still. It was trembling the whole time and I couldn't speak. I was in a right mess.

Wilf was moved to a Southport hospital for psycho-neurosis treatment where he spent 8 days before being transferred to Bedford for convalescence and finally to a Depot at Watton Camp, Nottingham. Here he waited for reposting.

Wilf Fisher...
One day, I'd been there about a fortnight, who should I see walking round the barrack square but Major Slater. He looked at me and said, 'You're just the bloke I'm looking for' and I said, 'How's that sir?' and he said, 'Coming back to the unit with me'. I said, 'When?' and he said, 'Tomorrow!'... Anyway, that's how I got back to the Hallams who were by now in the Venlo area of Holland... ...I was there in this forward position and I don't know what happened but ended up in a hospital at Eindhoven in a similar position to what I had been previously...

After being medically down graded Wilf ended up managing the Albert Hotel (leave centre) in Brussels. As was said earlier, Ivor Slater did not return to the Battalion.

It must have been on the 25th that Wilf Fisher conducted those reinforcements down through Fontenay because he talks about being in the next bed to 'Knocker' Lees who died of wounds on that day. It is thought that these reinforcements were members of 'B' Echelon which had been called forward by the C.O. when he was very short of men up front.

Dennis Townsend...
Later in the day, we went up a lane and there was a German sniper on the bank side and he'd been very seriously injured and his revolver was close by and he obviously knew that we were British. All he was saying was, 'Wasser! Wasser!' and he was in a bad way. Never-the-less, he was very young, he must only have been in the German Army for a few weeks and he was reaching for his revolver. One of the lads that I was with was very angry with the Germans because he had just heard that he'd lost his brother in Italy... ...this lad said, 'I'm going to shoot him,' and was prepared to, but I said, 'No! just leave him,' so we left him and that was it.

217

Ray Langdale...
Hart Dyke was really marvellous, in my opinion. We entered the village and came up this road as a Bn.HQ. and went into a farm yard where the half-track vehicle had arrived with 18 and 22 wireless sets going. We then pulled out of there because the barns had caught fire and went back down into an orchard near the stream. Then it started to rain and we were getting casualties left, right and centre.

George Learad was in this area at about the same time.

George Learad...
Freddy Ashmore was alive when I got to him and he'd got a very bad shrapnel wound across the front of his neck and I couldn't do anything for him. We were in these woods just to the side of the church so I went for the M.O. and the stretcher bearers at the bottom (probably near the stream). I asked them to come up and they were a bit scared, they wouldn't go up without me. So, I went up with them but when we got there, Freddy were dead. As far as I remember, he were one of the first of our lads to go. 'Mutty' Morton got it in't back the next day around the same area and I remember seeing an ambulance take him away from there with others who had been killed.

For all his responsibilities and anxieties of the day, Trevor Hart Dyke was able to find time in the next twenty-four hours to write letters of condolence to next of kin of those officers who had been killed. He wrote to Mary Lockwood.

B.W.E.F.
26 June, 1944

Dear Mary,
I cannot express my deep sorrow at the loss of your David. He was killed in action while leading his company headquarters to the attack. Visibility was almost nil and so the barrage was of little avail. I am writing in a slit trench under occasional mortar fire and I fear it is raining. I went out personally to see David was buried as we had to deal with snipers with automatics. David was shot through the head and would have known nothing about it. So much better than a mortar wound or something of that nature. The padre buried him. It was typical of David that he should have been leading his men. I told him not to go with the forward troops but when the mist and dust of battle made visibility under a yard one could only move by compass and hope that when the mist cleared one was not right on top of a Spandau. I fear we had bad luck with the fog. Otherwise we should have got in without many casualties. As it was we lost besides your David a number of other officers and other ranks killed or wounded. The most unpleasant part was being mortared all day after the night (or dawn) attack which your David was spared. There is a tank battle raging now right on our door step. Watson-Jones was killed yesterday and Ivor, John Brinton, Abbott and Jack Firth, wounded. Frank Tett and Noiseaux were killed and Dick Sandford seriously injured by a mine during our last operation. It is terribly tragic for us, but I fear we just cannot feel enough for you. I only wish I could do something... ...We enjoyed our rest for 5 days prior to yesterday as it was comparatively peaceful. It may be some source of pride for you to know that the Hallamshires were magnificent. Practically everyone deserved a decoration. They were simply wonderful and this of course was due to having such leaders as David. Our losses also were small compared to the other unit with the same task.
I felt you would like to know all about it. I cannot say how I feel. I can only say it happened through no lack of trouble on my part to ensure minimum casualties.

Yours ever,
Trevor Hart Dyke

218

As has already been said, the operations being conducted in this area by the 49 Division were only part of a much bigger plan to seize the city of Caen, some miles to the east. This had been an objective of Allied Forces on 'D' Day but had been stubbornly held and the attrition was now costing many lives and masses of material. It was soon to cost many, many more in this operation 'EPSOM', launched on the 25 June, with the attack on Fontenay le Pesnel being merely the prelude. None of those who fought in it would accept the Battle of Fontenay as a side show compared with that which was to come, but its purpose was to form a pivot and anchor point for the main thrusting attack centred on Cheux. It was hoped to punch a hole in the German front line and allow Caen to be encircled. That story is outside the scope of this book but see Bibliography. ('Hill 112' by Major J.J. How, M.C., would be a good place to start)

In order to consolidate a right flank for the main attack, the Hallams were now required to move forward and take up positions in fields just beyond Tessel Wood and a couple of fields in front of the village of Vendes which was strongly held by the Germans. Trevor Hart Dyke was at some variance with Brigade as to the means by which this might be achieved.

Trevor Hart Dyke...
In the middle of the night I was sent for, to attend a conference with the Brigade Commander and it was raining. I was told to try and advance to Juvigny and then get the high ground. I suggested the better route if I went up on the eastern side of Tessel Wood. I then had to find my way back at night and then collect the Company Commanders and give them their orders for the next morning. We decided that we would go just before half light and managed to get there before the Germans spotted us. We were able to deploy on the far side of Tessel Wood and then I sent for the Anti-Tank guns which came and took up positions which I had originally given them from the air photographs which were most helpful. I then sent a patrol down towards Vendes and they had a few casualties from anti-personnel mines and they reported that there were no enemy this side of the road running east and west at Vendes. I was then able to report to Brigade HQ.

Les Dalton...
There was a farm (probably Bejude) just in front of us and, I don't know his name, there was an old soldier with us and he used to crawl to this farm mostly in the morning just when it came light and pinch the eggs. He brought them back and we cooked them in a cigarette tin lid.

We put a raid in on this village and we was ambushed, the Germans were over a wall waiting for us and we lost four men as prisoners. As we moved out of Tessel Wood to occupy these fields, the Officer took all the Platoon towards this village and left me covering the corner of a cornfield with a Brengun with a No.2 man. I didn't see what happened but all of a sudden there was two almighty bangs and apparently a tank had fired at both groups, they'd split in two groups and that's when my two mates, Lovell and Eastwood, along with Cpl. Tipper and another were killed. There were about eight wounded and the next thing I saw was what was left, came running back over this cornfield. They brought Lovell out wounded but he died later in Aldershot. The others were left because we couldn't get to them.

This raid on Vendes, took place on the 27th June, confirmed by dates of death of some of the men named by Les Dalton. It is almost certain that Pte. Bill Jackson also took part in this patrol but he did not make it back to the Hallamshire lines. He was about to go out on this patrol when his Company Commander, Major Peter Newton, called him back to ask him if he was doing all right. The patrol by now had already set off and when the officer had finished talking suggested that Bill need not bother to catch up with them. Bill insisted on joining his mates but in his eagerness to catch up, must have taken a wrong turning which caused him to get past the patrol and into enemy territory.

Bill Jackson...
I went to catch the others up like and then I'd only gone a few yards and I was fired on against a stone wall. I was on the ground then and there was flak flying off the wall and I got a few ricochets...   ...I got onto this road and so I thought the best thing for me to do was to get into the open so I jumped over this hedge and was in a field and I could see all these tanks like! There were also some Germans so I'd had it then. The first one was all right and I was put in a motorbike and sidecar as I had superficial wounds and we went towards the interrogation place. When we got there I didn't go straight into the interrogation place. A young nazi officer came and started jabbering and said, 'I'll make you talk.' I couldn't say anything to calm him down like and he said, 'Come in here,' and we went into a small Nissen hut then and he had three men in there lying low and I was at the other end...

This intimidation was short lived and Bill was eventually moved away. He remembers spending one night in horse racing stables followed by four days travelling in railway cattle trucks. He later spent some time in a sugar factory where the main diet for prisoners was the by-product of sugarbeet and many of them suffered badly from diarrhea. He was finally moved to a cement factory in Hanover and was still there when liberated by the Americans in May, 1945. Bill was one of those men who settled in Leominster after the war.

Trevor Hart Dyke...
I was told that other units were to move through us and therefore I put my HQ. right up on the south side of Tessel Wood which was rather far forward for Battalion HQ. and we had two companies forward where I was along the hedgerows just north from the east-west road through Vendes and we were then told the attack was not going to come off from the other battalion.

Ray Langdale...
Bill Ashby was wounded when we were up at the forward position of Tessel Wood. There'd been an 'O' Group there and Bill had left it to return to his Company ('B') and he'd just got on the road when he got hit. It was at about the time when Capt. Young was killed and Lt. Turrell was wounded.

It is usual for officer casualties to be named in the War Diary but, curiously, the wounding of Capt. Bill Ashby is not reported at all. Trevor Hart Dyke says in his book that this occurred on the 27 June, the day before Capt. Phil Young was killed. To confuse matters, the War Diary places both 'D' and 'B' Coy. in the same place at this time (SW of Tessel Wood). All other points are covered by the other Coys. except the SE side and it is thought that this must have been where 'B' Coy. (Bill's new command after the death of David Lockwood) was actually placed. It is the only position that would require him to leave the field where the 'O' Group was and go onto the road where he was hit. This 'B' Coy. position has in fact, now been confirmed by notes placed on an aerial photograph by Chris Somers in a scrap book which he compiled after the war.

It is also thought that 'A' Coy. was placed on the east of the wood and not the west as stated in the War Diary. According to a K.O.Y.L.I. veteran (Pat Strafford), who was well placed on the NW corner to observe, the west face of the wood was not occupied! Chris Somers Diary gives backing to this theory but places 'A' Coy. in reserve.

Chris Somers (Diary)...
We had arrived at the south end of Tessel Wood without incident and began to dig in, in our allotted Coy. areas with 'D' Coy. on the S.W. corner, 'B' Coy. on the S.E. and 'C' Coy. in the middle. 'A' Coy. were back in reserve. Here we remained for three weeks in a spot which was never very

healthy, and casualties mounted day by day. The weather on the whole was fairly kind to us though. We walked into our allotted areas in comparative peace and quiet, but it didn't last long. The Boche must have watched us taking up our positions because the day had hardly elapsed when he began to lay down pretty accurate 'stonking' on Coy. positions and this continued for the next three weeks.

Our first casualty here was Bill Ashby. Only just promoted Major to command 'B' Coy., he had just arrived at Battalion HQ, a mere 20 yards from our position, when a burst of Spandau fire hit him in the back, badly wounding him. Mike Lonsdale-Cooper came to take over the Coy. almost at once which was a good thing as I was very busy trying to sort out our reinforcements and deal with Coy. affairs at the same time. I was also glad that he agreed with me about moving our Coy.HQ. slits from the side of the track into the open field. Very lucky because the next night my original slit received a direct hit. Early in the morning, forward Battalion HQ. received a severe stonking - one bomb killing Phil Young and wounding Raymond Jenkinson, Peter Turrell and the C.O. - slightly. To think that this was where we started to dig our Coy. HQ. till we were shifted by Battalion HQ.!!

Trevor Hart Dyke...
At about that time shells landed practically on my half-track where I had my HQ. It killed the Sniper Officer (Phil Young) who was dug in a yard or two in front of me and wounded two other officers. Fortunately it only just grazed me in one or two places and my command vehicle was a write-off. Anyhow, as the attack by the other battalion was not going to go through us, I realized that my headquarters was much too far forward so we moved back to the northeast corner of Tessel Wood where we stayed for some weeks.

Arthur Saunders was on the spot to witness what happened in this forward area where a very accurate stonk came down, right on top of the newly established Battalion Headquarters.

Arthur Saunders... (C.Os. Signaller)
I had started digging my trench near the halftrack at the side of the hedge and Bill Palmer was already dug in and he said to me, 'We're moving Sandy, tha can get in here, have you got any fags?' Well, I didn't smoke so I said, 'Here' giving him some fags. Well he and Jimmy Gallagher went round the hedge and both got killed there.

This was the 28 June and Bn. HQ. was still being established just south of Tessel Wood. The partly dug slit trench which Arthur Saunders had abandoned was the one occupied by Capt. Young (Sniper Officer) when a shell burst in the nearby hedge. The slit trench was too shallow to afford sufficient protection and the explosion severed his arm and caused other fatal injuries. Of the others in the immediate vicinity, both signallers died and Peter Turrell (Adj.) was badly injured. The C.O., John Mott and Ray Jenkinson were slightly wounded.

Arthur Saunders...
I've been back to Normandy about five times and I've always looked at that grave and thought, 'That should have been mine!' It's a funny thing that what crosses your life. In Norway, Lt. Young as he was then, he saved us. I was a Bren Gunner then and we were the last Platoon going back to Namsos. The Germans were there and we'd got to chop these fir trees down with us bayonets to block this big, long, tunnel. We would then have to cross a bridge to get to Namsos and Capt. Young came along and said, 'Who are you, you better get across that bridge they're going to blow it up! We would have still been there now if it hadn't of been for him.

MAP OF TESSEL WOOD AND SURROUNDING AREA.
(A) First Bn.HQ. in Fontenay. (B) Orchard where Cpl. Joe Penn was seriously wounded. (C) Where a civilian car was stopped near entrance to the repositioned Bn.HQ. (D) Knocked out Sherman tank used as cover for Regimental Aid Post (RAP) (E) Another knocked out Sherman tank. This one used as Forward Observation Post (FOP). It was here also that Ken Godfrey stumbled over the body of one of its crew members nearby. (F) Positions of Hallams front line Companies during three weeks of static warfare. (G) Positions held by 4th Kings Own Yorkshire Light Infantry (K.O.Y.L.I.). (H) Position of knocked out German tank that had been disguised to look like a small farm building. (DWS)

Bn. positions were often 'stonked' by what seemed uncannily accurate enemy gun and mortar fire. The RAP was never once targeted even though it was nearly always in close proximity of Bn.HQ. It was almost as though the enemy had an Observation Post in Fontenay itself which may very well have been the case, at least for the first couple of days. This might account for the perfectly aimed and timed stonk on the reinforcements and other targets. It would certainly account for a peculiar happening that occurred on the morning of the 28th, shortly after Phil Young died and the Bn.HQ. was pulled back to a rear position on the NE corner of the wood.

Ray Langdale...
Now, the C.O. had had the battle flag put up near the entrance to the field and this was guarded by a regimental policeman (L/Cpl G. Thwaite) with a stengun. He used to altinate between the gateway and the road and suddenly, one morning, a sten opened up and I ran out there. I saw this policeman still in an aiming position and when I looked, less than twenty yards from him in the Fontenay direction there was a French civilian motor car stopped with its windscreen smashed and the driver was shot up. The passenger you would have taken for a civilian but on closer inspection they both wore field grey from the waist downwards with jackboots on and 'civvie' shirts. The wounded driver and his passenger were taken away and we never knew where they came from or where they'd been.

Arthur Green...
We were stuck at Tessel Wood for about three weeks and I had to go forward (from B Echelon) *to Bn.HQ. every day with the wagon up this dusty track, carrying mail and hot meals and replacement equipment or whatever else was required. I used to try everything to get there without creating any dust and letting Gerry know you were there. When it was dry the dust would come up in great big clouds however slowly I went and if I stayed in first gear the engine would roar.*

Everybody remembers Sgt. Goodliffe (SBs) and he was forever shouting instructions to the lads to stop running about between slit trenches out in the open fields. They used to do this to get around their mates and in doing so they used to get wounded and would end up in front of him. He'd play merry hell as he stuffed a cigarette in their mouth and gave them hot sweet tea. There was always plenty of hot, sweet tea! I must say also that in the Second World War, they did look after the wounded and they were very quickly evacuated and they were never left unattended for any period of time.

Ray Langdale...
At Tessel Wood there was one rather humourous, well, I thought it was humourous because you had to have something to laugh at. It was there that the RSM joined us, Weatherall, and he came up and I had to brief him on what had happened and he got two of his regimental policemen to build an 'L' shaped slit trench. There was a 15cwt. truck brought a lot of timber up from Fontenay and it was a smashing slit trench. He said to me, 'Well, I'm going to get my head down here.' Now Gerry used to stonk us at night and there was a direct hit on this slit trench. There was bits of timber and soil and what have you, all blown up and I thought, 'Oh! He's had it!' Then through the murk staggered this CSM and the next time I saw him, he had a 'casualty' label on him and off he went.

The C.Os. trench was a smasher and it was built in the shape of a cross with a circular area (about three yards diameter) at the centre covered with beams and soil. When he had an 'O' Group (briefing) he would sit in the centre and the officers could crouch in the cross arms looking in. It was fairly bomb proof and that's where Ken Rispin, the C.Os. driver, had his Universal Carrier in the hedge. The Signals dugout was within shouting distance and likewise the Intelligence. In the adjoining field was the Regimental Aid Post (RAP) and there was a knocked out Sherman tank which they used. They'd dug a trench between the tracks and there was sufficient room to get two stretchers under there. They used to bring the food up in 15cwts. in hot boxes and on one occasion Cpl. Brooke came up and somebody shouted, 'Tanks! There's tanks coming!' Then he turned around and shot off back with all the food for a Rifle Company, but they got it back in the end.

Our first Bn.HQ. was at the forward end of Tessel Wood looking down towards Vendes. We had there a 22 set in this American White halftrack vehicle which was linked directly to Brigade and then we had 18 sets between Companies. It was said that the very long whip aerial for the 22 set had given our positions away there.

We had three adjutants in one day. The Col. wanted a message taken to 'B' Coy. in the next field and it only meant going four to five hundred yards and this new adjutant (Lt. Kesby) set off to deliver it and he'd just got to the entrance to the gate when he was hit by a mortar bomb. Major Mott shouted, 'Langdale, who's that over there?' Now, I never saw Major Mott out of his trench and I said, 'It was the Adjutant,' and he said, 'What do you mean?' and I said, 'He's dead!'

Bernard Kesby had been with the Battalion for less than 24 hours when he was killed and had taken the place of Lt. Turrell as Adjutant. However, the 'three adjutants in one day' does not quite add up if the War Diary and Commonwealth War Graves records and dates are correct. (see more information below towards end of Tessel Wood occupation - 15 July)

Chris Somers (Diary)...
Headcover was now being used by all - the timber being brought from the woods in Jeeps and Carriers. 'C' and 'D' Coys were most unpopular with us as their whining Carriers brought down a stonk on the track by us every time they fetched a load of wood, ammunition or food.

We pushed a small standing patrol forward to the crossroads 200 yards to our front. When I went up to pay them my first visit, they were being troubled by a sniper. I tried to spot him using my glasses and all the camouflage precautions as laid down in the Battle Drill Pamphlet, but a shot just over my head made me realize that he had the advantage and my field craft wasn't good enough. We fixed them up with a telephone which made a fiendish row every time it was used.

The next day I was up there, I was walking back down the hedge when I saw the N.C.O. in charge running down behind me with blood running down his face. Apparently a Boche must have been just over the other side of the road and threw a grenade which hit the N.C.O. smack in the face and blew his eye out. We stonked the orchard with 2 inch mortars and succeeded in killing the Boche in question and later got his papers. We moved the patrol back by a burned out tank about 20 yards from the cross track, where they could dig in without being heard too easily.

I went up to see how they were getting on the next day when some gunners unknown put a stonk down on the cross roads, most of it falling around us. Most unpleasant as we didn't have any real holes to get in. One chap was wounded so I withdrew the patrol down the track a bit while I checked up as to how much fire they intended putting down on our own troops!!

John Wollerton...
I was usually in a slit trench within yards of the C.O. and in the early period was being constantly sent for because of the wireless sets failing, which was mainly due to atmospherics. I reckoned that if I got three hours sleep a day, I was doing well. I was so involved mentally and so tired that I don't remember much about the early involvement. I went to an 'O' Group, sat in a corner, slumped down and fell asleep, I was so worn out through lack of sleep.

A lot of the time was boring and there was a lot of shell fire most mornings and late afternoons and I could sleep during them and ask my batman to keep a look out. It was very odd that machine gun fire could wake me up but considerable shell fire tended to put me to sleep.

By now, Capt. Tony Nicholson had replaced Ivor Slator as O.C. 'A' Coy. and Les Gill had replaced John Brinton as O.C. Sp.Coy. Les would now have plenty of opportunity to get to know the layout around Tessel Wood especially in view of the fact that the carriers would be buzzing back and forth supplying the demands of the various companies dug into the forward positions. 'A' Coy. was dug into the East of the wood, between the forward Coys. and Bn.HQ.

Les Gill...
In the field in front of where 'A' Coy. were dug in, there was a hell of a big shell, a huge shell that was there before we arrived. It was a naval shell and it must have failed to explode and bounced, coming to rest within a couple of hundred yards of 'A' Coy. HQ. We respected that shell and if a Gerry artillery shell had hit it, it could have blown the darn thing up. There were also three cows or bullocks in that field in front of us which had been killed one way or another and had become terribly bloated. They were virtually round and on one occasion a shell hit one of these cows. Now, you have never ever smelled anything like it in your life as the smell from that carcass. It was awful!

Arnold Whiteley...
About two fields in front of Tessel wood there was a road which ran across our front. It wasn't used in daylight but they (the Germans) used it at night time to bring food up but they must have taken a wrong turn at the crossroads and dropped it off on our forward positions. It was dished out and it were horrible stuff. We wouldn't have known anything but about half an hour later our own food truck came up from behind us lines. Our Sgt. Major said, 'That were bloody rubbish you brought us up earlier tonight!' It was obvious that the Germans had left it in the wrong place.

The men in the Intelligence Section had a rota system which saw them on various nights in Forward Observation Posts (FOPs) and then a night on the so called 'battlebox'. This was a large box that was carried everywhere the Battalion went and contained intelligence maps and various other operational documents and were usually kept in the vicinity of Battalion HQ. Ken Godfrey did duty in one FOP near a knocked out Sherman tank close to the Vendes cross roads, just forward of the Hallams front line (the same tank mentioned above by Chris Somers). Earlier, he had discovered the body of a dead crewman, forward of this tank and over the hedge in a field ditch, which must have been there for some time.

Ken Godfrey...
I was told to do a recce beyond this tank towards the crossroads to see if it was suitable for an OP and decided to make my way up on the field side of the hedge. I heard a ping and threw myself forward in the ditch and put my hand on this lad and I was so scared. He was burnt and I got up and threw myself up and over the hedge into the lane and carried on walking towards the crossroads. There was an officer coming the other way and he said, 'What you doing here?' I told him that I was looking for a spot to position an OP on the crossroads now that it had been captured. He said, 'Oh, no it hasn't!' So I had to turn around and come back. Later, I thought that if I had had any gumption, I would have removed this lad's identity tag but they must have found him after we finished there anyway. He definitely came from the tank because he still had his earphones on.

On duty at these FOPs we used to have a sniper with us as well, but he was usually laid up some distance away from our position. We would sometimes get a glimpse of the enemy, and they us, and I remember a story which I can't confirm related by one of our snipers, a cold blooded little devil. The Germans had got a latrine on the edge of a wood and this Sniper spotted it being used one day, waited till he'd finished and then shot him.

Whilst on the subject of sniping it might be the time to introduce a man, Harry M. Furness by name and a Battalion sniper by profession. Harry came to the Battalion at around the time of Fontenay, having previously served with the Green Howards during the first few days after 'D' Day. By all accounts, he would seem to have been very good at his trade. Of course, this was a requirement of such activities if a sniper wanted to stay alive. Harry has been able to provide a mine of technical information on the subject of sniping which is more fitted for inclusion into a book that might have been entitled 'The Snipers Manual'. Indeed, he has provided many people, both here, the U.S.A. and elsewhere with just that kind of material and his name is to be found in the acknowledgments of a number of expert volumes. Skills learned and perfected sixty years ago are still the basis for modern learning and Harry's knowledge has been much in demand all these years.

Harry Furness...

Landing in Normandy with the assault, I served as a Sniper with The Green Howards Regiment. But soon enough I was wounded by enemy mortar blast and fragments. I was first taken to our RAP (Regimental Aid Post), and from there to the FDS (Field Dressing Station) where, because I could still walk, was classified as 'walking wounded.' I was not sent back to the U.K. and received treatment near Bayeux, and after some days rest, I was informed that I was to be transferred to the Hallamshire Battalion. They had requested an urgent need for trained Snipers and so I reported in to the Hallams HQ. My memory after all these years of my joining them revolves mainly around the greeting I first received, for they didn't ask me where I had been trained and qualified or anything like that. Instead, I was asked, 'Where's tha from then?' I knew they meant my home town, so I told them Manchester, to which they replied, 'Well that's all reet then.'

Real Snipers were few and far between, they were all highly trained Specialists who did not engage in typical line infantry tactics. They never undertook harassment fire or shoot at everything that moved. They did not climb trees, hang out of windows, hide behind chimney pots, nor any place you might think they would be likely to be seen or found. All were highly trained in concealment techniques and camouflage and they were highly selective in target acquisition. It was quality of target that counted, never quantity.

We all had a priority listing of enemy targets we would engage and we provided a Sniper-Shield for our Battalion, which meant that mostly we operated well forward of our Bn. positions. We gave the highest priority to the elimination of enemy Snipers, followed by searching out and eliminating any battlefield leaders, mainly Officers and NCOs. In addition, anyone with a flame-thrower, bazooka, radiomen, tank commanders, anti-tank gunners, machine-gunners, and anyone else who looked likely to be dangerous to us. As a matter of course, we frequently held fire on private soldiers for a very good

Harry M. Furness was Mentioned in Dispatches for his sniping services. Here he wears special equipment and carries a telescopic rifle. He was very keen to point out that this was a publicity photograph and he would not have been quite so conspicuous in the field. Full camouflage was achieved by use of face veil, scrimmage and other coverings. (AFPU)

reason. Higher ranking soldiers, the preferred targets who might still be under cover, were emboldened to come out that way.

Les Gill...

The C.O. came up to me one day at Tessel Wood and he said, 'Gill! I understand that your latrines are something to behold!' I said, 'Oh! Yes they are, absolutely super-duper!' He said, 'What do you mean by super-duper?' and I said, 'Well, there's a safety factor in them' and he said, 'Oh! Yes. Are we near enough to one for you to explain in some detail?' I said, 'Oh! Yes Sir, there's one about fifty yards away,' and off we went. Now every hedge in Normandy is built on a bund and that little bund was a great blessing for us in many cases because at least if you were behind one, it gave some limited protection against enemy fire. Well, the idea of this

❖ *Road leading up towards Tessel Wood from Fontenay le Pesnel. The field on the immediate left here was the final position of Bn. HQ. The entrance was just short of the dark central group of trees and the RAP was just off picture to the left. A hedge once separated the road and field but has been removed in the recent past. (DWS)*

toilet or latrine as it's better known in the army was to put the latrine in a position behind the bund and low enough to use it as protection. So the C.O. said to me, 'How did you do that then? How have you got it so that your bum is so low.' I said, 'Well, you dig a strip out on your side of the bund which is where your feet are going to be so that it brings you down so much. Now, in order to get down, you need to use the hedge in front of you to get hold of so that you've got a solid thing to hang onto. Then, when you lean back, you don't fall back! So, he said, 'Why ever didn't I think about that! Consequently, the 'patent' was used in modifications to latrines surrounding Battalion HQ. so that in future you could 'operate' in a safe position with your head below the top of the bund!

Bert Murray took part in a patrol sent out towards the village of Vendes on the 2 July. The War Diary states that on that day Battalion casualties amounted to 3 killed, 5 wounded and 4 missing. Bert was one of the latter and witness to two of those who died.

Bert Murray...

My memory of the period between landing and being wounded and taken prisoner is not too clear after 50 years. I recall we cleared the beach and think we spent the first night in an orchard some miles inland. When we did move up to relieve (could have been the Green Howards) we seemed to spend most of our time ducking sniper fire or listening to the 'Moaning Minnies' hopefully passing over. I can remember being in 'B' Coy. and advancing one early morning into a valley of mist and smoke but were soon bogged down in crossfire with visibility down to about 5 yards and not knowing which was the 'friendly fire'. Shortly after this we stood down as I recall a bed and a haircut. Then we were up front again with quite a few strangers. I understand that we were now in Tessel Wood and it was from there that I went on my last patrol. I cannot be absolutely sure of the date but for 50 years I have had it as the 2nd July, 1944 (confirmed in the

War Diary). The letter to my mother from our O/C Major P.S. Newton was dated 13th July but I guess he had more things to do than write letters and 11 days to me seems reasonable.

I feel terrible about not remembering names but I recall our Sergeant coming to me the eve before and asking me if I fancied a walk in the woods. I cannot remember volunteering but nonetheless I was there early next morning. There would be about 25 to 30 in the patrol - An Officer, the sergeant and two privates all in 'light order' - followed by the rest of us a reasonable distance behind (20 yards maybe). We were told that the area or hamlet was clear of Germans (Recce Corps had confirmed it clear) and our job was to pass through and take up positions and hold until midday when the whole Battalion would be moving up to relieve.

I remember it was early light and we were progressing along the edge of a field behind a fairly thick, high hedge, beyond which I could see a tall barn type building running parallel to us. As we broke cover at the end of the hedge we came under intense automatic fire. At this stage I cannot recall what sort of cover the advanced party had, but from later evidence of the holes in my right trouser leg I was nicked by a least 3 shots. There was a little blood and worst of all my leg seemed to have gone dead and I thought it had gone. I now scrambled back behind cover, but had lost my Bren in the panic. By the time I had recovered myself the patrol had been ordered to get the hell out of it and at this stage picked up a Sten gun which had been dropped. The two privates from the advance party joined me behind the hedge and we started to crawl back towards base. We took stock and between us we had one loaded Sten, plenty of .303 rounds in Bren gun magazines, two 36 grenades and one smoke grenade.

At this time we were being fired on and they were lobbing the odd stick grenade over the hedge but we were always just ahead of them until we came to the edge of the field. At this stage we had to make a decision as to which way to go. The two 36 grenades were thrown in the general direction of the enemy followed by the 'smoke' - none of which exploded. Whether they hadn't been primed properly I don't know, but the smoke seemed our only hope at that stage and that had gone. The smaller of my two comrades whose name sounded like Pedley was leading when he was hit in the chest by a burst of automatic fire. His mate, whose name I can't recall, immediately made a dispairing run up the field and suddenly the enemy were all over the place and though he got some 30 or 40 yards he was hit a number of times.

I was taken into a barn and they put some sort of field dressing on my leg which to be honest was the least of my worries at the time. In this barn there seemed to be a number of Germans of high level and they probably had our patrol under observation for quite some time before opening fire. Later, I was taken to their HQ and soon found myself being lead away in the same direction from where I had just come from - there was little doubt I was going to be target practice before some argument took place and I was eventually locked in another outhouse for a few days. I queried my captors about my two comrades and they confirmed that they were dead.

As a P.S. to this story later in PoW camp, I was advised not to mention my injury even if I was in great pain as the German Medics experimented with amputation. Whether there was any truth in that I don't know but that dressing stayed put for a long, long time. When it was removed the wound had healed and I never thought about it again until 5 years later when a 9mm round worked its way to the surface. I had it removed in March, 1949, two years after demob at Preston Royal Infirmary.

So ended Bert Murray's war but his testimony, over 50 years later, sheds some light on one of the casualties whose name he thought was Pedley. It seems certain that this man was none other than George William Pedel, known as 'Jody' by his very close friend, Roy Simon. Having no known grave, his name is inscribed on the Bayeux Memorial to the Missing as he was subsequently declared as missing in action on 2nd July, 1944, which ties in exactly with the date remembered by Bert. The other man must have been one of two others subsequently confirmed as missing in action on that day. These were Ptes. Peter Pacey and Newton Snarr.

At about 1425hrs on the 3 July, an unusual incident occurred when a British Jeep containing four khaki clad figures was observed driving across the Hallams front on the road through Vendes. Where it came from or where it was going has remained a mystery but it passed without either side firing a shot. On the next day, another four officers joined the Battalion. These were: Lts. H.G. Lewis (GR), H.C.H. Chamberlain (WR), J.H. Court (NR) and H.S. Crowe (Canloan). On the 5th, Lt. S.A. Lucy (SWB) joined. These officers may well have thought that the Germans opposite had put on a special welcoming 'stonk' the next day which was particularly heavy but apparently there was another reason. A new German unit had just taken up positions in the line and was determined to make its presence felt. 2000 shells were sent back by the R.A. in a sort of welcoming reply.

At about 2100hrs on the 7 July, the ground to the east of the Hallams erupted when a carpet of 2,500 tons of bombs was laid on the northern district of Caen in an effort to reduce the resistance of the Germans who were holding this great city.

Arthur Green...
One summer evening there was a droning sound and we saw a wave of bombers coming over on their way to Caen. I always remember, we stood at the top of our trenches (in the relatively safe area of 'B' Echelon) on a lovely summers evening watching them go over and I was so relieved that something was being done because we were getting a bit disheartened with being shelled all the time and not moving one way or the other and at last they were doing something.

Whatever else may be said, this attack had the desired effect and the enemy eventually began to release it's strong grip on the area. The massive bombardment, sadly, had one other effect which should never be forgotten. Days later, the British and Canadians pouring over the rubble that had once been Caen, could not have known then that they were walking over the remains of up to 3,000 civilian men, women and children for whom they had brought liberation. With such knowledge, the word 'liberation' rings much less than hollow and it might be wondered how the decision was made for such devastation to be metered out. The criteria is said to have been based on the unacceptable casualties already suffered by the British 2nd Army since the landings. In round figures, the total casualties since 'D' Day (about 30 days) have since been estimated in excess of 20,000 (including over 3,000 killed), although there are probably conflicting figures elsewhere.

To put this into perspective, the British Army suffered approximately 60,000 casualties (including 20,000 killed) on the first day of the Somme Battle (1 July, 1916). Now that was unacceptable and so was the loss of 3000 civilian lives at Caen in just a few hours on that fateful day... C'est la Guerre!

More casualties occurred on the 10th when 'A' Coy. carried out a major raid on positions east of Vendes. Lt. H.E. Poynor was killed, Capt. P.H. Willis-Dixon and Lt. C. Pease were wounded.
Four ORs were killed, 16 wounded and 3 missing. Then on the 12th, the MO, Capt. A.A. Gregory - Dean and CQMS Jackson were both injured when three friendly, but defective, mortar bombs fell on Bn.HQ. The MO was replaced by Capt. J.D. Lavertime RAMC.

George Learad...
I didn't know Poynor myself but the padre asked me to help to dig his temporary grave. We didn't dig a deep grave of course, it was only about two foot and we'd take one of the identity discs and wrap their bodies in a blanket. That chap will always live in my memory, he couldn't have been very old and only looked about 18. I'll never forget how he had obviously died and he mustn't have felt a thing. He had a bullet clean through his heart and he couldn't have suffered, he must have died instantly. We buried quite a few lads and they were all buried with their heads towards the enemy, facing the enemy.

Lt. Harry E. Poyner had been brought back from the area where he had been killed, just to the south of Tessel Wood where the raid had taken place. George could not remember just where the burial took place but it must have been in the vicinity of Fontenay le Pesnel, just to the rear of Tessel Wood in a relatively safe area. Harry may have looked very young in death's repose but was in fact thirty years old.

The 13th brought some relief when no casualties were incurred and, in the evening, the Divisional Commander's prize of £5 was presented to the A/Tk. Pl. for being the first such unit in the 49th Division to knock out a German tank. This was the one that had been put out of action on the 25 June by Sgt. Palliser and L/Cpl Williams near the corner of the church in Fontenay. The tank had also managed to destroy the 6Pdr A/Tk. gun that these men were operating and the Cpl was wounded. He was awarded the Military Medal for this action.

Ray Langdale remembers a conversation with Jonnie Palliser, many years later, who told him that only one tank was knocked out and another came to the rescue of its crew members who managed to bail out. It may even have been some of these people that were shot up by Chris Somers in the same area. Trevor Hart Dyke mentioned that when he passed by the hulk one day on his way to Brigade, he chalked the word 'Hallamshires' on the side plates so as to claim credit for the Battalion and no doubt to prevent anyone else from 'bagging' it!

Chris Somers (Diary)...
As days went on, we got used to our holes in the ground, in fact we hated leaving them. The troops were settling down again having been rather shaky for a day or two after the big battle of Fontenay. I think this was mainly due to a lack of sleep and food and incessant stonking. There was quite a phase of 'bomb happiness' at one time, though I don't think many cases were genuine, except for perhaps one chap who ran down the track screaming his head off - a most unpleasant noise! Our Coy. HQ. Command Post was quite well laid out, the trench being dug in the shape of an 'H' with an adjoining small slit where Mike and I used to sleep. We had a large tarpaulin for a roof and felt quite safe - little did we realize!!

Water was always a problem as it had to come up in Jerry cans. There was just enough for shaving but no one had what you could call a wash for three weeks. The weather was reasonably good and on sunny days we would sunbathe by our slits. Luckily, our ears were so well-trained now that we could usually hear the bombs or shells start off and just had time to drop into our slits. We were only caught on the hop once when CQMS brought the lunch up and we were all sitting outside chatting. A small bomb landed about 20 yards away as we all dived in a heap into the Coy. HQ. Command Post!

Visiting the latrine was always a bit tricky as the Boche always seemed to choose this inconvenient moment to lob one over. Perhaps my luckiest escape in this position was when I was on duty and was just stepping out of the Command Post for a breath of fresh air and sun when the telephone rang. As I bent down by the signaller to answer it, there was a terrific explosion with a blinding flash. The air was filled with the dust and fumes and our ears were ringing. Our canvas roof had been torn in half and the glass of our hurricane lamp smashed. One of our own shells, as we discovered, had hit the parapet of our position about six feet from our heads. As it was the back of the trench we got the full blast our way. We never found out who fired the gun but it wasn't our own gunners. Luckily they didn't send another one after it!

Walking back across the open field to the rear platoon or Battalion HQ. was always an unpleasant job, as practically every time I went that way, Jerry lobbed one or two over in the vicinity and I and my runner had to flatten ourselves. I was once sitting on the end of a slit trench talking to a Cpl. of the rear platoon when some shells landed 50 yards to our flank. There was no room in the slit so there I had to sit with the Cpl. at the other end. A wicked piece of shrapnel wizzed between us and embedded itself into the side of the slit trench. It's all a matter of luck really!

I only did one very minor standing patrol in this area much to my relief. Then I had to lie up in a cold ditch with two other chaps to see if a Spandau used a certain position. It was a dull night and nothing happened. As we were getting a bit bored and stale, 'A' Coy. did a raid one day. At the same time we let fly with every weapon we possessed for a half an hour. I don't know if we did much damage. We got a little back in return and a visiting Leicestershire Cpl. got killed while helping us with a Bren, which was rather unfortunate.

I took most of the Coy. out of the line for a march one afternoon while the Carrier platoon relieved us. It was good to loosen the limbs and have a change of scenery. We went back over the old battlefields and I was able to check up where David and 'Happy' had been buried. It was the first time I had been out of the field for nearly three weeks. Casualties in the Battalion had mounted daily from stonking and occasional raids. Many officers had joined the Battalion but had gone back wounded before I even saw them.

Raids by our aircraft were always a good morale raiser. There was a big raid by Lancasters on Villiers Bocage when we had to stand to because of the dust. Then another on Caen sector. When the weather was clear, Typhoons were constantly strafing in front of us. Occasionally, Boche fighters came over low and at full speed. Invariably they lost one or two.

At last on July 15 we learnt that early next morning another Division (59th Staffordshire) was going to attack through us and at the same time we would launch an attack on Vendes to secure their right flank. That evening we changed places with 'A' Coy. as they were attacking before us. The idea was for each Coy. to move around into the other positions as they moved out. I had visions of being stonked like hell as we did it. Next morning proved I wasn't far wrong!

Lt. Bernard O. Kesby was killed instantly on the 15th by shellfire as he left Bn.HQ. to make contact with 'B' Coy. The C.O. had asked him to find out what was happening in their area when gunfire was heard from that direction. Such information could have been gleaned by telephone but he misunderstood the order, thinking that it was meant for him to make physical contact. This officer was a replacement for Peter Turrell (Adjt), who had been wounded on the 28 June. Lt. Kesby only joined the Battalion the day before he was killed which means that the C.O. had been without an Adjutant for 16 days. Lt. Kesby had been the eventual replacement but was lost within 24 hours of his arrival.

'D' Coy. of the 4 KOYLI, under the command of Major A. Dunnill, was now attached to the Hallams to add strength to an attack on Vendes which was to take place the next day.

Trevor Hart Dyke...

We were ordered to try and capture Barbee Farm and Vendes and I was given a Company of the KOYLI to support me in the attack. I think it was mainly because the new Brigade Commander was KOYLI and I had been told to carry out this attack which I was very hesitant in doing because I said I would like to do it with either smoke or with tank support and not just with my own soldiers. In fact, a KOYLI Coy. and one of mine did actually capture Barbee Farm but 'A' and 'D' Coys. were unable to capture Vendes as it was very heavily defended and, of course, the artillery support which we had, really did more harm than good because it merely collapsed some of the buildings in Vendes and gave the defenders extra cover.

So, the attack on Vendes actually was to take place in conjunction with the 59th Division on my left and my attack was just a support for the main attack by that Division. That was a failure, in fact I think their anti-tank guns did shoot up their own tanks which didn't help. So we were told by the Divisional Commander to withdraw our troops from Vendes and Barbee Farm and were given artillery fire to cover our withdrawal.

Chris Somers (Diary)...

Our final day around Tessel Wood had come at last, and what a day! In the early hours while it was still dark breakfast was being issued out to sleepy individuals - many missed it altogether. Everything seemed rushed that morning and before we knew where we were we were advancing from 'A' Coy's. position forward to our own position. However we had hardly got there when Mike gave the order to move across to 'C' Coy. position. Things were beginning to warm up already. As we crossed to their position small arms fire opened up on a gap which we had to make a quick dash across.

We quickly jumped into the slit trenches only just in time too. Very shortly afterward down came a mortar stonk. One landed on the edge of my slit where I was crouching with Mike, the signaller and 18 set. The 18 set landed on top of me plus a pile of dirt and logs! We had hardly changed to

the spare set when another bomb landed practically in the same place. The same shower of dirt covered us but this time we had the set in the bottom of the trench. Soon we began to move forward again to 'D' Coys. position. It was an unpleasant feeling having to get out into the open, knowing that the Boche had that area accurately registered. We were lucky however.

It wasn't long before we got the order to make for Barbee Farm to assist the Coy. of KOYLI who were already there. We followed the hedges down through the cornfields and some of the leading platoon succeeded in getting to the farm. But the Boche spotted them and covered a gap of 30 yards pretty thoroughly

❖ *Barbee Farm as it looked in the summer of the year 2000. It was taken and bravely held by a Company of Hallams and KOYLI under the command of Mike Lonsdale-Cooper and Derek Dunnill respectively, but the attack could not be followed through onto the main target which was the village of Vendes. In fact, the place was never captured as such because the German occupants, who had held the place so stubbornly for three weeks, chose to abandon it shortly after the attack was called off. (DWS)*

232

with Spandau fire, killing anyone who attempted to run for it or crawl through the corn. The Coy. was temporarily held up and the Boche opened up with small mortars. He seemed to follow us round the hedgerows - unfortunately there were no ditches. Eventually, after the Coy. had reorganized, the C.O. put down a goodly barrage on Vendes while we rushed across the gap and made for the farm.

I established the 18 set in an outhouse as they were too busy to dig in. Here, myself and the two signallers were lucky, because stonks rained down on the orchard where the two Coys. were digging in. Though many shells hit the farm buildings, I felt reasonably safe, a fools paradise perhaps. The platoons, particularly those of the KOYLI, were beginning to suffer many casualties, some from shells, many from snipers who had crawled up on either side of the orchard. As the day wore on it was realized that our position was becoming untenable owing to the shortage of men and the fact that the enemy was on three sides of us and could easily cut us off.

The situation elsewhere was not too favourable and after the padre had collected the wounded into the halftrack, a heavy barrage was put down to cover our withdrawal back to Tessel Wood, unfortunately leaving many grand chaps behind who had been killed during the fighting, including Cpl. Watkins, Pte. Crowther and MacIntosh, an SB who was shot while collecting in a wounded man. However, to make amends, a German prisoner went out and brought them in. It was a hot run back loaded up with spare shovels and helping to carry the 18 set, but if one goes the only thing is to go quickly. We learnt later that the Boche in that area were also at the end of their tether and had thrown in cooks and all sorts to hold out.

Arnold Whiteley took part in this abortive attack...

Arnold Whiteley...
On the 16 July, we went forward without any artillery, without any cover at all. We just went forward and crossed the two fields, crossed the road and then he had us where he wanted us. They opened up with shelling, mortar bombing and small arms fire and we were pinned down in the field. Me and me mate, we crawled to the side of this field and through a hedge where there was a bit of an irrigation ditch to give us a bit more cover. We got through the hedge and he was on my right and a young boy called Derek Hooley came and he was on my left. He had the Brengun and he put a magazine on and we knew which direction the fire was coming from. He opened up and he didn't get a magazine off when his head went down and he'd been shot clean through the head. He was only about twenty or so. I pulled the gun from him and I said to Sid, 'I'll get this thing going,' and he said, 'Don't mate, it's a sniper and he's seen the flash of the gun muzzle.' Then a shell came down nearly on top of us and it couldn't have come any nearer without doing something serious. We both got shell splinters and a terrific flash made us eyes go out of focus.

We laid there a bit then I heard the Coy. Commander shouting my name and he was at the other side of the hedge. He said that he wanted us to get back to the positions we had left and tell them that we were pinned down and we couldn't move and we want a lot of artillery put down. I crawled back through these two fields to Col. Hart Dyke who had brought Bn. HQ. forward and now taken over the slit trenches that we had left. So I went and I gave him my message and he said, 'We'll soon have them out. You don't go back, you've been hit,' and he sent me back to First Aid Post. So I finished up back at Bayeux in an ambulance with about a fortnight in hospital.

Doug Catley...
On the Vendes attack we went across one field and into the second towards the road and we got badly shelled and I remember getting blown over by the blast. Then Major Mackillop, who was

now our Company Commander, took us back to a great big ditch and that's where we got orders to contact the KOYLI officer on our right in Barbee Farm and liaise with him on the wireless.

We got back to our own trenches and then we got another signal to move back to the other end of Tessel Wood because we were being relieved. So we came out of the slit trenches and I was holding the 18 set for my mate to strap it on. All of sudden it was like an express train bearing down on us and we flattened and that's when we got hit. It had got my mate across the arse and all his trousers were ripped. We tended to him with these special bandages, you know, and they said to me, 'Are you all right?' and I said, 'Yes, I just got blown over again like I did this morning.' Ten minutes after that I fainted with a deep penetrating wound and Eric Goodliffe fetched us out and we got back to a tented hospital in Bayeux. A Canadian Doctor came round and tagged me for evacuation and I ended up at Sheffield Hospital via the Normandy Beaches, a landing craft, Portsmouth and London.

Whilst in Sheffield, Doug was visited by David Lockwood's mother and father who were eager to know anything about their son. Doug was moved to various places including Huddersfield and Dover and was eventually medically downgraded. Finally, he was sent for signals retraining at Catterick and then to Scarborough on a high speed signalling operators course which was still in progress there when the war ended. He never got back to the Hallams and was later demobilized at Strensall barracks near York.

Above: Vendes shortly after the war during repairs to the church tower which had been damaged by British artillery in an effort to prevent its use as an observation post. (THD) ❖Left: It has weathered sufficiently in the past 40 years or so to hide any evidence of repair, a credit also to the masons who carried out the restoration. (DWS)

Chris Somers (Diary)...

There was a welcome surprise for all of us when we got back to Tessel Wood. As soon as we had checked off the Coy., lorries and carriers were waiting to take us back out of the line, the Lincolns were taking over for the night. Every body felt jubilant, a peaceful sleep at last. Even a stray shell which landed in our rest area didn't deter anybody and we were soon sound asleep.

234

When the Hallams were withdrawn from the front-line they went into a rest camp near a little village called Ducy St. Marguerite which they had passed very closely on their right flank when moving into the line in front of Audreiu on 13 June.

This was a place later adopted by the Tyneside Scottish who erected a small memorial there (post war) on the right hand side of the road leading out of the village to Audreiu. The author has vivid memories of driving slowly through this village during the 50th Anniversary Tour to commemorate the landings in 1944 and seeing a huge, white bearded veteran in full highland garb. This ageing, 'Finlay Curry' sort of a man, was being led along the lane by two very small children of the village towards the memorial, one each side and holding his hands, carefully guiding his every step in a most endearing way.

On the 18th, the C.O. with Coy. Commanders and the Padre visited Vendes to identify and bury the dead. The attack had been very costly and the Hallams suffered five officers wounded. These were: Maj.G.J. Good, Capt. C.A. MacKillop, Lts. G.H.R. Jackson, L.F. Nobert and H.J. Allkins. Worse still, there had been 10 ORs killed and no less than 59 wounded. In the 33 days the Battalion had been on French soil the total casualties amounted to 33 Officers and 460 ORs. which represented well over half the Bn. strength.

❖ *Memorial to the 1st Tyneside Scottish in the small village of Ducy St. Marguerite. (DWS)*

John Wollerton...
After it had been finally cleared, I went back to Vendes with Mike Lonsdale-Cooper and one or two more to help with identification of the dead we had left behind there. It was a bit messy and nowhere to wash your hands. They were all lying where they'd fallen and hadn't been there for very long, but bodies soon went black and maggots attacked the eyes, ears, nose and mouth very quickly, in fact my batman's first remark on seeing a dead German earlier in Fontenay was how much he could get for the maggots down Attercliffe. The vulgarity of war!

During the Hallams rest period after Vendes many of the men were able to go to a concert put on for the troops which was held in a field near Ducy St. Marguerite. Ken Godfrey attended...

Ken Godfrey... (who 'sang' the words below to the author. It was 'captured' on audio tape!)
There was a woman singing a song and I got the music years later to do it in a show :-

> *All's Well, Madamoiselle, we're on our way to dear old gay Paris*
> *All's Well, Madamoiselle, we started off from Normandy, it won't be long till Victory*
> *France will love the happy day, France will ring with the Marseille*
> *So, All's Well, Madamoiselle,*
> *Soon we'll live again, love and romance again,*
> *Vive La France again, Madamoiselle.*

We went for our bath in a huge vat and they took all our clothes from us but we kept our own boots. We had a big swill round, a rough towelling and as we came out they gave us deloused clothing. There was great rejoicing as well because we had our first slice of bread since before Tessel Wood and Fontenay.

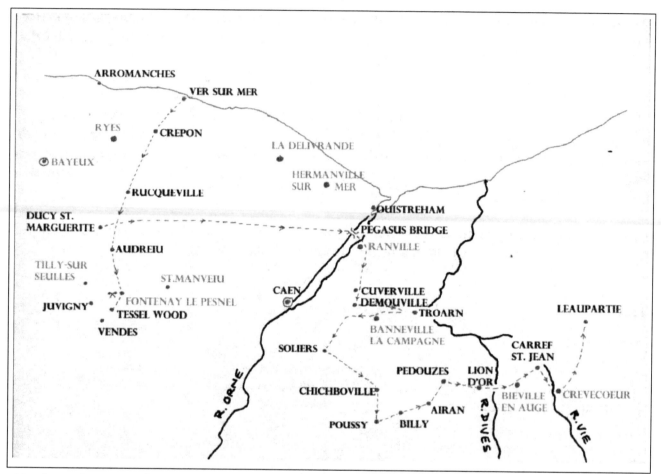

Map showing basic route of Hallamshire Battalion from Ver sur Mer to Leaupartie (places of Memorial in gray print) and some of the towns/villages through which they passed. A continuation of this map, Leaupartie to Le Havre, will be found in the next chapter.(DWS)

It was during this period that a man, far away from this place, but with the Hallamshire Battalion very much in mind, put pen to paper and wrote to Mary Lockwood from somewhere in Italy.

Major H.J.W. Marsh
6th Bn.The York & Lancaster Regt.
July 20th 44.

My dear Mary,
I cannot say how sorry I was to learn in a letter from Barbara yesterday of David being killed. Of course, learning the Hallamshires were in Normandy, I knew they must be having a lot of casualties but one always relies on ones own friends escaping.

I have known David from childhood, intimately in the Hallamshires for twelve years now; there was no one in the Battalion for whom I had more affection and respect. Until he came back home we all expected him to get command of our Battalion. I have continually heard tell of how well he was doing at Newton Chambers - he was one of Sheffield's 'coming young men' and he had a great career ahead of him.

236

If ever in the years to come (should I survive) there should be anything I can do for you or Benjamin, look upon me as one of David's, and your, warmest friends. Meanwhile all I can send is my deepest sympathy.

Yours very sincerely,
John Marsh.

It sounds almost by premonition that this man needed to qualify his promise to David Lockwood's wife with the words 'should I survive' because, sadly, he too was dead within two months of writing the letter.

The Hallamshires had now licked their wounds which were considerable. The reporting of casualty numbers in the June War Diary is not consistent and there are definitely some missing, at least for the 27th day. It was July before someone got into the habit of recording casualty figures as a matter of course at the end of each daily report. It can only be said that the figures 'reported' up to being pulled out of the line on the 16 July, stood at 5 officers killed and 17 wounded, 44 Other Ranks killed, 204 wounded and 12 missing. It must be remembered that subsequent deaths from wounds could obviously not be reported and therefore these on the spot reports can and do often differ from the later postwar official figures held by the Commonwealth War Graves Commission. So the total casualty figures 'reported' were 272 which was approximately one third of the whole Battalion and well over half the total number of its 'fighting' troops.

The Hallams remained at Ducy St. Marguerite where they re-equiped, reorganized and retrained until the 26 July, when they took part in a Divisional Route March. Next day, the Battalion moved out and took up positions in the Divisional Reserve area near Cuverville where it caught the aftermath of the battle for Caen in the form of heavy shelling and an air raid. The Bn. now moved in to relieve the 1/4 K.O.Y.L.I. in an area just East of Demouville and prepared for a new phase which would incure many river crossings and culminate in the capture of Le Havre.

❖ *A peaceful scene at Ducy St. Marguerite, Summer, 2000. (DWS)*

MANY RIVERS TO CROSS

Evidence for this book was collected over many years and from many sources, but it became apparent that few people were able to cast any light on the Hallams exploits between Ducy St. Marguerite and the River Seine. This was rather similar to the Norway Campaign where a lot of ground was covered in a relatively short period of time and where minds had some difficulty in registering events in this type of situation. It was far different in Tessel Wood, for instance, where the mind had many days to stamp images and events into the memory for much later recall. Almost miraculously, however, in each of the cases mentioned above, the gaps were filled by the works of two men. John Marsh and Chris Somers have filled both of those gaps that would otherwise have been left in this book. John left his works in the hope that it would 'help a future historian' and Chris revealed in a telephone conversation that he had kept a record of events, albeit related mainly to his own Company, but was pleased to allow its use for this book. His memoirs are the major source for this part, which covers the advance to the River Seine and beyond.

Chris Somers was born in Halesowen, Birmingham, on 13 May, 1916. His connection with the Hallamshire Battalion was as a direct result of moving to Sheffield where he lived in 'digs' whilst serving an apprenticeship in the steel industry during those few years leading up to the war. It was only natural that he should meet with others, like David Lockwood and John Marsh who were in the same business. It would not have taken him long to be attracted by the outdoor pursuits offered by the local Territorial Army in which a number of his contemporaries had commissions. This photograph was taken c.1942, probably on return from Iceland and at a time when he was about to marry his future wife, Doreene. Chris was one of the few Hallams officers to return home physically unscathed, after having served with the Battalion from the beginning. (ACS)

The 49th Division was now assigned to the Canadian 2nd Army and destined to take up a part of the left flank position in the Allied advance for many weeks to come. The move eastwards from Ducy St. Marguerite, so as to take up positions in that line, entailed the crossing of a bridge over the Caen Canal at a place called Benouville. At that time, it would have been passed over by the Hallams with little thought or knowledge of its significance in the general scheme of things. It would later figure largely in the story of 'D' Day, in that it became the first piece of France to be retaken in the very early hours of the 6th June, 1944. It was the now almost legendary, Pegasus Bridge.

❖ *Pegasus Bridge is guarded here by a 25 Pdr. Field Gun but no longer spans the Caen Canal. It has been saved for posterity and is now part of a purpose built museum close to the new bridge that replaced it. The Hallams and many others passed over this hallowed memorial during the summer of 1944.(DWS)*

Chris Somers (Diary)...
A week's rest at St. Marguerite was certainly welcome. I visited the dentist and had three days at the 1st Corps Rest Club by the sea where Michael Elliott was working. The Battalion moved the night before I got back but they sent a truck for me, and I joined them in the open plains near Demouville. The Coy. was dug in round the hedge surrounding a small field. The gun positions all

round drew counter battery fire pretty regularly. I had only been there a few minutes when a shell landed over the hedge and just about took the arm off the water truck driver.

Arthur Saunders was the C.Os. Signaller and was well acquainted with the nature of Trevor Hart Dyke. Without going into any detail, Arthur sums him up as being a fair and good officer but one who thought that his signaller was a man without the need for sleep. He was later transferred to a company of the South Staffs Regt. which formed a whole company within the Battalion when it became depleted through mounting casualties just before Le Havre. However, not all casualties were as a result of enemy action and Arthur, a man with a keen sense of humour, got himself into trouble on one occasion near the Bn. HQ. area near Demouville.

❖ *The open plains of Demouville (seen in the background) where the Hallams assembled ready to move a little further east and into the front line near Troarn, where they would soon have to deal with both snipers and mosquitoes. (DWS)*

Arthur Saunders...
I'd been out somewhere and when I came back Eric Goodliffe was doing something to this lad's toe as I was passing and I said, 'Why don't you cut it off?' Well, he came back to me and said, 'I'll have you Court - Marshalled Corporal Saunders,' and I said, 'What for?' He said, 'Don't you know what's happened?' So I said, 'No!' This lad had put his rifle to his foot, pulled trigger, and instead of hitting his toe it went between his big toe and the next and burnt him. He got four years hard labour, him!

It would be around this time that Arnold Whiteley was making his way back to the Battalion after recuperating from his shrapnel wounds sustained in the attack on Vendes. It was probably not a very good time to return because the Bn. was operating in an area during the last few days of the month, that was particularly unpleasant. Apart from the considerable attention that was being paid to this area by the enemy, one of man's more common enemies was making an appearance on the scene, just to add to all the misery - mosquitoes!

Arnold Whiteley...
There was one incident on our way back to Battalion from hospital. They stopped us at a Casualty Clearing Station, because there was an attack going in and they didn't want any vehicles on the road. There was a very big marquee there with the flaps rolled up and inside this marquee there were trestles all the way round and we were detailed to work with doctors. They started coming back in ambulances and they were carrying them in and they were shocking...   ...they'd only had First Aid up to that point and although I'd been in the field and although I'd seen a lot of men killed and wounded, I had to go out of that tent and spewed me heart out. Then I went back in straight away and could have carried on for ever and a day, you know. It was shocking to see what some of those doctors were doing and they never gave them enough praise for what they did...

Ken Godfrey...
Jim Metcalfe had been a Cpl. in the Intelligence Section but then he went into sniping and while we were in Troarn, you couldn't move for mosquitoes. Jim went out and laid up all day and he had been bitten so badly that he had to feel his way back to our lines. They sent him to the rear and what happened to him, I don't know. He was a big, tall and gently spoken countryman type and he'd been in Norway and Iceland. The first time we came under fire, he was the one who kicked my legs from under me and said, 'Get down you silly old so and so!'

Whilst Harry Furness could remember many incidents during the Allied advance, he was never able to pinpoint dates or places, probably because of the nature of his work. His mind must have been far too concentrated on fields, hedges, places of concealment and staying alive to bother much about where he was in relation to the broader geography, such as the surrounding townships, etc. He also had a pastime that was nothing like those indulged in by the ordinary rifleman. It could hardly have been described as a hobby but more like the pursuits of a pure professional who has no other choice if he wanted to remain in business! It involved the trading of his cigarette ration which was, in itself, not uncommon.

Harry Furness...
Whilst most soldiers learned to sew well enough for themselves, there was a soldier in HQ. Coy. who had been a tailor in civilian life, and he became the Battalion's unofficial 'Tailor.' The Officers managed to find him an old hand-driven table top sewing machine and he mainly carried out alterations and repairs for them and NCOs but in exchange for cigarettes, he was known to do sewing for anyone else, when he had the time.

Cigarettes could be traded for other things but the deals struck by non-smoker Harry Furness must have seemed quite bizarre to those people he approached in search of suitable ammunition for his task.

Harry Furness...
Snipers need the very best quality ammunition, and match grade was always the real requirement for one-shot kills. At any distance, only the best ammunition can provide that result. Wartime conditions though, often with fast advances, meant that selected supplies could be delayed for long periods, hence my constant search for the best ammo I could find for our Sniper Section, amongst other peoples' supplies. It helped that I felt no loss in handing over all my cigarette rations in exchange for ammo that would do the job.

A small number of the Hallamshires along with most other front line battalions were, by now, starting to suffer from a nervous condition which had been prevalent during World War I and known then as shell shock. The problem was not improved in World War Two, when reduced to a state of some derision by being given a different name by those who had, fortunately, not yet been caught in its grip. Being 'Bomb Happy' was a term used to encompass anyone who was becoming mentally unfit to carry on for any reason, and showing external signs by behaving in a peculiar manner. As in the Great War, there were both genuine and bogus cases with many grades in between which were often very difficult to classify. Almost all the men that helped with this book, who were involved in or near the fighting, admitted to experiencing fear to some degree or other and each had to cope with it in their own way. Some were able to contain that fear to the end, others were unable to do so and genuinely broke down. Then there were that very few who created a way out by sham, absenteeism or even self-inflicted injury.

Trevor Hart Dyke mentions the problem in his own book but it must have been extremely difficult to analyse the individual cases as they presented themselves and easy enough in the circumstances to cast doubt on some of the victims who did not appear to be obviously damaged. Where possible, he seems to have attempted to rehabilitate them and get them back into the line, or close to it, as quickly as possible. He certainly could never have taken the soft option of pulling every case out of the line on a permanent basis, otherwise the problem may well have become infectious. The ultimate deterrent used in the Great War which would have prevented many shams, must also have seen many brave and innocent young men strapped to a post or chair and 'shot at dawn'. Even though it was often threatened, such practice was not adopted in World War Two.

Late on the evening of 31 July, the Hallams were ordered to move with Brigade to an area west of Troarn, to take over from two battalions of the 3rd Division. This was a holding action on the left flank at a time when, away to the west, American Forces were about to seize the much needed port of Cherbourg on the extreme right flank. The relieved battalions had suffered considerably from sniper fire in this location and for that reason the Hallams Bn. HQ. was set up in a relatively safe gully by the side of a single track railway. Dugouts were built into the side of this and the nearby railway embankment. This was a relatively safe position except that it was infested with mosquitoes and a mini-war had to be waged against them. The surrounding undergrowth was cut down and small groups went into the attack with 'Flit'.

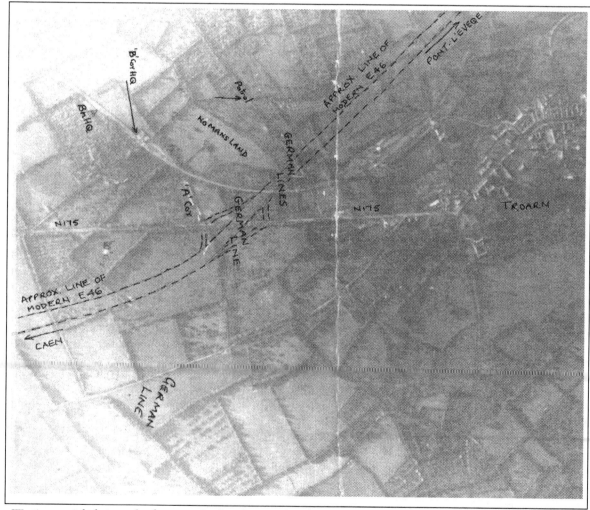

Wartime aerial photograph of poor quality but showing the Hallamshire positions (marked by Chris Somers) just west of Troarn on a single track railway, only a stones throw from German lines. No trace of the track could be found in Summer, 2000, and the more recent E46 Motorway cuts a swage right through the middle of the 'German Lines'. The area marked as Bn. and 'B' Coy. HQs. are now occupied by a strange assortment of what can only be described as semi-permanent dwellings and allotments. Line of the more recent motorway (E46) has been added to show its relative position to the old railway track and front line. (ACS)

242

Photograph taken (1960s) of the 'B' Coy. HQ. Position on the single track railway, west of Troarn. Part of the 'gully' falls away to the left in which the Bn.HQ. was sited further down the track. This view from German Lines looking west. (THD)

❖ *German Lines now completely obliterated by the E46 and its huge roundabout complex. This view from the N175 approach road, west of Troarn. The single track railway (no longer shown on modern road maps) would have been somewhere beyond the Motorway to the right. (DWS)*

'Flit' was a well known brand of insect killer at that time and kept in many homes as a 'cure all' remedy for any unwelcome creepy-crawly! It was dispensed in the home from a simple 'cycle' pump on the end of which was fixed the can of liquid. Each stroke of the pump drew liquid to the jet orifice and thus it was sprayed at the target. It is not known if a much bigger contraption was available to the British Army at that time but the author well remembers their use in Singapore, where mosquitoes are a particular nuisance and carriers of Malaria on the nearby mainland. The operator had what looked like an old lavatory cistern, containing the liquid, strapped high on his back and this had a pump lever on the top with a handled chain hanging down from the side. This was pulled down in a pumping action with one hand whilst the other brandished a long hollow rod with a jet nozzle on the end. This was fed by a pressure pipe from the cistern on the man's back. It was always quite amusing to see the operator walking along the Monsoon Drains pulling down the chain in a gentle rhythm that co-incided with each step and we always referred to these gentlemen as 'self flushing'. This will be better understood by those old sweats that remember the days when toilet cisterns were installed above head height.

Chris Somers (Diary)...
We eventually arrived at Troarn... I found everyone talking in whispers as we were supposed to be in very close contact. Luckily, this didn't apply to our Coy. We had a reasonable area with our Coy. HQ. in a railway cutting. Luckily, no shells landed in this area. The Boche was very close, a mere 200 yards separating us, but apart from odd patrols he kept very quiet in this area. Mosquitoes were now becoming a real trial, they buzzed all night in our dugouts and bit us constantly.

Over the night 6/7 August, a programme of raids was carried out over the whole 49th Divisional front which was a decoy to distract attention from the south of Caen, where operation 'TOTALISE' was being launched. This was intended to trap a large proportion of the German Army in a pincer movement to close the so called, Falaise Gap. At 0445 hrs. on the 7th, smoke screens were laid down across the whole front and the raiding parties went out. Snipers had cleared the area the night before to create the safest conditions for the raids. One party missed its way and its commander, Lt. R.V. Sankey, received burns when they walked into a field of friendly trip flares. One man was killed and three wounded in these operations, but the teams

Pte. Francis Carney. One of the twelve men to be officially recorded as Missing in Action during the period June, 1944 to May, 1945. (Photo provided by Relatives)

managed to withdraw in the heavy mist that tended to pervade this low-lying swampy area. During the morning, the Hallams were relieved by Nos. 41 and 47 Commandos and moved to Herouvillette where they spent the night.

Two men, Privates Mounsey and Carney, went missing at around this time. Although there were a number of such losses reported in the War Diary during this period, all have been subsequently lined through with an ink pen! These men are the only two to be later officially recorded as missing in action during the advance to the Seine. One of them, more probably Francis Carney, must have been the man mentioned by Les Sewell when speaking about the results of heavy shelling during that period.

Les Sewell...

I remember after Tessel when we were on the move (to the Seine), we lost a lad - he just disappeared. We all dived for cover in a ditch and when we got up he was missing. We had a search party out looking everywhere for him the next day, but as far as I know we never found him. I can't remember his name.

❖*Soliers, Summer, 2000. (DWS)*

On the 8 August, the Battalion moved into an area SE of Caen to the village of Soliers, with positions also held in the small hamlet of Fours. It took up these positions as they were being vacated by 51st Division which was now advancing in company with the 3rd Canadian Division towards Falaise. These new positions were infested with flies due to the previous bad sanitation and Chris Somers spent the night under some tanks for protection rather than digging in.

Chris Somers (Diary)...

Next morning (9th) we had to do one of the most unpleasant of marches up to our next position. I brought up the company as usual, Mike (Lonsdale-Cooper) having gone on another way with 'O' group. We had to cross a mile of open country down a track amongst the corn. There was no cover, not even a shallow ditch. As we started, a shell landed just over the wall and showered us with bits. We went in single file, 'A' Coy leading, then 'B' Coy. 'A' Coy got over all right and I, as leading man of 'B' Coy., had just cleared the cornfields into another field pitted with bomb craters. Then down came a mortar stonk right on the end of the track. With the leading men of the Coy., we ran like hell for the nearest bomb crater some 30 yards ahead and jumped into it. As soon as the stonk had finished I went back to inspect the damage. Lt. Bone, the leading platoon commander, had been killed and half a dozen others at least wounded. Luckily, two Jeeps soon appeared and carted them off fairly quickly. We had to wait here for the return of our company commanders.

The initial move from the area of Fours had been across open countryside in a southeasterly direction towards Chichiboville. The advance would pass a large wooded area on the right flank that lay SW of the village and the Battalion came under intense fire from that position. In addition to the death of Lt. J.W. Bone, 2 ORs. were killed and 15 others wounded. The village of

Chichiboville itself had been correctly reported as unoccupied and the Hallams moved in just after dark on the evening of the 9th, preceded by the Carrier Platoon.

Chris Somers (Diary)...
Tony (Nicholson) going back to join his Coy. in his jeep got blown up by a mine in the corn. Immediately afterwards, the Boche dropped some incendiary shells which set fire to the corn but Tony and the driver had managed to get out though a bit shaken. Bond (believed to be Chris's new batman - it will be remembered that his previous batman had been killed at Fontenay) also got blown up driving our Jeep in, but later we got our own kit back including my tin box and the Aquittance Rolls! We then went up to a larger wood on top of the hill, took over from 51 Division (again) and had a reasonably quiet night. There had been a little stonking around our HQ. in the village itself but only two chaps caught it badly when a shell landed on the edge of their slit. They staggered into our HQ. for attention, one with his eyes apparently blown in and the other with his arm practically severed through at the shoulder. Sitting there watching them being dressed up almost made me feel ill. About the first time this sort of thing had worried me.

❖ *Left : Entrance to Chichiboville from the north-west and probable route of the Battalion 'O' Group. The village was unoccupied but the Hallams were fired on from woods to the south-west as they approached.* ❖*(Right) Advancing towards Chichiboville from right to left, across these fields in the foreground, they came under intense fire (from wooded area seen in the background) and casualties were suffered, including Lt. Bone (killed) and Tony Nicholson who was blown up in his Jeep.(both DWS)*

The enemy had been reported in an area to the east of the village and a Pl. of 'B' Coy, under the command of Lt. Chamberlain, supported by two troops of tanks, moved towards these positions. Half of this Pl. had advanced across open ground, using the new infiltration tactics learned in retraining at Ducy St. Marguerite, when it was 'stonked' for ten minutes and all but one of the twelve men became casualties. The tanks neutralised the enemy LMG fire whilst the wounded were withdrawn. Another attempt was made under cover of a smoke screen, when Lt. Bardwell led a patrol across to the north of this open ground but also suffered casualties. The smoke screen was deliberately laid well to the side of where the actual attack went in and the War Diary states that the enemy was suitably 'hoodwinked' into placing its defensive fire (DF) in the wrong place. The deception was not completely successful because during action this day, 10 August, Capt. E.G. Wake was wounded, 6 ORs killed and 16 wounded. The Battalion was relieved of its positions in the evening by the 1 L.R. and moved to a rest area in woods to the West of Chichiboville. During this period, 10th/13th, Lt. H.C.H. Chamberlain and Padre Thomas recovered and buried the bodies of those killed in the recent disastrous actions.

Chris Somers (Diary)...
The Leicestershires then took over from us and we moved back to the South end of the big wood next to the Recce Regiment. We remained here till the 8th and I was able to get my Aquittance Rolls finished off and handed in to the CQMS. Bombing was still frequent at night, though little came

over by day. One of our platoon commanders (Lt. Chamberlain) *was shot accidentally in the knee by a recce sentry during his rounds at night.*

The Battalion now moved to the village of Poussy, a few miles directly south of Chichiboville, and once again took over positions being vacated by the 51st Division (5th Camerons) and the village was subjected to considerable shellfire and an air raid. On arrival, Chris Somers was led to believe that things were fairly quiet.

❖ *Above Left : Poussy. Above : The new church at Billy which replaced the shattered ruin in the old graveyard at the other end of the village. Left : Approach to the southern end of Airan and again the probable point of entry for the Battalion. Below Left : Picturesque setting in Pedouzes. (all DWS)*

Chris Somers (Diary)...

I was a member of a very unpleasant advance party to take over from 51 Division again. The big advance was now starting. We got slightly stonked as we drove down, but kept going. My opposite number i/c of the Coy. area I was taking over, assured me that his was a quiet area and they had only had one shell during the previous night. He must have forgotten to touch wood though, because later in the day they set about this area in no mean fashion and shells were falling all over the place. Two of his chaps received a direct hit on their slit trench and I think they were quite glad to go. I was

246

preparing our Coy. HQ. position with Bond when we heard the sound of a shell being fired and dived into cover just as it hit the roof of our shed. Being only a thin tile roof, the jeep underneath got the full blast which damaged the windscreen and punctured my tin box - recently recovered. We were covered in brick dust. Bond, still deaf from being blown up by the mine didn't hear it coming but luckily was out of harms way.

On 15 August, next day in fact, we made a quiet advance through Billy and dug in on a hill beyond. Next morning 'B' Coy did advance guard again at first light but didn't meet trouble till we got to Airan. Here our leading section ran into a Spandau position on a road junction, luckily without casualties. The Germans withdrew into some farm buildings where we stonked them with a P.I.A.T. after they had made our life rather unpleasant with rifle grenades. We eventually got about six prisoners and consolidated around the road junction. By mid day he had got rather fond of shelling this place and was landing them in the yard outside our HQ. So we weren't sorry when we moved on to Pedouzes (16th) - a mile or two to the North, where we dug in for the night. Mosquitoes were still as bad as ever. Next day found us at Mesnil and Lion D' Or with the KOYLI and Lincs ahead, having passed through us at Lion D' Or. We had a pleasant night in the back kitchen of a house here.

The P.I.A.T. (Projectile, Infantry, Anti-Tank), mentioned by Chris, was a weapon invented by Lt. Col. Blacker, R.A. It was an effective but clumsy affair that fired a bomb, the shape of which was reminiscent of a large, chubby dart. The bulbous front end carried the main charge and the hollow tail fin tube, contained the propellant cartridge. The weapon was initially cocked by standing with both feet on the shoulder pad and pulling up on the main body to compress a spring (an action rather similar to the way that some cross bows were cocked in days of old). The bomb was placed in the forward half cup of the launcher and it was ready to fire.

The operator pointed the weapon at the target, using the very crude sights, and pulled the trigger. This released the spring which drove a firing rod up the tail fin tube, fired the cartridge and the bomb was on its way. Some of the propellant gases drove the spring back into the cocked position so that it was immediately ready for another round to be loaded. It will be remembered that Bill Ashby used one of these at Fontenay, but failed to disable the 'Panther' tank he was aiming at. The P.I.A.T. had a range of up to 100 yards, was very unpleasant to use, and was also said to require nerves of steel in waiting for a tank to come that close. Bill Ashby's target must have been considerably less than half that distance!

The 49th Division was steadily moving East and now beginning to cross the River Dives. Much further upstream at this time, the river was becoming a nightmare to a part of the German Army which was attempting to escape across it through an ever narrowing gap being closed by the Allies and centred on St. Lambert. When this gap was finally closed, the terrible carnage was something to behold, where thousands of men and horses lay slaughtered amongst

❖ *Lion D'Or (looking east) just west of the River Dives, and where Chris Somers 'had a pleasant night in the back kitchen of a house'. Trevor Hart Dyke also remembered sleeping in a 'lovely country house' here and making use of the tomatoes in the back garden. (DWS)*

247

the piles of mangled wreckage. The Supreme Commander of Allied Forces, General Eisenhower, visited the scene afterwards and wrote later, 'It was literally possible to walk for hundreds of yards at a time, stepping on nothing but dead and decaying flesh.' The stench of the carnage was so great that it was said to have even penetrated the cockpits of aircraft flying over the area. Those who escaped the appalling destruction there, were now in full flight but the Germans in front of the 49th Division in the lower reaches of the Dives were still retiring in an orderly fashion and giving a good account of themselves as they fell back towards the Seine.

In the past few days, Major T. Nodwell had joined the Battalion and now on the 17 August, Capt. E.G. Smalley also joined as the new Adjutant. Meanwhile, the Hallams were helping to clear the areas between Lion D'Or and Mery Grepon, right up to the edge of the Dives. All bridges had been blown but a Bailey was placed across the gap downstream from Lion D'Or and the Battalion was now required to advance to the next obstacle, the River Vie.

Chris Somers (Diary)...
On 17 August, 'B' Coy was once again the left hand advance guard and were only just missed by Typhoons who stonked the road just ahead by mistake. It was a lovely hot day and seemed like a Battalion exercise in England as we advanced down a small lane which led across the valley to some wooded hills about a mile beyond. We guessed that the Boche would put up some resistance here. We were right! As our leading platoon neared the river half a mile from the hill, the familiar pop - pop - pop of a mortar firing could be heard. Almost immediately afterwards, these bombs fell near our Company. We halted temporarily and soon a message came from the leading platoon that they had contacted the enemy who were on the far side of the river. As we consolidated round a small farmhouse, more bombs fell amongst us. The signallers and I had a lucky escape as some fell near us as we crossed an open field. Unfortunately the place where I was hoping to establish the 18 set was under fire from enemy snipers, as I found out when walking down the wrong side of the hedge. I thought they couldn't see me till I saw the dust kick up just ahead of me. We eventually started to dig the set in on the edge of a track. As we were trying to dig it was rather slow going and very wet!

We now called for close support from our gunners as the Boche seemed rather well established and was giving us an unpleasant time. The first stonk came a little too close, one shell actually hitting the track a mere five yards away from us. Further stonks, however, failed to dislodge the Boche and we prepared to dig in for the night on the left flank of the Battalion, which had now advanced up to the river a mile to our right and were also held up. Our casualties were not too serious. I think only one killed and a Sergeant and Private seriously injured. They were both in great pain and losing a lot of blood. An old Frenchman and his wife whom we found in the cottage attended to them. Eventually we were able to evacuate them in the half track. After a rather miserable and half hearted attempt to dig in for the night, the C.O. sent up the Carrier to retrieve us and we moved half a mile across to the right in reserve for the night. 'C' and 'D' Coys. in front of us, were having a rather bad time during the night as they attempted to cross the river and fires raged in front of us.

Next day was Sunday and the padre held a small service in a little barn which we had made our company HQ. We had been told we should be here for a day or two so I took the opportunity to get the Coy's. clean laundry up. However, just as we were about to issue it, orders came that the Battalion was to attack the hill immediately in front; the Lincs were also battling away on our right flank. 'B' Coy. luckily were ordered to advance along the left flank of the Battalion through the scene of our previous day's battle. Patrols reported the enemy clear on the far bank of the river and it was possible to cross on a semi blown bridge. We advanced cautiously into the woods at the bottom of the hill and reached our objective without meeting trouble. We immediately pushed a patrol up a lane where it managed to pick up a prisoner. Other Gerries got away unfortunately. Meanwhile the Battalion had captured the hill top after quite a stiff battle and we consolidated once more with the Battalion flag flying from the top of the castle on the summit and the River La Vie was crossed on 20 August.

❖ *'Snig Hill' seen from a small bridge spanning the River Vie. (it must be said that many of these 'rivers' would be described by most people as little more than streams!). It was here or perhaps a little further downstream that the unorthodox 'bridge' of telegraph poles was used to get the Hallams across. The open ground on both sides of the river was well covered by harassing enemy fire but only one man was killed in the final attack. He is buried in a tiny civilian cemetery at the foot of the objective. The Chateau is still there, completely surrounded by mature trees and very private! (DWS)*

Most of the crossing points on this narrow river had been destroyed but rather than wait for Bailey Bridge equipment to be brought forward, the Hallams used their own device. This was in the form of four telegraph poles laid across the gap in two pairs to take stout planking, which had been salvaged from the top of German dugouts, laid on them to form two mini bridges set apart to accommodate the widths of both wheeled and tracked vehicles. Trevor Hart Dyke claimed that it could even take the weight of his captured German halftrack, which was probably the heaviest machine they were operating. The 'bridge' was laid across the Vie near 'B' Coy. positions and improvised by Major Peter Newton with the Pioneer Platoon. For their gallantry in constructing this bridge under intermittent shell and mortar fire, Major Newton was awarded the M.C. and Cpl. John Ellis, the D.C.M.

The Hallamshires had been given the task of capturing a feature named in the War Diary and by the C.O. as Butte de Haut Parc, on the east side of the river, but it was given the code name 'Snig Hill' in keeping with similar practice adopted in training, where objectives were given familiar Sheffield names. Today, this feature is easy to recognise physically as the southerly end, or Butte, to a ridge of hills that stretch away to the north. Curiously, it is named on modern maps as St. Pair du Mont. Be that as it may, 'Snig Hill' was a dominating landmark which had a thickly wooded, flat topped summit, surmounted by a chateau from which the sea could be seen to the north. All four companies had crossed the river and fanned out, with 'B' Coy on the left going for Carrefour St. Jean and 'A' Coy. (with Tony Nicholson back in command after having been 'blown up' a few days earlier) on the right, which reached Crevecoeur very quickly. 'C' and 'D' Coys. were between the two, but got held back and so 'A' Coy was now ordered to move

Pte. Arthur Linley, known to his friends as 'Bambino'. He was the only fatal casualty at Crevecoeur. Photograph taken in Iceland.(HFC)

against Snig Hill. It was supported by Churchill tanks of the 9 R.T.R. and managed to make it onto the wooded plateau with only one tank knocked out and very light casualties. The Chateau was cleared of the enemy, then 'C' Coy. arrived, followed by the Command Post. The building was now barricaded with furniture and all was got ready on the densely wooded summit, in the pouring rain and darkness, to repulse the expected counterattack which never materialised.

Trevor Hart Dyke had joined his men in the Chateau. Having left his Half-Track at the foot of the hill, he radioed back to 'B' Echelon for rations to be delivered to the vehicle and decided that he himself would lead a section down the hill to collect it.

Trevor Hart Dyke (Normandy to Arnhem)...
Everyone was in high spirits till the rain came down in torrents, and we realised that we had no hot food and we were tired. No one seemed to think that a runner would ever find his way to the road and back through the woods in the dark. Being the oldest soldier, I decided I had the most chance of getting the rations up, so I pushed off with my orderly, Stenton. We got down to the Carrier Platoon and I checked up on their dispositions and tasks, but there was no sign of the rations. HQ. swore they had been sent up ages ago, so after waiting for an hour, we pushed off down the road towards the village (Crevecoeur) and found the 15cwt. broken down.

I remember being extremely angry that the rations had not been manhandled up the road to my vehicle. I made up a carrying party and we eventually got going. The men found the receptacles very heavy and the uphill going was very difficult. It was raining hard and very slippery. I could not help, as Stenton and I were the only ones able to use our Sten Guns. I decided we would never get through the wood and that a circuit must be risked. I was soon hopelessly lost, but pretended I was not. The twenty odd men struggled on behind me, cursing under their breaths. I sat down and thought very hard. We were easy meat for any enemy we might bump into; we were obviously far beyond the Chateau in country said to be occupied by two hundred of the enemy; the party was exhausted and it was about 1a.m. I decided to cast back right handed and, just as I was giving up hope, we ran into a path and soon came to our posts. I always wonder whether that party of men ever knew how lost I was. The dinner went down like a house on fire!

Meanwhile, Chris Somers was a short distance to the north.

Chris Somers (Diary)...
We spent that night in a frail woodman's cottage but were soon on the move again next morning to a village which was probably Bonnebosq. We arrived as it was getting dark but just had time to dish out a meal and issue blankets while shallow slits were dug. Though all the men were rather tired, one or two stray 88 shells in our area spurred them into activity. The C.O. had had word that we might be here a week as we were now reserve Battalion. So next day we busied ourselves settling into some farmyard buildings. We all spent a lovely sunny day sitting in the orchard writing letters. Our rest didn't last long however, and the same day the order came around for 'O' groups. So, we knew we were on our way again.

The Hallams now moved away from 'Snig Hill' in a northeasterly direction and went into reserve at Leaupartie on the 21 August as the 1/4 K.O.Y.L.I. moved forward to clear Bonnebosq. 4 Lincs then moved on to take Le Breuil ready for the KOYLI to move through again to form a bridgehead over the River Touques, but mortar and MG fire brought things to a standstill. It was decided to exploit a bridgehead that had been secured further upstream near Coquainvilliers by 147 Bde. and so the Hallams came back into the fray, by being quickly transported to the scene.

Chris Somers (Diary)...
The Lincolns had passed through the KOYLI and were making a crossing at Pont l' Evergue. We moved up in reserve to an area near Drobec, the Coy. being in an orchard surrounding a small farmhouse. A flea ridden outbuilding served as Coy. HQ. 'O' groups were summoned again that night and we were loading up onto our own lorries at the crack of dawn next morning. Two of our men had gone absent and we never heard or saw anything of them again. Apparently the Lincolns crossing hadn't been too successful and they were having a bad time. We had been switched further south to Coquainvilliers to make a crossing on the left of 147 Bde, using small assault boats. I noticed that Mike Halford had joined the Battalion as we travelled in our transport to Coquainvilliers.

❖ *Above : Leaupartie, where the Hallams had a short rest.*
❖ *Below : Coquainvilliers, where they made a crossing of yet another river; this time by boat, leaving transport on the west side to follow downstream to the main objective, Le Breuil. Two officers and a number of men were soon lost in the advance down the far side. (both DWS)*

They crossed the River Touques by boat opposite the Chateau de Boutemont without casualties under the cover of smoke bombs and moved downstream on the opposite (east) bank towards Le Breuil. 'B' Coy. (on the road and accompanied by the Command Post) and 'A' Coy. on the higher ground on the right, led the way. Resistance was met along the way which resulted in the death of Lt. Lucy whilst leading a Pl. of 'A' Coy. 2/Lt. Pugh was killed shortly afterwards when 'D' Coy. now came between 'A' and 'B' Coys., in support. During this time, the Mortar and MMG Pls. had been moving along the river on the opposite bank, giving support fire to the Coys. in action. It is thought that this may have been the place where Arthur Saunders sort to borrow some spiritual help from an officer.

Arthur Saunders...
We'd got this 2 i/c Liverpool/Irish officer, he wore one of them cockades, and Hart Dyke left him and me together with the halftrack near the River Torques, saying that he'd call us down. We

could see 88mms miles across the top of the hill and they were ranging on us all the time and we had to keep moving. I got a message from 'Sunray' to go down and this Officer got his rosary beads out and started feeling them and I said to him, 'Gi' us a feel will tha?'........

'Sunray' was a code word used to identify the Battalion Command Structure and each one could be identified by a number - Sunray one, two, etc. The 88mm. guns were on the other side of the river, some distance to the east and the three Coys. on that same side, accompanied by the C.O. and Command Post, were now in trouble. An enemy AFV was reported to be shadowing them in the rear and 147 Bde. was being counter attacked. This meant that the Hallams group on the east bank were surrounded with no crossing point available to allow withdrawal. The situation improved when artillery support was brought down on enemy positions and 147 Bde. regained its ground. Chris Somers account adds a little extra detail, but conforms very closely with the above record which was researched from the official War Diaries in P.R.O.

❖ *Left : One house of Coquainvilliers can be seen in the background. Here the River Touques was crossed (in the trees just beyond the small building in the field on left). Then, this flat foreground (mentioned by Chris Somers) was crossed from left to right in order to reach the railway track (not mentioned in the War Diary but evident on contemporary maps).*
❖ *Right : From here, the Hallams advanced down stream, some along the valley floor and some up onto the steep higher ground to the right. The objective was Le Breuil. Both views looking north towards Le Breuil. The Chateau de Boutemont may well be another fine mansion but entirely obscured by trees away to the right and not actually seen during a tour of the area in Summer, 2000. (both DWS)*

Chris Somers (Diary)...
So, on 23 August, we crossed the River La Touques with 'A' Coy on the left and 'B' Coy on the right. The river was on our side of the valley too, so after leaving our boats we had to cross nearly a mile of flat open country. As each boat load of a section crossed, it formed up and made across the open in extended order at a fast speed. Strangely enough though, the Boche put down a few shells by us when we were forming up to cross, but he didn't bother us further. I think he was paying more attention to a bridge which was being erected on our right. Later in the day, our carriers found the crossing a bit hot on this bridge.

We soon had all 'B' Coy across and were joined by the C.O. who ordered us to advance northwards up to the main road to meet 'A' Coy. We went along with the normal advance guard, with Coy. HQ. and the C.O. with the rear of the leading platoon...Suddenly, as we came round a corner, a Spandau opened up at the leading men and the bullets went flying over our heads as we fell in the ditches.

Sergeant Davies was soon told to take his platoon up the hill and round the right flank. This was the last we saw of him and his platoon on this day and, as their radios failed, it made things rather difficult. As we could not advance down the road, Mike decided to follow Sergeant Davies with Coy. HQ. and the other uncommitted platoon, leaving the advanced one covering the road.

It was certainly a steep hill and no sooner had we got to the top than we ran into trouble and suffered a casualty or two. There was no sign of Sergeant Davies platoon. As we manoeuvred about this area with patrols, there was quite a bit of mortar stonking around and about. Another Coy. ('D') advanced up on our right but ran into a Boche LAA gun and suffered rather heavy casualties including an officer (Lt. Pugh).

Another platoon from 'A' Coy. advanced through but they suffered casualties almost before they had started, their officer platoon commander being killed (Lt. Lucy). As things quietened down, we reorganised and started to dig in and also gave the cross tracks across the fields a good pasting by the field gunners. Owing to the height of the trees, some burst among us but only inflicting a slight casualty.

As darkness fell food was brought up. Unfortunately we were too far from the road to get ours. So, I took a carrying party as a patrol down a lane in front of our Coy. area to 'A' Coy on the main road. Here we eventually located our food which had been dumped haphazardly on the roadside. Sergeant Davies platoon had also been located ahead on the road having carried its flanking task very efficiently. I gave each of my patrol a container and set off back up the lane after them. Somehow I missed the turning up to the Coy. and found myself going up a so far unexplored lane in pitch darkness on my own. I retraced my steps rather more quickly and luckily found the correct turning. It was some job issuing the food out as most chaps, apart from sentries, wanted to sleep instead of eat. The food was cold by now anyway!

❖ *The beautiful Chateau Le Breuil in a most tranquil setting and well worth a visit by the passing tourist today. In August, 1944, the surrounding area promised to be a place of well earned rest for a few days after a harrowing advance down the River Touques. It was not to be, however, and the Hallams were soon required to move off again in transport to catch up with the frontline. (DWS)*

Casualties included 8 ORs killed and 20 wounded. When the Battalion reached Le Breuil on the 24th, it was found that the enemy had withdrawn. The Carrier Pl. had proceeded into the village and now the rest of 146 Bde. was able to cross the Touques at this place. The Hallams were now ordered to rest and the Bn. HQ. moved back upstream to the Chateau de Boutemont, perhaps the most splendid of such quarters thus far in the war. The Battalion was to reside in a number of fine buildings during their trek from Normandy to Arnhem and it is thought to have been here that a small mishap took place, the cause of which was kept very quiet at the time.

Ray Langdale...
It was here that the HQ. command half-track caught fire (not the German Halftrack). It was very hot and sunny and we'd gone into this place and a certain man said to me, 'Don't forget Ray, I want a nice bedroom!' so I took him up to this bedroom and all the windows were open. He jumped on this bed, I can see him now, and he stretched himself out, took the cigarette out of his mouth and flicked it out of the window. Well, when we went to the window the truck was in flames and of course it was covered with a camouflage net and that was the first thing that had got alight. The whole lot had gone up but in less than twelve hours we had a new vehicle back with all equipment.

Chris Somers and 'A' Coy stayed further north in farm buildings and perhaps nearer to the Chateau Le Breuil, an equally fine mansion house, so may not have noticed the plume of smoke rising into the air in the direction of Bn.HQ. It must be said here that the book 'Normandy to Arnhem' gives a strong impression that Bn.HQ. was set up in the Chateau Le Breuil but the War Diary definitely states that it was Boutemont.

❖ *Left : A Sunday Market scene in Bonneville and (Right) a much quieter setting further north in Pont Audemer. Both of these places were passed through peacefully as the Battalion moved ever closer to the Seine. (both DWS)*

254

Chris Somers (Diary)...
After a miserable night, the morning brought forth sunshine and a departed enemy. We had soon joined our missing platoon on the main road and enjoyed a good breakfast at Le Breuil among some farm buildings. About seven days rest was again the order and all companies moved into farm houses, bathed in the river and issued N.A.A.F.I. packs and mail etc. I spent a very comfortable night on a feather bed in a farm. Unfortunately, I lost my watch next day when I went down to bathe. A day of rest and peace, then suddenly an 'O' group and everything was hurriedly packed and we were on the move once more! Very disappointing after expecting a good rest.

On a very sad note, it was in the grounds of Boutemont that the dead were temporarily buried but would eventually find a final place of rest in St. Desir Military Cemetery, just to the west of Lisieux. Otherwise, the 25 August was a day of bliss for the Hallams, but the long rest expected did not materialise as 146 Bde. was on its way again to catch up with the rest of 49th Division, which was now very close to the River Seine. The Hallams were transported a considerable distance via Bonneville and on to a crossing of the River Risle where they harboured at Le Plessis on the night of the 26th, just to the NW of Pont Audemer. It was here that 2/Lt. H.P. Toon joined the Battalion, just missing the holiday camp atmosphere of the previous day. The Hallams moved again, but still in reserve to another harbouring place, this time at Appeville, SE of Pont Audemer, on the evening of the 27th. During this period, the 4 Lincs and 1/4 K.O.Y.L.I. cleared the Quilleboeuf peninsular which was that large chunk of land sandwiched between the lower reaches of the Seine and Risle. Next day, the Battalion moved back into the line at Bourneville and moved up towards the River Seine.

Chris Somers (Diary)...
It was quite a long journey next day, crossing La Risle River on a pontoon bridge and spending the night in a Beechwood on the hillside. We were up at the crack of dawn the next morning and reached Bourneville. Here we sat for a bit waiting for orders. We were about to move into Coy. areas for the night when we got orders to move again.

After a short distance, we debussed at Tocqueville and 'B' Coy. set off as advance guard towards Aizier. It was a quiet and peaceful evening and once again it seemed more like an exercise as we followed the leading platoon down the narrow Lane. Soon we joined the main road and turned left to Aizier. The road ran down through some woods with a hill on our right and valley on our left. After about half a mile we passed some caves in the hillside in which a number of French civilians had taken refuge. It was all rather absurd! Here we were in the middle of an advance guard operation, advancing grimly and carefully down a road, when suddenly a mob of shouting and cheering French folk. They meant well no doubt but I felt they must have given good warning to any Boche waiting further down the road.

The peacefulness of the evening was soon to be broken as we came out of the wood hardly more than a quarter of a mile from Aizier. The front man of the leading section caught it as usual and the Cpl. was wounded. Mike decided to do a right flanking with the rear platoon along the wooded ridge which led around to the side of Aizier (the 3rd was already moving along the ridge). Once again as the leading section approached the nearest house there was a burst of Spandau and the two leading men caught it again. Men of the leading section are all heroes but they never get anything for it.

The country, apart from this leafy lane, was very open and as we were too far away from the Battalion and had no direct support, Mike decided to consolidate temporarily sending out patrols. We also managed to get in touch with the Battalion mortars who registered on the village. But as

❖ Top : Touqueville, where the Hallams debussed and moved on foot and downhill towards the edges of the River Seine. ❖ Below.: Aizier. Although some resistance was shown, the enemy were more concerned with making an escape across the very considerable expanse of water here. The Seine was the last in a series of many rivers that had to be crossed, but this one had a worthy prize awaiting on the other side. It was the much needed port of Le Havre. (both DWS)

we didn't know the strength and exact positions of the enemy, we couldn't bring down an effective stonk. One or two bombs came back near us but didn't do any damage. As it was getting dark, Mike sent me back down to the road to report the positions to the C.O. He had just arrived with his scout car and I walked down the road with him to where our leading section had first been shot up. We both walked forward ahead of it and recovered a Bren gun. All seemed quiet now and we were tempted to walk on down the road. However, 'A' Coy. came on the area saying that there leading platoon had just entered the village to find the Boche had flown.

We set off down immediately and I took the remainder of the Coy. through to the end of the village. I thought Mike was certain to follow down when he heard the noise of all the transport going downhill. I supervised the dishing out of a meal and then went back with Cpl. Hurford. We set off up the very dark little lane where they had been held up. The place stunk of dead animals, and not knowing what I was going to tread on next, moved out into the open fields where I could see better. I challenged what I thought was a man standing in the hedge but got no reply. I got Cpl. Hurford also to shout but whoever it was, we got no reply.

As I thought the Boche might still be there, I could not risk walking up to whoever I saw there. As he didn't answer me, I thought it rather strange so I moved on up to try to rouse the Coy. from somewhere else. Though I was standing only the other side of a thick hedge from where I left them, my shouts failed to attract attention. So I decided they had either moved or were enjoying a sleep, so decided to return and await daylight.

Luckily they arrived down just after breakfast. Mike wasn't very pleased about being up there all night, but I reckon if they'd been awake they must have heard all the Battalion transport moving down. Unfortunately, we had to start off on a Battalion wood clearing exercise almost immediately so that breakfast was rather a hurried affair. The plan was that 'B' Coy would travel eastwards through the woods, parallel to the River Seine and road which runs alongside, and form a stop across the road while 'A' and 'B' Coys. attacked a village between us and Aizier.

The 4th Lincolns were also clearing on our right. Soon after we started toiling up the hill through the woods there was a sound of a very heavy shelling in their area. I don't know if this was ours or the Boche, but it sounded very unpleasant and I hoped nothing would land our way. For the first half mile everything went smoothly and we picked up one German straggler. We came across a section of them in the next ravine, but they unfortunately saw us and fled down the road. We wondered if we had now lost our surprise.

However, we pushed on another mile and cautiously approached the road. We got down to the edge without being noticed and Mike dispersed the Coy. in all round defence while we laid two Brens to cover the road and get anybody who came along. Unfortunately, just as he stepped onto the road a German cyclist came around the corner. He saw what was happening and pedalled like hell down the road shouting for all he was worth. At the same time a German car came around the corner. They saw the cyclist and stepped on it. One Bren gun unfortunately jammed, but a following burst from the other made the car swerve into the ditch. Unfortunately, the driver got it under control again and they escaped.

❖ *The river road a short distance upstream from Aizier and possibly the place, or near to it, where Arnold Whiteley felt ill at ease when the officer he was with, took the rifle from him and killed a young German soldier on his bicycle. (DWS)*

This story is curiously similar to an account given by Arnold Whiteley who was also involved in the clearance of the wooded area along the banks of the river.

Arnold Whiteley...
Then we got near the River Seine towards these huge woods in Coy. strength. Going through this scrub land first, we came across these like gypsy covered wagons where the horses had just been left out to graze, paper strewn all over the place so we knew they hadn't been vacated for long. We went along a bit further to where the trees actually started and the Germans started coming out with their hands up, about seventy without a shot being fired. I was ordered to accompany an officer into this wood and we were going down hill and all of a sudden through the trees you could see the River Seine. At this side of the river there was a road and there must have been a steep banking down to the side and we must have been pretty close because we could hear Germans down there and they were shouting and bawling and playing hell with one another. Some had got across on a boat and some were playing hell because they weren't sending it back fast enough.

Then, a young German soldier came along this here road on this bicycle, rifle slung across his shoulder, cap pushed to the back of his head and he (the officer) said to me, 'Lend me your rifle,' and he shot this here boy. I'm grateful he didn't tell me. Then a German half-track pulling a big gun came along and as soon as he saw this boy, he stopped and dived to the other side. We then went back to the others.

Chris Somers (Diary)...
The noise of firing had woken large numbers of Germans in the area and bursts from Spandau whistled through the trees. Mike, thinking that we were badly outnumbered and without reserves of ammunition or bodies, decided to consolidate a hundred yards or so back out of sight. Here we dug in and all went quiet except for some mortaring where the other Coy. attack was going on. The Germans didn't waste much time in moving off eastwards. We had seen four cross in a boat

which they refused to row back for one of their pals, which was rather amusing to watch.(again similar to Arnold Whiteley's independent account)

Later in the day, the Carrier Platoon and another two Coys. pushed on up the road while we continued along the flank in the woods. We met opposition and mortar fire just where the woods ended but as it was getting dark and the troops hadn't had much sleep the last night or two the C.O. decided not to attack that night. So we moved back into the village just captured, where we had a meal and slept for the night in the open.

On the morning of the 30th, the Carrier Platoon went out along the river and recced via Flacq and la Vaquerie as far as Neuville. They brought back 39 prisoners and some considerable loot, some of which was said to be in the form of bank notes. Apparently, they had bumped into a German officer who was in the process of burning a vast quantity of money. He was unable to destroy all of it and rumour has always been rife that a great deal of money was rescued. Like all good rumours, it has been stretched to the tale that one member of the Hallams became a very rich man after the war. This is a good story but it hardly stands up to scrutiny, unless the money was of a currency that was able to retain its value when the war ended. Third Reiche banknotes, for instance, were virtually worthless, otherwise a good percentage of the British Army might have returned home as multi-millionaires! Now if the money had been French Francs and quickly deposited in a bank...

During this same day, the Battalion withdrew a short distance into Vieux Port for a brief but pleasant rest period. Next day, Capt. Cowell and Cpl. Harding were seriously injured when their Jeep struck a mine. The Cpl. died a few days later.

It was whilst resting here on the banks of the Seine, that David Lockwood's old 'B' Coy was now broken up and spread around the other companies. Chris Somers, with Mike Lonsdale-Cooper, were transferred to the re-formed 'C' Coy. with the latter in command. It was all part of a Battalion shake up when one whole Coy. from a battalion of the South Staffordshire Regiment arrived to make up the considerable losses. The Hallams had sustained these in the trek from Caen to the Seine during which a retreating enemy had the advantage of being able to use the tactic of kill and withdraw.

The new Coy. was from the disbanded 59th Division and came complete with its own officers in the form of Major G. Grey and Capt. Salmon. Rather than spread them throughout the other Coys. of the Battalion, they were allowed to stay together as a new 'B' Coy. They did, however, absorb a number of Hallamshire men, among whom were Sam Woolley and John Wollerton for example, the latter being relieved of his job as Signals Officer, after the Seine crossing. This was probably in order that these new men could be taught the finer points of how to conduct themselves now that they had become, in effect, Honorary Yorkshiremen! These men may not have been qualified to play cricket for the County but they did not need to be taught how to fight. Some of them now lie in military cemeteries between Le Havre and Arnhem, beneath headstones that declare them as being soldiers of the York & Lancaster Regiment, but their next of kin home addresses tell another story.

The Hallams, now at rest in Vieux Port (1 Sept), were ordered to cross the Seine and take up positions in the area of Auberville, which was only a few miles directly north of the present Hallams position but with the river in between. The idea was to travel miles upstream and get the marching troops across on patched up ferries and boats at Caudebec. The transport would have to go even further upstream to Rouen, about thirty miles, and gain a crossing over a temporarily repaired railway bridge. All the other bridges were down.

258

Trevor Hart Dyke...

We'd got to the River Seine and we were then ordered to move up the river to Rouen and cross over there with the idea of then proceeding to Le Havre. Well, it seemed to me rather unnecessary to go many miles up the river and then having to come all the way back, when we could see there were a lot of rowing boats and things at the far side of the river. So, I decided to get my Battalion across where it was, with the Divisional Commanders agreement. I sent one Company across ('C' Coy) and then my 'O' Group next and at the other side of the river there was a coal-burning vehicle which we boarded, bussed in that and liberated Lillebonne...   ...perhaps it was a bit foolhardy but anyhow, we were able to be the first Battalion to get to Le Havre.

❖ *Above: The very pleasant and popular little village of Vieux Port with people walking down to the edge of the River Seine where many others were picnicking on the far side of the church. The landing place at the end of the lane has now been stripped of its wooden landing jetty (seen top right in a photograph taken some years ago - THD), leaving only the large concrete base today.(top and bottom right - DWS)*

Chris Somers (Diary)...

We only managed to get two boats all together. Mike (Lonsdale-Cooper) set off in the first, followed by a section in another boat. It was one of the most amusing days I'd ever spent, watching troops circling around in their boats in mid stream. Two chaps nearly finished up in Le Havre bringing one boat back! Some civilians tried to gate crash one of the boats but the C.O. soon had them out at the point of his revolver. It took the whole day to get the company across plus Battalion 'O' group.

Trevor Hart Dyke also records that he had to fire a revolver shot across the bows of one small boat, which was being hi-jacked by civilians who were also wanting to get to the other side of the river. It had the desired effect and these people very quickly 'surrendered' the boat.

The steam driven vehicle was provided by the FFI and could only carry a small number of people. This antiquated lorry had to go by some circuitous, clockwise lowland route, as it could not negotiate the steep hills that lay on the direct route to Auberville. It was this that caused the C.O. and his small group to prematurely 'liberate' Lillebonne which had been vacated by the Germans, some of whom had only just left after attending the last cinema show!

Looking at the map, it can only be assumed that 'C' Coy. made its way, by the more direct route, to the designated concentration area of Auberville, where the C.O. and his O Group later joined them. The fact that 'C' Coy. got there first, on foot, can only be explained by the fact that there must have been some delay in the rapturous welcome received at each little village the lorry passed through, as the Hallams Command Post 'steamed' to the rescue. More French Resistance clung to the sides and onto the already overloaded lorry as it went along, waving flags and banners. Even though they might have been steaming into the jaws of the enemy and death, it was too much for some of the others on board. They were caught by the outrageously funny side of it all and folded in fits of laughter!

❖ *Touffreville, where the Battalion concentrated after crossing the Seine. The 'O' Group took a circuitous route via Lillebonne which was inadvertently liberated by the Hallamshires. This place had seen earlier 'sackings' (a different variety to that suffered by John Wollerton) when the Romans came to town, 2000 years earlier. Traces are still to be found of their occupation in the form of the now ruined Amphitheatre (below). (both DWS)*

Chris Somers (Diary)...
By this time, Mike had managed to get two lorries which we filled with petrol. The first loads went off and it was after dark by the time we were on the move and we had to rely on the French to take us to the right destination. Luckily, we had all met up okay and the Battalion 'O' group actually liberated Lillebonne by mistake. We managed to get a meal next morning although we had the wrong ration truck. Later in the day, the rest of the Battalion arrived at Touffreville (just east of Auberville) where we spent the remainder of the day.

John Wollerton...
I crossed the Seine with the C.O. and others in small boats and it was there that he asked me to get in touch with the rest of the Battalion who were crossing much further upstream at Rouen. Now this was an impossibility for an 18 set, so it turned out to be a good thing for me because it marked the end of my life as the S.O. when we reached Lillebonne. On our arrival, I remember the population came out in force and threw fruit at us as we passed. However, I was duly called in front of the C.O. there and marched in by the Adjutant and he told me that he had 'sacked' me as Signals Officer. I just saluted and said, 'Thank you sir.' I was 'about turned' and off I went to 'B' Coy. I was very, very relieved, because the pressure had been terrific and I had the first good nights sleep for I don't know how long. Even when I had been off duty, I was always being asked to do something. So that was that! and I was now in 'B' Coy. commanded by Major Grey.

By 0700 hrs. the next day, the bulk of the Battalion which had gone by way of the bridge at Rouen, under the command of Major John Mott, had still not arrived so the C.O. went to look for them. It was little wonder they were late. The bridge was only twenty-eight miles upstream from Vieux Port and although they had set off the previous evening, the first Bn. vehicles did not cross it until 1300 hrs.

Arthur Green...
The rest of the Battalion were transported right up the Seine to Rouen where there was a bridge that had been blown and collapsed in the middle but the Engineers had rigged a platform across so that transport could get over in single file. It was chaotic because everybody wanted to be across this bridge. There were Yanks, Poles, English and Canadians - everybody wanted to get across. There were every type of wheeled vehicles and tanks all going one way and the Red Caps were in a hell of a state trying to marshal it all and the traffic wasn't moving away on the other side, because they didn't know which way they were supposed to go. Anyhow, we'd had our instructions to keep to the river on the other side and go downstream to meet up with that part of the Battalion which had made the crossing further down.

Ken Godfrey...
I have memories of going along the banks of the Seine on my own and suddenly hearing these horrible shrieks and cries. I went round a corner and there were these two or three French women standing over a couple of men who the Germans had shot, not long before. It was around that time when I realised just how much Germany relied on horse drawn transport which was strewn around all over the place. Then there were the cows that had been killed and also those live ones that were dripping with milk and the lads milking them to relieve them. They did drink some of the warm milk but they also felt sorry for them.

All the Battalion was finally together by 1700 hrs, having had no sleep, then moved up behind 4 Lincs into a position at Routot, whilst the latter cleared their outpost positions up to Gainneville. Next day, 3 September, 4 Lincs and 1/4 K.O.Y.L.I. sent patrols forward to probe and discover the extent of defensive positions held by the German Garrison on the eastern outskirts of Le Havre.

Chris Somers (Diary)...
We were on the road again for Le Havre, the Coys. being carried on all types of vehicles. The 'O' group had gone on ahead to get a situation report and also select a billeting area. Just after passing through St. Romain I was surprised to see some of our advanced vehicles come back the opposite way. Apparently they had gone on so far that they found themselves in the middle of the Lincolns who were engaged in a battle. Eventually, however, the Battalion was fixed up in a small village (Routot) about two miles out of Le Havre, each company occupying a few small farm buildings. A plan was now being made for a full-scale attack on Le Havre and numerous patrols were sent out.

56 Bde were given the task of probing German defences from the north but as yet had only succeeded in getting one of its battalions across the Seine. Because of this, the Hallams now came under temporary command of 56 Bde and embussed on transport and tanks by way of Epretot and Epouville, to positions between Montivilliers and Fontenay (another Fontenay!). Here, they stopped for the night and sent out patrols to Montvilliers Station and various crossroads and a farm in the area. In the meantime, the German Commander in Le Havre had been given an opportunity to surrender the Garrison but this he refused.

Chris Somers (Diary)...
The Boche seemed rather fond of this place, a few copses and farm houses, as a target for his guns.
We soon dug in but there were a number of casualties in the Battalion. We had to send a patrol to
a farm about half a mile forward across the open cornfields. Enemy snipers were supposed to be
active just in front where there was a wood. 'D' Coy. was going to advance with tanks next
morning, the start line being just in front of us.

Trevor Hart Dyke...
Then we were used to try and get the Germans to surrender by advancing towards Le Havre and I
was told not to incur a lot of casualties if they decided to resist. When they started putting some
shell fire down, I decided to call it a day and a full attack went in some days later.

The Battalion was now relieved of its positions by the 2 G.R. and returned in pouring rain to 146
Bde. and the previous area of Routot, where it remained in reserve throughout the 5 September.
On this day, the City of Le Havre was bombed by aircraft of the R.A.F. Once again, the French
people were having to pay the high price of freedom. Over the previous two days, casualties
suffered by the Hallams amounted to ten ORs. wounded.

Chris Somers (Diary)...
The heavies raided Le Havre in daylight, a softening up raid, it was spectacular and burnt paper
etc. floated down in the Battalion area. Later we had a German officer out under the Flag of
Truce in connection with evacuation of civilians etc. Things remained as they were however till
the big attack started.

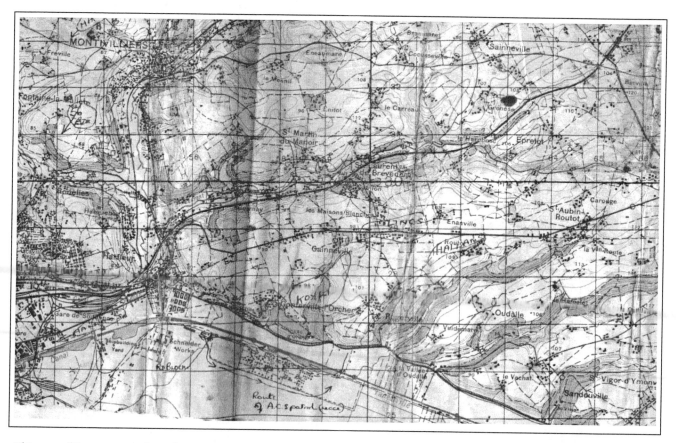

This map of the eastern outskirts of Le Havre is from Chris Somers Scrap Book and shows the route (marked by arrows) which he took when
required to patrol along the Tancarville Canal, prior to the advance into the Dock Area. The Schneider Works can be seen just beyond the
furthest extent of the patrol. Taking the dockyard area and this factory enabled the Hallams to claim later, that in addition to accepting the
surrender of over a thousand prisoners, they also captured three aircraft and one submarine! (ACS)

The Bn. remained at rest throughout the 6th and was now ordered to be ready for the assault on Le Havre from east to west along the Canal de Tancarville au Havre, which ran along the edge of the Seine from Tancarville to the main dock area. Col. Hart Dyke sent a patrol under command of Capt. A.C. Somers, to reconnoiter a bridge across the canal, south of Routot, and probe forward in a westerly direction towards the docks. The bridge was found to be blown.

❖ *Tancarville Canal at the point where Chris Somers crossed to start his patrol down towards the Schneider Works which would have then been situated some way down on this left bank (see map). The Dock Area was beyond this and the city of Le Havre can be seen on the horizon (centre). When the Hallams finally made their advance to the docks (this would be from right to left in the far distance, on this side of the city) they were fired on from high ground to their right rear. (DWS)*

Chris Somers (Diary)...
Most of the recce patrols were being done by the forward battalion but shortly before the attack itself, the C.O. asked me to take a recce patrol across the canal and down the far bank to discover what defences the Boche had in the area of the Schneider Works. It was thought possible that the Hallams might be asked to attack the dock area via this route.

I chose only one man to accompany me, a Cpl who had been with me on a previous patrol near Fontenay. A third man, though desirable in the event of casualties, I decided to do without as it simplified the canal crossing in the two man rubber boat. That evening we set out in a truck with our covering party who were going to carry the boat for us and await our return. It was pouring with rain (just the night for a patrol) but we were soon soaked through and our gym shoes made a rather loud squelching noise. The far bank, where we landed, was covered in thick rushes which we had to push through. We soon cleared these and came onto a good canal path alongside a big factory.

This factory was thought to be an area for German patrols and snipers, so I decided to move fairly carefully in view of the distance we had to cover i.e. about one and a half miles. Leapfrogging seemed to be the best method of advance and it worked quite well with only two of us. Soon we came to the end of the factory area where a small railway line started. I decided that it might be advisable to follow the line, so moved through the marsh and thick reeds between it and the canal. After some hard going we ran into some wire, the only gap being on the railway. Trusting to luck there were no mines and it wasn't booby trapped, we crept through. This, unfortunately, was only the outer ring of wire because as we crossed the road we saw a road block and line of double apron fencing.

Realising that they might have a sentry covering the road, I decided it would be better to crawl under the wire some 50 yards away in the open field and then make for a barn and some buildings. I don't know if this path was mined or not but we felt over the ground fairly carefully near the wire. Once under, we made a dash for the barn passing an empty slit trench en route. I felt much happier now that we were within the defences and also amongst cover of some buildings. The best route seemed to be along the back Gardens of some cottages. There was plenty of cover, but the fences made it difficult going. We came to the end of the group of cottages where there was an open field. The hedge running up the side of the road was thickly wired and we could find no way through.

I glanced at my watch to see how much longer we had got and decided that we ought to be pushing off back as we had to take a different route and also be back before daylight. We went back through the yard between the buildings and examined the road block from the enemy side and also upon one which appeared to be an O.P.. Back once more through the wire and road block. Here we fired our Stens to see if there was any Boche reaction. Luckily nothing came back although a heavy gun opened on the KOYLI position!! We were feeling a bit cold now, so I decided to take the risk and trot back, stopping only to examine the crater where the road had been blown. Finding our way back to the canal through six feet high reeds and marsh for 100 yards and more, proved rather strenuous. I was glad when we had found our dinghy and were safely back on the home side. We were soon onto the truck and back with the Battalion.

These were all that was left of the original Hallamshire Officers by the time they had reached Le Havre. The rest had been either killed, wounded or left the Battalion for various reasons. The remainder are from left to right, Gerry Bedward, Tony Nicholson, Peter Newton, Trevor Hart Dyke, Mike Lonsdale-Cooper, Lloyd Sneath, John Wollerton and Chris Somers. (THD)

During this period, Major J.A. Boucher (D.L.I.), Capt. C.B. Murray (D.L.I.), Capt. S.H. Smith (R.W.R.) and Lt. R.N. Judge (W.Y.R.) joined the Battalion. Major M.C.K. Halford now assumed the position of 2i/c, vice Major J.H. Mott who left the Battalion at about this time.

Another patrol, under the command of Capt. Pearce, made a further recce the next night and located the enemy posts just to the east of the Schneider works. Various recces were carried out on the 8th and another ultimatum was issued to the German Garrison. Again it was rejected,

Above : Padre Thomas after conducting a religious service in the field prior to the advance into Le Havre. The man in the background wearing the S.D. Cap with a stick under his arm, looks very much like Trevor Hart Dyke. (THD)

with the result that further aerial bombing took place at 1600hrs on the 10th. True figures may never be known, but it is believed that the total number of civilian dead was roughly equal to the number of tons of bombs dropped on the city and its defences, somewhere in the region of 3,000. This was a repeat of the tragedy which befell Caen and another case where words of explanation are totally inadequate.

No part was played by the Hallams in the immediate ground follow up. As the 56th and 147th Bdes. attacked from the NE, contingents of the 51st Division came down the coast from St. Valery where they had been settling an old score with the Germans to do with the action that took place there before Dunkirk. They attacked the city from the North. The Hallams stayed in reserve at 15 minutes readiness but the call never came for it to move forward during the day.

It was at about this time, during the lull and prior to the final assault on Le Havre, that a few photographs were taken.

Late in the evening of the 11th, the Bn. received ordered to move through the 4 Lincs, which had reached Harfleur, and clear the south side of the city which contained the dock area. The Hallams moved forward with 'D' Coy in Kangaroos (Sherman chassis adapted as armoured troop carriers) leading the Carrier Pl., backed up by 9 R.T.R. These were followed by a section of Mortars and one of Pioneers, all moving via the road from Routot to Gainneville and Harfleur and thence to the road leading into the dock area. The Pioneers had to start clearing this road of various obstructions with explosives and a bulldozer was sent for.

In the meantime, 'D' Coy. went forward on foot towards a number of road bridges that spanned a complex of railway loops and sidings that serviced the docks and factory areas. The first bridge was down and 'D' Coy moved to the next with 'B' Coy following up. The Command Post coming up from the rear now came under heavy concentrated 20mm (possibly A.A. guns) from high ground to the right and rear and were pinned down. These positions were effectively dealt with by 9 R.T.R. and 11 R.S.F. moved in to clear that area where a lot of white flags were now seen to be waving.

Chris Somers (Diary)...
'B' and 'D' Coys. were leading and encountered resistance as they approached the docks. The chief trouble was a German LAA gun on top of the cliff overlooking our road. This gun proceeded to pepper us with cannon shells on the road which was lined with troops, tanks and command vehicles. Our tanks had many direct hits on the Boche positions but it was some time before they gave in.

'B' Coy meanwhile had cleared their opposition and 'C' Coy. were passed through to go over the canal and clear the docks. Fortunately, there was one bridge which hadn't been blown and over we went. Much to our annoyance, the Brigade Signal Officer roared past in his jeep and rounded up some prisoners (plus their loot) before we could arrive on the scene. Even more unfortunate was the tragic death of Lt. McNeile who was with the leading platoon of our company.

While standing on a crossroad he was shot through the head by snipers. Luckily, the tanks got two snipers shortly afterwards. Just at this time, the C.O. ordered the company out of this area as the Germans were blowing everything sky-high, including the dock gate. We withdrew for a short time and then resumed our clearing which went on until darkness, without gaining much loot. 'B' Coy., who went to the Schneider factory, were more fortunate although they had a tiring trip!

❖Above : The Hallamshires would hardly have noticed as they moved down to the flat area of docklands that they were passing, on their left, the most picturesque little hamlet of Harfleur.(DWS)

Below : This road bridge was one of a series that had to be crossed in order to enter the dockland complex but which was damaged by enemy demolition charges during the operation. This photograph shows the bridge after post-war reconstruction. (THD)

Graham Roe...

I was with 'C' Coy on the road and to our right the German positions were well fortified and camouflaged. They allowed us to get right to the end of the road before they dropped the camouflage and then fired at us with 20mm cannon and machine guns. We were in a very, very bad position and at the end of the road there was a rolling mill, a steel rolling mill. I thought I would get between two or three of these heavy, metal rolls to take cover but unfortunately, I hadn't reckoned on ricochets. So, the position became more untenable than ever and it really was a matter of being finished off.

❖ Very bare example of the Churchill tank on display on the forecourt of the Bayeax Memorial Museum. (This place is well worth a visit). (DWS)

Then, a number of Churchill tanks appeared behind us, saw the position that we were in, and with great accuracy they were posting high explosive shells into the slits and hitting every one with the first shot and neutralised the problem. It took about twenty or thirty minutes, but whilst it was going on we were relieved from the pressure that was being put upon us and ultimately, we were able to carry on around the corner, clear a large area, and in so doing the Battalion took a thousand odd prisoners.

John Wollerton...

I remember flat ground as we got near to Le Havre by the river and I just crossed my fingers that we didn't get strafed by machine gun fire. We all ran across this land in a zig-zag fashion and then took cover at the end when we came under fire. I threw a hand grenade into a small building and there was an enormous explosion. I thought it must be an upgraded type of grenade but what I'd done was blow up a small ammunition dump. We proceeded very carefully into factory yards where we were cheered by the factory workers and we asked them to keep under cover. We knew they had had a hell of a bombing the night before, because we'd seen it going on for an hour and the burnt paper coming down afterwards. We went into an aircraft factory on the dockside. It was quite a big building and it looked as though they were building them in there.

It was now approximately 1130 hrs on 12 September, and some casualties had been sustained, including minor injuries to the C.O. and Major Peter Newton. Some opposition was met with from the south side of the canal and 'A' Coy. was sent across in boats to deal with it. Meanwhile, Cpl. John Ellis (Pnrs.) had managed to disconnect charges and plunger in a pillbox that had been set to blow one of the bridges. This enabled 'C' Coy to cross into the docks area but now there began a series of large explosions caused by demolition charges set by the German Garrison, which sent massive lumps of concrete and debris into the air. The C.O. ordered the forward troops to pull back in order to prevent severe casualties but it was at about this time that Lt. H.D. McNeile was shot, even though general hostilities had now ceased.

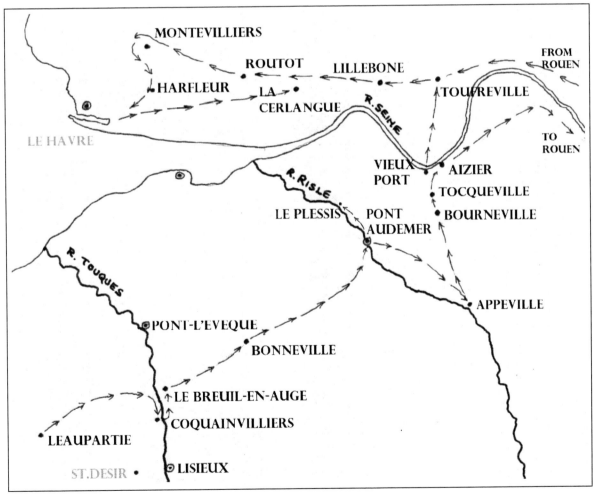

Map showing basic route of Hallamshire Battalion from Leaupartie to La Cerlangue (places of Memorial in gray print) and some of the towns/villages through which they passed. It should be remembered that the main contingent crossed the River Seine via the bridge at Rouen and only the 'O' Group and 'C' Coy. made the crossing at Vieux Port. (DWS)

Trevor Hart Dyke...
...there wasn't a great deal of resistance where we were going through and we advanced down to the dock. Major Newton and I came under a nasty bit of fire from the high ground on the right, both of us being hit by a bit of shrapnel before we got to the docks. Our pioneers managed to succeed in defusing a charge which had been put on the bridges into the docks. After that, we had to clear the dock area which was prickly because there were a lot of snipers and a few Germans holding out, and I'm afraid we lost one of our officers, McNeile, who had only recently joined us. He was shot through the head by a sniper and we had one or two other casualties.

Geoff Cooper...
We'd crossed this canal bridge and got about three hundred yards into the dockland when things started to blow up. There was all sorts of things flying through the air, big lumps of concrete, bunkers or some sort of demolition the Germans were doing in front of us. 2/Lt. McNeile was with our section and we were behind a concrete fence of some description and we got fired upon, so we got down behind this fence.

As Lt. McNeile was kneeling behind this fence to check on what the situation was, he was called on by Major Lonsdale-Cooper to come to a safer position. He hesitated a little while, and Major Lonsdale-Cooper had to shout again to him to come out. Then he called out the few of us that were with him to come out, but as he got up just to the edge of the wall he was shot and down he went.

Arthur Saunders...
After McNeile went down... ...The Recce Platoon brought a German individual and he looked a horrible man - arrogant! He was stood up in a carrier and there was bullets flying around and he never batted an eyelid. Anyway, this is where I differ from Hart Dyke. If Corporal Ellis were alive he'd tell you. I said, 'I'll shoot him!' and this Corporal Ellis said, 'I'll shoot him!' and Hart Dyke said, 'No! Not now.' McNeile were only three or four yards from Hart Dyke when he got it, right between the eyes.

Hart Dyke stayed on the docks and, eventually, when we came back at eleven o'clock at night there were no grub for us because they were all drunk on champagne. They were all bloody drunk when I got back! That's when I said, 'That's it. I'm finished.' We were on't docks all the time and the rest were flowing in champagne all over the place.

Arnold Whiteley...
We were stood around chatting and talking and this Lt. dropped down dead. They came out with these two men with sniper gear on so it must have been one of these two that fired the shot. At that point the Col. came up to see what the position was and he said, 'You shouldn't have taken those two men prisoners, they should have been shot,' because that was murder. Anyway they were taken away for questioning and you can draw your own conclusions. Throughout the war, I never saw a prisoner ill treated when they gave themselves up but in this case, there could have been an exception... I'm not prepared to say!

The Brigade commander now ordered the Hallams to clear all the remaining area on the south side of the canal, including the mole, which was an extension of the area already taken by the Battalion.

Trevor Hart Dyke...
Then there was the mole which had a lot of big pill boxes on it that was still held by the Germans but to get there you had to cross a railway bridge. So, I didn't want to have a lot of casualties doing that and managed to get permission to have an armoured car firing across the river while I led a

platoon across this bridge. Anyhow, by the time we got to the other end it was nearly dark and we moved forward to some of these pill boxes and, luckily, out came a German officer to surrender, which we were pleased about because we weren't looking forward to having to assault these pill boxes.

Les Sewell...
What I remember was all the civvies going into the German HQ. and looting it. First one chap came out with a side of beef, then another with a big pile of butter. I can remember the last chap who must have been disappointed because he came out with a big hat stand. We collected prisoners in the carriers and the next day we had quite a dinner in an orchard and the table was covered in wines and all sorts. I don't drink but I enjoyed some of those!

Above : This building was searched for during a visit to the Le Havre area in Summer, 2000. It shows the C.Os. American built International Half-Track on the left, and a White Scout Car on the right of the entrance to Bn. HQ. The Hallams 'Battle Flag' flies from a staff above the door. On good evidence (the Mayoress) this building is not in her town of La Cerlangue. It can only be assumed that this was part of the barracks used for the first nights rest after the clearance of the docks. (THD)

❖ *Right : The small town of La Cerlangue where the Hallams had a rest period that lasted five days and which was to leave them far behind the rapidly advancing front line. The Great War 1914 - 18 Memorial can be seen at the base of the steeple, which was the place where Trevor Hart Dyke tried to make peace between the local Resistance and their Mayor who, like many others in such thankless positions of authority towards the end of the war, stood accused of being a collaborator. (DWS)*

At the end of this action, by which time it was dark, the Hallams claimed to have captured one thousand and five prisoners, one submarine and three Dornier seaplanes, a peculiar 'bag' for an infantry battalion! Then shortly afterwards, the C.O. went back to the advance dressing station for treatment of a minor but painful shrapnel wound to his hand.Major Newton's wound, in the buttocks, must have been considerably more painful. The Battalion retired for the night into some barracks within the city but next day were moved two or three miles inland to a rest area in La Cerlangue to the east of Le Havre, to await its next assignment.

John Wollerton...
From this village, I went up the coast to get some Benedictine along with a group of other soldiers, many of whom tried to go round twice but were stopped by the nuns. We brought a bottle of this back to our Coy. and it really was very, very good.

Arnold Whiteley also did this trip to keep a friend company who had been given a 'chit' to collect one dozen bottles of that famous liquid but, before they got to the distillery at Fecamp, the figure twelve had been 'doctored' to read thirteen. When they got back to the Battalion area, an E.N.S.A. show had been put on for the troops and it was here that the ill begotten bottle of Benedictine was consumed.

Arnold Whiteley...
There were three or four of us sitting at the back drinking this stuff like pop and we didn't know whether we were on stage or at the back of the hall by the time we'd finished. We ended up in this cafe to buy more drinks and got a bit boisterous and I was going to stand on me head and sing 'Pratty Flowers'. Then two Gendarmes came and we couldn't understand each other, so my pal said, 'If my mate wants to F...... sing, he's going to sing!' Then six red caps turned up and sent us on our way without any more trouble and I remember us walking back to the Battalion through this village shouting, 'Vive La Churchill! Vive la France!' Then I was thrown into the back of this truck and carted back to camp.

Trevor Hart Dyke...
I was given two bottles of champagne by a farmer and one of them I later took out to Burma with me in my baggage and said I would get to drink it on VE Day, which I did but I had been sent back to India by then and I drank it at a place called Chas, near Ranchee in India, when we were under canvas there. Anyhow, it was a nice gesture from the farmer.

The Battalion now remained in rest for six days during which time Capts. L. Gill and C.A. MacKillop rejoined. News was also received that immediate awards had been approved as follows: Lt. Col. T. Hart Dyke - D.S.O., Majors J.A.H. Nicholson and L.M. Lonsdale-Cooper - M.C. An M.C. was also awarded to the M.O., Capt. P.G. Griffiths (R.A.M.C.). Some of these awards were later presented personally by Field Marshal Montgomery.

A celebration service on the 17th to mark the liberation of this area, held in the church at La Cerlangue, was marred at the end when the Mayor, who had attended the service, was denounced by local Resistance as being a collaborator. Col. Hart Dyke did his best to smooth things over by inviting everyone to celebrate with a glass of Champagne afterwards. The invitations were accepted but the Resistance group did not come to the party. It seemed that the war was not quite over for some people and old scores, for the moment, were being merely consigned to later settlement. It was no concern of the Hallamshires who were given a five day rest period before chasing after their own war, which had now left them well behind a very mobile frontline to the north.

❖ *The Benedictine Distillery at Fecamp. (DWS)*

BELGIUM AND BRAVERY

On 19 September, the Hallams began a three day journey with the remainder of the 49th Division to rejoin the 1st Canadian Army which by now, had reached almost to the Belgium/Holland border. The first part of the journey northwards was by way of St. Romain - Bolbec - Fauville-en-Caux - Cany-Barville - Crasville and along the coast road through Dieppe to a small village called Boscrocourt, about five miles SE of Le Treport. The convoy remained here for two nights and continued on the 21st to Phalesphin, three miles south of Lille by way of Eu - St.Valery sur Somme - Hesdin - St.Pol - Bethune - Lens - Lille. During this one night stay, Major Mike Halford made a detour to a place called Ennevelin where the 6th Battalion, The York & Lancaster Regiment, had stayed in 1940 as part of the British Expeditionary Force prior to withdrawal through Dunkirk and other French ports. The drums of this battalion had been left there during the withdrawal and it was hoped to be able to retrieve them, but they could not be located.

It must have been around this time that Roy Simon was being shipped back to Normandy, where he found himself in a transit camp near the beaches. His arm wound had healed and he was ready to make his way back to the Battalion, if he could find it, and if he wasn't going to be used as a gap filler in some other unit!

Roy Simon...
...we were in this assembly area and somebody shouted, 'Hallamshires?' and I turned round and there were this bloke and he were shackled. I said, 'What's the matter with you?' and it were that Gabbitas lad that played drum and he were limping after a bad leg wound had shipped him back the same time as me. I said, 'What you doing with them on?' He says, 'They've put me in Pioneer Corps and I'm not going. If I'm coming back over here I'm going back to Hallams. So if you see anybody can you tell 'em?' I said, 'Ay! I'll tell them.'

Meanwhile, the final stage of the journey, on the 22nd, took the Bn. to a place called Nijlen NE of Lier, just east of Antwerp by way of Menin - Courtrai - Harlebeke - Veichte - Audenarde - Alost - Termonde - Willebroack - Malines - Lier - Nijlen. All of the one hundred and five vehicles arrived safe and serviceable. The trip had been a long one and the route had taken them through many towns and villages where the Battalion was greeted ecstatically by crowds of people along the way. They were showered with fruit and flowers which caused some injuries, including a broken nose and one or two black eyes, to those who were sat in exposed positions on the transport. As if the Germans weren't enough!

❖ *Main street in Nijlen. (DWS)*

Chris Somers (Diary)...
...transport had been assembled to take us through France to the Antwerp area. Part of the company and myself travelled with an A/T Regiment as there were no troop carriers. It was certainly a cheerful trip, crowds of

civilians turning out to cheer us on our way, throwing us fruit and flowers. Eventually we arrived at a small Belgian village near Lier, fairly near the Dutch border. A mile or so and a canal separated us from the Boche but they were inactive and we were able to billet with civilians. A dance was organized that night by the Battalion though I didn't partake. I'd spent the day collecting the company pay and saw the Arnhem gliders passing overhead, a wonderful sight. Just as well I didn't go to the dance as we received a warning order to prepare to move during the night. Always the way!

The main parachute drops and glider landings for Operation Market-Garden had taken place on the 17 September when the Hallams were still at La Cerlangue. From here these flights could not have been witnessed by the Hallams as the nearest flight paths or 'corridors' (for the American drops and landings around Eindhoven) passed just south of Antwerp. The date that Chris witnessed what was obviously a large number of aircraft passing overhead was the 23rd, on the evening of which a dance took place. This dance is mentioned by Chris and confirmed in the War Diary. The aircraft seen by Chris were almost certainly one of the many, and no doubt spectacular, supply drops which took place during the whole of the ill-fated operation. On that same evening of the 23rd, the Battalion received orders that it would advance to the Antwerp-Turnhout Canal the next day.

❖ *Oostmalle - Turnhout road where Hallams debussed and moved through woods on left towards the canal. (DWS)*

Chris Somers (Diary)...
We passed through Oostmalle in troop carriers to cross the Antwerp - Turnout canal. We had a casualty en route when Cpl. Furness was hit in the face by an apple thrown by civilians. The bridge had been blown, so the Lincs had discovered, and we were turned off down the Turnout road. We debussed in some woods and advanced down under their cover to the canal. Opposition was supposed to be negligible on the other side but any movement by us brought small arms fire from the Boche. Luckily we were well concealed in the wood.

The designated Coys. were initially guided through these woods by an attached group of Belgian 'resistance'. 'C' and 'B' Coys. moved forwards through the woods and as they drew near to the canal it was reported by 'B' Coy. that enemy snipers were in evidence on the other side. An order was received from Bde. for the Hallams to make a diversionary crossing at this

❖ *The Hallams used canvas boats in an attempted diversionary crossing of the Canal from left to right bank. The action took place on a slight bend of the waterway at a point opposite the posts that can be seen on the other side. They were met by machine gun fire which seriously wounded Capt. Douglas Bell.(DWS)*

274

point, to coincide with an attempted main crossing on the left by 4 Lincolns and the R.E. using Bailey bridging.

'D' Coy. moved through 'C' Coy. on the left to attempt the crossing. The Hallams crossing point was immediately subjected to small arms fire when 'D' Coy. moved down to launch their canvas boats from the canal banking at 2330 hrs. The boats were riddled with bullets and the crossing was abandoned but it was here also, that Capt. Douglas R. Bell was severely wounded in the stomach (he was subsequently evacuated and died at home, more than three weeks later). Platoons from 'A', 'B' and 'C' Coys. remained on the canal side to maintain fire and keep the enemy busy on the right flank of the main attempted bridgehead crossing whilst the bulk of the Battalion was withdrawn.

4 Lincolns had been successful with their crossing and a small bridgehead had been gained across the canal during the night of the 24/25th by the R.E. using Bailey Bridging. These pieces of equipment are worth special mention and a simplified explanation of their use is given below.

Donald Coleman Bailey was born in the Clifton area of Rotherham, Yorkshire, on 15 September, 1901, and it was he who was destined to become the inventor of one of the most notable pieces of structural engineering of the 20th Century, the now famous Bailey Bridge. These bridges were designed to be easily portable in sections, the largest of which could be lifted by six men and all parts transportable in standard British Army 3 ton Trucks to almost any theatre of war. The structure was assembled using large steel pins and could be erected on site in varying degrees of strength depending on the required bridge span and/or weights of vehicle required to cross.

The basic design centred on open sided panels measuring 10ft. x 5ft (300cm x 150cm) formed by integral crossbracing and side struts. Two of these were spaced apart by cross girders and as many of these units or 'bays' pinned together as were necessary to span the river, ravine or other obstacle. The bridge structure could be strengthened by increasing the height (maximum of three side members high) and/or increasing the width of sides (maximum of three side members thickness at each side). The bridge was completed by laying a central roadway formed by laying heavy wooden sleepers across box-section steel panels laid on the cross girders.

The fascinating part of the design was in the method of launching the bridge across a river or other obstacle. The structure was built up on a series of rollers on one side of the 'gap' to be spanned (a river bank for instance) and slowly pushed out towards the other side. As it extended it had to be increasingly counterbalanced on the landward side by use of more structure or special weights to prevent the advancing free end from overbalancing and plunging into the river. Longer spans could be supported by floating structures.

So successful was the design and so rugged the structure that many of the bridges put in place in the post Normandy landings over 50 years ago are still in place today. There are a good number of these bridges still to be found in France alone. However, there is one fine example in perfect working order spanning the River Don at Eastwood, Rotherham, less than a mile from the York & Lancaster Regimental Museum. It was built in 1947 and refurbished by The Royal Engineers in 1991, a lasting and fitting tribute to one of Rotherham's famous sons.

It was now decided that the Battalion was to pass through the 4 Lincolns, who were probing east along the north bank, and join with 1/4 K.O.Y.L.I. who were already across with the Recce Regt. in an attempt to clear a way through Rijkevorsel and then advance east along the road towards Merxsplas.

Chris Somers (Diary)...
25 September : We had breakfast and I think did a bit of sleeping, but we were soon off again as the R.E. had quickly constructed a bridge. The bridge had actually been prepared before the Lincs attack. The bridge was under intermittent shell fire so I was glad when our own troop carriers had got clear. We travelled up the road towards Rijkevorsel which was being cleared by the KOYLI. The 56 Brigade were holding the left flank and later beat off some heavy counter attacks. Information was sorely lacking at this point and all our company troop carriers were sitting on the road with

fighting going on in the fields all around. Mike then got orders to take 'C' Coy. up a lane to the East, so we about turned and travelled back to the area of the bridge debussing by a brickworks at the start of the lane. A shell hit the road as we got out and troops were soon down in the ditch. At that moment, Mike told me to collect the company 'O' group so I had the unpleasant business of having to walk down the road while the Boche was trying to drop the odd shell or two on it. Luckily they all just cleared the road, landing in the field about 20 yards away.

❖ *Well maintained, Memorial Bridge to Sir Donald C. Bailey (its inventor) over the River Don near Retail World at Rotherham, South Yorkshire. All of the component parts can be clearly seen here including the distinctive side panels, cross girders, wooden sleepers that form the roadway and even the tails of the large steel pins holding the sections together. (DWS)*

They had crossed the Class 40 (load bearing capacity in tons) Bailey Bridge and moved up the road towards Rijkevorsel where there was quite a snarl up which resulted in the Hallams being sent back towards the canal. However, they managed to bypass the jam by moving along the sandy lane, mentioned by Chris (below), and then cut left with the intention of joining the road to Merxplas about a mile or so to the east of Rijkevorsel. The going was very tough!

Chris Somers (Diary)...
Eventually the Coy. got moving as an advanced guard to the Battalion up the sandy lane to reach the main lateral road (Rijkevorsel-Merksplas). We advanced up through pine woods and once again it felt for a moment as though we were on an exercise. All went well until after we had advanced

❖ *Loch position where Bailey Bridge was erected by 4 Lincolns and Royal Engineers to force a bridgehead over the Antwerp-Turnhout Canal. The red bricked building on the right is a restaurant called 'The Bridge' but the Bailey has long since been dismantled. (DWS)*

276

with 'B' Coy. on our left for about half a mile. Then we came upon an old German unexpectedly. He saw us first and dashed off before anybody could take a shot. No doubt he raised the alarm because a few hundred yards further our leading section was practically wiped out by Spandau fire, including Lt. Toon the platoon commander. Bullets were flying all over the place now and the leading platoon drew back round Coy. HQ. We temporarily consolidated and returned the Boche fire with our Bren. He also sent over a few mortar bombs but nothing much.

Unfortunately we had no reserve ammunition, our carrier not being able to travel through the wood, so got permission to withdraw into the Battalion area. 'D' Coy. too, had suffered very heavy casualties from shell fire and were reorganizing. It was quite a job disengaging from the enemy who began to follow us up and had also started firing from our left flank. We got the wounded out and gave them a good start and then got back in quick rushes. The Battalion was about quarter of a mile to our left and we were immediately given an order to dig in. A strong German patrol passed by without spotting us while we were engaged in getting ourselves underground.

❖ *Above : The pine tree lined, sandy lane described by Chris Somers is now a metalled roadway but still leads from the brick works by the canal to the main road between Rijkevorsel and Merxplas. Fierce fighting was encountered here and cost the life of Lt. Toon and others. (DWS)* ❖ *Right Above : Next day, Capt. Pearce (Canadian Army) was killed and Major Boucher wounded when they led 'D' Company down this road towards the Depot de Mendicite and Merxplas.(DWS)*

'C' Coy. had now fought their way to the road after having lost 2/Lt. Toon, but they were meeting even stiffer resistance. There seemed to be action taking place all around them with the rest of the Brigade fully deployed. 'D' Coy. had been brought up from positions near the canal, reached the road, and were ordered to proceed eastwards keeping well clear of the road itself. Unfortunately, they moved along its ditches and got caught in shell fire that was detonating in the canopy of trees above them. Capt. Pearce was killed and Major J. Boucher wounded and it was left to Capt. J. Hall to lead the now demoralised 'D' Coy. forward once again. Things came to a standstill for the night with casualties put at twelve ORs. killed and ten wounded.

Next morning (26th), the road was attacked from the north by a German 'bicycle' Coy. which threatened to cut the line between the Hallams and 1/4 KOYLI. further to the west but it was successfully repelled. During this action, 'A' Coy. was sent eastwards with tank support to clear the area where 'C' Coy. had fought the day before. 2/Lt. K.N. Hardy was wounded here, with one OR. killed and three wounded. More fierce fighting took place to the west, as the enemy tried to destroy the canal bridgehead which had been established earlier by 4 Lincolns and Royal

Engineers. They were halted and driven back by the 2 S.W.B. and 1 L.R. In the actions that had taken place over the past two days, seventy-eight enemy soldiers were captured or surrendered.

4 Lincolns were involved in confused fighting and having a hard time of it on the right of the Hallams between the road and the north side of the canal, almost opposite where Capt. Bell had been wounded a few days earlier. The Hallams had now begun to make their way in the direction of Merxplas towards the Depot de Mendicite which was down the road and off to the left. Whilst 'A' and 'C' Coys. moved cautiously down the road, 'B' Coy. was sent through the woods to the north for an attack on a farm house which was on the Battalion's left flank.
A fierce hand to hand battle took place here but the farm was eventually captured by a Platoon led by Lt. John Wollerton.

John Wollerton...
At the time of the attack on the Depot de Mendicite, I was given orders for an attack on a farm with the support of a platoon of carriers from 4 Lincolns and they suddenly pulled out without orders because things were getting too hot and we were left there holding the baby. We gave the Germans quite a strafing and my batman was marvellous. Ted was a good shot and got three in a row crossing a road there. I could trust that man implicitly and he never let me down. Whenever we were digging in under shell fire he'd take his helmet off his head and cover his private parts with it and I said to him once, 'Ted, you've been given that helmet to protect the most sensitive part of your body,' and he replied, 'Thee speak for thee sen Sir, tha don't know my Mrs. I'd sooner go home with 'at me heed!'

John Wollerton was operating to the left of the main attack and was alone with Sgt. Maj. Mackay at one point and shouting orders to his patrol when a group of Germans got up in front of him and scattered. He had no option but to open fire with his sten gun while shouting for the patrol, some distance away, to give him covering fire. He did almost all the firing himself because there wasn't time for the others to get to him and he apparently used up a number of magazines, fed to him by the Sgt. Major. He was reluctant to say if he had killed many of the enemy but, he must have done so because the others who were there with him, subsequently dubbed him with the nickname 'Killer' that has stuck to this day. It is true to say that the name lies heavy on his mind now, but the action then was courageous despite his misgivings. It has all to do with the taking of other men's lives, especially at such close quarters, and then being branded with an odious name tag even though it was, in its way, a mark of respect shown by the men under his command.

Chris Somers (Diary)...
We managed to get a bit of sleep that night (26/27) and next morning were given the job of clearing a large wooded area to the north of the main road, while 'A' Coy. cleared down the road and 'B' Coy. up to the end of the wood. We had a quiet trip down the wood. Mike spotted a Boche and picked him off at long-range - a good shot. We also found some Boche bicycles. At the far end of the wood, the leading platoon spotted a Boche but as we were on a semi-recce trip, we left well alone so that the Boche was unaware of our presence.

The C.O. asked us over the air to return to base via his HQ. which was behind 'A' Coy. I was leading the Coy. back with Mike in the rear along a ditch which traversed the field to our C.Os. house. I don't know if we got spotted from afar but shells started falling on either side of the ditch and much to my annoyance, the Coy. went to ground. I walked back to see what the hold up was and found that Mike had led the rear half of the men round the other way. So I got the others moving quickly out of the danger area and reported to the C.O. who gave me our new location for the night which was the previous evenings Bn.HQ. Here we got a reasonably good night's sleep and a double issue of Rum.

Irrespective of whatever 'liquids' might be carried in hip flasks for personal use, an official rum ration could be called forward by the C.O. whenever the occasion demanded which was usually before, during or after an action. A small amount was carried in the front line aboard one of the Bn.HQ. vehicles but to provide sufficient 'tots' for two or three companies necessitated a considerable amount being brought up from 'B' Echelon.

Arthur Green...
On one occasion around the time of the attack on the Depot de Mendicite, I was woken up at one o'clock in the morning to be told that the C.O. had requested that a rum ration be sent forward to Bn.HQ. after one or two skirmishes had taken place. Being woken up at that time was not very pleasant and I wasn't sure where the HQ. was, as I hadn't been up to that one yet. The REME Sgt. said he knew where it was and he'd go with me. He was a tough character was 'Jock' Henderson and we set off in this Austin Light Utility (Tilly) with the rum ration in the back and he said he would drive as he knew the way.

We went over tree roots and what have you and then he stopped and said, 'Ah! We turn off here.' As we turned, we went over this bank and got 'bellied' and we were stuck there. I thought, 'Oh! We're in a right pickle here.' Jock was strong as an ox and he said, 'You get in, put it in reverse, give it steady revs and I'll lift it up at the front.' Well, he got hold of the bumper bar of this 'Tilly' and the back wheels gripped and we sailed off the bank. We got there without any further trouble but it was a bit hair raising because I thought we were going to be stuck there all night. I wasn't very fond of rum - beer was more my line!

Such a rum ration was called forward on this, the night of the 27/28th and in the morning, the previous days work had to be repeated. 'A' Coy. reoccupied the houses on the south side of the main road opposite the earth wall and dike which protected the western approaches to the Depot de Mendicite on the opposite side. An enemy A/Tk gun, further down the road to the east, knocked out one of 'A' Coys. tank support but attempts to deal with it failed. 'C' Coy. reoccupied the woods on the north side of the road, right to its eastern edge where a clear view could now be had of the earthen bank, about three hundred yards away, in front of the Depot. 'B' Coy. took up positions in the NW corner of these woods and 'D' Coy. remained in the rear to provide a firm base.

Chris Somers (Diary)...
We moved up to our old wood again, to dig in at the far end in preparation for the attack on the Depot de Mendicite the following morning. 'D' Coy. had been split up and a platoon had reinforced us. We dug in near the top of the wood and prepared for the following morning and made recces etc. The Leicesters were coming through on our right in the early hours of the morning. A few shells fell near our company HQ. during the night but nothing much. In the pitch darkness of the early hours next morning we started to have breakfast and form up but I don't think many had breakfast. It was issued in one gallon containers (rum?) and it was all the poor Sergeants could do to find their men in the darkness. Of course neither our extra wireless or the Pioneers had turned up when we were ready to go. They just made it, however, though I told the Pioneers who had brought a heavy plank for crossing the dyke that they might as well stay behind! They wouldn't have got half way with it. Of course the Boche had to start shelling the wood at this point which was rather unpleasant in the darkness.

Bn. HQ. was now set up in a Hunting Lodge which was situated up a path through the woods on the north side of the road. This building belonged to a Mr. Van Bree, who had been a great friend of the late King Albert I of Belgium. It was in this very building that Ray Langdale was given two officers 'pips' and told to get them sewn onto the epaulettes of his battle dress. He was being awarded a field commission and was now 2/Lt. Langdale.

On the opposite side of the road from the path that led to the Lodge, there was a farmhouse and further down the road towards Merxplas, on the same side were a pair of villas which were now occupied by 'A' Coy. The scene was set for an attack the next day on the complex known as the Depot de Mendicite which was very strongly held by the enemy. The main assault was to be carried out by 1 Leicesters from the main road on the south side, but the Hallams were going to play a major role on the west side.

It is believed to have been around this time when Arthur Green came closer to the action than was usual, considering that in normal circumstances he would usually be operating in the 'relatively' safe area between Bn. HQ. and 'B' Echelon. However, anybody working immediately behind the sharp end was always in danger of residual or even direct shell fire.

Arthur Green...
I was part of a small convoy moving up to Bn. HQ. from 'B' Echelon with some stores and reinforcements. There was a petrol wagon, a water wagon, myself with some rations, another wagon behind me with reinforcements and behind them, three officers in a Jeep. I can't tell you the name of the village we were passing but it had been badly shelled and there was a big notice at the beginning of this village and it said, 'Do not pass beyond this point as you will be under enemy observation.' The transport officer said that we would wait until it got dark before we went any further but he got a little impatient because I think he was a bit afraid of what the C.O. might say if he was late arriving. Anyway, it still wasn't dark and he said, 'Come on, we'll risk it.' We set off along this track across fields and there were tapes on the left hand side and corn on the right. We were going as fast as we dare go and all of a sudden I could see shells falling, crump!, crump! and I thought, 'This is it! This is our lot!' One burst very close in front of my wagon and stopped the engine dead. I was feeling all over to see where I was hurt and fortunately I wasn't, so I just scrambled down and tried to get under my tin hat.

There was a slit trench at the side of the road with straw in the bottom and I'm thinking, 'Dare I get in here or will it be booby-trapped?' So, I thought I'd risk it and jumped down into it. I shuffled through me pockets to try and get a fag to cool me nerves because I was shaking like a leaf and it was remarkable that I hadn't been injured or anything. Anyhow, the QMs. Cpl., who had been sitting next to me, had got out of the wagon and run into the left hand side field through the tapes and suddenly realised that he was in a mine field. A Rotherham lad in the back, who was the Quartermaster's batman, had got out and was running up and down holding his arm across the front of him and shouting, 'Me arm's off! Me arm's off!' I was shouting, 'Get down you silly beggar, there's some more shells coming over.' The Cpl. must have shut his eyes and walked out of the field and survived.

Then I went and grabbed hold of this other lad who had only been going up to the front to see one of his pals and it wasn't necessary for him to go, but he would insist on coming with us. I noticed that the top of his battledress blouse was all blood and I could see he was going a bit funny coloured and grayish and I said, 'Come on, your only nicked, it's all right!' Then I put me left arm round his shoulders and I put me right hand across the front of him to stop the flow of blood and I squeezed about where the muscle was and me fingers just met through gristle and bone. I thought, 'Oh, my God, he has lost his arm.' I took him to the back thinking to put him in the Jeep to get him to the RAP, but I couldn't see any of the officers. Anyway, I found them all in a slit trench on top of one another. I don't know how they all got in but I could understand how they felt because they were new arrivals and this was their first taste.

On checking out the wagon after we'd got this lad away for treatment, there was only one area of damage and that was where the piece of shrapnel had passed through the tilt canvas and struck the lad in the arm. I found the fragment lying on the floor afterwards and kept it until the end of the war. Shortly after the war that wounded lad spotted me walking around Barker's Pool in Sheffield. He came and got hold of me, put his one arm around me and his head on my shoulder and cried like a child. He wanted to thank me for saving his life.

Trevor Hart Dyke...
The Depot de Mendicite I think was an asylum in peace time but the Germans had occupied it. It had a mound around it and then inside the mound was a ditch of fairly deep water. We had to attack that and the battalion on our right , I think it was the Leicesters from another Brigade, crossed the start line late and so all the German fire was directed on our soldiers. One of the leading platoon commanders was badly wounded in the neck and Corporal Harper took command and got the Victoria Cross later on for very gallant conduct in storming the mound and driving the Germans off. Unfortunately, he got killed just after he'd succeeded. Capturing that enabled the Polish Armoured Division to continue their advance.

The Depot de Mendicite, a huge complex of buildings, was originally established (c.1825) by a Dutch prince as a refuge for beggars, drunkards and social outcasts. It later took on more of a prison like stance when it began to accept criminals, mostly the seriously ill and deranged from other establishments. During the Second World War, parts of it were used by the German occupation forces where they housed various types of prisoner including those accused of being members of resistance movements. Many of these people were 'innocent' but still subsequently transported for use as slave labour. Today, it is a high security prison and better known to the local people as the Merksplas Kolonie. The asylum has now been converted to house illegal political refugees but there are plans to turn some of the buildings into a national museum telling the history of detention through the ages.

It was during the last decade of the nineteenth century that a decision was made to surround the 'Depot' with a moat or dyke in an attempt to stem the rising tide of escapes. The contents of the dyke was used to form a low earthen embankment, about two meters high, on the outer edge and this combination created quite a considerable barrier for those trying to flee the place. The work was never completed on the southern side but the western stretch of this barrier was that which the Hallamshires were now required to charge and breach, in conjunction with other battalions of the 49th Division, in order to clear the path for a Polish armoured unit to pass through.

Chris Somers (Diary)...
We reached our forming up place on the edge of the wood at Zero Hour. The leading platoon charged off into the darkness towards the moat surrounding the Depot de Mendicite taking with them the 18 set. Mike kept Company HQ. and another lot on the edge of the wood. The CSM, carriers and the No. 10 set were back where we spent the night. The first platoon reported casualties and asked for reinforcements so a second platoon was sent off.

❖ *The Hallams came in from the left over approximately 300 yards of open ground and were able to take some cover against the earthen bank. On the other side was a dike running parallel to it with various German defensive positions and a Victoria Cross was won here. In this same vicinity also, Roy Simon passed out after being shot in the chest. When he came round, two field grey clad figures approached and carried him to a brick barn, just within the complex known as the Depot de Mendicite. (DWS)*

Roy Simon had by now found his way back to the Hallams all right, and duly reported what had happened back at the beaches where Pte. Gabbitas had been demanding to be allowed to rejoin his own battalion. Roy had, of course, succeeded in finding his way back but he was not destined to stay for very long. An attack on the Depot de Mendicite was about to be launched from the edge of woods to the west of the complex and Roy was going to be very much involved in it as a rifleman of 'C' Coy. His story is enthralling.

Roy Simon...
...we stacked all us gear in one great big pile just prior to going onto positions through these woods and I was told to look after these two young lads who had never been in action before... (possibly some of those brought up by Arthur Green). We could see the objective some distance from our positions across open ground where there was little or no trees for cover. We were in a ditch on the edge of this wood and what happened next was real Errol Flynn stuff....

We were lined up and they were shelling us and Lonsdale-Cooper was at the side of me and he said, 'Right, get ready,' and he were looking at his watch. Then all of a sudden he blows his whistle and I gets half out of the ditch and nowt happens, nobody moved! and he says to me, 'Come on Simon,' he says, 'You're one of the old lads, show them how it's done!' So I gets up and I shouts, 'Come on the Hallams, let's go,' and I set off running and everybody moved with me you know. I said to these two young lads, 'Come on,' and we started across and everything seemed to be coming at us.

We got half way across and I was running like the clappers with nothing to fire at and I just glanced to my right and there was a German forward position in the middle of the field. This lad says, 'Look, there's some Gerries there,' and I said, 'Keep running,' and we got past them and we

282

went into this ditch (running parallel to the line of attack). We went down and I shouted, 'Right! Target four o'clock, take aim.' We were about to fire when these Gerries jumped up and I said, 'Don't fire!' because they were throwing their arms up and running towards the woods where we had come from.

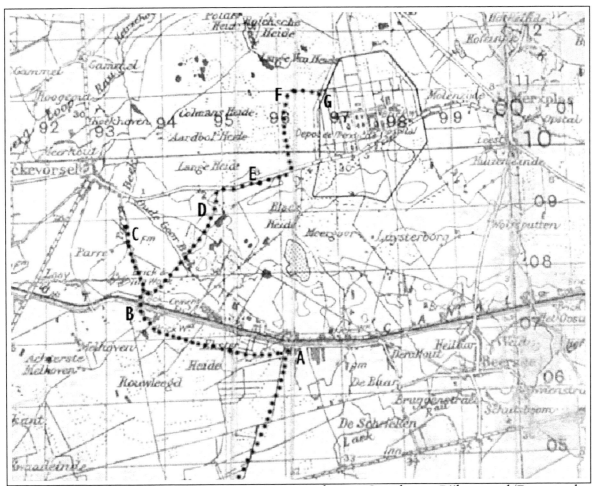

Map Showing advance over Antwerp-Turnhout Canal to Rijkevorsel/Depot de Mendicite/Merxplas.

Dotted line shows general direction of Hallams progress across the canal and on to the Depot de Mendicite. A = Companies led to this position by Belgian Resistance from Oostmalle-Turnhout road, down to edge of canal where Capt. Bell was seriously wounded in an attempted diversionary crossing. B = 4 Lincs and R.E. force bridgehead using Bailey Bridging. C = Hallams cross and attempt entry into Rijkevorsel in support of 1/4 K.O.Y.L.I. Unable to break through they come back to brickworks and make detour to main road near D = Position where Lt. Toon was killed. E = Capt Pearce killed in further advance along this road towards Depot de Mendicite and Merxplas. F = Roy Simon 'leads' the charge over 300 yards of open ground to earthen bank and dike at G = Position where Cpl. Harper was involved in action for which he was awarded a posthumous Victoria Cross. (PRO)

Arnold Whiteley...
We were lined up in the edge of a wood and we'd to cross about 300 yards of open ground to get to this Depot. It was a compound made up of a lot of buildings and I think it was a workhouse or something to that effect. There was a moat ran round and so there was only an entrance every so far and on the outside of the moat there was about 5 yards of soil and then banking. A lot of the German posts were outside the Depot and on this banking and they'd got the moat behind them. They tried to get the first platoon across just as it was coming light but Coy. HQ. hadn't got across and we found that the unit that should have been on our right were late onto start line so it left us open to fire from the right flank.

I remember a L/Cpl. bringing his section back and he approached Major Cooper and he said, 'Me nerves gone, I can't carry on.' He pulled his revolver out, did Major Cooper, and he stuck it in this fellows tummy and he said, 'Cpl. so and so, you're going back over there with your men or else I'm going to shoot you.' I knew it was no idle threat and the Cpl. did take them back.

Then we made our crossing and as we ran across you hear the bullets whizzing. We were well spaced out and it were only Major Cooper who got hit. Of course, when we got under cover of banking on the other side, I said, 'Thank God nobody got hit,' and he said, 'You speak for your bloody self!' He was shot straight through his left arm. Another six inches in and he would of been out of it!

Chris Somers (Diary)...
It was getting light now and a few shots were fired at them. Also the Boche had got wind of what was happening and had started to shell our part of the wood. Three prisoners were sent back under their own steam, being sniped at by their own troops. Mike going across to collect them got shot in the arm, only flesh wound luckily and I tied his field dressing around it and he was able to carry on.

The shelling of our part of the wood was now quite heavy. Luckily, however, each successive salvo either fell just beyond or just short of us. It was quite amusing in a way to see how much harder everyone scratched at the ground after each 'stonk' came down. Each time Mike and I had piled in on top of each other in our shallow slit trench which would hardly have given cover to a grasshopper. Once, I was thankful for my steel helmet when a minute fragment of shell splinter 'pinged' down on top of it. We told the three prisoners to get digging with their bayonets as we weren't going to lend them our shovels!

Roy Simon...
I looked around and our lads were going down and stretchers were being called for. Meanwhile we ran on up this ditch and got to this banking. There were about 15 of us in our group and we kept firing forward into the German positions. There were a bloke to my left with a Brengun and he wasn't firing it and I said, 'Why the hell don't you fire that Brengun?' The Corporal to his left shouted to him, 'Private, get that gun and fire it!' and he says, 'I'm not firing it. If I fire this they'll all come at me.' Just as he said that, something hit his helmet and he just went straight back and he were down on his back. The next thing he's shouting, 'I told you, I told you!' and he reckoned the shot had come from somewhere high up when another lad got hit.

Then there was a shot hit this tree next to me and I was looking around... ... someone were firing again and a shot ricocheted off this tree and suddenly I thought I'd seen him. I tried to get a bead on him from where I was laid down but there was another tree in my way so I moved round the other side of the big tree I was under, and raised my rifle to the left shoulder. I was just going to pull trigger when all of a sudden I heard this terrific bang at the side of my ear. I stood straight up and spun round and fell back towards the trench but this L/Cpl caught me. I were sat there and thought, 'Where have I been hit?' Then I felt all this warmth down me back and I said to this Lance Jack, 'What's me back like?' He said there were blood coming out and the same bullet had passed through and hit him in the wrist. One of the young lads came running over with both hands up in the air and he had been shot in both wrists while taking aim. I was now sat with my back against the trench side and then Gerry started mortaring us. Shells were falling in a pattern and bodies were going up all round.

Chris Somers (Diary)...
Soon the assaulting force asked for supporting fire and I managed to get the 3 inch Mortars on the air. They registered with smoke on the left flank and we had one or two rounds put down which may have had a little effect. I should imagine it was about midday when Mike went across with the remaining platoon and soon afterwards he asked for us to follow. We went over the open ground at the double and sniping started when we were about 100 yards short of the moat. No good going to ground, I thought, and finished very short of breath. Only one casualty luckily, a Cpl. shot through the head, though we didn't find his body till later that evening.

We all moved rapidly into the Depot de Mendicite and took over a position from the Leicesters who moved further into the grounds behind their leading troops. Mike was feeling a bit weak now no wonder, and allowed me to fix the company into a state of all round defence in an area of some farm buildings while he had a short sit down. We were soon fairly well established though troubled by some snipers which necessitated using the ditch instead of the track across our front.

Arnold Whiteley...
The lads who were in close proximity were eye ball to eye ball over this banking and they must have seen each other and killed simultaneously. There was only a few yards between our dead and theirs. We got into the compound and they started giving themselves up and I was with Major Cooper when the lads started to tell him about Cpl. Harper and his deeds. Then he said to them, 'I don't want you to talk about it amongst yourselves and I don't want to hear about it. I'll see you later.' I think what transpired was that he took each man's individual statement to see if it corroborated and he put him in for the V.C. and he got it, but of course he had been killed in the mean time.

Meanwhile, Roy Simon must have passed out or fallen asleep as the next thing he remembered was that German soldiers were moving towards him. Unknown to Roy, the fight in his sector was over...
They were coming closer to me, looked at two or three lads and came to me and I tried to raise my rifle. Then somebody said it was all right and that they'd do me no harm as they were stretcher bearers. One of them looked at me and he were nearly old enough to be me Granddad and then a thought registered in my mind, 'By Jingo! He's the double of Bob Shorthouse.' (Roy's brother's father-in-law!)

❖ *The barn to which Roy Simon was carried by two German Stretcher Bearers. (DWS)* ❖ *Back in the barn again after more than 50 years, he just sat down, closed his eyes and let the memories flood back.(DWS)*

One of our own stretcher bearers told me I would be all right with them and to just do as I was told. They picked me up and, using my rifle as a chair, carried me away along the earthen bank to the right and then turned left over a little bridge. We went into this kind of a barn and they sat me down. A German came over and treated my wound with my own field dressing and covered it with some of theirs. He put my battle dress blouse back on, took his own coat off and put it on me to keep me warm. I was sat with me back up against this support in this barn and when I looked round the place was full of wounded Gerries.

Some time later, Capt. Lonsdale-Cooper came in and Roy remembered him having his arm in a sling. Later still, Roy was stretchered away on a Jeep with another casualty who was in a bad way... *They strapped me on this stretcher and I'd got my arm round him and he were moaning and I said, 'Come on lad, you'll be all right,' and I'd got my arm round him and he did scream. Anyway we eventually got to the casualty clearing station and they laid us down. I was laid there and they're taking these lads tea to them and this, that and t'other; coming round giving blokes cups of tea and all kinds of stuff and passing me by. So, I didn't realise what was happening you see, and they never came anywhere near me. So then one bloke's coming towards me and this bloke says, 'Oh, you can leave him, he's a Gerry!' and I says, 'What the hell you talking about?' I didn't realise that I'd still got this Gerry overcoat on and they thought I were a Gerry. Anyway they took this coat off me and gave me a cup of tea!*

Roy was eventually taken to a hospital in Brussels where he had an operation and was placed in a recovery ward where things did not go well... *There was an incident where this lad in the next bed had a drip on his back and he died within twenty-four hours and the lad on the other side did same! There was an American in there demanded to be put in his own hospital and they took him away on the same morning as they came to me. They were going to put a drip in my back and I refused it. I said, 'No! I'm not having that!' and the bloke says, 'Why?' and I said, 'There's two of them 'deed' with them here,' I said, 'If I'm going to die, I'll die normal, I'm not going the same way as them lads, they went terrible.' So, he says, 'Well, yours might not be as bad.' Then they brought a big pickle bottle and on top a pump, like a football pump, brass, polished, and they put a big tube on it and on the end were a great big needle. It must have been a foot long and they put this blinking thing in me ribs and he said, 'You better turn away,' and I said, 'I'm not going to turn away otherwise I shall pass out.' I just watched it and they drew it all out and it were all colours, you know, green and a deep green. Then lighter green, yellow and then they'd half filled this thing with all this stuff off my chest and then they took it away. Then I were flown home and that was the end of my war!*

Author... In the summer of 1992, I had the pleasure of accompanying the Hallams Fontenay Club members on a trip to Roosendaal, Holland. Roy Simon also came along and I had promised him that I would hire a car and take him back to the place where he had been wounded along the earthen embankment and dike on the western side of the Depot de Mendicite. This we did in a brand new hire car but on approaching the place along a waterlogged path beside the earthen bank, we got stuck in the mud. I managed to drive out of it with much wheel spin, but the car became unrecognisable under a thick coat of mud - I had inadvertently discovered the perfect vehicle camouflage for that area but this would hardly have appealed to the car hire company! Getting it cleaned before returning it is quite another story.

We eventually reached the approximate spot where Roy had been wounded and then tried to retrace the steps of the German stretcher bearers who had carried him away. We walked along the bank which had changed little since the war and after a short distance, turned left at a crossing place over the dike. Roy was overwhelmed when he spotted the brick barn from his story and we both got through the field fence and went inside. He walked straight to the wooden post he had leaned against all those years before and sat down against it once more in the very dim light. I raised my camera and pressed the button, but this most likeable little man had already closed his eyes for a moment and allowed his mind to drift back in time, alone with his memories... ...'By Jingo! He's the double of Bob Shorthouse!'

During this action, an individual act of bravery had taken place along the earthen embankment which was one of those rare occasions in war, when a man sheds all fear or is able to suppress it to the utmost and carry out deeds which can only be held in awe by those who are a witness to it.

Cpl. John William Harper was the 13th and last member of the York and Lancaster Regiment to be awarded the Victoria Cross. He was also the only recipient of it, both in his Regiment and in the 49th Division during World War Two. Born in 1916, he had been a peat cutter before the war and lived in Thorne, near Doncaster. The citation, published in the London Gazette, will be found accompanying the Honours and Awards at the back of this book. (Page 389)

Extract from the 'Victor' comic of January, 1968, showing Cpl. John Harper in action at the Depot de Mendicite.

The story of Cpl. Harper's deeds were made the subject of a popular boys comic magazine, 'The Victor', in 1968, although the word 'comic' in those days was a general description of such magazines that told stories in picture or 'comic' strips and not necessarily meant to be funny. In the permissive and relaxed atmosphere of today's media it might be thought that such a document would appear rather tame. However, the captions that accompany the pictures, even by today's standards, would be seen by some to be in bad taste!

The York & Lancaster Regimental Museum, Rotherham, contains nine of the thirteen Victoria Cross awards to this Regiment. The medal awarded posthumously to Cpl. John William Harper is now a part of that Collection.

During the confused fighting, contingents of a number of units had taken part, both in and outside the compound. Elements of the Polish Armoured Division, for whom the Depot was being cleared for it to pass through to Merxplas, advanced too early along the road and had their leading tank knocked out by an A/Tk. gun, despite a warning to them that it was there. The enemy fought tenaciously but were slowly overwhelmed by tanks, Battalion carriers (with Capt. L.G. Sneath in command), flame throwing 'wasp' carriers and superior numbers.

Chris Somers (Diary)...
As we were rather down on our strength now, the C.O. said he would send the carrier platoon and some tanks down to clear the grounds northwards. Before they arrived however, the Leicesters, whom I was visiting, were having a bit of a scare. A lot of their leading men including an officer had been surrounded in a house and wiped out and others started drawing back towards us. I told the Sergeant in charge to hold firm with those coming back just in front of the buildings to the

east as he hadn't sufficient men left to look after this flank. The Carrier platoon arrived about this time and also our own carrier with the CQMS. They sent some sections up to the top of the grounds and drove the Germans back, although as they withdrew back to us the Gerrys followed them back again. I'm glad to say there was no shelling at this time on the Depot. I don't expect the Boche new quite what was what. There were a lot of potatoes in one of our buildings some of which I had loaded on our carrier for the CQMS.

As darkness began to fall the C.O. said he was going to withdraw our company, handing the Depot over to the Leicesters. I went off back to recce into our new area with the CQMS and Mike Halford, the 2i/c. To my disgust, I found that we were to go back into the wood again and to dig in near the top corner from which we had started our attack. To add to our enjoyment, the Boche started shelling the wood and we had to duck into holes every now and again. It was funny how he seemed to follow us around!

❖ *Some of the first buildings within the Depot de Mendicite that would have been encountered by the Hallams as they fought their way forward. (DWS)*

By the time I had recced the area the company arrived, also Mackillop who was taking over the Company. The evening was quiet while we dug in apart from two Boche A/Tk shells which cracked just over our heads. (Major C.A. Mackillop - referred to in future as 'Mac' by Chris)

At this point it might be of interest to look over the horizon for a moment and see what had been happening in another area of the conflict, the result of which was to effect the future operations of the 49th Division.

Operation Market-Garden was a very ambitious plan, basically meant to shorten the war and perhaps bring it to a conclusion before the end of the year. To put it simply, the idea was for airborne troops to be dropped and landed at the strategic points of Eindhoven, Nijmegen and Arnhem so as to seize and hold all the major river and canal bridge crossings. It was then the job of a strong armoured column (spearheaded by the Guards Armoured Division) to race up the road, from solid 'frontline' positions around Valkensward, to link and consolidate those three positions. The 'corridor' thus formed would then allow allied forces to drive quickly north to break and turn the enemy's right flank and strike into the vital, industrial heart of Germany.

Arnhem is history now and there are many theories and books to explain the ultimate reasons for failure. The fact is that the armoured column failed to reach Arnhem in the time allotted, the British 1st Airborne Division troops were all but over run, and finally had to be withdrawn after many casualties. It must be said, however, that this armour was entirely dependent on the ability of ground troops to take and hold a very wide corridor of land astride the road to enable speedy and secure progress along the main axis, to be known later as 'Hell's Highway'.

The Hallamshire Battalion was well to the left of this thrust but some idea of the difficulties involved in clearing a way forward can be understood when looking at the past few days in the 49th Divisional area of operations. The bridging of the Antwerp-Turnhout canal below Rijkevorsel on the night of 24/25 September, up to the action at the Depot de Mendicite on the 29th, represented less than five miles of ground gained in five days of hard fighting. The Guards Armoured Division would have had to travel 'sixty' miles in just three days to reach Arnhem, which would have been just possible if the German Army had stood aside and allowed it to happen!

It is strange to think that on the very day after the struggle at the Depot de Mendicite (almost directly west of the Guards Armoured Division start line at Valkensward), the bulk of escaped survivors of the broken 1st Airborne Division from Arnhem (more than seventy miles to the north east) had been pulled out and were already back in England!! This only goes to show how daring this far reaching operation had really been, but so far out on a limb that the branch had inevitably broken. The consequences of that failure were far reaching, not the least of which was to commit the Hallams and others to a very bleak winter in that area of low lying land between Arnhem and Nijmegen which was to become known as 'the Island'. For a while yet, however, the Hallams and others had their work cut out on the Belgium/ Holland border.

Chris Somers (Diary)...
Things seemed to have quietened down and the Polish Division, which had followed 49 Division, began to break out of the bridgehead and to push northwards. We were to hand over to the Duke of Wellington's Regiment next morning. I showed the C.O. and recce party around our area. Everything was so quiet that I think we exposed ourselves too much on the north of the wood and a few shells came over as a result.

Before the Poles moved out, they indulged in a bit of activity that verged on the knife edge between high spiritedness and indiscipline for which they were noted. Such behaviour was probably born of a far greater eagerness to get to grips with the enemy in a war that was, for them, much more personal and deep rooted. This did not deter them from having what they thought was the occasional bit of fun.

During the early hours of the 30 September, a report from the 1 Leicesters warned of a Spandau being fired close to the Hallams Bn. HQ. It was later discovered that a group of Leicesters had approached the area and been challenged by someone with a 'German' voice. This challenge had in fact come from a Polish officer in charge of a troop of 17 Pdr. guns that were camped nearby for the night. The Leicesters had turned on their heels and ran but the Poles, knowing full well that the men they had challenged were English, nevertheless put a burst of Bren Gun fire over their heads as a joke! After the previous day's fighting and losses, the Leicesters in particular would not have seen the funny side of it.

Since the bridgehead had been formed on the morning of the 25th, German resistance had steadily stiffened to the point where all the Brigades of 49th Division had been committed to the fray and now formed a long line north of the canal. Ryckevorsel had not been finally cleared until the 28th but now, with the added clearance of the Depot de Mendicite, the task was to hold the recent gains and extend positions by pushing further north. Up to this date, 1,119 prisoners had been taken in some very bitter fighting.

The Hallams remained in the woods to the west of the Depot de Mendicite throughout 1 October. During the next two days, with other units of the Brigade, they moved in conjunction with the Poles through Merxplas and then to the northeast.

Chris Somers (Diary)...

2 October : We boarded troop carriers on the main road and travelled on through Merxplas. Information from the Poles was a bit vague and we had a long halt in the sun by the roadside while our ultimate destination was determined. We eventually finished up in a very open area on the right flank of the Poles. The platoons of our Company were scattered over a wide area, the most forward one being nearly half a mile away which made feeding arrangements very difficult. We dug our usual slit trenches only as an emergency though, as this place seemed very peaceful and far from the battle. The C.O. announced that we should probably remain here a few days which was a pleasant thought. Mac, C.S.M., and I shared the night duty on the wireless and then slept high up on a pile of hay. I was rather frightened somebody would drop a cigarette in the place, but luckily we survived the night all right.

❖ *Weelde. (DWS)*

3 October : Next morning's 'O' group brought the news that we were to get on the move again immediately. Such is life. This time we marched as a Battalion advance guard along the route of the Poles. The burned out buildings and tanks marked the route, also many bodies of both the Poles and Germans showed the advance, though rapid, had been no picnic. It was a bit wet and cold when we halted on the outskirts of a small town on the Belgian /Dutch frontier. Our leading carrier went up on a mine at the crossroads, also another vehicle which went to its rescue. We were given a Company area to the right (left?) of the main road along the boundary. So I stepped into Holland for the first time in the campaign. We were half dug in and very wet when we got the order that we were to advance away to the right flank over some very open ground and clear the woods to the other side.

Nobody knew quite what to expect over this open ground which stretched half a mile to the woods. However, with another company we passed over without incident and commenced clearing through the wood with the platoon stretched out in extended order. Nothing to report however and we were told to remain the night in the village just the other side. Here we managed to get a roof over our heads for the night and had our cooks established with us. Platoon outposts had to be set up though as the last Jerry had only departed just before we arrived.

The Hallams provided flank cover through Keokhoven and Zondereigen and follow up to the village of Weelde and it was here at crossroads (051141) that Chris observed the loss of carriers which were two of those belonging to the Polish Armoured Brigade. They had been destroyed by mines concealed beneath paving stones at the side of the road. The Hallams were ordered to occupy the northern, and the 1/4 K.O.Y.L.I. the southern, half of this

❖ *This 'Chateau' between Weelde and Poppel was built as a resort for women in 1939 by a religious order known as Ancillae Ecclesia. For a very short time in October, 1944 it became the joint Brigade and Bn. HQ. for the attack on Poppel and surrounding area.(DWS)*

village which lay on the left of the road between Turnhout and Tilburg. The Battalion had not been directly involved in fighting here but were still able to take 13 prisoners, two of whom were found to be wearing civilian clothes. On the 4th they were ordered to advance from the village, with the K.O.Y.L.I. on their right, and take Poppel.

'A' Coy. followed up by 'C' Coy. were able to move through and establish themselves on the far side of the village but the carriers, which were attempting the same objective by a left flanking movement, were held up. 'B' Coy. were sent forward to assist, but the very open ground was not favourable and a troop of tanks was sent in to back them up. Three enemy strong points were met with on the western side of Poppel, one of which was in buildings about 800 yards to the west of the village and another about 250 yards further west again. The third was further west still at a place called Pont de Bedaf. Under very heavy covering fire from mortars, tanks and carriers, Lt. Gallagher and his platoon were able to drive the enemy out of the first two positions. As darkness fell, it was decided that the platoon and section of carriers should set up a defensive position for the night. The Battalion was reorganised for the night at a road junction (122206) with all round defensive positions set up as it was thought that an enemy counter attack would be put in very soon. The night was thankfully quiet. During that day Chris Somers, with 'C' Coy., had followed up behind and to the left of 'A' Coy. through the village. Casualties for this day were surprisingly light with one OR. killed and five wounded. Lt. D.C. Blake (Royal Fusiliers) arrived in the thick of it all to join the Battalion.

Chris Somers (Diary)...
4 October : 'O' groups were called for first thing next morning and we moved off on foot. We were to move up the main Turnhout/Poppel road with the object of clearing Poppel and pushing on to Tilburg with 49 Div. The Recce Regiment had already cleared the approaches so we were able to move up to a large chateau barely a mile from Poppel. The KOYLI were attacking on the right of the main road and Hallams on the left. So both Battalions and Brigade HQs. used the chateau (114134) as an advance HQ. The woods round about served as our start line, the carrier platoon watching the left flank. 'A' company were to go straight for the village capturing the road block (124195) en route. 'C' company on their left through the woods and 'B' company further over still on our left. Only 'A' company had artillery support unless called for.

The road block mentioned by Chris above was cleared by George Learad of the Pioneer Platoon. After having cleared many mines along the way both he and fellow pioneers had developed methods which could only be described as having been born of skilled knowledge developed through experience. However, such methods would no doubt have made the hair stand on end for anyone who might have been near enough to witness the crude basics of it all.

George Learad...
We were always there with the leading companies in the front line to clear mines. I must have cleared about a hundred mines altogether and I was mostly forward with Lonsdale-Cooper and Nicholson. I remember one 'do' when we had to clear these mines and Nicholson was in a doorway there and while I was working, Gerry was having a go at me. When I got back, he said to me, 'Didn't you hear the bullets?' I never heard these bullets because my mind was on the job of clearing the mines. I just said to him, 'They must have been bad shots!' After a bit, the mines didn't bother me and instead of removing them carefully I used to drag them out on a long chain with a hook on. I would just clip the hook on to one of the lifting handles, send everybody back and then pull the mine out to the side for later disposal by the Engineers.

This aerial photograph in Chris Somers Scrap Book is annotated to show the advance on Poppel. From (Route of Advance) at the bottom it leads to the 'Chateau' or 'Emmaus' as it was known then (Bn. & Bde. HQ. for attack). Above this was the Form Up Point (FUP) showing the path which 'A', 'B' & 'C' Coys. took, with the 1/4 K.O.Y.L.I. advancing on their right. The small dark triangular area just above the 'B' Coy. path, is the place called Pont de Bedaf where brave acts by John Wollerton would be rewarded with the Military Cross. Poppel is just off picture to the right in the top half. The Germans had created a (Road Block) marked with a 'X' just above the photo-join. This road block was cleared by George Learad. The place called Nieuwkerk was just off the top of the picture to the left and where the Bn. were to have some bad moments. (ACS)

292

Chris Somers (Diary)...

It must have been nearly lunchtime before the attack was launched. We followed our covered line of approach which led towards the farms on the left of Poppel. As we got out into the open, our leading elements came under slight small arms fire from Spandau. As Mac and I came up to them they were all standing together behind a farm building. Luckily, there were no shells or anything coming back or they would probably have suffered a few casualties. Apparently the hold up was due to the fact that the Boche had the next bit of open ground covered.

One section under the cover of 2 inch mortars got to a small copse half way across and then took cover behind a Canadian Sherman (27 C.A.R.) tank which had just arrived from the direction of Poppel. This tank sprayed the likely hedgerows for us while we all made a dash for it and got to the farmhouse which was our objective without casualty. Mac and I both had lucky escapes twice during the reorganisation as, while we were discussing the layout of our defence, two of our Bren gunners cleared their guns without looking which way they were pointing. I don't think either could have missed us by more than a foot or two.

The farmhouse had certainly been left in a hurry by the Boche, the chips were still cooking on the stove. We still had one platoon left at the other farmhouse so I ran back to collect them. John Hall, the mortar officer, had just arrived there so he walked back with me to see Mac. En route across the field I peered into a foxhole to see if there was any useful equipment but, to my surprise, saw a Gerry still in there. He looked very frightened and came out very peacefully and quickly - my first individual prisoner!

I had told the other platoon to follow as soon as they had collected their equipment. They weren't so lucky as the Spandau opened up again just as they were about to reach our farm. Only one man was hit, luckily, and I took S.B. Whiteley straight along with a stretcher and we had him in our HQ. in no time. We then set about the Spandau team with our 2 inch mortar and weren't troubled again. 'A' Coy. by this time had cleared Poppel though the place had been heavily stonked. 'B' Coy. were still having a lot of trouble away to our left. We then set about reorganising ourselves for the night.

On the morning of the 5th, Carrier Platoon was given the task of patrolling through Pont de Bedaf and drew no fire but 'B' Coy. complained of enemy fire coming from that direction. They were ordered to clear an area up to the Dutch Frontier and were given tanks in support to achieve this. It was obvious that the Germans had filtered back from woods (106201) into some of the positions they had been driven from the day before and 'B' Coy. had a difficult time of it. Lt. John Wollerton, with his platoon, moved towards the buildings around Pont de Bedaf to test the enemy strength there. Under covering fire from a Pl. of 'C' Coy. and supported by carriers and a troop of tanks, he succeeded in capturing and clearing these buildings under very heavy enemy fire. This small force was now withdrawn, still under heavy fire and Lt. Wollerton showed great bravery in returning to the already vacated buildings to retrieve some of his wounded men. For this and other previous acts of courage he was awarded the Military Cross.

'C' Coy. was ordered to follow 'A' Coy. up the road leading northwards to a village called Aerle so as to take over from the Recce Regiment who had cleared it the night before. As 'C' Coy. were approaching the village, a considerable amount of artillery fire was observed to fall on the village. This was 'friendly fire' called down by Recce Regiment on woods to the north of the village but their Forward Observation Officer had given the wrong co-ordinates and brought the stonk right down on top of themselves! Part of this came down on 'A' Coy. but, fortunately, no casualties were suffered.

Chris Somers (Diary)...
6 October : Mac went ahead (to Aerle) and I followed up with the Company on foot. We eventually arrived and platoons were allotted areas to the South and West of the village. 'A' Coy. to the North were having occasional trouble and had been shelled by our own guns. All was quiet in our part and remained so for the rest of the morning. After lunch, the C.O. wanted us to push on up to Nieuwkerk to take over from the Recce Regiment again, who had advanced there without opposition and now wanted relieving.

The most direct route through 'A' Coy. was blocked by the Boche, so Mac had to go right back through Poppel and up the main road past the Lincolns. I was told to take the company across country. There were few obvious landmarks but luckily we hit Nieuwkerk at the right place. All seemed quiet as we arrived apart from the noise of the recce armoured car and carriers warming up prior to departure. This noise, and no doubt the site of us arriving, spurred the Boche into activity. He opened up with light mortar on the crossroads where we were dispersing the platoons. No damage or casualties luckily.

Mac had had a lucky escape on his arrival having had a bullet through the windscreen of the Jeep as he got out on the northern cross tracks of the area. The platoons were quickly dispersed into their allotted areas, Company HQ. being in the centre near a small two roomed farmhouse. Being the only building apart from the shed or two we decided that we had better not use it as it was such an obvious target.

I started helping the signallers to dig the company HQ. position while Mac was fixing up the platoons. Almost immediately after the Recce. Regt. left, things began to hot up and we frequently had to crouch in our shallow slits as mortar bombs fell all around. Soon we struck water and realised that we should have to completely change our HQ. position or move into the cottage. Luckily the family inside the cottage decided to move into their outside shelter leaving us the whole building of two rooms and out house including the semi-cellar. We established the wireless in here as it was just below the level of the ground on the floor. The remainder of company HQ. had the room outside it. We hadn't been in long when a heavy stonk sent us flying in from outside, the blast of one bomb just about blowing Mac and I in a heap into the room as it burst near the door. Another one hit the tiled roof above our heads and showered us with bits of dust. A splinter went right through Mac's steel helmet which was lying on the floor. Mac also got a small splinter in his leg but luckily it did not handicap him in any way.

Sgt. Pollit (Porritt?) commanding our northernmost platoon reported enemy movement in the woods to his front. We repeatedly 'stonked' this area with very heavy artillery concentration till eventually the Boche showed signs of having had enough. Further concentrations soon persuaded him that he was right and we collected a bag of about 22 prisoners. Disaster followed this scoop however. The CSM collected them in the nearby barn for searching. Just as I was about to go out to join them a heavy mortar stonk came down right on the barn. I stayed put for the moment and as soon as it stopped, went over to find that one of our chaps had been killed and another, plus a prisoner, wounded. We sent them off soon afterwards under escort and got the SB half track up for the wounded.

❖ *Main street in Poppel showing the Town Hall. Just to the right of this building is a memorial to soldiers and civilians killed in this area. Most of the former (below left) are Hallamshires. (DWS)*

It was during this period that many of the enemy were choosing to come forward and surrender, often in small groups. There was seldom any problem with this as the Germans would attract attention by waving a white cloth and then be called forward in a controlled way. On one occasion, however, things went sadly wrong.

George Learad...
There were a lot of Germans coming forward to give themselves up and one of our younger ones panicked and fired on them. Of course they all scattered and I went down to the spot next morning with this officer called Hawkins. We came across this old fashioned push chair and there was this young German lad sat there in it, dead. The others had obviously been bringing him in wounded to surrender and for treatment and when they scattered they'd just left him. I searched in his pocket and took his wallet out and he'd got a photograph of his wife and two little kiddies at the bottom of a garden. It was then I thought, 'What the hell are we fighting for here then?'

❖ *Farm buildings at Pont de Bedaf. (DWS)*

294

Another aerial photo (the area called Nieuwkerk) from Chris Somers Scrap Book which illustrates the words from his diary. At the top of the picture, a crossroads is marked as being the position of 'C' Coy. HQ. It was here that a German Panther tank approached and crossed, not knowing that there was a 6 Pounder A/Tk. gun lying alongside the building. The gun was quickly trained on the rear end of the tank as it passed by and Sgt. Newman fired two or three shots which brought it to a halt. Then the tank crew attempted to traverse the turret to bear on the Hallams position but fortunately the barrel struck a tree and prevented the situation becoming very nasty. The tank then began to burn fiercely and the crew, some of whom were badly burned, bailed out. (ACS)

Chris Somers (Diary)...
A Boche stonk had set fire to the haystack on the cross tracks which was protecting our six pounder A/T from enemy observation. The gun team did a good job of work dragging the gun back behind an outbuilding where it was set up once again. 'B' Coy. were now established off to our right and we felt a little more secure. Meanwhile, the 4 Lincolns who had advanced within sight of Tilburg,

295

had been severely counter attacked and had been forced to withdraw, suffering many casualties, to the Brigade area. This now left us forward of the whole Brigade with two exposed flanks. Our company patrols were active throughout the night, particular good work being done by John Wollerton of 'B' Coy. Noises of tracked vehicles could be heard behind the woods and we repeatedly sent over heavy stonks.

At dawn next morning, the Boche really let loose with his mortars, our little cottage appeared to be the main objective and it wasn't long before he hit the chimney and bricks and mortar came showering down onto the S.Bs. filling the whole room with thick dust. They and the wounded were okay. However, I got them to move into our place. After the next stonk we heard the shout of 'fire' and rushed out to discover the end of the building was alight. A following bomb however, hit the same part bringing that part of the roof down and also putting out the fire. Our carrier, full of ammunition, miraculously escaped damage.

Arnold Whiteley...
Just outside Poppel we had a nasty time, the affair at Nieuwkerk. There were trees all round and we had no clear vision but we took about 30 prisoners. They were put in a barn when a shell hit a tree and burst and of all the German prisoners inside, it killed the one English lad who was guarding them.

While we were there, a German Panther tank came around a house and we'd an anti-tank gun at this side. We'd put it there because we thought it were faulty. However, they must have put it right because as this German tank came round they got him with it. Our position became untenable and it was evident that we'd got to withdraw and a shell actually hit the house we were in.

Chris Somers (Diary)...
It was apparent that something was in the air and sure enough there was suddenly a terrific burst of machine gun fire directed through the woods at our position. S.B. L/Cpl. Churchill, rushed in shouting that a tank was advancing up to our HQ. and a burst of fire followed him in. I got back to the wireless set and reported the fact to Mike Halford. It was indeed fortunate that the C.O. had sent up a section of Canadian Shermans which had arrived this moment. Suddenly there was a deafening crash. The A/Tk. gun had opened up by the wall of the house. From where I was sitting in the room it sounded as though the tank had opened up on the cottage. A few more of these deafening noises then I heard a shout of triumph go up followed by a series of internal explosions from the Boche Tiger (Panther?) tank now situated on the cross tracks some 20 yards from our cottage. I rushed out to see the Boche drivers staggering in, badly burned.

Apparently what had happened was that the Boche tank, seeing the Sherman up the track, had ignored our cottage and rushed to the attack. In doing so he had come right across the sights of the anti-tank gun, which we had hidden behind the cottage the previous night. The range being only 20 yards he couldn't miss and hit the Boche with three quick ones when she brewed up. The German infantry following the tank had all but overrun our forward positions when this happened but Mac had quickly put in a local counter attack with the reserve platoon and supported by a Sherman, had driven the Boche off.

John Wollerton...
The company I was with ('B' Coy.) were surrounded by the Germans and Major Halford was in charge at the time. I'd been out on a patrol and spotted enemy patrols and heard some tracked vehicles but luckily didn't make contact, so I came back and reported to Maj. Halford what I'd seen and heard. I suggested that he should prepare for a dawn attack supported by armour. In the

early hours the attack took place and a tank came down the track and was knocked out by one of our anti-tank guns. Eventually, we were relieved by the C.O.

It was during this period that John Wollerton ('B'Coy.) had done some very successful recce patrols. On one occasion, reported in the War Diary, his patrol was passed by a similar enemy unit using the same ditch going in the opposite direction. He spotted them first and was just able to evade their attention by lying low and got back safely to make his report. Due to casualties, 'B' Coy. now only consisted of two platoons with two sections in each. Now, both 'B' Coy. and the remnants of 'C' Coy. were in real danger of being cut off and overrun. To prevent this from happening, and as part of defensive fire laid down by the whole Brigade Artillery around the Nieuwkerk area, laid down a Defensive Fire. The 69 Field Regt. alone, fired over 3,000 rounds, purely in support of Hallamshire Battalion positions.

Chris Somers (Diary)...
In the excitement, our breakfast had been quite forgotten though no one had had anything to eat since the day before. When all was quiet, the civilian farmer appeared out off his dug out shelter to say that a little boy had been hit by a bullet. The two women with him were both in hysterics which became worse when they saw the state of their cottage which they had only walked out of the previous evening. (One of these women may have been the mother of the lady shown below). Now it was a shambles with holes in the roof, windows all broken and the floor covered in broken bricks and blood stained equipment from the wounded. Luckily the half track soon arrived and we shipped them all off together with our own wounded and the body of a dispatch rider, who had been hit while delivering a message. That afternoon, the C.O. gave orders for the two companies to be withdrawn as we were a mile in front of the Brigade and seriously reduced in numbers. Also there were indications that the Boche was working around behind us.

❖ *The crossroads at Nieuwkerk now. The Panther tank crossed just in front of camera position from right to left and was knocked out by the 6 Pounder A/Tk. gun which was sited along the side of the building. The lady, owner of the cottage today (right), lived in it throughout the war, but stayed with relatives down the road during the action which caused major damage. She remembered coming back later and seeing the knocked out tank in the lane. At that time, she thought it was a British tank because she had not seen many German ones previously. The house was rebuilt after the war but not to the original design. The fireside 'ornaments' she brought out to show us, are 25 Pounder artillery shell cases and nothing to do with the action which took place outside her door on the 7th October, 1944. Thousands of this calibre were expended in the Nieuwkerk area at that time. (DWS)*

All wheeled vehicles and carriers were to leave first, then 'C' Coy. followed by 'B' Coy. The vehicles all got away without incident. Then our first platoon moved out down the track which we had arrived up, though it should have been the one further into the woods which couldn't be seen by the Boche. The next platoon followed and then myself with Company HQ, leaving Mac to follow with the last platoon. We were walking in single file up the ditch and had just caught up with the rear of the other platoon when suddenly I heard the pop! pop! pop! of a small mortar. We all dropped to the ground but two chaps in the ditch on the opposite side of the track got hit. I left them in charge of the two S.Bs. with me, to get them onto the halftrack with 'B' Coy. and hurried up to the front of the column to get everybody moving before the next stonk arrived. On getting there, I found the Sergeant had lost contact with the front platoon and didn't know which route to take.

I heard firing down the track in front so decided to advance straight to our positions across country. I thought Mac and the rear platoon were following but apparently they had all gone to ground after the first stonk and Mac had difficulty in getting them all collected and on the move. It was fortunate that we didn't meet any trouble as there wasn't time to organise proper advanced guard and, anyway, I was the only one with a map and had to walk in front. On getting round the wood, I met Lloyd Sneath who showed me our new positions which was the forward Battalion position covering the road down which the others would be coming.

I quickly recced the area and put the forward platoon and Company HQ. in position and got them digging. A few mortar bombs gave them plenty of encouragement. Soon we heard the tanks firing at the Boche in the wood in front and realized the remainder were on their way back. Then they came into sight and we waved to attract attention, only to be met with the burst of fire from our own tanks. Most disconcerting, but we soon manage to establish friendly relations once again! Mac only had one platoon with him and had not seen the other one. So we got them in position and the last platoon turned up just before dark, so we were now all back safely. After some strenuous digging with our two signallers, Mac and I eventually finished our spacious HQ. position. This always consisted of two slits joined together at one end. In this gap at the end we always established the wireless and telephone, so that they would be reached by either us or the signallers. A tarpaulin formed the roof, enabling us to use a hurricane lamp for reading maps, etc. We had just got nicely established and the one off duty preparing for a little shuteye when we heard the familiar popping sound again. The first salvo of bombs landed almost directly on top of our Company HQ. dug out. We were showered in dirt, our roof was blown off and the lamp went out. We got up to rectify things once more and found that one bomb had landed just by the parapet badly damaging Mac's mess tins and equipment. Still, we were all OK which was all that mattered. Luckily, the next stonk wasn't quite so close. We tried to get bearings on the mortar with a compass and got our artillery to reply at likely spots. Not much rest was obtained this night either, after we had done our rounds of the Company position.

Next morning was quiet and we enjoyed a good breakfast. Chick Reid arrived soon afterwards and said that the C.Os. car was going to Brussels and Raymond, Sammy and self (3 2i/cs) were to go with it for a couple of days leave. What a wonderful surprise after such a hectic few days!

Meanwhile Les Sewell had been with the Carrier Platoon, but his story comes together with that of Chris Somers when he was called upon to move into woods and extricate some wounded from a house where the 'chimney' was brought down by enemy shellfire.

Les Sewell...7/10 Oct.
We were in some gardens near a hamlet with a large wood in front of us which I believe was Poppel Wood. I was in a hole with the Bren gunner and to the left was a Corporal, a new chap from the South Staffs and the driver was over on the right in another hole and out of sight was the

Sgt. and his crew. I was asleep and then I heard a big bang and then the driver called, 'Les! Les! get that Brengun out.' There were two figures passing me a few yards in front and I let off a burst and then the gun jammed. Anyway, one dropped and the other one went off. When we pulled ourselves together, this German Sgt. was dead, that's where I got the Schmeiser and the Luger. Before we got him, he'd chucked a bomb at us and the Cpl. on our left must have got it. I climbed out and went to him, I didn't know how badly he was hurt but I lifted him out of the hole and carried him back into the village where we had a First Aid Post and left him there. All I know is that my overcoat was covered in blood. Then I went and had a look at the German, and in the meantime our Sgt. had come and he said, 'That first bomb you heard was this patrol chucking a bomb into the hole where these two lads were.' They were L/Cpl. Johnny Green and Pte. Joe Clayton and both were killed. It must have been that bang that woke me up in the first place.

In the daylight we found a couple of Germans who had been part of the patrol, cowering in some holes near us. They had decided that they'd had enough. With the loss of our Corporal, I then became a carrier commander and my first task, volunteered, was to go into these woods to fetch our wounded out. We had to go through this village and back up the road then down a long, winding lane and it was getting stonked. We had to get to this house which was 'C' Coy. HQ. and waited quite a while in there as they collected these wounded together. They were laid all over the shop in this house and I sheltered in there. Then something hit the chimney and it came down, it was a real hot spot. Anyway I got a couple of stretchers on top of the carrier and I had to stand up in the middle holding them going back along this lane. We couldn't go very fast but we got out of that all right.

Next day the mail came and there was a parcel for Johnny Green, it was a cake and I can remember having a piece of that cake that his wife had sent him. We also had a chap in the platoon that was related in some way to Johnny and he told us that his wife had just had a baby.

Chris Somers (Diary)...
8 October : Our first night after the exciting two days at Nieuwkerk was spent a few miles behind the line at the house of a Roman Catholic priest. We all three shared a room and it was so strange to sleep between sheets again. Next morning we drove down to Brussels airport, delivered a man who was going on special leave, and carried on into Brussels itself.

We had great difficulty in finding accommodation for the night. They were preparing Brussels as a leave centre and all hotels were being taken over. The town Mayor treated us like dirt and hinted that leave hadn't officially started so that he couldn't fix us up. However, we managed to find a small hotel near the station, where they couldn't give us any food, but at least they gave us a bed. It was strange to be suddenly dumped in a large city where life appeared to be going on as normal while we realized that not so very far away, men were sitting cramped up in slit trenches out in the fields and woods, every now and again being mortared or shelled. It made one almost hate the calm way people went about shopping as though they didn't give a thought to those less fortunate. We heard all sorts of wild rumours about our part of the front having suffered a severe set back and we returned that evening wondering where we should find everybody. However, the rumours proved to be false and were only based on the Lincolns losses when they were heavily counter attacked and our own slight withdrawal to straighten the frontline.

On the 11 October the Battalion, having successfully withdrawn from and abandoned the Nieuwkerk area, was now required to exchange positions with the 11 R.S.F. at Zondereigen, a relatively safe spot and where no action was taking place. The men were able to relax a little and some were even able to take advantage of short leave pass periods in nearby Antwerp. The next few days activities were restricted to numerous patrols and the posting of snipers for observation purposes but it seemed as though the enemy were well drawn back from the areas being swept by the Hallams, leaving large stretches of 'no man's land'.

Chris Somers (Diary)...
The Battalion was just starting to move to Zondereigen, a quiet sector on the left of the Polish Division instead of the right. We three were sent on immediately as advance party. The Battalion was well spread out in little farms with Battalion HQ. in the village itself. We were about quarter of a mile away with a platoon outpost half a mile away and another watching the road near Battalion HQ. 'A' and 'B' Coys. were about half a mile in front of us. Feeding the outposts was my main problem but it was much easier than when we were in the front-line proper.

Our main job was to patrol into the Boche area anywhere in front of us. As no attack was expected, leave was permitted to Antwerp, and after some of the other officers had been, Raymond, Sammy and I were allowed to go for 48 hours staying in a very comfortable hotel. Rockets and Buzzbombs were just starting to fall but they didn't drop very near and arrived early in the morning. On our return to Zondereigen I had to take out a patrol, an ambush patrol. We had to take up position on a cross track some two miles inside the Boche area. I took a section with me and we passed through 'B' Coy. and down the dark narrow lane. As soon as possible, I moved off the lane in case the Boche had left a section outpost on it, and we advanced in open formation over the fields. Our final half mile was through scrub land and we made a terrible noise treading on twigs, etc., but found our cross tracks successfully.

I decided to have a group of three either side of the track leading to our own area with the idea of increasing the appearance of our firepower, and I gave the Cpl. the task of laying the necklace mines near his position on the left. Having done this we had to lie perfectly still in drizzling rain for the next 5 or 6 hours. The temptation to fall asleep was terrific and as the night wore on, I began to imagine all sorts of shapes appearing out of the wood in front. Then I really did see something crossing in front of us, I pushed forward the safety catch on my stengun and hoped that everybody was awake and ready. The ghostly figures moved slowly over the cross tracks between us. Just as I was about to fire, I realized that they were merely a few stray cows shuffling along one behind the other, yet they looked so like a section moving in single file. It was quite a relief to relax again.

Eventually it was time to return again, leaving the mines to do their work. We took a wide route back but encountered nothing, reaching the Battalion area just as it became light. In some ways I wish we could have achieved our object of ambushing some Boche but perhaps it was as well for us we didn't. Leslie Gill took a fighting patrol out to a suspected German billet a few days later and set the place on fire, but lost a very good Cpl. However, they wounded some Gerrys.

Only one real contact was made by the fighting patrol led by Capt. Les Gill when he was able to close on an enemy position, near enough for the use of grenades and inflicting a number of casualties. This occurred on the 13th and the War Diary states that one member of the patrol went missing. It is thought that this man may well have been the 'very good Corporal' mentioned by Chris Somers. Cpl. Arnold Worrell had led part of a patrol down a road and successfully flushed out an enemy position (possibly the grenade incident above). On recovering his steps he decided to investigate a house by himself, which the patrol had previously passed but which contained a number of German soldiers who were lying low. He was shot by them and was probably left behind in that way, to be reported as 'missing' on the day. His body must have been recovered later because subsequent, official, records do not show anyone missing or killed on that day. Cpl. Worrell is officially recorded as having died on the

17th when no casualties of any kind are reported in the War Diary. He is buried just to the north of Zondereigen in the Roman Catholic civilian cemetery of Baarle - Nassau.

Chris Somers (Diary)...
19th October : We got orders to move again and we were to follow in the wake of an Armoured Column heading for Roosendaal. The Battalion column moved back to the main road to Antwerp and headed in that direction finishing up for the evening in a monastery. I was allotted a very comfortable looking bedroom but had hardly dumped my kit there when our company received orders to cross the canal and occupy a village on the right of the advancing column. Much swearing and cursing by all the company!!

The concentration area to which the Hallams were drawn back, was a small town called St. Antonius and the monastery was almost certainly a Trappist establishment on its northern outskirts. The small village was Overbroek, to the north of St. Antonius. The journey entailed crossing the Antwerp/Turnhout Canal - again! (it will be remembered that the first crossing had taken place at St. Jozef on the 24 September). Just beyond the canal, the Carrier Platoon moved into positions vacated by a

❖ *Having successfully flushed out a German position about 200 yards up this road on the left, Cpl. Arnold Worrell was killed on coming back down the road, when he decided to clear the house seen here on the right. (DWS)*

Canadian Recce unit and a general clearance of the area was undertaken with the support of a Squadron of Churchill tanks. However, the only use to which these were put, was to rescue the C.Os. Half-track which had fallen into a deep ditch whilst trying to squeeze past a road block.

Chris Somers (Diary)...
Mac set off as advance party and I was left to follow with the company. We moved over the canal in vehicles and I reported to the Brigade Headquarters in whose area we were to go. They gave me my directions and said Mac would meet me. Unfortunately when we turned off the road up a track, one of the platoons lost contact and went straight on which meant we had to return to find them. Luckily, a sentry stopped them walking into the German lines!

Everywhere was muddy and wet and pitch dark. The guns were active all the time and little farmhouses blazing here and there. At last, we got established in a farmhouse complete with a Honey tank for wireless communication. After a short night we received orders to rejoin the Battalion who had also crossed over. We met up in better weather in a little village near some windmills.Temporary company areas were allotted as we expected to move. The peace was broken by an occasional shell landing near the bridge on the canal crossing about half a mile away.

21 October : After a boring but restful few hours we received orders to move up to Wustwezel by route march. As we moved off past Battalion HQ, shells began to drop either side of the road so I thought it was just as well we were leaving. It was a long and weary march up almost a dead straight road lined with trees, with traffic of the Armoured Column streaming past. As we neared Wustwezel we passed near the lines of the field gunners who were extremely active, but it was coming back too, so the noise was terrific. As we moved into the centre of the town, the Battalion column kept on stopping and starting as is always the case, especially as our company was on the crossroads just by the church tower, an ideal and usual target for Gerry gunners.

There was nobody back at Battalion HQ. to receive our company but the I.O. told me to wait for Mac at the crossroads in the centre of the town, a fine place I thought. I arrived there with the company to find no one to meet me so I took the precaution to tell the men to keep near the doorways to the houses for cover, while I looked around for Mac. I hardly crossed the road when down came a 'stonk'. I crouched against a garden wall while the shells hit the houses all round. At the same time, part of Division HQ. (Advanced) passed by in vehicles, much to my amazement. I think they regretted it too because although they got up the road without being hit they lost some vehicles in the night. Luckily, Mac turned up after one more 'stonk' and led us to our Company area about 300 yards down the road, just out of harms way.

The attack on Wurstwezel had been spearheaded by 'Clarkforce' which comprised two battalions of Churchills and the Recce Regt. To their left, the 4 Canadian Armoured Division had taken Achterbroek and all was now well placed for an attack on Roosendaal. On the evening of the 21st, the Hallams took up positions on the west side of the village where 'A' Coy. lines were approached by a Panther tank. Major Tony Nicholson took it on using rifle fire, the shots being so very accurately placed on various apertures, that the tank crew decided on a very hasty withdrawal!

❖ *Military Memorial Garden on the southern outskirts of Wurstwezel. Dedicated to the 49th (West Riding) Infantry Division, it was unveiled in 1984 (DWS)*

Chris Somers...
22 October : I thought we might have a peaceful day but word came early that we were to launch a counter attack northwards supported by Churchill tanks. We met OK after a rushed start and were soon advancing in extended order with the tanks. As we approached some scattered farm houses about half a mile from our start line, our leading platoons came under fire. SP guns also opened up on our tanks. Peter Hewitt, our gunner F.O.O. and self, moved up from the rear of the company with the wireless sets to see what was going on. We were narrowly missed once by a solid shot which bounced across a field, passing a few feet in front of us. As we reached one of our tanks it was hit and brewed up, the crew quickly bailing out, all except the commander who had his head blown off. Shots from this gun now proceeded to blow pieces off the farmhouses round about us while we crouched in the ditch.

Village of Steerthevvel : Meanwhile the leading platoon had gained the next block of farmhouses about 300 yards ahead and we had to make a speedy dash across the open to join them, shots were still flying about. Our right-hand platoon had done some good work in capturing an S/P team complete. The ground was very open from here onwards and further advance seemed pointless. Our gunners put down heavy 'stonks' where we suspected Boche SPs. might be lurking.

302

Later, we sent out a recce patrol but found the birds had flown. The C.O. arrived and told us to withdraw to a cross track about half a mile back while the carriers took over. We weren't very pleased about this as we had to give up a farmhouse and dig slit trenches for the night.

23 October : Next morning we had yet another job, clearing a wood on the left and advancing through the little village of Klooster which we stopped short of the night before. This was done without incident except that the wireless did not work too well in the woods. The ground for the next mile or two was flat and open right up to the Dutch border. The carriers later carried out a patrol without making any direct contact.

Belgium/Nederland border area showing locations of memorial and burial (grey print) of Hallamshire Battalion in relation to various towns and cities. Those not shown that belong to this group are Brussels (south of Antwerp), Arnhem-Oosterbeek (north of Nijmegen) and Munster Heath which is approximately fifty miles northwest of Dortmund in Germany. (DWS)

Chris Somers (Diary)...
25 October : The company was told to dig in once more in the woods which fringed the open expanse ahead. We stayed here a couple of nights - very quiet - and handed over to an American unit new to the line, early in the morning. Complete chaos as we had to have breakfast in the dark and be ready with all our equipment on for the Americans. The C.O. got very angry as we hadn't all got our steel helmets on and the hand over was rather a chatty affair.

This unit was the 1st Bn., 413th Regiment of the 104th (Timber Wolf) Infantry Division. It had arrived in Europe on 7 September and this was its first combat role. What happened next, according to Trevor Hart Dyke (Normandy to Arnhem), was nothing short of tragedy.

Trevor Hart Dyke (Normandy to Arnhem)...

...we were very impressed with their men, when they eventually arrived, in vast numbers. To our surprise we found their infantry battalions had very little transport, and the men had to carry on their backs, articles which we put on our carriers... ... Their companies were so large that they had to dig many extra slits, but otherwise they took over our dispositions as they stood, which was very complimentary of them. With the enemy three thousand yards away, it had been hoped that they would have an easy time in what was now a quiet sector, so as to get acclimatised to war before being put to the test.

I heard next day, to my horror, that they had advanced over the open plain and had lost heavily in their first taste of battle. I drove across to see them... ...I was sorry to hear when I arrived that the C.O. had been wounded and to see wounded still being attended to by their stretcher-bearers... ...They had gallantly advanced across the open plain... ...the enemy had reserved his fire and caught the defenceless battalion in the open with everything he had. It would have been contrary to our training, to advance across 3,000 yards of open ground without the friendly cover of either smoke or darkness. As I motored sadly back, I saw the pattern of enemy mortar bomb craters on the open ground over which the Americans advanced and thought, how many gallant lives had been unnecessarily wasted.

The 104th Division's 'motto' - 'Nothing in Hell can stop the Timberwolves' was a bold statement that was keenly challenged by the Devil himself in that terrible first taste of battle. This unit, however, continued to be unstoppable and took part in a number of further actions including the Remagen Bridgehead, Cologne, the Ruhr Pocket and others.

Having returned to the U.S.A. in July, 1945, the 'Timberwolves' began intensive training for an operation, code named 'CORONET', that would have been the final act of war in the Pacific. The 'motto' might then have been tested to the utmost but this fine Division, along with many others, was mercifully spared the total horror of what would have been the ultimate in beach assault landings. Invasion of Japan itself, the last island in the chain that stretched across the Pacific Ocean, which had already seen the massed slaughter of soldiers, sailors and airmen on both sides, was cancelled. Fate had decreed that others would have to pay the final price of peace, and this they did in their tens of thousands at Hiroshima and Nagasaki. The Devil had been robbed of the final opportunity to test that boastful motto, but found ample carnage to fulfil his blood lust in the two giant mushroom clouds that were to end the Second World War.

WATER! WATER! EVERYWHERE

Many members of the Battalion had recently placed the occasional foot over an invisible border line and stepped into Holland but now, the Hallams were about to make their last crossing, from a tactical point of view, via the hamlets and villages surrounding Essen which would eventually lead through Roosendaal. The chase was to continue on up to Willemstad, where it would end for them on the shore line of the lower reaches of the River Maas, a wide stretch of water known as Hollands Diep. So this was really the beginning of the end of operations in that part of the country as far as Polar Bears were concerned. For the moment, they were to be involved in many movements to the side of the main axis, which was being forced through from Wurstwezel to Roosendaal and where the main punch was still being provided by 'Clarkforce'. It was a messy, mopping up campaign where the enemy stubbornly held on here and there, and constantly caused casualties and a massive amount of damage in terms of equipment, by the use of some very cleverly sited SP Guns.

Chris Somers (Diary)...
We moved by transport to a Battalion assembly area on the line of advance where we were supposed to rest for a week. Most of 'C' Coy were given a day in Antwerp as a reward for their activities. On getting back to the Battalion we found that we were on the move again early next morning. Mike Cooper had also rejoined the Company and Mac became Liaison Officer.

26 October : We moved up on the right of the line of advance as flank protection and spent the night in a small farmhouse. On the 28th of October, we came once more up to the front taking over from the Battalion of another Brigade who were concentrating for the attack on Roosendaal. We spent the night of the 28th in the cellar of a burned out farmhouse. In fact the shell was still smouldering and the cellar was very warm.

29 October : We left our warm cellar and moved left across the general line of the front to launch an attack on the left flank of Roosendaal. Rocket firing Typhoons were busy on the strong points of Roosendaal in preparation for the attack by 147 Brigade. 'A' Coy carried out the first stage of our attack on Boeink and followed up the medium barrage so quickly that the Boche were caught just about to come out of their cellars. Meanwhile 'C' Coy had moved over the lateral railway line into a brickworks. As we had to advance over fairly open ground to our objective, a cross road at Vinkenbroek, we were supported by a squadron of Churchills.

The road down which a number of Churchills were knocked out by a well hidden gun. (IHD)

305

Our advance to the objective went off very satisfactory because the Churchills advanced up to the lateral road to cover our reorganization, five of them were quickly put out of action by a well sited and hidden gun some few hundred yards ahead. The remainder of the tanks were forced to withdraw. An Armoured car, which came down the road from the left was also dispensed with.

Our gunner O.P. tried to take up a position in the house opposite but they spotted him and made it a bit too hot for him. As I waited with the wireless set for Mike to decide on the exact position of his HQ. we happened to be in an unfortunate position behind the gunner O.P. and a tank which the Boche was endeavouring to 'brew up'. Although the misses were sizzling just over our heads and landing about 50 yards behind. In fact Mike was quite surprised to see us all in one-piece.

Soon transport such as A/T gunners moved up to the crossroads to support us. The company on our right became the centre of attraction for the Boche. We suffered a few casualties including two good Sergeants. Things quietened down somewhat and we were all able to get to dig in for the night in an open field covering the crossroads. There was a little cottage and barn nearby our company HQ. so we gave this to the SBs.

One of the other 'few casualties' of the day was 2/Lt. Ray Langdale, who had received his commission in the field only a month before, and just prior to the action at the Depot de Mendicite. He was about to receive some attention from an SP Gun, somewhere in the vicinity of Boeink.

Ray Langdale...
I was with Johnny Palliser in a forward gun position and from there we could see a water tower on the outskirts of Roosendaal. Suddenly, a carrier went past pulling a 6 Pdr. with a lad called Swift (D.R.) leading him to a good position as he thought and ended up with this gun between us and Gerry. I went to them and said, 'We've got to get you back because you're stuck out here on a limb.' On the road going back towards where Johnny's gun was, there was a farm about halfway down on the left hand side and I asked the Sgt. in charge of the gun to go like hell and turn quickly into this farmyard behind buildings and that we would follow.

I sat behind 'Swifty' on his motorbike and we just got to the entrance to the farm when Gerry got us. It was a Self Propelled 88mm and it poked its nose round the corner of a farm building and we were lucky in one respect, that the shell had fallen so close to us that the shrapnel hadn't spread sufficiently. Swifty got wounded and so did I but nothing above the hips so, that was more or less it. We were carried off in a stretcher jeep and the date was 29 October, a date that will stick in my mind as long as I live.

After evacuation and recuperation, Ray ended his army service whilst on the staff of a German PoW camp at Motcome Park near Shaftsbury, Dorset. His pre-war job at the Post Office was waiting for him when he got home but, after three years, it would seem that this no longer satisfied his temperament after the experience of war. Suffice to say that he retired in 1985 after thirty-one years service as a Police Officer.

Chris Somers (Diary)...
About midnight I was due to go on my rounds of the company positions when the Boche let fly with all he'd got in the mortar line. Bombs fell all around our HQ. position but luckily just straddled us each time. Neither we nor any of the platoons suffered any casualties. As soon as the noise died down, hoping for the best, I set off with Hicks my Batman. It was an unpleasant feeling crossing the open ground in pitch darkness thinking that any minute the Boche might open

again. I was thankful as we reached the cover of each platoon HQ. then we had a long trek into the unknown down the lateral road to contact the Recce Regiment. It was much further than I imagined, but eventually we were suddenly challenged by the wrong end of a Stengun barrel! It must have been nearly an hour after our departure before we got back to our night's sleep.

On 29th October, Boeink and Vinkenbroek on the outskirts of Roosendaal, were captured by the Bn., the main casualties being suffered by the supporting tanks who lost three in a few minutes at Vinkenbroek. Roosendall itself was taken by the 7 D.W.R. together with 1 L.R. and cleared by 11 R.S.F. and 1/4 K.O.Y.L.I.

Chris Somers (Diary)...
30 October : Our job was to force the roadblock into Roosendaal, but our luck was in because the Boche had flown, so all we had to do was to provide picks and shovels for the working parties. The remainder of us moved in on foot. Eventually, billeting parties including self were sent on ahead to fix up accommodation. A few days rest checking up on equipment was now the order of the day. Nevertheless we found time to play the local hockey team and beat them. Also to attend a party during these three days, 56 Brigade had taken up the chase.

Trevor Hart Dyke...(Normandy to Arnhem)
Before I could get my command vehicle and the fighting transport into town, a large crater had to be filled in. I shall never forget the amazement on the faces of the prisoners we had set to on the job when they saw the Colonel, officers and men of the Hallamshires take their coats off and join heartily in the work. British, German and some of the local population all worked harmoniously together until the huge crater was no more.

On the first two days of November, no less than six officers joined the Battalion. These were Capt. C.W. Reid, Lts. A.R.N. Brown and D. Simmil, 2/Lts.W.S. Tims, B.C. Conelly and one other whose name is indecipherable from the bad type in the War Diary but looks like B.J. Dawne. A serious loss occurred on the 3rd, when Lt. Kerner (MTO) received a facial wound from shellfire. Although he was not an original Hallamshire, he had been with the Battalion since shortly after landing in Normandy and had been responsible for the extremely high standard of transport serviceability.

Records kept in the field in the form of notes that would eventually form the basis for the monthly War Diaries and other returns could not have been wholly accurate but they do give at least some rough idea of what was happening and where. The figures in terms of casualties, etc. are also of interest but whilst the final list of war dead can hardly be disputed, it may never be known just how many people were wounded. Nevertheless, it might still be of interest to read the monthly total for October which was as follows... Hallamshire Battalion Casualties = 1 Officer wounded, 11 Other Ranks killed and 58 wounded. No comparative studies have been made of the final total of Hallams wounded as a ratio of those who died. Such studies in other documents often come up with ratios of approximately three men wounded for every one killed. The ratio here, for October, 1944, was a little over five to one.

German Prisoners of War taken during this month = 2 Officers and 271 Other Ranks.

Cpl. Arthur Furniss, who died on the 4th of November, 1944.(HFC)

In his farewell letter dated 30 November, 1944, Maj. Gen. 'Bubbles' Barker (O.C. 49 Division) stated that up to that date, the whole Division had taken a total of 140 Officers and 10,602 ORs. as prisoners of war, exclusive of the large number taken at Le Havre.

Chris Somers (Diary)...
Eventually, on the 4 November, what seemed more like an exercise in England took place, especially in these civilian surroundings. First we were given the order to be prepared to move out at an hour's notice and eventually at dusk we were off leaving behind much equipment in our billets. We were taken up in transport to the frontline, (nearly at any rate). Buildings were in ruins and still smoking where we debussed. We moved up the roads which were raised up above the flat low lying ground on either side, criss-crossed by dykes. Eventually we reached a point from where we were to launch the attack on Fijnaart straight down the main road.

'B' Coy. went first and reached their objective without incident. We passed through them and all went well till we were clearing the houses on our objectives, when a section commander caught a burst at close range and was killed (this must have been Cpl. Arthur Furniss). *We remained in the middle of the village for the night with Coy. HQ. in a cellar at the back of the row of houses on one side of the road. We shared this place with three Dutchmen, but did not have time for much sleep. As we were near a church and road junction we had one of two casualties next day from shelling.*

That evening we were ordered to advance another half mile down the road to a windmill. This was successfully carried out after dark. I made the mistake of going up with Mike and Coy. HQ. as we became out of touch with the C.O. having left two signallers in our old position on the telephone. I had only just reached the objective when a runner came down to tell me the C.O. wanted me on the phone. Back half a mile I had to go only to be told that the company had got to do an attack northwards to the River Mass which meant going back to Mike and bringing the company back to our old position. A special AA Platoon had continued to advance from our position.

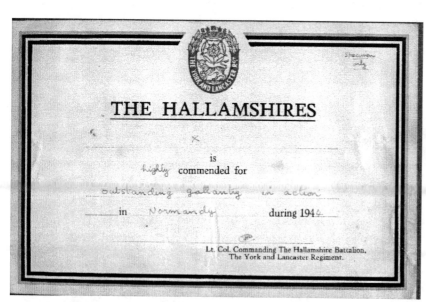

Specimen copy of Commendation Certificate devised by Trevor Hart Dyke and retained by him after the war. The introduction of such a document says a great deal about this officer and the care he had for those men under his command. (THD)

It should be said that this special A.A. Platoon was special only by the fact that it was now operating as an infantry unit. The role of A.A. units were becoming somewhat obsolescent in as much as there was very little to fire at in the way of German aircraft. For this reason many A.A. units were being broken up and men transferred to infantry units which were far from being obsolete and always able to absorb replacements.

On the 4/5th November, the 49th Division cleared small pockets of resistance as far as the Maas. The Hallams captured Fijnaart, Oude Molen and Zwingelspaan. This area was flat and featureless, giving no cover for troops who had to move about on raised roads edged with wide dikes. One incident was recalled by the C.O. which again involved the courage of Tony Nicholson (O.C. 'A' Coy.) during the advance on Oudemolen.

Trevor Hart Dyke (Normandy to Arnhem)...
...enemy machine gun fire along the road made further advance well nigh impossible. With indomitable courage, Tony Nicholson led his men forward arm-pit high in the dikes on either side. Firing their Bren Guns from the shoulder, they drove the enemy from the eastern half of the village.

Ken Godfrey...
Near the end, I was transferred to 'A' Coy. commanded by Tony Nicholson and became his Runner. He was the sort of man that if he'd said, 'Lads, I've got a 15cwt. here, we're going to Berlin,' you would have jumped in with him. To me, he inspired so much confidence, just the same as Hart Dyke. He was a bastard at times but we knew that no matter what, everything he could do to help his Battalion was done.

Above : Hallamshire Battalion 6 pdr. A/Tk gun position on a road junction just to the west of Fijnaart.(IWM) ❖Below : View from same camera position in Summer, 2000. The nearest of the twin bungalows has been modified to take a first floor with a flat roof and railed verandah. The building on the immediate right is no longer there and in its place there is now a high hedge. (DWS)

At one stage we were in a heck of a lot of woods. I was the only person in the Battalion who knew where a particular platoon was and all night I was walking up the rides through the forest finding my way to pass messages. I took a lot of officers up at different times all through the night and was later given a Hallamshire Battalion Commendation, which was an award devised by Col. Hart Dyke for men who were deserving of credit but had not been given recognition through normal channels.

Chris Somers (Diary)...
5 November : Mike left me with the company while he went a short way ahead with 'O' Group. Unfortunately, we were right by the church and, as I feared, shelling soon started. Luckily it was only slight but the roof of the house under which I was standing with the signallers was hit and we were showered with broken pieces. Eventually we started our advance up a raised track with no cover for miles around, to a forming up place in an area where 'A' Coy. had made an abortive attack. This time we were supported by a medium barrage. Our first objective, the main road, was quickly reached. The first house we entered we were met by frightened civilians who appeared from the cellar.

Here we turned right and advanced up the main road to our second objective. Resistance was only slight, probably one or two men with Spandaus. However, we only had the one road to advance along. Before daylight we had passed through the road junction to Zwingelspaan to our third objective. The Boche kept stonking this road junction throughout next day which made life a bit difficult when visiting the forward platoon, and one had to dash from house to house. We had a good O.P. from the top of our company HQ. position and were able to train the gunners onto retreating Boche who were moving along the Riverside a mile or so ahead.

George Learad...
Major Newton said to me, 'I want you to take the platoon and take that village!' So, I took two Brens and when I gets there, there's about thirty women come screaming out of this village, kissing us and what not and I'm trying to knock them away to get the Brens lined up. Of course, Gerry had scarpered, but we didn't know that. Anyway, these women gave us some coffee made out of acorns and there were no sugar in and that's what they had been drinking.

It was the same day that Johnny Ellis got killed. Major Newton sent for me to go and report to him. When I got there he said, 'I've got some bad news. Johnny Ellis has got killed.' I think that there must have been another mine underneath the one he was working on and when he pulled the top one off, it detonated the one below. Johnny was a bit of a dare devil you know.

Dare Devil or not, John Ellis had performed some very dangerous but vital work for the Battalion as a Pioneer Corporal in the last couple of months, for which he had already been awarded the D.C.M. He was one of only three Hallamshire men to receive it during World War Two. Some weeks previous to John Ellis being killed, George and he had acquired a Piano-Accordian and a suitcase full of American cigarettes which German troops had left behind in their withdrawal. John had bagged the musical instrument and George, the cigarettes but the latter had almost immediately been snatched by local civilians. After John's death, George sold the accordian and sent the proceeds to John's widow.

Trevor Hart Dyke with reference to his Pioneers (Normandy to Arnhem)...
It was a matter of pride with them never to ask for Engineer assistance. That this was the first time they had been caught when lifting an enemy mine was a high tribute to their technical skill. The death of Corporal Ellis was a sad blow to the Battalion. It was he who had got the bridge constructed under fire on the River Vie and who had saved the bridge into the docks at Le Havre. He was always at Hawkin's side when there was a particular sticky job to do. His courage was proverbial throughout the Battalion and he had already been awarded the Distinguished Conduct Medal (D.C.M.) for conspicuous gallantry.

Chris Somers (Diary)...
Unfortunately our gunner O.P. had met with a mishap while following up one line of advance. Apparently the crossroads which we had formed up on had been heavily mined. He had got a lift on our ration truck which got blown up. Luckily, no fatal injuries apart from a signaller getting covered in porridge! Our CQMS received a broken leg and our breakfast went west! Unfortunately, when our pioneers removed the mines, one was boobytrapped and a very good Cpl. (Ellis) was killed and the officer (Lt. Hawkins) wounded. As a result of this we were allowed to eat our emergency rations.

Later in the day, the Lincolns on our right took over our front and we were withdrawn once more back to Roosendaal where we spent another week before being moved south to the Weert area in order to help complete the clearing up to the Mass. A few days passed in the Weert area before recces were carried out and aerial photographs studied for clearing up to Venlo. Unfortunately, Major Newsome of the Lincs was killed by shell fire during one of those recces.

Les Gill...
We stopped for a week in Roosendaal and the people were marvellous. After all this chasing Germans, shooting Germans, it was a most wonderful thing to have a break from it. It was a complete break from the fierceness of it all and at Roosendaal, they gave us a breath of fresh air.

The steady advance had now come to a close in this area due to the fact that the enemy had withdrawn from their positions at Willemstad and crossed a wide expanse of water, known as the Hollands Diep. After having been asked to surrender, it was thought that they might have made a last stand in this old and picturesque little walled and moated town. However, they had quietly slipped away across the water during a short period of ceasefire intended to be used for the evacuation of civilians and casualties. To follow them across may have ended in a costly beach assault on the other side if the Germans had decided to oppose the landings. Many lives must have been saved by ending the chase here, for the time being. What is more, a pretty little

❖ *Willemstad and its harbour, now a very popular visitor attraction from both sea and land. Hollands Diep and far shore can be seen beyond the harbour entrance. (DWS)*

town and a fair proportion of its inhabitants, were spared from almost certain obliteration.

The Battalion was able to lick its wounds during the short rest in Roosendaal but numbers had been steadily dropping again due to casualties, accidents, etc. Peter Newton, for instance, was badly injured at this time when he was crushed between two carriers. At times also, there had been a considerable wastage of men due to sickness. Recurring bouts of Amoebic Dysentery, which had originally hit the Battalion in Normandy, took a steady toll and, along with other complaints, saw numbers dwindle as men were evacuated to England.

Trevor Hart Dike (Normandy to Arnhem)...
During the few days stay in Roosendaal, I enquired most carefully into the man-power problem. We had been very handicapped in the recent operations by having only three Rifle companies instead of four and this was not, by any means, the first time that our numbers had fallen so low that the elimination of one of the companies had been necessary. It put a great strain on the men and, naturally, gave them less rest. Reductions in our strength were by no means confined to battle casualties. Accidents, sickness, battle neurosis and absence were the causes of a constant drain on our man-power...

There comes a time when men, with prolonged service with the Rifle companies, or as a result of some particular stress, are no longer battle-worthy though their hearts might be too big ever to admit it. During our spell at Tessel Wood, I always had eight men per Rifle company and two men each from Signals, Carriers, Pioneers and Mortars living at 'B' Echelon. Each man went back for two days; one for a complete sleep round the clock; the other for a bath and in which to make up arrears in correspondence to the folk at home. The resultant deficiency in our fighting strength was well repaid by the increase in our morale and fighting efficiency. While we were at

Roosendaal, I changed over deserving Rifle company personnel with drivers and other administrative men, but there was a limit to this as special qualifications were often necessary.

That breath of fresh air, given to their liberators by the people of Roosendaal, was over all too soon and the Division was moved east into 12 Corps sector. Troops were concentrated in the area of Weert, poised for an advance eastwards through Maasbree to Blerick where a crossing of the River Maas would take place opposite the town of Venlo. The Hallams, like a number of other units in the 49 Division, proceeded to mop up as far as Blerick, encountering particularly nasty conditions in terms of rain, mortar fire and numerous mine fields.

Chris Somers (Diary)...
20 November : The Hallamshires were all set for a night attack across the canal passing through the Lincolns. However, main resistance came from shellfire and the Lincolns pushed on further than was expected. The battalion moved up just behind them but did not pass through until Maasbree had been taken and the Hallams were required to push on to Hout Blerick just short of Venlo.

22 November : I was proceeding up to an 'O' group for a company assembly area when our Jeeps were subjected to mortar fire which seemed to come from nowhere. Apparently the Gerrys had got an O.P. somewhere from which they could see our area. We baled out into the ditch as a precaution after a splinter had hit some equipment on a Jeep. We happened to stop by 'A' Coys. HQ., so collected Raymond Jenkinson before proceeding to a farmhouse which was to be temporary Bn. HQ. The Germans must have seen us again because they put down a 'stonk' which smashed a few of the windows. Our companies later consolidated in this area before starting the advance through the Lincolns.

23 November : I was granted a 72 hour leave in Brussels at this point, and left the company (perhaps luckily) just before they started the advance on Hout Blerick. I marched them up to Maasbree where I handed the company over. They were shelling the main street quite heavily when we arrived but we escaped casualties. Though I missed the attack itself, apparently it was quite successful as the Germans had retired. Progress was hampered by large quantities of Shue Mines and one of our officers lost his foot. Shelling also hampered the digging in that night. When I arrived back, they had just been drawn back again as another Division had taken over the final mile to Venlo.

George Learad...
We'd been in an attack at night and on guard during day and we were getting no sleep. This particular night I went to see Major Newton and I was shattered and so were my lads. He had a bed in a cellar and he was in bed when I saw him and I asked him could we have a break but he said he was sorry but we'd have to go on guard. Anyway, I fell asleep in the trench on guard and this officer came along and found me and said, 'You were asleep, weren't you?' And I said to him, ' and thou would be a f...... sleep if thou'd a been awake for a week!' He said, 'I'll have to put you on a charge,' and I said, 'I couldn't care bleeding less.' Anyway, I'd only just come round and I was told, 'You're wanted.'

I had to go and clear these mines on open ground in front of the River Maas at Venlo on me own. I was walking up and they were mortaring all the while and it were raining. The place was schnided with mines and I was going down with this mine-detector. As I leaned forward, I detected a tank mine but stepped on a schue mine just in front of it. I lost my left eye and it blew my right leg off. I would have lost my other eye but my right hand, being forward, shielded it from the blast but I was blinded and I had other shrapnel wounds to the arms and face. All I can remember was old Johnny Paget shouting, 'Come and fetch him then.' You can't clear mines if you're tired. You've got to have your sleep. I got some now and woke up in Swindon!

Les Sewell...
We moved over almost to the German border and I remember we stopped at a crossroads that was under fire from the Zeigfreid Line, it was as close as that. We came under fire and I jumped into the nearest hole and it was six or seven feet deep and I damaged my left leg. One of the pioneers Carriers had a direct hit there, which rather upset some of our lads that saw it. Then we got into a small town which I think was Maasbree? Anyway, our section had to make a recce towards Venlo to find out if a certain bridge was intact. We got well out and it seemed very quiet there except we were in a place where lots of spent bullets were dropping down. We got back from that and it was at that time when a number of promotions were due in the platoon, including myself to full Corporal. Then all at once the Col. cancelled it all because he was absolutely disgusted with the carrier platoon as they'd let him down. Apparently, his plans for going this way were based on the fact that the bridge was intact and it was reported as blown when in fact, he found out later, it was intact!

The use of tracked armoured 'Kangaroo' troop carriers enabled the Battalion to advance quickly in a sort of leapfrogging shuttle service which also saved many casualties from shue mines that had been sown like seeds in the area. Then, just when it seemed that it was poised for the final assault, the 49th were ordered to hand over to the 15th Scottish Division and proceed north to Nijmegen where it would relieve the 50th (Northumbrian) Division.

Les Sewell...
We went up the road through Grave and stayed at least one night in Eindhoven. We also passed through a number of villages, one of which I remember had four houses with forty children between them. At the farmhouse we stayed at, they had ten and you could see that they were particularly poor. They had a sort of porridge for their breakfast and porridge at night and, of course, we used to give them what we could and they thought it was marvellous, some bread or chocolate and things like that.

Building in Eindhoven used for Hallamshire billeting during the move from Venlo to Nijmegen. (THD)

Only a short distance to the north of Grave, the Battalion was to become involved in what would be the last phase of their war, albeit a rather cold, wet and drawn out affair. It was conducted on that low lying piece of land between Nijmegen and Arnhem which was to become known to all who were subjected to it as 'The Island'. More a delta than an island, that piece of land was, and is, closely hemmed in by the waters of the River Rhine which divides just east of Nijmegen at Millingen. The two parts then flow westwards through Nijmegen (Waal) on the south side and via the Pannerden Canal by way of Arnhem (Lower Rhine) to the north, creating an 'apparent' island.

The combined airborne/armoured Operation 'Market-Garden' has already been mentioned and that bold plan would have included capture of the 'Island' had it succeeded. In fact, its original purpose had been envisaged to drastically shorten the war and even see it ended by Christmas.

At the very least it may have made this new winter phase, which was to drag on through the winter and into the spring of 1945, unnecessary.

❖ *The prominent feature at Nijmegen, both then and now, was the bridge which only just escaped being destroyed when the main demolition charges set by German forces failed to blow. It would stand out in the memory of any Hallamshire man that served here during the winter of 1944/45 and they must have crossed it numerous times in the many change overs in the frontline 'Island' on the north side. This photograph was taken in a fine holiday atmosphere during the Summer of 2000, very different to conditions then.(DWS)*

Arthur Green...

We took over positions at Nijmegen and went over the bridge which had had a hole blown in the middle but this was now spanned by a wooden ramp. We occupied part of the island with the rest of the Brigade on the right hand sector in the area of Bemmel. We were there over the winter and the days were getting colder with ice and snow but we were very lucky and pretty comfortable in civilian houses at Nijmegen. Gerry had opened some of the sluice gates and flooded part of the Island. You couldn't drive everywhere because of it but those roads we could drive along in shallower water were marked by poles strung with tape.

Chris Somers (Diary)...

2 December : Found us up at Nijmegen after a tiring journey. Our Brigade was in reserve in the town itself and we were billeted in a large school alongside the railway line. The officers were billeted in houses just up the road.

8 December : We took over part of the line on the 'Island', 'C' Coy. going to Ressen. It was a very quiet sector and I preferred it to Nijmegen. After a week we were back in Nijmegen on the 14th December, in order to celebrate Christmas and have our dinner in the town. Nijmegen was a pleasant town, unfortunately all the shops had been destroyed by American bombing as they mistook it for another town! The Germans shelled it occasionally but nobody, not even civilians, took much notice and there were very few casualties.

314

Les Sewell...

Then we got to Nijmegen and I was billeted at 87 Jarvastraat. That was the better part of the town and not too far from the bridge. I was billeted with a nice family called Helb, I think the chap was an insurance man. There was his wife and two other elderly ladies he referred to as his sisters and a daughter aged about nineteen. They all slept in the cellar and the whole family spoke very good English. He put me up in his library and he said I could look at any book I liked. What interested me was one about Albrecht Dura, a well known artist.

I was now put in charge of both Coy. and carrier stores which was located in a locked building containing rations, spare parts, paraffin, etc. across the street from the billet.

Les Gill...

The type of life we had to contend with on the island needs very special attention because there are very few people realize that we were nothing else but a shooting gallery for the Germans. For instance, our area just over the Nijmegen Bridge and to the right through some gardens and things, we had trenches where we were within speaking distance of the enemy.

Les Sewell...

Battalion HQ. was on the 'Island' across the bridge as was the carrier platoon. To reach the latter you turned right over the bridge along a road to a house near the River Waal. The house which was the HQ. under Capt. Gill was cut off from the River by a 'bund' and the only way to get rations to it was to stop the vehicle by the bund and go on foot down to the right of it for so far and then go through a cutting in the bund to the house on the other side. (bund = linear earthen embankment/flood barrier)

You could only approach it in the dark and a previous rations party had been fired on by the enemy and dropped everything and run. So, I was detailed to guide a jankers party in the snow to the spot, collect the scattered items and deliver them to the house. I led them over this bank and walked down to pick up the various boxes and then we had to look for this opening. I was walking in front and they were all hanging back and I were terrified. We found this opening and we dropped everything off. They all started making their way back but Les Gill kept me talking for a long time and it was broad daylight when I went and I had to walk back on my own.

❖ *Above : Ressen, where the Hallamshire Battalion first took over reserve positions from 1/4 K.O.Y.L.I. on the 8th December, 1944. (DWS)*

❖ *Below : One company was sent forward into an area called Vergent which consisted of scattered farms. This area is not always identified on modern road maps but lies to the north of Bemmel. The poles and tapes below are reminiscent of the war time flood markers but these were to guide people to a horse show which was taking place on the day visited in summer, 2000. (DWS)*

Les Gill...
Some of the churches there had very narrow spires which were more often than not slated. I had one of my lads up in one just watching what was going on through a hole where a slate had been removed. Now where we were, we could see these V2 rockets lifting off from their launching pads away behind the German lines and one day one of these went out of control and crashed not far from the base of the church steeple. Well, it blew every bloody slate off and there was this lad up there and it looked as though there was nothing there to hold the spire up. It took me at least half an hour to get that bloke down. He just wouldn't budge and hung onto the slate laths.

Arthur Green...
The C.O. decided that some of the lads at the front ought to have a rest and brought some of 'B' Echelon up to replace them. I was told to leave my wagon and do a stint up front. I got as close as I'd ever been to small arms fire through this orchard and could see twigs flying and it put fear of death into me and was a bit unnerving. Anyway, I spent most of the time wondering about HQ. doing all sorts of jobs and driving for the M.O.

There was a White Halftrack at Bn.HQ. on the Island and it had a red cross painted on it and could carry four stretchers and I remember one day being ordered to take it out and retrieve the bodies of some lads who had been killed a few days ago and had been seen in the water. I drove to the place where they were with three or four stretcher bearers and the sight of them was ghastly. They'd been in the water for a few days and were bloated. It wasn't a pleasant sight. We brought them back and they were given a decent burial.

One day I was detailed to take six or seven of our lads, who were in detention for desertion and other misdemeanors, to help carry water, fuel, rations and stores to some forward positions in the dark and I was the only one with a weapon. These lads had probably gone off without permission because of home problems or they were 'bomb happy' and things like that and they were put on menial tasks like digging trenches, washing and cleaning, cookhouse fatigues, etc.

There was a bit of a scare around this time because Gerry had made one or two attempts to blow up Nijmegen Bridge by sending frogmen down the river with explosives. We were using a thing called 'Monty's Moonlight' at that time which was a means of lighting the area by bouncing searchlight beams off low cloud base. It wasn't very dark when we went along this riverbank after leaving the wagon parked up and as we moved along in about two or three inches of snow, I noticed these black patches at the edge of the water and even though I was the one with a weapon, I was shit scared! One of the lads who'd done the job before said that they were five dead Gerries and had been there a few days. We eventually dropped this stuff off further on and then came back, but I had to repeat the job a few days later and came to these dead Germans again and noticed there were now six black patches and thought that a live one might be lying amongst them waiting for us but when one lad took my sten gun and checked, he came back and said that one of the bodies had slid down the slope to another position making it seem that there were now six bodies. He said, 'Tha's a' reet, they're a' stone deerd!.'

There were now Cinemas and E.N.S.A. shows provided in the relatively safe area of Nijmegen. Even though there was the occasional long range shell falling on the city, the casualties were said to have been light and people tended to get on with their daily life. The Battalion had been withdrawn from the Island on 14 December after only five days in the line and it was soon learned that any official seasonal festivities would have to be celebrated earlier than usual. Christmas Dinner, in the Catholic School, had to be held on the 20th because they were due to go back into the line on the 22nd.

Chris Somers (Diary)...

The Ardennes offensive took place about this time and an attack was also expected in our area. (this occurred on the 16th and was later to become known as the Battle of the Bulge). Our Christmas Dance in Nijmegen was nearly spoiled as the Battalion was alerted just when it was due to start. Raymond and I were the organizers and I had the embarrassing experience of trying to persuade the Dutch girls not to leave before the officers (who were confined to the mess) arrived! Luckily the dance was allowed to go on.

22 December : On our return to the Island 'C' Coy went to Bemmel, a reserve company area but where most of the shells landed. Bemmel certainly came in for a packet at times. I always hoped I wouldn't get caught on the exposed road while visiting platoon areas. We spent most of our time building defences round houses. Most of us lived in cellars which were the only parts of most of the houses worth living in. We even got a piano down in ours for Christmas Day.

No temporary ceasefire was called on Christmas Day, which resulted in the death of Private Arthur Ellis during sporadic enemy shellfire. Boxing Day was business as usual although one occurrence was a little out of the ordinary.

On Christmas Day, a piano was manhandled down into the cellar of this house in Bemmel and 'C' Coy. celebrated as best they could on the 'Island'. The piano got stuck halfway down the stairs, so a corner had to be hacked off it without damaging the strung frame. (ACS)

❖ *These buildings are believed to be all that is left of the 'brickworks' to the west of the road bridge (Huis de Karbrug) north of Bemmel. They appear to be used for farm storage now but there are piles of bricks strewn all around. The Wetering can be seen in the foreground but no trace of the footbridge was found. (DWS)*

Trevor Hart Dyke (Normandy to Arnhem)...

Next day, an unusual incident occurred. At 11 o'clock, eleven Bosche presented themselves on the dike (this was most probably at or near the bridge across the Rijn Wetering to the north of Bemmel) with a Red Cross flag. We put 3 inch mortar smoke bombs behind them and this induced them to cross over. They consisted of four medical and seven infantry personnel, who stated that they had come over to collect the four men they had lost two nights earlier. In view of recent German activity, their broadcasts saying that they would be back in Nijmegen, and the constant rumours in that town of a coming attack, we regarded this act with the gravest suspicion and made prisoners of the whole party.

All three battalions of the Brigade were now told to try to establish outposts on the north side of the Wetering but the Hallams attempts were foiled by three German machine guns covering the bridge.

Trevor Hart Dyke (Normandy to Arnhem)...
The only hope of crossing the dike without a major operation was by a footbridge at the brickworks, two hundred yards to the west of the road bridge...   ...Before first light (27th) we installed our snipers there and they succeeded in wounding one and killing two of their snipers as they were opening the shutters of a house to set up shop on the far bank. From then on we always had snipers in the brickworks and definitely dominated the dike. Lt. Simmil took a patrol across the footbridge, shot up the houses on the far bank and returned via the main bridge without suffering any casualties. However, he was unable to get into the houses to secure a prisoner.

It was at about this time that the Hallams were visited by a journalist from the Sheffield Telegraph. Alfred Dow was able to send a number of reports back to the city which must have warmed the hearts of loved ones at that time of the year and, as much as censorship would allow, make them more aware of conditions that their menfolk were subjected to in Holland.

Alfred Dow (War Correspondent of The Sheffield Telegraph)...
9 January 1945 : When the Commanding Officer of the Hallamshire Battalion of the York and Lancaster Regiment learned I was going to Holland he wrote that he hoped my visit would coincide with active operations, so that I might take back a clear impression of life out there. His hopes were realized. I found Hallamshires right in the front-line, and while I was with them the operations seemed to me to be very active indeed, although I admit that to the hardened Hallamshires themselves the activity was probably just ordinary. And now my job is to try to give parents, wives, sweethearts and friends an account of how their men live and fight.

A Hallamshire officer met me at Eindhoven and drove me many miles along roads often lined with the wrecks of tanks, lorries, gliders and planes, both German and Allied. It was dusk as we reached the Battalion in the line. As we approached the command post the car had to pull up with a jerk and moved cautiously over the verge to avoid a dark figure in the roadway towards which soldiers were running. That was my introduction to the horrible side of warfare. A shell had fallen just before we reached this point and a solitary, unlucky, soldier had been killed.

We moved away - at increased speed I noticed gratefully - and we heard more shells bursting behind us. At the same time my companion pointed ahead to a flash like forked lightning shooting up vertically in the velvet twilight - a V2 being launched behind enemy lines he explained.

The command post was established in a picturesque Dutch farmhouse, substantially built and hardly damaged. Hear the Commanding Officer welcomed me into a cozy HQ mess with the tea table set, a hurricane lamp burning brightly, and a wireless set giving the background of dance music just loud enough to drown the noises of firing guns and falling shells.

During a well served and satisfying meal of ordinary army rations - minced meat, carrots and potatoes, jam tarts and custard, cheese, bread and butter - there were further developments. The meal was served in a room adjoining the operations control centre, where officers on unrelenting duty were in constant communication with the forward companies, patrols, snipers - and the dinner table. Many messages came through to us. The Colonel, the signals officer, the artillery major, the intelligence officer — all left a meal more than once and played a part in the developing situation.

318

A patrol reported noise of cracking ice in a certain specified area. A sniper heard whispers in the same quarter. Quickly the order was given for shells to be dropped on the precise point. The artillery major reassumed his dinner, making the unnecessary remark that the shells were being delivered - unnecessary because the noises of the firing two or three miles behind and of the shells dropping 1,500 or so yards ahead were already being heard. Later, acting on further reports from observation posts, the C.O. ordered mortar fire at certain points to deal with suspected enemy movements. His reaction to still more reported activity was to lay on machine gun fire, heavy bursts continuing for half an hour or so until it was decided that Jerry had enough. Sudden lulls, followed by sudden bursts of shelling and machine gunning, continued during the night. There was constant tension. About midnight I was persuaded to turn in, wrapping blankets and greatcoat and lying on blankets on the kitchen floor in a Dutch house occupied by the Regimental Aid Post. Hardened stretcher bearers and medical orderlies snored near me, but each time I dozed I was awakened by the crashing artillery and the muttering machine guns.

Hallamshire Officers at Nijmegen (very probably Dec./Jan. 1944/5). Back Row : Lt. Gerald Bedward (Intelligence Officer), Lt. John Wollerton ('B' Coy.), Mr. Alfred Dow (War Correspondent from the Sheffield Telegraph). Front Row : Major Geoffrey Grey (O.C. 'B' Coy.), Lt. Col. Trevor Hart Dyke (O.C. Hallamshire Battalion), Capt. W.S. Eade (Adjutant). (SNL)

Early in the morning I was aroused by ack-ack fire and went outside to watch several flying bombs roar over, with our guns trying to bring them down at the very outset of their journey. There were pieces of ice in the water I used for washing and shaving, and never have I known a mug of scalding hot tea so welcome as on that first morning in the line. But the reports on the past night's activities were warming too. Four Gerrys had been killed and the Hallamshires themselves had sustained no casualties. The first 12 hours had given me a very clear impression of how front-line

319

fighting is directed from the command post. My next duty was to go up to the men in the forward companies and to see the men who had been patrolling and sniping so successfully. To get from the command post to the forward companies of the Hallamshire Battalion in the line in Holland we had to use a much shelled road through a devastated village with a prominent church tower still standing.

On the morning the commanding officer took me to the advance positions, there had been quite a 'stonk' (present war term for heavy shelling) going on, but a lull had set in and we were taking advantage of it. Nobody loiters in this area, but as our jeep hurtled along, avoiding the latest shell holes, there was just time to notice the shops with their goods still displayed in their broken windows, the houses with their sides ripped open to reveal comfortably furnished rooms, the cottage kitchens with there religious statuettes and pictures visible to all passers-by. And never a building whole. (it is very probable that the place here described was Bemmel)

Quickly through the village and we reached the headquarters of the first of the companies of these York and Lancaster men. It was a big house standing slightly back from the road, substantially built and not yet badly damaged. Before the war it had been occupied by the family of a well-to-do Dutch businessman.

As we passed through the kitchen I noticed unbroken bottles of kidney beans prepared for winter by some prudent housewife. In a lounge there were big armchairs, dusty but still comfortable looking, pictures hanging awry... But these were not the quarters of the fighting men. Today there is no trench warfare of the last war kind, but in positions such as those the Hallamshires occupied during my visit to them, under constant harassing shell fire, underground accommodation is desirable. And the Hallamshires found safety in the substantial cellars of this and other similar houses.

When they first occupied the position there were high floods in the area and duck boards were necessary on the floors in the cellars, but when I was with them the waters had subsided and their quarters were both dry and cozy, lit by hurricane lamps. On the walls of most of the cellars were smashing pin-up girls and over the sleeping places of individual men were photographs of their wives, mothers, and sweethearts. Always ready 'mashed' (as the Sheffield boys called it) were cups of char, offered scalding hot to all visitors.

From these underground homes issued nightly the patrols and snipers, out into the freezing cold for their long vigil. This work of watching and contacting the enemy is exacting on the nerves. It demands tremendous patience to remain motionless and alone, waiting for the enemy to make the false move, it needs great endurance to withstand the cold in silence, there is great courage needed to penetrate the enemies lines and shoot him up.

Around most of the buildings occupied by the Hallamshire companies in the forward positions were orchards which offered good cover for any intruding Boche. I heard one story of the daring Gerry who came so close in that he was walking about our occupied farmyard before he was discovered. Then he disappeared quickly and quietly into the orchard, apparently unharmed by pursuing fire. With the commanding officer I climbed up to forward observation posts in the top stories of the ruined houses. He pointed over the flat countryside, white with hoar frost and shimmering in winter sunshine, to the enemy positions near a line of typical poplars. Only 500 yards away, Germans were peering back at us, but on the particular morning at that hour everything was quiet. Only in the distance was there the noise of shell fire.

Clambering down from one attic I kicked a legal-looking document which on examination proved to be the title deed for the damaged house. Nearby was a family photograph album with some of its treasures strewn on the floor, dirty and crumbled. An old neatly entered account book lay on the top of the debris in another corner of the room. Walking from one post to another we kept out of enemy observation by going behind the buildings and through the shielded orchards. In some positions we found the men having substantial meals. In others they were warming themselves beside fires, the smoke of which was carefully shielded. And some of the men were enjoying bottles of beer, Scotch ale, in pints which they said was very good.

Their spirits were high and confident. There was no pessimism here. Only one soldier did I find who said he was browned off. True, he made that admission in strong and by no means uncertain language, but I was much more impressed by the way two of his comrades followed me afterwards, took me on one side and apologized for him and earnestly reassured me that he was one in a thousand suffering from a hangover. Tell the people of Sheffield we are all right and full of fight they said. Don't take any notice of him indicating their browned off comrade.

As we hurtled back again along Stonk Ally the harassing shelling was resumed. Yet in the middle of the devastated village, to my amazement, we came upon an elderly civilian with a horse and dray, come - with permission, to try to recover some of his most treasured possessions from his ruined home. About this time one shell fell on the corner of a building which housed in anti-tank team, and there were three Hallamshire casualties, only slight, fortunately. The day spent going to the forward companies and with them in their cellars made me realize that Sheffield can be prouder than ever of 'Sheffield's Own' Battalion. These are grand soldiers who fought stubbornly at Caen, prized Gerry out of Le Havre, drove triumphantly through Belgium into Holland, and now hold firmly one of the most important salients in the north of Holland.

Chris Somers Diary)...
12 January : The weather had become very frosty and the Battalion was moved to Haalderen which was in very close quarters with the enemy and movement over most of the area impossible by day. There was plenty of shelling and mortaring in both directions, not to mention patrols. The reserve company lost a complete patrol one night, the officer i/c finding himself face-to-face with a Spandau at the end of the ditch he was crawling up!

Much of this month was taken up by attempts to capture individual enemy soldiers for intelligence purposes but to no avail. Good use of Battalion snipers gave them the edge in terms of harassment and protection of the forward companies against opposition snipers. Then disaster struck on the 15th when a patrol under the command of Lt. Godley ran into trouble when they were engaged by the enemy. Although Cpl. Stapleton and one other managed to crawl back wounded, the others were not heard from again except that it appeared that some action was still taking place tphe next morning. The War Diary for this day ended with one officer and eight ORs. reported missing in action. A later patrol was unable to find any trace of the earlier, ill fated patrol and all the signs were that they had been captured. This was subsequently confirmed after the war and one member of that patrol, 18 years old Pte. Reginald Wass, was known to have died but his body was never recovered.

George Pape indulges himself on what might be termed 'a busman's holiday' at a shooting gallery in Brussels. (Mr. Pape)

The Battalion was relieved by 2 E.R. on the 25th and came back to Nijmegen where the last few days of this month were taken up by resting, holiday and retraining. Life was relatively safe on the south side of the River Waal in the city and groups of men now began to take advantage of 72 hour leave passes to Brussels.

Arnold Whiteley...
You can imagine what it were like for us, you know, we were let go to a bath unit first and issued with nice clean clothes. We stopped in these big hotels and what they did, they provided these hotels with the food and the they did the cooking. I don't know what they charged for rent. It was fantastic to live in, like luxury in those hotels in the main square near the railway station.

There was a stretch of road there, maybe half a mile, and you couldn't walk ten paces before you were accosted by a woman with an invitation to go and have sex with her and they were well dressed. They must have made a hell of a lot of money because in appearance they weren't tramps. They'd have a good fur coat on, nylons and things, I mean, you could understand it were a big temptation for a young man. I never availed myself but the cost was a sliding scale depending on whether you wanted to sleep with her or if you wanted to go for just a short period.

I'll just tell you a story of what happened to one of the lads and he paid over a thousand francs. He went to sleep with this girl and he went to bed and, of course, he had a session and then he woke up and she wasn't there you see. So, he waited some considerable time and she came back. She said she'd been to the bathroom and they had another session and he woke up and she was gone again. It transpired that she was entertaining more than one man through the night.

As has already been said, there were entertainment's and other creature comforts to be had in Nijmegen itself without the need to travel to Brussels. Just to have a bath in those times was something of a luxury - if you could find one!

Arthur Green...
When I was going up to the front one day I saw an army Mobile Bath Unit at the side of the road and they were just ready for packing up. I said, 'Are you packing up?' and the bloke there said, 'We've been here for about six hours, where've you been?' I said, 'Well, is there any water left?' and he said, 'There might be a drop of warm left if you hurry up!' Anyway, I parked me vehicle up like and managed to get a quick bath and was I thankful to get a good scrub down.

One night I went to a dance in a hall where they had a 'dance orchestra' and you've never heard anything like it in your life. I was a reasonably good dancer in me youth but I couldn't pluck up the courage to ask anybody to dance. You used to just wander about in your best uniform and pass the time having a drink in a cafe or something like that. We started getting forty-eight hour leave passes to Brussels and I used to run them down there in the 3 tonner to this big hotel. I can't remember the name but it wasn't far from that little lad that used to urinate! Whilst they were there, they'd put their boots and laundry outside the door and the next morning it was there all cleaned for them.

John Wollerton...
I was taken out of the line at Nijmegen with Tony Nicholson and sent to a Battle School set up in a big house near Turnout and I think the C.O. was giving us a break as we were the only two original officers to have got to Holland unscathed. (there were two others in this category - Lts. Bedward and Somers, the latter of whom also attended the Battle School). I'm not sure whether that wasn't more dangerous than being on the Island though because the V1s (flying bombs) were

coming over and some new American anti-aircraft guns near us were bringing them down around us.

After Battle School, I was put in charge of the first Coy. of Belgian soldiers to be brought forward. We weren't in the front line and I got on with them extremely well. There was a lot of humour and they later presented me with a Scroll which proclaimed me to be, among other things, a Distinguished Linguist in that I had a job to say a short sentence in French. It was more dangerous training these lot than it was being in the front line.

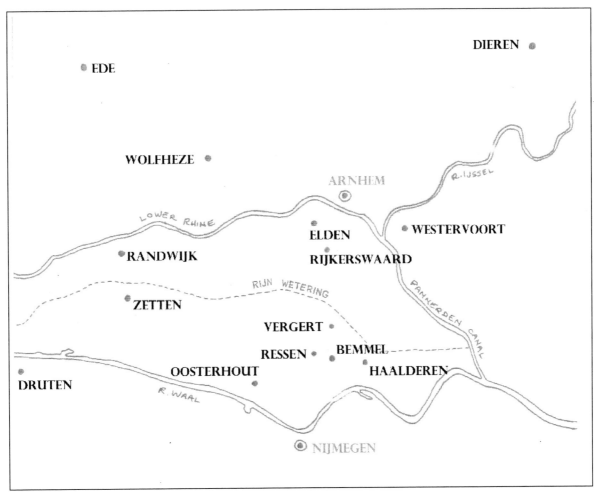

Map showing the 'Island' area in which the Hallams operated during the winter of 1944/45. (Places of Memorial and burial shown in gray print). Two distinct periods were centered on Bemmel and Zetten with the final advance via the Pannerdens Canal, Westervoort, Arnhem, Dieren, Wolfheze and Ede. On the 7 May, 1945, the Battalion left their dispositions at Ede and drove west to Utrecht. World War Two (Europe) was over. (DWS)

During the first week of February, the Hallams took part in training at Nijmegen but were back in the line on the 9th when they relieved the 11 R.S.F. around Zetten and Andelst. Pte. Banks was killed and three others wounded by shelling in this move. Deep snow in this area was now beginning to melt which caused flooding and a steady rise in water levels that forced the Bn. to concentrate positions on pieces of higher ground that were being turned into small islands. These now had to be serviced and supplied by amphibious craft such as DUKWs and Weasels which were based at the level crossing just west of Gekvoor. Patrols could be carried out by canvas boats but these were very vulnerable to under water obstacles.

Chris Somers (Diary)...

9 February : Found us on the opposite side of the front in the much flooded Zetten. D.U.K.W.s and Weasels were the only way troops and provisions could be brought up and to step off the edge of the road meant going up to the neck in water! The gunner officer and myself had the very unpleasant experience of being shelled while perched up in the belfry of the church. Luckily they missed although a direct hit was scored later. After a few days here, where I had been acting company commander while Mike was on short leave, I was sent back to Ryckworsel as Instructor to the Battle School run by Tony Nicholson.

Left : Loading stores into a collapsible canvas boat at the level crossing in the Zetten area. Two officers stand in the middle distance with hands on hips (on right is Jesse Mitchinson.) The officer standing in the water (right) is Raymond Jenkinson. A DUKW amphibious vehicle can be seen in the background.(SNL)

❖ *Above : Same area today and thought to be on or near the same spot where left picture was taken. (DWS)*

Left : Showing damage to spire of the Dutch Reform Church at Zetten. (HFC)
❖ *Right : John Swift returned to the scene of his lucky escape during a visit to Holland in 1992. The spire has been repaired but it may be noticed that it has been reduced in height from the original design. This appears to have been the case in a number of church tower rebuilds in the postwar years. (DWS)*

The *'direct hit scored later'* was an even closer call for John Swift of 'F' Troop, 69th Field Regt.. It will be remembered that John was closely associated with the Hallams in carrying out Forward Observation duties for his artillery and spent much of his time in the Battalion front line from where he could report back on target coordination. John had spent some period of time in the church tower at Zetten which he and his officer had been using as an O.P. And just minutes after he came down from his perch, the spire took a direct hit.

Patrols were sent north at this time to penetrate beyond the Rijn Wetering in an attempt to gain intelligence on enemy positions, but strong currents created difficulties. The Wetering was a considerable water channel which more or less cut the 'Island in half from east to west and, generally speaking, marked the dividing line between Allied and German forces during the stalemate winter period. Patrols did manage to probe as far forward as Indoomik including one led by Lt. Simmil but made no contact with the enemy other than hearing splashing noises! An opportunity was taken to install snipers in a house on the road just north of Talitha Kumi in the early hours of the 13th. Snipers installed in another house in this area were mystified by a man they reported moving about who was not one of theirs and a night standing patrol in the same house reported him again on the 15th. One patrol man had even tried to converse with him but was ignored!

This was soon forgotten when a German patrol in two boats came along and started clearing the houses by use of grenades and machine carbines. The patrol was accompanied by two men in a canoe and the whole group proceeded south towards Talitha Kumi, passing the house in which the two Hallams snipers and a signaller were installed, without clearing it. This patrol then retraced their steps and came back along the road minus the pair in the canoe and entered the sniper's house where they stayed for fifteen minutes. Although they did not detect the Bn. men who were concealed upstairs, they did find and remove a steel helmet and a No.18 Set battery which had presumably been left lying around and then they left the building. The sniper group waited until dusk and then came back to the Talitha Kumi area in time to warn Lt. Nicholson who was just about to lead a patrol through the danger area. He might have been walking into an ambush set up by the men in the canoe who must have still been in the vicinity. He was ordered by 'C' Coy. HQ. to proceed with his patrol anyway, but was shelled every time he approached the bridge over the Wetering, making it fairly obvious that he was being well observed.

Meanwhile, better progress was being made on the right of the Hallams sector where a patrol of six picked men led by Lt. Jesse Mitchinson had succeeded, on the night of the 14/15th February, in occupying a farm called De Hoeven which was well forward and about 1000 meters to the north east of Talitha Kumi. This position provided a very good outlook on part of the enemy Forward Defence Line at Randwijk and also views over the Lower Rhine (Neder Rijn) towards Renkum on the north side of the river. It may be remembered that Jesse Mitchinson was wounded in the action which took place at Fontenay le Pesnel in June the previous year. After recovery and various movements, Jesse found himself in Annan,

❖ *Bridge across the Wetering at Talitha Kumi. It is from here that Lt. Nicholson attempted his patrol (see above) and also Lt. Greens probable starting point (see page 302) when he set off on a relief patrol towards De Hoeven Farm which lies to the northeast, in the fields beyond the gap in the trees at left centre. It was here also, that a number of Hallams men died when their canvas boat was dragged over a large mine. (DWS)*

Scotland with the job of escorting a company of Black Watch soldiers across to the continent, to be handed over at a reception area. From there he made his way back to the Hallams, who were by now at Nijmegen, and was quickly integrated and given a platoon in one of the rifle companies.

Jesse Mitchinson...

My platoon did a number of successful patrols in as much as we reached our objectives and sustained no casualties. One of our tasks was to check farms along the Linge (Wetering) to see if they were being occupied by the Germans. There was nobody there but I remember stopping at one farm which was high enough to form a small island and there was still a couple of pigs and some chickens. Some of the lads were out of the boat like lightning and a few chickens were brought back to supplement our packed rations.

I did a patrol on the outskirts of Indoornik and again we were fortunate enough not to bump into the enemy. My instructions were to see if the end house was occupied and when we got there we found that it had been set up as a machine gun post but there was nobody in the building at the time we arrived. It was obvious that these places were being occupied only by day as observation posts and then, as was common German practice, being vacated at night.

De Hoeven was a two story farm house with a windowed attic and was at right angles to an avenue of poplar trees. To get there by way of Het Slop farm on the Wetering, in canvas boats and at night, I used a compass aiming for the middle of the row of trees and arrived at a point to the left of the buildings. I heard a door flapping in the wind and I thought, 'Well, there's nobody there.' I said to Cpl. Smith and another man, 'I want you to go up the road towards the house and we will cover you' but when they got out over the side of the boat, their feet wouldn't touch the ground. We'd got waders on so when they went down to their waist the water just flowed into their waders, so we had to pull them back into the boat which made a hell of a noise that broke the silence. It was obvious that there was nobody there so I decided to go in.

The front door was on the gable end facing north and it opened up into a very large room with stairs going up on the left hand side to the first floor. Unlike most of the other Dutch houses we had been in, it had been stripped of all its furnishings and the place was bare but when we got inside it was warm and you could smell the sweat of people having been there. I collapsed and sank the canvas assault boat so that if anyone came by they wouldn't spot it. We were all absolutely soaking wet but we went up into the attic because we could get a better wireless signal from there and it also had windows from which you could get the best views. We needed to be alert because it was obvious that the Germans were occupying this place only during the day, just as they had been doing in the house at Indoornik. Unfortunately, the rest of my platoon was sent up next morning in broad daylight so they must have been in clear view of the enemy who then shelled and machine gunned us all day but didn't do much damage. It wasn't a very easy place to defend but the C.O. had sent a message to ask for us to hold on to the place for another 24 hours when we would be relieved. When it came, I was quite glad to get out of the place.

On the 16th, a fighting patrol moved via De Taart to clear Talitha Kumi so as to become better established there and at dawn on the 17th, the patrol at De Hoeven was relieved. However, in the early evening the next day, a German officer in a canoe accompanied by four men in a boat were observed approaching the farm, who must have been unaware that the building was occupied. The Hallams held their fire too long, thus enabling the German patrol to infiltrate the barns and one man even managed to get through one of the windows in the farmhouse but was injured by a grenade. After some confusion, the German patrol managed to escape in their boat but were seen to have at least two casualties, one perhaps seriously. Sgt. Bradshaw decided to give chase but shortly afterwards, his boat ran aground in the mist that was developing and then another two boat loads of enemy were seen approaching, so the Sgt. withdrew his men back to the farm. His Platoon was relieved at 0730 hrs. on the 19th by another led by Sgt. Parkin of 'A' Coy.

It was now planned to build up strength north of the Wetering with a platoon permanently based at De Hoeven, one in a house on the northern tip of Indoornik and one in Talitha Kumi with a Company HQ. set up in this latter place, but in a house on the south side of the Wetering. This task was assigned to 'B' Coy. on the 20 February to be carried out in the next few days, but things went wrong from the start. The Indoornik position was found to be already occupied by the enemy so a house further south was adopted. Then one of the boats taking the platoon to Talitha Kumi ran aground just outside the building which they were about to occupy.

The men got out and whilst they were dragging it clear, a mine was detonated. The massive explosion killed two men, wounded three and another five were reported missing. These five men must have been identified at a later date, as subsequent Commonwealth War Graves Commission records do not show any Hallams missing in action on that day. Five Hallams men who did die on that day are, however, recorded as buried in Arnhem-Oosterbeek Military Cemetery. This is significant because if they had been recovered shortly after their death, they would probably have been buried in Nijmegen-Jonkerbosch Military Cemetery. They were Privates Antcliffe, Fellows, Locket, Peters and Yorke. The two reported killed (recovered) in the explosion, are among three men who died that day and buried in Nijmegen-Jonkerbosch, Privates Fletcher, Hutchinson and Lea. One of these must have been a sixth man reported missing on that day in the War Diary, but recovered not long afterwards.

❖ *De Hoeven Farm viewed from the north during Summer, 2000. This was the poplar lined road down which Cliff Campin's patrol set off to investigate the situation in the village of Indoornik. The old trees have been cut down and a new row planted. Look carefully at the animals in the field on the left hand side. There is a mixture of Deer, Lama and one of a number of Ostrich!! Can be seen on the extreme left of picture.(DWS)*

John Wollerton...
I went back to the 'Island' and had one or two unpleasant tasks to do. There was one where we took forward a boat with supplies and more men and at this time the Germans had mined the bridges and put holes in the middle so that you had to walk along the side. They'd taken this boat over, pulling it with about four to each side when suddenly this big mine went up and stripped the flesh off them from the knees up to the shoulders and one head went a hundred yards into the air. It was a mess!

In the meantime normal reliefs were being carried out and De Hoeven was taken over by a platoon of 'D' Coy. led by Lt. Green. During the evening of the 20th he carried out a patrol from there with one section, which was meant to scout the area prior to 'B' Coy. taking over all the positions north of the Wetering.

Lance Corporal Clifford G. Campin, had seen service with 10 D.L.I. and the 5 E.Y.R. 'A' Coy. of the latter had been part of the recently disbanded 50th Division in December, 1944, as a result of irreplaceable losses suffered by that unit and he had been finally transferred to the Hallamshires. In fact this company had enabled a new 'D' Coy. to be reformed. However, he was now part of Lt. Green's platoon and was chosen to go on the subsequent patrol. His description follows closely that reported in the War Diary for the 20 February.

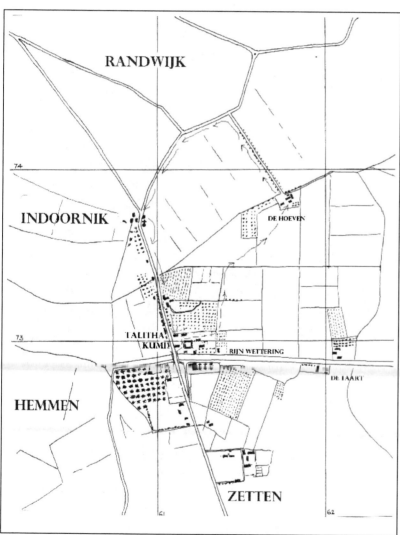

Cliff Campin...
With regard to life on the 'Island', from my recollection it was 'hell on water'. It may have been a little more acceptable in July and August, but in the winter of 1944-45 bearing in mind that it was the worst for many years, it was terrible. Patrolling in canvas boats was like being a sitting duck without wings. Nevertheless, if it was the intention of the 'powers that be' to gain ground by paddling your way forward and occupying the odd building, isolated or otherwise, then that is what you did.

It so happened that on one occasion during February 45, I set off with other members of a Platoon, for an isolated farm, well forward of our F.D.L. As far as I can tell we had two canvas assault boats, that held about 28 combatants, say 14 to each craft. For some reason our own Platoon Commander had been substituted for an inexperienced Lieutenant (Green) from the 2 Kensingtons, which normally fulfilled the role as Brigade M.M.Gs. using water cooled Vickers guns from behind the lines to provide harassing fire.

Map of area to the north of Zetten showing probable route (arrows) of patrol led by Lt. Green and in which Cliff Campin took part. The level crossing was just off picture at the bottom. (DWS)

328

The movement was carried out in daylight, and there is little doubt that on reflection we could be seen for miles as we paddled towards the so-called firm base. I have no idea from whence we embarked, but by looking at a fairly good map of the area printed in 1986, it would appear that it was north of Zetten, somewhere near the road leading to Indoornik. With further study, the only place that we could possibly have headed for was the farm at De Hoeven. It is isolated and shows a tree lined road leading from the farm towards Randwijk, this I remember quite clearly as I shall mention later.

As we approached the farm we noticed that it was possible to paddle into the open ended cattle shed, and conveniently disembark into the manger. As darkness began to fall we were busy checking communications and preparing defences, and I suggested that instructions would be given by the C.O. that a patrol would have to be launched from the base, and knowing my luck I would be on it. We didn't have to wait very long before this was confirmed, and the Lieutenant was to be the patrol leader. One section was earmarked for the task, and we eventually set off at about 2am in one of the boats, on what was to be an extremely 'hair raising' adventure. We paddled slowly and quietly down the avenue of trees, or should I say the poplar lined road, from the farm towards the German lines in the direction of Randwijk, and turned left to approach Indoornik from the north. The object of the operation was to determine whether the enemy were in occupation of the village, and as far as I know, they were using the church as an O.P.

Moving slowly down through the village, the church with it's large spire loomed up on this ghostly February night, on our left side. Perhaps I should have said port side! We were directly adjacent to the building when there was a swishing sound in the air followed by an explosion on the starboard side of the boat, to be followed quickly by a second exploding in roughly the same area. One or two of the chaps jumped overboard and there was a certain amount of panic which was not helped by the Lieutenant saying that we had hit a Teller mine. Had this been the case none of us would have been alive to tell the tale. We dragged 'the divers' back on board, the prime concern now being to get away as fast as possible. Without further hesitation, we set off to the north side of the church, keeping close to the side. We then headed in a SE direction in order to calm everybody down and skirt the village, just in case the enemy had established strong points farther down the road towards Zetten.

It is difficult for me now to understand the vulnerability of being in a canvas boat in such a situation, the enemy were obviously able to wipe us out, but they had no wish to give the position of their O.P. away, and so used grenades instead of machine guns to dispatch us. This they achieved, partly, but their presence was obvious, once the grenades were thrown.

I cannot say how we navigated our way back to our own lines but we did so, let us just say we were lucky. The Company HQ. seemed to be established in a Community building of some

❖ *The church at Indoornik, now completely rebuilt on the same site. It must have been in the then flooded foreground that the boat patrol paddled by from the left and 'abandoned ship' when two stick grenades were thrown at them in the darkness. They then doubled back behind the church and made their way down the back fields to Talitha Kumi. The steel framed bell tower is a very recent addition and was dedicated on 29 August, 1999 (DWS)*

sort, and as we approached through the gates, there were many dead bodies in the water at the entrance, victims of a land mine that had been detonated by the weight of a boat as it scraped along the ground. Again it is difficult to remember things that happened some 50 years ago, but as I entered the HQ. it appeared that the O.C. and his 2 i/c, were deeply distressed at the loss of men outside the building. My report on the situation at the church may not have appeared to be very significant, nevertheless Battalion HQ. was notified by RT and I was rather taken aback when told that my patrol was to return to the church. This to me was sheer suicide and I let my feelings be known, but who was I to argue? After all, I and my patrol were replaceable, at least this was the impression I had and still do for that matter.

If we were to return to the church I would decide how it was to be done. The boat spelled death so it was discarded and we waded forward towards the church from the south along the Zetten road. I had a 'pole man' in front of me to measure the depth of water so that we could avoid sinking into craters along the way. The water was chest high in some parts and never lower than three feet (1 Metre) as we waded forward. At this point I should say that we had to leave the Lieutenant at the Company HQ. as he was in no fit state to carry on. The water must have been like ice, but I suppose the adrenaline helped to overcome the effect of the water.

As we approached a group of houses on the right side of the road and south of the church, there was a clearing, and the patrol must have been silhouetted against the grey skyline, which presented an ideal target. Machine guns and sub machine guns from an enemy position inside the houses opened up, bullets sprayed through the water and we all dived below the surface, reversed our direction and struggled back to our Company HQ. By this time I think we may have convinced the C.O. that the enemy were in the village in some strength. As a result of our exploits we were ordered back towards Zetten. I cannot remember what we were told but we were pleased at the thought of finding a dry uniform. The business of wading back towards Zetten soon became a problem in as much that it became deeper and deeper. I therefore told my patrol to seek shelter in the upper floor of a nearby house whilst a volunteer and I attempted to seek help. This we must have achieved because I remember waking up in a Nijmegen hospital, my legs were all colours of the rainbow. I was given 48 hrs in which to recover before returning to my unit and I must have slept the whole time because I can't remember the nurses, eating food or anything about the place.

On return I learnt that the farmhouse had been blown up by the Dutch S.S. and that one of our platoons had either been killed or taken prisoner. This must have happened very soon after our patrol had left the building. So ends my story and, as a matter of interest, it is only in the last year or so that I've related such stories to anyone. I think there was a tendency after the war to forget but, oddly enough, as one gets older the past comes flooding back.

The remainder of Lt. Greens platoon at De Hoeven were still there at 1820 hrs. on the evening of the 21st when shells began to fall in the area and continued intermittently all evening. One shell made a direct hit on the farmhouse causing only one slight casualty and machine gun fire from the direction of Randwijk came through the windows. All was quiet at 2255 hrs. when part of the relief platoon of 'B' Coy. led by Sgt. Newman arrived. Some of his platoon had lost their way and didn't arrive until 0030 hrs. Shells again began to fall around De Hoeven at 0200 hrs. accompanied by machine gun fire. This was now counteracted by artillery fire put down on suspected enemy positions in Randwijk and on the roads north of the farm. Enemy firing ceased at 0341 hrs and Sgt. Newman reported in by RT that he thought the counter fire had been accurate but this was the last that anything was heard from De Hoeven. At 0440 hrs., 'B' Coy. at Talitha Kumi reported a large fire in the direction of the farm where ammunition could be heard exploding. A recce patrol led by Lt. Mitchinson was sent out and returned with the news that De Hoeven was gutted, with no sign of Sgt. Newman and his platoon of thirty men.

A few rumours rattled around about the reasons for the platoons demise, ranging from a direct hit by a stray flying bomb to the whole platoon having deserted! The latter was quickly dispelled by those who knew the character of Sgts. Newman and Potter and one other who is named in the War Diary as 'Spandau' Spencer! The truth came the following evening, care of Bremen Radio in Germany which announced, 'Troops of the Dutch S.S. eliminated an enemy strong point in Holland, capturing a number of prisoners from the 49 Division'.

De Hoeven had not been an easy place to defend. The two story house was surrounded by water up to two metres deep in places, except for a narrow muddy margin around its walls but it was flanked on the west side by two very large barns one of which they used as a boat house! These buildings badly obscured the very important field of view to the west and could not provide a suitable defensive position in themselves to give protection from that direction as there were no openings or windows in them.

Sam Woolley had joined the York and Lancaster Regiment as a regular in 1931. and when war broke out had been involved in the British Expeditionary Force operations in France. He had eventually escaped that ordeal through St. Malo and disembarked at Weymouth. Then, after being moved here and there which included a nights sleep on the steps of Wembley Stadium, he found his way to the Regimental Depot at Pontefract. He was later posted to the Hallamshires and joined them in Iceland in January, 1941, travelling in the same group as John Wollerton.

Collapsible Canvas Boat of the type used on many patrols by the Hallams beyond the Zetten area. This photograph is obviously posed in a relatively safe area but shows the way in which men would have been equipped for such duties. One man in the bow is armed with a Bren Gun and another (behind him nearest the camera) holds a Sten Gun. Although there are only five others providing the paddle power, it may have been possible to squeeze another five on board, but this would have tested capacity to the limits, especially when weapons, equipment and stores had to be carried. (SNL)

Sam was now part of the ill fated platoon that was captured by the enemy at De Hoeven Farm. His relief group had hardly settled after the shelling when they were attacked and taken very much by surprise. The Germans were apparently equally surprised as their attack had been planned to go in against the depleted platoon who had just been relieved. However, when they saw what was going on, they just delayed the attack.

Sam Woolly. This photograph was taken by the German press in Arnhem after his capture at De Hoeven..
(Mr. S. Woolley)

Sam Woolley...

It was about half an hour from Zetten to De Hoeven... ...I landed in the last boat and we went in through a cow shed which was attached to the house. There was one room on the left hand side and a small room on the right which I occupied near a window along with another youth and there was a passage straight down the middle.

The first indication of any trouble was when a great explosion and hole appeared in the wall. I'm sat taking these wellingtons off and putting me boots on and I'd only got one changed when this thing happened. Smirthwaite were sat there and of course he got the full blast. We had an oil lamp hanging up and the first thing I did was knock that out and dashed back to this window. It was already occupied by somebody else so, I went into one of the other rooms and that was when I saw Sgt. Joe Newton. Him and a Lance Sgt. were in there and I'd only been in there a few minutes when an explosion and hole appeared in that wall. I heard Joe gurgling and then go quiet and I thought, 'He's dead'. Shortly after that I thought I saw a machine gun barrel just come over the window ledge, you know, as though they were going to spray around the room. Anyway I told the lads to keep clear of the window. Shortly after that the signaller came from upstairs and said that the wireless were out of commission and he thought the place was on fire.

When the Germans came to the end of the cow shed they just shouted, 'Come out Tommy it's all over, we've surrounded the house and it's no good carrying on.' Cpl. Roberts (ex artillery man) said, 'What we going to do Sam?' and I said, 'We better get out, it's no good carrying on.'

One of these Germans spoke good English and he said, 'I'm very sorry for you blokes because we were actually surrounding this place ready to attack when we saw you coming up in the boats. So, we delayed it and let them get out, then we started at you.'

The following account of Sam's march into captivity was compiled from a few notes made in an earlier, untaped, conversation. He took part in a more detailed audiotaped interview at a much later date from which the above was extracted...

It was thought by Sam, at the time, that both Sgt. Newton and Cpl. Smirthwaite were both killed but it was confirmed at the end of the war that Cpl. Smirthwaite was taken alive but badly wounded and lost overboard in an attempt to escape. His body was never recovered and his name is recorded on the memorial to the Missing at Groesbeek.

The rest of the men were taken to a German R.A.P. on the south side of the river where one man (a South Staffs Regt. man according to Sam) was given treatment for an injured leg. This casualty was left behind and, according to Sam, was not seen or heard of again by them (this may have been L/Sgt. Potter who is known to have suffered a bad leg injury). The remaining 29 men continued their journey into captivity still in small craft and eventually arrived in Arnhem. Here they were placed in a church for the night and next morning marched away to the north under an armed guard of Dutch S.S. As the day drew to a close the group was halted and spent their second night in derelict houses by the side of the road. No food was provided up to this time. In the morning Sam and another prisoner, a signaller whose name he could not recall, were placed in a car and driven to a town, the name of which Sam could not remember.

It became apparent on arrival that they had been singled out for interrogation and to this end were treated separately. Little or no pressure was placed on Sam to divulge more than the usual number, rank and name and he was marched into a room where a very smartly dressed officer was sat at a desk. This man leaned forward and began to turn the pages of a very large book which Sam recognized as some sort of reference manual relating to British military insignia. Eventually the pages fell open to reveal the familiar Tiger and Rose cap badge of the York and Lancaster Regiment. 'This is your Regiment is it not?' said the officer. 'No comment,' replied Sam and so it went on for a while with questions that he didn't know the answers to anyway. Then an orderly walked into the room carrying a steaming hot plate of food which he placed on the desk. Sam was starving and wrongly thought that he was about to be enticed to reveal information. This was not to be, however, as he was then lead out of the building where he was reunited with the signaller. The pair of them were driven back to rejoin the other prisoners and the march continued.

At some time during this part of the trek, and not recalled by Sam, a photograph was taken as the group straggled along a tree lined road. (it was later used in a newspaper but the 'cutting' is in too bad a condition to be included here). It seems likely that the shot was taken from a stationary vehicle by the side of the road and in the path of the march. There are two guards, wearing peaked field service caps, and the prisoner in centre foreground is Sam Woolley. There are no more than 20 men, including guards, in the frame and therefore at least 10 have already passed out of camera shot. Sam Woolley is recognizable from another photograph, in the same series, taken of him as he passed through Arnhem and also published.

Some of the prisoners were occasionally allowed to ride bicycles belonging to the guards and Sam remembers once when he was using one, dropping back well behind the main group. He had a strong urge to break away and escape but the men had all been warned that any attempt to do so would result in three of the remaining prisoners being shot.

The guards were all Dutch S.S. and one of them spoke good English. Sam recollects that this man wore a remnant of silk parachute for a scarf, probably a relic of the 1st Airborne's abortive attempt to take the bridge at Arnhem in September of the previous year. When asked by Sam why he had become a member of the 'S.S.', the guard said that it had seemed the right thing to do in the earlier years when Germany was the dominant, all conquering power. Later, during the march, this same guard was greeted by a woman who came out of a house along the way. She flung her arms about him in such a way as to make Sam feel that this was the man's mother or some close relative. Previously, any attempt by civilians to come out of their homes to view the men as they passed by was met with raised Schmeisers and snapped orders to get back indoors, which the people instantly obeyed.

At one stage of the march Sam became aware of a Dutch civilian on a bicycle who repeatedly turned up whenever a road junction was reached. This man would stop and watch the group at the same time raising one hand to his face where he allowed two fingers to be laid across his forehead to form a secretive 'V' sign. On realizing this occurrence Sam mentioned it to another prisoner, telling him to watch out for the man at the next cross road. Sure enough, he was there again but although Sam felt sure the man was attempting to convey something more than just a sign of encouragement but, fearing he might give the game away he made no acknowledgment and walked on.

The captives eventually arrived in a town which Sam, on reflection, believed to have been Apeldoorn. They were refused entry to a small P.O.W. camp and spent the night in a building which Sam thought was either a school or hospital. Next day they boarded the carriages of a train which headed east. The train was attacked by aircraft as it passed through a cutting where the locomotive exploded. Everyone, including civilians, began to spill out onto the track in an effort to escape. The prisoners were rounded up and continued on foot. Eventually, they were placed in trucks and later transferred to another train which carried them into Germany. Finally incarcerated in Stalag X1B, north of Hanover, they remained in this camp until liberated by a British armoured unit at the end of the war. The audiotape, mentioned above, contains much more information about Sam's earlier exploits in France, 1940, as well as how he got back to his home in Catcliffe after being liberated in Germany, 1945.

Flood waters were now beginning to recede and on 26 February, 'A' Coy. was withdrawn from all positions north of the Wetering and the Carrier platoon was installed in the house that had previously been occupied by the Rifle company HQ. The rest of the month passed off fairly quietly with the Pioneer platoon making an unsuccessful attempt to bridge the Wetering at Hemmen, owing to the stream being still too wide and the currents too strong.

15 cwt. Truck negotiating flooded streets in Zetten area. This photograph was provided by Harry Portas, quite independently of the comments made by Les Sewell ! (Mr. Portas)

Les Sewell...
Later, when The Battalion was based on the left flank, the carriers were near Zetten. CQMS Peck and some Army reporters were shot up in this area by a German aircraft. This happened to Harry Portas whilst driving a truck and, of course, in that situation you can't hear them coming. I'd moved my stores into a boot factory, I remember seeing all these cobblers lasts lying around.

At this time I had a badly swollen leg and couldn't stand it any longer so I went to the doctors. I was put on an ambulance, then a Dakota, and ended up in a hospital near Tilberg. That was 1st of April and also Easter Sunday, 1945. Next morning I was put on another ambulance to a place near Brussels and then to a convalescence centre on the Belgian coast. I was granted 'Blighty' leave and at the time the war had just finished. On return I was sent to a selection centre and my leg still wasn't right, so I was given a job as a clerk. After some more leave I was finally demobbed in the September. After one or two jobs over the next ten years I got my old job back at Greenup and Thompsons and retired from there in 1973 and my last boss was a previous C.O. of the Hallams, a man called Hutton.

On 1 March, Jesse Mitchinson took a patrol out to the area of De Hoeven again and came under fire as he approached the ruined farm. The Germans withdrew in a boat but it was observed that they fired a red flare as they got clear, which was followed immediately by mortar fire being brought down on the vacated farm. A few days later, enemy positions in Indoornik were secretly infiltrated by the Hallams and a red flare was fired from the position. It had the immediate effect of bringing mortar fire down on the German forward position. This trick may well have been carried out by L/Cpl. Metcalfe and another sniper who were on the German side of the Wetering at this time. They were immediately surrounded by over a dozen Germans, but when ordered to surrender, made a dash for freedom by diving into the dike with their wellingtons on. They swam to the opposite side under fire and climbed out minus their wellingtons, then ran barefooted back to the Battalion area.

On 7 March, 1945, Lt. Col. Trevor Hart Dyke relinquished his command of the Hallamshire Battalion which passed to Major Michael C.K. Halford. The latter officer was in England at the time and temporary command was given to Major Barlow Poole (KOYLI), pending his return. Various attacks and patrols in the Talitha Kumi area were carried out by the Hallams under the commands of Lts. Davies, Kemp and Dyson but little contact was made. It appeared now that the enemy were pulling back and a great deal of activity was heard coming from the direction of Randwijk. At the time, 11 March, the Battalion was relieved by 2 S.W.B. and went into a rest area near Druten. Meanwhile, Chris Somers had returned from the Battle School in Belgium but did not stay long as he was granted a spot of U.K. Leave.

Chris Somers (Diary)...
After doing one course I returned to find the Battalion at Druten on the Nijmegen side of the Rhine. A safe spot apart from daily shelling. We had another dance in Nijmegen while here. Lieutenant Colonel Hart-Dyke had left us for India and Mike Halford now commanded the Battalion. I returned to England for leave and got back on the 3 April as they were clearing the Island capturing Rijkerswaad and Elden.

The Hallams remained in the rest area until the 26th March, when they moved back to the eastern sector of the 'Island'. Here they took over positions from the 1 L.R. at Haalderen. The area was relatively quiet and the Battalion did not stay long. It was relieved by 2 E.R. on the 29th and moved to Oosterhout where preparations and training were got underway for moves which would finally clear the 'Island'. A night patrol on the 30th was led by Lt. Jesse Mitchinson to reconnoitre enemy dispositions, prior to Operation 'DESTROYER' in which the Hallams were to clear the town of Zand.

❖ *Above: Part of the shopping precinct at Rijkerswoerd today.*
❖ *Right: Scene at a street Craft Fair in the village of Elden. (both DWS)*

In the first three days of April, clearance of the eastern side of the 'Island' via a bridgehead over the Wetering at Huis de Karbrug was swift and the small towns of Zand, Rijkerswaard and parts of Elden were quickly taken by 146 and 147 Brigades with the support of 'flail' tanks. These were equipped with a special anti-mine device which was crude but effective. A series of chains were attached to a high speed rotating drum held between brackets fixed to the front of the tank. As the machine moved forward, the free ends of the chains detonated mines in its path by literally beating the ground to create a safe 'carpet' for both itself and follow-up troops. It must be said that damage was regularly inflicted on these vehicles through being in close proximity to the many exploding mines and a number were knocked out in this instance.

Casualties were also inflicted on the Battalion during this phase including two officers but troops were now moving carefully right along the edge of the Lower Rhine where men of the 49th Division must have had a good view of Arnhem on the opposite bank. Although none of them knew it at that moment, it was to be the final prize which would have to be taken by force of arms as far as the Battalion was concerned. It would also be the final resting place for some of those involved, a particularly sad irony in view of the fact that the war was now virtually over.

Chris Somers (Diary)...
David Morris and Keith Robinson were wounded from 'D' Coy, so I took over 2 i/c of this company at Elden. Patrols crossed the Rhine near Arnhem the same night. We soon handed over this area and crossed the Rhine further eastwards ready for the attack, on Arnhem.

Left : George Pape and Dennis Townsend point to their final objective for the publicity cameras. (Mr. Townsend)
❖ *Above : Ferry crossing on the Pannerdens Canal at Huissen. Besides the pontoon bridge built across this obstacle, all manner of water craft were used to get troops, vehicles and equipment into position on the other side for the final assault on Arnhem (DWS)*

It was recorded in the War Diary that a Hallams patrol was the first of the 49th Div. troops to cross the Lower Rhine. The privilege of leading this patrol went to Lt. Farmer on the evening of 3 April and brought to an end the number of Divisional 'firsts' claimed by the Battalion.

These included first tank destroyed, first to cross the Seine and first to step over the Belgian/Holland border. The Battalion was now brought out of the line again and back to Oosterhout on the 5th in preparation for the final assault on Arnhem which was given the code word 'ANGER'. This was to involve a crossing of the Lower Rhine to the east of Arnhem (Pannerden Canal) which in turn would require a crossing of the River Ijssel westwards, to break into the city.

The initial assault, led by 56 Brigade was commenced at 2315 hrs. on 12 April. Operation 'ANGER' was underway and at 0500 hrs. the next morning, the Hallams were called to 146 Brigade concentration area in orchards just east Westervoort to be embarked on 'Buffalo' amphibious vehicles for the crossing of the Ijssel. At 1630 hrs. 'B' Coy. Took over positions from 4 Lincs on the railway track junctions about one mile east of Arnhem road bridge (now the famous Bridge Too Far) which had by this time been demolished by the Germans.

Les Gill...
As we moved towards Arnhem from the east through a small village (Westervoort?), we came across something that I felt was both disgusting and disappointing. There was a flat cart on top of which was a lass in a chair and her hair was being cut off so that she had no hair left and there were other women being held waiting for the same treatment. I took my own decision in this case to stop it.

We had three or four war dogs and they were most useful to us at Arnhem because there were big tenement buildings there which had been brought down by the use of our new thirty-six barrelled mortars. All barrels could be fired simultaneously and concentrated hits at a distance of about quarter of a mile shattered everything. So when we got to Arnhem we had to clear some areas and search through wrecked buildings with the dogs. The dog that I was with sensed that there was somebody in this building which allowed me to take extra care. The result was that one German died and I stayed alive, we were too close to use weapons and I killed him with my hands. The Alsatian dog had given me the advantage of knowing that someone was there.

The Battalion now moved in a northerly direction to secure pre-planned objectives which included a large army barrack complex and crucial road junctions beyond. It was during the action which took place at one of these road junctions that Lt. Ron Davies was killed, the last Hallamshire Battalion officer to be killed in action during this war. Three ORs. were also killed and 27 wounded in the taking of Arnhem.

Arnold Whiteley...
We crossed the Rhine (Ijssel) in Buffaloes (amphibious vehicles) to take Arnhem and it wasn't a vicious affair. When we got into it, it wasn't a long or hard job. We got a picture of how the Airborne must have fought, I remember just an ordinary house and in the backyard of this house there was a grave with twenty-five in it, It just said 25 British Soldat..

Many German soldiers were now giving themselves up as they had already taken a massive pounding from artillery with waves of Typhoon ground attack aircraft that delivered accurate rocket and cannon fire before the ground assault forces went in. For those bewildered men, some of whom may have witnessed the slaughter at Falaise (south of Caen), this would have been terrifying indeed and all too

❖ *Part of the Army Barracks (now Saksen Weimar Kazerne) that was captured by the Hallamshire Battalion on the 13 April. (DWS)*

much for them to bear. Surrender or capture, when it came, must have been a welcome release from it all. Add to this the fact that most of them would know in their minds by now, that they were fighting for a lost cause. In the miles of wartime film footage that is available today, the expressions on some of the individual faces of a beaten German Army must have, and did, draw compassion from all but the most hardened and bitter victors.

Chris Somers (Diary)...
This (the attack) took place on 13 April. We followed the Lincolns over, crossing in Buffaloes. We had to spend most of the first day sitting in full view of the Boche on the hill top. Needless to say we were heavily shelled. By night fall we had passed through the Lincolns and had reached the observation tower on top of the hill. Next morning our signallers found a party of Germans in this tower which we had been strolling past the night before!

John Wollerton...
At some time I was transferred to 'C' Coy. under Mike Lonsdale-Cooper and I stayed with him until the end of the war, including the crossing of the Rhine. Just before the crossing, we received quite a heavy stonking and one officer, who had newly joined us from an R.A. Regiment and complete with leather cane, disappeared I regret to say. Although being 2i/c of the Coy. by now, I had to take over his platoon without a slit trench, which didn't bother me but it was the fact that he had disappeared which still rankles me. I remember his name but I've no idea what became of him to this day.

We got off these DUKWs and marched into Arnhem and we proceeded to a high tower. I was sent on a patrol to eliminate a machine gun post on the southern end of the bridge and before I went out, was told not to fire on a top hatted gentleman and sure enough, before I left, a Jeep came racing in and with two men wearing top hats. They were men of the S.A.S. and that was the first time I'd met any of them in the war. We went out to the objective but it was found to be abandoned. There was no firing on us at all and then, coming down a road, a beautiful maiden shouted, 'The Germans have gone!' and then she put her arms around me and kissed me but I still made the lads dig in. I'd lost all trust in human beings by this time but now, thankfully, I was proved to be wrong and that was the end of the war for me.

Chris Somers (Diary)...
'A' Coy. had quite a hand to hand struggle in this part but we were lucky. We advanced through the graveyard next day in full view, we discovered, of a Gerry position in a field. Luckily, his gun must have jammed and we were able to capture him. There was much shelling during the night and some airborne passed through us in Jeeps, but did not get far until the Armoured Division went through.

The tower mentioned by both Chris and John was probably the same as that which stood on high ground near the barracks. It gave a commanding view of the battlefield and was obviously used as an O.P. by the Germans.(THD)

It is not known which graveyard Chris mentions here but the area just to the west of the barracks is dominated by large German and Russian burial grounds. A graveyard may already have existed there before the war.

Ken Godfrey...
I missed the Rhine crossing because I was in the team chosen to run the cross country race for the Division in the Corps Championships, and we were in training at that time. I rejoined the Battalion in Arnhem and they put me on guard the first night I was back, because they thought I had been idling off. I will always remember standing in the slit trench where we could hear some lions roaring that were still in the Arnhem Zoo and we felt more scared of them than we did of the Gerries!

Arthur Green...
I went over the Rhine on a pontoon bridge constructed by the R.Es. which was quite an experience. It was just wide enough to take tracked and wheeled vehicles and as you went along the bridge seemed to go down in front of your vehicle and came up again behind you. It was a funny sensation and you had to keep in the same gear all the way over. I noticed the Navy was there as well with motor-torpedo boats and other types and they were all getting people across.

When we got across, we turned left around the back of Arnhem. From what I gather, the Hallams were the first into Arnhem. I wasn't there with them, by the way, I was never the first in anywhere! Later on, we followed them through and I remember being billeted in a housing estate and there were no civilians about anywhere. Gerry had ripped the floorboards up and stacked sand bags around the hole to take shelter in and this place was a dentists house with the special chair in the front room and what have you. One day I jumped down into the hole, about four feet deep, when there was a bit of shelling going on and my tin hat came off and followed me in. It hit the back of my head and cut me and I thought I'd been seriously wounded!

The bridge that Arthur mentions above, is probably the one that spanned the Pannerdens Canal near Doornenburg and code named 'GREMLIN' which was used by a large proportion of the 49 Divisional build and follow-up in the crossings that led to the encirclement and final capture of Arnhem.

The Battalion was concentrated in the barracks on 15 April but the next day was given the task of clearing the road running parallel to the Ijssel through De Steeg and up as far as the town of Deiren. The trip was uneventful and the enemy along the road put up little

Hallams relax in the garden of a suburban house near the barracks in Arnhem. The man near the window (second from the left) is Arthur Saunders and all the men seem to be very absorbed by the magazines which must have been all Dutch to most of them! (Mr. Saunders)

or no resistance. At first glance, the War Diary for 16 April would seem to suggest a misprint or something not quite explained. The entry is quoted in full so as not to cloud the issue... '*The Battalion left at 0600 hrs. riding on tanks; at the same time two mattresses* (yes! Mattresses) *were brought down on ROSENDAAL* (an area on the NE outskirts of Arnhem) *where it was thought we might meet some resistance.*' The term was found to refer to the ground spread of the new multi-barrelled mortar weapon mentioned by Les Gill (page 337) and no more strange than if a 'carpet' of bombs had been laid, the latter term sometimes used in the context of aerial bombardment.

Battalion HQ. remained in the barracks until the 18th when the Hallams were moved to a concentration area at Wolfheze on the western edge of the city in the area which the 1st Airborne Division had used as a drop zone in September the previous year. Training was carried out here in preparation for a sweep to clear Western Holland but this was postponed when the Germans threatened to flood large areas. The Hallams remained at Wolfheze until the 26th and then moved further west to Ede.

Arnold Whiteley...
Then we got through Arnhem to a place called Wolfhese. After Arhnem it was more or less over for us, that was April the 13th and we moved up to a place called Ede. We held positions there and so the war finished for us a fortnight before the rest. There must have been a meeting between senior officers and the German Command. They (the Dutch) were starving and they'd agreed to let food go through on certain routes. There was also a threat that if we advanced any further they'd open flood gates and flood Northern Holland and it would have taken a lot to reclaim. So, we were stalemates about a fortnight before the war finished.

Chris Somers (Diary)...
After that quiet advance to Dieren, sitting on Sherman tanks, we moved to Ede in front of the Grebbe line. Here I acted as infantry instructor to our anti-aircraft unit but returned to the company in time for the end on the 4 May and we moved into Utrecht on the 7 May 1945. The war, in Europe at least, was over.

❖*Above : A peaceful and practical memorial set up to the 1st Airborne Division at Wolfheze in the form of a circular public resting place.* ❖*Right : Summer, 2000, outside the railway station at Ede where a sea of chained up bicycles await their commuter owners return from city jobs in Arnhem and Utrecht. (both DWS)*

Arnold Whiteley...
When it were announced that the war were finished, they started firing their weapons up in the air, just letting shots go off up in the air. The Germans agreed to go into certain areas themselves and one of the funny things was when we set off in convoy to Utrecht. As we went in, the people would be 'cheering' us and then you'd get a little convoy of German vehicles joining in on the same route then they'd be 'booing' them, then 'cheering' us. It seemed funny all of us going in the same direction. It was a fantastic scene, it was one mass of people all lining the roads, cheering, letting their hair down and throwing fruit. They really did appreciate being free.

Arthur Green...
We were soon on the move again to a place called Utrecht, as usual about five miles behind Bn. HQ. as a truce was called and I had to take some lads who were sick to the RAP which was in a farm house. I remember I was sat down in front of a big roaring fire in the kitchen and I'd had a bit of a sore throat and temperature and the M.O. came through. He knew me quite well as I'd

done quite a bit of driving for him and he said, 'Hello! Green. What you doing here?' and I told him that I'd brought some sick up from 'B' Echelon. He said, 'You look a bit on the hot side yourself, have you a temperature?' Anyway, they checked it and it was one hundred and four and I was evacuated to 146th Field Hospital with suspected diphtheria. By the time I got back to Battalion, about three weeks later, it had moved to Arnsberg in Germany. The war was all over and they'd given my vehicle to another driver.

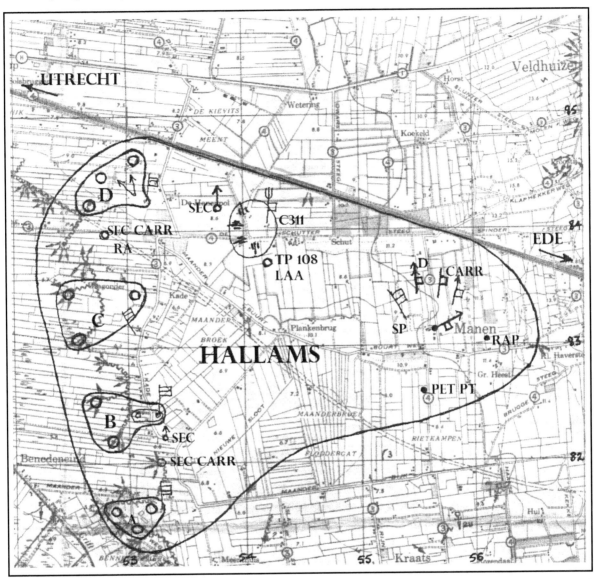

Final dispositions of the Hallamshire Battalion, just to the west of Ede railway station, although the war was physically at an end now. When the men were given news here of the ceasefire, all manner of weapons were fired into the air in celebration and a Rum Ration was issued. The overlay on this map shows the four Rifle company positions facing west towards the German lines. The symbols are translated as follows... Sec = Section. Carr = Carrier. RA = Royal Artillery. TP = Troop. LAA = Light Anti - Aircraft. Sp + Support. RAP = Regimental Aid Post. And it is thought that Pet Pt may = Petrol Point. The other symbols are not understood. (PRO modified)

John Wollerton started out on the last drive which would have allowed him to witness the final spectacle of the war, as the people of Utrecht welcomed their liberators, but destiny was lying in wait for him and a few others along the road, so they missed it all.

John Wollerton...
On our way to Utrecht we came across a car which had overturned in a ditch. There were three British soldiers badly injured in the back seat who had been given a lift towards town by a

Dutchman and his wife. The latter were hardly scratched but were terribly upset about these soldiers. One lad appeared to have a fractured skull and the others were critically ill so we stayed with them most of the night until help came along. At that time it was too late to go anywhere with them, poor devils.

It seems rather ironical also that another man should be denied the thing he most deserved. This was the undoubted pride and privilege it would have given him to lead the Hallams into Utrecht after having done so much to ensure their good training and preparation which had brought them through all the actions from Normandy to Arnhem. Just when the victory was in sight, it was now found necessary to remove him. This decision, made by those people of little sentiment who dwell in the corridors of power, must have come as a blow to this man. Trevor Hart Dyke would have been too proud to speak of it then or later and therefore his feelings on this subject will never now be known. He was not going to be allowed his 'triumph' as in ancient times, when the victor would be allowed to parade through the streets of Rome to a tumultuous welcome.

The 'triumph' now took place without him and the scenes of celebration in Utrecht were ecstatic, with singing and dancing in the streets, just like ancient times. Fruit and flowers, tears of joy, pride and gratitude, the people hardly knew what to do in order to welcome their liberators. They had, thankfully, been spared the dubious honour of their city becoming the final battleground and so, the worst horrors had not touched this place. Now, hundreds of redundant soldiers and their equally redundant war machines came trundling through the streets with more and more of the population climbing aboard for the carnival ride and to wallow in the new found peace.

The liberators are welcomed into the city of Utrecht on the 7th May, 1945. (ACS)

There were many, many others who should have been there on that day to share in the joy and wonder of it all, but they failed to arrive. These, of course, were those who had paid the greatest price of all to ensure that it happened, but never destined to take part. They now had a much more important role to play as they became part of those permanent stepping stones to victory, a role that would be never ending. Like their ancestors in past wars before them, they would now become the subject of annual memorial and pilgrimage, yet another warning to all mankind that such things must never happen again.

War Cemeteries have been likened unto the 'Silent Cities' (Rudyard Kipling) where none can speak but where each headstone speaks louder than words. The graves beneath contain the collective wisdom of every lesson learned throughout the history of mankind about the horror that is war, but even if the occupants could shout their warnings out loud, the words would still fall on so many deaf ears.

342

The nature of mankind is doomed to imperfection and even the best of his intentions are so often doomed to failure. Some of the most crucial lessons would seem to be the stuff of very short memory and have to be relearned by each generation in turn, at great cost. It will always be like that and the same conclusion is drawn in the aptly chosen passage by Mary Hart Dyke in her Foreword. They are King Arthur's dying words to Sir Bedivere after being carried by him, mortally wounded, from the battlefield in which all his other knights have died...

The sequel of today unsolders all
the goodliest fellowship of famous knights
whereof this world holds record. Such a sleep
They sleep - the men I loved.

Would that all the goodliest fellowship of our famous knights today, could be protected from the unsolderings of tomorrow. Now that would be the ultimate tribute to those who gave their lives in the wars of yesterday.

Such a sleep they then would sleep... ...all those brave young men.

Memorial at Utrecht which is simple and to the point. A Polar
Bear carved in stone stands on a plinth which carries a short
but sincere message from the people of that city. (HFC)

CONCLUSION

I have had the privilege over the past fifteen years or so of meeting, talking and travelling with a very small cross-section of Hallamshire Battalion veterans. Sadly, most of them have now passed on and I am left with some very fond memories of those people who belonged to the generation before mine. Most of them were members of a fraternity known as 'The Hallams Fontenay Club' and almost exclusively Hallamshires, who were involved in a battle which took place on the 25th June, 1944, in Normandy. On the 27th June, 1998, they made me an Honorary Member of that fraternity, a fine compliment equalled only by another Honorary Membership of the York and Lancaster Regimental Association itself which was acclaimed by its President to be unique. These have been my proudest moments and have to do with a sense of military 'belonging' which had been absent since I left the Royal Air force in 1973, after eighteen years service.

During World War Two, Eric Goodliffe, a well known and respected Sergeant/Stretcher Bearer with the Hallams, had been a great pal of Ray Langdale, both having always worked near to each other in the vicinity of Bn.HQ. After the war, they met up again and eventually did as they had always agreed - to go back to Normandy one day. They got in touch with Brigadier Trevor Hart Dyke and he kindly made his war maps of Normandy available for study purposes. Then they wrote to the Commonwealth War Graves Commission asking for literature on how to find the war cemeteries. They duly visited some of those places in Normandy and, on their return journey, called on Trevor Hart Dyke at his home where they presented him with some

Some of the founding members of the Hallams Fontenay Club at Endcliffe Hall, c.1970. From left to right : Doug Catley, Joe Penn, Arthur Saunders, Arthur Naylor, Doug Redmond, Bob Allinson (behind), Ernest Peck or Frank Priest, Bert Green, Walt Jackson, Eric Goodliffe, Ray Langdale, Arnold Bracewell, Tom Marsden, Stan Wild and Harry Dinnigan. (HFC)

champagne. The bottle was soon uncorked and the contents consumed as they reminisced and once more studied the war time maps spread out on the lounge carpet.

When they returned home, a discussion took place about their journey and how it had affected them, with the result that Eric proposed an idea of forming the fellowship mentioned above. In 1965, they organized a get together at the Union Hotel, Sheffield, in company with Bob Allinson, Ernest Peck, and a number of other Hallamshire Battalion Veterans and so the club was founded. Trevor Hart Dyke was invited to become its President which he was most pleased to accept. The Hallams Fontenay Club grew in numbers and organized many annual car and coach trips to France, Belgium and Holland as well as annual Reunion Dinners and get-togethers over the next thirty years. This fine brotherhood of men was formally disbanded in August, 2000.

Those who were 'left to grow old' have done so and numbers have dwindled, but at the time of writing there are still a good number of surviving veterans of whom few are to be found below the age of eighty years. Most, if not all, of these will count themselves to be amongst the lucky ones but there will have surely been a great deal of suffering for those who escaped death only to be left with mental and physical scars. As with any conflict, casualties of the Second World War did not cease with its termination and men and their families have continued to fall by the wayside as a direct result of it, right up to the present day.

The spinal injuries sustained by Bill Ashby at Tessel Wood consigned him to a wheelchair but he succumbed to them in 1954, as much a fatal casualty of that war as any man recorded in the official Roll of Honour. Joe Penn's brave spirit never left him but he finally gave way to all those years of personal suffering which he had borne in a quiet and dignified manner, with little complaint. He passed away on 5 July, 1991, a great loss to his family and many more besides. These are just two examples of the kind of pain and suffering that so often get left behind in the many stories of war. The sense of loss endured by loved ones is, in its way, even more tragic.

In war, the loss of thousands of young men is devastating to both family and country. In its wake, it can tear the heart out of each of them because of the love, the promise and potential that is lost. Those mainly youthful lives are gone forever and there are few religions that can stem the initial grief and trauma of it all, no matter what beliefs are held. I envy those whose religious faith allows them to believe in a life after death and often wonder why my mind has been denied the privilege of such conviction. I am left with my own inadequate beliefs that are born of simple and practical logic which tells me that nobody lives forever. If there is any kind of immortality, it can only be in the ability to live on in the hearts and minds of others when we die. The flaw in my belief, of course, would be the inability of such an individual to be aware of that continued existence. However, that same unawareness protects the dead from pain and suffering and it is for those who are left behind to bare such burdens. If and when that pain subsides, there is left a corner of the mind that harbours a wonderful storehouse. That storehouse is filled with memories and it is here where departed loved ones can, and do, continue to live.

Wars are not events to be revered or glorified but it is true to say that they invariably bring out the best and worst of mankind. The fellowship of servicemen that is developed in times of war is seldom, if ever, equalled in peacetime and it is this which bound the Hallams Fontenay Club together. For well over fifty years they have kept in touch and still meet together even though they may have had little else in common. They know the true meaning of comradeship and it extends to their war dead whom they have continued to visit on annual pilgrimages to military cemeteries in Normandy, Belgium, Holland and elsewhere. Such events are the result of emotions sustained through shared experiences in times of great danger. Civilians are rarely touched by this phenomena.

By the time this book is published, the Fontenay Club will have been brought to a very sad but dignified conclusion due to the advancing age of its membership and dwindling numbers. However, these quaint people and their stories, from what is now virtually another age, will not fade away as long as these pages survive to be read. The rich storehouse of their memories will linger long after those of the rest of us have faded into the dim and distant past.

Trevor Hart Dyke had this to say in the summing up of his long association with the Hallamshires...

Trevor Hart-Dyke...
I was very lucky to have commanded such a fine body of men and I'm sorry we had so many casualties. They were mainly from mortar and shell fire while we were around Tessel Wood although we did lose quite a lot at the Battle of Fontenay. We all realized we were doing an important job and after we'd left the Corps area, of course, it was very pleasant advancing with the people all throwing flowers and cheering us. Well, we felt like heroes then.

All I can say is that I am now eighty-seven and my memory is not awfully good. I hope that I haven't said anything that will upset anybody else when they hear it. I'm sorry that so many of my brother officers in the Hallamshires are no longer here, even those a great deal younger than myself and I'm also sorry that the Hallamshires no longer exist. It was a unit that had a very high Esprit de Corps and very well thought of in Sheffield. I'm very lucky to have been mixed up with them, they've given me a lot of pleasure and a lot of very good friends.

Three years later, this man passed away...

Life after death can mean all manner of things for those who believe. On 3 June, 1995, when the spirit of Trevor Hart Dyke was lifted up and carried away to that special place conceived by his religion, he would no doubt have been quite overwhelmed by the large number of people gathered there to greet him. Without the need for any word of command, those silent rows would have come quietly to attention in acceptance of their new arrival. That host of men paraded before him there, each one a real or honorary Yorkshireman, a veritable sea of familiar faces from his past... ...those Polar Bears from Sheffield...   ...The Hallamshire Battalion.

ROLL OF HONOUR

These Polar Bears from Sheffield 'neath the ground
In hibernation, sleeping, safe and sound
They sleep the sleep of heroes every one
So tread softly as you pass and then pass on

Memorial to the Missing. Bayeux.

AISTROP   4747403   Pte   23 Aug   1944
Cyril   Age 24
St. Desir War Cemetery, Calvados, France. Plot V. Row G. Grave 2.
Inscription : GOD SHINE THY BRIGHTEST STAR ON HIS GRAVE,
         FOR HE WAS GOOD. MOTHER.
Next of Kin (NoK) : A. Aistrop (Father) 115 Lansdowne Road, Sheffield.
Died in advance from Chateau le Boutemont to Le Breuil.

ALCOCK   4036726   L/Cpl   10 Aug   1944
Harry   Age 27
Bayeux War Cemetery, Calvados, France. Plot XXVII. Row C. Grave 10.
Inscription : AN EVENING STAR SHINES OVER THE GRAVE
         OF ONE WE LOVED BUT COULD NOT SAVE.
NoK : Gladys Alcock (Wife) 35 Charles Street, Hanley, Stoke on Trent.
Ex King's Shropshire Light Infantry. (Died of Wounds ?)

ANTCLIFFE   4719343   Pte   20 Feb   1945
Stanley   Age 21
Arnhem-Oosterbeek War Cemetery, Holland. Plot XII. Row C. Grave 1.
Inscription : HIS SMILING FACE, SUCH CAREFREE WAYS, REMAIN WITH US ALWAYS.
         DEVOTED MUM AND DAD.
NoK : Annie Antcliffe (Mother) 1 Hasland Place, Maltby, Yorkshire.
Ex King's Own Yorkshire Light Infantry.

ASHMORE   4747658   L/Cpl   25 Jun   1944
Fredrick   Age 34
Tilly sur Seulles War Cemetery, Calvados, France. Plot III. Row D. Grave 9.
Inscription : HOLD HIM LORD NOW HE IS THINE. LOVE HIM AS WE LOVED HIM
          WITH THY LOVE, DIVINE.
NoK : A. Ashmore (Wife) 115 Sturge Street, Heeley, Sheffield.

ASHTON   14655260   Pte   5 Nov   1944
Charles Ronald   Age 19
Roosendaal en Nispen Roman Catholic Cemetery, Netherlands. Row C. Grave 10.
Inscription : THE ECHO OF HIS VOICE, HIS EYES, HIS SMILE,
          ARE WITH US ALL THE WHILE.
NoK : D. Ashton (Father) Elton, Nr Matlock, Derbyshire.
Ex General Service Corps.

. Bayeux.   *Ryes*

BAKER   14547286   Pte   6 Feb   1944
Reginald   Age 19
Boston Cemetery, Lincolnshire. Section 6. Grave 161.
NoK : J. Thompson (Step Father) 10 Union Place, Boston, Lincolnshire.
Ex General Service Corps.

BAMFORD   14714302   Pte   25 Sep   1944
John Edward   Age 19
Leopoldsburg War Cemetery, Limburg, Belgium. Plot II. Row A. Grave 17.
NoK : Thomas Bamford (Father) 260 Alfreton Road, Nottingham.
Ex General Service Corps.

BANKS   14751072   Pte   9 Feb   1945
Reginald Ernest   Age 18
Nijmegen-Jonkerbosch War Cemetery, Netherlands. Plot VI. Row A. Grave 3.
NoK : F.W. Banks (Father) 198 Bromley Common, Bromley, Kent.
Ex General Service Corps.

BARKER   4748873   Pte   3 May   1940
William Pollock   Age 21
Brookwood Memorial, Woking, Surrey. Panel 13. Column 3.
NoK : (Father) 156 Seymour Road, Golcar, Huddersfield.
Died at sea on H.M.S. 'Afridi' (a 'Tribal' class destroyer) which was sunk by German aircraft during the withdrawal of troops from Namsos, Norway.

BARNARD   3854553   Cpl   20 Aug   1944
Frederick Joseph   Age 32
St. Desir War Cemetery, Calvados, France. Plot III. Row F. Grave 11.
NoK : W/12664 Pte. A. Barnard (Wife) c/o A.T.S. Records, Winchester.
Ex The Loyal Regt.

BATCHELOR   14692722   Pte   10 Aug   1944
Edward Frederick   Age 18
Banneville-la-Campagne War Cemetery,Calvados,France.Plot VI. Row E. Grave10.
Inscription : WE LOVED HIM WELL. IN HIS LOVE FOR US HE GAVE HIS LIFE.
    MUM, DAD AND BARRY.
NoK : Frederick Batchelor (Father) 11 Homefield Gardens, Mitcham, Surrey.
Ex General Service Corps.

BELL   89141   Capt   19 Oct   1944
Douglas Richmond   Age 35
Leominster Cemetery, Herefordshire. Sec. E Grave 67
NoK : Olga Patience Bell (Wife) Camberley, Surrey
       James Basil and Elizabeth Freeman Bell (Parents)
Died in England after sustaining wounds during the crossing of Antwerp - Turnhout Canal on 24 Sept. 1944.

BELL   4747660   Pte   3 May   1940
Sydney   Age 20
Brookwood Memorial, Woking, Surrey. Panel 13. Column 3.
NoK : (Father) 39 Crossland Street, Swinton, Yorkshire.
Died at sea on H.M.S. 'Afridi' (a 'Tribal' class destroyer) which was sunk by German aircraft during the withdrawal of troops from Namsos, Norway.

BELLWOOD   4745177   Pte   10 Oct   1944
George   Age 33
Brussels Church Cemetery, Belgium. Plot X. Row 23. Grave 29.
NoK : C. Bellwood (Mother) Water End, Brampton, Northallerton, Yorkshire.

BENE   4747551   Sgt   28 Aug   1944
Peter   Age 24
Bayeux War Cemetery, Calvados, France. Plot V. Row C. Grave 11.
Inscription : WE DID NOT HEAR YOUR LAST GOODBYE,
       SO IN OUR HEARTS YOU WILL NEVER DIE.
NoK : Andrew & Mary Bennett (Parents) 23 Bramley Street, Sheffield.
Died in hospital of Jaundice.

BENN. M.M.   4750381   L/Cpl.   30 Aug   1944
Eric Stanley   Age 27
St. Desir War Cemetery, Calvados, France. Plot II. Row C. Grave 3.
Inscription : DEARLY LOVED "SHELTERED BY THE ROCK OF AGES"
NoK : Ada Benn (Mother) 25 Charlton Place, Leeds.

BENNETT   6147555   Pte   25 Sept   1944
Edward William   Age 30
Leopoldsburg War Cemetery, Limburg, Belgium. Plot II. Row A. Grave 16.
Inscription : THOUGH MANY A SILENT TEAR,
            ALWAYS A BEAUTIFUL MEMORY OF YOU, MY DEAR.
NoK : Doris Lucy Bennett (Wife) Perivale, Greenford, Middlesex.
            Mr. & Mrs. Edward Bennett (Parents) Ex East Surrey Regt.

BENNISON   14741160   Pte   26 Nov   1944
Joseph Newton   Age 18
Nederweert War Cemetery, Netherlands. Plot I. Row B. Grave 1.
NoK : T.W. Bennison (Father) 'Lindholme' Runswick Bay, Saltburn-by-Sea, Yorkshire.
Ex General Service Corps.

BEWLEY   1528309   Pte   1 Mar   1945
John Bambridge   Age 29
Brookwood Memorial, Woking, Surrey. Panel 13. Column 3.
NoK :   Mary Grace Bewley (Wife) Woodend Farm, Lamplugh, Workington, Cumberland.
            Mr. & Mrs. T. Bewley (Parents) Moor Row, Cumberland.
Missing in Action. (confirmed in War Diary on 3/3/45 as known to have been killed)
Ex Royal Artillery.

BILL   14377521   Pte   5 Oct   1944
Frederick Thomas   Age 20
Leopoldsburg War Cemetery, Limburg, Belgium. Plot V. Row A. Grave 9.
Inscription : GREATER LOVE HATH NO MAN,
            THAN HE THAT LAYETH DOWN HIS LIFE FOR OTHERS.
NoK : F.J. Bill (Father) 25 Grove Crescent, Dudley Fields, Brierley, Hull. Ex General Service Corps.

BINDOTTI   14583935   L/Cpl   29 Sept   1944
Leslie   Age 19
Leopoldsburg War Cemetery, Limburg, Belgium. Plot II. Row A. Grave 18.
Inscription : TILL THE SETTING OF THE SUN, WE WILL REMEMBER.
NoK : May Bindotti (Mother) 187 Broad Oak Road, Brownley Green, Manchester.
Died at the Depot de Mendicite. Ex General Service Corps.

BISCOE   14666478   Pte   28 Aug   1944
Dennis Albert   Age 19
St. Desir War Cemetery, Calvados, France. Plot I. Row B. Grave 14.
Inscription : OUR DENNIS WE WILL NOT SEE UNTIL OUR RACE IS RUN.
            UNTO THAT MORN - OUR SON !
NoK : R.E. Biscoe (Father) Harrods Depository, Arundel Terrace, London SW13. Ex General Service Corps.

BONE   311495   2/Lt   9 Aug   1944
John William   Age 28
Banneville-la-Campagne War Cemetery, Calvados, France. Plot XVII. Row B. Grave 1.
Inscription : INTO THE MOSAIC OF THE WORLD WENT THIS PIECE
            THAT IS FOR EVER ENGLAND.
NoK :   Lena Bone (Wife)
            Francis William & Ellen Bone (Parents) Middlesborough, Yorkshire.
Notts & Derby Regt. - attached - 'B' Company. *Died in fields to the SW of Chichiboville. (shellfire)*

Hermanville   *La Deliverand*

BRADSHAW   4747863   L/Cpl   10 Aug   1944
Norman   Age 23
Banneville-la-Campagne War Cemetery, Calvados, France. Plot VI. Row E. Grave 5.
Inscription : AS THE DAYS GO BY YOU ARE IN OUR HEARTS,
       LOST BUT NOT FORGOTTEN. DAD AND FAMILY.
NoK : George Bradshaw (Father) 4 Jackson Terrace, New Street, Dinnington, Sheffield.

BRIDGES   14715294   Pte   5 Oct   1944
James   Age 18
Lier Belgian Milit. Cemetery, Lierre, Antwerp, Belgium. Plot IV. Row A. Grave 5.
NoK : Mr. & Mrs. F.A. Bridges (Parents) Blaclpool, Lancashire.
Ex General Service Corps.

BRISTOW   14670114   Pte   25 Jun   1944
Gerald Arthur   Age 18
Tilly-Sur-Seulles War Cemetery, Calvados, France. Plot III. Row D. Grave 12.
Inscription : THOUGH FAR AWAY HIS GRAVE MAY LIE,
       THOUGHTS OF HIM WILL NEVER DIE.
NoK : (Father) 23 Mill Lane, Belper, Derbyshire.
Ex General Service Corps.

BROADBENT   14696619   Pte   21 Aug   1944
Charles William   Age 29
Hermanville War Cemetery, Calvados, France. Plot II. Row H. Grave 11.
Inscription : HE GAVE HIS UNFINISHED LIFE, THE GREATEST GIFT OF ALL.
       MOM, DAD, BROTHERS AND SISTERS.
NoK : Thomas Leslie & Elsie Broadbent (Parents), Selly Oak, Birmingham.
Ex General Service Corps.

BROOK   4748019   Pte   16 Jul   1944
Horace   Age 33
St. Manvieu War Cemetery, Cheux, Calvados, France. Plot V. Row A. Grave 11
Inscription : IN MEMORY OF HORACE, A BELOVED FATHER AND HUSBAND OF
       ELIZABETH. EVER TO BE REMEMBERED.
NoK : Elizabeth Brook (Wife) 31 Bretton Street, Darton West, Nr. Barnsley.

BRUCE   4747418   Pte   3 May   1940
Walter   Age 29
Brookwood Memorial, Surrey. Panel 13. Column 3.
NoK : (Wife) 10 Kinglake Street, Sheffield.
Died at sea on H.M.S. 'Afridi' (a 'Tribal' class destroyer) which was sunk by German aircraft during the withdrawal of troops from Namsos, Norway.

BRUCE   14367900   Pte   13 Apr   1945
John Phillip   Age 20
Uden War Cemetery, Netherlands. Plot 2. Row A. Grave 8.
Inscription : PRAY FOR US " THERE'S ROSEMARY THAT'S FOR REMEMBRANCE;
     PRAY, LOVE, REMEMBER"
NoK : G.T. Bruce (Father) 139 Crofton Park Road, Brockley, London, SE4.
Ex General Service Corps.

BURRELL   4535227   Pte   25 Jun   1944
John William   Age 28
Tilly-sur-Seulles War Cemetery, Calvados, France. Plot III. Row D. Grave 3.
NoK : Mrs. A Wilson (Sister) 2 Leicester Street, West Hartlepool, Durham.
Died at Fontenay Pesnel. Batman to Sgt. Major Morton.
Ex West Yorkshire Regt.

CARNEY   3862972   Pte   7 Aug   1944
Francis   Age 32
Bayeux Memorial, Calvados, France. Panel 17. Column 1.
NoK : (Wife) 1 House, 5 Court, Mann Street, Liverpool, Lancashire.
Missing in Action west of Troarn.
Ex The Loyal Regt.

CATLEY   4747520   Sgt   16 Jul   1944
John Charles   Age 23
St. Manvieu War Cemetery, Calvados, France. Plot III. Row A. Grave 6.
Inscription : WENT THE DAY WELL ? WE DIED AND NEVER KNEW,
     BUT WELL OR ILL, FREEDOM, WE DIED FOR YOU.
NoK : S.M. Catley (Mother) 35 Western Road, East Dene, Rotherham.
Died in Attack on Vendes.

CHADWICK   1526011   Pte   13 Apr   1945
John   Age 30
Milsbeek War Cemetery, Netherlands. Plot II. Row E. Grave 2.
Inscription : IN MEMORY OF MY DEAR SON JOHN,
     GOD'S WILL SPARED FURTHER SUFFERING.
NoK : N. Chadwick (Wife) 19 Calf Hey, Littleborough, Lancashire.
Ex Royal Artillery.

CHAPMAN   14987110   Pte   23 Mar   1945
Peter Neilson   Age 21
Reichswald Forest War Cemetery, Germany. Plot DIV. Row C. Grave 17.
NoK : J.N. Chapman (Mother) High Dykehurst, Ewhurst, Surrey.
Ex General Service Corps.

CHORLTON   4748412   Pte   10 Sep   1945
Wilfred   Age 27
Reichswald Forest War Cemetery, Germany. Plot DIX. Row H. Grave 13.
Inscription : LOVING MEMORIES OF ONE SO DEAR, FAR AWAY BUT OH! SO NEAR.
    LOVED BY MAM AND FAMILY.
NoK : Timbercliffe Summit, Littleborough, Lancashire. Died in road accident (Carrier)

CHURCHILL   14679900   Pte   18 Aug   1944
Alfred Thomas   Age 18
Banneville-la-Campagne War Cemetery, Calvados, France. Plot III. Row E. Grave 17.
Inscription : GOD TAKES OUR LOVED ONES FROM OUR HOME,
         BUT NEVER FROM OUR HEARTS. MUM, DAD AND FAMILY.
NoK : Alfred Churchill (Father) 36 Chaucer Avenue, Richmond, Surrey. Ex General Service Corps.

CLARKE   7583770   Pte   21 Jun   1944
George   Age 36
Bayeux War Cemetery, Calvados, France. Plot VIII. Row E. Grave 18.
Inscription : EVER IN OUR THOUGHTS. WIFE WINNIE AND DERRICK.
NoK : Winifred Clarke (Wife) 6 Danadan Terrace, Gregory Boulevard, Nottingham.
Ex Royal Army Ordinance Corps.

CLAXTON   14670892   Pte   10 Jul   1944
Leslie   Age 18
St. Manvieu War Cemetery, Cheux, Calvados, France. Plot III. Row A. Grave 1.
Inscription : DEARER TO MEMORY THAN WORDS CAN TELL.
NoK : M.B. Barber (Mother) 42 Pelgrave Street, Sheffield. Ex General Service Corps.

Tilly-sur Seulles.   *Fontenay le Pesnel.*

CLAYTON   4750342   Pte   28 Aug   1944
Harry   Age 27
St. Desir War Cemetery, Calvados, France. Plot III. Row C. Grave 11.
Inscription : DEEP IN OUR HEARTS A MEMORY IS KEPT
         OF ONE WE LOVED AND WILL NEVER FORGET.
NoK : Hilda Clayton (Wife) Aldwarke Farm Cottage, Parkgate, Rotherham.

CLAYTON   4535749   Pte   7 Oct   1944
Joseph   Age not recorded
Leopoldsburg War Cemetery, Limburg, Belgium. Plot V. Row E. Grave 3.
NoK : (Mother) 28 George Street, Hipperholm, Nr. Halifax.
Ex West Yorkshire Regt.

CORDON   14714337   Pte   7 Oct   1944
Jack   Age 19
Leopoldsburg War Cemetery, Limburg, Belgium. Plot V. Row E. Grave 7.
Inscription : IN LOVING MEMORY OF MY DEAR SON JACK.
         MAM, DAD AND FAMILY 'THY WILL BE DONE'
NoK : Frank Cordon (Father) 14 Leicester Street, Nottingham.
Ex General Service Corps.

COUPE   4920812   Pte   23 Aug   1944
Harold   Age 28
St. Desir War Cemetery, Calvados, France. Plot V. Row C. Grave 11.
NoK : Ivy Sabina Coupe (Wife) 24 Slater Street, Sutton in Ashfield, Nottingham.
Died in advance from Chateau le Boutemont to Le Breuil. Ex South Staffordshire Regt.

COWELL   4806173   Pte   10 Mar   1946
Frederick   Age 25
Munster Heath War Cemetery, Germany. Plot IV. Row A. Grave 13.
NoK : John & Elizabeth Cowell (Parents) Spalding, Lincolnshire.
Ex Lincolnshire Regt.

COYNE   4748397   Pte   28 Aug   1944
Martin   Age 26
St. Desir War Cemetery, Calvados, France. Plot I. Row A. Grave 1.
Inscription : ETERNAL REST GIVE UNTO HIM O LORD
         AND LET PERPETUAL LIGHT SHINE UPON HIM.
NoK : Elizabeth (Mother) 19 Bent Street, Blackburn, Lancashire.

CROOKS   4745325   Pte   3 May   1940
Arthur   Age 30
Brookwood Memorial, Woking, Surrey. Panel 13. Column 3.
NoK : (Wife) 27 Havelock Street, Sheffield.
Died at sea on H.M.S. 'Afridi' (a 'Tribal' class destroyer) which was sunk by German aircraft during the withdrawal of troops from Namsos, Norway.

CROWTHER   4756330   Pte   16 Jul   1944
George   Age 31
St. Manvieu War Cemetery, Cheux, Calvados, France. Plot III. Row J. Grave 9.
Inscription : "THEMSELVES WILL FADE BUT NOT THEIR MEMORIES"
         LOVING WIFE GRACE AND DAUGHTER MAUREEN.
NoK : Grace Annie Crowther (Wife) 'Rose Bank' Great Cliffe, Grigglestone, Nr. Wakefield.

DALE   4750290   A/Cpl   23 Aug   1944
John   Age 27
St. Desir War Cemetery, Calvados, France. Plot V. Row D. Grave 13.
Inscription : HE DIED THAT WE MIGHT LIVE.
         LOVED ALWAYS BY HIS WIFE BETTY AND SON JOHN.
NoK : Elizabeth C. Dale (Wife) 'Somersey' West Ella, Nr. Hull.

DAVIES   6145716   Pte   2 Aug   1944
Frederick Alfred   Age 25
La Deliverande War Cemetery, Calvados, France. Plot IX. Row A. Grave 7.
NoK : G.M. Davies (Wife) 26A Stow Uplam Street, Stow Market, Suffolk.
Probably killed by sniper fire - SW of Troarn.
Ex East Surrey Regt.

DAVIES   315060   Lt   14 Apr   1945
Ronald   Age 31
Arnhem - Oosterbeek War Cemetery, Nederlands. Plot 7. Row A. Grave 7.
Inscription : RESTING WHERE NO SHADOWS FALL
NoK :   Dorothy Margaret Davies (Wife) Wakefield
            William & Annie Davies (Parents) Wakefield
Died at road junction to the north of Army Barracks on north side of Arnhem. He was the last Hallamshire officer to die in the conflict. Ex Cavalry of the Line.

DAVIS   5571562   CQMS   22 Nov   1944
Allan Walker   Age 25
Venray War Cemetery, Nederlands. Plot IV. Row D. Grave 11.
NoK : Walter Davis (Father) 288 Chester Road, North Sutton, Birmingham.
Ex The Wiltshire Regt.

DEMER   5056300   Pte   20 Aug   1944
Robert William   Age 31
St. Desir War Cemetery, Calvados, France. Plot III. Row E. Grave 1.
Inscription : SLEEP ON DEAR SON AND TAKE THY REST.
            THEY MISS YOU MOST WHO LOVED YOU BEST.
NoK : (Wife) 7 Aylmer Road, London, E11.
Ex North Staffordshire Regt.

DEVENNEY   14408223   Pte   25 Jun   1944
Michael Raymond   Age 18
Fontenay le Pesnel War Cemetery, Calvados, France. Plot IV. Row D. Grave 17.
Inscription : O GENTLE HEART OF JESUS, GIVE HIM ETERNAL REST.
            MAY HE REST IN PEACE.
NoK : (Mother) 1 Hill Street, Higher Bridge Street, Bolton, Lancashire.
Ex General Service Corps.

DICKER   6150809   Pte   1 Sep   1944
Stanley Walter   Age 28
Gloucester Old Cemetery. Plot B. Grave 371 5.
NoK : C.J. Dicker (Wife) 67 Theresa Street, Gloucester. Ex East Surrey Regt.

DURHAM   6147588   L/Sgt   23 Aug   1944
Jack Richard Harry   Age 28
St. Desir War Cemetery, Calvados, France. Plot V. Row D. Grave 6.
Inscription : IN LOVING MEMORY OF OUR DEAR SON.
            THOUGH ABSENT, ALWAYS IN OUR THOUGHTS.
NoK : Agnus Eileen Durham (Wife) 98 Baring Road, Lee, London, SE12.
Ex East Surrey Regt. (Died in advance from Chateau le Boutemont to Le Breuil)

EASTWOOD   4755840   Pte   27 Jun   1944
Harold   Age 30
St. Manvieu War Cemetery, Cheux, Calvados, France. Plot III. Row J. Grave 8.
Inscription : IN LOVING MEMORY OF HAROLD. HOLD HIM LORD
              WITH THY LOVE DIVINE. WIFE EDNA AND AUDREY.
NoK : (Wife) 9 Evans Street, Sheffield.

ELLIOTT   4535942   Pte   25 Jun   1944
George Isaac   Age 30
Ryes War Cemetery, Bazenville, Calvados, France. Plot II. Row J. Grave 1.
Inscription : HE GAVE THE GREATEST GIFT OF ALL, HIS OWN UNFINISHED LIFE.
NoK : (Wife) 'Ivydene' Main Road, Gedling, Nottinghamshire.
Died of wounds sustained at Fontenay le Pesnel. Ex West Yorks Regt.

ELLIS   14743344   Pte   25 Dec   1944
Arthur Oates   Age 19
Nijmegen - Jonkerbosch War Cemetery, Netherlands. Plot II. Row C. Grave 6.
Inscription : WE SHALL NEVER FORGET YOU DEAREST SON.
             MOTHER, DAD AND BROTHER
NoK : E. Thompson (Mother) 194 Belle Isle Road, Leeds.
Ex General Service Corps.

ELLIS   14684346   Pte   26 Sep   1944
Dennis Charles   Age 19
Lier Belgian Military Cemetery, Lierre, Antwerp, Belgium. Plot I. Row A. Grave 1.
NoK : George Ellis (Father) 52 Summerfield Field, Lee Green, Lewisham.   *Ex General Service Corps.*

St. Manvieu.

ELLIS D.C.M.   4756342   Cpl   5 Nov   1944
John   Age 30
Roosendal-en-Nispen Roman Catholic Cemetery, Netherlands. Row B. Grave 8.
Inscription : UNTIL THE DAY BREAK AND THE SHADOWS FLEE AWAY.
NoK : Ellen E. Ellis (Wife) 4 Newport Street, Leeds.
Died when defusing a mine on cross roads north of Roosendaal.

ELLIS   976437   Pte   30 Nov   1944
Thomas Carey   Age 29
Venray War Cemetery, Netherlands. Plot IV. Row A. Grave 8.
Inscription : I HEARD THE VOICE OF JESUS SAY "COME UNTO ME AND REST"
NoK : Mary Ellis (Mother) 'Hazelemere' Queens Road, Llandudno. Ex Royal Artillery.

ELSEY   6150810   Cpl   5 Nov   1944
John James William   Age 29
Roosendal -en Nispen Roman Catholic Cemetery, Netherlands. Row B. Grave 11.
NoK : Louise Elsey (Wife) 80 Hillside House, Dog kennel Hill, London, SE22.
Ex East Surrey Regt.

FELLOWS   14785802   Pte   20 Feb   1945
John Charles   Age 19
Arnhem - Oosterbeek War Cemetery, Netherlands. Plot XII. Row C. Grave 6.
Inscription : A DAILY THOUGHT, A SILENT TEAR, ALWAYS WISHING YOU WERE NEAR.
NoK : J.C. Fellows (Father) 17 Jenkinson Street, Sheffield. Ex General Service Corps.

FIELD   4748865   L/Cpl   5 Sep   1944
Wilfred   Age 25
St Maries Church Yard, Military Section, Le Havre, France. Grave 67
NoK : Hannah Field (Wife) 8 Wellgrove, Hove, Brighouse.

FIRTH   89409   Lt   1 Jul   1944
Jack   Age 34
Ryes War Cemetery, Bazenville, Calvados, France. Plot III. Row G. Grave 3.
Seriously wounded near St. Aubins Church in Fontenay le Pesnel on 25 June.

FISHPOOL   5190835   Pte   16 Jul   1944
Reginald Alick   Age 29
St. Manvieu War Cemetery, Cheux, Calvados, France. Plot III. Row H. Grave 8.
Inscription : IN LOVING MEMORY OF MY DEAR HUSBAND REG.
           FROM HIS LOVING WIFE AND SON DAVID.
NoK : M.M. Fishpool (Wife) 'The Cottage', Gorsey, Nr. Ross-on-Wye.
Attack on Vendes. Ex Gloucester Regt.

FLETCHER   5052517   Pte   20 Feb   1945
Norman Frank   Age 28
Nijmegen - Jonkerbosch War Cemetery, Netherlands. Plot VI. Row A. Grave 4.
Inscription : THERE'S SOME CORNER OF A FOREIGN FIELD
           THAT IS FOREVER ENGLAND.
NoK : F.E. Fletcher (Wife) Springfields, Mains Lane, Bishop Monkton, Harrogate, Yorkshire.
           Frank & Edith May Fletcher (Parents)
Ex North Staffordshire Regt.

FOSTER 14798279 Pte 13 Feb 1945
Albert Age 19
Nijmegen - Jonkerbosch War Cemetery, Netherlands. Plot II. Row C. Grave 8.
Inscription : DEEP IN OUR HEARTS A MEMORY IS KEPT
OF THE ONE WE LOVED DEARLY. GOD BLESS YOU.
NoK : Joseph & Elizabeth Foster (Parents) 6 Pashley's Yard, Howard Street, Rotherham. Ex G. S.Corps.

FOSTER 14410167 Pte 5 Apr 1945
Joseph Age 20
Nijmegen - Jonkerbosch War Cemetery, Netherlands. Plot XXI. Row B. Grave 4.
Inscription : HE DID NOT WEAKEN AT THE CALL.
FOR US HE GAVE HIS LIFE, HIS ALL.
NoK : Joseph & Edith Foster (Parents) 30 Woodland Street, Manchester. Ex General Service Corps.

FOTHERGILL 4753072 Pte 19 Jul 1944
John Age 29
St. Manvieu War Cemetery, Cheux, Calvados, France. Plot X. Row B. Grave 2.
NoK : H. Fothergill (Mother) 61 Duke of York Street, Wakefield, Yorkshire. (Died of Wounds ?)

FOZARD 4750441 Pte 25 Jun 1944
Willie Age 26
Ryes War Cemetery, Calvados, France. Plot VIII. Row H. Grave 5.
Inscription : HE THAT DOETH THE WILL OF GOD ABIDETH FOREVER.
WARS BITTER COST.
NoK : A. Fozard (Mother) 9 Flaxton Terrace, Pannal, Yorks.

FRANKS 6147910 Pte 22 Nov 1944
George Charles Frank Age 29
Venray War Cemetery, Holland. Plot IV. Row D. Grave 13.
Inscription : REST IN PEACE THY DUTY DONE.
UNTIL WE MEET AGAIN MY LOVING SON.
NoK : (Mother) 32 Moore Crescent, Dewsbury Road, Leeds. Ex East Surrey Regt.

FREEMAN 4747522 L/Sgt 20 Aug 1944
William Age 24
St. Desir War Cemetery, Calvados, France. Plot III. Row F. Grave 13.
Inscription : HE DIED THAT WE MIGHT REIGN FOR ALL,
WITH FAITH IN GOD WE MUST NOT FALL.
NoK ; W. Freeman (Father) 10 Leslie Road, Hillsborough, Sheffield.

FRY 6149139 Pte 26 Sep 1944
Leslie Ernest Age 29
Geel War Cemetery, Geel, Antwerp, Belgium. Plot II. Row C. Grave 11.
Inscription : ASLEEP. HE DIED THAT WE MIGHT LIVE IN PEACE.
NoK : T.N.V. Fry (Wife) 252 Botwell Lane, Hayes, Middlesex. Ex East Surrey Regt.

FURNISS 4747558 Cpl 4 Nov 1944
Arthur Age 25
Fijnaart-Heiningen Protestant Cemetery, Nr. Roosendaal, Netherlands. Grave 4.
Inscription : INTO THE MOSAIC OF VICTORY WE PLACE THIS PRICELESS GEM.
NoK : E. Furniss (Wife) 254 Maltravers Road, Wybourn, Sheffield.

GALLAGHER 4748860   L/Cpl   28 Jun 1944
James   Age 25
St. Manvieu War Cemetery, Cheux, Calvados, France. Plot V. Row A. Grave 15.
Inscription : YOU ARE GONE BUT NOT FORGOTTEN.
     STILL IN OUR HEARTS YOU WILL BE FOREVER. R.I.P.
NoK : A. Gallagher (Mother) 24A Cobden Street, Batley, Yorkshire.

GARNER   4748390   Pte   22 Nov 1944
Harold   Age 26
Venray War Cemetery, Netherlands. Plot VIII. Row C. Grave 3.
Inscription : AT THE GOING DOWN OF THE SUN, AND IN THE MORNING,
     WE WILL REMEMBER HIM.
NoK : D. Garner (Wife) 46 Lady Ann Road, Soothill, Batley, Yorkshire.

GILLOTT   4749129   Pte   11 Apr 1946
John Henry   Age 26
Rawmarsh (Haugh Road) Cemetery, Rawmarsh, Yorkshire. Section L. Grave 75.
NoK : John Henry & Nellie Gillott (Parents) Rawmarsh.

Ranville.

Banneville.

GODDARD 4380826   Cpl   3 May   1940
Albert   Age 42
Brookwood Memorial, Surrey. Panel 13. Column 3.
NoK : (Wife) 105 Liverpool Street, Sheffield.
Died at sea on H.M.S. 'Afridi' (a 'Tribal' class destroyer) which was sunk by German aircraft during the
withdrawal of troops from Namsos, Norway.
Ex Yorkshire Regt. (Green Howards)

GOLLIN   14660415   Pte   23 Jul   1944
John Henry   Age 19
Tilly-sur-Seulles War Cemetery, Calvados, France. Plot IV. Row A. Grave 5.
Inscription : IN EVERLASTING AND GLORIOUS MEMORY
     OF A DEAR AND BELOVED SON. R.I.P.
NoK : J. Gollin (Father) 392 Foxhill Road, Carlton, Nottingham.
(Died of Wounds ?) Ex General Service Corps.

GRAHAM   4268585   Pte   7 Oct   1944
John Wesley   Age 30
Leopoldsburg War Cemetery, Limburg, Belgium. Plot V. Row E. Grave 9.
NoK : 2/3542 Pte. E. Graham (Wife) c/o A.T.S. Records.
Ex Cavalry of the Line.

GRAY   3060374   Pte   22 Jul   1944
Ralph James   Age 27
Tilly- sur - Seulles War Cemetery, Calvados, France. Plot IV. Row A. Grave 10.
Inscription : HE GAVE HIS LIFE THAT OTHERS MIGHT HAVE FREEDOM.
NoK : E.V. Gray (Wife) 19 Hume Street, Stockton on Tees, Co. Durham.
(Died of Wounds ?) Ex Royal Scots Regt.

GREEN   4749613   L/Cpl   7 Oct   1944
John Arthur   Age 26
Leopoldsburg War Cemetery, Limburg, Belgium. Plot V. Row E. Grave 8.
NoK : E. Green (Wife) 32 Adelphi Street, Sheffield.

GREGORY   14531723   Pte   25 Jun   1944
Harry   Age 19
St. Manvieu War Cemetery, Cheux, Calvados, France. Plot III. Row B. Grave 1.
NoK : E. Gregory (Father) 2 St. Augustines Avenue, Chesterfield, Derbyshire.
Ex General Service Corps.

GRIFFITHS   4039703   Pte   4 Oct   1944
Horace   Age 33
Leopoldsburg War Cemetery, Limburg, Belgium. Plot 5. Row E. Grave 5.
Inscription : ONLY THOSE WHO HAVE LOVED AND LOST KNOW THE PAIN.
   REMEMBERED BY WIFE, SONS, MOM, DAD AND FAMILY.
NoK :   Emily Griffiths (Wife) 28 Wood Road, Smethwick, Staffs.
      Walter & Elizabeth Griffiths (Parents)
Killed in the attack on Poppel. Ex King's Shropshire Light Infantry.

GRITTON   1776317   Pte   25 Sep   1944
Bertram Ernest   Age 23
Leopoldsburg War Cemetery, Limburg, Belgium. Plot V. Row D. Grave 3.
NoK : (Wife) 117 Denman Street, Radford, Nottingham.
Ex Royal Artillery.

GUEST   4618881   L/Cpl   Sun   25 Jun   1944
Hubert Frederick William   Age 24
Fontenay le Pesnel War Cemetery, Calvados, France. Plot IV. Row D. Grave 11.
Inscription : BEAUTIFUL MEMORIES CHERISHED FOREVER,
      OF HAPPY DAYS WE SPENT TOGETHER.
NoK : P. Guest (Wife) 31 Milton Road, St. Marks, Cheltenham, Gloucestershire.
Ex Duke of Wellington's Regt.

HALFORD   14425335   Pte   25 Jun   1944
John Joseph   Age 19
Ryes War Cemetery, Bazenville, Calvados, France. Plot VIII. Row H. Grave 4.
Inscription : DEATH IS NOT A SLEEP, BUT AN AWAKENING TO LIFE.
NoK : J. Halford (Father) 19 Farm Drive, Field Lane, Ulverston, Derbyshire. Ex General Service Corps.

HAMPSON   5570669   Pte   16 Jul   1944
Edward Roy   Age 28
St. Manvieu War Cemetery, Cheux, Calvados, France. Plot V. Row A. Grave 12.
Inscription : A TRUE BRAVE HEART IN GODS KEEPING. FOREVER IN OUR THOUGHTS.
NoK : E. Hampson (Father) 101 Causley Heath, Warminster, Wiltshire.
(Attack on Vendes) Wiltshire Regt.

HANSON   4747143   Pte   25 Jun   1944
Ernest   Age 25
Ryes War Cemetery, Bazenville, Calvados, France. Plot II. Row H. Grave 2.
Inscription : LOVED BY ALL. FOREVER IN OUR THOUGHTS.
NoK : Ernest and Rose Ann Hanson (Parents)
        240 Greenland Road, Darnall, Sheffield.
Died shortly after being shot in the back whilst bringing up a No. 18 wireless set to Lt. Chris Somers in an orchard, 200 yards southeast of the church in Fontenay le Pesnel. Batman to Lt. Somers.

HARDING   4747584   Pte   7 Sep   1944
Ronald Lion   Age 25
St. Desir War Cemetery, Calvados, France. Plot II. Row A. Grave 1.
Inscription : SLEEPING IN HEAVENLY REST.
NoK : (Father) 35 Tom Lane, Sheffield.

HARDY   4537658   Pte   2 Jul   1944
Jack   Age 23
St. Manvieu War Cemetery, Cheux, Calvados, France. Plot III. Row H. Grave 6.
Inscription : HE DIED FOR THOSE HE LOVED AND THOSE HE LOVED REMEMBER.
NoK : D. Hardy (Wife) 27 Fairfax Road, Baghill, Pontefract, Yorkshire.

HARNON   3384956   Pte   29 Jun   1944
Owen   Age not recorded
Fontenay le Pesnel War Cemetery, Calvados, France. Plot IV. Row D. Grave 15.
NoK : (Mother) 10 Colning Place, Hastings, Sussex. Ex East Lancashire Regt.

HARPER. V.C.   4751678   Cpl   29 Sep   1944
John William   Age 28
Leopoldsburg War Cemetery, Limburg, Belgium. Plot V. Row B. Grave 15.
NoK : L. Harper (Wife) 25 Southend, Thorne, Nr. Doncaster.
Killed by machine gun fire in the attack on Depot de Mendicite, near Merxplas, Belgium.

HARPER   4749112   Pte   23 Oct   1943
Spurley   Age 24
Wadsley Church Yard, Sheffield. Row K. Grave 2.
NoK : (Father) 67 Leader Road, Sheffield.
(Accidentally killed by a mortar bomb in training when taking part in practice beach landings at Ardno, Loch Fyne, Scotland.

HATELEY   4748004   Pte   26 Jan   1942
Thomas Bernard   Age 22
Akureyri Cemetery, Iceland. Military Plot. Row A. Grave 6.
NoK : Mrs. Willis (Mother), 52 Harelaw Gardens, Annefield Plain, Co. Durham.
Isaiah and Sarah H. Hateley, of Bolton-on-Dearne (Grandparents)
Suffered a fractured skull in a 15cwt Truck accident at 1100 hrs near Horga Suspension Bridge in Northern Iceland. He died three days later in No.81 General Hospital at 2335 hrs. without regaining consciousness.

HATTERSLEY   4747636   Pte   25 Jun   1944
Ralph   Age 25
St. Manvieu War Cemetery, Cheux, Calvados, France. Plot III. Row A. Grave 4.
Inscription : A LOVING THOUGHT, TRUE AND TENDER,
                    JUST TO SHOW WE STILL REMEMBER.
NoK : R. Hattersley (Father) 33 Greenhead Lane, Chapeltown, Nr. Sheffield.

HAYNES   4748067   Sgt   1 Jul   1944
Robert Denver   Age 24
St. Manvieu War Cemetery, Cheux, Calvados, France. Plot I. Row G. Grave 9.
Inscription : A SMILING FACE, A HEART OF GOLD,
                    ONE OF THE BEST THE WORLD COULD KNOW.
NoK : A. Haynes (Mother) 71 Church Lane, Dinnington, Nr. Sheffield.

HEALD   4744094   Pte   26 Jan   1942
Frederick   Age 32
Akureyri Cemetery, Iceland. Military Plot. Row A. Grave 5.
NoK : Mrs. Lily Heald (Wife), 193, Springvale Road, Walkley, Sheffield.
Suffered severe burns in a Nissen hut fire at Krossastadir at 1200 hrs. on 23 Jan. He died at No.81 General Hospital. A small number of veterans had, in recent years, mistakenly believed that he and Pte Hateley (above) had died together in a snow storm but the only thing their accidents had in common was that they died on the same day in the same Hospital.

HEATH   14363248   Pte   25 Sep   1944
Daniel   Age 34
Leopoldsburg War Cemetery, Limburg, Belgium. Plot II. Row A. Grave 13.
NoK : S. Heath (Wife) Sandy Road, Sandyford, Dumfries & Galloway.
Ex General Service Corps.

HERROD   5891237   Pte   26 Jun   1944
John   Age 20
Ryes War Cemetery, Bazenville, Calvados, France. Plot III. Row J. Grave 2.
Inscription : FROM THE GROUND THERE BLOSSOMS RED.
                    LIFE THAT SHALL ENDLESS BE.
NoK : G.L. Herrod (Mother) 72 Pitt Street, Rotherham.
Ex Northamptonshire Regt.

HILL　　　　　　　　5622360　　　　　　Pte　　　　　　　16 Jul　　1944
John William　　　　　　Age 23
St. Manvieu War Cemetery, Cheux, Calvados, France. Plot III. Row H. Grave 4.
Inscription : LOVED AND REMEMBERED BY HIS DEVOTED WIFE
　　　　　AND DAUGHTER, WENDY. "FOLD HIM IN THINE ARMS".
NoK :　Nancy Elizabeth Hill (Wife) 'Cliffeholme' Corton, Surrey.
　　　George Henry & Eliza Jane Hill (Parents)
Attack on Vendes. Ex Devonshire Regt.

HINCHLIFFE　　　　4750504　　　　　　L/Cpl　　　　　12 Jul　　1944
Ernest　　　　　　　　　Age 27
St. Manvieu War Cemetery, Cheux, Calvados, France. Plot III. Row A. Grave 12.
NoK : H. Hinchliffe (Father) 20 Stubbs Road, Wombwell, Nr. Barnsley.

HINDLE　　　　　　14413310　　　　　　Pte　　　　　　　16 Jul　　1944
Ronald　　　　　　　　　Age 23
St. Manvieu War Cemetery, Cheux, Calvados, France. Plot III. Row H. Grave 13.
Inscription : AT THE SETTING OF THE SUN AND IN THE MORNING WE WILL REMEMBER.
NoK : R. Hindle (Grandfather) 6 Castle View, Barnoldswick, Yorkshire.
　　　Edith Hindle (Mother), Doris Bolger (Aunt) Burnley, Lancashire.
Attack on Vendes. Ex General Service Corps.

HOLMES　　　　　　14578392　　　　　　Pte　　　　　　　2 Jul　　1944
Joseph William　　　　　Age 19
St. Manvieu War Cemetery, Cheux, Calvados, France. Plot I. Row C. Grave 3.
Inscription : THOUGH YOU SLEEP IN A FAR OFF LAND,
　　　　　SOME DAY WE'LL MEET THEN UNDERSTAND.
NoK : G. Holmes (Father) 8 Marsden Place, Newbould Road, Chesterfield, Derbyshire.
Ex General Service Corps.

HOOKER　　　　　　5784200　　　　　　Pte　　　　　　　26 Aug　　1944
James Richard　　　　　Age 21
Banneville-la-Campagne War Cemetery, Calvados, France. Plot I. Row D. Grave 1.
Inscription : IN LOVING MEMORY OF JIM. SILENT THOUGHTS AND MEMORIES
　KEEP YOU FOREVER NEAR.
NoK : F. Hooker (Father) 31 Combe Gardens, New Malden, Surrey.
Ex Royal Norfolk Regt.

HOOLEY　　　　　　14407472　　　　　　Pte　　　　　　　16 Jul　　1944
William　　　　　　　　Age 19
St. Manvieu War Cemetery, Cheux, Calvados, France. Plot V. Row A. Grave 14.
Inscription : GOD MUST HAVE A BEAUTIFUL GARDEN. HE PICKS OUT ONLY THE BEST.
　MAM, DAD AND SISTERS.
NoK : J. Hooley (Father) 71 Marsh House Lane, Warrington, Lancashire.
Killed in action, probably sniper fire, in the attack on Vendes, whilst he was operating a Brengun with Arnold Whiteley. Ex General Service Corps.

HOUGHTON 14652358 Pte 20 Aug 1944
Thomas Randall Age 19
St. Desir War Cemetery, Calvados, France. Plot III. Row F. Grave 12.
Inscription : ONE OF THE DEAREST, ONE OF THE BEST,
GOD GRANT TO HIM ETERNAL REST.
NoK : E. Houghton (Mother) 5 Llanvair Road, Newport, Monmouthshire. Ex General Service Corps.

HUTCHINSON 14759760 Pte 20 Feb 1945
Colin Age 20
Nijmegen-Jonkerbosch War Cemetery, Netherlands. Plot II. Row E. Grave 1.
Inscription : THERE'S SOME CORNER OF A FOREIGN FIELD
THAT IS FOREVER ENGLAND.
NoK : John T.L. & Hilda Hutchinson (Parents) 22 Short Street, Sheffield. Ex General Service Corps.

JOHNSON 4750510 Cpl 25 Sep 1944
Charles Age 27
Leopoldsburg War Cemetery, Limburg, Belgium. Plot V. Row B. Grave 20.
Inscription : LOVED AND LONGED FOR ALWAYS. FOREVER IN OUR THOUGHTS.
LOVING MAM, EVA, RHODA AND LES.
NoK : E. Johnson (Mother) 13 Arthurs Terrace, Waterloo Street, Hull.

JONES 4747533 Pte 27 Jul 1944
Ernest Age 23
St. Manvieu War Cemetery, Cheux, Calvados, France. Plot III. Row J. Grave 12.
Inscription : FOREVER IN OUR THOUGHTS.
NoK : T. Jones (Father) 16 Mandall Street, Sheffield.

JONES 4750480 Pte 18 Feb 1945
John Alfred Age 27
Arnhem-Oosterbeek War Cemetery, Netherlands. Plot 12. Row C. Grave 5.
Inscription : LEST WE FORGET. HE DIED THAT WE MIGHT LIVE.
NoK : John & Ada Jones (Parents) 30 Arksey Lane, Bentley, Doncaster.

JORDON 4745945 Pte 25 Jun 1944
Thomas Age 28
Bayeux War Cemetery, Calvados, France. Plot VIII. Row A. Grave 1.
Inscription : FOR KING AND COUNTRY.
NoK : M.A. Jordon (Mother) 94 Tyne Close, Tyne Dock, South Shields.

JOYCE 5045718 Sgt 2 Jul 1944
Paterick Joseph Age 34
St. Manvieu War Cemetery, Cheux, Calvados, France. Plot III. Row J. Grave 3.
NoK : E.A. Joyce (Wife) 126 Knutton Lane, Knutton, Stoke on Trent. Ex North Staffordshire Regt.

KERR 4745300 Pte 25 Jun 1944
James Age 35
Banneville-la-Campagne War Cemetery, Calvados, France. Plot XIV. Row C. Grave 10.
Inscription : MY DEAR HUSBAND PADDY MADE THE SUPREME SACRIFICE.
REMEMBERED BY WIFE ELLEN. R.I.P.
NoK : Ellen Kerr (Wife) 7 Alexander Terrace, off Alexander Street, Leicester.
Mr. & Mrs. James Kerr (Parents).

KESBY   105267   Lt   15 Jul   1944

Bernard Oliver   Age not recorded

(Bedfordshire & Herefordshire Regt.)

St. Manvieu War Cemetery, Cheux, Calvados, France. Plot I. Row G. Grave 12.

NoK : Laura Kesby (Wife) South Norwood, Surrey

Edgar & Alice Kesby (Parents)

Died near entrance to Battalion HQ. on NE corner of Tessel Wood (shellfire).

KIRK   4748621   Cpl   22 Nov   1944

George Arthur John   Age 26

Venray War Cemetery, Netherlands. Plot IV. Row D. Grave 12.

Inscription : GOD TAKES OUR LOVED ONES FROM OUR HOME,

BUT NEVER FROM OUR HEARTS.

Nok :   G.E. Kirk (Wife) 4 Sherwood Street, Mansfield, Nottinghamshire.

Mr. & Mrs. George Kirk (Parents) Walworth, London.

Bieville en Auge.   *St. Desir.*   *Crevecoeur.*

LACK   4748737   Cpl   18 Aug   1944

William   Age 25

St. Desir War Cemetery, Calvados, France. Plot I. Row F. Grave 12.

Inscription : A SILENT THOUGHT BRINGS MANY A TEAR,

FOR ONE WE MISS AND LOVED SO DEAR.

NoK : (Wife) 63 Audrey Road, Sheffield.

LAMBERT   3858787   Pte   4 Jul   1944

Eric   Age 25

St. Manvieu War Cemetery, Cheux, Calvados, France. Plot VIII. Row A. Grave 15.

Inscription : NOW THE BATTLE DAY IS PAST, NOW UPON THE FARTHER SHORE,

RESTS THE VOYAGER AT LAST.

NoK : H. Lambert (Wife) 54 Langdale Road, Lancaster.

Ex Loyal Regt.

LAW   14414636   Pte   6 Oct   1944
Dennis Arthur   Age 19
Leopoldsburg War Cemetery, Limburg, Belgium. Plot V. Row E. Grave 5.
Inscription : IN LOVING MEMORY OF OUR DEAR DENNIS FOREVER
    REMEMBERED BY ALL AT HOME.
NoK : A. Law (Father) Hill View, Aughton Heath, Chester.
Ex General Service Corps.

LEA   1478340   Pte   20 Feb   1945
Frank   Age 18
Nijmegen-Jonkerbosch War Cemetery, Netherlands. Plot II. Row D. Grave 5.
Inscription : IN LOVING MEMORY OF FRANK.
            EVER REMEMBERED BY HIS MOTHER, BROTHER AND SISTERS.
NoK : Arnold & Alice Lea (Parents) 42 Waverley Street, Oldham, Lancashire.
Ex Royal Artillery.

LEAROYD   4745756   Pte   25 Jun   1944
Leonard   Age 31
Ryes War Cemetery, Bazenville, Calvados, France. Plot II. Row J. Grave 3.
Inscription : IN LOVING MEMORY OF A DEAR SON AND BROTHER.
    REMEMBERED ALWAYS. MAM, DAD AND JOYCE.
NoK : J. Learoyd (Sister) 27 Church Lane, South Owram, Nr. Halifax.

LEE   4747121   Pte   3 May   1940
Andrew   Age 27
Brookwood Memorial, Woking, Surrey. Panel 13. Column 3.
NoK : (Wife) 39 Victoria Street, Sheffield.
Died at sea on H.M.S. 'Afridi' (a 'Tribal' class destroyer) which was sunk by German aircraft during the
withdrawal of troops from Namsos, Norway.

LEES   4744035   Sgt   25 Jun   1944
William Henry   Age 37
Bayeux War Cemetery, Calvados, France. Plot VIII. Row A. Grave 4.
Inscription : SLEEP ON DEAR, GOD KNEW BEST. ON EARTH THERE'S TROUBLE,
IN HEAVEN THERE'S REST.
NoK : E. Lees (Wife) 91 Adisford Road, Sheffield.

LINLEY   4750299   Pte   20 Aug   1944
Arthur   Age 27
Crevecoeur-en-Auge Communal Cemetery, Calvados, France.
Inscription : I WAS NOT THERE WHEN YOU SAID GOODBYE
            BUT IN MY HEART YOU WILL NEVER DIE.
NoK : (Wife) 14 Olivers Mount, Pontefract, Yorkshire.
He is the only British soldier in this tiny civilian cemetery at the foot of 'Snig Hill'.

LOCKETT   4746326   Pte   20 Feb   1945
Sydney Noah   Age 24
Arnhem-Oosterbeek War Cemetery, Netherlands. Plot XXII. Row C. Grave 4.
Inscription : GONE BUT NOT FORGOTTEN. BILLIE.
NoK : Isabelle B. Lockett (Wife) Flat No.2, 28 Castle Bar Park, Ealing, London.
        William & Alice Lockett (Parents)

LOCKWOOD   4685738   Sgt   26 Jun   1944
Arthur   Age 37
Bayeux War Cemetery, Calvados, France. Plot XVIII. Row E. Grave 24.
Inscription : TOO DEARLY LOVED TO BE FORGOTTEN
          BY THE THREE THAT LOVED HIM.
NoK : I.L. Lockwood (Wife) 30 Beck Lane, Carlinghow, Batley, Yorkshire.

LOCKWOOD T.D.   47807   Major   25 Jun   1944
David Eadon   Age 33
St. Manvieu War Cemetery, Cheux, Calvados, France. Plot III. Row B. Grave 3
Inscription : TO THE PRECIOUS MEMORY OF OUR BELOVED DAVID,
          WHO GAVE HIS LIFE FOR US.
NoK : Mary Eliot Lockwood (Wife) 'Brookdean' Bamford, Derbyshire.
          Joseph Cyril & Dorothy Lockwood (Parents)
Died at Fontenay le Pesnel (sniper fire) in field just south of Tilley sur Seulles - Caen road.

LOCKWOOD   4748367   Pte   3 May   1940
Joseph   Age 20
Brookwood Memorial, Woking, Surrey. Panel 13. Column 3.
Died at sea on H.M.S. 'Afridi' (a 'Tribal' class destroyer) which was sunk by German aircraft during the withdrawal of troops from Namsos, Norway.

LONGFORD   4746873   Pte   25 Jun   1944
John Arthur   Age 25
Tilly - sur -Seulles War Cemetery, Calvados, France. Plot III. Row D. Grave 10.
Inscription : ALWAYS SMILING, ALWAYS CONTENT.
          LOVED AND RESPECTED WHEREVER HE WENT.
NoK : Mary Emma Longford (Wife) 4/3 Nandley Street, Pitsmoor, Sheffield.
          Eliza Longford (Mother) Sheffield.
Found (by Graham Roe) lying near edge of stream which runs through the village of Fontenay le Pesnel after Carriers had been destroyed by mortar/shellfire.

LOVELL   4754499   Pte   26 Jul   1944
Charles Victor   Age 29
Aldershot Military Cemetery, Hampshire. Row A. Grave 74.
NoK : Albert Edward & Sophie Lovell (Parents) 173 Stoneleigh Avenue, Worcester Park, Surrey.
Wounded in raid on Vendes, south of Tessel Wood, on 27/6/44.

LUCY   228599   Lt   23 Aug   1944
Stephen Alexander   Age 23
(South Wales Borderers - attached)
St. Desir War Cemetery, Calvados, France. Plot V. Row C. Grave 9.
Inscription : JESUS, MERCY ! MARY, HELP. LUX PERPETUA LUCEAT ET DOMINE.
NoK : Stephen & Brenda May Lucy (Parents) Trecynon, Aberdare, Glamorgan
Died in advance from Chateau le Boutemont to Le Breuil.

LUTON   5571418   Pte   10 Aug   1944
Roland James   Age 25
Banneville-la-Campagne War Cemetery, Calvados, France. Plot VI. Row E. Grave 9.
NoK : W. Luton (Father) Winscombe Hill, Winscombe, Somerset.
Ex Wiltshire Regt.

MACKIN   4748413   Pte   3 Jul   1944
Andrew   Age 26
Bayeux War Cemetery, Calvados, France. Plot VIII. Row B. Grave 13.
Inscription : OF YOUR CHARITY, PRAY FOR THE SOUL OF ANDREW
ON WHOSE SOUL, SWEET JESUS, HAVE MERCY.
NoK : J. Mackin (Father) 112 Windmere Road, Woodhouse, Whitehaven.

MACKINTOSH   4748761   Pte   16 Jul   1944
Charles William   Age 25
St. Manvieu War Cemetery, Cheux, Calvados, France. Plot V. Row A. Grave 10.
NoK : Dolly Mackintosh (Wife) 12 Duffield Road, Rotherham.
Stretcher Bearer. Killed when attending wounded man during attack on Vendes south of Tessel Wood.

Leopoldsburg.

McNEILE   189350   Lt   12 Sep   1944
Harold Dermot   Age 24
Ste. Marie Cemetery, Le Havre, Seine-Maritime, France. Plot 67. Row M. Grave 11.
Inscription : FROM THE UNREAL TO THE REAL. FROM DARKNESS TO LIGHT.
NoK : Revd. Alan Hugh McNeile D.D. & W. St. C. McNeile (Parents) South Kensington.
East Surrey Regt. - attached. (*Died in the Le Havre dock area - sniper fire*)

McNICHOL   14743644   Pte   22 Feb   1945
Edward   Age 18
Uden War Cemetery, Netherlands. Plot VI. Row D. Grave 13.
Inscription : EDWARD & MARIA. ETERNAL REST GIVE UNTO HIM, O LORD.
NoK : Edward & Maria McNichol (Parents) 2 Hartoft Street, York.
Ex General Service Corps.

MALONEY   4756417   Sgt   12 Jul   1944
William   Age 28
St. Manvieu War Cemetery, Cheux, Calvados, France. Plot III. Row A. Grave 11.
Inscription : DEATH DIVIDES BUT MEMORY CLINGS.
NoK : (Wife) 24 Oxford Street, South Shields.

MARSDEN 4756554 L/Cpl 16 Jul 1944
Albert Age 23
St. Manvieu War Cemetery, Cheux, Calvados, France. Plot III. Row H. Grave 7.
Inscription : IN OUR HEARTS YOU ARE NEAR. WE WHO LOVED YOU SADLY MISS YOU
AS IT DAWNS ANOTHER DAY.
NoK : E. Marsden (Brother) 35 Foxwood Avenue, Sheffield.
Attack on Vendes.

MARSH M.C. 53324 Major 13 Sep 1944
Harry John Wilson Age 34
Coriano Ridge War Cemetery, Italy. Plot V. Row F. Grave 11.
NoK : Alethea Barbara Marsh (Wife) Ridgeway, Sheffield
John Lockwood & Edith Maude Marsh (Parents)
Attached : 6th Bn. York & Lancaster Regt. *Died whilst accepting surrender of German troops in burst of automatic fire which also seriously wounded Capt. Tim Kewley, 6th Bn.*

MARSH 4748769 Pte 28 Jun 1944
Harold Age 25
Bayeux Memorial, Calvados, France. Panel 17. Column 1.
NoK : C. Marsh (Wife) 30 Greenwood Road, Sheffield.
Missing in Action between Tessel Wood and Vendes.

MARTIN 4746150 Pte 3 May 1940
John Age 27
Brookwood Memorial, Woking, Surrey. Panel 13. Column 3.
NoK : (Wife) 3/11 Shepney Street, Sheffield.
Died at sea on H.M.S. 'Afridi' (a 'Tribal' class destroyer) which was sunk by German aircraft during the withdrawal of troops from Namsos, Norway.

MAW 4756428 Pte 16 Jun 1944
Charles William Age 30
Bayeux War Cemetery, Calvados, France. Plot XIV. Row H. Grave 20.
Inscription : TREASURED MEMORIES UNTIL WE MEET AGAIN.
NoK : E.E. Maw (Wife) 64 Dunhill Road, Goole, Yorkshire.

MEARS 4748658 Pte 16 Jul 1944
Henry Charles Age 25
St. Manvieu War Cemetery, Cheux, Calvados, France. Plot III. Row H. Grave 3.
Inscription : NOT GONE FROM MEMORY, NOT GONE FROM LOVE,
BUT GONE TO THE FATHERS HOME ABOVE.
NoK : (Sister) 175 Tyers Street, Lambeth, London.

MERCER 4801628 Pte 16 Aug 1944
Thomas Victor Age 25
Banneville-la-Campagne War Cemetery, Calvados, France. Plot I. Row D. Grave 2.
Inscription : ONE WE SHALL NEVER FORGET, HIS MEMORY A TREASURE,
HIS LOSS OUR LIFETIME REGRET.
NoK : Thomas & Emma Mercer (Parents) 180 Cemetery Road, Low Brumby, Scunthorpe, Lincolnshire.
Ex Lincolnshire Regt.

MORGAN   4191496   Pte   12 Jul   1944
Thomas Ivor Val   Age 27
St. Manvieu War Cemetery, Cheux, Calvados, France. Plot V. Row A. Grave 8.
Inscription : ALWAYS SMILING, ALWAYS CONTENT.
             LOVED AND RESPECTED WHEREVER HE WENT.
NoK : (Mother) 3 Oakfield Terrace, Rhayder.
Ex Royal Welsh Fusiliers.

MORGAN   14714418   Pte   28 Aug   1944
George   Age 18
St. Desir War Cemetery, Calvados, France. Plot I. Row B. Grave 13.
Inscription : SWEET ARE THE MEMORIES SILENTLY KEPT
           OF A SON I LOVED DEARLY AND WILL NEVER FORGET.
NoK : E. Morgan (Mother) 103 Vale Road, Colwick, Nottingham. Ex General Service Corps.

MORLEY   4756558   Sgt   28 Jul   1944
George Herbert   Age 28
Banneville-la-Campagne War Cemetery, Calvados, France. Plot IV. Row F. Grave 20.
Inscription : BEAUTIFUL MEMORIES TREASURED EVER,
           OF HAPPY DAYS WE SPENT TOGETHER.
NoK : J. Morley (Wife) 11 High Street, Horbury, Nr. Wakefield.
Died of Wounds ?

MORTON   4744828   CSM   26 Jun   1944
Stanley   Age 33
Bayeux War Cemetery, Calvados, France. Plot XIII. Row F. Grave 22.
Inscription : IN LOVING MEMORY OF A DEAR HUSBAND AND DADDY.
           "LOVES LAST GIFT, REMEMBRANCE"
NoK : I.E. Morton (Wife) 14 Millfield Road, York.

MOUNSEY   3607648   Pte   9 Aug   1944
John Frederick   Age 21
Bayeux Memorial, Calvados, France. Panel 17. Column 1.
NoK : A. Mounsey (Wife) 8 Lewin Street, Leicester.
Missing in Action near Chichiboville. Ex Border Regt.

MUMBY   53539   Capt   27 Feb   1943
Richard   Age 35
Brookwood Memorial, Woking, Surrey. Panel 13. Column 3.
NoK : Margaret Mumby (Wife) Ley Hill, Buckinghamshire
        Frank Arthur & Eleanor Mary Mumby (Parents)
Died at sea in post of Ships Adjutant.

NEALON   14573591   Pte   25 Jun   1944
Patrick   Age 19
Ryes War Cemetery, Bazenville, Calvados, France. Plot II. Row J. Grave 5.
Inscription : HE NEEDS NO MEDALS, RIBBONS OR BARS,
           FOR HIS NAME IS WRITTEN ACROSS THE STARS.
NoK : E. Nealon (Mother) 10 Edmund Street, Collyhurst, Manchester.
Ex General Service Corps.

NEWMAN   4747883   Sgt   22 Feb   1945
Joseph   Age 37
Nijmegen-Jonkerbosch War Cemetery, Netherlands. Plot I. Row C. Grave 3.
NoK : M.A. Newman (Wife) 103 East Street, Dinnington, Sheffield.

NEWMAN   14714424   Pte   29 Sep   1944
Ronald Arthur   Age 18
Geel War Cemetery, Geel, Antwerp, Belgium. Plot II. Row B. Grave 24.
Inscription : GOD BE WITH YOU TILL WE MEET AGAIN.
NoK : (Mother) 22 Harley Street, Linton, Nottingham. Ex General Service Corps.

NICHOLS   4750406   Pte   25 Jun   1944
John   Age 27
Ryes War Cemetery, Bazenville, Calvados, France. Plot II. Row H. Grave 1.
Inscription : THE SON OF ROSE AND THE LATE JOHN T. NICHOLS OF
    WAKEFIELD, ENGLAND. GOD REST HIS SOUL.
NoK : M. Nichols (Wife) 13 Earl Street, Wakefield.

NIXON   5057873   Pte   7 Oct   1944
Ralph Dennis   Age 21
Leopoldsburg War Cemetery, Limburg, Belgium. Plot II. Row D. Grave 12.
Inscription : WE NEVER KNEW THE PAIN HE SUFFERED.
        ALWAYS REMEMBERED. DAD, MUM, STAN AND RON.
NoK : R. Nixon (Father) 33 Reynolds Road, Stansfields, Tunstall, Staffordshire.
Ex North Staffordshire Regt.

NOISEUX   CDN/182   Lt   14 Jun   1944
Joseph Arthur   Age not recorded
Bayeux War Cemetery, Calvados, France. Plot XI. Row F. Grave 22.
Royal Canadian Infantry Corps - attached.
Died just East of the village Audreiu.

NORMAN   14723112   Pte   13 Apr   1945
Eric Charles   Age 19
Arnhem-Oosterbeek War Cemetery, Netherlands. Plot VII. Row A. Grave 8.
Inscription : WHILE THE WORLD VIBRATES WITH JOY, I WITH AN ACHING HEART,
        WILL MOURN MY SOLDIER BOY.
NoK : Dorothy Norman (Mother) 17 Miora Crescent, Birmingham. Ex General Service Corps.

NUTTALL   2044892   Pte   10 Aug   1944
Percy   Age 26
Banneville-la-Campagne War Cemetery, Calvados, France. Plot VI. Row E. Grave 7.
Inscription : RESTING WHERE NO SHADOWS FALL.
NoK : E. Nuttall (Wife) 'The Hill' Holmfirth, Nr. Huddersfield. Ex Royal Engineers.

ODDY   4748833   L/Cpl   25 Sep   1944
Angus   Age 25
Leopoldsburg War Cemetery, Limburg, Belgium. Plot VI. Row D. Grave 12.
Inscription : IN LOVING MEMORY OF ANGUS, THE DEAR SON OF EMMA AND
    THE LATE EDWARD ODDY. BROTHER OF MARY AND FRED.
NoK : Edward & Emma Oddy (Parents) 200 Old Mill Lane, Birkinshaw, Nr. Bradford.

OXLEY	4745701	Cpl	18 Aug	1944

William Henry   Age 32

St. Desir War Cemetery, Calvados, France. Plot I. Row F. Grave 11.

Inscription : YOU DUTY DONE. WE CAN NEVER FORGET.
LOVE, ANN, MUM, DAD AND FAMILY.

NoK : (Father) 7 Northern Avenue, Arbourthorne Estate, Sheffield.

PACEY	14584792	Pte	2 Jul	1944

Peter   Age 20

Bayeux Memorial, Calvados, France. Panel 17. Column 1.

NoK : W. Pacey (Father) Toft House, Church Lane, Pudsey, Leeds.

Missing in Action between Tessel Wood and Vendes. Ex General Service Corps.

PALMER	4748496	Pte	28 Jun	1944

William Bransfield   Age 25

Tilly-sur-Seulles War Cemetery, Calvados, France. Plot IV. Row B. Grave 10.

Inscription : SADLY MISSED.

NoK : W. Palmer (Father) 15 Cooperative Street, Horsbury, Nr. Wakefield.

Died in mortar/shellfire at Forward Bn.HQ. on SE corner of Tessel Wood.

PARKER	4748876	Pte	10 Aug	1944

Norman   Age 25

Banneville-la-Campagne War Cemetery, Calvados, France. Plot VI. Row E. Grave 11.

Inscription : FOR ALL OF US HE DID HIS BEST. GOD GRANT HIM ETERNAL REST. R.I.P.

NoK : C. Parker (Father) 32 Albion Street, Morley, Leeds.

Roosendaal.   *Fijnaart.*   *Baarle - Nassau*

PARKIN	14624865	Pte	31 Aug	1944

Arthur   Age 39

St. Desir War Cemetery, Calvados, France. Plot III. Row C. Grave 1.

Inscription : PEACE PERFECT PEACE.

NoK : E. Parkin (Wife) 51 Old Park Road, Sheffield.

Ex General Service Corps.

PARKINSON   4748333   Pte   23 Aug   1944
Herbert   Age 26
St. Desir War Cemetery, Calvados, France. Plot V. Row C. Grave 3.
NoK : D. Parkinson (Wife) 222 Oxford Road, Gomersall, Nr. Leeds.

PARTNER   14683272   Pte   7 Oct   1944
Kenneth   Age 19
Leopoldsburg War Cemetery, Limburg, Belgium. Plot V. Row E. Grave 1.
Inscription : YOUR DEATH WAS SUDDEN KEN AND WE WONDER WHY
                YOU HAD NO CHANCE TO SAY GOODBYE.
NoK : R. Partner (Mother) 162 Milbourn Road, Ibstock, Leicestershire.
Ex General Service Corps.

PARTOON   4758040   Pte   26 Jun   1944
Thomas   Age 29
Ryes War Cemetery, Bazenville, Calvados, France. Plot III. Row G. Grave 4.
Inscription : HE GAVE HIS TODAY FOR YOUR TOMORROW.
NoK : (Father) 164 Weedon Street, Sheffield.

PAYNE   4976889   Cpl   15 Jun   1944
John William   Age 26
Bayeux War Cemetery, Calvados, France. Plot II. Row F. Grave 23.
Inscription : A DAY OF MEMORY SAD TO RECALL,
                WITHOUT FAREWELL HE LEFT US ALL.
NoK : W. Payne (Father) 12 Crossways, Bedford.
Ex Notts & Derby Regt. (Sherwood Foresters)

PEACOCK   4747621   Pte   3 May   1940
Cyril   Age 19
Brookwood Memorial, Woking, Surrey. Panel 13. Column 3.
NoK : (Father) 22 Maltravers Place, Wybourn, Sheffield.
Died at sea on H.M.S. 'Afridi' (a 'Tribal' class destroyer) which was sunk by German aircraft during the
withdrawal of troops from Namsos, Norway.

PEARCE   CDN/495   Capt   25 Sep   1944
Wilfred Arthur   Age 36
Leopoldsburg War Cemetery, Limburg, Belgium. Plot VI. Row D. Grave 14.
Inscription : LEST WE FORGET.
NoK : Mary Pearce (Wife) Calgary, Alberta, Canada
*   Fred Stanley & Emily Louise Pearce (Parents)*
Royal Canadian Infantry Corps - attached. *Died on the roadside (shellfire) between Rijkvorsel and*
Merksplas during the establishment of the Antwerp - Turnhout canal bridgehead.

PEARCE   5570547   Pte   7 Aug   1944
Wilfred Frank   Age 24
Warminster Baptist Chapel Yard, Wiltshire. Grave in West Portion.
NoK : (Wife) 56 Erlange Road, New Cross, London, SE 14.
Ex Wiltshire Regt.

PEARSON 14661111 Pte 27 Jun 1944
Norman Age 19
St. Desir War Cemetery, Calvados, France. Plot III. Row J. Grave 6.
NoK : J. Pearson (Father) 19 Park Avenue, Whiston, Nr. Rotherham.
Ex General Service Corps.

PEDEL 14590822 Pte 2 Jul 1944
George William Age 19
Bayeux Memorial, Calvados, France. Panel 17. Column 1.
NoK : E. A. Pedel (Father) 1 Beech Hill, Knaresborough, Yorkshire.
Missing in Action between Tessel Wood and Vendes.
Known to have been killed in fields to the south end of Tessel Wood during withdrawal from a raid on Vendes. Witnessed by Bert Murray who was captured in the same action. Ex General Service Corps.

PELLATT 6342345 Cpl 27 Aug 1944
Albert Edward Age 30
St. Desir War Cemetery, Calvados, France. Plot III. Row D. Grave 11.
Inscription : IN LOVING MEMORY OF MY HUSBAND. ALWAYS IN OUR THOUGHTS.
    WIFE ROSARIA AND MARGRETH.
NoK : M. Pellatt (Wife) 428 High Street, West Bromwich, Staffordshire.
Ex Royal West Kent Regt.

PENNINGTON 14715474 Pte 25 Sep 1944
Roy Age 18
Leopoldsburg War Cemetery, Limburg, Belgium. Plot V. Row B. Grave 18.
Inscription : DEARER TO MEMORY THAN WORDS CAN TELL,
        WAS THE ONE WE LOST AND LOVED SO WELL. R.I.P.
NoK : W.G. Perkins (Father) 67 Salthouse Road, Barrow in Furness.
Ex General Service Corps.

PERKINS 14533157 Pte 25 Jun 1944
Leslie Ronald Age 20
Ryes War Cemetery, Bazenville, Calvados, France. Plot VIII. Row H. Grave 3.
Inscription : SAFE IN GODS KEEPING. ONE OF THE BEST GOD EVER SENT.
        NOT GIVEN TO US, ONLY LENT.
NoK : G. Perkins (Father) 4 New London, Princetown, Devon.
Ex General Service Corps.

PETERS 14747834 Pte 20 Feb 1945
Albert   William Age 18
Arnhem-Oosterbeek War Cemetery, Nederlands. Plot XII. Row C. Grave 3.
Inscription : SAFE IN GOD'S KEEPING, PEACEFULLY SLEEPING,
        GOOD NIGHT, DEAR SON.
NoK : Albert & Edith Amy Peters (Parents) 27 Devonshire Road, Gillingham, Kent.
Ex General Service Corps.

PHIPPS 1154662 Pte 23 Aug 1944
Edward Walter Age 21
St. Desir War Cemetery, Calvados, France. Plot V. Row C. Grave 4.
Inscription : WE SHALL ALWAYS THINK OF YOU DEAR AND MISS YOUR FACE.
    YOUR LOVING MUM AND DAD.
NoK : F. Phipps (Father) 65 Henley Road, Edmonton, London, N 18.
Died in advance from Chateau le Boutemont to Le Breuil. Ex Royal Artillery.

PITCOCK 14673219 Pte 7 Aug 1944
Ernest   Graham Age 18
Ranville War Cemetery, Calvados, France. Plot VIII. Row B. Grave 3.
NoK : E. Pitcock (Father) 127 Broadway West, Walsall, Staffordshire.
Ex General Service Corps.

POTTER 5059009 Pte 29 Jul 1944
Eric Age 22
Banneville-la-Campagne War Cemetery, Calvados, France. Plot IV. Row F. Grave 23.
Inscription : PEACE PERFECT PEACE. HE DIED THAT WE MIGHT LIVE.
NoK : S. Potter (Father) 13 Oakville Avenue, High Lane, Burslem, Stoke on Trent.
Ex North Staffordshire Regt.

POYNOR 156757 Lt. 10 Jul 1944
Harry Edward Age 30
St. Manvieu War Cemetery, Cheux, Calvados. Plot III. Row A. Grave 10.
Inscription : IN PROUD AND LOVING MEMORY OF DEAR TED.
NoK : Isobel Dorothy Poynor (Wife) Dulwich, London.
        George Edward and Elsie May Poynor (Parents)
Killed in action at the southern end of Tessel Wood. Shot through the heart and buried by George Learad
in temporary grave.

PRESTON 4744722 Pte 25 Sep 1944
Herbert Age 32
Leopoldsburg War Cemetery, Limburg, Belgium. Plot II. Row A. Grave 15.
Inscription : NEVER SHALL HE BE FORGOTTEN OR HIS MEMORY FADE.
NoK : F.M. Preston (Wife) 27 Peel Street, Hunslet, Leeds, 10.

PUGH 302172 Lt 23 Aug 1944
Stanley Robert Age 20
St. Desir War Cemetery, Calvados, France. Plot I. Row B. Grave 1.
Inscription : SADLY MISSED BY THOSE WHO LOVED HIM.
NoK : Stanley Robert & Florence May Pugh (Parents) Bow, London
East Surrey Regt. - attached. *Died in advance from Chateau le Boutemont to Le Breuil.*

PYE 11002343 L/Cpl 7 Oct 1944
Arthur Neville Age 23
Leopoldsburg War Cemetery, Limburg, Belgium. Plot V. Row B. Grave 2.
Inscription : IN LIFE WE LOVED HIM DEARLY, IN DEATH SWEET MEMORIES CLING.
NoK : F. Pye (Mother) 178 Broom Lane, Levenshulme, Manchester.
Ex Royal Artillery (Anti-Aircraft Branch)

Venray.   Uden.

RAMSBOTTOM　　　　　4748383　　　　　Pte　　　　　25 Jun　　　1944
Arnold Robinson　　　　　Age 25
Ryes War Cemetery, Bazenville, Calvados, France. Plot II. Row G. Grave 7.
Inscription : ONLY LOVING AND BEAUTIFUL MEMORIES OF A GOOD SON.
　　　　UNTIL WE MEET IN HEAVEN.
NoK : H. Ramsbottom (Father) Sunnymount Terrace, Birstall. Leeds.

RAYNER　　　　　　　14746054　　　　　Pte　　　　　13 Apr　　　1945
Terence　　　　　　　　Age 19
Arnhem-Oosterbeek War Cemetery, Nederlands. Plot VII. Row A. Grave 9.
Inscription : IN LOVING MEMORY UNTIL WE MEET AGAIN.
　　　　MAY YOU REST IN PEACE. MUM.
NoK : A. Rayner (Father) East Row, Church Street, Headingworth, Huntingdonshire.
Ex General Service Corps.

REEVE　　　　　　　14327847　　　　　Pte　　　　　10 Jul　　　1944
Frank　　　　　　　　　Age 19
Bayeux Memorial, Calvados, France. Panel 17. Column 1.
NoK : A. Reeve (Father) 8 Hornsey Road, Kingstanding, Birmingham.
Missing in Action between Tessel Wood and Vendes. Ex General Service Corps.

RIGBY　　　　　　　11408278　　　　　Pte　　　　　22 Jul　　　1944
John Henry　　　　　　Age 23
Reichswald Forest War Cemetery, Germany. Plot DIX. Row H. Grave 12.
Inscription : HE DIED IN WAR BUT NOW RESTS IN ETERNAL PEACE.
　　　　TILL WE ARE RE-UNITED.
NoK : Robert Ernest & Florence Rigby (Parents) Southport, Lancashire.
Died of Wounds ?　Ex General Service Corps.

RILEY　　　　　　　3447780　　　　　Pte　　　　　4 Jul　　　1944
Jack　　　　　　　　　Age 31
Tilly-sur-Seulles War Cemetery, Calvados, France. Plot III. Row B. Grave 13.
NoK : Not recorded.
Ex Lancashire Fusiliers.

378

ROBINSON   14412764   Pte   10 Jul   1944
James Robert   Age 19
Bayeux Memorial, Calvados, France. Panel 17. Column 1.
NoK : A. Robinson (Father) 36 Napier Avenue, Southend on Sea, Essex.
Missing in Action between Tessel Wood and Vendes. Ex General Service Corps.

ROBSON   1676901   Pte   18 Aug   1944
John William   Age 36
St. Desir War Cemetery, Calvados, France. Plot I. Row F. Grave 13.
NoK : (Wife) 16 Hindle Street, Lancaster. Ex Royal Artillery.

ROSE   2183139   Cpl   16 Jul   1944
William Alfred   Age 36
St. Manvieu War Cemetery, Cheux, Calvados, France. Plot III. Row H. Grave 11.
Inscription : NO VERSE CAN SAY, NO WEALTH REPAY,
          FOR THE DEAREST ONE WE LOST THIS DARK DAY.
NoK : I. Rose (Wife) 105 Yew Tree Lane, South Yardley, Birmingham.
Attack on Vendes. Ex Royal Engineers.

ROWE   4968391   L/Cpl   26 Sep   1944
Jack Sydney   Age 37
Brussels Church Cemetery, Belgium. Plot X. Row 22. Grave 31.
NoK : (Wife) 9 Belle Lee, Portland Street, Daybrook, Nottingham.
Ex Nottinghamshire & Derbyshire Regt. (Sherwood Foresters)

SANDS   4748376   Pte   12 Jul   1944
Robert Edward   Age 26
St. Manvieu War Cemetery, Cheux, Calvados, France. Plot III. Row A. Grave 9.
Inscription : REST IN PEACE
NoK : M. Sands (Mother) 3 Blenheim Place, Eightlands, Dewsbury, Yorkshire.

SEAL   6342832   Pte   29 Sep   1944
George Henry   Age 30
Leopoldsburg War Cemetery, Limburg, Belgium. Plot V. Row B. Grave 16.
Inscription : "ABIDE WITH ME, FAST FALLS THE EVENTIDE"
NoK : W.M. Sands (Wife) 51 Alexandra Road, Ramsgate, Kent. Ex Royal West Kent Regt.

SEARLE   4747421   L/Cpl   7 Jul   1944
Walter   Age 24
St. Manvieu War Cemetery, Cheux, Calvados, France. Plot III. Row A. Grave 3.
Inscription : WITH HIS SWEET YOUNG LIFE HE PAID THE PRICE,
          THAT WE MIGHT LIVE. GOD REST HIS SOUL.
NoK : W. Searle (Father) 256 Buchanan Road, Parsons Cross, Sheffield.

SELBY   14508138   Pte   5 Nov   1944
Phillip John   Age 20
Roosendaal-en-Nispen Roman Catholic Cemetery, Nederlands. Row C. Grave 9.
Inscription : NEVER SHALL THY MEMORY FADE,
          SWEET THOUGHTS EVER LINGER WHERE THOU ART LAID.
NoK : (Mother) 9 Wallburgh Place, Shadwell, London, E 1.
Ex General Service Corps.

SELLIS 1627935 Pte 5 Nov 1944
Montague Age 33
Roosendaal-en-Nispen Roman Catholic Cemetery, Nederlands. Row B. Grave 10.
Inscription : TOGETHER THE HIGHWAY OF LIFE WE TROD,
            YOUR MEMORY BRINGS US NEARER TO GOD.
NoK : M. Sellis (Mother) 3 Acfold Road, London, SW 6.
Ex Royal Artillery.

SEYMOUR 4748715 Sgt 7 Jul 1942
Eric Douglas Age 23
Akureyri Cemetery, Iceland. Military Plot. Row B. Grave 7
NoK : Mr. & Mrs. A. Seymour (Parents) 49 Meopham Road, Mitcham, Surrey.
Accidentally shot whilst working in the 'butts' of a firing range near Bragholt.

SHAW 4748347 Pte 3 May 1940
Arthur Age 21
Brookwood Memorial, Woking, Surrey. Panel 13. Column 3.
NoK : (Mother) 53 Crescent Road, Birkley, Huddersfield.
Died at sea on H.M.S. 'Afridi' (a 'Tribal' class destroyer) which was sunk by German aircraft during the
withdrawal of troops from Namsos, Norway.

SHEPHERD 4746075 L/Cpl 3 May 1940
Sidney Age 23
Brookwood Memorial, Woking, Surrey. Panel 13. Column 3.
NoK : (Wife). 80 Ouse Road, Sheffield.
Died at sea on H.M.S. 'Afridi' during the withdrawal of troops from Namsos, Norway.

SHORROCK 14413614 Pte 16 Jul 1944
George Arson Age 19
St. Manvieu War Cemetery, Cheux, Calvados, France. Plot V. Row A. Grave 13.
Inscription : WILL ALWAYS BE REMEMBERED BY HIS MOTHER,
            TWIN BROTHER DON AND SISTER JESSIE.
NoK : Thomas and Annie Shorrock (Parents) Blackburn, Lancashire.
Attack on Vendes. Ex General Service Corps.

SINGLETON 4755733 L/Cpl 27 Jul 1944
Colin Age 31
Ranville War Cemetery, Calvados, France. Plot IV. Row F. Grave 24.
NoK : M. Singleton (Wife) Monks Wood, Upper Haigh, Rawmarsh, Rotherham.
Died of Wounds ?

SMIRTHWAITE 14759957 L/Cpl 22 Feb 1945
Ronald Age 22
Groesbeek Memorial, Canadian War Cemetery, Nederlands. Panel 5.
NoK : Mrs. Ada Baker (Mother) 51 Downham Road, Firth Park, Sheffield.
Missing in Action at De Hoeven Farm, Nr. Indoornik, Holland. Ex General Service Corps.

Milsbeek.   *Groesbeek Memorial*

SMITH   2596292   Pte   9 Aug   1944
Albert   James   Age 24
Le Deliverande War Cemetery, Calvados, France. Plot V. Row L. Grave 10.
Inscription : SLEEP ON DEAR SOLDIER, TAKE THY REST.
              MAY ALL THOSE DEAR TO THEE BE BLESSED.
NoK : (Father) 88 Cumber Lane, Whiston, St. Helens, Lancashire.
Ex Royal Corps of Signals.

SMITH   4746203   Pte   28 Jun   1944
Arthur Ray   Age 30
Fontenay le Pesnel, Calvados, France. Plot II. Row D. Grave 19.
Inscription : IN PROUD AND LOVING MEMORY OF A VERY DEAR HUSBAND.
              HIS LOVING WIFE ELIZABETH.
NoK : E. Smith (Wife) 87 Wilthorpe Avenue, Huddersfield Road, Barnsley, Yorks.

SMITH   14371376   Pte   16 Jun   1944
Harold Arthur   Age 33
St. Manvieu War Cemetery, Cheux, Calvados, France. Plot III. Row H. Grave 9.
Inscription : IN LOVING MEMORY OF MY PRECIOUS HUSBAND.
              GONE, NEVER TO BE FORGOTTEN. AMELIA.
NoK : A.S. Smith (Wife) 58 Kent Road, Grays, Essex.
Ex General Service Corps.

SMITH   14419850   Pte   16 Jul   1944
John William   Age 18
Bayeux Memorial, Calvados, France. Panel 17. Column 1.
NoK : J. Smith (Father) 51 Johnson Road, Croydon, Surrey.
Missing in Action during the attack on Vendes. Ex General Service Corps.

SMITH   7671645   Pte   27 Jun   1944
Reginald John   Age 27
St. Manvieu War Cemetery, Cheux, Calvados, France. Plot III. Row J. Grave 5.
Inscription : GOD GRANT HIM NOW ETERNAL REST.
NoK : K. Smith (Wife) 19 Liverpool Road, Watford, Hertfordshire.
Ex Royal Army Pay Corps.

| **SNARR** | 4745244 | Pte | 2 Jul | 1944 |
| Newton | Age 30 | | | |

Bayeux Memorial, Calvados, France. Panel 17. Column 1.
NoK : A. Snarr (Wife) 31 Morley Street, Goole.
Missing in Action between Tessel Wood and Vendes.

| **SNEYD** | 3607311 | Pte | 23 Aug | 1944 |
| Frank Dowell | Age 21 | | | |

St. Desir War Cemetery, Calvados, France. Plot III. Row F. Grave 8.
NoK : F. Sneyd (Father) 77 Worsley Road, Winton, Lancashire.
Died in advance from Chateau le Boutemont to Le Breuil. Ex Border Regt.

| **SOUTHWORTH** | 14715519 | Pte | 25 Sep | 1944 |
| James Leslie | Age 18 | | | |

Leopoldsburg War Cemetery, Limburg, Belgium. Plot V. Row B. Grave 17.
NoK : J. Southworth (Father) 20 London road, Preston, Lancashire.
Ex General Service Corps.

Nijmegen - Jonkerbosch.

| **SPENCER** | 14431357 | Pte | 29 Sep | 1944 |
| Charles Kenneth | Age 18 | | | |

Geel War Cemetery, Geel, Antwerp, Belgium. Plot II. Row B. Grave 23.
NoK : Charles H. & Emily E. Spencer (Parents) 3/110 Lupin Street, Birmingham.
Ex General Service Corps.

| **STAMFORD** | 14272269 | Pte | 5 Nov | 1944 |
| Roy William | Age 24 | | | |

Roosendaal-en-Nispen Roman Catholic Cemetery, Nederlands. Row B. Grave 9.
Inscription : R.I.P. WE WILL ALWAYS REMEMBER HE DIED A NOBLE DEATH.
NoK : L. Stamford (Wife) 7 High Street, Melbourne, Nr. Royston, Hertfordshire.
Ex General Service Corps.

STARKEY   4746559   Pte   3 May   1940
Douglas James   Age 19
Brookwood Memorial, Woking, Surrey. Panel 13. Column 3.
NoK :   2/Lt. T.R. Starkey, D.C.M., M.M. and Mrs. M.E. Starkey (Parents)
187 Darnall Road, Sheffield
Died at sea on H.M.S. 'Afridi' (a 'Tribal' class destroyer) which was sunk by German aircraft during the
withdrawal of troops from Namsos, Norway.

STOTT   14534339   Pte   22 Oct   1944
Enoch   Age 20
Geel War Cemetery, Geel, Antwerp, Belgium. Plot III. Row C. Grave 17.
NoK : E. Stott (Wife) 4 Glove Street, Attercliffe, Sheffield.
Ex General Service Corps.

TAGG   4685632   Pte   27 Jun   1944
William Edwin   Age 40
St. Manvieu War Cemetery, Cheux, Calvados, France. Plot III. Row H. Grave 5.
Inscription : ONE OF THE BEST, GONE FROM OUR HOME,
                 BUT NOT FROM OUR HEARTS.
NoK :   Mary Tagg (Wife) 43 Manor Oaks Close, Wybourn Estate, Sheffield.
Frederick & Eliza Tagg (Parents) Sheffield
Ex King's Own Yorkshire Light Infantry.

TETT   160584   Lt   12 Jun   1944
Frank Horatio   Age 26
Bayeux War Cemetery, Calvados, France. Plot XIV. Row K. Grave 17.
Inscription : IN LOVING MEMORY. HIS FACE, HIS VOICE, HIS SMILE,
                 WILL LINGER FOREVER. MOTHER.
NoK : Frank & Clara Eliza Tett (Parents) Surbiton, Surrey.
Died whilst attempting to clear woods to the east of Audrieu.

Arnhem - Oosterbeek.

TINDLE   14350148   Pte   25 Jun   1944
Robert Newton   Age 33
St. Manvieu War Cemetery, Cheux, Calvados, France. Plot III. Row B. Grave 2.
NoK :   A. Tindle (Wife) 11 South Street, Hemsworth, Nr. Pontefract.
Ex General Service Corps.

TIPPER   4618675   L/Cpl   27 Jun   1944
Lawrence Harold   Age 27
Bayeux Memorial, Calvados, France. Panel 17. Column 1.
NoK :   F. Tipper (Brother) 10 Darville Crescent, London, W 6.
Missing in Action at Tessel Wood Ex Duke of Wellington's Regt. (West Riding).

TOON   314153   2/Lt   25 Sept   1944
Harold Purday   Age 24
Leopoldsburg War Cemetery, Limburg, Belgium. Plot II. Row A. Grave 14
Inscription : DUTY NOBLY DONE.
NoK : Adrian & Evelyn May Toon (Parents) Hucknall, Notts.
Killed just south of the Rijkvorsel - Merksplas road approximately one mile east of Rijkvorsel. This officer was leading his Platoon along a track from the newly erected Bailey bridge during establishment of bridgehead across the Antwerp/Turnhout canal.

Left & right : Reichswald Forest

TURNER   4927158   Pte   16 Jul   1944
James Albert   Age 20
St. Manvieu War Cemetery, Cheux, Calvados, France. Plot III. Row H. Grave 10.
Inscription : WE LOVED HIM, WE MISS HIM, IN OUR MEMORY HE IS SO DEAR.
             HIS LOVING WIFE AND SON.
NoK : E.I. Turner (Wife) 30 Priory Road, Warwick, Warwickshire.
Attack on Vendes.
Ex South Staffordshire Regt.

TWIGG   4748767   Pte   16 Jul   1944
William John   Age 25
St. Manvieu War Cemetery, Cheux, Calvados, France. Plot III. Row J. Grave 13.
Inscription : FOR ALL OF US HE DID HIS BEST. GOD GRANT HIM ETERNAL REST.
NoK :   A. Twigg (Wife) 127 Carwell Road, Woodseats, Sheffield.
Attack on Vendes.

WADE   4748396   Pte   3 May   1940
Tom   Age 21
Brookwood Memorial, Woking, Surrey. Panel 13. Column 3.
NoK :   *(Father) 10 Park Lodge Crescent, Park Lodge Lane, Wakefield, Yorkshire.*
Died at sea on H.M.S. 'Afridi' (a 'Tribal' class destroyer) which was sunk by German aircraft during the
withdrawal of troops from Namsos, Norway.

WALTERS   1548900   Pte   25 Sep   1944
Charles William   Age 27
Leopoldsburg War Cemetery, Limburg, Belgium. Plot V. Row B. Grave 9.
Inscription : IN LOVING MEMORY OF DEAR CHARLIE.
                 DAD AND SISTER DORIS. JERSEY, CHANNEL ISLANDS.
NoK :   *R.W. Walters (Father) 18 States Houses, Greek-de-Ozette, St. Clements, Jersey.*
Ex Royal Artillery.

WARREN   4747653   L/Cpl   10 Jul   1944
Arthur   Age 24
Bayeux Memorial, Calvados, France. Panel 17. Column 1.
NoK :   *(Father) 97 Beighton Lane, Woodhouse, Sheffield.*
Missing in Action.

WASS   14743741   Pte   16 Jan   1945
Reginald   Age 18
Groesbeek Memorial, Canadian War Cemetery, Nederlands. Panel 5.
NoK :   *F.R. Wass (Father) 132 Myste Road, Heeley, Sheffield.*
Missing in Action near Bemmel. Ex General Service Corps.

WATKINS   4750508   Cpl   16 Jul   1944
Frank   Age 27
St. Manvieu War Cemetery, Cheux, Calvados, France. Plot V. Row A. Grave 9.
Inscription : TREASURED MEMORIES OF A DARLING HUSBAND.
                 TO LIVE IN LOVING HEARTS IS NOT TO DIE.
NoK :   *V. Watkins (Wife) 56 Holgate Crescent, Hordsworth, Nr. Pontefract.*
Attack on Vendes.

WATKINSON   14762224   Pte   16 Jan   1945
William Francis John   Age 20
Nijmegen-Jonkerbosch War Cemetery, Holland. Plot I. Row C. Grave 2.
Inscription : NO MORE YOUR VOICE WE HEAR, BUT YOU SEEM TO BE WITH US,
                 NEVER ABSENT, EVER NEAR. MUM, DAD & RON.
NoK :   *W. Watkinson (Father) 3 Tanners Hill, Abbots Longley, Watford, Hertfordshire.*
Ex General Service Corps.

WATSON - JONES   140486   Lt   25 Jun   1944
Oliver   Age 24
Ryes War Cemetery, Bazenville, Calvados, France. Plot II. Row J. Grave 2.
Inscription : THEY SHALL GROW NOT OLD, AS WE THAT ARE LEFT GROW OLD.
NoK :   *Flora Watson - Jones (Wife) York*
              Bernard & Aileen Watson - Jones (Parents)
Known to his fellow officers as 'George'. Died at Fontenay le Pesnel.

385

WEEDON   4751418   Pte   6 Oct   1944
Charles Samuel   Age 24
Leopoldsburg War Cemetery, Limburg, Belgium. Plot V. Row E. Grave 6.
Inscription : IN LOVING MEMORY OF A DEAR HUSBAND AND SON. 'MIZPAH'
NoK :   F. Weedon (Wife) 1 Holroyd Avenue, Tang Hill, York.

WEIGHT   14694571   Pte   29 Sep   1944
William Albert   Age 19
Leopoldsburg War Cemetery, Limburg, Belgium. Plot V. Row B. Grave 14.
Inscription : GONE FROM US BUT NOT FORGOTTEN.
          NEVER SHALL THY MEMORY FADE. R.I.P.
NoK :   M. Weight (Mother) 57 Ellenborough House, White City Estate, Westway, London.
Ex General Service Corps.

WILKINS   6403354   Pte   10 Aug   1944
Alexander Francis   Age 27
Banneville-la-Campagne War Cemetery, Calvados, France. Plot VI. Row E. Grave 6.
Inscription : MY BELOVED HUSBAND, ALWAYS.
          LOVE SO DIVINE DEMANDS MY SOUL, MY LIFE, MY ALL.
NoK :   J. Wilkins (Wife) 54 Dyne Road, Brondsbury, London, NW 6.
Ex Royal Sussex Regt.

WILLDER   4986998   Pte   16 Jul   1944
George Henry   Age 30
St. Manvieu War Cemetery, Cheux, Calvados, France. Plot III. Row F. Grave 1.
Inscription : REST, BELOVED, AND SLEEP. YOURS HAS BEEN THE SUFFERING.
THE MEMORY, OURS.
NoK :   (Wife) 13 Detlin Road, Northfleet, Kent.
Attack on Vendes. Ex Nottinghamshire & Derbyshire Regt. (Sherwood Foresters)

WILLIAMS   4754339   Pte   21 Aug   1945
Cyril   Age 32
Reichswald Forest War Cemetery, Germany. Plot DIX. Row H. Grave 14.
NoK :   E.A. Williams (Wife) 38 Raby Street, Tinsley, Sheffield.

WINSTANLEY   936675   L/Cpl   16 Jul   1944
Arthur   Age 24
St. Manvieu War Cemetery, Cheux, Calvados, France. Plot III. Row H. Grave 12.
Inscription : IN LOVING MEMORY OF A DEAR SON, ARTHUR
          WORTHY OF EVERLASTING REMEMBRANCE.
NoK :   Mrs. G.A. Winstanley 16 Carlton Avenue, Worsley, Wigan, Lancashire.
Attack on Vendes. Ex Royal Artillery.

WITHNALL   4928645   L/Cpl   23 Aug   1944
John   Age 29
St. Desir War Cemetery, Calvados, France. Plot V. Row D. Grave 12.
Inscription : WITH HIS RIGHT HAND SHALL HE COVER THEM,
          AND WITH HIS ARM SHALL HE PROTECT THEM.
NoK :   Mrs. Rodbottom (Sister) 151 Field Road, Bloxwich, Walsall, Staffordshire.
Died in advance from Chateau le Boutemont to Le Breuil. Ex South Staffordshire Regt.

WOOD   4535024   L/Cpl   18 Aug   1944
Bertram   Age 33
Bieville-en-Auge Churchyard, Calvados, France.
Inscription : THY WILL BE DONE.
NoK : Ann Wood (Wife) 54 Harborough Street, Denaby Main, Yorkshire
          Mr. & Mrs. Charles Robert Wood (Parents)
The only British soldier buried here. Ex West Yorkshire Regt.

WOOD   6342602   Sgt   22 Aug   1944
Eric William   Age 29
Bayeux War Cemetery, Calvados, France. Plot II. Row H. Grave 22.
Inscription : NOT JUST TODAY DEAR, BUT EVERY DAY IN SILENCE WE REMEMBER.
NoK :   *(Wife) 39 Queen Street, Worthing, Sussex.*
Ex Royal West Kent Regt.

WORRELL   4750424   Cpl   17 Oct   1944
Arnold   Age 27
Baarle-Nassau Roman Catholic Cemetery, Nederlands. Row B. Grave 1.
Inscription : EVER IN OUR THOUGHTS.
NoK : H. Worrel (Father) 67 Barnsley Road, Darfield, Nr. Barnsley, Yorkshire.
Died whilst on a patrol from positions near Zondereigen.

YORKE   14743765   Pte   20 Feb   1945
George Alfred   Age 18
Arnhem-Oosterbeek War Cemetery, Nederlands. Plot XII. Row C. Grave 2.
Inscription : ETERNAL REST GRANT TO HIM, O LORD;
          AND LET PERPETUAL LIGHT SHINE UPON HIM. R.I.P.
NoK :   *(Mother) 130 Tang Hall Lane, York.*
Ex General Service Corps.

YOUNG   73901   Capt   28 Jun   1944
Philip Mervyn   Age 24
St. Manvieu War Cemetery, Cheux, Calvados, France. Plot I. Row G. Grave 13.
Inscription : IN YOUR CHARITY, PRAY FOR THE REPOSE OF HIS SOUL.
          MAY HE REST IN PEACE.
NoK : John Joseph Baldwin & Margarita Young (Parents) Eckington, Yorkshire
Died at the Southeast corner of Tessel Wood from mortar/shellfire.

Memorial to the 49th (West Riding) Infantry Division at Fontenay le Pesnel.

HONOURS AND AWARDS

Corporal John William Harper V.C.
of 25 Southend, Thorne, Doncaster.

Citation.

In Northwest Europe, on September 29th, 1944, the Hallamshire Battalion of the York and Lancaster Regiment attacked the Depot de Mendicite, a natural defensive position surrounded by an earthen wall, and then a dyke, strongly held by the enemy.

Corporal Harper was commanding the leading section in the assault. The enemy were well dug in and had a perfect field of fire across 300 yards of perfectly flat and exposed country. With superb disregard for the hail of mortar bombs and small arms fire which the enemy brought to bear on this open ground, Corporal Harper led his section straight up to the wall and killed or captured the enemy holding the near side. During this operation the platoon commander was seriously wounded and Corporal Harper took over control of the platoon.

Corporal John William Harper V.C. (YLRM)

As the enemy on the far side of the wall were now throwing grenades over the top, Corporal Harper climbed over the wall alone, throwing grenades, and in the face of heavy close-range small arms fire, personally routed the Germans directly opposing him. He took four prisoners and shot several of the remainder of the enemy as they fled.

Still completely ignoring the heavy Spandau and mortar fire which was sweeping the area, once again he crossed the wall alone to find out whether it was possible for his platoon to wade the dyke which lay beyond. He found the dyke too deep and wide to cross, and once again he came back over the wall and received orders to try to establish his platoon on the enemy side of it. For the third time he climbed over alone, found some empty German weapon pits and, providing the covering fire, urged and encouraged his section to scale the wall and dash for cover. By this action he was able to bring down sufficient covering fire to enable the rest of the company to cross the open ground and surmount the wall for the loss of only one man.

Corporal Harper then left his platoon in the charge of his senior section commander and walked alone along the banks of the dyke, in the face of heavy Spandau fire, to find a crossing place. Eventually he made contact with the battalion attacking on his right, and found that they had located a ford. Back he came across the open ground and, while directing his company commander to the ford, he was struck by a bullet which fatally wounded him, and he died on the bank of the dyke.

The success of the Battalion in driving the enemy from the wall and back across the dyke must be largely ascribed to the superb self sacrifice and inspiring gallantry of Corporal Harper. His magnificent courage, fearlessness, and devotion to duty throughout the battle set a splendid example to his men and had a decisive effect on the course of the operations.

John Harper's Company Commander, Major L.M. Lonsdale-Cooper, in a letter of condolence to his wife said:-

'We were ordered to capture a position which was strongly held by the enemy. To be successful the attack had to be done in the dark. Your husband was leading a section in the forward platoon of my company, and he reached the enemy positions unnoticed. He rushed at the enemy, throwing grenades and firing his sten gun, and killed several of them. By this time the enemy had woken up, and a very fierce fight was raging on a steep embankment which was the Germans defence line. With complete disregard for his own safety, your husband went over the top of the embankment, and his men, fired by this splendid example, followed him and killed or made prisoners, all the enemy.

During this attack, his officer was severely wounded and Corporal Harper took command. While reorganizing the platoon on the objective he was shot by a sniper and killed instantly. It was entirely due to his magnificent leadership and example that we captured that enemy position. He was a very brave man and the best type of N.C.O. and it was an honour to have him with me in battle and out. He was always quietly efficient, always cheerful, and somehow gave everybody a feeling of confidence. I'm mourning the loss of a gallant soldier and friend, but I am very proud of him, and you must be too, for he upheld so very finely, all the best traditions of the fighting spirit of England's sons.

Unfortunately I was unable to attend the funeral, as I was myself wounded the same day. The padre tells me that your husband was buried close to the scene of his last triumph, which is what he would have wished. Please accept, on behalf of myself and all the company, our very deepest sympathy in your tragic bereavement. We too are mourning the loss of a brave soldier and a very fine man.'

Note: The number of VCs awarded since the outbreak of war is now 123. Of these, 43 have been won by the British Army.

Corporal Joseph Penn D.C.M.
(Le Havre, 1989) (DWS)

Corporal John Ellis D.C.M.
(Iceland, c.1942) (Mr. J. Ellis Jr.)

<u>THE DISTINGUISHED SERVICE ORDER</u>

Lieutenant-Colonel (temporary) Trevor Hart DYKE (30580),
The Queen's Royal Regiment (West Surrey).
- - - - - - - - - - - - - - - - - -

On the 25th June 1944, 146 Infantry Brigade attacked FONTENAY with a Battalion of Royal Scots Fusiliers of another Brigade on their left. The Hallamshire Battalion, Yorks and Lancs Regiment, was the left forward battalion of this Brigade and 'H' Hour was at 0415 hours. As a result of efficient and vigorous patrolling by the battalion and from Army Photographic Information Service photographs it was known that the enemy had strongly defended positions. Objectives were difficult to identify in good going owing to the many orchards and thick fences in and around the village, but on the morning of the attack a dense fog in the low ground limited visibility to a maximum of 5 yards. The fog necessarily caused a certain amount of disorganisation which was made more difficult by a considerable number of the R.S.F., who had lost direction, crossing the axis of the Hallams advance.

The enemy resisted strongly with spandau fire from houses and prepared positions, assisted by three Panther tanks, and the whole area was subjected to heavy mortar and shell fire. The Company Commander of their left forward company was killed and it soon became apparent that the forward company would not attain their objective. Lieutenant-Colonel DYKE therefore ordered his reserve companys forward and himself carried out a quick reconnaissance of the situation. He at once issued fresh orders which resulted in the right forward portion of the objective being captured thereby forming a firm base for phase II of the attack which entailed the passing through of a third battalion for the capture of a further objective.

Great trouble was being experienced by fire from the left flank owing to the R.S.F. being unable to get forward but this was successfully neutralised, the part of the village allotted to the battalion cleared of enemy, and the battalion's objectives all gained, as well as clearing a portion of the village allotted to

/the R.S.F. . . . .

the R.S.F. Two of the Panther tanks were knocked out by the Hallams 6 pounder anti-tank guns.

It was due to the leadership, initiative and personal example of Lieutenant-Colonel DYKE, who shewed a complete disregard to his own safety, that this difficult situation was cleared up and success achieved.

On the 27th June 1944 the Hallams successfully occupied the Southern end of TESSEL WOOD feature. Since then the Battalion has been in continued close contact with the enemy, and subjected to heavy mortar and shell fire. By excellent patrolling and use of snipers the battalion has succeeded in dominating the enemy.

Lieutenant-Colonel DYKE has throughout set a high example of courage and leadership under difficult conditions which has infected all ranks of the battalion and is responsible for the high state of morale and discipline which is evident to any visitor to the Battalion.

D.S.O. Citation to Lt.Col. Trevor Hart Dyke

Victoria Cross
Cpl J.W. Harper

Distinguished Service Order
Lt. Col. T. Hart Dyke
Lt. Col. M.C.K. Halford
Major D.B. Webster

Military Cross
Major P.S. Newton
Major L.M. Lonsdale-Cooper
Major H.J.W. Marsh
Major J.A.H. Nicholson
Major J. Wollerton
Capt. H.S.G. Thomas (Padre)
Capt. P.G. Griffiths, R.A.M.C.
Lt. R. Edgson

Distinguished Conduct Medal
C.S.M J.S. Simpson
Sgt. E.S. Longmore
Cpl. Joseph Penn
Cpl. John Ellis

Military Medal
Sgt. W. Newton
Sgt. E. Staniforth
Sgt. L. Smith
L/Sgt. J. Coutts
Cpl. A. Barker
L/Cpl S. Benn
L/Cpl H. Stones
L/Cpl Bryn Williams
Pte. S. Pearce
Pte. Arnold Whitely

Mentioned in Despatches
Capt. L.W. Sneath
Capt. J. Wollerton
Capt. H.S.G. Thomas
Lt. J.W. Mitchinson
Sgt. E. Goodliffe
Sgt. F.H. Mayoss
Sgt. A. Davis
Sgt L. Neal
Sgt. R. May
L/Sgt. E. Clifford
Cpl. W. Mundy

Cpl. J. Ellis
L/Cpl. G. Thwaite
Sgt. S. Nicholson

C-in-C's Certificate
Capt. G.A.G. Bedward
Capt. W. Ashby
Capt. A Cowell
Lt. P.C.L. Godlee
Sgt. S. Nicholson
Sgt. S.H. Thomas
Sgt. H. Oakley
Cpl. M.P. Ahern
L/Cpl. C.L. Nixon
L/Cpl. J. Metcalfe
Pte. W.L. Mawer
Pte. J.H. Gillott

Silver Star Medal (U.S.A.)
Major C.A. Mackillop

Croix de Guerre
Capt. L.G. Sneath (Gold)
Lt. L.H. Hawkins (Silver)
Pte. W. Mawer   (Bronze)

This list may not be exhaustive and there is none available for the considerable number of recipients of the C.O's 'Certificate of Commendation' instigated by Lt. Col. Trevor Hart Dyke for those he thought worthy of, but who had not been officially given, recognition for their outstanding services.

With sincere apologies for any omissions.

HALLAMSHIRE BATTALION
MUSTER ROLL (Feb./Apr.1940)

The precise date of this list is unknown but it must fall between 26 February and 12 April, 1940, the short period during which 2/Lt. C.G. Jurgensen (below) was with the Battalion. It follows that most of these men took part in the Norway Campaign. No similar list is available for the later war period (Normandy to Arnhem). Mounting casualties during this period resulted in men being drafted in from many sources, so it would be a marathon task for anyone wishing to compile any comprehensive list. The Army Medal Office might be a good place to start.

Underlined = Fatal Casualty

OFFICERS

Serv. No.	Rank.	Initials.	Surname.	
P/13950	Lt.Col.	C.G.	Robins.	C.O.
P/6900	Maj.	C.C.	Strong.	2 i/c
36971	Maj.	J.P.	Hunt.	
47807	A/Maj.	D.E.	Lockwood.	
53324	Capt.	H.J.W.	Marsh.	Adj.
53323	Capt.	K.W.	West.	
P/38217	Capt.	R.O.S.	Dimmock.	
53539	Capt.	R.	Mumby.	
85313	A/Capt	W.L.	Cave.	
72040	2/Lt.	S.	Martin de Bartolome.	
73883	2/Lt.	M.J.A.	Palmer.	
73901	2/Lt.	P.M.	Young.	
74027	2/Lt.	W.G.	Blake.	
79990	2/Lt.	L.M.	Lonsdale-Cooper.	
62413	2/Lt.	C.R.S.	Sandford.	
89141	2/Lt.	D.R.	Bell.	
89120	2/Lt.	C.A.B.	Slack.	
89104	2/Lt.	R.N.	Longridge.	
89123	2/Lt.	A.C.	Somers.	
89110	2/Lt.	S.J.D.	Moorwood.	
89131	2/Lt.	P.	Turrell.	
89409	2/Lt.	J.	Firth.	
88006	2/Lt.	H.W.	Ridley.	
P/103022	2/Lt.	G.J.	Good.	
	2/Lt.	P.H.	Willis-Dixon.	
	2/Lt.	W.R.	Jenkinson.	
	2/Lt.	J.	Randall.	
40885	Capt.	J.P.	Dobson, D.C.M.,M.M.	

ATTACHED OFFICERS

106325	Lt.	C.J.	Wells. (R.A.M.C.)
	Lt.	J.	Brown. (R.A.M.C.)
	Capt.	N.	Murray-Smith. (Chaplain)
	Capt.	D.G.	Carter. (R.A.P.C.)
	Capt.	R.H.C.	Windle. (R.A.S.C.)
	Capt.	A.P.	Currie. (Glasgow Highlanders)
	2/Lt.	**C.G.**	**Jurgensen.** (War Office General List)

WARRANT OFFICERS

4739822	RSM	A.	Burns.
4741007	RQMS	C.H.	McCredie.
4741157	CSM	F.	Colley.
4738053	CSM	G.	Grant.
4683828	CSM	J.	Howden.
4740147	CSM	H.	Marshall.
5493072	CSM	J.	Tanner.
4520182	PSM	T.F.	Bridges.
4604137	PSM	L.H.	Codd.
4606132	PSM	G.W.	Steel.
4739191	PSM	J.W.	Witham.
4742505	A/PSM	C.S.	Milner.

OTHER RANKS

'A' COMPANY

4747403	Pte.	C.	Aistrop.
4747392	Pte.	E.	Aistrop.
4747048	Pte.	E.	Badger.
4747873	Pte.	W.P.	Barker.
4748368	Pte.	A.	Barnsley.
4748617	Pte.	J.A.	Basford.
4748711	Pte.	J.W.	Benstead.
4748787	Pte.	E.	Benton.
4748348	Pte.	K.	Berry.
4747072	Pte.	F.W.	Billard.
4747784	Pte.	T.H.	Booth.
4379912	Cpl.	W.H.	Booth.
4747516	Pte.	R.T.	Bratley.
4748742	Pte.	J.S.	Broomhead.
4745068	A/Cpl.	W.	Burgin.
4748171	Pte.	H.	Cater.
4747520	L/Cpl.	J.C.	Catley.
4746319	Pte.	T.H.	Chandler.
4747530	Pte.	H.	Cliff.
4747580	Pte.	H.	Crooks.
4748352	Pte.	H.	Crowther.
4748751	Pte.	G.E.	Dagnall.
4687295	Pte.	H.	Danford.
4746724	Pte.	E.C.	Davies.
4746605	Pte.	R.	Dolman.
4744683	A/Cpl.	A.	Downs.
4747790	Pte.	W.G.	Dunning.
4748329	Pte.	C.M.	Farrand.
4748714	Pte.	J.	Fleming.
4748777	Pte.	G.	Ford.
4748779	Pte.	R.N.H.K.	Frith.
4747778	Pte.	A.	Fullerton.
4849634	Sgt.	E.	Gandy.
4746422	L/Cpl.	A.	Garner.
4746582	A/Cpl.	B.	Gee.
4748771	Pte.	A.R.	Geeves.
4748657	Pte.	A.	Gibbs.
4747770	Pte.	W.F.	Glove.

4748351	Pte.	A.E.	Gollick.	4749061	Pte.	H.M.	Stainrod.
4743913	CQMS.	A.E.	Grant.	4748307	Pte.	J.	Tidswell.
4749086	Pte.	L.	Gabbitas.	4747317	Pte.	P.	Turner.
4749021	Pte.	A.	Goodridge.	4748767	Pte.	W.J.	Twigg.
4747437	Pte.	H.	Hall.	4748782	Pte.	G.W.	Tyler.
4747584	L/Cpl.	R.L.	Harding.	4685632	L/Cpl.	W.E.	Tagg.
4746608	Pte.	A.E.	Harrison.	4748638	Pte.	J.E.	Tidmarsh.
4746597	Pte.	T.W.	Harrison.	4748778	Pte.	L.G.	Vale.
4747585	Pte.	H.B.	Heeley.	4747922	Pte.	H.	Vardy.
4747051	Pte.	F.	Jackson.	4748010	Pte.	J.	Vardy.
4748394	Pte.	G.H.	Jebson.	4748358	Pte.	J.	Varley.
4746315	Pte.	F.H.	Jones.	4748321	Pte.	A.	Walker.
4747394	Pte.	W.	Jubb.	4748831	Pte.	J.A.	Walker.
4748622	Pte.	C.W.G.	Kennan.	4746726	Pte.	E.H.	Watkinson.
4747545	Pte.	C.	King.	4745458	L/Sgt.	A.	Wheelhouse.
4747561	L/Sgt.	A.	Kirby.	4748322	Pte.	A.	Whiteley.
4748091	Pte.	H.	Lapish.	4746421	L/Cpl.	T.	Wilkinson.
4745831	Sgt.	C.	Laughton.	4746378	Pte.	A.L.	Williams.
4749133	Pte.	F.S.	Lambert.	4747860	L/Cpl.	A.L.	Wood.
4747563	Pte.	W.	Martin.	4748866	Pte.	G.	Wortley.
4748691	Pte.	F.S	Mayoss.	4749127	Pte.	A.	Wragg.
4747537	Pte.	C.	Milnes.				
4748636	Pte.	E.C	Mitchell.	**'B' COMPANY**			
4748757	Pte.	G.	Morritt.				
4749054	Pte.	E	Morris.	4747529	Pte.	R.	Anderson.
4744887	A/Sgt.	R.	McNaughton.	4747511	Pte.	D.	Appleyard.
4748857	Pte.	C.	Norgate.	4748439	Pte.	R.	Allinson.
4748833	Pte.	A.	Oddy.	4748062	Pte.	D.	Barber.
4749052	Pte.	J.	Ouldred.	4747476	Pte.	L.	Barton.
4748748	Pte.	D.	Parkin.	4746519	L/Cpl.	W.	Bassett.
4745535	Pte.	E.	Parkin.	4740501	Cpl.	T.H.	Bean.
4748618	Pte.	B.	Peacock.	4742829	L/Sgt.	A.E.	Beighton.
4748428	Pte.	J.	Pennington.	4743467	Pte.	W.	Binney.
4748028	Pte.	A.	Prigmore.	4744632	Sgt.	A.	Boater.
4749115	Pte.	F.	Pickersgill.	4748784	Pte.	A.	Bowes.
4748335	Pte.	F.	Ramsden.	4744669	Pte.	C.	Brahma.
4747591	L/Cpl.	W.	Reeve.	4748350	Pte.	B.	Brooke.
4747211	Pte.	W.H.	Robinson.	4745607	Pte.	AS	Brooks.
4748626	Pte.	R.J.	Roullier.	4748631	Pte.	J.	Brown.
4748370	Pte.	J.W.	Royal.	4746088	Pte.	J.	Caddie.
4746954	Pte.	W.A.	Russell.	4748700	L/Cpl.	WW	Chance.
4746610	Pte.	L.	Rycroft.	4748727	L/Cpl.	S.A.E..	Cooker.
4746612	Pte.	T.	Rycroft.	4746723	Pte.	V.	Coil.
4748376	Pte.	R.E.	Sands.	4748397	Pte.	M.	Cony.
4748319	Pte.	F.	Schofield.	4747913	Pte.	J.	Craig.
4747421	Pte.	W.	Searle.	4745475	Pte.	A.	Advise.
4748371	Pte.	F.	Senior.	4748685	Pte.	HA.	Drake.
4748715	L/Cpl.	E.D.	Seymour.	4748684	Pte.	WC	Drake.
4748409	Pte.	O.D.	Shepherd.	4748172	Pte.	CJ	Driver.
4747595	Pte.	C.	Smith.	1070366	L/Cpl.	A.C.H.	Due.
4748378	Pte.	E.	Smith.	4748776	Pte.	S.	Fardel.
4746474	Pte.	F.E.	Smith.	4748702	Pte.	A.M.	Finch.
4747891	Pte.	L.	Smith.	4746872	L/Cpl.	F.	Fletcher.
4747408	Pte.	S.	Smith.	4748173	Pte.	J.O.E.	Forster.
4748839	Pte.	S.	Smithson.	4748860	Pte.	J.	Gallagher.
4742012	Cpl.	L.	Sparham.	4748465	Pte.	W.	Gallagher.
4747336	L/Cpl.	E.	Strutt.	4748612	Pte.	W.C.	Garnham.
4748680	Pte.	A.E.	Stubbs.	4747706	Pte.	F.	Gibson.
4747407	Pte.	E.	Swann.	4747376	Pte.	W.	Gillott.

4748704	Pte.	A.E.	Gloster.
4746919	L/Cpl.	P.	Gough.
4747461	Pte.	V.E.	Green.
4748425	Pte.	B.	Grundy.
4748332	Pte.	P.A.	Haley.
4747977	Pte.	G.	Hall.
4746683	Pte.	H.A.	Harrison.
4746078	Pte.	B.	Hartley.
4744431	Pte.	F.	Hartley.
4682277	A/CQMS.	C.	Heath.
4747876	Pte.	B.	Hill.
4743474	Pte.	H.	Hopkins.
4745563	A/Cpl.	H.	Hughes.
2031037	Pte.	S.C.	Huttley.
4747220	Pte.	W.	Hadley.
4747984	Pte.	B.	Jackson.
4747586	Pte.	F.	Jackson.
4747885	Pte.	T.R.	Jones.
4748303	Pte.	T.	Kellyher.
4747560	Pte.	H.	Kent.
4748844	Pte.	F.	Kenyon.
4738812	Sgt.	J.	Killian.
4748621	Pte.	G.A.J.	Kirk.
4745221	Pte.	G.J.	Knowles.
4745384	Pte.	E.	King.
4748665	Pte.	R.	Labbett.
4748786	Pte.	E.	Leonard.
4609824	Cpl.	H.	Liversedge.
4744294	Pte.	L.	Laughlin.
4748567	Pte.	A.R.W.	Liptrot.
4744035	L/Sgt.	W.H.	Lees.
4748834	Pte.	J.W.	Machell.
4748761	Pte.	C.W.	Mackintosh.
4747588	Pte.	I.	Manning.
4742845	A/Sgt.	T.	Mason.
4748842	Pte.	R.	Middleton.
4747095	Pte.	H.A.	Mitchell.
4747096	Pte.	L.S.	Mitchell.
4748841	Pte.	T.S.	Morton.
4535532	Pte.	F.	Moffatt.
4748832	Pte.	W.	McQuinn.
4747606	Pte.	W.	Neil.
4744235	Pte.	W.	Newlands.
4747883	L/Cpl.	J.	Newman.
4748454	Pte.	A.E.	Newsome.
4747924	Pte.	E.	Newsome.
4743906	Pte.	T.W.	Oldershaw.
2031039	Pte.	L.A.	Oldfield.
4747509	Pte.	G.	Palmer.
4748078	Pte.	T.H.	Perkins.
4748417	Pte.	A.	Phillips.
4748624	Pte.	E.J.	Phillips.
4747888	Pte.	A.	Platts.
4748077	Pte.	J.	Porter.
4748496	Pte.	W.	Palmer.
4748876	Pte.	N.	Parker.
4748651	Pte.	V.E.	Putman.
4747098	Pte.	H.	Revill.
4748313	Pte.	S.	Rouse.

4748357	Pte.	C.	Russell.
4748556	Pte.	J.	Rothwell.
4748741	Pte.	A.	Saunders.
4747747	Pte.	B.	Savoury.
4748781	Pte.	N.H.	Scholey.
4746360	Pte.	E.	Scott.
4747733	Pte.	H.	Sharpe.
4745362	L/Cpl.	F.	Shaw.
4748664	L/Cpl.	C.W.	Smith.
4748543	Pte.	G.R.	Smith.
4747470	Pte.	J.	Smith.
4748365	Pte.	L.T.	Smith.
4748324	Pte.	A.E.	Stansfield.
4748081	L/Cpl.	W.	Sturman.
4744841	Pte.	A.	Shaw.
4747624	Pte.	G.	Slingsby.
4747526	Pte.	E.	Thompson.
4748828	Pte.	A.	Tinsdeal.
4748354	Pte.	J.E.	Tolan.
4748328	Pte.	F.	Topliss.
4747766	Pte.	A.	Turner.
4748647	Pte.	A.	Vine.
4748666	Pte.	H.C.	Walder.
4746406	L/Cpl.	H.	Watkinson.
4748600	Pte.	G.T.	Westall.
4746521	L/Sgt.	A.	Wiggins.
4747611	Pte.	A.	Wragg.
4747344	Pte.	A.	Yates.
4746599	L/Cpl.	W.	Yorke.

'C' COMPANY

4748086	Pte.	J.T.	Atkinson.
4747678	Pte.	A.	Barber.
4747792	Pte.	E.	Batham.
4745283	Cpl.	E.	Battle.
4748320	Pte.	G.H.	Bilton.
4746364	Cpl.	C.H.	Boot.
4748019	Pte.	H.	Brook.
4747631	Pte.	S.	Brookes.
4741162	CQMS.	N.	Brownhill.
4747721	Pte.	A.	Bunker.
4747499	L/Cpl.	H.	Butler.
4749125	Pte.	L.	Bamford.
4742666	Pte.	H.	Bower.
4749116	Pte.	G.J.	Brumby.
4748021	Pte.	A.	Cairns.
4746745	Pte.	C.	Cavanagh.
4749081	Pte.	J.T.	Cartledge.
4746981	L/Cpl.	W.H.	Chapman.
4748988	Pte.	G.	Coates.
4749146	Pte.	G.	Colley.
4749094	Pte.	P.	Cristanacce.
4747700	Pte.	A.	Daley.
4747975	Pte.	A.	Ellis.
4747617	A/Cpl.	H.	Ellis.
4747659	Pte.	W.	Ellis.
4744624	Pte.	F.W.	Eratt.
4738741	L/Sgt.	W.	Esplin.

4748157	Pte.	C.	Farr.
4749157	Pte.	S.	Fisher.
4747618	L/Cpl.	W.E.	Fisher.
4747531	Pte.	E.	France.
4749158	Pte.	J.	Flinders.
4749138	Pte.	G.	Foster.
4749057	Pte.	H.	Ford.
4748424	Pte.	H.	Graham.
4739984	Sgt.	A.W.	Green.
4746836	Pte.	D.	Greenwood.
4749129	Pte.	J.H.	Gillott.
4747143	Pte.	E.	Hanson.
4747619	Pte.	J.A.	Higgins.
4748362	Pte.	A.	Hirst.
4748139	Pte.	J.	Hirst.
4749010	Pte.	S.	Hirst.
4747758	Pte.	S.	Hodgson.
4747393	Pte.	W.G.	Holland.
4749189	L/Cpl.	T.J.R.	Hartley.
4747684	Pte.	W.	Johnson.
4747533	Pte.	E.	Jones.
2648139	L/Sgt.	F.R.	Judge.
4743938	Pte.	C.	Jameson.
4749140	Pte.	F.	Kirk.
4747502	Pte.	F.E.	Lee.
4746598	Pte.	G.W.	Lewis.
4739264	Sgt.	G.H.	Linley.
4745173	L/Cpl.	J.T.	Loxley.
4748413	Pte.	A.	Mackin.
4748102	Pte.	J.R.	Madden.
4748115	Pte.	G.H.G.	Moore.
4746591	L/Cpl.	J.H.	Musson.
4747354	Pte.	J.	Myers.
4749107	Pte.	R.	Marriott.
4745210	Pte.	S.	Mason.
4742731	Pte.	A.	Moore.
4742148	Pte.	H.	McGreavy.
4748148	Pte.	G.	Needham.
4748027	Pte.	W.R.	Newton.
4748316	Pte.	L.	Nield.
4747490	L/Cpl.	J.H.	Ogden.
4536214	L/Cpl.	A.	Othick.
4749178	Pte.	F.	Orton.
4746584	Cpl.	W.	Powell.
4748616	Pte.	T.V.	Pearce.
766467	L/Cpl.	D.	Piggott.
4749184	Pte.	J.	Peel.
4738009	L/Cpl.	F.	Quinn.
4737822	L/Cpl.	G.F.	Rhodes.
4746874	L/Cpl.	A.	Richardson.
4748356	Pte.	R.	Robinson.
4749072	Pte.	H.	Rodgers.
4746938	Pte	J.	Salt.
4747908	L/Cpl.	L.	Sewell.
4748054	Pte.	A.	Sharpe.
4747994	Pte.	E.	Shelton.
4748429	Pte.	J.S.	Simpson.
4747811	Pte.	F.	Smith.
4747463	Pte.	F.C.	Smith.

4748415	Pte.	L.	Smith.
4748744	Pte.	W.	Smith.
4746613	Pte.	E.	South.
4747258	Pte.	W.S.	Stephenson.
4746324	Pte.	W.	Stevenson.
4747525	Pte.	D.O.	Stewart.
4747038	Pte.	K.	Stimpson.
4747765	Pte.	H.	Stringer.
4747546	Pte.	R.	Stringfellow.
4748190	Pte.	V.	Stubbs.
4745752	A/Cpl.	H.A.	Styring.
4748863	Pte.	H.	Stapleton.
4748877	Pte.	G.R.	Strafford.
4749175	Pte.	G.	Sanderson.
4748380	Pte.	H.	Thorpe.
4746167	L/Cpl.	J.	Tonks.
4744662	Pte.	G.	Thwaite.
4747653	Pte.	A.	Warren.
4747944	Pte.	A.	Wathall.
4745171	Cpl.	E.	Wells.
4747379	Pte.	E.	Whittaker.
4748420	Pte.	T.	Whitter.
4748414	Pte.	F.T.	Wilson.
4747445	Pte.	F.D.	Woodhead.
4748372	Pte.	D.	Wyatt.
4748996	Pte.	S.R.	Waite.
4749120	Pte.	A.	Wheeler.
4748561	Pte.	C.	Whiteside.
4749087	Pte.	H.	Wildgoose.
4741141	Pte.	E.	Wilkinson.
4749078	Pte.	F.	Willert.
4744459	Pte.	F.	Wilson.
4749193	Pte.	A.	Wood.
4749128	Pte.	R.	Woodward.
4749027	Pte.	A.	Worthington.
4749064	Pte.	G.	Webb.

'D' COMPANY.

4746830	Pte.	W.	Acock.
4748289	L/Cpl.	G.	Allemby.
4747577	L/Cpl.	E.	Allen.
4748800	Pte.	G.	Barker.
4747553	Pte.	F	Barrott.
4747942	Pte.	F.	Baum.
4747551	A/Cpl.	P.	Bene.
4747554	Pte.	W.	Betts.
4748710	Pte.	F.	Birch.
4747500	L/Cpl.	A.	Bradford.
4747613	L/Cpl.	E.	Bradford.
4747823	Pte.	M.	Burke.
4747515	L/Cpl.	W.J.	Burnett.
4749168	Pte.	F.G.	Ball.
4749052	Pte.	G.W.	Booth.
4749172	Pte.	H.	Bramwell.
4747232	Pte.	D.M.	Carmichael.
4747579	Pte.	C.	Clark.
4745374	L/Cpl.	W.F.	Coukham.
4747945	Pte.	C.T.	Craven.

4747703	Pte.	J.	Duffy.
4748317	Pte.	C.	Ellis.
4747130	Pte.	W.	Facer.
4748871	Pte.	J.H.	Fawcett.
4748809	Pte.	J.	Faxon.
4748865	L/Cpl.	W.	Field.
4748610	Pte.	R.H.	Flowerday.
4747485	Pte.	R.	Fraser.
4747522	Pte.	W.	Freeman.
4747558	Pte.	A.	Furniss.
4748653	Pte.	S.T.	Gilman.
4747521	Pte.	L.	Glaves.
4748852	Pte.	W.W.	Goodall.
4747582	A/Cpl.	J.H.C.	Goodwin.
4747680	Pte.	C.	Greaves.
6087031	Pte.	H.	Green.
4748848	L/Cpl.	W.	Greenhough.
4748743	Pte.	E.	Griffiths.
3529052	L/Cpl.	J.	Handley.
4748231	Pte.	F.	Henshaw.
4747857	Pte.	L.	Holmes.
4746837	Pte.	M.	Humphreys.
4748639	Pte.	C.H.	Holland.
4748437	Pte.	J.	Haughton.
4744150	L/Cpl.	J.W.	Hudson.
4748754	Pte.	H.	Hunt.
4741504	L/Sgt.	G.	Innocent.
4747935	Pte.	H.	Jeffcoate.
4747952	Pte.	W.	Jeffcoate.
4746644	Pte.	J.	Jenkinson.
4748727	Pte.	W.	Lack.
4748701	Pte.	I.	Lewis.
4747836	Pte.	J.W.	Lewis.
4743914	Sgt.	G.W.	Lindley.
4748788	Pte.	W.	Lucas.
4748859	Pte.	S.	Leonard.
4747956	Pte.	F.	Male.
4743452	Pte.	Z.	Marsden.
4748769	Pte.	H.	Marsh.
4748729	Pte.	C.	May.
4748658	Pte.	H.C.	Mears.
4748850	Pte.	F.	Miles.
4742505	A/PSM.	C.S.	Milner.
4745501	Pte.	C.	Moore.
4748780	Pte.	T.	Moore.
4748718	Pte.	W.C.G.	Morris.
4746323	L/Cpl.	E.	Morton.
4748619	Pte.	J.	Martin.
4748864	Pte.	D.	Newton.
4748846	Pte.	H.	Newton.
4748670	Pte.	T.C.	O'Connor.
4748836	Pte.	A.S.	Overton.
4746671	Pte.	H.	Packard.
4747962	Pte.	A.	Peat.
4748334	L/Cpl.	C.	Peckett.
4748623	Pte.	F.	Perkins.
4748861	Pte.	A.	Porritt.
4748403	Pte.	S.	Prestage.
4748678	Pte.	C.G.	Purton.

4748825	Pte.	N.	Peel.
4748868	Pte.	H.	Pickles.
4748758	Pte.	J.	Porter.
4746746	Pte.	A.	Redfearn.
4747846	Pte.	S.	Ridge.
4748325	Pte.	D.F.	Riley.
4748856	Pte.	D.	Roberts.
4748717	Pte.	L.	Roberts.
4740503	CQMS.	J.G.	Rodgers.
4746741	Pte.	W.H.	Roe.
4748862	Pte.	G.	Raynor.
4749165	Pte.	A.	Reyolds.
4748418	Pte.	E.	Seddon.
4746106	Pte.	W.	Shaw.
4748643	Pte.	A.W.	Shead.
4747652	Pte.	E.	Smith.
4746655	L/Cpl.	F.	Smith.
4747456	Pte.	E.D.	Storr.
4748682	Pte.	W.R.	Sullivan.
4748750	Pte.	D.	Scamadine.
4748838	Pte.	T.B.	Seddon.
4748774	Pte.	M.	Shippham.
4748483	Pte.	S.G.	Straw.
4747547	Pte.	A.	Tate.
4747552	Pte.	W.	Tate.
6087827	L/Cpl.	V.	Taylor.
4746275	A/Cpl.	W.H.	Taylor.
4748668	Pte.	C.J.	Tedder.
4748630	Pte.	S.H.	Thomas.
4748835	Pte.	J.T.	Tierney.
4748327	Pte.	J.	Timlin.
4739016	L/Sgt.	G.H.	Turner.
4687483	Sgt.	H.	Turner.
4747851	Pte.	W.	Urquhart.
4748699	Pte.	C.R.	Warrener.
4748736	Pte.	H.	White.
4744542	A/Cpl.	G.D.	Wilkinson.
4747713	Pte.	A.E.	Williams.
4747853	Pte.	C.	Williams.
4743095	L/Sgt.	T.L.	Wing.
4748667	Pte.	G.A.W.	Wellham.
4748728	Pte.	W.	Whitaker.

'HQ' COMPANY.

4748287	Pte.	E.	Allen.
4747269	Pte.	T.E.	Allott.
4747576	Bdmn.	F.	Ashmore.
4747658	Bdmn.	F.	Ashmore.
4748387	Pte.	G.E.	Ashton.
4748366	Pte.	L.	Auty.
4743840	Pte.	B.	Barker.
4748323	Pte.	A.	Barraclough.
4743034	Pte.	J.	Baxter.
406890	L/Cpl.	W.	Baxter.
4746401	L/Sgt.	W.	Beever.
4746117	Bdmn.	R.	Beever.
4747679	Pte.	H.	Bell.
4747660	Pte.	S.	Bell.

4746910	Pte.	C.W.	Bennett.	4748390	Pte.	H.	Garner.
4748349	Pte.	R.	Berry.	4746082	Pte.	N.	Garner.
4747633	Pte.	J.A.	Bertram.	4747257	Pte.	G.W.	Garrett.
4747602	Pte.	L.	Biggin.	4748349	Pte.	E.	Gill.
4748169	Pte.	C.	Billups.	4747454	Pte.	J.A.	Gillott.
4746619	Pte.	T.	Birch.	4380826	A/Cpl.	A.	Goddard.
4746722	Pte.	W.	Bird.	4748314	Pte.	G.G.	Godfrey.
4746970	A/Sgt.	L.	Blankley.	4747405	L/Cpl.	A.	Graham.
4747505	Pte.	W.	Bond.	4748677	Pte.	A.R.	Graydon.
4744734	L/Sgt.	W.	Bradford.	4748066	Pte.	R.W.	Greaves.
4748385	Pte.	E.	Bradley.	4745896	L/Cpl.	H.	Green.
4743270	Sgt.	E.	Bramham.	4746842	Pte.	D.	Greenwood.
4746799	L/Cpl.	L.	Broadhead.	4748392	Pte.	H.	Greenwood.
4744216	Pte.	W.	Brockelhurst.	4748400	Pte.	H.	Gregson.
4748299	Pte.	B.	Brook.	4746759	Pte.	C.	Griffiths.
4745224	Sgt.	J.W.	Brown.	554568	A/Cpl.	E.	Goodliffe.
4746259	L/Cpl.	E.A.	Buttress.	4747455	Pte.	D.	Haddon.
4748692	Pte.	E.H.G.	Baker.	4748341	Pte.	J.W.	Haines.
4748628	Pte.	H.S.	Benson.	4744784	L/Sgt.	J.	Hale.
4744680	Dmr.	G.H.	Barron.	4748345	Pte.	J.	Harrop.
4748379	Pte.	W.	Calverley.	4748389	Pte.	A.	Hart.
4748382	Pte.	G.W.	Carr.	4743849	Bdmn.	L.	Hartley.
4740745	L/Cpl.	W.	Cawton.	4747231	Pte.	L.	Hartshorn.
4747435	Pte.	T.	Chappell.	4747636	Pte.	R.	Hattersley.
4748412	Pte.	W.	Chorlton.	4748067	Pte.	R.D.	Haynes.
4747603	Pte.	W.	Coe.	4744242	Pte.	W.	Heald.
4747765	L/Cpl.	J.H.	Cole.	4748393	Pte.	S.	Hicks.
4747615	Pte.	H.	Cole.	4743174	Cpl.	C.A.	Hides.
4747543	Pte.	J.	Cowley.	4746383	Pte.	A.	Hogg.
4747824	Pte.	H.	Cresswell.	4748359	Pte.	T.I.	Holdgate.
4745359	Cpl.	J.H.	Crompton.	4743994	Pte.	J.W.	Hopkinson.
4744516	Dmr.	A.	Crookes.	4748410	Pte.	J.	Hurst.
4745325	Pte.	A.	Crookes.	4743194	L/Sgt.	J.W.	Hurst.
4746675	Bdmn.	E.	Crookes.	4749112	Pte.	S.	Harper.
4747228	A/Cpl.	R.	Crookes.	4748816	Pte.	J.	Haslam.
4748805	Pte.	W.E.	Chambers.	4748738	Pte.	W.	Himsworth.
4748634	Pte.	A.S.	Clark.	4741426	L/Sgt.	C.W.	Hall.
4747436	Pte.	D.	Dalton.	4748374	Pte.	J.	Jackson.
4747616	Pte.	F.	Davenport.	4748426	Pte.	R.	Johnson.
4744736	Pte.	A.	Deakin.	4748178	Pte.	H.	Kemp.
4746148	L/Cpl.	N.	Denley.	4748401	Pte.	R.	Knight.
4745894	Pte.	J.W.	Dickinson.	4748411	Pte.	K.	Lawton.
4746434	Bdmn.	W.	Dickinson.	4742917	L/Sgt.	G.	Leaper.
4748398	Pte.	E.	Dodds.	4747605	Pte.	G.W	Learad.
4748312	L/Cpl.	S.J.	Dodman.	4747121	Dmr.	A.	Lee.
4746585	Pte.	C.E.	Downend.	4744541	L/Cpl.	S.W.	Legdon.
4748245	Pte.	F.W.	Dummer.	4744554	Cpl.	F.I.	Lennon.
4747646	Cpl.	B.L.	Dyson.	4744384	L/Cpl.	H.	Lewis.
4614351	Pte.	E.	Davies.	4747283	Pte.	T.N.R.	Lindsay.
4746312	Cpl.	H.	Eadon.	4743905	Pte.	F.	Linfitt.
4748399	Pte.	S.	Elliott.	4685738	Sgt.	A.	Lockwood.
4748353	Pte.	C.	Ellis.	4748367	Pte.	J.	Lockwood.
4972815	Pte.	J.E.	Fletcher.	4748338	Pte.	A.	Longley.
4746301	Pte.	J.W.	Fontana.	4748122	Pte.	D.	Love.
4748423	Pte.	J.H.	Foster.	4748688	Pte.	J.J.	Lambert.
4746327	L/Cpl.	A.	Furniss.	4744750	Pte.	E.	Machin.
4747705	L/Cpl.	W.H.	Furniss.	4748783	Pte.	H.	Maleham.
4749109	Pte.	B.	Frith.	4746687	Pte.	T.	Marley.
4747523	Pte.	A.	Garfitt.	4746150	Pte.	J.	Martin.

Number	Rank	Initials	Surname
4748629	Pte.	J.J.	Martin.
4746271	L/Cpl.	G.H.	Mason.
4748919	L/Cpl.	W.S.R.	Maunder.
4748330	Pte.	J.	Metcalfe.
4747802	Pte.	A.	Moorhouse.
4748599	Pte.	J.V.	Moran.
4380173	Pte.	A.	Murray.
4748687	Pte.	G.E.	Marjoram.
4748342	Pte.	T.C.	McGrath.
4748297	Pte.	H.	Naylor.
4748361	Pte.	A.	Naylor.
4747589	Pte.	W.	Naylor.
4739271	CQMS.	K.	Nelson.
4746387	Pte.	H.	Nicholson.
4748026	Pte.	D.G.A.	Nightingale.
4747663	Pte.	S.J.	Nowell.
4748373	Pte.	E.	Oldfield.
4743695	Pte.	L.	Oldfield.
4737676	Pte.	S.	Oldfield.
4746668	Pte.	R.	Packard.
4748333	Pte.	H.	Parkinson.
4742945	Pte.	W.	Patrick.
4747621	Pte.	C.	Peacock.
4745564	Dmr.	G.	Pears.
833362	A/Sgt.	J.	Pearson.
4748184	Pte.	F.	Peat.
4746921	L/Cpl.	E.	Peck.
4748315	Pte.	W.R.	Petty.
4748364	Pte.	W.	Pickles.
4748186	Pte.	L.	Platts.
4747355	L/Cpl.	H.	Postlethwaite.
4746846	Pte.	T.	Powell.
4746329	L/Cpl.	F.	Priest.
4749049	Pte.	J.	Padgett.
4749007	Pte.	G.H.	Presley.
4745565	Bdmn.	J.A.	Rastall.
4747358	Pte.	A.	Reed.
1843264	A/Sgt.	J.	Reilly.
4743088	Dmr.	H.	Reynolds.
4748293	Pte.	B.	Rochford.
4748384	Pte.	D.	Rodgers.
4748290	Pte.	J.E.	Rose.
4746449	Pte.	J.R.	Rose.
4748331	Pte.	E.	Rounding.
4747406	Pte.	C.H.	Rusling.
4747410	Pte.	H.	Rusling.
4747622	A/Cpl.	J.H.	Rayner.
4747666	Pte.	E.H.	Saville.
4737995	A/Cpl.	M.J.	Scanlan.
4746074	Pte.	J.T.	Searson.
4747539	L/Cpl.	D.	Seaton.
4748347	Pte.	A.	Shaw.
4748377	Pte.	J.	Shaw.
4746075	L/Cpl.	S.	Shepherd.
4748326	Pte.	H.	Sherratt.
4746972	Pte.	C.W.	Sherwin.
4746316	A/Cpl.	H.	Simmonite.
4741659	Pte.	C.E.	Simpson.
4748080	Pte.	L.W.	Skill.
4748294	Pte.	G.	Sladdin.
4748383	Pte.	A.R.	Ramsbottom.
4746017	L/Cpl.	L.	Smith.
4748030	Pte.	L.J.	Smith.
4746086	L/Cpl.	J.	Sorsby.
4747812	Pte.	J.E.	Staniforth.
4746559	Bdmn.	D.J.	Starkey.
4748336	Pte.	H.	Stephenson.
4748346	Pte.	A.	Stratton.
4746335	Pte.	A.	Strutt.
4744221	L/Cpl.	W.F.	Styring.
4739626	Sgt.	J.	Suckley.
4748295	Pte.	R.	Sutcliffe.
4748191	Pte.	S.G.	Swann.
4748419	Pte.	E.	Tatum.
4746793	Pte.	F.A.	Taylor.
4747748	Pte.	G.	Taylor.
4681156	L/Cpl.	N.	Taylor.
4746366	A/Cpl.	G.W.	Tillbook.
4746649	Pte.	M.O.	Tucker.
4742834	Sgt.	D.B.	Turner.
4747688	Pte.	J.	Turton.
4749102	Pte.	I.	Tazzyman.
4748381	Pte.	J.	Utley.
4748588	Pte.	H.	Vollum.
4748396	Pte.	T.	Wade.
4745970	Cpl.	R.V.	Wainman.
4745351	L/Cpl.	R.P.	Wainman.
4748355	Pte.	J.	Wakefield.
4745363	Cpl.	J.T.	Walker.
4747749	Pte.	R.	Walker.
4736716	L/Cpl.	C.D.	Waller.
4737713	L/Cpl.	W.	Waller.
4747626	Pte.	A.	Warburton.
4748033	Pte.	A.	Warren.
4744091	Pte.	W.F.S.	Watkinson.
4748889	A/Sgt.	J.	Welsh.
4746589	Dmr.	E.T.	Wharton.
4746020	Sgt.	B.	Whiting.
2214977	Pte.	W.	Widdowson.
4748298	Pte.	S.	Wild.
4746317	Dmr.	T.W.	Williams.
4747596	A/Sgt.	R.C.	Wingfield.
4747628	Bdmn.	J.B.	Witherspoon.
4745731	Pte.	C.	Wood.
4745751	Pte.	S.	Wood.
4747999	Pte.	J.	Worall.
4748430	Pte.	W.	Wright.
4747654	Pte.	S.	Warren.

ATTACHED PERSONNEL

Royal Army Ordinance Corps

Number	Rank	Initials	Surname
7583099	A/Sub/Cr.	A.P.	Cooke.
7609643	Pte.	J.	McKie.
7612336	Pte.	T.H.	Rowlands.
7608019	A/Sgt.	E.H.	White.

Royal Army Pay Corps

838047	Cpl.	K.	Eskrett.
7661919	Pte.	S.W.	Stewart.

Royal Army Service Corps

S/154010	Dvr.	D.E.	Farrar.
T/154823	Dvr.	G.	France.
S/54075	Cpl.	C.C.	Garnham.
S/158661	Dvr.	F.G.	Hillaby.
S/54591	S/Sgt.	N.S.	Mackay.
S/154827	Dvr.	E.B.	Robinson.

28 F.S.W. Corps of Military Police

1429271	Sgt.	A.J.	Blair.
7686231	L/Cpl.	K.	Hampson.
7686233	L/Cpl.	D.C.	Orback.
7686236	L/Cpl.	R.	Robson.

49th(West Riding)Divisional Signals. No.3 Section.

2310429	L/Sgt.	F.J.	Abrahams.
2573767	Sig.	J.	Armitage.
2572113	Sig.	D.	Baggley.
2579870	Sig.	H.	Bingley.
2571497	Sig.	J.E.	Boden.
7014233	Sig.	F.	Corkery.
2575966	Sig.	G.A.	Davis.
2572198	Sig.	H.	Endacott.
2575122	Sig.	F.E.	Noble.
2582470	Sig.	W.C.	Webb.

L/Sgt.	Lance Sergeant (3 stripes)
Sgt.	Sergeant (3 stripes)
CQMS	Company Quarter Master Sergeant
CSM	Colour Sergeant Major
RSM	Regimental Sergeant Major
A/	*Acting Rank*

Service numbers were allocated to Regiments in blocks and those for the York & Lancaster Regiment were Service Numbers 4736001 to 4792000.

Generally speaking, every man retained his Service Number no matter where he went. From this, a man's Regimental origins could be traced. That is, until Sept. 1942, when men were issued with a General Service Corps Number (14,200,001 to 15,000,000) which meant that they could have undergone initial training and service in any one of a number of Regimental Depots.

Thus, the Regimental origins of Roy Simon (14590846) could not be easily traced (although he is known to have received basic training with the Durham light Infantry). Les Sewell, on the other hand, has the Service Number 4747908 and therefore originates from the York & Lancaster Regiment.

ARMY RANKS

Commissioned

2Lt.	Second Lieutenant (1 pip)
Lt.	Lieutenant (2 pips)
Capt.	Captain (3 pips)
Maj.	Major (1 crown)
Lt. Col.	Lieutenant Colonel (1 crown + 1 pip)
(highest regimental rank)	
Col.	Colonel
Brig.	Brigadier
Maj. Gen.	Major General
Lt. Gen.	Lieutenant General
Gen.	General
Fld. Mar.	Field Marshal

Non - Commissioned

Bdmn.	Bandsman
Dmr.	Drummer
Sig.	Signaller
Pte.	Private
L/Cpl.	Lance Corporal (1 stripe)
Cpl.	Corporal (2 stripes)

'C' COMPANY MUSTER ROLL. This list was in force during service in Iceland. Precise date is unknown but probably between June 1940 and March 1941. (DEL)

Army No.	Rank.	Initials	Surname.	Army No.	Rank.	Initial.	Surname.
4748086	Pte.	J.H.	Allcock	4742148	Pte.	H.	McGreavey
4748168	Pte.	H.	Austin	4749706	Pte.	W.	Marsden
4742491	Pte.	J.T.	Atkinson	4750331	Pte.	W.L.	Mawer
4745283	Cpl.	E.	Battle	4750329	Pte.	E.L.	Morris
4747678	Pte.	A.	Barber	4750320	Pte.	A.	Metheringham
4747631	Pte.	S.	Brookes	4750515	Pte.	N.	Mulcahey
4747721	Pte.	A.	Bunker	4750438	Pte.	H.	Murphy
4748019	Pte.	H.	Brook	4748027	Pte.	W.R.	Newton
4747499	A/Cpl.	H.	Butler	4748316	U/B/Cpl.	L.	Nield
4748320	Pte.	G.H.	Bilton	4750501	Pte.	R.	Nicol
4749125	Pte.	L.	Bamford	4747490	L/Cpl.	J.H.	Ogden
4749116	Pte.	J.G.	Brumby	4749178	Pte.	S.	Orton
4750345	Pte.	J.A.	Briggs	4749184	Pte.	J.	Peel
4750358	Pte.	J.	Blakeley	766467	A/Cpl.	D.	Piggott
~~4750376~~	~~Pte.~~	~~V.~~	~~Barrett~~	4748315	U/L/Cpl.	W.R.	Petty
4746745	Pte.	C.	Cavanagh	4746584	Cpl.	W.	Powell
4748021	Pte.	A.	Cairns	4737822	L/Cpl.	G.F.	Rhode
4746981	U/L/Cpl.	W.H.	Chapman	4746874	Pte.	A.	Richardson
4749081	Pte.	J.T.	Cartledge	4748356	Pte.	R.	Robinson
4749094	Pte.	P.	Cristanacce	4749072	Pte.	H.	Rodgers
4749146	Pte.	G.	Colley	4750524	Pte.	R.	Ripley
4748988	Pte.	G.	Coates	4750443	Pte.	J.	Reilley
~~4750382~~	~~Pte.~~	~~A.~~	~~Clegg~~	4746938	Pte.	J.	Salt
4747700	Pte.	A.	Daley	4747463	Pte.	F.C.	Smith
4747975	Pte.	A.	Ellis	4747546	Pte.	R.	Stringfellow
4747617	B/Cpl.	H.	Ellis	4748190	Pte.	V.	Stubbs
4744624	Pte.	F.W.	Bratt	4748415	U/L/Cpl.	L.	Smith
4738741	A/Sgt.	W.	Esplin	4745752	Cpl.	H.A.	Styring
4747531	Pte.	E.	France	4746613	Pte.	E.	South
4747618	L/Cpl.	W.E.	Fisher	4747994	Pte.	E.	Shelton
4749057	Pte.	H.	Ford	4747811	Pte.	F.	Smith
4749158	Pte.	J.	Flinders	4747908	L/Cpl.	L.	Sewell
4749157	Pte.	S.	Fisher	4747765	Pte.	H.	Stringer
4750430	Pte.	A.T.	Farmer	4748744	Pte.	W.	Smith
4750278	Pte.	J.	Fletcher	4749175	Pte.	G.	Sanderson
4748424	Pte.	H.	Graham	4748863	Pte.	H.	Stapleton
4746836	Pte.	D.	Greenwood	4748877	Pte.	G.R.	Strafford
4748362	Pte.	A.	Hirst	4750301	Pte.	J.R.	Sharp
4749010	U/L/Cpl.	S.	Hirst	4750390	Pte.	D.H.	Stocks
4747143	Pte.	E.	Hanson	4746167	L/Cpl.	J.	Tonks
4747619	Pte.	J.A.	Higgins	4748380	Pte.	H.	Thorpe
4747393	Pte.	W.G.	Holland	4744662	U/L/Cpl.	G.	Thwaite
4749189	Pte. U/L/Cpl	T.J.R.	Hartley	773271	A/CQMS	H.B.	Tunstall
4747684	Pte.	W.	Johnson	4747653	Pte.	A.	Warren
4748938	Pte.	C.	Jameson	4748372	Pte.	V.	Wyatt
4750510	Pte.	C.	Johnson	4747445	Pte.	F.D.	Woodhead
4750480	Pte.	J.A.	Jones	4748414	Pte.	F.T.	Wilson
4750380	Pte.	E.	Jones	4748420	Pte.	T.	Whitter
4749140	Pte.	F.	Kirk	4745171	Cpl.	E.	Wells
4750521	Pte.	A.	Kay	4747379	Pte.	E.	Whittaker
4747502	Pte.	F.E.	Lee	4747944	Pte.	A.	Wathall
4739264	Sgt.	G.H.	Linley	4749128	Pte.	R.	Woodward
4750447	Pte.	E.	Leadley	4749084	Pte.	G.	Webb
4745173	L/Cpl.	J.T.	Loxley	4749087	Pte.	H.	Wildgoose
4750463	Pte.	T.	Lambert	4748561	Pte.	A.	Whiteside
4750287	Pte.	J.T.	Lees	4744459	Pte.	F.	Wilson
4748413	Pte.	A.	Mackin	4749078	Pte.	F.	Willert
4747354	Pte.	J.	Myers	4749193	Pte.	A.	Wood
4742731	Pte.	A.	Moore	4750508	Pte.	F.	Watkins
4749107	Pte.	R.	Marriott	4750493	Pte.	W.	Watson
4749129	Pte.	J.H.	Gillott	4750391	Pte.	C.	Walsh
4536214	L/Cpl.	A.	Ditrick				

(Continued on sheet

HALLAMS 'FONTENAY CLUB' PICTURE GALLERY

Trevor Hart Dyke at home in Bamford, Derbyshire.

Clockwise from Top Left : Arnold Whiteley, Bill Jackson, Arnold Bracewell, Doug Catley, John Swift, Ray Langdale, Arthur Saunders, Graham Roe. Tom O'Connor. Arthur Naylor. John Wollerton and Fred Andrew.

Top Row : Dennis Townsend, Les Sewell, Walt Jackson, Bunny Whiting. 2nd Row : Eric Bennett, Cyril Purton, Reg Bratley, Arthur Green. 3rd Row : Tom Garbett, Roy Simon, Albert Binns, Eric Scott. Bottom Row : Tony Jaques, Reg Westwood, Harold Newton, Sam Woolley.

The 49th (West Riding) Infantry Division.

This Division, originally formed in 1908, was one of a number of similar units existing within the British Army at the outbreak of war in 1939. As a First Line Territorial unit it was mobilised in September, 1939 and remained so for the duration. Divisional operations were temporarily suspended in April, 1940 when its Headquarters became 'Avonforce' for the Norwegian Campaign and 'Alabasterforce' during the occupation of Iceland. The Division was reconstituted when it returned home in April, 1942 and remained operational until disbandment in 1946.

The strength of an Infantry Division of that period rose from about 13,000 at the beginning of the war to approximately 18,000 men by the end. The whole force consisted basically of three Infantry Brigades each containing three infantry battalions. The nine Infantry battalions each containing approximately 1,000 men (but normally 800 - 900), therefore accounted for roughly half of the Divisional strength. The rest were other types of fighting or support units and individuals.

Structure of the 49th (West Riding) Infantry Division, 1939-45.

Infantry Divisions are best described as large battle groups formed by the amalgamation of other units to make up an almost self sufficient fighting machine. The fighting troops required a massive backup structure in terms of administration, organisation, support and supply. These backups, generally termed Divisional Troops, consisted of whole units, detachments and individuals with specialised skills and tasks.

Divisional Troops

This is not a history of the 49th Division but it might be of interest to list below some of the additional units which served within it. This vast array of other services was required in the form of attached Armoured Units (mainly elements of the 8th Armoured Brigade), Royal Artillery (R.A.), Royal Engineers (R.E.), Royal Electrical & Mechanical Engineers (R.E.M.E.), Royal Army Service Corps (R.A.S.C.), Royal Army Medical Corps (R.A.M.C.), Royal Signals, Pioneer Corps, Royal Army Ordinance Corps (R.A.O.C.), Corps of Military Police (C.M.P.), plus many more. Their tasks were varied but all with one aim in common, that of support, supply and backup for the infantryman at the sharp end in his quest to take and hold ground.

49 Regt. Recce. Corps	(9/42 —12/43)
49 Recce. Regt. R.A.C.	(1/44 ———————— 8/45)
69 Fld. Regt. R.A. (9/39 - 6/40)	(9/42 ————————————— 8/45)
70 Fld. Regt. R.A. (9/39 - 6/40)	
71 Fld. Regt. R.A. (9/39 - 6/40)	
79 Fld. Regt. R.A. (6/40)	
80 Fld. Regt. R.A. (6/40)	
143 Fld. Regt. R.A.	(4/42 ————————————— 8/45)

178 Fld. Regt. R.A.	(5/42 — 12/42)	
185 Fld. Regt. R.A.	(12/42 ——————————11/44)	
74 Fld. Regt. R.A.		(11/44 - 8/45)
58 A/Tk. Regt. R.A.(9-39 - 6/40)		
88 A/Tk. Regt. R.A. (6.42 ——————————11/43)		
55 A/Tk. Regt. R.A.	(7/43 ————————— 8/45)	
118 L.A.A. Regt. R.A.	(5/42 - 8/42)	
89 L.A.A. Regt. R.A.	(2/42 ————————— 8/45)	

The Infantry Brigades and their Battalions

No matter how sophisticated the weaponry used in war, it is almost invariably the task of infantrymen to occupy and hold any ground gained. This is the primitive end of conflict where mortality is high and reflected in the large numbers required. Within a WWII Infantry Division there were normally three Infantry Brigades. As has already been said, an Infantry Brigade contained three battalions, each with a strength of just under 1,000 men, bringing the total strength of the three Brigades to approximately 9,000. Not all of these were riflemen as each battalion was partially self sustaining with many of its own tradesmen such as cooks, clerks, drivers, signallers, etc. However, all were trained in the use of the rifle and could be called upon to fill such a role in an emergency. The following is a break down of the Brigades that made up the 49 Division and dates in service during the period 1939-1945. Numbers in the right hand column represent the Unit Serial Number which was carried on the front and rear off side of Brigade and Battalion vehicles. The numbers shown are those used during the period 1942-1945 and were normally painted white on a 9 inch (23cm), coloured square:- Red = Senior Brigade, Green = Second Brigade, Brown = Junior Brigade. Theoretically, every vehicle in the British Army could be identified by the combination of Divisional Sign and Unit Serial Number.

146 Infantry Brigade. (Senior) (9/39 - 4/40) (8/42 - 8/45)   81
4 Bn. Lincolnshire Regt.	(dates as Brigade)	55
1/4 Bn. Kings Own Yorkshire Light Infantry.	(dates as Brigade)	56
Hallamshire Bn. York & Lancaster Regt.	(dates as Brigade)	57

Support

The list of units below were those specifically allocated to 146 Brigade as and when required after the Invasion of Europe and therefore the most likely to be in support of the Hallams. However, a whole range of additional firepower was available on demand from Division for specific purposes including Tanks of 8th Armoured Brigade, Aircraft of the Royal Air Force and even the more powerful Naval guns of ships lying off the Normandy beach head in the case of the Battle of Fontenay le Pesnel.

218 Battery, 55 A/Tk Regt. (Suffolk Yeomanry), R.A.
2 Bn. The Kensington Regiment.
69 Field Regt., R.A.
294 Field Coy. R.E.
460 Coy. R.A.S.C.
146 Field Ambulance.
146 Infantry Brigade Workshops, R.E.M.E.

147 Infantry Brigade. (Second) (9/39 - 4/40) (8/42 - 8/45)   87
    1/5Bn. West Yorkshire Regt. (9/39 -4/40) (4/42 - 8/42)   60
    1/6Bn. Duke of Wellingtons Regt. (9/39 - 4/40) (4/42 - 1/43) (2/43 - 7/44)   61
    1/7Bn. Duke of Wellingtons Regt. (9/39 - 4/40) (4/42 - 1/43) (2/43 - 8/45)   62
    11 Bn. Royal Scots Fusiliers (9/42 - 8/45) (replaced 1/5 W.Y.R.)
    1 Bn. Leicestershire Regt. (8/44 - 8/45) (replaced 1/6 D.W.R.)

148 Infantry Brigade. (Junior) (9/39 - 4/40)   94
    1/5Bn. Leicestershire Regt. (9/39 - 4/40)   67
    2 Bn. South Wales Borderers. (9/39 - 4/40)   68
    8 Bn. Sherwood Foresters (9/39 - 4/40)   69

70 Infantry Brigade. (5/42 - 8/44) (replaced 148 Brigade)
    10 Bn. Durham Light Infantry. (5/42 - 8/44)
    11 Bn. Durham Light Infantry. (5/42 - 8/44)
    1 Bn. Tyneside Scottish. (5/42 - 8/44)

56 Infantry Brigade. (8/44 - 8/45) (replaced 70 Brigade)
    2 Bn. South Wales Borderers. (8/44 - 8/45)
    2 Bn. Gloucestershire Regt. (8/44 - 8/45)
    2 Bn. Essex Regt. (8/44 - 8/45)

Support Battalion (6/43 - 2/44)
    2 Bn. Kensington Regt.

Machine Gun Unit (2/44 - 8/45)
    2 Bn. Kensington Regt.

It can be seen here that the 49th Divisional structure did not remain static during the war. The 146th Brigade suffered little change except perhaps in fluctuations of men and material whilst the 147th saw movement, both in and out, in terms of some individual battalions. The 148th saw no further active service after the Norwegian Campaign in which it lost 1,402 men in dead and wounded. The Division was brought up to strength in October, 1940, when the 70th Brigade arrived in Iceland, the latter being replaced by the 56th Brigade in August, 1944.

Insignia.

The first pattern insignia of the 49th Division, a White Rose of Yorkshire, had been in use during the Great War (1914-18). In its most common form it was worn as a white metal badge on the upper sleeve of both arms. The diameter was a little under one and a quarter inches (3 cms) and was affixed to the uniform by a threaded post on the back of the badge. This protruded through a hole in the sleeve and the badge retained by a thin brass plate and a thin, rounded nut with a milled edge. The badge was still in use during World War Two even after a second pattern had been adopted in Iceland during the latter part of 1940. An order which took effect from 20 March, 1942, discontinued use of the old rose insignia.

It is reputed that the second pattern for a 49th Divisional Formation Sign was copied from the wrapper of a Foxes Glacier Mint! Be that as it may, it must be said that the design, a Polar Bear with head down and standing on an irregular shaped ice slab shows a strong resemblance and could have sparked the idea. It was adopted in Iceland and perhaps first used in late 1940

(August) as part of the front page header of a newspaper published within the Division called 'The Midnight Sun'.

The insignia was applied to the front and rear, nearside of most vehicles usually on a black background within a white circle. It was also worn as a cloth patch on uniform (battle dress blouse and greatcoat) below the shoulder on each sleeve. In this case they were used as a mirrored pair with both bears facing forward and set on a rectangular black background. Observed examples of this early design were produced in both the printed and embroidered form.

Shortly after returning from Iceland in April, 1942, a third pattern was devised, attributed to the new Divisional Commander, General 'Bubbles' Barker, still using the Polar Bear but now with head raised (see Cover). The idea was to make the bear appear more aggressive but apparently the natural posture for a charging, and presumably angry, Polar Bear is with head lowered! Examples of this cloth patch, once again, can be found in both printed and embroidered versions although the latter is believed to be more common in the post war period.

Component parts of the old 49th (West Riding) Infantry Division - White Rose Insignia, comprising the badge, backing disc and retaining nut. (approx. half size)

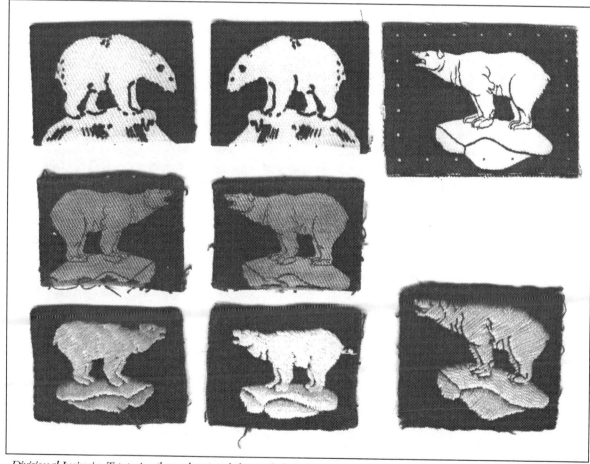

Divisional Insignia. Top pair - the early printed design (adopted in Iceland, 1940) with head down. Middle pair - Head up printed version (adopted at Leominster). Bottom pair - Head up embroidered version. Top right shows an unissued new patch with dots indicating the fold lines before stitching onto the uniform (newly issued insignia came as a matched pair on a single patch that had to be cut in half). Bottom Right - Embroidered patch of slightly different design to bottom pair. May be post war or from WWII officers uniform. The dull colour of some patches shown here is just ingrained dirt.

APPENDIX II

Battalion Structure.

Some difficulty has been experienced in asserting what numbers were assigned to the various Platoons. It is not even known for certain that all HQ. Coy. Platoons had numbers. Numbers have been 'allotted' below to fit in with the known numbering system within the Rifle Companies. It is known, for instance, that 12 Pl. was a part of 'B' Coy., 14 Pl. part of 'C' Coy. and 17 Pl. part of 'D' Coy. It is also fairly certain that Carrier Platoon was often referred to as No.4 Platoon. Otherwise, the information given below is provided as a rough guide only.

HQ. Company	Consisted of Clerks, Intelligence and Police Personnel, Stretcher Bearers, Snipers, etc.
No.1 Platoon	Signals. Maintained wireless and telephone communications.
No.2 Platoon	Motor Transport. Maintained all vehicles not allocated to other Coys.
No.3 Platoon	Administration.

Support Company

No.4 Platoon   Universal Carriers.

        Section = 3 x Carriers (1 fitted with wasp fame thrower)
        Section = 3 x Carriers
        Section = 3 x Carriers
        Section = 3 x Carriers

These vehicles in Iceland were named after pre Great War 1914 -18 Battle Honours and are contained in the list below. Drivers names (some missing) were drawn from the memory of Les Sewell, 50 years later :-

Vehicle Name	Drivers
Peninsula	Bill Killingbeck
Guadaloupe	Alec Mitchell
Tel el Kebir	Ralph Hattersley
India	John A. Longford
Arabia	Thomas Chandler
South Africa	A.A. Mitchell
Lucknow	W. Bramhall
Martinique	Ken Rispin
New Zealand	J. Jackson
Egypt	John Haynes
Nive	Arthur Barraclough
Relief of Ladysmith	

No.5 Platoon   Mortars.
Originally equipped 3" Mortars in 15cwt Trucks.
Later Equipped with 6 x 3" Mortars in Carriers.

No.6 Platoon   Pioneers. Mine detection and clearance. Constructional work.

No.7 Platoon   Anti-Tank.
Originally equipped with 2 Pounders that were carried in 15cwt. Portees
Later equipped with 6 x 6 Pounders towed by Carden Lloyd Carriers

<u>'A' Company</u> Rifle (approx. 120 men)

Coy. HQ.	Commander (Major), 2 i/c (Captain) and CSM.
No. 8 Platoon	Lieutenant and Sergeant.
	2" Mortar team
Section	Corporal, L/Corporal, five or six men
	Brengun, Rifles, Bayonets and Grenades
Section	Ditto
Section	Ditto

No. 9 Platoon As above
No. 10 Platoon As above

<u>'B' Company</u> Rifle (as above)
    Coy. HQ.
    No. 11 Platoon
    No. 12 Platoon
    No. 13 Platoon

<u>'C' Company</u> Rifle (as above)
    Coy. HQ.
    No. 14 Platoon
    No. 15 Platoon
    No. 16 Platoon

<u>'D' Company</u> Rifle (as above)
    Coy. HQ.
    No. 17 Platoon
    No. 18 Platoon
    No. 19 Platoon

Jesse Mitchinson was a Platoon Commander and carried in his pocket a small card index of the men under his wing. A Platoon consisted of about thirty-three men, ideally, but was often operated under strength. Jesse still has those cards which, relating to the winter period of 1944/45, have now become a little faded but they contain more information than is shown below. Some are more detailed than others but the best also include, age and date of birth, rifle number, clothing/cap/boot sizes, shooting proficiency on Bren and Rifle, civilian occupation, full next of kin address, religious denomination, etc.

Number	Rank	Name	Next of Kin	Employ.
4749711	L/Sgt.	Hughes, Dennis	Fulford Road, York	Pl. Sgt.
14425653	Cpl.	Smith, Frederick	Darnall, Sheffield	7 Sect. Comd.
14306152	L/Cpl.	Caddon, Christopher	Homerton, London	2i/c 7 Sect.
14670889	L/Cpl.	Calvert, James	Rollands Gill, Co. Durham	2i/c, 7 Sect. *
1083161	Cpl.	Marshall, Herbert	Friars Cres., Northampton	8 Sect. Comd.
2087776	L/Cpl.	Brennan	West Gorton, Manchester	2i/c Sect.
14692249	Cpl.	Treadgold, Harry	Kinver, Wiltshire	9 Sect. Comd.
14544543	Pte.	Dybell, Sydney High	Eresham St. Middlesborough	Bren No.1
14741046	Pte.	Johnson, D.	Richmond, Yorkshire	Bren No.1

412

1784873	Pte.	Donnelly, A.	Maxwell St., South Shields	Bren No.1
14334689	Pte.	Milton, H.	Stokes Croft, Bristol	Bren No.1
4746960	Pte.	Walker, Joseph H.	Southy Hill, Sheffield	Bren No.2
1775757	Pte.	Place, H.	Heaton Chapel, Cheshire	Bren No.2
5951845	Pte.	Horwood, C.W.	Aston Clinton, Aylesbury	Bren No.2
14743616	Pte.	Jipson, N.	Howden, East Yorkshire	Bren No.2 *
3458202	Pte.	Brierley, James	Patricroft, Manchester	Bren No.2 *
14724089	Pte.	Stephens, Reginald	Kingsdown Parade, Bristol	Bren No.3
14745877	Pte.	Cooper, Albert	Bath Street, Derby	Bren No.3
4748866	L/Cpl.	Wortley, George	Dewsbury, Yorks.	Mortar Comd. *
4736542	Pte.	Brockley, T.	Pepper Grove, Leeds	Mortar No.1
14427708	Pte.	Gregory, R.E.	Pollard Cres. Sheffield	Mortar No.2
14444677	Pte.	Gill, Robert	Birkinhead, Cheshire	Mortar No.2 *
4746577	Pte.	Saperia, Charles	Campers Road, Leeds	PIAT No.1
14587362	Pte.	Ogden	Richmond, Yorkshire	PIAT No.2
376704	Pte.	Martin, Cyril	Connaught Rd., Portsmouth	Rifleman
14775377	Pte.	Rogers, D.E.	Upper Pitt St., Liverpool	Rifleman
3783887	Pte.	Goodwin, W.L.	Greystone Rd., Liverpool	Rifleman
14986737	Pte.	Cooper, George	Sneyd St., Leek, Staffs.	Rifleman
468602	Pte.	Moore, Robert	Fulwell, Sunderland	Rifleman
14990064	Pte.	Bawdon, Emrys	Treorchy, Rhonda, S. Wales	Rifleman *
4736118	Pte.	Slater, W.	Dudley Hill, Bradford	Rifleman *
4538392	Pte.	Eardley, Joseph	Middleton, Leeds	Rifleman *
6207196	Pte.	Walker, Granville G.	Lyncroft Gdns. Ealing	Batman
14496307	Pte.	Handyside W.R.	Ashington, Northumberland	Pl. Runner
4747408	Pte.	Smith, Stanley	Bradbury, Sheffield	S.B. *

If this is a typical mix of those serving in a Hallams Platoon at the time these cards were in force (Early 1945), then the few details given here about this one tells its own story. Only five of these men have York & Lancaster Regiment Service Numbers with a further two having General Service Corps numbers but with addresses which fall within the Regimental Recruiting area of what is now termed South Yorkshire. The rest, as can be seen, are from all over the country. Those marked with an asterisk (nine) have been lined through, indicating that the man had left the Platoon and so it would seem that there were only twenty-six men on strength when the cards were last in use.

BIBLIOGRAPHY & ADDITIONAL READING.

NORMANDY TO ARNHEM : A Story of Infantry
(Primary source for this period)
Brigadier Trevor Hart Dyke, D.S.O.
Greenup and Thompson Ltd., Sheffield, 1966.

BATTLEGROUNDS in Normandy, Belgium & Holland.
An Album of post-war photographs compiled by Brigadier T. Hart Dyke, D.S.O.
(Mary E. Hart Dyke)

EXTRACTS from the letters of Major David Eadon Lockwood to his wife and mother
covering the period 15/10/39 to 23/6/44
(Mary E. Hart Dyke)

EXTRACTS from the Diary and Scrap Book of Capt. Alfred. Christopher Somers
covering the period June, 1944 - May, 1945
(Doreene Somers)

EXTRACTS from the Diary of Sgt. George Linley
covering the period 6 April, 1940 - 9 May, 1940

THE YORK & LANCASTER REGIMENT : VOLUME I & II
Colonel H.C. Wylly.
Gale & Polden, London,1930.
(Copy in Y & L Regimental Museum Archive)

THE YORK & LANCASTER REGIMENT : VOLUME III
O.F. Sheffield.
Gale & Polden, London,1956.
(Copy in Y & L Regimental Museum Archive)

THE YORK & LANCASTER REGIMENT
Donald Creighton-Williamson.
Famous Regiments Series, Leo Cooper, London. 1968.

THE YORK & LANCASTER REGIMENTAL MUSEUM
Guide and Short History
D.W. Scott.
English Life Publications Ltd. Derby.1985.

HALLAMSHIRE RIFLES : Handwritten Diary, May 1859 - Jan 1881
Hon.T.W. Best.
Y & L Regimental Museum Archives.

THE HALLAMSHIRE RIFLE VOLUNTEERS 1859 - 1989
A.J. Podmore.
4th Battalion Yorkshire Volunteers, 1991.

AUDIO TAPE RECORDINGS : by Officers & Men of
The Hallamshire Battalion, 1939-45.
Recordings produced by D.W. Scott between 1987 and 2000.
(now donated to the Y & L Regimental Museum Archive)

DOCUMENTS and PHOTOGRAPHS relating to the wartime and post-war activities of :
"THE HALLAMS FONTENAY CLUB" All members were present or in support at the
Battle of Fontenay le Pesnel and/or the occupation of Tessel Wood 25/6/44 - 16/7/44
Collected and Compiled by D.W. Scott and A. Green between 1987 and 2000.
(now donated to the Y & L Regimental Museum Archive)

LETTERS : to Lt.Col.W. Tozer, O.C. Hallamshire Bn.1934.
Y & L Regimental Museum Archive.

TIGER & ROSE : Regimental Journals and Newsletters from 1887 to 2000
Y & L Regimental Museum Archive.

A SHORT HISTORY OF 49TH WEST RIDING & MIDLAND INFANTRY DIVISION
TERRITORIAL ARMY.
Lt. Col. F.K. Hughes R.A.E.C.
The Stellar Press Ltd. Union Street, Barnet, Herts. 1957.

WARSHIPS OF WORLD WAR II.
H.T. Lenton & J.J. Colledge.
Ian Allan, 1973.

THE MIDNIGHT SUN a Services News Magazine produced in Iceland
(Y & L Regimental Museum Archive - incomplete series)

ARCTIC TIMES a Services News Magazine produced in Iceland
(Y & L Regimental Museum Archive - incomplete series)

HALLAMSHIRE HERALD a news magazine produced by the Battalion
(Y & L Regimental Museum Archive - incomplete series)

SHEFFIELD 'TELEGRAPH' AND 'STAR' NEWSPAPERS
Various extracts from wartime and post-war period
Sheffield Newspapers Ltd.

THE DOOMED EXPEDITION The Campaign in Norway 1940
Jack Adams.
Mandarin Paperbacks, 1990

NORWAY 1940
Francois Kersaudy.
Arrow Books Ltd., 1991

THE NORWEGIAN CAMPAIGN OF 1940
J.M. Moulton.
Camelot Press Ltd., 1966

SIX ARMIES IN NORMANDY
John Keegan.
Penguin Books, 1988

HILL 112
Major J.J. How, M.C.
William Kimber, 1984

NONE HAD LANCES
24th Lancers in World War Two
Old Comrades Association, 1986

PUBLIC RECORD OFFICE
War Diaries: Hallamshire Battalion 1939 - 1945 (some parts missing)
W.O. 166, W.O. 171, W.O. 176.

THE 'LOG' BOOK
A Diary of events and notes derived from various sources covering the History of the
Hallamshire Battalion, 1859 - 1934. Compiled by Lt.Col. W. Tozer, T.D.
Also contains update to 3 Sept. 1939.
(Y & L Regimental Museum Archive)

THE DEVIL'S BIRTHDAY
The Bridges to Arnhem 1944
Geoffrey Powell
Buchan & Enright Publishers Ltd. 1984.

BRITISH ARMY UNIFORMS & INSIGNIA OF WORLD WAR TWO
Brian L. Davis.
Book Club Associates. 1983

OPERATION MARTLET, JUNE, 1944.
The Battle for Fontenay and beyond.
Draft Copy printed in 1995. Unpublished.
Bill Ashby (son of Capt. W. Ashby)

STRUGGLE FOR SURVIVAL
The History of the Second World War
With good secondary book list on the subject.
R.A.C. Parker
Oxford University press, 1990

ABBREVIATIONS

AA	Anti-Aircraft
AB	Army Book
ACC	Army Catering Corps
ADCorps	Army Dental Corps
Adjt	Adjutant
AEC	Army Educational Corps
AEF	Allied Expeditionary Force
AF	Army Form
AFV	Armoured Fighting Vehicle
APTS	Army Physical Training Staff
A/Tk.	Anti -Tank
ATS	Auxiliary Territorial Service (women)
BD	Battle-Dress
Bde	Brigade
BEF	British Expeditionary Force
BEM	British Empire Medal
BHP	Brake Horse Power
BM	Brigade Major
Bn	Battalion
CBE	Commander of the British Empire
C-in-C	Commander-in-Chief
CIA	Chief Inspector of Armaments
CMP	Corps of Military Police
CO	Commanding Officer
Coy	Company
DCM	Distinguished Conduct Medal
DR	Despatch Rider, also known as 'Don Rs'
DSO	Distinguished Service Order
DUKW	Amphibious Vehicle - 'Duck'
ENSA	Entertainments National Service Association
FANY	Field Auxilliary Nursing Yeomanry
FS	Field Service
FSMO	Field Service Marching Order (refers to webbing equipment)
FUP	Form Up Point
GOC	General Officer Commanding
GS	General Service
GSO	General Staff Officer
HAA	Heavy Anti-Aircraft
HQ	HeadQuarters
i/c	in charge
IO	Intelligence Office
KD	Khaki Drill
KR	King's Regulations
LAA	Light Anti-Aircraft
MBE	Member of the British Empire
MC	Military Cross
MCC	Morris Commercial Cars
LMG	Light Machine Gun
MM	Military Medal
MP	Military Police
MT	Mechanical Transport/Motor Transport
NAAFI	Navy, Army and Air Force Institute
NCO	Non-Commissioned Officer
OC	Officer Commanding
OCTU	Officer Cadet Training Unit
'O' Group	Orders Group
OP	Observation Post
ORs	Other Ranks
PIAT	Projectile Infantry Anti-Tank
Pl	Platoon
PRI	President Regimental Institute
PTI	Physical Training Instructor
QM	Quarter Master
RA	Royal Artillery
RAC	Royal Armoured Corps
RAChD	Royal Army Chaplains Department
RAMC	Royal Army Medical Corps
RAOC	Royal Army Ordnance Corps
RAP	Regimental Aid Post
RAPC	Royal Army Pay Corps
RASC	Royal Army Service Corps
RAVC	Royal Army Veterinary Corps
RE	Royal Engineers
REME	Royal Electrical and Mechanical Engineers
RM	Royal Marines
RMP	Regimental Military Police
RTO	Railway Transport Officer
SAA	Small Arms Ammunition
Sam Browne	Officers Leather Belt/Straps
SAS	Special Air Service
SASC	Small Arms School Corps
SB	Stretcher Bearer
SC	Staff Captain
SD	Service Dress
Sec	Section
SO	Signals Officer
SnO	Sniper Officer
SOE	Special Operations Executive
TA	Territorial Army
TAF	Tactical Air Force
T.D.	Territorial Decoration
TO	Transport Officer
UK	United Kingdom
VC	Victoria Cross
WD	War Diary
WO	War Office
WVS	Womens Voluntary Service

ARMY RANKS

Commissioned

2/Lt.	Second Lieutenant (1 pip)
Lt.	Lieutenant (2 pips)
Capt.	Captain (3 pips)
Maj.	Major (1 crown)
Lt. Col.	Lieutenant Colonel (1 crown + 1 pip) (highest regimental rank)
Col.	Colonel
Brig.	Brigadier
Maj. Gen.	Major General
Lt. Gen.	Lieutenant General
Gen.	General
Fld. Mar.	Field marshal

Non - Commissioned

Pte.	Private
L/Cpl.	Lance Corporal (1 stripe)
Cpl.	Corporal (2 stripes)
L/Sgt.	Lance Sergeant (3 stripes)
Sgt.	Sergeant (3 stripes)
CSM	Colour Sergeant Major
CQMS	Company Quarter Master Sergeant
RSM	Regimental Sergeant Major

Regimental Abbreviations in the Text:

4 Linc	4th Bn.The Lincolnshire Regt.
4 KOYLI	1st/4th Bn.The Kings Own Yorkshire Light Infantry.
Hallams	Hallamshire Bn.The York & Lancaster Regt.
5 WYR	5th Bn.The West Yorkshire Regt.
6 DWR	6th Bn.The Duke of Wellingtons Regt.
7 DWR	7th Bn.The Duke of Wellingtons Regt.
11 RSF	11th Bn.The Royal Scots Fusiliers.
1 LR	1st Bn.The Leicester Regt.
5 LR	5th Bn.The Leicester Regt.
2 SWB	2nd Bn.The South Wales Boarderers.
8 SF	8th Bn.The Sherwood Foresters.
9 DLI	9th Bn.The Durham Light Infantry.
10 DLI	10th Bn.The Durham Light Infantry.
1 TS	1st Bn.The Tyneside Scottish.
2 GR	2nd Bn.The Gloucestershire Regt.
2 ER	2nd Bn.The Essex Regt.
9 RTR	9th Royal Tank Regiment

THE AUTHOR

Don Scott was born in the town of Hebburn upon Tyne, County Durham in 1938 and was educated at the Colliery Board and Clegwell Secondary Modern Schools. He joined the Royal Air Force in 1956 as an airframe fitter and saw overseas tours of service in  Germany, Persian Gulf and Singapore. On leaving the Service in 1973 he moved to the Sheffield area and indulged in various pursuits which included the manufacture of fibreglass mouldings, selling cookware, servicing cash registers and the production of aircraft parts.

In 1978 he became involved in the operation of a Mobile Museum Service run by South Yorkshire County Council, mainly on the grounds of being able to handle the very long Land Rover/Trailer combination. It was then that he decided on History/Museums as a second career and successfully applied for university entrance at the age of 40 years. After undergoing three years full time studies, he was awarded a B.A. Hons. Degree in Ancient History/Archaeology at Manchester University in 1982. This qualification was the key to allowing him the privilege of helping to set up the York and Lancaster Regimental Museum in its new home at Rotherham in 1984 where he became first, the Keeper of History/Antiquities and later of Militaria and enjoyed fourteen years of mostly historical research and enquiries until his early retirement in 1998.

During those years in the Regimental Museum, the author became involved with war veterans of both World Wars and travelled with them on a number of occasions to the battlefields of France, Belgium and Holland and in this way, was able to record the many personal stories to be found in this book.